Human Behavior in the Social Environment
A Multidimensional Perspective

Human Behavior in the Social Environment
A Multidimensional Perspective

José B. Ashford
Arizona State University

Craig Winston LeCroy
Arizona State University

Kathy L. Lortie
*University Medical Center
at the University of Arizona
Health Sciences Center*

Brooks/Cole Publishing Company
I(T)P® An International Thomson Publishing Company

Pacific Grove • Albany • Belmont • Bonn • Boston • Cincinnati • Detroit • Johannesburg • London • Madrid
Melbourne • Mexico City • New York • Paris • Singapore • Tokyo • Toronto • Washington

Sponsoring Editor: *Lisa Gebo*
Marketing Team: *Jean Vevers Thompson and Romy Taormina*
Editorial Assistant: *Terry Thomas*
Production Editor: *Laurel Jackson*
Production Assistant: *Mary Vezilich*
Manuscript Editors: *Jan McDearmon and Barbara Kimmel*
Permissions Editor: *Cathleen Collins Morrison*
Interior and Cover Design: *Roy R. Neuhaus*

Interior Illustration: *John and Judy Waller*
Cover Illustration: *Jose Ortega/The Stock Illustration Source*
Art Editor: *Lisa Torri*
Photo Editor: *Kathleen Olson*
Indexer: *Jane Farnol, Astor Indexing*
Typesetting: *TSI Graphics*
Printing and Binding: *R. R. Donnelley & Sons Co.,
    Crawfordsville Mfg. Division*

For more information, contact:

BROOKS/COLE PUBLISHING COMPANY
511 Forest Lodge Road
Pacific Grove, CA 93950
USA

International Thomson Publishing Europe
Berkshire House 168-173
High Holborn
London WC1V 7AA
England

Thomas Nelson Australia
102 Dodds Street
South Melbourne, 3205
Victoria, Australia

Nelson Canada
1120 Birchmount Road
Scarborough, Ontario
Canada M1K 5G4

International Thomson Editores
Seneca 53
Col. Polanco
11560 México, D.F., México

International Thomson Publishing GmbH
Königswinterer Strasse 418
53227 Bonn
Germany

International Thomson Publishing Asia
221 Henderson Road
#05-10 Henderson Building
Singapore 0315

International Thomson Publishing Japan
Hirakawacho Kyowa Building, 3F
2-2-1 Hirakawacho
Chiyoda-ku, Tokyo 102
Japan

Printed in the United States of America

10   9   8   7   6   5   4   3

Library of Congress Cataloging-in-Publication Data
Ashford, José B.
    Human behavior in the social environment: a multidimensional
  perspective / José B. Ashford, Craig Winston LeCroy, Kathy L.
  Lortie.
        p. cm.
    Includes bibliographical references and index.
    ISBN 0–534–14988–X (alk. paper)
    1. Developmental psychology.   2. Social psychology.   I. LeCroy,
Craig W.   II. Lortie, Kathy L., [date]   III. Title.
BF713.A82   1997
155.9'2—dc20

96–42497
CIP

To my wife, Nancy Disbrow,
for tolerating my unsociable working hours and for providing invaluable support
and counsel throughout my career.

— J. B. A. —

To my son, Skyler A. Milligan LeCroy,
who has taught me much about human behavior and development;
I love watching you grow!

— C. W. L. —

To my babies, Sarah, Susan, David, my first child, Shawn, and to Michael:
thanks for giving me the family I always wanted.

— K. L. L. —

About the Authors

José B. Ashford is a professor of human behavior and the social environment in the School of Social Work at Arizona State University. He is also a member of the faculty in the Interdisciplinary Ph.D. program in Justice Studies. Professor Ashford is a co-author of *Introduction to Social Work and Social Welfare* (with Mary Macht) and of the forthcoming books *Treatment of Adult and Juvenile Offenders with Special Needs* (with Bruce Sales and William Reid) and *Societal Responses to Mentally Disordered Offenders: Trends in Law and Policy* (with Bruce Sales). He is widely published in areas of offender justice and of law and mental health/social work interactions. In addition, Professor Ashford often testifies as an expert on the role of development and other human behavior considerations in the assessment of mitigating factors in capital murder cases.

Craig Winston LeCroy is a professor in the School of Social Work at Arizona State University. His previous books include *Social Skills Training for Children and Adolescents, Case Studies in Social Work Practice,* and *Handbook of Child and Adolescent Treatment Manuals.* He was previously Principal Investigator, National Institute of Mental Health Training Grant for severely emotionally disturbed children and adolescents; he is currently Principal Investigator for Youth Plus: Positive Socialization for Youth, a Center for Substance Abuse Prevention grant. Professor LeCroy has published widely in the areas of children's mental health, social skills training, risk and needs assessment with juvenile offenders, and adolescent treatment.

Kathy L. Lortie is a pediatric social worker at University Medical Center, University of Arizona, Health Sciences Center. She co-teaches Social Work in Health Care, a graduate course at Arizona State University. A certified childbirth educator, she has taught classes on childbirth, parenting, and infant care and has worked as a labor assistant. She is also the author of *Special Delivery: A Labor Guide for Expectant Parents.* Her current interests include child abuse prevention, infant mental health, and coping with chronic illness in adolescence.

Brief Contents

Contents

CHAPTER

6

Infancy   176

CHAPTER

7

Early Childhood   223

CHAPTER

8

Middle Childhood   265

CHAPTER

9

Adolescence   314

CHAPTER

10

Young Adulthood   363

Preface

We wrote this textbook to enhance social work students' knowledge and skills in the area of human behavior and the social environment. Although students of social work learn about many different theoretical concepts and perspectives, the connection between foundation knowledge and practice concerns is often weak. Students find it particularly difficult to apply the material learned in the human behavior and the social environment (HBSE) courses to direct practice. Most current HBSE textbooks introduce students to theoretical perspectives and concepts but do not connect this content to the practice process. This textbook will address this problem in several unique ways.

Up to now, textbooks in this area have focused either on development or on presenting knowledge about the range of social systems within which individuals live. Balance is rarely achieved between these two aims. Some traditional HBSE texts begin with an introductory look at systems and then embark on a coverage of development that does not substantially differ from what usually appears in developmental psychology textbooks. Others do a good job of reviewing major paradigms and describing the characteristics of key social systems, but they fail to provide comprehensive treatment of developmental content. As a result, students cannot integrate developmental considerations with their knowledge of social systems. With these issues in mind, we have adopted an integrated approach to exploring biopsychosocial development across the life span. We provide students with a multidimensional framework for assessing human behavior and apply this framework consistently throughout the textbook. To date, no other books in the field apply the same categories of information in their examination of human development.

We set out to write an applied, integrated, and comprehensive HBSE textbook that can be used in both undergraduate and graduate programs. We believe that few textbooks used in undergraduate HBSE courses are also adopted at the graduate level. The issue of comparability of content in foundation courses at the graduate and undergraduate levels is receiving increased attention at many levels of our profession, including CSWE—particularly in programs that allow students to use undergraduate courses to achieve advanced standing in graduate programs. Our comprehensive approach in this book will provide foundation material needed at both educational levels.

An additional goal of this book is to provide more foundation material from the biological, psychological and social sciences. Depending on their specific program, graduates and undergraduates may be lacking in at least one of those areas. Graduate students who reenter school after having been out for long periods need to review foundation material and strengthen their social and behavioral science backgrounds. Furthermore, both the professional journals and the accrediting body, the Council on Social Work Education, have demanded an increase in foundation information—especially biological, multicultural (that is, concerning racial and sexual orientation and populations at risk), and gender content. Many schools are criticized for deficiencies in these areas.

Although our profession has had a longstanding commitment to biopsychosocial considerations, the biological contributions to knowledge have been taken for granted. Students do coursework on human biology, but usually no one helps them to integrate this content in their assessments of human behavior. In fact, many textbooks in our field fail to discuss brain-and-behavior relationships, disabilities, and other relevant developments from the health sciences. Therefore, we include a chapter to describe fundamental concepts in the biological system that students can use to connect knowledge of human biology to social work assessment. This material covers many of the concepts included in certification examinations for social workers and deemed essential for practice in health and mental health settings.

All too often, the voices of the underrepresented are ignored in explorations of human development. Furthermore, when they are included, it is rarely in an integrated fashion. To address this omission, we have integrated multicultural (racial, ethnic, and gay and lesbian) and gender variables into our framework to ensure that this information is comprehensively covered.

We believe that the social worker must link an understanding of human behavior to the process of social work assessment. Making this connection is just as crucial as linking assessment to goal setting and treatment planning. A primary goal of this book is to give students information about social work assessment that incorporates knowledge about human behavior. We emphasize an applied perspective because, in our teaching experience, we have found the human behavior content too abstract for many students. Of course, abstract theories and concepts can be useful in social work, but if practitioners cannot apply theoretical material, its usefulness is lost.

To emphasize the application of human behavior content to social work practice, we include sections on implications for practice throughout the textbook. In addition, each life-span chapter ends with a case illustration that uses the multidimensional framework to demonstrate how knowledge of HBSE can be useful for practice.

It is important for students to understand that no single theory or level of analysis can address the range of issues they will encounter in social work practice. Rather, they need a multidimensional framework to guide their critical evaluation of human behavior concerns. Therefore, this book begins in Chapter 1 with an introduction to our multidimensional framework. We also introduce students to the social-functioning framework and a hypothesis approach to evaluating each dimension in the multidimensional framework. This approach suggests questions that will help guide students to explore client concerns from a holistic or multidimensional perspective.

In Chapters 2 through 4, we discuss the multidimensional framework for integrating knowledge of social functioning. This framework, rooted in ecological systems principles, is used to structure our presentation of life-span development. These three chapters examine the three dimensions in the multidimensional framework: biophysical, psychological, and social. Chapter 2 defines key concepts from the biological sciences that students will need to understand in the biological dimension: biophysical growth and development and biophysical hazards. Chapter 3, which covers theoretical themes from the psychological, cognitive, and behavioral sciences, introduces the student to subsystems of the psychological dimension: cognitive development and information processing, communication, attitudes and emotion, social cognition and regulation, and psychological hazards. Chapter 4 examines the range of social systems in which individuals live—the social dimension: families, groups, support systems, organizations, contexts, multicultural and gender considerations, and social hazards.

The rest of the book explores life-span development—from before birth to late adulthood—through the lens of the multidimensional framework. Our book, unlike any other, provides a framework for thinking about HBSE material. In *every* life-span chapter, we use the same framework for presenting the material. This framework is then applied to a case study at the end of each life-span chapter. This provides students with an improved template for viewing HBSE material and helps to focus their attention on applying the content.

Acknowledgments

This book is not merely the product of three individuals; rather, it is the work of many dedicated people whose help has been essential in completing this project. We have been fortunate to have many assistants who have contributed to the creation and development of this book. They include Julianne Azimov, Ellen Blessington, Audrey Brooks, Anna Cleveland, Annette Cline, Nancy Disbrow, Denise Gonzales, Eddie Gonzales-Santin, Cathy Jaworski, Hubert Johnston, Kelly Lovato, Ladona (Nonie) Maupin, Kerry Milligan, Marilyn Ramirez, Lou Reed, Linda Galdieri-Ryan, Jane Wenk, Nancy Young Wright, and Ellie Yepez. Special thanks to Rebecca Melin, who worked tirelessly on permissions and on all facets of the book.

We would like to acknowledge two chapter contributors, Jayne Cooper and Shirley Patterson. Jayne and Shirley accepted the task of learning our multidimensional framework and applying it to their areas of expertise—early childhood for Jayne and later adulthood for Shirley. We sincerely appreciate their work. Shirley Patterson would also like to acknowledge the work of Susan Cho and Chris Swenson-Lugo, both of whom provided invaluable assistance on the later adulthood chapter.

No book can be successful without the help of outside reviewers who offer useful suggestions, constructive criticism, and encouragement. These reviewers took the time to critique the book chapter by chapter and contributed to a final, improved version. We would like to acknowledge and thank them for their work; they include Eddie Davis, Buffalo State College; William R. Downs, University of Northern Iowa; W. David Harrison, University of Alabama; Kenneth L. Hobby, Harding University; Stephen M. Marson, University of North Carolina–Pembroke; Bernie Sue Newman, Temple University; Paula Nurius, University of Washington; Barbara W. Shank, University of St. Thomas; Serene Thornton, University of St. Thomas; Richard M. Tolman, University of Michigan; and Libby Zimmerman, Boston University.

Peggy Adams encouraged and recruited us to take on this endeavor, and the staff at Brooks/Cole have worked hard to produce an excellent end product. Lisa Gebo took the reins, worked closely with us, and guided us on every facet of the book. We appreciate her vision, critical thinking, and diligence, which were instrumental in moving this project forward. Additional staff at Brooks/Cole who worked on this book include Laurie Jackson, production editor; Cat Morrison, permissions editor; Roy Neuhaus, cover and interior designer; Kathleen Olson, photo researcher; Romy Taormina, advertising coordinator; Terry Thomas, editorial assistant; Jean Thompson, marketing manager; and Mary Vezilich, production assistant. We also wish to thank Jan McDearmon and Barbara Kimmel, manuscript editors; and Jane Farnol, indexer.

Finally, we would like to acknowledge and thank our families for their support and encouragement during this project.

José B. Ashford
Craig Winston LeCroy
Kathy L. Lortie

A Guide Through This Book

By its very nature, a human behavior in the social environment (HBSE) text presents difficult challenges to its authors. *How much of the book should focus on development and how much on presenting knowledge about the range of social systems in which individuals live? How much biological, psychological, and social theory should be included, and how should theories be integrated to help students assess human behavior?*

In this groundbreaking book, authors José B. Ashford (who specializes in the interrelationship of human development, crime, and psychopathology), Craig Winston LeCroy (who specializes in child and adolescent behavior), and Kathy L. Lortie (who specializes in infant mental health) offer a text that is more balanced, integrated, and applied than other texts for the course. In addition, the book's multidimensional framework, integration of the biopsychosocial dimensions for assessing social functioning, attention to foundation knowledge and diversity, and use of case studies to illuminate the applied aspects of HBSE content all combine to give readers an experience that is meaningful and exciting.

The next few pages illustrate the uniqueness of this book and show why a text written by social workers for social workers can make the difference in how well students learn and retain the material.

How Do Effective Practitioners Use Their HBSE Knowledge? How Can Complex Abstractions Take on Practical Significance?

As the reader moves through the pages of this book, the answers to these questions will become clear. The resulting knowledge provides a practical and theoretical understanding of biopsychosocial development across the life span—just what is needed to enter the profession of social work.

Using a multidimensional framework, Ashford, LeCroy, and Lortie demonstrate how no single theory or level of analysis can address the range of issues encountered in the practice of social work. This framework integrates knowledge and theory from the biophysical, psychological, and social perspectives on human behavior. It also provides a template for thinking about HBSE content, which focuses attention on the applied aspects of conceptual and theoretical materials. "Implications for Practice" sections are also used to help illuminate the practical significance of HBSE concepts.

In addition, the authors use a hypothesis approach to evaluate the multidimensionality of cases, challenging readers to be systematic in their evaluation of human behavior concerns. From this approach, readers develop a holistic view of development that directs their attention to the critical assessment of such issues as race, ethnicity, sexual orientation, gender, class, abilities and disabilities, and other pivotal dimensional considerations.

Brief Table of Contents

In Chapter 1, readers will find an introduction to the authors' multidimensional framework, to the "competence" and "social functioning" frameworks, and to a hypothesis approach for evaluating each dimension in the multidimensional framework. The hypothesis approach suggests questions that help readers view clients' concerns from a holistic or multidimensional perspective.

In Chapters 2 through 4, the authors examine each dimension in the multidimensional framework: biophysical, psychological, and social. This framework, rooted in ecological systems principles, is used to structure the presentation of content on life-span development and biopsychosocial theory.

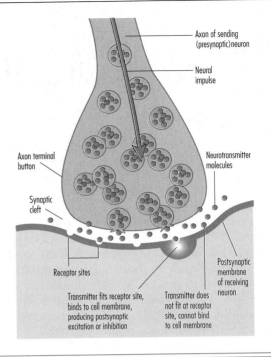

FIGURE 2.10   In Chapter 2, the authors define the key concepts from the biological dimension: biophysical growth and development and biophysical hazards. Figure 2.10, for example, demonstrates how messages are transmitted from one neuron to another.

FIGURE 3.3   In Chapter 3, the authors cover theoretical themes from the psychological dimension: cognitive development and information processing, communication, attitudes and emotion, social cognition and regulation, and psychological hazards. In Figure 3.3, for example, the authors illustrate how the psychological system processes information from the environment.

4. The Social Dimension for Assessing Social Functioning

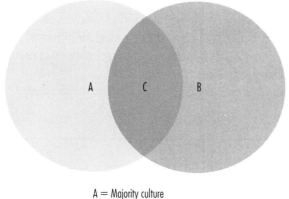

A = Majority culture
B = Minority culture
C = Shared values and norms

FIGURE 4.7   In Chapter 4, the authors introduce readers to information about the range of social systems in which individuals live—the social dimension: families, groups, support systems, organizations, contexts, multicultural and gender considerations, and social hazards. Figure 4.7, for example, illustrates how a member of an ethnic group can or is likely to become bicultural.

In Chapters 5 through 12, the authors examine life-span development through the lens of their multidimensional framework. Using the same framework to examine systematically each phase of the life cycle, the authors provide readers with a template for thinking about HBSE material. A case study at the end of each life-span chapter shows readers how the framework can be applied in actual practice.

5. **Pregnancy, Birth, and the Newborn**
6. **Infancy**
7. **Early Childhood**
8. **Middle Childhood**
9. **Adolescence**
10. **Young Adulthood**
11. **Middle Adulthood**
12. **Late Adulthood**

Appendix: Key Characteristics of Life-Span Development
The appendix presents an overview of key issues and characteristics of each phase of the life cycle.

I both enjoyed and felt I benefited from reviewing this manuscript. This is a well conceptualized and researched book. The application sections in each chapter are a real strength.

> Paula Nurius
> Social Welfare Doctoral Program Director,
> University of Washington

This text has coverage of all stages of the life span and also has excellent coverage of multicultural issues. I would recommend its adoption to a colleague over any other HBSE text I've seen, either at the BSW or MSW level.

> William Downs
> University of Northern Iowa

This text is a breakthrough. . . . The case examples are excellent. . . . Someone has finally gone beyond the status quo. . . . The major strength of the book rests with its juxtaposing the interfacing of the biophysical, psychological, and social dimensions as inextricable interacting variables in human behavior in the social environment. It confronts the diversity issues squarely.

> Eddie Davis
> Buffalo State College

[This text] is great! Very comprehensive! There is no question that there is overall coverage of all the areas that need to be covered for HBSE. There is certainly more on biology and medical issues than I have ever seen in a text.

> Jannah Hurn Mather
> Dean of Wilfred Laurier University

Be sure to check out the last page of this guide to find out more information about the accompanying Instructor's Manual with Test Items and Videos—available to adopting professors.

"Focus On" Sections Make the Material Easy to Learn

"Focus On" sections are visually stimulating and highlight multicultural issues, research, theory, history, ethics, gender, sexual orientation, and disability to reveal different voices and perspectives on the material.

"Focus on Multiculturalism: One Girl's Reflections on Being Biracial or of Mixed Race" shows readers the different challenges that individuals of mixed race confront in negotiating their daily lives.

The Social Dimension for Assessing Social Functioning   121

ter is called Indian Colored. Of course, many people categorized as Colored are of mixed Black and White ancestry. In fact, if you can prove having had a white grandparent or parent and are yourself very light skinned, you can even make an application to be reclassified from Colored to White. (Chapkis, 1986, p. 69)

Sociologists are interested in negative classification schemes that include beliefs about the abilities or traits of a racial group. They are also interested in studying any actions a society takes to use racial classifications to subordinate members of a group on the basis of color or other biological characteristics. These societal classifications change in time and are products of many social, historical, and political forces. In the United States, we have had shifting relations of power that have influenced our racial classifications. In 1860, the three classifications for the census were whites, blacks, and mulattoes; in 1890, five additions were added (quadroon, octoroon, Chinese, Japanese, and Indian); in 1990, five different groups were listed (White; Black or African American; Asian or Pacific Islander; American Indian, Eskimo or Aleut; and the ethnicity Hispanic). Each of these changes is indicative of key sociohistorical contingencies. The following Focus on Multiculturalism section poignantly describes one girl's reflections on being biracial or of mixed race.

FOCUS ON MULTICULTURALISM

One Girl's Reflection on Being Biracial or of Mixed Race

10:06 A.M. The buzz of an artificially lit classroom swarms around its third-hour occupants. Slouched in my chair at the back of the room, I try to ignore the sweat running into the collar of my T-shirt, the incessant tapping of my foot. I chew anxiously on my pen top, and the words on the paper before me swim around in a mocking blur.

No, I'm not struggling over a physics test, or an essay question in College English. This is simply a survey on student-teacher relationships given to the whole school, and I haven't made it past the first section.

Name _____. Okay, got that one. Age ___. Grade ___. Sex ___. Yeah, these are easy. Race ___. What? RACE. 1. White; 2. Black; 3. Oriental; 4. Hispanic; 5. American Indian. This is where my panic begins. I read my choices again, and my brow furrows. Basically, the problem is this: I'm racially mixed, and there is no option for me.

Now, this is not the first time this has happened. All my life, I've had to decide what race I am, which half of me to deny. I remember asking my sister one day in third grade which one I was. "We're mixed, Rach," she told me. Mixed. And for every survey, every technical form I received in every grade after, I looked for that word. The closest I ever found was "other." That always kind of amused me, but I tried it. Other; mixed. But my teachers came to me. "Mixed what, honey?" And they looked at me. "You're black. Next time, just put black, okay?" And I would go home to my mother, my single, cream-colored mother, who wanted nothing but to raise us well. Even as an intelligent 8-year-old, I was a bit confused.

My next practice, starting about seventh grade, was to circle both white and black. It made the most sense, really, but even here in high school I got in trouble. Again, the tender pressure: "Hon, you can't be *both*." So I ended up selecting "Caucasian" for the day. Recently, I went to my counselor and had that changed. See, I'm a junior, and considering colleges, and I know that as a "minority student" I'll be eligible for certain scholarships. Also, it will give me an edge at schools that are looking for a diverse student body. So I figure I'll be black for the next 5 years or so, and then go back to being myself.

But can I really go back? Can I really be comfortable with who I am if society ignores that people like me exist? Well, I can—but you must realize that I'm lucky. I grew up in Hyde Park (in Chicago), one of the most liberal integrated neighborhoods in America. My 14 years there taught me that I could exist as a mixed person, with both black and white friends. That I could be proud of my brown skin, even have fun with it. It's always great to see the look on people's faces when my mom and sister and I go out, especially with my white stepfather.

But for some kids, there is no joke. Only confusion, and the total lack of a sense of identity. These children are pressured to choose a group of friends, and in effect to choose a parent, a race, a way of life, a heritage—and

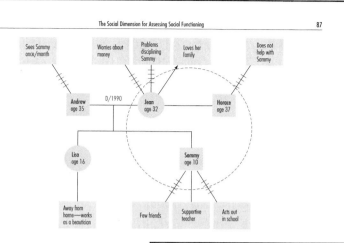

The Social Dimension for Assessing Social Functioning   87

⊢⊢⊢⊢ A conflicted or stressful relationship
————— A positive relationship
———➤ An unequal relationship; direction of the
     arrow indicates who "gives" the most

FIGURE 4.2 An ecomap Source: Jordan & Franklin, 1995.

ior: obtaining and using social work resources, adapting to life transitional problems and needs, and influencing the social environment. Recall that the social worker's task is to match clients' coping behaviors with qualities associated with the impinging environment.

According to Carol Germain (1991, p. 15), "ecology is the science that studies the relations between organisms and their environments." Critical to the ecological perspective is its holistic view of people. The ecological perspective is a metaphor that provides an understanding about the reciprocal transactions that take place between people and the social environment in which they

In this "Focus On" section, readers are exposed to the theoretical foundations underlying ecological systems theory.

86   Chapter Four

think about the experiences of a multitude of previously silenced groups (Andersen & Collins, 1995). Material and symbolic culture influences all facets of our behavior, and it is given significant attention in the analysis of social systems by most practice frameworks in social work.

Bronfenbrenner used the prior four systems to describe the environmental contexts of human development. Figure 4.1 presents Bronfenbrenner's model of the social environment. These same systems have been adopted by social work scholars to conceptualize the environmental component of our professional focus on person-and-environment transactions. Prior to the emergence of ecological systems thinking in social work, there were many simplistic views of the environment in our profession. These views frustrated most practitioners' efforts to achieve any objectives involving "environmental modification" (Grinnell, Kyte, & Bostwick, 1981). Grinnell and colleagues pointed out that these earlier concepts of environment represented: "(1) social structures (e.g., social class system, ethnicity); (2) social conditions (e.g., unemployment, discrimination); (3) social systems (e.g., economic, health, and educational networks); and (4) specific neighborhood or community resources (e.g., schools, churches, day-care centers, job training programs)" (1981, p. 153). Many other dimensions and classifications have been used in social work to categorize the environment. However, ecological systems thinking, unlike the other approaches, enhanced our ability to look at the environment in a way that allowed for its modification. This perspective redirected the attention of workers to the transactions between persons and environment, not to either person or environment variables.

Principles from systems theory direct social workers to identify relevant systems, their subsystems, and the suprasystems of which they are a part (Anderson & Carter, 1984). Social workers often achieve these ends by drawing an **ecomap.** Hartman and Laird (1983) are known in social work for having originally developed this tool for use by social workers in the field of child welfare. Their ecomapping highlights the points of connection between systems influencing a person's life and allows for the identification of points of conflict and points of support in a person's life space. Figure 4.2 presents a case example to illustrate the application of an ecomap to a social work situation.

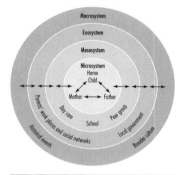

FIGURE 4.1 Bronfenbrenner's ecological model Source: Adapted from Kopp & Krakow, 1982.

To apply ecomaps and other systems-oriented concepts, you need to understand how to define the key social systems and their characteristics. We begin this process by describing the dimensions and characteristics of the family system. The family is a pivotal microsystem that influences many forms of social behavior.

FOCUS ON THEORY

Ecological Systems Theory

Social work focuses simultaneously on the person and the social environment. Figure 4.3 presents the major ideas of ecological systems theory in social work. This figure stresses the need for understanding people's coping behavior in relation to the quality of their impinging environment. It represents three types of coping behav-

A Case Study at the End of Each Life-Span Chapter Shows Students How the Framework Can Be Applied in Actual Practice

In Chapter 5, the authors help readers understand the influence of multiple factors (such as the environment, attitude, emotions, and physical state) on a couple's reaction to their premature infant.

APPLYING THE FRAMEWORK

The Family of a Premature Infant

Jessica and Travis[1] asked to see the hospital social worker to discuss their concerns for their 2-week-old infant who was in the hospital NICU. The baby had been born nine weeks premature. The couple was displaying some fear and apprehension in interacting with their baby during his stay in the NICU. They were apprehensive about their ability to parent their infant. They were worried about how they would ever be able to care for the baby on their own at home. They were also concerned about future developmental problems for their child.

Developmental History

Travis and Jessica had been attempting to have a baby for several years. Two previous pregnancies had ended in miscarriage. Fifteen months after her last miscarriage, Jessica became pregnant for the third time. She did not use alcohol or drugs during the pregnancy, but she did continue to smoke. After learning she was pregnant, though, she had managed to cut down to four or five cigarettes per day. Preterm labor began for Jessica in week 26 of her pregnancy, and she was placed on bed rest and medications at home to stop her labor. Several weeks later her cervix started to dilate, and she was hospitalized in the high-risk obstetrics unit for the duration of the pregnancy. Eric was born at 31 weeks gestation and weighed 1134 grams (2 lb. 8 oz.). The Apgar scores were 6 at one minute and 7 at five minutes. Immediately after birth, Eric began to experience respiratory distress. After a brief viewing by his parents, he was transferred to the neonatal intensive care unit.

Biophysical Considerations

Upon admission to NICU, Eric was placed under an oxygen hood. He required cardiac and respiratory monitoring. Because he was too small to maintain his body temperature, he was placed in an incubator. He required intravenous lines for maintaining fluids and administer-ing medications. Eric's very low birth weight and gestational age placed him at potential risk for continued respiratory difficulty, anemia, infection, intraventricular hemorrhage, jaundice, and retinopathy of prematurity.

Fortunately, Eric's condition improved quickly. His lungs were mature enough that his need for supplemental oxygen ended when he was removed from the oxygen hood three days after birth. He then developed jaundice (hyperbilirubinemia), but that was successfully treated with phototherapy (being placed under lights). Because he was born before his sucking reflex was well established, he required oral gavage feedings. Eight days after birth, he was transferred to the area of the NICU for "growing preemies," where he would remain until he had developed coordination to nipple- or breast-feed and had gained enough weight for discharge home.

Psychological Considerations

Jessica and Travis reported that upon entering the NICU for the first time, they found themselves totally unprepared for the sight of their baby. Alongside the machines and other technology, he appeared weak and vulnerable. Travis described his thoughts on that day: "We had lost control of the situation, and felt completely intimidated. There were machines everywhere and he just looked so small." Travis and Jessica began to worry about possible complications for their baby. As with many families when faced with high-risk perinatal situations, Jessica and Travis became focused on possible medical outcomes instead of on their new baby.

Worry and uncertainty over their child's fate began to interfere with parental attachment and bonding. Jessica and Travis found it difficult to bond with a baby they feared might die or be severely handicapped. Jessica   *(continued)*

[1]The cases in this book are loosely based on several actual cases. Names and other identifying details included in the cases in this book are fictitious.

Failure to Thrive

(continued) She reports that she experienced persistent vomiting throughout the first half of the pregnancy. Until her sixth month of gestation, she was almost unable to hold down any food or drink, and she was hospitalized three times for dehydration. She states that she and her husband, Raul, very much wanted a baby. Although she was very happy to be pregnant, she was so sick that she was glad when it was over.

At 15 months, Roberto is only now beginning to pull to stand. His mother is not sure whether he says any words other than "mama" and "dada."

Biophysical Considerations

Since he was 2 months old, Roberto has suffered from almost constant ear infections. Roberto was bottle-fed, and his mother reports that he was a very slow eater, sometimes taking over an hour to finish a bottle. Often he would only take a couple of ounces at a feeding. Roberto is especially hard to feed when he is ill. Then he has a very poor appetite. The doctor believes that Roberto's failure to gain weight makes him more susceptible to illness.

Psychological Considerations

Cognitive Development

Roberto's development seems delayed; he does not walk alone yet. His mother reports that he did not sit alone until he was 9 months old. Roberto appears to be thin and sickly and quite wobbly on his feet even when holding on to something.

Communication

Roberto says no words other than an occasional "mama" or "dada." He does startle to loud noises. He sometimes appears to comprehend basic requests, but often ignores them. He communicates mostly by pointing and grunting.

Attitudes and Emotions

Roberto's mother reports that as a baby he was loud and intense. He was very unpredictable in daily habits. He never has liked cuddling very much and has always been difficult to calm. On observation, when Roberto looks to his mother, she looks past him. When asked to hold the baby in her lap, she faces him away from her. He squirms to get down and screams until she lets him go. He plays well with his father. They make eye contact and smile at each other. His father talks to him, shows him interesting objects, wrestles on the floor with him, and changes his diaper when needed.

Social Cognition and Regulation

Roberto makes few social overtures to his mother or to the social worker during the interview. He ignores all requests from anyone. He seems interested only in exploring the room, and he can be distracted only by physical

Teen parents and their infants may need additional support. Often, teen parents do not understand developmental milestones and offer limited cognitive stimulation to the baby.

sion, increase their self-esteem, and understand their infant's temperament.

Implications for Practice: The Importance of Social Support

Infants need a safe and stimulating environment and nurturing, responsive caregivers. Several difficulties may interfere with a caregiver's ability to provide an adequate environment or to interact with an infant. As we have seen, these problems include poverty, drug and alcohol addiction, mental illness, marital difficulties, adolescent parenthood, and developmental delay. In all these situations, we have stressed the importance of social support. Mothers interact more positively with their infants if fathers are supportive and help with child care. Single, teen mothers do better with the help of involved grandparents. Parents of handicapped infants and of difficult infants fare better when they have friends who call to ask how the parents are coping or who offer to sit for the child to give the parents a break.

New parents need the help of other people—family, friends, neighbors, churches, agencies, and community programs. You may hear this African proverb often in your career, but it describes social support so well: "It takes a whole village to raise a child."

APPLYING THE FRAMEWORK

Failure to Thrive

Roberto was referred to the Growth and Nutrition Clinic by his pediatrician. The social worker in the clinic completed the initial psychosocial assessment. The baby is a 15-month-old Hispanic male who weighs 19 pounds, 2 ounces. His rate of growth has been dropping since he was 2 months old and is now well below the 5th percentile for his age. Roberto's parents both have a history of developmental delay. His pediatrician is concerned about Roberto's lack of growth and his parents' ability to adequately care for him. For this reason, he has referred the case to Child Protective Services (CPS) for failure to thrive.

Developmental History

This was the first pregnancy for Roberto's mother, Angelica. She carried the baby to term and had a normal vaginal delivery. Roberto weighed 5 pounds, 12 ounces at birth with Apgar scores of 8 and 9. Angelica denies any drug or alcohol abuse during the pregnancy. *(continued)*

In Chapter 6, the authors help readers make the connection between developmental theory and actual problems they will encounter in child welfare.

Dynamic Ancillaries

Instructor's Manual with Test Items
(ISBN: 0-534-34581-6)

Includes a special section that uniquely describes the history of HBSE in social work, multiple-choice and essay questions, ideas for class projects, guidelines for teaching the course, transparencies, and discussion questions.

Videos

Adopters of this text are provided with at least one video rental voucher from the Brooks/Cole Counseling and Social Work Video Library. Please call Brooks/Cole Marketing at (408) 373-0728 for more information.

The following videos are available for your use:

HUMAN NATURE AND DEVELOPMENT

The Social Brain
The Nature of Human Nature
Nature and Nurture

CRIME AND VIOLENCE

Domestic Violence, Street Violence
Society's Problems in Children's Lives
Juveniles and the Death Penalty

SUBSTANCE ABUSE

Addiction: The Family in Crisis
Altered States: A History of Drug Use in America

MENTAL HEALTH

No More Shame (3 tapes—choose one)
1. Understanding Schizophrenia
2. Depression
3. Addiction
Depression: Back from the Bottom
Schizophrenia: Out of Mind
Post-Traumatic Stress Disorder
Self-Image and Eating Disorders

HUMAN/CHILD/FAMILY DEVELOPMENT

The Psychology of Jung (4 tapes—choose one)
1. Carl Gustav Jung: An Introduction
2. Mind and Matter
3. Symbols and Symbolism
4. Self Knowledge
Abandoning the Elderly
To Be Old, Black, and Poor

SOCIAL PSYCHOLOGY

Racial and Sexual Stereotyping
The Differences Between Men and Women

A Multidimensional Framework for Assessing Social Functioning

Case A: Jean Davis

Jean Davis[1] is a 19-year-old woman who started experiencing difficulties in college. She moved out of the dorm because she thought other students were out to ruin her life. Her former roommate said that Jean would stay up all night reading the Bible and laughing inappropriately. Jean claims that other students in the dorm were jealous of her because of her special powers. She will not tell anyone what these powers are; when asked, she just smiles strangely. Her mother recently learned that Jean stopped attending classes. Neighbors have complained about hearing Jean pace the floors of her apartment throughout the night. Whenever the mother talks to her daughter, Jean tells her mother that she

needs to prepare because the end is near. Jean told the social worker that God speaks to her all the time, telling her that she needs to be prepared. But Jean says that she cannot tell anyone what she is preparing for. Her mother is frightened because this is not like the Jean she previously knew. She is concerned because Jean is not eating and is disturbing her neighbors.

Which statement offers the best understanding of Jean's situation? Explain your choice.

(a) Jean is suffering from schizophrenia.

[1]The cases in this book are loosely based on several actual cases; names and other identifying details included in the cases in this book are fictitious.

(b) Jean has developed an extreme fear of others and is seeking refuge in her spiritual beliefs.

(c) Jean has learned to adapt to the stresses of college and young adulthood by withdrawing from others.

(d) The lack of support in Jean's school environment caused her to seek refuge in fantasy and other escapist activities.

(e) Jean is acting irresponsibly so that she can avoid the stressful expectations in her everyday life.

Case B: Jeff Johnson

Jeff Johnson is a 27-year-old man who was arrested for two counts of sexually inappropriate behavior. He was accused of having sex with two boys from his scouting troop. Jeff was previously arrested and convicted for sex with minors but was placed on conditional probation for treatment. Jeff has virtually no relationships with persons his own age. He lives with his parents and is currently employed as a truck driver for a company that collects old newspapers. His probation officer eventually learned that Jeff kept this low-paying job primarily because it is near an area with underprivileged children whom he often paid for sexual favors. When Jeff was 12 years old, he became involved in a sexual relationship with an older man. He was in this sexual relationship for approximately five years. He also recalled being fondled in a closet by an older boy at his school when he was around 8 years old and recalled being ambivalent about the experience. Jeff reports never developing a relationship with a female or a male over 16 years of age since he stopped seeing the older man. He prefers having sex with young boys and presents vivid descriptions of what stimulates him about them physically.

Which statement offers the best understanding of Jeff's situation? Explain your choice.

(a) Jeff is suffering from a mental disorder called paraphilia of the pedophilia type.

(b) Jeff's inappropriate sexual orientation is due to his immature personality.

(c) Jeff learned his interest in molesting children from his own experience of molestation.

(d) Jeff's social situation does not provide him with effective social outlets.

(e) Jeff's behavior is morally "disgusting" or bad.

Case C: Tim Lad

Tim Lad is a 7-year-old boy who was referred by the school counselor for running away from school and for constantly fighting with other students. Tim lives with his brother, sister, and mother in a poor section of a small southwestern town. Tim's father deserted the family when Tim was 2½ years old. His father was an alcoholic and had a history of trouble with the law. Tim is very impulsive and has difficulties controlling his behavior. His teachers say that he often misinterprets the actions of others. For instance, he bumped into a boy the other day in class, and the boy told him to be careful. Tim responded with "no one tells me what to do" and proceeded to attack the other youth. Tim also has difficulties reading and sitting still in class. Tim's mother works long hours and says she is exhausted when she gets off from her restaurant job. She reports that she is not sure she can control him any longer. Ms. Lad reported that Tim has always had a bad temper but is generally sorry for whatever he does. When the social worker met with Tim, he was very cooperative and friendly throughout the interview.

Which statement offers the best understanding of Tim's situation? Explain your choice.

(a) Tim has attention deficit hyperactivity disorder and a possible conduct disorder.

(b) Tim is acting out his need for love.

(c) Tim has learned that the only way to get what he desires is to act on impulse. He has not learned to reflect on his actions.

(d) Tim is acting out because he is in a school system without adequate special education resources. His school situation needs to provide him with a substitute father figure to replace the loss of his father.

(e) Tim is a bad child who needs to learn discipline and responsibility.

In selecting appropriate responses for each of the preceding cases, some of you may have believed that all the responses correctly applied. Others may have thought that none applied. All responses were taken from established approaches for assessing human behavior with roots in biological, psychological, and social theory. Each of these theories contains concepts that are of use to the assessment process in social work.

Why Do Social Workers Study Human Behavior and the Social Environment?

What influences our behavior? What makes us act in certain ways? Is it our biological makeup, our psychological characteristics, or our social setting? As you will learn in this book, human behavior takes place in a diverse array of physical, psychological, and social contexts. In these contexts, people confront biological, psychological, and social demands that require effective human responses. The ability to respond effectively to these demands on individuals, families, and groups is known as **adaptation.** Understanding the process of adaptation is vital to practice in any human service profession. In the field of social work, Human Behavior and the Social Environment (HBSE) is the curriculum area that provides the foundation of knowledge needed for a basic understanding of the process of human adaptation.

Most of you have taken courses in anthropology, sociology, psychology, human biology, political science, and economics. These courses present a variety of approaches, concepts, and frames of reference for understanding human behavior, the social environment, and problems in living. In addition to this knowledge, you will need a framework for social work practice to help you organize the rapidly expanding knowledge from the behavioral, social, and health sciences.

This book will introduce you to a multidimensional framework for integrating knowledge and theory from biological, psychological, and social perspectives on human behavior. We stress the need for social workers to take into account the interactions of three dimensions in assessing social functioning: biophysical, psychological, and social.

The presenting problems of clients can be very complex. Any single theory will almost certainly be incapable of accounting for the whole range of forces influencing a person's behavior in the social environment. Various approaches to assessing human behavior have guided the activities of social work professionals—medical, psychoanalytic, social learning, social group, community and organizational, normative, and ecological systems. These approaches direct the way practitioners define problems and seek solutions. Focus on History: Charlotte Towle's Common Human Needs presents a historical perspective of human behavior.

FOCUS ON HISTORY

Charlotte Towle's Common Human Needs

Towle's *Common Human Needs: An Interpretation for Staff in Public Assistance Agencies* (1945) is a seminal work in our profession's clarification of its knowledge base. In this publication, Towle explained that social workers must have an understanding of basic motivations and adaptations in normal human behavior. She wrote:

> These motivations and adaptations serve all individuals throughout life in all kinds of situations. We encounter them in our clients and in our colleagues. We experience them ourselves in our professional lives as well as in our personal lives. Recognition of them in ourselves, as well as in others, may help us to function more effectively, particularly if we can see them as normal responses about which we need not be anxious and defensive or condemning. (p. 11)

In her view, workers need to understand how their emotions determine their thinking and behavior as well as the thinking and behavior of their clients. She accepted the assumption in psychoanalysis that emotions are the primary determinants of human relationships and behavior. Her book had profound implications on social work thinking because it identified needs common to all persons, not just persons in need of public assistance (Brieland, 1987). It was also considered a seminal work in the field of public assistance because it shifted the focus of assessments of human needs from physical needs to emotional needs.

Dimensions of Human Behavior and the Social Environment

What are appropriate measures for assessing human behavior? Are there different measures for assessing the social environment? Social work practitioners must be clear about how they will systematically measure or describe the characteristics of their clients. These descriptions are significantly influenced by one's perspective. As Anderson and Carter (1984) note, any viewpoint is relative to one's own perceptions and to the system being described, and its environment. Social work professionals seek a perspective of human behavior that is consistent with the principles of their professional code of ethics and their commitment to respecting individual uniqueness.

Many terms can be used to classify or define the dimensions of individuals or their situations. Sciences also have systems for classifying and measuring areas of interest. The science of social work practice is no exception. Practitioners from this profession are expected to use empirically validated classifications of behavior that transcend the biases associated with "common sense" and other forms of "conventional wisdom." These scientific classifications are needed to make important distinctions about client functioning. If practitioners lack categories or classifications for making such distinctions, they are unlikely to understand their clients' individual characteristics. Practitioners' ability to assess these differences is highly correlated with the validity of their classification system. Although social work has not established a unified system of human behavior classification, it has advocated the use of a biopsychosocial approach to understanding human behavior.

The framework that we use in this textbook subscribes to this approach. It is conceived of as a perspective and not as a theory. This perspective offers practitioners a way to consider various points of view and to integrate these points of view in their assessments of client concerns. The biopsychosocial approach is based on principles from systems thinking that assume that "Each person is composed of molecules, cells and organs; each person is also a member of a family, community, culture, nation and world" (Eisendrath, 1988; p. 36). The fundamental assumptions underlying this framework are as follows:

1. There are three dimensions for assessing human behavior and the social environment: biophysical, psychological, and social.
2. These three dimensions are conceptualized as a system of biopsychosocial functioning.
3. This system involves multiple systems that are organized in a hierarchy of levels from the smallest (cellular) to the largest (social).
4. This ascending hierarchy of systems is in a constant state of interaction with other living systems and with other nonliving components of the system's physical environment.

We assume that the multiple systems in this framework are needed to guide practitioners in understanding human development. These dimensions provide perspectives on human behavior that form the bases for various kinds of intervention strategies. They also ensure that practitioners take into account client strengths. Practitioners all too often focus on presenting problems and fail to zero in on areas of strength that can facilitate change in the person's situation (Saleebey, 1992b). A comprehensive framework is more likely to see individuals in their totality. This holistic view is especially useful in assessing social functioning.

Norton and colleagues (1978) recognized the need for a comprehensive framework that would also capture the experiences of racial and ethnic minorities. They introduced the concept of a "dual perspective," which has been influential in the integration of minority content into a social work perspective on human development. Focus on Diversity: The Dual Perspective describes this approach.

FOCUS ON DIVERSITY

The Dual Perspective

The dual perspective is a cognitive approach for understanding the behavior, attitudes, and response patterns of minority clients within the context of the dominant culture. This approach seeks to acknowledge the fact that every person is a member of two systems: the dominant

Diversity can be understood from a dual perspective that suggests that people are part of two cultures—the dominant society system and the person's own immediate social environment.

societal system and the system involving the client's immediate emotional, physical, and social environment. These two systems are referred to in this perspective as the *sustaining system* and the *nurturing system*. The duality of perspectives created by these systems is what social workers need to understand.

Social workers must understand normal expectations for behavior, attitudes, and values in the sustaining system as well as in the nurturing system. Normal expectations for childhood in the sustaining system may differ from expectations in the nurturing system. For example, children from ethnic minority homes and children in the majority culture will experience different processes that influence self-development. These different developmental tasks affect childrens' view of themselves and how they evaluate themselves against their peers to establish a sense of self-esteem. If these differences are ignored, interventions are not likely to address the child's real psychosocial needs. They are also likely to inhibit the child's engagement in an appropriate intervention plan. Latino children live in the Latino community and the wider American community. The problems they and other minority group members encounter require social workers to be sensitive to the dual perspective. It provides a cognitive device for increasing awareness of the differential experiences, values, and beliefs of oppressed persons. This framework cannot be implemented without a solid foundation of facts, events, and issues about various ethnic and racial groups. The developers of this system assumed that this content should be provided in Human Behavior and the Social Environment courses.

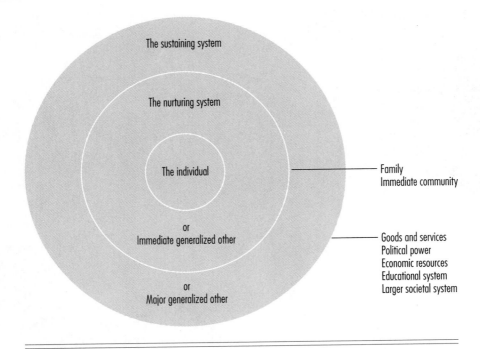

FIGURE 1.1   **Key systems in the dual perspective**   Source: Norton et al., 1978.

Figure 1.1 represents the key systems in the dual perspective. These systems represent the experiences of all minority persons. Practitioners have the duty of assessing the degrees of convergence and divergence between these systems.

What Is Social Functioning?

Werner Boehm (1958) made a major contribution to social work's knowledge base by clarifying social work's focus. Prior to the late 1950s, the profession lacked an explicit focus for understanding *persons, problems, and behavior* that was different from that of other human service professionals. Boehm (1958, p. 14) wrote that "both the complexity of man's functioning and the increase of scientific specialization have made it necessary for each profession to take one aspect of man's functioning as the primary focus of its activities." In Boehm's view, whereas the physician focuses on enhancing the client's physical functioning, the social worker should focus on enhancing the client's social functioning.

Social functioning is a technical term in social work that supports the profession's focus on person-in-environment transactions. Social functioning "involves addressing common human needs that must be adequately met to enable individuals to achieve a reasonable degree of fulfillment and to function as productive and contributing members of society" (Hepworth & Larsen, 1993, p. 5).

The concept of social functioning developed by Boehm had roots in social interaction theory and role theory. Accordingly, it directs the social worker to focus on factors relevant to the performance of roles expected of individuals by virtue of their participation in various social groups. This emphasis on social functioning helped shift the focus of social work away from the individual and toward the interaction of the individual with the environment. Such a shift had important implications for a multicultural perspective, as described in Focus on Diversity: Curriculum Changes.

FOCUS ON DIVERSITY

Curriculum Changes That Emphasize Multicultural Perspectives

With the emphasis on integrating social science in social work during the 1960s, there was also a recognition among social work educators that students needed to appreciate diversity. The urban crises of the 1960s and the Civil Rights movement also encouraged educators to explore perspectives in the social and the behavioral sciences that were sensitive to gender, racial, and ethnic variations. By 1971, the Council on Social Work Education (CSWE) instituted specific standards for accreditation that encouraged faculties to enrich their programs by including racial and cultural diversity in the student body, faculty, and staff. During the 1970s, there was also considerable discussion in the social work literature about what social workers needed to know about ethnic and racial diversity. By 1984, the CSWE's Curriculum Policy Statement required that students understand the consequences of a person's ethnicity, race, class, and gender on behavior. This knowledge area is now considered a key component of the HBSE curriculum.

During the 1970s, William Ryan (1971) published his book *Blaming the Victim*, which criticized the application of pathological orientations to social problems. This book had a major impact on many social workers. It sensitized them to the limitations in individually oriented views of behavior that placed responsibility for social problems on individuals rather than on defective so-

cial institutions. Blaming the victim generally occurs when well-intentioned practitioners set out to identify the causes or differences in the individual that explain problems or deviations from established expectations. Approaches that adhere to a blaming-the-victim ideology generally avoid the wider social origins of problems. Individuals are assigned responsibility for a situation that was essentially out of their control. Recognition of the dangers of a blaming-the-victim ideology and of preoccupation with pathology prompted movements in social work toward alternative models.

During the early 1960s, Charlotte Towle (1960) made a passionate plea to social workers to take responsibility for curricula in Human Behavior and the Social Environment. Her challenge for social workers to speak with authority on dealing with content on growth and behavior was consistent with many of the forces that propelled social workers to develop their own orientation to assessing social functioning. Social work educators devoted substantial resources to clarifying social work's distinct orientation to growth and behavior content during this period of its development. One key outcome that emerged from this history was the social functioning framework. This framework focused on enhancing individuals' *potential for social functioning* rather than correcting their deviations. This shift in focus was essentially a shift from preoccupation with defects or deficits to a focus on positive social competencies.

Social Work's Social Competence Model

Boehm's (1959, p. 31) social functioning framework led to the formulation of five major educational objectives for social workers in the curriculum area of Human Behavior and the Social Environment:

1. Understanding endowment as the source of the potential for human functioning
2. Understanding environmental forces that may enhance or endanger the potential for social functioning
3. Understanding interaction of endowment and environmental forces as enhancing or endangering the potential for social functioning

4. Understanding the person's response to change and stress
5. Understanding assessment of the potential for social functioning

This social functioning framework is often reflected in social competence models of human behavior. Wine and Smye (1981) pointed out that, in competence models,

> humans are seen as growing, changing, learning and in continuous interaction with their environments. While defect models tune their users to the observation of pathology, the users of competence models are more likely to be alert to positive behaviors and capacities in individuals. . . . People are seen as at least potentially capable of setting goals, identifying needs, and developing skills that will allow them to cope more effectively with stress. (pp. 24–25)

Competence models focus on helping people achieve their potential and on understanding the normal stresses and demands that environmental transactions place on people. "The defining characteristic of competence approaches is a concern with the effectiveness of the individual's interactions with the environment" (Wine & Smye, 1981, p. 24). Exponents of competence models are more likely to subscribe to what Garvin and Seabury (1984) have termed a *nature metaphor*. In this metaphor, the focus is on issues of growth and decay and not on deviations. Interventions derived from this metaphor focus on balancing, fitting, and matching human capabilities with environmental demands (Garvin & Seabury, 1984). (Focus on Theory: Life Models and Nature Metaphors discusses this view.) This metaphor differs from disease metaphors, which stress treatment and the elimination of causes of disease. The social functioning framework developed by Ruth Butler (1970) is highly compatible with the nature metaphor. In fact, it was developed to replace linear causal frameworks that involve disease and pathology metaphors. Focus on Theory: Medical and Disease Metaphors describes the most widely used pathology metaphor in social work: the *Diagnostic and Statistical Manual of Mental Disorders, Fourth Edition* (DSM-IV).

FOCUS ON THEORY

Life Models and Nature Metaphors

The life sciences recognize that living organisms cannot be understood piece by piece because they are greater than the sum of their parts. The complexity of living systems also rules out single causal and unidimensional explanations of behavior. Unlike machines, the functioning of an organism cannot be predicted using simple "if-then" modes of thought because living systems are constantly in a state of change. For instance, if you drink a specified amount of alcohol today and again tomorrow, we cannot predict that the alcohol will have the same effect on your behavior tomorrow that it does today. Tomorrow, your food intake may be different. This will influence the effects of alcohol on your behavior. From a life science perspective, the human organism can be understood only if changes in its multiple subsystems and in its environment are taken into account. A system cannot be understood by separating it from its internal and external environment. This living systems orientation is similar to the person-in-environment focus, which has been a thread running through much of the thinking in our profession since its inception. This is a major reason living systems principles have been adopted in social work to understand the complexity of human behavior.

FOCUS ON THEORY

Medical and Disease Metaphors— The DSM-IV

The medical approach is concerned with the identification and treatment of illnesses, diseases, and disorders. Its use is based on many of the biological assumptions that we will examine in detail in Chapter 2. Because its focus is on the identification of medically relevant conditions, social workers need to understand terms like *illness, disease,* and *disorder.* Although practitioners often use these terms interchangeably, it is best to define them separately (Nurcombe & Gallagher, 1986).

Illness refers to a person's subjective perception of being unwell (Nurcombe & Gallagher, 1986). If a person is feeling significantly distressed, then this subjective feeling may be properly assigned the label of illness. It is possible to feel *distress* after failing an important examination or losing a member of one's family. These examples demonstrate that a person can feel distress and label it an illness without having a disease. Although it is true that persons with diseases generally feel ill, there are many circumstances when a person will have a disease and not feel ill at all. For instance, many women and men have contracted cancer and are not aware of it. In fact, many women are often shocked at a diagnosis of breast cancer because they have not experienced any ill feelings. Because illness refers to subjective states, it is a concept that has been applied to many distressful circumstances not attributable to underlying diseases. The validity of how this label is applied to persons is controversial.

Disease, on the other hand, refers to "a classifiable set of symptoms and signs stemming from disturbed bodily function and associated with characteristic paraclinical findings, course and etiology" (Nurcombe & Gallagher, 1986, p. 11). Paraclinical findings include laboratory tests, psychological tests, and so forth. To appreciate the definition of disease, it is also necessary to provide definitions of symptoms, signs, and syndromes. **Symptoms** are in essence subjective complaints. They represent the subjective labels clients employ to describe their problems, distress, or dysfunction. "As such, they are greatly influenced by culture, socioeconomic status, intelligence, and symbolic capacity" (Ludwig, 1986, p. 5). The goal in a medical approach is to identify clusters of symptoms that are associated with specific diagnostic categories. If the client is presenting the symptoms associated with a diagnosis, then the clinician can use this information to define the client's problem. An

example of a symptom is feeling anxious or having a pain on the left side of your head. These symptoms involve complaints that cannot be directly verified or observed by the clinician.

In the medical approach, **signs** refer to objective findings that can be reliably observed by the trained clinician (Ludwig, 1986). These include findings from tests and other devices for measuring or quantifying the person's presenting problems. It is generally assumed in medical approaches that signs should take precedence over symptoms in the diagnostic process because they are more reliable and less susceptible to the influences of social and cultural factors. A cluster of signs and symptoms is technically referred to as a **syndrome.** If the signs and symptoms are associated with specific bodily dysfunctions, then this syndrome is considered a disease. The same reasoning applies to mental diseases and diseases affecting behavior. A mental disease involves signs and symptoms associated with defects in physical processes that contribute to mentally related impairments. By the logical extension of this reasoning, impairments in behavior not associated with underlying defects in physical functions could not be accurately classified as mental diseases.

The term **disorder** refers to a syndrome of behavioral, physical, or psychological dysfunctions less clearly defined than a disease primarily because the etiology of the dysfunctions are unknown (Nurcombe & Gallagher, 1986). In a disorder, there may be physical impairments or physical defects. However, the causal relationship between these defects and the presenting dysfunctions cannot be established. For example, many hyperactive children have a form of brain dysfunction. This is why hyperactivity used to be called Minimal Brain Dysfunction, or MBD. Yet, no corresponding etiology can be established between the observed minimal brain dysfunction and either attention deficit disorder or hyperkinetic syndrome. Many children presenting with these dysfunctions do not have any observable brain damage. Today, the metaphor of a disorder is applied widely in social work to address problems in living and social functioning. It is particularly used by practitioners who use the current *Diagnostic and Statistical Manual* (DSM-IV). The DSM-IV is the most widely used classification

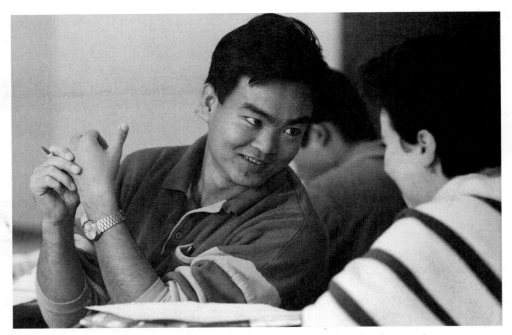

Asian American youth must adapt to unique demands in their environment, and social workers must be sensitive to the special tasks confronting such youth.

system in mental health for understanding and classifying mental disorders.

Practitioners subscribing to an approach for assessing social functioning that relies on the DSM classification system must determine whether deviations observed in thought, mood, or behavior are consistent with an established diagnostic category in the DSM classification system. Classifications are included in this system only if they comply with the system's definition of a mental disorder. Nurcombe and Gallagher (1986, p. 232) have summarized the key assumptions underlying the definition of a mental disorder in the DSM system:

1. A psychological or behavioral syndrome
2. Causing distress or disability
3. Stemming from physical, psychological, or behavioral dysfunctions
4. And not solely a reflection of disturbance between the subject and society

Many categories included in this system address either excesses or deficits in behavior, thought, or mood.

Implied in this approach is that effective social functioning involves the absence of a disorder or a disease.

Tasks and Life Demands

The emphasis in a social competence model is on helping clients realize their potential. Social workers need to understand the demands and life tasks people encounter if they are to help people realize their aspirations. To this end, Bartlett (1970) suggested the concept of *tasks* to assist workers in assessing their clients' life situations. The concept of tasks plays a key role in social functioning and in social competence frameworks. By asking the question "What tasks are confronting my client?" the worker can focus on key biopsychosocial demands. For instance, what biopsychosocial demands confront a half-Asian youth in achieving a sense of identity during adolescence? What tasks confront a 16-year-old girl who is losing her hair while undergoing chemotherapy? Each adolescent is confronting distinct biopsychosocial demands. The worker must understand each of these demands to help the youth adapt to the social environment. Besides having knowledge of life tasks, social workers also need an understanding of how people respond to problems in living. Bartlett (1970) refers to these common responses to life tasks as **coping,** and they are considered a key component in any approach to assessing social functioning.

Maluccio (1981) points out that competence is a theme present in the writings of several pioneers in social work education, including Mary Richmond (1917) and Bertha Reynolds (1942). Although these pioneers addressed competence concerns, competence was primarily an implicit component of their approaches. In response to this lack of specificity, Maluccio (1981) introduced an ecological approach to competence that supercedes many of the other prior conceptual frameworks on this topic in social work. His ecological competence model has three major components: capacities and skills, motivational aspects, and environmental qualities. These components represent Maluccio's attempt to conceptualize the multiple dimensions of competence and their dynamic interplay. For many social workers, this model provides an excellent conceptual approach for assessing person-and-environment transactions. In fact, we believe that the ecological systems theory is the best overall framework for social work practice.

If social workers are to focus their activities on enhancing individuals' responses to their life tasks, should they also understand disease and pathology metaphors? That is, should practitioners direct their activities toward treating and correcting client deviations? In this text, we have assumed that the answer to this question is yes. We take this position because illnesses and pathology often affect a person's social functioning.

For instance, clients with schizophrenia have significantly impaired effectiveness in role functioning. The practitioner must understand how this disorder affects the clients' abilities. Equipped with this knowledge, social workers can better focus their activities on enhancing clients' skills to meet the demands of their environment. The social worker's duty, regardless of the particular field of practice, is to select the right view of behavior for the right circumstance. Focus on History: Medical and Psychiatric Contributions looks at how the fields of medicine and psychiatry have affected social work's view of human behavior.

FOCUS ON HISTORY

Medical and Psychiatric Contributions

The influence of medical professionals on social work education was especially significant in early curriculum development. Courses on medical and psychiatric information were made part of the required minimum curriculum for several reasons. The medical information presumably exposed social workers to needed information from the biological sciences that improved social work services. For instance, family caseworkers needed to understand normal growth processes in children if they were to properly assess the effects of social relationships on a child's health and welfare needs. Similarly, psychiatric knowledge was presumed essential because it equipped the social worker to deal with behavior concerns. Herman Adler and his colleagues (1932) presented a forceful argument at the National Conference of Social Work about the need for welfare personnel to be trained in human behavior. He pointed out that the one common denominator underlying most social problems is human behavior. He stated:

> Just as in the field of public health a medical education is almost essential, and in the field of education training and experience in pedagogy is necessary, so in the field of public welfare a thorough knowledge, both theoretical and practical of the nature and treatment of behavior disorders should be regarded as a prime requisite. (Adler et al., 1932, p. 435)

This quotation clarifies how human behavior knowledge emerged as an essential foundation for practice in social work and how it is rooted in psychiatric thought.

In this period of history, psychiatric knowledge did not focus just on illness, "behavior disorders" were also considered a part of the psychiatric knowledge base. The prevention of behavior problems fell under the province of psychiatry during the mental hygiene and child guidance movements. These movements assumed that illnesses and problems resulting from behavior could be prevented by early identification and intervention. Adolf Meyer, the psychiatrist who coined the term *mental hygiene*, included social workers in his holistic approach to psychiatry (Macht & Ashford, 1991). His approach directed psychiatrists and social workers to have "knowledge from biology, physiology, psychology and sociology to understand human behavior" (Blashfield, 1984, p. 16). Social workers were to investigate aspects from each of these knowledge areas in performing a comprehensive case history.

The Person-in-Environment System

The person-in-environment (PIE) system was designed to assess problems in social functioning. It provides social workers with a common classification system for communicating about client problems (Williams, Karls, & Wandrei, 1989). This system presents four factors used in describing client problems:

Factor I: Social-role problems
Factor II: Environmental problems
Factor III: Mental disorders
Factor IV: Physical disorders

All four factors are considered necessary for describing a client's problems. The first two factors address the components in a social functioning assessment handled primarily by the social work practitioner. In this system, social functioning refers to the client's ability to accomplish the tasks necessary for daily living (such as obtaining food, shelter, and transportation) and to fulfill his or her major social roles as defined by the client's community or subculture (Williams, Karls, & Wandrei, 1989). This system sets up explicit categories for identifying problems in social-role functioning and for establishing a list of environmental systems and problem areas. Factor III addresses mental disorders, and Factor IV includes any medical conditions that might affect social functioning.

In the PIE framework, the social worker describes the problems, their severity, and their duration. This framework uses the established categories and codes defined in the manual for describing client problems. As in the DSM-IV, this system operationally defines the categories, terms, and codes used in classifying client problems. Use of this system might increase social workers'

reliability in defining social functioning concerns. Without reliable definitions of social functioning problems, we cannot accurately assess whether problems are increasing or decreasing. We also lack a shared system for communicating about problems. The PIE system is presently undergoing field tests similar to those applied to the DSM-IV. With the benefit of a universal definition of social functioning, researchers will have an easier task trying to assess the prevalence rates of problems in social functioning typically found in the practice of social work.

The following example illustrates how a complete case would look when applied to the PIE system (based on Williams, Karls, & Wandrei, 1989). This case involves a 68-year-old woman who was admitted to the hospital with fever and confusion. Neighbors reported that the confusion had been increasing over the last few weeks. The patient was diagnosed with a urinary tract infection and was treated with intravenous antibiotics. When the medical problem was resolved, however, the confusion and disorientation was not. Because of this increasing confusion, the hospital staff determined that the woman would be unsafe returning to her apartment alone. Because the woman had no savings and only a limited income from social security, she was unable to afford in-home care. The woman's son wanted to help out, but because of his lifestyle as a musician and single father, he was unable to care for his mother in his own home. The patient was adamant about returning to her own apartment. The social worker obtained a psychiatric evaluation of the woman, which determined that she was suffering from dementia and was unable to make her own decisions. On discharge from the hospital, the social worker and the son, against the patient's wishes, placed the woman in an assisted-living home that was willing to accept the social security payments in exchange for care. Over the next two weeks, the woman, who had always been proud of her independence and strength, became increasingly despondent over her living arrangements.

Factor I
Social-role category: other nonfamilial (tenant)
Social-role problem: status/status change
Severity: 4, high
Duration: 5, two weeks or less
Coping skills: 4, inadequate

Factor II
Environmental system: economic/basic needs
Environmental problem: shelter and care (unable to care for self in own apartment)
Severity: 4, high
Duration: 5, two weeks or less
Factor III
Dementia
Factor IV
Urinary tract infection, resolved

On Factor I, the worker indicates the role relationship in which the client is having a problem. The worker also establishes the type of role problem, its severity, and its duration. On Factor II, the worker identifies the physical or social environmental systems affecting the client and the type of problem, its severity, and duration. A key benefit anticipated from this system, besides research, is a shared approach for communicating and defining client problems that results in improved treatment effectiveness. Focus on History: Medical and Psychiatric Contributions examines how medical and psychiatric contributions evolved in social work.

The Biopsychosocial Interaction

Individuals and their environment represent multiple systems that extend from the biochemical to the psychosocial realm (Nurcombe & Gallagher, 1986). The biological realm of an individual extends from the molecular to the molar; the psychological realm extends from the emotional to the behavioral. The social realm of an individual includes the family and groups, the neighborhood, the cultural setting, and the context of society. Such multiple sources of influence can be described as a person within a body, within a family, within a state, within a country, within the world, within the solar system, within the galaxy, and within the universe.

A person's constitution is who he or she is individually (genetic makeup, past learning, and so forth) and socially or environmentally (the social forces in the environment). Behavior is the result of interactions between the person and the environment. A person's biological makeup can limit his or her capacity to respond to the environment in certain ways.

It is important to understand that no single factor can be solely responsible for causing a behavioral response. Multiple factors, within a complex system, interact to produce specific behaviors. When we think of the biopsychosocial interaction, we recognize that certain biological problems, cognitive processes, or certain environments can increase our prediction that a particular behavioral response will develop.

Human behavior has a multidimensional aspect. For example, attention deficit disorder in children can have a strong genetic component. However, some children that possess this genetic component will not develop attention deficit disorder, indicating that biological factors do not completely determine who will develop the disorder. We must also consider psychological and social or environmental variables in accounting for people's behavior. A parent's interaction with a child can exert a profound amount of influence. A child with a small tendency toward hyperactivity may be influenced by a parent in such a way as to reinforce and promote more hyperactive behavior. A child exposed to high amounts of lead, through lead-based paint, can develop symptoms of attention deficit disorder.

As a social worker, you must understand that explanations of human behavior need to be multidimensional to adequately explain human behavior. This, however, makes it difficult to plan treatments. Systems explanations are useful for understanding the total picture of the client but are not specific enough to be helpful for designing an intervention. Social workers must break the system into separate parts, considering each part's contribution to the client's problem while at the same time keeping in mind the total system.

In social work we seem to either emphasize the total picture through a systems model or focus on specific components for assessing and planning treatments. Unfortunately, neither is adequate. You must take into consideration the broad picture in assessing a client and then move to an understanding of some of the relevant factors that could be influencing your client's behavior. To become more adept at examining independent factors, we suggest that you learn how to formulate hypotheses, within a framework for understanding human behavior. In our framework we move from individual factors to social and environmental factors. It is our expectation that this will help you think about human behavior from a more multidimensional perspective.

Multidimensional Framework

The **biophysical dimension** of this framework consists of the biochemical systems, cell systems, organ systems, and physiological systems (Nurcombe & Gallagher, 1986). This dimension looks at an individual's physical growth and development and is described in Chapter 2. The functioning of this system refers to the balanced exchange of energy among its biophysical components. Any change in this dimension will have corresponding changes in the other dimensions inside and outside this system. Therefore, this dimension also considers physical hazards that may affect an individual's behavior.

The **psychological dimension** represents the systems that contribute to the organization of the individual's mental processes. This dimension involves several functions designed to help the person achieve a sense of satisfaction of his or her needs. These psychological functions involve the systems of information processing and cognitive development, communication, attitudes and emotions, regulation and social cognition, and psychological hazards. These systems are described in detail in Chapter 3.

The **social dimension** refers to the systems of social relationships that a person interacts with individually or in a group (Nurcombe & Gallagher, 1986). This final dimension is described in Chapter 4. The social groups and relationships included in this system are families, other support systems, gay and lesbian relationships, cultural groups, ethnic groups, and other social contexts such as churches, political parties, schools, and health care and welfare institutions.

Applying the Multidimensional Framework

To understand a person's total functioning, the social worker makes an assessment of all aspects of the person's life and experience. It is helpful to take a hypotheses approach to each primary dimension and its underlying functions. Hypotheses from the biophysical, psychological, and social dimensions are posed in order to examine possible etiology and explanations of the client's functioning. Using a hypotheses approach can help guide the questioning and data gathering of social workers during the assessment phase.

The following outline suggests specific areas of potential questioning to consider for each hypothesis in making an evaluation of a client.

I. Biophysical hypotheses
   a. Biophysical growth and development
   b. Biophysical hazards
II. Psychological hypotheses
   a. Cognitive development and information processing
   b. Communication
   c. Attitudes and emotions
   d. Social cognition and regulation
   e. Psychological hazards
III. Social hypotheses
   a. Families, groups, support systems, and contexts
   b. Multicultural and gender considerations
   c. Social hazards

We expand on this outline by presenting a brief overview of how this framework can be applied in gathering data in an assessment. But first, we provide examples of some potential assessment considerations to use in making your evaluation. This is not a conclusive list of assessment questions, other information can and should be considered. Each of the developmental chapters in this book goes into further detail and provides other considerations for you to use. When reading the case study at the end of each developmental chapter, keep these suggested considerations in mind. Also, think of other questions you would want to ask or obtain answers to when evaluating the client's problem in each case study.

Biophysical Hypotheses

Physical or biological hypotheses refer to assumptions about the client's functioning as a result of a biological catalyst. Examples include influences from the autonomic nervous system, the neuroendocrine system, physical dependence on a drug, or a biological reaction to an environmental event. The social worker should seek to understand the client's general physical condition. Assess information about the client's medical history including any diseases, neurological impairments, physical impairments, current physical condition, and any medications being taken. A client's problem may be related to or a direct result of the following biological determinants.

Biophysical Growth and Development

Prenatal Growth and Development Assessment considerations include mother's nutritional status during pregnancy, mother's health status, father's health status, length of gestation, prenatal substance abuse by mother, pregnancy complications, family genetic history, genetic abnormalities, chromosomal abnormalities, and physical birth defects (cleft palate, heart defects).

Client's History of Attaining Developmental Milestones Assessment considerations include when did client take first steps, say first word, feed self, dress self, achieve toilet training, have first menses or first wet dream, and develop sex characteristics.

Client's General Health Status Assessment considerations include stability of weight; regularity of menstrual periods; regularity of sleep-wake cycle; level of physical activity and level of nutrition; presence of biochemical imbalances; presence of physically handicapping conditions; use of substances such as tobacco, alcohol, and drugs; assessment of client's general appearance (does client look his or her stated age); and client's ability to perform activities of daily living (ADLs).

Biophysical Hazards

Problems with General Health Status, Including Problems with Any Major Organ System Assessment considerations include family history of heart disease, respiratory problems, cancer, diabetes; health status of close relatives; cause of death of close relatives and age of death of those relatives; client's current and past health status; and presence of symptoms related to a major illness.

Psychological Hypotheses

The social worker must consider many relevant psychological hypotheses when making an assessment in this dimension. Psychological data can be gathered through a variety of means. Most relevant to the social worker is the individual or family interview. In addition to the tra-

ditional psychosocial interview, social workers are making use of semistructured interviews as well as psychological tests, behavioral observations, personality tests, and rapid assessment instruments.

A client's problem may be either related to or a direct result of the following psychological determinants:

Cognitive Development and Information Processing

Client's Attention Span, Memory, Concentration, and Capacity for Abstract Thought Assessment considerations include ability to focus attention, ability to complete tasks appropriate to age, and capacity for memory.

Client's Learning Abilities and Performance Assessment considerations include school performance, problem-solving abilities, and capacity for insight and reflection.

Communication

Client's Language Ability and Vocabulary Assessment considerations include bilingual expectations, use of language, and general verbal and nonverbal abilities in self-expression.

Attitudes and Emotions

Client's Self-Perception Assessment considerations include negative and positive perceptions of self, view of self with others, comparison of self with expectation of others, and perception of what others think about the person.

Client's Emotional Responses Assessment considerations include full range of emotions evident and excessive emotions such as anger, sadness, or frustration.

Client's Self-statements Assessment considerations include content of self-talk, amount of irrational ideas present, and relationship between self-talk and problem behavior (e.g., fear and hopelessness).

Client's Perception of Others Assessment considerations include client's view of others, view of others' expectations of client, and extent to which perception is reality based.

Social Cognition and Regulation

Client's Social Knowledge About Others   Assessment considerations include client's understanding about social interactions, client's view of friendship, and client's expectations of others.

Client's Capacity For Empathy   Assessment considerations include client's capacity for perspective taking, client's sense of morality, and client's interpersonal understanding of others.

Client's Reality Base   Assessment considerations include client's cognitive functioning, client's ability to discern reality, and content of client's thoughts and perceptions.

Client's Social Skills   Assessment considerations include appropriateness of client's social interactions, client's knowledge of social skills, and client's ability to communicate effectively.

Client's Social Problem-solving Skills   Assessment considerations include client's ability to generate solutions to problems, client's ability to think of consequences, and client's means-ends thinking (steps needed to solve problems).

Client's Maladaptive Behavior Patterns   Assessment considerations include client's behavioral response to problem situations; client's patterns of behavior that lead to difficulties for self, others, or society; and client's desired behavior changes and patterns.

Psychological Hazards

Client's Experience of Past Life Events   Assessment considerations include client's description of significant events in childhood, client's experience with parents and other adult figures (especially whether any physical or sexual abuse occurred), client's experience with peers, client's psychosocial living environment, client's history of past diagnosis of a mental disorder, and history of use of antidepressants or antipsychotics.

Client's Experience with Recent Life Events   Assessment considerations include client's description of significant life events in recent years, client's recent experiences with adult and peer figures in his or her life (especially events such as divorce or parent's divorce, death of a loved one), present use of antidepressants or antipsychotics, and use of other prescription drugs.

Social Hypotheses

The social worker's assessment extends beyond the biological and the psychological to include the social. Social factors include the family, social support systems, access to resources, and the impinging social environment. What are the client's social relationships? And what is the environmental context of the client's social relationships? For example, does the client live in poverty or does the client face racism on a daily basis? It is important for the social worker to assess how the client is viewed by society, by the social systems he or she interacts with, and by the individuals directly involved with the client on a daily basis, such as friends and family.

A client's problem may be related to or a direct result of the following sociological or environmental determinants.

Families, Groups, Support Systems, and Contexts

Family's Boundaries, Systems, and Subsystems   Assessment considerations include open or closed family system, family structure (e.g., enmeshed or disengaged), and how the family defines itself.

Family's Patterns of Communication   Assessment considerations include content and process of interaction, patterns of conflict, and verbal and nonverbal expressions of affect.

Family's Roles   Assessment considerations include role assignments within the family, satisfaction with roles, expectations and definitions of roles, allocation of power, and role strain and support.

Groups the Client Interacts With   Assessment considerations include patterns of interaction in peer and work groups, influence of group norms and other group dynamics, and behavior of the individual in the group.

Support Systems Available to the Client Assessment considerations include social supports (family, friends, extended family, social support or self-help groups), institutional supports (child support, welfare, health benefits), access to resources (day care, recreational facilities, police protection), barriers to support systems, and need for new resources and support systems.

Environmental Context of the Client's Problem Assessment considerations include who in the external environment perceives the client's responses as maladaptive, external factors likely to influence client behavior (such as loss of job, aging, relocation), and stressful factors in the environment (poverty, racism, underemployment).

Multicultural and Gender Considerations

Cultural and Gender Context of the Client's Life Assessment considerations include ethnic or gender identity; degree of acculturation; sexual orientation; language barriers; amount of interaction within and outside the ethnic group; and expectations influenced by cultural, gender, or sexual-orientation considerations.

Social Hazards

Social Context of the Client's Life Assessment considerations include high rates of unemployment, divorce, poverty, discrimination, inadequate social institutions, and impoverished neighborhoods.

Hypotheses Help You Select Interventions

When you select a hypothesis as a way of explaining a person's behavior, it should help you select an appropriate intervention. For example, if your assessment suggests that the best hypothesis for understanding a person's behavior is based on his or her biochemical makeup or brain chemistry, then an intervention that changes an individual's physiology should be considered. If a client is diagnosed as having a schizophrenic disorder that you believe is due to biological factors, then that person should be referred for psychotropic drug treatment. Of course, the client might also need psychosocial treatment as well.

If you develop a hypothesis that a person's difficulty is due to inappropriate social learning, then the intervention will focus on providing the client with a new learning experience. For example, if the person has developed a serious phobic disorder of open spaces (agoraphobia) and you believe this is related to some negative learning experiences, then the intervention will attempt to provide the client with some new positive learning experiences. The intervention might use contact desensitization, where the goal is to induce a state of relaxation and then expose the client gradually to the feared stimulus. This procedure provides a new learning experience for the client.

If you develop a hypothesis that the person's problems are related to the environment, then the intervention should be one that focuses on environmental changes. For example, you may be working with a child who has come to your attention because of extreme withdrawal behavior and discover that the child is suffering from serious physical abuse. The determinant of the child's problem is primarily environmental. Here, the intervention is to change the child's environment. You may make arrangements for the state child welfare department to remove the child from his or her home environment. By giving the child a new environment—placement into a foster home, for example—you control the child's environment and provide new experiences to meet the child's needs for safety and proper development.

Behavior can also be changed by helping the client access new resources. Often clients simply need information and resources. For example, a client may need help in obtaining housing or material resources. The intervention is either providing the information or resources or making a referral so the client can access the resources.

In summary, hypotheses help you think about the various determinants of human behavior. We encourage you to think about human behavior in terms of different hypotheses. In this way, you will become better skilled in assessment. And the better you are in assessment, the more effective you will be in providing services.

Overview

In the first part of the book we describe theoretical and conceptual themes that influence development within the biophysical, psychological, and social dimensions. In the second part of the book, the life-span development portion, each life stage is introduced with a review of developmental themes. These sections reflect Erik Erikson's view that each stage contains certain life tasks that need to be achieved for optimal development (see Chapter 3, Focus on Theory: Erikson's Psychological Development). Each developmental chapter then discusses in-depth factors that affect behavior in the biophysical, psychological, and social dimensions. Each of the dimensions in this framework provides a distinct outlook on problems in social functioning. Each dimension also suggests different strategies for intervention that must be synthesized for an appropriate response to a client's problem. For example, a client suffering from a severe psychosis needs interventions directed at multiple levels. Biological concepts from neurobiology suggest psychopharmacological interventions to address the psychotic systems, psychological concepts to deal with the client's expectancies regarding his or her condition, and social concepts to address the supportiveness of the individual's environment. These multiple strategies are needed because of the complexity of the problem situations encountered in the practice of social work. Social workers do not have the luxury of limiting their description of problems to a single dimension. Using a single dimension to assess social functioning ignores the total person. It also implies the existence of a unified theory of human behavior. Because there is no unified theory of social functioning, we assume that it is inappropriate for practitioners to adhere to a single explanation of social functioning.

Our multidimensional framework cannot be considered comprehensive. Other dimensions can be used to assess social functioning concerns. However, we will review only dimensions that have received the profession's sanction and are supported by established scientific disciplines. This does not mean that you should ignore other dimensions in your evaluations of client functioning. In fact, careful evaluation of information from these specified dimensions will sensitize you to issues requiring the development of other dimensions relevant to assessing social functioning concerns.

Keeping in mind the multidimensional influence of these systems, it is important to recognize that a person is more than the sum of his or her parts. Each aspect is in constant interaction with the other dimensions.

Chapter Summary

Social workers need a multidimensional framework for integrating the knowledge and theory from biological, psychological, and social perspectives on human development. No single theory or approach to intervention can account for the whole range of forces influencing social functioning. A multidimensional framework was presented that includes the following assumptions: (1) There are three dimensions for assessing human behavior—biophysical, psychological, and social; (2) these dimensions compose a system of biopsychosocial functioning; (3) these multiple systems are organized in a hierarchy of levels from smallest to largest; and (4) this hierarchy of systems is in constant interaction with other systems.

Social functioning is the primary focus of a social worker's orientation to human development. Social functioning takes a person-in-environment perspective, which suggests that common human needs must be met for individuals to function effectively in society. How individuals perform their roles in order to participate in society represents the interaction of the individual with the environment. The social functioning framework is similar to social competence models. In the social competence model, the focus is on helping people achieve their potential and on understanding the normal stresses and demands on people in their interactions with the environment. A useful way of looking at this is by examining the tasks that confront people in adapting to their environmental situation. In addition, how people respond to these tasks can be better understood by looking at their coping abilities. The PIE system was specifically designed by social workers to assess problems in social functioning.

System explanations are useful in alerting us to the multidimensional nature of human behavior. When combined with a hypotheses approach, a multidimensional perspective allows us to systematically evaluate the impact that different dimensions and their complexity have on client functioning. This perspective also ensures that practitioners focus their attention on the person's whole situation, including his or her personal and environmental hazards and strengths. The multidimensional framework includes the following:

I. Biophysical dimension
    a. Biophysical growth and development
    b. Biophysical hazards
II. Psychological dimension
    a. Cognitive development and information processing
    b. Communication
    c. Attitudes and emotions
    d. Social cognition and regulation
    e. Psychological hazards
III. Social dimension
    a. Families, groups, support systems, and contexts
    b. Multicultural and gender considerations
    c. Social hazards

KEY TERMS

adaptation	disorder	social dimension
biophysical dimension	illness	social functioning
coping	psychological dimension	symptoms
disease	signs	syndrome

The Biophysical Dimension for Assessing Social Functioning

What biological processes affect human growth and development? Exactly how do these processes affect aspects of an individual? What information do social workers need in order to understand how biology affects behavior? Since the inception of social work as a profession, biological knowledge has been recognized as a fundamental foundation for effective practice (Schwitalla, 1930). Yet the knowledge base of social workers in clinical and other areas of practice has been virtually unaffected by the veritable explosion of knowledge in the biological sciences (Saleebey, 1985). Social workers tend to be better versed in the psychological and social facets of the profession's biopsychosocial framework (Johnson et al., 1990).

Yet, many functions performed by social workers require biological knowledge. These functions include screening, referral, collaborating services with medical and psychiatric caregivers, case monitoring and advocacy, and psychotherapy (Johnson et al., 1990). It follows that without relevant biological knowledge, practitioners can make bad referrals or engage in inappropriate screening and other caregiving activities. Most reviews of social work curriculum during the 1980s revealed minimal evidence that the profession was translating biological knowledge into assessment, intervention, prevention, and education strategies (Saleebey, 1985). This problem was particularly acute in the area of clinical practice (Cohen, 1988; Gerhart & Brooks, 1983; Libassi, 1990).

As a result, the Council on Social Work Education took specific actions aimed at increasing the social work student's knowledge of adverse effects of psychotropic medication on patients (Libassi, 1990). Of course, there are other reasons social workers need to understand brain and behavior relationships and their biochemical substrates.

This chapter reviews the biophysical dimension that is included in our multidimensional framework for assessing social functioning. It looks at aspects of cell systems and organ systems involved in human growth and development. It also explores the biochemical aspects of neuroanatomy relevant to current explanations of alcoholism, depression, schizophrenia, impulsivity, and violent behavior. Also included are characteristics of neurotransmitters that are important in psychopharmacological interventions. Each component of the biophysical dimension contributes to the physical maturational and developmental concerns examined in our development chapters. This chapter also examines several theories concerning the biological aspects of development, beginning with Focus on Theory: Evolution and Inherited Behaviors.

FOCUS ON THEORY

Evolution and Inherited Behaviors

Evolution is an early biological theory that has played a significant role in creating a biological basis for behavior. This theory seeks to help us understand the mechanisms and factors that have contributed to the development of humans as a species. Evolution tries to identify how much the species has changed over time and to explain why these changes have occurred. A key concept in this field of study is *variation*.

Variations are differences between individual organisms that affect their functioning. Some variations in organisms are due to outside conditions involving the physical and social environment—for example, the weather, rich soil, availability of nutritious food, effective social supports, presence of predators, and other external

factors. The variations or differences in individuals produced by these factors are considered acquired developmental characteristics.

Lamark, an early evolutionary theorist, assumed that these acquired traits could be passed from generation to generation. In other words, as an explanation for why a particular tribe of people eats a certain plant, Lamark's theory might assume the people in the tribe learn to eat the plant because it is abundant and tastes good. The knowledge to eat this food would then be inherited by offspring of the tribe.

Lamark's thesis was challenged by Charles Darwin in his book, *The Origin of Species* (1859/1958). Because of Darwin's work, we now know that acquired developmental characteristics cannot be inherited. Instead, Darwin established the principle of natural selection as the key mechanism underlying variations observed in species. This mechanism selects traits that are useful to the survival of the species. According to natural selection, a tribe would eat a certain plant not only because it is plentiful and tastes good but because the tribe possesses an enzyme that allows them to digest that plant and use it as food. This ability to digest would be inherited, and persons who possess this enzyme would have a more plentiful food supply and therefore a greater chance at survival than would those who do not possess the enzyme.

The principle of natural selection offers a general explanation of how humans changed from lower to higher forms. Yet natural selection does not offer an explicit description of the specific mechanisms involved in the process of inheritance. This mechanism was not discovered until Mendel's (1866) work on inheritance was rediscovered (Vale, 1980). It was not until we understood genes that the actual explanation for variations in organisms were understood. For example, people in a tribe choose a particular plant as food because tribe members possess a gene that produces the enzyme that allows them to digest the plant. They would pass that gene to their offspring, giving them a survival advantage over another group of individuals who did not possess the gene and could not eat this plentiful food source. Thus, Darwin's major contribution to science was his identification of a principle that explained why species vary.

Darwin's theory was not easily accepted by some. Before Darwinism, humans were perceived as being special creatures who could be distinguished from animals on the basis of their intelligence. This fundamental notion was turned upside down when Darwin linked the development of humans to the development of animals. This linkage involved the connection of animals to intelligence, and by logical extension, of humans to instincts (Vale, 1980). Darwin's contribution then not only added to our understanding of human development but also challenged cherished conceptualizations of human nature.

Biophysical Growth and Development

In the study of human behavior, the growth and development of the biophysical aspects of a person play a central role, and social workers are expected to understand how changes occur in biophysical processes. **Growth** is the technical term that refers to the addition of new biophysical components, such as new cells, or an increase in body size (Schuster & Ashburn, 1992). **Hyperplasia** refers to the type of growth observed in the fetal and early phases of development, which involves an increase in the number of cells (Schuster & Ashburn, 1992). It is eventually replaced by **hypertrophic growth,** or growth involving an increase in the size of cells. In fact, most of our growth after adolescence involves hypertrophic growth.

In a biological sense, development can be studied from a hierarchical perspective. The biophysical dimension in our framework is part of the larger biopsychosocial system. This larger system represents the person in the social environment and is organized in a hierarchy from the smallest (biological) to the largest (social). Biological systems can also be organized from the smallest to the largest, beginning at the cellular level and progressing to tissues, organs, and organ systems. Physical development can be studied from this progression.

Cells are the smallest unit of living matter known to scientists. Most cells are too small to be seen without the aid of a microscope. When cells are grouped together, they form *tissues*, which have varying characteristics according to their function. Examples include connective tissue, muscular tissue, nervous tissue, and epithelial tissue (the outer surface of the skin) (DiMatteo, 1991). Tissues also combine to form organs. Organs serve specific

functions in the body's system but do not work independently of one another. They combine to form systems that serve various functions in maintaining life forms. Each of our organs is assumed to contain optimal growth periods. If in an optimal growth spurt the organism is subjected to adverse conditions, then there is a danger of serious impairment. That is, body tissue is most sensitive to permanent damage in these periods of rapid growth (Schuster & Ashburn, 1992).

Development refers in the biophysical dimension to the refinement or improvement of body components. Most adherents of a maturational view of human development assume that any species will follow a typical path of development that is determined by genetic processes. The process by which persons inherit general pathways that constrain their growth and developmental processes is referred to as **canalization.** Some aspects of human development seem to be canalized, or genetically determined, and regardless of environmental conditions, these predetermined pathways limit the degree of variation observed in a species. For instance, most normal human infants will learn to walk. This ability is genetically determined and only a severely deprived environment would alter the development of walking in a normal infant.

We will begin our discussion of how biophysical growth and development can affect human behavior by looking first at genetic transmission and then at specific biochemical processes in the nervous system. First, though, Focus on Theory: What Is Sociobiology? looks at what this discipline has contributed to our knowledge of human behavior.

FOCUS ON THEORY

What Is Sociobiology?

The discipline of sociobiology involves studying the biological contributions to the social aspects of behavior observed in animals. In 1975, E. O. Wilson published *Sociobiology.* This book has as its primary focus the objective of understanding animal behavior, but it also offers some controversial speculations about the contributions of biological processes to the social aspects of human behavior. Wilson summarized his book in a well-quoted phrase: "Genes hold the culture on a leash." Wilson and other sociobiologists believe that there are important similarities between the way people act and the unthinking behavior of animals. Did you ever wonder why animals and even insects display courtship rituals before mating? Lower animals also commit "crimes" similar to those committed by humans. Mallard ducks commit rape, chimpanzees form groups that conduct warlike raids on neighboring tribes, and ant colonies have a social hierarchy that includes slaves. Lower animals also commit acts of altruism not unlike those of people. For example, bees will die to save the beehive, and birds will often warn of an oncoming predator even though the warning most likely will result in the bird's death. Wilson's work was significantly influenced by the principle of *genetic altruism*. William D. Hamilton, an entomologist, put forth this principle in 1964 (Maxwell, 1991), which is referred to elsewhere in the literature as the "selfish gene." "The key point is that altruism is not 'really' performed for the good of others, it is performed for the good of the gene that selfishly 'wants' to be included in future generations" (Maxwell, 1991, p. 6). For entomologists, this principle explained altruistic behaviors observed in insects and animals. Thus, when a mother runs back into a burning house to save her two sons, sociobiologists believe she is compelled at a biological level. This self-sacrificing, altruistic behavior is simply a gene's way of working toward continued existence. This perspective, sociobiologists argue, is the result of billions of years of evolution. Basically, we got to where we are today on the basis of our genes through the process of natural selection. This explains how altruistic behavior may have evolved as an adaptation (Kalat, 1995).

Wilson's *Sociobiology* was initially seen as a new form of social Darwinism. Social Darwinism refers to the social theoretical movement that ascribed the domination of one group over another to the selection by nature of the fittest group, commonly referred to as "survival of the fittest." As a consequence, many researchers approached it with grave suspicion. Yet, it stimulated them to explore a number of issues involving the relationship between genes and culture. It eventually led to Wilson collaborating with Charles Lumsden (1978) in develop-

ing a theory of gene-culture coevolution. This theory addressed a number of interesting problems. Why do very distant cultures have many characteristics in common? How did cultures originate? The emphasis was on trying to understand the genetic bases for many cross-cultural universals observed in human behavior.

Ideas stimulated by this theory have been some of the most controversial issues of the nature-versus-nurture debate. Some argue that the theory is too simplistic, that genes do not plan and scheme on their own accord. Instead, it could be argued that people learn new ways to behave in response to situations and they pass these learned behaviors on. Also, if selfish genes do exist, social norms would be likely to conquer them. Other theories, like behaviorism, contend that people act certain ways based on what they have learned from the environment. The ideas of coevolution bring the nature-nurture controversy into perspective. People are not all genes. Yet, a "gene's eye" view of behavior suggests the power of genes to influence behavior but not directly control it. Genetic evolution occurs because a form of behavior is selected for its adaptive function. In the end, behavior is a combination of genes, culture, and environment—and in what proportion will receive continued debate.

Genetics and Human Behavior

Social workers require some basic knowledge of cellular growth because they encounter many people with dysfunctions or defects in cellular processes. These breakdowns in natural growth processes can occur in formative or growth phases of development or after the organism has reached maturation. Such defects can play a significant role in many aspects of a person's behavior. Inadequate growth can place the person at definite risk for behavioral dysfunctions and for disease. For this reason, we will provide a brief overview of cellular growth processes from a genetic perspective. A genetic perspective is chosen primarily because it represents one of nature's key control mechanisms for directing the kinds and amounts of cells needed for effective adaptation.

Genetic information is contained within each cell of the human body. This information is located on chromosomes—threadlike structures found in the nucleus of the cell (see Figure 2.1). Specific traits of an individual,

FIGURE 2.1 The top portion of the figure shows chromosomes during mitosis. The bottom portion shows matched and sorted chromosomes.

such as hair color, eye color, and height, are coded in genes located on the chromosomes. Each body cell contains 46 chromosomes.

Mitosis is the cellular process by which a body cell reproduces itself by dividing and producing two new daughter cells, each with 46 chromosomes. When cells reproduce themselves, they do so at varying rates. For instance, blood cells reproduce as rapidly as every 10 hours (Schuster & Ashburn, 1992), whereas muscle cells can wait several years before reproducing and nerve cells do not reproduce at all once a full complement has been established. It is through these processes of cell division that growth and development occur.

The cell division that creates the reproductive or sex cells is called **meiosis.** The sperm and egg cells (also known as gametes) formed in this process have only half of the parent cell's genetic material, or 23 chromosomes. At conception, the mother and father each provide 23 chromosomes through each gamete. The offspring then develops from a single cell formed by the union of these two gametes—one from each of the parents—a sperm and an egg. The single cell formed from this union contains 46 chromosomes, or 23 pairs of chromosomes. Of these pairs, 22 pairs are **autosomes.** Autosomes are any chromosomes other than sex chromosomes. The pair of sex chromosomes consists of two X chromosomes in females and one X and one Y chromosome in males (so named because of their shape). Each of these autosome and sex chromosome pairs consists of many genes, which represent the basic units of inheritance.

If the human species has evolved through variations caused by genetic inheritance, how have these variations occurred? One source of variation observed in humans involves problems in cell division. In this variation, one parent contributes "something other than exactly one copy of each chromosome" (Kalat, 1995, p. 462). Any process that affects this copying of chromosomes from each of the parents contributes to major variation in an organism's characteristics. Chromosome disorders occur when an alteration takes place either in the structure or the number of chromosomes.

As we have discussed, in the process of fertilization, male and female gametes should unite 23 single chromosomes from each parent and produce a single cell containing 46 chromosomes. However, errors can occur in which the offspring has more or fewer than the normal 46 chromosomes. Problems with chromosomes that affect growth and development are discussed in the section on chromosome disorders.

Problems that affect development can also occur with the genes located on the chromosomes. When two parents unite in a reproductive effort, there are approximately 1 million genes available for forming a new progeny (Beck, Rawlins, & Williams, 1988). This potential for the recombination of genes is why offspring have a new combination of genes that differ from their parents. *Recombination* is a major source of the variations observed in offspring. Variations in organisms can also be due to changes in a gene. This process is referred to as **mutation.** Mutations are random events that can distort key characteristics in an organism's growth and development.

Problems with genes can also occur in the expression of particular traits associated with specific genes. We know that many inherited characteristics involve genes that follow simple Mendelian ratios in trait expression (Kalat, 1995). (Mendelian refers to Gregor Mendel, whose work in 1865 involving inheritance of attributes in flowering sweet peas laid the foundation for modern genetics.) These Mendelian ratios of expression are determined by analyzing the combinations of gene pairs. At conception, when the 23 chromosomes from each parent unite to form a single cell, the chromosomes pair up; the genes for specific traits found on these chromosomes also pair up. Individuals inherit a great variety of gene pairs. In a gene pair, each individual gene for a specific trait is known as an **allele.** In other words, each person inherits one allele for a trait such as eye color from the mother and one allele for eye color from the father. These alleles form gene pairs and determine the eye color of the individual.

Some alleles are dominant and others are recessive. When both alleles for a given trait are identical (for example, both for brown eyes), they are **homozygous.** When the two alleles are different (one for brown eyes and one for blue), they are **heterozygous.** A **dominant gene** (brown eyes) produces the same characteristic (brown eyes) in an offspring regardless of whether it pairs with an allele that is the same (brown eyes) or different (blue eyes), whereas a **recessive gene** (blue eyes) requires the presence of another recessive allele (blue eyes) for the expression of that trait (blue eyes) in the individual.

We will use the following notations to indicate whether a gene pair is homozygous (*AA* or *aa*) or heterozygous (*Aa*). "By convention, geneticists refer to Dominant Alleles with capital letters and to Recessive Alleles with small letters" (Rauch, 1988, p. 137). If two heterozygous (*Aa*) persons mate, they each contribute a dominant *A* gene to 50% of their offspring and a recessive *a* to 50% of their offspring. See Figures 2.2 and 2.3 for a diagrammatic representation of this process. These ratios would produce 25% *AA* offspring (with two dominant genes for a particular trait), 50% *Aa* offspring (with one dominant and one recessive gene), and 25% *aa* offspring (with two recessive genes for a particular trait).

The type of genes inherited (*AA, Aa, aa*) is the **genotype.** The characteristic actually displayed in the individual (hair color, eye color) is the **phenotype.** So a person may have a heterozygous genotype (*Aa*) of one gene for brown eyes (dominant) and one gene for blue eyes (recessive), but the phenotype or displayed eye color would be brown. A person with a genotype of two dominant genes for brown eyes (*AA*) would have a phenotype of brown eyes, and a person with a genotype of two recessive genes for blue eyes (*aa*) would have a phenotype, or displayed characteristic, of blue eyes. In this way, dominant and recessive genes contribute factors to dominant- and recessive-based disorders.

Social workers involved in pediatric settings, child welfare, developmental disabilities, health care, and other forms of practice involving young children must have an understanding of the relationship between genetics and various developmental disabilities and birth defects. That is, social workers need to have a fundamental understanding of the basic types of genetic disorders. The genetic component of a variety of other problems is also gaining substantial support. For instance, many mental health problems have genetic components. We will explore various types of genetic disorders and their causal mechanisms in the following sections of this chapter. This discussion is intended to sensitize you to the types of disorders commonly encountered in direct practice. Basic knowledge of these disorders is needed to counsel family members and make appropriate referrals for genetic counseling.

The three fundamental types of genetic disorders are single gene, multifactorial, and chromosomal. **Single-gene disorders** refer to inherited dysfunctions or defects that result from dominant, recessive, or X chromosome–linked genes.

Dominant Single-Gene Disorders

Huntington's chorea is a disorder involving a dominant autosomal gene. This disorder has a 50-50 chance of occurrence in an offspring. Because the gene for Huntington's chorea is dominant, we will refer to that gene as *H* and the recessive or non-Huntington's gene as *h*. An affected individual will have a genotype of *Hh* and a phenotype of having the disease. When this affected individual produces a child with another person, the chance of that child inheriting the dominant or *H* gene is 50%.

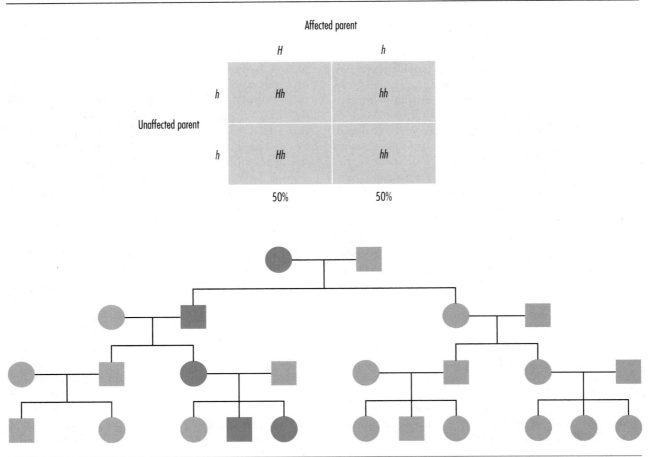

FIGURE 2.2 Autosomal dominant transmission   Source: Rauch, 1988.

Each parent contributes a gene to the offspring. The affected person with the genotype of *Hh* might contribute the dominant *H* or the recessive *h* gene to the offspring. When the parent with this allele contributes a recessive *h* rather than the dominant *H*, the child will have an *hh* pair and avoid the disorder. However, when the parent with the *Hh* allele contributes the dominant *H*, then the offspring will have this condition. Huntington's chorea is a serious disorder that is characterized by progressive chorea (purposeless motions) and the eventual development of dementia (mental deterioration). This disorder is of particular concern because it often does not manifest itself until the fourth decade of life. By this time, the affected individual most likely will have already had children before discovering that he or she has the disease. And half of these children may also have the disease.

Another example of a dominant genetic disorder is *Apert syndrome*. This syndrome involves mental retardation and structural abnormalities in a person's cranial bones. Persons with this syndrome have a towerlike skull and total fusion (**syndactyly**) of their fingers and toes. *Myotonic dystrophy* is another example of a disorder believed to be due to a dominant gene. Persons with this condition have difficulty in relaxing their contracted muscles. In fact, this disorder is considered one of the most common forms of muscular dystrophy (Abuelo,

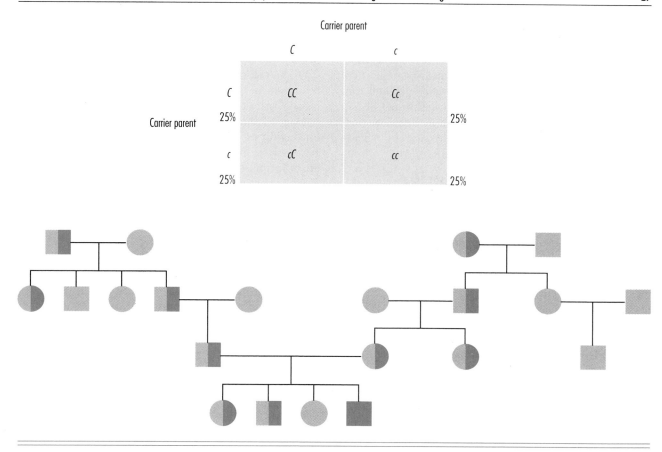

FIGURE 2.3 Autosomal recessive transmission   Source: Rauch, 1988.

1983). Persons with this disorder become progressively weak and are highly susceptible to respiratory infections.

Some dominant genes when present with a recessive gene do not entirely control the inherited characteristic. This condition is called *incomplete dominance*. For instance, the dominant gene for red blood cells that are round does not totally mask the effects of a recessive gene for *sickle-cell disease*. Individuals with sickle-cell disease have sickle-shaped blood cells that tend to clump together. This clumping causes severe pain for the individual. These sickle-shaped cells also cause problems because they distribute less oxygen through the circulatory system than normal cells (Sigelman & Shaffer, 1991).

Sickle-cell disease occurs most often in African Americans and does not have a cure (Rauch, 1988). Some individuals who are carriers of this disease can have many round cells but are likely to also have some sickle cells. These sickle cells do not have an impact on the person's functioning except in stressful circumstances. In stressful situations, persons with this condition of incomplete dominance may experience some symptoms of the disease.

Sickle-cell disease is often encountered by persons working with members of the African American community. One out of every 12 African Americans carries the gene for this condition (Rauch, 1988). This condition also occurs in persons of Mediterranean extraction, from

Greece, Italy, and Turkey, and has been found in persons from malarial regions of the world such as Indo-China and China. A prominent feature of this disease is anemia. A person with sickle-cell disease has a life expectancy that is significantly compromised, but many adults with this condition have lived well into their seventies. Social workers involved with persons affected by this condition seek to reduce the stresses that place the affected individuals at risk for serious health complications.

Recessive Single-Gene Disorders

Most single-gene disorders affect some aspect of the body's structure and are often serious and life threatening (Rauch, 1988). Single-gene disorders are not limited to those caused by dominant genes. Autosomal recessive genes also contribute to genetic disorders. We all carry abnormal recessive genes. These genes will cause no ill effects unless we mate with a person who is also carrying an abnormal gene. If two persons carry the same abnormal gene, the chance is 1 in 4 that their offspring will inherit two of these recessive genes (Abuelo, 1983). For example, Figure 2.3 displays the probability of inheriting a recessive disorder such as cystic fibrosis (CF). Between 1 in 20 and 1 in 30 whites carry the recessive gene for CF on chromosome 7. If two people with this recessive gene marry and have a child, each parent has a genotype of *Cc*, one dominant gene that does not cause the disease and one recessive gene that does. Because the dominant gene overpowers the recessive gene, the parents do not have this disease. When these parents have a baby, there is a 25% chance that the child will have a genotype of two dominant genes *CC* and will not have the disorder; a 50% chance that the child will have the genotype *Cc* and, like the parents, not have the disease; but a 25% chance that the baby will inherit two recessive genes *cc* and have cystic fibrosis.

Cystic fibrosis is a serious disease of the exocrine glands that causes secretion of excess, thick, body fluids. The disease occurs in 1 out of 1600 to 1 out of 3600 live births. The affected individual has difficulties with lung function and digestion, among other problems. In years past, many children died of cystic fibrosis, but with improved medical care, children with this disease are living into adulthood. The average life span in 1993 was 29.4 years. As adults, individuals with CF are still quite ill and often are limited in their ability to function. These indi-

viduals may require the services of a social worker, especially in coping with chronic illness and reduced life expectancy as a young adult.

The risk of both parents carrying a recessive abnormal gene is increased for persons who are related by blood. First cousins are at a substantially higher risk of having a child with birth defects because they have one-eighth of their genes in common (Abuelo, 1983). For example, the risk in the general population of having an offspring with mental retardation is approximately 3–4%, whereas the risk of mental retardation for the offspring of cousins is approximately 6–8% (Abuelo, 1983). (Please note that this is a population statistic, however, for individuals whose genotype is unknown. The risk for those related by blood of each having a recessive gene is higher, but for any two individuals, related or not, where each are known to have a recessive gene, the risk of the offspring having the disorder is 25%.)

The prevalence of abnormal recessive genes is often higher in certain ethnic groups. For instance, Ashkenazi Jews have a 1 in 30 chance of being a carrier of the recessive disorder **Tay-Sachs disease.** Tay-Sachs disease is a neurodegenerative disorder characterized by progressive mental and physical retardation. Most children with this disease die between 2 and 4 years of age. The chances of occurrence of this disorder are 1 in 300 in the general population (Abuelo, 1983).

Whenever social workers encounter a rare genetic disorder, they should take a genetic history and explore whether the parents are related. In isolated rural areas and on islands, the gene pool is reduced, which results in individuals running the risk of sharing a common ancestor without knowing it. Careful questioning is needed to discern any indication of potential consanguinity. Also, it should be noted that the risk for abnormalities in offspring from an incestuous relationship rises as much as 30%, whether it involves father and daughter or brother and sister (Abuelo, 1983). Thus, social workers should rule out the possibility of incest whenever there is a negative history for a rare recessive disorder and a teenage mother is involved.

X Chromosome–Linked Disorders

The third form of single-gene disorders involves any condition that is associated with X chromosome–linked genes. That is, these disorders are influenced by a single gene that is probably located on the X chromosome. Y chromosomes are shorter than X chromosomes and, as a result, have fewer genes. The genes on the X chromosome then have no corresponding allele on the Y chromosome that could possibly overpower the effects of a harmful gene on the X chromosome. For instance, red-green color blindness occurs most often in males. This scenario is most probable if a male has a recessive gene for color blindness on his X chromosome, because it cannot be overpowered by a matching dominant gene on the Y chromosome. Thus, males are more likely to have red-green color blindness because they lack a gene for this trait on the Y chromosome. Females can have this condition only if they have recessive genes for color blindness on both of their X chromosomes (Sigelman & Shaffer, 1991).

Hemophilia is a condition due to a defective gene on the X chromosome that causes a problem with blood coagulation. This condition is often referred to as the bleeder's disease. Hemophilia also occurs mostly in males, who have no corresponding gene on the Y chromosome to overcome the effects of this X chromosome–linked gene. *Duchenne muscular dystrophy* is another form of X-linked genetic disorder. However, "Not all types of muscular dystrophy are X-linked recessive; some are *autosomal dominant* or *autosomal recessive*. In other cases, there is no family history of muscular dystrophy; these so-called sporadic cases are thought to be due to a change in a gene (mutation)" (Rauch, 1988, p. 62).

Lesch-Nyhan syndrome is another disorder that involves a gene on the X chromosome. It is characterized by mental retardation, spasticity, and self-mutilation (Abuelo, 1983). Children with this condition often bite their fingers and lips and have abnormal physical development. This genetic disorder creates an inborn error in the metabolism of purine. Infants with this condition appear normal at birth. In fact, the first sign of difficulty emerges when the primary care-giver discovers orange sand in the infant's diapers. This sand is crystals of uric acid that result from the infant's inability to metabolize purine (Abuelo, 1983). Children with this condition often stand out in terms of their aggressiveness. *Fragile X syndrome* is another disorder linked to the X chromosome. However, it is considered a chromosome disorder and therefore will be discussed in that section.

Multifactorial Disorders

This second major group of disorders is characterized by the interaction of multiple genes and environmental factors. The mechanisms underlying these disorders are poorly understood. It is difficult to isolate the effects of environmental factors on these conditions. The environment can play a significant role in the presentation of multifactorial disorders. If the environment buffers the person from reaching a given threshold, then the person will not develop the characteristics of the genetic aberration. There is an increased incidence of persons contracting these conditions who have relatives with the condition. However, if they have this genetic liability, it does not mean that they will get the disorder (Rauch, 1988). An excellent example of this principle is seen in cancer. Many individuals with relatives that have had cancer do not develop the condition.

A group of disorders known to be associated with multifactorial inheritance is neural tube defects. These disorders involve conditions in which a child has an open defect in the brain or spinal cord. Included in this group are anencephaly, encephalocele, and spina bifida (neural tube defects are described in more detail in Chapter 5). These are serious conditions that are usually accompanied by severe mental retardation and sometimes result in death (Abuelo, 1983). The risk for neural tube defects is 1 in 500 for persons in the United States. The condition with the best prognosis among neural tube defects is spina bifida. In fact, smaller percentages of persons with this condition have developed severe mental retardation in recent years. Surgical advancements have greatly improved the prognosis for persons with this condition. Although some anencephaly and other neural defects may have a genetic basis, others may be due solely to environmental causes, such as lack of folic acid in the mother's diet during pregnancy.

In effect, multifactorial disorders have a genetic component, but this component is dependent upon the environment for its presentation. For instance, some persons may be at risk for developing structural abnormalities that will be triggered by less exposure to alcohol during prenatal care than others. Thus, the interaction of many variables are involved in the causation of disorders, and one, two, or more of these variables will be genetic. Careful assessment is needed, as it is difficult to isolate the genetic component for many forms of multifactorial conditions.

Chromosome Disorders

Chromosome disorders represent the last major class of genetic disorders. The development of these disorders is due to a variety of problems in cell division of which translocation and nondisjunction are the most common.

Meiotic errors, during the process of forming gametes, can occur in the formation of either the sperm or the egg and are not hereditary. Remember that during meiosis the pairs of chromosomes must separate to form sex cells with only 23 chromosomes each. During this process, a piece of a chromosome may break off and attach to another chromosome. This is called *translocation* or *deletion*. The chromosome lacking genetic material results in defects that are contingent on what genetic information was deleted from the chromosome.

Chromosome disorders are often a result of too many or too few chromosomes—45 or 47 chromosomes rather than the normal 46. Failure of paired chromosomes to separate during meiosis is called *nondisjunction*. Nondisjunction can contribute to three chromosomes for one cell (trisomy) or only one chromosome for a cell (monosomy). These types of abnormalities underlie many of our identified chromosomal disorders.

Down syndrome or *Trisomy 21* was the first chromosome abnormality identified by scientists (Foster, Hunsberger, & Anderson, 1989). About 95% of Down syndrome cases result from an extra number 21 chromosome. At conception, the newly formed cell has three number 21 chromosomes because chromosome 21 did not separate during meiosis. Thus the offspring received one number 21 chromosome from one parent and two number 21 chromosomes from the other. Risk for this problem is highly associated with advancing maternal age. After age 35, the risk increases and remains about the same up to about age 40. At 40, the risk increases dramatically. The reason for this association between age and increased risk for Down syndrome is unknown. One plausible explanation is associated with the aging of the body's system. That is, the body fails, as a result of age, to recognize and spontaneously abort chromosomal abnormalities. Another explanation often given in the literature is that the eggs are exposed to environmental threats for longer periods of time and accordingly are more likely to encounter errors in the meiotic process.

Down syndrome is not the only type of disorder resulting from an additional chromosome. There are two syndromes with a lower frequency of occurrence that are associated with extra chromosomes: Trisomy 18 (Trisomy D) and Trisomy 13 (Trisomy E). Trisomy 18 is the second most common autosomal disorder with an incidence of 1 in 3000 live births. It is characterized by multiple deformities and severe mental retardation. This disorder is more prevalent in females, and survival is generally for no more than three months. Trisomy 13 occurs in approximately 1 in 5000 births and is present on rare occasions on chromosome 14 or 15. This disorder is associated with many types of central nervous system abnormalities. Newborns with this syndrome rarely live beyond six months of life.

The last major type of chromosomal disorder that we will discuss in this overview involves the X chromosome. The first syndrome that we will discuss is called **fragile X syndrome.** It is a form of serious mental retardation that is identified in karyotype studies (microscopic study of the chromosomes) by a constriction at the end of the long arm of the X chromosome. In some circumstances, the portion below this constriction is broken, which is why the disorder is labeled fragile X syndrome. Although the exact incidence of this condition is unknown, fragile X is believed to be second only to Down syndrome as a genetic contributor to mental retardation. This syndrome, which occurs in males, is characterized by nonspecific mental retardation, large testes, speech defects, and large protuberant ears (Foster et al., 1989).

Many sex-linked defects in chromosomes are undetected until early adolescence because some of these disorders are identified only by an individual's failure to develop secondary sex characteristics. Klinefelter's and Turner's syndromes are excellent examples. In **Klinefelter's syndrome,** the most common of the sex chromosome disorders, the child is born with an extra X chromosome (XXY). Males with this condition have gynecomastia or femalelike breasts, mild mental retardation, underdeveloped testes, and attendant personality difficulties involving body-image problems. It is the most common condition associated with male infertility.

Turner's syndrome is the chromosomal disorder resulting from only one X chromosome, and it occurs in 1 out of 3000 live female births. That is, females with this condition have an XO genotype and a number of physical stigmata that are correlated with a lack of secondary sexual characteristics (Lemeshow, 1982). Women with this condition are short in stature, have a webbed neck, and often have congenital heart problems and kidney difficulties. However, mental retardation is not necessarily a characteristic, and when present, it is generally mild. Doctors have begun treating these women with estrogen during adolescence to enhance their development of secondary sex characteristics. Most persons with Turner's syndrome will achieve an adult height of 5 feet. Genetic counseling is needed when a mother has a child with this condition to identify future risk (Foster et al., 1989).

Implications for Practice

Social workers often confront clients who have irrational beliefs about the causes of disabilities observed in their children. They may unnecessarily blame their mate for their child's problem or blame themselves for behaviors that have no bearing on the true cause of their child's problem. Social workers must understand the different types of genetic disorders in order to make effective referrals and dispel many of the misconceptions clients hold. In fact, many parents operate on a number of false assumptions that are easily addressed by exposing the parents to relevant educational materials. It is shocking how many families have been destroyed by misinformation about developmental and physical disabilities.

Social workers are also operating more and more in autonomous capacities (Lebassi, 1990). In these situations, social workers end up determining, for many of our indigent clients, whether these clients are referred for genetic counseling. Genetic counseling is an essential service from which many clients can benefit. This counseling helps family members identify the risk of occurrence of a given genetic disorder. Families need this information to make plans about having additional children. Genetic counseling also provides information and advice about options available to a couple given each partner's family history. When parents have a disabled child, some of the stress about having additional chil-

dren can be minimized if they learn that their child has a disorder with a low probability of occurrence. Often, parents are in a state of shock when they are given the initial diagnosis. Thus, the genetic counselor or social worker can play a major role in clarifying information that is unintentionally distorted by family members.

Social workers also need to focus on genetic issues in their assessments to help clarify the etiology of many of the problems encountered in practice. If social workers do not consider family genetic history in their investigations, they may fail to identify patterns that can provide essential clues to the causes of various behavioral and developmental disturbances. Many conditions with a genetic basis often follow similar patterns among family members. (See Focus on Genetics: Genetic and Environmental Effects on Human Behavior.) This information may be overlooked unless the worker pursues family background information. Thus, the genetic and biological bases for behavior are essential components of human functioning that cannot be ignored by practitioners in assessment of human behavior functions and dysfunctions. Focus on Genetics: Prader-Willi Syndrome takes a close look at an interesting genetic defect.

FOCUS ON GENETICS

Prader-Willi Syndrome

Prader-Willi syndrome (PWS) was introduced to medical literature in 1956. This syndrome results from a deletion of a portion of the long arm of chromosome 15 (Chu, Cooke, Stephenson, & Tolmie, 1994). Prevalence is estimated to be 1 in 15,000 births. Characteristics of this syndrome include infantile hypotonia (deficient tone or tension), early childhood obesity, mental deficiency, short stature, small hands and feet, and hypogonadism (small genitalia). In addition, behavioral disorders primarily associated with food and eating occur in older children and adults affected by this disorder. Because symptoms of PWS become more noticeable as the child ages, infants and young children display fewer

Our knowledge of the developmental needs of children with Prader-Willi syndrome has developed over time. As this picture illustrates, not all children with Prader-Willi syndrome need early hospitalization or become grossly overweight.

symptoms than do older children and adults. Many features of PWS are nonspecific or are expressed subtly, and significant variations can be observed in individuals with this syndrome. Diagnostic criteria were recently developed (see Holm, Cassidy, et al., 1993).

The Prenatal, Neonatal, and Infancy Stages   Decreased fetal movement and abnormal fetal positioning are often reported (McCamman, Rues, & Cannon, 1988). An absent or weak, kittenlike cry is also noted (Holm, Cassidy, et al., 1993). The most distinguishing characteristics of infants with PWS are extremely poor muscle tone, tendency to sleep most of the time, and unresponsiveness to internal and external stimuli (Neason, 1994). Decreased muscle tone in the neck and facial areas results in a weak or absent sucking reflex and contributes to poor weight gain during the first year of life (McCamman, Rues, & Cannon, 1988). Neuromuscular studies are normal, although motor landmarks such as sitting independently and walking are delayed (Holm, Cassidy, et al., 1993). Parents benefit from referrals to a pediatric physical therapist for information on handling, positioning, and exercise to assist their infant through developmental stages (Neason, 1994). Although hypogonadism at birth may go unrecognized in females, in male infants the penis is quite undersized and the testicles are small and undescended.

Childhood   The hallmark of early childhood for a child with PWS is excessive weight gain between 12 months and 6 years of age (Holm, Cassidy, et al., 1993). The PWS Association (PWSA) describes this as "thriving too well" after a period of "failure to thrive." However, this compulsion for food correlates with improved muscle tone. Parents are often encouraged when their child begins to eat and gain weight, but this feeling fades when the appetite is seemingly insatiable and weight gain leads to obesity (McCamman, Rues, & Cannon, 1988). Suggested interventions include locking the refrigerator and the food cabinets, supervising food preparation and meals, promptly clearing food items after meals, and alerting friends and neighbors to not overfeed the child (Neason, 1994). Speech and language difficulties are common, and although the cause is unclear, speech therapy is recommended to assist with the communication problem of poor articulation. While developmental delay is apparent in children younger than 6 years of age, older children have a range of cognitive functioning from learning disability to mild mental retardation (Holm, Cassidy, et al., 1993).

Adolescence and Adulthood   Obesity remains the primary problem of individuals with PWS as the person matures and food-seeking problems persist. These problems are compounded by temper tantrums and outbursts, oppositional behavior, manipulation, rigidity, and obsessive and compulsive behaviors (Holm, Cassidy, et al., 1993).

According to the PWSA, sexual development is deficient, and fertility of either sex has not been documented. Secondary sex characteristics do not develop, and hormonal replacement is necessary (Holm, Cassidy, et al., 1993).

Family Involvement and Social Work   The PWSA was established in 1975 to assist in educating parents and professionals about the disorder. The PWSA's suggestions for families include taking legal steps to secure guardianship of the individual as an adult prior to the age of 18 to prevent conflicts in decisions about living arrangements, contracts, and medical care. Behavioral problems tend to escalate during the teenage and adult years, and higher-than-average incidence of psychosis occurs in adult PWS individuals. The PWSA recommends that the individual be placed in a group home between the ages of 18 and 20 for socialization, behavior modification and food control, and adjustment to a different living situation before an emergency arises, such as the death of the parents, intolerable behavior, or life-threatening obesity.

Source: Written by Cathy Jaworsky.

FOCUS ON GENETICS

Genetic and Environmental Effects on Human Behavior

Jim Springer and Jim Lewis are identical twins, separated just 6 weeks after they were born. Reunited 39 years later in a study of twins conducted at the University of Minnesota, they discovered that they had married and divorced women named Linda, married second wives named Betty, and named their first sons James Allan and James Alan, respectively. That's not all: They both drove the same model blue Chevrolet, often vacationed at the same small beach in St. Petersburg, Florida, and owned dogs named Toy (Begley, 1988, p. 80).

Are the striking similarities between these two brothers the result of similar environmental influences, pure coincidence, or the fact that they share the same genes? And what accounts for their differences? To what extent does one's genetic makeup influence behavior, and to what extent is the environment a factor? This issue is commonly referred to as *nature versus nurture*.

There are two major methods for studying whether family resemblance is a result of shared heredity or shared environment. The first method is *twin study*, in which researchers examine whether identical twins raised in the same environment are more similar to each other on particular attributes than are fraternal twins raised in the same environment. If heredity is an important prerequisite for the occurrence of a trait, identical twins, because they share the same genotype, should be more alike than fraternal twins (Plomin, 1990).

The other common family study is *adoption study*, which focuses on siblings who are adopted and reared apart from each other. An example would be our identical twins who were adopted apart at birth and raised in different environments. The degree to which these raised-apart twins are alike reveals the impact of heredity. The resemblance these twins would have to members of the family in which they were raised reveals the impact of environment.

Family researchers suggest that about 50% of the differences between people on IQ scores are genetic (Plomin, 1990). Personality characteristics, such as extroversion and neuroticism, show heritability of about 40%. Various forms of psychopathology, such as schizophrenia, show evidence of genetic transmission—about 30%. Genetics also seems to influence such behaviors as delinquent and criminal activity.

Recent research by Robert Plomin (1994) indicates a significant genetic influence in human social development for such attributes as empathy, attachment, and social competence. In fact, Plomin predicts that, by the turn of the century, researchers will no longer have to rely on twin and adoption studies but will be able to pinpoint specific genes that directly affect genetic variability among individuals. Just recently, in fact, scientists have found a link between a particular gene and the personality trait of novelty seeking. Persons with a gene for novelty seeking score higher on such traits as impulsiveness, excitability, quick temper, and extravagance (Ritter, 1996).

According to recent research, therefore, one-third to one-half of all differences in behavior can be attributed to genetics. This means, however, that most differences in human behavior are a result of the environment. How, then, does the environment shape behavior?

Previously, researchers believed that shared environment contributed to similarities among family members. Shared environment refers to the physical environment of the home, the family's socioeconomic status, parents' style of parenting, and so on. Research now seems to indicate that shared environment has almost no influence on differences in behavior among siblings (Tellegen et al., 1988). Thus, when family members resemble each other, this resemblance is due to genetics.

Family members are different because of their nonshared environment—those aspects of the environment that they do not share. Examples of nonshared environmental influences include parental response to a child's gender, birth order, and temperament. In other words, parents respond differently to an easy-going, first-born female than they do to an intense, demanding younger son. Another source of nonshared environmental influence is the interaction among siblings. An older sibling with the responsibility for caring for younger siblings may develop more assertive, responsible behaviors; a younger sibling may learn to be more passive and cooperative. Other examples include outside influences particular to each family member, such as interactions with teachers and peers.

According to this research, you are similar to your siblings because you share similar genes. You are different from your siblings because you experience different environmental influences through your interactions with parents, siblings, peers, and others.

To what extent, then, do genetics and environment interact in determining human behavior? A current popular belief is that genes influence behavior by determining the type of environment that people choose. People seek out environments that match their genetic preferences (Bouchard et al., 1990; Scarr & McCartney, 1983). As children grow older, they are less influenced by their parents and freer to choose their own environmental influences. In reality, research shows that siblings become less alike the longer they live together (Plomin & Daniels, 1987). Athletic, outgoing children may choose team sports, whereas more withdrawn children may choose reading or playing computer games by themselves. Because of genetic preferences, these two types of children experience very different environments.

Research by Scarr and McCartney (1983) indicates that the nonshared environmental influences that children experience may also result from the fact that their different genetic make-up causes them to elicit different reactions from others. Parents may respond more positively to an alert, smiling baby than to a fussy, demanding one. An extroverted child may have more positive interactions with peers than a shy, withdrawn child. It would appear then, that a child's genetic make-up determines, to some extent, that child's nonshared environmental influences.

Research by Thomas Bouchard and his colleagues (1990) seems to indicate that twins reared apart are similar because their genetic make-up causes them to choose similar environments. This research states that, although it does indeed appear that most psychological variance is due to learning through experience, those experiences are self-selected. We choose our environment based on our genetic preferences. According to this theory, the twins in our story are alike not because of coincidence or because they ended up in similar homes, but because they have the same genes, which caused them to choose similar environments and experiences and to elicit similar responses from the people in their environments. Therefore, it is less appropriate to distinguish between nature versus nurture than to study "nature via nurture" (Bouchard et al., 1990).

Biochemical Systems and Behavior

After exploring biophysical growth and development at the cellular level, we will now turn to biochemical processes in the nervous system that can have a significant effect on behavior. We will first focus on the brain because it is the key organ in our nervous system. In addition, we will review the characteristics of our autonomic nervous system and the structure and function of nerve cells. This should provide you with the necessary foundation for understanding biochemical subsystems that contribute to the functioning of key psychological processes.

Anatomy of the Brain

It is difficult to understand brain functions without some fundamental understanding of neuroanatomy (study of structure and function of the nervous system). The brain's cerebral cortex (its covering) is divided into two hemispheres, and each of these hemispheres is divided into four lobes. These four lobes were named after bones in the human skull: frontal, parietal, occipital, and temporal (see Figure 2.4). The **frontal lobe** involves the portion of the brain that participates in body movements, thinking, feeling, imagining, and making decisions. It is the lobe that includes the largest portion of the brain. It also plays a critical role in social inhibitions and emotional expressiveness (Kalat, 1995). Persons with impairments in this area of brain functioning may have marked changes in personality and in planning abilities. The left side of the frontal lobe also contains an area known as Broca's area, which plays an important role in speech production (see Figure 2.5).

The **parietal lobe** is that portion of the brain that is primarily involved in the process of integrating sensory information. This lobe is located next to the motor components of the frontal lobe. When individuals have damage in this area, they generally have some type of difficulty involving the ability to interpret sensory information. For instance, they may not be able to identify objects by touch, and may have a poor sense of coordination. The **occipital lobe** is located below the parietal lobe and is involved in the receiving and sending of visual information.

Last, the **temporal lobe** is the area of the brain that is easiest to detect by nonneuroscientists. Sometimes lay observers cannot detect the occipital and parietal lobes without assistance from experts. These lobes do not possess such clear structural demarcations as the temporal lobe does. The temporal lobe is involved in emotions and human motivation. "Damage to the temporal lobes can lead to unprovoked laughter, joy, anxiety or violent behavior" (Kalat, 1995). The left side of the temporal lobe contains an area referred to as Wernicke's area, which has been identified as being important for language comprehension (see Figure 2.5).

The brain has three major divisions besides the four lobes: the forebrain, midbrain, and hindbrain (see Figure 2.6). The *forebrain*, or cerebrum, is the largest portion of the human brain. This area of the brain contains important structures, such as the pituitary gland, which regulates certain hormones; the basal ganglia, which control certain aspects of movement; and the limbic system, which regulates such behaviors as eating, drinking, sexual activity, anxiety, and aggression (Kalat, 1995). The *midbrain* is the portion of the brain that includes aspects of the brainstem (that portion of the brain above

FIGURE 2.4   The parts of the brain   Source: Heller, 1996.

FIGURE 2.5   Broca's area and Wernicke's area   Source: Goldstein, 1994.

the spinal cord). The midbrain also includes the reticular system. This system monitors the state of the body through connections with the motor and sensory tracks. The third and final division of the brain is the *hindbrain*. This portion of the brain includes the *medulla oblongata* and the *cerebellum*. The medulla is considered a portion of the spinal cord and is involved in controlling heart rate, vomiting, salivation, and other vital reflexes (Andreasen, 1984; Kalat, 1995). The cerebellum is the portion of the brain concerned with a person's sense of bal-

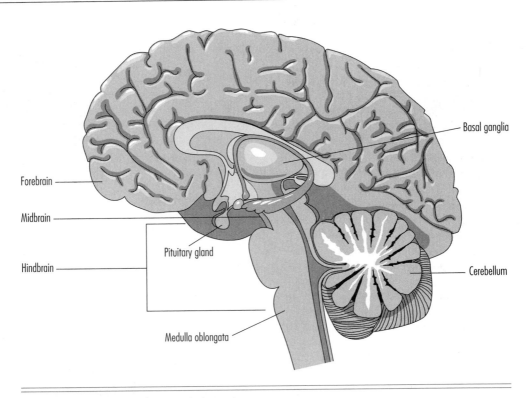

Basal ganglia

Forebrain

Midbrain

Pituitary gland

Hindbrain

Cerebellum

Medulla oblongata

FIGURE 2.6   Structures and areas in the human brain

ance. The following Focus on Theory section considers the relationship between the mind and the body and the distinction between the mind and the brain.

FOCUS ON THEORY

Neuroscientific Approach to the Mind-Body Problem

What is the mind? What is the body? How are the two related? This dilemma is referred to as the mind-body problem and is approached differently by neuroscientists and traditional psychologists. Neuroscientists study the mind by analyzing various aspects of the brain and define the brain in terms of chemical and other physical properties (Hoyenga & Hoyenga, 1988). But how do we define the mind? The answer is quite controversial. Many psychologists consider the mind to be a nonphysical entity defined in terms of meanings and values. In such a view, the mind is not defined on the basis of physical substances; rather, the mind consists of all the nonphysical properties of signs and symbols that we associate with mental events. Given these definitions, neuroscientists confront a fundamental problem in developing an appropriate perspective for their research. How are the physiochemical aspects of the brain related to the nonphysical aspects of the mind (Hoyenga & Hoyenga, 1988)? "This problem is aggravated by the fact that our very idea of what causation is has been derived from observations of physical events and not from observations of mental events . . ."

(Hoyenga & Hoyenga, 1988, p. 7). This historical artifact has prompted significant controversy in the philosophy of science and among neuropsychological researchers. The question is, do we need different methods of science for understanding mental events?

There have been a number of solutions to this mind-body problem: functionalism, dualism, and monism. *Functionalism* refers to any approach that describes the mind and body and the interactions between them in terms of their functions. In recent years, functional approaches have relied heavily on images derived from the computer sciences in which distinctions are made between hardware and software. The hardware refers to the brain and its components and the software refers to the brain's system of programming. This imagery has generated a specific solution to the mind-body problem: "Mental states are defined by their causal relation to other mental states and to states of the body" (Hoyenga & Hoyenga, 1988, p. 7). This solution is not as widely used as the other two recognized solutions to the mind-body problem.

Dualism is the second and most popular solution to the mind-body dilemma of neuropsychology. In this approach, the mind and body are perceived as different types of phenomena. Although they are viewed as separate systems, their relationships present a fundamental problem for scientists. Some dualists assume that these parallel systems involving mental and physical events can influence one another (interactionists), whereas other dualists assume that mental events can have no direct influence on brain events. In this latter view, the direction of the influence is viewed as being primarily in one direction: Brain events cause mental events. This is not to suggest that the mental events have no importance in the mental system of events or in a person's conscious sense of self. Instead, this view holds that mental events are what philosophers refer to as *epiphenomena*. An epiphenomenon would be described in this context as a mental event that occurs with brain events but has no influence on the causal process itself. For example, a false belief that a person is being controlled by television may result from an underlying biochemical dysfunction, but this belief in no way has a direct influence on the biochemical events causing these abnormalities. Exponents of this kind of dualism assume that mental events will be properly understood when we can reduce them

to their appropriate physical events. This viewpoint has important implications for practice. It suggests that mind interventions may be ineffective in addressing the causes of many biologically based mental disturbances.

Monism is the approach to the mind-body problem that conceives of the mind as a part of the physical world. In this approach, "the mind is part of the physical and chemical properties of the brain, just as our electrical recordings of brain function are" (Hoyenga & Hoyenga, 1988, p. 8). In addition, the mind is a subset of the brain that indirectly represents various aspects of the brain. Every individual mental event is viewed as an aspect of a physical event. Thus, "the physical events of the brain (ones that can be electrically recorded and chemically analyzed) and the mental events of the mind are simply two different ways of knowing and experiencing the same event" (Hoyenga & Hoyenga, 1988, p. 9). This solution to the mind-body problem has also been referred to in the literature as the "identity theory" (Figel, 1960). In this theory, there are no fundamental distinctions made between mind and body. Mind and body simply represent different vocabularies that refer to the same set of events in the material world (Stevenson, 1981).

Autonomic Nervous System

The autonomic nervous system involves the **sympathetic** and the **parasympathetic nervous systems** (see Figure 2.7). The autonomic nervous system controls glands, internal organs, smooth muscles, the stomach, and intestines. It is the system that plays a significant role in the human stress response. It is also the system that contributes to many of the symptoms and signs observed in persons with anxiety disorders. Under stress, the sympathetic nervous system prepares the body to participate in the fight-or-flight response. This system speeds up the heart rate, increases the blood supply to the body's organs, and prepares the body to respond to a perceived sense of threat (DiMatteo, 1991).

The parasympathetic system counteracts the stimulatory effects of the sympathetic system; that is, it serves the opposite function (DiMatteo, 1991). This system is called the parasympathetic nervous system because it consists of nerves that are next to the sympathetic nerve pathways.

Sympathetic		Parasympathetic
Pupils dilated, dry; far vision	**Eyes**	Pupils constricted, moist; near vision
Dry	**Mouth**	Salivating
Goose bumps	**Skin**	No goose bumps
Sweaty	**Palms**	Dry
Passages dilated	**Lungs**	Passages constricted
Increased rate	**Heart**	Decreased rate
Supply maximum to muscles	**Blood**	Supply maximum to internal organs
Increased activity	**Adrenal glands**	Decreased activity
Inhibited	**Digestion**	Stimulated

FIGURE 2.7   The autonomic nervous system   Source: Goldstein, 1994.

Biochemical Processes in the Nervous System

We currently know that the brain consists of various groupings of neurochemical systems (Andreasen & Black, 1991). These systems vary depending on the function they perform in the nervous system. The social work practitioner cannot directly assess these biochemical systems and is not expected to do so. However, the social work student should understand how these systems operate and how they relate to various forms of human behavior.

The structural organization of any true living system has the cell as its basic unit of organization. This fundamental unit consists of two kinds of molecules: proteins and nucleic acids. Proteins are the fundamental substances involved in the building of cells, muscles, skin, and internal organs. In fact, the term *protein* is derived from the Greek word *proteious*, "of first rank" (Page, 1981). **Proteins** are defined as any organic compound that has a large combination of amino acids. Scientists have identified over 100 amino acids, 20 of which are the building blocks for forming proteins. Eight of the amino

acids must be obtained from dietary sources: isoleucine, leucine, lysine, methionine, phenylalanine, threonine, tryptophan, and valine. These eight amino acids are referred to as *essential amino acids*. Any dietary deficiency in these amino acids contributes to many of the problems observed in social work involving delayed growth and development, emotional disturbance, and various physical conditions. Protein molecules also include a class of bio-

FIGURE 2.8   The central and peripheral nervous systems   Source: Goldstein, 1994.

chemical catalysts called *enzymes*. Enzymes facilitate chemical reactions in cells and aid proteins in achieving their structural and transport functions in the cell processes of human organisms (Steiner & Pomerantz, 1981). The other key molecules in living organisms are the *nucleic acids*. The two kinds of nucleic acids important in the study of development are deoxyribonucleic acid (DNA) and ribonucleic acid (RNA). These nucleic acids are important in the transmission of genetic information and in the synthesis of proteins (Steiner & Pomerantz, 1981, p. 3). In this section, we will explore the influence of biochemical processes by examining the biochemical aspects of our nervous system.

Although proteins are involved in all processes of growth and development, social workers need to understand their functions in the **central** and **peripheral nervous systems** (see Figure 2.8). The central nervous system (CNS) consists of the neural cells and their attendant chemical processes that are located within the brain or the spinal cord. The peripheral nervous system (PNS), on the other hand, involves all the neural cells and cell processes that lie outside of the brain and the spinal cord (Hoyenga & Hoyenga, 1988). Our entire nervous system consists of thousands of nerve cells, and each nerve cell receives information from about one thousand other nerve cells (Hoyenga & Hoyenga, 1988).

There are two kinds of cells in our nervous system: **glia** and **neurons.** Glia cells make up the bulk of our brain. There are various kinds of glia in our nervous system. They are often referred to as "supporting cells" (Kalat, 1995). Their exact nature and function are still being debated (Hoyenga & Hoyenga, 1988). However, we know that they do not covey information from one cell to another and are not as plentiful in the brains of nonhuman species (Kalat, 1995).

Neurons are generally what people refer to when they speak of nerve cells (see Figure 2.9). Neurons are the cells involved in conveying information from one cell to another. These cells are long and have branched extensions that diverge from their bodies. The single longer extensions are called axons and the short extensions dendrites (Lickey & Gordon, 1983). **Axons** are long fibers that carry the impulses from the cell body of a neuron to other cells. **Dendrites** perform the opposite function. They are the branched fibers on a cell body that bring messages to the cell body of the neuron. Neurons are the only cells in the human body that are separate from one another (Maxmen & Ward, 1995). Since neurons are separate, they need to communicate across the open spaces between individual neurons and between neurons and other cells. The space between any two neurons or a neuron and another cell is called the

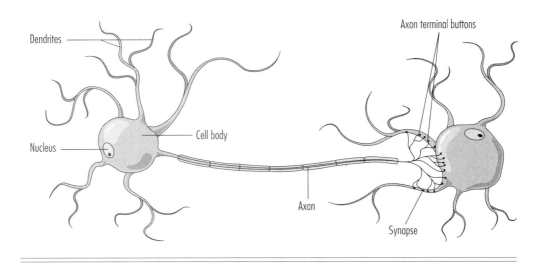

FIGURE 2.9   The neuron and neurotransmitter   Source: Goldstein, 1994.

synaptic cleft (see Figure 2.10). How are messages transmitted across this synaptic cleft from one cell to another?

At the tip of the axon is a small bulblike swelling called the *axon terminal* (Lickey & Gordon, 1983, p. 18). An axon terminal is generally found near a dendrite of another cell body. The axon terminal of the neuron sending the message is referred to as the *presynaptic terminal*, and the receiving portion of the neuron is referred to as the *postsynaptic membrane*. Conveying information from the transmitting cell to the receiving cell across the synaptic cleft requires mechanisms, known as synapses, for communicating the impulse or message. There are different types of synapses, some chemical and some electrical (Grebb, Reus, & Frimer, 1988). Chemical synapses involve the signaling of information from one cell to another by means of chemical substances. Different cells in the nervous system release different kinds of chemical substances to transmit the information across the synaptic cleft. In our discussion, we will focus on the actions of one type of chemical substances, the neurotransmitters, because they play a central role in current treatments of mental disorders.

Neurotransmitters are chemicals that are synthesized inside the neuron. These neurotransmitters are released from the axon's end or presynaptic terminal where they swim across the synaptic cleft and bind onto receptors on the membranes (or edges) of adjacent cells (the postsynaptic terminal) (Maxmen & Ward, 1995). Neurons actually act like a wet sponge. When they fire, they contract to release neurotransmitters; when not firing, they expand and reabsorb the neurotransmitters (Maxmen & Ward, 1995).

Receptors are located on postsynaptic membranes and are the special protein molecules on which neurotransmitters will attach. When a neurotransmitter is released from one nerve cell, swims across the cleft, and attaches to a receptor site on another cell, that process is called *binding*. This binding process activates chemical changes in the receiving neuron. Sometimes the chemical change encourages the production of a nerve impulse, and other times it discourages nerve impulses. When the chemical process encourages the production of a nerve impulse, this is called *synaptic excitation*. However, when the chemical process in the membrane discourages an impulse, it is called *synaptic inhibition*. In sum then, a transmitting neuron releases a chemical

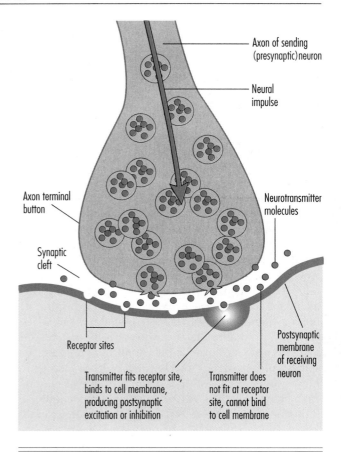

FIGURE 2.10   The synapse   Source: Weiten, 1995.

substance known as a neurotransmitter from the presynaptic terminal. This chemical crosses the space between the cells and binds onto the postsynaptic membrane of the receiving cell. The chemical then either encourages the receiving cell to fire a nerve impulse or discourages the cell from firing an impulse.

Transmitter Systems

Researchers have identified a number of neurotransmitter systems that play an important role in current psychopharmacology. Different areas of the nervous system use different neurotransmitters for conveying nerve impulses. Problems related to neurotransmitters depend on which area or pathway in the nervous system that partic-

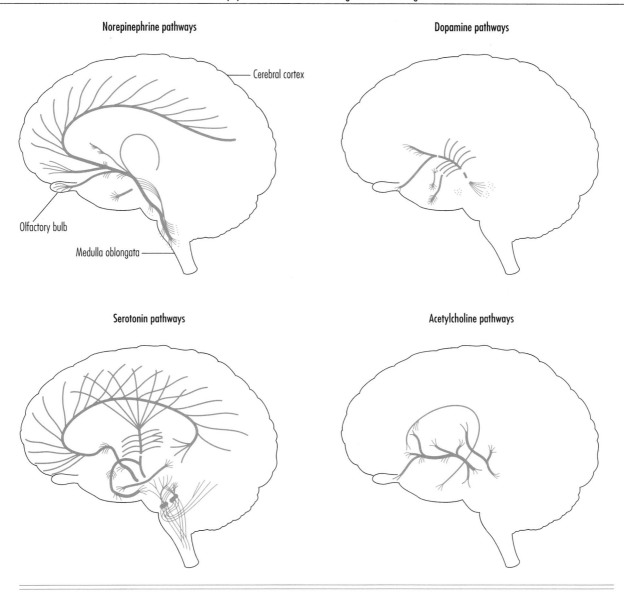

FIGURE 2.11   Neurotransmitter pathways   Source: Based on Valzelli, 1980.

ular neurotransmitter is prominent (see Figure 2.11). We will begin our discussion of neurotransmitter systems with *acetylcholine*, a transmitter that is part of a neuron system located throughout the brain, in spinal motor neurons, and in the basal ganglia (the lower nerve knots). This transmitter can have both excitatory and inhibitory effects, but it is generally involved in the process of stimulating muscles. Let's explore how problems with too much or too little of this neurotransmitter can affect behavior.

After the neurotransmitter acetylcholine has passed across the synaptic cleft and either encouraged or discouraged a nerve impulse, the transmitter is either removed, deactivated, or reabsorbed by means of enzymes. The enzyme *acetylcholinesterase* is generally involved in the process of deactivating acetylcholine. Without this enzyme, acetylcholine will build up, and the neuron will remain stimulated and continue firing electrical impulses (Jones-Witters & Witters, 1986). In fact, this is exactly how nerve gases used in earlier warfare operated. These gases blocked the production of acetylcholinesterase in the postsynaptic terminal, so the acetylcholine released from the transmitting neuron continued to build up and remain active and the receiving neuron continued to fire impulses.

Besides being involved in muscle stimulation, acetylcholine plays a major role in memory (Andreasen & Black, 1991). Individuals with a diagnosis of Alzheimer's disease show significant losses of portions of their brain involved in the acetylcholine system. However, this chemical's specific role in memory processes is still unclear. It would stand to reason that if Alzheimer's disease is related to a lack of acetylcholine, then finding a way to help the body produce more acetylcholine would help cure the disease. Choline is the substance necessary for the production of acetylcholine, and choline is found in cauliflower and milk and can be made from lecithin, which is found in egg yolks, liver, soybeans, peanuts, and other foods (Kalat, 1995). Persons with Alzheimer's disease have been given large doses of choline in an effort to stimulate production of acetylcholine. However, the choline supplements are not being properly transformed into acetylcholine, and so these experiments have not been successful.

Another major group of neurotransmitters is called the *catecholamines*. The catecholamines include three major neurotransmitters: dopamine, norepinephrine, and epinephrine. *Dopamine* (DA) is synthesized from tyrosine, an amino acid. Dopamine serves as a neurotransmitter in several areas of the nervous system. One prominent area or pathway of dopamine activity is in that portion of the brain involved in the motor system. Loss of nerve cells in this region is correlated with Parkinson's disease. Persons with Parkinson's disease shake, especially in their extremities, and have a tendency to become stiff, rigid, or even paralyzed (Andreasen, 1984). A lack of dopamine then seems to result in this disease.

Two other key portions of the brain share dopamine: the basal ganglia and the limbic system. The functions of dopamine pathways within these areas are poorly understood. However, we know that dopamine receptors are related to emotional behavior and to the psychiatric disorder schizophrenia. One theory of schizophrenia, the dopamine hypothesis, assumes that schizophrenia is a result of excessive activity in the dopamine receptor systems (Maxmen & Ward, 1995). In other words, schizophrenia could be the result of too much dopamine. Dopamine has also been associated with other motor and tic disorders. In Huntington's chorea and Gilles de la Tourette's syndrome, it is believed that there is a dopamine excess and an acetylcholine deficiency (Grebb et al., 1988). That is, one current hypothesis is asserting that we should expect a dynamic balance between dopamine and acetylcholine. An imbalance in these substances is generally correlated with disorders such as Gilles de la Tourette's syndrome. This syndrome has received substantial attention in recent years by the popular media because of its odd verbal and motor tics. Sufferers of this syndrome may uncontrollably bark or shout out obscenities.

Norepinephrine and epinephrine essentially follow the same pathways as dopamine. *Norepinephrine* (NE) is a system in the brain that is involved in regulating mood, learning, memory, anxiety, and the sleep-wake cycle (Grebb et al., 1988). The catecholamine hypothesis of depression attributes this disorder to insufficient norepinephrine. This theory began with the observation that certain drugs used for nonpsychiatric purposes affected mood. For instance, reserpine, a blood pressure medication, was found to have the side effect of depression (Lickey & Gordon, 1983). After studying the effects of this medication, it was found that it acted as a depleter of the neurotransmitter norepinephrine.

On the other hand, the drug iproniazid, used to treat tuberculosis, was found to improve a person's mood. This drug is now considered the original monoamine oxidase inhibitor. Monoamine oxidase is the enzyme that deactivates norepinephrine. Iproniazid inhibits monoamine oxidase, thereby increasing the amount of norepinephrine that is available in the presynaptic terminal. In other words, drugs that are monoamine oxidase inhibitors suppress the production of enzymes that destroy the transmitter norepinephrine. Thus, these drugs increase the activity of norepinephrine and thereby alleviate depression.

Imipramine, otherwise known by its trade name Tofranil, is known as one of the first antidepressants. It is believed that this drug operates by blocking the reuptake or reabsorption of norepinephrine into presynaptic endings (Lickey & Gordon, 1983). This action would therefore increase the levels of norepinephrine.

If decreased levels of norepinephrine are associated with depression, then it is logical to conclude that increased activity of its receptors or too much norepinephrine results in mania. Drugs that decrease the action of norepinephrine would help alleviate disorders involving mania.

Epinephrine, or adrenaline, uses pathways in the nervous system that have adrenergic receptors. These receptors respond to the action of epinephrine. This neurotransmitter is assumed, however, to play less of a role in central nervous system functions. Epinephrine is synthesized by means of the conversion of norepinephrine. Epinephrine is being considered a correlate of some forms of panic disorders; that is, too much epinephrine or adrenaline may cause these types of disorders. However, less research has been involved in developing medications from this neuronal system.

Serotonin is a neurotransmitter that has been identified as playing a significant role in depression. It is classified as an indolemine rather than a catecholamine. In the literature, distinctions are often made between the catecholamine and indolemine hypotheses of depression. Like norepinephrine, serotonin is located in many parts of the brain (see Figure 2.11). Serotonin is synthesized from the amino acid tryptophan.

Serotonin is also thought to play a significant role in circadian rhythms (biological cycles recurring at approximately 24-hour intervals), the perception of pain, obsessions, and the sleep-wake cycle (Grebb et al., 1988). As with norepinephrine, antidepressants are thought to increase the activity of serotonin in its synapses. Similarly, overly high serotonin levels are assumed to be associated with manic-oriented moods. Focus on Research: Diet and Violence looks closely at how substances in the foods we eat might affect our behavior.

FOCUS ON RESEARCH

Diet and Violence

Is eating too much corn dangerous to members of your family? Researchers (Mawson & Jacobs, 1978) have found that the murder rate is highest in countries where people consume substantially high amounts of corn. Corn is deficient in the amino acid tryptophan, which is considered the precursor of the neurotransmitter serotonin. The rate at which a person turns over serotonin is correlated with violence (Kalat, 1988), and low levels of serotonin are associated with high levels of aggressive behavior. When people eat lots of corn, they are decreasing the synthesis of serotonin in their system (Lytle, Messing, Fisher, & Phebus, 1975). Although these speculative assumptions are appealing, findings of increased violence in communities whose residents consume high amounts of corn may be explained by other factors. Obviously, further research is needed. Scientists are exploring other aspects of our diets that reduce serotonin production in our brains. For instance, the chemical phenylalanine (NutraSweet) competes with tryptophan for entry into the brain (Kalat, 1988). Because a number of studies have found that people with a history of violence have lower serotonin turnover, future research about the role of diet in influencing this process may provide deeper insights into processes contributing to violent behavior.

Implications for Practice

Competence in understanding biochemical processes is a new skill required of autonomous social workers (Libassi, 1990). Social workers are currently involved in monitoring medications, making referrals to psychiatrists, and educating patients about potential side effects (Davidson & Jamison, 1983; Wise, 1986). In order to fulfill these role requirements, social workers need a basic understanding of some of the topics discussed in the preceding section of this chapter. They will also need to acquire a working knowledge of the brain in order to understand the targets of existing drugs and appreciate current etiological explanations of major mental dysfunctions from a biochemical perspective (Johnson, 1980). In fact, this perspective currently is playing a dominant role in a wide variety of mental health settings.

Given the foundation of biochemical concepts discussed in the prior section, you will need to apply these concepts to understand psychopharmacology. In particular, you will need to familiarize yourself with common terms used in discussing various forms of medications. For instance, clients receiving antipsychotic medications for schizophrenia also may be given drugs referred to as *anticholinergics*. At first glance, these appear to be drugs involved in processes with which you are not familiar. However, this term refers to a neuronal system that you are already acquainted with. **Cholinergic** refers to any nerve that releases the neurotransmitter acetylcholine at its synapse. Thus, anticholinergic drugs are any chemical substances that block acetylcholine receptors. They block these receptors by binding onto them and inhibiting the transmission of nerve impulses through the neurotransmitter acetylcholine. The action of these drugs would lower the level of acetylcholine activity.

Propranolol is a drug widely encountered in practice. It is classified as a beta blocker and is used in the treatment of heart conditions and anxiety disorders. How would knowledge of neurotransmitter systems help you understand the action of this drug? Remember, too much epinephrine or adrenaline can contribute to anxiety and panic disorders. There are two receptors that respond to epinephrine—the alpha adrenergic receptor and the beta adrenergic receptor. Propranolol binds onto the beta receptor in the postsynaptic membrane and blocks the absorption of epinephrine. By lowering the available level of epinephrine or adrenaline, the anxiety disorder is lessened. Thus, knowledge of the basic principles discussed in the prior section leads to a basic understanding of the processes involved in the use of these drugs.

You should try to read the *Physician's Desk Reference* (PDR) to test whether you understand the basic properties and processes of drugs used in the treatment of your clients. Some common drugs are listed in Table 2.1 to assist you with this exercise. Focus on Research: Racial and Ethnic Variations in Responses to Medications considers how different ethnic and racial groups experience side effects of various medications.

FOCUS ON RESEARCH

Racial and Ethnic Variations in Responses to Medications

Medications designed to treat psychic forms of distress are commonly encountered in social work practice. These medications are designed to target specific biochemical systems in our nervous system. Although medications are targeted to hit specific biochemical systems, they also affect unintended elements and systems in our bodies. These side effects vary from individual to individual and vary among ethnic and racial groups. The sparse research in the area of racial and ethnic variations in medication responses reveals a few noteworthy distinctions. Compared to whites, Asians require lower dosages of a variety of psychotropic medications, including lithium, antidepressants, and neuroleptics. Hispanics also require lower dosages of antidepressant medications and report more side effects at half the doses considered therapeutic for whites. Thus, whites require larger dosages of sedating drugs than do individuals from other racial and ethnic groups. A variety of interpretations of these differences have been proffered in the literature. For instance, these variations can be due to inherent biological differences; however, cultural explanations are equally compelling. Further research is needed to understand the factors underlying observed variations in ethnic and racial responses to medications. For instance, why do African Americans have better responses than whites do to phenothiazines and tricyclic antidepressants? Are these variations due to different factors in their metabolism, diet, or symptoms? Until these questions are answered, persons on medications need to be closely monitored by practitioners involved in observing their behavior in the community. In addition, social workers should begin developing practice principles that will help ethnic clients comply with treatment. For instance, increased follow-up and probing about side effects may be needed to guide workers involved in cases in which Hispanic clients have been placed on antidepressant medications (Lawson, 1986).

TABLE 2.1 Widely Used Drugs in Mental Health

Class and Generic Name		Trade Name	Class and Generic Name		Trade Name
Anticholinergics (Antiparkinsonian)	Benztropine mesylate	Cogentin		Doxepin	Sinequan, Adapin
	Trihexiphenidyl	Artane		Trimipramine	Surmontil
	Piperiden HCL	Akineton		Clomipramine	Anafranil
	Procyclidine	Kemedrin		Desipramine	Norpramin, Pertofrane
				Nortriptyline	Aventyl, Pamelor
Adrenergics (Antiparkinsonian)	Caffeine sodium benzoate	Caffeine		Trazodone	Desyrel
	Amantadine HCL	Symmetrel			
Phenothiazines (Antipsychotic)	Chlorpromazine	Thorzaine	**Hypoanxiolytics** (Antianxiety)		
	Thioridazine	Mellaril			
	Mesoridazine	Serentil	**Barbiturate-like**	Chloral hydrate	Noctec
	Perphenazine	Trilafon		Ethchlorvynol	Placidyl
	Trifluoperazine	Stelazine		Meprobamate	Miltown, Equanil
	Fluphenazine	Prolixin			
Butyrophenones (Antipsychotic)	Haloperidol	Haldol	**Benzodiazepines** (short-acting)	Aprazolam	Xanax
				Estazolam	ProSom
				Lorazepam	Ativan
Thioxanthenes (Antipsychotic)	Chloprothixine	Taractan		Oxazepam	Serax
	Thiothixine	Navane		Temazepam	Restoril
Miscellaneous (Antipsychotic)	Clozapine	Clorazil		Triazolam	Halcion
	Loxapine	Loxitane	**Benzodiazepines** (long-acting)	Chlordiazepoxide	Librium
	Molindone	Moban		Clonapazepam	Klonapin
	Risperidone	Risperdal		Clorazepate	Tranxene
Unicyclics (Antidepressants)	Bupropion	Wellbutrin		Diazepam	Valium
				Flurazepam	Dalmane
Bicyclics (Antidepressants)	Selective Seratonin Re-uptake Inhibitors (SSRIs)			Prazepam	Centrax
	Fluoxetine	Prozac		Quazepam	Doral
	Sertraline	Zoloft	**Miscellaneous**	Buspirone	BuSpar
	Paroxetine	Paxil		Propranolol	Inderal
Tricyclics (Antidepressants)	Imipramine	Tofranil		Zolpidem	Ambien
	Amitriptyline	Elavil, Endep			

Biophysical Hazards

We currently know that any deficits or dysfunctions in physiological structures will have some bearing on a person's social functioning. The social workers's duty is to assess how these physiological impairments influence the person's capacity to meet life tasks. Before appropriate support services can be identified, the social work professional must have a general understanding of the person's disease, impairment, or disability. This generalized understanding is not possible without a basic understanding of key human biological systems.

This understanding of biological systems is markedly improved whenever the social worker has a basic understanding of disease and health terminology. In fact, many social workers, in addition to health social workers, are expected to review the client's health status and history when doing background studies. This common expectation requires a requisite understanding of human biosystems and health-related concepts. This section provides a brief overview of biologically related concepts encountered in multiple practice contexts. However, the diseases and other biological hazards addressed in this section are not intended to be compre-

There are many psychosocial aspects of having cancer. For example, adjustment to hair loss is difficult both for people with cancer and for those around them.

hensive. Further discussion of these topics is systematically provided in each subsequent chapter on developmental content under the heading "Biophysical Hazards" in our framework. Our multidimensional framework seeks to make you aware of the need for having a developmental perspective on relevant biological hazards. This knowledge is needed for assessment in direct practice and in planning contexts involved in preventive programming. This section cannot cover all the relevant biosystems; that task is beyond the scope of this book. Instead, we hope to sensitize you to the various types of medical and physical information you will need in your practice. Additional information on biosystems is addressed in the biophysical sections of our chapters on life-span development.

Cancer

Any living organism can get cancer. Cancer is a serious disease that involves improper cell growth, considered the purposeless growth of cells. Our cells grow by the orderly process of cell division known as mitosis. Mitosis involves one cell dividing into two and two cells becoming four and so forth. The process of cell division is normally controlled by natural processes. Any process that interferes with nature's controls can lead to massive cell growth. Cell growth that leads to the buildup of masses of purposeless tissue is referred to as a **tumor**. Self-contained tumors are called *benign* tumors; tumors that are spreading, or are not self-contained, are generally referred to as **malignant tumors.** The spread of these cells to other areas of the body is known as *metastasis*. When cancer metastasizes, the cells then begin to grow in other organs and the disease is much more difficult to cure.

Though progress has been made in the diagnosis and treatment of cancer, this disease remains a leading cause of death, surpassed only by heart disease.

Cardiovascular System Problems

The heart is a hollow "muscular pump" that provides the energy needed to force a person's blood through the body. It is one of the few human organs that works constantly. This necessity for continuous work makes the heart vulnerable to a wide variety of injuries and abnormalities (Meyers, 1972). The heart is divided into four chambers, two atria and two ventricles (see Figure 2.12). The wall that runs down the center of the heart is called the septum. There are two chambers on each side of the septum. The top chambers are atria and the bottom chambers are the ventricles. The structures that control the flow of blood through these chambers are valves. Blood gets into the heart by means of *veins.* The *arteries* carry blood from the heart to the rest of the body.

The heart is about the size of a human fist. It is enclosed in a thin sac, called the **pericardium,** that covers the middle muscular layer of the heart. This important muscle is known as the *myocardium.* The function of the heart and its valves may be impaired by a variety of processes. For example, the heart or any of its components may be malformed at birth, a condition known as a congenital heart disease. Numerous factors may contribute to a congenital heart condition. Many of these factors will be discussed in our presentation of prenatal development. Also, the heart can be exposed to infec-

tions or other factors that damage or injure the heart's muscle (**myocarditis**) or its valves (**endocarditis**) (Meyers, 1972). There is also a technical term used when the sac surrounding the entire heart is diseased, *pericarditis.*

The most common lesion in valvular heart disease involves a condition known as *mitral valve insufficiency.* In this condition, the valve fails to prevent the regurgitation of processed blood. *Mitral stenosis* is another valvular disease involving the hardening or narrowing of the mitral valve, which is located between the left atrium and left ventricle. Social workers in mental health may encounter persons with severe anxiety symptoms that result from a condition known as **mitral valve prolapse.** This valvular disease involves the protrusion of one or both cusps of the mitral valve back into the left atrium. This protrusion can contribute to a backflow of blood. Common symptoms are chest pain, palpitations, fatigue, or dyspnea. This is one of the conditions that a mental health worker should be aware of in performing differential assessments. The worker may need to make a referral to have this condition ruled out by a physician because it is often confused with anxiety disorders and other forms of psychological distress.

The force of the blood through the heart may also injure any component of the cardiovascular system: heart, arteries, veins, or capillaries. This force of the blood through the body is known as *blood pressure.* Normal blood pressure is expressed in two numbers, the **systolic pressure** and the **diastolic pressure.** The systolic pressure involves a measure of the heart when it is contracting and pumping blood out and through the body. This is the highest number or measure of the blood's force through the heart. Normal blood pressure in a young adult is about 120 mm Hg systolic and 70 to 90 mm Hg diastolic (DiMatteo,1991, p. 25). Diastolic pressure is the measure of the blood's flow during the relaxation, or diastole, of the heart. When a person's systolic pressure is above 140, or if the diastolic pressure is above 90, the person is considered to have *hypertension.* Essential hypertension refers to having a chronically elevated blood pressure over a long period of time.

Angina pectoris is a coronary condition involving pain and a tightness in the chest. This condition results when the heart muscle does not receive sufficient oxygen. When insufficient oxygen is directed to the heart's muscle, resulting in the death of part of the heart's tissue,

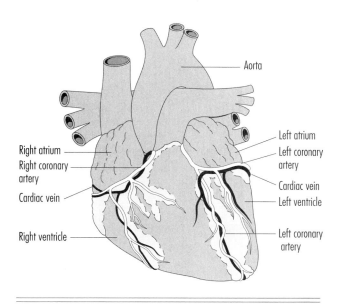

FIGURE 2.12   **The cardiovascular system**   Source: Brannon & Feist, 1997.

this is referred to as a **myocardial infarction,** or heart attack. A number of processes can contribute to the blockage of arteries and to a myocardial infarction. For example, arteriosclerosis, a condition contributing to decreased blood supply, is a common condition that contributes to heart attacks. This condition is often associated with aging and may be referred to as hardening of the arteries. It is due to the buildup of plaques in the walls of the arteries. These plaques are produced by a fatty substance known as *cholesterol.* They clog up the arteries and impede appropriate blood flow.

The heart beats at a rate of 60 to 80 beats per minute. A heart beat of 100 beats per minute or above following normal activities is an indicator of potential difficulties. This elevated heart beat can indicate structural or functional impairment or the influence of some type of psychoactive substance. The heart rate or *pulse* must change to respond to the body's demands for oxygen. The heart generally beats faster when an individual is involved in a strenuous activity. However, it also beats faster when a person is angry, anxious, or emotionally excited. During pregnancy, the heart works harder because it is also having to handle the needs of the fetus. This is one of the major reasons some women experience secondary heart complications during pregnancy.

The blood flowing through the heart and cardiovascular system consists of several formed elements—red cells (erythrocytes), white cells (leukocytes), and platelets (thrombocytes)—in a liquid medium known as plasma. The number of red blood cells ranges from about 4.5 to 5.5 million per cubic milliliter of blood (Meyers, 1972). If a person has a blood count of below 4 million or a blood hemoglobin (protein compound in the blood) below 12 grams, then they are considered to have anemia. Anemia is a condition that involves inadequate red blood cell production. Red blood cells are responsible for carrying oxygen from the lungs to various tissues in the body. Anemia then may result in less oxygen being available to the body and cause fatigue and dizziness.

White cells number about 5000 to 10,000 per cubic milliliter and protect the body against infections and other foreign substances. The platelet number is approximately 200,000 to 400,000 per milliliter. Platelets play a critical role in blood clotting. Platelet problems can result in difficulties with excess bleeding.

Respiratory System Problems

The respiratory system handles the taking in of oxygen and the giving off of carbon dioxide. This system consists of the lungs, diaphragm, major air pathway (trachea or windpipe), and other air pathways (Meyers, 1972) (see Figure 2.13). The chief organ involved in the respiration process is the lungs. The lungs are two pyramid-shaped structures that lie in the chest cavity. The lungs consist of spongy tissue that is divided into numerous small air sacs called alveoli. These air sacs have in their walls a network of tiny blood vessels called capillaries. These capillaries cover the alveoli and take the oxygen from the air into the bloodstream. *Bronchial asthma* is a condition of the lungs characterized by intermittent attacks of shortness of breath. The cause is often an allergic response associated with the constriction of the bronchioles (tubes that carry air from the trachea to the air sacs or alveoli). During an asthma attack, the bronchial mus-

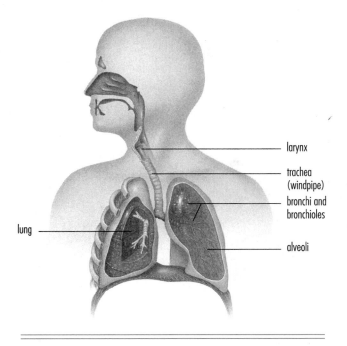

larynx

trachea (windpipe)

bronchi and bronchioles

lung

alveoli

FIGURE 2.13   **The respiratory system**   Source: Ingraham & Ingraham, 1995.

cle constricts and a thick, sticky mucus is produced. This mucus further obstructs air pathways. Air intake may be normal, but only partial expiration is achieved. In severe attacks, mucus can plug or block the bronchi.

Acute bronchitis is a disorder involving a bacterial infection of the bronchi, whereas *chronic bronchitis* is a progressive inflammatory disease that is caused by exposure to irritants (Wilson, 1987). Chronic bronchitis is a disorder that develops in middle age, often in persons with a history of chronic smoking. This disorder contributes to an extreme difficulty in breathing called dyspnea. The condition is aggravated by damp and cold. If the alveolar walls are ruptured because of chronic bronchitis, the person will develop emphysema or chronic obstructive pulmonary disease. This condition destroys the walls between the alveoli and decreases the surface within the lung that can be used to exchange gases (DiMatteo, 1991, p. 29).

Endocrine System Problems

The endocrine system is a system of glands without ducts (ductless) that is controlled by the autonomic nervous system. The endocrine system consists of the pituitary, the thyroid, the adrenal, the sex glands (or gonads), the pancreas, and others (Meyers, 1972) (see Figure 2.14). These glands release chemical substances called hormones into the bloodstream. The stimuli that release these hormones are controlled by the nervous system, which is linked to the endocrine system by means of the

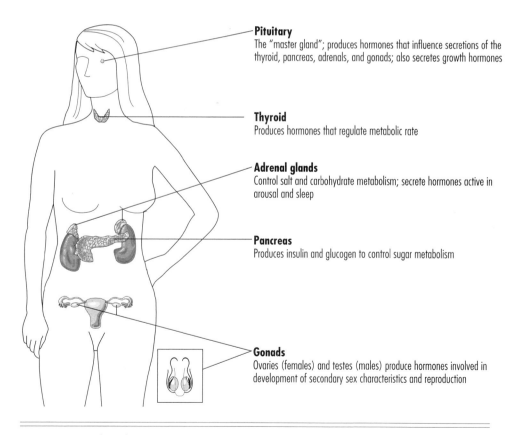

Pituitary
The "master gland"; produces hormones that influence secretions of the thyroid, pancreas, adrenals, and gonads; also secretes growth hormones

Thyroid
Produces hormones that regulate metabolic rate

Adrenal glands
Control salt and carbohydrate metabolism; secrete hormones active in arousal and sleep

Pancreas
Produces insulin and glucogen to control sugar metabolism

Gonads
Ovaries (females) and testes (males) produce hormones involved in development of secondary sex characteristics and reproduction

FIGURE 2.14   The endocrine system   Source: Goldstein, 1994.

pituitary gland and its connections with the hypothalamus (DiMatteo, 1991). DiMatteo (1991) has summarized this process in relation to stress.

> When the sympathetic nervous system becomes aroused in response to an emergency, the hypothalamus chemically stimulates the pituitary to release ACTH (adrenocorticotropic hormone) into the blood. ACTH stimulates other hormones in response to stress. The adrenal glands, located on top of the kidneys, are stimulated to produce epinephrine and norepinephrine (adrenalin and noradrenalin), which speed up the heart and respiration and increase the liver's output of sugar to the muscles. Cortisol is also released by the adrenal glands during perceived emergencies to help control swelling should injury occur. (p. 36)

The role the pituitary plays in stress is just one example of the important roles played by endocrine glands in human emotions and behavior.

The pituitary gland consists of three lobes and is located just below the hypothalamus. The posterior pituitary collects vasoprine, an antidiuretic hormone, and oxytocin. Vasoprine is involved in the regulation of water reabsorption by the kidneys and oxytocin with contraction of involuntary muscles in the uterus (Green, Beatty, & Arkin, 1984). The thyroid gland is located at the front of the neck and secretes the hormone thyroxin. This hormone is essential for normal body growth and development. Hyperthyroidism is a condition that results from overactivity of the thyroid gland. The gland in this condition is generally enlarged. Hyperthyroidism is clinically characterized by nervousness, tremor, constant hunger, heat intolerance, hyperactivity, and insomnia. The pancreas is another important ductless gland that is located below the stomach. It secretes substances such as digestive enzymes, insulin, and glucagon.

Problems with insulin production and utilization lead to the disease diabetes mellitus. Insufficient production of insulin or inadequate use of insulin results in body cells being unable to absorb glucose or sugar from the blood for metabolism. As a result, glucose builds up in the blood and causes high blood sugar and the problems associated with diabetes melitis. This disease occurs in two forms, Type I or juvenile onset diabetes (insulin dependent) and Type II or adult onset diabetes. Type I diabetes is caused by failure of the pancreas to produce sufficient insulin. Persons with this type of diabetes must have daily insulin injections to replace what the body fails to produce. In adult onset diabetes, the body has decreased ability to utilize the insulin produced, so the pancreas must produce more insulin to compensate. Blood sugar also builds up, causing problems. Diabetes, especially juvenile onset, can lead to many complications, including blindness, renal failure, and infections in the lower extremities that can result in amputations. Persons with diabetes must pay careful attention to diet and weight and must carefully regulate their blood sugar levels. Regulation of blood sugar often requires finger sticks to check the blood. Social workers may be involved in helping diabetes mellitus sufferers adjust to the lifestyle changes necessary to maintain good health.

The other hormones produced by the endocrine system also play vital roles in human functioning. Researchers are exploring the role played by hormones in sexual and aggressive behavior.

Abnormalities in these systemic processes can be major contributors to emotional disturbances and should not be ignored by social work practitioners in assessing dysfunctions in the affective domain.

Implications for Practice

Health status is significantly related to a person's sense of well-being. As a result, practitioners must be aware of conditions that threaten key health functions. They must also seek an understanding of the effects of various conditions on a person's sense of self, behavior, and expectations. Biological defects in organ systems or diseases can significantly change how people perceive who they are and how they relate to others. For instance, persons who have had a heart attack will make substantial changes in how they approach many aspects of their everyday lives. They may (1) develop new approaches to handling stress, (2) change their lifestyle, (3) eliminate previous coping behaviors that contributed to their heart attack, and (4) change diet and exercise practices. They also may develop new maladaptive responses to fears that have no realistic basis in their recovery process. Thus, it is essential for the social worker to appreciate these conditions as well as develop a basic understanding of the organ systems affected by common disease processes. With this information, social workers are better equipped to engage in effective education, prevention, and treatment.

In health social work, practitioners also need to have a basic understanding of illness behavior. Illness behavior refers to how people respond to their subjective realization that they have an illness. Illness behavior can vary directly with the biological systems involved in the client's illness. For instance, some clients have more adaptive coping skills for dealing with physical disorders, whereas others have developed poor coping responses for dealing with physical distress. Although some people do not handle physical illnesses well, these people may have excellent skills for handling mental disorders. The social worker must understand how basic biological systems function and how these systems affect human behavior processes in order to enhance client responses to physical and mental disturbances. The following Focus on Research section examines how a substance produced in the body affects eating behavior.

that blocks the effect of GLP-1 was also tested. The blocker more than doubled the food intake of rats that were already full.

Thus, scientists believe the blocker was interfering with the rats' GLP-1 signal to stop eating. Also, the research found that the blocker had no effect on rats that were starving because the hungry rats had no GLP-1 signal to be blocked. To create a medication for people, researchers will create a substance that acts like GLP-1 but can reach the brain after being orally taken, or they might devise a drug that can slow the natural breakdown of GLP-1. Such a drug would be effective if the person is full and has the GLP-1 signal. This could be groundbreaking research if such a medication can help obese people eat less and prevent people with anorexia (an eating disorder where the person doesn't eat) from starving themselves.

Source: From *USA Today* (1996).

FOCUS ON RESEARCH

Research on the Brain May Help You Be Thinner in the Future

An attempt is under way to produce a medication that could be used to fight obesity. The latest research published in Nature reports a study that identified an effective appetite suppressor that made rats eat 95% less because they felt full. How would such a medication work on the brain? Scientists were working with a substance called glucagon-like peptide-1 or GLP-1. This substance may be the key to how the brain regulates food intake.

In the hypothalamus, which regulates appetite, researchers found GLP-1. When researchers injected GLP-1 into the brains of rats that had not eaten in 24 hours, the rats reduced their food intake by up to 95%, depending on the dosage. After receiving the GLP-1, the rats acted the way we do after a big meal—they became sleepy and didn't move around much. The GLP-1 made the rats feel full, suppressing their appetite. A substance

Conclusions

In efforts to understand human behavior, social workers who ignore the contributions of the body will compromise the quality of both their theory and their practice (Saleebey, 1992). As Saleebey has argued, "the profession of social work has given only superficial attention to taking into account the body's urges, promptings and energies" (1992, p. 112). We have attempted to compensate for this limitation by examining key biophysical systems that play a fundamental role in understanding human behavior. We assume that the body-mind-environment connection requires the integration of each of the biological subsystems examined in this chapter.

Individual variations in biological systems must be identified in social work assessments. Social workers must not hold biological variables constant in their practical assessments, and practitioners must be as diligent about assessing biological dimensions as they are about assessing social and psychological dimensions. If social workers do not take into account these biological variations, they run the risk of subscribing to abstract conceptions of client concerns and run the additional risk of ignoring vital biological sensations or needs that make up the fundamental characteristics of the human experience.

Chapter Summary

Biophysical Growth and Development

Any understanding of human growth and development must take into account key biophysical systems. Human growth includes all the processes that contribute to the addition of new components of a person's physical structure, including added biophysical components like cells that result in increased size of a person's body. Growth differs from development, which refers to all the processes that contribute to the improvement or change in body components.

Cells represent the smallest unit of living physical matter. Basic cellular functions are under the control of DNA and RNA, the nucleic acids that determine our hereditary characteristics. A gene is a small portion of the DNA molecule that provides the blueprint for the other nucleic acids that control the fundamental properties of human organisms.

Chromosomes are located in the nucleus of every cell and contain sets of genes from each of the parents. The mother and father each provide 23 chromosomes to the zygote or fertilized egg. These chromosomes contain many genes that influence our inherited characteristics.

Social workers must understand the fundamental processes that influence variations in inherited characteristics in order to help clients understand inherited physical and developmental processes. The fundamental kinds of inherited disorders encountered by social work practitioners include single-gene (dominant, autosomal recessive, sex-linked recessive), multifactorial, chromosomal (Down syndrome, Trisomy 18 and 13), and sex chromosomal disorders. Cell division problems occur in both meiotic and mitotic processes. Translocation and nondisjunction are the most common problems in cell division. Each of these problems influence biophysical growth and development.

Biochemical processes, especially those in the central and peripheral nervous systems, influence many aspects of human behavior. The central nervous system (CNS) consists of the nerve cells (neurons) and their attendant chemical processes located within the brain and spinal cord. The peripheral nervous system involves all the nerve cells and cell processes that lie outside the brain and spinal cord. The nervous system consists of thousands of nerve cells, and each nerve cell receives information from about one thousand other nerve cells through biochemical substances called neurotransmitters.

Our nervous system has many neurotransmitter systems: acetylcholine, dopamine, norepinephrine, epinephrine, and serotonin. The acetylcholine system has implications for memory processes and is associated with Alzheimer's disease. Dopamine is associated with Parkinson's disease, schizophrenia, Gilles de la Tourette's syndrome, and other motor and tic disturbances. Norepinephrine regulates mood, learning, memory anxiety, and the sleep-wake cycle. Epinephrine is correlated with anxiety states and disturbances. Serotonin plays a major role in depressive disorders, violence, eating, and the sleep-wake cycle.

Biophysical Hazards

Impairments in any organ or physiological system have significant implications for social functioning. Cardiovascular system problems are a major concern at various stages of the life cycle. There are many ways to measure the cardiovascular organ system's functioning. Blood pressure represents the force of blood through the body, and it is expressed in two numbers: systolic pressure and diastolic pressure. Social workers should know the ranges of normal blood pressure at various stages of development and in various social situations. The heart rate, which is typically 60 to 80 beats per minute, changes to respond to the body's demands for oxygen and is measured as a pulse. Abnormalities in the heart, respiratory, and endocrine systems can contribute to many forms of emotional disturbance. Social workers need a basic understanding of the range of physical conditions that contribute to emotional and behavioral disturbances in each of the key organ systems outside the nervous system.

KEY TERMS

allele
angina pectoris
autosomes
axon
canalization
central nervous system
cholinergic
cystic fibrosis
dendrite
development
diastolic pressure
dominant gene
endocarditis
fragile X syndrome
frontal lobe
genotype
glia
growth

hemophilia
heterozygous genes
homozygous genes
Huntington's chorea
hyperplasia
hypertrophic growth
Klinefelter's syndrome
Lesch-Nyhan syndrome
malignant tumor
meiosis
mitosis
mitral valve prolapse
mutation
myocardial infarction
myocarditis
neurons
neurotransmitter
occipital lobe

parasympathetic nervous system
parietal lobe
pericardium
peripheral nervous system
phenotype
protein
recessive gene
single-gene disorder
sympathetic nervous system
synaptic cleft
syndactyly
systolic pressure
Tay-Sachs disease
temporal lobe
tumor
Turner's syndrome

3

The Psychological Dimension for Assessing Social Functioning

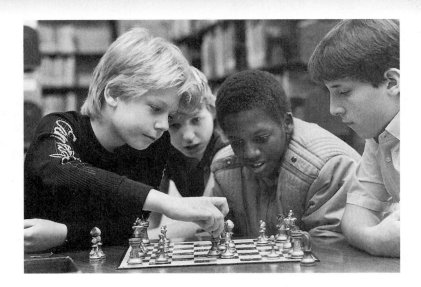

What do we mean by the term *psychological?* Although we can have an intuitive understanding of psychological processes, we often find it difficult to define our psychological characteristics and functioning. Although the discipline of psychology is relatively new, questions and concerns about the mind's operations have interested humans since the inception of human history (Hothersall, 1984). Our ancestors explored dreams, memory, ideas, perception, and other key mental functions. They were also curious about what we would refer to today as personality or individual differences.

What factors account for patterns we observe in our character or behavior? How are we unique? Can we differentiate ourselves from others around us? These are questions commonly addressed by psychologists with an interest in personality concerns. What is the role of intuition and subjective experience in understanding the mind or cognition? What determines the formation of our individual personalities? What are common human needs and emotions? How do people learn and forget information? What motivates people to behave as they do? How is information represented and stored in our minds? There are a multitude of questions that reflect the psychological dimension.

This chapter addresses the psychological dimension of psychosocial functioning. The psychological system serves the purpose of mobilizing our biological and social resources to attain goals (Anderson & Carter, 1984). Anderson and Carter (1984) have pointed out that the function of goal attainment is what differentiates the psychological system from the other major systems of psychosocial functioning. The psychological system also plays a critical role in helping avoid danger. This dimension includes many subsystems with key concepts of use to social workers in assessing the psychological contributions to problems of social functioning.

Each of these subsystems contains concepts that are useful in assessing psychological contributions to human behavior. They are also useful in differentiating the psychological system from the social and biological systems in our multidimensional framework. Several theories pertain to how the psychological system affects functioning. The following Focus on Theory sections examine Freud's psychodynamic theory and Erikson's psychosocial development approach, which expanded Freud's ideas by covering the entire life span.

FOCUS ON THEORY

Psychodynamic Theory

Sigmund Freud, a physician and neurologist, developed the first major theory of personality during the late 19th century. He became interested in patients with mental problems and encouraged his clients to explore their childhood experiences. He believed that all behavior was determined by events that happened in childhood. His contributions to psychology are perhaps unmatched in terms of their overall influence (Leahey, 1987). His concepts and views of human nature are incorporated in popular culture, most areas of social science, literature, and the humanities. He clarified for practitioners how we can study the unconscious by observing its clinical manifestations.

All human behavior, according to Freud, is driven by a special kind of energy referred to as the **libido.** The libido is in constant search of pleasure. This "libido theory" is considered the cornerstone of contemporary psychoanalysis (Gaylin, 1986). "With this theory, all human behavior could be related to the driving force of the sexual instinct and the counterforces that kept it in check" (Gaylin, 1986, p. 47). The libido is associated with in-

stinctual drives like hunger, elimination, and sex, which are biologically determined. These drives must be released in order to reduce tension, and this release is experienced as pleasure. These drives operate according to the *pleasure principle*, which insists on immediate gratification of urges. Even an infant's behavior is motivated by these unconscious, pleasure-seeking urges (Frosh, 1987). The **id,** one of the three components of personality, is the instinctive component and operates from the basis of the pleasure principle. The id is often referred to as the storehouse of psychic energy. This psychic energy is limited to **primary process thinking,** which is based on irrational, illogical, and fantasy-oriented notions—it is disconnected from reality.

The **ego** saves us from being victims of our own pleasure. It is the executive branch of one's personality and makes rational decisions. It is able to postpone pleasure until an appropriate time. The ego operates within the context of the *reality principle* by bringing individual pleasure within the boundaries of reality. The ego must create balance between the other two personality components, the id and superego. In attempting to create a balance, the ego is sensitive to the desires for immediate gratification and also acknowledges social realities such as norms, rules, and customs that influence behavior. The ego is responsible for mediating between the id and superego. Mastery of this task leads to more mature and adaptive behavior. Such adaptive behavior is referred to as **secondary process thinking,** which is based on realistic and rational approaches to problem solving. The ego desires to avoid any negative consequences from society and thus helps the person conform to society's rules. The ego is an abstract concept that is often defined by its functions. These functions represent the way a person adapts to his or her environment (Goldstein, 1984).

The **superego** is the moral guidance that helps balance the drives associated with the id. It represents the social standards derived from society and the family. As children grow up they are exposed to moral standards for behavior. The id and superego are not too friendly with one another—they are each oriented toward a different goal—one pleasure and the other moral standards. Luckily, the ego mediates between these two components, taking into account instinctual impulses and moral values. Freud assumes that the superego emerges from the ego at about 3–5 years of age.

From a Freudian perspective, how does personality develop? Psychoanalytic theory is based on a stage theory of development. We move through various stages, and how well we master those stages forms the basis of our personality. As children mature, their sexual energy (urges for physical pleasure) is invested in biologically predetermined areas of the body. Each stage in Freud's psychosexual development represents a different area of sexual focus that influences our adult personality. Infants are dominated by an oral focus, early childhood moves through an anal and phallic focus, middle childhood is represented by a latency focus, and the psychosexual stages end at puberty when the focus is on one's genitals.

Personality depends on how each of these stages are handled. Children may experience excessive gratification or excessive frustration while in one of the stages. When this happens, *fixation* occurs whereby the child cannot move on to the next stage of development. Experiencing fixation would be apparent during the adult years. Many people are familiar with the label "anal." A person is referred to as "anal" because his or her fixation is exhibited by compulsiveness. Table 3.1 presents Freud's stages of psychosexual development.

According to Freud, early childhood development is critical in the development of personality. In fact, personality is laid down by the age of 5 or 6 as the child completes the primary psychosexual stages. The last two phases of development are latency and genital. During the latency stage, a child's sexual energy subsides. During the genital stage in adolescence, the conflicts of early childhood are revived. If they have been mastered appropriately, then the child moves into normal heterosexual relationships. This foundation of one's personality is reexperienced in adulthood such that adult conflicts are related to early crises that occurred in childhood. Many theorists did not like Freud's notion that personality development is confined to the early years. Most notable is Erik Erikson, who believes that personality evolves across the life span. His work, as well as Freud's, is criticized for its emphasis on heterosexual relationships.

FOCUS ON THEORY

Erikson's Psychosocial Development

Erik Erikson is noted for having developed a psychosocial approach to human development. Before immigrating to the United States in 1933, Erikson worked with Sigmund Freud. But Erikson's work includes several key departures from the thinking of Freud. In Erikson's view, Freud attached far too much emphasis on the role of biological and sexual forces on human development. This resulted in Freud's neglect of development after adolescence. Erikson, on the other hand, was interested in explaining development from birth through death.

TABLE 3.1 Freud's Stages of Psychosexual Development

Stage	Sexual Focus	Key Tasks	Fixations
Oral (0–1)	Mouth	Weaning from breast or bottle	Obsessive eating, talking, smoking, drinking
Anal (1–3)	Anus	Toilet training	Obstinacy, compulsiveness, possessiveness
Phallic (3–6)	Genitals	Oedipal crisis, identification with adult role models	Homosexuality, narcissism, arrogance, flamboyance
Latency (6–12)	None	Focus on social relationships	
Genital (puberty)	Genitals (intercourse)	Development of intimate relationships	

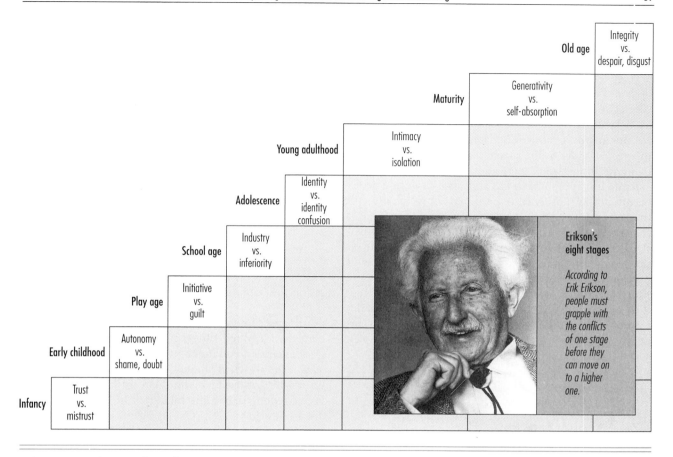

FIGURE 3.1   Erikson's psychosocial stages   Source: Erikson, 1976.

Erikson assumed that people follow a sequence of stages of development from birth through death. These developmental stages include tasks that result from both biological forces and age-related social or cultural expectations. The biological forces follow a built-in plan that governs when and how aspects of the biological system arise. This plan is technically referred to in the literature as the **epigenetic principle.** It refers to the biological blueprint that dictates how the organism grows and reaches maturity. This plan guiding the biological forces combines with the changes in the social expectations of a society to structure the person's adaptation to his or her environment.

Erikson has identified eight psychosocial stages of human development, as shown in Figure 3.1. Each of

these stages is marked by differential tasks. "They are patterned sequences of stages encompassing appropriate physical, emotional, and cognitive tasks that the individuals must master in the struggle to adjust to the demands of the social environment." (Okun, 1984, p. 16). This patterned sequence of changes is not considered complete in adulthood; it continues across the life span. A fundamental issue underlying this sequence of changes is how individuals define their sense of identity.

For Erikson, each of the eight stages of development should be viewed as a psychosocial crisis or psychosocial conflict. "Whether the conflict of a particular stage is successfully resolved or not, the individual is pushed by both biological maturation and social demands into the next stage" (Sigelman & Shaffer, 1995, p. 269). These conflicts involve bipolar tasks, such as trust versus mistrust. With the successful resolution of each of these conflicts, the person acquires new ego strengths. For instance, a person develops a healthy balance during the first stage of development between trust and mistrust. For our survival, we cannot be too trusting or distrusting but need an appropriate balance between these opposite life tasks.

In many of our discussions of developmental themes, we refer to the psychosocial tasks from Erikson that have influenced theory and research on human development. His approach has appealed to social workers because of its sensitivity to the impact of social and cultural variables on processes of human development. But the age-grading associated with many of his identified stages is not without controversy. Many individuals do not adhere to the age-grading implied in his stages of psychosocial development. Furthermore, his stages reflect a historical bias toward heterosexuality, marriage, dual-parent families, and other social formations that differ from many of our current realities. Nonetheless, his approach directs us to look at the influence of historical, social, and cultural factors on human development.

Cognitive Development and Information Processing

Cognitive psychologists investigate processes involving human sensation, perception, and cognition. **Sensation** refers to the processes by which the organism detects internal and external stimulation at its various receptor sites. **Perception,** on the other hand, refers to the interpretation of this sensory input. It involves the use of signals and symbols to understand and differentiate among sensations. **Cognition** is the process of obtaining, organizing, and using sensory and perceptual information from the environment, from past experience, and from other mental activities such as plans and strategies (Kietzman, Spring, & Zubin, 1985). All these processes are examined by cognitive psychologists. Prominent among cognitive psychologists is Jean Piaget, whose concepts about cognitive development are widely used in various areas of cognitive science and impact many areas of social work practice.

Jean Piaget's Structural Approach to Cognition

Piaget was formally trained as a biologist, and his biological perspective influenced his eventual work in cognitive psychology. He published his first scholarly work at age 10 on an albino sparrow that he observed in a park (Cohen, 1983). An important benefit of this accomplishment was his introduction to Paul Godet, a zoologist and a curator of the Museum of Natural History in Neuchatel, Switzerland. After Godet saw his one-page article, he invited Piaget to go with him on walks in the countryside where Godet showed Piaget how to make observations. By age 16, Piaget was given the job of curator of mollusks at the local museum of natural history. He continued research in this area and completed his doctoral thesis on the habits and habitat of Valais mollusks (Cohen, 1983).

Piaget's interest turned to psychology, and he collaborated with Alfred Binet on the development of intelligence tests. In conducting these tests with children, Piaget was intrigued about how children reason about their wrong answers. Rather than study how to measure intelligence, he became interested in how children *use* their intelligence.

Piaget built his career on studying the relationship between how we develop and how we learn. He believed that we mature into logic rather than learn it. This important distinction is one of the reasons that some of his early works were ignored by American psychologists. According to many behaviorists, logic and other knowledge skills are products of learning. Many behaviorists consider the mind at birth to be a blank slate that is written on by experience. But Piaget assumed that there are inborn, invariant processes in humans that play a fundamental role in understanding reality. These processes are *adaptation* and *organization*.

The concepts of adaptation and organization are critical components of Piaget's theory of cognitive development. People use schema (plural schemata) or cognitive structures in the process of adapting to and organizing their world. A **schema** is a unit of information that an individual possesses; **adaptation** deals with the individual's relation to the external world and the ability to change or adapt to that world. The process of adaptation involves the twin processes of **assimilation** and **accommodation.** According to Piaget, what we perceive in the external world does not always fit our internal schema or what we know. So we can assimilate new information into our existing schema or thought structures and thereby change what we perceive (assimilation). Or we can accommodate our thought patterns to what we perceive, in other words, change what we think (accommodation).

Organization is the other invariant feature of human cognition. "Organization is the tendency for all members of a species to systematize their processes into coherent systems, physical or psychological" (Ginsburg, 1985, p. 180). It is the way we make sense out of what we perceive. To understand this concept, it is often helpful to keep in mind Piaget's biological perspective on the role of heredity in human development. In Piaget's view, individuals are endowed with physical structures that are species specific. Each species has distinctive physical structures, and as humans, we inherit several key physical structures that are specific to our species. In other words, through heredity, everybody possesses the same basic nervous systems, perceptual structures, and other similar attributes (Ginsburg, 1985).

This suggests that the *specific heredity* of humans guarantees that they have in common a universal potential for acquiring a specific type of cognitive development. The expression of this potential requires an adequate environment. For instance, humans have the inherited potential for abstract thought, but they will not develop this psychological function without an environment that stimulates the need for the development of abstract adaptations.

This tendency toward organization is what Piaget's theory of cognitive development seeks to explain. He provided a stage description of the developmental variations in the systems or structures of thought observed in humans. In his approach to cognition, he proposed that individuals go through a series of mental stages: (1) the sensorimotor period (from birth to about age 2), (2) the preoperations period (ages 2 to 7), (3) the concrete operations period (ages 7 to 11), and (4) the formal operational period (ages 11 and above). These stages illustrate why we observe variations in knowledge between children and young adults. These variations are not due merely to children lacking facts, experience, or information; chil-

dren think differently because of the mental structures that define their stage of development. The role played by mental structures in his theory of cognitive development is why Piaget is considered a *structuralist.*

Piaget's structural approach has significantly impacted how clinicians approach working with children. In the past, minimal attention had been given to a systematic approach for working with children from a cognitive developmental perspective. Today, cognitive development is gaining recognition as a critical consideration in choosing appropriate interventions for children.

Although adults recognize that children lack the capacity to understand many events in their lives, Piaget's work provides an invaluable base for explaining observations that are often taken for granted. For instance, throughout history the limitations in the abilities of children have been recognized. But these developmental abilities are often ignored in actual interventions. An excellent example of the dangers associated with ignoring cognitive developmental abilities is addressed in the work of Berrick and Gilbert (1991) on the child sexual-abuse prevention movement.

Berrick and Gilbert argue that prevention services were created to respond to the perceived epidemic of sexual abuse without regard for the potential consequences and age appropriateness. In fact, the first child sexual-abuse prevention program relied heavily on principles from rape prevention programming developed for adults (Ashford, 1994). In these adult programs, the concept of empowerment was a key organizing principle. This principle, coupled with the now well-recognized "good and bad touches" continuum, were incorporated into the early child sexual-abuse prevention programs. Berrick and Gilbert's assessment of these prevention strategies indicate that efforts to sensitize preschool children to be assertive in their responses to good and bad touches is developmentally inappropriate. The researchers offer a different approach to this problem that takes children's developmental needs into account. Many of these needs involve cognitive considerations requiring actual prevention efforts by adults. Their suggestions are consistent with many of Piaget's propositions. It is now becoming widely known among clinical professionals that they should use a cognitive developmental approach when developing interventions for children. In addition, social workers are often asked to counsel children about very complex emotional or traumatic events. In fact, this was a key role played by social workers following the bombing of the federal building in Oklahoma City in 1995. Members of the media asked mental health specialists, including social workers, to provide consultation to parents about how they should explain this horrible event to their children. Piaget's theoretical approach offers some general guidelines for this type of practice task. It cautions practitioners to be sensitive to children's cognitive abilities. In his theoretical approach, it is assumed that the preoperation child cannot understand notions of cause and effect commonly understood by adults. In fact, one of the fundamental aims of many of Piaget's experiments was to understand how children develop these fundamental notions of causality. These developmental differences in understanding the causes of events must be taken into account in trying to explain complex issues (such as why people would kill children with a bomb) to children.

At what age is it reasonable to assume that children can self-monitor their own behavior? Do preschool children have understandings of death, divorce, war, and other events similar to those of adolescents and adults? The answers to many of these questions will be covered in the developmental chapters of this book, and propositions from Piaget's cognitive theory of development are useful in answering these questions.

Though Piaget's work provides valuable insight into cognitive development, more recent research has shown that we cannot make accurate assessments of key cognitive functions without understanding the information-processing system. This system and its subsystems play a fundamental role in most of our cognitive activities. Today, social workers cannot rely on just one theory of cognition to address the multifaceted problems they encounter in their practice situations. We will explore information processing in the next section.

Information Processing

For social workers to assess the mental functioning of their clients, they must have a basic understanding of human **information processing.** The goal of most human information-processing approaches is to under-

stand how stimuli generated internally or externally enter the perceptual awareness of individuals and result in some kind of response. Information processing examines the uptake, selection, coding, and storage of information (Weinman, 1987). This perspective assumes that a sequence of stages takes place between the initial stimulus and the subsequent response. These stages follow procedures analogous to those followed by the computer, as shown in Figure 3.2.

Each stage of information processing contains many substages and concepts that must be understood by social workers. Deficits or problems in any of these areas will contribute to impairments in cognitive functioning. For this reason, we will briefly review several key functions in the information-processing subsystem: (1) consciousness and orientation, (2) perception, (3) attention, (4) learning, (5) memory, (6) comprehension, and (7) reasoning and judgment (Nurcombe & Gallagher, 1986).

Consciousness and Orientation

Consciousness is considered the most fundamental and essential element of our cognitive activities, and it is defined as our awareness of internal or external stimuli. This includes awareness of self, others, and various aspects of the physical environment (Ludwig, 1986). Healthy individuals experience a wide zone of awareness in their day-to-day activities, from alertness to sleep. Although consciousness can be described in many ways, it is difficult to operationalize.

One approach, other than the sleep-wake cycle, for dealing with the definitional problems associated with consciousness is to examine levels of consciousness along a continuum from coma to full alertness. Coma represents a mental state in which verbal, motor, or other responses cannot be elicited even with noxious stimuli. Alertness, on the other hand, refers to the ability to respond to any emotionally meaningful, noxious, or novel stimulus (Ludwig, 1986).

Social workers can test a client's level of consciousness by evaluating the individual's response to various types of stimuli. Have you ever called out the name of a person who is seriously intoxicated? Such persons may respond to your efforts to arouse their awareness, but immediately after your efforts they drift back into a state of unawareness of their surroundings. Persons in deep

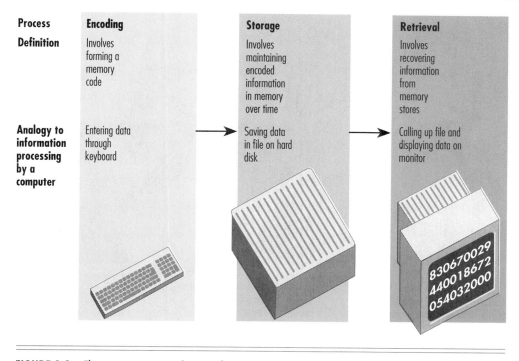

Process	Encoding	Storage	Retrieval
Definition	Involves forming a memory code	Involves maintaining encoded information in memory over time	Involves recovering information from memory stores
Analogy to information processing by a computer	Entering data through keyboard	Saving data in file on hard disk	Calling up file and displaying data on monitor

FIGURE 3.2   The computer as an analogy to information processing   Source: Weiten, 1995.

sleeps can also experience difficulties in being made aware of their surroundings. These states of low alertness affect a person's potential for many kinds of cognitive processes. These states of consciousness are called **disoriented states** whenever individuals experience significant deviations in their levels of awareness. In a disoriented state, a person loses specific levels of awareness: awareness of time, place, and person. Disorientation can be indicative of an organically based mental disorder. Generally, if a person's sensory registers are clouded or restricted, then the individual is likely to have problems in orientation. Social workers employed in nursing facilities and in situations where they encounter persons suffering from serious mental disorders often see orientation difficulties. Orientation, therefore, is a form of consciousness that social workers assess in determining the status of a client's mental processes by asking clients questions about the time, hour, day, date, month, year, place, city, and so forth.

Perception

Our knowledge of our physical and social realities rests on the functioning of our senses. Can we have pure knowledge of these sense experiences? This puzzle has intrigued philosophers and scientists throughout human history. What are the differences between sensations and perceptions? Sensation refers to the process in which receptors detect information that is transmitted to the brain. We currently know that infants detect light, sound, and other stimuli at birth, but they do not understand what this information means. They cannot make sense of this information. Perception is the interpretation of this sensory input (see Figure 3.3). There are very few things people do that do not involve perception. As a result, a number of theories about perception have developed in the field of psychology. We will briefly discuss two of these theories: enrichment theory and differentiation theory.

Light waves

Sound waves

Sensation		Perception
Sensory organs absorb energy from physical stimuli in the environment.	Sensory receptors detect stimulus energies and convert them into neural impulses, which are sent to the brain.	The brain organizes this input and translates it into something meaningful.

FIGURE 3.3   The distinction between sensation and perception   Source: Weiten, 1995.

Enrichment theory is often associated with Jean Piaget. In Piaget's view, the information received by our sensory receptors is formless. For this reason, Piaget assumed that we must enrich this fragmented information to make sense of it. Figure 3.4 illustrates this point. At first glance you will probably see a young woman looking back over her shoulder. However, you might also see an older woman with her chin placed on her chest (the young woman's ear becomes the older woman's eye). People who are led to expect to see a young woman or an older woman generally end up seeing what they expect (Weiten, 1995). Our cognitive expectations enrich this visual sense experience. That is, our perceptions help us construct interpretations of our reality. In social work, many individuals we encounter in practice situations have faulty perceptions that are rooted in negative life experiences. For instance, many children of abuse often misperceive the actions of other children. They will per-

ceive hostile intentions from neutral acts like someone accidentally bumping into them.

On the other hand, **differentiation theory** contends that all the information we need is contained in the sensations themselves. Our task is to differentiate the various aspects in the stimulations that were there all along. These two theories hold different understandings of how we make sense of reality. Many factors can influence human perceptions. In fact, the same situation will trigger different perceptual responses among different individuals. Our aim is to understand what factors are contributing to these different perceptions. As social workers, we must understand how individuals perceive objects and persons. Different factors can be involved in each of these processes. Social psychology devotes substantial attention to trying to discern the factors that influence our perceptions of other human beings in our environment. Other areas of psychology focus on per-

A famous reversible figure

Unambiguous drawings of the young and old woman

FIGURE 3.4 **An exercise in perception** Source: Based on Boring, 1930.

ceptual difficulties in dealing with physical objects in reality.

Attention

Attention is a fundamental cognitive function that plays an important role in memory. Although clients can demonstrate levels of alertness in their functioning, this does not mean that they are attentive. **Attention** differs from alertness in that "it pertains to the ability to focus on a specific stimulus without distraction by irrelevant stimuli" (Ludwig, 1986, p. 17). Attention is often evalu-

ated in clinical practice by having clients perform what is known as serial 7s. Serial 7s give an indication of the client's ability to attend and indications of special memory functions. The client is asked, on interview, to subtract 7s in a repeated fashion from 100. To accomplish this task, the client must focus on the remainder while performing the serial subtractions. Some workers prefer to have clients spell words like "world" backward to test an individual's attentional abilities. Another test is to ask a client to recite the months of the year backward. Clinical scientists have identified other aspects of attention

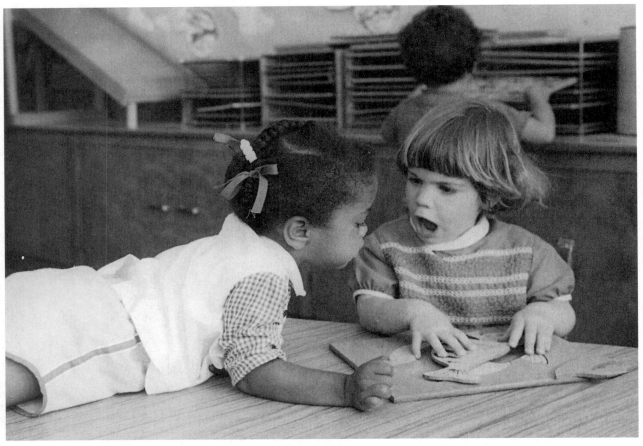

Aggressive children have been found to perceive events in such a way that they overattribute the actions of others as hostile.

with significance in human behavior assessment—vigilance and concentration.

Vigilance differs from attention in that an individual must be able to sustain outward attention over a prolonged period of time. In dangerous or unpredictable situations, this is a very important cognitive function. Individuals must be able to scan the environment with a high degree of vigilance to guard against potentially harmful events. Individuals with disorders like post-traumatic stress disorder and other anxiety disorders often engage in this process in circumstances where it serves no function. **Hypervigilance** refers to an excessive focus on outward factors in the environment. For example, persons suffering from post-traumatic stress disorder are hypervigilant about scanning their environment for danger.

Concentration is another cognitive function that involves attentional abilities. It refers to a person's ability to sustain inner mental operations without disruption (Ludwig, 1986). When social workers encounter persons with attention problems, it is important for them to distinguish the type of deficit in the client's attentional processes in describing the problem for other professionals.

Learning

The issue of how people learn new information has fascinated humans since the time of Aristotle. In fact, Aristotle is noted for having instituted a special tradition in philosophy that continues to have influence on the field of learning psychology—**associationism.** Association is probably one of the oldest and most influential constructs in the field of psychology (Bourne, Ekstrand, & Dominowski, 1971). It involves the formation of mental associations that are registered or stored in the mind (Richardson, 1988). These associations are due to three fundamental factors: continuity, similarity, and repetition.

Continuity refers to associations occurring in the mind because two events occur together in time or space. For instance, if a person connects the sense experience of furriness with a dog, this can lead to the lasting association between furriness and the concept dog. Other associations occur in memory because of the principle of **similarity.** This principle refers to associations being formed because events or ideas that occur close together have features that are similar. Associationists also believe that ideas are likely to become associated when they occur together often. This process is referred to as **repetition.**

Some associationists have made a distinction between sensory association and stimulus-response association. Sensory association assumes that there is a direct connection between the experience of an event and the sensation of that event in the brain. This sensation of the event in the brain is called an idea or *image.* This viewpoint suggests that the connection in the brain is what contributes to ideas being associated with one another. This form of associationism was eventually replaced by stimulus-response associationism. It was felt that stimulus-response associations were easier to study. In a stimulus-response approach, learning involves the development of chains of stimulus-response associations or connections in the mind.

Interests in studying processes of association led researchers to discover another major factor contributing to the learning process—reinforcement. **Classical conditioning** and instrumental or **operant conditioning** are two fundamental models of learning that employ a slightly different definition of reinforcement. In classical conditioning, reinforcement involves the strengthening of an association between a stimulus and a response through the presentation of a second stimulus. For example, a dog can learn to flex its paw in response to a bell (first stimulus) that is associated with a second stim-

ulus (a shock). In operant conditioning, reinforcement refers to the acquisition of new responses because of their effect on the environment. For instance, if a response solves a problem for a child, the child will repeat that response if provided with a similar situation because of the associated result. (See Focus on Theory: Learning Theories.)

Other factors besides reinforcement contribute to learning in humans. A close relative of instrumental conditioning is learning through observation, or **social learning theory.** In this approach, individuals learn by observing events that they do not directly experience. Bandura (1977) is one of the most noteworthy contributors to this learning theory. He has identified four fundamental components of observational learning: attentional, retentional, motor reproduction, and motivational processes. These processes explain how people can learn information without experiencing themselves the consequences or reinforcement for their behavior. (See Focus on Theory: Social Learning Theory.)

FOCUS ON THEORY

Learning Theories

John B. Watson brought behaviorism into the forefront of psychology in 1913 when he asserted that psychology must abandon its focus on subjective "mentalistic" concepts and instead focus exclusively on behavior. Watson is recognized as the father of *behaviorism,* a learning theory that is based on observable behavior. Watson was extreme in his position that we are born *tabula rasa*—as a blank slate. A well-known statement of his represents his thinking:

> Give me a dozen healthy infants, well formed, and my own specified world to bring them up in and I'll guarantee to take any one at random and train him to become any type of specialist I might select—doctor, lawyer, artist, merchant, chief, and ye, even beggar-man and thief, regardless of his talents, penchants, tendencies, abilities, vocations, and race of his ancestors. (Watson, 1925, p. 82)

Clearly, Watson believed that development depends on learning. Given the proper experiences, learning will proceed. This theory is quite different from the theories of Freud or Piaget, which assume that changes in behavior take place as children move through different stages. Furthermore, behaviorists reject notions like the id, ego, and superego because these mental functions cannot be observed and studied. Instead, they focus on studying observable stimuli and observable responses to the stimuli.

Watson demonstrated the importance of learning in an experiment designed to prove that children's fears are learned and not inborn. A child named Albert participated in an experiment where he learned to fear cute little white rats. The procedure was simple: Albert was presented with a stimulus, the cute white rat, and at the same time was exposed to a second stimulus, a loud, frightening sound. Through repeated associations Albert learned to associate the white rat with the frightening noise. It did not take long before just presenting Albert with a white rat led to a fearful reaction. Thus, Watson demonstrated that fears can be learned through experience.

This learning is referred to as *classical conditioning*, the term used to explain learning that occurs when a neutral stimulus acquires the capacity to elicit a response that was originally elicited by another stimulus. Classical conditioning is a widely accepted explanation for the acquisition of certain emotional responses, such as fear and anxiety. You can easily see how a phobia or fear could be developed in this manner. For example, if you got into a serious automobile accident you could develop a fear of driving. The previously neutral stimulus of driving a car is now associated with your frightening accident. So when you recover from the accident and get into the driver's seat again, you may not be able to drive the car without a heightened sense of fear and panic.

Although John Watson's name may not have been familiar to you, B. F. Skinner, who built on Watson's learning theory, is probably a familiar name. Skinner (1953) advanced the study of *operant conditioning*, a form of learning that occurs when responses are controlled by their consequences. Skinner observed that behavior is repeated when followed by positive consequences and that behavior is not repeated when followed by neutral or negative consequences. When consequences such as rewards and punishments are made contingent on behavior, they can have a powerful influence on behavior.

Two critical concepts in operant conditioning are *reinforcement* and *punishment*. Reinforcement refers to anything that follows a behavior and increases the likelihood of that behavior. Punishment is anything that follows a behavior and decreases the likelihood of that behavior. It is really quite simple, and part of the attraction of operant conditioning is that it is a straightforward theory about behavior.

Two other learning processes contribute to how behavior is acquired. *Negative reinforcement* occurs when a behavior increases because it is followed by the withdrawal of an unpleasant stimulus. *Extinction* occurs when a conditioned response that was previously reinforced stops producing positive consequences.

Consider the following example: A child begins to whine at his mother, begging for a cookie prior to dinnertime. The child continues to whine and nag the mother until she eventually gives in and gives the child a cookie. In this example, the child's whining will be strengthened through positive reinforcement—the whining was followed by a positive consequence, the cookie. On the other hand, the mother's behavior is influenced by negative reinforcement. The child's whining, an aversive event, is terminated by the mother's giving in and rewarding the child with the cookie. The mother's giving-in behavior is an example of negative reinforcement because this response is strengthened by the termination of the aversive event.

From a developmental point of view, Skinner's theory of operant conditioning provides an understanding of how learning takes place. Our behavior can be influenced—over the life course—by the positive and negative consequences that we experience. Many theorists, while agreeing with Skinner about the influence of the environment on behavior, have argued that our beliefs or thought processes can also influence how we learn. Watson would be surprised today to learn that many modern day behaviorists have acknowledged a role for cognition in understanding behavior.

Social Learning Theory

Foremost among these new cognitive behaviorists, or more appropriately referred to as social learning theorists, is Albert Bandura. Bandura attempts to understand people as conscious, thinking beings who can have an influence over their environment. What is distinctive about his perspective is that unlike Skinner, who believes learning is passive, Bandura believes that people can process information to actively influence how the environment controls them.

Bandura's cognitive emphasis in learning becomes obvious when we examine his perspective on how observation can lead to learning. *Observational learning* occurs when people observe role models and learn new behavior as a result of those observations. In this context, learning occurs without any reinforcement for imitating what is being observed. In essence, observational learning is a kind of indirect learning. The learning process is considered cognitive because people must pay attention to the role models and process this information in their memory.

According to social learning theory, models are critical in the development of personality. How do children learn to develop aggressive tendencies? Bandura thinks it has a lot to do with the kind of social role models children are exposed to. In perhaps his most famous research experiment, Bandura demonstrated the dramatic influence of observational learning. He and his colleagues (Bandura, Ross, & Ross, 1963) exposed one group of children to a film that showed children displaying aggressive behaviors and another group of children to a neutral film. Following the film, children were taken to a playroom and allowed to interact freely. Children who had seen the aggressive film and had been exposed to aggressive models engaged in more aggressive behavior than did children who had been exposed to the neutral film. This study became a classic because it demonstrated the negative influence that media can have on children's behavior.

An important aspect to Bandura's approach to social learning theory is the notion of *self-efficacy* (Bandura, 1989). Self-efficacy refers to a person's belief about his or her ability to perform behaviors that lead to expected outcomes. When people have a strong belief in their ability to perform certain behaviors, their confidence is high. This confidence means they are likely to persist in their endeavor. When people have low self-efficacy, they are not very confident and so are likely to give up easily. Thus, the decision to engage in a situation as well as the intensity of the effort expended in the situation is determined by a person's self-efficacy.

From a human development perspective, self-efficacy is helpful in understanding how individuals adjust and adapt to new situations and roles. A strong sense of self-efficacy can help a person engage in new situations and persist. For example, if a person, say a single woman, moved to a new city and did not know anyone, a strong sense of self-efficacy may be helpful in her adjustment to the move. If she is confident in her ability to meet new people (a strong sense of self-efficacy), she is more likely to pursue situations that give her the opportunity to meet people. Furthermore, her efficacy may be helpful in her persistence to find new friends—that isn't an easy task and may take repeated attempts.

Memory

Besides the various reinforcement theories of learning, there are cognitive approaches, including information-processing theories. In the information-processing model, memory is considered the most critical component of the learning process. Clinical professionals have come up with specific ways to describe the various components of our memory processes. These descriptions help practitioners identify areas of impairment in people's memory functions that are impeding their capacity to learn new information. We have already reviewed this approach for understanding memory in our discussion of information processing. We will now discuss some specific concepts used in the mental-status evaluation to assess human memory functions.

The first distinction made in clinical assessment is between **immediate memory** and **short-term memory.**

Immediate memory refers to information that is retained for up to ten seconds. Immediate memory is generally tested by having a person perform digit span. *Digit span* is administered by having a person repeat a list of numbers given forward and backward. An unimpaired individual should be able to repeat five to six digits forward and up to four or five digits backward. Intermediate memory can also be tested by having the person repeat back three pieces of information. Andreasen and Black (1991) offer the following example—the color green, the name Mr. Williams, and the address 1915 High Street. The objective is to assess whether the client can recall this information immediately after being told by the practitioner. This clinical test examines whether the client has any problems registering this information. If so, the person will not be able to recall the information.

In the information-processing approach, memory involves four stages: registration, rehearsal, retention, and recall. Ludwig (1986) refers to these four stages as the "Four Rs." Registration cannot occur without receptor elements being intact—we register or receive information through our senses (sensory registration). Injuries in the brain caused by a stroke or by a physical trauma can injure portions of the brain that play a major role in the registration of information. Short-term memory loss generally is due to an impairment in some areas involving registration, rehearsal, or consolidation of information (Ludwig, 1986), whereas long-term memory loss is generally due to a problem in recall or in the retrieval of the needed information. When assessing memory, workers often warn clients that they will ask them within 5 minutes to tell them the same three items they were given. After 5 minutes of pursuing other topics in the interview, the client will be asked to recall the objects.

Short-term memory has definite limits. It can maintain unrehearsed information for about 20 to 30 seconds; with rehearsal, it can last between 5 and 10 minutes. Rehearsal, a critical strategy for retaining information, refers to the process of repeating by verbalization, imagery, or thought the information received from stimuli. When individuals cannot rehearse unfamiliar information, this information is easily lost from their short-term memory.

Short-term memory is also limited in the number of items it can hold. George Miller (1956) wrote a famous paper on this topic called "The Magical Number Seven, Plus or Minus Two: Some Limits on Our Capacity for Processing Information." As a result of Miller's research, we now have a better understanding about short-term memory capacity. When additional information is added, some of the older information will have to be displaced. For instance, if you are reciting a telephone number to yourself provided by the operator (see Focus on Psychology: Information-Processing Functions in Remembering a Phone Number) and stop to ask yourself where you placed your pencil, the additional information about where you placed the pencil will displace some of the information already in your short-term memory. In fact, Miller discovered that if you are memorizing ten items, the ninth or tenth item will knock out earlier items in your memory.

Think of short-term or working memory as containing seven slots or drawers. Each drawer can handle only a single item of information (Howard, 1983). This means that we cannot add additional information to these drawers without displacing the information already contained in them.

Long-term memory refers to the retention of information for days to months to years. Most individuals easily remember events from their past. In assessing long-term memory, clients may be asked to recall the last five presidents. Social workers can also ask about personally relevant information that was obtained before the interview. For example, they can ask about significant childhood experiences that they learned about from relatives.

Long-term memory has an unlimited capacity for storing information. There are many views on the length of time that memory can be stored in our brains. One view is that memory in this store, unlike memory in the other areas, is permanent. Evidence of its permanence is often illustrated in cases of "flashbulb memories," memories involving vivid and detailed recollections. Examples include persons remembering explicit details about where they were and how they felt when they learned of the bombing of Pearl Harbor, the assassination of President Kennedy and of Martin Luther King, Jr., and the explosion of the *Challenger* spacecraft. Additional evidence of the permanency of memory is often found in cases involving exceptional forms of recall triggered by hypnosis. Penfield and Perot (1963) provided additional evidence in some of their early brain research. They found that they could trigger long-lost memories in experiments in which subjects had portions of their brains electrically stimulated.

Even with these different forms of evidence, many scientists are not certain that long-term memory is permanently stored (Weiten, 1995). Some scientists use the analogy of a barrel to illustrate how memories are lost. The permanency view holds that memory is stored as if we were placing small stones in a barrel. In this view, none of the stones placed in the barrel will leak out. When people forget information, it is because they cannot retrieve or pull out the desired stones contained in the barrel. They have a problem in how the information is organized in their memory store. This organizational problem makes it difficult to locate the stone or bit of information. The other view assumes that some memories can vanish because the barrel is leaky and allows some of the stones to leak out of the storage area (Weiten, 1995).

Figure 3.5 provides an illustration of the key memory systems in our psychological system: sensory registers, short-term or working memory, and long-term memory. In particular, note that we register many forms of information in our sensory registers, but because our attention can focus on only a few items at a time, much of this information is not committed to our long-term memory.

Practitioners also make distinctions between recent and remote memory in their evaluations of clients. **Recent memory** refers to retention of information individuals need to perform their daily functions. It is usually tested by asking a person about events occurring within the last 24 hours. Individuals should be able to recall, for example, what they did on the day prior to the interview, how they got to the interview, what they had for breakfast, or other more immediate happenings in their daily life. **Remote memory** refers to information occurring several weeks or months in the past.

In assessing memory functions, social workers should consider in their evaluation recall of both auditory and visual information. Most of our prior examples focused on testing auditory memory capabilities. *Visual memory* is usually tested by having a person reproduce simple designs. The clinician will draw a simple design and ask the client to reproduce the same design. At points, the social worker will need to capitalize on memory capacities that are still preserved. For instance, some individuals lose the capacity to remember verbal infor-

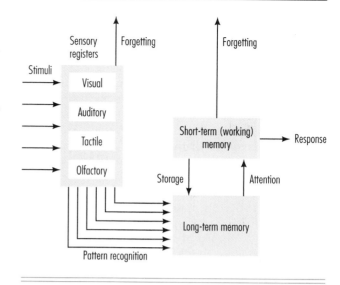

FIGURE 3.5 A diagram of short-term and long-term memory
Source: Howard, 1983.

mation but can remember how to read. If reading is preserved, this can be used to help the person remember.

The assessment of memory functions has always played an important role in assessing psychological functioning. Social workers will probably experience increased demands for their expertise in handling memory impairments. As our population ages, social workers will have increased contact with persons suffering from various kinds of dementia. To assess the functioning of these individuals, they will need to determine the extent to which their client's memory has deteriorated.

FOCUS ON PSYCHOLOGY

Information-Processing Functions in Remembering a Phone Number

Let's look at the stages involved in the process of memory by considering the example of remembering a telephone number told to us by an operator. The first stage of information processing is referred to as *sensory reg-*

istry. At this stage, the phonetic sounds on the phone provided by the operator stimulate the listener's acoustic nerve. This information is then transmitted to the appropriate cortical area for auditory information in the brain. Initially, this phonetic information is not necessarily categorized as a number or as any other signal or symbol value. The assignment of symbolic value does not occur until the second stage of processing. A sizable proportion of auditory sensations that we receive are not processed beyond the stage of sensory registration. Individuals must attend to the specifics of the sound in order to progress to the other stages (Kietzman et al., 1985).

The next stage in information processing involves perception and is often referred to in the literature as *pattern recognition*. The attachment of meanings or symbols to the auditory sounds indicates that pattern recognition has taken place. When the sounds of the operator are recognized as numbers, then pattern recognition has occurred. Language and other factors associated with experience are located in our long-term memory storage and play a significant role in this process. The pattern recognition stage is followed by the short-term memory stage. Any deficits in these three processes can influence how information is stored in our long-term memory.

The digits of the phone number fill up our short-term or working memory. (Remember there are only seven drawers, the addition of any more information will knock one of the numbers out of its drawer.) Many people hold the number in their working memory by reciting (rehearsing) the number to themselves until they have dialed it.

Remembering the phone number long enough to dial it is a working memory issue only. Committing the number to long-term memory will require other memory functions such as association or learning through repetition.

Comprehension

Practitioners confront many problems that are due to deficits in comprehension. For instance, social workers often encounter clients experiencing difficulties in the comprehension and expression of language. These processes are closely associated with memory impairments. In fact, Nurcombe and Gallagher (1986) point out some of the key areas in which comprehension and expression overlap. They both depend on the following:

1. The amount of information in long-term memory (storage)
2. The amount of information that can be retrieved from long-term memory (retrieval)
3. The arrangement of information in long-term memory (organization)
4. The capacity to apply to problems the schematas, structures, scripts, or maps in long-term memory (p. 46).

Although comprehension and expression are intimately related, they are often kept separate by practitioners in doing clinical assessments.

Deficits in human comprehension are represented in various forms of disorders commonly encountered in social work practice. For example, clients suffering from brain damage caused by stroke, Alzheimer's disease, or trauma experience *aphasia*, which is a disorder that involves deficiencies in the comprehension or expression of language. There are two fundamental types of aphasia: *sensory* and *motor*. Sensory aphasia refers to language deficits that are due to problems in the receptive mechanisms of the brain, whereas motor aphasia refers to an inability to express one's thoughts through language. This is why motor aphasia is also referred to in the literature as an expressive form of aphasia. Motor aphasia is often due to some form of neurological impairment.

Reasoning and Judgment

Although persons can understand stimuli in their environment, this does not mean that they will interpret this information effectively. Our mental functions also involve a number of other cognitive abilities. For example, *problem solving* and *abstract reasoning* differ in many ways from the cognitive functions previously discussed in this chapter. Scientists make important distinctions between thinking and other cognitive functions like remembering and comprehending. Although they define these other functions differently, thinking cannot occur without them. In the field of cognitive psychology, thinking is often divided into three areas: problem solving, reasoning, and conceptual thinking.

We will begin this description of human thought processes by discussing problem solving. Social workers are interested in understanding why people cannot solve their problems in living. This problem cannot be understood without a conceptual understanding of what we mean by the term *problem*. A problem is assumed to exist under the following conditions: "First, there is some initial state in which the person begins. Second, there is some goal state that is different from the initial state and which the person wishes to achieve. Third, the actions that are necessary to convert the initial state into the goal state are not immediately obvious" (Howard, 1983, p. 407). If any of these conditions are not present, then the situation is not considered a problem. We often desire to move from an initial state to another state, but the solution is obvious. These forms of behavior would not fall under what is considered problem-solving activities because they do not meet the third condition described above.

Much of our everyday life involves a need to change our state of being. Cognitive scientists are interested in understanding why people fail to arrive at adequate solutions to these problems. One common factor is *rigidity*. We currently know that people often use a solution from their past that worked well in other situations to solve problems even though there might be a better way of solving the new problem. This represents a special form of rigidity referred to as a response set, so called because the person continues to use a response that worked well in other situations (Howard, 1983).

Rigidity in problem solving can also occur in other ways. All too often humans use only one perspective to perceive a problem. This represents a form of perceptual rigidity called a **perceptual set.** This type of set occurs whenever people perceive objects as having only their most common or recent functional significance. Duncker (1945) is known for a famous problem in psychology that illustrates this point. He asked individuals to figure out how to mount a candle on a plywood board so that it could act as a lamp. They were asked to solve this problem with a group of common items placed on a table. The items included candles, a box of matches, string, and some tacks. To solve this problem, the subjects needed to change their perspective about the objects on the table. The correct solution to this problem is illustrated in Figure 3.6.

People often have difficulties solving Duncker's problem because they fail to see the matchbox as having another potential function besides holding the matches. It is interesting that when this experiment is repeated

FIGURE 3.6 The solution to Duncker's problem

with the matches outside the box, subjects generally encounter less difficulties solving the problem. They have problems solving the initial task because of the common barrier in problem solving known as *functional fixedness.* We cannot solve many problems in living without finding novel uses for known objects.

Another key barrier to problem solving in humans is the use of irrelevant information. This has been clearly illustrated in a number of psychological experiments. See if you can solve the following problem (Weiten, 1995):

> Fifteen percent of the people in Topeka have unlisted telephone numbers. You select 200 names at random from the Topeka phone book. How many of these people can be expected to have unlisted phone numbers? (p. 281)

The correct answer to this problem is none, because you will not find anyone with an unlisted phone number in the phone book. If you had trouble answering this problem correctly, it was probably because you committed a common error in the human reasoning process. You focused on irrelevant information in the problem statement. In this problem, numerical information is not relevant to its solution.

Also, whether we can solve a problem depends on how it is mentally represented. We can represent a problem in many ways: verbally, visually, mathematically, or spatially. In fact, some problems are incapable of being solved unless we can properly represent them in our minds. This point is often illustrated by having individuals try to solve the Buddhist monk problem:

> At sunrise, a Buddhist monk sets out to climb a tall mountain. He follows a narrow path that winds around the mountain and up to a temple. He stops frequently to rest and climbs at varying speeds, arriving around sunset. After staying a few days, he begins his return journey. As before, he starts at sunrise, rests often, walks at varying speeds, and arrives around sunset. Prove that there must be a spot along the path that the monk will pass on both trips at precisely the same time of day.

Research has demonstrated that subjects who represent this problem verbally or mathematically have tremendous difficulties arriving at the correct solution. However, it is easy to solve this problem by using graphic representation. See Figure 3.7 for the solution to this problem.

Humans have a number of problem-solving strategies. One of the most widely written about strategies is **trial and error.** This approach involves the sequential application of possible solutions to a problem. These solutions are tested and eliminated when they do not work. Other approaches include means-ends analysis, changing the representation of the problem, searching for analogies, and many others. In clinical practice, it is difficult to assess these mental functions. To this end, practitioners often examine special types of problem-solving abilities. In particular, it is common for clinicians to ask their clients mathematically oriented problems involving the need for the client to complete a series of numbers. These problems are often referred to as series-completion problems (A, 3, B, 6, C, ?). To answer this question correctly, clients must have the ability to sort out relevant from irrelevant information and adopt a strategy or plan to solve the problem. They must also detect a pattern in this sequence of numbers. In fact, **problem solving** is defined as the "ability to sort out relevant from irrelevant information and to adopt a strategy or plan for completing the task" (Ludwig, 1986, p. 21).

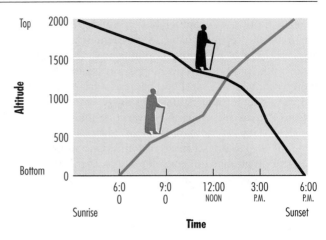

FIGURE 3.7 Solution to the Buddhist monk problem
Source: Weiten, 1995.

Abstract thinking is another cognitive function that is difficult to assess. **Abstraction** involves the ability to recognize the meaning of symbols. For this reason, it is often tested by asking clients about similarities and differences among objects. This is also why psychiatrists often ask their clients to interpret commonly known proverbs. For example, they may ask clients if they have ever heard the saying "People in glass houses shouldn't throw stones." These simple tasks can help the clinician determine whether the client can handle abstract tasks. Without the ability to abstract or problem solve, a person will have severe impairments in judgment. Clinicians often test this function by asking clients to solve a simple problem in living like, "What would you do if someone jumped in front of you in line at the movies?" Persons with serious impairments in abstract thought processes will have serious difficulties solving this problem.

Communication

Communication is considered one of the most important elements in human affairs. It involves oral and written language, nonverbal gestures, and other forms of exchanging information. Throughout this book, we will examine various aspects of linguistic and nonlinguistic forms of communication. In particular, social workers need to have an understanding of speech and language acquisition. These two forms of communication play a pivotal role in understanding human behavior. We will assume in this discussion that when we communicate with language it involves two basic activities: speaking and listening. These two activities hold important clues about a person's psychological makeup and implications for his or her ability to interact with other human beings.

We cannot have any form of culture or civilization without some form of speech and language. Brown observed that language "is nothing less than an inventory of all the ideas, interests, and occupations that take up the attention of the community" (Brown, 1958, p. 156). Although this is a very figurative description of the term, it does not provide a clear definition. Before providing a definition of language, it is important to point out that language and speech are not synonymous (DeVito, 1970). People can fail to develop speech but possess a system of symbols and rules that make up what we would call language. As Saussure (1959) has pointed out, language is a social thing shared by an entire community, whereas speech is considered an individual product. (Saussure is a famous linguist who has significantly influenced many theoretical approaches to the study of language. He is one of the major contributors to the field of modern linguistics.)

Speaking and listening are not the only way in which individuals communicate. We also communicate nonverbally and by writing. *Nonverbal communication* includes the facial expressions, gestures, and other actions intended to send a message to a receiver. These forms of communication have many characteristics in common with language systems. However, unlike verbal communication, nonverbal communication has multiple channels for the transmission of messages. That is, information can be transmitted through gestures, facial expressions, eye movements, and other channels, whereas verbal communication is limited to one fundamental channel of communication (Weiten & Lloyd, 1994). In effect, human communication consists of four basic components: (1) the source, (2) the message, (3) the channel used to send the message, and (4) the receiver. In addition to these fundamental elements, communication theorists have added feedback as another major consideration. Clinical social workers are particularly interested in the role of feedback in understanding human communication.

Moreover, spoken and written language are the two key elements in the human communication process of interest to social workers. To understand these components, several subfields of study have developed in the language sciences: phonology, semantics, syntactics, and pragmatics. **Phonology** examines the system of sound in languages. Every language is made up of two basic units: **phonemes** and **morphemes.** The basic identifiable sound in the language system is known as a phoneme. We currently know that the simplest language has about 15 phonemes and the most complex about 85. In English, each letter of the alphabet has a related phoneme, and some letters have more than one. For example, the letter *i* in pipe is different from the *i* in pit. This is also true of other alphabets. Every word in the English language can be broken down into sound patterns or phonemes. In English, we have a total of 45 phonemes. The smallest unit of meaning in any language system is called a morpheme. An excellent example of a morpheme is *-ing.* There are approximately 50,000 morphemes in the English language.

Semantics is the area in language studies that deals with meaning. It is concerned with understanding how signs and symbols signify actual referents. Because speech and language serve the important function of communicating meaning, this an important area of interest to most social work professionals. We often are asked to decode client communications. In doing so, we must understand the role of symbols and signs within the individual's language system, culture, class position, and nationality. A **symbol** stands for other things or ideas but does not necessarily have a direct relationship with them. The Spanish word *cielo* serves as a symbol of the referent "sky." This word does not directly represent aspects of this object. The same is true of the symbol or word *sky* in English. That is, the symbol sky is not any more blue than the symbol cielo. A symbol does not relate directly to the object it is describing. In fact, the attribution of a symbol in a language is often arbitrary. DeVito illustrated this point clearly: "the word *small* is actually larger than the word *big* and the symbol green—on this paper—is just as black as the symbols black and white" (DeVito, 1970, p. 7).

Signs differ from symbols in that they do bear a valid relationship with the thing for which they stand (DeVito, 1970). When we say a person has a fever, some linguists assume that there is a real rather than an arbitrary relationship between a sickness and the sign—fever. Although this viewpoint is controversial, it clarifies an important distinction that linguists often make between signs and symbols. Symbols are seen as being arbitrary and lacking clear relations with objects they describe. Also, symbols are not limited to speech. They can include other substances like cloth, rock, metal, or sound, and these symbols are used in conjunction with clearly defined rules. Recall that language is considered a structured system that enables the speaker to produce an infinite number of messages with a set of agreed-upon rules.

In the study of language, **syntax** is the component that focuses on the rules that govern the way words are combined to form sentences. Human speakers learn these rules quickly. With the exception of a few salutations and clichés, most of the sentences expressed by a person are made for the first time. Would any speaker of the English language accept the following string of words as fitting the rules of the English language? *Time break heard about and.* Even very young children intuitively recognize this as not a legitimate communication. Linguists assume that children recognize that this phrase violates the fundamental rules of their language system. In fact, many linguists predict that children would show little hesitation in accepting a word string like *All mimsy were the borogoves, and the mome raths outgrabe* as being strange but would consider it a potential utterance from their language (Vetter, 1969).

Grammer is the element of language that provides its coherent features and makes language a predictable process. The role of grammar in language studies has had a long and extensive history. In fact, grammar was considered a fundamental component of early Greek philosophy (Taylor, 1976). Most early linguists set out to uncover the units in each language system. However, the views of Noam Chomsky on transformational generative grammar (TGG) have revolutionized the field. TGG captures an element about language that is distinctive to human communication processes—generativity. When linguists state that human language is generative, they mean that humans can use a limited number of symbols in infinite ways. Although chimps can use symbols to communicate, very few studies have uncovered

evidence of a generative grammar in their communication competence. Chimps have been taught to use symbols, but their messages often lack spontaneity.

The complexity of language acquisition has triggered significant investigation into a variety of issues. One topic that is gaining in popularity is the study of bilingualism. A *bilingual* individual is someone who can speak two languages that differ in sounds, vocabulary, and syntax (Taylor, 1976). Although Americans have seen bilingualism as an unusual occurrence, it is a more pervasive characteristic in the world community than many Americans realize. Many educated individuals from other countries speak more than one language. For instance, many people in Holland speak Dutch, English, and German. Moreover, English is becoming a major second language in many parts of the world. The demand for bilingual skills in New York, Chicago, Los Angeles, Miami, Phoenix, San Francisco, and other major cities is on the increase. The social worker should understand how having two systems of grammar can influence basic psychological functions.

Pragmatics, the final major area in the language sciences, is the study of the rules that specify how language is used across social contexts. All human speakers must master what can and cannot be said to people in their environment. Grammar relates words to words, whereas pragmatics involves the study of the relationship between words and behavior in the social environment. What is polite or appropriate language behavior in relating to one's boss? Many clients fear contact with individuals that communicate with them in a fashion suggesting a lack of respect. Issues of respect and politeness vary from language system to language system and from era to era. This area of linguistics crosses into social concerns often examined by sociolinguists and anthropologists.

Implications for Practice

Social workers must reflect constantly on the content of messages conveyed by the language and words used in all aspects of direct and indirect practice (Schriver, 1995). What should we call the place for providing services to persons with mental disorders? If I want to target a program for new mothers to prevent child abuse and neglect, then what should we call this program? Some names contain meanings that can alienate the very persons who need the services most. What is the best way to tell parents about their child's future? Why do foreign-born individuals often regress to their first language system following a stroke? What is the best way to enhance language acquisition in bicultural environments? The answers to these questions require knowledge of human communication processes, including aspects of speech and language development. Throughout this book, we will examine key developmental milestones that involve these basic communication functions.

Attitudes and Emotions

In the prior discussions, we looked at factors that play a critical role in cognitive development. However, we did not look at parts of the psychological system that play a role in motivating behavior. With this goal in mind, we will explore the role of attitudes and emotions in human behavior. Attitudes and emotions have been subjected to substantial empirical and theoretical scrutiny by researchers in both social work and psychology. Students of human motivation are interested in solving many motivational puzzles: Why do some people have greater propensities toward altruism? What motivates individuals to be achievement oriented? Why do some people prefer antisocial over prosocial activities? We will begin this discussion of motivational subsystems by examining the role of attitudes in human behavior.

The Nature and Function of Attitudes

What are attitudes? How do we form them? What purpose do they serve in our day-to-day activities? An **attitude** is defined as "a learned evaluative response, directed at specific objects, which is relatively enduring and influences and motivates our behavior toward these objects" (Lippa, 1994, p. 214). Gordon Allport (1935) considered attitudes "the keystone in the edifice of American social psychology" (p. 708). Social psychology is a branch of psychology that links the behavior, attitudes, and emotions of the individual to the broader social context of which the individual is a part. Language is one way of making this connection between the individual and so-

ciety, and attitude is a common element of everyday language. All of us have at some time heard or made comments about other people's positive or negative attitudes.

Some social psychologists attempt to distinguish attitudes from other mental structures like values and beliefs. **Values** are considered abstract goals that do not have specific objects or reference points (Deaux, Dane, & Wrightsman, 1993). Examples of values include abstract judgments about topics such as beauty, freedom, or health. These values can contribute to the development of attitudes and other belief systems. We also use values to evaluate information in making many of our decisions. In fact, attitudes play a mediating role in turning our values into action (Deaux et al., 1993).

We also need to be able to distinguish **beliefs** from attitudes. Beliefs include information about objects. But what distinguishes a belief from an attitude? Technically speaking, beliefs are observations about the qualities of objects (Feld & Radin, 1982). For instance, we can have information or beliefs about the harmful consequences of smoking. Are these beliefs the same thing as an attitude? As this example points out, it is difficult to make distinctions between attitudes and other mental structures. Although we may hold beliefs, it does not mean that we will not smoke or behave in a particular fashion. It is assumed in social psychology that attitudes are more likely to influence behavior than general beliefs.

Fishbein and Ajzen (1975) addressed this issue directly in their *theory of reasoned action*. They set out to determine what factors, in addition to attitudes, influence our behavior. In their approach, they make an interesting distinction between *attitudes* and **subjective norms.** They suggest that attitudes refer to our evaluative feelings; for instance, negative internal feelings you may have about smoking reflect your attitude about this activity. Subjective norms would be your beliefs about what important people or significant others think about smoking (Lippa, 1995). That is, you may learn scientific information about smoking and its negative consequences, but this does not mean that you will develop a negative attitude. In Fishbein and Ajzen's (1975) theory, attitudes and subjective norms combine to influence our behavioral intention.

Behavioral intention refers to our subjective estimate of how likely we are to engage in a specific behavior. For instance, what is the likelihood that you will smoke in the next month? Fishbein and Ajzen's (1975) theory predicts that, in many circumstances, people's internal attitudes will better predict their behavioral intention than will their subjective norms. This theory allows for a comparison of internal and external influences on our behavior: Our attitudes represent the internal influences on our behavior, and our subjective norms represent the social or external influences.

Fishbein and Ajzen's theory is useful in understanding intentional behaviors: Do you intend to have a baby? Do you intend to increase your study time? These behavioral questions are influenced by some combination of your attitudes, subjective norms, and perceived behavioral control. But, in examining these factors, you should also consider the consequences of the behavior you are trying to predict, and you should personally evaluate these consequences. For instance, two people might agree on the consequences of increased studying—improved grades and less time with friends—but each may evaluate these outcomes differently (see Figure 3.8).

From research on Fishbien and Ajzen's (1975) theory, we know that attitudes are most likely to predict smoking among adults. Subjective norms, however, are more likely to predict the smoking behavior of adolescents; adolescents are more likely to be influenced by the subjective norms of their peers. Information of this nature is useful to social work professionals who assist in the development of preventive interventions. With the benefit of theories on attitudes, social workers are better equipped to develop effective programs intended to change client attitudes.

Attitudes differ from emotions in several important ways. Unlike attitudes, emotions do not have to be directed at a specific target or object. Furthermore, attitudes tend to be enduring. If you are opposed to racism today, you probably will be tomorrow. Emotions, on the other hand, can come and go in a matter of seconds. Although you are angry at your best friend today, this does not mean that you will be angry at him or her tomorrow. Attitudes differ in many respects from emotional responses.

However, there is a feeling or affective component to attitudes that we cannot ignore. Feld and Radin (1982) point out that there are definitions of attitudes that emphasize this point. Fishbein and Ajzen's (1975)

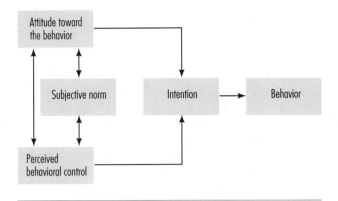

FIGURE 3.8   The relationship between attitudes and intentional behavior   Source: Ajzen, 1987.

theory includes a definition of attitudes that stresses emotional reactions. In their theory, attitudes are considered emotional responses to objects in the form of favorable or unfavorable feelings. People have favorable feelings toward many objects in their environment. In fact, this is what many scientists attempt to capture in their research.

Regardless of how we define attitudes, social workers must be able to modify or change attitudes. While social psychologists debate about the best definition of attitudes, social workers need validated theories to guide their change efforts. In *Social Psychology for Social Work and the Mental Health Professions*, Feld and Radin (1982) have identified theories in social psychology that social workers may find helpful in achieving their practice objectives (for example, cognitive dissonance theory and self-perception theory). Social workers need to develop a strong competency in understanding attitude formation and change. For this reason, we provide systematic coverage of factors in human development that contribute to the formation of attitudes. These attitudes are assumed to play a fundamental role in human motivation and development. (See Focus on Theory: Theories of Attitudes and Their Change.)

Theories of Attitudes and Their Change

In social work, we assume that if we change the attitudes of our clients, it will influence their behavior. This assumes that we can predict behaviors from attitudes. It also assumes that attitudes influence behavior. Although many studies have uncovered a relationship between attitudes and behavior, this relationship is not consistent. At an intuitive level, people expect consistency between attitudes and behavior. This assumption has contributed to the development of an entire group of theories on attitudes known as consistency theories.

Consistency theories in social psychology refer to the idea that people strive to maintain consistency in their views of themselves, their environment, and in their relations with others (Lindgren, 1969). People are motivated to keep their attitudes and behaviors consistent (Deaux et al., 1993). This implies that if people have attitudes inconsistent with their behaviors, they feel uncomfortable. This sense of discomfort will motivate them toward reestablishing some form of balance or consistency between their attitudes and behavior.

Leon Festinger (1957) is known for proposing another important consistency theory known as *cognitive dissonance theory*. Cognitive dissonance describes the feelings of anxiety that arise when a person is aware of two inconsistent cognitions, or a cognition and a behavior that are inconsistent. In his theory, whenever an attitude and a behavior are inconsistent, this inconsistency generates dissonance. Festinger assumes that this distress motivates individuals to reconcile the inconsistencies in their cognitions or between their cognition and their behavior. However, Festinger found that subjects would not always experience dissonance from conflicts between attitudes or cognition. In his view, they experience a sense of dissonance only if the thoughts or attitudes are relevant to one another. Conflicting cognitions that are not related to one another do not trigger a sense of personal dissonance.

Festinger's theory initially focused on inconsistencies in cognitions and predicted that dissonant cognitions would motivate a person to change one of his or her cognitions. In his early research, he discovered that change in behavior could trigger changes in attitudes. In fact, his theory predicts that people will change their attitudes to be consistent with already-performed behaviors. In his now-famous forced compliance experiments, this finding occurred on a regular basis. He subjected individuals to dull tasks and paid them to lie to other students about how interesting they found the tasks. The individuals who participated in the dull tasks were then given a questionnaire to determine their private attitudes about the tasks. Some individuals had been paid $1 and others $20 to engage in these tasks. The individuals who were paid $1 experienced greater dissonance; dissonance theory suggests that they became more motivated to believe that the tasks were really interesting because the justification for their actions—a measly dollar — was insufficient.

Self-perception theory, another theory about attitude changes, was developed by D. J. Bem (1967). It seeks to explain the same types of behavior addressed by cognitive dissonance theory. However, it offers a different explanation for why a person might change an attitude after performing a behavior (Feld & Radin, 1982). Self-perception theory suggests that when we are not sure of our attitudes about a certain topic, we infer them from our behaviors and from the context within which those behaviors occur. Using this theory, Bem set out to offer an alternative explanation of what occurred in Festinger's experiment. In Bem's view, the subjects defined the tasks as interesting not because of dissonance but because they had merely inferred their attitude from their actual behavior. "That is, one dollar is not enough money to induce someone to lie, so subjects in that condition looked back at their behavior and decided they must have enjoyed the experiment because they had said they enjoyed it; no inconsistency, no discomfort, no dissonance" (Deaux et al., 1993, p. 170). In his view, the individuals in the experiment were essentially asking themselves: "What must my attitude be if I am willing to behave in this fashion?"

Bem's theory has led to important findings widely used to obtain the cooperation of clients. His theory has also led to the discovery of what is known as the *foot-in-the-door effect*, or the tendency for individuals who have complied with a small request first to agree to a larger request later. Researchers thought this phenomenon occurred because of individuals' changes in self-perception. Bem's theory predicts that "if individuals observe themselves doing something out of free choice, the behaviors are attributed to their disposition, not to external forces, and the conclusion reached is that 'I am that sort of a person'" (Feld & Radin, 1982, p. 175). Some theorists also predict that persons who comply with small requests are also likely to conclude that "I am the type of individual who agrees to socially desirable requests." Thus, there are competing theories of why changes in behavior can result in changes in attitudes.

Emotions

What are *emotions*? How can we explain our emotions and their role in human behavior? Are emotions caused by internal and bodily changes or by some form of cognitive appraisal? The answers to these questions are quite controversial. In this section, we will provide a brief overview of some of the different theoretical perspectives in psychology on human emotions.

The word *emotion* in its early history meant to move or agitate in a physical sense (Petri, 1986). It later came to mean an agitated or aroused mental state. Although there is no commonly accepted definition of the term, there are a number of widely debated theories or models on human emotions.

The first person to write about the topic of emotional expression was Charles Darwin (1872), in his book *The Expression of Emotions in Man and Animals*. Darwin was the first theorist in modern times to assume that both emotions and their expression are innate. The bulk of his writings on the topic focused on the manner in which emotions are expressed. Today, there is still controversy as to whether there are universal ways to channel the expression of our emotions.

Although humans have expressed concerns about the control of emotions since ancient times, Ross Buch (1988) recently proclaimed that "psychology has rediscovered emotions." As we pointed out earlier, psychology shifted during the 1950s and 1960s to investigating

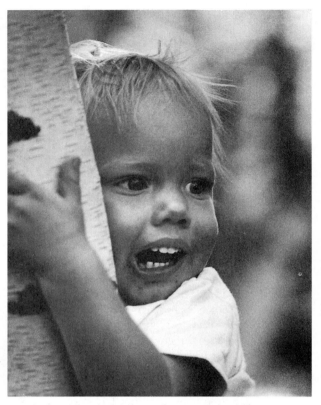

Fear plays an essential role in human functioning. This child appears frightened by something in his environment.

cognitive functioning. This did not, however, include studying emotions. Emotions were relegated to a second-class position in the psychological sciences. Shame, guilt, and anger were studied, but much of the research in this area was motivated by clinical or neuropsychological interests. Much of the controversy in this area of study dates back to the writings of William James (1884).

William James and Carl Lange arrived at a similar conclusion about emotions that challenged traditional assumptions. They identified the following order for describing emotions: perception-to-bodily change-to-emotion (Hilgard, 1987). This theory turned common sense upside down. "Everyday logic suggests that when you stumble onto a rattlesnake in the woods, the conscious experience of fear leads to visceral arousal (the fight-or-flight responses)" (Weiten, 1992, p. 363). This means that the order of events is: perception-to-emotion-to-bodily expression (Hilgard, 1987). Independent of one another, James and Lange arrived at views that contradicted this assumption. James placed greater stress on perception of change in striate muscles, and Lange emphasized changes in heart rate and blood pressure. Their approach to emotions is referred to as the James-Lange theory of emotions, and it emphasizes the role of physiological determinants in the expression of emotions.

Stanley Schachter is noted for developing a two-factor theory that includes physiological explanations in looking at the experience of emotion. In his theory, the experience of emotion requires two factors: autonomic arousal and cognitive interpretation of the visceral or autonomic arousal. In his approach, a person will experience physiological arousal and then search his or her environment for an explanation. If you are in a threatening situation, then your explanation of your arousal will probably fit the situation. Schachter's model was the first to stress the important role played by cognitive appraisal in experiencing emotions, but it stressed the need for both factors to be present.

Lazarus has argued, however, that cognition alone is sufficient for a person to experience emotions. In his experiments, he was able to alter the intensity of subjects' responses by modifying their appraisal process (Petri, 1986). He showed subjects movies and could change their emotional responses by changing the nature of the sound track. With the benefit of these findings, Lazarus has argued for the primacy of cognition in experiencing emotions. Zajonc (1980) has argued for the primacy of affect in experiencing emotions.

Zajonc (1984) bases his theory on observations of animals. He contends that emotion is a universal phenomenon in the animal kingdom. But the cognitive processes and systems observed in humans are not transferable to animals. "Indeed, as Zajonc noted, a rabbit would rarely have time to assess all the attributes of a snake in order to decide whether to fear it; the rabbit feels fear and reacts. Such reactions may also occur in people" (Petri, 1986). That is, people probably acquired the same emotional mechanisms prior to the development of cognitive systems. Thus, Zajonc assumes that the emotions of humans have much in common with the emotions of animals. Another argument that he provides in support of the primacy of affect is that we cannot avoid emotions. If logic appears prior to emotions, then

logic should affect our emotional responses to stimuli. Yet this is not always what occurs. Overall, Zajonc argues that emotions are innate reactions that are part of our evolutionary makeup.

Evolutionary theories of emotion are once again regaining popularity in psychological research. The theorists in this area include Silvan Tomkins, Carroll Izard, and Robert Plutchik, who set out to identify the fundamental human emotions. These emotions are considered to be innate and to have evolved prior to cognition. Tomkins, Izard, and Plutchik assume that people exhibit between eight and ten primary emotions. A summary of these emotions is presented in Table 3.2. Note the similarities between the elements in their lists. These theorists do not assume that our emotions are limited to these primary emotions. Plutchik has pointed out that we can develop many secondary blends of emotions from our primary emotions.

Implications for Practice

Without emotions, individuals cannot develop meaningful responses to their environment. Social workers need to develop practical ways for describing changes in their clients' emotional states. From the theories discussed, we can distinguish between the *expression* of emotions and the *experience* of emotions. We experience our emo-

TABLE 3.2 Summary of Emotions According to Different Theorists

Silvan Tomkins	Robert Plutchik	Carroll Izard
Fear	Fear	Fear
Anger	Anger	Anger
Enjoyment	Joy	Joy
Disgust	Disgust	Disgust
Interest	Anticipation	Interest
Surprise	Surprise	Surprise
Contempt	Sadness	Contempt
Shame	Acceptance	Shame
Distress		Sadness

Source: Based on Mandler, 1984.

Understanding a person's mood and affect is an important clinical skill. What emotion is the person displaying in this photograph?

the role of social cognition in controlling our emotions and behavior.

Social Cognition and Regulation

How do we acquire social knowledge? Is there a difference between social and nonsocial cognition? Does social knowledge acquisition differ from the acquisition of other forms of knowledge? These questions have helped psychologists clarify the nature of **social cognition.** Theorists in the field have devoted substantial ink to topics like, Do we employ different processes in acquiring knowledge about things than we employ in acquiring knowledge about people? These debates have led to some general conclusions. Now social cognition is widely considered cognition about people. It includes "thinking and knowledge about self and other individuals, about social relations between people, about social customs, groups, and institutions" (Flavell,1985, p. 159). In fact, substantial attention is now being devoted to understanding the role of the self-system in all areas of human cognition.

In the mid-1970s, it was rare to encounter theorists with identified interests in social cognition. Social cognition is considered a newly discovered convergence of two distinct disciplines: social psychology and cognitive psychology. Developments in each of these disciplines have created major shifts in traditional approaches to scientific inquiry in psychology.

Social psychologists began identifying many deficits in their approach to studying human behavior and judgment processes. Most of their early research focused on understanding the effects of situational and individual differences on various forms of social behavior. As disenchantment with stimulus-response models mounted, social psychologists started to realize that this approach to research was not clarifying the fundamental psychological processes that underlie *social* behavior. To rectify this problem, they turned to cognitive theory (Wyer & Srull, 1984).

Many of the concepts introduced in this chapter to examine cognitive functions are now being employed in psychology to address a number of social processes. These same processes are examined in sociology and other fields of inquiry. We have included social cognition in our psychological dimension primarily because it employs a psychological orientation to studying social

tions within our central nervous system and its attendant cognitive structures, but we express these emotions through our somatic and autonomic response systems.

Clinical social workers also distinguish between mood and affect. **Mood** can be defined as a prevailing and enduring emotional state. **Affect** refers to a person's instant emotional state. In assessing affect, social workers focus on determining the presence or absence of specific types of emotional states. For instance, **lability** is a technical term that refers to the rapid shift from one emotion to another within a very brief period of time. If these shifts are very extreme, some clinicians label these states as representing a form of emotional "incontinence" (Ludwig, 1986). Social workers must learn the characteristics of normal and abnormal presentations of emotion. They must also have an understanding of how people learn to use their emotions and behavior. In the last subsystem of our framework, we will look more closely at processes. The fundamental aim of social cognition, as a field of inquiry, is to understand the interdependence between cognition and social behavior (Ostrom, 1984). Isen and Hastorf (1982) refer to this field as "cognitive social psychology" instead of social cognition. This area of study in psychology focuses on individual-level explanations of social behavior. Anthropology and sociology also examine various aspects of social behavior but rely primarily on group-level explanations (Lippa, 1995).

In this book, we will explore various factors in social development that influence individuals' sense of self, their ability to control their behavior, and their sense of social competence. Because social cognition is a useful framework for examining each of these concerns, we cover topics from that field in each of the chapters.

Researchers in the field of social cognition have recognized that a significant component of social behavior is motivated by our innate need to control various aspects of our environment. Robert White (1959) refers to this as a form of *competence motivation.*

Competence is the capacity to interact effectively with one's environment. In essence, the goal of this motive is to bring about a sense of efficacy for the individual. This assumption is also acknowledged by social workers in models of interaction that take into account principles of social cognition (Brower & Nurius, 1993).

This need for a sense of control has received further scrutiny by Richard deCharms. In his view, the primary motive at the root of most social behavior is the need to be effective in producing changes in our environment. He refers to this as a need to achieve a sense of personal causation.

> As deCharms noted, we typically describe motivation in relation to the goals toward which a behavior leads: When hungry, we seek food; when thirsty, we seek water; and so on. Though we speak of the hunger motive, personal causation is the force requiring that we be able to respond in ways that will get us food. Thus, deCharms saw personal causation as the underlying principle of all motivated behaviors. (Petri, 1986, pp. 298–299)

Regulation of behavior, emotions, and cognition is an important area of research developing in the field of social cognition. By employing principles of social cognition, it is possible to link processes of social regulation with individual cognitive processes. This linkage allows for the identification of external and internal factors con-

tributing to the regulation of our emotions and behavior. Regulation is an important human behavior function and will receive substantial attention in our developmental chapters. We now know that humans learn considerable information from others that helps in regulating various aspects of their behavior. The focus in social cognition research is on understanding how people acquire this information from other individuals.

Implications for Practice

Brower and Nurius (1993) have written on the utility of social cognition in what they have termed a cognitive-ecological model for direct practice. In their view, social cognition and social transactions serve as "the backdrop for understanding our clients' presenting problems and for developing change strategies that will positively build upon these normative processes" (Brower & Nurius, 1993, p. 3). They believe that social cognition plays an important mediating role between people and their environments. They contend that if we integrate our knowledge of the self-system with information-processing knowledge and knowledge of human problem solving, we can deal more efficiently with the presenting concerns of our clients.

By using their cognitive approach, we can better evaluate the impact of immediate and distant factors on specific forms of human behavior. Ecological and broader social influences are important, but the concepts of social cognition enable us to isolate key personal factors that play unique roles in an individual's behavioral choices. That is, social cognition is an approach that allows us to bring together important person-and-environment factors. In particular, it places tremendous emphasis on self-constructs that recognize the highly interdependent relationship between self and society. Unlike personality constructs, the self-system in social cognitive approaches does not artificially isolate persons from key social realities. Moreover, concepts and principles in the social cognitive approach are highly useful in achieving social work's commitment to making person-and-environment interactions central in its approach to understanding human behavior. It allows us to understand individual processes underlying our tendency to make selective appraisals of situations based on our personally constructed schemata and life images.

Psychological Hazards

Our psychological system facilitates our processing of information from our internal and external world and helps us communicate and respond to the demands of everyday life. It includes many processes and functions that are vulnerable to many kinds of hazards occurring at the biophysical, psychological, and social levels of functioning.

Psychological hazards include events, experiences, abilities, skill deficits, cognitive impairments, emotional impairments, and behavioral impairments that compromise the mental processes and functions employed by individuals to control their biopsychosocial system.

Individuals are exposed to many experiences that constitute risks to their mental functioning. A risk occurs whenever there is a lack of harmony in the person's psychological system. Individuals are also at risk when there is a lack of opportunity to develop mental and motor processes that enable them to meet the demands of their life circumstances.

A crisis presents a problem in living that requires more than habitual coping (Nurcombe & Gallagher, 1986). Whenever an individual cannot cope with problems, he or she is at risk for many kinds of psychological harm. This harm has many different forms of presentation: learning disabilities, mood disturbances, abstract reasoning deficits, perpetual disturbances, and many others.

Conclusions

This chapter provided a description of key developments in the cognitive and psychological sciences that help us understand individual-level explanations of human behavior. We reviewed concepts from major theoretical perspectives that assist us in understanding the cognitive and individual bases for human behavior. These factors play a critical mediating role between our biological and social systems. They involve many functions that people need to engage in planned behavior intended to resolve their problems in living. Each of the subsystems in our psychological system also provides internal motivation for many of our activities. The psychological system consists of several key functions employed by humans in directing their behavior to achieve desired ends. These individual processes differ significantly from the social processes that will be described in our next chapter.

Chapter Summary

The objective of the psychological system is goal attainment. This system consists of many functions associated with our mental processes. These processes are needed to help people achieve their desired goals.

Cognitive Development and Information Processing

Cognitive development is an approach to assessing cognitive functions. Piaget's structural approach is useful for social workers. It explains how cognition is organized or structured at various phases of development. Different mental structures direct cognitive processes for individuals at different stages of development.

The information-processing subsystem of the psychological system includes seven major functions: consciousness and orientation, perception, attention, learning, memory, comprehension, and reasoning and judgment. Information processing is not only a major function in the psychological system but also an established approach in psychology for studying human cognitive processes. Information processing resembles a computer and explains the uptake, selection, coding, and storage of information.

Consciousness involves the processes that allow us to be aware of internal and external stimuli. Orientation is a form of consciousness assessed by clinical professionals in evaluating the status of a person's mental functioning. Perception refers to the interpretation of information detected by our senses. Attention is the component of our information-processing system that pertains to the ability to focus on a specific stimulus without distraction by irrelevant stimuli. Vigilance involves the ability to sustain outward attention over a sustained period of time. Concentration refers to a person's ability to sustain inner mental operations without disruption.

Memory is considered a key component of the learning process in our information-processing system. It consists of four stages: registration, rehearsal, retention, and recall. There are definite limits on our capacity for processing information. Our short-term or working memory is limited to the number of items it can hold (seven plus or minus two). Unlike short-term memory, long-term memory has unlimited capacity to store information. Key processes, besides memory, assessed by social workers include problem solving, abstract reasoning, and judgment.

Communication

Communication involves oral and written language, nonverbal gestures, and other forms of exchanging information. Language is a social product, but speech is an individual product. Human communication consists of four basic components: the source, the message, the channel used to send the message, and the receiver.

Attitudes and Emotions

Attitudes and emotions play a fundamental role in motivating behavior. Attitudes refer to our evaluative feelings and other evaluative responses directed at specific norms. There are several different theories of what influences changes in attitudes: consistency theories and self-perception theories. Emotions are difficult to define, but there are several noteworthy theoretical conceptualizations of emotions: the James-Lange theory, Schacter's two-factor theory, and evolutionary theories. Without emotions, individuals cannot develop meaningful responses to their environment.

Social Cognition and Regulation

Social cognition refers to knowledge about people. Social and cognitive psychologists assume that acquisition of social knowledge differs from acquisition of other forms of knowledge. The norms learned from social cognitive processes constrain and regulate our behavior in social situations.

Psychological Hazards

Psychological hazards include anything that compromises mental functioning. A risk to mental functioning occurs when there is disharmony in the psychological system or a lack of opportunity to develop mental and motor processes needed to cope with the demands of life. When people have a crisis and cannot cope with life demands, they are at increased risk of psychological harm.

KEY TERMS

abstraction	epigenetic principle	recent memory
accommodation	hypervigilance	remote memory
adaptation	id	repetition
affect	immediate memory	schema
assimilation	information processing	secondary process thinking
associationism	lability	semantics
attention	libido	sensation
attitude	long-term memory	short-term memory
behavioral intention	mood	signs
beliefs	morphemes	similarity
classical conditioning	operant conditioning	social cognition
cognition	organization	social learning theory
concentration	perception	subjective norms
consciousness	perceptual set	superego
continuity	phonemes	symbol
differentiation theory	phonology	syntax
disoriented states	pragmatics	trial and error
ego	primary process thinking	values
enrichment theory	problem solving	vigilance

4

The Social Dimension for Assessing Social Functioning

The aim of this chapter is to define and describe how social systems guide the multidimensional framework employed in this book. A whole host of debates occur in the social sciences about the merits of micro versus macro approaches to social analysis. This kind of dualism, along with the dualisms of agency versus structure and individual versus society, is avoided in this chapter by using systems principles to describe the dimensions of social life.

For purposes of clarity, we treat the social systems and categories included in our framework as if they were independent of one another. However, you should keep in mind the following principles:

1. Any analysis of a social system must take into account the interactions of that system with other systems.

2. All social systems and structures are highly interrelated and have many points of intersection that are critical to understanding processes of social domination and other forms of social inequality.
3. Social structures are both sources of support and sources of oppression.
4. Any analysis of social, cultural, and individual experience cannot ignore key multicultural foundations.

In the preceding chapter, we discussed the role of psychological systems in human development. However, these psychological processes do not occur in a vacuum. All forms of goal-directed activities involving humans take place in an established environment. If we are going to understand how the environment influences behavior, we need to have a framework that allows us to compare elements in one social context with those of another. To this end, our multidimensional framework provides a description of ways to conceptualize the key systems making up the social system. It also identifies variables and concepts that are useful for looking at different levels of social organization. We begin this description of the social dimension by defining the social system and its utility in studying human development.

Our approach to human behavior in social work deals not only with developmental events but also with the context in which these events take place. The term *context* in the social work literature is often used interchangeably with *space, setting, situation, territory, locus, milieu,* and *environment.* In this book, we define many forms of contexts in terms of systems principles. We subscribe to this approach because we assume that social workers must adhere to a *people-in-systems* approach to understanding human behavior. Focus on Theory: Ecological Systems Theory describes the relationship between ecological systems theory and social work practice.

You need a deep understanding of the social system in order to understand the structure of various social contexts. A system represents any set of elements that affect or influence one another. We cannot solve the problem of any system without taking into account all the factors that influence the system and its components. A social system is one in which the components are people. These people participate in a number of social systems that influence their development—family, school, work setting, neighborhood, community, nation, and so forth. We cannot understand human development by focusing merely on the psychological dimensions of individuals or what transpires in them. For this reason, we need to develop knowledge of the key dimensions of social systems, their interrelations, and their environment.

Brim (1975) and Bronfenbrenner (1977) identified four categories or levels of **systems** that are useful to social workers: microsystems, the mesosystem, the exosystem, and the macrosystem. **Microsystems** represent any systems that involve face-to-face or direct contact among the system participants. As social workers, we are interested in having categories that enable us to classify behavior that takes place in these systems. This type of analysis is limited, however, if it neglects the relations between the microsystem of primary attention and other

key microsystems. If we have an understanding of how our multiple microsystems are interconnected, we can have a more informed understanding of the behavior in a particular microsystem. The **mesosystem** is the category systems theorists use to address this level of analysis. It refers to the network of personal settings in which we live our social lives. Each of our clients lives in a similar, but different mesosystem. It is critical to have an understanding of the network of personal settings affecting a particular microsystem under investigation.

Individuals are members of a number of different microsystems. What happens to them in any one microsystem can influence their behavior in other settings. For example, if you are working with an adolescent, you should not ignore the fact that events in his or her peer group can influence the degree of conflict observed in his or her school or family setting. The makeup of the mesosystem must be taken into account in analyzing any identified microsystem issue.

The **exosystem** in Bronfenbrenner's scheme refers to the larger institutions of society that influence our personal systems. This includes institutions like government agencies in which we do not directly work but that have profound effects on our lives. Exosystems are considered any of the systems in which an individual is not directly involved. For instance, parents' work settings can affect the life of their child in many ways, yet the children have no direct involvement in the work settings of their parents. An exosystem level of analysis stresses the need to take into account the broader social environment of our clients by examining the influence of significant social institutions.

Last, the **macrosystem** represents the larger subcultural and cultural contexts in which the microsystem, mesosystem, and exosystem are located. This system has the most pervasive level of influence on social activities. **Culture** is defined as a system of meanings and values shared by a population and transmitted to future generations (Sigelman & Shaffer, 1995). It includes all the key artifacts developed during the history of a population—all its material and nonmaterial (symbolic) products. Every sociocultural group has its own history, but in recent years scholars of race, class, and gender studies are pointing out through the voices metaphor that many of these histories have been silenced. The goal of much of current multicultural scholarship is to help people think about the experiences of a multitude of previously silenced groups (Andersen & Collins, 1995). Material and symbolic culture influences all facets of our behavior, and it is given significant attention in the analysis of social systems by most practice frameworks in social work.

Bronfenbrenner used the prior four systems to describe the environmental contexts of human development. Figure 4.1 presents Bronfenbrenner's model of the social environment. These same systems have been adopted by social work scholars to conceptualize the environmental component of our professional focus on person-and-environment transactions. Prior to the emergence of ecological systems thinking in social work, there were many simplistic views of the environment in our profession. These views frustrated most practitioners' efforts to achieve any objectives involving "environmental modification" (Grinnell, Kyte, & Bostwick, 1981). Grinnell and colleagues pointed out that these earlier concepts of environment represented: "(1) social structures (e.g., social class system, ethnicity); (2) social conditions (e.g., unemployment, discrimination); (3) social systems (e.g., economic, health, and educational networks); and (4) specific neighborhood or community resources (e.g., schools, churches, day-care centers, job training programs)" (1981, p. 153). Many other dimensions and classifications have been used in social work to categorize the environment. However, ecological systems thinking, unlike the other approaches, enhanced our ability to look at the environment in a way that allowed for its modification. This perspective redirected the attention of workers to the transactions between persons and environment, not to either person *or* environment variables.

Principles from systems theory direct social workers to identify relevant systems, their subsystems, and the suprasystems of which they are a part (Anderson & Carter, 1984). Social workers often achieve these ends by drawing an **ecomap.** Hartman and Laird (1983) are known in social work for having originally developed this tool for use by social workers in the field of child welfare. Their ecomapping highlights the points of connection between systems influencing a person's life and allows for the identification of points of conflict and points of support in a person's life space. Figure 4.2 presents a case example to illustrate the application of an ecomap to a social work situation.

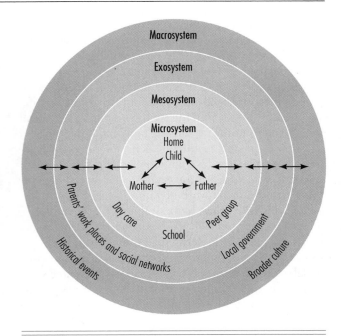

FIGURE 4.1   Bronfenbrenner's ecological model   Source: Adapted from Kopp & Krakow, 1982.

To apply ecomaps and other systems-oriented concepts, you need to understand how to define the key social systems and their characteristics. We begin this process by describing the dimensions and characteristics of the family system. The family is a pivotal microsystem that influences many forms of social behavior.

FOCUS ON THEORY

Ecological Systems Theory

Social work focuses simultaneously on the person and the social environment. Figure 4.3 presents the major ideas of ecological systems theory in social work. This figure stresses the need for understanding people's coping behavior in relation to the quality of their impinging environment. It represents three types of coping behav-

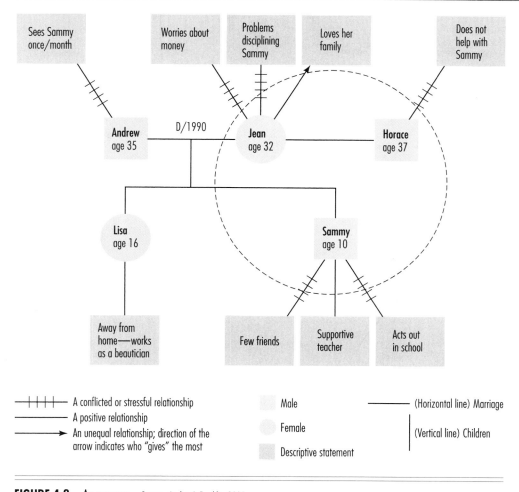

FIGURE 4.2 **An ecomap** Source: Jordan & Franklin, 1995.

ior: obtaining and using social work resources, adapting to life transitional problems and needs, and influencing the social environment. Recall that the social worker's task is to match clients' coping behaviors with qualities associated with the impinging environment.

According to Carol Germain (1991, p. 15), "ecology is the science that studies the relations between organisms and their environments." Critical to the ecological perspective is its holistic view of people. The ecological perspective is a metaphor that provides an understanding about the reciprocal transactions that take place between people and the social environment in which they

function. Therefore, people and environments are part of a holistic system in which each shapes the other (Germain, 1991). Some of the basic ideas from the ecological systems perspective are presented below (Germain, 1991; Hearn, 1979):

Social work practice is based on a dual focus. This focus includes the person and situation and the system and its environment.

Social work practice occurs at the interface between the human system and its environment.

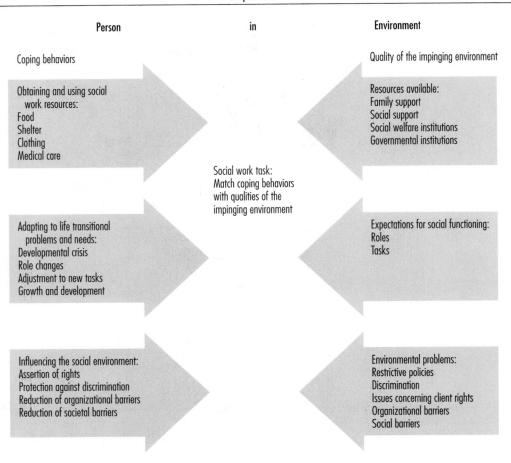

Person   **in**   **Environment**

Coping behaviors   Quality of the impinging environment

Obtaining and using social
   work resources:
Food
Shelter
Clothing
Medical care

Resources available:
Family support
Social support
Social welfare institutions
Governmental institutions

Social work task:
Match coping behaviors
with qualities of the
impinging environment

Adapting to life transitional
   problems and needs:
Developmental crisis
Role changes
Adjustment to new tasks
Growth and development

Expectations for social functioning:
Roles
Tasks

Influencing the social environment:
Assertion of rights
Protection against discrimination
Reduction of organizational barriers
Reduction of societal barriers

Environmental problems:
Restrictive policies
Discrimination
Issues concerning client rights
Organizational barriers
Social barriers

FIGURE 4.3   Ecological systems and social work practice   Source: Based on Monkman (1982), Maluccio (1992), & Germain (1991).

Transactions occur at the interface between the system
   and the environment.

In transactional relationships, both systems are influenced by change efforts.

Social work practice is best conducted when the transactions promote growth and development of the organism while simultaneously being ameliorative to the environment, thus making it a better place for all systems that depend upon the environment for sustenance.

Families, Groups, Support Systems, and Contexts

The **family** is increasingly being recognized as a "social system"—a whole composed of interrelated parts, each of which affects and is affected by each other, and each of which contributes to the functioning of the whole. This "systems perspective" helps us recognize that understanding a family is not as simple as understanding the mother-and-child relationship. Indeed, the family is

Carol Germain was a noted social work theorist who developed the ecological perspective for the practice of social work and furthered the understanding of human behavior in multiple environments.

influenced by many factors: the father and his relationship with the mother and baby, the grandparents and their relationship with the parents and the infant, the environmental context—what kind of support does the family have from friends, church groups, and neighborhood? The important point about understanding families as systems is to recognize how different interactions within and outside of the family system affect the family. Garbarino and Abramowitz (1992, p. 16) discuss an ecological approach to human development that emphasizes the *interaction* between the individual and environment:

> This view sees the process of development as the expansion of the child's conception of the world and the child's

ability to act on that world. An individual organism and the environment engage in reciprocal interaction: each influences the other in an ever-changing interplay of biology and society—with intelligence and emotion as the mediators, and identity and competence as the outcomes.

Belsky (1981) describes the family as a social system, wherein the family is bigger than the sum of its parts. Parents can influence the infant who can influence each parent and the marital relationship (see Figure 4.4). Consider the following example. An infant is interacting with its mother and is involved in a process of **reciprocal interaction.** It is reciprocal because the infant can influence the mother and the mother can influence the infant. If the mother responds to the infant's smile with a corresponding smile and high-pitched talk, the infant is likely to reciprocate with laughter. When the father walks into the room, the mother-infant dyad is transformed into a family system (Belsky, 1981). The family system can be impacted by any pair in the family. For example, mothers are less likely to play with their infants when the fathers join the dyad. Further complicating the understanding is that the marital relationship affects the relationship between the parent and child, and, in turn, each parent's relationship with the child affects the quality of the marriage.

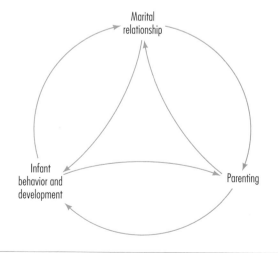

FIGURE 4.4   A diagram of the family as a social system
Source: Belsky, 1981.

Family practitioners and clinical social workers use a systems perspective to help them understand the social context of a family problem. When a family is seen for a child's problem, the assumption is that the child's problem cannot be understood separate from the family system. The problem is related to how the person is treated in the family system, and as such the solution to the problem involves changing the other members of the family system as well, not just changing the "problem" child.

No family system can be completely understood without also considering external factors and influences. So to the already complex family system we must add influences such as the extended family, the school system, the neighborhood, the church or religious affiliation, the friends, the work environment, and so forth.

Defining the Family

A difficult question is, what is a family? How you answer this question can have important implications for how you practice social work. Indeed, how we as a society define family has important implications for the benefits and rights that family members receive. For example, if gay and lesbian couples are not considered a family, then certain legal implications are effected. For example, they may not be able to get married, make medical decisions for each other when the other person cannot do so, and receive shared benefits from health and life insurance companies. What about single-parent families? Shouldn't they be included in any definition of a family? The changing norms of society suggest that we must have changing definitions of families.

Schriver (1995) uses the term "familiness" to broaden what is the traditional concept of family. He states that "this concept reminds us as individuals and as members of particular families to think always about possible alternative structures and sets of functions that constitute *family* for others" (Schriver, 1995, p. 220).

Garbarino and Abramowitz (1992) refer to the family as the "headquarters for human development." Families do make up the thread necessary to weave human society together. "Through our families we are connected to the past—the distant times and places of our ancestors—and to the future—the hope of our children's children"

(Garbarino & Abramowitz, 1992, p. 72). Most discussions about the family include two related aspects of family: the family as the "headquarters for human development" and the family as a social institution.

Sociologists who attempt to answer the question "what is a family?" stress three functions: getting married, having children, and developing kinship ties. Reiss (1980, p. 29) summarized a global perspective regarding the family as "a small kinship-structured group with the key function of nurturant socialization." Duvall's (1971, p. 5) definition of the family is: "a unit of interacting persons related by ties of marriage, birth, or adoption, whose central purpose is to create and maintain a common culture which promotes the physical, mental, emotional, and social development of each of its members." A less traditional definition of the family is offered by Hartman and Laird (1983, p. 576), who state that a family is created when "two or more people construct an intimate environment that they define as a family, an environment in which they generally will share a living space, commitment, and a variety of the roles and functions usually considered part of family life." Therefore, a family is a composition of people who decide to act as a family. This definition takes into account diverse forms of the family that might include homosexual couples, single-parent families, elderly persons not related by blood but living together as a family group, and other extended family groupings. Although the family is clearly changing, it remains a strong thread that ties together society as it functions to help provide socialization and companionship for diverse groups of people.

The Family Life Cycle

One way of understanding family life is to consider the family life cycle—a sequence of developmental stages that families typically move through. Carter and McGoldrick (1988) have described a six-stage model of family development. An overview of the model is presented in Table 4.1.

As couples move through the family life cycle they have different sources of satisfaction and frustration. Some researchers have attempted to examine the effect of the life cycle stage on various behaviors and attitudes. For example, how does the stage of the family life cycle

TABLE 4.1   The Family Life Cycle

Stage of the Family Life Cycle	Key Developmental Task	Changes in Family Status Required to Proceed Developmentally
1. Between families: the unattached young adult	Accepting parent/offspring separation	Differentiation of self in relation to family of origin Development of intimate peer relations Establishment of self in work
2. The joining of families through marriage: the newly married couple	Commitment to new system	Formation of marital system Realignment of relationships with extended families and friends to include spouse
3. The family with young children	Accepting new members into the system	Adjusting marital system to make space for children Taking on parenting roles Realignment of relationships with extended family to include parenting and grandparenting roles
4. The family with adolescents	Increasing flexibility of family boundaries to include children's independence and grandparents' frailties	Shifting of parent-child relationships to permit adolescent to move in and out of system Refocus on midlife marital and career issues Beginning shift toward concerns for older generation
5. Launching children and moving on	Accepting a multitude of exits from and entries into the family system	Renegotiation of marital system as dyad Development of adult-to-adult relationships between grown children and their parents Realignment of relationships to include in-laws and grandchildren Dealing with disabilities and death of parents (grandparents)
6. The family in later life	Accepting the shifting of generational roles	Maintaining own functioning, couple functioning, or both, and interests in face of physiological decline; exploration of new familial and social-role options Support for a more central role for middle generations Making room in the system for the wisdom and experience of the elderly; supporting the older generation without overfunctioning for them Dealing with loss of spouse, siblings, and other peers and preparation for own death; life review and integration

Source: Adapted from Carter & McGoldrick, 1988.

affect marital satisfaction? In general, researchers (Belsky, 1990; Rollins & Feldman, 1970) have found a U-shaped relationship between life cycle stage and marital satisfaction. Marital satisfaction starts high with the newly married couple and decreases to its lowest point at the stage where families have school-aged children. The next stage, families with teenage children, begins the upward incline to the final stage, the aging family, where satisfaction reaches a level similar to that of the newly married couple. Figure 4.5 presents the U-shaped relationship across the family life cycle stages.

Although the family life cycle is a useful perspective to use in understanding how families change over time, it is important to recognize that it presents common patterns of the typical family. However, families today are not easily described using typical norms. Therefore, transitions from one stage to the next may depend on the unique aspects of the family and the family's previous experience. Indeed, changes in the "typical" family such as divorce, working mothers, delayed childbirth, and blended families add different sets of tasks and challenges that may be different from those of the traditional family.

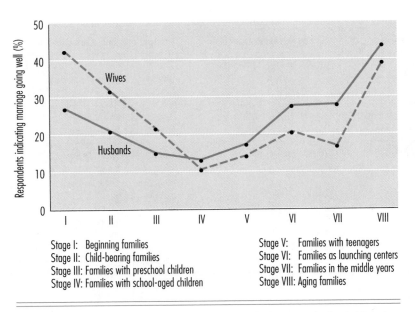

Stage I: Beginning families
Stage II: Child-bearing families
Stage III: Families with preschool children
Stage IV: Families with school-aged children

Stage V: Families with teenagers
Stage VI: Families as launching centers
Stage VII: Families in the middle years
Stage VIII: Aging families

FIGURE 4.5   The U-shaped relationship of marital satisfaction across the family life cycle
Source: Rollins & Feldman, 1970.

Key Concepts of Family Structure and Function

Family systems theorists have developed a number of different models for understanding how families interact and function. Across a number of these models are consistent concepts about the qualities of family functioning that are important to evaluate. Jordan and Franklin (1995) discuss the following key concepts that they believe are useful in understanding family assessment.

Family Structure

Examining **family structure** and function can help us understand how families work. All families have different structures; for example, is the family a *nuclear family* or an *extended family*? Family structure refers to the manner in which each family organizes itself into interactional patterns (Minuchin, 1974), including the type of family (single, blended, or intact) and the number of

family members (nuclear or extended). The family structure can influence the nature of family patterns. Jordan and Franklin (1995) present an example of a recently divorced father who remarries and enters a new family structure, a blended family. Because the father previously relied on the children's biological mother to provide discipline, he does not assume the role of disciplinarian. When the stepmother attempts to step in and enforce some rules, the children resist because she is not "our mother." In this case the father can be seen as "underfunctioning" because he is not performing his proper role, and the stepmother can be seen as "overfunctioning" because she is assuming the father's role in order to take up the slack.

Subsystems of the Family

The family as a system can be conceptualized as a series of subsystems. The major subsystems in a family are the couple subsystem, parental subsystem, sibling subsys-

It is increasingly recognized that "family" does not mean two heterosexual parents and a child—families represent great diversity, as this lesbian family demonstrates.

tem, and parent-child subsystem (Janzen & Harris, 1986). Each subsystem in the family has different functions (Aponte & Van Deusen, 1981) and should be evaluated separately (Jordan & Franklin, 1995). For example, the parental subsystem could be evaluated to assess how a couple is adapting to parenting roles and responsibilities. Is the family socially isolated or do they have social support from an extended family or from friends? Many family therapists evaluate the hierarchy in the parental subsystem. For instance, Jay Haley (1990) believes that families must acknowledge their adult roles and responsibilities and take appropriate control and direction of the family.

Families function best when the subsystems maintain their own unique roles, identities, and boundaries (Jordan & Franklin, 1995). Jordan and Franklin (1995) present examples of subsystem dysfunction that social workers are likely to encounter:

- A child taking sides with one parent against another parent
- Children providing ongoing nurturing, emotional support, and parenting to a parent
- Parents being overly intrusive into the private lives of their children
- Parents asking their children to take sides in an argument between them
- The adults in one generation forming a prolonged coalition with a member of another generation against a certain family member
- Parents refusing to interact with or negotiate with their children
- Children shutting themselves off from guidance, interactions, and relationships with their parents
- Parents forming a prolonged coalition against a child or children forming a prolonged coalition against their parents

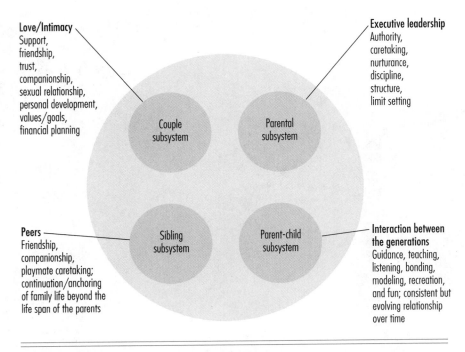

FIGURE 4.6   Family subsystems and normative roles   Source: Jordan & Franklin, 1995.

Figure 4.6 presents a visual graph of the family system with corresponding subsystems and information about normative roles.

Homeostasis, Information, and Feedback

Homeostasis can be defined as the self-regulating mechanism of a family system. Family members have an adaptive tendency to maintain this homeostasis—a steady state—in their relationships. From a family systems perspective, a child's dysfunctional behavior serves as a homeostatic mechanism (Jordan & Franklin, 1995). Thus, a common viewpoint about a child's misbehavior in a family system is that it serves an important function in the family—it keeps the conflicted marital subsystem focused on the common goal of helping the child and binds the family together in a steady state.

The flow of information that impacts the family system can be "open," allowing a free flow, or "closed," restricting the flow of information. Kantor and Lehr (1975) use these system concepts to define families as either open or closed. The open family is characterized by flexibility; for example, family events are adaptable, based on the different needs of the family members. In general, *open family systems* are adaptive and use consensus for decision making. The *closed family* is rigid, with well-defined boundaries. "The closed family is based on a 'family comes first' philosophy, regulated by conformity to family goals, strict family events, family-defined reality, and an emphasis on stability" (Garbarino & Abramowitz, 1992, p. 83).

The family system uses feedback mechanisms to identify and respond to environmental changes. If an open system is confronted with new environmental conditions, it has the capacity for adaptive self-organization. Feedback, thus, provides information that can help a system become self-correcting and allow for a deviation in the system to be corrected. There can be both *positive and negative feedback loops* that influence interactions within the system. Jordan and Franklin (1995, p. 208) provide an example of negative feedback based on a battering husband's plea for forgiveness. "By pleading for forgiveness and promising to never hit his wife again, the husband may convince the wife to give the marriage another try, thus returning the system to its former steady state." The example continues with the impact of positive feedback, which accelerates the deviation in a system. "If the woman in our previous example comes to a battered women's shelter and insists her husband get help or she will end the marriage, the system will not be allowed to return to its former steady state, and further change in the system will be initiated" (Jordan & Franklin, 1995, p. 208).

Communication and Relationships

Communication and relationships are critical to understanding families. A family systems perspective suggests that all behavior in the family is important in understanding individual problems. Therefore, how family members relate and communicate with one another is critical in an assessment. "The focus of a family assessment therefore is to understand the nature of relationships in the family" (Jordan & Franklin, 1995, p. 208).

An example of family systems relational concepts is the idea of **triangulation.** The process of triangulation occurs when parents experience conflict and "triangulate" a third member to regulate the stress and conflict between them. The parent generally demands that a child ally with him or her against the other parent during parental conflict. Bowen (1978) believes that a triad is fundamental to understanding family relationships. Thus, families are seen as a series of interlocking triangles that can extend across generations and that lend stability to the family system.

Similarly, a healthy family system must have effective communication between the members. Indeed, a lot of family systems work grew out of family communication theory, which developed at the Mental Research Institute in Palo Alto. Here, well-known family practitioners and researchers such as Don Jackson, Paul Watzlawick, Jay Haley, and Virginia Satir highlighted the importance of family communication in understanding family problems. These researchers based their notions on the idea that children learn and develop by responding to verbal and nonverbal communication. Therefore, they reasoned that how children perceive themselves and their environment depends on the mes-

sages they receive from their parents. Because children must depend on parents for survival, these messages are critical.

Rules and Myths

All families are governed by various rules within the family. Some family rules are explicit, whereas others are implicit. For example, the requirement that everyone must be at the dinner table for dinner may be an explicit rule that is understood by all family members. An implicit rule might be that only certain topics are to be discussed at the dinner table. Family rules, whether implicit or explicit, form prescriptions for behavior that define relationships and organize the manner in which family members interact. In assessing families, it is critical to evaluate which rules are functional and which are dysfunctional (Hepworth & Larsen, 1993). An example of a dysfunctional rule would be that family members cannot discuss any serious problems. An example of a functional rule would be that when conflicts arise between family members, it is important to work out the disagreements.

Family myths are shared cognitive perceptions that refer to members' shared beliefs and expectations concerning one another (Janzen & Harris, 1986). The family often subscribes to family myths to help shape, maintain, and justify interactional patterns and relationships (Hepworth & Larsen, 1993). An example of a family myth might be as follows: "Over the past four years, 10-year-old Jeffrey Richards has been in constant difficulty with his teachers at school because of open defiance of classroom rules, argumentative behavior, and physical skirmishes with other children. As a result of these problems, Mr. and Mrs. Richards have changed Jeffrey's enrollment from one school to another several times during the past three years. Sharing the cognitive set that 'the world is out to get us,' Mr. and Mrs. Richards view teachers and principals alike as punitive and vindictive and their son as 'misunderstood'" (Hepworth & Larsen, 1993).

Problem Solving, Negotiation, and Decision Making

Families are functional to the extent that they have good problem-solving, negotiation, and decision-making skills. Problem-solving skills reflect the family's ability to generate alternative solutions to problems, evaluate the different alternatives, and carry out decisions. Problem solving is also enhanced when families have a structured approach to meeting and discussing problems, coming up with solutions, and monitoring the progress of solutions (Dinkmeyer & McKay, 1983; Robin, 1994). In addition to problem solving, the process of negotiation is critical to the functioning of family systems. Jordan and Franklin (1995, p. 210) state that "couples in particular must learn to negotiate roles and power between them and model these behaviors to their children." Last, the process of decision making is central to the healthy functioning of families. What is the pattern of decision making in the family? The family may share decision making in an egalitarian manner, or the family may divide the decision-making functions depending on the nature of the tasks being confronted.

Individual Dynamics and Biological Systems

In concert with the systems perspective, social workers should keep in mind psychological and biological factors when attempting to understand the functioning of families. Because many problems are increasingly being recognized as having biological determinants, social workers need to consider interventions in the biological system as well as in the family system (Jordan & Franklin, 1995). As part of their assessment, social workers need to identify the psychological and biological dysfunctions along with considerations about the family.

The Changing Family

As we have seen, the family is a complex system; but it is not static, and as a developing system the family reflects a changing world. As we noted earlier, even the definition of "family" is changing to accommodate rapid changes that are taking place in our society. Therefore, understanding the family includes staying informed about the numerous changes that have taken place with regard to families. Some recent changes include the following trends (Sigelman & Shaffer, 1991):

- More adults are living as singles today than in the past.
- Many young adults are delaying their marriage while they pursue educational and career goals.
- After marriage, couples are having fewer children.
- An increasing number of couples are deciding to remain childless.

- Most women, including those who have children, work outside the home.
- Up to 50% of young people are expected to divorce sometime in their marriage.
- Up to 50% of children born in the 1980s will spend some time in a single-parent family.
- Because more couples are divorcing, more adults, about 75%, are remarrying.
- Adults today are spending more of their later years as couples or as single adults without children in the home due primarily to people living longer.

Postmodernism and the Family

Tommy needs to eat at 6:00 because of a school function at 7:00. His sister, Martha, must be picked up from her field hockey game because their mother, Sarah, has an office function and can't get home until after 8:00—thus, no dinner and no transportation. Sarah asks her husband, Rick, to come to the rescue, but he has to work late to prepare for a flight to Dallas the next morning. It is also Sarah's mother's birthday the next day, but Sarah is not prepared. Urgent messages await on the answering machine, one from a longtime friend of Rick's, in town for a day and wanting to drop by, and another from a close friend of Sarah's in tears because of her floundering marriage. (Gergen, 1991, p. 29)

This description of the modern family portrays what Gergen refers to as the "saturated family." Unlike family life a century ago, new technologies have infiltrated our lives and become necessities. The impact has been that the individual's experience of the cultural and social world has expanded and become more complex. In this electronic age, which brings new forms of communication—fax machines, copy machines, internet connections, electronic mail—there is a new reality concerning our abilities to interact. At the social level, we confront a multiplicity of relationships. One result of all this, Gergen points out, is that it is increasingly difficult for people to discover what they believe in. This experience of the world and the self is referred to as "social saturation" (Gergen, 1991). We are simply bombarded with new causes, different inner voices, and mixed opinions, and it is increasingly difficult to get a sense of the "right way."

The above example of typical family life is characterized by what Gergen refers to as a "slapstick style of turmoil now so pervasive that it seems unremarkable" (Gergen, 1991, p. 29). Do families have consensual goals that provide direction in their lives? Gergen believes that the technologies of social saturation make this very difficult. "The ordinary, daily confluence of multiple lives within one household makes for a sense of fragmentation, as if the members of the family were being scattered by the centrifugal force of postmodern life" (Gergen, 1991, p. 29). This predicament leads to the inability to define "family." In fact, Gergen refers to the **floating family,** which is a formless array of familial relationships that are in a continuous state of flux. Such a lack of boundaries leads to a blurring of ideals, whereby there is no sense about what it means to be a "good" family. Because there is no shared sense of reality, the family often becomes the site of multiple confrontations and conflicts. Furthermore, the floating family must adapt to a loss in power structure. Traditional notions of hierarchy and authority structure are becoming increasingly less relevant.

Such changes have led to more intense discussions about what a family really means and how to function within a family. Gergen believes that in this new world "the postmodern family can provide a kind of emotional sustenance that seems uniquely suited to the needs of people in a saturated world" (p. 34). The home is not just a place where one can "be oneself," but it is a place where one can "be their many selves." So although the family is undergoing many new adaptations, it remains an adaptive self-system.

Groups as Social Subsystems

How many groups do you belong to? To answer this question you need to think about what makes up a group. When you are together with your friends, is this a group? What about the members of the Human Behavior and Social Environment class you are presently taking; is this a group? Are all the college students from your hometown a group?

A group can de defined as "two or more persons who are interacting with one another in such a manner that each person influences and is influenced by each other person" (Shaw, 1981, p. 8). Brown (1991, p. 3) defines a group as "a small, face-to-face collection of persons who interact to accomplish some purpose." There-

fore, although you have a lot in common with all the college students from your hometown, they do not constitute a group because the people don't depend on each other to accomplish shared goals.

Groups are often classified as either formed or natural groups. **Formed groups** are created through an outside influence or intervention and are convened for a particular purpose, whereas **natural groups** are created by naturally occurring events, interpersonal attraction, or the mutual needs of the individuals involved (Toseland & Rivas, 1995).

Belonging to a Group

People belong to particular groups for a variety of reasons. Why would you want to be a member of a particular group? Clearly, there are a variety of reasons. Schein (1980) suggests that these reasons revolve around five essential goals we want to accomplish in groups:

1. To fulfill our need for affiliation
2. To increase our sense of identity and our self-esteem
3. To obtain a source for social comparisons between ourselves and others
4. To obtain a greater sense of security and power
5. To accomplish a particular task or set of tasks

We need groups to function effectively in society. All of us have special needs for affiliation and want to enhance our self-esteem. Groups also help us achieve important goals, like developing a greater sense of security and power.

Treatment and Task Groups

In social work, an important classification of groups is whether they are treatment or task oriented (Toseland & Rivas, 1995). In general, **treatment groups** serve a different purpose than **task groups** do. In treatment groups the purpose is to meet members' socioemotional needs. Different types of treatment groups include groups for support, education, therapy, growth, or socialization. In task groups the primary purpose is to complete the work for which the group was convened (Toseland & Rivas, 1995). The task group is not specifically linked to the needs of the members of the group. Using selected characteristics, Toseland and Rivas provide a comparison of treatment and task groups, as shown in Table 4.2.

TABLE 4.2   A Comparison of Task and Treatment Groups

Selected Characteristics	Type of Group	
	Treatment	**Task**
Bond	Members' personal needs	Task to be completed
Roles	Develop through interaction	Develop through interaction or are assigned
Communication patterns	Open	Focused on the discussion of a particular task
Procedures	Flexible or formal, depending on the group	Formal agenda and rules
Composition	Based on common concerns, problems, or characteristics	Based on needed talents, expertise, or division of labor
Self-disclosure	Expected to be high	Expected to be low
Confidentiality	Proceedings usually private and kept within the group	Proceedings may be private but are sometimes open to the public
Evaluation	Success based on members meeting treatment goals	Success based on members accomplishing task or mandate, or producing a product

Source: Toseland & Rivas, 1995.

Although we have presented a distinction between two types of groups, treatment and task, there are many different group purposes within these two types of groups (Toseland & Rivas, 1995, p. 20):

Rehabilitation: Restoring members to their former level of functioning
Habilitation: Helping members grow and develop
Correction: Helping members who are having problems with social laws or mores
Socialization: Helping members learn how to get along with others and do what is socially acceptable
Prevention: Helping members develop and function at an optimum level and helping them to prepare for events that are likely to occur
Social action: Helping members change their environment
Problem solving: Helping members resolve complex issues and concerns
Developing social values: Helping members develop a humanistic approach to living

Understanding How Groups Function

Groups can have a powerful influence on human behavior. What factors can account for this influence? To answer this question, we must obtain an understanding of *group dynamics* or *group process*. These factors can influence the behavior of both the individual in the group and the group as a whole. In social work we direct our attention to the helpful influences of group dynamics. However, it is important to recognize that group dynamics can unleash harmful as well as helpful forces (Galinsky & Schopler, 1977). The group dynamics that help explain these forces include *norms* that guide the behavior of group members; *roles* that members play in groups; *communication patterns*, which influence the manner in which people interact; *power and status*, which affect the influence members have on each other;

and *cohesiveness*, which determines how much sharing takes place in the group.

Roles and Norms

Norms are expectations and beliefs regarding appropriate behavior in a group. When you are with your group of friends, there are certain informal, unwritten laws about what is appropriate behavior. For example, name-calling may or may not be appropriate depending on the norms of your particular group. In some groups, this is a sign of affection or expected behavior, and in other groups, this would be considered inappropriate and rude behavior. How you decide whether to engage in behaviors like name-calling will depend on the norms of your group. Rosenblatt (1962) notes that the influence of norms on behavior will depend on the extent to which they are considered binding. In general, however, group norms exert powerful influence over the behavior of individuals. As Toseland and Rivas (1995, p. 81) point out, "soon it becomes clear that sanctions and social disapproval result from some behaviors and that praise and social approval result from other behaviors." The development of group norms can be helpful to the individuals and to the group itself. Norms provide a predictable group environment and add stability and security for members. Through the development of group norms, groups can develop procedures for coordinated action to reach goals (Toseland & Rivas, 1995). Alternatively, norms can develop destructive patterns of behavior that are harmful or unethical to others.

A **role** is a pattern of behavior that a person acts out in a group. It is a shared expectation about the functions of the individuals in the group. For example, there are role expectations about your status as a student, a mother, a spouse, and the many other roles you have in society. In groups, individuals also act according to certain roles, which can be important contributors to the group's effectiveness. "Roles are important for groups because they allow for division of labor and appropriate use of power" (Toseland & Rivas, 1995, p. 82). By accepting a particular role, individuals agree to behave in a certain manner.

Roles, like norms, can vary from very explicit roles to vague and informal ones. Bales (1958) has identified two categories of roles: *task-related roles* and *socioemotional roles*. Task-related roles refer to actions that move

the group toward the completion of its goals. Socioemotional roles refer to actions that keep the interactions in the group positive, friendly, and supportive. Box 4.1 shows seven different task roles and seven different socioemotional roles that are used in groups.

Communication Patterns

Communication patterns reflect the nature of how the members in the group communicate—in both verbal and nonverbal ways. A communication process is always occurring in the group because people communicate whenever they are together in a group. Communicating in a group has a number of functions (Kiesler, 1978):

- Understanding people and finding out where they stand in relation to other people
- Persuading others
- Gaining or maintaining power
- Defending oneself
- Provoking a reaction from others
- Making an impression on others
- Gaining or maintaining relationships
- Presenting a unified image to the group

Communication patterns vary within a group and may be either centralized, in which the leader is usually the central figure, or decentralized, where members share equally in communication and the pattern of interactions is more group-centered. What kind of communication pattern is best for groups? Research by McGrath (1984) found that when problems are simple, centralized groups are very efficient in resolving the problems. "Group-centered communication patterns tend to increase social interaction, group morale, and members' commitment to group goals" (Toseland & Rivas, 1995, p. 74). However, when problems are more complex, a decentralized pattern of communication is more effective. Group members have greater satisfaction in more decentralized groups.

Status and Power

How do some group members obtain more status and power than other members? **Status** refers to the ranking of each group member's position in the group relative to the other members. **Power** refers to the potential ability of a member to influence the group's decision or the behavior of individuals in the group. Although status and power often go hand in hand, this is not necessarily the case. A person's status is based on two different factors. First, what is the person's prestige or position outside of the group? Is the person recognized as a leader in the community? Second, what kinds of roles does the person assume when he or she becomes a member of a group? Is the person a coordinator and standard setter, influencing how the group achieves its goals? Because status is defined relative to other group members, a person's status is influenced by how others in the group perceive the person.

Power is a difficult concept to define, but French and Raven (1959), in a classic analysis, identify five sources of power in groups:

Reward power: Based on the person's ability to reward others as a means for obtaining power

Coercive power: Based on the person's ability to apply sanctions such as punishments and threats toward others

Expert power: Based on the person's ability to demonstrate superior skills and abilities as a means of influencing others

BOX 4.1

Tasks and Socioemotional Roles in Groups

Task Roles

Information seeker: Emphasizes "getting the facts" by calling for background information

Opinion seeker: Asks for more qualitative types of data, such as attitudes, values and feelings

Elaborator: Gives additional information—such as rephrasing, implications—about points made by others

Coordinator: Shows the relevance of each idea and its relationship to the overall problem

Orienter: Refocuses discussion on the topic whenever necessary

Evaluator-critic: Appraises the quality of the group's efforts in terms of logic, practicality, or method

Energizer: Stimulates the group to continue when discussion lags

Socioemotional Roles

Encourager: Rewards others through agreement, warmth, and praise

Harmonizer: Mediates conflicts among group members

Compromiser: Shifts his or her own position on an issue in order to reduce conflict in the group

Gatekeeper or expediter: Smooths communication by setting up procedures and ensuring equal participation

Standard setter: Expresses or calls for discussion of standards for evaluating the quality of the group process

Group observer and commentator: Informally points out the positive and negative aspects of the group's dynamics and calls for change if necessary

Follower: Accepts the ideas offered by others and serves as an audience for the group

Source: Adapted from Benne & Sheets, 1948.

Referent power: Based on the person's personal characteristics, such as likability and respect, that give them influence over others

Legitimate power: Based on the person's perceived legitimate right to make demands of other people

Cohesiveness

A **cohesive group** is one in which individual members have strong bonds with one another and to the group itself. Group cohesion is the dynamic that compels individuals to remain part of the group (Festinger, 1950). Therefore, cohesive groups are often emotionally close, loyal to each other and to the group, and have a strong sense of camaraderie.

Fundamentally, the factors that would make a group cohesive are those that promote positive, caring relationships among the members—for example, groups that are more similar in attitudes, have greater liking and respect for one another, and that are successful in achieving goals (Ridgeway, 1983). When members are attracted to a group, there is a greater likelihood of developing group cohesion. Attraction to the group is influenced by people's desire for affiliation, the group's access to resources and incentives, the expectations group members have about the outcomes that can be achieved in the group, and the relative comparison to other groups (Cartwright, 1968).

Group workers believe that an important skill for a group leader is the ability to influence group cohesion (Rose, 1989). This skill is important because a cohesive group has a number of benefits (Cartwright, 1968; Dion, Miller, & Magnan, 1970; Evans & Dion, 1991; Rose, 1989; Yalom, 1985):

- Members are more likely to stay in the group.
- Members are more likely to persevere in attempts to accomplish group goals.
- Attendance is higher.
- Members accept more responsibility for group functioning.
- Members are more satisfied.
- Members are less likely to feel psychological distress.
- Members are more likely to have increased self-esteem and greater self-confidence.

Impact of Gender on Groups

How does gender influence small group interactions? Not surprisingly, the small group is similar to what we experience in society. Therefore, status and power differentials in the larger society are reflected in the small group. As a result, gender roles can play an important function in how individuals and groups behave. Kanter (1977) believes that when men and women are in mixed-sex groups, tension exists that places many women at a disadvantage. In essence, because men and women do not have equal power and status in society, there is little reason to believe that equal power status would exist in the small mixed-sex group.

Indeed, research on mixed-sex groups has found that, in line with traditional gender-role expectations, men are more likely to assume task-oriented roles and women are more likely to assume socioemotional roles (Eagly & Wood, 1991; Wood, 1987). Wood (1987) further discovered that when groups confront problems that require a task orientation, all-male groups do better; but when problems are based on complex social interactions, all-female groups do better.

Decision Making in Groups

Whatever the composition of the group, its members often have to confront group decision making, and social psychologists have discovered interesting theories about group decision making. In a classic study, Stoner (1961) asked individuals and groups to make decisions under conditions of uncertainty. For example, one scenario involved an electrical engineer with a small family to support. He makes an adequate income and has good job security. After attending a conference, he is offered a job at a small new company with an uncertain future. However, if he takes the job, he can participate in a share of the ownership. Stoner compared how individuals and groups decided about such dilemmas and found that, overall, groups made riskier decisions than individuals did. This observation became known as *risky shift.*

Further research found that the shift can occur in either direction. A group may start out mildly opposed to an idea, and, after discussion, the sentiment against the idea is stronger. On the other hand, a group may start out favorable toward an idea, and after discussion, this sentiment becomes stronger. This shift toward the more extreme position is referred to as *group polarization*. Group polarization results when discussion strengthens a group's perspective and then shifts toward a more extreme position in the same direction.

Another important group phenomenon is **groupthink**. Groupthink is the result of a cohesive group emphasizing consensus at the expense of critical thinking when attempting to problem solve. Groupthink is based on the keen observation skills of Irving Janis (1972; 1982), who described groupthink in an effort to explain how President John Kennedy and his advisers could so mistakenly decide to invade Cuba at the Bay of Pigs in 1961. Janis was amazed at what a horrible attempt the invasion turned out to be. "How could bright men like John F. Kennedy and his advisers be taken in by such a stupid, patchwork plan as the one presented to them by the CIA representatives?" (Janis, 1973, p. 16).

From this experience, Janis developed his model of groupthink, which is described in Box 4.2.

When groupthink sets in, members of the group fail to use their own critical judgment. Because the group is cohesive, members develop group norms against dissent and the pressure to conform becomes great. Also, the group's viewpoint is protected by "mind guards," who shield information from the group if it contradicts the group's perspective.

If the group's view is challenged from the outside, then an *ingroup* and an *outgroup* are created. The in-

---

BOX 4.2

Janis's Model of Groupthink

Antecedent Conditions

High cohesiveness
Insulation from the group
Lack of methodological procedures for search and
    appraisal
Directive leadership
High stress and a low degree of hope for finding a better
    solution than the one favored by the leader or other
    influential groups

Concurrence-Seeking Tendency

Symptoms of Groupthink

Illusion of invulnerability
Collective rationalization

Belief in inherent morality of the group
Stereotypes of outgroups
Direct pressure on dissenters
Self-censorship
Illusion of unanimity
Self-appointed mind guards

Symptoms of Defective Decision Making

Incomplete survey of alternatives
Incomplete survey of objectives
Failure to examine risks of preferred choice
Poor information search
Selective bias in processing information at hand
Failure to reappraise alternatives
Failure to work out contingency plans

Source: Janis & Mann, 1977.

group includes everyone who agrees with the group perspective, and the outgroup is everyone who is not part of the ingroup. By perceiving the outgroup as very different from the ingroup, the outgroup can easily become the enemy, and an "us versus them" mentality develops. An additional symptom of groupthink is a biased approach to examining information and facts. Everything is seen from a viewpoint of supporting the group perspective.

The groupthink theory suggests that the way individuals in groups process information may not be the best approach to problem solving. Janis reports that groupthink was an underlying problem in President Roosevelt's lack of preparation for Pearl Harbor, President Johnson's continued involvement in the Vietnam War, and in President Nixon's cover-up of the Watergate scandal. However, as Weiten and Lloyd (1994) note, groupthink is likely to be observed in everyday life as groups struggle with the many decisions they have to make.

What would be the likely causes of groupthink? Janis notes three critical factors: first, the isolation of the group; second, the influence of directive leadership; and third, the use of unsystematic procedures for generating and evaluating decisions. Additional factors include the stress present in the situation, the *particular* characteristics of certain leaders, and the level of cohesiveness in the group. Although research has found that groupthink is not inevitable, it can occur and can lead to profoundly negative consequences (Weiten & Lloyd, 1994).

Research like Janis's has led to the implementation of new procedures in approaches to group decision making. For example, the Institute for Cultural Affairs, a nonprofit organization designed to empower people to facilitate change, has developed a method called the Technology of Participation (Spencer, 1989). This process teaches people a specific method for focused conversation that systematically follows four steps for groups: to be objective, reflective, interpretive, and decisional. Then the members use five steps of the Technology of Participation in decision making: (1) set the context, (2) brainstorm data and ideas, (3) order the data, (4) name the categories, and (5) evaluate the work and its implications.

Support Systems

Children and families do not develop in isolation. They grow and develop in interaction with many other systems such as school systems, neighborhood systems, and extended family systems. These systems can offer a needed source of *social support*. Caplan (1974, p. 4) defines **social support systems** as "continuing social aggregates that provide individuals with opportunities for feedback about themselves and for validations for their expectations about others, which may offset deficiencies in these communications within the larger community context." Germain (1991) classifies support systems into five different types: formal organizations, formed groups, self-help groups, social networks, and natural helpers. For our discussion, we are concerned primarily with informal support systems, which include self-help groups, social networks, and natural helpers. Understanding social support is important in social work because the notion of *social* support expresses the person-in-environment perspective and is critical to making a social work assessment (Germain, 1991). Silverman (1987) notes that social support groups are important for people who are undergoing transitions in certain roles, as this can be a critical time for change. Often such mutual aid helps people develop appropriate expectations and learn appropriate role behaviors for obtaining a new integration into society.

Self-Help and Mutual Aid Groups

Social support is offered through self-help or mutual aid groups. These groups seek to offer mutual aid through the exchange that occurs when people share a common problem. Such exchanges may have strong biological and social roots. People are often drawn to small groups, and this may be because of the evolutionary benefit of being in such groups; groups provide emotional and physical security. As Dubos (1978) points out, evolution took place in the context of small groups, which provided security from predators. The impact of this connection to small groups is felt in contemporary life where we "experience urbanized mass society as stressful, despite its attractions and advantages. We protect ourselves by maintaining noninvolvement through depersonalized, detached interactions with those outside our own 'band'" (Germain, 1991, p. 77).

In self-help groups, people join together to help each other cope more effectively with shared problems. These groups are often a part of voluntary organizations where members control the resources and policy decisions. In this sense, they are self-help organizations. Silverman (1987) uses the term *mutual help* to describe these organizations, noting that the help goes two ways.

Mutual aid groups can be classified into two basic types: social change and personal coping groups (Germain, 1991). Social change groups may be involved in changing public laws or attitudes, such as groups that support gay and lesbian life issues or groups for parents with disabled children. These groups are often involved in awareness campaigns or efforts to ensure that group members receive the kind of services and treatment that they are entitled to. Personal coping groups focus on getting help for individual members that will influence their behavior or personal growth. The best example is Alcoholics Anonymous, the oldest self-help organization of its kind. Both of these types of groups represent examples of mutual help organizations because the "members retain control of resources and are actively involved in helping programs built on their own experience" (Silverman, 1987, p. 171).

Characteristics of Self-Help or Mutual Aid Groups

What makes a self-help group different from other types of groups? One of the fundamental differences is that in **self-help organizations,** it is the members that control the resources and policies—the groups are self-governing and self-regulating (Silverman, 1987). However, the nature of the organization's structure varies considerably. For example, some very informal organizations have little or no organizational structure, and the members that participate control the organization. Other groups emulate voluntary organizations, using parliamentary procedures, establishment of committees, and election of officers (Silverman, 1987). For example, the La Leche League is a service organization for mothers that breastfeed, and local offices follow national leaders for directives in running the local chapters. Typically, such groups use dues from affiliated chapters that support the national office. Other self-help groups are less formally organized and use a consensus model in managing the activities of the group.

Functions of Self-Help Groups

Silverman (1987, p. 173) identifies three primary functions in a mutual self-help organization: "(1) receive information on how to cope, (2) obtain material help when necessary, (3) feel cared about and supported." Self-help groups are fundamentally based on the idea that people with like experiences can offer the best information regarding these three functions. Silverman (1987, p. 173) describes the functions this way:

> The helper and the beneficiary become peers, if only in the sense that they share a common problem. As they discover that what seemed unusual is common to others in a similar situation, people no longer feel alone with their problems. Their emotions and experiences are legitimated, and a framework is provided for coping with the situation. They receive specific guidance on how to implement change, thus expanding their repertoire of appropriate coping strategies.

Each self-help group or organization has its own approach to helping its members. Alcoholics Anonymous is the best-known self-help organization, and its basic structure and philosophy are used as a model for other similar self-help groups for addictive behavior and other personal problems. Examples of such groups include Overeaters Anonymous and Incest Survivors Anonymous.

The relationship between self-help groups and professional organizations has not always been cooperative. Indeed, self-help groups may be reluctant to associate with professionals, fearing their autonomy may be compromised. Furthermore, many people who use self-help groups may have had poor experiences with formal helping systems. Many professionals have attempted to intervene with self-help groups in an effort to impose their professional knowledge. As a result, there is often tension between professionals and the self-help organization. However, some research (Toseland & Hacker, 1982) has found strong connections between self-help groups and professionals. Social workers increasingly recognize that self-help groups can be an important resource that is often more flexible and responsive than formal service systems (Toseland & Rivas, 1995).

The number of self-help organizations has grown so rapidly that many people now refer to self-help as a movement. Box 4.3 presents only a sample of self-help groups that were available in one community. Germain (1991, p. 74) notes that "the rapid expansion of self-help reflects the readiness (always present, but until recently not acknowledged nor recognized) of people in all segments of society to solve their own problems, in concert with others like themselves." Libraries, grocery stores, and community organizations list information about self-help groups. Computer access through the Internet has greatly increased people's ability to find people with like problems and join self-help groups electronically (Finn, 1995). Indeed, there are many computer-based self-help groups, such as those for sexual abuse survivors and for recovered substance abusers (Finn, in press).

Why is the self-help movement gaining such popularity? Part of the answer to this question lies in the evolutionary benefit achieved by such groups. The growth may also be due to the expanding professionalism and the depersonalization of care being offered (Gartner & Riessman, 1977). Perhaps the rapid changes taking place in society are limiting the opportunities for people to ob-

tain needed social support. The growth also parallels the consumer movement, which advocates greater personal involvement in one's care and less reliance on outside professionals. Silverman (1987) believes the growth in self-help reflects the fact that people want a different form of help that is simply not available in the existing service system. People often seek help that can be made available to them only through association with others who are similarly afflicted.

Natural Helpers

Closely related to self-help organizations are **natural helpers**—"central figures in a social network or in a neighborhood who have gained recognition for their unique wisdom, resourcefulness, and caring qualities"

BOX 4.3

Some Support Groups and Anonymous Organizations

Adult Children of Alcoholics
Adult Children of Sex Addicts
Adults Recovering from Incest (women's group)
Alcoholics Anonymous
Al-Anon
Child Abusers Anonymous
Chronic Pain Outreach
Cocaine Anonymous
Coc-Anon
Concerned United Birth Parents
Eating Disorders
Emotions Anonymous
Families Anonymous
For Accountability in Religion
Gamblers Anonymous
Men for Sobriety
Depressive and Manic-Depressive Association
Narcotics Anonymous

OURS (for adoptive parents)
Overeaters Anonymous
Parents Anonymous
Pills Anonymous
PMS Peer Support group
RESOLVE: Infertility Education Support
Sex Addicts Anonymous
Sex and Love Addicts Anonymous
Sex-oholics Anonymous
Co-Sex-oholics Anonymous
Shoplifters Anonymous
Smokers Anonymous
Spenders Anonymous
S-Anon
Survivors of Incest Anonymous
Twelve Steps for Christian Living group
Women for Sobriety
Women with Multiple Addictions

(Germain, 1991, p. 81). Pancoast, Parker, and Froland (1983) describe mutual help groups as natural helping networks, and Collins and Pancoast (1976) describe neighborhoods where natural helpers are a critical resource, providing social support to families at risk for child abuse and neglect.

Developing and using natural helpers may be critical in efforts to help people who are isolated and without access to traditional support services. For example, Patterson, Brennan, Germain, and Memmot (1988) found that natural helping in rural communities is characterized by reciprocity—helpers provide for friends and are in turn cared for by them. Germain (1991, p. 82) quotes a natural helper's description of her role:

> He was abusive and very, very abusive of their son. When the divorce was finally completed, it made her very sad because it all started because of alcohol. She really still liked the guy, but she was determined this was it. As a result she was badly in need of friends. And that's where I thought I helped her—more for listening than anything else because I couldn't do anything else.

Interest in natural-helping networks has grown as part of the larger interest in prevention, self-help, and community building at the local level (Pancoast & Collins, 1987). Informal helping is now a legitimate part of the continuum of helping strategies (Whittaker & Garbarino, 1983). This interest and the growth of such interventions has led to the development of a new role for the social worker. The social worker is expected to be not an expert but instead a partner with the natural helpers. As Pancoast and Collins (1987, p. 180) point out, "it is important for social workers to be careful not to usurp the position of the natural helper or to take on a customary professional position of leadership and direction."

Contexts: Organizations and Institutions

Organizations are a special context in which humans live. Social workers and other social scientists assume that organizations can be studied apart from the people who make them up because organizations continue even after their members die, quit, or retire (Ferrante, 1995). Much of our life takes place within these imper-

sonal structures. Most of us begin life in a hospital; attend school in a formal organizational setting; eventually work in a bank, factory, office, or corporation; have contacts with members of governmental agencies; and depend on multinational organizations for meeting many of our other needs. **Formal organizations** differ significantly from situations in which people have most of their needs met by primary groups. For instance, it was rare in many parts of traditional China for members of a rural village to ever come in contact with a governmental official or nonprimary group member (Giddens, 1989). They lived their lives for the most part in small group settings without the influence of formal organizations.

What Is a Formal Organization?

A formal organization is any large social group that is designed to rationally achieve specific objectives. Organizations have carefully designed structures that coordinate the activities of their members with an end in view of achieving the greatest possible efficiency. The relationships among the members of a formal organization are based on their position or location in the organization. The duties and rights associated with their position are attached to the office itself and not to the individuals. For most formal organizations, we can draw a chart that reflects the relationships of the various positions in this social system without making any reference at all to the actual individuals working in the organization.

Without a doubt, our way of life in a postindustrial society is still highly dependent on the existence of formal organizations. Although fewer and fewer individuals are working in large factories, most individuals have some form of affiliation with a formal organization, such as a governmental agency, multinational corporation, telecommunication organization, or educational system. In fact, formal organizations appear very natural to most individuals who were born and raised in an industrial society. During their lives, they have had very few opportunities to escape the influence of these designed social systems, which employ highly impersonal structures to achieve their specified aims.

In the preindustrial era, families and neighbors provided for most of an individual's needs. Primary groups were responsible for providing the food, instructing the children, and managing the leisure-time activities. Today, most of our needs are handled by persons whom we have never had an occasion to meet. In this type of social context, there is a need for extremely effective coordination of actions and resources. The most common structure used for achieving this objective is a bureaucracy.

What Is a Bureaucracy?

When organizations are large and complex, they often adopt what is known as a bureaucratic structure. Most modern organizations have bureaucratic qualities. The word **bureaucracy** was first coined in 1745 by Monsieur de Gournay. "He added to the word 'bureau,' meaning both an office and a writing table, a term derived from the Greek verb 'to rule.' 'Bureaucracy' is thus the rule of officials" (Giddens, 1989, p. 277). As Giddens points out, the term has been used in disparaging ways since its inception. De Gournay questioned the emerging power of governmental officials and even alluded to them as having an illness that he called bureaumania. Today, *bureaucracy* still carries negative connotations, and these connotations are not limited to governmental organizations. *Bureaucracy* conjures forth many images of excessive red tape, inefficiency, and alienation of its participants. Yet, Max Weber, who is the most influential writer on the topic, defined it as representing, in theory, a "rational organization" (Ferrante, 1995).

For Weber, rationalization was the master trend taking place in the modern world. He identified four fundamental types of social action: instrumentally rational action, value-rational action, affective action, and traditional action (Waters, 1994). Focus on Theory: Weber's Topology of Rational Action provides a description of each of these forms of action. Weber used these hypothetical types as ideals against which to evaluate any kind of intentional action. It was his view that instrumentally rational actions were, in the modern world, replacing actions guided by traditions, emotions, and other nonrational processes. He was interested in the transformation in Western societies from power structures based on claims of tradition to structures based on claims of reason. Weber extended this view of rational actions to his theory of bureaucracy and his widely known theory of authority relations.

For Weber, the bureaucracy is considered an **ideal type.** An ideal type refers to an abstract description derived from real cases that were analyzed to determine their essential features. A real agency will not necessarily conform in all respects to this type.

In Weber's view, a bureaucracy is an ideal type that has the following features:

- Its activities are governed by rules.
- It has a specific sphere of competence.
- It is organized hierarchically.
- Its members are specifically trained for their occupations.
- Its officers do not own the means of production.
- They do not own their jobs, but can be dismissed from them.
- Its actions are recorded in files. (Waters, 1994, p. 224)

For Weber, an organization with features that resemble these is likely to be efficient at coordinating the activities of its members and in achieving specific objectives.

FOCUS ON THEORY

Weber's Topology of Rational Action

In the theory of Max Weber, the meanings and intentions of actors play a central role. He is noted for the development of *Verstehen* (understanding) sociology, an approach to sociological analysis that focuses on actors' reasons for their actions. Weber recognized that our reasons can vary, and he developed a well-known typology that classifies various forms of social action:

Instrumental rationality: Involves action that is rational in relation to a goal. The individual selects the best means available to achieve an intended goal. It is also referred to as goal-rational action.

Value-rational action: Involves action that is considered rational in relation to a value. The individual acts in terms of what is right: for instance, acting in relation to a commitment to a higher-order value like beauty, justice, or God.

Affective action: Action that is determined by feelings, passions, psychological needs, or other emotional concerns.

Traditional action: Any action that is dictated by custom. That is, it is performed because that is the way it has always been performed.

Source: Waters, 1994.

Scientific Management Traditions in Human Organizations

Shafritz and Whitbeck (1978) point out that any theory must be evaluated in the context of its time. This is also true of organizational theory. Early management theory, in this tradition, originated before workers began to enjoy even limited rights. Times were harsh and workers were seen merely as interchangeable parts in a highly impersonal "industrial machine." "Consequently, the first theories of organizations were concerned with the anatomy or structure of formal organizations. This is the hallmark of classical organization theory—a concern for organization structure that is premised upon the assumed rational behavior of its human parts" (Shafritz & Whitbeck, 1978, p. 1).

Within this context, the first notions of organizational principles were developed. It is often customary to begin discussion of the origins of management theory with the early writings of Adam Smith. In his famous work, *An Inquiry into the Nature and Causes of the Wealth of Nations* (1776), Smith looked at the optimum functioning of a factory in the chapter "Of the Division of Labor." This chapter clarifies how increased specialization of labor contributed to the enhanced productivity of a pin factory. In Smith's view, the factory represented the "most appropriate means of mass production." This view was shared by Frederick Winslow Taylor, who believed that factory workers could be even more productive if their jobs were scientifically designed. Taylor is

considered by most authorities as the founder of *scientific management*.

For Taylor, there is "one best way" of accomplishing a job task, and the goal of the scientific manager is to ensure that the best way is followed by the employees of the organization. Taylor is noted for instituting time-in-motion studies and piece-rate wages. In 1954, Peter Drucker observed that scientific management "may well be the most powerful as well as the most lasting contribution America has made to Western thought since the Federalist Papers". (see Shafritz & Whitbeck, 1978, p. ix). In some sense, the major focus in the writings of Taylor was on issues of technology.

Management, as a separate discipline, emerged in the United States after World War I and was heavily influenced by scientific management principles. In fact, this approach is often referred to as "Taylorism." In 1937, Luther Gulick introduced the famous mnemonic *POSDCORB* that defined the elements required to manage an organization: planning, organizing, staffing, directing, coordination, reporting, and budgeting. These elements are still examined today by modern organizational theorists.

Formal and Informal Relations in Organizations

Weber's approach to understanding organizations focused primarily on issues of formalization and structure. The more an agency is bureaucratized in its organization, the more formal its relationships are. In fact, Weber has very little to say about the role of informal relations in the operations of modern organizations. We now know that informal relationships and networks exist in most formal organizations. People in organizations know each other in many ways besides their official positions. They develop informal procedures for handling problems, negotiating their way through the hierarchy, and achieving assigned tasks. The Hawthorne studies at the Western Electric Company in 1932 documented these processes. In fact, the results of this research led to a specific approach in organizational studies known as the **human relations school**. This tradition in organizational studies focuses on understanding the influences of informal networks on all forms of organized activities.

The human relations school was in many senses a reaction to the overemphasis on structural rationality in the writings of Weber and members of the scientific management school (Netting, Kettner, & McMurtry, 1993). Chester Barnard (1938) proposed the first real theory on human relations that challenged the other classical approaches. He pointed out the important role of cooperation and other social processes in organizations. He is noted mostly for introducing researchers to the study of "natural groups within the organization, upward communication, authority from below rather than from above, and leaders who functioned as a cohesive force" (Perrow, 1978, p. 315). His focus on cooperative processes was well-timed because he was writing around the period of the Great Depression (Perrow, 1978), when there was significant labor unrest and conflict between labor and management.

The human relations school ushered in a wealth of research on the traits of effective leaders in organizations. Also, social psychologists in this tradition studied task groups to determine the impact of social factors on human efficiency. However, this school has not been without its critics. Netting and colleagues (1993) argue that several studies have shown that informal organizational structures might not be as prevalent in organizations as many human relations writers suggest. Furthermore, democratic leadership may have less to do with productivity than with other factors in human motivation, such as economic benefits. Nonetheless, this school has introduced many concepts in organizational research that encourage more humane treatment of organization members. In fact, it directs us to look at the assumptions about human nature contained in any theory of organizations.

Douglas McGregor's work (1960) is an excellent example of theoretical work resulting from the shift from analysis of structure to analysis of participants' behavior in organizations. His work focused on understanding the factors that motivate employees. He identified two distinct approaches to leadership or management in organizations: Theory X and Theory Y. Theory X approaches to management assume that managers must adopt coercion in their style of leadership because coercion is necessary to obtain good work performance by employees. McGregor (1960) argues that the theories of Taylor and Weber were highly supportive of this type of management style. He assumes that workers need to be controlled by the structure of the organization because: "(a) people have an inherent dislike for work; (b) they must be coerced in

order to work; (c) the average worker prefers to be told what to do; and (d) monetary reward is the worker's primary motivator" (Netting et al., 1993, p 133). Theory Y approaches assume that, in trying to motivate workers, management needs to take into account many of the higher-order needs identified by Maslow. Theory Y's assumptions are:

1. Work is as natural an activity as rest or play, thus people do not necessarily have to be forced to do it.
2. Workers will commit to organizational goals if they are able to meet their own needs in so doing.
3. Workers will accept responsibility for meeting goals that are congruent with their needs.
4. Organizational tasks should be structured to allow workers to exercise creativity and imagination in fulfilling these responsibilities (Netting et al., 1993, p. 133.)

Theory Y approaches are sensitive to individual worker needs but ignore the motivational needs of persons. To this end, William Ouchi (1981) developed an approach that he terms Theory Z. "Theory Z had its roots not in traditional Western assumptions about humans, but in assumptions about humans based on Japanese culture and reflected in many Japanese organizations and approaches to management" (Schriver, 1995, p. 421). Ouchi contrasted these approaches to management in Japan with approaches in the United States. They are presented in Table 4.3.

Thus, workers need knowledge not only of theories of organizations but also of management. But views of management cannot be limited to U.S. viewpoints. The United Nations estimates that there are approximately 35,000 multinational corporations worldwide. A disproportionate number of their headquarters are in the United States, Japan, and Western Europe. Corporations in Japan and Western Europe may subscribe to distinctly different approaches to management and views of human nature, a fact that social workers cannot ignore. Multinational corporations are a special type of organization having characteristics that can contribute to many social problems encountered by social work professionals. When students are asked about how their lives are affected by our increased global contexts, we often learn the impact that multinational corporations are having on them and their families. That is, they can point out how

TABLE 4.3 Japanese and U.S. Management Approaches

Japanese Organization	U.S. Organization
Lifetime employment	Short-term employment
Slow evaluation and promotion	Rapid evaluation and promotion
Nonspecialized career path	Specialized career paths
Implicit control mechanisms	Explicit control mechanisms
Collective decision making	Individual decision making
Collective responsibility	Individual responsibility
Holistic concern	Segmented concern

Source: Ouchi, 1981.

their lives have changed because of some connection with a corporation that has significant international ties.

Social Institutions

Every society requires the formation of institutions in order to survive. Giddens (1989) considers these institutions the cement that holds together all forms of social life. They constitute the basic social arrangements within which people live most of their daily lives. A society, like any other system, is composed of many parts or subsystems. These subsystems are interrelated, bounded, and have environments. The most basic parts from which these subsystems are built are a society's status positions, roles, and norms (Turner, 1972).

In social work, we rarely assess individuals without taking into account their behavior in larger social contexts, including key social institutions. In particular, we are interested in understanding the primary institutional arrangements that contribute to the health and welfare of our clients. Most societies have large social institutions that encompass and cut across many segments of their members' social life. The institutions of economy, kinship, education, law, polity, and religion are observed in most industrial or postindustrial societies. These institutions contribute to the stability of statutes, roles, and norms observed in the behavior of people in these communities. This relationship of structure to human behavior is what social scientists grapple with when they examine human behavior in terms of its structural or in-

stitutional properties (see Focus on Theory: Modern Functionalism).

William Graham Sumner (1906), in his classic work *Folkways*, examined how social institutions are formed in nonindustrial societies. He contends that the first task of life is to survive, stating, "Need was the first experience and it was followed by some blundering effort to satisfy it" (Sumner, 1906, pp. 17–18). In Sumner's view, the yardstick for measuring the success of these blundering efforts is pleasure and pain. Pleasure and pain underlie all of our trial-and-error methods of testing solutions to our survival needs. Our early ancestors tried to profit from the successful experiences of other group members. The most expedient ways for achieving survival ends were generally adopted by the group, and these ways turned into what are known as customs. In effect, successful ways of doing things become institutionalized in any society. In Sumner's view, this is how **folkways** arise in natural group processes.

This concept of folkways is a key foundation underlying most of Sumner's theoretical observations (Cotterrell, 1984). For Sumner, folkways represent group ways of solving problems and of doing things. These ways are handed down through tradition, imitation, and authority. They "provide for all the needs of life: they specify the best way to make a fire, to cook meat, to greet one's neighbor, and to raise one's children" (Cotterrell, 1984, p. 20). Folkways are sanctioned in many premodern societies by fear of ancestors. That is, the ghosts of ancestors will seek vengeance if members of the community deviate from the ancient ways of doing things. This implies that folkways are transformed at some point in societal evolution from representing merely utilitarian ends to having a position of right or truth. When folkways start to be viewed in terms of right and wrong ways of doing things, they are elevated to what Sumner termed **mores.**

Folkways and mores prescribe the rules that govern the behavior of people in primary group relations. These rules exist prior to a person's birth and structure how life is to be lived. As societies change and become more modern, traditional rules are replaced by formal law. Formal law is considered to be the type of system capable of maintaining moral order in a complex society with a high division of labor. In this system, "All citizens are, in theory, formally equal under the law. Law is also autonomous from other social institutions" (Horwitz, 1990,

p. 2). That is, the law is to maintain a culture and set of norms that are distinct from the rules of religion, political systems, and economic interests. This view differs from the views of law espoused by Sumner.

In Sumner's view, the law needs to be rooted in the mores of the society, an assumption that has been challenged by other legal scholars. Many aspects of law are in opposition to the customs and mores of people. Civil rights law in the United States is an excellent example: The customs and mores of southern society were in violation of laws in modern case law that made segregation illegal. The law is a very important social institution that has a pervasive effect on our lives and the lives of our clients. For this reason, we will discuss the characteristics of this system to illustrate the role of major social institutions in social life.

FOCUS ON THEORY

Modern Functionalism

Talcott Parsons and Robert Merton are two of the major contributors to functionalist thought in American sociology. Their work was significantly influenced by the early sociologists and the first functional anthropologists—Malinowski and Radcliffe-Brown. Talcott Parsons is considered "the most dominant theorist of his time" (Turner, 1991, p. 51), known for having established a general theory of social systems. Before developing this dominant analytical approach to the social system, he viewed social life as a matter of agency. *Agency* is a technical term in sociology that includes the idea that goal-oriented people act in intentional ways (Waters, 1994). Any theory of social behavior that examines the process of acting in relation to a set of meanings or intentions is referred to as a theory of agency.

To this end, Parsons considered action systems as being patterned by a series of alternative courses of action called *pattern variables*. These pattern variables prescribe the limited choices available to individuals in social situations.

In Parsons's scheme, actors can choose only one of the options in a pattern variable. For example, a person confronting another person in a situation can choose only one option from each pattern variable to judge the other person by—in terms of his or her performance (achievement) or in terms of his or her qualities (ascription). Because these choices influence the social arrangements in any given society, they were widely used to classify differences in social structures among societies.

Parsons modified his approach to studying the structure of social systems to give them a stronger functional focus, which led him to emphasize the importance of social systems. This change in his theory became known as *structural functionalism*. In this phase, Parsons identified four functional imperatives that are essential to the survival of any social system. These four requisites are referred to as the AGIL scheme after its initials:

Adaptation
Goal Attainment
Integration
Latent Pattern Maintenance

Any social system must meet these requisites if it is to survive. These requisites also help us understand the role played by key social systems in society. To illustrate this point, we will use the AGIL scheme to provide a conceptual description of the needs of the social system (Waters, 1994). These needs are represented below.

Social system need	Fulfilled by
1. Adaptation	The economy—money
2. Goal Attainment	The political system—power
3. Integration	The social system—social controls, norms, and legal rules
4. Pattern Maintenance	Socialization—family, schools[1]

This classification scheme helps us make sense of the major social institutions in our society. Functional principles help us study our social institutions, and social institutions represent the final step in the process in which cultural values are translated into customary behavior. A social institution is technically defined as an

[1]Source: Waters, 1994.

"integrated set of social norms organized around the preservation of a basic society value" (Leslie, Larson, & Gorman, 1973, p. 109). Parsons and his followers identified five basic institutions: family, religion, education, economy, and government. Each of these institutions plays a critical role in the social system's survival. A common assignment for social work students is to examine the social welfare system using principles from Parsons' institutional conceptualizations.

How can we analyze social systems? Parsons also contributed a useful conceptual scheme for classifying the four layers of social organization that underpin the social system (Layder, 1994). This scheme is described below.

System or level	Aspect of experience
1. The physiological system	The body
2. The personality system	Individual psychology
3. The social system	Norms, roles, and positions
4. The cultural system	Knowledge, literature, art, and other human products[1]

Robert Merton also looked at the functions of social structures, but he extended his study of social systems to include dysfunctions. For instance, he would analyze a system such as poverty in terms of its dysfunctions but would also seek to uncover any of its alternative functions. According to Merton, we need to examine the manifest and latent functions of any social institution.

For example, Herbert Gans, a noted sociologist, set out to discover why poverty exists. To the surprise of some, he uncovered 15 functions that were served by poverty, including the provision of job opportunities for individuals who serve the needs of the poor. Some functionalists assume, therefore, that balanced approaches to understanding problems cannot be arrived at merely by looking at their functions. Instead they argue that questions should also be asked about the manifest and latent functions, as well as the dysfunctions of any social system (Ferrante, 1995). These concepts provide social workers with a conceptual approach for thinking about the influence of social systems that identifies the key units in social systems. These units are included in the multidimensional framework presented in this textbook.

The Legal Institution

Many conservative legal scholars recognize that legislation and other forms of modern law can diverge from the mores of a community. They are troubled by these processes because they believe that the law should reflect the customs and sentiment of a community. For instance, the conservative legal jurist Karl von Savigny (1831) assumed that law should be allowed to develop spontaneously. He did not support a view of formal law in which legislatures had the authority to design laws that did not reflect the spirit of a people. In his view, if law became too divorced from the people, it would lose its legitimacy or authority. Today, many of these views seem strange because legislatures and other modern legal institutions play such a conspicuous role in most areas of our life. But some scholars today are also questioning the role of formal law in many aspects of modern life (Abel, 1982).

The form taken by a legal system is not a natural occurrence. Different societies have different types of legal institutions that approach issues of what is right, wrong, permissible, and not permissible in different ways. For instance, in many preliterate societies, kin are responsible for enforcing violations of law, whereas, in modern systems, these same tasks are assigned to specialized law enforcement agents and agencies. Are the rules governing the resolution of disputes in our current lives in the hands of too many legal specialists? What should we do when we have a conflict with a boss? Should we file a lawsuit against him or her to have our rights protected? When should we use more informal methods of control for handling deviant acts?

Many of the things we take for granted about the role of law in our lives are relatively recent phenomena. In earlier periods of history, formal law was less influential in people's lives; most of their private areas of life were regulated by informal mechanisms of social control. Today, however, formal law guides our work relations (administrative law and labor law), mental health practices (mental health law), child welfare practices (child welfare law), and most of the areas influencing the practice of social work. In fact, there are very few areas in

---

[1] Layder, 1994.

social work that are not regulated by some form of administrative rules or legislative policy.

Horwitz (1990) points out that even if the law is not directly involved in the settlement of disputes, it can still have a significant symbolic presence. Legal cases often speak to issues of great social significance in a society. In addressing these issues, legal rulings are providing normative levels of influence far beyond the persons involved in the cases. In fact, the ethics of practice in many social work contexts are driven by how the courts responded to a particular party in a case. Although the ruling in this case might not apply to a practitioner's jurisdiction, the reasoning can serve as a normative guide for the practitioner's future behavior. Law is penetrating more and more of social work and other areas of social life.

Horwitz states: "Private forums such as families, schools, clubs, and businesses that were immune to law in the past are now subject to more legal control than ever before. This has resulted in the perception of a 'litigation crisis' where people are becoming ever more likely to bring lawsuits to realize their goals" (1990, p. 7). Furthermore, access to lawyers has increased significantly in many sectors of the society. However, social theorists contend that the use of the law will vary with the person's location in social space (Black, 1993). That is, there are social or institutional factors that influence how the law as an institution will affect the lives of people in a society. This is a critical issue that social workers need to understand.

We are interested in understanding the effects of variations in social organization or other variables on changes in social space. Our location in social space has important implications for many areas of social analysis, including the study of social institutions like the law. In fact, it is a pivotal concept in social ecology, social geography, sociology, and other areas of social science.

Social Space in Institutional and Structural Modes of Analysis

Social workers and social scientists are interested in understanding space because it provides a useful concept for studying the organization of social relations. Social organization refers here to any relatively stable pattern of relationships between individuals. Many types of social organization are of interest to social workers. In assessing these forms of social organization, we need to evaluate how the location of people in their social space influences their patterns of organization. To this end, social scientists have established a number of technical terms to describe the variations in a person's location in his or her social space.

Black (1976, 1993) has adopted several social terms about space to aid in understanding the behavior of law. A major dimension of social space explored in study of law is **social distance.** Distance refers here to the nearness in relationships between people. "Different individuals are more or less close to one another as indicated by the strength of bonds between them, their investment in the relationship, and their frequency of contact" (Horwitz, 1990, p. 11). Some of these relationships are what Horwitz (1990) terms **uniplex relationships.** These relationships are characterized by a single limited type of exchange. A social worker–client relationship is an excellent example of a uniplex relationship. Social work ethics caution against having dual or **multiplex relationships** with our clients. In a multiplex relationship, a person has more than one type of exchange with other individuals. For instance, people on a reservation who live in the same community and are both kin and in a client-professional relationship, is an excellent example of multiplex relationship. These relationships are characterized by multiple ties or bonds.

Social integration is a technical term that refers to a special form or type of multiplex relationship. It measures the quantity of ties that a person has to major social institutions. We can determine a person's degree of integration if he or she has many ties to family, kin, work, education, religion, and other formal and informal organizations in a society. **Social marginality** refers to "the absence of these same ties" (Horwitz, 1990). Each concept captures some aspect of a person's **relational space.** They both measure a person's relational distance in terms of "the degree of intimacy between people as indicated by factors such as the number and type of interactions between them, the intensity and length of their relationship, and the nature of their ties" (Horwitz, 1990, p. 12).

Another major dimension of social space that predicts variations in law and other forms of social organization is **hierarchy.** This dimension consists of all the elements involved in a society's system of social stratification. "Individuals have higher or lower ranking positions that indicate their prestige and power within the hierarchical systems of the group" (Horwitz, 1990, p. 13). These rankings vary from social system to social system—class position, race, gender, socioeconomic status. With knowledge of these rankings, Black (1993) predicts that we can account for variations in the application of the law. That is, the amount of law applied in a dispute will depend on whether the victim is offended by a person in a higher, lower, or equal rank.

For instance, we know that an African American who victimizes a white or Anglo American will be treated differently by the law than an African American who victimizes another African American. It is not the race of the offender, but the relationship between the victim and offender that accounts for variations in outcome. In sum, if we know a person's social location in any form of legal dispute, we can use this relational information to predict the quantity and direction of law in these situations.

We assume in social work that families, groups, communities, organizations, race, class, and gender are different but are interrelated axes of social structure. Social structure refers here to the institutional or structural bases for all forms of social behavior and relationships. In our view, social workers must recognize that social systems are not features of human experience that can be examined separately. Any analysis of social behavior must take into account how systems and their structures are interrelated. For example, we cannot look at just the influences of race on the experiences of our clients without also taking into account how these same experiences are also being structured by the categories of gender and social class. Similarly, an analysis of one race without taking into account other races and social contexts can be equally misleading. The social worker must recognize that every system and its social categories intersect with other systems and their categories.

By using a structural analysis, we can understand behavior in many social institutions besides the law. We can use it to examine how the welfare system responds to clients, how the health care system offers services to societal groups, and other institutional responses of interest to social work planners and policy analysts. Thus, social workers must become familiar with concepts that enable them to understand the institutional and structural aspects of all forms of social behavior.

Multicultural and Gender Considerations

One of the most interesting aspects of the human species is its diversity. Yet this diversity contributes to significant intergroup conflict and social inequality. All societies have some way of making distinctions among its members. But some of these distinctions are used for purposes of **discrimination.** Discrimination is applying prejudice or bias to a person based on some particular characteristic. Discriminations are often based on physical characteristics or cultural traits. In the United States, physical and cultural differences influence the life chances and experiences of many women and persons of color. As a consequence, race, ethnicity, gender, sexual orientation, and able-bodiness are key variables in assessing social and interpersonal relations.

Racial and Ethnic Considerations

The United States is witnessing many demographic and cultural changes. "People of color constitute the fastest growing population in the United States" (Comas-Diaz & Greene, 1994, p. 3). If current trends in immigration and birth rates continue, the Hispanic/Latino population will increase by an estimated 21%, the Asian American population by about 22%, and the African American population by approximately 12%, whereas projections for growth rates in the white population are for an increase of about 2%. By the year 2056, it is projected that typical residents of the United States will trace their ancestry to Africa, Arab nations, Asia, Latin America, or the Pacific Islands (Takaki, 1993). These trends in birthrate projections and immigration patterns suggest the arrival of increased cultural pluralism within the United States.

The United States has had pluralism since its inception. Yet this fact is often overlooked in discussions about multiculturalism. Many early ethnic groups immigrating to this country maintained their original group identities but incorporated customs and practices from other cultures into these identities to adapt to their new environment. In fact, this process is referred to in the West Indies and in Spanish and French settlements in the Americas as **creolization** (Ancelet, Edwards, & Pitre, 1991). Ancelet and colleagues point out that "migration,

Our society is becoming increasingly multicultural.

whether voluntary or not, caused a break in ancestral patterns. While individual cultures did preserve some of their old ways in the New World, the frontier environment also provided the opportunity for them to create new ways based on the old" (1991, p. XIV). These new ways contributed to many of the rich cultural traditions observed in Cuba, Haiti, Puerto Rico, Mexico, and Louisiana that include a blending of many different cultural influences.

Throughout American history, groups have interacted and intermarried with neighbors of different cultures and races. This blending produced some interesting cultural variations that make up our current ethnic landscape. *Cajuns* are a distinct ethnic group in this country that we will use to illustrate the process of creolization. When Cajuns were exiled in 1755 from the region of Canada known as Acadia, some migrated to the French settlements in Louisiana. In Louisiana, they encountered new groups of Native Americans with tradi-

tions and customs different from those they were accustomed to in Canada. They also encountered persons born in Louisiana who were direct descendants of French-born individuals (Creoles). Some of the Acadian immigrants attempted to join the French plantation society. Others isolated themselves from this group and intermarried and interacted with Native Americans, African Americans, and many different immigrants to this region, including German Alsatians, Spaniards, Anglo Americans, the Irish, and the Scots. This blending of cultures and races produced a new cultural group with its own distinctive identity.

Today, many individuals in Louisiana identify with the Cajun ethnic group but can trace their ancestry to other groups outside of Canada. "This is why one finds people who call themselves Cajuns yet who have last names like Hoffpauir and Schexnayder, Ortego and Romero, Johnson and Reed, and McGee and Melancon" (Ancelet et al., 1991, p. xv). The Acadians had significant interaction with Africans born in the region, who influenced their music, dancing, and cooking practices. Cajuns are members of an ethnic group whom many modern French-speaking Canadians and Europeans find difficult to understand. In fact, their culture has minimal points of commonality with persons from other more dominant French regions of the world. In particular, European and Canadian French "are surprised at the Cajun's love of fried chicken and iced tea, forgetting this is also the American South; at their love of hamburgers and Coke, forgetting this is the United States; at their love of cayenne and cold beer, forgetting this is the northern tip of the West Indies (Ancelet et al., 1991, pp. xvii–xviii).

In efforts to define America, history has tended to ignore the experiences of Cajuns and other groups who don't support the *Anglo-conformity ideology* that underlies our espoused national identity (McLemore, 1991). This identity, although false, has supported the assumption that an American is a white person of European origin who has abandoned language ties and adopted a distinctive American culture. Ronald Takaki's (1993) book *A Different Mirror: A History of Multicultural America* points out that the histories of Asian Americans, African Americans, and other persons of color are not included in existing constructions of the American identity. He begins the book by describing an incident widely shared by Americans who are nonwhite and of non-European origins. He was riding in a taxi to a conference on multiculturalism in Norfolk, Virginia, when the taxi driver asked him how long he had been in this country. For Takaki, this situation illustrates the narrow view shared by many Americans about its history and its people. Takaki's family had lived in this country for well over 100 years, yet this driver adhered to a very narrow but commonsense definition of the American identity as "white" and primarily European in ancestry.

The changing racial and ethnic makeup of the country is threatening the identity of many Americans. As Takaki (1993) points out, the country has been racially diverse since its inception, but evidence of increased diversity is triggering fearful responses in many sectors of our society. Some long for "a more cohesive culture and more homogeneous America" (Takaki, 1993, p. 3). However, this view ignores the significant diversity in our country's past that was systematically purged from most major accounts of America's history. Because of this oversight, many universities are introducing curricula to assist students in obtaining a more accurate view of their country's history (Schoem, Frankel, Zuniga, & Lewis, 1993). This approach to history has not been without controversy. In fact, the demands for increased multiculturalism in education are starting to retest the legitimacy of valued notions of tolerance previously considered the hallmark of most Western liberal societies (Horton, 1993). This is clearly seen in students' objections and protests to multicultural courses that have been required on many college campuses.

Most modern liberal societies celebrate diversity and other forms of difference. In fact, this country considers tolerance of difference an important element underlying its reason for existence. Yet, "it has become an increasingly urgent issue of theory and practice as to how tolerant liberalism is, or can be, of cultural and religious groups which do not themselves subscribe universally or without qualification to what have been taken to be the basic values of liberalism" (Horton, 1993, p. 1). These values include liberty, equality, rights, neutrality, and autonomy. That is, all modern liberal societies are experiencing immigration patterns that involve cultures with distinct value traditions that are in opposition to the values of modern liberal thought. Does this mean that there are limits to what are considered acceptable or tolerable forms of cultural diversity in these societies?

Steven Lukes (1991) points out that liberalism was born out of religious conflict, and toleration was central to the development of liberalism. At the heart of this toleration is the notion that one will not interfere with other groups' cultural beliefs and behaviors. Does this view also apply to Jewish, Buddhist, and Islamic traditions? Muslims in France and England have asserted that Muslim girls ought to be educated in a context that prepares them for roles in Muslim society rather than in the values of secular liberalism. Muslims were also in violent disagreement with the kinds of free speech that permitted the vilification of their culture's most sacred beliefs with the publication of *The Satanic Verses* by Salman Rushdie. These examples illustrate situations in our liberal societies in which issues of tolerance are being reexamined. Current multicultural scholars are noticing that much of the acclaimed tolerance is not being extended to non-Christians or nonwhites.

As Gundara (1991) points out, if we assume that the imposition of a single culture or value system in a country like Trinidad is improper, then these same principles should apply to American, British, and other European countries. Liberal critics have vigorously attacked countries that advocate a single-value orientation in Africa, Latin America, and Asia because of their totalitarian implications. Yet many new writings are emerging in our own society that promote intolerance toward ethnic, religious, and linguistic variations. In fact, a number of politicians are arguing for English as the official language in the United States. What is the implication of this from a multicultural perspective?

The "Intelligence Report," a publication of the Southern Poverty Law Center, chronicles the recent increases in violence toward immigrants in our society. The center reports that hostility toward immigrants is at the highest level it's been in 70 years. This view is supported by the findings of Jack McDevitt, associate director of the Center for Applied Research at Northeastern University and an expert on hate crimes. He has stated that attitudes toward immigrants in recent years are "frighteningly similar to those of the mid-1920s when the United States passed restrictive laws to halt massive immigration from southern Europe" (Southern Poverty Law Center, 1994, p. 3). Examples of hate crimes the Southern Poverty Law Center is tracking include the following:

- A 19-year-old Vietnamese American pre-med student in Coral Springs, Florida, was beaten to death by a mob of white youths who called him "Chink" and "Vietcong."
- A Hispanic man in Alpine, California, was beaten with baseball bats by six white men at a camp for homeless migrant workers. The assailants later reportedly bragged about "kicking Mexican ass."
- A Hispanic immigrant activist in Davis, California, was assaulted twice in April 1993 by white men who wrote "wetback" on her body.
- An Indian immigrant in New York City was beaten and burned with a cigarette by three teenagers who reportedly told him they did not like Indians.
- Two lesbians organizers were killed in Medford, Oregon, by presumed hate groups.

Official government statistics are not completely accurate, but 4558 hate crimes were reported in the United States in 1992 (FBI, 1993). Nakagawa (1993) reports that the number of hate crimes in Los Angeles increased about 31% between 1991 and 1992. Hate crimes are not on the increase only in the United States; there were approximately 2,000 reported hate crimes in Germany in 1992, a remarkable number given the relative size of that country's population compared with the United States (Baldwin & Hecht, 1995).

The shameful intolerance of ethnic differences is a frightening but all too prevalent characteristic of our times. Understanding intolerance is, therefore, a significant issue that social workers in all areas of practice need to understand. Baldwin and Hecht (1995) have adopted what they refer to as a *layering metaphor* for describing how intolerances develop. In their view, layering is a useful metaphor for illustrating that there are alternative ways of experiencing the world that "are continually juxtaposed and played off of each other and/or blended together (Hecht, 1993, p. 76). For instance, "the perception of a certain group begins at a young age, when people around the individual speak of group members in terms of their distinctiveness from the person's own group. Images and messages from parents, media, friends, textbooks, and teachers, as well as personal experiences with members of the 'other' group layer upon each other and interplay with one another to form the person's own, often inconsistent view of the 'others'" (Baldwin & Hecht, 1995, pp. 61–62). By examining these layers, we can get a better perception of what is happening at different levels of a person's experience. Each level of experience provides another clue to the puzzle of how prejudicial and hateful attitudes develop.

Prejudice and Discrimination

Although there has been much progress in human affairs during this century, it has been marked by horrible episodes of prejudice (Lippa, 1994). This century has seen the mass murder of Armenians by Turks, the Nazis' final solution in Europe for Jewish and other non-Aryan peoples, the ethnic cleansing by Serbs in Bosnia, the mass lynchings of African Americans in the first half of this century in the United States, and vicious attacks in New York at the Stonewall Bar that triggered the gay rights movement. **Prejudice** is a generalized negative attitude directed toward another person's membership in a socially defined group. Like most attitudes, it occurs at

Intolerance is mounting among white racist groups who perceive the advances of many racial and ethnic groups as a threat to their own interests.

the cognitive (beliefs), behavioral (overt action), and affective (emotional) levels. It can include negative emotional responses to a group of people resulting from intolerant, unfair, or unfavorable attitudes toward the targeted group (Deaux et al., 1993). It also can involve discriminatory actions or practices.

The cognitive component of prejudice involves the beliefs we hold about a target group. A structured set of beliefs about any identifiable social group is referred to as a **stereotype.** Stereotypes can be either positive or negative. A negative stereotype is highly interchangeable with what is known as prejudice. That is, stereotypes represent an important foundation upon which prejudices are built.

Basow (1992) uses a familiar story to demonstrate the pervasiveness of stereotypes in modern life:

A boy and his father were involved in a serious automobile accident. The father was killed instantly, the son was severely injured. An ambulance rushed him to the nearest

hospital, and a prominent surgeon was called in to perform the operation. Upon entering the operating room, however, the surgeon exclaimed: "I can't operate on this boy. He's my son." Question: How can this be? (Basow, 1992, p. 2)

If you came up with the answer of a stepfather, adopted father, or some other similar response, then you are not unlike most Americans. Most Americans see surgery as a predominately male field. As a result, you would have ignored the fact that the surgeon probably was the boy's mother. Stereotypes of this nature are highly prevalent in our society and can contribute to various types of discrimination. Stereotypes can be directed at any group: Hispanics, short people, physically disabled people, gay men and lesbians, and fundamentalist Christians. When individuals act on their prejudicial stereotypes, this leads to what is known as individual or attitudinal discrimination. *Individual discrimination* involves overt acts that treat members of a target group in an unfair manner. Generally, the bases for these discriminatory treatments have roots in negative stereotypes.

Some forms of discrimination in society are legal. In addition, many individuals justify discriminatory practices on what they consider moral grounds. For instance, in many societies "senior citizens" are allowed to pay cheaper rates for using public facilities: movies, buses, public parks, and museums. Publishers of some professional journals also engage in differential treatment of customers when they provide different subscription rates for people from different income categories. Are these practices unlawful or without moral justification? Although these forms of differential treatment are considered lawful, they are always open to moral challenge. This raises the important question of whether there are circumstances when it is legitimate to make differentiations in treatment of people in terms of race, sex, class, or age. What distinguishes differentiation from discrimination?

Most religions of the world do not think it is discriminatory to bar women from holding positions of leadership in their hierarchy. Yet many members of these same communities assume that these practices are without moral justification and are discriminatory. How do we determine whether this form of differential treatment is considered discriminatory? In most modern industrial societies, disputes involving issues of discrimination are handled by our legal institutions. However, this is a relatively recent historical phenomenon. Notions of unlawful discrimination took a long time to develop in Western legal systems. Banton (1994) points out that the first recorded use of the term *discrimination* was in a speech by President Andrew Johnson in 1866. He used this term in discussing debates surrounding the denial of the benefits of full citizenship to African Americans. Robert MacIver (1948), however, is known for educating the public "to distinguish between discrimination as a form of behavior and prejudice as an attitude" (Banton, 1994, pp. 6–8).

Most early considerations of discrimination in the United States involved issues of race; *discrimination* was not used in a more general sense to include other groups until around 1958. In that year, the International Labour Office (ILO) defined discrimination as "any distinction, exclusion or preference made on the basis of race, colour, sex, religion, political opinion, national extraction or social origin" (Banton, 1994, p. 7). In recent years, discrimination law has been extended to many other areas of life. However, the issue of discrimination in law focuses primarily on protecting people from unfair treatment in public life.

Discrimination law does not apply to private life or private decisions. "In Great Britain and the United States the main protected fields are those of the administration of justice, employment, education, housing, and the provision of goods, facilities and services" (Banton, 1994, p. 8). For instance, people may limit invitations to parties on the grounds of race or gender. As you might imagine, the legitimacy of such actions is a major societal concern. Still, there is substantial controversy about what ought to be considered private versus public spheres of life. Should the law protect individuals from unfair treatment by private clubs or other organizations? Should the law of discrimination apply to treatment in voluntary organizations like churches? For instance, should the law address actions within churches regarding issues of equality for women? Churches and other religious institutions are organizations that presently do not fall under the legal protections of antidiscrimination law. But this does not mean that these institutions do not violate moral definitions of discrimination shared by many members of a society.

In social work, we encounter many forms of discrimination that contribute to a diverse array of social disadvantage and other forms of inequality. For this reason, it is important that the social worker have a fundamental understanding of race, ethnicity, sex roles, and other areas in which persons can be subjected to unfair social practices. Our goal as social work professionals is to engage in activities that will reverse structural contributions to harmful discriminatory practices in voluntary social organizations and in public social institutions.

Institutional discrimination is a special type of discrimination derived from structural arrangements in the society. It refers to inequalities rooted in the normal operations of society and its social institutions. This form of discrimination has little to do with attitudes or prejudices. Even when we eliminate prejudice in a society, the inequalities between groups often remain because they are rooted in the everyday operations of existing social institutions. That is, discrimination can continue in a society even though its members are not intent on discriminating. For instance, a Mexican

American family can be denied access to housing leading to better schools not because of intentional bigotry by realtors but because their previous restriction to low-paying jobs inhibits their ability to purchase a home with access to superior schools. Institutional discrimination has much more subtle characteristics than the more visible forms of attitudinal or individual discrimination. For example, in social service agencies, institutional racism may be present when supervisors assign low-income clients of color to MSW students and middle-income whites to senior staff. This is particularly problematic because low-income clients of color have higher drop-out rates and may benefit more from an experienced social worker.

Race and Everyday Social Relations

What are the differences between race and ethnicity? **Race** is a social term used to refer to groups that are defined in terms of their physical characteristics. It is important to recognize that the characteristics used to define a racial group are socially defined; the word *race* is a fundamentally meaningless biological concept. Although humans can be traced back well over a million years, the racial differences of today are quite recent in origin (Robertson, 1977). "Whatever the seeming diversity of races in the modern world, all contemporary human beings trace their origin to ancestral populations that lived in east Africa about 200,000 years ago" (Green, 1995, p. 11).

People attach meanings to physical differences that are either real or imagined. "From a sociological point of view, then, a race is a large number of people who, for social or geographical reasons, have interbred over a long period of time; as a result, they have developed visible physical characteristics and regard themselves and are regarded by others as a biological unit" (Robertson, 1977, p. 262). However, it is not easy to classify humans into different races. In fact, determining race by blood sample would be impossible because human population groups are not distinct; rather, they form a continuum. This is why physical anthropologists prefer using terms like *population* or *gene pool* to explain physical differences to using terms like *race* (Green, 1995). For these scientists, "The genetic diversity within populations that share certain visible physical traits is as great as those between groups" (Giddens, 1989, p. 246). Accordingly,

many scientists argue that race is not a useful concept and should no longer be used (Giddens, 1989).

The Anglo ideology of assimilation has always emphasized that immigrants should conform to the dominant culture and leave behind their ethnicity. "Full assimilation, in this view, is achieved when the descendants of the immigrants blend into the majority group and are no longer distinguishable from it" (McLemore, 1991, p. 106). But this ideology has not applied to persons of Indian, Asian, and African decent. Persons of color cannot blend into the societal matrix as do white ethnics. As Rushdie (1982) points out, there are two different worlds in Anglo societies and which one you inherit depends on the color of your skin.

In Germany, individuals are entitled to citizenship, regardless of their country of origin, if they can prove that they are of German ancestry. That is, the criterion for German citizenship is biological. This law makes life very difficult for persons who have lived their entire lives in Germany but who do not look German or who lack German biological ancestry (Ferrante, 1995). Turks, Arabs, and East Indians are subjected to serious discrimination in Germany because of this emphasis on biology. Even though some African Germans can demonstrate German ancestry, they are still discriminated against because they do not fit the German biological stereotype. Biracial individuals also have a confusing identity in the United States.

Although, by convention, people are assigned to one of three racial categories—Caucasoid, Mongoloid, or Negroid—many people do not easily fit into one of these groups. Even though these classifications are difficult to implement, people continue to apply them. In South Africa, the classification of races was still a major societal enterprise in the late 1980s. The following quotation illustrates the difficulties this society encountered in trying to classify persons racially. A woman classified as "Colored" reports:

> Under South African law, I am officially considered Colored. But so is my light-skinned sister with brown hair and my brother who has kinky hair and skin even blacker than mine. The state determines what color your are. At sixteen, you have to fill out some forms, attach a photograph and send them to a state authority where your race will be decided. Differences in color are noted by official subdivisions. For example I am a Cape Colored whereas my sis-

ter is called Indian Colored. Of course, many people categorized as Colored are of mixed Black and White ancestry. In fact, if you can prove having had a white grandparent or parent and are yourself very light skinned, you can even make an application to be reclassified from Colored to White. (Chapkis, 1986, p. 69)

Sociologists are interested in negative classification schemes that include beliefs about the abilities or traits of a racial group. They are also interested in studying any actions a society takes to use racial classifications to subordinate members of a group on the basis of color or other biological characteristics. These societal classifications change in time and are products of many social, historical, and political forces. In the United States, we have had shifting relations of power that have influenced our racial classifications. In 1860, the three classifications for the census were whites, blacks, and mulattoes; in 1890, five additions were added (quadroon, octoroon, Chinese, Japanese, and Indian); in 1990, five different groups were listed (White; Black or African American; Asian or Pacific Islander; American Indian, Eskimo or Aleut; and the ethnicity Hispanic). Each of these changes is indicative of key sociohistorical contingencies. The following Focus on Multiculturalism section poignantly describes one girl's reflections on being biracial or of mixed race.

FOCUS ON MULTICULTURALISM

One Girl's Reflection on Being Biracial or of Mixed Race

10:06 A.M. The buzz of an artificially lit classroom swarms around its third-hour occupants. Slouched in my chair at the back of the room, I try to ignore the sweat running into the collar of my T-shirt, the incessant tapping of my foot. I chew anxiously on my pen top, and the words on the paper before me swim around in a mocking blur.

No, I'm not struggling over a physics test, or an essay question in College English. This is simply a survey on student-teacher relationships given to the whole school, and I haven't made it past the first section.

Name _____. Okay, got that one. Age ___. Grade ___. Sex ___. Yeah, these are easy. Race ___. What? RACE. 1. White; 2. Black; 3. Oriental; 4. Hispanic; 5. American Indian. This is where my panic begins. I read my choices again, and my brow furrows. Basically, the problem is this: I'm racially mixed, and there is no option for me.

Now, this is not the first time this has happened. All my life, I've had to decide what race I am, which half of me to deny. I remember asking my sister one day in third grade which one I was. "We're mixed, Rach," she told me. Mixed. And for every survey, every technical form I received in every grade after, I looked for that word. The closest I ever found was "other." That always kind of amused me, but I tried it. Other; mixed. But my teachers came to me. "Mixed what, honey?" And they looked at me. "You're black. Next time, just put black, okay?" And I would go home to my mother, my single, cream-colored mother, who wanted nothing but to raise us well. Even as an intelligent 8-year-old, I was a bit confused.

My next practice, starting about seventh grade, was to circle both white and black. It made the most sense, really, but even here in high school I got in trouble. Again, the tender pressure: "Hon, you can't be *both*." So I ended up selecting "Caucasian" for the day. Recently, I went to my counselor and had that changed. See, I'm a junior, and considering colleges, and I know that as a "minority student" I'll be eligible for certain scholarships. Also, it will give me an edge at schools that are looking for a diverse student body. So I figure I'll be black for the next 5 years or so, and then go back to being myself.

But can I really go back? Can I really be comfortable with who I am if society ignores that people like me exist? Well, I can—but you must realize that I'm lucky. I grew up in Hyde Park (in Chicago), one of the most liberal integrated neighborhoods in America. My 14 years there taught me that I could exist as a mixed person, with both black and white friends. That I could be proud of my brown skin, even have fun with it. It's always great to see the look on people's faces when my mom and sister and I go out, especially with my white stepfather.

But for some kids, there is no joke. Only confusion, and the total lack of a sense of identity. These children are pressured to choose a group of friends, and in effect to choose a parent, a race, a way of life, a heritage—and to completely deny the other. But do black people really want a friend who's only half black, and vice versa?

That was the problem facing the first mixed kids—the children born of slaves and their owners. It should not exist now. In this age, the so-called "modern civilization" we're supposed to have reached, being racially mixed shouldn't be a dilemma, it should be considered a blessing. We are graced with the best of both worlds, exposure to two entirely different walks of life. In fact, our parents should be congratulated for creating a higher, enlightened race with such a large sphere of influences and possibilities. Instead, they have been scolded. God forbid we should pollute one race by adding another to it.

The world is a box of crayons. Though they're all different colors, they're all made of the same thing. And even though yellow and blue are combined to make green, once the wax has set, it's a green crayon, and that's all. It's never asked to made a choice between blue and yellow. One of the things my sister and I did together was draw pictures of the family, coloring them from our big box of Crayolas. And I always thought it was neat that a drawing of four people could use up three crayons—peach, light brown, and dark brown, when the other kids only got to use one.

Source: Morris & Leighninger, 1990.

Forms of Racism and Privilege

Racism is technically defined as "any attitude, action or institutional structure which subordinates a person because of his or her color" (U.S. Commission on Civil Rights, 1969, p. 1). Today, it is less socially acceptable to show blatant forms of racism than was once true. However, racism has remained in other more symbolic or subtle ways, which are termed in the social psychology literature as *modern racism*. Modern racists convey their negativity toward others by opposing issues that promise equality for the races. They do not blatantly attack persons on racial grounds, but they defend practices that maintain social privilege. For instance, they may oppose equal-opportunity hiring by arguing against the use of quotas, rather than by directly attacking individuals on presumed notions of inferiority (Deaux et al., 1993).

The systemic features of racism are a key part of social structures that social workers must understand. "In a racist system, well-meaning White people benefit from racism even if they have no intentions of acting or thinking like 'racists'" (Andersen & Collins, 1995, p. 60). That is, they might not question the built-in system of privilege for whites in our social system. Peggy McIntosh (1995) has pointed out in her groundbreaking essay "White Privilege and Male Privilege" that systems of privilege become invisible to the persons benefiting most from them. In her view, people are carefully socialized not to recognize these privileges.

After experiencing significant frustration with men who did not recognize male privilege, Peggy McIntosh set out to understand her own privileges as a white female. She wanted to know what advantages she had as a white person in our society. Through this exercise, she realized that her own difficulties facing privilege as a white person were similar to the difficulties faced by men in experiencing their own privilege. She wrote, "Only rarely will a man go beyond acknowledging that women are disadvantaged to acknowledging that men have unearned advantage . . ." (McIntosh, 1995, p. 77). In her view, white women and men have many layers of denial that prevent them from examining their unearned advantages. McIntosh (1995) identified these special circumstances and conditions as part of her day-to-day privileges as a white woman:

1. I can, if I wish, arrange to be in the company of people of my race most of the time.
2. I can avoid spending time with people whom I was trained to mistrust and who have learned to mistrust my kind or me.
3. If I should need to move, I can be pretty sure of renting or purchasing housing in an area which I can afford and in which I would want to live.
4. I can be reasonably sure that my neighbors in such a location will be neutral or pleasant to me.
5. I can go shopping alone most of the time, fairly well assured that I will not be followed or harassed by store detectives.
6. I can turn on the television or open to the front page of the paper and see people of my race widely and positively represented.

7. When I am told about our national heritage or about "civilization," I am shown that people of my color made it what it is.

8. I can be sure that my children will be given curricular materials that testify to the existence of their race.

9. If I want to, I can be pretty sure of finding a publisher for this piece on white privilege.

10. I can be fairly sure of having my voice heard in a group in which I am the only member of my race.

11. I can be casual about whether or not to listen to another woman's voice in a group in which she is the only member of her race.

12. I can go into a book shop and count on finding the writing of my race represented, into a supermarket and find the staple foods that fit with my cultural traditions, into a hairdresser's shop and find someone who can deal with my hair.

13. Whether I use checks, credit cards, or cash, I can count on my skin color not to work against the appearance that I am financially reliable.

14. I could arrange to protect our young children most of the time from people who might not like them.

15. I did not have to educate our children to be aware of systemic racism for their own daily physical protection.

16. I can be pretty sure that my children's teachers and employers will tolerate them if they fit school and workplace norms; my chief worries about them do not concern others' attitudes toward their race.

17. I can talk with my mouth full and not have people put this down to my color.

18. I can swear, or dress in secondhand clothes, or not answer letters, without having people attribute these choices to the bad morals, the poverty, or the illiteracy of my race.

19. I can speak in public to a powerful male group without putting my race on trial.

20. I can do well in a challenging situation without being called a credit to my race. (McIntosh, 1995)

Although race is not a fact of nature, it continues to structure many aspects of social reality. Moreover, many Americans consider it to be an unchanging part of the natural world sanctioned by God (Green, 1995). These views sanction negativity toward the mixing of the races and the ascription of rank along selected racial lines. As social workers, we cannot ignore the fact that race influences social relations at all levels of social life. Also, people's experience with race will depend on their location in social space. That is, it will also vary with their social class, gender, age, sexuality, and other markers of social location (Andersen & Collins, 1995).

Ethnicity and Its Social Consequences

Ethnicity, like race, focuses on differences in people. But it is not always easy to identify true ethnic differences: "When we try to determine what differences mean, the idea of ethnicity becomes complex and frequently troublesome" (Green, 1995, p. 16). There are many definitions of ethnicity in the social sciences, and each definition captures a different layer of an ethnic group's experiences. Some definitions stress distinctive values underlying the behavior of group members, whereas others focus more on the association of ethnicity with social class, political processes, or other forms of social experience. Although these approaches to difference may be useful in many forms of social analysis, they often lead to the formation of needless stereotypes. For this reason, we subscribe to a more process or transactional definition of ethnicity developed for social service professionals by James Green.

Green (1995) contends that we should study ethnicity in terms of boundaries, control, and meaning construction. "Ethnicity has less to do with distinct and enduring groups than it does with the perceptions of boundaries, with how contrasts are manipulated, managed, denied, asserted, and proclaimed. With ethnicity, we are dealing, first, with meanings that define separateness, and, second, with the enforcement of meanings and separateness through power" (Green, 1995, p. 19). In other words, we need to understand how individuals assert their sense of ethnicity and how others treat this ethnicity in various social contexts. In particular, we need to understand how dominant-group individuals use ethnic differences to isolate or exclude individuals from inclusion in the most valued segments of social life.

Focus on Multiculturalism: Biculturalism discusses how individuals must function in two systems: the minority culture and the majority society.

Core Versus Surface Features of Ethnicity

Many surface aspects of ethnicity are used to identify various ethnic groups in our society. These include "clothing preferences, speech pattern, behavioral styles, physical characteristics, housing locations and types, living arrangements and decor, food items, and family and community rituals and celebrations" (Green, 1995, p. 19). These manifestations of ethnicity are used to distinguish outsiders from insiders. As Green (1995) points out, these aspects are what many Americans think of when making references to ethnic differences. But they should not be confused with what is truly ethnic about ethnicity. Pinderhughes provides one of the more descriptive definitions of ethnicity that includes these core elements. She states: "Ethnicity refers to connectedness based on these commonalities that have evolved as a result of shared identity and history based on religion, nationality and so on" (Pinderhughes, 1994, p. 265).

Nash (1989) has also tried to differentiate between surface and core elements of ethnicity. Core elements refer to the real grounds upon which all forms of boundary maintenance rest. They represent the central psychic and social foundations that underlie human identification with group relationships. Nash has broken down these core elements into three fundamental components: kinship, commensality, and a common cult. He provides a definition of each of these components in his book *The Cauldron of Ethnicity in the Modern World.* He states:

> The most common ethnic boundary markers, in the ethnographic record, and the most pervasive, in any system of ethnic differentiation, are *kinship*, that is the presumed biological and descent unity of the group implying a stuff or substance continuity each group member has and outsiders do not; *commensality*, the propensity of eating together indicating a kind of equality, peership, and the promise of further kinship links stemming from the intimate acts of dining together, only one step removed from the intimacy of bedding together, and a *common cult*, implicating a value system beyond time and empirical circumstance. . . . (1989, pp. 10–11)

The prior description of the core elements of ethnicity indicate the levels at which sentiments surrounding ethnic identity occur. They describe the dimensions that define people's sense of connection to their social context. Obviously, these senses of bondedness will vary with a person's position in the social structure and his or her life experiences. These fundamental elements of ethnicity can play a major role in how clients respond to social work interventions.

FOCUS ON MULTICULTURALISM

Biculturalism

When examining ethnic groups in America, classical theorists in the social sciences treated ethnic groups as independent and internally consistent cultural systems. De Ande (1984) and others in social work termed these approaches *culture deficit* or *cultural difference* models. In these models, scientists commit the common fallacy of ignoring the influence of the dominant culture on the socialization processes of persons from other cultural groups. Members of ethnic groups in the United States are exposed to dual, and in some instances multiple, socialization processes. In De Ande's view, "the bicultural model holds the most promise for understanding the process by which an individual learns to function in varying degrees within two systems—the minority culture, and the majority society" (De Ande, 1984, p. 101).

Scientists from Latin America have tuned in on this issue of multiple socialization processes for quite some time. Jose Vasconcellos (1927) spoke of the Mexican culture as reflecting a mix of the Hispanic-European and Native American cultures *(mestizo).* He took significant pride in the fact that Mexicans represented what he termed a people of the world *(la raza cosmica).* Similarly, Ramos (1975) urged Mexicans to adopt a notion of a "living culture" to capture the influence of diverse social and historical events on the socialization process of Latinos. Ramirez (1978) even introduces the notion of pluralistic identities in his writings to reflect similar interests. Each of these writers recognized that people can move in and out of cultures that appear outwardly different from one another. That is, the diversity provided by two cultures represents an opportunity for enriched and diverse experiences, rather than a barrier or problem. But the important empirical question is, how does this happen?

De Ande (1984) points out that the bicultural experience is made possible by some degree of overlap between cultures. In fact, this overlap is what facilitates whether people can anticipate the behavioral expectations of two distinct cultures. De Ande uses this logic to explain the variations in the rates of inclusion of members of various ethnic groups in our society. In her view, the levels of inclusion are contingent on the degree of overlap between cultures on six factors:

1. Norms, values, beliefs, perceptions, and the like
2. Availability of cultural translators, mediators, and models
3. Amount of corrective feedback regarding appropriate behavior provided by each culture
4. Overlap in styles of problem solving between the cultures
5. The person's degree of bilingualism
6. Degree of dissimilarity in physical appearance from majority culture

The overlap of these factors between cultures is the process used to explain why the melting-pot theory of assimilation never worked for many ethnic groups in our society (see Figure 4.7). It also clarifies the processes influencing whether an individual will be competent in two cultural settings.

Communal Versus Individualistic Styles of Intervention

Green (1995) and many other cultural theorists in social work are uncomfortable with providing practitioners with a laundry list of differences between and within ethnic groups. However, there are general variations in values that do translate into marked differences in responding to many social situations. Anthropologists have made distinctions as to whether groups have individualistic or communalistic value orientations. This type of distinction has been examined extensively in the social sci-

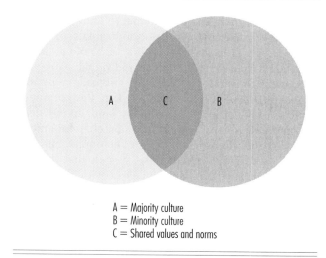

A = Majority culture
B = Minority culture
C = Shared values and norms

FIGURE 4.7 **Biculturalism** Source: De Ande, 1984.

ences. Horwitz has formulated a specific proposition about therapeutic systems: "The style of therapeutic control reflects the degree of group bondedness" (1990, p. 86).

In Horwitz's view, groups with very tight social bonds are more likely to develop what he refers to as communal styles of *therapeutic control*. By therapeutic control, he refers to all responses to deviance that involve a therapeutic rather than a punitive response. In therapeutic responses, the focus is typically on using some method of changing something about the person, whereas a punitive response to deviance focuses on punishing or sanctioning the deviant act itself. Horwitz states: "Communal styles of therapy emerge in groups that grip each member in a tight network of social relationships and bind them to communal purposes. These styles deemphasize the exploration of the personality and deal with problems of normality through strengthening the ties of individuals to groups" (1990, p. 86). This style of treatment is widely employed by many Indian peoples. For example, they employ group "sings" and other communal ceremonies to reconnect the person to the group.

Societies with values that stress the individual and that are highly heterogeneous tend to pursue more individualistic interventions. "Individualistic therapies arise when people are freed from group ties. They strive to enhance the autonomy of afflicted individuals" (Horwitz, 1990, p. 86). Thus, in tribal groups we would anticipate that less emphasis is placed on individual symbols or modifying individual motivations. Instead, a person's problems are seen as being rooted in the communal symbols of the group. On the other hand, an individual from an individualist culture draws on different cultural symbols, ones that stress notions of autonomy and individual reformation. These ideas suggest that the core elements of a culture may intersect with deep-seated communal or individual notions of therapy that are characteristic of a particular cultural group. Social workers must be cognizant of these context features in order to respond in a meaningful way to the needs of their clients.

Pinderhughes (1994, pp. 293–294) points out that "culture determines what clients see as a problem, how they express it (that is, whether symptoms are somatic, behavioral, or affective; what specific symptoms clients manifest), who they seek out for help, what they regard as helpful and the intervention strategies they prefer." To respond to each of these levels, the social worker must be exposed to the life experiences of many different ethnic groups and to multiple representatives from these groups. This is critical because there is as significant a diversity within ethnic groups as there is between ethnic groups.

In this book, we assume that culture influences many aspects of behavior. For this reason, we will systematically review documented variations in human development involving cultural variables. We will not, however, provide a laundry list of key historical events or characteristics of ethnic group members. We believe that clients will situationally define and manage their ethnic boundaries and identity, ethnic boundaries being how individuals define their own sense of ethnicity. The relevance of historical events is contingent on individuals' current boundary maintenance needs. That is, time and other historical factors will be used differentially by clients in setting their ethnic boundaries. Some clients will seek a sense of revival of ethnic ties; others will struggle with their significance in current situations and contexts. Thus, our aim as social workers is to assess the factors contributing to how contrasts are asserted by persons with ethnic differences and how dominant group members respond to these differences.

Gender and Sexism

Can women perform on an equal basis with men as firefighters or police officers? Why or why not? Many women are currently employed in these and other professions previously dominated by men, including the military. The current debate about the role of women in the military reflects a larger debate about sex roles in our society. To place these debates in context, it might be useful to review recent history about the roles of women in our society.

As recently as the 19th century, women were denied the right to vote, to be a member of a jury, to have sole custody of their children, and to attend most institutions of higher education. Many of these practices were justified on false beliefs about differences between males and females. In fact, a major area of research in the social sciences focuses on the existence or nonexistence of sex differences between males and females. Social scientists use the word **sex** to refer to the biological status of being female or male. These scientists research the structural and other biophysical characteristics that distinguish females from males. **Gender,** on the other hand, refers to the social definitions of male and female. It represents a socially constructed concept and not a fact of nature with specific biological imperatives.

In assessing human behavior, social workers need to have a good understanding of the consequences of gender roles and beliefs. Gender issues incorporate all the factors that structure the relationships between women and men. This includes all the social processes that dictate how women are to behave in their social life. In work and other social contexts, the relations of women are structured differently from those of men. The specific structures that establish how they should behave are also a part of each of the other major social institutions in their lives. Sandra Lipsitz Bem (1993) has termed this process **gender polarization,** which refers to "the organizing of social life around the male-female distinction" (Bem, 1993, p. 192). In fact, in a gender-polarized society, every aspect of a person's life is connected to his or her sex in some way. This includes "modes of dress, social roles, and even ways of expressing emotion and experiencing sexual desire" (Bem, 1993, p. 192).

Gender differences, like racial and cultural differences, can be used to distort many aspects of social life.

"Anthropologists, for example, use the term *exotic bias* to refer to the investigators' tendency to focus only on those aspects of a group or society that differ from their own group or society" (Deaux et al., 1993, p. 350). This type of bias is often found in situations in which actual differences are noted in women. For instance, many studies have shown that the average male is more aggressive than the average female. But our biases can influence how we interpret the findings from these studies. Figure 4.8 presents a graph of male and female distributions of aggressiveness. As you can see, many of the females in these studies have aggressiveness scores that are higher than those of the males. Also, these distributions indicate that many of the women and men have similar aggressiveness scores. The information on averages can be used to distort the realities of many of the women and men in these studies by supporting the bias toward an assertion of fundamental difference between males and females.

Hooyman (1994) has identified three conceptual frameworks in social work for examining women's content: women's issues, nonsexist perspectives, and feminist perspectives. The *women's issues* approach has also been referred to as "add the women and stir," and it is probably the most dominant approach to education in social work. In this approach, separate attention is devoted to understanding the distinct issues that pertain to women. This approach is typically criticized because in many circumstances it perpetuates the treatment of women as "others". This means that they are treated as a special population in knowledge discourse rather than as a pivotal group representing 51% of the world population (Hooyman, 1994). As a group with special consideration, they are judged in relation to male criteria, and this perpetuates the structural features of many of their problems.

The second approach is the *nonsexist* or *equal rights* model. This approach does focus on structural factors within systems that maintain sexist practices and it assumes that "the range of problems experienced by women are rooted in and influenced by societal expectations for women's behavior and in societal restrictions of life possibilities" (Hooyman, 1994, p. 321). In such a view, problems should not be assessed in terms of culturally prescribed sex-role behaviors. This view has important implications for practice because it indicates that

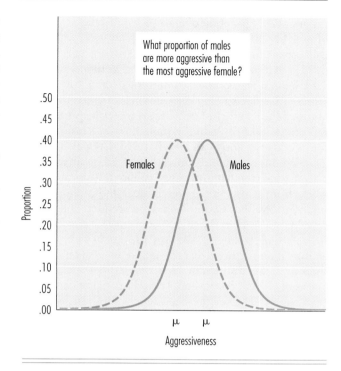

FIGURE 4.8 Overlapping distributions on aggressiveness for males and females   Source: Deaux, Dane, & Wrightsman, 1993.

behaviors by women that do not conform to traditional role expectations should not be considered deviant. For instance, women who choose not to care for their parents, but who leave the task to their brothers instead, should not be viewed as deviant or pathological.

The *feminist* model, on the other hand, rejects many traditional notions about gender and starts from the assumption that current knowledge of human behavior is for the most part sexist. Social reality as we know it is shaped by the male perspective known as **androcentricity** (man as norm) (Hooyman, 1994). Essentialist thinking about gender is challenged in this approach. In essentialist approaches, gender is often considered absolute, or fixed in nature as a biological fact. The feminist perspective rejects the binary conceptualizations of males and females, or of white men and women, and sees gender as one "strain" among others in our layered experiences. This point of view "opens up the possibility of diversity among men and women in specific historical, social and cultural constructs" (Hooyman, 1994, p. 325). It also allows analysis and action to focus on the experiences of women without neglecting the other "isms"—like racism and ageism—that threaten the well-being of humanity. In fact, feminism sees its fundamental aim as that of ending domination and resisting all forms of oppression (Van Den Bergh & Cooper, 1987).

Feminism is more than an analytical approach; it is also an ideology that involves a "call for transforming the world from competitive, hierarchical and authoritarian relationships to a world based on gender and racial equality" (Van Den Bergh & Cooper, 1987, p. 611), and it has a long history in Western society. In fact, gender stratification is more deeply rooted in human history than are class distinctions and many other social categories of current oppression. Like class, gender stratification has varied over the ages, as has feminist ideology (Calvert & Calvert, 1992). The following Focus on Theory section discusses conflict theory, which is critical in understanding the role of power in social relationships.

FOCUS ON THEORY

Conflict Theories

Conflict theories focus on issues involving conflict, coercion, and the role of power in social relations. The most well-known conflict theorist was Karl Marx—without a doubt the most influential thinker from this group of early 19th-century social theorists. His theory assumes that all of human history represents a struggle over material or monetary resources involving conflicts between the classes, and it places significant emphasis on understanding the material structures of production. For Marx, the relations of production are the fundamental organizing principles of human society. To illustrate this point, we need to review his key assumptions and theory of structural contradiction.

Marx considers production to be a fundamental quality of human nature. He contends in his materialist view of history that the first act of human history is to produce the necessary materials for survival. To achieve this end, humans enter into social relationships that are "independent of their will." "These are the relationships which surround the production process and which will vary according to the particular historical stage of development of the system of production—technically referred to as the *mode of production*. These relations of production are the foundation of society, its economic base" (Waters, 1994, p. 101). In Marx's view, this economic base is the fundamental determinant of the structure and development of social life. The social organization of production (referred to as the economic substructure) plays the determining role not only in the productive processes but also in the formation of the society's superstructure. The superstructure in Marxian theory includes all the idealist structures in society, such as religion, law, and philosophy (Timasheff, 1967). In his view, the characteristics of these superstructures are determined by the economic base of the society.

For Marx, social change occurs as a result of the contradictions between the material forces of production and the relations of production. He defines the forces of production as all the factors required in the production process—raw materials, technology, and so forth. The relations of production refer to the social organization of the production process, especially the relations surrounding ownership of the means of production. Waters (1994) contends that this conflict between the material forces of production and the social relations is the key form of structural contradiction within societies that Marx assumes contributes to changes in social relations.

Other conflict theorists identify other forms of conflict between groups that contribute to harmony and change in social systems, including interest-group conflicts, value conflicts, and conflicts in authority relations. Denisoff and Wahrman (1979) provide an overview of some of the basic assumptions in more modern conflict approaches:

1. Interests are basic elements of social life.
2. Social life involves coercion.
3. Social life involves groups with different interests.
4. Social life generates opposition, exclusion, and hostility.

5. Social life generates conflict.
6. Social differences involve power.
7. Social systems are not united or harmonious.
8. Social systems tend to change.

This summary of assumptions indicates that stability is not of primary concern. In addition, it illustrates that an important issue in conflict is who is benefiting from a particular form of social arrangement. This perspective invites social workers to ask questions like, whose interests are involved and who will benefit or suffer from the existing social conditions? For social workers, this perspective is most helpful in studying issues of social inequality. Conflict theorists do not assume that inequality exists because it is functional for the society as a whole. Instead, they assume that these inequalities result from some group's ability to achieve power over another.

Sexual Status and Forms of Oppression

The ideology of sexism takes on many forms, but regardless of its form, sexism supports a system of oppressive gender relations for women. "Like racism, sexism is a system of beliefs and behaviors by which a group is oppressed, controlled, and exploited because of presumed gender differences" (Andersen & Collins, 1995, p. 67). For this reason, we need to approach issues of gender difference with extreme caution. Sexism pervades all aspects of our cultural symbols and ways of doing things. In fact, our language itself has supported the dominance of males in human relations. Until the 1960s, few questioned the use of terms like *mankind* when referring to humans or humanity. We also used the pronoun *he* when speaking of a person whose sex was unspecified, because our language did not have a pronoun representing "he or she." Sexist language is being challenged, but its existence reflects the extent to which sexism is deeply rooted in our cultural traditions.

Sex-Role Stereotypes

What are sex-role stereotypes? Sex-role stereotypes involve beliefs about men and women that describe not how men and women *actually* differ but how societal members *believe* they differ (Rothblum & Franks, 1983). Baumgartner-Papageorgious (1982) asked a group of elementary and high school students how their lives would

be different if they were a member of the opposite sex. These students' responses reflect many of the stereotypes within our society. In particular, it is interesting to note that boys perceived that the change would result in more negative consequences. This is a sample of some of their responses:

- "I would start to look for a husband as soon as I got into high school."
- "I would play girl games and not have many things to do during the day."
- "I'd use a lot of make-up and look good and beautiful . . . I have to shave my whole body."
- "I'd have to know how to handle drunk guys and rapists."
- "I would not be able to help my dad fix the car and truck and his two motorcycles." (pp. 2–9)

Girls, on the other hand, anticipated more activity and less restrictiveness in their life if they were a member of the opposite sex:

- "I would have to stay calm and cool whenever something happened."
- "I could sleep later in the mornings since it would not take [me] very long to get ready for school."
- "My father would be closer because I'd be the son he always wanted."
- "I would not have to worry about being raped."
- "People would take my decisions and beliefs more seriously." (pp. 5–13)

Baumgartner-Papageorgious (1982) found similar beliefs among college students. This study points out how much of our lives are organized around male-female distinctions. In fact, the quotations from respondents in these studies indicate that there is even a gender belief system that influences how people make decisions (Ferrante, 1995).

The pressure to conform to established sex-role stereotypes can contribute to many psychological problems: depression, sexual dysfunction, obesity, and other clinical concerns (Rothblum & Franks, 1983). Women confront many dilemmas in the face of sex-role stereotypes. Their strategies for coping with these dilemmas are important for social work practitioners to understand. A number of other consequences should be taken into account as well. Gender influences self-esteem, psychological well-being, and physical health. In addition, it structures how and with whom we establish friendships and introduces many barriers in the social relationships between males and females. It also has important consequences for family relationships and forms of labor force participation. Throughout our discussion of human development, we will treat gender as a social category that affects each of these areas of social behavior. Also, we will try to provide a diverse sample of experiences that women encounter in their development. Without this knowledge, social workers cannot engage in activities designed to remove the key structural barriers that affect the liberty and life chances of women in our society.

Homophobia

Gender oppression is also closely linked with the other system of oppression involving gender: sexual orientation. **Homophobia** refers to the fear and hatred of sex with a same-sex partner. In our society, power and privilege are structured in terms of sexual preferences, and our system has institutionalized heterosexual forms of gender identity. In fact, a heterosexual gender identity has been considered the yardstick for determining normality and has contributed to the isolation and oppression of gays, lesbians, and bisexuals.

As feminists point out, women and men are not monolithic groups; they have significant within-group diversity. One key within-group variation in gender relations is *sexual orientation*. Sexual orientation is a critical life-span issue that has multiple dimensions and layers of experience that constitute an integral part of the human experience (Newman, 1994). For this reason, we will examine this topic using a life-span perspective. From this perspective, equal time should be allotted to the issue of sexual orientation as will be given to other gender issues like gender identity and gender roles. But biases in our research institutions have contributed to some regretful deficiencies in this area of our knowledge base, making this task more difficult.

Longres (1995) points out that gays and lesbians are not socialized into roles, values, and positions in society the way that heterosexuals are. As a consequence, gay males often have more in common with heterosexual males before they "come out." After coming out, gay males can learn the customs and ways of the homosexual community. The stigma associated with their sexual orientation also structures how they relate with gay and nongay persons in heterosexual (straight) interactions. How they negotiate this marginalization by the dominant society at various phases of their life becomes an important knowledge issue for social work professionals.

In sum, issues of diversity are highly complex and require close scrutiny by members of the social work community. You will be exposed to many studies in this book that suggest fundamental differences between males and females, between racial and ethnic groups, between heterosexual and homosexual persons, and between able-bodied people and people with disabilities. You must always approach the interpretation of the findings from these studies with extreme caution. Some researchers have a bias toward finding differences that perpetuate many forms of insensitivity or oppression. Thus, we advise that you take a critical stance in evaluating the social consequences of any findings suggesting behavioral tendencies that are attributable to any form of human difference. This is not to imply that there are not important physical, psychological, and social differences. Instead, our aim here is to sensitize you to the fact that you are responsible for making distinctions between real and false differences in people that are supported by compelling and unbiased evidence.

Social Hazards

Many social and cultural conditions in our lives place us at risk for many forms of harm. These include conditions of poverty, inequality, injustice, dependency, relative deprivation, segregation, powerlessness, underrepresentation, postindustrialism, postmodernism, and others.

Our economy has become more global in scope and is experiencing a major social transformation. Unemployment is rising in many industrial sectors of our economy, and technology is eliminating many positions in manufacturing and service sectors. These economic pressures reduce available resources for sustaining our welfare systems. In fact, debates about the viability of welfare systems and of the welfare state are increasing in our society. Crime, substance abuse, domestic violence, homelessness, poverty, and urban decline are also increasing at exponential rates. Rivers and other sources of drinking water are diminishing, and pollution of our waterways and our air are threatening the well-being of individuals and communities.

Other quality-of-life concerns are gaining the attention of more and more people in our major metropolitan areas. Natural resources are being depleted, and food shortages are increasing in sectors of our society and the world at large. Immigration is increasing, and public tolerance of difference is decreasing. Racial and ethnic tensions are mounting, and peaceful relations between the straight sector and gay and lesbians is in jeopardy in many communities. These conditions differ from the conditions encountered by other birth cohorts in our society's history and will contribute to distinct variations in life-span development.

One way of understanding how critical such factors can be to the well-being of the child is to examine them in the light of sociocultural risk. Garbarino and Abramowitz (1992, p. 35) define sociocultural risk as "the impoverishing of the child's world so that the child lacks the basic social and psychological necessities of life." Children need many things to grow up happy and competent—for example, the basic necessities of food, water, and shelter; affection and love; proper medical care; proper educational stimulation; and positive social interactions. Without these things, children may end up "at risk" for impaired development (Garbarino & Abramowitz, 1992). Adults are also at risk for impaired development or other deficiencies if they are deprived of needed resources.

Two significant sources of sociocultural risk include *social impoverishment* and *cultural impoverishment*. Social impoverishment is the lack of critical social resources in a child's life, and cultural impoverishment refers to the values that undermine the child's healthy development. "Both of these forms of impoverishment find their most significant expression in the day-to-day content and structure of formal and informal support systems in a family's environment" (Garbarino & Abramowitz, 1992, p. 65).

Impoverishment of this nature is the result of unavailable, dysfunctional, eroded, or destroyed support systems. When institutional and community forces prevent supportive relationships from becoming established and being maintained, children and families are placed at increasing risk. This risk transcends the material re-

Many children grow up in impoverished conditions, which include physical, social, and cultural forms.

sources and, in fact, is particularly destructive when accompanied by social deprivation. The combination of social deprivation and poverty produces devastating consequences (Garbarino & Abramowitz, 1992).

Sociocultural risk for children revolves around the extent to which parents' functions are supported (Garbarino & Abramowitz, 1992). If parents are supported, encouraged, and helped by others who have a significant investment in the child's long-term future, then sociocultural risk is significantly reduced. Community efforts to create healthy living environments for children need to examine the support net the community provides for parents and children. Reducing sociocultural risk is part and parcel of community development.

For example, community efforts to reduce child abuse need to examine the available support that can be offered to offset the sociocultural risks families face in their daily existence. Pregnancy complications can be reduced when support systems are made available to women (Nuckolls, Cassel, & Kaplan, 1972). Infant development can be enhanced for infants at high risk due to poverty, maternal depression, and caretaking inadequacy when offered support through home visitors (Lyons-Ruth, Connell, Grunebaum, & Botein, 1990). Turner and Avison (1985) found that maternal adaptation to the parental role is distinguished, in part, by social support. In essence, women who do not obtain the needed level of social support have difficulty providing the most positive and healthy environment for their children. Social support enhances parental functioning by providing feedback about children and parenting, norms for nonabusive child-rearing, and increased opportunities for reducing stress and problem solving. Living in today's society has its challenges, as we will see in the following Focus on Sociology section.

FOCUS ON SOCIOLOGY

What Is Postmodernism?

Many scholars define postmodernism by contrasting it with modernism. Postmodernism is considered the new phase of history that follows the period known as modernism. Brown (1994) argues that many scholars assume that there were two great events in human history: the appearance of horticulture and the emergence of "modern societies." We are now on the verge of a third major event, which involves the appearance of a "yet unnamed 'post modern' social and cultural formation" (Brown, 1994, p. 13).

Modern societies are characterized by industrial economies, territorial states, mass culture, and scientific rationality (Smart, 1993). Other theorists differentiate modern societies from other social formations by focusing on the relationship between modernism and the spirit of Enlightenment, or what is known as the *Age of Reason*. In this historical period, instrumental rationality replaced tradition and religious dogmas as the grounds for truth and knowledge. Modernity promotes instead the pursuit of innovation, novelty, and dynamism through the process of instrumental rationality (Kellner, 1990). This highly rational, changeable, and instrumental way of life associated with modernism did not emerge in human history until after feudalism, or the Middle Ages, around 1600.

The postmodern age, by contrast, is a "time of troubles" marked by the collapse of rationalism and the ethos of the Enlightment (Kellner, 1990). It is considered a pe-

riod in which social engineering and other forms of scientific thought are looked upon with great suspicion. Most postmodernists are critical of views that support the notion that social work can solve the problems of social life with the aid of principles of science. In their view, this is an arrogant belief that is doomed to failure.

One of the major formulators of the postmodernist perspective is Jean-Francois Lyotard. Lyotard (1984) wrote *The Postmodern Condition*, wherein he states that "the status of knowledge is altered as societies enter what is known as the post-industrial age and culture enters what is known as the postmodern age" (p. 3). In the modern age, science is elevated to a position of high status because it replaces the fictions and myths of tradition with facts derived form the scientific method. For Lyotard, the idea of postmodernity represents a fundamental change in the ways in which we relate to science and knowledge. In the postmodern period, we relate to science as another language game of mythical narrative. The goals and values of Western culture are no longer considered universal; nor are they considered the primary points of reference for any form of social organization or knowledge. In the views of many postmodernists, the decentering of Western knowledge and values is reflected in many of the controversies of our times.

Conclusions

This chapter presents a way of conceptualizing the key systems that make up our social system. This is the system that integrates and regulates how we relate to one another. It also involves all of the processes and structures that contribute to various forms of social organization. In discussing these elements that make up the social system, we presented traditional and nontraditional concepts from the social work and social science literature. We also examined structures in social relationships that contribute to various forms of oppression and social support. The content covered on these topics described how these social structures are interrelated and have many points of intersection. This form of knowledge is essential in trying to individualize the experiences of clients. It is essential to understanding the consequences of race, class, and gender on each aspect of human behavior. In the next section of the book, we begin applying each of the dimensions in our framework to the many phases and events associated with the process of human development.

Chapter Summary

The social system serves the function of integrating people into a life shared with other people. Its key components are people in interaction with one another. The various contexts in our lives can be analyzed as separate systems, and there are four levels of systems: microsystems, mesosystems, exosystems, and macrosystems. These systems can be used to examine the environmental contexts of human development.

Principles from systems thinking help us identify relevant systems, subsystems, and the suprasystem of which problems, persons, and behaviors are a part. This approach is aided by drawing an ecomap. An ecomap highlights the points of connection between systems influencing a person's life and allows for the identification of points of conflict and points of support in the person's life space.

Families, Groups, Support Systems, and Contexts

The family is a key system within the larger social system. By treating the family as a system, the social worker can better understand the social context of family difficulties. The family is a system that is considered bigger than the sum of its parts. There are traditional and nontraditional definitions of the family. A useful definition that takes into account the conditions of our times is: A family is a composition of people who decide to act like a family. Families, like individuals, experience a sequence of developmental stages. Carter and McGoldrick have described a six-stage model of family development that is useful in understanding how families change over time.

Examining family structure and function helps us understand how families work. Family structure refers to the manner in which each family organizes itself into interactional patterns. The key subsystems in a family are the couple subsystem, parental subsystem, sibling sub-

system, and parent-child subsystem. Families function best when the subsystems maintain their own unique roles, identities, and boundaries. Family systems involve a number of key processes, such as homeostasis, information, and feedback, and communication plays a major role in family relations. Families are functional to the extent that they have good problem-solving, negotiation, and decision-making skills.

Another key context for understanding human behavior is the group. Groups are any small face-to-face collections of persons who interact to accomplish some purpose. Groups are often classified as (1) formed or natural, or (2) treatment or task groups. Understanding how groups function requires knowledge of group dynamics and processes, including knowledge of norms, roles, communication patterns, power and status relationships, and cohesiveness. Most groups must resolve the issue of how they will make decisions.

Support systems are a special type of social context. They represent continuing social aggregates that provide individuals with opportunities for feedback about themselves and for validation of their expectations about others. There are five different types of support systems: formal organizations, formed groups, self-help groups, social networks, and natural helpers. Self-help groups are a major social trend. Closely related to self-help groups are natural helpers. Natural helpers are considered central figures in a social network or in a neighborhood who have gained recognition for their unique wisdom, resourcefulness, and caring qualities.

Organizations and institutions are other types of contexts within which humans live. A formal organization is any large social group that is designed to rationally achieve specific objectives. Some formal organizations develop bureaucratic structures. All forms of organization meet critical goals necessary for the survival of a society.

Another key social context that influences our lives is our social institutions. These include the institutions of economy, kinship, education, law, polity, and religion. They contribute to the stability of status, roles, norms, and power in our relationships. Our location in social space is significantly influenced by our social institutions. There are many terms employed by social scientists to describe variations in a person's location in social space: social distance, social integration, social marginality, and hierarchy.

Multicultural and Gender Considerations

We live in a multicultural world. This requires knowledge of factors contributing to tolerance and intolerance
in social relationships. Prejudice refers to a generalized
negative attribute directed toward another individual's
membership in a socially defined group. Discrimination
involves overt acts that treat members of a target group in
an unfair manner. Race is a social and not a biological
concept, and it can be used to make distinctions that
have unfair consequences. Ethnicity also focuses on differences in people, but it is not as easy to identify ethnic
differences as it is to identify racial and sex differences.
Ethnicity, gender, and sexual orientation should be examined in terms of acquired meaning. These meanings
have little to do with distinct differences that can characterize each of these social categories.

Social Hazards

Many social conditions place people at risk for many
forms of harm, such as poverty, inequality, and postindustrialism. Major transformations in society continue
to take place, affecting the social condition. Examining
sociocultural risk is one way of identifying and understanding such conditions. It occurs when a child's world
is so impoverished that the child lacks basic social and
psychological neccessities. Sociocultural risk includes
two aspects: social impoverishment and cultural impoverishment. Community efforts can be designed to increase support and reduce the risks families face.

KEY TERMS

androcentricity
bureaucracy
cohesive group
communication patterns
creolization
culture
discrimination
ecomap
exosystem
family
family structure
floating family
folkways
formal organization
formed groups
gender
gender polarization

groupthink
hierarchy
homeostasis
homophobia
human relations school
ideal type
macrosystem
mesosystem
microsystem
mores
multiplex relationship
natural groups
natural helpers
norms
power
prejudice
race

racism
reciprocal interaction
relational space
roles
self-help organizations
sex
social distance
social integration
social marginality
social support systems
status
stereotypes
system
task groups
treatment groups
triangulation
uniplex relationship

5

Pregnancy, Birth, and the Newborn

Developmental Themes

It has been said that pregnancy is an act of faith until the actual birth, when nine months of waiting culminate in a new life. Upon seeing their infant for the first time new mothers have been actually heard to exclaim, "Oh my God, it really is a baby!" Whether planned or unplanned, confirmation of pregnancy is often a shock. The first task for the expectant parents is to accept that the pregnancy is real and involves the growth of a real fetus (Reeder, Mastroianni, & Martin, 1983). Reva Rubin, who has researched the developmental tasks of pregnancy, describes two questions women ask throughout **gestation** (the length of pregnancy): "Now?" and "Who, me?" (Rubin, 1970). If the pregnancy is unplanned, the mother may have to decide whether to terminate or continue it (see Focus on Ethics: Abortion—A Difficult Decision). Even if the pregnancy is expected, the mother may still wonder whether it is such a good idea at this time. She may have thoughts such as, "Wait, am I really ready for this?" Even the most wanted pregnancy can be a source of anxiety. The mother may worry about the birth process and wonder, "How is this baby going to get out and how much will it hurt?" A young, single mother may ignore the reality of the pregnancy for months, refusing to admit even to herself she may be expecting.

As the pregnancy progresses and the mother feels the fetus move, hears the heartbeat, and perhaps sees the fetus via ultrasound, she usually becomes more reconciled to the reality of the pregnancy. At this point, she may begin to integrate the baby as part of herself. Baby and mother become one. During this phase, the mother turns inward and becomes narcissistic and self-centered. She becomes preoccupied with her own thoughts and feelings. In later pregnancy, the baby begins to become a real and separate person. Now the mother begins to plan for the birth. She fantasizes about her baby, dreams about her baby, and plans for her baby. She may begin to think of her own childhood and her relationship to her family. Pregnancy can reactivate unresolved developmental conflicts for a woman (Schuster & Ashburn, 1992) and lead to the task of resolving identity confusions and assuming the role of mother. She may analyze her own identity, her relationship to her mother, and her relationship to her partner. She may worry about balancing career and family and about being a good mother without losing her own identity.

Pregnancy for the father is as much of an adjustment as it is for the mother. He also has many worries about his ability to parent, to provide for a family, to live up to his wife's expectations. The pregnancy is even less real for him, and his task often is to assimilate the fact that the fetus is real and is his. Feeling fetal movement, hearing the heart beat, attending childbirth preparation classes, and being present at the birth all help include the father in the process.

One example of a cultural practice that may serve to establish the man as father of the baby is couvade. In certain tribal societies, the father behaves as if he were giving birth. While his wife is delivering the infant, the father goes to bed and may even complain of labor pains. This custom symbolically establishes the man as father of the baby and gives him legal rights as the parent. In modern societies, up to 65% of men report symptoms of pregnancy during their partner's gestation (May & Perrin, 1985), including nausea, fatigue, back pain, and even abdominal pain. Though many different reasons have been suggested for this phenomenon—an expression of underlying biological changes in the male, envy of the pregnant woman, somatized anxiety—its prevalence is not entirely understood. Could this modern version of couvade be the result of the male identifying strongly with his mate and thereby symbolically assuming responsibility for his role as father of their child? Could these symptoms help make the pregnancy more real for him?

Through the nine months of pregnancy, then, the couple faces the tasks involved in becoming a mother and a father. When the baby is born, both must give up the fantasy baby each has dreamed of for nine months and accept the very real baby that has been born. The following Focus on Ethics section discusses the difficulties a woman faces when deciding whether to keep or abort a fetus.

FOCUS ON ETHICS

Abortion—A Difficult Decision

See when you do something like that [have an abortion], you do it because for you it is your only choice. The sad thing is you really want to be able to feel bad about it without feeling wrong.

— Kathy Najimy —

For a woman of any age, the abortion decision is often one of the most difficult and distressing choices in her life. Abortion is a complicated and controversial issue with strong arguments both for and against. At one extreme, some pro-life advocates feel that termination of a pregnancy at any point for any reason is murder and is morally wrong. On the other hand, pro-choice advocates feel that a woman has the right to control her own reproductive process and determine her own fate.

The abortion question has a long history. In 1973, the Supreme Court in *Roe* v. *Wade* decided that states could not deny a woman her right to have an abortion. Since that time, however, several other laws and rulings have eroded that right. As early as 1976, the Hyde amendment stopped Medicaid funding for abortions, which made it more difficult for poor women to obtain abortions. Before that time, 33% of abortions were paid for by federal funds. In 1989, a more conservative Supreme Court ruled on *Webster* v. *Reproductive Health Services*, allowing states once again to limit abortions. The *Webster* ruling allowed states to ban abortions in public hospitals and clinics and prohibit public employees from assisting in abortions. Since then, the Supreme Court has accepted even more cases with the result being that abortion is still legal but less available, especially to young, poor women. For instance, more than 30 states require girls under 18 to notify or get permission from their parents in order to obtain an abortion—in some states permission is required even from a noncustodial parent. And employees of federally funded family planning clinics cannot discuss abortion with clients; only the doctor can mention abortion as an alternative or even offer abortion counseling (Guernsey, 1993). And fewer and fewer doctors are available who perform abortions. Some simply are untrained in the procedure, whereas others become discouraged over the violence associated with abortion protests. However, as of this writing, many women still have a choice.

How does a woman make such a difficult decision? She needs to honestly explore how she personally feels about abortion. She needs help in exploring alternatives such as putting the baby up for adoption, raising the child herself, or allowing a family member to raise the child. She needs to think through what each choice means for her now and in the future. She needs to look at what is going on in her life. Is the father of the baby involved? Does she have any support? Are there other chil-

dren involved? What are her plans for the future? (Eisen & Zellman, 1984). What are her moral and religious views regarding the abortion question? Can she afford an abortion? Estimates are that first-trimester abortions cost on average $300. Can she afford to raise a child?

A social worker can play an important role in helping a woman make the abortion decision. But this is one instance in which it is vital to be able to separate personal from professional values. The most important consideration is that the woman needs to make the decision herself. No one can make it for her. Though many women feel some guilt and depression after an abortion, most women have less regret and fewer emotional problems when the choice has not been forced upon them by other people (Reeder, Mastroianni, & Martin, 1983). In fact, fewer than 10% of women experience psychological problems after an abortion (Lemkau, 1988; Olson, 1980). Women who do have a high incidence of emotional problems following abortion were more ambivalent before the procedure, felt coerced, or already had symptoms of personality problems (Schuster & Ashburn, 1992). On the other hand, women who have been denied an abortion may have more problems with the child born as a result of that denial. One study in Czechoslovakia (Matejcek, Dytrych, & Schuller, 1979) found that at the age of 9, children born to women denied an abortion had more hospitalizations, poorer school grades, poorer relationships with peers, and more irritable dispositions than other children.

A woman who is encouraged to take some time and carefully analyze her options before coming to a decision will be better able to live with that decision. Counseling before and after the abortion can help a woman deal with her feelings about her choice. The goal is to help a woman make a decision that—whether she feels good or bad about it at the time—she ultimately believes is the right one.

Biophysical Dimension

Biophysical Growth and Development

What will eventually become a baby begins as a single cell. About midway through her menstrual cycle, a

Sperm and egg: A magnified image of the process of conception.

woman produces a mature ovum, or egg, in a fluid-filled sac on one of her ovaries. At ovulation, the sac bursts and the mature ovum is swept into the fallopian tube to begin the journey to the uterus.

When the ovum enters the fallopian tube, it is swept along to about the lower one-third of the tube. Sperm deposited in the vagina during intercourse swim up through the cervix, into the uterus, and then into the fallopian tube, where one sperm fertilizes the ovum.

The fertilized ovum is known as a *zygote*. After a brief rest of 24–36 hours, the zygote begins the process of regular cell division (see Table 5.1). It then takes three days for the zygote to travel down the fallopian tube and into the uterus. By the time the zygote enters the uterus, it has developed into a fluid-filled sphere of about 150 cells. The inner layer of cells develops into the embryo, and the outer layer of cells forms the chorionic villi— fingerlike tendrils that give the zygote a shaggy appearance. These chorionic villi burrow into the uterine lining (implant) and provide early nutrients. This process of implantation of the zygote, known as the *germinal period*, takes about two weeks. After implantation, the zygote, now known as an embryo, begins to secrete human chorionic gonadotrophin (HCG) to maintain the pregnancy. HCG can be detected in the mother's blood six to eight days after conception, and presence of this substance is the basis for early pregnancy testing. An at-home early pregnancy test can detect HCG in the mother's urine one day after the missed menstrual cycle.

The next few weeks after conception, from two to eight weeks, is the *embryonic period*.

Physical Development of the Fetus

no one, not even the rain, has such small hands

— e.e. cummings —

After eight weeks, the embryo begins to look quite human; it is 90% formed, with most of the basic structures, including a face, arms, legs, feet, and hands. From this point on, the embryo is referred to as a fetus, and this period is called the period of the fetus. Between 8 and 12 weeks, the chorionic villi develop into a functioning placenta attached to the mother's uterus, and the fetus is connected to the placenta by the umbilical cord. For the remainder of the pregnancy, the placenta acts as the fetus's lungs, digestive tract, kidneys, and liver. Oxygen and nutrients from the mother pass through this semi-permeable membrane to the fetus, and carbon dioxide and other wastes pass from the fetus to the mother. It was once thought that the placenta acted as a barrier and protected the fetus from any harmful substances ingested by the mother. Now, however, we know that what the mother eats, drinks, sniffs, or inhales is passed on to the developing baby. The effects of these substances on the fetus will be discussed in a later section.

The fetus floats in amniotic fluid inside the amniotic sac, or bag of waters. This fluid regulates the temperature, cushions the fetus from injury, and allows freedom of movement. After 12 weeks, the fetus begins to move in this fluid, to drink this fluid, and to urinate into it. By this time, also, it is possible to determine the sex of the fetus.

By 20 weeks, the mother feels the first fetal movements—commonly described as butterflies fluttering in her lower abdomen. Often this is the time when the expectant parents first hear the fetal heart beat on a prenatal visit. The fetus is covered with fine, downy hair called *lanugo*. Some babies are born with a substantial amount of this hair on their bodies, although many babies lose most of this body hair before birth.

By 24 weeks, the fetus resembles a tiny baby. This baby appears to be rather red and wrinkled, though, because it has not put on much fat. At this time, the fetus is covered with a substance called vernix, which looks a lot

TABLE 5.1   Summary of Major Changes from Conception to Birth

Period	Age	Height	Weight	Notable Changes
Germinal	(0–2 weeks)			Rapid cell division; ovum attaches to uterine wall; inner and outer mass formed
Embryonic	(2–8 weeks)	2.5 cm	14 g	Human form takes shape; internal organs begin to develop; placenta and umbilical cord form
Fetal	(8–37 weeks)	50 cm	3.2 kg	Growth and change to sustain independent life
Third month	12 weeks	7.5 cm	28 g	Activity, movement; head growth; facial features
Fourth month	16 weeks	15 cm	110 g	Reflexes become brisker; growth spurt in lower part of body; mother feels movement
Fifth month	21 weeks	30 cm	450 g	Skin structures form; fetus has characteristic life
Sixth month	26 weeks	36 cm	900 g	Eyes, eyelids formed; fine layer of hair on head; grasp reflex; irregular breathing
Seventh month	30 weeks	40 cm	1.4 kg	"Age of viability"
Eighth–ninth months		50 cm	3.2 kg	Rapid weight gain; fatty tissues develop; organ system activity (e.g., heart, kidneys) steps up

Source: Santrock, 1983.

like shortening. This substance protects the skin from prolonged exposure to the amniotic fluid. Babies at term are sometimes born with some of this vernix still covering their skin. A fetus at 24 weeks makes breathing motions, hiccoughs (sometimes felt by the mother), responds to sound, and sleeps and wakes in noticeable cycles. With the advanced technology now available in high-level neonatal intensive care units (NICU), babies born at 24 weeks have a chance for survival.

If born at 28 weeks, the fetus has a good chance of survival. Now the fetus opens and closes its eyes and may even suck its thumb. A fetus usually assumes the head-down position in the uterus at this time, because the head is the heaviest part of the body.

During the last two months of pregnancy, the fetus stores fat and gains weight. The fetal lungs undergo important development, and each week the fetus remains in the uterus now increases its chances of survival. Although a premature baby has improved chances of survival at earlier and earlier stages of pregnancy, other problems related to low birth weight and prematurity remain.

The fetus is full term and ready for life outside the uterine environment between 38 and 41 weeks. How is this "due date" determined? If pregnancy is defined as beginning at the time of conception, then birth occurs after 266 days or 38 weeks. The mother's due date, however, is usually calculated according to Nagele's rule. To determine a woman's due date, count back three months from the first day of her last menstrual period and add seven days. According to this procedure, pregnancy begins on the first day of the last menstrual period and lasts 280 days or 40 weeks. In most clinical situations, pregnancy is calculated in this way, so for our discussion of prenatal development, pregnancy is based on menstrual dates and lasts 40 weeks.

The Birth Process

Doesn't it seem that in popular media depictions of birth, labor begins with the woman doubling over in sudden, intense pain? This is followed by a frantic rush to get to the hospital in time for the birth. Although some cab drivers have delivered babies, in reality most women find that labor begins a little more slowly, allowing ample time to make it to the hospital.

Labor is divided into three stages (see Figure 5.1). During the first stage, the cervix opens up or dilates to 10 centimeters to allow the passage of the baby's head. The average length of the first stage of labor is 12–14 hours. In early labor, the contractions can be up to 20 minutes apart and usually last less than 1 minute. Most women are pretty comfortable in the early part of labor and are excited about having the baby at last, though a little anxious over the process. As labor progresses, toward the end of the first stage, the contractions may come one right after another and last up to 2 minutes. During this phase, a laboring woman needs a lot of support and encouragement. And if she has not gone to the hospital or birthing center yet, now is the time to rush or hope the cab driver knows what he or she is doing.

When the cervix has fully dilated to 10 centimeters, the second stage of labor begins. During this stage, the baby is born. A woman can now actively participate in the birth process by pushing the baby down the birth canal. This process can take from 10 minutes to over 3 hours, depending on how many previous births the woman has had and how much medication she has been given.

During the third stage of labor, the placenta is delivered, which usually takes from 5 to 30 minutes. At this time, the mother and her partner or support person are busy marveling over the baby. Sometimes a fourth stage of labor is included; this is the recovery time, the 1 to 2 hours after birth. During this time, the mother is watched for excessive bleeding or other recovery problems. This is usually the time for the new family to get to know each other.

The following Focus on History section discusses significant changes that have taken place in preparing for childbirth.

| Before labor begins | Just before the baby's head enters the birth canal | The baby's head before crowning |
| The head crowning | The head emerging | The placenta coming loose and about to be born |

FIGURE 5.1   The birth process   Source: Adapted from Moore, 1989.

At birth, babies leave the comfort of the uterine environment and must immediately adapt to the outside environment.

FOCUS ON HISTORY

Prepared Childbirth

Having a baby involves some degree of pain. A popular comedienne describes the pain of childbirth: "Take your lower lip and pull it up over your head." Physically the pain comes from cervical dilation and the sensation of the baby's head pushing through the pelvis. Through the years, different methods have been used to help ease this pain.

Many of the early drugs given to relieve the pain of childbirth rendered most women unconscious during delivery. Because the mother was not awake and could not help push the baby out, the baby was usually delivered with a high degree of medical intervention. Her partner would wait in the fathers' waiting room. After birth, the baby was kept in the hospital nursery and brought to the mother only at scheduled feeding times. Understandably, women began to want more control over and participation in their birth experiences. Also, such a heavy reliance on drugs for pain relief during birth had major side effects for the baby. In response, other methods of pain relief without drugs were developed.

The most popular method of prepared childbirth was developed by a French obstetrician, Fernand Lamaze. In the Lamaze method, the father or other support person stays with the mother through her labor to provide help and encouragement. The mother and her support person attend classes where they learn about the birth process and specific relaxation techniques. Knowledge and relaxation help reduce fear and thereby reduce pain. The woman is taught to replace the normal responses to pain of fear and tension with more useful and distracting responses, such as patterned breathing and relaxation.

More recently, studies have shown that women who walk and move around during labor have shorter labors, experience less discomfort, and need less medication than women who lie down (Balaskas, 1992). Studies have also shown that the presence of a supportive female birth attendant, or *doula*, during labor results in less medication, less medical intervention, fewer birth complications, and a shorter labor (Klaus, Kennell, & Klaus, 1993).

Over the years, hospitals have attempted to make birth more family centered. Many hospitals have special birthing rooms, which resemble a regular bedroom. The mother is allowed to have any number of attendants present for the birth. Siblings may even be included. After the birth, the baby is handed to the mother, and she can keep the baby in the room with her and feed on demand. Birthing centers, outside the hospital setting, allow for homelike birth with the possibility of medical intervention if necessary. Some women choose to have their babies at home, but in case of last-minute complications, most obstetricians prefer to deliver babies in a hospital or birthing center.

Medications for Labor and Delivery

Development of prepared childbirth methods (see Focus on History: Prepared Childbirth) has allowed women to be awake and active participants in the birth process. Being rendered totally unconscious with drugs is now usually only an option during an emergency cesarean section. However, prepared childbirth does not eliminate the pain of labor. Today, "natural" childbirth does not necessarily mean unmedicated childbirth.

The most commonly used medications in labor today are narcotics and regional anesthesias. Narcotics, such as Demerol, are given before the end of the first stage of labor so that most of the drug will pass out of the baby's system before birth. If the baby is born with the narcotic in its system, it may experience difficulty breathing or sucking. Because the narcotic is sometimes given with a tranquilizer, the baby may also be sleepy at birth in contrast to unmedicated babies, who are more alert.

Regional anesthesias include the epidural. In the epidural, an anesthetic is injected into the mother's lower spine. Though little of this drug reaches the baby, its long-term effects on the baby are still unknown. Some studies show mild effects on early newborn behavior (Sepkoski, 1992), whereas others have found little or no effect. The epidural can lower the mother's blood pressure (Pritchard, MacDonald, & Gant 1985); this hypotension may lead to reduced oxygen to the fetus. Over the years, some studies have indicated there are effects on the birth process itself. For instance, the epidural may increase the length of labor and the need for medical intervention, including use of forceps (a pair of instruments that resemble salad tongs used to guide the baby out of the birth canal when the mother is not able to push the baby out), and the possibility of a cesarean section (birth through an incision in the mother's abdomen) (Cohen, Yeast, & Hu, 1994). On the other hand, preliminary reports from a study conducted by a group of anaesthesiologists suggest that the epidural relaxes women, helps labor progress, and has few complications (Erikson, 1996).

Implications for Practice: Effects of Medication on the Baby

Although most women who are prepared for childbirth use less medication than those who are not, the use of medication in labor in many hospitals remains quite high. In fact, in some hospitals the rate of epidural use approaches 85 to 90%. All obstetric medications given to the mother cross the placenta and alter the baby's environment in the uterus (Balaskas, 1992). Conclusive evidence on the long-term effects of these drugs is not yet available. Thus, use of medications during birth may still be an important factor to consider in making an assessment.

Characteristics of a Normal Newborn

How does a newborn infant look? Bill Cosby describes the experience of seeing his new baby for the first time, at which point he tells his wife, "Congratulations, dear.

A striking comparison of the baby at birth and at 4 weeks. The newborn's head is elongated, and the baby's face shows the pressures that occurred during the birth process.

You have just given birth to a . . . lizard." Although most newborns bear little resemblance to reptiles, they are not exactly the "Gerber Baby."

Normal newborns at term weigh between 5 1/2 pounds (2500 grams) and 9 1/2 pounds (4300 grams). The head of a vaginally delivered newborn is often elongated or cone-shaped. This molding of the head results from the fact that the bones in a newborn's head are not fused together. These bones shift during birth, allowing the head to mold to fit through the birth canal. (Infants delivered by cesarean section have well-shaped, round heads.) Passage through the birth canal can also cause facial bruising and swelling. Many newborns have a bluish color to their skin until they begin breathing. After birth, the newborn's skin may be red, wrinkled, and scaling. But to the new parents, their newborn is usually a beautiful sight.

Newborn Evaluations

One of the first questions asked by new parents at delivery is, "Is my baby OK?" One objective exam that looks at whether or not a newborn is OK is the **Apgar score** (see Table 5.2). In 1953, Virginia Apgar developed a scale that looks at the infant's adaptation to life outside the womb. A newborn is given an Apgar score at 1 minute and 5 minutes after birth. At these times, the physician evaluates the baby on skin color, heart rate, response to stimulation, muscle tone, and breathing effort. In each area, the physician gives the baby a score of 0, 1,

TABLE 5.2 The Apgar Score

	Score		
Sign	**0**	**1**	**2**
Heart rate	No heart beat	Under 100 beats per minute	100 to 140 beats per minute
Breathing	No breathing	Irregular shallow breathing	Strong breathing and crying
Reflex	No response	Weak reflexive response	Strong reflexive response (sneezing, coughing, grimacing)
Muscle tone	Limp	Weak flexion of arms and legs	Strong flexion of arms and legs
Color	Blue body	Body pink, blue extremities	Body and extremities pink

Source: Based on Apgar, 1953.

or 2. Normal newborns usually lose a point or two for skin color, in that the hands and feet remain somewhat blue for a time after birth. There is an old joke that only fellow obstetricians' babies receive a perfect score of 10. At any rate, a score of 7–10 is considered good. A score of 5–7 is poor, and the baby may need some medical intervention. A score of 0–4 is very poor; the baby very likely requires resuscitation and has increased risk of mortality. A score of 0–4 at 5 minutes is significantly associated with increased risk of mortality and neurological defects.

Biophysical Hazards

Birth is as safe as life gets.

— Harriette Hartigan —

As discussed in Chapter 2, when gathering developmental data about a client for a psychosocial history, it may be helpful to obtain prenatal information about the client, including any problems or complications that occurred during the pregnancy or birth. These complications may have an impact on the individual's postnatal development. For instance, some research (Colletti, 1979) suggests that children with learning disabilities had a significantly higher incidence of pregnancy and birth complications than did normal children. Other evidence suggests a link between attention deficit disorder and pregnancy, birth, and neonatal complications (Sprich-Buckminster, 1993). In the next sections, we will discuss some of the possible complications of pregnancy and birth.

Complications of Pregnancy

Many women experience nausea, or morning sickness, during early pregnancy. This nausea and occasional vomiting usually clear up by the fourth month of gestation. If a woman vomits several times a day for a long period of time, however, she runs the risk of nutritional problems and dehydration. This frequent vomiting during pregnancy is called **hyperemesis gravidarum.** Some women have vomiting so severe that they require hospitalization.

A complication that can have serious consequences is **vaginal bleeding.** In early pregnancy, this bleeding can be due to spontaneous abortion. Seventy-five percent of spontaneous abortions occur in the first 12 weeks of pregnancy. Not all incidences of first-trimester bleeding end in loss of the pregnancy, though. Sometimes the bleeding abates, and the pregnancy is carried to term. But, because many spontaneous abortions are the result of fetal abnormalities, it may be helpful to note instances of early-pregnancy bleeding.

Vaginal bleeding in later pregnancy may be an indication of placental problems. This bleeding is usually the result of a placenta located low in the uterus and covering the cervix (placenta previa) or a placenta that begins to separate from the wall of the uterus (abruptio placentae). Significant bleeding in late pregnancy due to these conditions can be very serious and threaten the survival of the mother and baby.

Toxemia or eclampsia can also be a serious complication of pregnancy. Early stages of toxemia are referred to as preeclampsia. In *preeclampsia*, the pregnant woman exhibits elevated blood pressure, swelling (especially of the hands and face), weight gain, and protein in her urine. These symptoms are not always easily noticed by the mother and are often caught at a prenatal visit. This is one reason that regular, consistent prenatal visits are so important to pregnancy outcome. If these early signs are not detected and treated, the condition can advance to eclampsia and serious complications, including maternal death, fetal death, and fetal brain damage.

Sometimes the pregnant woman has too much amniotic fluid, or **polyhydramnios.** This excess fluid can signal problems with the baby. Remember, the baby drinks the fluid. If for some reason the baby cannot drink the fluid, it builds up in the uterus, causing the mother to exhibit an overly large abdomen.

A good example of a complication of pregnancy that can be caused by factors in the maternal environment is **intrauterine growth retardation (IUGR).** This condition occurs when the fetal weight falls below the 10th percentile for gestational age. Many factors can affect the quality of the maternal uterine environment and result in this growth slowdown, including the mother's nutrition, weight gain, age, number and spacing of previous pregnancies, health status, level of environmental stress, and her ingestion of substances such as cigarettes, alcohol, and drugs. In many instances, this growth reduction is in some way due to intrauterine deprivation. Because of this deprivation, IUGR increases the risk of fetal death and the risk of problems for the infant after birth.

Environmental Effects on Prenatal Development

The child is born into a family environment that will shape and influence his lifelong development. Even before birth, however, human development occurs in an "environment" that exerts significant influence on the growing fetus. The fetal environment exists inside the mother's uterus, and this environment can be influenced by numerous factors, such as the mother's health, her diet, her ingestion of substances such as alcohol and drugs, and her emotional state and level of stress. In this section we will discuss maternal health factors and practices that can adversely affect prenatal development.

Maternal Age   Problems in pregnancy attributable to maternal age arise in mothers under 18 and over 35.

Older mothers have an increased risk for illness and for pregnancy complications. Specifically, the incidence for chromosomal abnormalities such as Down syndrome goes up significantly for older women. The risk of Down syndrome for a 21-year-old woman is 1:1600, whereas the risk for a woman at age 41 is 1:83.

On the other hand, teenage mothers also have more problems with pregnancy, including increased risk of infant death, pregnancy complications, and mental retardation. One contributing problem for young mothers may be that teenage mothers are less likely to obtain prenatal care (Eberstadt, 1991).

For either end of the age spectrum, good medical management of the pregnancy through prenatal visits increases the likelihood of a successful outcome. Some outcomes, however, may not be what we expect. The following Focus on Diversity section presents some research results that indicate that teens with lower socioeconomic status (SES) may actually have healthier babies than teens with higher socioeconomic status.

FOCUS ON DIVERSITY

Lower-SES Teens May Have Healthier Babies

One researcher (Geronimus, 1991, 1992) has discovered some interesting information about lower-socioeconomic-status teens. This researcher found that economically disadvantaged women who give birth as teens have healthier babies than do comparable older women. In particular, when looking at birth outcomes for low-SES African American sisters, those who gave birth as teenagers had healthier babies and more family support than did the sisters who gave birth in their twenties. One suggested explanation for this outcome is that lower-SES women are healthier as teenagers. As they enter their twenties, the health of these women declines as a result of poor living conditions and unsafe health habits.

Multiple Gestations   A pregnancy involving more than one fetus increases the risk of complications of pregnancy, especially for IUGR and premature labor. Whereas the average gestational age for single fetuses is 39 weeks, for twins it is 35 weeks, triplets 33, and quadruplets 29. Multiple gestations are twice as likely to have birth defects (Feinbloom, 1993).

Women who have several closely spaced pregnancies also experience more problems with fetal health.

Maternal Nutrition   A pregnant woman needs an extra 300 calories a day of high-quality food for good nutrition. Physicians used to advise pregnant women to limit their weight gain to 15 to 18 pounds. Physicians now advise their patients to "eat to appetite" and to gain 25 to 30 pounds. Poor nutrition can result in IUGR and a low-birth-weight baby. Lack of certain vitamins and minerals can cause problems; specifically lack of folic acid has been linked to neural tube defects. Severe malnutrition increases the likelihood of congenital defects and fetal death. A good diet adequate in protein is most important during the last three months of pregnancy, when the baby is gaining weight and developing brain cells.

To help ensure adequate nutrition for low-income women during pregnancy, the government developed the Supplemental Food Program for Women, Infants and Children (referred to as WIC). This program provides vouchers to pregnant women and new mothers with children to age 5 for high-protein, iron-fortified food. The program also provides nutritional education and counseling.

Pica During Pregnancy

A nutritional problem for women in some communities is pica—the ingestion of nonfood substances such as paint chips, starch, dirt, clay, and ice. Sometimes the pregnant woman may ingest enough of these substances to interfere with her appetite for normal food. As a result, she may experience nutritional problems that can affect fetal growth and development. Though pica can be a craving for a particular substance, it can also be a cultural phenomenon. In some ethnic communities, women ingest nonfood substances with the belief that these substances will relieve the symptoms of pregnancy or benefit the fetus.

A study at a prenatal clinic in Washington, D.C., found that 8.1% of the African American patients engaged in a form of pica called *pagophagia*—the ingestion of ice or freezer frost. These women ate up to two cups of ice a day and as a result showed a tendency toward anemia. This study suggested that these urban women ate ice chips to help alleviate stress. In fact, the authors found that pica was higher among women who had a poor social support network (Edwards et al., 1994). And, interestingly, the women who ate ice chips used fewer illegal drugs.

Maternal Illness   Several illnesses can cause serious problems with the pregnancy or for the fetus at birth. In particular, several nonbacterial infections referred to as the *TORCH complex* can cause multiple complications, including blindness, deafness, brain damage, miscarriage, fetal death, and mental retardation. These infections include *toxoplasmosis*, a parasite found in raw meat and cat feces; *rubella or German measles*, if contracted during the first three months of pregnancy; *cytomegalovirus*, a viral infection; and active *herpes*, a sexually transmitted disease.

Sexually transmitted diseases, such as syphilis, gonorrhea, and HIV, can have a profound effect on the fetus. Syphilis can be passed to the fetus through the placenta. Fetal infection with syphilis can result in miscarriage or eye, ear, bone, or brain damage. A woman with gonorrhea can pass the infection to her newborn during birth, which can cause blindness in the infant. As a safeguard, most hospitals treat a newborn's eyes with erythromycin ointment or silver nitrate. About 50% of mothers infected with HIV transmit the virus to their babies. In these babies the disease progresses rapidly and kills 95% of infected infants by the age of 3.

Diabetic mothers have increased risk of pregnancy and birth complications. Uncontrolled diabetes can result in miscarriage, fetal death, and birth defects. Also, babies born to diabetic mothers tend to be large, with an increased risk of birth injury because of their size. For this reason, infants of diabetic mothers are often delivered early, resulting in problems associated with prematurity.

Another problem that can have serious effects on pregnancy outcome is not a maternal illness but is related to a maternal characteristic—the mother's blood type. This problem is known as **Rh incompatibility.** This problem arises when a mother with Rh negative blood has a partner with Rh positive blood, bringing about the possibility that their fetus will have Rh positive blood. During pregnancy, the blood of the mother and fetus can sometimes mix through small tears in the placenta. If an Rh negative mother is exposed to fetal blood that is Rh positive, the mother forms antibodies against the fetal blood. During a first pregnancy this is usually not a problem. But in subsequent pregnancies, Rh negative mothers who have been sensitized to Rh positive blood will have these antibodies in their system. If these antibodies enter the fetal blood supply, they destroy fetal red blood cells, resulting in fetal anemia and possible death. A fetus that survives to birth is at risk for mental retardation. For this reason, Rh negative mothers are given Rho Gam, a drug that counteracts the Rh antibodies, within 72 hours of a delivery or miscarriage to prevent sensitization. A fetus with this Rh problem can sometimes be saved by a blood transfusion.

Maternal Drug Use   Substances that cause birth defects are known as **teratogens.** The serious effects of drugs as teratogens can be illustrated with the story of thalidomide. Thalidomide was a mild tranquilizer sold over the counter in the early 1960s for symptoms of morning sickness. The drug had been tested on pregnant laboratory rats and deemed safe for use by pregnant women. Although thalidomide was widely used in West Germany and Britain, the FDA never approved its use in the United States, "pending further study." Unfortunately, thousands of women who used the drug in early pregnancy gave birth to babies with birth defects. The most striking defect was short or missing limbs, so that hands and feet were attached to the torso. This story illustrates that the effects of a substance on a developing fetus cannot always be accurately assessed in the laboratory. A pregnant woman is now advised not to take any over-the-counter medications without consulting her physician. Table 5.3 lists several other drugs that have been identified as teratogens.

Drug-exposed infants differ significantly in appearance and behavior from normal newborns and require extensive care immediately after birth.

Though the long-term effects of illegal substances on development are still questionable, mothers addicted to street drugs, such as cocaine, heroin, and barbiturates, can give birth to addicted infants. These infants suffer the withdrawal problems associated with these drugs, including seizures, vomiting, agitation, tremors, and sleep disturbances. In addition, illicit drug use can increase the incidence of miscarriage, fetal death, hemorrhage, and low birth weight.

FOCUS ON SOCIOLOGY

Mandatory Drug Testing of Pregnant Women—Does It Work?

Laura arrived at the hospital emergency room in early labor. On questioning, Laura admitted that she had received no prenatal care. When the nurses requested a urine sample, Laura left. Three days later Laura returned, hemorrhaging, and an emergency cesarean section was performed. Because of the lack of prenatal care, Laura

TABLE 5.3   Drugs That May Affect Prenatal Development

Alcohol	Prenatal/postnatal growth retardation, developmental delays, facial anomalies, microcephaly (small head), heart defects, hyperactivity, behavioral problems, mental retardation
Amphetamines	Premature birth, stillbirth, neonatal irritability, poor feeding in newborn

Antibiotics
   Streptomycin
   Tetracycline
	
	Hearing loss
	Premature birth, stained teeth, short arms or legs, webbed hands, inhibited bone growth

Aspirin	Bleeding problems in mother or infant
Dilantin (seizure medicine)	Head and facial abnormalities, heart defects, cleft palate, mental retardation
Barbiturates	Fetal addiction with subsequent withdrawal symptoms, including seizures, vomiting, agitation; also can cause neurological problems
Hallucinogens (LSD, mescaline)	Possible chromosomal damage, miscarriage, possible behavioral abnormalities
Lithium	Heart defects, lethargic newborn
Cocaine	Low birth weight, seizures, microcephaly, SIDS, premature birth, IUGR, miscarriage
Heroin (methadone)	Toxemia, IUGR, miscarriage, premature birth, low birth weight, stillbirth, SIDS, neonatal addiction with withdrawal symptoms, including restlessness, vomiting, tremors

Hormones
   DES
   Estrogens
   Androgens
	
	Reproductive system anomalies, cancer of reproductive system
	Feminization of males
	Masculinization of females

Tranquilizers Valium	In first trimester, can cause cleft palate, respiratory distress, poor muscle tone, lethargy in newborn
Tobacco	IUGR, premature birth, stillbirth, low birth weight, miscarriage, SIDS, possible hyperactivity, possible learning problems
Vitamin A Accutane (acne medicine)	Cleft palate, heart defects Microcephaly, blindness, heart defects, miscarriage, fetal death
Caffeine	Low birth weight, IUGR, premature birth
Antihistamines	Anomalies, fetal death
Corticosteroids	Anomalies, cleft palate, IUGR

was screened for drug use, and her lab results showed positive for methamphetamines. Laura's baby was born lethargic, with low muscle tone and an irregular heart beat. He was immediately transferred to the neonatal intensive care unit for further evaluation. The hospital notified Child Protective Services.

The effects of drug use in pregnancy take their toll on innocent infants. To help eliminate the occurrence of situations such as the one described above, many people favor laws that allow a pregnant woman to be tested and treated for substance use without her consent. These people believe that if the mother does not comply with treatment, she should be jailed. Although there can be little dispute over protecting unborn children from maternal drug abuse, how effective are mandatory testing and threatening a mother with possible jail as preventive measures? Jannke (1994) questions the ethics, legality, and effectiveness of these punitive laws.

First of all, is it ethical to test a woman without her consent? Such practices may undermine the relationship of health care providers with drug-using families. Such families often mistrust medical workers and fear these workers are trying to take their children away. Testing a woman without her consent with the intent of jailing her only further reinforces this fear and may lead these women to become more distrustful and ultimately to avoid contact with health providers (Jannke, 1994).

As to the question of legality, it should be noted that many of the women who would be tested for drugs or jailed are African American. Although a study conducted in Florida found little difference in rates of abuse between private insurance patients and those on public assistance or between white and black clients, providers are less likely to suspect white, middle-class women with health insurance of drug abuse. In fact, a booklet produced by the U.S. Department of Health and Human Services states, "Reports indicate that a pregnant woman's race, ethnicity, and socioeconomic status have an overwhelming impact on whether or not she is screened" (Mitchell, 1993, p. 48). So poor, ethnic minority women may be singled out by these laws.

How effective are these laws? Women who use drugs during pregnancy often know the risks to the fetus but are unable to stop the abuse because of the nature of addiction. Threat of prosecution only makes women avoid prenatal care. In fact, as described above, the mother may avoid reporting to the hospital when she is in labor, hoping that a delay will give her some time and reduce the possibility of a positive drug screen.

Is jail the answer? Drugs are readily available in jail, so imprisoning the mother may not protect the fetus at all. Also, adequate medical care for pregnant high-risk mothers is not available in most jails. Few prisons provide education for expectant mothers on childbirth and parenting (Jannke, 1994).

What about treatment? Often, even when the mother agrees to drug treatment, the treatment options are inadequate or not available. In fact, only 11% of pregnant addicts get into treatment (Cronin, Ludtke, & Willwerth, 1991). Many treatment programs have a long waiting list, many do not take pregnant women, and those that do often do not allow the woman to keep her other children with her during treatment. For an addicted mother, residential treatment, when available, can mean up to a year's separation from her family. Sometimes her children are placed in foster care. If the woman's partner is also abusing drugs, treatment for him is even more difficult to find. Programs that consider the needs of whole families are rare. Even in communities that do not prosecute and jail pregnant substance abusers, the women often experience neglect from the health care and service delivery systems.

The report entitled "Pregnant, Substance-Using Women" written in 1993 by a panel for the U.S. Department of Health and Human Services states, "The Panel does not support the criminal prosecution of pregnant, substance-using women. Furthermore, there is no evidence that punitive approaches work" (Mitchell, 1993, p. 2). This report recommends that individuals who work with addicted mothers should provide counseling and education, drug treatment, and assistance in general living skills.

Maternal Alcohol Abuse Though much attention has recently been given in the media to "crack babies," the leading known preventable cause of irreversible mental retardation in the Western world is a common legal drug—alcohol (Abel & Sokol, 1987). In the past, doctors recognized that some infants were born with an unidentified syndrome of facial abnormalities and behavioral problems. Having no other term to describe this particular set of abnormalities, physicians would enter "FLK" in the infant's chart. These initials did not specify a particular medical diagnosis, but reflected the doctors' bewilderment at the nature of the disorder; FLK stands for "Funny Looking Kid." Today, this set of abnormalities has been associated with infants born to alcoholic mothers. Mothers who drink heavily during pregnancy may give birth to newborns with that particular set of birth defects now recognized as **fetal alcohol syndrome (FAS).**

FAS is a set of birth defects with lasting consequences. As previously stated, it is the leading known preventable cause of mental retardation. The physical signs include facial abnormalities such as a small head, small eyes or short eye openings, poorly developed philtrum (that part of the face between the nose and upper lip), thin upper lip, short nose, and flattened mid-facial area (Warren, 1985) (see Figure 5.2). Children with FAS have problems with learning, attention, memory, and problem solving along with lack of coordination, impulsiveness, and speech and hearing impairment. Adolescents and adults with FAS exhibit impulsiveness, lack of inhibitions, poor judgment, and a lack of understanding of socially appropriate sexual behavior. These behavioral characteristics make it difficult for these individuals to hold a job or establish successful peer relationships.

Less severe birth defects that may be related to alcohol use are termed fetal alcohol effects (FAE). The characteristics of FAE include low birth weight, irritability, and hyperactivity in the newborn, and short attention span and learning disabilities in the child (Little & Ervin, 1984). Having an abnormality that can be attributed to alcohol use is termed an alcohol-related birth defect (ARBD).

Maternal Smoking   Inhaling cigarette smoke increases the level of carbon monoxide in a pregnant woman's blood. This increase in maternal carbon monoxide blood level decreases oxygen to the fetus. Smoking increases the risk of prematurity, infant death, miscarriage, low birth weight, and other complications of pregnancy and birth. Smoking has also been implicated as causing a higher risk for sudden infant death syndrome (SIDS). A growing number of studies now are showing that the effects of smoking during pregnancy may be long-term. Children of smokers are smaller and show problems with cognitive development and educational achievement. Infants of smokers show differences in responsiveness by 1 week of age. Through the preschool years, these children scored lower on verbal tests than children of nonsmokers (Newman & Buka, 1991).

FIGURE 5.2   Facial characteristics of fetal alcohol syndrome
Source: Zigler & Stevenson, 1993.

Maternal Stress   In the *New England Journal of Medicine,* Davidson (1992) states that we need to assess the role of stress in pregnancy as a contributing factor to premature and low-birth-weight infants. Other studies have shown a significant relationship between IUGR and stress (Goldenberg, 1991). In what exact ways does maternal stress contribute to complications of pregnancy?

A mother's physical response to stress could result in reduced blood flow to the uterus. This reduced blood flow, in turn, could decrease the amount of oxygen and nutrients to the fetus.

More important, however, are the effects that stress can have on the mother's coping responses. Pregnant women may cope with environmental stress by engaging in poor health behaviors such as smoking, drinking, and using drugs—activities that have all been shown to increase the risk of premature birth and low birth weight (Brooks-Gunn, McCormick, & Heagarty, 1988).

Prenatal Testing

Several prenatal tests have been developed in recent years that allow for genetic screening during pregnancy. It is now possible to determine before birth the sex of the fetus and whether the fetus has a specific genetic anomaly. This ability to obtain information about the sex and health of the fetus before birth brings up several legal and ethical issues (see Focus on Ethics: Selecting for Perfection—Important Questions to Consider).

Ultrasound is used almost routinely in prenatal care now. During an ultrasound, or sonogram, high-frequency sound waves are passed through the mother's abdomen to form a picture of the developing pregnancy. The procedure is used often during pregnancy, in particular to determine the gestational age of the fetus, location of the placenta, and whether there are multiple pregnancies and to assess the growth and development of the fetus. Ultrasound can identify anomalies of the fetus and other pregnancy complications.

Another noninvasive procedure is **alpha-fetoprotein blood screening.** This procedure is used to detect neural tube defects including spina bifida, an opening in the spinal column. Alpha-fetoprotein (AFP) can leak out of this opening and be absorbed into the mother's bloodstream. The test is done at 16 weeks gestation and detects the presence of AFP in the mother's blood.

A much more invasive procedure is **amniocentesis.** During this procedure, a needle is inserted through the mother's abdomen into the amniotic sac to collect a sample of amniotic fluid. This fluid contains fetal skin cells, which can be grown in a culture for genetic screening. The skin cells are used for a karyotype—a genetic picture of the fetal chromosomes. This procedure can detect chromosomal abnormalities such as Down syndrome and Trisomy 13. Amniocentesis can also determine the sex of the fetus.

Amniocentesis is usually performed at 15–16 weeks gestation. Growing the cells for genetic testing takes another 3 weeks. This means that by the time the mother receives the test results, she could be almost halfway through her pregnancy. She may have already felt the baby move. The decision to terminate the pregnancy for genetic reasons is a difficult one at this point because termination requires a second-trimester abortion. By the time the mother has the abortion, the baby may almost be viable, or able to live outside the womb. Another problem with amniocentesis is the slight risk of spontaneous abortion brought on by the procedure.

In contrast, a **chorionic villus sample (CVS)** can be performed at 8 weeks of gestation. In this procedure, the physician inserts a catheter into the uterus through the cervix and obtains a piece of the chorionic villi—the developing placenta. These cells contain the same genetic material as the fetus. Because these cells are growing rapidly, chromosomal test results are available within a couple of days. The decision to terminate the pregnancy can be made early in the first trimester. CVS is thought to have a slightly higher risk of spontaneous abortion than amniocentesis.

FOCUS ON ETHICS

Selecting for Perfection—Important Questions to Consider

Most parents who find out they are carrying a fetus with a major birth defect choose to have an abortion. This elective abortion of defective fetuses brings up many questions that social workers need to address.

Does this practice of elective abortion mean that living with a disabling condition is now unacceptable? How do these practices reflect our society's attitude toward people with disabilities? For example, there has been a recent increase in "wrongful life" and "wrongful birth" lawsuits allowed by courts. These suits are filed by parents who claim that the physician failed to recommend prenatal testing, which would have detected a genetic abnormality. As a result, the parents want to hold the physician responsible for the birth of a child with disability and require the physician to pay damages. Do these actions endorse the notion that defective fetuses should be aborted and that life with a disability is not worth living?

Critics claim that decisions to terminate a pregnancy because of a birth defect should not be made without adequate counseling. Yet, what constitutes genetic counseling? These critics claim that what passes for genetic counseling does not include adequate information concerning the range of disability associated with a particular condition. Children with Down syndrome have a wide range of intellectual ability, and those with spina bifida have a wide range of physical impairment, from a slight limp to life in a wheelchair. The critics contend that most genetic counseling consists of discussing the problems of a particular condition and does not include information from people living with that condition. What other information is necessary for couples to make an informed decision?

To what extent should prenatal testing be used to determine which characteristics are desirable? In some parts of the world, where male infants are preferred, prenatal testing is used for sex selection. If prenatal sex selection becomes acceptable in the United States, what other undesirable characteristics may be weeded out? A poll of New England couples showed that 11% would abort a fetus predisposed to obesity. How many couples would choose to abort a fetus destined for short stature or low IQ?

Another question that needs to be addressed concerns who receives prenatal testing. The tests are expensive and may not be available to lower-class families. Will this result in more disabled individuals among the lower classes?

Activists and ethicists urge us to carefully consider these questions concerning the use of prenatal tests before coming to the decision of who does and who does not live.

Source: Adapted from Lamb, 1994.

Complications of Birth

Birth complications have been linked with everything from schizophrenia (Verdoux, 1993) and violent crime (Raine, Brennan, & Mednick, 1994) to sleep disorders (Coren & Searleman, 1985) and left-handedness (Van Strien, Bouma, & Bakker, 1987). Other studies have failed to conclusively establish a connection between difficulties of birth and later problems. As we have already stated, some evidence exists, however, that suggests a link between learning disabilities and attention deficit disorder and pregnancy and birth complications. Further research may yet turn up relationships between abnormal development and problems during the birth process, so complications of birth may be an important factor to consider in making an assessment.

One birth complication that has an effect on development is **anoxia,** or insufficient oxygen to the fetus during delivery. Oxygen loss to the fetus can be caused by

such problems as maternal blood loss, maternal overmedication, or umbilical cord compression. Lack of oxygen to the fetus during labor can cause fetal distress, which can be detected by an electronic fetal monitor that records the baby's heart rate during labor and birth. When the baby is in distress, the heart rate drops or fluctuates. Lack of oxygen can cause brain damage or, in some instances, death. One consequence of anoxia is cerebral palsy—a condition that can result in movement and speech problems. Even mild reduction in oxygen to the fetus during delivery has been shown to produce problems with early development. However, with an adequate and stimulating home environment, these problems associated with mild anoxia usually clear up by the time the child is ready for school (Corah, Anthony, Painter, Stern, & Thurston, 1965).

Meconium aspiration can cause problems for the newborn baby. Meconium is the waste material in the baby's bowels at birth. It is black and tarry. If problems occur during delivery, the baby may have a bowel movement into the amniotic fluid during labor. If the baby inhales or aspirates amniotic fluid containing meconium, the baby can have respiratory problems at birth.

Another problem of birth is **malpresentation** (see Figure 5.3). In 95% of deliveries, the fetus is in a head-down, or vertex, position, with the result that the head is the first part of the baby to be born. In 5% of births, however, some other part of the fetus presents for delivery. In a breech presentation, the feet or buttocks of the infant is the first part through the birth canal. Breech presentations carry a higher risk of injury and death for the baby. For this reason, many physicians deliver breech babies by **cesarean section** (birth through an incision in the mother's abdomen). Another presentation that requires a cesarean birth is transverse lie. Here the infant is across the mother's abdomen (see Figure 5.3) with a shoulder or arm presenting into the pelvis.

A **prolonged labor** is one lasting more than 24 hours for a first-time mother or more than 12 hours for a woman who has previously given birth. Long labors can leave a woman exhausted and dehydrated. The baby faces a risk of intracranial hemorrhage (bleeding in the brain) from prolonged pressure to the head during the long labor. A baby with severe intracranial bleeding can be stillborn or suffer from mental retardation or cerebral palsy.

Vertex presentation   Transverse presentation

Breech presentation   Breech presentation

FIGURE 5.3   Birth presentations   Source: Zastrow & Kirst-Ashman, 1990.

FOCUS ON BIOPHYSICS

Cesarean Section

Jane and Gary were anticipating that their first child's birth would be an uncomplicated vaginal delivery. Gary had actively participated with Jane in childbirth classes. As a graduation present, she had presented him with a dark blue T-shirt with COACH printed on the front. Jane's labor was long and slow. She spent most of her labor in bed with an epidural for pain relief. She never dilated beyond 6 centimeters. After 18 hours of labor, the baby was delivered by cesarean section. Now, six weeks after the birth of a beautiful baby girl, Jane is tired and weepy. In addition, she feels guilty about her sadness because she thinks she should be happy just to have a normal, healthy baby.

In the past, some of the complications of birth could result in fetal death or injury. Today, however, many babies are saved through birth by cesarean section (an incision in the mother's abdomen). Though a c-section can be a life-saving solution to a birth complication, the procedure itself carries increased risks for the mother and baby. A cesarean birth increases the mother's risk of pain, trauma, and surgical complications and has two to four times the risk of maternal mortality as a vaginal birth (Mutryn, 1993).

In addition, some studies have shown that women who give birth by cesarean suffer from depression more than do women who give birth vaginally (Edwards, Porter, & Stein, 1993; Gottlieb & Barrett, 1986). Depression is a common consequence of major surgery (Mutryn, 1993), and a c-section is major surgery. A woman who gives birth by cesarean not only must recover from surgery but also must care for a newborn infant. This experience may leave her feeling tired and drained, and her fatigue and depression may interfere with maternal-infant interactions.

Many fathers or support persons now attend cesarean births. It has been said that a c-section is the only circumstance in modern medicine where an individual watches a loved one undergo major surgery. The support person may be a bit overwhelmed.

The rate of c-section birth has increased over the past 30 years from around 5% to 25–35%. This means that in some hospitals, more than one-third of all babies are delivered surgically. Mutryn (1993) claims that in recent years, because of the increased incidence of surgical births, cesarean delivery has been trivialized. Even childbirth educators describe a cesarean as "just another way to have a baby." This attitude may overlook the fact that surgery is one of life's most frightening experiences.

Neonatal Complications—The High-Risk Infant

One of the major risk factors for the newborn infant is low birth weight. A low-birth-weight infant is one born weighing less than 2500 grams, or 5 1/2 pounds. A low birth weight can be the result of **prematurity**—being born before the 38th week of gestation—or intrauterine growth retardation (IUGR)—having some sort of prenatal deprivation that retards growth. In the past, all babies born weighing less than 5 1/2 pounds were considered premature. However, a baby born before 38 weeks to a diabetic mother can weigh 5 1/2 pounds but still be premature and still encounter problems associated with early birth. A baby born at 40 weeks weighing less than 5 1/2 pounds is mature but will encounter the problems associated with retarded fetal growth and development.

Intrauterine Growth Retardation (IUGR) Growth retardation can occur at any point in the pregnancy. A fetus is considered growth retarded or small for gestational age (SGA) if its weight is less than the 10th percentile of the normal weight of an infant at that particular stage of gestational development. *A premature baby whose weight is normal for gestational age is low birth weight because of being born too early; but a small-for-gestational-age baby is low birth weight because of abnormal growth.* As we have already seen, this abnormal prenatal growth can be caused by factors such as maternal illness, poor nutrition, and drug and alcohol abuse.

The problem for growth-retarded infants is not just that they are born small—they are small because some sort of prenatal deprivation affected their growth and development. In terms of long-term developmental problems, these children exhibit more abnormal brain-wave patterns and an increased risk of learning disabilities (Reeder, Mastroianni, & Martin, 1983).

Prematurity   Seven percent of births occur before the end of the 37th week of pregnancy and are classified as premature. Though these babies may be growing and developing at a normal rate, they face the problems associated with low birth weight due to being born too early, such as respiratory difficulties, feeding problems, and jaundice. The lower the birth weight and the earlier the gestational age, the more likely these problems will occur.

Problems Associated with Premature Birth   During the last month of pregnancy, the fetal lungs mature in preparation for birth. A baby born before the lungs are fully mature can suffer from respiratory distress syndrome (RDS). The baby may need supplemental oxygen, which needs to be carefully monitored, as it has been discovered that high oxygen levels can cause blindness (retinopathy of prematurity).

A baby with RDS may need a ventilator to assist with breathing. A baby on a ventilator has a breathing tube placed down his airway, or trachea. If the baby requires this breathing tube for a long period, scarring and narrowing of the airway may occur. If the narrowing becomes severe enough to prevent normal air intake, then in order to breathe on his own after being removed from the ventilator, the baby will require a tracheostomy. In this procedure, a small opening is made in the baby's throat and a small tube is placed in this opening so that the baby breathes through this tube instead of through the nose or mouth. Taking home a baby with a tracheostomy can be a scary experience for new parents. A baby with a tracheostomy cannot make a sound, so the parents cannot hear their baby cry. Long-term placement of a tracheostomy may interfere with development of speech.

Another breathing problem of premature infants that can cause distress to new parents is *apnea*, or periods when the baby stops breathing. Apnea is common among premature babies after periods of exertion, such as following a feeding. Babies experiencing apnea may need to be on a monitor to signal when breathing has stopped, so the baby can then be stimulated to resume respiration.

The reflexes of a premature infant are often weak or lacking. In particular, the sucking reflex is not well established until 34 weeks gestation. A baby born before 34 weeks, then, may have feeding problems and not be able to nurse or take a bottle. These babies must be fed through a tube passed through their noses, down their throats, and into their stomachs (gavage feeding). The baby then has to learn to suck to feed from a bottle or the breast.

Preterm infants have more problems with *jaundice* than do full-term infants. Before birth, the fetus has extra red blood cells circulating in the blood. After birth, when the baby begins to breathe, these extra red blood cells are not necessary and are broken down in the baby's body. As these cells break down, they produce a by-product known as bilirubin. In a normal newborn, this bilirubin is broken down by the liver and excreted. A preterm infant's immature liver cannot effectively break down the excess bilirubin, so the substance builds up in the baby's system. Because bilirubin is orange-colored, this buildup results in a yellowish orange tint to the baby's skin, called jaundice (also known as hyperbilirubinemia). High levels of bilirubin deposited in the infant's brain can lead to a form of brain damage that can result in mental retardation. Babies with jaundice, or hyperbilirubinemia, are usually placed under lights because the light helps break down the bilirubin. A baby under these bili lights must wear a mask because the light can harm the baby's eyes.

Developmentally, premature babies need to be assessed according to their expected due date instead of their actual birth date. Therefore, babies born two months early will have the capabilities of newborns when they are two months old. With good care, many of the problems of premature infants discussed up to this point resolve in the first few years after birth, allowing the children to develop normally. But the smaller and more immature the infant, the greater the risk of long-range problems. With the high technology now available in neonatal intensive care units (NICU), smaller and smaller babies are surviving. With good care, 67% of infants born weighing between 750 and 999 grams (1 lb. 10 oz. to 2 lb. 3 oz.) live. What is even more amazing, up to 44% of babies weighing between 500 and 740 grams (1 lb. 2 oz. to 1 lb. 10 oz.) can be saved. What are the long-term developmental consequences of being born so small?

These very small babies run a higher risk of central nervous system bleeding or infection, which can result in permanent disabilities such as mental retardation, seizure disorder, and cerebral palsy (Jason & van de Meer, 1989). Sometimes parents and practitioners face the very difficult decision of whether to use high-technology procedures and knowledge to save a very small infant, who may later have severe handicaps, or to let the baby die.

Implications for Practice: The Premature Infant

A premature birth can be a difficult adjustment for new parents. Depending on gestational age and weight, the baby may spend several weeks or months in an isolette to regulate temperature and guard against infection. New parents may feel intimidated by the high-technological and medical atmosphere of the NICU. They may hesitate to interact with a small, fragile infant hooked up to an intravenous line, a feeding tube, and a ventilator. When the parents do interact with the baby, they may find the experience frustrating. It may be hard to attract and keep the baby's attention. Yet, too much stimulation can cause the baby to withdraw. Parents need help in learning to read their baby's cues and in learning to know when to interact and when to back off. The combination of an immature nervous system and a lengthy stay in an overstimulating hospital environment may make the baby irritable and difficult to parent (Jason & van de Meer, 1989).

In addition, many premature infants are born to young, poor, uneducated, single mothers. In fact, low-birth-weight births "are often associated with poverty and its cofactors (e.g., low maternal education, high unemployment, and teenage motherhood), which are themselves associated with decreases in child well-being" (Fong-ruey & Brooks-Gunn, 1994). For these infants, it is hard to separate the effects of deficits in the home environment from those of problems caused by prematurity.

Recent research by Bradley and colleagues (1994) has underscored the importance of the home environment in the development of low-birth-weight children. Overall, the researchers found that low-birth-weight children born into poverty function poorly in all areas of development (Bradley et al., 1994). However, they also found that babies who did well had stimulating toys and materials available, responsive parents who understood and accepted the baby's behavior, and space for play and exploration. The low-birth-weight infant, then, may ben-efit from a home where parents are sensitive and attentive and provide a rich array of objects and persons for the child to interact with (Bradley et al., 1987).

FOCUS ON PSYCHOLOGY

Handling Death Issues in NICU Settings

Newborn death is a reality in the neonatal intensive care unit. Bereavement programs are often utilized in these settings as a way for the staff to support family members who are dealing with issues surrounding the death of their infant. Several programs are available and share features that have been helpful in assisting parents, other family members, and hospital staff in coping with the grief that accompanies this unexpected loss (Heiney, Hasan, & Price, 1993; Johnson et al., 1982; Limbo & Wheeler, 1986).

Infant loss programs that assist families in dealing with grief issues often include the following features.

A Team Approach to Support Parents and Staff Members   The environment of a neonatal intensive care unit necessitates that all staff members have a general understanding of death issues, but not everyone is comfortable assisting families in dealing with their grief. Interested nurses, social workers, and others are specially trained in issues of perinatal death to function as grief counselors. Hospital pastoral care or clergy are also involved, and a blessing or baptism is usually offered.

Provision of a Private Place and Time for Parents to Be with Their Infant   Visualizing, touching, holding, bathing, wrapping, and just spending time with the infant allow the process of closure to begin for the family. Honoring this as a special and private time further acknowledges the family as a group. Parents sometimes choose to name their child at this time.

Creation of a Keepsake for the Parents to Take Home   A keepsake can be as simple as a baby book adapted into a scrapbook containing photographs of the baby and family, a lock of hair, handprints and footprints, hospital identification bracelet, crib card, certificates of birth and death, or anything else that parents wish to keep. Blankets and clothes the baby wore are also given to the family.

Sharing of Grief Information/Bereavement Packet These packets contain booklets on infant loss, sibling issues, and family coping strategies during the grieving process. Handouts and pamphlets on additional reading material, as well as lists of community support services, are also provided.

Assistance with Final Arrangements The family is supported in whatever decisions they make concerning how they choose to memorialize their child. Planning a memorial service, contacting the mortuary, or other arrangements can be organized by members of the team.

Family Follow-Up A sympathy card is usually sent to the family by the nurse and staff who were caring for the infant at the time of death. The parents are also contacted either by telephone or by written correspondence after discharge and at significant anniversary times. Parents can contact members of the bereavement team at any time for answers to remaining questions, emotional support, or counseling referrals to assist in further grief resolution.

Source: Written by Cathy Jaworski, RN.

Birth Defects and Developmental Disorders In spite of all of the possible things that can go wrong in the prenatal period and during the birth process, most infants are born normal and healthy. About 3 babies out of 100, however, have some kind of anomaly or malformation at birth. Many of these congenital disorders or anomalies can affect the individual's development.

Congenital heart defects include hearts with openings between the chambers and hearts that are malformed. Sometimes heart disease is associated with other genetic anomalies such as Down syndrome. If the heart defect is severe, it can interfere with growth and development. The baby may need corrective surgery at some point.

Spina bifida is a **neural tube defect** that occurs in 1 out of 500 births. In this condition, one or more vertebra do not close over the spinal cord, leaving the cord uncovered in a portion of the spinal column. When the cord bulges through the opening, the baby has a meningocele, which increases the risk of fetal death and paralysis.

Several congenital conditions affect the infant's brain. *Hydrocephalus* is a condition in which there is excess fluid in the baby's head. Because of the pressure of this increased fluid, hydrocephalus can result in mental retardation, paralysis and incoordination, and seizures. For these babies, a shunt can be placed in the head to drain off the excess fluid. Infants with *microcephaly* have a much smaller than normal head. Because of a small brain, these infants can be mentally retarded. In *anencephaly*, the baby is lacking all or part of a brain, and the life expectancy of these infants is very short. The question has arisen regarding the ethics of using these infants as donors for organ transplants. Should an infant with no brain who will die in a matter of days or weeks be sacrificed to save the life of another child?

Several *chromosomal abnormalities* can affect development. The most common is Down syndrome or Trisomy 21, which results from an extra chromosome. Infants born with this disorder are at higher risk of heart defects and have increased infant mortality. Babies with Down syndrome also have some degree of mental retardation, but the degree of retardation varies with each child. Early intervention programs can help these children reach their full potential. Many learn to read, hold jobs, and live in group housing. Babies born with other problems involving extra chromosomes, such as Trisomy 13 and Trisomy 18, usually do not live beyond 6 to 12 months.

Problems in metabolism include *phenylketonuria* (PKU). In this condition, the baby cannot metabolize a substance known as phenylalanine found in protein. This substance builds up and can cause mental retardation. For this reason, babies are tested for PKU at birth. Children with this condition must eat a restricted diet and avoid foods containing phenylalanine.

Babies who acquire brain damage from lack of oxygen or intracranial bleeding, either prior to or during birth, can develop **cerebral palsy.** The major problems with this condition are paralysis, muscle weakness, and incoordination. Some children with cerebral palsy also have mental retardation. A high portion, 70–80%, have

Children with Down syndrome often are not as active as normal newborns.

some combination of speech and hearing problems, visual problems, learning problems, or seizures.

FOCUS ON SOCIOLOGY

When the Baby Isn't Perfect

You know it's like my baby died twice. Once on the day she was born and then last week when she got pneumonia.

— Mother of a Down syndrome infant who died at the age of three months —

Birth of an infant with a disability can be a time of grief and loss for new parents. These parents have lost the baby they dreamed of and expected throughout the pregnancy. The perfect, fantasy baby died at birth, and they must now adjust to the reality of a less-than-perfect infant.

Parents of a child with a disability often go through an initial phase of grief, shock, and denial. Though faced with indisputable medical evidence of their child's condition, many parents attempt to minimize the seriousness of the disability (Jackson, 1985). One mother remembers thinking as the nurse checked her wristband before handing the baby over at discharge, "Please God, let her tell me I have the wrong baby."

As the parents develop a sense of awareness of the problem, they are often overcome by a sense of guilt and failure. They may feel they are being punished for past indiscretions or for wanting the baby to be of a particular sex instead of just a healthy baby. They may agonize over what they could have done to cause the disability. They may feel that they are biological failures for not being able to make a baby "right" (Jackson, 1985).

The sorrow and grief that accompany the birth of a child with a disability is chronic and pervasive (Kowalski, 1985). Parents of a child with a disability are faced with their loss every day. Each new crisis renews the feelings of intense sadness and guilt.

All this contributes to increased stress for the family at a time when the family is also often faced with added financial burdens. Families can feel lonely and isolated and cut off from former friends and acquaintances. The divorce rate in families with children with mental retardation is three times the national average (Kowalski, 1985). Investigators have found that families with children with developmental disabilities experience problems with adjustment, poor health, and family relations (Schilling, Gilchrist, & Schinke, 1984).

Research indicates that families with children with developmental disabilities need personal coping skills and an adequate social support network. Personal coping skills include problem-solving abilities, relaxation techniques, self-praise, and so forth. Adequate social support includes physical assistance, information, and emotional support. Supportive social networks are associated with increased personal well-being for the parents and enhanced development for the child (Dunst, Trivette, & Cross, 1986).

Psychological Dimension
Cognitive Development and Information Processing

True or False?
Psychosocial development is a continuous process from about the 12th week of intrauterine life through the preschool years.

There is a high correlation between intrauterine fetal activity and a newborn's level of activity.

Babies of stressed mothers have higher levels of fetal activity and exhibit more problems after birth than babies of nonstressed mothers.

Mothers with a fetus who becomes very active at bedtime should place a flashlight under the covers.

A fetus prefers Mozart over the Rolling Stones.

Fetuses of all cultures really like the music of Boy George.

A newborn responds to its mother's voice.

Most newborns do not respond to their father's voice.

Surprisingly enough, recent research indicates that all the preceding statements are true. And yes, researchers have found that individual fetuses, not yet born into any culture, really do prefer the music of Boy George (St. James, 1987). It was once thought that before birth the fetus could not experience sensation, emotion, learning, personality, or thought. New ways of studying fetal behavior, however, have revolutionized thinking about the prenatal period. Advancements in ultrasound, intrauterine photography, measurement of fetal movement and heart rate, and the survival of infants at earlier and earlier stages of development in neonatal intensive care nurseries have provided valuable insight into prenatal behavior. Information is gained through ultrasound; by recording changes in fetal movement, heart rate, and breathing motions; and by noting changes in swallowing and sucking behaviors in response to stimulation. Noting the responses of infants as early as 24 weeks gestation in an NICU has provided information on the behavior of the fetus during the last 16 weeks of intrauterine development.

Because of this new information, psychosocial development is considered to be a continuous process from the 12th week of intrauterine life through the preschool years. And enough research now exists to allow us to look at the unborn child's various responses and capabilities.

Cognitive Development and Information Processing

There is much evidence that a fetus responds to various types of stimulation. For instance, the fetus has been observed to react to invasive obstetrical procedures. During amniocentesis, doctors have noted the fetus to respond by drawing away from the needle, decreasing breathing motions, and exhibiting an erratic heart beat. Also, during intrauterine blood transfusions, doctors have noted signs of fetal distress, including vigorous body and breathing movements and increased fetal cortisol and B-endorphin levels, an apparent sign of hormonal stress response to needle invasion (Giannakoulopoulos et al., 1994).

The fetus also responds to light. Shining a bright light on the pregnant abdomen causes an increase in fetal heart rate. In fact, it is now believed that the fetus may see light through the abdomen as a rosy glow. Many mothers report that the fetus becomes more active at bedtime; this increase in activity could be due to the darkness in the womb when the mother turns out the light and goes to bed. Placing a flashlight under the covers could serve as a night-light for the fetus (Schuster & Ashburn, 1992).

The fetus seems to respond to touch. By the 17th week of gestation, almost all parts of the fetal body will react to being stroked by a hair. Many fetuses will kick back at a spot pressed on the abdomen. Mothers report that a fetus will kick at a book or an arm resting on the pregnant abdomen.

In addition, babies in the womb show a preference for certain tastes. Fetuses will increase their swallowing of amniotic fluid when drops of a sweet tasting substance are introduced into the womb, and they will stop swallowing when a bitter substance is introduced (Chamberlain, 1994).

Communication

Much anecdotal evidence suggests that a fetus responds to sound. When a mother laughs or coughs, fetal movement increases. Many mothers report that the fetus startles to loud noises such as a door slamming. Mothers at loud concerts or viewing violent movies report increased fetal activity during this time. Researchers have found that babies seem to become more active in response to loud rock music, whereas classical music has an apparently calming effect (St. James, 1987). Research has shown that at 26 weeks gestation, a fetus will respond to a sound vibration. After several repeats of the sound stimulus, the fetus will stop responding. This failure to respond after repeated stimulation is evidence of the ability of the fetus to habituate—a form of learning (Chamberlain, 1994).

Evidence of fetal learning ability also comes from the fact that a newborn responds to her mother's voice over another woman's and to music heard in the womb. Newborns also prefer to hear their native language (Mehler, cited in Chamberlain, 1994). The fetus hears these familiar sounds, learns to distinguish them from others, and prefers those sounds after birth. In fact, studies by DeCasper and Fifer (1980) found that newborns who had heard their mothers read *The Cat in the Hat* twice a day in utero, preferred that story over *The King, the Mice and the Cheese*, which they had not heard (see Focus on Research: How Do We Know Babies Like Boy George?).

Attitudes and Emotions

The mother's emotional state also seems to affect the fetus. Some evidence suggests that depressed or highly anxious women give birth to children with lower birth weights, higher levels of crying, and more neurological problems (Creno, 1994). Excessive crying and inconsolability of newborns has been linked to the mother's score on a depression scale during pregnancy (Zuckerman, cited in Chamberlain, 1994).

Chamberlain (1994) reports that "current research reveals prenatal pain, preferences, interests, learning, memory, aggressive behavior, fear, crying, smiling and affection. . . . Observation from conception to birth reveals a continuum of prenatal and postnatal behavior in which sensory, motor, emotional and cognitive features are constantly intertwined" (p. 19).

A small but growing number of parents and mental health professionals now believe that a child's emotional health begins at conception. These parents and professionals believe that prenatal meditation and communication with the fetus increase bonding and result in the child's better emotional well-being (Creno, 1994). Whether or not these beliefs hold up under closer examination, these ideas can be used in working with expectant parents.

New parents can be introduced to the capabilities of their fetus. The practitioner can encourage the parents to talk, play music, read, and sing to their unborn child. Parents who see that the baby will kick back at a spot pressed on the mother's abdomen can experience the fetus as a real, interactive being. These activities can help the parents relate to the baby and may increase their level of attachment to their child. Some researchers believe that this early attachment may help prevent later child abuse.

FOCUS ON RESEARCH

How Do We Know Babies Like Boy George?

Researchers have come up with some ingenious ways to determine what very young infants prefer. Here's how DeCasper and his associates found out that babies prefer sounds heard in the womb. In one of their studies, these researchers had pregnant women read a passage from *The Cat in the Hat* twice a day during the last six weeks of pregnancy. When the baby was born, the researchers set up an experiment using a pacifier hooked up to a tape recorder. By sucking faster or slower the baby could control what was heard through a set of earphones. Some of the babies heard *The Cat in the Hat* when they sucked fast and heard *The King, the Mice and the Cheese* when they sucked slowly. For some babies, this was reversed so that they heard *The Cat in the Hat* when they sucked slowly. The researchers found that the babies would change their rate of sucking to hear the familiar story. This was true even when a woman other than the baby's mother read the story. In similar studies, newborns would vary the rate of sucking to hear their mother's voice, their native language, and certain types of music.

Researchers have also devised a method using sucking to determine what an infant likes to look at. In these studies, an infant sucks on a nipple hooked up to a slide projector. Whenever the infant sucks, a new picture is projected for the baby to see. So if the infant wants to look at a particular picture, he or she quickly learns to stop sucking. The researchers can gauge an infant's interest in a picture from the length of time the infant pauses in sucking to look at that picture.

Social Cognition and Regulation

At birth, a newborn infant is sensitive and responsive. During the first hour after delivery, the baby is usually in a state of quiet alertness and spends most of this time quietly listening and looking around with eyes wide open. A newborn can focus on objects about 8 to 12 inches away—the distance from a mother's arms to her face. In fact, studies have shown that newborns prefer looking at contrasting, complex patterns with curves—especially faces. Newborns will orient toward a sound and they prefer high-pitched sounds, such as a female voice. They recognize their mother's voice and prefer it to that of another woman's; they do not, however, prefer their father's voice over another man's. Low-pitched sounds, such as a man's voice, may be more difficult to hear in utero than the higher-pitched mother's voice. Newborns can discriminate tastes and prefer sweet over salty, acidic, or bitter. A 6-day-old baby knows its mother's smell and can distinguish her breast pad from another woman's.

Infants interact with their environment and begin learning from birth. Newborns imitate facial expressions such as sticking out the tongue. They also move in response to speech in a sort of rhythmic dance. In studies, 1-day-old infants were trained to turn their heads to the right upon hearing a bell for a reward of sugar water. They learned to discriminate the bell from a buzzer and to not turn at the sound of the buzzer. They were then trained to turn for the buzzer and not the bell (Klaus & Klaus, 1985).

Newborn States

A newborn infant spends most of its time in one of six states. Ten percent of each 24 hours is spent in the quiet alert state, listening and looking around. This time is a good opportunity for making eye contact and interacting with an infant. The infant may also be in an active alert state—moving, looking around, and making small sounds—which occurs when the infant is beginning to get hungry or fussy. When really hungry or uncomfortable, the infant enters the crying state—not at all hard to recognize. After feeding and before falling asleep, the infant is in the drowsiness state—relaxed and moving a little with eyes half-closed and unfocused. Then the newborn has two periods of sleep, which alternate every 30 minutes. In quiet sleep, the baby is relaxed, moves little, and breathes regularly. During active sleep, the baby's

eyes move under the eyelids and may even flutter open; the baby moves around making faces and breathing rapidly. This state of sleep is also referred to as rapid eye movement (REM) and is comparable to adult REM sleep in which dreaming occurs, although it is not known whether infants dream.

An infant spends most of its time in sleep states, though sometimes it does not seem that way to tired new parents. Infants also use sleep to control their environment. When overstressed or stimulated, the infant copes by going to sleep.

Newborn Reflexes

Babies at birth are equipped with many reflexes and survival skills. When placed face down, infants will turn their head to the side or will turn away from something obstructing their breathing. If a scarf is placed over their face, infants will swipe at it with their hands and arms in an effort to remove the scarf. If you touch the side of a baby's face, the baby will turn toward the touch and open its mouth, displaying the *rooting reflex*. By touching the appropriate side of an infant's face, a breast-feeding mother can get the baby to turn toward her breast and open its mouth in preparation for feeding. Infants also have sucking and swallowing reflexes, which allow them to take in food and swallow it.

When pricked on the foot, babies will withdraw the limb to avoid the prick. When placed in an upright position with feet touching a hard surface, infants will place one foot in front of the other in a walking pattern. The crawling reflex is similar: When placed on their stomach, infants will push against something placed next to their feet. Babies also have a palmar grasp reflex, and will grasp hold of a finger or object placed against their palm. This reflex would allow a newborn to grasp the mother's hair for security when being carried. When pulled to a sitting position, babies will open their eyes the way a baby doll does. This is a good way to wake a sleepy baby for a feeding. When startled, babies exhibit the *Moro reflex*—arching their back, throwing out their arms, and grasping with their fingers. When stroked on the bottom of the foot, babies exhibit the *Babinski reflex*, fanning out their toes. An interesting reflex is the tonic neck or fencing reflex, which occurs in the following way. Babies' neck muscles are very strong to prevent the baby's head from falling, and these strong neck muscles are linked to the babies' arms. So when babies turn their head to the side, as happens when the babies lie on their back, they extend the arm and leg on that side while flexing the arm and leg on the opposite side. Try to imagine what purpose this reflex might serve. If you look closely at babies in this position, you will see that their hand is now directly in their line of sight. In fact, one of the first moving objects babies study closely is their hand. So regardless of the evolutionary significance of this reflex, by turning the head to the side and extending the arm, a baby at least has something interesting to look at.

The Brazelton Neonatal Assessment Scale

The Brazelton Neonatal Assessment Scale (BNAS) can be used with infants up to 1 month of age, assessing such items as the newborn's muscle tone and reflexes and how the infant responds to and controls stimulation (see Table 5.4). For instance, the practitioner pulls the baby to sit

TABLE 5.4   The Brazelton Neonatal Assessment Scale

Items Assessed	Examples	Scoring
Neurological Items		
Elicited reflexes and movements	Plantar grasp Hand grasp Ankle clonus Babinski Standing Automatic walking Crawling Tonic neck reflex Moro Rooting Sucking Passive movements of both legs and both arms	These neurological items are rated on a three-point scale for low, medium, and high intensity of response; asymmetry and absence are also noted.
Behavioral Items		
Specific behaviors observed or elicited	Focusing and following an object Reaction to an auditory stimulus Reaction to persons Reaction to a voice Reaction to a person's face and voice	These behavioral items are rated on a nine-point scale. The midpoint of the scale denotes the expected behavior of a 3-day-old normal baby.
General behaviors observed	Degree of alertness Motor maturity Cuddliness Consolability with intervention Peak of excitement Irritability Amount of startles Self-quieting activity Hand-to-mouth facility Number of smiles	

Source: Based on Brazelton, 1973.

and notes whether the baby holds the head steady or lets it fall back, or the practitioner also holds the baby upright on a table to elicit the walking reflex. In another test, the practitioner rings a bell to see whether the baby will turn toward the sound. Then the practitioner rings the bell to see how long it takes the baby to habituate and stop turning toward the bell. In all, the baby is evaluated on 37 behavioral items and 18 neurological reflexes.

The exam is especially helpful in looking at how babies use different responses and states of consciousness to control their reactions to environmental stimulation. A baby who has had too much stimulation may respond by averting his or her gaze, falling asleep, or crying. The practitioner can help the parents understand their infant by pointing out the baby's needs and preferences in interactions. The practitioner can frame the baby's response in a positive light: "Look at how she is telling you she has had enough; that's amazing." The parents can learn to look for signs that the baby is stressed or that the baby is ready for more interaction, and they can learn to vary the level of stimulation to make the interaction pleasant for both parents and baby.

Implications for Practice: Using the BNAS

Several studies have highlighted the benefits of using the Brazelton Neonatal Assessment Scale with new parents. After participating in the BNAS, mothers of high-risk infants show more responsiveness to their babies (Widmayer & Field, 1980). Other studies have shown that use of the assessment increases the parents' confidence in their caregiving abilities, increases the effectiveness of parent-child interactions, and increases the parents' understanding of their newborn's behavior (Myers, 1982). Fathers who participate in the assessment have shown more involvement in the care of their babies and more confidence in their parenting skills (Myers, 1982). Some studies tentatively conclude that use of the BNAS increases later cognitive development in infants (Tedder, 1991).

The assessment is inexpensive, and parent's seem to enjoy participating. Some hospitals use the BNAS as part of their discharge teaching for new parents. Use of the assessment is a good way to introduce new parents to the individuality of their baby and to help them appreciate their newborn as a unique human being with strengths and resources.

Psychological Hazards

In the past, hospital routine separated mother and infant at birth. During the hospital stay, they were reunited every 4 hours for a feeding. Then, in 1972, pediatricians John Kennell and Marshall Klaus published a study indicating that mothers who received extra contact with their infants beginning immediately after birth exhibited better mothering skills than did mothers who received the routine hospital mother-infant contact. These pediatricians concluded that human mothers experienced a "sensitive period" just after birth for bonding with their infants in the same way that other species, such as goats, cows, and sheep, do.

Over the years, many articles have been published on the importance of early mother-infant contact. These findings have been important in changing hospital birthing practices to allow more contact between mothers and babies. In most hospitals now, healthy, full-term infants are handed to their mothers at birth for skin-to-skin contact. Face-to-face eye contact and breast-feeding are encouraged immediately after delivery. Many clinicians involve new parents in newborn examinations such as the BNAS in an effort to enhance parent-child interactions by introducing the parents to their baby's characteristics. Nurses in the NICU are trained to encourage interactions with premature and sick infants and their families. Some believe that early bonding can reduce child abuse and neglect.

These ideas of early contact helped change the way women give birth, but have these ideas set up unrealistic expectations for new families? What implications does this bonding issue have for the woman who has an emergency c-section and is not conscious immediately after birth? Or for the woman who lives in a remote area of an Indian reservation and has no transportation to come for regular visits to her infant in the NICU? Or for the woman who adopts a much-wanted infant when the baby is several weeks or months old?

Some practitioners now believe that the importance of early bonding should not be overemphasized to the exclusion of other social and emotional factors that can affect the mother-infant relationship (Eyer, 1994). For example, some of our now-accepted bonding practices may be in conflict with childbearing practices and rituals of other cultures (Symanski, 1992). In some cultures, other female family members assume the major care of the newborn while the new mother recovers from giving birth. In some Native American and Hispanic cultures, women do not attempt breast-feeding until their milk comes in. And for cultural reasons, some mothers may not engage in extended eye contact with their newborns.

Research has failed to show that early contact has any long-term benefits for forming attachments (Goldberg, 1983; Grusec & Lytton, 1988). In fact, many researchers now believe that forming an attachment is an ongoing process and that the immediate postpartum period is not the only opportunity for establishing lifelong ties. Mothers of premature infants or adopted babies can and do love and care for their infants. And although evidence exists that early interventions such as introducing the baby to the mother by doing the BNAS enhances subsequent mother-infant interactions, this immediate postpartum period is not the only opportunity to enhance family relationships. Finally, early bonding is not the magical answer to child abuse and neglect. Bonding should not be overemphasized at the cost of dealing with the complex social and emotional problems of the family, such as poverty and social isolation (Eyer, 1994, p. 90).

The Baby's Experience of Birth

The use of medications has made labor and delivery less painful for the mother, but to what extent have obstetrical interventions made the process more painful for the baby? Potentially painful procedures for the infant include internal fetal monitoring, in which an electrode is placed under the baby's scalp, and fetal blood scalp sampling, in which blood is taken from the baby's head during delivery. Babies born by forcep delivery often have forcep marks on their faces for several hours after birth. Babies delivered vaginally often have elongated heads and facial bruising and swelling caused by the birth process. Is being squeezed through a small opening into a bright, cold world traumatic for the baby? What effect, if any, does birth trauma have on later development?

In 1929, Otto Rank described birth as a traumatic event that affected an individual's ability to cope with stress later in life. In particular, he believed that a long, complicated labor led to an anxious and neurotic adult. In 1975, Frederick LeBoyer, a French obstetrician, wrote a book called *Birth Without Violence*, in which he advocated reducing the trauma of birth. At that time, infants were routinely delivered in brightly lit, cold operating rooms. After birth, the baby was struck to stimulate breathing and was often separated from the mother for several hours. LeBoyer suggested that the newborn receive gentle handling for the first 15 to 30 minutes of life. In the LeBoyer method, the infant is born in a quiet, warm, dimly lit setting. The physician places the newborn on the mother's abdomen and waits until the cord stops pulsing before cutting it. Shortly after birth, the baby is given a warm bath to simulate the amniotic fluid of the uterine environment.

The benefits of a gentle birth, however, are questionable. It is difficult to regulate the temperature of the bath, and it is hard for the physician and nurses to see in a dimly lit room. In addition, there is no evidence that these gentle techniques result in a happier, more well-adjusted child. One study looked at 385 neonates at a hospital in Quebec and found no evidence that gentle birth techniques or other perinatal circumstances, such as use of medication or delivery by c-section, had any effect on infant temperament in the first year of life (Maziade, 1987).

Despite the controversy over the benefits of gentle birth, many hospitals and physicians have adopted some of these techniques for routine births. As was previously described, in many hospitals, babies are born in homelike birthing rooms. Physicians no longer strike the infant to start breathing, and immediately after delivery, the baby is placed on the mother's abdomen. The mother can ask for delay in silver nitrate or erythromycin drops in the baby's eyes to facilitate eye contact in the minutes following birth. The baby is often weighed and examined in a warm bed with the mother and father watching. Hospital procedures now encourage early contact between the new parents and the baby. But most hospitals do not give the baby a bath until several hours after birth.

Implications for Practice: The Birth Experience and Development

Actually, the birth process may be beneficial to the baby. The contractions of labor help clear the lungs of mucous. Babies who are born by cesarean section have more respiratory difficulties than do babies born vaginally. One study suggests that the increase in catecholamines—presumably caused by the stress of birth—enhances the neonate's chance of survival (Lagercrantz, 1986). However, some therapists believe that prenatal and birth trauma have a profound effect on psychological development. Some research has suggested that a relationship exists between near-death experiences at birth and later suicide, and between barbiturate and opiate use in labor and later drug addiction (Jacobson, 1987; Roedding, 1991). Although these notions are controversial, it may be helpful to note the method of delivery and occurrence of any birth trauma when making an assessment.

The Neonatal Intensive Care Unit Experience

What are the long-term developmental consequences of spending the first three months of life in an NICU? Do the stresses of painful procedures, separation from parents, and overstimulation have an effect on later personality development? At this point, there are no clear answers to these questions.

Some studies have shown that infants who spent time in special-care nurseries were at higher risk for child abuse (Lynch, Roberts, & Gordon, 1976). This increase in risk was attributed to the fact that the infant and parents were separated and did not form an attachment. Although Klaus and Kennel (1976) emphasized the importance of early contact for bonding in the postpartum period, other studies have failed to establish the existence of this "sensitive period." Numerous studies have shown the importance of touch for the preterm infant, however (Harrison, Leeper, & Yoon, 1991; Harrison & Woods, 1991). Parental touch results in increased weight gain, a better-developed nervous system, and more rapid development. Other studies have indicated that the high levels of stress and stimulation in the NICU affect the infant's blood oxygen level and contribute to chronic lung disease. The increased level of stimulation to the premature infant brain may also affect early brain development (Als et al., 1994).

Implications for Practice: Changes in NICU Practices

For these reasons, NICUs now allow more parent-infant interaction. NICU staff are encouraged to promote parental involvement in the baby's care. An innovative concept in the care of premature infants is Kangaroo Care. Instead of spending most of the time in an isolette, the baby lies in skin-to-skin contact with the mother's or father's chest while still receiving NICU care. Proponents of Kangaroo Care claim that this procedure improves the baby's temperature regulation, heart rate, breathing patterns, weight gain and growth, behavioral states, emotional states, and interactions with parents (Ludington-Hoe & Golant, 1993).

A concept for reducing the high levels of stress and stimulation in preterm infant care is individualized developmental care (Als et al., 1994). Nurses are specially trained to recognize signs of stress (changes in skin color, pauses in breathing, finger splaying, arching, averting gaze) in premature babies and to help the infant with self-calming techniques. For instance, babies are placed in a flexed position for sleep to promote restfulness, and they are comforted before and after taxing or painful procedures. Babies are allowed to sleep, wake, and feed on their own individual schedules. The unit is kept relatively dark and quiet. Special equipment such as a hammock, soft nipple on a terry-cloth strip, and a terry-cloth bunting is also used to help soothe the infant. These researchers found that these measures resulted in calmer infants with better medical and developmental outcomes than did routine care.

Social Dimension
Families, Groups, Support Systems, and Contexts

Each child is born into a family environment. What is the impact of that environment on development? What is necessary for optimal development? Research by Bradley (1987) indicates that stimulation and support are the most important requirements in the home. New babies need parents who respond to them and talk to them. They need a structured, safe home with stimulating play and interesting toys. And new babies especially need a small group of adults who are warm and nurturing and eager to meet the infants' needs. In the next chapter, we will further explore infants and families.

Prenatal Intervention Programs: Every Birth a Healthy One

Adequate prenatal care is vital in ensuring the best pregnancy outcome. Yet in many poor communities access to health care is still a problem (Brooks-Gunn, Mc-Cormick, Heagarty, 1988). Barriers to health care in poor neighborhoods include the large number of pregnant adolescents, the high number of non-English-speaking clients, and the prevalence of low literacy skills. In addition, cultural ideas about health care practices may be hard to overcome, so that even when health care is available, pregnant women may not understand the need for early and regular prenatal care.

How then do we encourage pregnant women to seek care? One answer is programs that focus on recruiting pregnant women into prenatal care by using indigenous lay workers. The idea behind such programs is that community members can have more influence on the health practices of their neighbors than can a health care professional. An example of this type of prenatal outreach program is Woman to Woman in Tucson, Arizona. This program uses trained lay health care workers in disadvantaged neighborhoods to locate and educate expectant mothers. These lay workers, or promotoras, are volunteers who receive 40 hours of training. Following the formal training period, the promotoras attend regular group meetings for ongoing training, case review, and support. Outreach workers recruit clients in the community by distributing flyers, putting up posters, and setting up booths at health fairs and other neighborhood events. After a woman is enrolled in the program, other workers visit her in her home to offer emotional support, help in getting to medical and agency appointments, prenatal education and information, help with community resources, and services and information on problem-solving skills. Ideally, outreach workers in these programs can overcome some of the barriers to prenatal care in poor communities and help get better care for their neighbors.

Postpartum Early Intervention Programs

Many new families may be facing less-than-ideal conditions, and few programs exist to help them. After an uncomplicated vaginal birth, if the mother isn't bleeding and the baby is stable, both are discharged from the hospital to home after a 48-hour stay, whether or not they actually have a home. These new families can be dealing with problems such as homelessness, domestic violence, stress, poverty, and unemployment. A two-day hospital stay does not allow much time to deal with these problems, and unfortunately, taking a baby home to

such an environment increases the risk of abuse and neglect (Belsky, Gilstrap, & Rovine, 1984).

Some researchers believe that early intervention programs that include home visitation can greatly benefit new families at risk for abuse and neglect. Evidence suggests that these programs improve poor children's cognitive development and school performance and reduce the incidence of delinquent behavior and conduct disorder (Fong-ruey & Brooks-Gunn, 1994; Zigler, Taussig, & Black, 1992). Seitz and colleagues (1985) found that ten years after conducting a comprehensive early intervention program using home visitation, lasting positive outcomes could be observed in parental socioeconomic status, childrens' behavior and social adjustment, and parent-child relationship in comparison with a control group.

An example of a program with home visitation is Healthy Families Arizona (LeCroy, Ashford, Krysik, & Milligan, 1996). Healthy Start/Healthy Families began as a three-year demonstration project in Hawaii in 1985 with the primary goal of supporting the family's optimal functioning. Results from the Hawaii program showed that out of the 241 intervention families, none had reports of child abuse or neglect.

The Arizona program screens families at the time of the birth of an infant for risk factors that can cause high stress levels. Families at risk for abuse and neglect are then visited weekly by paraprofessional workers. The worker attempts to reduce the family stress level by providing support, assisting parents to identify needs and solve problems, and coordinating with community services appropriate to the family's needs. Practical assistance is provided for obtaining food, housing, diapers, utilities, child care, or transportation.

The workers also seek to strengthen family functioning. They provide information and activities designed to improve the parent-child relationship and enhance parents' understanding of child development and appropriate discipline techniques. The worker encourages parents to provide the child with adequate nurturance and stimulation and helps parents find appropriate toys and other play materials.

The family support worker assists parents in developing social supports, managing stress and anger, and developing skills to avoid and resolve crises. The worker maintains contact with the family until the target child is 5 years old and ready to attend school.

Multicultural and Gender Considerations

Up to this point, we have looked thoroughly at the biological birth of the infant. But many cultures include another aspect of birth—the social birth of the child as a new member of the community. In fact, many cultural and ethnic groups have specific rites or ceremonies that welcome the child into the group. For instance, in many cultures during a special ceremony, someone other than the parents receives the child into the society and expresses the desire to help raise the child. In some cultures, godparents accept responsibility for the child. During a baptismal ceremony, an entire church congregation welcomes the child and vows to oversee the teaching and nurturing of the infant.

In some cultures, circumcision is used as a birth ceremony. Removal of the foreskin of the penis is a symbolic act that establishes the child as a member of a particular culture or religion.

Many cultures have naming ceremonies to welcome the child into the community. In some Native American naming ceremonies, the new infant is held up to the rising sun as described in this passage from Byrd Baylor:

> And high on a mesa edge in Arizona they were holding a baby toward the sun. They were speaking the child's new name so the sun would hear and know that child. It had to be sunrise. And it had to be that first sudden moment. That's when all the power of life is in the sky.

Infant Mortality: The African American–White Disparity

Although medical advances have reduced the overall infant mortality rate in the United States, the current rate is still higher than that in many other developed nations. This disparity is due in part to the powerful racial disparities that exist in U.S. infant mortality rates. The infant mortality rate for white infants is 6.9 per 1000, whereas the rate for African American infants is over twice as high, at 16.5 per 1000. What factors are causing this alarming disparity?

For white infants, the leading cause of death is congenital anomalies, whereas for African American infants, it is low birth weight. Although many consider poverty and lack of prenatal care to be contributing factors for low birth weight, after controlling for sociodemographic factors, the proportion of low-birth-weight babies is still twice as high for African Americans as for whites (Eberstadt, 1991).

Interestingly, several studies have found that the Hispanic infant mortality rate is as low as or, in some instances, lower than Caucasian infant mortality, even though Hispanics have a lower socioecomonic status and encounter language and cultural barriers to prenatal care (Rogers, 1989). So even though Hispanic women have to deal with poverty and lack of prenatal care, their infant mortality rate is significantly lower than that of African American women. Why?

It has been suggested that Hispanic women have favorable birth-weight distributions in part because of their low rates of smoking and drinking and their strong familial, cultural, and social ties (Rogers, 1989). In other words, Hispanic women have a strong social support network, which seems to mediate the effects of poverty and lack of prenatal care (Mason, 1991). If socioeconomic factors and lack of prenatal care fail to account for the infant mortality disparity, what then is the cause?

Over 90% of the excess risk of low birth weight among African American infants is related to the mothers' increased risk for high blood pressure, placental problems, or premature labor (Davidson, 1992). These factors can all be seen as related to maternal health and behavioral practices that can be affected by stress. African American women are segregated into black neighborhoods, lack social support, and experience increased problems due to their ethnicity. All these factors increase the pregnant woman's level of environmental stress, and this increased stress can lead to poor health habits, such as abusing substances and failing to obtain adequate health care. These poor health habits, in turn, affect pregnancy outcome.

In conclusion, then, to reduce the infant mortality of African American infants, the United States may need to address more social than medical problems. This implies taking measures to increase the social support and decrease the environmental stress in an African American woman's life.

Cultural Differences of Newborns

How much of the cultural difference in temperament is learned and how much is inherited? Daniel Freedman tested infants from different cultures on their "defense reaction," measured by

The babies' reaction to a cloth pressed over their noses
How quickly the babies stopped crying when picked up
How long it took the babies to adapt to a light shown in their eyes
How they reacted to a sudden loss of support of the head and neck

In response to the cloth pressed over their noses, the white and African American babies fought the cloth by turning away and swiping at the cloth with their hands. In contrast, the average Chinese baby did not try to remove the cloth, but lay on its back and breathed through its mouth. Crying Chinese babies stopped crying immediately upon being picked up, whereas white babies cried for longer periods. In response to the light shown in their eyes, white babies took longer to adapt than Chinese babies. In response to having head and neck support withdrawn, white babies became agitated and began crying, whereas Navajo babies remained calm and unconcerned.

This researcher concluded that what we consider cultural conditioning may in fact have a biological basis. Although we have assumed that Asian and Native American mothers conditioned their children to be quiet and compliant, these children may actually have just been born that way.

Source: Adapted from St. James, 1987.

Circumcision

Circumcision of newborn males is a controversial issue. For years, removing the foreskin of the penis shortly after birth was standard procedure in the United States. Circumcision was done for religious reasons, for hygienic purposes, and because many parents wanted their baby boy to resemble his father and most of the other men in the United States. Other countries, though, had much lower circumcision rates. In 1975, the American Academy of Pediatrics decided to no longer endorse circumcision of newborns. Their policy stated that there was no proven medical rationale for newborn circumcision.

Many began to argue against routine circumcision. Critics brought up the possible hazards of strapping a newborn baby boy down and removing a part of his anatomy while using no anesthesia. These critics also pointed out the possible complications of circumcision, including infection and bleeding. Some insurance plans began to refuse to pay for routine circumcision at birth. And the rate of circumcision of newborns began to decline.

However, the American Academy of Pediatrics has lately revised its policy on newborn circumcision, stating that the procedure does have some benefits. Uncircumcised males are at higher risk for urinary-tract infections, sexually transmitted diseases, and inflammation and infection of the penis (Robson & Leung, 1992). Circumcision reduces these risks and therefore has some preventative health benefits.

There is still the question of anesthesia, though. Physicians used to believe that newborns did not feel pain and that, even if they did, anesthesia carried too much risk for a newborn. Babies do feel pain, and the procedure is painful. Some physicians are now recommending the use of a local anesthetic (Fontaine & Toffler, 1991), oral pain medications, or a pacifier for the procedure (Schoen & Fischell, 1991).

Social Hazards

In this chapter, we have focused mainly on the biological risk factors that can affect prenatal and perinatal development: gestational age, prenatal environment, genetic anomalies, and so on. Throughout the discussion, though, you may have noticed a strong undercurrent of associated risk—the social factors that can have a negative impact on developmental outcomes. Social risk factors include poverty, unemployment, lack of maternal education, parental mental illness, large family, absent father, adverse neighborhood, economic recession, and inadequate health care systems (Fong-ruey & Brooks-Gunn, 1994). Many of these risk factors have a common denominator—that of poverty.

Children born into poverty have a higher risk of health and developmental problems (Kliegman, 1992). Poverty is a factor in lack of prenatal care, low birth weight, prematurity, and poor maternal health habits. In particular, low income is strongly associated with child maltreatment (Jones & McCurdy, 1992), and children who are abused and neglected have a higher risk for developmental problems (Goldson, 1991). Of course, this does not mean that poor families love their children any less than affluent families do. The high levels of environmental stress associated with poverty inhibit good parenting by preventing parents from providing a stimulating and nurturing environment (Bradley et al., 1994). In later chapters, we will further explore the effects of poverty on development.

Drug-Exposed Infants

Newborns who were prenatally exposed to drugs have a very low sensory threshold due to their fragile and disorganized nervous systems. These infants have trouble actively engaging in their environments. They very rarely reach and maintain a quiet and alert state. In response to stimulation, these infants spend a lot of time either sleeping or crying uncontrollably. Interactions with these infants can be difficult as they are most easily overwhelmed by the sight of a human face (Griffith, 1988).

The mother of the drug-exposed infant is or has recently been a drug user. Drug-addicted women often come from dysfunctional homes, and, as a result, the mother may have very low self-esteem and an exaggerated need for affection. She may have become pregnant to have someone—the baby—who will love her unconditionally (Griffith, 1988).

So what happens when this mother tries to interact with this baby? The mother approaches the baby expecting love and acceptance or at least a smile, and the baby, upon seeing a human face, begins to cry uncontrollably. The mother now feels rejected and inadequate, and the baby is at risk for abuse and neglect. The mother may stop trying to interact with the infant and let him sleep all the time, or she may become angry when her attempts to soothe him fail to stop his constant crying.

Implications for Practice:
Long-Term Effects of Prenatal Drug Use

There has been little research to verify the long-term effects of cocaine and other illegal substances on infants. Griffith (1992) describes the major risk factors for drug-exposed infants as being related to the fact that chronic substance-abusing women receive inadequate prenatal care and have poor prenatal nutrition. Postnatally, the major risk to the infant is having parents who continue to abuse drugs. Chronic drug abuse is also associated with an increased incidence of child abuse or neglect. Drug-abusing parents may fail to provide the child with adequate nutrition, appropriate medical care, or a stimulating learning environment.

Children who are removed from the home do not necessarily fare any better. These children may be shifted between foster homes for the first several years of life and may be at increased risk for failure to thrive and other attachment problems.

Mothers of drug-exposed infants can be taught how to interact with their babies. Swaddling, use of pacifiers, vertical rocking, and control of intensity of stimulation can help these babies reach a quiet, alert state (Griffith, 1988). Although the effects of prenatal drug exposure are still unclear, some research (Griffith, 1992; Newman & Buka, 1991) suggests that with early recognition, early intervention, and the benefits of a stable home environment, these children can achieve normal development.

Fetal Alcohol Syndrome

Children with FAS are at high risk for physical and sexual abuse, abandonment, and neglect. These children are hard to care for, even for nonalcoholic parents. FAS babies may be hyperactive, irritable, and may need to be fed hourly. An alcoholic home is often characterized by few economic resources and little emotional support.

However, only a small percent of FAS children remain in their own homes. A study of FAS individuals revealed that by the age of 6, 64% of FAS children were no longer with their biological mother. In this study, many of the mothers of FAS children had died from alcohol-related problems, and many FAS children were in the foster care system, where they experienced multiple home situations (Streissguth, LaDue, & Randels, 1988). For these babies, although early intervention can help with development, no amount of social services can reverse the devastating effects of prenatal alcohol abuse.

Implications for Practice: Preventing FAS

Prevention of fetal alcohol syndrome involves teaching pregnant women about nutrition and the harmful effects of drinking during pregnancy. Practitioners should screen for alcohol problems at the first prenatal visit and work with women through support groups and education classes to promote healthy pregnancy outcomes.

A manual from the U.S. Department of Health and Human Services states, "The birth of a child with FAS can be a pivotal point in a family's decision to seek alcoholism treatment" (Streissguth, LaDue, & Randels, 1988, p. 46). The authors note that extensive support services are needed for these families to help them deal with the tasks of overcoming alcoholism and parenting a child with a disability.

FOCUS ON SOCIOLOGY

Domestic Violence

Teri arrived in Labor and Delivery in premature labor brought on by cocaine use. Teri is 33 weeks pregnant and has had no prenatal care. Upon further questioning by the social worker, Teri disclosed that although she has been abusing cocaine during the pregnancy, her contractions started shortly after her husband shoved her against the refrigerator. She claims that he often becomes violent after drinking and sometimes pushes or shoves her. Teri and her husband live in the desert in a pop-up trailer with no heat, no running water, and no indoor toilet. They have no car. Teri's husband makes it to his five-dollar-an-hour job during the week and often helps at night with the kids. But after work on Fridays, he starts drinking and, by the end of the weekend, usually ends up pushing Teri around some. Teri copes by using cocaine.

Domestic violence is a risk factor for a pregnant woman and her fetus. For many women, battering starts or becomes worse during pregnancy. Studies indicate that up to one in four women are physically abused at some point during gestation. Physical abuse during pregnancy increases the risk of miscarriage, preterm labor, and low birth weight. Because of social isolation, battered women have less access to prenatal care (Chambliss, 1994). In addition, because of the increased stress experienced in a violent relationship, battered women have a high incidence of poor health habits, such as cigarette use and drug and alcohol abuse, all of which can have adverse effects on a developing fetus (Newberger et al., 1992).

As illustrated in the above example, women do not usually volunteer information about abuse; they need to be asked. During the interview, the woman should be separated from her male partner. A woman is more likely to disclose abuse to another woman offering sympathy, help, and support. With a hesitant client, the interviewer should use open-ended questions such as, "When I see injuries like yours, often it is because someone has done it on purpose. I'm wondering if that's what happened to you."

The home situation also needs to be assessed. What is the level of violence? Are there any weapons in the home? Is the woman afraid of her partner? Is she afraid for her children? What previous experiences has she had with the police and courts?

The woman needs to develop a safety plan. Whom can she call? Where can she go? Can she put some money away? The battered woman needs information about shelters and emergency housing and referrals to legal and medical care and to counseling and support groups. Most of all, a battered woman needs to be reassured that no one deserves to be hurt by someone they love.

Implications for Practice: Prenatal Considerations

In this chapter, we attempted to look closely at those pre-natal and perinatal factors that can affect lifelong devel-opment of an individual. Complications of pregnancy and birth, hazards in the prenatal environment, mater-nal habits, prematurity, genetic abnormalities, and social influences are all risk factors for developmental prob-lems. An adequate assessment of prenatal and perinatal risk factors may sometimes provide a clue to possible contributions to an individual's problem.

Hopefully you have begun to see the importance of prevention. Early prenatal care, identification and treat-ment of substance abuse, parent education, promotion of good health practices, and adequate social support can go a long way in optimizing development and deal-ing with problems before they start.

For high-risk infants and families, early intervention programs that are "intensive, comprehensive, well inte-grated into other community services and flexible in re-sponding to a family's unique needs produce the most consistent and impressive outcomes" (Daro, 1991).

With all of its hazards and complications and all that can possibly go wrong, the birth of an infant truly is a miracle.

BOX 5.1

Prenatal Information to Obtain in Making an Assessment

Gestation
Duration of pregnancy—was baby full term or premature
History of maternal substance abuse
Medications taken by mother during pregnancy
Mother's nutritional status
Maternal illness during pregnancy
Maternal exposure to radiation, toxic wastes
Other maternal factors during pregnancy: fever, acci-dents, diabetes, toxemia, threatened abortion (vagi-nal bleeding), previous stillbirths

Birth
Presentation of infant—was baby breech or normal
Type of delivery—cesarean or vaginal
Birth weight
Multiple or single birth
Complications—prolonged labor, fetal anoxia (fetal dis-tress)

Newborn
Problems with newborn—hyperbilirubinemia (jaun-dice), hypoglycemia (low blood sugar), cerebral he-morrhage, infections
Duration of hospitalization (more than 24 hours or less)

Source: Adapted from Willis & Holden, 1990.

APPLYING THE FRAMEWORK

The Family of a Premature Infant

Jessica and Travis[1] asked to see the hospital social worker to discuss their concerns for their 2-week-old infant who was in the hospital NICU. The baby had been born nine weeks premature. The couple was displaying some fear and apprehension in interacting with their baby during his stay in the NICU. They were apprehensive about their ability to parent their infant. They were worried about how they would ever be able to care for the baby on their own at home. They were also concerned about future developmental problems for their child.

Developmental History

Travis and Jessica had been attempting to have a baby for several years. Two previous pregnancies had ended in miscarriage. Fifteen months after her last miscarriage, Jessica became pregnant for the third time. She did not use alcohol or drugs during the pregnancy, but she did continue to smoke. After learning she was pregnant, though, she had managed to cut down to four or five cigarettes per day. Preterm labor began for Jessica in week 26 of her pregnancy, and she was placed on bed rest and medications at home to stop her labor. Several weeks later her cervix started to dilate, and she was hospitalized in the high-risk obstetrics unit for the duration of the pregnancy. Eric was born at 31 weeks gestation and weighed 1134 grams (2 lb. 8 oz.). The Apgar scores were 6 at one minute and 7 at five minutes. Immediately after birth, Eric began to experience respiratory distress. After a brief viewing by his parents, he was transferred to the neonatal intensive care unit.

Biophysical Considerations

Upon admission to NICU, Eric was placed under an oxygen hood. He required cardiac and respiratory monitoring. Because he was too small to maintain his body temperature, he was placed in an incubator. He required intravenous lines for maintaining fluids and administer-

ing medications. Eric's very low birth weight and gestational age placed him at potential risk for continued respiratory difficulty, anemia, infection, intraventricular hemorrhage, jaundice, and retinopathy of prematurity.

Fortunately, Eric's condition improved quickly. His lungs were mature enough that his need for supplemental oxygen ended when he was removed from the oxygen hood three days after birth. He then developed jaundice (hyperbilirubinemia), but that was successfully treated with phototherapy (being placed under lights). Because he was born before his sucking reflex was well established, he required oral gavage feedings. Eight days after birth, he was transferred to the area of the NICU for "growing preemies," where he would remain until he had developed coordination to nipple- or breast-feed and had gained enough weight for discharge home.

Psychological Considerations

Jessica and Travis reported that upon entering the NICU for the first time, they found themselves totally unprepared for the sight of their baby. Alongside the machines and other technology, he appeared weak and vulnerable. Travis described his thoughts on that day: "We had lost control of the situation, and felt completely intimidated. There were machines everywhere and he just looked so small." Travis and Jessica began to worry about possible complications for their baby. As with many families when faced with high-risk perinatal situations, Jessica and Travis became focused on possible medical outcomes instead of on their new baby.

Worry and uncertainty over their child's fate began to interfere with parental attachment and bonding. Jessica and Travis found it difficult to bond with a baby they feared might die or be severely handicapped. Jessica (continued)

[1]The cases in this book are loosely based on several actual cases. Names and other identifying details included in the cases in this book are fictitious.

The Family of a Premature Infant

(continued) described her bonding process with Eric as a roller-coaster ride. "I loved him, but it felt like a risk."

Jessica felt she did not know her infant—that she had lost control of the baby to the NICU staff. She felt inadequate and incompetent in her ability to care for her very ill child. Jessica remembered those early moments following Eric's birth. "He was taken away so quickly, and we had no idea where they were taking him. I looked at Travis and started crying. It wasn't what we expected." Just minutes after finally becoming a new mother, Jessica had relinquished her role of primary caregiver to the nurses and medical staff. This feeling was further reinforced when Jessica attempted to hold her baby. He slept most of the time, and when he was awake he was irritable. When Jessica held him, he would cry, put up his hands, and turn away from her. Jessica felt that the baby was rejecting her.

Social Considerations

Family Situation

Jessica and Travis were in their mid-twenties and had been married to each other for six years. Travis worked as a manager in a supermarket. Jessica worked as a medical transcriptionist in a hospital. They had recently purchased their first home. Jessica had planned to take three months off from work to care for her new baby, but because she was on bed rest for five weeks before the birth and had been visiting her baby in NICU daily since his birth, Jessica had already used up half of her maternity leave. Jessica was afraid of losing her job, but she did not see how she could return to work full-time with such a small baby to care for. On the other hand, the couple did not see how they could make their mortgage payments on just Travis's salary. They had little savings. There was a possibility that Jessica could work part-time and perhaps do some transcription at home.

Jessica's parents lived in town, and she reported having a warm and close relationship with them. Her mother had expressed a desire to help with the baby's care, but because of back problems, her participation would be limited. But her mother stated she might be able to come and watch the baby while Jessica was working at home.

Groups, Social Supports, and Contexts

Travis and Jessica attended a Methodist church in their neighborhood. They had many church friends and neighbors who had offered support and prepared meals for them throughout the past six weeks. Jessica's friends from work had also helped out by throwing a baby shower a few days after the baby's birth and providing her with needed baby items.

The community in which the couple lived provided an early intervention program for low-birth-weight babies. The program offered weekly in-home visits as well as regular developmental follow-up in a clinic.

Summary and Impressions

From the assessment, this family had the following problems:

1. Low-birth-weight infant due to prematurity
2. Medical complications of hyperbilirubinemia and respiratory distress with need for supplemental oxygen
3. Problems with parent-infant interactions
4. Unknown long-term prognosis for the infant
5. Family financial problems

Looking at the couple's strengths and resources showed that they had a stable home life with an adequate environment for a low-birth-weight baby. They had family and friends who were supportive and caring. The parents were interested in and willing to be involved in learning to care for and interact with their infant. The hospital staff was very supportive of the new parents and willing to be involved in enhancing positive parent-infant interactions. The community provided an early intervention program for parents of low-birth-weight infants.

The Family of a Premature Infant

After meeting with the social worker, Jessica spent time every day with Eric, initially just observing others caring for him. His primary nurse explained his capacity for interaction, "time out" signals, proper handling, and positioning. The nurse showed Jessica how to swaddle the baby and hold him quietly for a feeding. She taught Jessica to wait until the baby began to look around searchingly before trying to make eye contact and talk to him. The nurse explained that when Eric held up his hand and spread his fingers, he was signaling that he was tired and needed some time alone. Given information and support from the nurses and from the social worker, Jessica was able to interact positively with her infant.

As time went by, both parents learned about and participated in Eric's care. Their involvement helped establish and enhance their bond to the baby. They kept a calendar of events and took photos of Eric's days in the NICU—the transition from incubator to open crib, first tub bath, first attempts at feeding. Thus they were able to share their tiny son's struggles and accomplishments with friends and family.

After five weeks in the hospital, Eric weighed 1843 grams (4 lb. 1 oz.), was breastfeeding well, and was ready to go home. Jessica and Travis were ready to accept the responsibility for him at home, but the excitement of discharge was still tempered with apprehension about the transition. The long-term effects of the baby's prematurity were still unknown. And though they were now independent in their caring for Eric, they still felt "dependent on the NICU staff for backup." They admitted to still feeling a bit incompetent and unsure of their ability to adequately care for their small son. Travis recalls that "leaving the hospital was almost as stressful as being there, but we were glad to be taking our baby home. Finally!"

Source: Written by Cathy Jaworski, R.N.

Chapter Summary

Developmental Themes

During pregnancy, the couple goes through several stages in preparation for the baby's birth. At first, the couple must accept the reality of the pregnancy. As pregnancy progresses, the woman integrates the fetus as part of herself. She turns inward and begins to resolve her own identity crisis. Toward the end of pregnancy, the woman begins to prepare for the birth and to see the fetus as a separate being. At birth, the couple must reconcile the real baby with the fantasy baby.

Biophysical Dimension

Biophysical Growth and Development

Conception occurs with the union of sperm and egg in the fallopian tube. From conception to implantation (about two weeks), the fertilized egg is known as a zygote. From two to eight weeks, it is an embryo. During the period of the embryo, most major organs and features are formed. At eight weeks, the embryo becomes a fetus. From this time until birth, the fetus grows and puts on weight. The birth process is divided into three stages. The first stage lasts 12–14 hours and ends with the cervix (opening to the womb) fully dilated (opened) and the woman ready to push the baby down the birth canal. The second stage is the actual birth and can last from minutes to three hours. The third stage is the delivery of the placenta, or afterbirth. Many births involve some form of pain-relieving medication, but long-term effects of these medications are still unknown. A normal newborn weighs between 5 1/2 and 9 1/2 pounds. Full-term pregnancy lasts 38–41 weeks. The Apgar score is an objective exam of the newborn's adjustment to life.

Biophysical Hazards

Complications of pregnancy may affect development. These complications may include persistent vomiting, vaginal bleeding, toxemia or preeclampsia, and intrauterine growth retardation (IUGR). Several environmental factors may affect pregnancy outcome, including maternal age (mothers under 18 or over 35), multiple births, poor nutrition, illness, drug use, alcohol use, cigarette use, and stress. Alcohol use during pregnancy may cause the child to suffer from fetal alcohol syndrome (FAS), the leading known preventable cause of mental retardation in the Western world. Several tests screen for fetal problems, including ultrasound, alpha-fetoprotein blood screening, amniocentesis, and chorionic villus sample (CVS).

Birth complications may also affect later development. Such complications include anoxia, meconium aspiration, malpresentation, and a prolonged labor. Birth complications can necessitate birth by cesarean section, or birth through an abdominal incision. A major risk factor for newborns is low birth weight, either from intrauterine growth retardation (prenatal deprivation) or prematurity (birth before 38 weeks). Premature babies face many problems, such as breathing problems, feeding problems, and jaundice. Birth defects that may affect development include heart defects, neural tube defects, chromosomal abnormalities, phenylketonuria, and cerebral palsy.

Psychological Dimension

Cognitive Development and Information Processing

Research indicates that the fetus responds to stimulation. The fetus can see, hear, taste, and respond to touch.

Communication

Research by DeCasper found that newborns recognize their mother's voice, indicating fetal learning in utero.

Attitudes and Emotions

Research suggests that the mother's emotional state affects the fetus. Some professionals now believe that a child's emotional health begins at conception and that prenatal experiences affect emotional development.

Social Cognition and Regulation

Newborns are interacting with and responding to their environment. They recognize their mother's voice and her smell. They imitate facial expressions, and they can learn. Newborns have several states, ranging from quiet alertness to fussiness to sleep. Babies are also equipped with reflexes and survival skills. The Brazelton Neonatal Assessment Scale measures a baby's responses to stimuli and ability to regulate those responses.

Psychological Hazards

In the past, many believed there was a sensitive period for maternal-infant bonding in the first few hours after birth. This belief led to changes in hospital practices. However, many now feel that the first few hours after birth are not so critical and that bonding is an ongoing process. Gentle birthing procedures were developed by LeBoyer to make the birth process less traumatizing for the baby, but the benefits of gentle birth are questionable. The long-term effects of spending the first weeks or months of life in a neonatal intensive care unit are still unknown, but many NICUs now encourage parent-infant interaction and developmental care procedures.

Social Dimension

Families, Groups, Support Systems, and Contexts

Babies need adequate stimulation and loving, caring adults for optimal development. Prenatal intervention programs attempt to get women into prenatal care. Postpartum intervention programs provide support to new families.

Multicultural and Gender Considerations

Many societies and cultures have welcoming rituals and rites to include the baby as a new member. Although the overall mortality rate is decreasing, the rate for African Americans in this country is still quite high. This high rate is attributed to risk factors that are influenced by environmental stress. The solution to this problem may need to include social as well as medical considerations. Even though the circumcision rate is falling, the majority of male infants in this country are circumcised at birth. New research indicates medical benefits from the procedure. But many now question the practice of performing the procedure without anesthesia.

Social Hazards

Drug-exposed infants are disorganized and may have a low sensory threshold. They are difficult to care for and may be at risk of abuse and neglect. Early intervention may benefit these babies. Infants with fetal alcohol syndrome are also at increased risk for abuse and neglect. Parents who continue to abuse drugs and alcohol after the baby's birth may not provide an adequate environment for development. Poverty is also a risk factor for infant development.

KEY TERMS

alpha-fetoprotein blood screening
amniocentesis
anoxia
Apgar score
Brazelton Neonatal Assessment
   Scale (BNAS)
cerebral palsy
cesarean section
chorionic villus sample (CVS)

fetal alcohol syndrome (FAS)
gestation
hyperemesis gravidarum
intrauterine growth retardation
   (IUGR)
malpresentation
meconium aspiration
neural tube defects
polyhydramnios

prematurity
prolonged labor
Rh incompatibility
sensitive period
teratogens
toxemia
ultrasound
vaginal bleeding

Infancy

Developmental Themes

Biophysical Dimension
    Biophysical Growth and Development
    Biophysical Hazards

Psychological Dimension
    Cognitive Development and Information Processing
    Communication
    Attitudes and Emotions

    Social Cognition and Regulation
    Psychological Hazards

Social Dimension
    Families, Groups, Support Systems, and Contexts
    Multicultural and Gender Considerations
    Social Hazards

Applying the Framework: Failure to Thrive

Developmental Themes

Before modern times, the major developmental task of infancy was simply to survive it. In premodern Europe, 40% of all children died before they were 5 years old. And babies who did survive were not exactly treated like cherished little bundles of joy. Many families, hesitant to invest in someone with such a high probability of dying, sent their babies to be raised by wet nurses (a woman hired to breast-feed the baby) for the first two years of life—until the babies had survived their infancy. With improved nutrition and control of infection and childhood disease, the infant mortality rate improved dramatically. Over the years, there has been an accompanying increase in interest in babies and their development. Ideas of infant development have changed during this century, from the early belief that babies were "blobs" that could not see, hear, think, or feel to the more recent belief that babies are highly sensitive creatures whose experiences in early infancy affect personality and other characteristics for the rest of life. The first two years of life are now regarded as a special time of growth and development.

According to Erikson, infancy is the stage of trust. Infants are born totally dependent on their caregivers. They must receive appropriate and consistent care in order to develop a sense of security. Infants who have their needs met consistently in a warm and nurturing manner learn that the world is a safe place and that people are dependable. They learn trust. This trust allows babies to develop positive emotional bonds or social attachments to their caregivers. Babies who are neglected, rejected, and inconsistently cared for learn to be suspicious and fearful of the world around them. These babies develop mistrust, which can prevent or delay cognitive development and hinder movement into other stages (Schuster & Ashburn, 1992). A baby must also de-

Attachment between infant and mother is crucial for healthy development.

velop a sense of self, form an attachment to caregivers, and acquire knowledge (Kagan, 1984). These tasks will be explored in depth in this chapter as we consider the physical, cognitive, emotional, and social development of a child from birth to age 2.

Biophysical Dimension

Biophysical Growth and Development

Here's how to have some fun with a 2-year-old—measure him and predict his future size. In two years a child has already grown to half his adult height. During those years, the infant quadrupled his birth weight and now weighs between 27 and 30 pounds. As you can see, the first two years of life are a time of rapid growth and development. Several processes occur to take the child from being a sedentary infant to a busy and active toddler.

At birth, the bones of an infant are soft and pliable. Over the period of infancy these bones harden, or ossify, to allow the child to stand and walk. The infant's skull is made up of several bones that are not fused together to allow molding of the head for a vaginal birth. An infant's head has *fontanelles*, or soft spots, where these skull bones do not join. By the age of 2, these soft spots fill in and harden.

The brain of the infant grows to more than half of its adult size by 1 year. The infant brain is growing so rapidly that between the seventh month of gestation and the age of 1, the brain gains 1.7 grams per day (Shaffer, 1993). Diet during this period of rapid brain growth is crucial. It takes a good amount of high-quality protein to sustain this rate of growth. Inadequate nutrition in infancy can have a detrimental effect on brain development.

Another concept of brain development is **myelinization,** which begins in the prenatal period and continues after birth. Myelin is a substance that forms around neurons and acts as insulation, allowing faster and more efficient transmission of nerve impulses. Myelinization occurs from the brain downward and from the spinal cord out to the extremities. Motor development follows the growth of this myelin sheath. Therefore, a baby's development is referred to as **cephalocaudal** (from the head to the feet) and **proximodistal** (from the spine to the ex-

tremities). So the baby gains control of its body in a downward and outward direction. For example, first the baby gains control of his head and neck and can lift his head up. Then the baby gains control of the trunk and can roll over. A baby can grasp an object in his palm before he can pick up an object with thumb and forefinger.

Motor development follows this sequence: hold up head, roll over, sit, roll from back or stomach to sit, crawl or creep, move from sit to crawl and back again, pull to stand, stand alone, cruise (walk holding onto furniture), walk. Table 6.1 lists typical ages for attaining motor development in infancy.

Although there are cultural variations in age norms, infants the world over obtain these motor milestones in the same sequence. This is evidence of a maturational theory of development—that developmental achievements are genetically programmed to occur in a particular sequence as the baby grows.

Implications for Practice: Recognizing Developmental Delay

How can you tell whether a baby is developmentally delayed? This is where knowledge of developmental norms becomes so important. To make an accurate assessment of developmental problems, you have to be able to contrast a child's current level of functioning with what is expected of typical children her age (Johnson & Goldman, 1990). Basically, infants may need developmental assessment if they fail to demonstrate a skill at an age when 90% of babies can perform that skill (see Table 6.1).

FOCUS ON DEVELOPMENT

Early Intervention for Developmental Delay

Margaret's first baby was born with a severe neural tube defect. The baby had a meningocele, or opening in the back of her head. Unfortunately, the problem was not detected prenatally, and after a long and difficult labor, the baby was delivered with forceps. The baby suffered brain

TABLE 6.1 Age Norm for Motor Development

Skill	Age (in months) at which:	
	50% of Infants Have Mastered Skill	90% of Infants Have Mastered Skill
Lifts head 90° while lying on stomach	2.2	3.2
Rolls over	2.8	4.7
Sits propped up	2.9	4.2
Sits without support	5.5	7.8
Stands holding on	5.8	10.0
Walks holding on	9.2	12.7
Stands alone momentarily	9.8	13.0
Stands well alone	11.5	13.9
Walks well	12.1	14.3
Walks up steps	17.0	22.0
Kicks ball forward	20.0	24.0

Source: Adapted from Frankenberg & Dodds, 1967.

damage. Margaret's doctor told her that the baby would be severely mentally retarded and would never learn to walk or talk or feed herself. He suggested placing the baby in an institution, but Margaret took her daughter home. The community in which Margaret lived provided an early intervention program for infants with disabilities, and the baby started a formal program at the age of 3 months. Margaret spent hours each day doing exercises and activities with her infant. And although the child would never be completely normal, at the age of 6, Margaret's daughter could not only walk and talk and feed herself, but every day after school she would go outside and roller-skate around the block.

In the 1970s, there was an increase in infant stimulation programs for infants with disabilities. Prior to this time, parents were encouraged to institutionalize babies with mental retardation. But then information began to accumulate on the abilities of very young babies. Researchers learned that infants could process information from birth; newborns could see and hear and understand (Pines, 1982). So programs were developed to begin interventions for children with disabilities in infancy. In 1986, PL99-457 (Part H), Services for Infants and Toddlers with Handicapping Conditions, was enacted to provide special services to children with disabilities from birth.

Most communities now provide infant stimulation or early intervention programs for infants with disabilities and their families. In most cases, the parents are involved as the infant's teachers. The parents are taught exercises and activities to perform with the child at home to enhance the child's development. For instance, babies with Down syndrome have weak muscles and poor muscle tone. For this reason, these babies have delayed motor development. So at an age when typical babies are lifting their heads, grabbing at interesting objects, and learning from these interactions, the Down syndrome babies, who because of weak neck muscles cannot lift their heads, receive less stimulation and interaction. By exercising the baby's neck, parents can help strengthen the baby's muscles so the baby can lift its head. Helping babies with mental retardation lift their heads, reach for objects, move around, and interact with the environment enriches their experiences and enhances their cognitive development as well as their physical development (Zausmer, 1978).

What about other disabling conditions? Infants with visual impairments are delayed in their ability to reach for objects, crawl, and walk. Blind infants will not begin to crawl until their second year (Zigler & Stevenson, 1993). Parents of blind infants can be taught to use auditory and other forms of sensory stimulation to enhance their infants' development. Infants with hearing-impairment often appear to develop normally for the first few months. These babies begin to vocalize and babble at the same age that unimpaired infants do. However, after nine months these infants show problems in learning language. The language deficit affects acquisition of other cognitive skills, and parents who do not know that their baby is deaf may think the child has some mental retardation. Early detection of and intervention for a hearing impairment can enhance this child's development.

Biophysical Hazards

To new parents, babies may often seem like accidents just waiting to happen. Infants climb on chairs that topple over, fall down stairs, eat poisonous plants, choke on small objects, and fall headfirst into buckets of water. Infants require constant attention to protect them from injury. Parents need to carefully babyproof the house and anticipate possible hazards to their child. Table 6.2 lists some considerations for preventing accidents and injury.

Illness

Illness and disease are a particular concern to infants. Although babies are born with some natural immunity to rubella, measles, mumps, polio, and diphtheria, this immunity does not last past the age of 3 to 6 months. In addition, the baby can contract chicken pox, tetanus, whooping cough (pertussis), and strep infections during this time (Foster, Hunsberger, & Anderson, 1989). As stated at the beginning of this chapter, in the past many children did not survive infancy because of these diseases. It is important, then, for parents to have their children immunized. Table 6.3 lists the immunization schedule for childhood.

Babies are also very susceptible to upper respiratory infections (colds). Exposure to tobacco smoke can increase the risk of respiratory problems for infants—placing them at higher risk for bronchitis and pneumonia.

TABLE 6.2   Preventing Accidents and Injury in Infancy

Hazard	Prevention
Falls	Don't leave infant unrestrained on any surface. Even very small infants can move and fall off a bed or couch. Don't place a baby in an infant seat on a table. The baby may wiggle the seat off and fall. Avoid use of infant walkers.
Poisoning	Lock up all hazardous materials, including cleaning supplies and medications. Use childproof caps on medications. Keep poisonous plants out of reach. Keep number of poison control near phone.
Choking	Keep small objects out of reach. Don't tie anything around baby's neck, including the pacifier. Cut food into small pieces. Avoid hard foods such as nuts, hard candy. Parents should learn the Heimlich maneuver.
Suffocation	Don't prop the bottle to feed. Keep plastic bags out of reach. Remove doors of old refrigerators. Don't shake baby powder onto baby (put in your hand and apply). Avoid use of pillows and several blankets in crib. Use approved crib. Watch for drapery or blinds cords near crib.
Drowning	Never leave baby unattended in bathtub. Keep toilet seat down. Be careful of all containers of water. Babies can drown in only a few inches of water in a bucket. Use pool safety gates. Never leave baby unattended near pool or any water. Parents should take a CPR class.
Burns	Lower temperature of water heater to 120°–130°. Check temperature of bathwater with elbow. Push pot handles toward back of stove. Use nonflammable clothing. Install smoke detectors. Don't heat bottles in microwave.
Auto accidents	Always buckle child into approved car seat.

Source: Foster, Hunsberger, & Anderson, 1989.

TABLE 6.3 Immunization Schedule for Infants

Age	Immunization
Birth	Hepatitis B (Hep-B)
2 months	Hep-B Diphtheria, tetanus, pertussis (DTP) Polio (OPV) Hemophilus influenza (Hib) (for meningitis)
4 months	DTP, OPV, Hib
6 months	Hep-B, DTP, Hib, OPV
12–15 months	DTP Hib Measles, mumps, and rubella (MMR) Chicken pox
4–6 years	DTP, OPV, MMR

Source: Based on data from the Immunization Action Coalition, 1995.

Meningitis, a bacterial infection of the lining of the brain, is especially hazardous to infants. This illness can result in a 1–5% death rate or in neurological complications, including learning disabilities. Babies with meningitis are irritable, run a fever, have a high-pitched cry, and often have bulging fontanelles (the soft spots on their heads).

Colic can develop between 2 and 6 weeks of age. Colic refers to patterns of sudden and unexplained outbursts of inconsolable crying. You are cuddling your 3-week-old baby one evening and suddenly, out of nowhere, it starts—inconsolable crying. The baby shrieks, stiffens her body, arches her back, and begins a pattern of crying that occurs at about the same time each day. Nothing you do to comfort her seems to work for longer than a few minutes. A quick trip to the pediatrician confirms that you have a colicky baby. Colic has been attributed to food allergies, an immature digestive system or immature nervous system, and to a nervous caregiver. To the relief of parents, babies outgrow this condition by about 3 months of age.

FOCUS ON BIOPHYSICS

Sudden Infant Death Syndrome

At 4:00 in the morning, Dana woke sweating. Something was wrong. She had put her 2-month-old baby to bed at 7:00 PM the previous evening and he was still asleep. He had never slept longer than six hours before. In fact, lately he had been sleeping poorly because he had a cold and had been waking often with a stuffy nose. Dana went to check on the baby and found him lying on his stomach, wedged up at the top corner of his crib. The sheet was crumpled, his blankets were kicked off, and there was a little blood on the mattress. Dana put her hand on the baby's back and discovered he was not breathing. Dana's screams woke her husband, John, and he called the paramedics. Unfortunately, efforts to resuscitate the baby failed, and he was pronounced dead at the hospital.

Sudden infant death syndrome (SIDS) refers to the unexpected death of an infant, for which no physical cause can be found. SIDS is the most common cause of death in the first year of life (Krugman et al., 1994). SIDS occurs in approximately 1 in 400 babies and results in 7000 deaths each year. Although investigators still do not know what causes SIDS, several risk factors have been identified. SIDS occurs more often in male infants, low-birth-weight infants, premature infants, babies with low Apgar scores, babies whose sibling previously died of SIDS, and babies who sleep on their stomachs (Martinez, 1996).

Several maternal factors also increase the risk of SIDS; these factors include young age, multiple births, smoking, prenatal drug abuse, low SES, no prenatal care, and closely spaced pregnancies (Martinez,1996).

Several theories on what causes SIDS have been proposed, but none of these theories is conclusive. The latest evidence suggests that babies who die of SIDS have a problem with their lungs. Autopsies of SIDS babies often reveal changes of the airway. Many babies who die of SIDS had a viral infection prior to death. The majority of babies had blood-stained frothy secretions in their mouths and in the bed, which showed signs of a struggle (Berry, 1993). These clues—an infection, signs of a struggle, and changes in the airway—suggest that the babies do not just stop breathing in their sleep, but that something may be going on in the babies' lungs (Martinez, 1996). Other evidence contributes to this notion. Premature babies have more respiratory problems and a higher risk of SIDS. Breathing secondhand smoke can contribute to respiratory problems, and babies of mothers who smoke have a definite increase in risk of SIDS.

What about putting babies to sleep on their stomach? Babies have been put to bed this way for many years. Although there is no evidence that this sleeping position is a cause of SIDS, babies who sleep on their stomachs are at a higher risk. In countries where this position has been discouraged in the last several years, the death rate from SIDS has been reduced by 50% (Willinger, Hoffman, & Hartford, 1994).

Other evidence suggests that babies who fall into deep sleep may be at higher risk. As an example, babies who sleep alone can go into deeper sleep, but infants who sleep with their caregiver adjust their sleep patterns to synchronize with the caregiver's. So as the caregiver drifts in and out of deeper and lighter sleep, the infant's sleep patterns follow. In fact, rates of SIDS are lower in countries where infants routinely sleep with their mothers (Stipp, 1995).

As yet, no one knows what causes babies to die unexpectedly, but parents who lose an infant this way often blame themselves and try to determine what they did wrong to cause the death. The parents may believe that putting the baby down alone in the room with a cold for that long nap was the cause. Their grief is almost unimaginable. Parents coping with the loss of an infant to SIDS need much support. Although finding a cause for SIDS may help prevent future deaths, at present no particular cause has been identified. Parents should never be made to feel that anything they did or did not do resulted in their baby's death. They need reassurance that they did the best they knew how.

Psychological Dimension

Cognitive Development and Information Processing

Suddenly a piece of space stands out.
It's a pillar, thin and taut.
It stands motionless and sings out a bright melody.

Now, from close by, different notes drift in.
There is nearby another pillar of space.
It, too, sings—but in harmony with the first.
The two melodies mingle in a tight duet,
One melody loud, the other quiet . . .
Then from somewhere else, sounds a different note.
A shooting star, it flashes past and quickly disappears.
(Stern, 1990)

In this passage from *Diary of a Baby* (1990, p. 32), Daniel Stern is describing a 6-week-old infant turning his head and seeing first one crib bar and then another. Try to imagine what the shooting star could be. It is the baby's hand passing through his line of vision.

People have long been intrigued with trying to determine what babies think about, what they perceive, and how they process information. In the past, theories of infant development were based on the clinical infant—a construct developed by the therapist working with adult clients trying to remember early experience. Theories of infant development from developmental psychology are based on the observed infant. In this case, researchers set up experiments and observe babies to determine their responses and capabilities (Stern, 1985). Jean Piaget was well regarded for his ability to observe human development.

Piaget's Sensorimotor Stage

Piaget developed his theories of cognitive development by closely observing first his own children and then others. He classified the time from birth to age 2 as the sensorimotor stage. During this stage, the infant goes from having mostly random reflex actions to displaying **goal-directed behavior.** Instead of just watching a hand shoot past her eyes, she learns to use that hand to push a chair over to the kitchen counter so she can climb up on the counter and get cookies. Goal-directed behavior, then, is putting together a series of actions to achieve a desired result. The infant in this stage also develops **object permanence**—the ability to hold an image of an object or person in one's mind. According to Piaget, very young infants forget an object as soon as they can no longer see it. For instance, if you show a 4-month-old infant a toy and then place that toy under a cloth, the baby will not lift the cloth to find the toy even if the baby saw you put it there. But 2-year-olds remember that those cookies are on the counter even though they can't see them. They hold the image of the cookies in their mind and thoughtfully solve the problem of how to get to them.

Piaget's sensorimotor stage is divided into six substages.

1. *Reflex activity (birth to 1 month).* Piaget believed that the reflexes present at birth are the basic building blocks for intelligent behavior. Touch the baby on the cheek and the baby will turn toward the touch with open mouth. Place a nipple in the baby's mouth and the baby will suck. Place an object in the baby's palm and the baby will grasp it. Ring a bell and the baby will look for it. These actions are not intentional but are the result of inborn reflexes. The baby quickly begins to learn about the environment through these random reflex actions.

2. *Primary circular reactions (1 to 4 months).* During this stage, the baby learns that certain reflex actions bring about pleasurable results. The baby then begins to repeat those actions. For instance, babies learn that sucking to eat reduces hunger and gives comfort. If babies accidentally place their hand in their mouth, they will suck on it and find this sucking comforting. They will then repeat placing the hand in the mouth for comfort. Through accidental reflex activity, the baby acquires new patterns of behavior. The baby is focused on its body (primary) and on repeated actions (circular). Piaget believed that babies in this stage could repeat actions only they themselves initiated and could not imitate actions of others.

3. *Secondary circular reactions (4 to 8 months).* Now babies' focus shifts from their own body to objects in the world (secondary). They learn to control not just their body but other things as well and will repeat random actions for their results. For instance, if a baby is lying in a crib looking at a mobile and the baby kicks its feet and the mobile moves (and the baby finds this movement interesting), the baby will kick its feet again to see whether the mobile will move. Babies at this stage will re-create actions to see interesting results.

4. *Coordination of secondary schemes (8 to 12 months).* In this stage, the baby learns to take several random activities and put them together to achieve a goal. This is known as **intentional means-end behavior.** Now the baby can begin to solve problems. The baby also begins to develop object permanence. If you hide a toy under a cloth, a 9-month-old baby will lift the cloth to find the toy. But if you then hide the toy under a different cloth, the baby will continue to search for the toy under the original one. Even if you show the baby you are hiding the toy in a new place, the baby will still look in the original hiding place. Another aspect of this stage

is that babies are able to imitate actions performed by others. If you show babies how to clap, they can repeat the action after watching you but cannot initiate the action on their own.

5. *Tertiary circular reactions (12 to 18 months).* Babies at this age are little explorers. They no longer rely on random activity but can now think up activities on their own. If you show babies at this age that you are hiding the toy under one cloth and then show them that you are hiding it under a second cloth, they will be able to find the toy. But if you put the toy under a box and then place the box under a cloth, then tip the toy out of the box and leave it under the cloth and return the box to its original location, the babies will search for the toy under the box. They will not look under the cloth even though they can see the bulge the toy makes in the fabric. Babies at this stage are said to be unable to understand **invisible displacements.**

6. *Beginning of representational thought (18 to 24 months).* Here babies make a transition from being action oriented to being symbol oriented. Babies now have full object permanence and can hold an image of an object or person in their mind and solve problems. So they will search for a toy even if they didn't see you hide it. Babies will look for cookies in the cookie jar on the counter because they remember that is where they are kept, even though they didn't see you place them there. Babies can keep the image of cookies in their mind and figure out how to get to them. Now babies can repeat actions without having to watch someone else, so they can clap for themselves when they are pleased with their accomplishment.

Information Processing

New research is finding that babies may be more competent than Piaget ever imagined. Innovative techniques make it possible to observe infants much more closely than Piaget did. These techniques look at how babies actually process the information they receive through sensory stimulation.

One way of observing babies is by studying their attention. Infants display **obligatory attention;** that is, they will look intently at or fixate on something interesting and not be distracted from it (Stern, 1990). Researchers can determine how babies process information by looking at how long it takes a baby to stop paying attention to the same stimulus (**habituation**) and how long it takes the baby to become interested in a new stimulus (**dishabituation**). Babies will look longer at something they

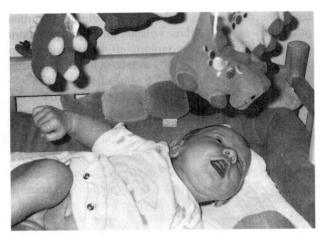

Mobiles are excellent devices for getting a baby to focus attention on objects in the external environment.

find interesting. After becoming familiar or bored with that stimulus, they stop looking at it, or habituate; then they will pay attention to a new stimulus, or dishabituate.

Researchers have discovered that babies not only pay attention to stimuli they have never seen before, but they also pay more attention to events they have some control over, such as watching a mobile they can shake by kicking, and to events they did not expect to happen. Using this information, researchers have discovered amazing capabilities of young infants.

Cohen and Strauss (1979) found that 30-week-old infants were able to categorize (place objects into groups) on the basis of similarities. They habituated one group of infants to a single individual (Sally) by showing the babies a picture of a female face until they became bored with it and looked away. They habituated another group of infants to a series of individuals (Sally, Mary, Barbara, and Joan). These infants paid less attention to each subsequent picture of a new female face. Then each group was shown a picture of a new face (Elizabeth). The infants who had seen only Sally dishabituated to Elizabeth and looked intently at that picture. The infants who had seen the series of faces (Sally, Mary, Barbara, and Joan) were not interested in another female face and remained habituated—they would not look at the new face. Although the individual stimulus was new,

these infants had formed a category for the series of female faces and were then habituated to the category. Research has shown that infants as young as 6 or 7 months display **categorization** (Bjorklund & Bjorklund, 1992).

Some research suggests that very small babies can transfer information gained from one sense to another sense. This process is referred to as **cross-modal transfer.** An example would be exploring an unseen object with your hands and then trying to recognize a picture of that object. Piaget had argued that babies learn this capability gradually through repeated associated actions such as watching their hands grasp objects. But more current research suggests this ability may be present in very young infants. In one study (Meltzoff & Borton, 1979), 3-week-old infants were blindfolded and given a nipple with an unusual shape to suck (see Figure 6.1). The nipple was then removed and placed next to another unusually shaped nipple. When the blindfold was removed, the babies would look longest at the nipple they had sucked. These babies were able to detect the shape of the nipple in their mouths and then, based on that information, determine the visual appearance of the nipple. Other research by Gibson (1984) has supported the idea of cross-modal transfer in young infants.

Other research has found that infants have better memories than believed. Rovee-Collier (1980) placed 2 1/2-month-old infants in a crib and attached a mobile to a leg or arm with a ribbon. The babies learned to shake the mobile by moving that arm or leg. Two weeks later, when placed back in the crib with the same mobile, the babies tried to shake the mobile by moving the correct limb, even though the ribbon was not attached.

Indeed, studies seem to show that babies have an innate sense of how the world works. For example, in experiments conducted by Spelke (1994), babies attended more to unexpected physical actions, such as a ball seeming to roll through a solid barrier or a ball hanging in midair. Spelke found that babies can also recognize the position of a moving ball when it leaves their view and then look to where they expect the ball to be when it comes back into sight. Another researcher, Wynn (1992), discovered that babies seem to have a sense of addition and subtraction. In these experiments, researchers would show a 5-month-old baby a doll and then place the doll behind a screen. Then they would show the baby another doll and place that one behind

FIGURE 6.1 Pacifiers used to test cross-modal transfer
Source: Meltzoff & Borton, 1979.

the screen. They would then remove the screen to reveal either two or three dolls. The babies would look longer at the unexpected result of three dolls instead of two.

Sophisticated technology has also contributed to knowledge on information processing. Haith and Canfield (1991) had babies lie in a black box and look at a TV screen. The babies would see a sequence of colorful objects appear in different positions, while the researcher watched the babies' eye movements with an infrared camera hooked up to a computer. After seeing a particular sequence five times, the babies would begin to predict where the next object would appear and look to that position. With practice, babies as young as 3 months could remember a four-step series. Two weeks later, they still remembered that series when placed in the box.

This new research indicates that object permanence may occur much earlier than Piaget hypothesized—by the fact that babies show surprise when objects disappear behind a screen or behave in unexpected ways (Baillargeon, 1987; Spelke, 1985)—and that babies may be able to imitate others earlier than Piaget believed possible (Meltzoff & Moore, 1977, 1983).

What does all of this mean? Spelke (1994) suggests that in addition to basic reflexes, babies are born with an innate core of knowledge of the world and how it works that begins to emerge very early in life. As more sophisticated methods for observing infants are developed, more knowledge about their information-processing capacities will become available (see Focus on Research: IQ Testing in Infancy).

Implications for Practice: Should Babies Learn to Read?

If babies are so brilliant, should parents devote time and energy to teaching young children to read or perform math problems? Should parents place note cards naming items around the house to encourage language development?

Parents who attempt structured teaching of young babies may become invested in the success of their endeavors. Such attempts at early enrichment may turn into stressful parent-child interactions. Babies involved for long periods in a structured teaching session may miss out on opportunities for free play and exploration. Most young babies do not need to know how to read or add—they have better things to do. In addition, no evidence exists that suggests enrichment programs create Superbabies (Zigler & Stevenson, 1993). Parents should be encouraged to provide an interesting environment for the child to explore; to provide stimulating play materials; and to talk to, play with, and enjoy their baby.

FOCUS ON RESEARCH

IQ Testing in Infancy

Do the capabilities of young infants have any predictive value for later cognitive performance? In general, scores of mental development in the first months of life are not predictive of later IQ. Prediction of later IQ becomes much more reliable after the baby is 2 years old and no longer an infant. Predicting future functioning in infants is most accurate for those who score significantly below average (Honzik, 1976). In other words, a baby who walks at 9 months may not be brighter than one who walks at 13 months; but a baby who does not walk until 22 months may have cognitive delays.

To date, the Bayley Scales of Infant Development (BSID) is one of the best measures of infant development available (Culbertson & Gyurke, 1990). As already stated, this measure does not predict later cognitive ability if the scores are average to above average. However, the measure is predictive of cognitive problems if the scores are significantly below average. Tests such as the BSID, then, are valuable in identifying developmental problems. The BSID tests cognitive and motor skills of infants aged 2 months to 30 months. The infant is assessed on scales that cover memory, perceptual abilities, problem-solving skills, object permanence, verbal skills, gross and fine motor skills, and personal-social skills. Test administration requires special equipment and a trained clinician to administer.

Interestingly, recent research suggests that measures of information processing in infancy may be more predictive of future learning problems than are tests such as the BSID. For instance, infants who fixate visual stimuli briefly and habituate quickly have been found to do better on cognitive scores at age 2 and 4 (Bornstein & Sigman, 1986) and at age 12 (Sigman, 1991). When shown a series of pictures, these infants will study a new picture for a brief time only and then look for a new picture. As just stated, babies who do this score higher on later cognitive measures. So brighter babies may be able to process visual information more quickly—to learn more about the stimulus and retain the information in a briefer period of time.

There is also some evidence that the ability to demonstrate cross-modal transfer and object permanence predicts later IQ (Rose, 1991). In fact, Rose (1992) found that 6-year-old children at risk for learning disabilities had demonstrated low scores on processing visual information at 7 months of age and on performing cross-modal transfers at 1 year. Further research may make it possible to use information-processing measures to identify children at risk for later learning problems.

Communication

Infancy comes from the Latin word *infantia*, the inability to speak. Although newborn babies cannot speak words, they can communicate and are born ready to respond to the human voice. Babies will move in synchrony to human speech in a kind of dance that is slow and rhythmic (Condon, 1975). Neonates prefer human speech over noise, they prefer their own language to others, they prefer baby talk over adult speech, they prefer a female voice over a male voice, and they prefer their mother's voice over another woman's. By the end of infancy, the baby begins to learn to speak a language. Anyone who has tried to learn a new language as an adult knows how hard this can be. But a baby does it quite well and in a consistent and predictable fashion. Babies all over the world and throughout time have developed speech in the same sequence.

Crying and Cooing

The newborn communicates primarily by crying. At first crying is unintentional, simply a response to discomfort or need. But as the caregiver responds to the infant's cries, the baby learns to cry for specific reasons. New parents often ask, "Why does the baby cry?" Babies cry when they are hungry, tired, cold, wet, hot, scared, lonely, in pain, bored—whatever. Most caregivers learn to distinguish between cries, such as the loud, piercing cry of pain or the fussy, whiny sound of tiredness or boredom.

By the end of the first month (3 to 5 weeks), babies begin to coo or make vowel sounds such as "aaaaah" or "oooooh" (see Table 6.4). At around 3 or 4 months, the baby throws in some consonants such as "b" or "k."

Babbling

Between 3 and 6 months, the baby puts the vowel and consonant sounds together, repeats them over and over, and begins **babbling.** Common first babbling sounds include "mamama," "papapa," and "dadada." It is probably no coincidence that in many languages the common names ascribed to infants to refer to their mother and father are mama, dada, and papa.

Babies all over the world begin making these repetitive sounds at this age. Babbling seems to be a maturational process, because even deaf babies who have never heard language will begin to babble by 6 months; however, with no auditory reinforcement, they stop babbling by 8 months. (But if the hearing impairment is caught early and the parents communicate with the baby through sign language, the baby will repeat some signs over and over and "sign babble.")

Why do infants babble? Babbling may be a form of practice to develop the throat, lips, and tongue for producing sounds (Zigler & Stevenson, 1993). Or it may be a way for infants to begin to relate socially with family members and to learn the basic social skills of communication (Bjorklund & Bjorklund, 1992). For the first 6

TABLE 6.4 Developmental Milestones for Speech and Language

Age (in months)	Milestone
2–3	Coos
3–6	Babbles
9–17	Says "mama" and "dada"
12–15	Uses two to three words besides "mama" and "dada"
15–18	Uses many words and can point to body parts
20–24	Uses two- to three-word sentences
24	Refers to self by own name

Source: Adapted from Willis & Holden, 1990.

months, infants vocalize at the same time as someone talking to them. By 7 or 8 months, though, the baby begins to take turns in vocalizing. Now the baby will listen while someone else is speaking and then respond with babbling. By 8 months, the infant takes on the accent of the native language, matches the speaker's tone of voice, and ends phrases with upward or downward inflection (Bjorklund & Bjorklund, 1992). The baby is learning the basics of communication.

The infant then begins to make sounds that refer to specific objects, people, or actions. For instance, the baby may make an "rrrrr" sound when seeing a truck or "mmmmm" when seeing food. Babies also accompany their speech with gestures and pointing to get their message across. A popular form of this type of communication is the scream-and-point method. Babbling increases until the age of 9 to 12 months, when babies say their first word.

Holophrastic Speech

Babies begin to say their first words by 10 to 13 months. At this point, their receptive language is better than their expressive language; in other words, they understand more words than they can say. By the time babies speak their first word, they can understand almost 100 words (Benedict, 1979). The baby begins to add new words slowly, one at a time until she has a vocabulary of 10 words

(Shaffer, 1993). Then the baby has a vocabulary spurt, or naming explosion, where new words are added rapidly (Zigler & Stevenson, 1993). By 20 months, a baby has a vocabulary of about 50 words and by 24 months, of about 180 (Shaffer, 1993).

During this phase, the baby uses one word to express the meaning of a whole sentence. This is referred to as **holophrastic speech.** For instance, a baby may point to a pitcher, whine, and say "juice," meaning "I would like some juice to drink." When you pour a cup and hand it to the child, the baby may smile and happily say "juice," meaning "Oh good, some juice to drink at last." When the cup tips and spills juice on the baby's shirt, the baby may grab the shirt, cry, and say "juice," meaning "I've spilled juice all over me and now I'm wet and uncomfortable and I want a clean shirt." Babies at this age use one word in a fashion referred to as an **overextension.** This means that the word becomes generalized to include a larger category. For instance, babies often use the word "dog" to refer to any furry animal, but this overextension does not mean that the baby can't tell the difference between a dog and a cow. The baby can often accurately point out animals in a book before being able to name them. Remember, babies know more words than they can say. But when your usable vocabulary consists of four words and you know the large mooing animal is not mommy, daddy, or ball, then dog is your best guess. Often the adult will then provide the proper name of the animal for the baby: "That's a cow. A cow goes moo. Can you say cow?" By mislabeling the animal, the baby has gained more knowledge and an increased vocabulary. So the baby now points to the cow and says . . . "dog." It may take a few tries.

What are the first words babies learn? Babies learn words that refer to things that interest them—often people or objects important to them, such as caregivers (mommy, daddy), toys (bear, doll), food (milk, cookie), and animals (dog, kitty). They also like things that move or make noise (airplane, truck) or that can be acted on (ball).

Telegraphic Speech

Between 18 and 24 months, babies begin to put words together to form simple phrases or sentences. Because these sentences are like the message in a telegram, they are referred to as **telegraphic speech.** When you have to pay for each word you use, as you do when sending a telegram, then you only want to use words that are absolutely necessary to convey your message. So in telegraphic speech, babies use nouns, verbs, and adjectives. They omit auxiliary verbs, prepositions, articles, and pronouns. For example, 18-month-old Sarah had never said more than one word at a time. One day she was sitting quietly at her mother's feet looking at a lamp. After a few minutes, she climbed into her mother's lap and said, "Mommy, lamp, hot, burn, ouch." With a few words she had communicated the message that if you touched a hot lightbulb you would burn yourself and it would hurt.

This period of development is an exciting time. Parents begin to get a glimpse of what is going on in their children's mind. But what *is* going on in an infant's mind? Again, infants use words that are important to them: words that convey action (throw ball), possession (my truck), recurrence (more juice), nonexistence (all gone), location (doggie out), and naming and labeling (cow—finally).

Implications for Practice: Recognizing Speech Problems

Although infants develop speech in a predictable sequence, the amount of speech individual children evidence at age 2 can vary greatly. Some 2-year-olds speak in simple two-word phrases, whereas others speak in longer sentences. Both are normal. But as we mentioned earlier, it is important to recognize delays in speech. This is especially important for children with hearing impairments. If the hearing loss is caught early, children can learn sign language in the same progression as they would learn spoken language. The problem is identifying hearing loss in an infant. Hearing loss is often undetected because the infant begins to babble on schedule. Parents should instead note how the infant responds to loud noises. A baby who does not startle when hearing a loud noise, or does not look to find the source of a noise, may have problems with hearing.

As we have seen, in order to develop speech, infants need to hear spoken language. But even some infants without hearing impairments can have problems with adequate verbal stimulation. Parents with a lack of developmental information may assume that a 7-month-old infant doesn't understand speech and may thus fail to

verbally interact with the baby. This can be a particular problem with teenage parents. Adolescent parents need to be encouraged to speak to the baby even if the essence of the speech is silly nonsense (see the following Focus on Development section).

How's My Little Schnookums?

What happens to mature, sophisticated adults when they see a baby? All of a sudden they begin speaking in a sing-song, high-pitched voice, using short phrases, asking lots of questions, using many repetitions, and adding exaggerated emphasis to certain words.

"How's daddy's little schnookums? What do you see? Is that a *doggie*? Yes? Where's the *doggie*? Hello, *doggie*. Nice *doggie*."

This kind of speech directed toward infants occurs in other cultures, among both sexes, and in various age groups, from elderly gentlemen to 4-year-olds. Some parents attempt to avoid talking to their baby using this infant-directed speech, or baby talk, fearing that their baby will end up talking this way. But new research suggests that this failure to use baby talk may be a mistake. Babies love to listen to this type of speech and actually seem to learn language better when addressed in this fashion.

Anne Fernald (1987), the leading researcher in infant-directed speech, has suggested that babies prefer baby talk. She trained babies to turn their heads to hear different types of speech, and these babies turned to hear infant-directed speech over regular adult speech. As one explanation for why babies prefer baby talk, Fernald is studying the musical qualities of infant-directed speech. The sounds in baby talk cover a whole two octaves. The sing-song quality of this speech may help modulate infants' emotions and may better attract the infants' attention. This type of speech may help teach babies language, because it engages the babies' attention (babies hear high-pitched sounds better than low-pitched ones) and better communicates emotions and desires (they are able to respond to emotions in the voice before they can respond to facial expressions of emotions). In addition, certain sounds in baby talk have different meanings, with high-pitched sounds being used to stress the importance of a particular word. In another study by Fernald (1991), when an adult who used either baby talk or adult talk asked babies under 18 months to look at a picture of an object, the babies would recognize the name of the object only when the adult emphasized that word using baby talk (Adler, 1990). According to Fernald, then, baby talk is important for normal infant development. In fact, instead of just being silly chatter, it may be music to their ears.

Source: Adler, 1990.

Attitudes and Emotions

In the past, research concentrated on cognitive development, with emotion being seen as the outcome of cognitive activity. The baby would engage in activities and learn that some were pleasant and some were sad and some were scary (Bremmer, 1988). Recent research, however, indicates that emotions have a strong biological component. If this is true, then babies do not learn to be afraid of unfamiliar situations; they enter a developmental stage in which they begin to exhibit fear of strange people and places.

Research by Izard (1982) and associates suggests that babies all over the world develop emotions at the same ages in a predictable sequence. Izard videotaped infant expressions during various situations, such as being separated and reunited with their mothers, being approached by a stranger, hearing a balloon pop nearby, tasting lemon rind, and receiving scheduled inoculations. He then had independent observers classify infant expressions. This type of research has found that at birth babies display interest, distress, disgust, and happiness. Between age 2 1/2 and 6 months, infants display other primary emotions of anger, sadness, surprise, and fear.

Fear is one of the emotions that develop during this phase. At 5 to 6 months, babies begin to show **stranger anxiety.** Before this age, if given time to warm up, babies will smile at anyone. At 8 months, though, babies will cry and turn away from an unfamiliar face. Between 8 and 10 months, babies begin to display **separation anxi-**

ety; the baby now cries at being left by the primary caregiver. This fear begins to diminish at about 13 months, when the baby has acquired object permanence and can remember the mother when she is away and anticipate her return. At this time, the baby may also have developed a **transitional object**—a blanket, toy, or teddy bear the baby uses for comfort in the caregiver's absence. During the second year of life, babies add complex or secondary emotions of embarrassment, shame, guilt, and pride. These later emotions may require that the child have a sense of self and knowledge of appropriate conduct; in other words, the baby would realize that "Baby has done something wrong." By 18–24 months, babies are fairly accomplished in the emotional area, being able to display a wide range of emotions and even to fake certain emotions, such as sadness, in order to manipulate others (Shaffer, 1993).

Research suggests that emotional expression in infancy is predictive of later childhood emotional characteristics. Shy babies grow up to be shy children (see Focus on Psychology: Shy Children Are Born, Not Made). Huebner (cited in Trotter, 1987) had babies look at a human face, a mannequin face, and an inanimate object with scrambled facial features. Five years later, the babies who had looked longest at the human face were the most sociable, whereas those who had looked the least time at the human face were shy and withdrawn.

Many researchers have wondered whether babies can read facial expressions. Research on younger infants is inconclusive, but there is clear evidence that by 8 to 10 months of age, babies are affected by the moods of others (Shaffer, 1993). Termine (1988) found that babies of sad mothers exhibited a similar expression and showed less exploratory and play behavior than did babies of happy mothers. When confronted with strange situations, babies at this age look to the mother for emotional cues. For instance, if the baby sees a new toy that looks like a pink bunny noisily beating a drum, the baby will look to see how the mother feels about this object. If the mother smiles, the baby may approach the toy. By 12 months, babies will even look to strangers for cues on how to react. Looking to others for emotional information is known as **social referencing.** In a study by Klinnert and colleagues (1986), 12-month-old babies would play with an unfamiliar toy if a nearby stranger smiled at them but would not approach the toy if the stranger showed fear. Older babies, then, take cues from others as to which situations are safe or not.

Greenspan and Greenspan (1985) have described a developmental sequence for emotions from birth through age 4. The infant first takes an interest in the world, then in people, then falls in love with the caretakers, and later learns to dream, imagine, and fantasize.

FOCUS ON PSYCHOLOGY

Shy Children (and Uptight Monkeys) Are Born, Not Made

At a preschool in Silver Spring, Maryland, a mother tries to drop her 2-year-old son off at a Mother's Morning Out program only to find that he clings to her leg, cries, and adamantly refuses to enter the room, whereas other children rush into the room and begin playing with the toys. An hour away, on a five-acre wooded lot, a mother rhesus monkey is separated from her 2-month-old infant. This infant becomes very upset, shows signs of depression, and stops eating, whereas other monkey infants adjust easily to periodic separation from their mothers.

Jerome Kagan studies human infant development, and Stephen Suomi conducts developmental studies of monkeys. These researchers have found that extremely inhibited children and uptight monkeys often behave in similar ways when faced with novel situations. They found that these species have similar physiological reactions as well. Kagan believes that the limbic system—particularly the amygdala and hypothalamus—in these children and monkeys is activated more easily and that this overactivation is inherited. Kagan found that timid children show a pattern of excessive physiological responses to mildly stressful situations that do not occur in more easygoing children. Under stress, these children have dilated pupils, an increased heart beat, and elevated blood cortisol. Suomi's uptight monkeys, when stressed during infancy by brief separations from their

mothers, showed the same rise in blood cortisol and increase in heart rate. The researchers found that neither the monkeys nor the children tend to outgrow these abnormal physiological responses to stress.

Suomi and Kagan agree that this extreme timidity seems to have a genetic foundation. The monkeys were reared together in nurseries and in peer groups, so parenting was not influencing their individual reactions to stress. Research by Robert Plomin and David Rowe indicates that identical twins tend to exhibit the same reaction to strangers, supporting the notion that humans possess a biological predisposition to extreme shyness. About 20% of monkeys and 15% of children seem to be genetically predisposed to timidity. However, being born shy does not doom a child or monkey to lifelong social difficulties.

Suomi found that monkeys can be helped to overcome their stress responses through changes in how they are reared. Environmental influences such as having a nurturing mother can offset the genetic tendency toward shyness. Surrounding a monkey with friendly, outgoing peers and a nurturing foster mother or grandmother helps the monkey learn coping strategies. When stressed, this monkey can seek out a nurturing friend or mother figure. This activity prevents the normal highstress physical response. Growing up with a nurturing mother figure often helps these monkeys respond better than their peers and become leaders in their group.

Kagan's studies of human children provide evidence that although timid toddlers tend to stay shy, these children can overcome this tendency with help from their parents. Social workers can help parents of very shy children recognize the problem early, protect the child from too much stress, and help the child learn coping skills. Parents can help the child by inviting other children to the home to play with the child and by teaching the child how to cope with the physical response brought on by stressful situations.

The work of Suomi and Adler has helped to clarify how heredity and environment interact to influence behavior and development. Some children may be born shy, but a supportive and nurturing environment can help them to later social success.

Source: Adler, 1989, 1990; Asher, 1987.

Infant Temperament

Though all babies seem to possess primary emotions at birth, those emotions vary in how they are exhibited among individual newborns. Some babies are easily comforted and sleep and eat on a regular schedule. Some babies are more difficult to comfort and have very unpredictable daily patterns. The characteristic pattern in which an infant responds to and interacts with the environment is referred to as **temperament.** Some consider temperament to be the basis of later personality development. And for the most part, temperament is thought to be biologically determined (Thomas & Chess, 1989).

In an extensive study of temperament, Alexander Thomas and Stella Chess conducted the New York Longitudinal Survey in the mid-1970s. They looked at 133 individuals from infancy through adulthood and identified nine dimensions of temperament, including activity level, rhythmicity, approach or withdrawal, adaptability, threshold of responsiveness, intensity of reaction, quality of mood, distractibility, and attention span and persistence. These dimensions are further explained in Box 6.1.

Based on the data obtained from their work, Thomas and Chess (1977) determined that the combination of these nine dimensions described three types of children: the easy child, the slow-to-warm-up child, and

BOX 6.1

Dimensions of Temperament

Activity level: Active babies are in motion most of the time, even while sleeping. Quiet babies can be placed almost anywhere, as they will not move much.

Rhythmicity: Some babies are very regular in the times they eat, sleep, and have bowel movements. Others are very irregular and unpredictable.

Approach or withdrawal: When presented with a new toy, some babies respond positively by smiling, vocalizing, and reaching for it. Other babies cry, turn away, or push the toy away.

Adaptability: Some babies adapt to changes in routine easily and quickly. They may be shy with a new sitter at first but accept the sitter after a brief time. Some babies become very upset at even slight changes. They may cry for days even if their familiar sitter changes hairstyle.

Threshold of responsiveness: Some babies sleep through loud noises and cry briefly when they fall down. Others wake easily in response to sounds and cry long and loud when even slightly hurt.

Intensity of reaction: Some babies cry softly and giggle gently. Others scream and kick and laugh out loud.

Quality of mood: Some babies are pleasant and contented most of the time. Others are fussy and irritable.

Distractibility: Some babies can be easily distracted from something they want. If you offer them a toy, they will stop trying to turn on the TV. Other babies are intent on figuring out how the TV works no matter what you do.

Persistence and attention span: Some babies are very persistent in their activities. If they are looking at a book, they need to turn every page before they will let you put on their shoes. Other babies turn a few pages of the book and move on to something else.

the difficult child. Approximately 40% of the children in their sample fit the description of the easy child. This baby is characterized by regular, positive responses to new stimuli, high adaptability to change, and mild or moderately intense mood, which is usually positive. In other words, this infant is apt to easily accept new toys, foods, individuals, and settings. This baby has predictable eating and sleeping schedules and is usually happy and pleasant.

Fifteen percent of the children studied were classified as slow to warm up. As babies, these children exhibit a more sedate and less exuberant orientation to the world. They have more negative responses and are slower to adapt to new situations. Like the easy child, the slow-to-warm-up child usually has predictable eating and sleeping schedules. Although these infants are wary of new experiences, such as visiting a new house, they are able to adjust over time, if not hurried or pushed during the transition.

In contrast to the other types, the difficult child has unpredictable daily habits. As babies, they wake up at a different time every day and do not establish a regular napping schedule. Their appetite also varies from day to day. These infants exhibit negative responses to new stimuli, adapt slowly or not at all, and usually express an intense, negative mood. These babies protest loudly when introduced to new toys, foods, people, or situations; throw temper tantrums when agitated or frustrated; and squeal loudly when excited. Ten percent of the children in the sample fit this description.

Since the work of Thomas and Chess, much research has been conducted to examine the validity of inborn temperament. Studies of twins have found temperament to be biologically determined to some extent (Emde et al., 1992). Our review of studies by Kagan found that shy babies grow up to be shy children (see Focus on Psychology: Shy Children Are Born, Not Made), and difficult babies grow up to be difficult adults. In Thomas and Chess's study, 70% of the difficult infants entered psychiatric treatment later in life, but only 18% of the easy infants did so (Zigler & Stevenson, 1993).

Implications for Practice: Goodness of Fit

Although research has found that a certain degree of personality difference seems to be genetic, the development of the remainder of one's personality is due to environ-

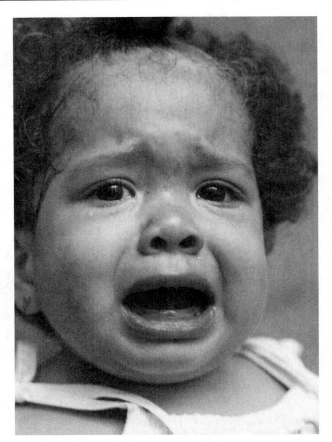

Some children are temperamentally "difficult," displaying negative moods and sleep, eating, and elimination irregularities. These children are less adaptable, more vulnerable to adversity, and more likely to produce and elicit adverse responses.

ment. One way that environment can affect personality development is through goodness of fit. Goodness of fit refers to how well the demands of the environment match the child's behavioral style. An active, intense baby with outgoing, high-energy parents who encourage loud play and exploration will have a better fit than will such a baby born to quiet, introspective parents who expect the baby to sit and look at books.

Research indicates that the family environment can play a role in the child's later development. Maziade and colleagues (1990) discovered that all 38 of the children in their study, who were identified at age 7 as having a difficult temperament and a poorly functioning family with little behavioral control, were diagnosed as having a clinical disorder in preadolescence or adolescence. A slow-to-warm-up baby may experience stress if the parents are highly sociable and always on the go. An easy child with a more difficult sibling may be ignored while the parents concentrate their energy on their other child.

Parents can be helped to understand their babies' different temperament styles and to alter the environment to fit that style and enhance the child's development. Researcher Alicia F. Lieberman (1993), author of *The Emotional Life of the Toddler*, focuses on all three temperament types described by Thomas and Chess as well as an additional type, which she calls the *active child*. Lieberman makes recommendations as to how to best interact with each type of child. Parents of difficult children should not take the children's behavior personally, should keep a sense of humor about the children's behavior, should be patiently available to the children, should have clear guidelines for behavior, and should develop a support system that allows the parents time away from the children. Parents of active children should structure the house and yard to allow for robust play. Parents of slow-to-warm-up children should take special measures in introducing their children to new situations. Parents should essentially stay near the children until their mood has changed from caution to enjoyment, then step back. Lieberman reminds parents that easy children can be taken advantage of. They may not demand attention or complain even when they should and may therefore be ignored in the hectic pace of everyday life.

Attachment[1]

Anyone who has had the privilege of a friendship with a small child may have noticed changes in how the child interacts with you as he grows. Before 3 months, the baby will come to you, smile, and make eye contact. Around 4 months, the baby may frown at seeing your face, look to mother's face, and then back at you. It may take a few minutes of coaxing to get the baby to come to you. By 8 months, the baby may whine and turn away to hug mother when you approach. You may have to resort to bribing with a toy or treat to get the baby to come to you. But the baby may still refuse, obviously preferring mother

now. Because of these actions, you may begin to feel the child no longer likes you. Then one day you go to visit your active toddler friend and you are greeted with a big grin. The child takes your hand, waves goodbye to mom, and wants to go home with you (see Table 6.5).

This scenario illustrates the process of **attachment,** or forming a strong emotional tie to a caregiver. Researchers have long been interested in what motivates a baby to form this close bond with a caregiver and to prefer that caregiver over other people. Early theories held that attachment was the result of need satisfaction. In other words, babies love their mother because she feeds and takes care of them. But classic research by Harlow on infant rhesus monkeys failed to support this idea. These monkeys were separated from their mothers at birth and raised in a cage with an inanimate surrogate mother made of either wire or cloth. Some monkeys were fed by the wire surrogates and some by the cloth ones. But when the infant monkeys needed someone to cling to, they preferred the cloth mother even when they had been fed by the wire mother. These monkeys showed no preference for the wire surrogate who had fed them.

Today, attachment theory is most closely identified with psychiatrist John Bowlby (1958). According to his theory, attachment has a biological, evolutionary basis. A baby forms a close, intimate relationship with a caregiver to ensure its survival. In an evolutionary sense, when a predator threatens, someone needs to protect the vulnerable young. And infants need a particular caregiver to remember to pick them up when everyone else is running away.

This theory suggests that parents and infants may be biologically programmed to form an attachment. The caregiver and the infant each exhibit specific behaviors that facilitate the process of forming a bond.

The Parents' Behaviors   Parents of an infant engage in several activities meant to engage the baby's attention. They position their faces directly within the infant's visual field, about 22.5 cm away from the baby's face (Papousek & Papousek, 1992). This is a very interesting phenomenon considering that a newborn can focus on objects no more than 30 cm away. Parents seem to instinctively know how

[1]This section was written by Ellen Blessington, MSW.

TABLE 6.5 Bowlby's Phases of Attachment

	Age	Behaviors
Phase 1	Birth–2 or 3 mos.	Displays indiscriminate smiling, cooing, clinging toward anyone.
Phase 2	2–3 mos. to 6–7 mos.	Begins selective interactions. Develops a true social smile directed at preferred caregivers. Compares a stranger's face with caregiver's.
Phase 3	6–7 mos. to 1 year	Clearly attached to primary caregiver. Cries when caregiver leaves. Crawls after caregiver. Wary of strangers and strange situations.
Phase 4	Second year of life	Has full object permanence. More secure in knowledge that caregiver exists when not in sight. More sociable with other people.

far the baby can see, so they attempt eye contact within that range. Parents also attempt to get the infant's attention through a series of facial expressions known as the "greeting response." In this response, parents tilt their head back, open their mouth halfway, and raise their eyebrows (Papousek & Papousek, 1987). Parents also use "baby talk" when addressing the infant (see Focus on Development: How's My Little Schnookums?). Research suggests that these behaviors are not conscious but may be intuitive in nature (Papousek & Papousek, 1992). Parents just seem to know what babies like and respond that way.

The Infant's Behaviors The biggest contribution the infant makes in the attachment process is having "the look." Babies are cute. Adults just cannot seem to resist the rounded facial features and "babyishness" of infants. Adults are also drawn to babies' responsiveness. Parents like to feel recognized and needed, and newborns seem equipped to meet that need. Babies show a particular fondness for a human face and respond to adults with smiles and vocalizations. As we have already seen, babies recognize their mother's voice at birth. Newborns also respond by imitating facial expressions.

The infant's reflexes—in particular grasping, sucking, rooting, and turning—serve as responses to parental caregiving and also reinforce parental interaction. These infant behaviors make the parents feel needed. In addition, infants quickly learn who is caring for them and make responses that reinforce that care. For instance,

within three days of birth, a newborn will respond to being placed in the feeding position by moving in the direction of the mother, turning toward the breast, and opening the mouth (Call, 1964).

Other Attachment Ideas Mary Ainsworth added information to ideas of attachment. According to Ainsworth and colleagues (1978), the infant uses the primary caregiver as a secure base from which to leave to explore the environment and to return to for comfort and security. Using this idea, Ainsworth developed a method for measuring attachment by observing the infant's response to various events occurring in a strange situation. This laboratory assessment procedure, known as the Strange Situation Procedure, involves eight structured episodes occurring over about 25 minutes:

Episode 1:   Mother and baby are introduced to a playroom.
Episode 2:   Mother and baby are left alone to explore the contents of the playroom.
Episode 3:   An unfamiliar woman joins them.
Episode 4:   The mother leaves the room and the stranger attempts to play with the baby.
Episode 5:   The mother returns.
Episode 6:   The child is left completely alone.
Episode 7:   The strange woman returns.
Episode 8:   The mother returns.

Analysis of the responses of infants in the strange situation led to a classification of attachment patterns.

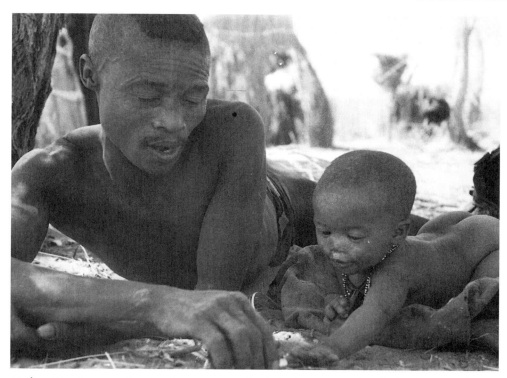

Attachment to primary caregivers is an important aspect of early development regardless of cultural or historical context. This !Kung father is establishing a connection with his child.

Ainsworth identified three levels of attachment.

• *Secure attachment.* These infants utilize their mothers as a secure base from which to explore the playroom. They are aware of their mother's presence and keep checking to make sure she is available if needed. When their mothers leave them, these infants cry or protest. When the mothers return, these infants seek them out for comfort and physical contact.

• *Anxious attachment.* These infants are clingy and reluctant to explore the playroom even with their mother present. When their mothers leave, these infants become extremely upset and cry for long periods of time. When their mothers return, these infants seek physical contact but also hit their mothers or pull away. They are not easily soothed by their mothers. According to Ainsworth, these infants do not trust their mothers to meet their security needs.

• *Avoidant attachment.* These infants demonstrate a marked indifference toward their mothers. They do not use their mothers as secure bases but actually act as if their mothers are not present. They do not seek eye contact or attention from their mothers. They are not distressed when their mothers leave and show indifference upon their return.

Sixty-five percent of middle-class infants display secure-attachment behaviors. What factors influence the attachment process? How do 35% of infants end up not securely attached?

Risk Factors Associated with Attachment Failure   Factors involving the baby, the mother, and the home can interfere with attachment. First of all, characteristics of babies can affect the mother-infant relationship. For instance, premature babies are at risk for attachment problems—these babies are not as "cute" as full-term infants and also not as responsive. In addition, preterm infants are less engaged with their mothers and receive less enjoyment in mother-involved play activities (Field, 1983). Other infant-related factors that can affect attachment include drug exposure (Lester, 1992) and difficult temperament.

A parent-related problem that affects the attachment relationship can occur with adolescent mothers. These mothers on average engage in less verbal exchange with their children and have trouble interpreting and responding to their infant's cues (Crockenberg, 1981; Field, 1981; Hann, Osofsky, Barnard, & Leonard, 1990). Another problem arises with depressed mothers, who may have more problems bonding with their babies (Radke-Yarrow, Cummings, Kuczyski, & Chapman, 1985). A depressed mother is wrapped up in her own feelings and may not be responsive to an infant. She may be so busy concentrating on her own pain that she misses the baby's social cues. The baby then tends to match the mother's mood even with other nondepressed adults. Other parental factors that may affect attachment include alcoholism, childhood abuse and neglect, and an unplanned pregnancy.

Factors in the home can also affect attachment. A mother with lots of small children may not have time to respond to a new infant. The marital relationship has an effect on the primary caregiver's interactions with an infant. When spouses or partners are supportive, mothers are more responsive and affectionate toward their babies (Crnic, 1984). And a mother's level of social support is critical, especially when she is parenting an irritable infant. A secure attachment is more likely when a mother has an adequate social support network (Crockenberg, 1981). High levels of environmental stress also influence mother-baby interactions (Booth, Barnard, Mitchell, & Spieker, 1987). Mothers dealing with poverty, domestic violence, and their own personal trauma may not have enough emotional energy to engage an infant.

In fact, a new category of attachment failure has been suggested by Main and Soloman (1986, 1990), termed *disorganized/disoriented attachment*. Children in this category exhibit unclear, inconclusive, or contradictory attachment patterns. This category can include children who are hard to classify and do not fit into one of Ainsworth's three attachment patterns. Children with this pattern often come from families with the above-mentioned problems.

Implications for Practice: Assessing Attachment Problems

Bowlby believed that a warm, intimate, and continuous relationship with a mother was vital for a child's later personality development. Recent research suggests that the quality of a child's attachment with a primary caregiver is an excellent predictor of later functioning (Cicchetti & Wagner, 1990). Securely attached children exhibit a healthy mix of self-reliance and the ability to ask for help from others (Stroufe, Fox, & Pancake, 1983). Children with secure attachments relate better to their peers than do those with insecure attachments (Lieberman, 1977; Matas, Arend, & Stroufe, 1978). A strong parent-child bond also seems to result in better self-knowledge (Pipp, Easterbrooks, & Harmon, 1992) and in better school performance (Jacobsen, Edelstein, & Hoffman, 1994).

If attachment is so important to development, what are the signs to look for in assessing children that would point to attachment problems? Children with attachment problems are believed to exhibit the following problems in interactions. They do not show a preference for a particular adult; they may seek affection and attention from anyone and run up to and hug total strangers. They will wander away from their caregiver—the caregiver is frequently losing the child in crowds and in public places. The child may be reckless and accident-prone, and excessively clingy or aggressive toward the caregiver. The type of behaviors that Zeanah and Emde (1994) believe are suggestive of an attachment difficulty in young children are listed in Table 6.6.

FOCUS ON MULTICULTURALISM

Cultural Considerations in Examining African American Attachment Patterns

It is important for practitioners to be aware that the cross-cultural validity of identified attachment behaviors has been called into question. As stated by attachment researcher Jacquelyne Faye Jackson (1993), "Both execution of the 'strange situation' procedure and unequivocal classification of infant attachments have been technically difficult in cultures outside the USA (Sagi et al.,

TABLE 6.6 Assessing Attachment Problems in Young Children

Behaviors	Signs of Attachment Disorders
Showing affection	Lack of warm and affectionate interchanges across a range of interactions; promiscuous affection with relatively unfamiliar adults
Comfort seeking	Lack of comfort seeking when hurt, frightened, or ill; comfort-seeking in odd or ambivalent manner
Reliance for help	Excessive dependence, or inability to seek and use supportive presence of attachment figure when needed
Cooperation	Lack of compliance with caregiver requests and demands by the child as a striking feature of caregiver-child interactions, or compulsive compliance
Exploratory behavior	Failure to check back with caregiver in unfamiliar settings, or exploration limited by child's unwillingness to leave caregiver
Controlling behavior	Oversolicitous and inappropriate caregiving behavior, or excessively bossy and punitive controlling of caregiver by the child
Reunion responses	Failure to reestablish interaction after separations, including ignoring/avoiding behaviors, intense anger, or lack of affection

Source: Zeanah, Mammen, & Lieberman, 1993.

1985; Takahashi, 1986), and no transcultural distribution of types has been found (van Ijzendoorn & Kroonenberg, 1988)" (p. 91).

Jackson (1993) presents a compelling argument that the African American practice of sharing child-care responsibilities among relatives results in a negative misinterpretation of African American infant-attachment patterns. Jackson explains that, as a consequence of discrimination, African American mothers have, historically and currently, needed to work outside the home. As a result of this economic reality, African American culture has developed a distinct, adaptive, cultural pattern to ensure that their children receive the nurturance and care they require.

This cultural pattern includes the exposure of the child to a multitude of extended-family caregivers. Jackson (1993) notes research (Young, 1970) indicating that, because of a cultural context that encourages the acceptance and development of caring interactions with a number of different caregivers across a variety of settings, African American children develop an independent and out going orientation. Hence, she asserts that, when African American children are assessed utilizing the Strange Situation, they may be mistakenly viewed as not being securely attached because of their greater confidence in examining novel environments and their high level of trust as to the comings and goings of caregivers in general.

Jackson (1993), therefore, maintains that it is not surprising that a relatively high proportion of African American children appear to be insecurely attached when assessed according to the standards for majority children. In support of her contention, she cites the work of Hansen (1980), who also questioned whether the African American children he had examined when employing the Strange Situation had experienced the degree of stress necessary to elicit attachment behaviors. The children he studied actively explored the playroom, did not demonstrate noteworthy distress at times of separation, and were not specifically solicitous of maternal attention at times of reunion. Furthermore, these children had an overall, genial demeanor during the procedure. Thus, it can be argued that these children did not experience the Strange Situation in the same fashion as do majority children, both in terms of their expression of distress and their reunion behaviors. Moreover, given the infants' observed pleasant attitudes toward their mothers, it is also questionable whether these infants could be seen as fitting Ainsworth's typology for resistant or avoidant infants.

Because she believed that the Strange Situation is inadequate in assessing African American infant-attachment patterns, Jackson (1993) conducted an exploratory study that employed a laboratory assessment procedure developed by Kotelchuck (1976). Kotelchuck's playroom strategy includes two attachment figures as opposed to the Strange Situation, which includes only one. Jackson found that African American infants utilize both their mothers and secondary attachment figures as secure bases from which to explore the environment. She also found that the majority of the African American infants she studied were simply not upset by being left in a playroom for a brief time period with an amicable stranger. As a result of her exploratory study, Jackson believes that, although Kotelchuck's procedure is an improvement in assessing African American infant attachment by the inclusion of multiple caregivers, it is not sufficiently stressful to activate distress reactions in African American children. Hence, she concludes that culturally relevant assessment instruments need to be developed and that researchers should be cautious in arriving at negative conclusions regarding African American infant-attachment patterns.

Source: Courtesy of Ellen Blessington, MSW.

Social Cognition and Regulation

At what age does a baby know that she is a baby? Lewis conducted experiments to test babies' awareness of self (Lewis & Brooks-Gunn, 1979). He put a spot of rouge on the baby's nose and had the mother sit with her infant in her lap in front of a mirror. If the babies recognized themselves in the mirror, they touched their own nose. Babies under 1 year looked in the mirror but did not touch their nose. Some babies at 15 months would touch their nose; but by 18 months, 75% of the babies recognized themselves in the mirror and touched their nose. Further research by Lewis has suggested that most babies have a sense of self by 18 months.

Margaret Mahler felt that developing a sense of self as being separate from others was a major developmental process with a significant impact on personality development. In Mahler's view, the infant grows from being a newborn with no sense of self as separate from her care-

taker to being an autonomous, independent individual. She termed this process **separation-individuation.** During the first month of life, infants are in the *normal autistic phase*, unaware of self, other people, or the world. At 1 to 5 months, the babies are in the *normal symbiotic phase*, aware that someone is caring for them but unaware of that person as being separate from themselves. At 5 to 9 months, in the *differentiation phase*, babies begin to get a sense of self and nonself. At this age, babies will sit in their mother's lap and explore the mother's face visually and tactually. As babies begin to crawl and then walk between 9 and 14 months, they enter the *practicing phase*. Now they can move away from the mother but they need to check back often for emotional refueling (a look, a smile, a hug). The *rapprochement phase* occurs between 14 and 24 months. Babies know they are separate from the mother but still need to check back regularly. The *consolidation phase* occurs between the age of 2 and 3. Now babies can separate from the mother without becoming too upset.

Remember that Mahler's theories of separation-individuation are based on the *clinical infant,* the adult recalling the past in psychotherapy. In experiments involving information processing, Daniel Stern (1985) has done extensive research on the *observed infant.* On the basis of data from these experiments, Stern believes that infants have a sense of self from birth, that babies are always able to differentiate self from others. How? As we discussed in the Information Processing section of this chapter, babies are able at birth to accurately discriminate sensory input. Even newborns seem to have an innate core of knowledge about the world. They can tell when they are sucking their own or someone else's fingers. They can tell when they are moving their own arm or having it raised by someone to play "How big is baby?" And they can tell when they are causing actions or when someone else is.

In any case, by the end of infancy, children have a well-established sense of self as separate and independent. This notion of self is important for later development. For instance, as you may remember, a baby must have a sense of self before being able to express more complex emotions, such as guilt and shame. More important, a sense of self is a necessary foundation for social development. "The acquisition of the self by the end of the second year not only facilitates the acquisition of social knowledge, but underlies social competence, peer relations, gender identity, and empathy" (Brooks-Gunn & Lewis, 1984, p. 234). Some important milestones in social development are listed in Table 6.7.

Regulation

Somewhere around the age of 2, the baby learns to say "No!" This is a statement of independence and autonomy. The baby now has a sense of self and what that self wants and does not want. The ability to know right from wrong, good from bad, and want from not want begins to develop after the age of 18 months. Regulation can begin when the infant has adequate language skills, a sense of self, more complex emotions of guilt and shame, and a sense of autonomy (Lyons-Ruth & Zeanah, 1993). Even babies who have been "easy" up to this point may not be as compliant now. They are more difficult to distract. They can formulate certain goals and realize whether or not they have obtained them (Lyons-Ruth & Zeanah, 1993). And in terms of moral development, they have internalized certain standards and become upset when those standards are not met. Where did they get these standards and ideas of right and wrong, good and bad?

These standards and ideas are based on the previous responses of others. Remember, babies engage in social referencing, or looking to an adult for how to respond in new situations. Babies learn through experience that when they throw things on the floor and break them, mother becomes upset. They learn that when they pour their juice on the floor, father becomes upset. So now when babies break or spill something, they become upset. At this age, babies will often reach out for an object and then look to mother to see if she is going to stop them.

Babies at this age are also unsure of many standards, and they test parents to determine which actions are acceptable and which are not—usually more than once. "Will mother get mad at me if I eat the food in this bowl on the floor? She lets the cat eat it. But mother yelled at me last time I ate it. Why? Let's see what happens this time."

Through repeated experimentation, babies learn to be reasonably obedient in the presence of parents. But they do not possess the ability to obey when parents are not watching until about 36 months (Lyons-Ruth &

TABLE 6.7 Developmental Milestones for Social Behaviors

Age (in months)	Milestone
0–2	Smiles in response to a voice or touch
3–5	Smiles spontaneously
3–5	Reaches for familiar people
9–11	Plays pat-a-cake and peek-a-boo
9–11	Becomes upset when separated from caregiver
20–23	Plays near but not with other children
28–31	Is aware of differences between sexes
32–35	Can identify own sex
32–35	Can separate easily from caregiver

Source: Adapted from Willis & Holden, 1990.

Zeanah, 1993). To the 2-year-old, it's OK to eat cat food unless mom catches you. In this context, the reason to be good is to avoid displeasure from mom.

Implications for Practice: The Terrible Twos

During the second half of the second year of life, babies can become much more difficult. They begin to develop a sense of autonomy and independence. They want to do things for themselves, they want to do it now, and they want to do it their way. No becomes their favorite word. Even when asked whether they want ice cream, children may reply, "No," and then cry when the parents don't provide the ice cream. Some parents become locked in power struggles with their children, sometimes erupting into food battles. Parents may try to force the child to eat only to discover that some children would rather starve than eat when coerced. On the other hand, some parents allow the toddler to run the house. They hesitate to provide any structure for the baby, failing to set limits or establish regular routines. Even though toddlers struggle to obtain it, they are often afraid of their growing independence. Parents should be encouraged to set limits and provide structure and routine for the child but to allow independence where appropriate and avoid power struggles.

Psychological Hazards

What exactly are the effects on psychological development of losing a caregiver at a young age or even of failing to establish a bond with a primary caregiver at all? Loss of a primary caregiver has often been referred to as maternal deprivation, which can occur through separation from the caregiver or if the caregiver fails to interact with the infant and neglects or abuses the baby. If the loss occurs before 6 months of age, it can interfere with the baby's forming an attachment to a caregiver. If the loss occurs after 6 months, it can disrupt an existing attachment (Bremmer, 1988).

Failure to Form an Attachment

What happens to babies who fail to form an attachment? Research on this issue has to rely on separations that occur naturally and usually involves babies who have been institutionalized. A classic study was conducted by Spitz (1945) on children in orphanages in the United States and Germany. These babies received adequate medical attention, food, and physical care but they received little social interaction. Most of their time was spent in cribs with a sheet over the rails. The death rate for children under 2 in these institutions was high; many died from childhood diseases such as measles. The babies were emotionally apathetic and retarded in physical, mental, and social growth.

What about institutions that offer more stimulation than just lying in a crib? Tizard and Rees (1974) looked at good British orphanages that had a high caregiver-to-baby ratio and lots of interaction. These institutions provided stimulating toys and materials but had a high staff turnover. Some babies experienced 50–80 caregivers before preschool age. These children were normal in intellectual development but had problems socially and emotionally. At the age of 8, many were restless, disobedient, and unpopular with their peers and constantly sought attention. Tizard found that the longer the babies were in the institution, the more trouble they had with peer relations.

Infants who move from one foster home to another can have attachment problems. What happens when these children grow up? Bowlby (1980) looked at adolescents who had spent their infancy and childhood in institutions or foster care, often with repeated moves. These adolescents, who were not loved consistently as babies, were unable to love as teens. They displayed a lack of empathy and affection for others. Many children who fail to form attachments as infants grow up to exhibit disturbed behavior such as delinquency, disregard for life, and lack of empathy. These are the children who kill animals—the ones who would stomp a cat to death (Trout, 1995).

So, early deprivation of a consistent caregiver can affect cognitive, emotional, and social development. But can these effects of early deprivation be reversed with good care at a later age? Quite by accident, Skeels (1936) had an opportunity to explore this question. Two infant girls aged 13 and 16 months from neglectful families were admitted to an overcrowded orphanage in Iowa. Because they appeared retarded and functioned at the age of 6 or 7 months, they were placed in a home for women with retardation. Six months later these girls were alert, lively, and functioning normally. Why? They had become the "darlings" of the women in the home and received a great deal of stimulation and interaction. Skeels followed these girls' development and found that they remained normal. He then conducted a study comparing children in the orphanage with children placed in the home for women with retardation (Skodak & Skeels, 1945, 1949). Even as adults, the children who had been placed with the attentive women functioned better than did those who had been in the orphanage.

Other work has been conducted on rhesus monkeys by Suomi and Harlow (1972), who raised infant monkeys in social isolation for six months. These isolated monkeys displayed lack of social skills. For "therapy" these monkeys were placed with a 3-month-old monkey for two hours a day, three days a week. Young monkeys were used as "therapists" because they would not know that the behavior of the isolated monkeys was abnormal and would not be as aggressive toward them as older monkeys would have been. Because the young monkeys learned social skills from the regular monkey colony in which they spent most of their time, they taught the isolated monkeys how to interact. After six months of this type of therapy, the isolated monkeys learned social skills similar to normal monkeys.

So it appears that the effects of early deprivation can be reversed to some extent. But what happens to infants who form an attachment to a caregiver and then lose that caregiver?

Separation after Attachment

Babies who are separated from their primary caregiver show immediate effects (Rutter, 1981). At first, they display acute distress by crying and complaining loudly. This is known as the *protest phase*. Then babies go into the *despair phase*, showing general misery and apathy. When the caregiver fails to return after a period of time, the baby becomes unconcerned and relatively peaceful once again. This is the *detachment phase*. The amount of distress a baby displays depends on the circumstances. For example, there is a difference between going to grandma's for a week and being admitted to the hospital for surgery. In the hospital, the baby may be separated from the whole family and experience scary and painful procedures. Children who are in another family situation—especially if with a sibling or other family member—adapt more easily (Bremmer, 1988).

How does loss of a caregiver affect the child after these immediate responses? Recent studies have corroborated what Anna Freud suggested, "that separation is always traumatic in one way or another, but that it is particularly so for the young child" (Gerard & Dukette, 1954). The most profound responses occur if the separation takes place when the child is between 6 and 28 months (Trout, 1995). These responses include a drop in developmental quotient (the child scores lower on standard developmental tests), low frustration tolerance, eating disturbances, depression, social withdrawal, inconsolability when left alone, and repeated efforts to make the lost object reappear (opening cabinet doors, waiting by doors). In particular, a *sudden* loss can be overwhelming for a small child and have long-lasting effects (Trout, 1995).

So which is worse, to have loved and lost (separation from a primary caregiver) or to have never loved at all (failure to form an attachment)? Rutter (1981) looked at children from homes broken by divorce and children from homes where the mother had died. For children, the effects of these two circumstances (death and divorce) can result in similar short-term and long-term consequences (Kastenbaum, 1977). Rutter found that children from broken homes displayed higher rates of delinquent behavior than did children from intact homes. But what was causing the behavior problems—the breakup or difficulties in the home that led to the breakup? Rutter found that there was more delinquency in children from homes with family problems that caused the breakup than in children from stable homes where the mother had died. So it may not have been the loss of the caregiver that caused the behavior problems but difficulties in the broken homes. In general, there appear to be more problems for children who fail to form an attachment than for those who lose their primary caregiver (Bremmer, 1988).

Implications for Practice: Fostering Secure Attachment

Labeling early loss or separation as maternal deprivation implies that the mother is solely responsible for her infant's well-being. In actuality there are few effects from the lack of attachment to a biological mother (Bremmer, 1988). What is important is the quality of stimulation the child receives and some sense of continuity. A baby needs care that is consistent and continuous (Zigler & Stevenson, 1993). Consistent care means that one caregiver is predictable and reliable over time so that the baby can form a bond with that person. The mother is not the only person qualified for this role. Fathers, grandmothers, adoptive parents, aunts, and friends can all serve as primary caregivers. In fact, babies can form attachments to more than one person. A baby who receives nurturing care from a few people can form several attachments (Bremmer, 1988).

But this care needs to be consistent during infancy. Separations from the caregiver should be well planned, because babies tolerate separations better if they are prepared for the separation in advance. Trout (1995) suggests that even a very young infant be given information about a pending separation over and over. The child should be told that he may feel afraid, lonely, and sad. Children in foster care should receive regular visits with parents unless the parents are dangerous or there is no possibility of a reunion. Babies separated from caregivers do better if they are placed in a family-like environment. In fact, spending some time away from the caregiver with someone they are close to—at grandma's or a friend's home—may help children deal with later, more difficult separations (Stacey, Deardon, Pill, & Robinson, 1970).

In general, recovery from early separation and loss depends on the child, the circumstances of the loss, and what occurs after the loss. With good, loving care, children may be able to overcome the effects of early deprivation. Although it was once believed that trauma and deprivation in infancy would scar a person for life, research shows that infants are extremely resilient. With an adequate environment, appropriate intervention, and care provided in an enduring fashion, children may recover from early loss and deprivation (Emde, 1987).

Failure to Thrive

By definition, **failure to thrive** occurs when a child's weight falls below the 5th percentile for his age. Many failure-to-thrive babies begin life at normal weight but then decrease their rate of weight gain significantly. Some babies may be constitutionally small and naturally fall into this weight range. But for these babies, their height and weight drop simultaneously. For failure-to-thrive babies, weight drops before their height or head circumference begins to decline (Frank, Silva, & Needl-man, 1993).

Cases of failure to thrive are usually divided into two classifications—organic and nonorganic. In organic failure to thrive, there is an underlying medical condition such as congenital heart disease, cystic fibrosis, or renal disease that causes the growth decline. In nonorganic failure to thrive, no medical cause can be found. Cases of nonorganic failure to thrive have usually been attributed to emotional deprivation. Selma Fraiberg (1980) states that nonorganic failure to thrive "is almost universally associated with the impairment of the mother's capacity to nourish, both in the material and in the psychological sense of the word" (p. 104). In this instance, then, failure to thrive can be considered to have a psychological cause—maternal deprivation. And in fact, many mothers of failure to thrive infants are found to have been deprived in some way in their own childhood. Many of these mothers report an unhappy childhood and a difficult relationship with their own mothers. These factors may interfere with a woman's ability to emotionally respond to her infant and adequately meet his needs. Some believe that this emotional deprivation causes a decrease in the amount of growth hormone produced in the infant's pituitary gland, resulting in slow growth. Emotional tension also may increase the likelihood of the infant having vomiting and diarrhea or loss of appetite (Schuster & Ashburn, 1992).

Deborah Frank (1993) states, however, that emotional disturbance in itself does not cause slow growth. According to Frank, although emotional stress may be a contributing factor, failure to thrive is a problem of inadequate caloric intake. And it is not helpful to label the condition organic or nonorganic. Babies with heart or lung disease may have a medical cause for slow growth, but they may have also developed a feeding problem. And babies with nonorganic failure to thrive may have a genetically determined temperament that makes them difficult to feed. Failure to thrive, then, would not just be the result of maternal deprivation but of an interaction between biologic and environmental factors.

Failure to thrive can happen in families where parents obviously care about their children. Some babies are very difficult to feed—for instance, babies with cerebral palsy. An example would be the feeding scene from the movie *My Left Foot*, where a harried mom, in a very stressful family situation with a nondemanding child with cerebral palsy, spoons a couple of bites of mush into her child's mouth and then goes off to do a mountain of chores. Another situation occurs among premature babies. Twenty to forty percent of failure-to-thrive infants started out with low birth weight (Zigler & Stevenson, 1993). Low-birth-weight, premature babies can be difficult to feed. Remember, premature babies can be irritable and hard to care for. Also, some babies have chronic ear infections or sore throats. These babies may not feel well enough to eat most of the time. Because they have inadequate nutrition, they are more prone to be sick; and because they are sick, they are less likely to eat.

Family situations can contribute to failure to thrive. Families with high levels of stress may have a chaotic lifestyle and may fail to establish regular mealtimes. Family members may be too preoccupied with problems of living to notice that the child is not eating. They may feed the child in front of the TV, which can be very distracting. Some parents may be too controlling and get into "food battles" with their toddler. In this situation, the child gains power by not eating. Some weight-conscious parents may think that fat is bad and switch the baby to low-fat milk. Some mothers may be struggling with their own eating disorder, such as anorexia nervosa or bulimia, and may fail to understand the caloric needs of small children. Some families are dealing with depression, substance abuse, or domestic violence. Parents with a history of developmental delay may have trouble understanding nutritional requirements for babies. And of course, another contributing factor may be poverty. The Supplemental Food Program for Women, Infants and Children (WIC) provides only enough formula to meet 75% of an infant's daily needs. Some families may run out of money for food before the next AFDC check, packet of food stamps, or paycheck comes. Poverty also contributes to overcrowding, disorganization, and increased distractions in the home, all of which can interfere with feeding an infant (Frank, 1993).

Implications for Practice: Treating Failure to Thrive

Infancy is a time of rapid growth, and good nutrition during this time is vital for optimal development. Nutritional deficits during infancy can have long-lasting effects, including later personality problems, learning disorders, and mental retardation (Fraiberg, 1980). But blaming the mother for her infant's slow growth only makes her defensive and resistant to help. Ephross (1982) states that failure to thrive is not maternal emotional deprivation but a problem of family dysfunction with multiple causes. Failure-to-thrive families are not "bad" families but people with problems who need help.

These families may need counseling to deal with depression, substance abuse, grief and loss issues, and environmental stress. Parents may need help in establishing techniques to deal with a difficult, hard-to-feed infant. Many parents need help in improving parent-child interactions, especially in establishing positive, rewarding feeding experiences, free from coercion, food battles, and the distraction of television. Information on infant developmental norms and the nutritional needs of babies can benefit many new parents.

Infants with severe failure to thrive may require hospitalization, but many families require intensive outpatient and in-home treatment from a team of professionals including a pediatrician, nutritionist, and social worker for many months (Frank, 1993).

Infant Mental Health

On hearing the term *infant mental health*, many people laugh and ask how you do therapy with a baby. Does he lie in a crib and free-associate? Actually, in the last 20 years there has been a significant increase in the knowledge of the emotional, social, and cognitive functioning of infants. Along with this knowledge has come an interest in working with the problems of infancy. Infants are vulnerable creatures subject to abuse and neglect. Infants may withdraw from interactions and even seem to suffer from depression. They can also develop problems with feeding, sleeping, and behavioral regulation (Emde, 1987). But as we have seen, they are very resilient and can respond to appropriate intervention.

Out of the concern for the psychological problems of infancy has come the multidisciplinary specialty of infant mental health. This specialty is concerned with the factors that affect the psychological health of infants and with development of methods to assess and treat these small clients (Lieberman, 1985). The traditional knowledge base and intervention skills of social workers are especially suited for work in this field (Bonkowski & Yanos, 1992). Passage of the Education of the Handicapped Act Amendments of 1986 requires that states provide family-based services for at-risk children from birth to age 3. This requirement opens opportunities for social workers to become actively involved in providing services to infants and their families.

Social Dimension
Families, Groups, Support Systems, and Contexts

A baby is no longer seen as a passive creature controlled by his basic instincts but is viewed as an active participant in the family environment (Emde, 1987). Treatment of an infant cannot be separated from treatment of the family. Interventions with infants require a systems approach, because problems with a baby do not reside in the baby but in the interactions between the baby and a caregiver or the baby and the family. So in working with infants, you do not concentrate on the baby alone or the parent alone but on their relationship and on relationships among other family members (Jennings, Wisner, & Conby, 1991).

In fact, many researchers now feel that an infant needs to be viewed less as an individual and more as a social product. Sameroff (1993) describes a transactional model of infant development: ". . . the development of the child is seen as a product of a continuous dynamic interaction between the child and the experience provided by his or her family and social context" (p. 6).

Family Influences

Factors in the family that can affect development include parental personality and temperament, parental mental illness, major family transitions such as death and divorce, and periods of parental unresponsiveness such as occur with depression (Crnic & Harris, 1990). Intergenerational patterns also often impact the family environment. Parenting styles are passed on from parents to children, who then use the same style with their own children (Lyons-Ruth & Zeanah, 1993). Parents who abuse their children were often abused as children themselves.

Interactions in the family seem to occur in a circular pattern. Parents who are satisfied with the marriage may interact positively with the baby and have a responsive infant. Stress in the relationship can preoccupy the parents and affect the quality of their interaction with the infant. Marital problems, then, can negatively affect the baby's development.

Ironically, one of the major sources of stress in the relationship can be the babies themselves. A demanding infant can increase the family stress level, which can then interfere with the parents' interactions, which in turn can affect the baby's responses.

Belsky (1981) describes these interactions as **circular influences.** He states that "what transpires between husband and wife might affect a parent's caregiving attitudes and/or behavior, which in turn could influence the infant's functioning, which, coming full circle, might affect the marital relationship." And Clarke-Stewart (1978) looks at this circular influence still another way. The mother's stimulating involvement with the infant enhances the infant's development. This responsive infant increases the father's participation in parenting. The father's interest in the infant further increases the mother's involvement with the baby.

Other family relationships can also play an important role in determining the quality of the family environment. In general, a mother's relationships affect how she cares for the infant, and this care affects the infant's development (Crockenberg, Lyons-Ruth, & Dickstein, 1993). The more support the caregiver receives, the bet-

ter care the infant receives. As we have seen, social support is especially important for caregivers of handicapped infants, premature infants, and for caregivers with problems such as depression. Caregivers deal with stress better—whether it is from the infant, or other factors of life—if there is adequate support (Crnic & Harris, 1990).

If we consider that the mother is usually the caregiver, where does she receive most of this support? A study by Levitt (1986) asked mothers of 13-month-old infants to identify individuals who supplied support for them. The top two people on the list were family members—the father of the baby and the maternal grandmother. These two family members, then, can indirectly affect the infant's development by supplying support for the mother, but what direct influence might they also have on the infant?

Fathers and Babies   One of the authors of this book asked on the birth of his first son, "When do I get to throw him in the air?" Studies have found that this is a usual male response to interacting with an infant. In general, fathers spend less time with the baby than mothers do. When they do spend time with the baby, that time usually involves playing more than caregiving. Mothers actually play more with babies, but that is because they spend more overall time with the infant. And the quality of the play that fathers engage in with the infant differs from that of mothers. Mothers involve the infant in verbal interactions, whereas fathers are more physical and rough with their babies. They tend to move the infant's limbs and bounce and lift the infant in the air (Yogman, 1982).

Belsky, Gilstrap, and Rovine (1984) found that fathers also spent more time reading and watching TV with infants, whereas mothers spent more time nurturing and caring for the infants. This does not mean, however, that fathers cannot be nurturing and sensitive caretakers. Fathers who do spend more time with babies and engage in caretaking activities can be sensitive to an infant's cues (Lamb, 1982). What happens when the father is the primary caregiver? The father is just as competent in giving care as the mother is (Parke & O'Leary, 1976), but the father still plays in a more physical way with the infant (Field, 1978).

Fathers, then, can be competent primary caregivers. Babies can form an attachment with fathers much the

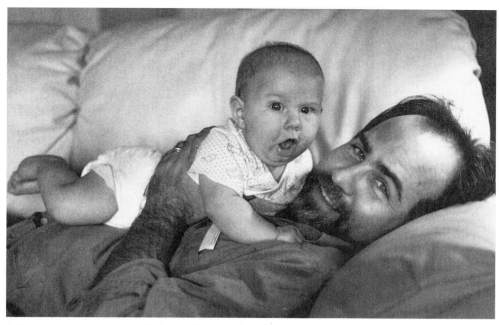

Fathers are an important source of sensory, affective, and social stimulation for infants.

same as they do with their mothers (Lamb, 1982). The more fathers interact with infants, the greater impact they can have on development.

Grandparents and Babies Next to the baby's father, the maternal grandmother is the main source of support for most mothers. For single mothers, the maternal grandmother is often the first source of support. For teenage mothers, the grandmother can even step in as the infant's primary caregiver.

Three out of five children see their grandparents at least once per week (Tinsley & Parke, 1987). Studies have found that infants who have frequent contact with their grandparents interact with grandparents in the same manner they do with their parents (Crockenberg, Lyons-Ruth, & Dickstein, 1993), and babies whose grandparents interact with them show higher developmental scores (Tinsley & Parke, 1987), much as they do when they have highly responsive parents. When the mother is struggling with difficulties that interfere with her ability to care for a baby, the grandmother can medi-

ate the effect these maternal problems have on the infant. When the mother is young, single, mentally ill, addicted to drugs, or unable to care for the infant, the grandmother can provide consistent and nurturing care for the baby.

In addition, with so many mothers returning to work after the birth of their babies, many grandmothers are assuming childcare responsibilities (Lewis, 1987). This is especially true for lower-SES families. In some cases, because of parents' substance abuse, poverty, hopelessness, and disability from AIDS, grandparents are serving as primary caregivers and are raising the children. Oyserman, Radin, and Benn (1993) suggest that grandfathers can fill the role of absent fathers for children of single mothers. In fact, the American Association for Retired Persons (AARP) now publishes a newsletter for grandparents raising grandchildren and provides a grandparent information center.

Siblings and Babies Often the mother of an infant with an older sibling, when asked the age of her baby, will reply with something like, "He's 18 months, but he thinks he's 4." Infants with an older sibling may spend a large portion of their time in the company of that sibling. Spending so much time with another person can certainly influence development. Infants tend to imitate their older siblings. If the interactions with the sibling are positive, the baby can learn sharing and cooperation (Dunn, 1991). However, 25% of all interactions between 18-month-olds and their siblings involve conflict and aggression. Dunn and Munn (1986) found that the level of aggression of an older sibling was correlated to the level of aggression of the younger child six months later.

Crockenberg, Lyons-Ruth, and Dickstein (1993) state that because infants imitate older siblings, it is important to understand how siblings influence infant development. More research is needed in this area. Can a sibling help provide comfort and support when parents are emotionally or physically unavailable? On the other hand, can an aggressive sibling teach the baby to be more aggressive in interactions with others?

Babies and Their Peers   Young babies often interact by curiously poking each other in the eyes. Actually, babies really do interact with each other—at least to some extent. In the first year, babies look, smile, touch, and vocalize with each other (Mueller & Vandell, 1979). In the second year, toys become more important in interactions. Of course, many of these interactions involve taking toys away from each other. But babies can also play some simple games together (Mueller & Lucas, 1975). Babies will play contingency games, in which one will perform an action and the other will respond to it; say, one baby will throw a doll up in the air and the other will scream. At 20 months, babies begin to more fully interact with each other. They begin to take turns in an activity and may be able to roll a ball back and forth without running to retrieve the ball before it reaches the other baby.

Adoption

"California couple, financially secure, with much love and affection to offer, wishes to adopt white newborn to age 1. Suburban home, lots of pets. Can provide a secure and rewarding life for your baby."

Newspapers are full of such ads placed by couples looking for a baby to adopt. Many ads specify white newborns, but with the number of young girls who choose abortion or single parenting, the search for a white infant can be long and frustrating.

Adoptions can be arranged through an agency or a private source. Most states have agencies that handle adoptions in the state welfare department or department of children's services. Children can also be adopted through private agencies that are regulated by the state. The wait for an infant through an agency, though, may take years, so some couples seek other adoption options.

In some states, private adoptions can be arranged through a physician or lawyer. Adoptions can even be started through ads placed in the newspaper and then processed privately by a lawyer. There are more problems connected with these private adoptions, however. Parents pursuing this type of adoption may receive less background information on the birth parents than they would through an agency, and birth mothers receive less counseling. The financial costs to the adopting couple can be high. And private adoptions may have more legal problems than agency adoptions (Costin, Bell, & Downs, 1991).

Because the supply of white infants is so limited, some parents choose to adopt older children, special-needs children, or foreign infants. One-half of children adopted are over 2 years old. Special-needs children include those who have disabilities, and the state may provide a subsidy to these parents to help cover medical expenses. Ten percent of adoptions are international adoptions (Schuster & Ashburn, 1992).

Open Adoptions   In years past, parents who adopted children as infants often debated whether or not to tell the child about the adoption. Many children grew up not knowing they were adopted, and for those who knew of the adoption, the birth mother's identity was kept secret. Parents are now encouraged to be honest with the child from the beginning. In 1975, laws changed to allow adults who had been adopted to obtain information about their birth parents if those parents did not object. This change in attitude toward adoption information has led to **open adoptions.**

In this type of adoption, the birth mother and sometimes the birth father participate in choosing a family for their baby. That family may choose to attend childbirth preparation with the birth mother and be present at the baby's birth. The birth mother may stay in contact with the family as the child grows, exchanging letters and photographs. Sometimes visits are arranged between the birth mother and the child. In some cases these visits are arranged through the adoption agency and are limited to once or twice a year, whereas in other cases the birth mother may serve as the child's baby-sitter (Foster, Hunsberger, & Anderson, 1989).

Open adoptions can lead to problems, though. What about families with adopted children from different birth parents? What if one birth mother stays in contact with the child and the other does not? What if the birth mother ceases contact with the child at a later time? In addition, adoptive parents may agree to any conditions of the birth mother in order to have a baby. How does this affect their parenting abilities (Costin, Bell, & Downs, 1991)? On the other hand, the birth mother may change her mind after the baby is born, leaving a couple—who may have waited through the pregnancy, furnished a nursery, and attended the birth—without a child. But when both sets of parents agree on the conditions of the open adoption, this arrangement can be satisfactory to all involved.

Transracial Adoptions   Adoption of children of a different race from the adopting family—**transracial adoption**—is highly controversial. The majority of couples looking to adopt a child are white, but many of the children available for adoption are not. This means that without transracial adoption, many white couples remain childless while minority children wait in foster care for permanent homes twice as long as white children do (Smith, 1995). But the National Association of Black Social Workers (NABSW) is opposed to transracial adoptions. They believe that African American children raised in a white home will lose connection with their race and culture—that the children will grow up not fitting into either culture.

The Multiethnic Placement Act of 1994 prohibits adoption decisions based solely on race, color, or national origin. This law was developed in order to reduce the amount of time minority children wait to be adopted. (This law does not affect the Indian Child Welfare Act, discussed in the next section.) The National Association of Social Workers (NASW) still states that efforts should be made to place a child in the home of

Many families choose to adopt. This family has adopted two children of mixed race.

parents who are of similar racial and ethnic background. The NABSW now recommends that transracial adoptions be considered, but only as a last resort.

Prospective foster and adoptive parents need to become familiar with and understand racial and cross-cultural issues before adopting a child of different race. Efforts need to be made to increase the number of prospective foster and adoptive parents from all races and cultures (Smith, 1995).[1]

Native American Adoptions Another controversy surrounds the adoption of Native American children. In the 1950s and 1960s, 25 to 35% of all Native American children were removed from their families. Many of these children were taken from parents who were poor and lived in homes with no indoor plumbing. After adoption, these children were often raised in circumstances that deprived them of their culture and heritage. Many believed that this practice was threatening the future of Native American tribes (Doyle, 1995).

In 1978, Congress passed the Indian Child Welfare Act, giving tribes control over adoption of Native American children. Adoptions involving Native American children require not only a release from the birth parents but also a release from the tribe. Even when the parents agree to the adoption by a non-Indian family, the tribe can veto the process and place the child with a Native American family. Critics claim that children have been removed from adoptive parents and returned to a tribe even when the birth parents did not live on a reservation and had no tribal affiliation. Tribes argue, however, that to preserve heritage, Native American children need to be raised by Native American families.

Birth Fathers The rights of birth fathers is another area of concern. The well-publicized case of Baby Jessica illustrates this problem. Jan and Roberta DeBoer adopted a 1-week-old baby girl after the baby's birth mother agreed to the adoption and signed the release. However, the birth mother lied about the identity of the baby's father, claiming the father was her present boyfriend. She changed her mind about the adoption after several weeks and told the real father of the baby—her ex-boyfriend, Dan Schmidt. He then petitioned for custody of the baby on the grounds that he had not signed a

[1]Written by Jane Wenk, MSW.

release for the adoption as the father of the infant. The DeBoers challenged the petition in court for two years. Finally, the Supreme Court refused to hear the case, upholding a lower-court decision giving custody of the baby to the birth parents, who had in the meantime married and given birth to another child. As the nation watched on television, Jessica, then 2 years old, was removed, crying, from the arms of her adopted mother and turned over to her birth parents.

In 1972, the Supreme Court ruled that unwed fathers could not be denied custody of their children unless they were proved unfit as parents. But how long a time period should an unwed father have to assert his parental rights? Some states allow six months, which is a long time for a baby to wait for a home. Some agencies will not consider an adoption unless the birth mother names the father of the baby so his release may be obtained. But some birth mothers will not name the father out of fear or because they do not want him to be involved (Foster, Hunsberger, & Anderson, 1989). Many men do not learn of the birth of a child until the child has been placed in an adoptive home. At that point, should the baby be removed from a home the child may have lived in for several months and be turned over to the birth father? On the other hand, if the man is not an unfit parent, should the birth mother be allowed to decide the fate of his child without his consent?

In 1983, the Supreme Court ruled that men could not claim rights to a child unless they had established a relationship with the child. How can a man establish a relationship, though, if the birth mother keeps the pregnancy and birth a secret from him? In response to this problem, New York and other states have established a putative father registry for unwed fathers. An unmarried man must register so that he can be notified of any adoption proceedings involving a potential offspring.

Implications for Practice:
Making Difficult Decisions in Adoption Practices

Adoption brings up the question of what takes precedence: the best interests of the child or the rights of the birth parents, ethnic group, or tribe? Children have been removed from homes they have lived in for months because of issues of paternal rights, same-race placement, and tribal affiliation. Some claim that the children's rights should be considered first and that they should remain in homes where they have come to consider the adoptive parents their family. But the issue is very complicated. For instance, many were appalled that baby Jessica was removed from the only home she had ever known to total strangers who just happened to be her parents. But her birth father had petitioned for parental rights when she was only 3 weeks old. The DeBoers fought a long battle that lasted two years, but some believe that the best interest of the child would have been to surrender the baby in the beginning instead of keeping her until she was attached to her adoptive family.

Social workers need to carefully consider these issues. What are the rights of birth fathers? Should children be raised in same-race homes? How long should children wait in foster care for same-race families? Should tribes have the right to protect cultural heritage?

Another issue concerns children placed in foster care because of abuse or neglect. These children may wait for years for parental rights to be terminated to release them for adoption. Many believe that these children should be permanently removed from their parents and placed for adoption. Others favor family preservation efforts with the ultimate goal of reuniting children with their birth families (Foster, Hunsberger, & Anderson, 1989). They feel that poor people are penalized by having their children removed. Many birth mothers are poor and single, whereas couples wishing to adopt are financially secure and married. And sometimes children love their parents even though those parents are inadequate.

FOCUS ON SOCIOLOGY

How Are Adoptive Families Doing?

Approximately 25% of adopted children, as compared to 15% of nonadopted children, require clinical intervention for severe behavioral problems. However, research by psychologists reveals that adopted children and their adoptive families are doing quite well.

David Brodzinsky at Rutgers University has been studying adoption for more than 20 years, and he reports that approximately 75 to 80% of adopted children are well within the normal psychological range. Adopted children are most often referred for clinical treatment for problems such as acting out or aggression starting at age 5 to 7 years, when children are just beginning to understand that they've lost their birth family as well as having gained their adoptive family. Brodzinsky found that coping styles affected their experiences—children in adoptive families that had a problem-focused, assistance-seeking style of coping fared much better than did those with an avoidant style of coping. He also found that adopted children have neither more nor less serious problems than do nonadopted children when their parents divorce—it affects both groups "in a serious way." Anu Sharma and her colleagues at the Search Institute in Minneapolis conducted a study of 181 adopted adolescents and found that most of the teens were functioning within the normal mental health range and that the teens described themselves as attached to their parents. Children from open adoptions, in which birth mothers have contact with their children, also seem to lack the confusion many had feared they would have about their parents' identity. Harold Grotevant at the University of Minnesota and Ruth McRoy at the University of Texas at Austin found that the children view their adoptive mother as their mother and view the birth mother as an aunt or friend. The experience of adoption also brings adoptive parents closer together. Cornell University researcher Jeffrey Haugaard finds this to be especially true in cases where the child has problematic behavior, because the parents come together to deal with this behavior. Haugaard also found that older adoptees form stronger attachments to their adopted fathers than to their adopted mothers; he speculates that this may be because they feel abandoned by their birth mother. Ellen Pinderhughes at Vanderbilt University is developing a family-systems model to research situations such as this where birth mothers' maternal rights have been terminated due to abuse or neglect.

Source: Adapted from DeAngelis, 1995.

Day Care

In Chapter 11, we discuss the fact that, in general, maternal employment may have a positive effect on children's development. But what about infants under a year old whose mothers work full-time outside the home? Does maternal employment in the first year interfere with attachment? Do babies who grow up in day care suffer any ill effects? Many researchers have tried to answer these questions.

Belsky and Rovine (1988) looked at attachment in infants with working mothers. Their research suggested that babies whose mothers worked more than 20 hours a week were at risk of forming insecure attachments. Clarke-Stewart (1989) argues, however, that such studies run into problems because they use the Strange Situation procedure to assess attachment. Children in day care may be more used to strangers and may not exhibit apprehension in a stranger's presence. When assessed using the Strange Situation procedure, then, these children would not be wary of the strange situation or the stranger and would therefore not receive secure attachment rating. In fact, other studies (Chase-Landsdale & Owen, 1987) have found no difference in attachment for children in day care. In relation to day care affecting attachment, Belsky and Rovine (1988) concluded that it is too hard to say what the effects are because it depends "on the child, the family, and the particular day care arrangements" (see Focus on Research: Who's Minding the Baby?). In fact, some professionals are beginning to think that day care gives children a secure caregiver with whom to form an attachment when the home lacks a secure, reliable caregiver.

Implications for Practice: The Realities of Day Care

Although it is interesting to discuss the effects of day care on child development, many mothers do not have much choice about whether or not they return to work after the birth of a baby. Financially, many women need to work to pay the bills and buy the food. Some women return to work within weeks of giving birth. They must find care for their infants, and there just are not enough federally subsidized day-care centers for low-income women (Specht & Craig, 1987). Some studies have suggested that good day care can increase the cognitive and social functioning of disadvantaged children (Brock, 1980), but many jobs available to low-income women do not pay enough for them to afford good day care. Without federally subsidized care, these women must rely on

other arrangements that may not be as beneficial to the baby's development.

FOCUS ON RESEARCH

Who's Minding the Baby?

More than half of the children living in the United States are in the care of someone other than their mother for significant periods of time. What type of child care is best in terms of a child's healthy psychological development? Until now the answer wasn't clear, but a study of child care conducted by the National Institute of Child Health and Human Development (NICHD) provides some revealing data.

In 1990, a team of NICHD researchers recruited 1364 infants from two-parent and single-parent families across the United States representing a range of socioeconomic and sociocultural backgrounds. The study included a random sample of which approximately 60% had mothers who worked or attended school full-time, 20% had mothers who worked or attended school part-time, and 20% had mothers who stayed at home full-time. Parents of the infants studied chose a variety of child-care situations, including child care provided by the fathers and grandparents of the child, child care in a home setting, and child care in a day-care center.

Researchers find that children are most likely to receive higher-quality caregiving when there are fewer children being cared for and the child-to-adult ratios are low. This study also revealed that less authoritarian beliefs about child-rearing on the part of caregivers, as well as the provision of stimulating physical facilities, were most likely to result in higher-quality caregiving. According to the research, the highest quality of caregiving was provided by fathers and grandparents as well as in-home caregivers, whereas the lowest quality of caregiving was provided by child-care centers. However, regardless of care type, an adult-child ratio of 1 to 1 was the best predictor of high-quality caregiving.

Source: Adapted from Azar, 1995.

Multicultural and Gender Considerations

When feeding their infants, mothers in Yorkshire, England, tell their children something about the spoonful of food "going to Auntie Mary's in Bradford." Mothers in Newfoundland tell small children that if they don't eat the crusts of their bread, the Crust Man will steal the children away. Many American mothers fly spoonfuls of food like airplanes into their childrens' mouths. In other cultures such as the Malay, as soon as children learn to walk they are expected to feed themselves when they get hungry with no encouraging comments from mother (Dettwyler, 1989). These various feeding practices illustrate the fact that parents in different cultures bring different beliefs, attitudes, and practices to the raising of their children. Even in the United States, the child-raising practices and beliefs of ethnic groups can be quite different from those of the majority culture.

In addition to having differing parental beliefs, minority infants also experience different family contexts. Minority infants are more likely to live in homes with younger mothers, single mothers, and large extended families (Coll & Myer, 1993). Minority families face problems including socioeconomic disadvantage, inadequate access to health care, residential segregation, substandard housing, and unemployment. Coll and Myer (1993) state that "if we recognize that these minority and ethnic families experience different cultural expectations, family constellations and access to economic and social resources, in addition to being subjected to prejudice, racism, classism, sexism, and segregation, we would expect that their world view and their infants' developmental outcome would be profoundly affected by these life experiences" (p. 60).

Developmental Assessment of Minority Infants

Of particular concern is the developmental assessment of minority infants, because the norms established for developmental assessment instruments are based on the majority of children in this country, who are Anglo. Compared with these norms, some minority children may appear abnormal. In particular, African infants appear developmentally advanced whereas Native American and Asian infants may be a bit reserved on standard measures. You may remember from the last chapter that there is some evidence that these characteristics may be ge-

netic, but infant-care practices among these cultures also vary and may contribute to this difference. African infants are handled vigorously by their mothers from birth. Their mothers place them in an upright position for most of the day and encourage early sitting, standing, and walking (Cintas, 1988). Native American and Asian infants, on the other hand, are more protected by their parents.

Cintas (1988) cautions that practitioners "working among a heterogeneous population such as that in the U.S. need to be cognizant that cultural variations in developmental patterns do exist. Further, since infant care practices appear to have some influence on neuromotor performance, North American therapists and families can perhaps benefit from knowledge of parent care methods in other cultures" (p. 17).

FOCUS ON MULTICULTURALISM

Understanding Different Cultural Beliefs

Understanding different cultural beliefs is important when working with minority families with infants. Coll and Myer (1993) discuss the clinical implications of working with families from minority cultures. First, the family with different attitudes and beliefs may not feel that a "problem"—whether biological, psychological, or social—exists. For instance, in some cultures, having a baby as a teen is a way to gain status and respect in the community. Dealing with the "problems" of teenage motherhood in this community, then, could be difficult if the community does not see it as a problem. In fact, Burton (1990) found that in one African American community with a high level of male unemployment, teenage childbearing was encouraged; because the maternal grandmother would be caring for the infant, she (as the mother of the teenager) would be young enough to take care of and enjoy the baby. Families have different ideas as to the origin of a problem as well (Coll & Meyer, 1993). Some families may see a developmental problem as an act of God, as punishment for past sins, or as a test of faith. Some may turn to faith healers or religious leaders for a cure. Families also differ in their expectations of treatment. Play therapy to facilitate parent-infant interactions may be inappropriate for cultures that do not see the mother's role as including playing with her children. In those cultures, grandparents, siblings, and other children are expected to interact with infants. Asian mothers often take on the role of teacher of their infants (Coll & Meyer, 1993).

Coll and Meyer (1993) suggest a series of cultural assessment questions that can help provide an idea of how a family views a problem—what the problem is, how it originated, and what the family expects in terms of treatment.

1. What do you think caused your child's problem?
2. Why do you think it started when it did?
3. What do you think the problem does to your child? How does it work?
4. How severe is your child's problem? Do you expect it will have a short- or long-term course?
5. What kind of treatment do you think your child should receive?
6. What are the most important results that you hope to have your child receive from treatment?
7. What are the main things that the problem has caused for you and your child?
8. What do you fear most about your child's problem?

Source: Adapted from Coll & Meyer, 1993.

Gender Issues

Some mothers joke that the first time you hand a baby boy a truck, he will push it on the floor and say, "rrrrrrr" or some other appropriate truck noise, whereas a baby girl will try to feed it her bottle. Just how different are baby boys and girls and how much of that difference is learned from their parents?

Although children do not label themselves as boys or girls until they are 2 1/2 to 3 years old, they display gender differences in behavior from birth (Coll & Meyer, 1993). As summarized in Bjorklund and Bjorklund (1992), boys are more aggressive, more active, take more chances, are more demanding of parental attention, and get into more mischief as toddlers. Girls are more nurturing and more compliant at this age.

In the second year of life, infants begin to show toy preferences. By 18 to 22 months, boys play more with trucks and cars and girls play with dolls and soft toys (Smith & Daglish, 1977). But to what extent do parents and others encourage children to play with these sex-appropriate toys?

Babies actually are treated differently from birth. Parents are more rough and active with baby boys and more verbally interactive with baby girls. Studies by Fagot (1978, 1991) show that fathers give fewer positive responses to boys who play with cross-sex toys and mothers give more verbal instructions to girls. Parents encourage girls to participate in dancing, playing dress-up, and playing with dolls, whereas they encourage boys to play with blocks, trucks, and push-and-pull toys. Interestingly, children of parents who encourage sex-type toy play can accurately label themselves as boy or girl sooner (Fagot, 1989, 1992).

Even parents who want to be non–gender specific in interactions with their infants may unconsciously alter their responses. For instance, consider a 14-month-old girl who brings a truck to show to her mother. Her mother wants to encourage her daughter to play with typically male toys, so she says, "What have you got there, a truck? That's good, honey." Then the baby approaches her mother with a doll and mother says, "What a pretty baby. Is she your baby? Is she hungry? Are you her mommy? Maybe you should feed her. Go get her bottle and give her some milk. You be the mommy and feed your baby." Which toy do you think the little girl has been rewarded for playing with? With the interactions that occur between babies, parents, and others, children may refuse to play with cross-sex toys by the age of 18 to 24 months (Shaffer, 1993).

Coll and Meyer (1993) offer this conclusion from the literature on gender and infants: "Gender differences in behavior from birth have been documented in a variety of cultures. . . . But more important than actual sex differences in behavior may be the caregivers' interpretations of an infant's behavior, development, and needs as a function of the infant's gender" (p. 59).

Social Hazards

As we discussed in the last chapter, poverty can have a detrimental effect on development. Infants in poor families are more likely to have inadequate nutrition and are also more likely to have increased blood lead levels (see the section on lead poisoning). Poor infants have more health problems and more injuries, and when abused or neglected they are more likely to be removed from their homes. Seventy percent of children in foster care are from poor families (Halpern, 1993).

Infants living in poverty are more likely to have an impoverished environment with irregular daily routines, overcrowding, little attention for the baby, and lack of parental responsiveness (Halpern, 1993). Poverty adds to the caregiver's stress, making it difficult to care for an infant. The effects of prenatal poverty may have resulted in a premature birth or a baby with complications. This infant may need extra care and parental responsiveness, but the energy of the mother must go to dealing with the problems of living and not to the infant. Halpern states that "a fussy, disorganized, low birthweight infant is likely to overtax the limited physical and emotional resources of an already overstressed mother" (p. 75). The mother may then avoid interacting with the infant.

Homeless infants are at highest risk. Having no home makes it very difficult to meet the needs of an infant. How does a homeless caregiver prepare bottles, store infant food, wash clothes, provide a safe environment to explore, find toys? Because of poverty, then, a difficult-to-care-for infant may be born to an overstressed mother with few resources. The infant adds to the mother's stress, and the baby is at increased risk of abuse and neglect.

Environmental Context and Child Development

So far, in considering factors that can affect development, we have looked at the characteristics of the child and then of the family. A third variable that is important for optimal development is the type of environment the child experiences—in other words, the child's home. The quality of the home environment affects the health and development of an individual, and a poor environment may result in poor development. Halpern (1993) discusses aspects of the infant's environment that contribute to good developmental outcomes, including the cognitive, socioemotional, and physical environment of the home.

Cognitively, infants develop well if they receive rich and varied verbal interaction from their caregivers. The caregivers should place an emphasis on learning and provide a variety of stimulation for the baby. In the socioemotional realm, infants need parents who are responsive, warm, and nurturing. Harsh punishment can have negative effects for the baby. The physical environment should be safe and well organized. The baby should have adequate areas to explore. Appropriate and stimulating toys and play materials should be available for the infant to investigate and manipulate.

Taking these factors into consideration, what is an impoverished environment? This would be a home that is overcrowded, noisy, and disorganized. The baby would have no set routine or predictability. Multiple caregivers would come and go. Someone may calm the baby by handing the child a bottle filled with cola. The baby may be confined to a small area with few toys or interesting objects to manipulate. The baby would receive little or no verbal interaction or warmth from caregivers. Caregivers may fail to respond to or meet the baby's needs.

Implications for Practice: Assessing the Home Environment

Quality of the home environment should be considered when making an assessment. Researchers have developed various methods for measuring the quality of a child's home. The most widely used measurement is the Home Observation for Measurement of the Environment Inventory, or HOME Inventory (Caldwell & Bradley, 1984). This instrument is designed to measure the quality and quantity of stimulation and support available to the child in the home. It consists of 45 items separated into 6 subscales: parental responsivity, acceptance of child, organization of environment, play materials, parental involvement with child, and variety of stimulation (see Box 6.2). Assessment of the environment consists of observation of the home and a semistructured interview conducted in the child's home with a primary caregiver (Bradley & Brisby, 1990).

Infant Abuse and Foster Care

One-third of the child victims of abuse are less than 1 year old. A common injury to babies at this age is head trauma. Infants who are difficult to soothe and who cry uncontrollably are at particular risk of this type of injury (Mrazek, 1993). Head trauma may occur from someone hitting the baby's head against a hard object, but a head injury can also occur if someone shakes the infant. This form of abuse is known as **shaken infant syndrome.** Some parents who would never dream of hitting a baby's head against a wall will pick a crying infant up and, out of sheer frustration, shake the baby. Difficult and demanding infants may be at a higher risk for this type of abuse. It is not hard to imagine that, after a long day when you are tired and trying to get dinner and the baby has been crying for the last 2 hours and nothing you do will make the crying stop, even a gentle person may pick up the baby and give a good shake. Many parents do not realize, however, that shaking an infant can cause severe injury. Babies have weak neck muscles and cannot con-trol their head well. When shaken, their head moves back and forth rapidly and their brain hits against the skull. This action can result in bruising and bleeding of the brain and in subsequent brain damage.

Parents at risk of physically harming their infants need help. They need to understand that the baby's responses are not intentional; the baby is not out to get them. They need help in learning to control and modify their infant's responses, and they may need to adjust the level of stimulation the baby receives. They need to understand differences in temperament—that a difficult, demanding baby cannot help being that way. They may need help in dealing with stress in their lives and in finding adequate resources and social support. These parents need to know that when they are at the end of their rope and on the verge of lashing out at the infant, they should put the baby in the crib, close the door, and take a break.

BOX 6.2

Sample Items from the HOME Inventory (Infant-Toddler Version)

Emotional and Verbal Responsivity of Parents
Parent responds to the child's vocalizations with verbal response.
Parent caresses or kisses child at least once during visit.

Acceptance of Child
Parent does not shout at child during visit.
Parent does not interfere with child's actions or restrict child's movements more than three times during visit.

Organization of the Physical and Temporal Environment
When parent is away, care is provided by one of three regular substitutes.
Someone takes child to grocery store at least once a week.

Provision of Appropriate Play Materials
Child has some muscle-activity toys or equipment.
Parent provides toys or some interesting activities for child during visit.

Parental Involvement with Child
Parent consciously encourages developmental advance.
Parent structures child's play periods.

Opportunities for Variety in Daily Stimulation
Father provides some caretaking every day.
Family visits or receives visits from relatives once a month.

Source: Adapted from Bradley & Brisby, 1990.

They can call someone else to come over and deal with the baby for awhile. They especially need to know to *never shake a baby.*

Another possible form of infant abuse is **Munchausen's syndrome by proxy.** In this form of abuse, the caregiver (usually the mother) induces symptoms of illness in her child. The mother may administer syrup of ipecac to the baby to induce vomiting or may place drops of blood in the infant's urine. Of particular concern are babies who seem to be suffering from apnea (episodes where breathing stops). This apnea may be a result of efforts by the mother to fabricate illness in the child.

Infants who are abused or neglected may be removed from their parents and placed in foster care. In many cases, the aim is to return the child to the parents when the abusive or neglectful situation changes. Some children, though, remain in foster care for a long time, waiting to return home or to be placed for adoption. And some children move from one foster home to another. This lack of permanence and continuity of care can have detrimental effects on an infant.

Fahlberg (1991) suggests the following guidelines for children placed in foster care. The child's previous caregivers should participate in the placement decision. The caregivers should be included in a separation interview to help determine what type of placement would be best for the child. Caregivers should continue visiting the child in foster care—visitation allows the attachment relationship to continue and allows the caregivers to practice more positive interactions with the child. Whenever possible, siblings should be placed in the same foster home.

Lead Poisoning

In older buildings, constructed before 1950, walls were painted with paint that contained up to 50% lead. As the buildings aged, the paint began to peel off the walls. In poor areas, many neglected, run-down dwellings have problems with peeling lead-based paint. Infants will put anything in their mouths, including these paint chips. Eating this paint causes lead to build up in their systems. Children with high lead levels in their blood may have problems with learning and with delayed growth and hearing loss. One out of six children in the United States has toxic blood lead levels that can affect intellectual functioning. The percent of poor children with high

lead levels is nine times higher than that of more affluent children. The lead levels of African American children are six times higher (Bellinger & Needleman, 1985).

In fact, the lead does not even have to be ingested. Even in homes where the paint is not peeling off the walls, the house dust can contain lead. Studies have shown that daily exposure to even low levels of lead in the environment can result in inattention, hyperactivity, and irritability (Marlowe, 1985). Although older housing is the main source of lead exposure, lead in the environment is also produced through industrial emissions and from the exhaust of leaded gasolines. Drinking water can also contain lead.

Social workers need to be aware of programs to remove lead-based paint from older dwellings. But that is only part of the problem. Because lead is present in the environment from other sources, many children are at risk of lead poisoning. And now researchers are finding that even low lead levels can affect learning. For this reason, it is now being recommended that all children with learning disabilities or behavior problems be screened for lead exposure. Early identification and treatment reduces the risk of permanent damage, and an inexpensive blood test can identify lead exposure (Marlowe, 1985). The child should then be removed from the source of the exposure. If the lead level is high, medications can help remove lead from the body.

Parents with Mental Illness

Children whose parents have a mental illness are more at risk of developing mental illness themselves (Seifer & Dickstein, 1993). Some of this risk is genetic, but some risk comes from the parents' behavior. The risk is particularly high if the parent has bipolar disorder or schizophrenia, is addicted to alcohol or drugs, or is depressed. These types of mental illness can interfere with parent-infant interactions.

For example, a depressed mother may fail to make eye contact when feeding the infant, may be less inclined to play with the infant, and may be less responsive to the infant. To a depressed mother, the infant may seem demanding and troublesome. Because the mother is more likely to be negative in her interactions with the baby, the baby then reflects the mother's mood and is more negative in interactions both with the mother and with other adults. As a toddler, the child of a depressed mother seems more negative and impulsive, engages in more conflict with the mother, and may exhibit an insecure attachment (Seifer & Dickstein, 1993).

Maternal depression is of particular concern because some women seem to suffer from a form of depression after giving birth. A large percentage of women experience some low feelings after having a baby; these feelings are usually attributed to changing hormones or fatigue. This *postpartum depression* clears up in a few days or weeks. But some women may display clinical signs of depression that last for months. There is some question as to whether this type of postpartum depression is any different from other forms of depression (Seifer & Dickstein, 1993). In fact, the DSM-IV classifies postpartum depression as Major Depressive Episode with Postpartum Onset if the depression occurs within four weeks of delivery. Women who experience postpartum depression should not pass the depression off as "baby blues" but should be encouraged to seek treatment.

Parents with a History of Developmental Delay

Several problems can arise for infants of parents with a history of developmental delay. Many mothers with mental retardation have low self-esteem (Bromwich, 1985). They may not be emotionally available to the infant, and they may lack skills in reading and responding to the baby's cues. They may lack judgment about what is safe handling of an infant and may be rough with the baby. They may lack the ability to be flexible and adapt their responses to the changing needs of a growing child (Bromwich, 1985).

In-home help and parenting programs can benefit many parents who are developmentally delayed. Having another adult in the home can make a critical difference (Bromwich, 1985). Some parents with mental retardation live with their own parents, who provide support and help with child care.

Several issues need to be considered in this situation. Federal and state laws have assured equality to people with disabilities, including the right to have children (Bromwich, 1985). But what is in the best interests of the baby? Should a baby who is not growing be removed from the home? What if the baby is attached to the parents? What happens as the unimpaired child grows up with parents with mental retardation? Perhaps more pro-

grams need to be developed that address the needs of children living with such parents and that can help those parents provide adequate care for their children. Bromwich (1985) suggests that as we protect the rights of parents with a history of developmental delay to have children, we must also protect the rights of those children "to be exposed to social and educational experiences that will foster their healthy growth and allow them to develop their own capabilities to the fullest" (p. 12).

Teen Parents—Children Having Children

Nancy, a hospital social worker, was surprised to receive a request from the nurses on the postpartum unit for a social work visit to an 11-year-old new mother. She thought there must be some mistake. But on entering the room, she found a young girl holding a beautiful baby boy, watching *Barney* on TV.

Teen parents come with their own set of risks and problems. Adolescent parents are more likely to be living in poverty. In addition, they are at risk of developmental problems themselves that can interfere with their ability to interact with an infant. As we shall see in the chapter on adolescence, teens are in the developmental stage of identity formation. And as above, some teen mothers are still just children themselves and may have problems with establishing an identity while trying to care for an infant.

Compared to adults, teen parents are more prone to depression (Osofsky, Hann, & Peebles, 1993). In addition, as parents they are less verbally interactive with the infant and less responsive and so offer the baby less cognitive stimulation. Many teens lack knowledge of developmental milestones. For instance, some adolescents may have unrealistically high developmental expectations for the baby, whereas some may fail to recognize developmental problems. In general, compared to adults, adolescents perceive their infants as being more difficult and engage in more punitive child-raising practices. With toddlers, teens are less sensitive, more intrusive, and more negative in interactions. Infants of adolescent parents may have more problems with attachment (Osofsky, Hann, & Peebles, 1993).

Osofsky, Hann, and Peebles (1993) discuss factors that help teens succeed as parents of an infant. These factors include having support, being able to complete their education, and receiving help to cope with depres-

Teen parents and their infants may need additional support. Often, teen parents do not understand developmental milestones and offer limited cognitive stimulation to the baby.

sion, increase their self-esteem, and understand their infant's temperament.

Implications for Practice: The Importance of Social Support

Infants need a safe and stimulating environment and nurturing, responsive caregivers. Several difficulties may interfere with a caregiver's ability to provide an adequate environment or to interact with an infant. As we have seen, these problems include poverty, drug and alcohol addiction, mental illness, marital difficulties, adolescent parenthood, and developmental delay. In all these situations, we have stressed the importance of social support. Mothers interact more positively with their infants if fathers are supportive and help with child care. Single, teen mothers do better with the help of involved grandparents. Parents of handicapped infants and of difficult infants fare better when they have friends who call to ask how the parents are coping or who offer to sit for the child to give the parents a break.

New parents need the help of other people—family, friends, neighbors, churches, agencies, and community programs. You may hear this African proverb often in your career, but it describes social support so well: "It takes a whole village to raise a child."

APPLYING THE FRAMEWORK

Failure to Thrive

Roberto was referred to the Growth and Nutrition Clinic by his pediatrician. The social worker in the clinic completed the initial psychosocial assessment. The baby is a 15-month-old Hispanic male who weighs 19 pounds, 2 ounces. His rate of growth has been dropping since he was 2 months old and is now well below the 5th percentile for his age. Roberto's parents both have a history of developmental delay. His pediatrician is concerned about Roberto's lack of growth and his parents' ability to adequately care for him. For this reason, he has referred

the case to Child Protective Services (CPS) for failure to thrive.

Developmental History

This was the first pregnancy for Roberto's mother, Angelica. She carried the baby to term and had a normal vaginal delivery. Roberto weighed 5 pounds, 12 ounces at birth with Apgar scores of 8 and 9. Angelica denies any drug or alcohol abuse during the pregnancy.   *(continued)*

Failure to Thrive

(continued)   She reports that she experienced persistent vomiting throughout the first half of the pregnancy. Until her sixth month of gestation, she was almost unable to hold down any food or drink, and she was hospitalized three times for dehydration. She states that she and her husband, Raul, very much wanted a baby. Although she was very happy to be pregnant, she was so sick that she was glad when it was over.

At 15 months, Roberto is only now beginning to pull to stand. His mother is not sure whether he says any words other than "mama" and "dada."

Biophysical Considerations

Since he was 2 months old, Roberto has suffered from almost constant ear infections. Roberto was bottle-fed, and his mother reports that he was a very slow eater, sometimes taking over an hour to finish a bottle. Often he would only take a couple of ounces at a feeding. Roberto is especially hard to feed when he is ill. Then he has a very poor appetite. The doctor believes that Roberto's failure to gain weight makes him more susceptible to illness.

Psychological Considerations

Cognitive Development

Roberto's development seems delayed; he does not walk alone yet. His mother reports that he did not sit alone until he was 9 months old. Roberto appears to be thin and sickly and quite wobbly on his feet even when holding on to something.

Communication

Roberto says no words other than an occasional "mama" or "dada." He does startle to loud noises. He sometimes appears to comprehend basic requests, but often ignores them. He communicates mostly by pointing and grunting.

Attitudes and Emotions

Roberto's mother reports that as a baby he was loud and intense. He was very unpredictable in daily habits. He never has liked cuddling very much and has always been difficult to calm. On observation, when Roberto looks to his mother, she looks past him. When asked to hold the baby in her lap, she faces him away from her. He squirms to get down and screams until she lets him go. He plays well with his father. They make eye contact and smile at each other. His father talks to him, shows him interesting objects, wrestles on the floor with him, and changes his diaper when needed.

Social Cognition and Regulation

Roberto makes few social overtures to his mother or to the social worker during the interview. He ignores all requests from anyone. He seems interested only in exploring the room, and he can be distracted only by physical play with his father. According to his parents, Roberto is very hard to feed. He often refuses to eat. Roberto will sit in his high chair only for a few minutes before wanting to get down. His parents have been so worried about his lack of weight gain lately that they now spend over an hour trying to force the baby to eat. Mealtimes have become a nightmare for everyone. When Roberto does eat, he refuses to eat from his own plate but takes food from his mother's. In other areas, the baby seems to have no set routine. He has no regular bedtime or bedtime routine. His parents allow him to stay up until he falls asleep on the living room floor.

Social Considerations

Family

Roberto's parents are married and live in a one-room apartment in a poor section of town. They are both Mexican American. Roberto's father is from Mexico and does not speak English. On standardized tests, both parents

Failure to Thrive

show a history of developmental delay. Roberto's father works as a food server in a Mexican restaurant, and his mother stays at home to care for the baby. Though she has poor reading skills, Angelica graduated from high school. Raul completed the sixth grade in Mexico. Angelica's mother and sister live in town, but all of Raul's family live in Mexico. Angelica thinks her baby is doing well. She says he is just not that interested in eating, but she feeds him when she can. As a child, Angelica says that she didn't have much of an appetite either, but that was good because her family did not have much to eat. She doesn't understand why everyone is so worried about her son's weight.

On observation, Angelica is a small, thin woman who looks sad most of the time. She does not even brighten when her baby comes up to her. Even when he smiles at her, Angelica avoids eye contact with her son.

Although they have a history of developmental delay, Angelica and Raul have been doing well on their own. They maintain an apartment, hold a job, and pay the bills. Though they live in a poor neighborhood, the apartment is clean; but the baby has few toys to play with. Also, they have no transportation and rely on public transportation, which is somewhat lacking in their town. This lack of reliable transportation makes getting to appointments a long ordeal. Lunchtime is often spent in waiting rooms or on the bus.

Social Support

Angelica has a close relationship with her mother and sister. They baby-sit for her sometimes and come over to help out. Angelica and Raul attend parenting classes through the Department of Developmental Disabilities. They have an in-home parent aide who visits them once a week. They really don't have any friends, and although they are religious, they do not attend church on a regular basis. The local Child Protective Services has a day-care program. CPS will pay for the child to attend a day-care center full-time where he can experience a set routine,

can receive up to three meals a day, and can observe other children eating and enjoying mealtimes.

Multicultural Considerations

When Roberto has been sick with ear infections, his parents have often used folk remedies. They say he doesn't like to take his antibiotics; in fact, he tries to spit out the medication. So Raul's grandmother suggested they feed the baby sweetened manzanita tea. He likes it and will drink it, and his parents think it helps with his fevers.

When asked what she thinks is wrong with the baby, Angelica replies emphatically that she had "nervous" during pregnancy. When asked to elaborate, Angelica explains that Raul lost his job when she was five months pregnant and they had no money until Raul found his present job three months later. Angelica was under a lot of stress during this time and worried constantly about how they would support a baby. She is sure this is why Roberto is so irritable and hard to feed.

Because they are unable to get him to eat enough, the parents often light candles and recite prayers asking that they will get to keep their baby and not lose him to CPS. They pray that he will soon eat well, and grow, and walk on his own, so that everyone will think they are good parents and they can keep their son.

Raul is the higher-functioning parent, but he does not speak English. Because no one at the clinic speaks Spanish, communication with Raul is through a volunteer interpreter. The interpreter often seems to be changing what was originally intended in the messages to Raul. The staff suspects that the interpreter is giving his own advice to the parents. On one occasion, a staff member with some understanding of the language thought she heard the interpreter tell Raul not to worry, that he just needed to make sure the baby drank "la leche" (milk). It is often difficult to tell whether the parents understand instructions about their baby.   *(continued)*

Failure to Thrive

(continued)

Summary and Impressions

Roberto seems to have the following problems:

1. Failure to thrive
2. Possible developmental delay, possibly due to inadequate food intake
3. Chronic ear infections, which may contribute to lack of appetite
4. Difficult temperament
5. Behavioral problems with feeding

Additional problems:

1. Parents with a history of developmental delay
2. Poverty
3. Possible poor environment
4. Lack of routine and order in care
5. Possible poor mother-infant interactions
6. Possible maternal depression

The parents have many strengths and resources. They are able to maintain an apartment on their own. Angelica and Raul obviously love and care for the infant. Though Angelica in particular may have some problems in interactions with the baby, she is very concerned about his health and development. The parents have kept all of their appointments at the clinic. They cooperate well with the parent-training program and with the parent aide. The baby seems to be especially attached to his father.

Both parents are highly motivated to do whatever is necessary to keep their baby. They can follow simple written instructions regarding care and feeding of their child. They are keeping clear and accurate food logs about what Roberto eats each day. They are willing to work at establishing a schedule for the baby—to feed him six times a day and to establish a regular bedtime routine. They are also considering the day-care program for Roberto. The baby has been referred for developmental assessment. Several members of the clinic staff have signed up for an accelerated Spanish course.

Chapter Summary

Developmental Themes

According to Erikson, infancy is the psychosocial stage of trust versus mistrust. During infancy, babies learn to trust, they develop a sense of self, they form an attachment to a caregiver, and they acquire knowledge about the world and how it works.

Biophysical Dimension

Biophysical Growth and Development

In the first two years of life, the infant grows to half his adult height. The infant brain also grows to more than half its adult size. Diet is important for optimal growth and development. Motor development follows the formation of the myelin sheath and progresses in a cephalocaudal and proximodistal direction. Motor development seems to be maturational. Infants may be developmentally delayed if they fail to demonstrate a skill at an age when 90% of infants that age can perform.

Biophysical Hazards

Accidents, illness, and disease are hazards of infancy. Babies should receive regular immunizations in the first two years.

Psychological Dimension

Cognitive Development and Information Processing

According to Piaget, infants are in the sensorimotor stage of development. During this stage, infants go from having mostly random reflex actions to displaying goal-directed behavior. Babies also acquire object permanence during this stage. The substages of this stage are reflex activity, primary circular reactions, secondary circular reactions, coordination of secondary schemes, tertiary circular reactions, and representational thought. Research using measures of information processing suggests that babies have more capacities than Piaget imagined. They can categorize objects into groups, transfer information from one sense to another, remember, and imitate. Recent studies seem to show that babies have an innate sense of how the world works.

Communication

The acquisition of language occurs in an orderly and predictable fashion, from crying and cooing to babbling, to the development of holophrastic and then telegraphic speech. Babies need to hear speech in order to acquire it. Hearing impairment and parents who fail to communicate with the baby can affect language development.

Attitudes and Emotions

As with motor development and language acquisition, the development of emotions seems to follow a maturational sequence. Babies first develop anger, sadness, surprise, and fear. Then in the second year, complex emotions—such as embarrassment, shame, guilt, and pride—develop. Emotional expression in infancy seems to

predict later emotional characteristics. Babies display different temperaments from the easy child to the slow-to-warm-up child and the difficult child. Some add the classification of the active child. Goodness of fit can affect personality development. Babies attach or form an emotional bond with a caregiver. Bowlby's theory of attachment suggests that parents and infants are biologically programmed to form this attachment. Ainsworth developed the Strange Situation procedure to assess attachment. Her classifications of attachment include secure attachment, anxious attachment, avoidant attachment, and, more recently, disorganized/disoriented attachment.

Social Cognition and Regulation

Research suggests that most babies have a sense of self by 18 months of age. According to Mahler, development of a sense of self was a process that went through stages: normal autistic phase, normal symbiotic phase, differentiation phase, practicing phase, rapprochement phase, and consolidation phase. More recent research suggests that babies have a sense of self from birth. Regulation of self can begin when the infant has language skills, a sense of self, complex emotions, and a sense of autonomy.

Psychological Hazards

Failure to form an attachment and loss of or separation from a caregiver can have long-lasting effects on the child, some of which can be mediated by intervention and adequate nurturing. Repeated moves from one foster home to another can be detrimental in infancy. Failure to thrive has been described as a problem of attachment but is ultimately a problem of inadequate nutrition, often a result of a combination of biological, psychological, and social factors. Different family situations can contribute to the occurrence of failure to thrive.

Social Dimension

Families, Groups, Support Systems, and Contexts

A baby cannot be studied only individually but must be looked at in the context of the family. Problems with an infant arise in the interaction with caregivers and other significant people. Interactions between infants and caregivers are referred to as circular influences. Social support enhances parent-infant interactions. Adoption procedures have changed over the years; many people now opt for open adoptions. Some question the ethics of adoption practices, especially in transracial adoption, Native American adoptions, and those involving the rights of birth fathers. It is difficult to discuss the effect of day care in infancy. Ultimately it depends on the child, the family, and the particular day-care arrangements. However, quality day care is a necessary and important consideration.

Multicultural and Gender Considerations

Cultural and ethnic practices may affect development. Cultural variations in development exist. Male and female infants behave differently from birth, and they are treated differently.

Social Hazards

The home environment can affect development. Infants need verbal interaction; a variety of stimulation; warm, responsive caregivers; a safe, well-organized home and freedom to explore it; and appropriate and stimulating toys. Poverty can have a detrimental effect on development. Infants born in poverty to overstressed caregivers are at increased risk of abuse and neglect. Forms of infant abuse include shaken infant syndrome and Munchausen's syndrome by proxy. Lead poisoning from eating paint chips or absorbing environmental lead can cause learning problems and delayed growth and development. Children born to parents with mental illness, parents with a history of developmental delay, or teenage parents may be at increased risk for developmental problems. Early intervention and social support can mediate problems in these families.

KEY TERMS

attachment
babbling
categorization
cephalocaudal
circular influences
cross-modal transfer
difficult child
dishabituation
easy child
failure to thrive
goal-directed behavior

goodness of fit
habituation
holophrastic speech
intentional means-end behavior
invisible displacements
Munchausen's syndrome by proxy
myelinization
object permanence
obligatory attention
open adoption
overextension

proximodistal
separation anxiety
separation-individuation
shaken infant syndrome
slow-to-warm-up child
social referencing
stranger anxiety
telegraphic speech
temperament
transitional object
transracial adoption

Early Childhood

Jayne E. Cooper

223

Developmental Themes

When Skyler's parents ask him a question, his response is a predictable "No, no, no!" "Skyler, you like ice cream?" "No, no, no!" He continues to shake his head. Grabbing his father by the finger, Skyler pulls him into the family room and demands that he put in a *Sesame Street* video. His father reluctantly complies. Afterward, Skyler is ready for refueling—obtaining some emotional closeness before moving on to his next activity.

Early childhood often represents a struggle for independence and self-mastery. Children expend a lot of energy striving for inner control. They are pushing for independence, yet at the same time, they are overwhelmed with feelings of dependence. A critical task at this age is achieving a balance between these two forces. Perhaps one of the most amusing phases of development is the toddler/preschool years. The "terrible twos" are a result of this desire to establish autonomy. Even when offered something desirable, the toddler, like the child in the paragraph above, exclaims, "No!" demonstrating how strong the desire to be in control is. The "No!" also confirms the toddler's ability to make his or her own decisions. Erikson refers to this stage as autonomy versus doubt. Children who successfully master this stage develop a sense of self-control and adequacy. Children at this age are fast becoming more independent, trying out all kinds of activities for themselves, as well as learning many self-care skills that facilitate their autonomy. Children who do not realize a sense of independence and self-control at this age are likely to have feelings of shame and self-doubt about themselves instead.

During the preschool years, from age 3 to 5, children are transformed from infants and toddlers into little boys and girls. Physical and cognitive changes continue to unfold. Yet, perhaps the most profound changes during this period occur in children's social and emotional growth and language acquisition. Preschoolers are honing the skills they will need in preparation for formal education in the middle childhood years.

Children in this stage increasingly demonstrate greater autonomy, physical ability, and language skills in their activities and relationships. They revel in their sense of accomplishment and mastery. They are achieving mastery in the areas of basic self-help skills such as toiletry, dressing, and hygiene and in recreational skills such as running, jumping, and bike riding. This mastery also extends to verbal skills used in expressing thoughts, singing, playing pretend games, and playing social games.

Older preschool children, ages 3–5, face the psychosocial crisis Erikson referred to as initiative versus guilt. Children at this period ideally initiate all kinds of activities for themselves, including motor, cognitive, fantasy, imaginative, and language, and they achieve some proficiency and mastery in these areas. Perfection is not important as a goal; however, feeling that their efforts will be encouraged and praised is crucial to developing a healthy sense of initiative. Children who feel that they can take on and participate in a task with the expectation that they will achieve some degree of mastery will be more ready to meet the challenges involved in learning at school.

The primary tasks of this period include developing more coordinated gross motor skills, acquiring social skills to enhance relationships, and achieving immense growth in cognitive abilities and expressive language skills, all of which are fostered during play. Play is crucial to physical, cognitive, and emotional growth for preschool children. Learning and relationship skills are acquired through daily, active play. By the end of the preschool period, most children will have developed the necessary attention, coordination, and social skills to successfully make the transition to middle childhood, where school and peers will become the primary focus of children's days.

Biophysical Dimension

Biophysical Growth and Development

Physical development refers to two processes. The first involves actual physical growth, and the second involves an increase in the ability to perform various motor tasks. The average preschool child grows 2.5 inches and gains 5–7 pounds a year. Girls remain only slightly smaller and lighter than boys, a pattern that lasts through most of childhood until puberty. During early childhood, both boys and girls slim down, with their body fat percentages declining slowly. Girls tend to have more body fat than boys overall, whereas boys tend to have more muscle tissue than girls, even at this young age. As their body fat decreases and trunks lengthen, preschoolers lose their babyish look, although their heads are still relatively large compared with their bodies. By the time children turn 3 years old, they have doubled in height and are four times heavier.

Of course, as with almost all aspects of development, there is a wide range of normal growth. Outside of genetics, most differences in growth among children are attributed to nutrition and ethnic factors (Meredith, 1978). Overall, urban, middle-class, firstborn children tend to be taller than rural, lower-class, later-born children. Furthermore, in the United States, African American children tend to be taller than white children. Nutritional needs of preschoolers will be discussed in a later section.

Gross Motor Skills

Early childhood is an exciting time for physical growth and motor development. At this age, children run, jump, climb, and tumble repeatedly for the sheer joy derived from challenging their bodies. They are stimulated and delighted by their accomplishments. The typical 3-year-old child can ride a tricycle, walk up and down stairs, throw a ball overhand, and catch a ball that is bounced. Many can even turn a forward roll and gallop. Catching a ball thrown through the air will still be a relatively difficult feat, but one they begin to practice with large balls. By age 4, children refine their coordination of large muscle groups and can jump higher and farther, run faster, throw a ball with more speed and precision, and hit a ball off a tee. They can hop on one foot, and descend stairs with one foot on each stair. Five-year-olds can hit a ball pitched to them, jump rope, and roller skate (Skinner, 1979). Girls tend to develop both gross and fine motor skills slightly ahead of boys. Just as "peekaboo" is an invigorating game for infants, preschoolers never tire of "chase" and "hide-and-seek," games that allow them to shriek and run at high speeds with anyone and everyone in hot pursuit.

Three-year-olds exhibit the highest activity level of any age group. Just watching a 3-year-old play can be an exhausting experience for any adult. These children are seldom still even as they eat and sleep. The high levels of physical activity characteristic of this age span necessitate daily physical exercise that emphasizes large muscles.

Fine Motor Skills

Fine motor coordination during early childhood progresses rapidly as well. However, children in this age group can be frustrated by the limitations in their precision and dexterity. Some projects are frustrating to preschoolers because the child can cognitively conceive of the goal but cannot achieve the intended result due to fine motor limitations. For example, a child might want to make a beautiful necklace but struggles to loop tiny beads on a string. That same child might want to build a tower as tall as his or her brother's only to watch it wobble and topple. We can imagine the frustration.

The average 3-year-old likes to build tall towers and enjoys large-piece puzzles and manipulating figures in cars and playhouses. Three-year-olds also strive to conquer zippers, snaps, and scissors. Four-year-olds enjoy building more complicated towers and buildings and begin to understand basic structural and design requirements to accomplish the task. Four-year-olds can manage buttons and draw stick figures. Five-year-olds can print capital letters, simple letters, and numbers. Preschoolers learn to master scissors, paints, pencils, and crayons quite

This girl has developed the fine motor skills to brush her teeth. This skill will be refined as her development progresses.

readily. They enjoy the tactile and creative expression afforded by these media.

Preschoolers are often more adept at operating video players than are their parents. With the proliferation of CD-ROM players in home computers, many children also learn to successfully and fearlessly navigate educational and recreational software games. For this age group, computerized programs that are interactive and "speak" to the child, without requiring any reading, are preferred sources of play and learning. Although children in this age group typically do not formally read, they can recognize letter patterns and logo designs as meaningful symbols in much the same way as they will later recognize letters and words.

Nutrition

Nutrition in the preschool years continues to be vital to skeletal growth, body shape, and immunity to disease. The average preschool child needs between 1700 and 2300 calories a day. These calories should be derived from about 16 ounces of milk, 2 ounces of protein, whole grain bread or cereal, and fruit. A multivitamin may be provided if the child is a picky eater (Brazelton, 1992). According to the American Heart Association, preschool children should receive 35% or fewer of their calories from fats.

Implications for Practice: Nutrition and Exercise

Preschool-age children need daily, physical exercise to accommodate their large muscle growth and high energy levels. When provided with plenty of free-play experiences, children will stretch their imaginations as well as their bodies. Children should not be confined for very long or unreasonable amounts of time. If a child plays physically over the course of the day, quiet time, eating, and sleeping habits will be much easier to regulate.

Preschool children can begin to take responsibility for food choices and the health of their bodies. This knowledge enhances their sense of self and competency. They are also learning the connection between the physical need for food as nutritional fuel and the emotional and social pleasures of eating and socializing with food. The goals of autonomy and independence will be thrust into the feeding arena for preschool children. Parents should refrain, despite the difficulty entailed, from turn-

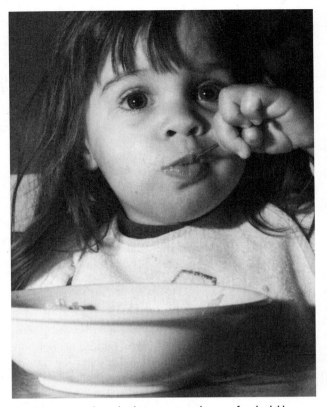

The ability to eat independently—a major milestone of early childhood—is a task that challenges the fine motor skills of the child and the patience of her parents.

ing mealtime into a battleground. Many problems in eating and food selection, short of failure to thrive (see Chapter 6), will work themselves out as children establish their place in the family and a more secure sense of personal identity. A sense of personal identity and role in the family develop over time as the child continues to explore and test limits amid the security and comfort of trusting family relationships.

Biophysical Hazards

The fatal disorders of early childhood include birth defects, cancer, and heart disease. Fortunately, the number of deaths have recently been reduced as a result of improvements in health care and treatment (Garrison & McQuiston, 1989). Prevention strategies to reduce the fatality rates for children under age 5 include adequate birth spacing, prenatal care, breast-feeding, immunizations, and special feedings before, during, and after serious illnesses.

Asthma

Asthma is another health concern for preschool children. Almost 4 million children under the age of 18 suffer from asthma, the leading chronic illness among children. With recent advances in the knowledge and treatment of asthma, children are no longer restricted in activity and can anticipate leading normal lives. Learning to manage the asthma prevents serious medical and psychological complications.

What is asthma and how do we recognize an asthma attack? Asthma is a respiratory illness that makes breathing difficult by narrowing the bronchial tubes. The lung tissues swell, the muscle surrounding the bronchial tubes spasms, and mucus accumulates within the air passages. Asthmatic children can be recognized typically by the wheezing sound produced when the air is squeezed out through the narrowed tubes. They also experience a congestion or tightness in the chest, difficulty exhaling, and rapid breathing.

Although most incidences of asthma in early childhood are triggered by viral illnesses, other allergens such as dust mites, mold, pollen, cold air, tobacco smoke, and smoke from a wood-burning fire can trigger or exacerbate future episodes. Treatment includes bronchodilators, or nebulizers in young children, to relax the muscles around the bronchial tubes, and anti-inflammatory drugs to treat the swelling of the lung tissues. A first or serious asthma attack is not something that can be managed without the care of a physician.

Although asthma is not a psychosomatic disorder, psychological complications can arise if the disease is not managed well. Children experiencing an asthma attack can feel fearful, helpless, and anxious. Most people feel anxious when they cannot breathe, and the anxiety often exacerbates the breathing difficulty. Prevention in the form of adequate rest and avoidance of known allergens, coupled with quick and effective treatment, can help reduce the child's fears. By involving children in the early stages of detection and treatment, they can learn to help manage their illness, promoting a sense of control and decreasing a sense of helplessness. When

symptoms are not recognized or treated effectively, children's psychological symptoms are likely to surface. With proper treatment, however, asthmatic children can lead happy, active lives.

Psychological Dimension
Cognitive Development and Information Processing

Early childhood is a time of fanciful, creative, and imaginative thought. Children can think about themselves and others in new and important ways. Imaginative thought leads the way for the development of humor, empathy, and altruism. These features of psychological development will be discussed in following sections.

Three-year-old children can use abstraction and symbols in increasingly complicated ways. They can classify objects according to one feature, such as color or shape, and recognize that cats and dogs fit into different categories. At about age 4, children can begin to categorize objects along two dimensions and understand that both cats and dogs fall into the larger category of animals. Numbers symbolize more than just words for the preschool child. They learn to understand the meaning and function of numbers and to use them in everyday tasks. For example, a child may count three books to read at nap time or ask for five more pitches before dinner.

Preschoolers can understand objects as ideas that exist mentally when the object is not physically present. Until children reach the age of about 5, they have little concept of time, past or future. They have difficulty imagining something they have never experienced before. Without a concept of time, they cannot think logically about cause and effect. As a result, consequences of actions cannot be abstracted. However, around the time a child turns 5, a sense of time and logical thinking begin to take shape. Five-year-olds begin to imagine likely outcomes of their behavior. In addition, they have more experience upon which to base these logical consequences.

Piaget's Preoperational Stage

Piaget's work laid important foundations for our thinking about what children know (Piaget, 1967). Piaget labeled the early childhood years, roughly from the age of 2 to about 7, the *preoperational stage* of cognitive development. Children in the preoperational stage cannot perform certain tasks mentally that older children can. Preoperational children cannot understand the meaning of properties like weight, volume, size, or height without a physical representation of the concept. More about the meaning of operations according to Piaget will be discussed in the chapter on middle childhood, when children enter the stage of concrete operations. *Operations* conform to rules and principles of logic that preschool children do not comprehend. During the preschool years, mental reasoning, stable concepts, egocentrism, and magical beliefs emerge in children's thoughts as they make the transition from a simple use of symbols to more sophisticated use.

Piaget described two substages of preoperational thought, *symbolic function* and *intuitive thought*. What can we expect of children during these stages of development? Children between the ages of 2 and 4 typically possess abilities characteristic of the symbolic function substage. This means that they can now represent objects mentally that are not present in their immediate environment. At this stage, children can draw scribbles that represent an object or person (Gardner, 1980), play pretend games alone and with other children, and talk about people and things not present. They can begin to imagine whole scenarios about other people and themselves and incorporate these ideas into their play and language. For instance, children in the symbolic function stage can play "house" or "school," taking the roles of mom, dad, student, or teacher. Because they can now conceive of and share more complex thoughts and ideas, their social interactions move to a deeper level of involvement and satisfaction.

Egocentrism is another characteristic feature of the symbolic function substage, according to Piaget's theory. Egocentric children cannot distinguish between their perspective and that of another's. For example, preschool children playing hide-and-seek will think that if they cannot see us, we cannot see them. They cannot understand that we have a vantage point different from their own. Another familiar example is that of preschoolers nodding their head on the phone without speaking, not realizing that the person on the other end cannot see them.

Animism, as Piaget described, refers to the belief that inanimate objects have lifelike qualities and abilities. Some developmentalists disagree that this is a general concept the child holds about the world. Instead, they argue that animism represents a child's lack of knowledge and understanding about features of the world (Dolgin & Behrend, 1984). We should also consider that many children's movies and stories depend specifically on this notion. So we must ask ourselves, do children think this way independently, or is animism a function of the way we portray the world to them at this age?

Piaget's second substage of the preoperational stage, intuitive thought, develops between the ages of 4 and 7. Children in this substage can use primitive reasoning, but not formal logic. During this substage, children typically ask a lot of questions, want to know the "how" and "why" of everything, are sure of what they know, but not certain of how they came to know something. As we have described above, some of Piaget's conclusions may be erroneous because they relied on assumptions made about children's thinking based on adult-oriented tasks and interpretations. Challenges to Piaget's theoretical assumptions are currently being examined in research labs.

Information Processing

Research in the field of information processing focuses on how children come to know something rather than on what they know when. This emphasis complements that espoused by Piaget and other stage theorists who are interested in the latter concerns. Examples of information processes include developmental changes in attention and memory. During early childhood, children make great strides in both abilities.

As you will remember, toddlers' attention spans tend to be relatively short and wandering. Preschoolers on the other hand, develop the capacity to attend for longer and longer periods of time if they are motivated by the activity. For example, children at this age are interested in books that tell a story, especially about a favorite topic, can watch about a half-hour of a show such as *Barney* or *Aladdin*, and can play simple board games. By the time they begin school at age 6, children can attend for increasingly longer periods of time. This increased attention span is necessary for the child to benefit from formal education.

One of the limits in attention that preschool children demonstrate is an inability to attend to the relevant aspects of a task. This deficit imposes limits on children's problem-solving abilities because children attend to the more exciting aspects instead, such as bright colors, lights, movement, and novelty. Developmentalists describe the process of learning to attend to relevant aspects as children's acquiring cognitive control of their attention. When this change occurs, preschool children act less impulsively and engage in more reflective thought (Paris & Lindayer, 1982).

A second important process in children's cognitive development involves retention of information over time. The process of information storage and retrieval depends heavily on how children understand and represent information (Ornstein, 1995). As you will recall, infants as young as 7 months old are capable of conscious memory.

However, most children have little or no memory for specific events before the age of 3. This phenomenon is known as **infantile amnesia**. Researchers believe that several cognitive developments in children during early childhood are responsible for changes in memory capabilities. These include a sense of self, which allows children to represent autobiographical material and is held largely responsible for the resolution of infantile amnesia (Howe, 1995).

Robin Fivush (1995) found that starting at age 3, children begin to embellish their stories and recitation of memories. This embellishment adds details and feelings and puts the memory into context. These recountings enhance the child's organization of memories, which, in turn, promotes memory abilities. Although the methodology for this research has been criticized because of the reliance on correlational data (Brewer, 1995), defenders retort that, by nature, most work with memory must be retrospective and correlational.

Stein (1995) has found that when a particular event is relevant and meaningful to a child, children as young as 3 can recount the memory with as much description and complexity as a 14-year-old. Stein's work generally relies on memories of salient events for children that made them feel happy, sad, or scared. Stein concludes that emotionally charged events can be stored accurately by even young preschool children.

Memory processes involve both the storage and retrieval of information. Howe (1995) has found that for children age 1 year to 11 years, problems in storage were three times greater than retrieval failure rates. In addition, preschoolers' memories fade faster than those of older children and adults. Researchers believe that either young children's memories are not completely stored or their ability to organize autobiographical events is not sufficient to guarantee storage.

The speed of processing information increases during early childhood, as do the abilities to rehearse, repeat, and identify items. These factors promote storage and increase short-term memory functions. These abilities have been assessed in children using the digit span task. The average 3-year-old child can repeat two digits in succession. Short-term memory functions increase during early childhood, so that by age 7, the average child can repeat five digits. Of course, individual differences in aptitude and IQ will influence a child's performance (Dempster, 1981).

Task Analysis

Task analysis is another way to study what children know. This method identifies the various components of the task the child is performing. Researchers have found that when tasks are made simpler and more interesting, children tend to show greater cognitive maturity than revealed by the studies of Piaget (Hawkins, Pea, Glick, & Scribner, 1984). Nonsense words in syllogisms were used to demonstrate this position. Children were presented with two true statements and were asked whether the conclusion was then true. The use of nonsense words prevented children from answering based on previous experience with the items and appealed to the children's sense of fun. This study showed that preschool children do use reasoning, which Piaget had concluded was beyond their capacity (Hawkins et al., 1984). The numerous and varied questions preschool children ask provide clues about their cognitive efforts to reason and understand themselves, other people, and their world.

Developmental Waves

Until recently, developmentalists pictured children's cognitive development as proceeding in stages or steps. But the step model has posed problems in explaining the great variability in children's development and the change process of development. Questions still remained about how children shift from the use of one strategy to another and how to account for the fact that children seem to use so many different strategies to complete the same task at any given time.

Traditional theories are being challenged by new models suggesting that "overlapping waves," as opposed to steps, better account for how children learn and use strategies (Siegler, 1995). This theory is referred to as **developmental waves.** The waves represent the natural ebb and flow portraying the natural continuity and transitions in children's thinking. Siegler (1995) advocates a shift from emphasizing how children think at different ages to examining how many and what kinds of strategies children use at any age. This focus provides a means of analyzing a strategy by task framework. In addition, information about how children change the use of strategies can be gleaned from this focus.

Siegler's theoretical suppositions are supported by evidence from his research. These findings include that children learn a new strategy slowly and frequently revert back to using the old strategy as they are learning the new; they tend to use older, more time-consuming strategies for difficult tasks; and they choose a correct strategy more often when approved by their partner while working in pairs. Also, children tend to use three or more strategies to solve problems such as telling time, and as many as seven strategies when faced with moral-reasoning problems. Numerous studies support that children always use more than one strategy to solve all kinds of problems. Although Siegler's work has introduced new ways of thinking about how development advances, his work does not discount the previous work put forth by stage or level theorists. The theoretical viewpoints may complement one another to broaden our understanding of children's cognitive development.

Communication

Preschool children's comprehension precedes their speech. They can understand much of what is said around them and to them before they can verbally express their ideas on the subject. The process of acquiring language skills proceeds in a relatively uniform way for most children, although the time frame may vary. Language acquisition during the preschool years is quite re-markable when we think of children advancing from putting one and two words together to forming complex sentences and questions incorporating the correct morphology, syntax, semantics, and pragmatics of conversation in just a few months' time.

What kinds of speech can we expect from preschool children? Three-year-old children have a vocabulary of about 900 words. By age 6, their vocabulary will have increased to between 8000 and 14,000 words. In other words, they will have learned an average of 5–8 words a day since they were 1 year old (Carey, 1977). At about age 3, children can also converse about people, objects, and places not present. Once children have matured cognitively to achieve mental representation of things not physically present, they can think about them and talk about them.

Once children put two words together consistently, they begin to use morphological rules. We hear children at this age use plurals, possessives, and verb tenses—including the present-progressive tense (-ing endings). Children will make grammatical mistakes at this age and overuse the rules, referred to as overregularization. Examples include saying "mouses" for "mice" and "he goed" instead of "he went," which children may have said correctly earlier. These mistakes and overuse problems imply that children "know" the rules yet their perception and understanding of the world is limited by their developmental level (Santrock, 1992). Berko (1958) demonstrated knowledge of morphological rules by asking preschool and first-grade children to read fictional words, recall the correct word, and apply the correct ending. Because the words were fictional, the children were forced to rely on rules and not memory. Preschool children could complete this task as could first graders. During early childhood, children also learn to use pronouns such as "a" to refer to something initially and "the" for later references to the same noun.

Children also learn to apply the rules of syntax as their language skills progress. They first learn to add "wh" words, such as *where* and *what*, to the beginnings of sentences to form questions. Later, they learn to invert the subject and verb. Early preschool children will ask, "What we are going to do now?" and "Where my ball is?" As they approach the elementary school years, children speak in more complex ways, such as combining ideas in one sentence (Santrock, 1992). Negatives are learned in much the same manner. First, they place the negative marker at the beginning of the sentence, then place the negative close to the verb, and finally, use auxiliary verbs such as *was, do,* and *is* to modify the verb as adults do.

Children's semantic skills improve readily as well. We see children at this age learning the meaning of relationship words, such as *big/little, fast/slow, I/you,* and using them accurately in sentences. However, they do not use these words in a true comparison until about age 4 or 5, when they can articulate comments such as, "I am bigger than you." To carry on an effective conversation, children must know to use "I" as the speaker and "you" as the object. This semantic relationship appears to be one of the first that young children come to know.

In addition, children become increasingly skilled at the pragmatics of conversation during early childhood. Recent research suggests that preschool children are more adept at communicating comprehensible messages than earlier studies indicated (Revelle, Wellman, & Karabenick, 1985). For example, preschool children speak differently to younger children than to adults. Shatz and Gelman (1973) found that 4-year-olds spoke in short sentences to toddlers and elaborated, using more polite diction, when speaking to adults. Also, we see children at a very young age recognizing that they are more likely to get their requests met if they speak patiently and politely (Bates, 1976). Savvy 3-year-olds quickly rephrase "I wanna go now!" to "Please, can we go now?" We even see preschoolers correcting their own ambiguous messages when they are not understood. They will also let a speaker know when a message has not been clear enough for them to respond (Revelle et al., 1985). Clarifying ambiguous messages as both the speaker and the listener are skills that develop more fully in middle childhood.

Language development also appears to be encouraged by the frequency and type of responses verbalized to children by adult speakers. Parents who ask their children lots of questions and initiate frequent verbal interaction tend to promote syntactical rule learning and longer utterances in their preschool children. These children tend to recognize more letters and numbers by age 5–6, and score higher on second-grade reading profi-

ciency tests compared with children of parents who are less conversant (Hoff-Ginsberg, 1986).

In addition, children exposed to adults who speak in slightly more complex and longer sentences than the children do and both expand and recast the child's telegraphic statements into new grammatical forms, acquire syntactical principles faster than other children (Hoff-Ginsberg, 1986). So we can glean from these studies that, although children do not learn language simply by imitating adults, environmental exposure to slightly more advanced language provides an opportunity for language expansion in young children. The following Focus on Social Development section looks at language as a form of social reinforcement.

FOCUS ON SOCIAL DEVELOPMENT

Language as a Social Reinforcement

Language for the preschooler not only represents a means of expressing needs, but it also becomes a social reinforcer. Language allows children to share and interact with others in ways not previously available to them. Language opens up a whole new world of secrets, jokes, cooperative play, and positive reinforcement. Furthermore, language skills facilitate independence, allowing children to respond to and initiate verbal requests.

The peer group is already a powerful socializing agent. Never mind that parents are mortified when their child screams at the top of his lungs to a departing friend, "Bye-bye, butthead!" The other child roars with delight at the compliment and returns the salutation. Such is the social language of the preschool child.

Communication Disorders

Language develops rapidly during the preschool years. For the most part, children learn language in an orderly, sequential fashion. Developmental delays can occur, however. Communication disorders we are likely to see in preschoolers include expressive language disorder, phonological disorder, and stuttering.

Expressive language disorder can be either developmental or acquired. The acquired type generally follows some known neurological insult, whereas the developmental type does not. The identifying features of this disorder will vary according to age of the child and severity of the disorder. These features include limited speech and vocabulary, shortened sentences, difficulty learning new words, misuse of words, limited and simple grammar, and slowed language acquisition. Language comprehension is usually normal (American Psychiatric Association, 1994).

Developmental expressive language disorder is usually evident by the time a child is 3 and occurs in 3–5% of children. About half of these children outgrow the problem, whereas the remainder suffer complications that are more long-term. Fewer children also exhibit mixed expressive-receptive language disorder, in which they experience difficulty understanding language as well (APA, 1994).

Phonological disorder affects at least 2.5% of preschoolers and is more prevalent in males. The defining characteristics include difficulty articulating speech sounds, especially those learned later in the developmental sequence (such as l, r, s, z, th, ch), and errors in the order of sounds in syllables or words, such as "aks" for "ask." Most children with mild cases recover by the early elementary years without intervention (APA, 1994).

Attitudes and Emotions

No two preschoolers would ever be described exactly alike. As they wind their way through the early developmental years, most children are a mix of positive and negative attributes. However, some children possess qualities that make them easy and fun to be around, whereas appreciating other children requires more tolerance and work. The old axiom "Beauty is in the eye of the beholder" also applies to preferences in personality types. We cannot exclude the interpretive bias of the person ascribing value judgments to children's behaviors and qualities. For instance, some adults would describe a very active child with a mind of his own as exuberant and determined, whereas others would describe him as aggressive or hyperactive—terms that are pejorative and re-

flect, to a large degree, the qualities preferred by the adult speakers more than the "true" characteristics of the child.

Fears

Preschool children enjoy wonderfully exciting imaginations and fantasy lives. Firstborn children often invent an imaginary friend at this age to serve many purposes. An imaginary friend can try out negative, risky, and even miraculous behaviors and feelings, provide companionship, and foster creativity. Children's imaginary friends should be respected, and, for the most part, allowed to be just that—the child's own imaginary friend.

A preschool child's emerging cognitive abilities and imagination also promote empathy and humor. However, the downside of these new cognitive abilities is the onset of fears and phobias. Fears and **phobias** become issues for preschool children, as do nightmares and **night terrors.** Fears of the dark, monsters, loud noises, and strange places crop up in imagination in ways that were not possible before the child was capable of symbolism and abstraction. Most children try to squelch these fears and strong emotions while awake, holding in their reactions so others will not be displeased. As a result, these fears will often surface at night when the child's conscious guard is down, especially during REM dream sleep. The dreams may be terrifying to the preschool child because they may portray aggressive feelings and actions the child has been trying to control in response to fears while awake.

Several steps can be taken to help children learn to handle negative feelings and fearful thoughts adaptively. Children benefit from discussions to prepare and reassure them about their fears and strong emotional responses. We can also teach children to talk about their feelings and act out their aggressive energy in safe ways, such as hard play, hitting something soft, and taking some time alone. Preschool children may not be able to act on these suggestions but will benefit from the discussion and may generate some healthy coping strategies themselves through the process (Brazelton, 1992).

Aggression

Our connotations of aggression are usually negative and call up various images of violence. But how do we define **aggression** when we think of this concept in developmental terms? What forms might aggression take as children mature? What are the meanings of aggressive acts? And do these forms and meanings change over time with development?

In order to grow, develop, and survive, we must be equipped with a biological drive for aggression. Researchers have divided aggression into two forms, labeled **hostile aggression** and **instrumental aggression** (Shaffer, 1989).

The most accepted definition of aggression by researchers today includes an element of intention. Baron and Byrne (1984) refer to aggression as all acts intended to hurt another and include among these acts that were not successful. For example, a child knocking over another in the midst of a pillow fight would not be considered aggressive. Yet, a child who strikes at a friend who has taken his ball, but misses, would be considered aggressive. Behaviors designed to hurt another are referred to as hostile aggression. Behaviors designed to achieve a nonaggressive end but, nonetheless, hurt someone in the process are referred to as instrumental.

In general, preschool aggressive acts diminish after age 4 as children learn better negotiating skills. They also learn to resolve differences verbally in tandem with the increased expectations of parents and teachers preparing children for elementary school.

What can research tell us about preschool children's aggressive behaviors? Studies by Florence Goodenough (1931) and Willard Hartup (1974) provide us with most of our knowledge of aggressive behaviors in preschool children. Goodenough's work analyzed mothers' diaries of their 2- to 5-year-olds' angry episodes and suspected causes and outcomes. Hartup observed interactions of 4- to 6-year-olds and 6- to 7-year-olds, recording the causes and consequences of interpeer aggression. Their findings of normal preschool aggressive behavior are summarized below.

- The total amount of aggression tends to peak at about age 4, and then decreases. Temper tantrums with no recognizable antecedent tend to decrease during the preschool period and are almost nonexistent after age 4.
- At about age 3, preschoolers increase their retaliatory aggression in response to frustration or attack.
- Young preschoolers, age 2–3, tend to behave aggressively after parents have set limits. Older children tend to act aggressively in response to peer conflict.

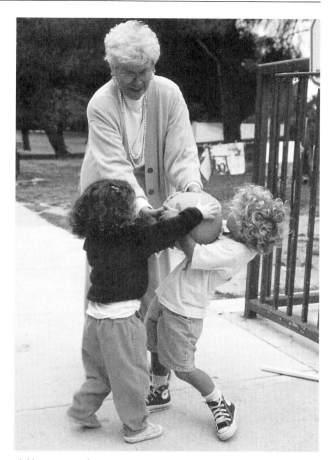

Children express their aggression and unwillingness to share in many ways. Preschool children have not yet become socialized to adopt alternative ways of controlling their aggressive behavior.

- Young preschoolers tend to kick and hit to get something they want, like a toy. Their aggression is primarily instrumental. Older preschoolers tend to use verbal aggression in the form of teasing, name-calling, and tattling. They still argue over objects, but their aggressive acts become more hostile, designed to hurt another.

Implications for Practice: Curbing Aggression

Several strategies for decreasing hostile aggressive acts have been researched. We will describe each of these procedures briefly. Remember, the goal is not to deny or negate the preschool child's very real emotional experience. Rather, the goal is to help the child find adaptive ways of expressing and asserting needs and interacting with others.

• *Incompatible-response technique* (Brown & Elliott, 1965; Slaby & Crowley, 1977). This technique promotes prosocial behaviors and reduces aggressive acts by simultaneously ignoring all but dangerous, aggressive interchanges while positively reinforcing acts incompatible with aggression. This method has been shown to reduce verbal and physical aggression while promoting helpfulness. Another advantage lies in the avoidance of punishment and attention paid to aggressive acts. Therefore, children are not reinforced for attention-seeking aggressive acts, and aggression in the form of punishment is not modeled to the children.

• *Time-out procedure* (Parke & Slaby, 1983). This technique allows adults to attend to and prevent harmful acts of aggression in nonpunitive ways by removing the child from the activity and providing a safe place for the child to regain control of behavior. The adult does not unwittingly provide reinforcement for attention-seeking behavior because attention is withdrawn until appropriate behavior can be maintained.

• *Modeling and coaching strategies* (Richard & Dodge, 1982). This method relies on adults and other children to serve as models and teachers of nonaggressive conflict resolution strategies. Children are more likely to use these alternative strategies if they see someone else obtain success using these methods. This technique has proved effective with chronically aggressive children who have poor problem-solving skills.

• *Creating nonaggressive environments* (Feshbach, 1956; Hartup, 1974; Smith & Connolly, 1980). This method relies on the ingenuity of adults to create play spaces that minimize conflict and the need for physical contact. Large play spaces allow children to play vigorously without physically contacting each other. Play environments that have enough equipment for all the children also prevent conflict. Also, when aggressive toys are provided, children tend to get into more fights. Keeping aggressive toys out of the play areas of young children can prevent aggressive behavior in the form of play and real fights.

The following Focus on Development section examines what happens to children who were aggressive in preschool.

FOCUS ON DEVELOPMENT

Handling Preschool Aggression—Do They Grow Out of It?

When he was 2, Doug's mother took him to a play group. He was not a popular addition to the group. After only two weeks he became known as "the biter." The other mothers would run to pick up their children whenever Doug approached them. When he was 3, his mother enrolled him in a preschool program. After the first month, the teacher called his mother in for a conference because Doug had pushed another child off the slide. When he was 4, his mother took him to Sunday School. The first day, someone came to get her out of the church service because Doug had gotten in an argument with another child and punched the child in the nose.

What happens to aggressive preschoolers? Research has shown us that aggression in preschoolers tends to be associated with aggression in middle childhood (Emmerich, 1966) and even adolescence (Olweus, 1980). Although stability in aggression has usually been considered a male attribute, recent research has documented stability of aggressive tendencies among females as well (Caspi, Elder, & Bem, 1987; Huesmann, Eron, Lefkowitz, & Walder, 1984). Males tend to be more aggressive physically and verbally than females (Maccoby, 1980; Maccoby & Jacklin, 1974). In addition, aggressive attacks are likely to be less intense if the target of the aggression is a female (Barrett, 1979).

Yet, despite biological differences, families, society, and even the individuals themselves play a large role in the development and maintenance of aggressive characteristics and behavior (Olweus, 1980; Patterson, DeBarsyshe, & Ramsey, 1989). Olweus (1980) found that highly active, impulsive boys tended to be the most aggressive. Mothers of these boys were found to be more tolerant of their aggression, but when they could no longer ignore the behavior, they reacted with physical punishment to get their sons in line. Parents who fail to monitor and supervise their children effectively are frequently the parents of deviant adolescents, as discussed in a later chapter.

In addition, Patterson and colleagues (1989) researched parent-child interactions in families with at least one aggressive child and found these home environments to be characterized as coercive. The researchers described coercive interactions as ways of making someone stop irritating another and included crying, whining, complaining, yelling, and hitting. Negative reinforcement, the removal of a noxious behavior, was also used to control family members. Social reinforcement, affection, and approval were rarely articulated in these families as a means of achieving and rewarding desired behavior. Children are also exposed to numerous incidences of violence in society via the television, sports, and superheroes. We will consider the impact of these social systems in a later section.

How can we alleviate the propensity for aggressive acts among preschoolers in our society? Assertive aggression often takes the form of separating from parents, achieving independence, and striving to master new skills, all of which are necessary if a child is to survive in the world. Hostile aggression, on the other hand, is often intended to hurt or coerce, physically or verbally, another child into doing what the aggressor wants. This kind of aggression is not favorably regarded, yet, for children, the meaning of the act must be understood before we can help them achieve their goals any other way.

There is always an underlying message when children use aggression of any kind. Say, for example, we see a preschooler wrestle another child to the ground to retrieve a toy. The meaning of the behavior may be to say to the other child, "See what I can do" or "I'll show you who I am" or "I'll do what I feel like doing." The child may be making a plea for attention from the other child or adults. All in all, preschoolers' aggressive behaviors are ways of defining themselves and asserting their independence.

Even when preschoolers cannot verbalize their rationale, we can model other appropriate, and more effective, ways of asserting ourselves. These include asking the children about their feelings and needs, acknowledging their feelings, and redirecting their energies toward more helpful ways of expressing negative feelings. Children should be encouraged to assert themselves in ways that help define themselves as unique individuals and establish their autonomy by setting personal limits, needs, and wants to maximize their own growth and development, not to exploit or take advantage of another.

FOCUS ON RESEARCH

Children's Coping with Background Anger

E. Mark Cummings has systematically explored how young children cope when exposed to anger—especially anger in the home. In one such study, Cummings (1987) exposed pairs of 4- and 5-year-old same-sex friends to a series of 5-minute interchanges enacted by two adult women. The women were first friendly and greeted each other warmly. Then they simulated anger at each other and yelled but were not physically aggressive. Last, they reconciled, apologized, and parted amicably. In between each simulated session were 5-minute spaces without the adults present. The children watched from an adjoining room as they played. Following the angry sequences, the children were interviewed about their feelings and were observed playing together.

Cummings (1987) found that preschoolers showed increased arousal following the exposure to background anger. This increased arousal took the form of positive and negative behaviors, including more sharing and smiling as well as verbal and physical aggression. The children were classified into four groups based on their behavioral responses to the simulated-anger episodes. The groups were labeled (1) ambivalent, (2) concerned, (3) unresponsive, and (4) unclassifiable. Ambivalent responders were found to engage in positive and negative behaviors following the simulated anger. They also reported feeling happy during the fight and also admitted to feeling most aroused. Concerned responders showed negative emotions following the quarrel and reported feeling sad and wanting to mediate the fight. Unresponsive responders stated they wanted to ignore the fight and that they felt angry. They did not show positive or negative behavioral responses following the simulated anger, perhaps as a way of hiding their emotional response.

Cummings (1987) concluded that children as young as 4 and 5 responded aggressively and with heightened arousal to a relatively tame incidence of anger. He underscores the implications of these findings for children living with marital conflict, which would have a much greater impact on the children. Cummings also concluded that children's coping responses to background anger are complex. The observational and interview data combined to provide a richer picture of children's coping behaviors. Further studies of stress and coping should consider the need for multimethod approaches to understanding coping responses.

Altruism and Empathy

Altruism (helpful behaviors that arise out of a concern for the welfare of others) begins with sharing for young children. Learning to share becomes much of the focus of social interactions during the child's first years. Eisenberg (1982) has studied children's sharing behavior extensively. She concludes that by age 3, children generally share because sharing promotes fun in play. By age 4, children show more empathic sharing as they develop an ability to recognize and understand the feelings of others. In addition, through parental encouragement, 4-year-olds have internalized the belief that they have an obligation to share. This does not mean they always act on this knowledge, however. Sharing is a difficult concept to grasp, one that takes many years to develop. Still, children at this age do not share in an altruistic sense. Rather, they are usually motivated to share as a means of getting their way.

How do children learn to share and develop a sense of altruism? For the most part, peers provide the primary influence in this arena, above and beyond adult recriminations to share and give. Peers accomplish this by providing reinforcement through their responses to the give and take of social play (Eisenberg, 1982). When a child happily hands over the treasured race car, there is nothing more powerful than the exuberant smile of the friend to reinforce sharing.

Each of us has an innate capacity for **empathy** (the ability to understand the feelings and attitudes of others). Children are predisposed to empathize with the emotions of others from a very young age. Even infants demonstrate this capacity to detect and model the feelings of another when they use social referencing. Children need adult encouragement to develop their natural capacity for empathy, however.

Preschool children cannot cognitively understand another person's feelings. Yet, they are equipped with the emotional ability to sense another's feelings and match them with their own experiences. In order to match another's feelings, first a child needs to be able to identify the feeling. Preschoolers feel the basic emotions of happiness, sadness, and anger intensely and can empathize quite readily with these feelings in others.

Altruism has been found to be a highly stable attribute, similar to its counterpart, aggression (Rushton, 1980). Children who act prosocially in one setting are likely to do so in others also. When sex differences are found, girls tend to be more helpful, but sex difference findings in general tend to be controversial (Radke-Yarrow, Zahn-Waxler, & Chapman, 1983). Preschoolers also tend to act more altruistically toward other children of the same sex (Hartup, 1974), but need becomes a determinant as children develop. One factor found to contribute to children's altruistic behavior was opportunities to provide compassionate, helpful care to younger siblings (Radke-Yarrow et al., 1983). Compared with other societies, Western society places a higher value on competition and individual achievement. As a result, children from industrialized societies often score lower on measures of altruism compared with cultures in which the group is valued over the individual (Whiting & Whiting, 1975).

Implications for Practice:
Helping Children Develop Empathy

How do we, as adults, encourage the development of empathy in children? First, we need to help children understand a range of emotions and to be able to identify and label them accurately. To accomplish this task, we can express honestly our own emotions and provide children with word labels for their own future experiences. Praising prosocial behavior and talking to children about their feelings increases their emotional and cognitive understanding. When children do something that pleases us, we should be quick to let them know our feelings. We can also let children know that their concern for us makes us feel better. Sometimes children will laugh, not because seeing someone feeling bad strikes them as funny but because they do not understand more complex emotions like frustration and embarrassment. They have usually felt this way at one time, too, but cannot identify or label the emotion when they see it in another.

Social Cognition and Regulation

Preschoolers' self-concepts are largely determined by their physical characteristics and physical abilities. They learn to classify themselves and others according to age first, gender second, and then by what they can actively do, such as play baseball or climb a tree, and sometimes by what they physically possess. This method of classifying themselves is referred to as the **categorical self.**

During the preschool years, children become increasingly able to make finer distinctions between physical attributes. Yet, not until middle childhood do they consistently attribute psychological characteristics to themselves or to others. We should note, however, that parents tend to describe their children along these same dimensions, both to the children and to other adults. We can observe behavioral attributes of our children and only infer the psychological components. Furthermore, adults may describe children in this way to the children themselves in accordance with their perception of the children's understanding. In other words, children may be demonstrating cognitive limitations when they describe themselves along physical and activity dimensions, or they may be reflecting the characteristics they have always heard applied to themselves.

We hear 3- to 5-year-olds refer to themselves as little or big boys and girls, depending on how independent they feel at the moment. Edwards (1984) demonstrated through the use of photographs that preschoolers can recognize distinctions in other age groups such as babies, little boys and girls (ages 2–6), big boys and girls (ages 7–13), mommies and daddies (14–49), and grandmas and grandpas (50+). They are also likely to know that they are either boys or girls, although they may still believe these are transitory properties they could change if they wanted to (Kohlberg, 1969). By school age, children recognize gender as a fixed feature of identity and have some ideas of culturally sanctioned roles that parallel one's sexual identity. Gender development will be more fully addressed in a later section.

Preschool children can make basic distinctions between their private selves and public selves. They can understand that others do not know everything they think or feel. Preschool children have been shown to fake an emotion to manipulate another, demonstrating their belief that only they have access to some personal information (Bretherton, Fritz, Zahn-Waxler, & Ridgeway, 1986). They recognize that their own private talk, which accompanies many problem-solving tasks, is not the same as speaking to another, as Vygotsky (1962) highlighted in his theory. Four- and five-year-olds, especially, know that thinking goes on in their heads, others cannot "see" what they are thinking, and inanimate objects do not think (Johnson & Wellman, 1982). The following Focus on Psychology section looks at a contemporary debate: Should we encourage self-esteem or competency in children?

FOCUS ON PSYCHOLOGY

Self-Esteem Versus Competency Debate

A recent debate has raged about the utility of promoting self-esteem versus competency. In fact, some developmental psychologists would argue that self-esteem is not the important ingredient in children's success (Damon, 1995) and that false praise can actually do some harm. Critics of the self-esteem movement offer several points in contention of praising kids indiscriminately for any effort put forth (Damon, 1995; Seligman, 1995; Stevenson, 1995).

First, they argue, the data legitimately show positive self-esteem to be highly correlated with academic achievement; positive social skills; and resistance to drug involvement, early sex, gangs, and delinquency. However, they strongly assert that proponents of self-esteem as a panacea for social ills misinterpret the data to infer causality. Instead, the reverse conclusion is just as likely, but that cannot be inferred from existing data either.

That conclusion states that self-esteem increases as a function of increased competency, better skills for dealing with problems, and an improved ability to evaluate oneself accurately.

Their second argument pertains to the practice of dispensing praise liberally and with no real basis in reality. This practice can actually produce the opposite effect, causing children to distrust both adults' opinions and their own judgment. Furthermore, as a result of unwarranted praise, children do not learn to assess their strengths and weaknesses accurately.

Vanguards of the self-esteem movement regard a child's sense of worth and value as critical to motivation, success, and protection against depression and suicidal ideology (Dwyer, 1995; Harter, 1995; Pfohl, 1995). However, none of the proponents advocates the use of indiscriminate praise. They emphasize building self-esteem in the context of building competency skills, but they assert that a child's sense of cooperation, contribution, and effort lead to success and mastery of skills. They feel the unique needs of the child must be considered before learning can take place. Self-esteem enhancement must be tailored to each child to be truly meaningful and cannot be effective as a package deal applied identically to all children.

So how are we to interpret these arguments as we interact with children every day? Although these viewpoints appear to be at odds with one another, the real target of complaint for both appears to be the parenting and educational packages that rely on building self-esteem as the sole means of preparing children for the real world. This practice is not supported by the data. However, even in the controlled research lab, let alone the real world, causality is difficult to measure. Many researchers would condone drawing conclusions based on strong inference without making any claims to causality.

In the case of the self-esteem debate, a lot of correlational evidence exists. Positive self-esteem has been related to almost everything else parents, teachers, and clinicians would want to bolster in a child. From this standpoint, building self-esteem as a part of skill-based learning certainly seems merited. An important caveat is added by the researchers, however. Self-esteem and competency skills are both maximized through honest interchanges between adult and child.

Sociability of Preschoolers

As children age, they naturally come into contact with a larger social audience that includes other adults, teachers, peers, siblings, and older children. Two- and three-year-olds still stay physically close to adults and seek physical affection. Older preschoolers tend to seek the attention and approval of their peers through antics and playful gestures (Hartup, 1983).

Researchers have examined the question of sociability among preschoolers from several angles. Baumrind (1971) has focused attention on features of parent-child relationships that promote sociability. She has found that warm, supportive parents who set reasonable standards and expectations for their children's social interactions tend to raise well-adjusted, socially competent children. Permissive parents, on the other hand, who do not set or enforce social rules, tend to raise children who are more rebellious, aggressive, and uncooperative.

Shea (1981) observed 3- and 4-year-old children attending preschool over a period of about ten weeks. He concluded that children's social skills were enhanced by their participation in preschool. They began to interact more with each other than with the teacher and became more playful and outgoing as opposed to forceful and aggressive over the course of the observational period. Although preschool experiences have typically been shown to bolster a child's sociability, children who are less sociable tend to miss more school (Pennebaker, Hendler, Durrett, & Richards, 1981). Social skills training (see Focus on Sociology: Social Skills Training for Preschool Children) becomes essential to bring these children up to speed, so to speak, so they too can reap the benefits of the preschool social environment.

Longitudinal studies have produced data suggesting that sociability is a highly stable trait. By the age of 2, children's social behaviors are fairly predictable. The social behaviors assessed include reactions to play sessions, initiation of social interactions, and time spent interacting with other children. Measures of children's sociability at age 2 predicted sociability at age 3½ in preschool (Bronson, 1985). These findings are particularly salient when considering the long-term effects on unsociable children. Later on, in middle childhood and adolescence, peer rejection becomes a forceful determinant correlate of behavioral and emotional difficulties.

Social Skills Training for Preschool Children

To develop sociability skills in children, we must first consider exactly what skills we would like to improve. Asher and Dodge (1986) defined these skills as initiating play activities; communicating effectively; cooperating; giving help, affection, and approval to their peers; and resolving conflicts. The development of effective social skills is exceedingly important because poor peer relationships are often the result of poor social skills. Poor peer relations, especially rejection by peers, have been linked steadily with increases in delinquency, psychopathology, and low self-esteem.

Several therapeutic approaches have been designed to remediate social skills problems in children. These approaches include reinforcement, modeling, and cognitive strategies. Reinforcement and modeling strategies may be necessary at first to make immediate gains and motivate children to pursue more complicated strategies, such as problem solving and role play, that are associated with longer-term gains.

To implement positive reinforcement strategies, two essential elements must be present. First, positive reinforcement in the form of verbal praise, attention, and even tangible rewards can be used to shape socially appropriate responses. For example, every time a child shares, praise can be bestowed. This works best if the praise is awarded consistently to every child that demonstrated desirable social behavior according to a group reinforcement plan (Combs & Slaby, 1977). In this way, unsociable children can see others rewarded for positive behavior as well. While positive social behavior is being rewarded, less desirable behaviors like solitary play and aggressive behaviors are ignored as much as possible so as not to inadvertently reinforce them.

Second, the environment often requires slight manipulation to provide and instigate social contact that can then be reinforced. We can structure a play setting relatively easily by introducing social games like tag and duck-goose that draw in the less sociable children. In addition, children deficient in social skills can be given a valuable commodity such as treats to give out to playmates. This strategy creates a social interaction in which everyone will want to interact with the unsociable child.

Modeling techniques have also been shown to help socially shy or withdrawn children enter the play group with less fear. Models that work best are those who are like the unsociable children in that they appear initially hesitant to engage others socially. When the models' positive social behaviors and natural benefits are pointed out to the group, undersocialized children more often imitate the positive behaviors (Asher & Renshaw, 1981). Another unexpected gain was found by this practice. Not only did the shy children engage in positive social behaviors like smiling, helping, and initiating contact, but so did the other children in the room. The benefits were reciprocal in that all the children responded in socially positive ways to each other (Cooke & Apolloni, 1976).

More complex social-skills-training approaches, such as teaching cognitive strategies, require more activity on the part of the unsocialized child. The child actively participates in thinking about, practicing, and problem-solving likely scenarios to develop helpful tools for prolem situations. In coaching, the therapist both demonstrates and provides the rationale for particular socially desirable behaviors. The child then practices the behavior with the therapist and, even better, in live settings where interaction and cooperation are encouraged (Oden & Asher, 1977).

Role-playing techniques represent another cognitive therapy strategy. In this case, children discuss hypothetical problems and generate potential solutions for them. Myrna Shure and George Spivack (1980) developed a ten-week program aimed at preschoolers. The children used puppets to act out problem scenarios and helpful solutions. Then the preschoolers were guided in discussing the feelings of all the characters involved in the problem situation. Gains were made not only in the puppet exchanges, which became less aggressive, but also in the kinds of solutions worked out by the students themselves in the classroom.

Regulation

Young preschool children rely on physical means of expressing their emotions, both positive and negative.

When preschoolers are happy, they are happy with their whole bodies, from smiling faces down to dancing feet. When they feel angry or frustrated, they strike out physically as well. They throw tantrums, hit, kick, throw objects, and even bite. These behaviors assert their autonomy in the only way they know how.

As preschoolers develop better and better language skills, and as their adult role models set reasonable limits and model social cooperation as well as acceptable ways of expressing negative emotions, children begin to incorporate these skills into their repertoire of self-assertive techniques. They are displaying the first signs of self-control when they use words and not physical aggression to communicate their feelings (Spitz, 1966). However, the preschooler's first choice of words are rarely those that would win a peace prize. They use fighting words, words chosen to arouse a reaction in another child, not mediate the problem. Not surprisingly, for young preschoolers, much of the vocabulary of the day revolves around body parts and bodily functions. Verbally aggressive preschoolers will use "bathroom talk," use swear words and "I hate you" (Wolfgang, 1977). The content of the remark is not what is important at that moment, but rather the emotion conveyed. The content may be dealt with another time when the child is calm enough to hear what we say. We can tell them those words hurt others' feelings, but they can't cooperate when their emotional energy is high.

Children who learn to use words instead of physical aggression will, eventually, learn to use more socially sanctioned verbal approaches as well (Wolfgang, 1977). The process of internalizing self-control takes time over the course of early and middle childhood (Fraiberg, 1968). Schuster and Ashburn (1992) have noted that children whose parents acknowledge the children's feelings and teach them to use alternate behaviors and means of expressing their feelings also learn cooperation and internalize self-control. Children who are taught to obey and comply regardless of how they feel do not learn to internalize cooperation skills. They may strike out, engaging in less mature behaviors when the threat of punishment is not there.

Psychological Hazards

Many disorders of childhood affect behaviors in very specific domains, such as eating, sleeping, eliminating, speaking, paying attention, and learning. Mood disorders, including anxiety and depression, and even the beginnings of antisocial conduct can be seen in children as they attempt to cope with normal developmental issues as well as situational and traumatic stressors. These disorders are considered developmental in that they represent an aberration in the normal course of development.

The disorders of childhood generally fall into one of three categories: developmental delays, developmental disorders, and developmental psychopathology. Developmental delays represent a slowed rate of skill acquisition, or normal behaviors such as bed-wetting that occur at an inappropriate age. Delays can occur in almost any area of functioning; however, most children catch up before any real damage is done. Delays in critical areas, such as speech, tend to be more readily recognized and produce more profound negative effects for the child.

Developmental disorders occur in the areas of eating, sleeping, speech, eliminating, and attending (Bootzin, 1988). These disorders are characterized by a disruption in the performance of these skills. As such, they tend to cause problems for those caring for the children as well as for the children themselves. Children with developmental disorders are more likely to be referred for treatment than are children who show delays in the acquisition of normal behaviors, unless the delays are extreme. Examples of developmental disorders include enuresis, encopresis, stuttering, attention deficit disorder, and night terrors.

Developmental psychopathology results when a child's healthy adaptation is impeded by an inability to rally resources and cope with stressors. Although the child's response may, in fact, be a reasonable response to an identifiable stressor, the child's functioning becomes impaired by an inability to cope with and recover from trauma. Instead of one behavioral domain being affected, multiple areas of the child's life are compromised, including peer and family relationships, school performance, activities, and developmental goals. In this sense, developmental psychopathology is pervasive. Examples of developmental psychopathology include mood disorders such as anxiety and depression. Although these disorders have counterparts in adult psychopathology, the etiology, course of the disorder, and prognosis are different for children.

Diagnostic and Assessment Issues

Age is a critical factor in determining whether a particular behavior falls within an expected and normal developmental range. Children develop and change rapidly compared with adults, making a diagnosis of problem behavior difficult for parents and professionals. This difficulty is confounded by the fact that many normally developing children experience transitory problems from time to time and frequently adjust and grow out of the problem behavior just as quickly.

Children are dependent on adults not only to recognize the existence of a problem but also to seek help for them. Parents who have grown accustomed to a child's usual pattern of behavior, and those who do not have the opportunity to observe their child in the company of agemates, may not possess the requisite understanding of normal developmental behavior patterns to ascertain whether their child needs help. Furthermore, treatment of childhood disorders frequently involves the cooperation and participation of parents and family members, only some of whom are capable and willing.

In the following sections we will examine childhood disorders involving elimination, speech, attention, anxiety, and depression.

Elimination

Problems in toilet training can arise from unreasonable parental expectations, because children must be physically, emotionally, and cognitively mature enough to master the task. In our culture, children are generally daytime toilet-trained by the time they enter the preschool years and nighttime trained about one year later. Girls' ability and motivation generally precede that of boys, and a wide normal range exists between children.

Enuresis is defined as a lack of bladder control after age 5 (American Psychiatric Association, 1994). Primary enuresis refers to bladder control that was never achieved by age 5, and secondary enuresis refers to a loss of ability after first achieving control. Secondary enuresis frequently occurs when feelings of jealousy or insecurity are triggered, such as following the birth of a sibling or a similar stressor. After a period of adjustment, toilet-training skills return to normal. Other times, the problem becomes more serious. Thirty percent of enuretic children were found to be aggressive, unresponsive to discipline,

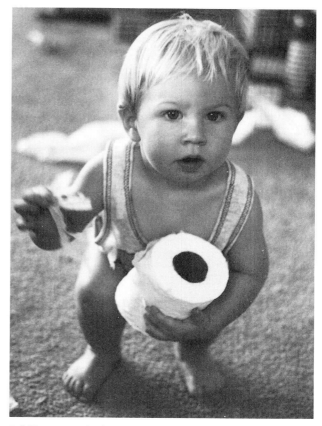

A child's mastery of toilet training requires coordination of biophysical, psychological, and social domains of development.

and have low frustration tolerances (Kaffman & Elizur, 1977). Fewer children showed signs of poor motivation, depression, and lack of assertiveness. During the normal course of the disorder, about 5–10% of children spontaneously recover each year.

Encopresis is defined as a lack of bowel control after a normal age and is distinguished as either primary or secondary. Encopresis is not diagnosed before age 4. The disorder is more common in boys than in girls and occurs in about 1% of the 5-year-old population. About one out of four encopretic children are also enuretic. Factors associated with encopresis include inconsistent toilet training and psychosocial stressors, such as entering school or the birth of a new sibling. Encopresis rarely becomes chronic.

Anxiety Disorders

Separation anxiety disorder, characterized by severe anxiety about leaving home or separating from the child's primary attachment figures, is not uncommon, occurring in about 4% of the population. Children typically fear harm will come to them or their family if separated, and they go to great lengths to prevent separations. Children develop somatic complaints, refuse to attend school, and behave in clingy, demanding ways with parents to ensure their closeness. These children also experience sadness, loss of interest in activities, withdrawal, and difficulty concentrating on school or play. In the course of normal development, separation anxiety peaks at about 1 year and gradually lessens with age. Separation anxiety is most frequently seen in very tight-knit families and following some sort of trauma for the child. In the general population, separation anxiety is more prevalent in females than males; however, gender rates are about equal in clinical samples (APA, 1994).

Avoidant disorder, commonly called a fear of strangers and strange or new situations, can be socially debilitating to a child. This response is normal between the ages of 8 months and 2–3 years, but it may continue into childhood for some children. A child may severely limit involvement in social and academic settings to avoid this fear. As a result, the child may feel lonely and depressed and lose self-confidence, causing further avoidant behavior (Bootzin & Acocella, 1988).

Overanxious disorder or generalized anxiety disorder is distinguished from separation anxiety in that the child's fears have no specific focus. In the case of overanxious disorder, children anticipate something going wrong in almost any situation and worry about the possibility. Children with these unfocused worries doubt themselves and their abilities as well. Worries often center on school and sports performance, and children frequently redo tasks in an attempt to make sure they are good enough. Children living in homes where love and acceptance are granted for good behavior tend to be approval seeking and perfectionistic (APA, 1994). A vicious cycle unfolds when children's performance is handicapped by worries and anxiety, which, in turn, causes them to fail and produces even more anxiety (Bootzin & Acocella, 1988).

Childhood Depression

Depression in children tends to co-occur in the presence of other psychological disorders (Garmezy & Rutter, 1983). The symptom pattern differs from that exhibited by adults. Children tend to display more than one symptom and can act clingy, disobedient, irritable, sad, and hopeless; refuse to attend school; and show a decreased interest in usual activities. Children are rarely suicidal, although this possibility increases in adolescence. Children who experience depression tend to have mood disorders as adults (Cantwell, 1982). Prevalence rates for prepubertal males and females are about equal, however, by the time girls reach adolescence and adulthood, they are twice as likely to report depression as males (APA, 1994). Depressive episodes often result from a severe psychosocial stressor in a child's life, such as the loss of a loved one, separation, or other trauma. A more serious psychological disorder is discussed in the following Focus on Psychology section.

FOCUS ON PSYCHOLOGY

Childhood Autism—A Severe Developmental Disorder

Kevin's parents thought he was a little odd as a baby. He was rather fussy. When they fed him and tried to stroke his back, he would stop eating and fuss until they stopped the stroking. When they picked him up for play, he would often avert his gaze or look past them. As a toddler, he liked to play by himself. He would sit for long periods of time just watching a patch of sun on the floor or dropping blocks over and over. His language development seemed especially slow, but he was their first baby and they had no expectations for language acquisition. The pediatrician told them Kevin would learn to speak soon. When he went to preschool at the age of 3, however, the teacher called the parents in for a conference because Kevin would not play or interact with any of the children in the class.

He spent most of his mornings sitting and rocking and he rarely spoke to anyone. In fact, the only thing the teachers had heard him say was "water" when he needed a drink.

Childhood **autism** is a pervasive developmental disorder with profound implications for the child's ability to function (APA, 1994). Children with autism suffer psychological, cognitive, and social deficits that impair their functional capacities in nearly every realm of their lives.

Although the disorder is typically present at birth, autism is often not diagnosed until the child is about 3 years old, when language deficits can be distinguished from speech delays.

Language deficits are prominent in autistic children. More than half do not speak at all, whereas others whine, scream, or demonstrate **echolalia,** repeating songs and phrases from others' conversations. These verbalizations are distinct from social communication because they are rarely intended as a means of interacting with or communicating information to another person. More often, verbal expression is used as a means of self-stimulation or for getting a simple need met. The severity of language deficits has been found to be the best predictor of the child's overall prognosis. Children who have developed recognizable speech by the age of 5 fare the best in terms of leading independent lives.

Mental retardation appears to be a stable feature of autistic disorder, with more than 70% of children testing at an IQ level below 70. Furthermore, their mental retardation does not improve with therapy (Rutter, 1985). Boys are three to four times more likely to develop autism than are girls.

Significant social deficits and poor relationship skills also characterize autism. These children typically react to others not as people but as objects in their environment. They do not relate physically, seek comfort, communicate, or otherwise interact with other people unless they need something they cannot manage themselves (Bootzin & Acocella, 1988). They prefer the company of inanimate objects, and when with other people, autistic children frequently do not respond to their own names, make eye contact, smile, initiate communication, or respond when spoken to. More often, autistic children will not acknowledge the presence of another human being.

We see autistic children play in rigid, unimaginative ways. They do not use make-believe or imitative play.

Furthermore, they do not engage in social play, instead preferring to occupy themselves alone. They also engage in nonfunctional routines and rituals (APA, 1994). These children demand sameness and predictability in their environments and daily routines. They also exhibit distorted body movements. Autistic children can be seen flapping their arms, hands, and fingers, banging their heads, and twisting their bodies in unnatural ways.

Parenting an autistic child can be extremely difficult, frustrating, and sad. When a child does not respond or relate, the quality of parental and sibling interactions and stimulation can taper off. Treatment efforts result in slow, minimal gains. Behavioral therapy techniques have documented empirical support. These techniques include token economy strategies, modeling, social skills training, and language and speech training. B. J. Freeman (1993) proposes an individually based program, in which each child's developmental profile is considered and treatment components are designed accordingly.

Social Dimension
Families, Groups, Support Systems, and Contexts

By the time a child reaches the period of early childhood, the family has undergone numerous changes. These changes are noted in the marital relationship, parent-child relationships, work, and family systems dynamics. The couple has become a family, and that family may continue growing again with the birth of another child. The developing child plays an active role in promoting healthy change in the family structure and dynamics and, at the same time, must adjust to the changes as well.

For the preschooler, parents and family remain the primary socializers and sources of companionship and comfort. However, as children progress through the preschool years, they relate to and rely on a larger circle of adults and peers because their needs no longer center so much on physical care. Preschoolers are growing, exploring, investigating, and refining motor, social, and emotional skills at an exhilarating and enthusiastic pace. They also discover new sources of anger, frustration, jealousy, and elation as they interact within a wider social environment.

Parenting roles and tasks shift from those involving physical care to setting limits, encouraging increasing amounts of independence in self-care and play skills, and using language and reason as methods of social control. Throughout all these very profound changes in the preschooler's social environment, the family continues to provide the basis for support, attachment, and exploration. Children need their parents to be there for them whenever they need them.

Family Influences

As we mentioned briefly, parenting roles begin to take on a different color as children traverse the preschool years. Children still need their parents as the primary sources of attention, care, love, encouragement, and security. Children living in homes where their changing needs are provided for can attend to their developmental tasks unencumbered with worries or fears for their safety and for that of their family members. Parents who are too preoccupied with their own identity issues, ambitions, or survival will struggle with child-rearing tasks that seem extremely demanding because they compete for energy with their other pressing needs.

Parents of preschoolers begin to shift their focus from physical care to encouraging self-care, greater independence, and compliance with rules of social systems such as the family, peer group, preschool, and society. Effective parents allow their children to try out new activities, develop some self-sufficiency, and set reasonable limits with their children. Parents who are too rigid or demanding impose unrealistic expectations on their children, causing them to feel as if they cannot measure up and to feel guilty for failing to accomplish something on their own.

According to Erikson's theory, the psychosocial crisis facing children during the preschool years is one of initiative versus guilt. The parent of a preschooler, much like the parent of the adolescent, must help the child discover personal and social abilities and limits while enjoying their accomplishments and sense of self-reliance. In this way, measured against the backdrop of peers and society, children continue to learn about themselves.

Diana Baumrind has investigated parenting styles over several decades (1971, 1991), and her research has described three styles of parenting and their consequent effects on children: *authoritarian, authoritative,* and *laissez-faire permissive.* Maccoby and Martin (1983) have further differentiated the permissive parenting style to include two distinct types, *permissive indulgent* and *permissive indifferent.* Erikson (1968) also theorized that parents differ along two dimensions of parenting he considered fundamental during the preschool years as parents begin to restrain and socialize their children. He labeled these dimensions parental warmth (warmth-hostility) and parental control (permissiveness-restrictiveness).

Parental warmth refers to the acceptance and approval shown to children across a number of different occasions. These parents offer their children encouragement and praise and are generous with affection. Hostile parents, on the other hand, tend to criticize, reject, or ignore their children and their bids for attention. Parents tend to be characterized as either warm and approving or hostile and rejecting, and these styles tend to be mutually exclusive.

The construct of parental control taps into the number of demands, restrictions, and limits that parents place on their children. Permissive parents encourage their children to explore and make independent decisions. Restrictive parents impose more demands and enforce more rules on their children, controlling their actions and decisions. Parents tend to become more permissive as children age and develop the experience and ability to make healthy decisions for themselves. All children need guidance and monitoring, which can be flexible and change according to the developmental needs of the child.

What effects do we see on children reared within the context of these distinct parenting models? Parents need to adapt their style of relating and interacting, as well as discipline, to their child's developmental level. As children enter the preschool years, parents can begin to rely on verbal exchanges, reasoning, moral sanctions, and giving and withholding of special privileges. Table 7.1 highlights the features associated with each parenting style and the behavioral effects on the children.

Discipline strategies that invoke logical and immediate consequences for preschool children tend to be the most effective because children are beginning to understand cause and effect. They also help a child develop an ability to think logically about actions and to make choices based on likely outcomes. Furthermore, the use

TABLE 7.1   Effects of Parenting Styles on Children

Parenting Style	Characteristics	Effects on Children
Authoritarian	Restrictive, punitive style; sets firm limits and controls; encourages obedience; values work and effort; few verbal exchanges allowed	Average social, cognitive competencies; fearful, unhappy, vulnerable to stress, passively hostile, aimless, irritable, conflicted
Authoritative	Warm, nurturant, accepting; encourages independence, but with limits; verbal exchanges using negotiation, compromise, and reason also encouraged; responsive to needs of child	High social, cognitive competencies; cope well with stress; curious, self-controlled, cooperative with adults, energetic, friendly, self-reliant
Permissive Indulgent	Very involved in child's life; few demands placed on child; lax control; allows freedom of expression, encourages creativity, confidence	Low self-control; difficulty focusing own behavior; expect to get their own way; allow poor social, cognitive competencies; not popular with other children; domineering, impulsive, aggressive
Permissive Indifferent	Very uninvolved in child; few demands placed on children; lax control; allows freedom of expression and impulses	Low self-control; poor social, cognitive competencies; rebellious, impulsive, aggressive

of logical consequences helps avoid power struggles between parents who impose discipline (Dreykurs, 1964). Logical consequences just happen, because of their very nature, and the child begins to learn about problem solving in the real world.

Several researchers found few differences between mothers and fathers when disciplining their preschool-aged children. Mothers tend to verbalize more while fathers give more commands (McLaughlin, 1983; Yogman, Cooley, & Kindlon, 1988). Differences did emerge when researchers examined the interaction between parents and sons and daughters. Sons were provided more task-oriented, directive, and approval instructions than were daughters by both parents (Frankel, 1983). Girls, on the other hand, were taught to be more cautious and cooperative and were provided feedback about their performance more than were boys. The subtle, but clear, messages to boys and girls from both parents convey stereotypical gender-role expectations. More aggressive behavior is tolerated, if not encouraged, in boys, whereas girls are taught cooperation and empathy through parental play and teaching (Power & Shanks, 1989). The following Focus on Multiculturalism section examines cultural differences in parenting styles.

FOCUS ON MULTICULTURALISM

Cultural Differences in Parenting Styles

Many researchers have documented the positive effects on children raised by parents who are warm and affectionate and who set consistent, reasonable rules for their children as opposed to those that behave in a punitive or aloof manner (Baumrind, 1971). Of course, most of this research has been conducted on middle-class, white families. These findings may neglect the fact that not all children are raised to participate and succeed in the same environment as the middle-class children represented in these studies.

Research studies of lower-income and lower-educational-status families suggest that these parents tend to be more authoritarian in their child-raising practices; they expect more obedience from their children, engage in less verbal exchange, and exhibit less warmth (Maccoby, 1980). But does this make lower-income parents less desirable or effective parents? Shaffer (1989) reviews several reasons why lower-SES parents may be more authoritarian with their children. They may be facing more stress, which makes it harder for them to be warm and caring. They may be preparing their children for the types of jobs the parents themselves hold, in which obedience and respect are positive attributes. The children themselves may be more difficult to parent. Many lower-income mothers are young and may not have received adequate prenatal care. As a result, these mothers may have delivered premature, low-birth-weight, or drug- or alcohol-exposed babies. As we have discussed, such babies are more difficult to care for. Also, lower-SES parents may feel that authoritarian parenting is necessary to protect their children from environments that are full of risks. These risks increase the likelihood of delinquency, school dropout, early pregnancy, and substance use. Children from risky environments may not be permitted the luxury of experimentation without dire consequences that children from more affluent environments are afforded.

As a result, children from lower-SES families may play by and adopt a different set of values according to the roles, goals, and relationships they aspire to. These ecological constraints are not always incorporated into the interpretations of findings on the most effective parenting style for children. We must remember that as the cultural context changes, so do expectations of behavior and beliefs. Ethnocentric biases prohibit us from understanding which parenting styles promote competent children in differing cultures and subcultures (Laosa, 1981). But regardless of the parental style, or the reasons for that particular style, parental warmth and approval remain important ingredients in the parent-child relationship.

Mother's Role　Although preschool children need their mothers less for physical care than they did as infants, the need for emotional support and encouragement is just as great as ever (Hartup, 1989; Sears, Maccoby, & Leven, 1957). Still, much of a mother's time with her preschooler revolves around child-care duties (seven

times more than fathers), whereas fathers tend to spend much less time in direct care and more time playing (Robinson, 1977).

What kinds of things do preschoolers learn from their mothers? Studies reveal that mothers tend to introduce soothing activities to their preschoolers, such as reading, drawing, and music. In this way, children are learning how to soothe and comfort themselves. Children also learn a great deal about feelings and relationships from their mothers. During play, mothers tend to be more verbal and visual with their preschoolers than fathers (Power, 1985). This interaction style during play may contribute to the child's understanding of relationships and coping strategies.

In addition, preschoolers are attuned to learning about the meaning of their gender and begin to identify with the same-sex parent, all the while learning how to relate to the opposite-sex parent. Preschoolers observe that males and females act differently. Research has supported the idea that males and females rely on different strategic approaches to solve problems. Males tend to focus on only one relevant aspect of the problem and base their decision on that aspect alone. Females, on the other hand, tend to gather lots of information and attend to the context of the situation before determining a solution. In this way, children learn about diversity and alternative approaches to events in their lives.

Maternal employment has become a necessary part of everyday life over the past few decades. What effects do we see on preschool children whose mothers work outside of the home? Children tend to become more independent and may be socialized into the larger community faster when their mothers work. Preschoolers of working mothers tend to be as socially confident and even more gregarious with peers than do children of stay-at-home mothers (Schachter, 1981). In addition, girls, in particular, and boys develop less stereotypical and rigid impressions of the roles of men and women in our society (Hoffman, 1989).

Father's Role　The relationship between preschoolers and their father broadens the children's perspective on the world. For the most part, even today, preschool boys and girls are raised in almost exclusively female environments. They spend most of their time with mothers and with baby-sitters and teachers, who are usually female.

The child's father may be the only male figure with whom contact is regular.

As we discussed in the last chapter, fathers play differently with their children than mothers do. Remember, father play has been described as more provocative and vigorous, and less conventional and verbal than mother play (Yogman et al., 1988). These differences were found to be especially true of play with preschoolers, and with sons more so than with daughters. Fathers who play physically and roughly with their children tend to raise children with increased social competencies (MacDonald, 1987; Parke, MacDonald, Beital, & Bhavangri, 1988). This physical play is important to children in that how they learn to cope with the exhilaration, challenge, and unpredictability of their fathers' physical play prepares them for later life experiences.

By watching and interacting with their fathers, children also learn that there are numerous ways to complete a task. The father may not do things exactly the way the child's mother does, and the child is shown another way to solve a problem. Of course, family structures and parenting styles vary. Mothers and fathers may assume complementary but nonstandard roles that work just as well for their children and family.

Around age 4 or 5, both boys and girls find their relationship with their fathers especially appealing and important, and they seek him out as a playmate more often than they seek their mother (Lamb, 1981). Adult males help young boys define their own developing masculinity by encouraging and supporting their accomplishments. Boys will model themselves after their fathers at this age. Girls also seek out fatherly attention and time. The father's role helps girls define their feminine side. Also, preschool girls may tend to be resentful and jealous of their mother's special relationship with their father. Involved fathers help preschool children understand more about themselves and the larger world.

Siblings   Most children grow up in a family enriched and complicated by the presence of siblings. In the United States and Britain, this figure is estimated to be about 80%. The birth of a sibling often occurs when the first or previous child enters the preschool years. The exact influence one sibling wields over another depends on many factors, including birth order, birth spacing, number of siblings, and gender.

Sibling rivalry tends to begin early. Frequently, an older child will have to make adjustments and concessions, willingly or not, as soon as the next baby arrives. Even before the birth of a sibling, mothers can be incapacitated during pregnancy and not able to perform all of their usual child-care responsibilities. For most children, the period of adjustment to a new sibling is relatively short. As the youngest becomes capable of responding to an older child, positive interactions between siblings soon begin to dispel the initial reaction of anger and resentment. The children also develop a relationship of their own, not contingent on the parents' involvement.

For the firstborn child, adjustment issues are magnified because the arrival of a second child represents the first time a family must contend with sibling rivalry and expanding relations. Preschoolers and older toddlers receive less attention from their mothers after the birth of a sibling (Dunn & Kendrick, 1982; Stewart, Mobley, Van Tuyl, & Salvador, 1987).

Of course, from the children's point of view, suddenly having to share the love, affection, and attention of parents that was once reserved only for them seems to be an awfully overwhelming task. An infant demands and requires more time and physical attention than an older child does. Furthermore, mothers were found to play less and act in more coercive and restraining ways with the firstborn after the birth of the second child, although an especially intense relationship tends to continue with the oldest child (Dunn & Kendrick, 1982).

What do we know about sibling relationships? Aside from exploring all possible combinations of sibling dyads, we will consider differences compared with the parent-child relationship, age, and gender. The sibling relationship was found to differ from that of the parent-child relationship (Baskett & Johnson, 1982). In-home observations supported the contention that both parent-child and sibling-sibling relationships favored more positive than negative interactions. However, children demonstrated more affection, compliance, and positive social responses to parents than to their brothers and sisters. Instead, children directed more negative behaviors, such as teasing, hitting, and yelling at their siblings, than at parents. Older siblings were found to be both more aggressive and domineering as well as helpful and nurturant with younger siblings (Abramovitch, Corter, Pepler, & Stanhope, 1986). Fighting and rivalry among siblings

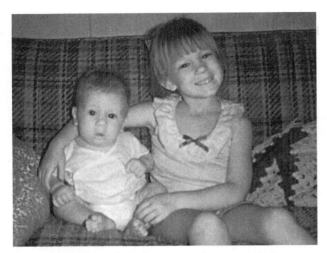

Siblings offer challenges to the development of interpersonal relationships. They must learn to get along with each other while competing for their parents' time.

provides a safe opportunity to practice resolving conflicts and, in fact, may toughen up children, making them less vulnerable to the pain and hurt that can be a part of peer relationships.

Same-sex siblings were found to be more aggressive and struggle more over dominance than were cross-sex siblings (Minnett, Vanell, & Santrock, 1983). However, several other investigators found opposing results, concluding that same-sex siblings showed more prosocial behaviors to one another than did cross-sex siblings (Abramovitch et al., 1986; Dunn & Kendrick, 1982; Furman & Buhrmester, 1985a, 1985b).

When children live together as siblings, they contribute to each other's development in unique ways. They serve as teachers and models of both prosocial and negative behavior, communication partners, playmates, and rivals. Even children as young as preschoolers provide valuable and attentive emotional support to younger siblings, especially when they have been shown basic care skills and can identify the baby's source of distress (Stewart, 1983).

Siblings benefit from assuming the role of teacher or learner. Firstborn children with younger siblings, compared with only children, have been shown to excel in academic achievement, believed, in part, to stem from playing the role of tutor to younger siblings (Zajonc &

Markus, 1975). Younger siblings benefit from instruction in social skills, negotiation, and learning academic basics like ABCs and 123s by playing games like "school." Only children display solid social adjustment gained through social interactions with peers and extended family.

Peer Relationships   During the early childhood period of development, children continue to rely heavily on their parents for social and emotional support, care, and companionship. However, the security fostered by healthy family relationships provides children with the stability necessary to confidently initiate play and friendships with peers (Hartup, 1989; Pettit, Dodge, & Brown, 1988). Throughout this period of development, peers play an increasingly important role in the child's life.

Just how important are peer relationships in early childhood? We see peers providing a different learning environment from that of the family. Compared with the nonegalitarian family atmosphere, peer relationships tend to be of equal status. Preschoolers need other peers close in age to compare skills and their own abilities, learn social skills and information, and try out ways of interacting in a safe environment. Through this comparison, children find out more about themselves and others (Shaffer, 1989). Peer relationships have been associated with normal social development, whereas peer isolation and rejection have been linked to a host of behavioral problems in children, including delinquency and schizophrenia (Cairns et al., 1989; Kupersmidt & Coie, 1990). Peer rejection has been shown to predict more deleterious effects than peer isolation (Cowen et al., 1973).

In a classic study epitomizing the importance of peer relations, Anna Freud (Freud & Dann, 1951) studied six children found in a concentration camp after World War II. The children had all lost their parents and had reared themselves with very little consistent contact from adults. The children were each other's constant companions and refused to tolerate separation. They shared easily and were more concerned for the others than for themselves. After 35 years, the children had all grown to lead successful lives, with no evidence of psychosis or criminality. The companionship, nurturance, and skills they learned from each other supplanted those received from adults in their early years.

Researchers have found that children as young as 5–6 years of age spend as much free time with peers as with adults (Ellis, Rogoff, & Cromer, 1981). How would we characterize preschool children's peer groups? Preschoolers typically play with children of the same sex, a pattern that develops as early as age 1–2 and continues through middle childhood (Ellis et al., 1981). This observation should not come as a surprise to us, given that children are socialized by parents who may think boys should play with boys and girls with girls. Furthermore, because gender-role development and stereotypical behaviors and interests peak during these years, we would expect children to play with others who share their interests.

What kinds of influence do preschool friends exert on each other? Even preschoolers distinguish preferred playmates from acquaintances. They share more readily (Masters & Furman, 1981), are less hostile (Hinde, Titmus, Easton, & Tamplin, 1985), and make more personal sacrifices for the benefit of a friend (Kanfer, Stifter, & Morris, 1981). They also reinforce sex-appropriate behavior and extinguish behavior that does not conform (Lamb, Easterbrooks, & Holden, 1980). Preschoolers have also been observed to imitate and mimic a friend to instigate a positive social encounter and influence the other child (Dollinger & Gasser, 1981; Grusec & Abramovitch, 1982).

In addition, several factors were found to contribute to the popularity of preschoolers with their peers. These factors included secure attachment to authoritative parents, having an athletic build, facial attractiveness (Lan-glois, 1986), higher intelligence (Hartup, 1983), a pleasant name (McDavid & Harari, 1973), and behavioral characteristics such as outgoing, cooperative, and supportive (Langlois & Stynczynski, 1979). Obviously, children born without some of these innate characteristics may benefit from developing compensatory social skills to achieve positive status within their peer group.

Preschoolers' Play

As we have stated in previous sections, play is the primary medium for learning for preschool children. Play, for all ages, is a pleasurable activity, rewarding in its own right for the positive feelings engendered. In addition, frustrations, tensions, conflict, and anxiety can be reduced through play experiences. Play increases children's peer affiliations, social contacts, conversation, and social skills. Piaget (1967) observed that children's cognitive skills are exercised and promoted during play. Conversely, children's play is also limited by their cognitive abilities. Vygotsky (1962) also emphasized the importance of imaginative play for preschoolers in developing symbolic functions. Berlyne (1960) described how play fulfills a child's need for exploration, curiosity, surprise, and novelty. These opportunities provide children with information about themselves and their world.

Mildred Parten (1932) observed and categorized preschool children's play according to the amount of social interaction. Her findings are described in Table 7.2.

TABLE 7.2   Preschool Children's Play Styles

Play Type	Child's Behavior
Unoccupied play	Unengaged with other children or activities, not goal directed, least frequent type of play.
Solitary play	Child plays alone, engaged in task but not with other children, typical of 2- to 3-year-olds.
Onlooker play	Child watches other children play and talks, asks questions, and participates verbally but does not engage in the play directly. Interested, but not involved.
Parallel play	Child plays with toys like those others are using, but does not play with other child. More common among younger children than older ones.
Associative play	Children play actively together. The interaction is more important than the task or organization of the play. Social skills such as turn–taking, follow-the-leader are objects of the play.
Cooperative play	Children play an organized activity with a lot of social interaction. Social games, formal activities arranged by a teacher, competitive games fall into this category. Not as frequent among preschoolers.

Parten concluded that 3-year-olds engaged in more solitary and parallel play, whereas 5-year-olds were more frequently seen playing associatively and cooperatively. Barnes (1971) replicated Parten's study to find that play styles of children had changed over the decades. He found that children spent less time playing associatively or cooperatively than the children in the 1930s, perhaps due to the effects of TV and technological toys that require a single operator and less imagination.

Current research now looks at play as a function of both social interaction and cognitive ability (Bergin, 1988). Preschoolers were found to engage primarily in pretense/symbolic play (Bergin, 1988; Singer & Singer, 1987) and constructive play (Hetherington, Cox, & Cox, 1979). These current representations of children's play are described in Table 7.3.

Effects of TV on Preschool Children

Television has been noted as an important socializing agent and influence on children's behavior. American children spend more time watching television than with their parents or in school, an average of 25 hours per week (1988 survey by *Weekly Reader Magazine*, cited in Jaffe, 1991). The television has become a convenient baby-sitter. Parents often use television to hold children's attention so they can accomplish household chores. Many parents find that in today's fast-paced world, they have less time to interact with their children. Bronfrenbrenner (1986) commented that TV becomes a negative influence not because of what is provided but, instead, because of what is prevented. He suggests that the presence of TV decreases the amount of time families spend actively participating in mutual activities requiring discourse, argument, and reciprocity—such as playing games, going on outings, and talking—which promote children's learning.

Television has been criticized for negatively influencing children's lives. These criticisms include promoting increased passivity because television is not an interactive method of learning. Another criticism is that television perpetuates unrealistic views and expectations incompatible with real life, such as fairy-tale endings. A third criticism is that television promotes aggressive behavior (see Focus on Research: Television and Aggression) and flaunts gratuitous sex. Finally, television casts women, older people, and ethnic minorities in stereotypical roles, often unfavorably as victims, villains, criminals, and incompetents (Brody, 1987). In addition, Condry (1989) found that ethnic minorities tended to be underrepresented compared with whites.

Television has no doubt brought advantages to children's lives as well. These advantages include educational programs that expose children to information, knowledge, and alternative lifestyles and points of view to which they would not normally have access. The images and themes of entertainment television often erode these advantages, however.

Originally, educational television shows such as *Sesame Street* were developed and marketed to reach underprivileged children. The goal was to prepare children for school by helping them learn letters, numbers, colors, counting, classifying, and simple problem solving. Evaluations of *Sesame Street* confirmed the intentions of the show. Children who watched *Sesame Street* often made cognitive gains that lasted into the early elementary years. This finding was especially strong for 3-year-olds compared with 5-year-olds, who already had some of the skills taught on the show (Bogatz & Ball, 1972). The only criticism logged against *Sesame Street* is that children from advantaged homes tend to watch the show more than do underprivileged children for whom it was originally intended.

How children are affected by television viewing is determined, to a large extent, by what they are watching. In addition, parents can discuss the themes, staging, cultural biases, and peddling of consumerism depicted by television with their children. Open, nonjudgmental discussions can teach children to be informed viewers and not just consumers of television hype.

FOCUS ON RESEARCH

Television and Aggression

Bandura (1965) was one of the first researchers to study the effects that watching television violence has on children. In his experiment, one group of children watched a violent television show, and one group did not. He

TABLE 7.3   Development of Children's Play

Play Category	Activity Description
Sensorimotor play	Typical of infancy, to explore sensorimotor abilities.
Practice play	A means of practicing new skills, developing motor coordination, mental mastery. A skill or behavior is repeated until the skill is mastered. Important for sports and other games. Common throughout life and accounts for about one-third of preschoolers' play time (Rubin, Fein, & Vandenberg, 1983).
Pretense/symbolic play	Sociodramatic play when children use the physical environment as symbolic of something else, pretend play, try out fantasy, and role play. Begins between 9 and 30 months of age and peaks at about age 4–5.
Social play	Social interaction with peers, rough-and-tumble play, running, chasing, wrestling, and jumping are examples.
Constructive play	Combines sensorimotor and symbolic play, games that are created by the children, or projects developed by the children themselves. Organized games with rules are more common in elementary school–aged children.

found that children who had been exposed to the violence on television were later more likely to hit a doll repeatedly than were those who had not.

In another study, Steuer, Applefield, and Smith (1971) observed preschool children playing outdoors at nursery school and paired these children according to how much aggressive behavior, like hitting and kicking, they displayed. One child in each pair was shown a violent television program every day for two weeks. The other child was shown a television show free of aggressive and violent acts. The researchers found that those children shown the violent show, despite their previous level of aggressive behavior, became more aggressive in their play.

From these studies, we can conclude that television violence promotes increased levels of aggressive behavior in the play of preschool children. Friedrich and Stein (1973) demonstrated that this effect was strongest for children who engaged in more aggressive behaviors prior to viewing violence on television. Children who were not rated as aggressive to start with were hardly affected by the television violence. So, although violent television may contribute to aggressive acts in children, it is only one of many factors.

Preschool Environment

Today, many preschoolers will attend preschool or day care for three to five years. The emphasis of preschool programs varies greatly, with some focusing primarily on cognitive, academic development and others focusing almost exclusively on social and emotional development. However, for a child to fully appreciate a preschool setting, the curriculum should closely match the child's developmental goals.

Ideally our choice of preschools would include a large space for outdoor play and exploration of the natural environment; opportunities for unstructured free play; opportunities for semistructured group play involving cooperation and social interaction; opportunities for creative expression through art, dance, movement, and music; and verbal stimulation from both peers and adults to gently expand children's verbal skills. Perhaps most important, our ideal preschool would cherish each child for his or her own unique strengths and weaknesses, providing a safe, nurturing place to experiment with new feelings, behaviors, and ideas. All in all, our ideal preschool should be both age-appropriate and individually appropriate (Santrock, 1992).

Clarke-Stewart and Fein (1983) found numerous positive effects of early childhood education for children. They comment that these effects are all positive even though some may seem negative, because these effects are all in the direction indicative of healthy development for preschoolers. These effects include the following:

1. More interaction with peers, both positive and negative
2. Less cooperation with and responsiveness to adults
3. More social competence and maturity; also increases in confidence, assertiveness, and self-sufficiency; more verbally expressive; confident in social and stressful situations
4. Better adjusted when they begin elementary school—more leadership, goal-directed and persistent
5. Less socially competent—not as polite and compliant, but louder, more aggressive, and bossier if both the family and school support these behaviors

Overall, preschool children tend to perform well in school when they have learned some self-control and self-discipline. These skills allow them to work with others, delay gratification, and handle the frustration inherent in problem solving that accompanies school tasks. The family environment, and parents in particular, can create situations in which the child experiences frustration and mastery, as well as learns to accept "no" for an answer. Children will learn internal self-control by first learning to accept external control of their behavior imposed by parents. As a side effect that is beneficial to the child-teacher relationship, children learn to respect and cooperate with adults and those in authority, but not to fear them. These skills make the transition to formal educational settings much smoother for children.

Kindergarten

The concept of kindergarten was first developed by Freidrich Froebel in the 1840s. He conceived of kindergarten as a "garden for children," where they would be carefully nurtured, like plants. However, over the course of shifting trends in social and educational practices, some kindergartens have become too focused and concerned with success and achievement as opposed to nurturing the developing child (Elkind, 1987, 1981). This approach also worries some developmental experts who

fear that too much pressure is placed on children to succeed and achieve at the expense of real learning.

In response to this debate over delineating the most effective kindergarten environment, Ballenger (1983) described a child-centered kindergarten, organized around the child's needs, interests, and learning style. Ballenger's guidelines emphasize teaching the whole child, including the physical, cognitive, and social being. He argues that kindergarten programs should concentrate their efforts on the process of learning, not on what is learned. Ballenger stresses that kindergarten children learn most effectively through play incorporating direct experience with objects, people, and materials. He further describes excellent kindergarten programs as those that focus on the child's state of being, not becoming, through speaking, listening, experimenting, exploring, and discussing.

Today, kindergarten is mandatory in some states and optional in others. Although kindergarten curriculums may vary considerably, the primary goals remain fairly consistent across programs. These goals include developing good work and listening habits, learning to play and work independently, cooperating with peers, and forming a positive opinion about school. Because kindergarten is designed to prepare children for success in elementary school, kindergarten also provides an opportunity to assess a child's readiness for school. Children with adequately mature language, motor, and perceptual skills will benefit from entering first grade. However, the less prepared child will benefit from participating in a transitional class designed to bring skills up to par with other classmates. Assessment for school readiness becomes important to prevent unprepared children from falling behind academically and struggling with the negative emotional consequences of academic failure. Although preschool and kindergarten are among the resources available to assist in preparing children for formal education, many developmentalists reiterate the fact that the parents play the largest and most critical role in preparing their children for school. Only when parents are prevented from doing so do the other resources become especially important (Schuster & Ashburn, 1992).

Project Head Start

Project Head Start was spearheaded in 1965 as part of Lyndon Johnson's Great Society initiative. The overall goal was to break the cycle of poverty by providing a preschool experience for children from economically disadvantaged families at risk for school failure. Krown (1974) and Smilansky's research (1968), as well as Seligman's theory of learned helplessness (Seligman, 1975), have documented that children from disorganized, helpless families perform poorly in school. According to this research, parents in these families feel helpless to control events in their lives and, as a result, are detached from their environment and are unresponsive to their children's needs. They fail to teach their children ways of mastering their environment, and the children are, in essence, handed down the attitude of helplessness. When the children cannot fulfill their own expectations to perform well in school, they become detached as well, and feel helpless to succeed. Their natural curiosity and motivation are stymied from the beginning.

To counteract this phenomenon, the program was first offered to 4- and 5-year-olds during the summer preceding their kindergarten year. Now the program is available for an entire year prior to enrollment in kindergarten. Head Start shares many features of other early intervention programs (Richmond, Stipek, & Zigler, 1979), yet it makes unique contributions in the areas of parent participation, health, and nutrition. The specific curriculum for each Head Start program is determined by the individual program, with about 2000 programs existing in slightly different forms. However, all Head Start programs are committed to bettering the quality of life for the children and family participants.

Head Start programs are guided in their approach to intervention by several philosophical underpinnings. All Head Start programs include health, nutrition, education, parent involvement, and social services components. Children receive a physical exam, including vision, hearing, and dental checks, with referrals for immunizations and follow-up services as needed. Children also receive one hot meal and one snack each day to counter the effects of hunger on a child's ability to learn. Education focuses on the children's learning about themselves and the larger world, as well as on practical ways to care for themselves, which helps improve their self-esteem. Head Start program curriculums are guided by an understanding that children will perform better in school if they feel good about themselves and others, are motivated to succeed, and are healthy, as well as have improved verbal skills (Zigler, 1973).

Head Start directly involves parents in planning, administration, and delivery of services as opposed to relying only on professionals. In this way, the cultural background and diversity of the participants is respected and incorporated into the program, not rejected as inferior to white, middle-class traditions (Zigler & Valentine, 1979). Parents and children demonstrate positive gains in that they improve intellectually, and have increased self-esteem and better sense of control over their lives (Coleman et al., 1966).

Research evaluations of the Head Start program promoted a shift in the field of developmental psychology. Prior to involvement in Project Head Start, most researchers simply strove to accumulate knowledge. Following their efforts to evaluate Head Start, many realized they could also participate in developing social policy by fostering a deeper understanding of factors that both promote and hinder healthy development in children (Zigler & Finn-Stevenson, 1992).

What have we learned over the past 30 years of administering Head Start and other early intervention programs? First, we have refined our evaluation skills. We have learned that specific goals must be outlined for any project in order to ensure a proper evaluation of the program's intended effects. Initially, the effects of Head Start were evaluated only in terms of increases in children's IQ scores. But this represents only one small factor in determining school success. Effects on the health and motivation of the children and parent component were not examined, although they clearly influence school achievement as well (Zigler & Trickett, 1978). As a result, the evaluation failed to measure change in the most prominent areas of the program and caused undue disenchantment with the program. An example of this dissatisfaction stemmed from the Westinghouse Learning Corporation's (1969) evaluation, which showed that even after a full year of Head Start, children's IQ scores were initially increased, only to decrease a short while later in elementary school. Head Start proponents have had to battle for funding and acceptance ever since. Fortunately, more comprehensive, better-designed follow-up evaluations of Head Start have shown that children who participated in this program were more likely to succeed at school and less likely to be placed in remedial education programs (Consortium for Longitudinal Studies, 1983).

Although Project Head Start has served about 7.5 million children during the first 15 years of operation, this number represents only about 20% of those eligible (Schuster & Ashburn, 1992). The program is still under-funded and cannot provide enrollment for all eligible children. Federal and local monies fund the program, which is provided free to all eligible children.

An effective evaluation of early intervention programs must also include a cost-benefit analysis. A cost-benefit analysis is an important consideration because policy makers usually depend heavily on this figure. The Committee on Economic Development (1987) has determined that every dollar spent on preschool intervention programs saves $4.75 in later expenses for remedial education, welfare, and crime.

The Perry Preschool Program is another good example of the money-saving benefits of preschool intervention programs. Although the program appeared expensive at first, costing about $6000 per child per year, the achievements were notable. Evaluations revealed that after 19 years, children who had participated in the high-quality program, compared with other low-income students who did not, were significantly more successful in school, work, and personal lives and less likely to have dropped out of school, received public assistance, or engaged in criminal activities (Berrueta-Clement et al., 1984). From these studies, we learn that money spent initially on quality preschool programs not only saves on future expenditures to support undereducated, disadvantaged individuals but also greatly improves the quality of life for all. Society in general benefits when more members are able to contribute to and participate in established social institutions. To realize these gains and to prepare children for school, the integrity of high-quality programs must be maintained. The positive results documented by evaluation studies were found in high-quality programs with clearly established goals that addressed the whole child in the context of family and culture.

Multicultural and Gender Considerations

The preschool years are important for developing a positive and unique sense of self (Proshansky & Newton, 1968). Preschool children begin to recognize ethnic characteristics in appearance in themselves and in oth-

ers. One of the early classic studies on racial awareness was conducted by the Clarks in 1939 (Clark & Clark, 1939). The researchers asked three 5-year-old African American children to identify themselves from a series of drawings that included various animals, a clown, a white boy, and an African American boy. They discovered that by age 4, children would begin to identify the African American boy and by age 5, their identification with the African American boy was well developed.

Young preschoolers may not understand ethnicity as a fixed personal attribute until they have developed the concept of conservation, which occurs close to age 5. Preschoolers do not understand that these features may have a social significance beyond what is visible to the eye. Just as children cannot cognitively understand the meaning of sexuality, they cannot understand the social meaning of membership in one culture or another. As soon as they identify with one ethnic group, children learn who they are in comparison with others. They learn to evaluate themselves along the dimensions of appearance, ability, group membership, and hopes for the future (Proshansky & Newton, 1968).

What preschool children come to know about their own heritage is largely determined by their parents and extended families. They have not branched out into the larger community unprotected by caregivers very often. Children who feel valued in their own right learn to respect themselves and others. In addition, parents who teach their children the truth about racial inequality and discrimination may be preparing them to deal squarely with problem situations when they are encountered.

Gender-Role and Sexual Identity Development

Gender-role development and sexual identity development are separate yet intrinsically linked processes. What factors contribute to gender and sexual identity development? As we discussed in the last chapter, babies show gender differences from birth, and certainly, social and cultural expectations permeate child-rearing from a very early age. Parents, families, teachers, peers, and physical and cognitive development all contribute to a child's sexual identity formation.

By the preschool years, boys will play with boys and girls with girls (Hartup, 1983). This represents the beginning of gender-role identity in that boys and girls tend to play differently during the preschool years. Preschool boys and girls already have strong notions of sex-typed play (Kuhn, Kohlberg, Langer, & Haan, 1977). They can identify whether boys or girls cook, play with cars, fight, climb trees, and kiss. Gender-specific toy preferences are also evident at this young age (Weinraub et al., 1984), and parents encourage sex-typed play in young children as well. This is especially true of fathers who tolerate tomboyish activities for girls but tend to express more concern about cross-sex activities for boys (Langlois & Downs, 1980). Boys adopt sex-typed behavior and toys earlier than girls do (Blakemore, LaRue, & Olejnik, 1979).

At this time, children also develop stronger identification with the same-sex parent. They will dress like them and engage in sex-stereotypic behaviors. They are busy exploring what it means to be a boy or girl in their world. Before age 4–5, preschool children may think their sex is changeable. After this time, however, children realize they will always be either a boy or a girl. By age 3, children know what gender they are. By age 4, they can identify and recognize differences in boys and girls based on styles of behaving, playing, and dressing.

Sex play becomes more common in this age group and is usually nothing more than a healthy curiosity about their bodies. Children at this age are fascinated with everyone's body and bodily functions. Modesty and privacy are not concepts that have any meaning to them; curiosity wins out. Masturbatory play is also common during this period. Parents may have different personal beliefs about this activity, but they should try to convey to their children that their bodies are sources of pleasure to them but that certain activities are done in private. We should try not to overreact too strongly or shame the child who is simply engaging in exploratory behavior. The preschool years are an excellent time to introduce the notion of "private" and "public" selves. In addition, these concepts become useful in talking about safety and in preventing child sexual abuse for children.

Although many gender-role qualities are learned, two characteristics appear to be genetically transposed: aggression and nurturance. Boys tend to be more aggressive than girls and engage in more aggressive play, from rough-and-tumble sports to "fights" with guns and superheroes (Maccoby & Jacklin, 1974). Girls display more

nurturance than boys do and play more games oriented to relationship themes (Maccoby, 1980). These qualities do not describe every boy or girl, but they do tend to remain fairly constant over the course of development for most children.

FOCUS ON GENDER

The Effects of Sex-Stereotyping

Tyrone's mother was determined to raise her children in a non-gender-specific way. In particular, she wanted her son to develop characteristics of warmth and nurturance, free from the constraints of sex-stereotyping, so she discouraged aggressive play and aggressive toys. Tyrone spent most of his time at home with his mother and sister playing quietly. He often joined his sister in playing with her dolls and stuffed animals. Tyrone's mother did not become worried about him until he began wearing a dress-up skirt and pretending his name was Tara. Then she took him to a therapist who told her to forget the dolls, throw out the skirt, and buy him a cowboy outfit.

Many argue that parents should not raise gender-neutral children because gender differences have real meaning and value in our society and to the children themselves. Studies by Fagot (1989, 1991) suggest that young children whose mothers have stereotypical attitudes toward sex roles in the family more easily learn labels for boys and girls; and children whose parents encourage sex-typed toy play can accurately label sex at an earlier age. Children may need to identify as one sex or the other not only in a physical sense as they learn about their bodies but also from a role standpoint, as they learn about who they are in the larger society.

But what exactly are children learning about their sex roles in this society? By early childhood, children have been found to attribute more competency to boys than girls. In one study, 3- to 5-year-old children, when asked who was smart, pointed to the baby that was labeled the "boy" (Haugh, Hoffman, & Cowan, 1980). And parents tolerate a girl acting like a boy more readily than they do a boy acting like a girl. In fact, Emmerich (1959) suggested that girls spend their developmental years trying not to be babies, but boys spend these years trying not to be girls. Even children's literature makes being a boy more interesting than being a girl. In traditional literature, boys have adventures while girls get rescued and clean up after dwarfs.

Many believe that these attitudes have contributed to inequality of women in our society, and they argue for teaching children to be androgynous. **Androgyny** refers to a combination of feminine and masculine attributes in the same individual. Advocates for androgyny argue that many girls and women have suffered from a loss of opportunity due to traditional sex stereotypes. Bem (1974) suggests that well-adjusted people possess qualities that are both masculine (assertiveness, competitiveness) and feminine (cooperation, nurturance).

However, preschool children have been found to be very rigid in their sex-type behaviors and attitudes (Maccoby, 1980). Maybe this rigidity is necessary for the child to develop a gender identity. After this identity has been well established, children can then alter their ideas about sex roles and characteristics. In fact, Hall and Halberstadt (1980) found that 27–32% of 8- to 11-year-olds could be classified as androgynous.

Perhaps the real problem is not in gender-role differences but in the value assigned to those roles and sex-type characteristics by the culture.

Social Hazards

As discussed in the previous chapter, poverty and social class impact children's lives even before they are born. For preschool children, effectiveness, exposure to language, mastery, and motivation are highly affected aspects of development (Kagan, Kearsley, & Zelazo, 1978). Kagan and colleagues (1978) report that by age 5, middle-class children have a better sense of efficacy than lower-class children do. Their sense of efficacy has been instilled by parents who respond to their needs and ameliorate them. Children of lower-class families receive less exposure to language than do middle-class children. Children whose parents do not talk to them directly are hindered in their ability to use and understand language

(Kagan et al., 1978). Mastery experiences in the early years provide children with the confidence and motivation to try new experiences and expect to succeed. A positive sense of mastery is directly related to success in school (Kagan et al., 1978). Hungry children cannot learn, and children who are not consistently cared for do not learn to care about themselves or to trust others. The fundamental questions of preschool children center on their developing sense of mastery and worth. Through their behavior they ask, "Can I make a difference in my world?" and "Am I valued and loved for myself?" Children growing up in poverty depend heavily on their parents' ability to attend to their children's needs despite their own pressing worries (Pavenstedt, 1965). This is a formidable task, not easily met by any class of parents.

Too often, the symptoms of poverty are considered personal faults of the child (Segal & Yahraes, 1978). This conception of the problem results in faulting children while failing to recognize social causes. Social workers who effectively evaluate the context of the family and child in the larger community stand a much better chance of addressing the causal agents affecting the child's development.

Child Abuse[1]

Child abuse,[1] or the maltreatment of children, implies a range of conditions that violate social norms regarding the care, security, and safety of minors. Although state laws regulating the treatment of children vary, each state defines child maltreatment to include one or more of the following: physical abuse, sexual abuse, physical neglect, educational neglect, and psychological abuse (Pecora, Whittaker, & Maluccio, 1992).

Physical abuse involves injuries such as broken bones, serious and minor burns, and bruises. In addition, there may be physical contact that does not cause noticeable injuries. Slapping, punching, and striking a child with a belt or paddle not always result in a visible injury.

Sexual abuse typically refers to various forms of touching, penetration, and exploitation. *Molestation* is the term used to describe inappropriate touching of minors, which may or may not involve genital contact. *Ex-*

---

[1]This section was written by Linda Galdieri Ryan.

4 out of 5 convicts were abused children.

Child abuse, a serious problem in the United States, has far-reaching consequences for the healthy development of the child.

ploitation refers to involving a child in sexual activities such as prostitution or pornography. Penetration includes oral, anal, or genital contact and can involve the use of body parts (fingers, penis) or objects.

Child neglect can include less explicit forms of abuse because it can include both active and passive behaviors from adults. Physical neglect includes abandonment, delay or refusal of health care, inadequate supervision, and inadequate provision of basic care such as food, housing, clothing, and personal hygiene. If each of these areas of neglect are to be avoided, then parents need continuous support, resources, and initiative in caring for their children. Often, child neglect is the result of severe lack of resources.

Educational neglect includes not enrolling a child in an educational program, allowing frequent absence from school, and refusing to respond to special educa-tional needs. At times, parental values surrounding the role of formal schooling and the problems of handicapping conditions may come into conflict with the mandates of education laws and the values of special-education providers. These potential conflicts cloud the issues of educational neglect, thereby creating difficulty in substantiating negligence in some cases.

Psychological abuse refers to physical restraint, repeated threats, exploitation, rejection, and degradation. Although less concrete in its definition, descriptions of psychological abuse suggest that verbal messages are considered behaviors that should be regulated with regard to their impact on children's well-being. For example, negative labels and name-calling are forms of degradation.

People often think of child maltreatment as abusive behavior from a parent. In fact, the mistreatment of children can include any relationship in which an adult is responsible for the general well-being and supervision of minors. Thus, the adults potentially involved in child maltreatment may include parents, members of extended family, teachers, child-care providers, clergy, and so on.

Factors that Contribute to the Incidence of Child Abuse Several factors that contribute to child maltreatment have been identified, including family stress, child and family characteristics, interaction style, parent problems, and the value of violence. But with the realization that factors such as stress, social isolation, and parent history of abuse can also be noted in nonabusive relationships, speculations about what contributes to child abuse are weak (Belsky, 1980). Furthermore, Widom (1989) noted that the long-range impact of abuse has not been determined because of the difficulty in measuring variables such as ability and predisposition. These variables may influence both children and adults involved in child abuse cases.

Incidence of Child Abuse With the help of television and newspaper reporting, widespread awareness of child abuse and neglect has been promoted in recent years. It is not uncommon to learn of someone's personal experiences as a victim via a television talk show. As a result of this increased reporting, there appears to have been an alarming increase in physical abuse, sexual abuse, and neglect in the last two decades (National Center on Child Abuse and Neglect, 1994; Strauss & Gelles, 1986). But increased reporting is difficult to distinguish from actual increases in new cases of child maltreatment. Incidence rates may vary depending on how the data is collected and on the channels used for reporting. Formal reports to child protective service agencies may only partially represent the actual rates of abuse (Strauss & Gelles, 1986).

Reports of child maltreatment include people from all educational, economic, and ethnic backgrounds. However, poor people and minorities are more likely to be reported (Pecora, Whittaker, & Maluccio, 1992).

A decision to report child maltreatment may be one of the most challenging situations that people face. Although individual perceptions may vary, concerns about false reporting and the potentially negative or stigmatizing outcome for the children and families involved may create a predicament for the person deciding whether or not to notify child protection authorities.

Investigation of Child Maltreatment   Child abuse is often very difficult to substantiate. Confirming the history of child maltreatment requires comprehensive, time-consuming assessments, but child protection workers must often make immediate decisions with limited data. The child's safety must be ensured while also protecting the rights of the parents and children involved (Besharov, 1985).

Workers making child placement decisions are often faced with competing values—keeping the family together and protecting the child (Pecora, Whittaker, & Maluccio, 1992). Often the worker has a poor history, little information, and limited time in which to come to a decision about whether to remove the child from the home.

The continued mobility of society also contributes to the difficulty in substantiating abuse that has supposedly occurred over a long period of time. A family's mobility may result in lack of continuity from one agency to another in compiling necessary information. Mobility may also contribute to the delay of interventions and to their effectiveness in helping families.

Child protection organizations use an assessment system that addresses the nature and severity of child maltreatment and the further risk to child safety. This information is used to determine what services are needed and what services are available, as well as the intervention's chances of producing a successful outcome (Pecora, Whittaker, & Maluccio, 1992).

Thorough interviews of adults and children involved in child maltreatment take extensive time and skill. Often, the adults involved are not willing to divulge information concerning individual and familial history, the nature and extent of stress present in the family, negative feelings toward the child, and possibility of irresponsible behavior on their part. Parents may be reluctant to fully discuss their situation for fear that the only outcome is losing their child.

Interviewing children to confirm abuse is very difficult because of several developmental concerns, including language, cognition, emotional growth, and attachment to significant adults. Before age 5, children's expressive language is still developing, and a child may not have the expressive vocabulary and sentence structure to describe experiences with accuracy and detail. The details concerning how the child felt, and what happened where and when may be extremely difficult or impossible for many children to express. In particular, very young children have difficulty distinguishing real events from imagined ones. Children who are awakened from a deep sleep during an abusive incident may have difficulty orienting to time, place, and the authenticity of abusive behavior.

Feelings of guilt about the abuse are common among victims. Children who have been convinced that they are somehow responsible for an adult's reactions may internalize the blame or assume responsibility for abusive conditions. Some children may believe that if they could just be "good" the abuse would stop. The loyalty and bond between children and the significant adults in their lives may also contribute to a child's feeling guilty about disclosing abuse. Children may realize that disclosure of the abuse may break up the family. If dad is the sexual-abuse perpetrator and goes to jail as a result of the disclosure, the family may lose its main source of income.

Implications for Practice: The Child Welfare Worker

Social workers have a long history of interest in the welfare of children and families. In recent years, the profession has shifted away from casework and has developed specific goals and interventions (Wells, 1995). But selecting and implementing these interventions for child abuse and neglect require highly skilled professionals (Brissett-Chapman, 1995), and in the field of child abuse, these services are more often provided by paraprofessionals (Wells, 1995).

Collaboration among social workers, other human services providers, law enforcement, and the family's social support system is important when dealing with the complicated and multifaceted problems of child abuse. But few comprehensive and coordinated prevention and treatment programs exist, creating a vacuous situation for child protection workers and for families in crisis (Brissett-Chapman, 1995). In most child welfare organizations, the reality of shrinking financial resources results in few staff managing larger caseloads. The workload often leaves little time for supervision or staff development. But in spite of the stress and difficulties associated with the job, children need protection, families need help, and people need support; and the role of the child welfare worker is an important and challenging opportunity for social work professionals.

Risk and Protective Factors

Research has identified risk factors that play a clear role in child development. These factors include exposure to parental psychopathology, low socioeconomic status, low IQ, large family size, marital discord and divorce, poor parent-child relationships, poor social support, perinatal trauma, biological disabilities, difficult temperament, and being born male (Pellegrini, 1990). This list puts many children at risk. Yet, in the face of such difficulties, some children thrive (Werner & Smith, 1982). These children are said to possess **resiliency,** the ability to recover from or adjust to stress. What factors influence the development of children who demonstrate resiliency? What helps some children of single, teenage mothers, or alcoholic mothers or depressed mothers, grow up to be well-adjusted and productive?

The following have been identified as factors that act as protection for children against the traumas and adversities of life:

1. They have good social skills—these children have a positive mood and are friendly. Other people like them.
2. They are able to interact with and engage other people. They approach and interact with adults outside the home. As a result, these children receive encouragement and support from teachers, other relatives, baby-sitters.
3. They possess good problem-solving skills. As a result, they acquire a sense of mastery and learn to think for themselves.
4. They have specific interests and are usually very creative.

Research has also identified protective factors that affect these children's early development:

1. They had a good relationship with at least one caring adult, especially in the first year of life. Children cannot raise themselves.
2. They faced challenges and were not overprotected.
3. They did not have to deal with overwhelming stress. Children with one risk factor may do well, but with each added risk the likelihood of problems for the child increases (Pines, 1979).

Implications for Practice: Resiliency

For some children, physical, psychological, and social stressors may impede their growth and development. Fortunately, most children are highly resilient, and with the help of knowledgeable and supportive adults in their environment, they can develop adaptive mechanisms for coping with adversity. For others, the adversity may be too great, causing them to fall behind their peers developmentally. Accurate assessment and timely intervention are critical to healthy development in distressed children. When too much time goes by, children suffer complications that prevent them from learning new skills and catching up with peers. Prevention efforts include providing identified high-risk children with medical and educational programs to combat an unstable home environment.

Developmental Delay in a 4-Year-Old

Developmental History

Missy, a 4-year-old white girl, was referred to the Speech and Language Center by her pediatrician. Missy's mother, Mrs. Jones, stated that she was not concerned about Missy until her relatives started commenting about her speech. She reported they would say things like, "Well, she'll probably be talking in whole paragraphs once she gets going." Other than this small problem, Mrs. Jones stated that Missy had been "pretty much average, just like my first daughter" in development. She reports no pregnancy or birth complications she can remember. She added that she has not found her daughter to be a problem and that they get along well and "understand each other just fine."

Biophysical Considerations

Missy is rather small for her age, appearing thin and tired. She has some trouble with gross motor coordination and cannot skip or throw a ball yet. Her fine motor coordination appears to be normal, although she is hesitant to initiate tasks and slow to complete them. At the teachers' request, Mrs. Jones had Missy's hearing tested a year ago. The examination concluded that Missy's hearing was within normal limits.

Psychological Considerations

Information Processing

Missy exhibits difficulties with information-processing tasks. Specifically, she is inattentive at times, staring out into space rather than paying attention to the task at hand. She appears easily distracted during conversation, but she plays the same games for hours on end at home, according to her mother. Her memory is poor in testing; however, her mother says she can replay events over and over days after they happened. Mrs. Jones related that

Missy attended preschool last year for a brief time, but she removed her because the school "wasn't right for her." When asked to elaborate about this, Mrs. Jones added that there was not enough structure in the school program, and Missy would just play imaginary games by herself all day. The teachers asked Mrs. Jones about hearing and speech difficulties. Mrs. Jones followed up with her pediatrician and had Missy's hearing tested.

The Wechsler Preschool and Primary Scale of Intelligence was administered to Missy, and she achieved a Full Scale IQ score of 92, placing her in the average range. Her Performance IQ score was 97 and her Verbal score was 80. Assessment of Missy's intellectual functioning revealed that her scores for expressive language development were below her overall intellectual functioning scores. Also, her scores on tests of her ability to understand language were in the normal range, significantly above her expressive language scores. Furthermore, her performance on the visual-motor tasks showed slight impairment.

Communication

Missy speaks when spoken to, hardly ever initiating communication. During the interview, her speech was slow and quiet. Her mother reports that she responds to questions at home but does not carry on lengthy conversations. Her mother added that Missy's older sister often completes sentences for her. Testing revealed Missy's vocabulary was limited for her age. In addition, she used the wrong tense in her responses to questions. Missy tended to hesitate when speaking, as if waiting for someone to help her. She nodded her head or gestured whenever possible.

Attitudes and Emotions

Missy's mother reports that Missy is a compliant child, who usually does what she is told and does not argue or "sass back." Missy's demeanor is quiet, but she can become quite animated and insistent when playing with

Developmental Delay in a 4-Year-Old

her dolls. Missy rarely cries or calls attention to herself in the family, Mrs. Jones recalls. To her, Missy looks content most of the time and is never demanding of attention. Her mother completed the Child Behavior Checklist (Achenbach & Edelbrock, 1983), and Missy's scores were in the normal range, with no elevations. However, her scores for internalizing behaviors were significantly higher than her externalizing behavior score.

When asked, Missy reports that she feels "fine." She states she rarely has upsets but admits to feeling sad much of the time, except when playing with her dolls. When asked if she cries very often, Missy says that she does not. She plays with her dolls or goes to the neighbor's house when she feels sad. When asked about her favorite activities, she listed playing with dolls and playing with the family dog alone outside in the backyard.

Missy agreed to draw a picture of herself for formal assessment. She did so hesitantly and slowly. Her picture was developmentally appropriate, although very small and in one corner.

Social Cognition and Regulation

Mrs. Jones reports that Missy has one friend she plays with in the neighborhood. Together, they play dolls. Usually Missy visits the friend's house and brings her dolls along. She is quite willing to share as long as her game is being played. Missy does not often play with her sister or her brother, but instead plays alongside them. Mrs. Jones noted that her oldest daughter spends a lot of time at her aunt's house next door. Mrs. Jones commented that Missy usually talks "baby talk" when playing dolls and her older sister complains about this when they do play together. Missy's older sister is often rude to Missy, too, according to her mother. She calls her names and teases her.

Missy relates that she likes her older sister but also likes it when she is away from home at her aunt's house, stating she doesn't have to "worry so much." Missy never argues back with her sister. Neither Missy nor Missy's

mother report any incidences of verbal or physical aggression instigated by Missy. Her friend does not seek out her company but will usually play when asked. Missy often tries to convince the friend to play dolls when the friend wants to play another game instead.

In terms of Missy's self-care skills, she generally has no difficulties. She feeds herself, brushes her teeth, and dresses herself but does not fasten her own buttons. She sometimes has difficulty choosing clothing to wear and will wait until her mother comes in her room to ask for help. Mrs. Jones states that Missy goes to bed easily but often lies in bed for over an hour before falling asleep. Missy denies nightmares or fears associated with sleep. She admits to worrying about her family and says she "sometimes just waits and listens." She says she likes to have her dog sleep in her room with her at night. Mrs. Jones reports that Missy is not a big eater but will usually nibble at whatever she is served. Missy states her appetite is adequate but that she doesn't feel like eating very often.

Social Considerations

Family Situation

Missy lives with her mother, father, older sister, and younger brother in a small house owned by her father's sister. Mrs. Jones reluctantly admitted that her marriage is not perfect. She stated that she and her husband argue frequently about money, his help in the family, and the children. She added that he blamed her for the children's problems because she "partied too much and did too many drugs in high school." Neither she nor her husband finished high school, and both are currently unemployed. Mrs. Jones reported that her husband does not spend much time with the children, even though he is home most of the day. He yells at them when they are too loud, but he has never struck the children. She described the home as usually quiet, without *(continued)*

Developmental Delay in a 4-Year-Old

(*continued*)   anybody talking to each other unless something is wrong. Mrs. Jones stated she has thought about leaving her husband but has nowhere else to go. Mrs. Jones added that she often feels trapped in the house; her husband will not let her go out without him very often, except to take the children to their appointments. Mrs. Jones conceded she spends little time recreating with her children because most of her time is spent performing house-hold duties, child care, and taking her children to their appointments.

Missy stated she was closest to her mother but was afraid her father would be angry if he knew. In vague terms, Missy admitted to worrying about what will happen to her family. She says she likes to play at the neighbor's house and was happy going to school. Missy states she plays dolls most of the time and stays in her room when home. She is not allowed outside to play very often, even though she lives near a school.

Groups, Social Supports, and Contexts

Missy's family interacts primarily with social welfare institutions. Her family receives assistance in the form of aid for dependent children and food stamps. Her mother goes with the children to the appointments because her father will not attend, nor will he baby-sit the children when she is out.

Multicultural and Gender Considerations

Missy lives in a fairly homogeneous neighborhood and rarely has contact with others of a different ethnic background. Her family does not participate in community events, and the preschool she had attended briefly was also primarily white.

As for her gender development, Missy plays with stereotypical girl toys when she has the opportunity. She identifies herself as a girl and drew long hair and a bow on herself in her figure drawing.

Summary and Impressions

Missy has several problems that became evident during the assessment.

1. Expressive Language Disorder—mild (APA, 1994)
2. Poor peer relations and lack of social skills
3. Excessive worries interfering with sleep and appetite
4. Possible childhood depression
5. Inadequate self-system
6. Possible problems with coordination

Additional difficulties include the following:

7. Poor family communication
8. Inadequate social and peer opportunities
9. Marital conflict and possible abusive behavior directed toward her mother by her father
10. Inadequate gross motor play opportunities

Missy was cooperative with the social worker. However, her limited verbal skills, including poor vocabulary, inaccurate sentence structure and grammar, and reluctance to engage in conversation made information gathering a difficult task. Some concern also exists about Mrs. Jones's ability to attend to Missy's physical and emotional needs. Furthermore, the Jones family does not appear capable of providing a sufficiently interactive and stimulating environment to promote healthy growth and remediate Missy's language delays.

On a positive note, Missy possesses adaptive skills in the sense that she can adjust her behavior to minimize the damage her environment imposes on her. She is quiet and does not make demands on a family already stressed by unemployment and marital conflict. In addition, she and her mother appear to have a close relationship compared with other family members. She also has a friend with whom she enjoys spending time and with whom her feelings are reciprocated to some degree. Last, she would most likely develop more friendships and improve her motor skills if given the opportunity.

Chapter Summary

Developmental Themes

Children in early childhood are developing greater autonomy. This is the Eriksonian psychosocial stage of autonomy versus shame and doubt (age 2–3) and also of initiative versus guilt (age 3–5). Children in this stage develop coordinated gross motor skills, acquire social skills, and achieve growth in cognitive and language abilities.

Biophysical Dimension

Biophysical Growth and Development

Preschool children run, jump, climb, and tumble. They can ride a tricycle, walk up and down stairs, throw a ball, and catch a bounced ball. Fine motor skills also increase. Children learn to handle buttons and zippers and by age 5 can print letters. These children need time and room for physical activity.

Biophysical Hazards

Asthma is a leading chronic illness among children. Risk factors for asthma include having a family history of asthma, allergy problems, and a mother who smokes.

Psychological Dimension

Cognitive Development and Information Processing

Preschool children have increased attention spans. As they progress through this stage, they develop cognitive control of their attention and can attend to the relevant aspects of a task. Children usually do not remember much before the age of 3. As children develop a sense of self, their memory for past events increases. Speed of information processing increases during early childhood. Preschool children are in Piaget's preoperational stage. The substages of this stage are symbolic function and intuitive thought. Characteristics of thinking in this stage include egocentrism and animism. According to task analysis, when the task is interesting to the child, the child shows greater cognitive maturity. Other researchers feel development occurs in overlapping waves instead of discrete steps.

Communication

Children of this age understand more than they can express. They begin to learn the basic rules of language and communication. Language development is enhanced when the child receives appropriate verbal interaction from adults. During this time, communication disorders such as stuttering can arise.

Attitudes and Emotions

Preschool children have vivid and active imaginations. They may develop fears and phobias. Some experience nightmares and night terrors. Aggression can be described as either instrumental or hostile (with intent). Preschool aggressive acts diminish after age 4 as children learn to negotiate. In an effort to reduce aggression, children can be taught ways of expressing needs and interacting with others. When encouraged to identify and express their own emotions, children learn to be more empathic.

Social Cognition and Regulation

Preschool children learn to classify themselves by their physical characteristics and abilities. They usually know their gender and have some idea of cultural roles. Children begin to learn self-control at this age. They learn to use words instead of aggression. Children in this age begin to develop social skills. Having warm, supportive parents who set reasonable limits and having opportunities to interact with peers enhances children's social skills.

Psychological Hazards

Children in early childhood may encounter developmental delays, developmental disorders, and developmental psychopathology. Age is a crucial factor in assessing developmental problems. Some problems are normal, transitory behaviors for a particular age. Children may exhibit problems of elimination such as enuresis and encopresis. They may have anxiety disorders such as separation anxiety, avoidant disorder, and overanxious disorder. Children may become depressed from stressors in their life.

Social Dimension

Families, Groups, Support Systems, and Contexts

Parenting styles fall into the categories of authoritarian, authoritative, and permissive (permissive indulgent and permissive indifferent). These styles have different behavioral outcomes for children. Parental warmth is an important consideration in any style. Mothers, fathers, siblings, and peers play important roles in the socialization of children. Play is the primary method of learning in early childhood. Play styles can be categorized according to the amount of social interaction occurring. Younger children engage in more solitary play, whereas older children play more cooperatively. Television is seen as an important socializing influence on children. Preschool programs should consider the developmental needs of the child. Project Head Start was developed to give underprivileged children a preschool experience and to enhance later school performance.

Multicultural and Gender Considerations

Children develop a racial identity as a fixed attribute by the age of 5. Parents and extended families influence children's knowledge of ethnicity and heritage. Preschool children learn gender identity and tend to play with same-sex peers and with sex-appropriate toys. Boys tend to be more aggressive, and girls more nurturing.

Social Hazards

Divorce results in particular stressors for children. These stressors can be taxing for children. Children of divorce must make many adjustments and benefit from support during and after the divorce. Child abuse includes physical abuse, sexual abuse, neglect,. and psychological abuse. Family stress, social isolation, and parental history of abuse as a child all contribute to the risk of child abuse. Child welfare workers face difficult decisions regarding appropriate placement of abused children. Safety of the child must be weighed against family preservation. Poverty can affect children's sense of mastery and their ability to learn. Though many children face risk factors for development such as parental mental illness, poverty, large family, divorce, poor parent-child interactions, lack of social support, perinatal trauma, disability, and difficult temperament, many display resiliency and overcome these early stressors. In general, resilient children possess social skills and problem-solving abilities. These children had a nurturing caregiver in the first year of life. They faced difficulties, but were not overwhelmed by them.

KEY TERMS

aggression
altruism
androgyny
animism
autism
avoidant disorder
categorical self
child abuse

developmental waves
echolalia
egocentrism
empathy
encopresis
enuresis
hostile aggression
infantile amnesia

instrumental aggression
night terrors
overanxious disorder
phobias
resiliency
separation anxiety disorder
task analysis

8

Middle Childhood

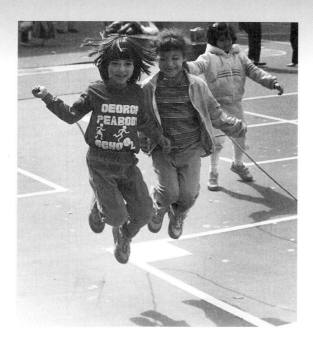

Developmental Themes

A white 1970 Volkswagen Beetle passes by. "Slug bug," says the 7-year-old sitting next to me, and punches me in the arm. Ten minutes later, an old VW bug with a sunroof goes by. "Double slug bug." I get two more punches.

"I pinch you, you can't pinch back, for I see a man in a white straw hat."

"Oh, wow! Check it out! Made you look! Made you look!"

"Roses are red,
violets are blue,
I'm going crazy
just like you."

Middle childhood is characterized by a child culture—a whole reality of rules, reciprocity, and fairness (Konner, 1991). "Slug bug" is a very popular game for children in middle childhood, and its appeal comes from a long tradition. The game "I pinch you, you can't pinch back, for I see a man in a white straw hat" was a well-known game in the 1950s in England (Opie & Opie, 1987). "Made you look!" has been around as long as we can remember. It is great fun for kids because they can trick you into doing something, and they love that. "Roses are red, violets are blue"—this line fills many pages of yearbooks and provides an opportunity for wonderful poetic expression.

All these examples probably sound familiar to you. Although the exact nature and style changes, such play is universal for children in middle childhood. Why are such games so familiar? In middle childhood, games and play form a common children's culture—a culture that children can control and that belongs to no one but them (Konner, 1991). As children move from early childhood to middle childhood, their capacity to play such games unfolds. Their focus is on developing rules, ensuring fairness, and creating sanctions for rule-breakers. Children at this age can be in charge of the rules—in fact, they can create their own new rules. Piaget learned a great deal from children's games, referring to them as "the most admirable social institutions." Rousseau, the philosopher, said that the work of children is play. Play is their work and they learn and grow from it. Such play seems particularly critical in the middle childhood years.

Middle childhood is the stage in life that begins at age 6 and ends at age 12, where adolescence begins. Children at this stage are ending their preschool years and beginning to learn new skills and competencies. This stage is often referred to by Erikson as one of industry, which means "to build," versus inferiority. Children in this stage develop competence in intellectual, social, and physical skills. Children who fail to gain this sense of competence may develop feelings of inferiority.

Many of the most important skills to children at this age are reflected in their daily pursuit of games, sports, reading, writing, and other school-related skills. This is a critical time for the development of coordination, physical strength, and flexibility. During this stage, children continue to make impressive cognitive gains in their intellectual functioning. As they move closer to adolescence, they develop some sophisticated logic and problem-solving abilities. The development of role-taking abilities becomes important as their interaction with peers becomes more critical. Successful adaptation to friendships and peer groups is a major developmental task for the middle child. Much of this adaptation is played out in our school system, as this is where the child now spends half of his waking hours. Successful adaptation can be complicated by psychological problems associated with learning or communication or by social problems such as peer difficulties or family disruption and divorce.

Biophysical Dimension

Biophysical Growth and Development

Throughout middle childhood, we see a slow but consistent growth pattern. This slow growth is sandwiched between the rapid growth of early childhood and the forthcoming growth spurt in the prepubertal years (10–13 years old for girls, 12–16 years old for boys). For instance, during the early and middle childhood years, children grow an average of 2 to 3 inches per year. The average 6-year-old child reaches almost 4 feet. Girls are actually shorter than boys at age 6, but by age 10, girls are slightly taller than boys. They continue to be taller through age 13. In terms of weight, girls weigh less than boys until age 11, when they have a growth spurt and end up weighing 3 pounds more than boys within the span of only one year. By age 14, boys exceed girls in weight and height and continue to do so throughout adulthood.

In middle childhood, fat tissue develops more quickly than muscle tissue, although through middle childhood there is a decrease in the growth of fatty tissue and an increase in muscle development. Girls retain the fat tissue longer, and boys develop muscle tissue more quickly. In physical appearance, girls are rounder, softer, and smoother than boys because of their greater amount of fatty tissue.

Motor development in middle childhood continues, and children become more coordinated and smoother in their responses. Development in both the large and small muscles facilitates changes in the child's coordination, agility, and smoothness. Whereas only one child in a thousand can hit a tennis ball over the net by age 4 (a good reason not to play tennis with your 4-year-old), by age 11 most children can learn to play tennis well (Santrock, 1986). Elementary school children become fascinated with many sports activities, such as climbing, throwing and catching a ball, swimming, skateboarding, and in-line skating. At this age there is full exercise of gross-motor activity. Often school-age children have difficulty controlling their impulses—they jump, run, bicycle, and climb everywhere. This activity can sometimes lead to unrecognized fatigue that becomes exhibited in quarrelsome or crying behavior (Schuster & Ashburn, 1986). By 7 and 8 years of age, children, although still very active, develop more interest in sit-down games as they have an increased attention span and better cognitive abilities. By 8 and 10 years of age, children are involved in activities that require longer and more concentrated attention and effort, such as baseball, gymnastic skills, or soccer. As children get to the end of middle childhood, they become more interested in peer-related physical activities.

During middle childhood, boys' motor development exceeds that of girls'. However, girls are better than boys at fine motor skills. Boys' greater motor development may partially explain why boys are more interested in physical activity than girls are (Lefrancois, 1989).

Although children become increasingly adultlike, they are not miniature adults. Many of the child's physi-

cal elements are not completely developed. The child's optic nerve is not developed, and therefore the child cannot see as well as an adult. The child's bone growth and muscular development are far from complete. It is important to understand the child developmentally, because without such an understanding, we may expect certain behaviors at an age that the child is not physically or intellectually prepared for. The result is likely to be to discourage the child when he or she is not ready for learning the behavior. **Readiness** is an important concept in understanding human development. If we give a child special reading lessons at the age of 4, he or she can learn over the course of one or two years, whereas the average 6-year-old will learn to read in a matter of weeks.

Biophysical Hazards

Most of the children we see and interact with demonstrate the strong innate capability to grow in an orderly sequence that shows healthy development. However, both the rate and pattern of growth can be altered by adversity. When the child's environment is not meeting the child's fundamental needs, growth can be affected. Nutrition, amount of rest and sleep, opportunities to learn, amount of affection, extent of security—these and other factors can determine how fast and to what degree a child develops.

If we take a worldwide perspective, it is easy to discover that children suffering from poverty and lack of food are unable to achieve healthy development. Also, conditions that exist during times of war, such as lack of food, constant fear, and loss or separation from parents, can lead to permanent physical damage. Although human development is marked by great resilience, there are environmental conditions that will produce marked changes in growth. Consider the following conditions and their impact on development: Lack of iodine in community drinking water will lead to an increase in **cretinism,** a chronic disease characterized by physical deformity and dwarfism. **Rickets** is due to a deficiency in vitamin D and will produce permanent damage to the bones in the body, resulting in a flat chest, deformed pelvis, or a crooked back.

Psychological Dimension

Cognitive Development and Information Processing

Middle childhood represents an exciting period of study in terms of cognitive development. Piaget classified children in this age group as operating from concrete operational thought. This stage is characterized by becoming less egocentric. The child can begin to decenter and demonstrates the operation of **reversibility**. Children at this stage also show **conservation** skills. We will examine these concepts in more detail in this section.

Piaget described the concrete operational stage as a series of operations or mental actions that are reversible. Such an operation is characterized by rules of logic. This stage is referred to as concrete because the child's thinking is limited to real objects. A child at this stage cannot use the logic of formal operations—to compare the ideal with the actual or to think hypothetically.

The best way to understand these concepts is through the mind of Piaget himself. Piaget was a great observer of children, and he devised many ingenious experiments or tasks to test his ideas. His task of conservation is one of the most famous and is a hallmark of the concrete operations stage. Conservation has to do with the quantitative aspects of objects or things that do not change unless something has been added to or subtracted from the object, although other changes may lead to perceptual differences.

The beaker task will clarify what we mean by conservation. A child is presented with two identical beakers of liquid filled to the same level. The child is asked whether the beakers are equal in the amount of liquid, and the child says yes. Then, the liquid from one beaker is poured into a third beaker that is much taller and thinner than the first two beakers (see Figure 8.1). The child is asked whether the tall, thin beaker contains the same amount of liquid as the original beaker. A child who is 5 or 6 years old will say no, pointing out that one beaker is obviously higher than the other, indicating more liquid. The child's error in this example is his or her inability to conserve. A child of 7 or 8 will say the beakers have an equal amount (conservation). He or she will reason that although the beakers are different, they both contain the same amount.

Figure 8.2 shows different tasks that can be used to measure conservation of number, mass, length, and

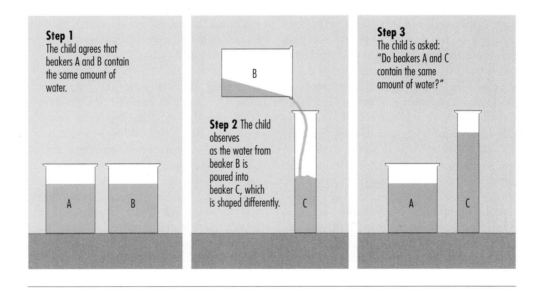

FIGURE 8.1   Piaget's beaker test   Source: Weiten, 1995.

	Typical tasks used to measure conservation	Typical age of mastery
	Conservation of number Two equivalent rows of objects are shown to the child, who agrees that they have the same number of objects.	6–7
	One row is lengthened, and the child is asked whether one row has more objects.	
	Conservation of mass The child acknowledges that two clay balls have equal amounts of clay.	7–8
	The experimenter changes the shape of one of the balls and asks the child whether they still contain equal amounts of clay.	
	Conservation of length The child agrees that two sticks aligned with each other are the same length.	7–8
	After moving one stick to the left or right, the experimenter asks the child whether the sticks are of equal length.	
	Conservation of area Two identical sheets of cardboard have wooden blocks placed on them in identical positions; the child confirms that the same amount of space is left on each piece of cardboard.	8–9
	The experimenter scatters the blocks on one piece of cardboard and again asks the child whether the two pieces have the same amount of unoccupied space.	

FIGURE 8.2   Tests of conservation   Source: Weiten, 1995.

area. Let's look at an example of conservation of mass. Suppose we gave a child two equal balls of clay, then took one ball and rolled it out into a long and narrow shape (see Figure 8.2). The child is asked whether the snakelike object contains the same amount of clay as the original ball of clay. A child who is 5 or 6 will say that the long, narrow piece of clay contains more. However, a child of 7 or 8 is likely to reason that although one ball of clay was rolled into a snakelike shape, it could be re-formed into a ball and it would still contain the same

amount of clay. This task also shows the child can use the operation of reversibility. Rather than focusing exclusively on the physical characteristics of the objects, the child is able to coordinate information about both shapes of the clay, demonstrating concrete operational thinking (thought processes governed by rules of logic).

Although Piaget's influence on and contribution to understanding cognitive development is unmistakable, there are some important new developments in the field. In particular, Piaget argued that children's cognitive development proceeded according to a predetermined sequence of stages. Recent research has discovered that there is tremendous individual variation in the performance of children of the same age and supposedly the same stage. In addition, researchers have found that when the instructions for the task change even slightly, it can throw the results off considerably. As a result, many of the researchers who continue in the Piagetian tradition now refer to "levels," which are considered less specific developmental milestones than "stages."

Intelligence and Intelligence Tests

Although we discuss and refer to intelligence often in our everyday world, the concept of intelligence is quite complex and difficult to measure. However, most people are familiar with Alfred Binet's concept of **mental age,** which is the age level at which the child scored on the test. Binet developed the first intelligence test in 1905. The Stanford-Binet is a well-known, widely used **intelligence quotient** or IQ test. Most of us think of the IQ test in terms of the following formula:

$$IQ = \frac{\text{mental age}}{\text{chronological age}} \times 100$$

IQ is calculated by comparing the child's mental age with the child's chronological age. Because IQ tests can have important implications when planning services with children, let's examine the two IQ tests you're likely to come across in school reports or case records, the Stanford-Binet and the Weschsler.

The Stanford-Binet   This test must be administered individually by a trained person. It is most often used with young children, although it is designed for individuals 2 to 18 years old. The Stanford-Binet is considered a verbal test of intelligence because it contains a large number of items that rely on verbal abilities. Table 8.1 gives examples of representative tasks used in the test.

The Stanford-Binet is composed of four areas: *verbal reasoning, quantitative reasoning, abstract/visual reasoning,* and *short-term memory.* The IQ score is a composite score that is referred to as a measure of "adaptive ability." The Stanford-Binet has been administered to many people during the years, and the results show that peoples' IQ scores form a normal distribution. Most of

TABLE 8.1   Sample Tasks from the Stanford-Binet Test

Age	Sample Tasks
2	Identify parts of the body on a large paper doll. Place a circle, square, and triangle in the appropriate three holes of a form board.
5	Complete a drawing of a man. Fold a paper triangle in a manner similar to that modeled by examiner.
8	Answer questions about a story that has been read by the examiner. Indicate how objects are similar and different.
12	Define a number of words. Repeat five digits backward.

the cases fall in the middle of the distribution. The Stanford-Binet has a mean of 100 and a standard deviation of 16. The mean refers to the average score, and the standard deviation is a measure of how much the scores vary. Reviewing some basic statistical concepts, one standard deviation from the mean constitutes 68% of the cases. The 68% is considered the average range, with scores ranging from 84 to 116.

The Wechsler Tests   Another very popular test developed for use with children is the Wechsler Intelligence Scale for Children, third edition (WISC-III). This test is different from the Stanford-Binet in that it groups the items into subsets that make up separate verbal and performance scales. The WISC-III is also unique because it taps both verbal and performance abilities, producing three values: a verbal IQ, a performance IQ, and a full-scale IQ. The verbal scale samples the degree of knowledge about general information; the ability to master concepts, think abstractly, and concentrate; use of judgment; and memory. The performance parts sample visual-motor skills, planning ability, attention to detail, and other attributes. The various subtests of this test allow the examiner to determine particular areas of strengths and weaknesses. In addition to this test, there is the Wechsler Preschool and Primary Scale of Intelligence–Revised (WPPSI-R), which has been developed for children between the ages of 4 and 6½.

The Kaufman Assessment Battery for Children (K-ABC)   The K-ABC battery of tests is a new method of assessment based on a particular model of functioning referred to as the **Das-Luria model of cognitive functioning** (Das, 1984). The model is based on the notion that there are two modes of processing information: simultaneous processing and successive processing. Simultaneous processing is concerned with the immediate processing of related stimuli, whereas successive processing is concerned with the processing of stimuli that reflect a sequence or ordering. From this perspective, intelligence is based on the ability to use both simultaneous and successive strategies effectively in goal-setting and planning behavior.

This test, like the WISC-III, is composed of various subtests, each related to various abilities. However, some general scores are derived, including the Mental Processing Composite Index, which assesses general intellectual functioning, and the Achievement Index, which assesses knowledge of facts, language concepts, and other school-related skills such as arithmetic, reading, and vocabulary. The developers of this test have provided extensive data in support of its reliability and validity.

The K-ABC may be of particular interest to social workers in the school because one of the test's specific functions is to provide information to help plan teaching and remediation, especially with learning-disabled children. Central to the model is the ability to construct a cognitive map of a particular child so that specific strengths and weaknesses can be identified. Instructional strategies are then based on the results of the cognitive mapping.

Intelligence Tests: Good or Bad?

Since their inception, intelligence tests have been controversial. Early concerns over the IQ test centered on the use of the tests to label and classify children. It was common to find children labeled "average" if they scored 105 on a Stanford-Binet, "mentally retarded" if they scored 65, and "genius" if they obtained a score of 150. Such labels should not come from the results of a single test. Indeed, additional information should be carefully gathered and assessed if a child is going to be classified. Unfortunately, many children are still being classified by the results of a single test and will receive a label from their classification that will stay with them for many years.

Another major issue with the use of intelligence tests is whether they can be considered culturally biased.

Many of the tests rely heavily on verbal intelligence that reflects a middle-class bias. Adrian Dove dramatized this point when he developed the Chitling Test. Sample items from this test included defining such things as a "gas-head," a "blood," and "Bo-Diddley" and knowing how long to cook chitlings. His point was clear: The emphasis on verbal abilities in many IQ tests reflected an environment that was familiar to white, middle-class children. Many of the IQ tests have attempted to improve their cultural fairness. For example, the Stanford-Binet, known for its emphasis on verbal abilities, is considered less accurate for children whose language development is different from or slower than the average middle-class child. The latest edition of the test has been designed to reduce this problem. The more recently developed *Kaufman Assessment Battery for Children* is being promoted as more culturally fair than existing intelligence tests (Kaufman & Kaufman, 1983).

Are intelligence tests good or bad? Often it is not the intelligence test that is problematic but the misuse of the test that leads to serious problems. We must remember that intelligence is a very complex concept. It is not fixed, and it cannot be measured easily. If a child is despondent and unmotivated when tested, this could easily influence the results. If an IQ test is administered in English and that is not the person's native language, the results are not likely to be accurate. Intelligence tests are not easily linked to success, and therefore their use should be carefully scrutinized. Social workers must ensure that children receive fair and accurate assessments. Understanding the benefits and weaknesses of intelligence tests is a start in this direction.

Information Processing

Researchers are beginning to study how children process information about their social world. For instance, information processing may be linked to aggressive behavior. Consider the following scenario: Justin walks by Sean's desk and accidentally knocks a book off of his desk. Sean immediately jumps up and pushes Justin. The teacher runs over to break it up. The teacher is familiar with this scenario because Sean often gets into fights. Sean immediately responded to Justin as if Justin's actions were hostile, and this led him to an aggressive reaction. Kenneth Dodge is studying boys like Sean because he believes they have skill deficits in their ability to detect social cues.

In his study (Dodge, Pettit, Murphy, & Buchsbaum, 1984), children viewed videotaped vignettes that depicted a social interaction in which one child provokes the other. Three different scenes were used that showed different intentions—hostile, prosocial, and accidental—and children were asked to differentiate among the intentions. The study found that children who were identified as being socially rejected did not perform as well as did children who were popular or average. Children who are deficient in **intention-cue detection** are likely to make errors and view acts that are prosocial or accidental as hostile.

How we process information can be critical to our mental health and well-being and has become a major approach to understanding the developing child. Three things are fundamental to the information-processing approach. The first is how knowledge develops—its creation. Second is the processes and strategies that become part of the knowledge base or the processes used to retrieve from the knowledge base. Third is the child's awareness of self as a knower able to use and evaluate strategies, also referred to as **metacognition**, which is knowledge about knowing. As we progress with the developing child, we will return to these early notions of information processing to examine the role of cognitive development. The following Focus on Assessment section examines the cognitive ability of children to testify.

FOCUS ON ASSESSMENT

Assessing Childhood Competency to Testify

Are children in the period of middle childhood cognitively competent to testify as a witness? Children are sometimes needed as witnesses to acts of crime and negligence. They are also victims of abuse, crime, or neglect. To testify in these matters, they must be able to truthfully and accurately communicate their personal knowledge of relevant facts. These expectations of a witness are presumed to exist for any adult who lacks a mental disorder

or defect. However, the law presumes that children under 10 or 12 years of age, depending on their jurisdiction, are incompetent to testify (Weithorn, 1984). The justification for this presumption is the child's developmental immaturity. Although this presumption is refutable in most jurisdictions, it requires a solid understanding of a child's individual development. The validity and reliability of a child's testimony has been challenged on a number of grounds: memory, cognitive development, moral development, and suggestibility (Melton, Petrila, Poythress, & Slobogin, 1987). The memory issues relate to children's capacity to communicate their recollections of an event in response to questions presented in court. Will children describe "true memory" of an event, or will their memory of an event be the product of the suggestions from others with whom they have discussed the event? Will the child describe actual occurrences or occurrences based on fantasy? As you recall, fantasy and language are schemata used by preoperational children to adapt to their environment. Although there is concern that children may confuse fact with imagined experiences, a recent study indicates that children are no more likely than adults to confuse what is observed with what is imagined. Child abuse workers further recognize that "very young children do not fantasize or lie about having experienced sexual abuse" (Weithorn, 1984). These findings suggest that children's capacity to recall events is not limited by their development. They possess the capacity to recall events when given direct questions. However, research does support the viewpoint that children's developmental immaturity limits their capacity for free recall. Their memory of events must be prompted by objective questions.

Cognitive development issues involve concerns about the child's conceptualization or comprehension of events. Can a child conceptualize complex acts and order these acts in time and space? Does the child understand the meaning of terms and behaviors of relevance to a legal inquiry? The answers to each of these questions are influenced by knowledge from cognitive development. Children acquire cognitive competencies in each of these skill areas at different ages. Developmentalists also note inconsistencies in the application of these capacities across situations and tasks encountered by children in middle childhood.

Will children's immaturity influence their likelihood of being truthful in their testimony? This issue involving moral development is often raised in spite of current findings to the contrary. Melton and his colleagues (1987) point out that children are no more prone to lying than are adults. How development affects children's morality is in their ability to provide reasons or justifications for their behavior. It also affects children's comprehension of terms such as oath, truth, and court. However, this comprehension has no bearing on their propensity to tell the truth. It is a much better indicator of their intellectual development.

"Data on suggestibility are less clear, but seem to indicate fewer age differences than might be suspected" (Melton, Petrila, Poythress, & Slobogin, 1987, p. 105). The primary fear is that children's testimony will be determined by their perceptions of adult expectations of how they should behave — that is, the type of testimony that the adult examiner is expecting of them. There is also a fear that children are more susceptible to leading questions. However, research by Marin, Holmes, Guth, and Kovac (1979) demonstrates that children were no less affected by leading questions than adults are. (Further research is needed, however.)

Each of these issues presents interesting assessment objectives for practitioners. Assessment objectives require a solid understanding of developmental processes and their assumptions. Melton and his colleagues have provided the following guidelines for evaluating children's competency to testify.

Evaluators should assess the child's

1. Understanding of the obligation to tell the truth
2. Reliability of memory
3. Ability to perceive reality accurately
4. Vulnerability to suggestion

These guidelines cannot be implemented without understanding the key cognitive developmental milestones for early and middle childhood.

Source: Adapted from Melton et al., 1987.

Communication

Middle childhood is the period of linguistic refinement. In early childhood, the focus in language development is on such things as correcting past tenses for irregular verbs. Children's use of language becomes more grammatically correct and complex than the simple yes or no questions or the big why questions (Shaffer, 1993). Language develops in deaf children much as it does in hearing children. The Focus on Development: Developmental Aspects of Sign Language gives a description of how sign language develops. As children develop, they become increasingly aware that words can have multiple meanings, and they understand the notion of abstract connotations. This ability to "go beyond the information" is referred to as **metalinguistic awareness** (Shaffer, 1993). As this ability develops, children begin to appreciate the humor in jokes, riddles, and puns. At about age 10, children can begin to understand and use metaphors such as "people who live in glass houses shouldn't throw stones" (Reynolds & Ortony, 1980). In studying language and middle childhood, the relationship between language and knowledge becomes important.

Language development is central to healthy development in children. (See Focus on Development: Speech Disorders in Children for a description of the impact of speech disorders.) Language is the door to obtaining information from others. It allows you to make requests of other people and makes a wealth of information accessible. In fact, early language researchers believed that language was necessary for thought (Whorf, 1956). However, most child developmentalists now believe that thought is a prerequisite to language.

Piaget's research led him to the conclusion that many logical concepts are learned before the development of the language that corresponds to those concepts (Lefrancois, 1989). For example, a child first learns the concept of bigger and then begins to use the language that describes the concept.

Recent research has found that difficulties in communication can result from listeners who fail to detect **uninformative messages** or who don't ask for clarification of a message (Beal, 1987). This shows up developmentally as well, where 6- to 7-year-olds will clarify an uninformative message they judge to be problematic. However, younger children, having at least some idea of what is meant by a statement, will overlook the problem in the message and assume that the speaker's intentions are clear. For example, "Bring me that toy" is an ambiguous statement when there are two toys placed next to each other. A young child will hear the request and assume the speaker wants the toy closest to the child, whereas 8- to-10-year-olds will question the ambiguity and ask for clarification.

We can teach children with communication difficulties better communication skills by having them learn to focus on the differences among the stimuli in their conversations (Pratt, McLaren, & Wickens, 1984). Also, we can teach children to be better listeners by having them evaluate what they hear and ask questions to clarify statements they don't understand.

Another important aspect of communication is the developmental theory of **verbal control** that came from the work of Russian psychologists Vygotsky and Luria (Luria, 1961; Vygotsky, 1962). They believe that speech develops through three successive stages: other-external, where the behavior of a child is controlled through the verbalizations of others; self-external, where the child's own overt verbalizations provide control over his or her behavior; and self-internal, where the child's behavior is controlled by his or her own covert *self-verbalizations*. This early work on the role of speech and behavior was groundbreaking because it suggested the relationship between self-verbalizations and self-guidance. An important developmental aspect of speech and behavior was also discovered: Luria observed that as children got older, they were able to inhibit behavior not only by following adult instructions (other-external) but also in response to their own self-instructions (self-internal). If, as the Russian researchers suggest, internal speech can control overt behavior, then why not teach children who lack self-control to use their own speech to gain more control over their actions? Their work laid the groundwork for the development of self-instructional training, a popular treatment approach for impulsive children who lack self-control.

Implications for Practice: Self-Instructional Training

Self-instructional training has become a major treatment modality for practitioners working with children who have difficulties with self-control. Researchers have developed a fairly specific sequence of training activities that include the following: (1) The therapist performs the task while asking questions aloud about the task, giving self-guiding instructions, and making self-evaluations of the performance; (2) the child imitates the therapist's overt self-instructional sequence while doing the task; (3) the therapist repeats the task, only this time using a whisper; (4) the child imitates the therapist's performance and self-instructions using a whisper; (5) the therapist models covert self-instructions while performing the task; (6) the child imitates the therapist's covert self-instructions and performance. Research has found that it is important to perform tasks in ways that are not perfect and then teach children how to cope with errors in their performance (Kendall & Braswell, 1985).

One program (Camp, Bloom, Herbert, & Van Doorninck, 1977) developed a "think-aloud" approach to working with aggressive, impulsive children. The approach uses the cognitive-behavioral techniques outlined in the previous paragraph to teach self-instructions for solving problems. Children were taught to ask and answer four questions: (1) What is my problem? (2) What is my plan? (3) Am I using my plan? and (4) How did I do? The practitioners used various cognitive problems and interpersonal problem-solving games requiring the children to control their impulses to teach the self-instructional skills. In a similar manner, Kazdin and Frame (1983) worked with an aggressive 11-year-old boy and taught him to use problem-solving steps that could be used in everyday situations. Their training focused on the following set of questions and statements: What am I supposed to do?; I need to look at all of my possibilities; I have to focus in (concentrate); I have to make a choice; and How well did I do?

Social workers interested in applying such techniques should keep in mind the following recommendations (Kazdin & Frame, 1983). First, self-statements should be ones that children can understand and retain. The statements should be committed to rote memory, and practitioners need to keep them simple to not overburden the child. Research has found that general self-statements ("I need to look at all my possibilities") are better than specific self-statements ("Just kick the ball and don't get mad"). Last, keep the self-instructions geared to problems that represent difficulties in real life.

Developmental Aspects of Sign Language

Although we normally think of communication as exclusively verbal, this is not necessarily so. Many people communicate using sign language. Children who are born without the ability to hear and who therefore cannot communicate with an oral language often learn the American Sign Language (ASL), an advanced system of communication that includes the use of both hands in various gestures, like the ones in Figure 8.3.

Children learn ASL just as they would an oral language (Shaffer, 1993). Children who are born to deaf parents begin to learn to communicate with signs at a very early age. Most deaf children will learn their first sign at around 9 months of age, which is 3 months before hearing children begin to use words (Bonvillian, Orlansky, & Novack, 1983). Like hearing children, deaf children begin to communicate by "babbling," but they do it in signs that they have observed their parents using. As the children develop, they begin to use the equivalent of one-word phrases—a single sign that communicates several messages. Interestingly, the kinds of signs that children first begin to use are essentially the same as the categories of words that speaking children first learn. Deaf children's ability to communicate continues to develop as they begin to combine signs, like the telegraphic statements made by speaking children. Communication becomes increasingly refined as deaf children learn the complex rules inherent in communicating their thoughts and feelings.

ASL is a creative and advanced system of communication. Similar to oral language, signs combine to form declarative statements and ask questions. ASL users are fond of making a play on words (pun) just as oral communicators do. Many people argue for "total communication" among the deaf, so that they can use ASL and oral language. Perhaps you remember the movie *Children of a Lesser God*, which portrayed some of the issues involved in learning and using "total communication." Learning oral communication and ASL does not make it easier for children to learn the spoken language, but many people believe it enhances the quality of interactions between deaf and hearing people.

FIGURE 8.3   Sign language   Source: Courtesy of Ohio School for the Deaf.

Speech Disorders in Children

The development of a speech disorder can have a negative effect on a child's healthy development. It is not un-

common for children with speech disorders to have difficulties with intellectual and academic achievements, as well as emotional difficulties. Such children may be teased and as a result have low self-esteem. Family problems can also develop, especially if family members pressure the child.

There is a wide variation in the nature of speech disorders. Some are extremely mild and almost unnoticeable; others can be so serious that they affect day-to-day living. We don't know what causes the majority of speech disorders, but there can be a combination of physiological, psychological, or environmental circum-

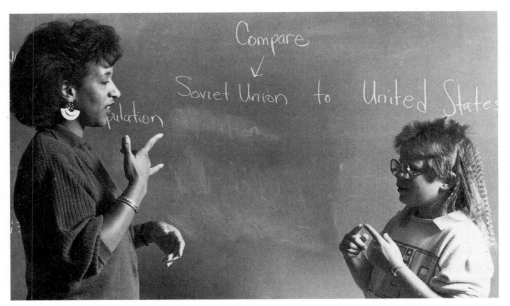

Not all communication is verbal; many children must communicate using sign language. These children learn American Sign Language (ASL), a system of communication based on hand gestures.

stances. Speech disorders manifest themselves in a variety of forms, including articulatory problems, voice abnormalities, stuttering, or aphasia, the inability to speak. Speech disorders are more common among children who have hearing impairments, physical impairments (such as in cerebral palsy), mental retardation, and emotional disturbances. Two of the more common speech disorders are stuttering and faulty articulation.

Stuttering refers to interruptions in communication produced by repetitions, hesitations, or other forms of "blockages" of sounds or words. Some children with more serious forms of stuttering also have overt indications of tension. Stuttering is four or five times more common in boys than in girls, and an estimated 5% of all children may suffer from a stuttering problem for various periods of time. Most cases of stuttering begin early—by age 4 or 5—and usually clear up spontaneously, but professional speech therapists are sometimes needed.

Most experts now believe that stuttering develops as a result of biological and environmental factors. Re-

search from a biological perspective has found that the incidence of stuttering is higher when there is a family history of stuttering. Furthermore, research on brain laterality has demonstrated that the neural organization of stutterers is different from that of nonstutterers. However, other research supports environmental factors; for example, stuttering varies quite dramatically across cultures. Anthropologists have noted the relative absence of stuttering in cultures with permissive child-rearing practices. In contrast, industrial cultures that stress competition, pressure to speak at an early age, and standards of achievement have produced a higher incidence of stuttering. Most speech disorder experts believe that the causes of stuttering develop from an interaction between biological and environmental factors.

Bilingual Children

Language and communication are difficult skills for children to develop. What happens when a child is spoken to in one language at home and taught another language in school? Researchers have found that there can be both negative and positive outcomes for bilingual children. For minority children whose first language is a minority language, learning a second language is a disadvantage for them. However, when children's first language is the majority language, learning a second language can be an advantage (Lefrancois, 1990).

Many Hispanic children in the United States have a negative experience with bilingualism because they become less functional in Spanish, their first language, as their language skills improve in English. Lefrancois (1990) believes that there are three reasons for this problem. First, the majority language, in our case English, is the dominant language used in the media and larger community, so Spanish receives little reinforcement outside the home. Second, the minority language (Spanish) is often discouraged in the home or by the children themselves. Third, the minority language (Spanish) used in the home is sometimes not a model of good use, especially when characterized by such factors as colloquialism and improper grammar. If Spanish is not part of the children's schooling, they are not likely to write or read it. For minority children, the minority language should be taught and the majority language should be the second language (Lefrancois, 1990).

In other circumstances, when children's first language is the majority language, learning the second language has distinct benefits (Bialystok, 1988). Consider, for example, English-speaking children enrolled in Spanish-immersion programs. As Lefrancois (1990, p. 271) notes, "although most students who go through immersion schooling don't develop as high a level of proficiency as do native speakers, their language deficiencies don't seem to interfere with their use of the second language."

The results of a good bilingual program can be both a proficiency in the second language and a strengthening of the first language. Evaluation of bilingualism is complex, but Cummins and Swain (1986) argue that bilingualism can have positive advantages for both minority and majority children.

Other Cultural Influences on Language Abilities

A child's language abilities can be influenced by cultural experiences. Disadvantaged children have a restricted vocabulary and construct sentences that are less grammatically correct than middle-class children's. Although lower-class children score lower on tests of vocabulary and sentence structure, the questions about the appropriate use of grammar is controversial. An important distinction to make is between language performance and language competence (Ashburn, Schuster, Grimm, & Goff, 1986). Grammatical "correctness" may be a relative or arbitrary issue. Children whose dialect differs from white, middle-class children may be using "structured grammatical systems through which they can express both emotional and logical thoughts" (Mussen, 1974).

When a child says, "Me and him ain't goin' to no movie," the child is speaking an imperfect sentence according to the American school system of the larger middle-class society. However, this construction is typical in African American dialects where the verb "to be" incorporates a tense, referred to as *habitual* (Seymour, 1974). The habitual tense expresses an action that occurs frequently or continually. Therefore, "He be playin' " in standard English is "He's still playing," "He's always playing," or "He's been playing." "He playin' " means he is playing currently. Such nonstandard grammar might sound reasonable when spoken to other members of this person's culture. As Ashburn and others (1986, p. 270) argue, "such children are not necessarily deficient in the ability to learn to speak standard English, nor are they necessarily cognitively inept; they are merely the product of their socioaffective environment." So how should a child from this culture speak? When the child is in his or her cultural environment, it is appropriate and adaptive to speak using nonstandard grammar. When attempting to be biculturally adaptive, the child will need to speak "correctly," especially if the child is seeking socioeconomic advancement.

Disadvantaged children do use nonstandard grammar, but the more controversial question is, does nonstandard grammar lead to substandard language competence? According to the language deficit theory, this language is deficient and inferior. This deficiency affects students' academic achievement and their intellectual development. Subsequently, students' opportunities for employment advancement are limited. These deficiencies are the result of impoverished environmental circumstances. The language difference theory argues the opposite—that nonstandard grammar does not reflect

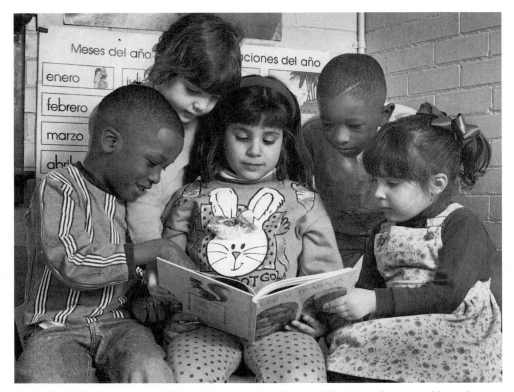

People often think that exposing a child to two languages will confuse the child and cause linguistic problems. These fears are unfounded.

deficient language development. As noted earlier, the dialect represents a well-ordered and highly structured language that differs from standard English.

Some studies have found that children from a lower-socioeconomic demographic background are more competent in language than their speech would indicate. For example, one study (Robinson, 1965) compared lower- and middle-class children on the task of writing a formal and an informal letter. Social class differences were not found in the formal letters, but they were in the informal letters. Many children learn to be **bilingual,** using one language in school and speaking another language at home and in the neighborhood. Teachers and others who are critical of a child's use of dialect may succeed only in reducing the child's positive self-concept.

Attitudes and Emotions

As children enter middle childhood, they begin to have changing self-concepts, fueled by their increasing ability to understand how other people view them. Remember the theory of the looking-glass self where one's self-concept is the image seen in the "looking glass"? This theory helps explain how children's self-concept begins to change in middle childhood because they have a much better ability to look into that glass and see how their behavior can elicit certain reactions from others. Children begin to control their own actions depending on what kind of social self they want to display.

In early childhood, conceptions of self were limited to primarily physical qualities—motor skills, sex-type, and age. In middle childhood, conceptions of the self expand to include such things as ideal self, ethnic awareness, and conscience development (Konner, 1991). In addition to an expanded self-concept, children at this age begin to have a more differentiated self-concept, a more individuated view of themselves, and their self-concept becomes increasingly more stable (Santrock, 1986).

This differentiated view of themselves is a less global view than they had previously. Children who earlier thought of themselves as "not talented" might now recognize that although they are not very good at sports, they are better than most at playing a musical instrument. Children's self-concept also becomes more individuated, so that they begin to see themselves as different from others, as unique: "I am the fastest person in my school." Their self-concept is developing into a more integrated sense of who they are. This self-concept will continue to change, but the early threads of the self are being sown as children continue to develop their more complete self.

Self-concept is complex and difficult to measure; however, Harter (1985) has developed a unique measure of self-concept called the Self-Perception Profile for Children (see Table 8.2 for examples of sample items). Her measure is based on children's evaluations of four areas of competence:

1. *Cognitive competence.* Being good at school work, remembering things, doing well in school, understanding what is read.
2. *Social competence.* Having a lot of friends, having other people like you, feeling well liked, being important to one's classmates.
3. *Physical competence.* Doing well at sports, being chosen for team games, liking games and sports.
4. *General self-worth.* Being sure of self, feeling happy the way I am, feeling like a good person, wanting to stay the same.

This measure has received a lot of praise because, unlike other measures that ask about a child's perceptions regarding his or her abilities in a variety of areas, Harter's scale breaks up the notion of self-concept into four areas. Each area then measures a child's self-concept in that domain.

Research using this scale has led to some interesting findings (Harter, 1982). Most important is that children make distinctions about their competencies in different areas, therefore, a child's self-esteem depends on the situation or circumstance. A measure of a child's overall self-concept could be misleading because it may depend on the area being assessed. Children may have positive self-esteem in the classroom but a poor self-concept on the playground where sportslike games are played.

Also important is the finding that children's evaluations of themselves pretty much resemble the way other people perceive them. For example, a child whose self-rating was high on social competence was in fact found to have a lot of friends who considered that person a good friend. In a similar manner, a child's self-evaluation of cognitive competence was related to how teachers evaluated the child's academic achievements. These research results provide continued support for the idea that how other people perceive us has a lot to do with who we are (Shaffer, 1993). In this case, the "looking glass" was how others perceive a child's self-esteem, and as the looking-glass theory would predict, it accurately reflected the child's self esteem.

These findings also lend support to Erik Erikson's notion that the psychosocial crisis that 6- to 12-year-olds confront is *industry versus inferiority.* At this age, children measure themselves against their peers to establish a sense of who they are. The focus is on personal and social competence, or, according to Harter's research, on cognitive and social competencies. Children work hard to develop their cognitive skills—writing, reading, and arithmetic—as well as their social skills—cooperation, fairness, and receiving approval from others. Erikson's theory predicts that children who develop these skills will successfully master a sense of "industriousness," and they will be able to move on to the next stage of development, the identity crisis of adolescence.

Social Cognition and Regulation

One of the most important concepts in understanding human behavior comes from the field of social cognition. **Social cognition** refers to the level of awareness one has regarding other people's thoughts, feelings, and intentions. Social cognition has a tremendous impact on how

TABLE 8.2   Sample Items from the Self-Perception Profile for Children (measuring social competence, cognitive competence, physical competence, and general self-esteem)

Really True	Sort of True				Really True	Sort of True
☐	☐	Some kids find it hard to make friends.	BUT	For other kids it's pretty easy.	☐	☐
☐	☐	Some kids like school because they do well in class.	BUT	Other kids don't like school because they aren't doing very well.	☐	☐
☐	☐	Some kids feel they are better than others their age at sports.	BUT	Other kids don't feel they can play as well.	☐	☐
☐	☐	Some kids think that maybe they are not a very good person.	BUT	Other kids are pretty sure that they are a good person.	☐	☐

Source: Harter, 1985.

children relate to other children and adults. As children mature and develop, their cognitive growth gives them a new understanding of themselves and other people. Perhaps most critical is the child's developing capacity concerning **role-taking abilities,** or perspective-taking skills.

Social role-taking ability, or the reduction of egocentric thought, is viewed as a critical aspect of healthy social development. Based on the early work of Piaget (1928), this concept refers to children's inability to decenter the focus of their conceptual efforts. In other words, children without role-taking abilities just can't see things from another person's perspective. Young children cannot empathize with the feelings of other people, but this social cognitive capacity develops as the child grows older.

How does a child develop such role-taking abilities? This skill matures through exposure to role-taking opportunities that involve an exchange of differing perspectives. Role-taking is related to moral development, which depends on a person's ability to perceive and comprehend the differing perspectives of other people. Role taking should be considered a parallel stage to moral development—it is a necessary but not sufficient condition for moral reasoning. The next chapter discusses in greater detail aspects of moral development. For now, let's see why an understanding of role-taking has important implications for understanding and working with children.

Role-taking ability begins to change around 12 years of age, when the ability to think about oneself and one's social relations becomes more advanced (Selman, 1980; Shantz, 1983). As the middle child grows older, he or she can begin to infer others' feelings, thoughts, and intentions. Although cognitive abilities begin to expand during this developmental period, this period is still characterized by egocentrism, or the inability to assume another person's role or viewpoint.

Role-taking ability is closely related to the development of social skills in children. Role taking is a prerequisite for the emergence of many social behaviors, such as cooperation and altruism. Many researchers (Piaget & Inhelder, 1969; Staub, 1984) have suggested that a variety of social behaviors are strengthened by a child's ability to take the role of another. One researcher, Robert Selman, has expanded the concept of social-role taking to help explain how children's friendships and peer relationships develop.

Interpersonal Awareness

Robert Selman's work has focused on what he refers to as interpersonal awareness, how the child conceives his or her own interpersonal relationships, particularly friendship and peer group relationships. Can distinctive ways of reasoning about such relationships be ordered along a developmental continuum? Furthermore, do children who have social and emotional problems reason at a different level when compared with better-functioning peers? These are the questions that Selman sought to answer in his research. Before we reveal the answers, lets look a little closer at his theory of interpersonal awareness.

As we have been learning from the classical work of Piaget, children's physical-cognitive development proceeds according to specific stages:

0—preoperational
1—transitional preoperational
2—consolidated concrete operational
3—transitional concrete/early formal operations
4—consolidated formal operations

In a similar manner, Selman (1980) suggests that developmental levels can account for social perspective-taking abilities:

0—undifferentiated and egocentric perspective-taking skill
1—differentiated and subjective perspective taking
2—self-reflective and reciprocal perspective taking
3—third-person and mutual perspective taking
4—societal/symbolic perspective taking

At the first stage of perspective taking, children cannot differentiate between the physical and psychological aspects of people. Beginning with level 1, children (ages 5–9) begin to differentiate the physical and psychological characteristics of individuals. For example, they can differentiate between intentional and unintentional behavior. By level 2 (ages 7–12), major advances occur and children can take a self-reflective view of the self. Chil-

dren recognize that there can be a difference between the physical self and the psychological self. Level 3 is known as the mutual perspective-taking level (ages 10–15) because here children can take a third-person perspective; that is, they can truly see things from different perspectives. Level 4 emerges after age 12, but it may not be present until adulthood. At this level, one can think abstractly about the various levels of understanding and can recognize that each level can have a different point of view. Although this material is theoretically complex, you will see in the following section how it can be useful in understanding and working with children.

Interpersonal Awareness and Interpersonal Relationships

Continuing with Selman's theory (1980; 1990), we can take interpersonal awareness and examine how the child conceives his or her own interpersonal relationships, particularly friendship and peer group relations. As Table 8.3 indicates, there are stages of friendship and peer group formation that relate to the physical-cognitive stages of development. For example, in the consolidated concrete operational stage, the corresponding stages are one-way assistance in friendship and unilateral relations in the peer group.

Selman's research sought to answer the question, can distinctive ways of reasoning about relationships be ordered along a developmental continuum? From his research, he came up with the stages identified in Table 8.4. Let's look even more closely at how to apply his work.

TABLE 8.3 Developmental Stages Across Impersonal and Interpersonal Awareness

Impersonal		Interpersonal	
Stage	Cognitive	Friendship	Peer Group
0	Intuitive preoperational	Momentary physical playmate	Physical connections
1	Transitional preoperational/concrete operational	One-way assistance	Unilateral relations
2	Consolidated concrete operational	Fairweather cooperation	Bilateral partnerships
3	Transitional concrete/early formal operational	Intimate-mutual sharing	Homogeneous community
4	Consolidated formal operational	Autonomous interdependence	Pluralistic organization

Source: Adapted from Selman, 1980; Selman, Jaquette, & Lavin, 1977.

TABLE 8.4   Stages of Friendship Showing Sample Responses

Stage	Friendship	Sample Responses
0	Momentary physical playmate	Alan, age 4, said he trusted his friend, Eric. When asked why, he said, "If I give him my toy he won't break it . . . he isn't strong enough."
1	One-way assistance	"I trust a friend if he does what I tell him."
2	Fair-weather cooperation	"Trust means if you do something for him, he will do something for you."
3	Intimate-mutual sharing	Trust is "when they can get it off their chest if they talk with you; things that are going on in your life and in the other person's life."
4	Autonomous interdependence	"Trust means that you've got to grow, the more you hold on to, the less you have. You have to have confidence in yourself as a good friend, then you'll have trust in your relationship."

Source: Based on Selman, Jaquette, & Lavin, 1977.

We can take one issue that is relevant to friendship—interpersonal trust—and see how the developmental stages of friendship apply (Selman, Jaquette, & Lavin, 1977). Table 8.4 shows the stage, level of friendship, and sample responses that would indicate the stage the child is in.

As Table 8.4 indicates, children reason very differently about trust, depending on their level of interpersonal awareness. The researchers gathered these sample responses by presenting children with different dilemmas and then asking a series of questions, such as: What is trust? Why is it important for friends to trust each other in order to stay friends? With this kind of interviewing, they established the different stages of interpersonal awareness.

By studying the levels of interpersonal awareness of normal and emotionally disturbed children, Selman hopes he can develop a set of therapeutic and educational goals oriented to developing greater maturity of interpersonal awareness. Selman's research suggests that children who have experienced extremely inconsistent or disruptive interpersonal experiences, and who manifest severe difficulties in their interpersonal relations, do not develop through the domain of social reasoning as steadily as do children with more consistent, dependable, and mutual relations with friends or peers. A 15-year-old who defines a friend as "someone who does what I want him to do" is going to have difficulty establishing friendships with other adolescents, who perceive friendship as cooperation and reciprocal affection (Selman, Jaquette, & Lavin, 1977).

Implications for Practice: Pair Therapy

Given this conclusion, how can we help children develop better ways of reasoning about friendships and peer relations? The key is providing children with role-taking opportunities and encouraging them to think in ways that expand their social reasoning.

Recently, Lyman and Selman (1985) have described *pair therapy* as a means by which to enhance the social reasoning of children who are experiencing peer conflict. Pair therapy is a method whereby two children with interpersonal difficulties meet together for weekly sessions with an adult who provides a forum for negotiation. The therapist helps the peers reflect on their different ideas and strategies. When children experience repeated negotiation, taking into consideration various and different perspectives, they are being given new opportunities to develop insight and skills.

Pair therapy involves three basic dimensions: stage setting, structuring, and facilitating reflection. Stage setting is simply the development of specific opportunities for conflict within a conducive environment. The stage should be an atmosphere of acceptance and safety in which the children are free to express themselves, share ideas and fantasies, and try out new ways of dealing with conflicts. Structuring involves mediating peer negotiations, providing incentives, setting limits, and becoming less involved as necessary. The structuring should provide the opportunity and the motivation to experiment with new and better ways of negotiating conflicts. To facilitate reflection, the therapist encourages the children to reflect on their own and their partner's behavior, helps facilitate peer feedback, and uses role modeling and problem solving to encourage alternative strategies for conflict resolution. Reflection is encouraged both *in vivo*, while they are together working on problems, and after the fact so they develop retrospective reflection.

Psychological Hazards

Most childhood disorders can be classified into one of two categories: problems of undercontrol and problems of overcontrol. Undercontrol problems are often referred to as **externalizing problems,** and overcontrol problems are referred to as **internalizing problems** (Achenbach & Edelbrock, 1983). Externalizing problems consist of behaviors that reflect a tendency to "act out"; for example, aggressive behavior like fighting, acting defiantly, and overactivity. Internalizing problems consist of behaviors that reflect an "inner state," such as anxiety, loneliness, shyness, social withdrawal, and depression. Two of the most common problems of middle childhood are hyperactivity, an externalizing problem, and depression, an internalizing problem.

Hyperactivity or Attention Deficit Hyperactivity Disorder

Carlos was referred to the outpatient mental health clinic by his teacher, who demanded that Carlos get some help to control his behavior. Carlos, age 7, demanded the attention of almost everyone around him and constantly disturbed the other children in the class. The teacher noted that Carlos could not sit still, concentrate on his work, or complete his tasks. He was always on the move. Even when sitting in his seat, Carlos fidgeted and moved about, which disturbed other students next to him. His mother reported that he was a motormouth; was unable to stick to any one chore, task, or game; and was often found away from the house where he was not allowed to be. She described several examples of Carlos's poor judgment and problem-solving abilities.

Carlos, of course, is a typical 7-year-old boy who suffers from **attention deficit hyperactivity disorder** (ADHD). Carlos has three important characteristics of the disorder: excess motor activity, impulsiveness, and inattention. Box 8.1 presents the criteria as defined by the most recent edition of the *Diagnostic and Statistical Manual of Mental Disorders* (DSM-IV).

Although most researchers and clinicians who work with children like Carlos agree that there is a true syndrome or disorder in which you can classify such children, to do so in a reliable manner is problematic. Schwartz and Johnson (1985) point out some diagnostic problems. For example, the criterion "has difficulty sitting still or fidgets excessively" assumes that everyone will agree on what it means to fidget. But what is excessive fidgeting? Without any normative criteria (recorded observations of how much the average child fidgets), applying this criterion is difficult. Consider, for example, that in one study teachers of 8-year-olds classified 43% as having short attention spans (Werry & Quay, 1971). Children at this age are often considered "bundles of energy," and a certain amount of overactivity occurs in children who would be considered "normal." Therefore, behavior problems in children must be considered within the context of developmental norms. A child with ADHD is developmentally abnormal; otherwise, many average children with "bundles of energy" would be classified as having hyperactivity.

Despite these problems, checklists have been developed that can help in identifying children who are likely to suffer from ADHD. Usually parents or teachers are asked to fill out a checklist indicating which behaviors are characteristic of the child. Box 8.2 is an example of a rating scale used in assessing ADHD in children.
It is estimated that about 3% of children can be diagnosed as having ADHD and that of those with the disorder, there are three ADHD boys for every one ADHD girl (American Psychiatric Association, 1994).

Researchers are still unclear about the causes of hyperactivity. (See Focus on Research: Can Diet Reduce Hyperactivity in Children?) It used to be thought that hyperactivity was due to some form of brain dysfunction; in fact, hyperactivity used to be referred to as minimal brain dysfunction. Much research has been conducted to investigate the role of brain dysfunction and hyperactivity. A lack of activity in the frontal cortex and the basal

BOX 8.1

DSM-IV Diagnostic Criteria for Attention Deficit Hyperactivity Disorder

A. Either (1) or (2):

1. Six (or more) of the following symptoms of inattention have persisted for at least 6 months to a degree that is maladaptive and inconsistent with developmental level:

    Inattention

    a. often fails to give close attention to details or makes careless mistakes in schoolwork, work, or other activities
    b. often has difficulty sustaining attention in tasks or play activities
    c. often does not seem to listen when spoken to directly
    d. often does not follow through on instructions and fails to finish schoolwork, chores, or duties in the workplace (not due to oppositional behavior or failure to understand instructions)
    e. often has difficulty organizing tasks and activities
    f. often avoids, dislikes, or is reluctant to engage in tasks that require sustained mental effort (such as schoolwork or homework)
    g. often loses things necessary for tasks or activities (e.g., toys, school assignments, pencils, books, or tools)
    h. is often easily distracted by extraneous stimuli
    i. is often forgetful in daily activities

2. Six (or more) of the following symptoms of hyperactivity/impulsivity have persisted for at least 6 months to a degree that is maladaptive and inconsistent with developmental level:

    Hyperactivity

    a. often fidgets with hands or feet or squirms in seat
    b. often leaves seat in classroom or in other situations in which remaining seated is expected
    c. often runs about or climbs excessively in situations in which it is inappropriate (in adolescents or adults, may be limited to subjective feelings of restlessness)
    d. often has difficulty playing or engaging in leisure activities quietly
    e. is often "on the go" or often acts as if "driven by a motor"
    f. often talks excessively

    Impulsivity

    g. often blurts out answers before questions have been completed
    h. often has difficulty awaiting turn
    i. often interrupts or intrudes on others (e.g., butts into conversations or games)

B. Some hyperactive-impulsive or inattentive symptoms that caused impairment were present before age 7 years.

C. Some impairment from the symptoms is present in two or more settings (e.g., at school [or work] and at home).

D. There must be clear evidence of clinically significant impairment in social, academic, or occupational functioning.

E. The symptoms do not occur exclusively during the course of a Pervasive Developmental disorder, Schizophrenia, or other Psychotic Disorder and are not better accounted for by another mental disorder (e.g., Mood Disorder, Anxiety Disorder, Dissociative Disorder, or a Personality Disorder).

Source: American Psychiatric Association, 1994.

ganglia has been observed in people with ADHD (Zametkin et al., 1990) Other researchers (Riccio, Hynd, Cohen, & Gonzales, 1993) have found evidence that the right hemisphere may be malfunctioning. However, research has failed to demonstrate a clear relationship between ADHD and any neurological impairment. Researchers have turned their attention to an investigation of genetics and ADHD, and although the studies are not conclusive, the evidence does suggest there are genetic factors in ADHD.

Implications for Practice: ADHD and Medication

Many people are familiar with the pharmacological treatment of children with ADHD. A high percentage of children diagnosed with ADHD receive some form of medication (e.g., Ritalin, Dexedrine, Cylert, Benzedrine). The majority of children are helped by the medication, which increases the child's ability for sustained attention. However, medications do not necessarily reduce activity levels, and they have little effect on school performance. Although it is clear that medication helps ADHD children in the short term, the long-term

benefit of medication has been questioned. In addition, many practitioners are concerned about the side effects of medication on children. Two common reactions to medication for hyperactivity are appetite reduction and sleep disturbance (Loney & Ordona, 1975). In spite of these problems, medication seems to make children less distractible and less disruptive in class (Dulcan, 1986; Swanson et al., 1993). It also enhances the way classmates perceive the hyperactive child, and this may produce important social benefits.

Most experts believe that medication should be supplemented by behavioral treatment. This hunch was confirmed by a study (Chase & Clement, 1985) that found the combination of medication with cognitive-behavioral treatment produced the most benefit. Thus it seems necessary to provide treatment beyond medication that will address academic performance, an aspect of behavior not affected by medication. Chase and Clement (1985) found that having children set goals for reading assignments and give themselves points to exchange for reinforcers increased both the amount of work completed and its accuracy.

BOX 8.2

The Conners Rating Scale for Assessing Hyperactivity

Not at all (0)	Just a little (1)	Pretty much (2)	Very much (3)	
0	1	2	3	1. Constantly fidgeting
0	1	2	3	2. Excitable, impulsive
0	1	2	3	3. Disturbs other children
0	1	2	3	4. Cries often and easily
0	1	2	3	5. Stubborn
0	1	2	3	6. No sense of fair play

Source: Conners, 1989.

Can Diet Reduce Hyperactivity in Children?

A study by Gross, Tofanelli, Butzirus, & Snodgrass (1987) was designed to answer the question, does diet affect the behavior of hyperactive and learning-disordered children? Much excitement had resulted from the claim by Feingold (1975) that hyperactive behavior could be reduced by controlling the chilren's diet—in particular, eliminating foods with preservatives, artificial flavors, and artificial colors. Many parents formed "Feingold Clubs" with the promise that a controlled diet will reduce their child's hyperactive behavior. Therefore, an important question is whether or not diet can indeed have a positive influence on the behavior of hyperactive children.

This experiment involved 39 children who were attending a two-week summer camp. All the children had learning disorders, and 18 of the children had attention deficit hyperactivity disorder. The cook for the camp was instructed in the Feingold diet, and he meticulously followed the diet for the first week. Because the children were not allowed to bring their own food, the cook had complete control over their diet. After one week, the diet was completely changed, emphasizing whatever foods the children desired, with as much food with artificial coloring and flavoring as possible. The canteen was also stocked with snack foods such as soft drinks, cakes, candies, and chips—most of which include artificial colors and flavors.

To assess the impact of the diet, a television camera in operation at each meal in the dining hall recorded the children's behavior for 4 minutes. The dining hall was used because it required the children's maximum self-control. These tapes were later reviewed by teachers who had not been at the camp. The time segments were presented to the raters in random order, and they rated the following behaviors on a scale from 1 to 10: motor restlessness, disorganized behavior, and misbehavior. After interrupter reliability was established, the results were

statistically analyzed comparing week 1 with week 2. The results revealed no differences. Therefore, the researchers concluded that a diet rich in additives and food coloring does not produce or aggravate symptoms of hyperactivity.

Social Dimension

Families, Groups, Support Systems, and Contexts

Family strength is an important concept that has dramatically influenced social work practice. Social workers are increasingly concerned about offering families opportunities to use their strength. For too long, social workers did not recognize family strength and instead were concerned only with a family's pathology. Today, family strength is emphasized because we recognize that the family environment holds the key to unlocking a child's capacity to grow and develop in a healthy manner.

A child can grow up in many different family contexts—as one of ten other children with little or no individual parental attention; in a family with an alcoholic parent; as the recipient of a stepparent's physical and sexual abuse; or in poverty where gang warfare and drug abuse are a part of everyday life. In contrast, children can also grow up in large families that care deeply about each other and work together to provide for themselves; in families where alcoholism afflicts one of the parents, but an abiding love exists between the parents; in situations where child abuse has devastated and torn apart families, but they have worked to create a new context in which they can live peacefully together; and in situations where poverty and drug abuse are all around but where enough love between a mother and her child protects against such negative influences.

It is within this context that children are embedded. They are subjected to the complex web of family relationships that significantly shape their future.

Normal Family Process

By the time children reach late childhood, they are spending much less time with parents and more time with peers. One study (Hill & Stafford, 1980) found that parents spend less than half as much time with their children between the ages of 5 and 12 than they did before. Although less time is spent with the family, it continues to be an extremely important influence on the child. A parent's attitude about a child's ability is a more important influence than is the child's past performance (Parsons, Adler, & Kaczala, 1982).

At this age, the family provides an important base for the child to continue growing and developing. Children need the safe, authoritative structure that parents can provide. Although children show less love and respect for their parents, they depend on parents for unconditional love and as sources of information and authority (Rapalje, Degelman, & Ashburn, 1986). The role of discipline continues to be critical for good parenting.

Parental Discipline

Three major parental disciplinary strategies identified by Hoffman (1970) are **power assertive discipline**, which includes physical punishment, threat of punishment, and physical attempts to control the child's behavior; **love withdrawal**, which involves withdrawing love when the child's behavior is viewed as inappropriate; and **induction**, which involves the use of explanation and rationality in attempting to influence the child's actions.

What effects do these different strategies of parental discipline have on children? Research studies have shown that parents who use power assertion (punishment) increase their children's aggressive tendencies. There are several possible explanations regarding why punishment would lead to aggressive behavior in children. As you learned earlier, parents who act aggressively toward their children provide a model of aggressive behavior for the child to imitate. Also, children involved in physical confrontations with their parents learn that this is how disputes are resolved—through fighting, arguing, and threats of punishment. Have you ever observed a child being physically punished by his or her parents? You may also have noticed the child is embarrassed and ashamed, which demeans the child. Children with low self-esteem may be more likely to respond with aggressive behavior in the absence of more appropriate social skills.

Parents who use love withdrawal do so by verbally discounting children, threatening to send the children away, and indicating to the children that they are not loved because of their actions. Love withdrawal also includes such parental actions as persistently ignoring the child, refusing to talk with the child (the silent treatment), and generally not interacting with the child. Of course, this behavior is unfair and often makes the child fearful. Research has found that this form of parenting can lead to excessive anxiety in children and inhibit needed expression of emotions (Hoffman, 1970).

Consider the difference between these two types of parental discipline strategies: "Chen, get in this house right now! If you don't do as I say, I'll take the paddle to your butt" and "Chen, you need to come in and get ready for dinner. Your aunt is expecting us later tonight and we don't want to be late." How would a child feel in response to these two statements? The first response is likely to elicit anger and resentment, whereas the second response is more likely to elicit cooperation and understanding. The use of induction helps the child develop an understanding of why he or she should act in the requested manner. Other examples include telling a child, "Please don't climb on that wall because it isn't strong enough to hold your weight" (appeal to prevent injury); "You can't watch TV tonight because you broke our rule about no more throwing temper tantrums" (appeal to fairness); "Don't chew food with your mouth open—that's not appropriate at the dinner table" (appeal to standards of conduct).

Induction is an important parental strategy because it helps children develop internal moral standards (Lickona, 1983). Children disciplined by induction methods gain experience in exercising self-control and learn to display more consideration and generosity toward others when compared with children who have been disciplined with power assertion techniques (Dlugokinski & Firestone, 1974). Induction is really a strategy based on principles of moral development. Understanding a child's social cognitive and moral development is critical in successfully using such discipline strategies. An understanding of parental discipline is pivotal in helping parents learn effective parenting techniques.

Implications for Practice: Parent Training

Many social workers are called upon to do some form of parent training. They may run parent-training groups for parents of noncompliant children, work directly with foster parents, or conduct parent-training classes to help prepare pregnant adolescents to become better parents. Indeed, parent-training courses have been introduced everywhere—in schools, hospitals, community mental health centers, and churches. Professionals approach parent training from many different perspectives, ranging from humanistic to psychoanalytic, and although there are some similarities, there are also some important differences. Let's examine four of the more popular approaches to parent training that you will likely come across in your work: P.E.T. (Gordon, 1970), behavior modification (Gerald Patterson, 1982; Dangel & Polster, 1988), P.I.P. (reality therapy for parents, inspired by William Glasser), and STEP (Adlerian therapy for parents, originated by Dreikurs and best represented by the work of Dinkmeyer & McKay, 1982). Briefly, let's examine some of the fundamental principles involved in each of these approaches (based on Brown, 1976; Jaffee, 1991).

Parent-Effectiveness Training (P.E.T.) This humanist approach to parenting emphasizes the need for respect between parent and child. Central to Gordon's ideas about parenting is his complete rejection of parental power. P.E.T. encourages parents to give up, forever, the use of power. He argues two reasons for this. First, it is damaging to people and relationships, and second, power undermines P.E.T.'s no-lose method of resolving conflicts. Another interesting concept in P.E.T. is the different conceptualization of children's behavior. P.E.T. says there is no such thing as children's misbehavior; children simply behave. All behavior is aimed at getting needs met. The driving ideas behind P.E.T. are summarized in Table 8.5.

The first strategy is to encourage parents and children to enlarge the no-problem aspect of their relationships. This can be accomplished by such things as environmental modification—putting things where children can't reach them—or minding your own business or relaxing and staying calm.

When this doesn't work, the parent turns to the critical techniques of P.E.T. The parent is taught to first ask the question "Who owns the problem?" If the child owns the problem, the parent learns to use active listening. For example, the child comes home and is upset because the homework was lost and so wasn't turned in to the

TABLE 8.5   The P.E.T. Approach to Parenting

Behavior acceptable to parent	Child owns problem	Use active listening
	No problem	
Behavior unacceptable to parent	Parent owns problem	Use I-messages and, if necessary, the no-lose method of problem solving

Source: Gordon, 1970.

teacher. The parent is taught to help the child understand, accept, and deal with his or her own feelings: "You really look upset—it means a lot to you to get your homework turned in on time." Often a parent's inclination is to use other ineffective strategies, including getting mad at the child, attempting to reassure the child, or presenting rationalizations or solutions.

When the behavior is unacceptable to the parent, the parent owns the problem and the first strategy is to use I-messages: "I really need some quiet time—could you please turn off the stereo?" Parents are taught to use this rather than the familiar You-message: "You always have to turn the stereo up too loud." These messages, according to P.E.T., only demean the child and can be damaging to the child's self-esteem.

When active listening and I-messages do not resolve the problem, the parent turns to the no-lose method of problem solving. The parent elicits the child's cooperation in problem solving and follows these six steps: (1) Define the conflict, (2) use brainstorming with the child to generate solutions, (3) evaluate the solutions on the list, (4) see if there is a solution that satisfies both parties, and if so, (5) decide how to implement it, and (6) evaluate the solution later to see if it worked.

Parent-Involvement Training (P.I.T.) A large part of the P.I.T. program focuses on getting parents involved. The P.I.T. theory says that no behavior change can take place without a helping relationship based on trust, warmth, and respect. You must believe in your child in order for any behavior or self-concept to change. P.I.T. uses very direct strategies for getting kids involved, including teaching parents to stop what they are doing and attend to their children, especially if the children are upset. Other strategies involve specific instructions for such things as dinnertime conversations, games to play, and so forth. The program is based on the following seven steps:

1. Establish and maintain involvement. Strongly recommended is conversation—talking about topics of mutual interest.
2. Help the children see what their current behavior is and understand that it is something they have chosen. Although feelings are important, behavior is critical.
3. Suggest that the children evaluate their behavior. Self-judgment is stressed by asking the children whether what they are doing is helping them.
4. Help the children plan for increasingly responsible behavior. Help the child set realistic goals and have a successful experience.
5. Get the children to make a commitment to the plan. Contracts like this increase the children's motivation and involvement.
6. Accept no excuses, and if the children fail to meet the commitment, start again with step 3.
7. Don't use punishment. This can cause the children physical or mental pain and may lead to loneliness, isolation, or hostility. Instead, use praise for successes—it will encourage involvement.

Behavior Modification   The use of *behavior modification* in parent training involves teaching parents how to apply the principles of behavior to their children. The principles of behavior include such concepts as reinforcement, punishment, extinction, differential reinforcement of other behaviors, and stimulus control. Parent-training programs usually start out by teaching parents how to define the behavior they would like to see changed. After learning how to precisely define behavior, parents choose a home project to begin to put the principles to work. Parents must choose a behavior, define it, and develop a method of tracking and record-keeping. If parents are working on reducing the number of temper tantrums, then they must define what a temper tantrum is and record this behavior. Often they chart the behavior for a week or more with graph paper in order to assess the ex-

tent of the problem and to have a comparison after introducing an intervention.

Parents are then taught ways to either increase behaviors or decrease behaviors. Most parents choose to implement a reinforcement program based either on praise (social reinforcement) or on a home-style token economy, where points are exchanged for tangible reinforcement (money, prizes, or special privileges). When working to decrease behaviors, parents are taught to use various forms of punishments. For example, a parent working on reducing bedtime crying may use extinction, which involves ignoring the behavior (because the parent's attention was what kept the child crying night after night). Two of the most widely used punishments are time-out and the withdrawal of privileges. Time-out is time without reinforcement, and the child must sit quietly in a chair in the corner of a room for 2–6 minutes. The strategy is to make the time-out boring and unrewarding to the child. Withdrawal of privileges is often used on older children in conjunction with token economies. When unacceptable behaviors continue, the child loses a predetermined privilege. For example, a parent trying to reduce sibling fights would withdraw the privilege of watching TV that night for any instance of fighting.

Most behavior modification programs work hard to teach parents the hidden value of using praise and reinforcement with their children. Parents are encouraged to dramatically increase the use of praise. They are taught to rewrite rules using positive language, to record and increase the number of times they use praise, to make and display cards to encourage praise (like "catch your child being good"), and to display charts proudly showing the progress that the child is making.

Systematic Training for Effective Parenting (STEP)   This approach to parent training rests on the belief that a misbehaving child is a discouraged child. The STEP program teaches parents that there are four goals to a child's misbehavior: attention, power, revenge, and inadequacy. STEP teaches parents to use techniques of encouragement and discipline. Encouragement strategies emphasize giving the child a lot of responsibility and avoiding overprotection and unnecessary service. Whereas most parents will serve the child by pouring the child's milk, STEP recommends letting the child pour his or her own milk. If the child spills it, wipe it up and let the child try it again. STEP strongly recommends that parents not be overprotective but allow children to learn from their own behavior. This is well demonstrated by the STEP approach to discipline.

Discipline involves the use of natural and logical consequences. Again, the idea is to get parents to allow children the opportunity to experience the effects of their choices and behavior—good and bad. Unlike behavior modification, in which parents reward and punish the child's behavior (which means the parents are responsible for the child's behavior), STEP says children should be allowed to make their own decisions. If their choice is good, they experience the benefits; if their choice is bad, they suffer the consequences. This encourages children's actions to become more responsible and adult oriented, guided by natural outcomes, not parental interference.

The idea behind natural consequences is that they follow directly from the child's behavior in the absence of parental intervention. For example, children who arrive home late and miss dinner will have to prepare dinner for themselves. Children who leave the house without a coat will have to deal with being cold. Children who miss the bus are expected to walk to school. These are natural consequences because they follow directly from the behavior. When this is not possible because natural consequences are not available or would be dangerous, STEP teaches parents to use logical consequences. For example, if the parent cannot trust the child to play outside, the child must play inside; or if the child colors on the wall with a crayon, the crayons are taken away. Natural and logical consequences are considered preferable to rewards and punishments because they avoid power struggles and give children the opportunity to learn from real-life consequences.

Groups, Support Systems, and Contexts

In middle childhood, children begin to have an increasing preference for spending time with their peers. This shift is clearly illustrated by Figure 8.4, from a study by Ellis, Rogoff, and Cromer (1981). The figure reveals the dramatic increase of child companions from age 1 to age 8. This increase is accompanied by a similar decrease in the number of adult companions. Also interesting is the fact that these children actually spent less time with age-

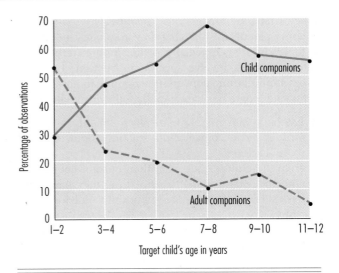

FIGURE 8.4   Developmental changes in children's companionship with children and adults   Source: Ellis, Rogoff, & Cromer, 1981.

mates (children within one year of their age) than with children who were either younger or older.

What makes a peer group? Is it just a few children who are similar in age and who hang out together? Apparently not, as researchers have defined **peer groups** in a specific manner: a group of age-mates that is durable and composed of interactions based on an established set of social relationships. Peer groups are defined by their shared values and goals. Often, children in cliques are identified by their similar social prejudices, speech, or clothing styles. Within the group, an individual will have a certain role or status. Although formal groups often elect individuals to certain roles, like team leader, similar roles emerge naturally in informal peer groups. Let's examine the ways that peer groups are formed, the social interactions within peer groups, and how they might influence the behavior of their members.

Group Formation

As children increase the number of stable encounters with age-mates, they begin to form groups. These groups often start when the child enters school and has increased and regular contact with peers. Peer groups are important in the child's development throughout the life

Peer groups are important throughout a child's development. In early middle childhood, they are informal and lack structure, but by late middle childhood, peer groups become more formalized, with distinct roles and social rules that govern the group.

course, but their nature and function change as children get older. In early middle childhood, children are involved in informal groups that lack much structure. There are few rules that govern the behavior of the members, and there is a high turnover in membership. As a result, the influence of peer groups is reduced until the child reaches late childhood. Beginning with the junior high school years, group formation becomes increasingly important as peer relationships take on a new importance. At this age, groups become more formalized and roles emerge more clearly, as do the social rules that govern the groups—for example, "We only allow girls from our soccer group." Children begin to feel a cohesiveness that binds them to the group's values.

The most famous study of group formation was done by Sherif and colleagues (Sherif et al., 1961), who conducted a fascinating experiment with boys in a camp setting. The children were divided arbitrarily into two groups, and many of the boys resented being separated from their friends; each group had friends who had been assigned to the opposite group. As the groups participated in separate activities, their cooperation and cohesiveness with each other developed. Soon each group had developed its own rules of conduct, leadership hierarchy, and status relationships. The children in each group now identified more closely with peers from their own group. The experiment continued by bringing the two groups together for an intergroup conflict phase. The children were exposed to win-lose competition and planned frustration to increase the tension between the groups. These activities increased the level of animosity harbored by the two groups. In the last phase of the experiment, the researchers explored ways to reduce the intergroup conflict. When Sherif and colleagues sought to reduce the conflict, they brought the two groups together under noncompetitive conditions. However, this only heightened the conflict. When the two groups were brought together to work on a common goal that required cooperation (the researchers deliberately broke a water line so both groups would have to help), the boys were able to reduce the conflict.

This study has many important implications. First, the study illustrated the importance of cooperation and common goals in the formation of cohesive groups. The study also showed that groups independent of any prior shared interest can develop bad feelings and learn to discriminate against an out group. Second, the study found that competition and frustration can increase hostility between groups. Third, the study found that such hostility can be reduced when a common goal is introduced and groups are required to work together.

The Power of Peers

Early research by Merrill Roff (1963) was groundbreaking in its discovery of the importance of peers for healthy psychological development. Roff conducted a number of follow-up studies that examined children who had poor peer relationships and found that years later, as adults, these people had more than usual mental health adjustments, had more problems adjusting to military service, and had more serious mental health problems.

Numerous studies now confirm Roff's early hunches that difficulties in social adjustment are likely to lead to poor mental health. Research by Cowen and others (1973) demonstrated the predictive power of not getting along with peers. His well-known study began by identifying first-grade children who were having poor peer relationships and were thought to be at greater risk for mental health problems. To test his idea, he followed several first-grade classes until the children reached early adulthood. He found that the children identified to be at greater risk because of poor peer relationships were disproportionately represented as suffering from psychiatric problems as adults.

Even more interesting for social workers was his finding that assessments of children's social competence by their peers is a more powerful predictor of later behavior problems than assessments of parents, teachers, or mental health practitioners. Indeed, we now realize that peers are critical to the healthy development of a child—perhaps second in importance only to the influence of parents.

Peers have always been considered an important aspect of childhood, but in the last 10–15 years we have learned much more about the impact that children can have on one another—both positive and negative. One thing is clear—peer friendship is an important part of a child's development. People have an innate desire for human companionship, and peer friendship is critical if we are to feel connected and socially involved with one another. The absence of peer friendship speaks clearly to how important it is for healthy development. The following letter is from an adult who was deprived of peer friendships while growing up (Hartup, 1979, p. 155):

> I am an only child, now 57 years old and I want to tell you some things about my life. Not only was I an only child but I grew up in the country where there were no nearby children to play with. My mother did not want children around. She used to say, "I don't want my kid to bother anybody and I don't want nobody's kids bothering me."
>
> From the first year of school I was teased and made fun of. For example, in about third or fourth grade I dreaded to get on the school bus to go to school because the other children on the bus called me "Mommy's baby." In about the second grade I heard a vulgar word. I asked what it meant and they made fun of me. So I learned a lesson—don't ask questions. This can lead to a lot of confusion to hear talk one doesn't understand and not be able to learn what it means. . . .
>
> I never went out with a girl while I was in school—in fact I hardly talked to them. In our school the boys and girls did not play together. Boys were sent to one part of the playground and girls to another. So, I didn't learn anything about girls. When we got into high school and the boys and girls started dating I could only listen to their stories about their experiences.
>
> I could tell you a lot more but the important thing is I have never married or had any children. I have not been successful in an occupation or vocation. I believe my troubles are not all due to being an only child . . . but I do believe you are right in recommending playmates for preschool children and I will add playmates for the school

agers and not have them strictly supervised by adults. I believe I confirm the experiments with monkeys in being overly timid sometimes and overly aggressive sometimes. Parents of only children should make special efforts to provide playmates for [their children].

This letter supports various research studies that have documented the significance of good peer relationships. In reviewing this literature, Hartup (1979; 1983) summarized the importance of peer relations on child development:

- Poor peer relations are associated with discomfort, anxiety, and a general unwillingness to engage the environment.
- Children master their aggressive impulses within the context of peer relations.
- Sexual socialization cannot take place in the absence of peer interaction.
- Peer relations are related to role-taking ability, empathy, and moral reasoning.
- Children who are rejected by their peers are at greater risk for delinquency, school dropout, and mental health problems.

Children offer each other important knowledge and skills that are often unavailable from adults. Friendships are critical because they provide opportunities for learning social skills and a beginning sense of group belonging. The recent emphasis on peer relationships has stimulated research and program development in two areas, social skills training and social cognition. (See the following Focus on Research section.)

Culture and Cooperation

Cooperation is a critical concept in understanding peer interactions. Do children from different cultures respond to cooperation in different ways? When put in certain circumstances—for example, when there is an element of competition—there are differences. Researchers have found that children from small Mexican villages are more cooperative than urban Mexican, Mexican American, African American, and white American children (Madsen & Shapira, 1970). Other similar studies have found differences between urban and rural children. These results point to the influence of simple, agrarian cultures that foster cooperation in children. Urban cultures that are more complex reward competition more.

FOCUS ON RESEARCH

Can Isolated Children Be Taught the Social Skills Needed for Friendship Making?

A study by Oden and Asher (1977) was designed to assess coaching as a method of training socially isolated children in social skills for gains in peer acceptance. Children (ages 9–10) were selected for this study on the basis of the results of a sociometric assessment. The sociometric assessment used a roster-and-rating questionnaire. Children rated each other in answer to two questions administered separately during the same session: "How much do you like to play with this person at school?" and "How much do you like to work with this person at school?" The children used a rating scale consisting of five points from 1—"I don't like to" to 5—"I like to a lot." Based on these results, children who were rated as low-accepted children became the participants in the study. The children were then randomly assigned to one of three groups: coaching, peer pairing, or control. The coaching group included instructions from an adult in social skills for friendship making; playing games with peers to practice social skills; and a postplay review session with the coach. In the peer-pairing group, isolated children played the same games with the same peers but did not receive instruction or review. In the control group, isolated children were taken out of the classroom with the same peers but did not interact or receive verbal instruction or review. To measure the effectiveness of the intervention, the researchers used the sociometric measure previously described and a "best friends" peer-nomination inventory in which children were asked to name one, two, or three of their best friends in the classroom. The overall results of the research found that the coaching procedure was effective in increasing isolated children's peer acceptance. In particular, the coaching group showed significant increases on the play sociometric rating from pretest to posttest when compared with the peer-pairing and control group. Also impressive in this research was the finding that the coaching group continued to make gains far above the other two groups at a one-year follow-up. With regard to friendship nominations, the results found that the coaching group did increase the number of best-friend nominations, but this gain was not enough to produce statistical significance. The researchers point out that this measure would not be expected to show large differences since many children are unlikely to substitute a recently trained child for a long-standing friend. This study points to the potential for enhancing children's peer relationships when a direct intervention is implemented for isolated children.

Implications for Practice: Assessing Friendship Skills

The absence of friendships may increase the risk of psychiatric disorder; conversely, having friendships may provide protective factors against stress. Social workers must consider a child's friendship patterns when making assessments of children. As we have seen, a child with poor peer relationships is more likely to have problems throughout his or her development. The following semistructured interview was developed to assess friendship capabilities in children (Goodyer, 1990):

1. Do you have friends near your home?
2. Do you have friends at school?
3. Do you play out with friends or see them in the evening?
4. Do friends come and see you at your house?
5. Do you go to friends' houses?
6. Do you have a special friend or person whom you can share a secret with?
7. Do you belong to a team, club, or gang?
8. When something troubles or worries you, do you talk to anyone about it?
9. Are your friends the same age as you?
10. How long do you usually keep your friends?

Helping children develop friendship skills and get along with one another is critical for their successful socialization. The following Focus on Research section examines interventions designed to reduce prejudice in children.

Can We Reduce Prejudice in Children?

The development of prejudice in children is a serious concern among parents, teachers, and mental health professionals. Is there a way that we could help reduce prejudice in children? This is exactly the question two researchers, Katz and Zalk (1978), sought to answer in their study. The study compared four different ways to reduce the racially biased attitudes of white second- and fifth-grade children. Children who participated in the study were selected on the basis of having scored high on tests of prejudice. These children were then randomly assigned to one of four groups: (1) increased positive racial contact—children worked on interracial teams to solve a puzzle and were praised for their work; (2) vicarious interracial contact—children were told a story about a sympathetic and resourceful African American child; (3) reinforcement of the color black—children were reinforced every time they chose a picture of a black animal instead of a white one; (4) perceptual differentiation—children were shown slides of an African American woman whose appearance and name were varied and, the children were then tested to see how well they remembered the names and different appearances; and (5) a control group where no intervention took place. Two weeks following the experiment, the researchers measured the children's prejudice again. Children who participated in any of the four experimental groups showed less prejudice than did the children in the control group. The researchers found that different techniques can be effective in changing children's prejudice level.

School Influences

School is a major socialization agent for our children. Children begin school by age 6 and spend five hours every weekday interacting with teacher and peers in ways that will affect their social and emotional development. When most of us think of schools, we think of the three Rs—reading, writing, and arithmetic. However, schools go far beyond academic basics. Children must learn to conform to the rules set forth in their school, respond to teacher demands, interact successfully with age-mates, and manage their day-to-day responsibilities. Schools often invite such opportunities as ganging up on our peers, involvement in drugs, and new experiences with sex. Clearly, schools have a major responsibility in the proper socialization of children.

Designing More Effective Schools   Research on the effects of different schools has produced some evidence that we can do a much better job at designing good and effective schools. Rutter and others (1979) gathered extensive data from schools on such factors as achievement tests, attendance records, and classroom behavior and found that schools differ in effectiveness. Students in the "better" schools attended school more regularly, exhibited fewer behavior problems, and made better academic progress than did students from the less effective schools. Particularly interesting was the finding that the initially poor students who attended the "better" schools scored just as high on the measure of academic progress as did the initially good students who attended the least-effective schools. Schools can and do make a difference in students' successes.

Perhaps surprising to many was the finding that many traditional measures of a good school did not enhance the school's effectiveness. Not important were factors such as monetary support, size of the school, staff-pupil ratios, or quality of the buildings.

What does make for a good school? Most important to a school's effectiveness is the atmosphere of the school and its quality as a social institution (Rutter et al., 1979). Rutter (1983) summarizes what to emphasize in designing a more effective school: academic emphasis, where students focus on clear academic goals, are regularly assigned homework, and receive teacher feedback; classroom management, where there are clear expectations and students receive clear and unambiguous feedback about their academic performance; discipline, where schools enforce rules on the spot but do not resort to corporal punishment or other forms of physical sanctions, which appear to create a negative unproductive atmosphere; and staff organization and teacher morale, where the school staff work together as a team and teachers believe they have a say in school policies and decision mak-

ing. Getting students motivated to learn appears critical as Rutter (1983, p. 23) concluded in his review that "good pupil outcomes were [nearly always] dependent on pupils *wanting* to participate in the educational process."

Teacher Expectations   One of the most famous educational research studies documented the well-known influence of teacher expectations on student performance. Rosenthal and Jacobson (1968) gave a group of students an IQ test and convinced their teachers that this test could predict which students would rapidly develop in intellectual growth. Teachers were then given the names of students who were likely to show such bursts of intellectual growth. In reality, the teachers had been given the names of ordinary students who were chosen at random. When the researchers retested these children, the "brightest" students showed significantly greater gains in IQ and reading achievement than did other students in the class. The impact of the teacher expectations was incredible—their expectations became self-fulfilling prophecies.

Other research studies (see Harris & Rosenthal, 1985) have found similar results; therefore, it is clear that teachers can transmit their expectations in ways that either promote learning or discourage it. Yet, it is not well understood how teachers communicate such messages. Chaikin and his associates (1974) studied how teachers and students interact nonverbally. They found that teachers interact with students perceived as bright with more smiling, leaning toward the student, head nodding, and greater eye contact than they do with students perceived as ordinary or inferior.

Self-Expectations and School Performance   Although the influence of teacher expectations has been considered important for a long time, more recent concern has focused on students' self-expectations (Lefrancois, 1989). Research by Dweck (1986) examined students who could be classified as either mastery oriented, likely to attribute their successes to ability and effort; or helplessness oriented, likely to attribute their failures to luck or the difficulty of the task—causes that they have no personal control over. Studies that have looked at the differences between these two types of students have found that mastery students are confident in their performances on various tasks, whereas helpless students see themselves as helpless, lack confidence in their abilities, and think they will likely confront failure in the future (Diener & Dweck, 1980). In one study (Dweck & Reppucci, 1973), the helpless children gave up after a single failure, although they had both the ability and the motivation to perform on subsequent tasks.

Although many children have **learned helplessness,** research has demonstrated that these children can be taught to attribute their failures to insufficient effort rather than a lack of ability. This affects their sense of *self-efficacy,* and they learn to persist in spite of a failure.

Disadvantaged Children and the Public School System The public school system is a middle-class institution, and as a result, it can have a negative impact on disadvantaged children. Shaffer (1989) outlines three barriers that low-income and minority students face in the school system: low parental expectations in school performance, lack of culturally relevant educational materials, and low teacher expectations for school performance.

Academic expectations may be quite different when we compare middle-class parents with low-income and minority parents. Whereas middle-class parents put value on the idea of "getting ahead," parents of disadvantaged children are often more concerned with "staying out of trouble." These varying expectations are likely to influence the academic behavior of children—working hard to get ahead or working just enough to get by. Sometimes the influence from disadvantaged parents is inadvertent; they simply participate less in school activities, and their children place less value on school as a result. It is important to recognize that when parents of disadvantaged children do get involved and expect good school performance from their children, their children are likely to do well (Hess & Holloway, 1984). Social workers should keep in mind that parental involvement and interest in their child's school performance can make a difference.

The "relevance" of school material can also be a barrier that low-income and minority children must face. Imagine reading only stories about well-to-do white children when you are African American and live in a low-income neighborhood. The stories might not be of much interest because they lack any cultural relevance. One study that examined this issue found that Hispanic

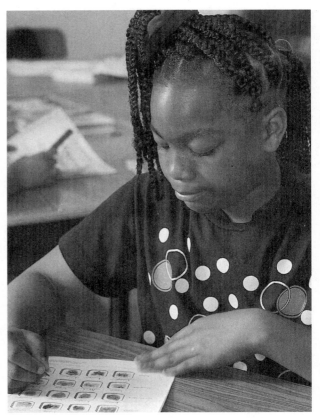

In the public school system, low-income African American students can face significant barriers, including low parental and teacher expectations regarding school performance and lack of culturally relevant educational materials.

Americans (who spoke only English) scored far below Anglo classmates in reading proficiency. The reading material dealt mostly with middle-class interests and values and was not culturally relevant. However, these same Hispanic American students performed much better in comparison with white students on mathematical ability—where there is less culturally oriented material. Our schools need to do a better job at providing minority students with culturally relevant material.

Earlier we presented information about the importance of teacher expectations. This can be a critical barrier to academic success if teachers hold negative expectations about low-income and minority children. Unfortunately, it appears that teachers do have lower expectations for children from low-income families (Minuchin & Shapiro, 1983). A common practice in many schools is to advance students to the next grade regardless of their accomplishments. This may represent teachers' negative expectations that these children are not going to do well anyway. According to Shaffer (1989) such "social promotions" may perpetuate social inequality by depriving children of the opportunity to acquire needed academic skills.

Implications for Practice: Enhancing School-Community Relationships

Social workers, in particular school social workers, often have the opportunity to influence the way in which school systems, teachers, and school officials interact with community members. One goal of a school social worker working in a low-income community might be to reduce barriers, like those just described, that low-income and families of color confront. The social worker could act as a consultant to the school system and work with teachers to help them encourage better performance from minority students, work with families to help them get more involved in school activities and have more of a say in school materials, or work with school officials in an attempt to examine their school policies, such as "social promotions," to evaluate whether they truly benefit the children involved.

Often the primary role of the school social worker is to enhance school-community relations. Constable (1983) describes some of the remedial tasks school social workers are likely to perform in addressing school-community relations:

- Identify children or target groups of children needing alternative educational planning or programs and support services.
- Consult and collaborate with community representatives to identify the effects of interacting school/community/pupil characteristics and develop resources to meet needs of child or target group.
- Collaborate with community agencies in the development of alternative education programs and support services.

- Clarify and interpret specific roles and responsibilities of the community in promoting school attendance.
- Set objectives, monitor progress, and measure outcomes of service.

School social workers are often a vital link between the community and the school. Often the child and his or her family need specialized services from other agencies — for example, health services, counseling, and respite care. School pupils also are sometimes involved in other major socialization agencies, such as the juvenile justice system or the child welfare system. The school social worker must interact with community agencies in efforts to provide for needed planning (Constable, 1983).

The School and Public Law 94-142 One of the most significant changes in schools was the adoption and implementation of Public Law (PL) 94-142, the Education for All Handicapped Act. This law has been referred to as a "bill of rights for the handicapped" because it established the right to a free, appropriate, public education for all "handicapped" children aged 3 through 21.

Children falling under the provisions of this law are evaluated according to a multidisciplinary team. The team develops their objectives, and together with special education and related services, each child receives a written Individualized Educational Plan (IEP). This law guarantees children the right to special education and related services, including any service that helps the child benefit from special education. Services that are recommended in the IEP must be provided to the child and his or her family at no cost. Of particular interest to social workers is the fact that seriously emotionally disturbed children fall under the category of disabled.

This law has provided, in essence, a legal mandate for school social work services. School social workers find themselves quite involved in the development and coordination of the Individualized Educational Plan required for every student (Timberlake, Sabatino, & Hooper, 1982). The multiple tasks required of the school social worker point to the importance of understanding the school environment and its influence on children's development. Indeed, it is critical to understand the school as a social organization. School social workers often must act as change agents within the

Public Law 94-142 and other developments in education have contributed to the mainstreaming of children with physical disabilities and developmental disabilities in the schools.

school, working toward organizational change to meet the needs of the students they serve.

Multicultural and Gender Considerations

Imagine a child who turns on the TV Sunday morning and becomes engrossed in a TV series. He or she begins to identify with one of the characters on the show and imagines being that person. However, the characters in this TV program are all white. Suddenly, one day the child is not really sure he or she can be like this person, and begins to realize that many people will consider him or her an outsider. The child is African American, un-like the character in the TV program. The pervasive and subtle effects of racism are beginning to be felt in the everyday life of this child.

By middle childhood, racial identity is beginning to be formed. Children begin to think about who they are in terms of similar peer groups, their appearance, and their aspirations. How is the development of a child's self-concept affected by a society that portrays negative meanings about being African American? Do these children as a consequence develop feelings of self-doubt, inferiority, and low self-esteem? Many social scientists believe this may not be an adequate explanation. Indeed, research has found that the self-esteem of African American children is not significantly lower than that of white children—in fact it is higher (Rosenberg & Simmons, 1971). Researchers have suggested several explanations for this observation. African American children may develop their sense of self-esteem within an African American culture. Their identity is developed from an African American perspective. In situations where the African American child must confront an almost all-white school, his self-perceptions may take into account the idea that society is racist and irrational rather than developing an attitude of self-blame (Rosenberg & Simmons, 1971).

During middle childhood, parents can no longer protect their children from the hostility caused by prejudice because of a child's color, appearance, attitudes, ethnic background, or neighborhood. However, parents and teachers can accentuate the child's strengths and abilities. In their study of ghetto children, Silverstein and Krate (1975) observed African American and white children from Harlem as remarkably self-reliant and independent. These children clearly grew up fast and developed functional characteristics to help them adapt to many of the hardships in life. Unfortunately, many teachers rarely recognize these abilities as strengths. Still, much progress has been made by parents, teachers, and others who recognize the strengths evident in all children. The benefits are clear: Children's identity and self-esteem can be strengthened by providing them with a sense of belonging and reassurance about their difference (Rapalje, Degelman, & Ashburn, 1986). Their differences need to be associated with positive attributes, not with the societal projections that attribute different with "bad" or "less worthy."

Primary Prevention for Traumatized Khmer Children

In an innovative program to resettle Khmer refugee children in Tacoma, Washington, Duncan and Kang (cited in Williams & Berry, 1991) describe a creative and culturally sensitive treatment program. These children lived through the Pol Pot atrocities in Cambodia and were forced from their families when they arrived by themselves in Tacoma. They experienced trauma and loss that included the separation from families without the resolution of grief and loss. In addition, these children experienced serious acculturative stress. Post-traumatic symptoms emerged soon after their arrival and included sleep disturbances, nightmares involving family members, and disturbing visits of spirits, including parents and grandparents.

The primary prevention program included three Theravada Buddhist ceremonies and rituals to honor the children's dead family. These included *Ban Skol*, a memorial for absent family members; *Pratchun Ban*, an annual family reunion of living and deceased relatives, and religious observances for absent family members that took place during the Khmer New Year's celebration. Also included was special consultation with Khmer Buddhist spiritual leaders. Last, the program included placements in ethnically similar foster homes.

The Ban Skol ceremony was a joint effort between the foster parents and the social service agency that was held at the child's foster home. A special meal was provided to the monks, family, guests, and agency staff. The child prepared a list of the family members and was instructed to burn it and to douse the ashes slowly with water. This symbolic cremation was prepared for those children who had witnessed dead bodies that were simply left to rot, and the refugee child was the primary focus of the ceremony. This ritual was intended to provide protective functions to the child. As Williams and Berry (1991, p. 637) point out, "through the process of the ceremony, the child was able to begin seeing the foster family, their friends, and the agency's caseworkers as sources of support."

During the ceremony, many of the children were either withdrawn or overcome with feelings of loss and grief. This allowed the foster family and others to console the children and offer support. There were anecdotal reports after the ceremony of decreased sleep problems, fewer spirit visits, increased bonding with the foster family, and greater grief resolution.

Source: Adapted from Williams & Berry, 1991.

Sex Roles in Middle Childhood

During middle childhood, girls and boys begin to learn about their different roles. With increasing expectations about what a boy or girl should think or do, children at this age must begin to incorporate such information into their self-concept. Middle childhood begins to have a significant impact on children's **sex-typed behavior**. Sex-typed behavior is the developmental process by which culturally assigned values and behaviors are considered appropriate for members of that sex.

With their increased ability to understand other people's expectations of themselves, children, especially boys, begin to show some changes in sex-typed behavior. The behavior and attitudes of boys become increasingly masculine oriented. However, girls at this age do not show a corresponding change toward femininity; in fact, they have a preference for masculine interests and activities (Richardson & Simpson, 1982). (Remember, this tendency began in the preschool years.) For example, in examining the Christmas wish list of boys and girls, Richardon and Simpson (1982) found that most requests were sex-typed but that more girls than boys asked for "opposite sex" items. What can account for this tendency for girls to show interest in masculine-oriented behavior? Shaffer (1993) suggests three possible reasons: (1) girls are becoming increasingly aware that masculine behavior is more valued, (2) girls are allowed more permission to engage in cross-sex play when compared with boys, and (3) masculine games may simply be more fun because they are action oriented as opposed to the more passive activities of playing with dolls and doll houses.

Children at this age also begin to develop **sex-role stereotypes**. Sex-role stereotypes reflect how we categorize people according to our general impressions of what we consider "male" and "female." What do you consider to be the major differences between men and women? Do you believe that women are more submissive, passive, less competitive, more home oriented, less adventurous, or less confident? Do you believe that men are more aggressive, more objective, more active, more competitive, or more direct? The ideas you have about such differences between men and women reflect your stereotypes. In previous chapters, we pointed out that sex differences exist from birth and are noticeable through the preschool years. However, disagreement exists about whether these differences result from biology or from socialization. In other words, how much of the early difference between sexes is due to genes and how much due to sex-role stereotyping? What are the true differences between men and women?

A famous review of over 1500 studies by Maccoby and Jacklin (1974) attempted to set the record straight. The results are surprising, because most of us have grown up with many myths about gender differences that reinforce our sex-role stereotypes. The results found only four gender-related differences:

1. Females have greater verbal ability.
2. Males have better visual/spatial ability.
3. Males have better mathematical skills.
4. Males are more aggressive.

Our myths about gender differences are quite strong, but as stated earlier, only four differences can be accounted for. The following list describes some of the more common myths about gender differences that you should review and consider changing. If you find these ideas difficult to believe, then you know firsthand how difficult it can be to change stereotypes.

Boys are more active than girls.
Girls are more suggestible than boys.
Boys are more competitive than girls.
Girls are more sensitive than boys.
Boys are more dominant than girls.
Girls are more social than boys.

One of the reasons it is hard for us to change our views about gender myths is because sex-role stereotyp-

ing begins at a very early age. Recall the study by Haugh, Hoffman, and Cowan (1980) in which 3- and 5-year-olds watched a film with two babies playing, one identified as male and one as female. When asked to point to the baby that was "smart," the children almost always chose whichever one had been labeled a boy.

We learn to develop such stereotypes at home and at school. Parents often have very different expectations of boys than of girls. In addition to reinforcing gender stereotypes, we are learning how parents can even affect their sons' and daughters' attributions about their academic achievements. Not surprisingly, one study (Parsons, Adler, & Kaczala, 1982) found that parents expect their sons to do better in math than their girls. However, these attitudes also affected their children's own assessments of their math abilities and their belief that they can be successful in the future. In other words, children's beliefs about their own math abilities were better reflected by their parents' beliefs in their math potential than by their own past experiences in math. A child's academic self-concept is strongly influenced by his or her parents' stereotyped notions about that child's academic potential. Add this type of influence to findings in the classroom that show teachers praise a boy's ability when he is successful but praise a girl's neatness and effort when she is successful (Dweck, Davidson, Nelson, & Enna, 1978), and you can see why we have a long way to go before changes occur in our sex-role stereotypes.

Social Hazards

The experience of childhood takes place in a social context—in the neighborhood and community where the child lives. The neighborhood is perhaps most critical to the middle child in molding the child's experiences and shaping how the child adjusts to the social world. The neighborhood opens up an important arena for exploration and social interaction and contributes to the child's physical and social development (Garbarino, Galambos, Plantz, & Kostelny, 1992). As the child moves beyond the boundaries of the front yard, the child is impacted by who is in the neighborhood and how safe the neighborhood is. Consider the multitude of neighborhood factors that contribute to the child's development—neighborhood safety, available health and social services, recreational activities, quality of the local schools, the surrounding economic conditions—all are influences in the lives of children.

The notion of a "community" becomes increasingly critical to the child's healthy development. The nature and types of social interactions available influence the quality of life for families. Consider the difference between the types of social interactions that occur in a housing project in Chicago and in an upper-income suburb in Chicago. As you can see, consideration of the social hazards alerts us to how the community affects the development of the child. Indeed, studies have shown that when a community's economy is negatively affected, there is an increase in rates of domestic violence (Straus, Gelles, & Steinmetz, 1980). Families that exist in high-risk neighborhoods and communities must face a large number of stresses. As the number of stresses increase, the available support for the family becomes eroded. This loss of support is often related to family disruption such as divorce.

Marital Conflict and Divorce

Marital conflict and divorce constitute major impediments to the adjustment of children of all ages. Divorce rates of about 50% reflect increased societal acceptance of divorce. Nearly 1 million children will experience divorce each year. By the year 2000, 1 out of 4 children will live in stepfamilies. Half of all children will live in single-parent families for some part of their childhood (Jaffe, 1991).

In this section, we will focus on the experience of divorce from the child's point of view. Although we tend to think of divorce as occurring at a fixed point in time, for the child and family, the reality of divorce looks and feels more like a succession of painful experiences (Hetherington, 1989; Wallerstein & Blakeslee, 1989). In fact, Kalter (1987; 1990) proposed that children experience a series of stressors when their parents divorce. The stressors outlined by Kalter and Schreier (1994, p. 308), in order of significance, are described in Table 8.6. In the presence of such extreme stressors, children's energy is diverted from their own needs to worries about security, safety, and survival for themselves and their loved ones.

Wallerstein (1988) describes three stages of divorce, all of which affect children's ability to focus on their developmental tasks. The *acute phase* is characterized by parental fighting, conflict, anger, depression, and the actual separation, which is often not mutual. This phase extends from months to over a year and is particularly difficult for children because they witness arguments and must live amidst household instability and parental neglect. Parents do not often consider the effects of their behavior on their children when they are embroiled in a heated, prolonged battle. During this phase, children usually bear the brunt of poor parenting, although the quality generally improves after a year (Hetherington, Cox, & Cox, 1982).

The second phase is described as the *transitional phase*, in which parents and children try to adjust to their new life in a restructured family. The transitional phase usually lasts several years before the family settles into new roles and routines. In the third phase, the *stabilizing phase*, the family has typically adapted to the shifts in roles and allegiances. An optimal level of functioning is regained, and the family has moved on to tackle new changes. Not every family experiences each of these stages, however. Individual family members will vary in the level of functioning they achieve postdivorce.

Divorce is especially taxing on children because it disrupts one of the core relationships in their lives and dissolves the family structure they depend on for secure development (Wallerstein & Blakeslee, 1989). More often than not, children of divorce face adjustment issues throughout the course of their lives. As is true of the divorce process, the stresses evoked by divorce are not time-limited and will resurface in different forms as children develop. Although research has cited marital conflict as contributing more to children's distress than the actual divorce (Long & Forehand, 1987), many factors have been identified as determinants of children's adjustment (Kalter, Kloner, Schreier, & Okla, 1989). These factors include the personality and temperament of the child, the quality of the parent-child relationship pre- and postdivorce, stability of the custodial parent's household, financial security, and the postdivorce relationship between the ex-spouses (Hetherington, 1989; Wallerstein, 1988).

For all children, regardless of age or gender, the loss of a parent dredges up feelings of insecurity, loss of self-worth, loss of love and feeling lovable, anxiety, loneliness, anger, resentment, guilt, fear of abandonment, depression, and helplessness (Wallerstein & Blakeslee, 1989). To compound these painful feelings, children face issues of relocation to new homes and schools; ma-

TABLE 8.6   Stressors That Occur with Divorce

Life Changes	Consequent Effects on Children
Hostilities between parents	Sadness, anger, loyalty conflicts
Distraught custodial parent	Anxiety, put in roles of parent, co-parent to custodial parent
Loss of relationship with noncustodial parent	Self-blame, low self-esteem, depression
Parent dating	Competitive feelings with parent's new partner, fear of loss of parent's affections, curiosity (for older children) about parent's sexuality
Remarriage	Sharing parents, accepting parents' intimacy, forming relationships with stepparents and stepsiblings, accepting new parent as authority, resolving issues of loyalty to new stepparent and parent of same gender
Poverty, associated	Downward economic mobility, emotional stresses, changes in residence, loss of peer relationships and familiar school environment, change in consistent caregivers

ternal employment; custodial parents who are themselves under stress, impatient, and overburdened; disorganization and unpredictability in daily events such as meals and bedtime; and difficulties in school performance and peer relationships. Unfortunately, just when children need their parents the most, parents are compromised in their ability to attend to their children effectively (Wallerstein & Blakeslee, 1989).

So how do children fare when marital conflict and divorce become part of their life history? The age of the child at the time of divorce influences short- and long-term adjustment. Younger children initially suffer more fear because they are more dependent on their parents and are more limited cognitively in their ability to understand the reasons for divorce; they tend to blame themselves. Because they are working on separation issues during the early childhood years, fears of abandonment become heightened with the reality of divorce (Hetherington, 1989). Wallerstein (1988) found that young children's adjustment tended to worsen during the year and a half following the divorce and continued to be poor even after five years. This was especially true

for boys, who were more aggressive and disruptive at home and at school. Young children's development rests more completely on the quality of care in the home. Consequently, they suffer more than older children when the quality is diminished. Older children possess a larger coping repertoire with direct access to more resources than do younger children, which can buffer them from the initial hardships imposed by divorce (Cicchetti & Schneider-Rosen, 1986).

However, younger children tend to have better long-term prognoses for adjustment when assessed ten years later. This finding may be due to their limited recollection of specific traumatic events and consequent fears and their inability to incorporate the experience into their belief systems (Masten et al., 1991). Interestingly, children who were young at the time of the divorce fantasized about their parents reuniting even ten years after the divorce. These children reported feelings of sadness over the loss of their family and worries about future relationships and commitments, especially with the opposite sex. Younger children reported feeling more hopeful about relationships than did their older siblings. Adolescent girls reported the most anxiety (Wallerstein, Corbin, & Lewis, 1989).

Differences in adjustment outcome for boys and girls have also been noted and depend, to a large extent, on the sex of the custodial parent. Overall, girls tend to fare better following divorce than do boys. Most girls tend to adapt faster and better to divorce with the exception of those who mature early at puberty. These girls were found to be less compliant, more argumentative, have lowered self-esteem and more problems in heterosexual relationships than on-time and late-maturing girls (Hetherington, 1988). Boys who resided with mothers who never remarried tended to experience the hardest adjustment from preschool through adolescence. Generally, children living with custodial parents of the same sex demonstrated increased self-esteem, social competencies, independence, security, and maturity (Santrock & Warshak, 1986).

These findings may be attributed to the fact that most children reside in the custody of their mothers and are provided with role models and sources of support. Some hold beliefs that sons need fathers more than girls do. In truth, girls may find role models in their mothers and learn relationship skills from them that boys need to learn from fathers. These findings may also reflect the difficulty many single mothers of teenage boys confront when disciplining and controlling their sons. The power structure embedded in many cultures within our society places more value and autonomy on males compared with females. As a result, mothers have little authority over their sons, and daughters have fewer rebellious aspirations. In addition, many studies of divorce do not employ a control group. This limitation constrains conclusions we can draw about children of divorce compared with children of intact families. We cannot rule out that children from nondivorced families experience some of the same adjustment problems as do children of divorced families (Demo & Acock, 1988).

Implications for Practice: Smoothing the Aftermath of a Divorce

Sigelman and Shaffer (1991) identify five factors that can help smooth the path in the aftermath of a divorce:

1. *Adequate financial support.* Research studies confirm the notion that families do much better in adjusting to divorce when their finances are not seriously depleted (Menaghan & Lieberman, 1986). The challenge is helping single-parent households retain a reasonable amount of financial support. Social policy experts have been helping through their work to encourage states to pursue noncustodial parents who do not pay their child support.

2. *Adequate parenting by the custodial parent.* Because parents are under increased stress and pressure, their parenting usually becomes less effective. However, if parents can be supported in these stressful times and encouraged to continue a relationship based on warmth and consistent discipline, their children will be less likely to experience problems (Kline, Tschann, Johnston, & Wallerstein, 1989).

3. *Emotional support from the noncustodial parent.* One serious consequence of many divorces is the intense hostility and anger that the spouses feel and express. As a result, children suffer feeling insecure, being torn between each parent, and are more likely to experience behavior problems (Kline et al., 1989). Also, many children lose contact with their noncustodial parent. In fact, about a third of the children lose contact with their fathers (Seltzer & Bianchi, 1988). Research suggests that regular contact with supportive fathers can help children adjust to the divorce, particularly sons (Rosen, 1979). When children have supportive relationships with both parents and there is an effort to reduce the conflict between parents, they are more likely to make a positive adjustment to a single-parent household.

4. *Additional social support.* Social support also plays an important role in helping both parents and children adjust to the negative effects of divorce. Parents who have close friends are less depressed (Menaghan & Lieberman, 1986). Children who participate in divorce groups have an opportunity to share their feelings and learn positive coping skills (Pedro-Carrol & Cowen, 1985). Another interesting finding is that adolescents in single-parent homes commit fewer delinquent acts when a relative helps with the child-rearing and supervision (Dornbusch et al., 1985). Helping a family find social support can buffer the effects of the divorce.

5. *A minimum of additional stressors.* The divorcing family may face many new changes—lower income, moves to new neighborhoods, legal battles, and extended family complications. Not surprisingly, the ability to cope successfully with the divorce can be facilitated by reducing the amount of stress (Buehler, Hogan, Robinson, & Levy, 1985).

Many factors influence how a family reacts to a divorce. The five factors just described are a beginning

APPLYING THE FRAMEWORK

Attention Deficit Hyperactivity Disorder

Developmental History

Tommy is a 7-year-old African American child who was referred to the Child Guidance Clinic by his teacher. Tommy's mother, Ms. Paul, reports that Tommy's birth was not planned and that Tommy's father was not pleased about her pregnancy. She was upset that Tommy's father did not want the child and concerned about what would happen. Ms. Paul reported that she was in labor for a very long time and that she was given Demerol during the birth process. Complications in pregnancy were mostly a result of her failure to dilate properly.

Ms. Paul noted that Tommy developed "normally" and began walking and talking at developmentally appropriate times. She noted that at about age 5 Tommy became much more difficult to manage. She began getting complaints about his behavior at school.

Biophysical Considerations

At about age 5, Tommy developed problems with his eye muscles. He received optometric treatment for about a year. Ms. Paul reports that she had a very difficult time getting him to do his required eye exercises. Tommy stopped receiving treatment last year when Ms. Paul changed jobs and lost her health insurance.

Psychological Considerations

Cognitive Development and Information Processing

Tommy has difficulties with information processing. In particular, his attention span is exceedingly short. This has led to his diagnosis of **Attention deficit hyperactivity disorder** (ADHD). Teacher reports indicate that constant supervision is required to keep Tommy from bothering the other children. Also, his teachers state that he "cannot sit still" and that he "cannot concentrate." Tommy's school performance has gotten much worse over the last year. His teacher reports that he is at least one full school year behind. Achievement tests suggest this is true, but that his poor performance may be due to his impulsivity.

The parent interview supported similar conclusions. Ms. Paul has difficulty managing him because he is "all over the place." She also indicated that his judgment is lacking. He will apparently do things that disturb other children and not be aware he is offending them. She says that he does not come in from play when he is supposed to and that she cannot get him to take responsibility around the house. Ms. Paul completed a Child Behavior Checklist (see Focus on Assessment: Empirical Assessment—The Achenbach Child Behavior Checklist), and Tommy received an "often true" or "sometimes true" rating in 9 of the 11 items that assess hyperactivity. The items included point for thinking about how to help families who must face this crisis. Sigelman and Shaffer (1991, p. 465) remind us of how these factors demonstrate that "the family is a social system embedded in larger social systems. Mother, father, and children will all influence each other's adjustment to divorce, and the family's experience will also depend on its interactions with the surrounding world."

Attention Deficit Hyperactivity Disorder

the following: can't concentrate, can't pay attention long, can't sit still, confused, daydreams, destroys his own things, impulsive or acts without thinking, poor school work, and prefers playing with younger children. Tommy scored well above the clinical cutoff score for hyperactivity.

Tommy was referred for a psychological evaluation, and the psychologist noted that Tommy could not maintain his attention, although he did stay in his seat. During an IQ task, Tommy gave up quite quickly, making the assessment difficult. He also had difficulty maintaining his focus in conversations with the psychologist.

The Wechsler Intelligence Scale for Children-III (WISC-III) indicated that Tommy's overall intelligence is in the average range (FSIQ = 98), with similar verbal (VIQ = 101) and performance ability (PIQ = 99). Tommy's achievement scores show he is slightly below average for his age.

Communication

Ms. Paul reports that Tommy can communicate appropriately for his age. She complains that at times Tommy can become a "motormouth" and will not stop after repeated requests for him to do so. Although Tommy has difficulty getting along with peers, he does appear to be able to communicate with them in an age-appropriate manner.

In the clinical child interview, Tommy spoke clearly and loudly to the social worker. Although his language appeared normal, Tommy had difficulty completing his thoughts when responding to questions.

Attitudes and Emotions

Ms. Paul describes Tommy as an unhappy child who has many social problems and gets angry easily. She says that Tommy does have difficulty "controlling his emotions." Ms. Paul reports that Tommy had numerous temper tantrums when he was younger and that he has problems with his anger. As an example, she described a recent incident when Tommy got angry and began throwing his toys against the wall. Ms. Paul noted that it took her at least 20 minutes to get Tommy under control. Ms. Paul reports that Tommy does not easily admit to feelings of sadness; however, he does get into crying spells that last for a long time. She reports no specific fears, saying that at times he appears "fearless." Ms. Paul believes that Tommy is very upset over his father's leaving the family, although he never wants to talk about it. She feels that much of Tommy's current difficulties stem from her divorce.

In the interview with Tommy, he denied feeling lonely or being sad about anything in his life. When asked if he was sad that his parents were no longer together, he said, "They just want to go off and be by themselves." He agreed that sometimes his anger (continued)

Attention Deficit Hyperactivity Disorder

(continued) gets him into trouble. "I can really get mad," he said with some pride. Tommy reported that he did have difficulty in school and that he was "bad at school most of the time." He also did not see himself as able to please his mother at home: "I don't do what she wants me to do." When asked about games and sports, Tommy said, "I am sometimes the best on the team." In general, in many of the domains in Tommy's life, he sees himself as "bad" or "unsuccessful," which is affecting his sense of self-esteem. Themes in the semistructured interview indicated problems with anger, low self-confidence, poor peer relationships, and a lack of interest in school.

Social Cognition and Regulation

Ms. Paul reports that Tommy does not have good judgment. Often it appears that Tommy does not think through the consequences of his actions. On several occasions, Tommy has been excessively cruel to their pet dog. Ms. Paul has consistently tried to explain to Tommy that it is wrong to inflict pain on the dog, yet Tommy does not refrain from being cruel toward the dog. Ms. Paul also reports that Tommy has difficulty getting along with peers partly because he sees them as mean and always bugging him. Tommy has a difficult time having successful long-term interactions with his peers.

Tommy does not appear to have reciprocal friendships. For example, he does not know anything specific about his best friend's likes or dislikes. When asked "what is a friend?" Tommy stated, "When you are over at someone's house playing with their things." In the interview with Tommy, he recounted an incident that occurred between himself and a neighborhood boy. Tommy was asked how his actions might have made the other boy feel. Tommy could not identify the feeling the other boy would have been likely to have. Tommy's social knowledge of others and his sensitivity to other people's feelings is apparently not well developed.

With regard to adaptive and self-help skills, Tommy seems to have no difficulties. Tommy functions well in terms of daily living skills—he feeds himself, brushes his teeth, and cares for his health. Ms. Paul states that sometimes Tommy has difficulty going to sleep at bedtime and has difficulty getting up in the mornings.

In the semistructured interview, Tommy was presented with a conflicted social situation and asked how he would resolve the problem. He generated two impulsive solutions and could identify only a few of the consequences associated with his solutions. In a role-playing situation that could easily incite a fight, Tommy was asked what he would say or do. His response showed he lacks the skills needed to avoid situations likely to lead to conflict.

On the social competence measure of the Child Behavior Checklist, Tommy scored within the normal range on the activities scale but above the clinical cutoff point on the social and school scales.

Social Considerations

Family Situation

Ms. Paul and Tommy live together in a low-income African American neighborhood. Ms. Paul and Tommy's father divorced two years ago. Tommy is an only child. Tommy sees his father about every two weeks. Ms. Paul states that she believes Tommy and his father have a good relationship. Ms. Paul characterized her marriage before the divorce as always in a conflict or fight over something. She reports that Mr. Paul was not abusive toward her or Tommy. Currently, Mr. Paul is contributing

Attention Deficit Hyperactivity Disorder

money toward child support, although sometimes his payments are late.

Ms. Paul recently got a new job as a sales clerk. She reports that she is happy with her new job and that she has been in good spirits lately. Ms. Paul reports frequent episodes of depression in the past. She has never been hospitalized or received treatment for depression. Although Ms. Paul is involved with her extended family, she states she feels lonely and without close friends. Ms. Paul states she loves to cook and enjoys having others over for dinner. Weekends are often spent with the relatives, fishing, or other planned activities.

Ms. Paul sees Tommy's problems as a result of his poor adjustment to the divorce. She thinks Tommy may be "hyperactive" but is not sure and does not want to put Tommy on "any drugs." Although she has problems with his behavior at home, she believes the school has not really worked with Tommy to help him. Ms. Paul made it very clear that she is not happy with Tommy's school and how it has treated him. She has become increasingly concerned about her ability to manage Tommy. She feels "completely exhausted at having to deal with him after work" and complains of extreme tiredness.

Ms. Paul and Tommy spend a lot of time with Tommy's grandparents. Ms. Paul's mother has "pitched in and helped a lot." Ms. Paul says she doesn't know what she would do without her. However, Tommy's grandfather is a concern. Ms. Paul reports that he has a long-term drinking problem and that she does not like to see Tommy around him when he has been drinking. Although she has discussed this many times with her parents, her father continues to sometimes drink when Tommy is around.

When Tommy was asked to do a family drawing, he stated, "I don't have a whole family." Tommy drew a picture of his mother cooking and him watching TV. He then drew a solid black line and drew a picture of his father. He stated that he and his father don't get to watch TV much.

Groups, Social Supports, and Contexts

Ms. Paul describes Tommy as not well liked by his peers, although he does have a few good friends. She believes Tommy's aggressive behavior affects his ability to get along well with peers. Tommy was rated above the clinical cutoff for aggressive on the Child Behavior Checklist. Ms. Paul noted the following items were of concern: aggressive, brags, cruel to others, demands attention, destroys others' things, disobeys at home, disobeys at school, poor peer relationships, impulsive, shows off, excess talk, teases, temper, and loud. Teacher reports confirm Tommy's difficulty with aggressive behavior.

Ms. Paul and Tommy interact with several social institutions that are of significance. As already noted, Ms. Paul is concerned about Tommy's school. She has gone to a number of teacher conferences, and each time she has felt that the school is unresponsive to her. She believes the school teacher is angry because she has not put Tommy on any medication for his hyperactivity. Ms. Paul perceives the school as too large to respond effectively to the needs of the students. Ms. Paul describes Tommy's class as unstructured and too large for one teacher to handle. She also believes that the expectations of students there are extremely low because of where the school is located. Tommy's school is in a low-income neighborhood and is well known for having many social problems. Drug abuse is not uncommon.

Ms. Paul and Tommy regularly go to church. Ms. Paul states this is a very important part of her life. She sees a few of her friends there but wishes she could spend more time getting to know others in the church.

(continued)

Attention Deficit Hyperactivity Disorder

(continued)

Ms. Paul would like to bring better role models into Tommy's life. She is concerned that he will never have a chance at a decent life unless he sees the success some people can attain. Ms. Paul has friends, but without child care she cannot afford to spend much time away from Tommy.

Multicultural and Gender Considerations

Ms. Paul and Tommy live in an old house that is badly in need of repair in a poor, urban African American neighborhood. Ms. Paul reports that much of the paint inside and outside of the house is cracked and peeling. The paint could be lead-based and might account for Tommy's hyperactive behavior (recent research has found a relationship between high lead levels and attention deficit hyperactivity disorder).

Many of Tommy's peers in the neighborhood have already had associations with the law due to drug use and vandalism. This leaves very few male peer models for Tommy. Ms. Paul is concerned about his lack of "appropriate friends and acquaintances." Much of Tommy's free time appears to be spent playing aggressive sports or watching violent TV shows. Ms. Paul reports she does not monitor the type of TV programs Tommy watches. Ms. Paul feels many of the types of activities and games Tommy plays contribute to his problems because there are no "normal recreational activities for him to play in the neighborhood."

Although Ms. Paul and Tommy live in a primarily African American neighborhood, Ms. Paul is concerned about Tommy's experiences of prejudice and discrimination. There have been long-standing conflicts between several of the ethnic groups in the nearby neighborhoods. Tommy has been in a number of fights that have occurred because of racial issues. Ms. Paul is also angry that Tommy's school is underfunded and that the teachers have such low expectations of the students.

FOCUS ON ASSESSMENT

Empirical Assessment—The Achenbach Child Behavior Checklist

An empirical approach to assessment gathers systematic ratings of children from significant others, parents, teachers, or practitioners. One well-known approach to empirical assessment is the Child Behavior Checklist devel-oped by Thomas Achenbach. The Child Behavior Checklist is a standardized rating scale that is typically filled out by parents and teachers. It examines behavior across a number of domains or syndromes, such as depressed, obsessive compulsive, social withdrawal, aggressive, and so forth. The items include statements such as "Can't concentrate," "Can't pay attention for long," and "Disobedient at home." The parent circles 2 if the item is very true or often true; 1 if the item is somewhat true or sometimes true; 0 if the item is not true.

The checklist is scored on the Child Behavior Profile (see Figure 8.5). Each of the syndromes of the profile (e.g., anxious/depressed, aggressive behavior) were

Attention Deficit Hyperactivity Disorder

Ms. Paul and Tommy have limited access to a number of needed resources. Although Ms. Paul has a full-time job, the minimal pay has not allowed her to receive needed health care for Tommy. Their house is crowded, and the peeling paint may be a significant health hazard. Ms. Paul's income level does not allow her to adequately meet her and Tommy's needs. Mr. Paul's late and inconsistent child support payments make budget planning difficult.

Summary and Impressions

Tommy has several problems that have become evident from the assessment:

1. Impulsive and overactive behavior—apparently attention deficit hyperactivity disorder
2. Aggressive behavior—possibly conduct disorder
3. Poor school progress
4. Poor peer relationships and lack of social skills

Additional difficulties include the following:

5. Inadequate health care for Tommy
6. Inadequate and possibly unhealthful living environment
7. Inadequate recreational opportunities
8. Lack of role models

Ms. Paul and Tommy do have a number of personal strengths and resources. Ms. Paul is clearly concerned and motivated to do her best in providing for Tommy. She displays caring and concern over his difficulties. Ms. Paul has successfully provided for Tommy, to the best of her ability. She is perceived as an intelligent, hardworking person who has a lot of concern for others. Ms. Paul has better-than-average parenting skills. Tommy continues to have a successful relationship with his father following his parents' divorce. Ms. Paul also has some social support—especially from the extended family. She is involved in her church and continues to maintain a number of friendships.

developed through extensive research (see Achenbach, McConaughy, & Howell, 1987). To score the profile, the 1s and 2s under the syndrome are summed to obtain a total score. This score is then charted on the profile. For example, on the profile for Jenny, there were several 1s and 2s under the withdrawn syndrome. When these scores are summed, Jenny receives a score of 8 which is entered as the total on the bottom of the profile and then charted. The Child Behavior Checklist is normed, which means you can compare scores against the scores obtained from a normal population of children. For example, Jenny's score of 8 on the social withdrawal scale is around the 98th percentile (normal range is marked on the left of the profile, and the dotted line represents the upper boundary of normal). This means that a score of 8 on the social withdrawn scale is higher than the scores obtained by 98% of the 4- to 18-year-old girls in the normative sample.

The behavior profile for Jenny led to the following observations: Jenny's mother completed the Child Behavior Checklist during her intake visit to the Child Guidance Clinic. Two of the scales from the Child Behavior Checklist suggest problems: social withdrawn, anxious/depressed. The anxious/depressed scale showed scores on all of the items. A score of 2 was listed on four items: lonely, worthless, sad, and worries. The social withdrawn scale had

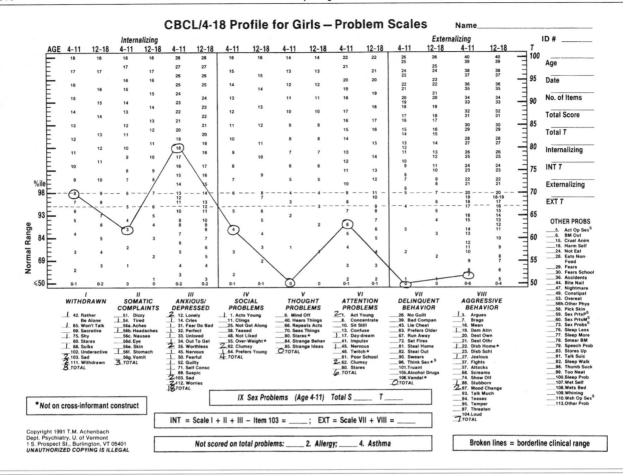

FIGURE 8.5 Revised Child Behavior Profile   Source: Achenbach, 1991.

scores on six items: rather be alone, won't talk, shy, sulks, sad, and withdrawn. These results suggest some serious problems for Jenny, especially in the areas of depression and social withdrawal. The practitioner would want to seek additional information (teacher reports, observations, clinical interviews) to corroborate these results before reaching any conclusions (Achenbach & Edelbrock, 1991).

Chapter Summary

Developmental Themes

As children end their preschool years, they begin to learn new skills and competencies. Middle childhood represents a stage of "industry," which means "to build." Children are building skills by playing games and are making large gains in their intellectual functioning. Successful adaptation to peer groups is a major developmental task.

Biophysical Dimension

Biophysical Growth and Development

In middle childhood, boys and girls exhibit a slow but consistent growth pattern. Girls retain their fat tissue longer than boys do; boys develop muscle tissue more quickly. Continued development in the large and small muscles enhances the child's coordination, agility, and smoothness. Sports become popular as boys and girls enjoy climbing, throwing, swimming, skating, and in-line skating. Boys have greater motor development, and girls are better than boys at fine motor skills.

Biophysical Hazards

Environmental conditions can affect the child's health and development. Poverty and a lack of food can be very damaging. Impoverished conditions can lead to such problems as cretinism and rickets.

Psychological Dimension

Information Processing

Children at this age operate from concrete operational thought; that is, thought processes are governed by rules of logic. This stage is characterized by becoming less egocentric. Children can show reversible thought and conservation skills. For example, they understand that certain transformations do not change the quantitative features of objects. Although Piaget's ideas have withstood the test of time, it is now recognized that cognitive changes do not proceed according to predetermined sequences of stages. As a result, *levels* is a better conceptual notion than *stages*. Information processing is also relevant to a child's social relationships. Research has found that skill deficits in how children process information may influence their behavioral interactions. Children's intelligence is often measured with an IQ test. IQ is measured by dividing mental age by chronological age and multiplying by 100. The Stanford-Binet is a widely used IQ test that has four areas: verbal reasoning, quantitative reasoning, abstract/visual reasoning, and short-term memory. Other similar tests used with children include the Wechsler tests and the Kaufman Assessment Battery for children. Concerns with the use of IQ tests include the labeling and classification of children and whether the tests are culturally biased.

Communication

Middle childhood is considered a period of linguistic refinement. As children develop their language skills, they become capable of metalinguistic awareness and appreciate humor in jokes, riddles, and puns. Children who are deaf learn language in much the same manner as hearing children. As communication becomes increasingly important for the social life of children, deficits in communication have social consequances. For example, speech disorders like stuttering can lead to academic as well as emotional difficulties.

Children's verbal control develops as children move from external control to covert self-verbalizations. Self-instructional training is a major treatment approach for children who have difficulties with self-control. Bilingual children can have both positive and negative outcomes, depending on how the two languages are used. A child's language abilities can be influenced by cultural experiences. Disadvantaged children have a restricted vocabulary and construct sentences that are less grammatically correct when compared with sentences of middle-class students.

Attitudes and Emotions

Conceptions of self extend to include such things as ideal self, ethnic awareness, and conscience development, and a more differentiated self-concept emerges. This self view is less global and more specific to who the child is as a unique being. One measure of children's self-concept is the Perceived Competence Scale for

Children. Research has found that children's evaluations of themselves are pretty much the way other people perceive them.

Social Cognition and Regulation

Social role taking is the reduction of egocentric thought—egocentric thoughts being children's inability to de-center the focus of their conceptual efforts. Role-taking ability—to see things from another person's perspective—changes around 12 years of age when a child can think about himself or herself and social relations become more advanced. A child's interpersonal awareness can be ordered along a developmental continuum, and concepts such as friendship and peer groups can be viewed as a series of steps through which children progress. How children think and reason about such concepts can influence their adjustment. Children may benefit from training, like pair therapy, that helps facilitate such reasoning.

Psychological Hazards

Childhood disorders can be divided into two categories: externalizing problems of overcontrol and internalizing problems of undercontrol. ADHD, an externalizing disorder, is a common disorder that affects a child's attention and activity level. Medication is commonly used to treat this disorder.

Social Dimension

Families, Groups, Support Systems and Contexts

By the time a child reaches late childhood, he or she is spending much less time with parents and more time with peers. Still, the family provides children with a safe, authoritative structure that children need. Discipline continues to be critical for good parenting. Three major parental disciplinary strategies are power-assertive discipline, love withdrawal, and induction. Parent training is recommended by social workers for families that are having problems. Four approaches to parent training include parent-effectiveness training, parent-involvement training, behavior modification, and systematic training for effective parenting. Children begin to have an increasing preference for spending time with their peers. They begin to form peer groups, which are often referred to as cliques. The process of group formation can have important implications for peer cooperation and respect and peer conflict and/or discrimination. Children who are rejected by their peers are at risk for adjustment problems. The importance of friendships and positive peer relationships has been uncovered by several studies. Friendships may provide for unique learning of critical social skills. Children who are rejected by their peers can be taught the social skills needed for friendship making. Schools are a major socializing agent. Effective schools can be differentiated from less effective schools on the basis of their atmosphere and quality as a social institution. Teacher expectations and a child's self-expectations can influence school performance. Schools have not made very many accommodations for disadvantaged students. School social workers must sometimes act as advocates in school-community relationships. For example, Public Law 94-142, the "bill of rights for the handicapped," or people with disabilities is a case in point.

Multicultural and Gender Considerations

By middle childhood, racial identity is beginning to form. The effects of racism can influence a child's sense of identity. Sex-typed behavior begins at this age. Children also begin to develop sex-role stereotypes. Although there are many stereotypes about differences between the sexes, one review study found only four gender differences.

Social Hazards

As with early childhood, in middle childhood divorce is a significant social hazard. Divorce leads most families into a period of crisis and reorganization.

KEY TERMS

attention deficit hyperactivity
  disorder (ADHD)
bilingual
conservation
cretinism
Das-Luria model of cognitive functioning
externalizing problems
induction
intelligence quotient

intention-cue detection
internalizing problems
learned helplessness
love withdrawal
mental age
metacognition
metalinguistic awareness
peer groups
power assertive discipline
readiness

reversibility
rickets
role-taking ability
sex-role stereotype
sex-typed behavior
social cognition
uninformative messages
verbal control

9

Adolescence

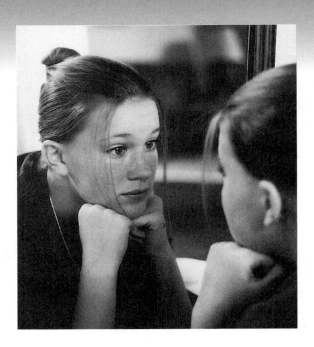

Developmental Themes

Biophysical Dimension
    Biophysical Growth and Development
    Biophysical Hazards

Psychological Dimension
    Cognitive Development and Information Processing
    Communication
    Attitudes and Emotions

    Social Cognition and Regulation
    Psychological Hazards

Social Dimension
    Families, Groups, Support Systems, and Contexts
    Multicultural and Gender Considerations
    Social Hazards

Applying the Framework:
    A Depressed Adolescent

Developmental Themes

On a beautiful spring evening in San Francisco, I stood at the intersection of Sutter and Polk streets, a cheerful, crowded jumble of boutiques and bookstores, head shops and bead shops, restaurants, and bars. The corner was thronged with students and tourists, straights and gays, and bunches of teenagers leaning against the window of a pizza shop. They wore uniforms and insignia of their various tribes: leather-clad punks, California surfers, Eastern preppies, suburban gypsies, and born-again hippies. Boys and girls laughed and joked together, jostled and pushed one another with the rough physical affection with which kids treat their friends and fellow tribespeople. (Hersch, 1990, p. 19)

America's adolescents attract a lot of attention in their exuberance to establish an identity. Adolescence represents the journey of discovery—Who am I? How am I different from others? What do I want to do with my life? Erikson's theory of adolescent identity recognized this almost universal phenomenon.

But what is life like for today's adolescents? Our society offers a wealth of opportunities for young people to explore their place in society—modern technology has brought endless hours of watching MTV, Internet connections to the world, better physical health, and improved education. Yet, young people must also face head-on the ills that modern society brings with it—AIDS, violence, exposure to alcohol and drug abuse, bombardment of media images, and hopelessness.

In spite of our changing society, the tasks adolescents face have remained stable. In essence, they must carve out their place in the world. And many of the problems young people face are not with the youth themselves but a result of reduced opportunities and a neglect of support from a caring adult (Santrock, 1990).

Adolescence is typically defined as the period of growth beginning about 10–12 years of age and ending around 21–22 years of age. Researchers studying adolescent development believe it is important to consider adolescence in terms of early and late periods. Early adolescence begins around ages 10–15 and is characterized by important physical changes and significant cognitive and social changes (see Box 9.1). In particular, early adolescents place great importance on peer approval. Late adolescence begins around the ages of 16–18 and continues up to approximately 22 years of age. During late adolescence, two developmental tasks are considered important: independence from the family and the development of personal identity. Erikson refers to this stage as one of identity versus identity confusion.

Adolescence is a period when young people become concerned about their physical appearance. In addition, they are concerned about how other people perceive how they look. They become aware of the fact that their bodies are developing—girls will have their first menstrual cycle, and boys may have their first wet dream.

Biophysical Dimension

Biophysical Growth and Development

Boys and girls at this stage of development both experience what is referred to as an adolescent growth spurt, where there are rapid gains in height and weight. However, the growth spurt occurs two years earlier for girls than for boys. The growth spurt for girls begins at about age 10 and lasts for about two years. For boys, it begins at age 12 and also lasts about two years.

There is considerable individual variability, so girls could begin the growth spurt as early as 7 and boys as early as 9. Adolescents gain weight following the same timetable as the rate at which they gain height.

The Pubertal Process

Biologically, adolescence begins with the onset of the pubertal process. This process defines sexual maturity or the capacity to make babies. **Puberty** is identified by the combination of the growth spurt, maturation of physiological mechanisms, and the development of secondary sex characteristics, such as pubic hair and breasts (Adams & Gullotta, 1989). Although menstruation is one indication of puberty for girls, there is no clear indication for boys. Wet dreams and facial hair can indicate puberty in boys, but they may go unnoticed. Table 9.1 summarizes the changes that take place for both boys and girls in the pubertal period.

The onset of puberty for girls has been getting earlier since it was first recorded in the 1800s. In particular, records from Norway in the 1840s show **menarche,** the first menstruation, occurred at age 17, whereas today it occurs at age 13. In the United States, the average age for menarche has declined to 12.45 years of age. This dramatic change in the age of menarche has decreased an average of four months every ten years for the past century. Why are girls prepared for childbirth at an earlier age today? Although there are no clear answers, most experts believe the earlier onset is a result of a better standard of living, medical advances, and improved nutrition. The following Focus on Multiculturalism section examines how the Apache ceremony honors the changing woman.

The Apache Ceremony of the Changing Woman

When an Apache girl reaches childbearing years, she is honored with a traditional ceremony of the changing woman. This ceremony comes from the Apache goddess White Painted Woman, who declared this event significant in the lives of the people: "Let all the people come together. Let them eat and dance and have a good time. The Masked Dancers will come forth at night and then the People will dance with each other, side by side and face to face."

The four-day ceremony is one of the tribe's most private ceremonies. In preparation, the father sends announcements to friends and family. The girl undergoes instruction from an attendant who guides the maiden in proper behavior. A special dressmaker constructs the clothes based on the original garments worn by the White Painted Woman. The garments are dyed pollen yellow, a symbol of fertility. Food is made and gathered to accommodate all the guests.

The ceremony begins in the morning with the washing of the maiden's hair with yucca roots. The attendant gives traditional advice (Mildred & Hooper, 1993, p. 64):

> Be happy so your people may be happy. Don't talk too much or you'll always be a talker. Don't be cross or you'll always be a nag. Don't laugh too much or your face will wrinkle soon. Don't allow water to touch your lips, or the skies will weep and everybody will not have a good time. Don't think bad thoughts or you'll have evil to the end of your days.

BOX 9.1

Developmental Changes of Early Adolescence

Puberty	Adult appearance and size	School	Changing school structure and format
	Reproductive capacity	Parents	Parental responses to adult size of adolescent
	Timing (especially if off-time)		
	Internal endocrine changes		Sexual stimulation of newly pubertal child
	Asynchrony (among body parts, among adolescents		Implications for parent's aging
Cognition	Capacity for abstract thought		Impending separation
Peer groups	Conformity	Society	Hope and expectations for youth
	Pressure to try new experiences		Occupational choices and opportunities

Source: Petersen, Kennedy, & Sullivan, 1991.

TABLE 9.1   Physical Changes of the Pubertal Period

Step	Females	Both Sexes	Males
1		Apocrine gland development	
2	Increased diameter of internal pelvis	Pelvic changes	Thickening and strengthening of bone structure
3	Growth of ovaries and uterus	Growth in gonads	Growth of testes and scrotum
4		Breast enlargement	
5		Appearance of pubic hair	
6	Growth of labia and vagina	Growth of external genitalia	Growth of penis
7	Menarche	External puberty	Nocturnal emissions
8		Axillary hair	
9	Oogenesis, ovulation	True puberty	Spermatogenesis, sperm in urine and semen
10	Broadening of hips	Broadening of body frame; vocal changes throughout	Broadening of shoulders

Source: Schuster & Ashburn, 1992, p. 499.

The White Painted Woman's holy home, or wickiup, is made of four spruce poles that are lashed together. The maiden enters her home and is now the personification of White Painted Woman. She now has supernatural powers. She lies down on deerskin and is massaged to become supple and possess good health. The shaman and special dancers perform rituals. As the sun rises, the woman faces east and the shaman paints her face with white clay, using an eagle feather. She becomes "White Painted Woman" and is again painted with pollen and runs in four directions. As she leaves the wickiup for the last time, it is pulled down and pushed to the east. Favors are tossed to the children, and her parents can now accept marriage proposals.

Source: Mildred & Hooper, 1993.

Hormonal Changes in Adolescence

During adolescence, the **endocrine glands** produce **hormones** that create different bodily changes in the young person. Table 9.1 outlines the physical changes that take place in males, in females, and in both sexes. Hormones are powerful chemical substances that regulate various organs in the body. The endocrine glands that secrete the sex hormones are the pituitary gland and the sex glands, or gonads, referred to as testes in the male and ovaries in the female. The pituitary gland, or master gland, regulates a number of the other glands. Control of the pituitary gland rests with the **hypothalamus,** which "instructs" the pituitary gland on the optimum level of hormone secretion. The hormones secreted by the pituitary gland are known as **gonadotropins,** and they activate the **testes** and **ovaries,** which are the parts of the endocrine system called the gonads. The gonads secrete hormones; **androgen** from the testes, and **estrogen** from the ovaries. These hormones have an important effect on puberty in adolescence. Their effect is gradual as the hormones are gradually secreted, and the child moves toward physical and sexual maturity. The hormonal changes take place about a year before changes in the body and sex organs are visible (Daniel, 1983).

Implications for Practice: Physical Changes and Psychological Consequences

Physical changes have psychological consequences for developing boys and girls. With girls, menarche is associated with greater social maturity, improved status among peers, higher self-esteem, greater self-awareness regarding one's body, and increased self-consciousness (Brooks-Gunn, 1986; Petersen, 1987). These psychological reactions are convincingly described in this diary entry of Anne Frank (1952):

> I think what is happening to me is so wonderful, and not only what can be seen on my body, but all that is taking place inside. I never discuss myself or any of these things with anybody; that is why I have to talk to myself about them.
>
> Each time I have a period—and that has only been three times—I have the feeling that in spite of all the pain, unpleasantness, and nastiness, I have a sweet secret, and that is why, although it is nothing but a nuisance to me in a way, I always long for the time that I shall feel that secret within me again.

However, puberty can be related to both positive and negative emotions. In one study (Petersen, 1987), an early-maturing girl exclaimed, "I tried to hide it. I was embarrassed and ashamed." A study by Brooks-Gunn and Ruble (1983) found that an equal percentage of the girls had positive emotions about menarche, negative emotions, mixed emotions, or neutral emotions. One factor that influences whether a girl's reaction will be positive or negative is early or late maturation.

Studies have found that, in general, it is better to be an early-maturing rather than a late-maturing boy. Research has found that the early-maturing boys perceived themselves more positively, had more successful peer relationships, and were more confident when compared with late-maturing boys (Petersen, 1987; Simmons & Blyth, 1987). For girls, early maturation seems to have mixed effects. Early-maturing girls (maturity defined as onset of menstruation) did not do as well academically and were more likely to have behavior problems. However, early maturity was an advantage in terms of independence and opposite-sex relationships. Early development was initially related to a positive body image, but this pattern was reversed when the girls entered the

ninth grade. This may be due to the fact that early-maturing girls are shorter and stockier, whereas late-maturing girls are often taller and thinner.

These studies clearly demonstrate that the physical changes that take place in boys' and girls' bodies can lead to positive or negative reactions. An explanation for many of the negative reactions is that the young people were not prepared for the changes they were experiencing (Brooks-Gunn & Ruble, 1983). Most girls describe their first period as "a little upsetting." Although girls often receive some preparation, boys receive little or no preparation for their experiences of nocturnal emissions and spontaneous erections. What can be done to better prepare young people for these impending changes in their bodies? Better information from sex education programs or from parents could be helpful in creating a more positive adjustment for adolescents. A cross-cultural perspective indicates that for girls menarche is a sign of womanhood (Weideger, 1976); therefore, it is surprising that in the United States we do not treat a girl's first menses as a **rite of passage**. A ritualized recognition may be beneficial in helping young persons experience their bodily change as positive (Adams & Gullotta, 1989). Consider the ritual one girl reported in her family's reaction to her period (Shipman, 1968):

> When I discovered it, I called my mother and she showed me what to do. Then she did something I'll never forget. She told me to come with her and went to the living room to tell my father. She just looked at me and then at him and said, "Well, your little girl is a young lady now." My dad gave me a hug and congratulated me, and I felt grown up and proud that I really was a lady at last. That was one of the most exciting days of my life. I was so excited and happy. (pp. 6–7)

Although puberty clearly has an impact on adolescent development, many researchers are concluding that the effect is not as strong as it was once believed to be (Brooks-Gunn & Warren, 1985; Petersen, 1987). Looking at this period within the overall framework of the life cycle, it clearly has an impact; but so do other facets of the life cycle. Puberty may be no different. For some young people it is a significant stress, but for most it is not. New challenges result from the biological changes, but there are also cognitive, social, and environmental changes to be dealt with. Biological change may not be the single source of significant change we once thought it was.

Biophysical Hazards

Although adolescence is typically a period of good general health, it is also the beginning of some potentially serious health concerns. In particular, many adolescents experience problems with nutritional needs and eating habits, weight concerns, dysmenorrhea, acne, and headaches.

Nutritional Needs and Eating Habits

A familiar sight is the hungry teenager wolfing down a burger, fries, and a large shake. Adolescents need to increase their calorie intake to match their rate of growth. Their calorie intake can be so enormous that it often angers parents who have to provide the food they need. An adolescent male who is involved in sports may need as many as 6000 calories in one day (Schuster & Ashburn, 1992). Given this large need for food intake, a critical question is whether the adolescent is getting his or her nutritional needs met. Often, adolescents do not get the proper nutritional diet. They frequently miss a meal, usually breakfast, and may fill up on high-energy snacks rather than eating a proper meal. In fact, it is estimated that up to one-third of a young person's calories come from snack foods (Marrale, Shipman, & Rhodes, 1986). Although adolescents may get the calories they need, it is not uncommon for them to be lacking in the proper amount of fluid, protein, iron, and calcium.

Adolescents should have enough protein to comprise 12% to 16% of their total daily energy intake (Schuster & Ashburn, 1992). Adequate calcium intake is also a concern. Boys may not get enough calcium during periods of rapid skeletal growth, and girls, when weight-conscious, may unknowingly reduce their calcium intake. Also, overconsumption of soft drinks may interfere with obtaining enough calcium. Studies have found caffeine and sugar in a soda can cause a 30-mg calcium loss 3 hours after consumption (Marrale, Shipman, & Rhodes, 1986). The female adolescent's iron levels may be low from blood loss during her menses. An iron supplement is often recommended.

Weight Concerns

Obesity can be a serious problem for adolescents. **Obesity** can be defined as a body weight of 20% or more above the recommended weight for one's height. It is a serious health problem that is associated with certain diseases, high blood pressure, and social and psychological problems. In adolescence, obesity is a serious social problem because of the name-calling, stigma, and rejection from peers that many young people receive. Many children prior to adolescence develop extra fat in response to the adolescent growth spurt. Once additional cells are formed, they may predispose the person toward obesity (Schuster & Ashburn, 1992).

Dysmenorrhea

Dysmenorrhea is the experience of painful menstruation. It occurs in approximately 33% of adolescent females once ovulation occurs (Schuster & Ashburn, 1992). Dysmenorrhea is experienced as spasmodic uterine or lower abdominal and back pain during the first 12 to 24 hours of the menstrual flow. Dysmenorrhea is probably due to contraction of the smooth muscles and lack of oxygen of the uterine muscles (Schuster & Ashburn, 1992). It often disappears either after the female reaches 24 years of age, when the uterus is completely mature, or after the birth of a baby.

Acne

A common problem in adolescence is acne, occuring in more than 80% of adolescents. Acne is the result of increased androgen levels at puberty, which stimulate the production of sebum by the sebaceous glands of the body, usually the face. Most adolescents start to experience a decline in acne sometime after their twentieth birthday. Acne is associated with genetic predisposition, but it is also related to accumulated oils in the body. Acne can be a concern because it can lead to scarring of the tissue and can create embarrassment and social withdrawal. In recent years, antibiotics have been used to greatly control the spread of acne.

Headache

By the time people reach adolescence, they most likely have experienced a headache. In fact, headaches can begin to occur with some frequency—29% of boys and

32% of girls have at least one headache per month during adolescence (Linet, Stewart, Celentano, Ziegler, & Sprecher, 1989). Approximately 5% of boys and girls experience migraine headaches during adolescence.

Psychological Dimension
Cognitive Development and Information Processing

Cognitive development in adolescence is identified with Piaget's last intellectual stage—formal operations. This period of development generally begins at around age 11 or 12. At this stage of development, the adolescent is capable of abstract thought; prior to this stage, the child could use only **concrete thinking.** Now a whole new world is opened up within the adolescent's mind— flexible and abstract thinking. Adolescents begin to understand abstract propositions and try to reason logically about them. This kind of logical problem solving is referred to as **hypothetical-deductive reasoning.** This problem-solving process uses hunches, or hypotheses, to solve a problem and follows a planned manner to test and evaluate the hypotheses until the best solution is discovered.

In fact, adolescents may begin to ponder the nature of their own thinking. They can think about why they were thinking about certain things. This kind of abstract thinking is also associated with idealism and thoughts about future possibilities.

Why do adolescents often concern themselves with such things as future life plans, their internal life, or developing their own ideology? Piaget (1972) would argue that this thinking is caused by the characteristics of formal operational thought. It is the nature of this thought that leads adolescents to ponder about such thoughts. They can now think beyond the real to the possible and reflect on the nature of thought itself. For example, an adolescent girl might think, "What would it be like if Jack and I were married?" "I shouldn't think about Jack that way; I should think about what I want from him now."

Formal operational thought is believed to occur in two distinct stages during adolescence. The first stage is characterized by a focus on the ideal, with unlimited possibilities. This stage is referred to as assimilation, in which the adolescent consolidates new information into existing knowledge. During middle adolescence, a better balance is obtained through the process of accommodation; the adolescent must adjust to the cognitive changes that have occurred. As adolescents gain experience, they incorporate their formal operational thinking (Lapsley, 1989). Table 9.2 presents a summary of the five major changes that occur with formal operational thinking (Keating, 1980).

Although Piaget's theory emphasizes a universal understanding of thought, it is important to recognize the individual variations that occur in adolescents' cognitive development. For example, research by Strahan (1983) found that only 1 out of 3 eighth-grade students is capable of formal operational thinking. A critical factor in such thinking is the adolescent's experience and knowledge in certain areas (Flavell, 1985). In this manner, children and adolescents gradually build up knowledge through experience and practice in different areas (Santrock, 1990).

FOCUS ON MULTICULTURALISM

Racial Differences and Intellectual Ability

Block and Moore (1986) conducted a study using the Armed Services Vocational Aptitude Battery, which is a measure of intellectual potential. Items from the test are based on general knowledge and information and problem-solving abilities. The test involved over 12,000 male and female adolescents from a national sample. The data provide a good comparison among the three largest sociocultural groups in the United States: Whites, African Americans, and Hispanics. The results found considerable differences across the three adolescent racial groups; however, the minority adolescents scored, on the average, lower than the majority adolescents. When socioeconomic status was controlled for, more similar results were discovered. The authors present a

TABLE 9.2 Examples of Formal Operations and Logic in Adolescence

Major Changes in Thinking	Examples
Thinking about possibilities	"I would like to get to know her even better—she could be a good friend, or I might decide she'd be good as a girlfriend. We like each other. We can work out a closer relationship."
Testing hypotheses	"She told me she wasn't interested in being my girlfriend. After that I thought girls just don't like me, that I'm not good-enough looking or cool enough. But I've had other girlfriends and other girls have shown interest in me. Not all girls are going to like me—I just need to find the right girl for me."
Thinking about the future	"I have a girlfriend now, and we get along really well, but if we stay together, I won't know what it's like to be with other girls. In order to marry the best person, it seems like you need to have a lot of girlfriends."
Thinking about thoughts	"I keep thinking about how much other people like me. Am I really popular with other kids? But even if I'm not that popular, I've got a lot of good friends. I shouldn't worry so much about whether I'm popular and just keep the good friends I have."
Expansion of thought	"I was invited to a party, but my best friend, Tyler, wasn't. John, who's giving the party, doesn't like Tyler. If I tell Tyler, then he'll be mad at John—and John told me not to let him know. But if Tyler asks me, I don't want to lie to him. I don't know if I should keep my promise to John and lie to Tyler."

community-norm theory to explain any of the observed differences. They believe that critical to understanding differences is the observation that schools are part of a local community or ecological system. Community standards set a limit on what schools can achieve. Block and Moore (1986, p. 175) state:

> Children whose horizons are limited respond primarily to the norms of the community in which they play their part. These norms determine most of their speech, conduct, interests, aspirations, and motivations. The average effect of such determinants of behavior can be greatly different in communities that, for historical reasons, have been separated from the majority culture by barriers of communication and cultural interchange for many generations.

The differences observed between the different groups can be understood by the different local norms that influence performance.

Communication

Along with an improvement in thinking abilities in adolescence comes a greater capacity for effective communication. The manner of a person's thinking is logically related to his or her ability to use language. For example, the use of metaphors increases during this time period. To understand metaphors, one must think beyond concrete operations; therefore, fables or parables are not of interest to elementary school children (Elkind, 1976). Metaphors refer to a comparison of two ideas, such as "he has a heart of stone."

Also of particular interest in adolescence is the use of satire or ridicule (Santrock, 1990). Adolescents typically invent satirical labels for teachers, parents, and peers. For example, peers may be better known by such labels as "klutz," "brain," or "Mr. Heavy Metal" than by their real names.

Writing becomes much more meaningful in adolescence. Indeed, this is the age when many young people begin a journal to record their inner thoughts and personal experiences. Younger children have difficulty writing because they do not have the type of logical thought processes needed to organize their ideas. Adolescents are able to accentuate the important points they are trying to communicate because they can think logically about what they want to say before they write it down.

During adolescence, the nature of boys' talk and girls' talk begins to become increasingly differentiated, as described by one adolescent boy (Eckert, 1990, p. 91):

> I think girls must talk too much, you know, they—they—talk constantly between themselves and about every little thing. Guys, I don't think we talk about that much. (*What kinds of things do you talk about?*) Not much. Girls . . . cars, or parties, you know. I think girls talk about, you know, every little relationship, every little thing that's ever happened, you know.

In general, it appears that boys talk more in terms of competitive conversation, comparing knowledge and experience, whereas girls talk more about themselves, their personal feelings, and their relationships.

Attitudes and Emotions

Adolescence is an important period for the developing self-concept. Young people set out to discover "who they are" and "what they want to become." A significant part of this process results from a focus on self-reflection and thought. And indeed there is much for the young adolescent to think about. Adolescents obtain greater freedom in behavior and decision making, increased opportunities for both acceptance and rejection by peer groups, experience in dating and the awareness of their sexuality, and major decisions affecting their movement into adult life. As these experiences are explored and reflected upon, the adolescent develops a more integrated self.

The founder of developmental psychology, G. Stanley Hall, is well-known for his characterization of adolescence as a time of "storm and stress." In her writings, Anna Freud argued that such storm and stress is simply a part of normal adolescence. Psychoanalyst Peter Blos also believed that adolescence was a period of uncontrolled sexual and aggressive impulses. However, these early notions about the craziness of the teenage years is now considered a myth. Experts in adolescent psychology (see, for example, Adelson, Douvan, Offer, and Bandura) are increasingly concerned because the widespread idea that adolescence is a normal period of serious difficulty has mischaracterized the lives of millions of healthy adolescents. Daniel Offer, an adolescent psychiatrist, brought attention to this myth when he declared a "Defense of Adolescence." Although it is diffi-

cult for many people to believe, research has empirically supported the fact that the majority of adolescents are well-adjusted, get along well with peers and parents, and cope well with their emotional processes and external environments.

Adolescent Self-Esteem

What does research on adolescent self-esteem tell us about adjustment in adolescence? In general, we find that self-esteem can vary depending on the stage of adolescence. It is during early adolescence (age 12 to 14 years) that self-esteem appears to be at its lowest point (Simmons, Rosenberg, & Rosenberg, 1973). During these years, young people are highly self-conscious, and their self-perceptions are more easily influenced. This is especially true of girls making the transition to junior high school. The lowest self-esteem occurred among girls who had matured early and had started to date. Also interesting is that the change from junior to senior high school is not associated with a similar drop in self-esteem. It is important to emphasize that, overall, most adolescents emerge from this developmental phase with about the same amount of self-esteem as they had at the outset (Dusek & Flaherty, 1981). The following Focus on Multiculturalism section discusses African American adolescents' sense of self-esteem.

One interesting study attempted to examine the emotional life of adolescents during their daily life. Researchers Csikszentmihalyi and Larson (1984) asked 75 adolescents to wear electronic pagers for one week. When they were signaled, about every two hours, they completed a log about where they were, how they felt, and what they were experiencing. One conclusion derived from the study was that adolescents experience a remarkable amount of diversity. They may be a student, a helper, an employee, a commuter, a child, a teammate, a friend, and more. Also remarkable is that the average adolescent can come down from extreme happiness or up from extreme sadness within 45 minutes.

This is in contrast with adults, who often take hours to change from one mood to the next. The researchers suggest that adolescents must learn to come to terms with the downs as well as the ups. Instead of allowing the down to completely overtake them, they need to strive for greater balance and perspective. Many of the youth, in response to boredom, became involved in less produc-

In early adolescence, young people who are self-conscious can easily develop negative self-perceptions. These self-perceptions sometimes lead to depression, a common problem in adolescence.

tive and less satisfying activities like watching television. However, youth who took up more challenging activities learned the positive feelings of personal fulfillment that can result from such challenges.

FOCUS ON MULTICULTURALISM

Do African American Adolescents Have Low Self-Esteem?

Although growing up as an African American adolescent might suggest low self-esteem when compared with majority white youth, such a finding is complex and not clear-cut. During the period of school desegregation, it was believed that African American children suffered damage to their self-esteem because they were in segregated schools. However, research that examined this issue found there are no differences in self-esteem between African American children in segregated and desegregated schools (Cook, 1979). Adolescents of color do experience greater discrimination, poverty, and social

and educational barriers than white youth do, and as a result, we can predict more negative outcomes for African American adolescents. However, as Gibbs (1990) points out, social workers must be careful about over-pathologizing and stereotyping all African American youth as victims of their racial identity or social class status. The majority of African American youth cope effectively with their ethnicity and social class status. Furthermore, research has found no differences in self-esteem between nonclinical samples of African American youth and white youth (Gibbs, 1985; Rosenberg & Simmons, 1971). Chestang (1980) suggests there is a dichotomy between "personal identity" and "racial identity." Self-esteem is more related to the various characteristics the adolescent subscribes to the self. Such things as physical attractiveness, peer popularity, and pride in identification with a religious or racial group have a strong influence on self-esteem.

Implications for Practice: Enhancing Adolescents' Self-Concept

Adolescents can improve their self-concept so that it moves closer to their ideal self. Many young people need to challenge the realism of their ideal self. Is it realistic to hope for such high standards? Many adolescents begin the process of insisting on irrational standards of behavior. These "shoulds" and "musts" can take the place of recognizing actual accomplishments. Adolescents who are taught to recall positive thoughts and feelings about past events show an increase in self-esteem (Anderson & Williams, 1985).

Adolescents can be guided to emphasize the areas in which they are more likely to succeed. A less physically coordinated young person can become more skilled in playing a musical instrument or in playing a game that requires more intellectual skills. Assertiveness-training studies with young people have found results that show an increase in self-esteem (Stake, DeVille, & Rennell, 1983). Sometimes adolescents need to work harder at achieving their standards of excellence or to accept a good as opposed to a perfect performance (Schuster & Ashburn, 1992).

Self-esteem is also related to other factors such as peer group formation. One study found that self-esteem was improved by participation in community and school experiences (Brennan, 1985). Such experiences through participation can enhance an adolescent's self-esteem.

Social Cognition and Regulation

Adolescence is believed to be an important time for the development of identity. Young people seek to answer important questions about themselves. Who am I? What is important to me in my life? These types of questions represent the stage of life that Erikson characterized as identity versus identity confusion. Young people enter what Erikson calls a **psychological moratorium**—a gap between childhood security and adult autonomy. Erikson's ideas were extended by James Marcia (1966), who developed a classification system for adolescent identity statuses, or modes of resolution:

• *Identity diffusion.* This is the least mature status for the adolescent to be in. These adolescents have not yet experienced a crisis; that is, they are not exploring meaningful alternatives. No commitments have been made to important attitudes, values, or plans for the future.

• *Identity foreclosure.* In this stage, adolescents have made a commitment to particular goals, values, and beliefs but have not yet experienced a crisis. Most often, in identity foreclosure, parents push a commitment on their adolescents in an authoritative manner (you will go to college or the army). Yet adolescents have not had the needed opportunities to adequately explore their own perceptions, ideologies, and beliefs.

• *Identity moratorium.* This status describes adolescents who are currently experiencing a crisis—actively exploring values, ideologies, and beliefs. Their commitments may be either absent or only vaguely defined.

• *Identity achievement.* At this final stage, adolescents have undergone and resolved their crisis by making strong commitments to such things as an occupation, a sexual orientation, or a religious ideology.

Although the identity status theory has had an enormous influence on the field of adolescent psychology, it has become increasingly criticized (Cote & Levine, 1988; Lapsley & Power, 1988). Most of the criticism revolves around Erikson's notions of crisis and commitment. Erikson emphasized questioning perceptions and

expectations and developing an autonomous position within one's society, whereas the identity status approach is concerned with simply evaluating whether one has thought about such issues. In their search for identity, young people are struggling with unresolved questions. Adams and Gullotta (1989) present a variety of questionnaire items that represent an alternative to Marcia's interview technique in assessing identity status. Table 9.3 presents examples of the questionnaire items used in measuring ego-identity status.

Recent work in identity development suggests several important considerations. The idea of *crisis* may be misleading in that identity development appears to be a lengthy process. The complexity of identity formation is becoming more recognized (Marcia, 1987), as is the notion that such a process does not begin and end in adolescence. Identity development is significant in adolescence because this is when physical development, cognitive development, and social development converge, creating the opportunity for a synthesis as the young person charts a path to adulthood (Santrock, 1990).

Marcia (1987) notes that critical issues for early adolescence are gaining confidence in parental support, the development of a sense of industry, and a self-reflective perspective about the future. However, research (Meilman, 1979) is finding that many of the most important identity changes are taking place in later adolescence, between the ages of 18 and 21. Furthermore, researchers (Adams, Abraham, & Markstrom, 1987) have found that changes toward a more advanced identity status are related to personality development and to social cognitive development. The following Focus on Multiculturalism section examines identity considerations of Native American youth.

Identity and Native American Youth

Consider the following story about a conversation between a Native American and an Anglo youth (Coles, 1986). "In school, I drew a picture of my father's horse.

TABLE 9.3   Examples of Questionnaire Items Used in Measuring Ego-Identity Status

Status	Item
Diffusion	I haven't chosen the occupation I really want to get into, but I'm working toward becoming a _____ until something better comes along.
Foreclosure	I've never really questioned my religion. If it's right for my parents, it must be right for me.
Moratorium	I just can't decide how capable I am as a person and what jobs I'll be right for.
Identity Achievement	A person's faith is unique to each individual. I've considered and reconsidered it myself and know what I can believe.

Source: Adams & Gullotta, 1989, p. 241.

One of the other kids wouldn't believe that it was ours. He said, 'You don't really own that horse.' I said, 'It's a horse my father rides, and I feed it every morning.' He said, 'How come?' I said, 'My uncle and my father are good riders, and I'm pretty good.' He said, 'I can ride a horse better than you, and I'd rather be a pilot.' I told him I never thought of being a pilot."

The boy is clear about the differences between himself and the Anglo youth he knows. "The Anglos I've met, they're different. I don't know why. Anglo kids, they won't let you get away with anything. Tell them something, and fast as lightning and loud as thunder, they'll say, 'I'm better than you, so there!' My father says it's always been like that."

This poem of a 12-year-old youth reflects the development of his peaceful identity as a Native American youth (Coles, 1986):

Rivers flow.   The sea sings.
Oceans roar.   Tides rise.
          Who am I?
A small pebble on a giant shore;
Who am I
To ask who I am?
Isn't it enough to be?

Source: Coles, 1986.

Youth of Color and Adolescent Identity

Identity in adolescence is a significant developmental task, and often it is an even more critical task for the adolescent of color. During adolescence, youth must integrate their image of being from an ethnic group while being exposed to values and images of the mainstream white culture. Young people often perceive a negative image from the white majority and then face the task of developing a positive identity as a member of an ethnic group (Spencer & Dornbusch, 1990). Because of their cognitive maturity, adolescents of color are often quite aware of how others are evaluating their minority status.

Issues that such youth face as they focus on identity development include racial stereotypes that affect their "looking-glass self"; cultural devaluation of the symbols and heroes of their group; and lack of successful role models with whom to identify (Spencer & Dornbusch, 1990). Identity development during adolescence leaves many young people making comparisons between themselves and others. Eventually, adolescents of color must reconcile their lives from the standpoint of two contrasting cultural systems—their own ethnic and cultural values and the white majority cultural values. This often leads to three options: alienation, where youth reject the majority culture and the opportunities it provides; assimilation, where youth reject their ethnic values and strive to conform and assimilate to white majority values; and biculturalism, where youth learn to negotiate both their ethnic values and the values of the dominant culture. In this case, the value structures of both groups are available, and the young people must negotiate which standards to use depending on the situation (Spencer & Dornbusch, 1990).

Implications for Practice: Identity and Independence

Independence is a related aspect of developing an identity. To help a young person successfully develop an identity, issues of independence need to be carefully reviewed. Young people face many challenges as they attempt to establish an identity—making new commitments to friends, gaining greater independence from parents, and developing more intimate friendships and relationships. Also at this time, the young person is increasingly learning to reflect on his or her actions as he or she makes increasingly important life decisions.

Parents can be important influences in the adolescent's development of identity (Cooper & Grotevant, 1989). Research has found that the adolescent's connectedness to parents and the presence of a family atmosphere promotes individuation in the adolescent's identity development. **Connectedness** refers both to the adolescent's sensitivity to and respect for others' views and to the adolescent's openness and responsiveness to others' views. **Individuation** has two parts—separateness and self-assertion. Separateness is the expression of the individual's distinct self from others. Self-assertion refers to adolescents' expression of their viewpoints and their clear communication.

Consider the situation in which the adolescent's mother has not "let go" of her daughter. The girl is tied to the mother financially and emotionally in ways that do not let her mature independently. Under these circumstances, the girl could develop difficulties in developing mature intimate relationships and in career choices (Santrock, 1990). She may turn down important opportunities for more responsibility, doubting her abilities to be independent. Similarly, rather than confronting difficulties in her intimate relationships, she may turn to her mother for support and comfort. In working with adolescents, social workers need to be aware of their need for independence and help young people chart a course of increased maturity. This may involve working with parents or school staff on independence-granting skills in order to encourage responsibility and maturity. Too often, society sees the young person as immature and not ready for adult roles rather than systematically encouraging the young person to take increasing responsibility for mature behavior.

Social Cognitive Monitoring

Social cognitive monitoring is a person's ability to monitor and make sense of his or her social thoughts. This development of conscious self-awareness increases during middle childhood and adolescence. Such social awareness is indicated by thoughts like "I don't think I'm easily influenced by others" or "I'm going to have a difficult time talking to and getting to know this person." These kinds of thoughts exemplify how adolescents monitor their social world. As young people develop, they begin to recognize that social thoughts are difficult to assess. Also, experiencing different aspects of others can decrease their accuracy in assessing social thoughts. For example, witnessing another person expressing strong emotions may lead to an inaccurate understanding of that person. As this process develops, children learn that people sometimes do not think accurately about others because they have caught them in a bad mood (Flavell, 1981). Flavell (1979, p. 910) states that "In many real-life situations, the monitoring problem is not to determine how well you understand what a message means but rather to determine how much you ought to believe it or do what it says to do."

Regulation

A woman was dying of a particular type of cancer. However, there was one drug that doctors believed could save her. A druggist in the town where the woman and her husband lived had discovered this drug. Although the drug was expensive to make, the druggist was charging ten times what the drug cost him to make. He paid $200 for the drug and was charging $2000 for a small dose of it. The woman's husband, Heinz, went to all their friends to borrow money for the drug; however, he gathered only $1000—half the cost. He told the druggist that his wife was dying and asked him to sell it more cheaply or let him pay later. The druggist said, "No, I discovered the drug, and I am going to make money from it." So Heinz got desperate and broke into the druggist's store to steal the drug for his wife (Kohlberg, 1969).

This story about Heinz and the drug raises a number of difficult moral questions. Should Hienz steal the drug? What is the right and wrong thing to do in this situation? Does the husband have a duty to steal the drug for his wife if he cannot get it in another way? Did the druggist have a right to charge so much for the drug?

This story and these types of questions are a common method of investigating adolescents' moral judgments. The attempt is to find out how the adolescent thinks about moral dilemmas where there is no clear right or wrong answer. How a person reasons about whether to steal or not steal the drug would be an indication of his or her stage of moral development. **Moral development** refers to the rules of conduct people use in their interactions with others. For example, the adolescent could reason that he or she should not steal the drug because stealing is against the law. However, another line of reasoning might be that stealing the drug is acceptable because it is unfair to charge such a high price for the drug and it is worse to have the wife die from not receiving the drug than it is to steal.

Kohlberg believes that rules of conduct develop as individuals progress through stages. Each stage represents a different way of reasoning about various rules of conduct. In this model, there are six separate stages of moral development that people can progress through. The stages, summarized in Box 9.2, begin in the preschool years and continue through adulthood. These stages can be thought of as theories of right and wrong that we carry around with us. Each stage has a different idea of what's right and a different idea of the reason a person should be good (Lickona, 1983). As people progress through each stage, they get closer to a fully developed morality. The stages, correspond to the preconventional and postconventional stages of moral reasoning as described by Kohlberg.

Critique of Kohlberg's Moral Development Theory

Although Kohlberg's theory of moral development has received considerable support, there have been a number of criticisms. Major questions have been raised concerning the link between moral thought and behavior, the quality of the research, and gender bias. To what extent is moral judgment associated with behavior? Do people who reason differently also decide to act on the basis of their judgments? These are difficult questions, and researchers have not found consistent results (see Emler, Renwick, & Malone, 1983; Lapsley et al., 1984). Perhaps moral reasoning does not directly affect behavior but may provide a sense of direction and ethical standards.

Criticism concerning the quality of the research in this area tends to focus on a couple of aspects. Most critical is how moral development is measured. Kohlberg uses a series of moral dilemmas, like the one presented

earlier, and interviews subjects in order to arrive at a stage of moral development. Some researchers (Rest, 1986) would like to see alternative methods used in assessing moral development. Also, concerns have been raised about the content presented in the moral dilemmas—that is, the dilemmas do not reflect the subjects' lives. One developmentalist (Yussen, 1977) had adolescents generate their own moral dilemmas, and, indeed, the focus was more oriented toward friends, acquaintances, and other issues as well as toward family and authority.

Another issue involving moral development has to do with gender bias. Most moral development research has been conducted with males. Carol Gilligan (1982, 1985) is well-known for her criticism of Kohlberg. She contends that his theoretical perspective is based on a **justice perspective,** in which the focus is on the rights of the individual. People are characterized as standing alone in their decision making. In contrast, Gilligan offers a theory based on a **care perspective,** in which the focus is on people's connectedness to others. There is more of a focus on interpersonal communication. According to Gilligan, Kohlberg has underestimated the care perspective underlying moral development for both males and females. She believes that the highest level of moral development involves a search for moral equality between oneself and others.

Implications for Practice: Adolescent Moral Development

To further illustrate how moral development can be used to better understand adolescence, we will use independence as an example. Most young adolescents are in stage 3, interpersonal conformity, according to Box 9.2. At this stage, young people seek to be nice people—so that others will think well of them and they can think well of themselves. A significant challenge for parents is confronting the typical conformist reasoning apparent at this stage. This is best done by teaching the value of independence and strengthening the young person's ability to be her or his own person and resist the pressures of the peer group (Lickona, 1983). Lickona presents a parent's perspective on how to challenge adolescent thinking at this stage. He presents six ways to help adolescents break free of typical conformist reasoning:

1. *Be an independent person yourself.* Parents need to model independent thinking and behavior. When young people suggest the old standby "Other parents let their kids do . . . ," parents need to resist the pressure to conform to parent peer pressure. Parents should suggest that what is important is not what others are doing but what they think is right.

2. *Talk about the value of being independent.* Par-

BOX 9.2

The Stages of Moral Reasoning

Ages indicate reasonable developmental expectations for a child of normal intelligence growing up in a supportive moral environment.

Stage 0: Egocentric reasoning (preschool years—around age 4)

What's right: I should get my own way.
Reason to be good: To get rewards and avoid punishments.

Stage 1: Unquestioning obedience (around kindergarten age)

What's right: I should do what I'm told.
Reason to be good: To stay out of trouble.

Stage 2: What's-in-it-for-me fairness (early elementary grades)

What's right: I should look out for myself but be fair to those who are fair to me.
Reason to be good: Self-interest: What's in it for me?

Stage 3: Interpersonal conformity (middle to upper elementary grades and early to mid-teens)

What's right: I should be a nice person and live up to the expectations of people I know and care about.
Reason to be good: So others will think well of me (social approval) and I can think well of myself (self-esteem).

Stage 4: Responsibility to "the system" (high school years or late teens)

Stage 5: Principled conscience (young adulthood)

What's right: I should fulfill my responsibilities to the social or value system I feel part of.
Reason to be good: To keep the system from falling apart and to maintain self-respect as somebody who meets my obligations.
What's right: I should show the greatest possible respect for the rights and dignity of every individual person and should support a system that protects human rights.
Reason to be good: The obligation of conscience to act in accordance with the principle of respect for all human beings.

Source: Lickona, 1983, p. 12.

ents need to help adolescents see that it is in their own interest to be independent. Lickona (1983) recommends that parents say such things as, "Be your own person. Do what you like to do, what *you're* interested in. If you're true to yourself, you'll be happy with yourself. You can't be happy trying to be what you're not."(p. 189).

3. *Help young people think of words to say.* Parents should help young people role-play the exact words they might use in resisting peer pressure—for example, to a boyfriend who's interested in sexual relations, the young person might respond to a statement such as "Everybody's doing it" with "Well, if everybody's doing it, then you shouldn't have any trouble finding somebody else."(Lickona, 1983, p. 189)

4. *Help young people understand themselves.* Young people will be better prepared to be independent if they understand the feelings that cause them to conform. Many young people experience feelings of inferiority, and those feelings lead them to seek peer approval through conformity.

5. *Help young people put popularity in perspective.* Peer popularity is what often keeps adolescents from being more independent. It is important for young people to realize that values change. Having a winning personality is valued at age 14 but may be less important in three or four years. Later, such values as sensitivity to others and being able to accomplish their goals will become increasingly important.

6. *Challenge the "group morality" of stage 3.* Parents can challenge adolescents' conformist reasoning by helping them see that "group morality" isn't a very good way to solve moral problems. Lickona (1983, p. 190) presents an example of how parents can do this:

> Will, who was on the junior high school baseball team, told his mother that the coach had kicked a kid off the team. Kids who thought it was unfair were talking about boycotting practice.
>
> "Do *you* think it was unfair?" his mother asked.
>
> "I'm not sure," Will said. "I just heard about what happened from some other kids. I didn't see it. According to them, Mr. Thompson accused Eric Miller of goofing off when he wasn't doing anything wrong. Then he just told him he was off the team."
>
> "I see," his mother said, "So it's hard to be sure exactly what happened. What do you think of the boycott idea?"
>
> "I don't know," Will said.

> "How will you decide what to do?"
>
> "I'll find out what other kids are going to do."
>
> Will's mother tried to get him to examine the inadequacy of this kind of moral thinking. "What will you do then?"
>
> Will sighed and shrugged his shoulders.
>
> "So can you decide what's right on the basis of what the other kids are doing?"
>
> "I guess not," Will said.
>
> "Right," his mother said. "You have to use your own judgment. Think about what's fair, and what's going to help you, the coach, and the team. Would a boycott help matters?"
>
> "No, not really."
>
> "What else can be done?"
>
> Together, Will and his mother came up with the idea that he could go to Mr. Thompson privately the next day and ask if he would call a meeting of the team to talk about what happened.

Moral Development: Three Theoretical Perspectives

Adams and Gullotta (1989) describe three common theoretical perspectives used to help explain and understand moral development: cognitive-developmental, learning-theory, and psychoanalytic. The cognitive-developmental perspective is based on the notion of re-ciprocity between the individual and society. There is a norm of reciprocal respect that guides the individual in his or her moral conduct. A person's moral behavior is based on the manner in which the person justifies his or her actions. Therefore, the way a person reasons directly affects his or her behavior. In the learning-theory perspective, moral behavior results either from the re-inforcement of behavior or through the observation of others' behavior (modeling). Individuals learn moral behavior through direct reinforcement and indirectly through observation of models. In the psychoanalytic perspective, moral behavior is the result of people's personalities, primarily their instinctual drives. People's instinctual drives are moderated by their ego development. Moral behavior is the result of people's personality—their early childhood experiences that have influenced their ego development.

The perspective provided by each theory would lead the practitioner to emphasize different things. For example, in understanding a young person's violent action, a cognitive-developmental perspective would seek to examine the person's reasoning—the person's moral justification for his or her actions. A learning-theory perspective would seek to examine what elements present in the young person's environment may be reinforcing his or her actions or what role models provide vicarious reinforcement. Last, a psychoanalytic perspective would focus on parental relationships, sense of guilt, and ego development to understand how desires and impulses are controlled.

Egocentrism

"I hate eating at the swimming pool. Everyone just stares at you, I never know if I've got ice cream all over my face or if guys are just trying to look at my body," Janna said with a sense of desperation. Her friend, Anita, has a similar reaction: "I know, you can never look right at this place. I mean with wet hair and no makeup I think people are looking at me and saying, gosh I didn't think she looked that bad. I keep thinking that guys who might think I'm reasonable looking will come here and see me and never give me a second look."

This conversation between Janna and Anita at the local swimming pool represents what David Elkind (1978) refers to as adolescent *egocentrism.* Egocentrism refers to a type of thought that is characterized by preoccupation with one's behavior, feeling, or thoughts in a self-conscious manner. It is the onset of formal operational thinking that is believed to lead to such egocentric thought. Elkind discusses two aspects of egocentric thought—the imaginary audience and the personal fable.

The **imaginary audience** is the belief that others are as preoccupied with the adolescent's behavior as he or she is. Adolescents harbor this notion that they are "on stage" and that everyone is their audience. Adolescents' preoccupation with their own bodies may be a result of their egocentric thinking. In the conversation above, both Janna and Anita believed that everyone's attention was directed at them, and therefore they were very concerned about their appearance.

The **personal fable** reflects adolescents' sense that they are indestructible and unique. In fact, they are so unique that no one can understand what it is like to be them. In their self-focus, they also come to believe that they are indestructible. Things simply are not going to happen to "them."

Recent work in adolescent egocentrism suggests that this phenomenon may be due not only to formal thought, as Elkind hypothesized, but also to the adolescent's interpersonal understanding (Lapsley, 1985; Laps-ley & Rice, 1988). Such an understanding reflects the ability to step out of oneself and perceive reactions from others in imaginative circumstances. This theoretical notion is similar to the perspective-taking theory presented earlier by Robert Selman (1980). As you will recall, Selman discusses how a child's perspective taking or role taking develops across five levels. By examining the way a child reasons according to different perspective-taking levels, you can better understand the child's behavior.

Psychological Hazards

A majority of psychological problems for boys and girls in adolescence involve *externalizing disorders.* This is particularly true for boys, but is also true for girls. Between the ages of 12 and 16, over 25% of all boys and girls are referred to mental health clinics for problems of delinquency or conduct disorder (Achenbach & Edelbrock, 1983). *Internalizing disorders* are also well-known in adolescence, as many young people become depressed and turn to suicide. (See the following Focus on Research section.) Depression will be discussed in the chapter on young adulthood. Social workers interested in community mental health with children and adolescents need to become quite familiar with the problems associated with conduct disorder and delinquency because these are major psychological hazards for young people.

FOCUS ON RESEARCH

Identifying Risk Factors for Suicide Attempts Among Navajo Adolescents

Suicide is the third most common cause of death in adolescents. The suicide rate for youths has tripled over the past 30 years. American Indians and Alaskan Natives have the highest suicide rates of all ethnic groups; it is more than double the rate for adolescents of all races. In a study conducted to identify the risk factors for self-reported suicide attempts by Navajo adolescents, over 7000 students in grades 6 through 12 on the Navajo reservation were surveyed. The study found that 15% of the sample ($N = 971$) reported a previous suicide attempt; over half of those admitted to more than one attempt. The researchers wanted to discover what factors are more likely to predict suicide attempts. Controlling for age, they used a regression model and found the following factors predict the risk of suicide: history of mental health problems, alienation from family and community, having a friend who attempted suicide, weekly consumption of hard liquor, a family history of suicide or attempts, poor self-perception of health, history of physical abuse, female gender, and sexual abuse. The authors conclude that efforts to prevent suicide attempts in Navajo adolescents should target individuals with the identified risk factors.

Source: Grossman, Milligan, & Deyo, 1991.

Conduct Disorder

Debbie was very active as a young child. Her parents complained that she was difficult to manage as early as 4 years old. At that time, they believed that Debbie just would not listen and follow their instructions. Both parents used reprimands and spanked Debbie but to no avail—she was her own boss. As she got older, Debbie became argumentive and increasingly noncompliant. When requested to be home at a certain time or to do a chore, Debbie would often just exclaim, "I don't have to if I don't want to." Easily "set off," Debbie would yell at her parents and scream, "I hate you." She has been increasingly absent from school. School officials claim she is involved in a gang that sells and uses drugs. One of her girlfriends is now on probation after having been arrested for shoplifting.

Debbie's pattern of behavior would easily fit into the category of **conduct disorder** (see Box 9.3), which is a constellation of behaviors that range from oppositional and noncompliant behavior to delinquent behaviors such as stealing, robbery, and physical assault.

It is difficult to estimate the prevalence of conduct disorder because it represents a fairly large heterogeneous group. For example, some researchers distinguish between nondelinquent conduct problems, and others refer only to delinquent behavior. The estimate of prevalence is as high as 8% when considering a broad pattern of conduct disorder (Yule, 1981). We know that each year, between 4% and 5% of young people are referred to the courts for suspected offenses other than traffic violations (White, 1989). However, twice as many young people come in contact with the police but are not arrested. Also, studies of "normal" children indicate that most (up to 75%) have engaged in illegal behavior (Johnson & Fennell, 1983).

Although many young people may engage in illegal behavior, conduct disorder behaviors in some youth begin early in life and follow them into adulthood. One well-known study (West & Farrington, 1973) found that the aggressive and difficult behavior of 8- to 10-year-olds was a strong predictor of later delinquent behavior. For some, youth conduct disorder or delinquency is strongly related to psychological factors or personality. Of course, there are many causes of delinquent behavior. Conduct disorder may be related to such factors as temperament or personality, deficits in moral development, family structure and environment (divorced parents, absent fathers, uncaring and abusive parents), and negative modeling. Biological factors could come into play, as conduct disorder may arise from biologically driven arousal deficits that lead to stimulation-seeking behaviors. What theories do you think best explain delinquency?

Implications for Practice: Approaches to Treating Delinquent Youth

The approach to treatment of delinquent youth has gone through much change over the last 20 years. In general, treatment has moved away from a psychiatric model focusing on intrapsychic conflict, emotional disturbance, and diagnosis to treatment models based on growth, behavioral change, skill acquisition, social learning and modeling, and responsibility for one's actions (White, 1989). In particular, behavioral approaches have been applied and evaluated with such youth. Treatment techniques emphasize reinforcement for appropriate behaviors, learning new social skills, token economies, modeling, and goal setting. Perhaps one of the best-established treatment models is Patterson's parent-training model for aggressive children (Chamberlain & Patterson, 1985).

This approach teaches child-management techniques to the parents. Parents learn to define, pinpoint, monitor, and apply consequences to various child behaviors. Feldman, Caplinger, and Wodarski (1983) found support for behavioral methods in a community-based setting, and Alexander and Parsons (1982) integrated family systems and behavioral methods for delinquent youth. Behavioral methods became quite well-known through the notoriety of Achievement Place, behavior modification programs for delinquent youth in a home-based residential setting (Fixsen, Phillips, Phillips, & Wolf, 1976). In the Achievement Place model, parents are taught to apply the principles of behavior modification with the young people. The young people follow a set of rules based on a token economy where they earn privileges based on their daily behaviors. Six treatment methods appear to be the most

widely used with delinquent youth: restitution and community service (teaches responsibility through direct or symbolic repayment of the victim); family intervention; token economies; fear, emotional shock, and avoidance training; wilderness training; and social skills training (White, 1989). Family intervention and social skills training appear to have the best results in reducing recidivism.

Social Dimension
Families, Groups, Support Systems, and Contexts

The transition into adolescence involves some stress in most families, for both adolescent and parent. This stress

BOX 9.3

DSM-IV Diagnostic Criteria for Conduct Disorder

A. A repetitive and persistent pattern of behavior in which the basic rights of others or major age-appropriate societal norms or rules are violated, as manifested by the presence of three (or more) of the following criteria in the past 12 months, with at least one criterion present in the past 6 months:

Aggression to people and animals
  1. Often bullies, threatens, or intimidates others
  2. Often initiates physical fights
  3. Has used a weapon that can cause serious physical harm to others (e.g., a bat, brick, broken bottle, knife, gun)
  4. Has been physically cruel to people
  5. Has been physically cruel to animals
  6. Has stolen while confronting a victim (e.g., mugging, purse snatching, extortion, armed robbery)

  7. Has forced someone into sexual activity

Destruction of property
  8. Has deliberately engaged in fire setting with the intention of causing serious damage
  9. Has deliberately destroyed others' property (other than by fire setting)

Deceitfulness or theft
  10. Has broken into someone else's house, building, or car
  11. Often lies to obtain goods or favors or to avoid obligations (i.e., "cons" others)
  12. Has stolen items of nontrivial value without confronting a victim (e.g., shoplifting, but without breaking and entering, forgery)

may be due in part to the rapid developmental changes that take place—more occur during adolescence than any other period of the life cycle (Smetana, Yau, Restrepo, & Braeges, 1991). Three key developmental tasks for the family include the development of autonomy, resolution of parent-adolescent conflict, and parent-adolescent attachment (Steinberg, 1990).

Family Influences: Development of Autonomy

Consider the following interaction between a mother and daughter:

Daughter: Mom, get off my back! I know what I'm supposed to do around this house. I don't need you telling me every second.

Mother: I have to tell you every second or it just doesn't get done. If I could trust you to do it, I wouldn't have to keep after you.

This common interaction reveals an essential theme of the parent-adolescent relationship: control versus autonomy. Much of the stress in parent-adolescent relationships is related to struggles that revolve around control and autonomy. As young people move into adolescence, they begin the process of acquiring more independence, and parents need to begin the process of granting more independence. Because parents have had full responsibility for their children up to now, the process becomes a difficult balance between letting go and still having some control. Some parents successfully adapt to the adolescent's need for independence and are able to grant the young person more decision-making

BOX 9.3

DSM-IV Diagnostic Criteria for Conduct Disorder

Serious violations of rules
13. Often stays out at night despite parental prohibitions, beginning before age 13 years
14. Has run away from home overnight at least twice while living in parental or parental surrogate home (or once without returning for a lengthy period)
15. Is often truant from school, beginning before age 13 years

B. The disturbance in behavior causes clinically significant impairment in social, academic, or occupational functioning.

C. If the individual is age 18 years or older, criteria are not met for Antisocial Personality Disorder.

Specify type based on age at onset:
    Childhood-Onset Type: onset of at least one criterion characteristic of Conduct Disorder prior to age 10 years
    Adolescent-Onset Type: absence of any criteria characteristic of Conduct Disorder prior to age 10 years
Specify severity:
    Mild: few if any conduct problems in excess of those required to make the diagnosis and conduct problems cause only minor harm to others
    Moderate: number of conduct problems and effect on others intermediate between "mild" and "severe"
    Severe: many conduct problems in excess of those required to make the diagnosis or conduct problems cause considerable harm to others

Source: American Psychiatric Association, 1994.

authority. However, other parents do not acquire the needed skills involved in independence granting and remained locked into a need for control over decision making. What is the result of these two different styles of parenting? Parents who hold tightly to their control and are authoritarian in their decision making are more likely to produce young people who have difficulty with autonomy. A democratic family structure, where there is equal involvement of parents and adolescents with parents retaining the final authority, appears to produce a young person with a healthy sense of autonomy.

Parent-Adolescent Conflict   The parent-adolescent relationship is not viewed as one of stress and storm, rebellion against parents, or a generation gap the way it was in the past. The current thinking about the parent-adolescent relationship is that it is a transitional period characterized by minor conflicts and disagreements about the details of everyday life (Galambos & Almeida, 1992; Montemayer, 1983). It is important to recognize that, contrary to popular notions, most adolescents have warm and satisfying relationships with their parents, turn to parents for advice, and feel loved and appreciated by them (Offer, Ostrov, & Howard, 1981; Rutter, Graham, Chadwick, & Yule, 1976). What is common are parent-adolescent disagreements; in fact, this appears to be a normative and adaptive aspect of the transition to adolescence (Smetana, Yau, Restrepo, & Braeges, 1991).

Researchers have discovered that it is during early adolescence when the conflict between parents and adolescents begins and is characterized by bickering and negative interactions, fewer shared activities, and less frequently expressed affection (Steinberg, 1990). Such conflicts often occur around the time of puberty. This is interpreted by some to represent the family's adaptation to the adolescent's physical development (Hill, Holmbeck, Marlow, Green, & Lynch, 1985). The prevalence of conflict between parent and adolescent is about two times weekly—twice as often as a typical married couple (Montemayer, 1983). Contrary to many popular notions, conflicts are not about values, politics, or social issues but about mundane everyday issues such as curfew, chores, and school—the same issues since studies began 60 years ago (Montemayer, 1983).

Is there a functional reason that adolescents and parents have this increase in conflicts? Many researchers believe there is, and they base their ideas on the following theories (Steinberg, 1990):

1. Steinberg (1990) suggests that, based on a sociobiological perspective, conflict during adolescence ensures that young people will spend time separated from their family of origin and mate outside the natal group. This theory is based on the observation that conflict intensifies at puberty in other species of primates and that the underlying tension may be derived from an evolved basis. The adolescent is forced, through the bickering, to search for intimate companionship outside the family.

2. Holmbeck and Hill (1988, cited in Steinberg, 1990) explain the conflict from both psychoanalytic and social-learning theories. From an intrapsychic perspective, the conflict may facilitate the process of individuation. Furthermore, this intrapsychic emancipation allows the young person to develop a more realistic and mature appraisal of his or her parents. This leads to a more mutual relationship with them. The function of the disagreements is that adolescents must come to terms with their parents' fallibility and, as a result, release their dependence on their parents.

3. Smetana (1988) presents a cognitive-developmental perspective suggesting that parent-adolescent conflict can be best explained by the different manner in which adolescents and parents define family rules, events, and regulations. From a cognitive-developmental perspective, conflict in adolescence is related to the development of social reasoning. For example, instead of seeing an issue as one of social convention (everyone in this family must keep his or her room clean), it is perceived by the adolescent as an issue of personal choice (this is my room and I should decide how clean I want to keep it). Because parents maintain a conventional stance regarding such issues, conflict is the result. Also significant is that at this early and middle adolescent period, young people tend to perceive social conventions as arbitrary.

Parent-Adolescent Attachment   Is it better for adolescents to become detached from parents as they move toward independence, or is it better for them to remain attached? Just as it has been in infancy, secure attachment is becoming increasingly recognized as critical to adolescent healthy development. Yet, the psychoanalytic notion has been that adolescents who remain close to their parents will not show healthy developmental progress. Research has found that adolescents with secure attachments to their parents do better than their peers in terms of self-reliance and independence, behavioral competence, and psychosocial well-being (Hill & Holmbeck, 1986; Maccoby & Martin, 1983; Steinberg & Silverberg, 1986). Furthermore, adolescents with secure attachments score lower on measures of social and psychological problems such as drug abuse, depression, and delinquency (McCord, 1990). As Steinberg (1990) points out, this finding is robust across socioeconomic and ethnic groups. He also points out that, contrary to some clinical notions, there is no research to support the hypothesis that the parent-adolescent relationship can be so cohesive that it is enmeshing.

Parenting Styles and Adolescent Development Baumrind (1989) has identified three types of parenting styles: authoritative, authoritarian, and laissez-faire. She has found that the type of parenting influences the adolescent's behaviors. **Authoritative parenting,** where there is warmth and affection coupled with demandingness, leads to adolescents with greater psychological health. Authoritative parents expect adolescents to be independent but still place limits and controls on their behaviors. Authoritative parenting is related to the young person's development of social competence, particularly self-reliance and social responsibility. **Authoritarian parenting** is characterized by being demanding, restrictive, and punitive while showing low levels of warmth. This type of parenting is associated with anxiety concerning social comparison, ineffective social interactions, and inability to initiate activities. **Laissez-faire parenting** has been recently suggested as representing two types—permissive indifferent and permissive indulgent. *Permissive indifferent* parents are uninvolved in their child's life such that they are neglectful and unresponsive. This type of parenting is associated with a lack of self-control on the part of the adolescent. *Permissive indulgent* parents are warm, accepting, and responsive but are undemanding. Such parents are actively involved in the adolescent's life but do not enforce rules and allow extensive freedom. Adolescents learn from this type of parenting that anything goes—they do not have to abide by rules. Research has found that responsiveness was the most important factor related to adolescents' social competence and, con-

versely, that parents who are indifferent or uninvolved are associated with adolescents with the greatest risk for psychological and social problems (Baumrind, 1989).

Implications for Practice: The Power of Authoritative Parenting

Steinberg (1990) suggests that the power of authoritative parenting can be taught. The most relevant work in this area is based on the research of Patterson and colleagues at the Oregon Social Learning Center. They have developed specific treatment methods for working with families with aggressive, delinquent, and noncompliant children. Their social-learning model embraces many of the aspects of authoritative parenting—monitoring, supervision, clear limit setting and rules, and a warm relationship built on positive reinforcement. The focus of the program is on child management, not on interpersonal and underlying psychodynamics. The model teaches parents to communicate clear expectations for acceptable and unacceptable behavior, to carefully monitor target behaviors selected for modification, to consistently and contingently apply discipline (time-out), and to reinforce acceptable and positive behaviors. Research results have shown improvement in the target behaviors of children and improvement in the behavior of siblings as well (Patterson, 1986).

Peers and Adolescent Development

The notion of the "teenage" years is practically synonymous with peer relationships and peer groups. If we asked you to picture the first thing that comes to your mind when you hear the word *teenager* or *adolescent*, you'd probably picture one of the following scenes: a teenager talking on the telephone, two girlfriends sitting and talking with one another, a couple out on a date, a group of peers at the mall, or a group of teenagers at the movie theater. Such is the reality of most adolescents, who spend an increasing amount of time in the company of peers (Berndt & Ladd, 1989). Research has documented that by the sixth grade, adults (excluding parents) account for only 25% of early adolescents' primary social network and even less (10%) when adolescents mature early (Garbarino, Burston, Raber, Russel, & Crouter, 1978).

However, this time with the peer group is well spent. Adolescents are at a point in their development

In adolescence, an increasing amount of time is spent with peers, which is critical for personal and social competence development. By spending time with their peers, adolescents learn about sexual relations, leadership, conflict, and mutual problem solving.

where they need to spend time with peers. This interaction provides important information that is usually not available within the family. Indeed, peer interaction is a critical source for personal and social competence development. Through interaction with peers, young people learn about sexual relations, compassion, leadership, conflict, and mutual problem solving, to name just a few. Locating a peer group that is supportive and compatible with one's interests is a psychological task of early adolescence. As discussed in earlier chapters, the impact of peer rejection and isolation can be critical to the adolescent's healthy development.

Good peer relations are also critical to one's popularity, and popularity is keenly sought after in adolescence. Young people strive to behave in a manner that will enhance their popularity. There are many factors that contribute to one's popularity: attractiveness, athletic ability, intellectual ability, social class, ethnic group membership, and special characteristics or talents. Attractiveness is a powerful force in determining one's popularity. This appears most critical at the extremes—either very attractive or very unattractive—and is a determinant of social acceptance or rejection (Coleman, 1980).

Peer Pressure and Conformity   As one 15-year-old stated: "Kids need to look at peer pressure and ask, 'Do I want to do this?' Whether the answer is yes or no, they need to ask why" (Clasen & Brown, 1987). Peer pressure and conformity are strong processes in adolescence. Peer pressure and conformity are the greatest in early adolescence, especially from the sixth to the ninth grades (Berndt, 1979). Adolescent thinking is often characterized by "if the group is doing it, it must be good and right." By late adolescence, conformity to antisocial behavior decreases and parents and peers begin to experience greater agreement. As young people move toward independence, they rely less on peer and family influence. Perhaps this period of strict conformity to peers is a normal and important task of adolescence—to gradually come to terms with the influence of groups (Minuchin, 1977). We all have to learn to balance the need for personal autonomy with the desire for group participation.

Conformity, agreeing with the group opinion when pressured, can be both positive and negative (Santrock, 1990). Although we often view adolescent peer pressure and conformity through a negative lens, it is often positive or neutral. For example, many young people conform to dress, music, and hairstyle norms. Perhaps the greatest conformity is spending time with the peer group itself. Positive conformity and constructive peer pressure are exemplified by Students Against Drunk Driving (or SADD), where students promise themselves, peers, and parents not to drink and drive (Clasen & Brown, 1987).

Friendships   In adolescence, more complete friendships begin to develop. Perhaps most significant is the capacity for intimacy in friendship. Intimacy in friendship refers to the sharing of personal thoughts. This personal knowledge about others leads to a greater sense of closeness. Although the intimacy of friendship is highly valued in adolescence, there are other important functions of friendship. Research by Parker and Gottman (1989) outlines six critical functions of friendships: companionship, stimulation, physical support, ego support, social comparison, and intimacy/affection. Consider the following description of a close friendship between two boys:

> I know everything about John and he knows everything about me. We know where the secret places are in each other's house, and that my mother cooks better but his father tells funnier jokes. . . . We always stick together because I'm good at fights, but John's the only one besides my family who knows that I sleep with my light on at night. He can jump from the high diving board but I know he's afraid of cats. . . . He saw me cry once and the day he broke his arm I ran home and got his mother for him. We know what's in each other's refrigerator, which steps creak on each other's stairs and how to get into each other's house if the door is locked. I know who he really likes and he knows about Mary too. John is my best friend and I am his. (Zolotow, 1968)

This quote clearly outlines the six functions of friendship described above.

Implications for Practice: Social Skills Training

An increasing emphasis is being placed on a social skills or social competence model for understanding, preventing, and remediating the problems experienced by ado-

lescents. **Social skills training** assumes that problem behavior in young people can be understood in terms of their not having acquired skills needed to cope with various situational demands. The focus is on discovering effective responses for resolving the demands of problem situations while minimizing the likelihood of future problems. This approach perceives human development as a process of confronting a series of tasks and situational demands rather than as movement through stages. The treatment model focuses on teaching the prosocial skills and competencies that are needed for day-to-day living, rather than on understanding and eliminating pathological responses. The emphasis is on new learned behavior that leads to positive consequences rather than on past behaviors that may have elicited negative consequences.

Promoting social competence in young people can be an effective strategy for helping them confront stressful and problematic situations. Adolescents need to acquire numerous social skills, because during this stage of life they develop new patterns of interpersonal relationships, confront new social experiences, and need to learn new behavioral responses. Social skills training has been applied to many different problem areas—for example, the specific problems Native American adolescents face (Schinke et al., 1985), school adjustment problems (LeCroy & Milligan, 1996), preventing unwanted pregnancy (Gilchrist, Schinke, & Blythe, 1985), and prevention of substance abuse (Elias, 1991). Without adequate social skills, these experiences can become avenues to such problems as pregnancy, drug use, social isolation, and loneliness.

Depending on the goals of the program and the type of problem situations being addressed, different skills would be appropriate. For example, in a program for juvenile offenders, Hazel and colleagues (1981) focused on the following skills: giving and receiving feedback, negotiating and resisting peer pressure, and problem solving. A program for pregnancy prevention might focus on skills such as discussing birth control, asking for information, refusing unacceptable demands, and problem solving.

All social skills programs break down the skills into component parts for easy teaching. For example, beginning conversational skills might include four parts: greeting the other person, making small talk, deciding whether the other person is listening, and bringing up the main topic.

In teaching social skills, it is also important to construct social situations that demand the types of social skills you want to teach. For example, LeCroy (1994) uses the following situation in a social skills program:

> You went to spend the afternoon with some friends but agreed to be home by 4:00 P.M. since your family has plans to have dinner with some friends. You lost track of time and did not get home until 4:45 P.M.

The process of teaching social skills includes seven basic steps that leaders should follow. Box 9.4 presents these steps and outlines the process for teaching social skills (LeCroy, 1992). In each step, there is a request for group member involvement, because it is critical that group leaders involve the participants actively in the training. This keeps the learning process interesting and fun for the group members.

Adolescent Peer Groups

Adolescent peer groups provide important functions that extend beyond friendship. Groups provide an organized means of participation, a collective sense of camaraderie, and group support for mastering the tasks of adolescence. Group membership allows young people to assess their individuality in light of group pressure and norms. As young people continue their search for identity, choosing to participate in a group helps answer the question "with whom do I belong?" Groups provide experience with difficult social expectations of inclusion and exclusion as well as conformity and independence.

It is during this period, late childhood through adolescence, that peer groups have their greatest importance. As adolescents prepare for increasing independence, peer groups can provide needed support. For example, during this time sexual and emotional development are critical, and peer groups help young people address these challenges. Ethnographic research by Fine (1980) reveals that sexual concerns are prominently dealt with in 9- to 12-year-olds.

Cliques and Crowds Adolescents typically form small interaction-based groups in which they spend a great

---

BOX 9.4

Seven Basic Steps for Teaching Social Skills

1. Present the social skill being taught.
   a. Solicit an explanation of the skill.
   b. Get group members to provide rationales for the skill.
2. Discuss the social skill.
   a. List the skill steps.
   b. Get group members to give examples of using the skill.
3. Present a problem situation and model the skill.
   a. Evaluate the performance.
   b. Get group members to discuss the model.
4. Set the stage for role playing the skill.
   a. Select the group members for role playing.
   b. Get group members to observe the role play.

5. Have group members rehearse the skill.
   a. Provide coaching if necessary.
   b. Get group members to provide feedback on verbal and nonverbal elements.
6. Practice using complex skill situations.
   a. Teach accessory skills, e.g. problem solving.
   b. Get group members to discuss situations and provide feedback.
7. Train for generalization and maintenance.
   a. Encourage practice of skills outside the group.
   b. Get group members to bring up their own problem situations.

Source: LeCroy, 1992.

deal of time and develop close relationships. These groups are referred to as a **clique.** In contrast, **crowds** are larger reputation-based collectives of similar young people who do not necessarily spend a lot of time together. *Reputation-based* refers to the adolescent's crowd affiliation, which suggests the attitudes or activities with which one is associated by peers (Brown, 1990). Typical crowds are commonly known as jocks, brains, partners, nerds, and druggies. Crowd norms reflect the stereotypic image that peers have of crowd members (Brown, 1990). These different types of crowds are commonly described in various studies and may be related to two basic dimensions on which adolescents could be rated—commitment to the formal reward system of the school (adult controlled) and commitment to the informal status system (peer controlled). This notion lead researchers Rigsby and McDill (1975) to identify four generic peer cultures: well-rounded, studious, fun culture, and uninvolved.

Gangs   Increasingly familiar are the gangs of the big cities—the Crips and Bloods of Los Angeles or Chicago's Vice Lords and Black Gangster Disciples. The recent increase in gangs across the United States has received increasing attention from the media, popular writers, and scholars. Recent films such as *Colors*, about the Crips and Bloods, and *Boyz in the Hood* have put the topic of gangs on the front pages of many newspapers. No longer are gangs associated only with New York, Chicago, and Los Angeles (Huff, 1993). How can we tell whether a person is a gang member? Defining what constitutes a gang is difficult. For example, what is the difference between a gang and a group? Gangs are usually differentiated from other groups on the basis of their delinquent activity, but the distinction is not just limited to delinquency. Huff (1993, p. 4) provides a comprehensive definition of a youth **gang:**

> A collectivity consisting primarily of adolescents and young adults who (a) interact frequently with one another; (b) are frequently and deliberately involved in illegal activities; (c) share a common collective identity that is usually, but not always, expressed through a gang name; and (d) typically express that identity by adopting certain symbols and/or claiming control over certain "turf" (persons, places, things, and/or economic markets).

Gangs seem to be related to the developmental need for young people to associate with peer groups. In-

deed, adolescents who have difficulties with peer relationships are often maladjusted (Huff, 1993). Because adolescence is a time when intense peer involvement is typical, it is not surprising that gangs are an outgrowth of that involvement. According to Huff (1993), because group experience is a normal part of the adolescent subculture, gangs can be considered an extreme manifestation of the need for peer group involvement and acceptance. Gangs often play a very important function for young people by providing social support, bonding, and protection from rival gangs (Huff, 1993).

Growth in gang numbers is considerable. In Los Angeles, it is estimated that there are approximately 100,000 Crips and Bloods who account for more than 500 homicides every year. These two groups are the most discussed gangs because of their size, the extent of their violence, and their role in drug trafficking. Also, these gangs now exist throughout the United States and are not limited to Los Angeles. These gangs began as primarily African American and Hispanic street gangs in the late 1960s. The Crips are the original gang and the Bloods formed as a means of protection against the Crips.

Gang members range in age from 15 to 30 years old. There is no centralized leadership, but groupings are based on different factors, such as location. Gangs are often discussed in terms of three primary groupings: (a) leaders or original gangsters; (b) hard-cores, members committed to the gang and its criminal activities; and (c) wannabes, usually younger youth who want to be hard-core gang members. Gangs can often be identified by their symbols, clothes, or other ways of showing affiliation.

The following Focus on Diversity section discusses another serious problem that youth face: the hopeless path of the runaway.

FOCUS ON DIVERSITY

Runaway Youth: A Hopeless Pathway

Tim, at age 16, knows what it is like to be homeless. He's lived that way for the last five years. Where would you be most likely to find him? Look in abandoned buildings in downtown Phoenix, under highway overpasses, or in alleys filled with homeless men and women in the worst parts of the city. Tim is only one of an estimated 2 million runaway youth. What kinds of difficulties do these youth face? Are there common problems that most runaway youth have?

According to recent research, such homeless youth are frequently afflicted with drug and alcohol abuse, prostitution, and thoughts of suicide. In an attempt to better understand runaway youth, Robertson conducted research interviews with youth, searching out abandoned buildings, fast-food restaurants, and the boulevards known to harbor such youth—Hollywood and Santa Monica. The interviews were conducted with youth aged 13 to 17, with an average age of 16.1 years. The majority were white (60.2%) and male (61.3%), and most had completed the ninth grade. The interviews revealed that these adolescents had previous experience with hopelessness (79%), and more than half had lived in foster homes or group homes. This history suggests a pattern of residential instability that began as early as age 5 or 6. Most of the youth were receiving money from friends, family, or short-term jobs. Young people are not eligible for welfare benefits, and shelters are not required to take them in. Additional sources of income included dealing drugs and prostitution.

In a profile of the runaway youth, almost 50% met the criteria for alcohol dependence; however, co-morbidity was common. All the alcohol-dependent youth met the criteria for conduct disorder based on criteria from the DSM-IV. Robertson further found that more than one-fifth met the criteria for major depression. Nearly half of the sample had attempted suicide at least once, and over 50% had attempted suicide within the previous 12 months. Most of the adolescents in the sample had engaged in sex at least once. Moreover, only about half of the sexually active adolescents reported that they had used a condom the last time they had sex. Almost half of the girls reported one or more pregnancies.

Clearly, runaway youth face many health and social problems. Unfortunately, very few of the youth have the needed resources to address the problems they face. Over two-thirds of the sample had no medical coverage. Although many of these youth were in state care, they had fallen out of care and were not receiving benefits they were entitled to through the state.

Source: Robertson, Ropers, & Boyer, 1985.

School Influences

A functional match between schools and the adolescent is becoming an increasingly recognized idea that needs attention and reform. Indeed, many researchers and professionals believe that the middle school is not an effective institution for young people. Eccles and Midgley (1989) argue that a serious mismatch exists between the organization and curriculum of middle schools and the intellectual, social, and emotional needs of young adolescents. To address many of the educational issues of adolescents, we will examine three themes: the effect of schooling on adolescent development; the ecology of the schools; and a life-course perspective about schools (Entwisle, 1990).

Schooling has played an important role in influencing adolescent development. Perhaps most significant was the movement to make secondary schooling compulsory, putting adolescents in a submissive position and keeping them from the workforce in order to make employment more manageable. Although the emphasis in schools has changed over time, the basic function has remained stable since the 1900s (Sizer, 1983). That function is to provide a comprehensive curriculum to prepare young people for the diverse aspects of life. How this "comprehensive curriculum" is structured is a source of debate. For instance, the back-to-basics movement has gained prominence, but opponents argue that schools must also be responsive to young people's social and emotional lives.

Whatever the curriculum, the numerous hours that young people spend in school expose them to significant and life-changing events and experiences. Their identity formation, competence in social and academic abilities, career paths, and social relationships are all affected by their experience in school. In spite of this influence, many people have questioned whether schooling is effective. This question is evaluated from two vantage points: Does school affect cognitive abilities? and Can schools compensate for the negative effects of poverty?

(Santrock, 1989). Research suggests that schooled children can outperform unschooled children (Wagner & Stevenson, 1982). However, it is also true that average achievement-test gains are small in high school (Jencks, 1985). With regard to the second question, there is evidence, although not without controversy, that schools have little impact on the cognitive development of students in poverty. Furthermore, the effect of school quality produces small differences in students' achievements (Jencks, 1985).

Although students of color must confront institutional and individual discrimination, it is important to acknowledge diversity in the educational experience of different cultures and races. Some groups (e.g., Asian Indians and Chinese) perform better on the average in school and attain higher levels of formal education than whites do, whereas other groups (e.g., Puerto Ricans and Mexicans) do not compare as well (Mare & Winship, 1988). A significant predictor of educational success for youth of color is parents' level of education and father's occupation.

Our previous discussion focused on how young people's backgrounds and personal characteristics influence their school success, but also important are the social and organizational characteristics that influence adolescent development (Entwisle, 1990). One of the major organizational factors that influence the relationship between school and adolescent development is the transition from elementary school to middle school and the transition from middle school to high school.

From 1970 to 1987, there was a 160% increase in the number of middle schools and a corresponding decline of 53% in the number of junior high schools (Alexander & McEwin, 1989). In most schools, the ninth grade has been included in the high school system, and most school systems now have middle schools that include either the seventh and eighth grades or the sixth, seventh, and eighth grades. The transition from elementary school to middle school is often a stressful one. As the Carnegie Council on Adolescent Development (1989) points out, it often represents a move from a small neighborhood school with the stability of one classroom to a large and impersonal institution, often more complex and bureaucratic. This shift may disrupt important support and comfort from peer groups and caring relationships from school teachers and staff. Furthermore, this transition occurs in tandem with puberty and other emotional and social changes (e.g., concerns about body image, decreased dependency on parents, changes in social cognition).

This stressful transition may be explained in part by the top-dog phenomena observed by Simmons and Blyth (1987) in their study on the transition into adolescence. These researchers found that stress is increased for young people as they move from being "top dog" (biggest, oldest, most powerful) in the elementary school to being "bottom dog" (smallest, youngest, least powerful) in the middle school. This study also compared the self-esteem of seventh-grade girls who had transitioned to junior high with girls who remained in a K–8 school. The junior high students were negatively affected by the transition: They had lower self-esteem, negative attitudes toward school, fewer leadership roles, and more victimization by boys. Despite the trend toward middle schools, there is no good evidence to support this change; in fact, some research suggests it would be better to keep the old school system of grades K–8 and 9–12.

The Carnegie Council on Adolescent Development has been extremely critical of the organization and curriculum of middle schools. The Council finds that middle schools fall short of meeting the educational, health, and social needs of young adolescents. They identify three essential qualities schools need to create a community for learning: (1) schools need to be restructured to a more human scale, which means creating smaller learning environments; (2) schools need to create a small group of caring adults who work with each other to develop coordinated, meaningful, and challenging educational experiences and provide some stability with peer groups; and (3) schools need to create opportunities for each student to interact with at least one adult who can provide the youth with advice about academic matters and personal problems and emphasize the importance of succeeding in the middle school.

The high school also is not beyond criticism. One of the most prevalent images of the high school is that of the "shopping mall" (Powell, Farrar, & Cohen, 1985). As many shoppers wander aimlessly in the mall, the average high school student is lost within the corridors and classrooms of the high school. This image was the result of an extensive study of 15 diverse high schools. Although the high schools offer variety and choice, the result is a curriculum that is watered down and lacking in substance for most of the students. The researchers claim that the average students—neither on a "high" track nor a "low" track—are the forgotten students in the high school. Thus the shopping mall high school promotes individualization but does not provide personalization.

High School Dropouts   Although high school dropout is considered a serious problem, the percentage of youth that do not finish high school has decreased considerably over the years. Fifty years ago, over 60% of students had not finished high school. Today that percentage is approximately 14% (U.S. General Accounting Office, 1986). However, it is important to realize that this figure varies dramatically depending on the city and region of the country. In Chicago, the dropout rate is 55%. Dropout rates of minority groups in urban cities, while declining, are still above levels of white students. It is important to recognize that when students of color and white students with similar test scores and high school grades are compared, students of color may be somewhat *more* likely to graduate from high school (Entwisle, 1990). The poor academic preparation and disadvantaged economic background of students of color appear to account for their high dropout rate when compared with white students.

Studies of the characteristics of dropouts have found several factors that predict dropout: living in poverty, single-parent families, parents who do not participate in decision making concerning the youth, delinquent behaviors, grade retention, poor grades, pregnancy, more than 15 hours of work per week, and urban lifestyle (National Research Council, 1993). Dropout prevention programs have focused on targeting at-risk students and improving academic performance, changing attitudes about school, and reducing absenteeism. Very few dropout prevention programs have been evaluated for their effectiveness. However, the trend is to begin dropout prevention strategies earlier than high school by focusing on middle schools and elementary schools. Also, because dropout rates in some schools are so high, the strategy is to improve the overall school in order to prevent dropout. It is estimated that 25% of urban schools have dropout rates of approximately 50% (National Research Council, 1993); therefore, an individualized approach is no longer feasible. The current focus of prevention is on schoolwide practices that can reduce alienation from the educational process and increase motivation and interest in learning.

Multicultural and Gender Considerations

There are many multicultural and gender considerations in adolescence. As young people experience a broader world, they become more aware of their unique qualities—what it means to be a person of color, an immigrant from another country, a boy or girl, a heterosexual or homosexual.

Peer Relationships and Adolescents of Color

In adolescence, young people of color begin to interact with a more heterogeneous population, and as a result they become more aware of their ethnic status. Also, adolescents of color often have two sets of peer relationships—at school and in their neighborhoods (Santrock, 1990). Neighborhood peers are more likely from their own ethnic group. In a study by Brown and Mounts (1989) of multiethnic high schools, between one-third and one-half of students of color were associated by peers with ethnically defined crowds—for example, rappers or African Americans, or Hispanics. The remaining students, two-thirds to one-half, were classified into reputation-based groups such as populars or new wavers. Because adolescents of color may have two sets of peers, it is important to inquire about relationships both in school and in the neighborhood. Adolescents who may be isolated and rejected in school could be neighborhood stars (Gibbs & Huang, 1989).

The Adolescent Immigrant

Thousands of adolescents immigrate to the United States with their families each year from countries all over the world—Mexico, Thailand, Vietnam, and Haiti, to name a few. How does immigration affect their long-term adjustment to a new country? A five-year longitudinal study (Arrendondo, 1984) suggests three factors that are important for a satisfactory adjustment. Adolescents must address the issue of belonging versus estrangement. Many adolescent immigrants get quick exposure to racial and ethnic discrimination. Their minority status is heightened by differences in appearance, dress, and language. A sense of belonging can be developed through participation in their immediate community or through participation in educational and political activities. Critical to their adjustment is reliance on their earlier primary group's cultural values because this can provide a foundation for their adjustment. By using their identification with earlier values, they can make new accommodations without the need to reject basic values. Last, supportiveness of family relationships is necessary to provide positive expectations about their new adjustments to a different way of life. Encouragement that they can be successful and achieve reduces the sense of self-doubt and feelings of being marginal and provides a basis for them to realize their aspirations. Immigrating adolescents face many unique challenges in successful acculturation.

Regardless of their cultural background, adolescent girls are confronted with special problems that arisesolely because of their gender.

The following Focus on Gender section explores the unique challenges that adolescent girls face.

FOCUS ON GENDER

Meeting at the Crossroads: A Study of Adolescent Girls

Carol Gilligan is well known for her feminist work *In a Different Voice*, which changed the way researchers view women's development. In her new work, *Meeting at the Crossroads*, with Lyn Mikel Brown, she examines the lives of adolescent girls and provides a new perspective about young girls' development. The central question the researchers sought to answer was, "What, on the way to womanhood, does a girl give up?" The way to womanhood was found to be accompanied by a falling away of the self. The researchers found that younger, preadolescent girls perceived conflict as a sign of healthy relationships, and they could more easily speak about their thoughts and feelings. At this stage of development,

these girls were comfortable with feelings of anger, fighting in relationships, and disagreements. In contrast, girls approaching adolescence struggle with a preoccupation with perfection and are engulfed with idealized relationships. At this age, girls desire attention, love, and popularity, and in their pursuit to build relationships, they are expected to give up something—for example, expression of their real feelings of anger. These girls' accounts are documented with vivid anecdotes as they describe their losses and their inability to express themselves. The researchers refer to this phenomenon as a form of psychological repression. For example, Gail reflects on her life over the past year: "I think I've gotten along better with people . . . I don't disagree as much . . . and I don't get into fights as much. Like arguments with my friends." When the interviewer asks why, she responds, "Maybe because I can understand how they think now and accept them . . . accept what they think, instead of being just one-minded . . . I realized that I went along with that and I realized I was experienced I guess, because I realized that I should understand what they think also." Then the interviewer asks, "Do you think fighting or arguing is worthless?" and Gail offers a confusing statement and then concludes that yes, fighting is worthless because she's stopped fighting and she doesn't "have to think." In this example, Brown and Gilligan (p. 93) comment: "Gail's response to her interviewer's questions about arguing exemplifies the intricate and subtle relationship between Gail's developing capacity to understand and appreciate and take in viewpoints different from her own and the fear that by continuing to speak in the presence of difference she will lose her relationship with her friends." Brown and Gilligan encourage practitioners to help strengthen healthy resistance and courage in girls. The major lesson is the importance of helping girls discover their lost voices.

Source: Brown & Gilligan, 1992.

Gender Roles

What does it mean to be a boy or girl in today's society? In the past, there were more clear indications about what a boy did compared with a girl—boys played rough and got dirty, whereas girls played quietly and kept clean. In today's culture, there is greater diversity about gender roles and an increasing emphasis on equality or role sharing. Much of this change in gender roles is characterized as a move toward androgyny, which is the combination of masculine and feminine behaviors in the same person (Bem, 1977). An androgynous male adolescent is someone who is both assertive and sensitive to others; an androgynous female is dominant and assertive as well as nurturing. Various research studies on gender roles suggest that, in general, changes are taking place in the direction of greater role sharing.

Do you think you are an androgynous person? A widely used measure of sex roles, the Bem Sex Role Inventory, is presented in Box 9.5, so you can make an assessment of yourself. There are four major gender-role classifications: androgynous, masculine, feminine, and undifferentiated. We have already defined *androgynous*, you are familiar with the notions of masculine and feminine, and the undifferentiated classification refers to a person who has neither masculine nor feminine characteristics. Although androgyny is a useful concept, researchers

BOX 9.5

The Bem Sex Role Inventory

Instructions: Rate each item on the scale from 1 (never or almost never true) to 7 (always or almost always true).

1. self-reliant
2. yielding
3. helpful
4. defends own beliefs
5. cheerful
6. moody
7. independent
8. shy
9. conscientious
10. athletic
11. affectionate
12. theatrical
13. assertive
14. flatterable
15. happy
16. strong personality
17. loyal
18. unpredictable
19. forceful
20. feminine
21. reliable

22. analytical
23. sympathetic
24. jealous
25. has leadership abilities
26. sensitive to the needs of others
27. truthful
28. willing to take risks
29. understanding
30. secretive
31. makes decisions easily
32. compassionate
33. sincere
34. self-sufficient
35. eager to soothe hurt
36. conceited
37. dominant
38. soft-spoken
39. likable

40. masculine
41. warm
42. solemn
43. willing to take a stand
44. tender
45. friendly
46. aggressive
47. gullible
48. inefficient
49. acts as a leader
50. childlike

51. adaptable
52. individualistic
53. does not use harsh language
54. unsystematic
55. competitive
56. loves children
57. tactful
58. ambitious
59. gentle
60. conventional

Scoring: Masculinity score—add up ratings for 1, 4, 7, 10, 13, 16, 19, 22, 25, 28, 31, 34, 37, 40, 43, 46, 49, 52, 55, and 58. Divide the total by 20. The result is your masculinity score.

Femininity score—add up ratings for 2, 5, 8, 11, 14, 17, 20, 23, 26, 29, 32, 35, 38, 41, 44, 47, 50, 53, 56, and 59. Divide by 20. That is your femininity score.
Note: If your masculinity score is above 4.9 (the median score) and your femininity score is above 4.9 (the median score), then you would be classified as androgynous on Bem's scale.

Source: Hyde, 1985.

have had a difficult time specifying the concept. Also, we must consider how the concept reflects the developmental level of the child (Santrock, 1990). What is feminine for a 4-year-old girl will be quite different from that of a 15-year-old. What aspects do you think best characterize masculinity and femininity during adolescence?

Recent work on gender roles has led to a greater understanding of the concepts involved. For example, Ford (1986) defines masculinity in terms of the concept of self-assertion and defines femininity in terms of integration. Self-assertion is composed of leadership, dominance, independence, competitiveness, and individualism. Integration refers to sympathy, affection, and understanding. An androgynous person has a high degree of both self-assertion and integration.

Body Image and Adolescent Depression for Girls

Body image in adolescent girls may explain higher rates of depression. Depression is twice as high for girls as it is for boys. This may be the result of girls' significant unhappiness with their body image. In childhood up to puberty, more boys are depressed than girls. Suddenly, in late adolescence, twice the number of girls as boys are depressed—a finding that continues through adulthood. Some research (Girgus, 1989) has examined a number of possible factors that could account for such differences, including body dissatisfaction, life events, popularity, and sex roles. However, the most significant factor related to depression is body image. Girls interpret their maturing bodies negatively because they desire to become thinner than they have been in the past. But whereas girls see their rounded curves as negative, boys perceive their body changes as positive—as developing more muscles.

Girls and boys were equally likely to be depressed because of life events, but girls unhappy with their body images were more likely to be depressed. Also, girls who spend more time in "feminine activities"—such as makeup, cooking, shopping—were more inclined to be depressed. Girgus (1989) suggests that because feminine stereotypical activities tend to be passive and may provide less mastery and autonomy, they may contribute to a tendency to depression. The following Focus on Research section presents an example of a common research method used to study adolescent behavior.

FOCUS ON RESEARCH

Conducting Ethnographies to Study Adolescent Behavior

Ethnographic-type assignments can be used to learn how to integrate theories and information about human development. Peggy Quinn (1992) uses this technique in her Human Behavior classes. An ethnography is a study of people; the researcher studies how people make sense of their world. It has also been referred to as taking the client's perspective from the inside out (Watts, 1985). Students are asked to select theories they perceive as appropriate for a given developmental stage. For example, some students chose to study young teens. One good observational setting was the mall, where young people spend a fairly large percentage of their time. Students selected what aspect of the mall they would use—for example, the food court or the video arcade. Next, they developed a framework for observing teenagers' behavior, such as noting greeting behaviors, dress, conversational patterns, and so forth. Student observations included notes on peer pressures, efforts at differentiation, and the girls' flirtatious behavior. Students were expected to discuss their observations as reflecting various theories of human development. As you read through this text on human development, take the time to conduct mini-ethnographies—observe a group of people and study their interactions. How does their behavior fit with various theories? What aspects of their behavior are difficult to understand? What meanings, besides the obvious, might explain their behavior? By asking questions and observing behavior, you can learn a great deal about people's unique behaviors and social relationships.

Adolescent Heterosexuality

No discussion of adolescence would be complete without a section on adolescent sexuality. In adolescence, formation of a sexual identity is a major developmental task. From adolescence to young adulthood, young people begin the process of sexual exploration—a search for their sexual identities. Although this may sound like a sexual stereotype, it is during this time that boys aggressively search for sexual experience with girls and girls eagerly desire romantic involvement with boys. For example, Cassell (1984) found that more girls than boys report being in love as the main reason for engaging in sexual intercourse. Adolescent boys recognize this socialization, and as a result, profess to be "in love" with a large number of girls. However, changes in sexual behavior in the last 20 years do show a decline in the sexual double standard. Sexual intercourse for adolescent girls has increased more rapidly than for boys, indicating greater acceptance of girls being sexually active. However, research on attitudes and feelings about sexual intercourse has found that twice as many boys as girls report positive feelings about their sexual experiences (Gordon & Gilgun, 1987). A related study found that both male and female adolescents accept that the role of the male adolescent is to be the aggressor in sexual relations and that the female adolescent's role is to set the limits of this behavior (Goodchilds & Zellman, 1984). Many aspects of adolescent sexuality have undergone rapid and considerable change, yet many other aspects have remained unchanged.

How sexually active are adolescents? Recent data suggest that they are quite active. Table 9.4 presents data from a sample of more than 46,000 youth in 25 states (Benson, 1990). As the table indicates, starting in the seventh grade, 22% of the boys and 10% of the girls have already experienced sexual intercourse. By the twelfth grade, 77% of the boys and 66% of the girls have experienced sexual intercourse. Contraceptive use shows a gradual increase from 33% at first intercourse in the seventh grade to 53% in the twelfth grade. Not quite half of the eighth- through twelfth-grade adolescents use contraceptives consistently after the first intercourse.

As might be expected, several factors influence the incidence of sexual activity among adolescents. For example, sexual activity is lowest for white adolescents, followed by Hispanic, and then African American adolescents. The following factors have been found to significantly influence adolescents' sexual activity (see, e.g., Miller, McCoy, & Olson, 1986; Newcomb, Huba, & Bentler, 1986):

- Living in a single-parent household is related to a higher incidence of sexual activity.
- Attending church and doing well in school discourages sexual activity.
- Good parent-adolescent communication discourages sexual activity.
- Early dating experience encourages sexual activity.
- Parental discipline—either too permissive or too strict—encourages sexual activity.

Petersen and Crockett (1992) identify four influences that they believe are associated with early sexual behavior and subsequent pregnancy:

1. *Biological influences.* Puberty is hypothesized to have a major influence on adolescent sexual behavior, leading to greater risk of pregnancy and childbearing. Pubertal development may affect adolescent sexual behavior in two ways: directly through hormonal effects on the brain, and more indirectly through somatic changes that stimulate a more mature physical appearance, which in turn suggests expectations about more mature sexual behavior.

2. *Sexual abuse.* Prepubertal sexual abuse may have a significant effect on girls' subsequent sexual behavior. It is hypothesized that prepubertal sexual abuse is linked to earlier sexual behavior, earlier pregnancy, and earlier childbearing and that it is related to difficulties with child-rearing skills. The reasons for this connection are complicated and not well understood.

3. *Deviance or problem behavior.* Adolescents that are involved in problem behaviors are more likely to have earlier sexual behavior and earlier pregnancy. Jessor (1992) identifies sexual behavior as one part of the problem behavior syndrome. Jessor speculates that involvement in problem behavior is related to psychological readiness to participate in adult behaviors. Or participation in one problem behavior may bring young people into contact with peer groups where additional problem behaviors are modeled and encouraged. More simply, pregnancy and the sexual behavior of adolescents appear to be part of a "deviant lifestyle" characterized by multiple problem behaviors (Elliot, 1993).

4. *Normative expectations.* Transitions to subsequent life stages may be influenced by societal expectations. In other words, if an adolescent is expected to complete college, then marry, and then have children,

TABLE 9.4   Sexual Behavior, by Grade and Gender

| Grade | Percentage Sexually Active | | | | If Sexually Active, Percentage Using Contraceptives | |
| | One or More Times | | Four or More Times | | At First Intercourse (Partner or Self) | All the Time Now (Partner or Self) |
	Boys	Girls	Boys	Girls		
7	22	10	7	3	33	36
8	32	17	12	4	38	42
9	41	27	17	14	45	45
10	50	43	26	27	49	47
11	58	54	37	41	53	51
12	77	66	51	54	53	53

Source: Benson, 1990.

these expectations are likely to influence the course of such events. Petersen and Crockett (1992) found that girls who are sexually active in junior high school anticipate making several adult transitions, such as finishing their education, starting a job, and marrying, at earlier ages than do girls who are not yet sexually active. Also interesting is the finding of familial transmission of these expectations. Several studies have found a relationship between mothers' sexual experience as adolescents and the sexual experience of their adolescent child. This may be due to a permissive attitude toward sex, or it could be due to early maturity by both mother and daughter. The following Focus on Narrative presents several adolescents' viewpoints about sex.

FOCUS ON NARRATIVE

Adolescents' Views on Sex

Santrock (1990, p. 426) quotes several adolescents about their sexual experiences:

I am 16 years old and I really like this one girl. She wants to be a virgin until she marries. We went out last night and she let me go pretty far, but not all the way . . . It's getting hard for me to handle . . . I feel I am ready to have sex. I have to admit I think about having sex with other girls too . . . (Frank C.)

I'm 14 years old. I have a lot of sexy thoughts. Sometimes just before I drift off to sleep at night I think about this hunk who is 16 years old and plays on the football team. He is so gorgeous and I can feel him holding me in his arms and kissing and hugging me . . . (Amy S.)

Is it weird to be a 17-year-old guy and still be a virgin? Sometimes I feel like the only 17-year-old male on the planet who has not had sex. I feel like I am missing out on something great, or at least that's what I hear. I'm pretty religious and I sometimes feel guilty when I think about sex . . . (Tom B.)

I'm 15 years old and I had sex for the first time recently. I had all of these expectations about how great it was going to be . . . We were both pretty scared about the whole thing. It was all over in a hurry. My first thought was, "Is this all there is?" It was a very disappointing experience. (Claire T.)

AIDS Prevention and Adolescent Males

Given the high rate of sexual intercourse among adolescent boys, there is a great need for AIDS prevention among this population. AIDS, or acquired immune deficiency syndrome, is caused by the **human immunodeficiency virus (HIV)**. This virus destroys the human immune system and leads to opportunistic infections. These infections are caused by agents such as bacteria and viruses that are usually harmless to a healthy individual. In the immune-compromised individual, however, these agents produce illness and, ultimately, death. Infection with HIV leads to a classification of the person as HIV-positive. The rate of infection from this virus has been increasing at an alarming rate over the past several years.

It appears, however, that AIDS prevention is responding to the AIDS epidemic. From 1979 to 1988, the proportion of sexually active adolescent boys using condoms has doubled. A study reported by Sonenstein, Pleck, and Ku (1989) surveyed adolescent boys, ages 15–19, about their levels of sexual activity, use of contraception, and knowledge of AIDS. Using a comparison sample from 1979, they found that, despite the AIDS dilemma, the number of sexually active adolescents is on the rise. The researchers found almost a 20% increase from 1979 to 1988 in the number of 17-year-olds who say they had sexual intercourse. However, in 1979 only 21% of the sexually active adolescents used a condom the last time they had sex, whereas in 1988 58% reported using a condom. Furthermore, the percentage of adolescents who said they had used no protection during their last sexual intercourse fell from 51% in 1979 to 21% in 1988.

More encouraging is the level of knowledge the adolescent males had about AIDS. For example, most of the adolescents surveyed were knowledgeable about the way the virus is transmitted, and 82% realized that AIDs is not so uncommon that they don't have to worry about it. Also, most of the adolescents—75%—disagreed with the statement "using condoms to prevent AIDS is more trouble than it's worth." There are still some misconceptions; for example, 40% thought you could get AIDS from giving blood. However, progress in AIDS prevention appears to be paying off. As Ellen Stark (1989) reminds us, the trend of a round indentation in the wallet from carrying a condom is making a comeback.

Less encouraging is that young gay men aren't consistently practicing safe sex, although a majority of older gay men have changed to safe sex behavior. In one study of young gay men, 36% indicated they had unprotected anal sex during the prior two months. Younger gay men see AIDS as something that happens to older gay men. Other subgroups that represent high risk include youths in juvenile detention, where in one study, all the jailed adolescents had experienced sex and 78% had had two or more sex partners in the past year. Also, 13% had admitted using intravenous drugs. In a similar manner, homeless and runaway youth are at higher risk for AIDS. Because they are more concerned with daily survival, protecting themselves against AIDS is not seen as a priority (Sonenstein, Pleck, & Ku, 1989; Youngstrom, 1991).

Adolescent Homosexuality

Consider the following quotes from gay and lesbian adolescents (Hersch, 1990):

> When all the guys are discussing their latest crushes, I play along. What a body Carol has. Look at those great tits on Marge. How can I tell them I dream of Dave? It would be all over the school in a flash. I'd be dead meat.

> It's difficult to know what to wear, what to say, how to act with different people. You are so scared of being found out that you never know if you will ever be able to be yourself.

> I don't understand what is going on with me. I want to kill myself. I'm scared of who I am. There is no one else like me. What am I going to do? It's not normal to be gay— normal is a man and a woman. Am I the only one?

These are the words of gay and lesbian adolescents. They are also words of secrecy and fear—a world that homosexual adolescents must learn to live within. Life is difficult, if not dangerous, as many homosexual adolescents experience violence because of their sexual orientation. Indeed, adolescent homosexuality presents our society with many challenges. As Hersch (1990) aptly puts it, "to a culture already uncomfortable about adult sex, worried about adolescent sex, and downright hostile about homosexual sex, gay and lesbian adolescents pose a compounded threat—children who are sexual *and* deviant." Society has a difficult time accepting adolescents as sexually active and would rather deny the existence of homosexual adolescents. (See Focus on Diversity: Guide-

Often, in adolescence, young people decide on a homosexual or heterosexual expression of their sexuality. Homosexual adolescents often experience alienation and face developmental problems because they may repress their identity, face peer rejection, and feel the pressure of cultural sanctions against intimate homosexual relations.

lines for Adolescents Who Want to Consider Coming Out.)

Yet, homosexual adolescents do exist. Chilman (1979) found that 3% of boys and 2% of girls report participating in ongoing homosexual relations during adolescence. However, that was more than 15 years ago. Today most experts estimate the gay and lesbian population at about 10%. The estimated 4 million homosexual adolescents must confront many social problems.

Perhaps of most concern is the isolation, depression, and potential for suicide. These young people are two to three times as likely to attempt suicide as are other youth. In a study (Remafedi, Farrow, & Deisher, 1991) of homosexual adolescents, 30% reported at least one suicide attempt. Twenty-one percent of the suicide attempts re-

sulted in medical or psychiatric hospitalization, but almost three out of four attempts did not receive any medical attention. A significant number of the suicide attempts were related to personal turmoil about homosexuality. Many of these young people have a difficult time confronting the social isolation they experience, their concern about secrecy, and their fear of violence.

In addition to the concern about depression and suicide, homosexual adolescents face a number of increased risks. Destructive alcohol and drug abuse, being victims of crime, sexual diseases including AIDS, and school dropout are some of the more prevalent risks associated with adolescent homosexuality. These risks can be compounded if the youth is a minority. Gay and lesbian youth of color live within three communities: their ethnic community, the gay and lesbian community, and the majority community (McManus, 1991). They are thus susceptible to two types of prejudice: racism and homophobia. This lifestyle can require "a constant effort to maintain oneself in three different worlds, each of which fails to support significant aspects of a person's life."

FOCUS ON DIVERSITY

Guidelines for Adolescents Who Want to Consider Coming Out

Many gay and lesbian adolescents will confront the decision about whether or not to come out and discuss their homosexuality. This is a difficult decision with a lot of serious consequences. Sauerman (1984) has produced a pamphlet for the Federation of Parents and Friends of Lesbians and Gays, Inc., that presents a series of questions that need to be considered before coming out:

1. Are you sure about your sexual orientation?
2. Are you comfortable with your gay sexuality?
3. Do you have support?
4. Are you knowledgeable about homosexuality?
5. What's the emotional climate at home?
6. Can you be patient?

7. What's your motive for coming out now?
8. Do you have available resources?
9. Are you financially dependent on your parents?
10. What is your general relationship with your parents?
11. What is their moral societal view?
12. Is this your decision?

Social Hazards

How can we understand the various factors that play a significant role in leading to adolescent risk behaviors or

lifestyles? For several years, Richard Jessor (1987, 1992) has been studying adolescent problem behavior. Figure 9.1 shows five protective and risk factors that influence adolescent risk behavior: biology/genetics, social environment, perceived environment, personality, and behavior. It is important to point out that the influence of these concepts is bidirectional.

Adolescent Pregnancy and Childbirth

A significant social hazard of the adolescent years is teenage pregnancy—a topic that many people in our society discuss. Teenage pregnancy has become a national

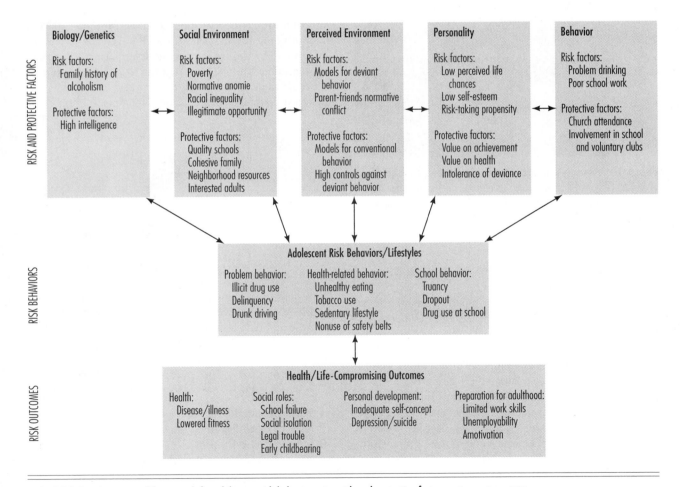

FIGURE 9.1   A conceptual framework for adolescent risk behavior using risk and protective factors   Source: Jessor, 1992.

concern. Indeed, the act of being sexually active can take a young person down many new roads. Once an unplanned pregnancy occurs, there are many difficult decisions to confront: Should I have this baby? Should I give this baby up for adoption? Should I consider an abortion? The result of an unplanned pregnancy has many implications for the future of the young woman: involving the father, getting married, finishing school, parent relationships—all of these things must be attended to. It is as if the young person is thrust into a completely new reality. This section will examine the prevalence of adolescent pregnancy, the consequences of adolescent pregnancy, the adolescent father, and implications for reducing adolescent pregnancy.

Prevalence of Adolescent Pregnancy   When examining the prevalence of adolescent pregnancy, several factors come into play. First, how many adolescents are sexually active? Second, how many of the sexually active adolescents are effectively using contraception? Third, if early pregnancy does occur, how many adolescents are obtaining abortions? When all these factors are taken into consideration it is easier to understand that the actual rate of births to adolescent parents has been decreasing over the last several years. Table 9.5 presents data on what changes have taken place for adolescent sexual behavior and outcome. As the data point out, sexual activity has clearly increased over the years, but so has the use of contraception. This has had an impact of slightly lowering the overall pregnancy rate (−1%). This lower rate, coupled with a small increase in abortion, has resulted in an overall decrease in the birthrate. Table 9.5 also makes clear that there are important racial differences in these outcomes.

In general, there have been more than 1 million teen pregnancies in the United States since 1973, and about 1 out of every 9 adolescent females conceives every year (Dryfoos, 1990). It is estimated that about 1 in 4 sexually active adolescents experience a pregnancy during the year. Pregnancy of very young girls, under age 15, represents only 2% of the births of girls aged 15–19; thus it is considered a rare event

Consequences of Adolescent Pregnancy   The consequences of early pregnancy impact both the mother and the child. For the infant, low birth weight and an increased likelihood of infant mortality are consequences. Prenatal care is obtained by only 1 out of every 5 mothers during the critical first three months of pregnancy. For the mother, especially young mothers, there are increased risks of complications and mortality. There is also a greater likelihood for young mothers to experience such complications as toxemia, anemia, and prolonged labor (Dryfoos, 1990).

The long-term consequences of early pregnancy find teenage mothers suffering many critical disadvantages. Not surprisingly, there is reduced educational achievement due mostly to early dropout from school. This may

TABLE 9.5   Percent Change in Rates of Sexual Behaviors and Outcomes for Girls 15–19 Years Old

	Sexual Activity 1982–88	Contraception at First Intercourse 1982–88	Pregnancy 1982–87	Abortion 1982–87	Birth 1982–87
Total	+13%	+36%	−1%	+1%	−4%
White	+16%	+26%	−5%	−5%	−7%
Nonwhite	—	—	+4%	+11%	−1%
Black	+3%	+50%	—	—	+3%

Source: Hamburg & Dixon, 1992.

Adolescent pregnancy is an important risk factor because it decreases the likelihood that the mother will complete school and significantly reduces her chances for economic self-sufficiency.

contribute to the additional problems of low-status jobs, lower income, and welfare dependency. There are equally critical disadvantages in social relationships—high divorce rates, unstable relationships, and more subsequent unintended births. Long-term consequences for children of adolescents can include lower educational achievement, behavioral and emotional problems, a greater likelihood of themselves becoming teenage parents, and an existence based in poverty (Dryfoos, 1990).

Young women who terminate their pregnancy experience few negative consequences, although the later in the pregnancy the abortion occurs, the greater the risk of complications. The literature has not found significant psychological consequences associated with abortion. Similarly, there appear to not be any serious psychological

consequences associated with adoption, although adoption is rarely an alternative selected by teenage mothers.

Adolescent Fathers   The adolescent father is gaining increasing attention from society. What do we know about the adolescent father? In general, he is much more involved in parenting than previously thought. Research (Danziger & Radin, 1989) has found that fathers are willing and interested in participating in parenting. Most adolescent fathers have daily contact with their children, and 3 out of 4 contribute some financial support. (See the following Focus on Gender section.)

Being an adolescent father is associated with several disadvantages. For one, many adolescent fathers decide to provide financial support, and often this means quitting school. Having quit school, these fathers are eligible only for low-paying jobs.

Only recently have social service agencies recognized the need to respond to adolescent fathers. However, programs are springing up around the country that are specifically designed to help adolescent fathers cope and function effectively in their new role. One such program focuses exclusively on African American fathers; the young men get together to take their children out for the day, provide emotional support to one another, and receive education about fathering and being an effective parent.

FOCUS ON GENDER

Including Adolescent Fathers

Social workers have been working with teenage mothers for many years now. The mother is often the one who has made all the decisions regarding the baby. Teenage fathers have been left behind when decisions are made about their baby. Often the fathers face hostility from their girlfriends' parents, and it has been the myth that teenage fathers don't want anything to do with their girlfriends or the baby once they find out about the pregnancy. Recent findings, however, are showing that an increasing number of fathers do not want to abandon their baby. Therefore, social workers need to consider including teenage fathers when decisions are being made.

Teenage fathers face the same emotional struggles and dilemmas that teenage mothers do, and many fathers want a baby for the same reasons that teenage mothers want one. Like teenage mothers, fathers often imagine only the good times that lie ahead when they think of being a parent. And, not unlike teenage mothers, fathers often feel trapped once the reality sets in and they understand the totality of what is involved in raising a child.

Many fathers truly want to help support their girlfriends and their babies. Most fathers, even though they don't marry the baby's mother, tend to stay close during the first year of the baby's life. Social workers need to take this fact into account when working with teenage mothers and their children, as it is no longer just the two of them in the picture.

Unfortunately, fathers' involvement tends to taper off after the first year of the child's life, when the demands of hard work (required for supporting the child and girlfriend) and raising the child become too much for them to handle. It is important, therefore, that social workers pay attention to teenage fathers and offer them services during the second year of the baby's life as well. New programs are being offered that teach teenage fathers about nutrition and child care. Previously these classes were offered only to mothers; however, a recent trend is to offer coed classes.

Prevention is an important factor when looking at the problem of teenage pregnancies. Children need to be taught sex education early, which should include the proper use of contraceptives and a section on abstinence. Again, these classes are just as important for boys as for girls. One strategy in preventing teenage pregnancies is to have teenage fathers talk to the community about their experiences and encourage other teenagers to be more careful.

Source: Adapted from Robinson & Barret, 1985, by Marilyn Ramirez.

Implications for Practice: Reducing Adolescent Pregnancy

The consequences of adolescent pregnancy point to the need for a more effective means to reduce the incidence of unwanted adolescent pregnancy. How can it be done? A comprehensive approach at several levels is needed. The following are a few of the suggested approaches:

1. *Expanded sex education efforts.* The best model for sex education and the best data supporting the influence of the model on rates of pregnancy comes from efforts outside the United States. The adolescent pregnancy rate in this country is the highest in the Western world. For example, the adolescent pregnancy rate in the United States is twice as high as it is in England or Canada. It is three times as high as it is in Sweden. Yet, the adolescents in the United States are not any more sexually active than adolescents in these other countries. In fact, adolescents in Sweden are more sexually active at an earlier age and are more exposed to sexual activities through television. One difference may be that all children in Sweden, beginning at age 7, are exposed to a sex education curriculum. The majority of parents appear to favor sex education in the schools. In addition to sex education, there is the need for a specific emphasis on decision-making skills, life skills, and life planning. Schinke and Gilchrist (1984) have designed a school-based prevention program that emphasizes the need to teach young people problem solving and assertiveness skills in addressing situations where there is risk for pregnancy.

2. *Increase access to birth control.* Many people believe that increased access to contraceptive devices would likely reduce the number of unwanted pregnancies. School-based clinics appear to be ideal because they can be community based, they can reduce stigma by providing a wide range of services, and their staff can work closely with other school officials and outside social service workers. A well-known example is Health Start, where primary and preventive services (physicals, emergency care, mental health, social work counseling) are offered during school hours at four schools (Dryfoos, 1990).

3. *Provide greater "life options" for young people.* Because a lot of adolescent pregnancy is associated with social disadvantage, the implication is that changes in the social environment may be needed in order to enhance "life options" (Dryfoos, 1990). Increasingly, professionals are recognizing that adolescents have to be-

come motivated to reduce their risk of pregnancy (Santrock, 1990). Edelman (1987) states the point succinctly: "the best contraceptive is a future."

4. *Enhance community involvement and support.* Too often, sex education and advice is seen as the parents' responsibility or the school's responsibility. In an important survey, Thornburg (1981) found that only 17% of adolescents' sex education comes from mothers and 2% from fathers. Yet we know that contraceptive use increases when there is greater communication between parent and adolescent about sex. But our efforts must go beyond the parents to a communitywide level. If we can change attitudes about sex education, we can enhance access to family planning services. When we compare European countries where sex education is more open and without such conflict, adolescent pregnancy rates are much lower.

Sex Education and Adolescent Development

Does the adolescent's cognitive development have an influence on the success of sex education? Joan Lipsitz (1980) believes it does, because giving adolescents contraceptives is not enough. What does matter is adolescents' cognitive development—their acceptance of themselves and their sexuality. This level of acceptance depends on young people's emotional and cognitive development, or maturity. The prevention of adolescent pregnancy embraces some very complicated features, including the ability to approach problem solving in a planned and organized way, the ability to anticipate consequences, the ability to delay gratification, and the ability to communicate in a direct manner.

However, many of these capabilities require the ability to solve problems and anticipate consequences—cognitive abilities that many adolescents are just beginning to develop. As a result, a lot of what is being used in prevention programs may not be appropriate for early adolescents. In late adolescence, there is some realistic and future-oriented thinking about sexual experiences. In middle adolescence, there is often much romanticizing about sexuality. And in early adolescence, sexuality is depersonalized in a manner that gives way to anxiety and denial.

The following Focus on Gender section presents information for mature adolescent boys about sexual assault.

FOCUS ON GENDER

Sexual Assault Information for Guys

Increasingly, attention toward sex education is being devoted to males as well as females. So *What's It to Me?* is an informational guide about sexual assault for guys written by Gayle Stringer and Deanna Rants-Rodriguez. These authors recognized the need to address sexual assault prevention from the male side of things. In their booklet, they describe how men get socialized into negative thinking and behavior patterns. For example, men can't be caring, sympathetic, or emotional; or to be tough means getting what you want by being pushy. This booklet presents direct thoughts from teens about relationships, sexual exploration, and the problem of sexual assault. Real-life examples are presented about sexual confrontations, and young people are encouraged to think about prosocial alternatives. Below is one example:

> It's Saturday morning. All the guys are hanging out in the weight room and comparing Friday night dates.
>
> "Who was the fox you were with?"
> "Did you score?"
> "What's wrong with you, Smith? Doesn't sex turn you on?"
> "Was she any good?"

It's pretty easy to feel like you have to be as successful as the other guys are claiming to be. If you listen carefully to what these guys are saying, you'll see that they aren't very concerned about young women as people—only as performers in their story swapping. It's difficult to be one of the guys and still show that you don't treat women as they do, or at least like they say they do. It isn't necessary to put other guys down, but it is possible to respond positively without looking bad to your friends.

Who was the fox?	Janice is the girl I was with.
Did you score?	Hey, I wasn't playing a game!
Was she any good?	We always have a great time . . . (or) . . . She's a lot of fun to be with.
What's the matter, doesn't sex turn you on?	Sure, it turns me on, but my private life is my own business and it's not something I want to talk about with everybody.

Relationships with friends, with other young men and young women, which are based on respect for one another can be great. Friendships based on competition and a need to prove something can be difficult.

Source: Stringer & Rants-Rodriguez, 1987.

Sexually Transmitted Diseases

Sexually transmitted diseases are an increasing concern among adolescents, particularly with the development of AIDS (acquired immune deficiency syndrome). AIDS is a disease for which there is no known cure. It is caused by a virus that attacks and destroys the body's immune system. The effects are both devastating and deadly. It is difficult to understand the incidence of AIDS in adolescence because it has a long incubation period that can last eight years from contraction of the HIV virus to clinical manifestation. We do know that the rate of AIDS is doubling every year and that the current number exceeds 60,000—more than the number of American lives lost in the entire Vietnam War. Two minority groups, African American and Hispanic, represent more than 50% of all adolescents with AIDS and 75% of all children with AIDS (Steel, 1988, cited in Dryfoos, 1990). According to the Centers for Disease Control, over 90% of the adolescents surveyed understand that AIDS can be transmitted through sexual intercourse and sharing of needles; however, adolescents are also misinformed about contraction of the disease through blood tests and public toilets. More detailed information about other sexually transmitted diseases is discussed in the chapter on young adulthood.

Alcohol and Other Drug Use

No discussion of adolescent social hazards would be complete without a section on alcohol and other drug use. For many—parents, teachers, and human service professionals—this is the number one social issue facing young people today. Drinking is a big part of being an adolescent in today's world. One study found that almost all, 93%, of the high school class had begun drinking before graduating and that over half, 56%, had begun drinking between the sixth and ninth grades (Johnston, O'Malley, & Bachman, 1985, 1988). The majority of seniors have experimented with other drugs, particularly marijuana. After observing large increases in drug use by high school seniors, we have been seeing the rates leveling off and in some instances declining. Figure 9.2 shows the percentages of high school seniors using various drugs.

What causes young people to be more likely to abuse drugs? This question has undergone extensive research, and several different factors play a significant role in drug use. In general, drug use by peers, drug use by parents, the belief that drugs lead to tension reduction, delinquent behavior, stress, a sense of power, and low self-esteem are often cited as key factors. Jessor (1987) suggests that problem behavior like drug use is linked to adolescents' attempt to assert their independence and become more adultlike. Also, drinking may be a learned mechanism for coping with frustration at the failure to attain more conventional goals.

In a 12-year longitudinal study of problem drinking among adolescents, Jessor (1987) found that three factors differentiated problem drinkers from other adolescents— their personal qualities, their social environment, and their other patterns of behavior.

In terms of personal qualities, problem drinkers were clearly alienated from conventional values. For example, they did not value academic achievement, religion, or conventional nondeviant behavior. In terms of their social environment, they perceived large differences between their parents' values and their friends' values, were more influenced by friends than parents, and had peers who also engaged in problem drinking.

Thus, problem drinking occurs within the context of other problem behaviors. In other words, problem drinkers were more likely than other adolescents to engage in additional problem behaviors, such as sexual activity and delinquency. Their behavior is part of a larger syndrome of norm-breaking problem behaviors. Therefore, adolescent drinking would also predict other adolescent problem behaviors as well.

Delinquency

A chapter on adolescence would also not be complete without a discussion about juvenile delinquency. How many of the individuals in your class do you think committed a delinquent act as a youth? If you guessed quite a lot, you're right. Studies have found that over 80% of

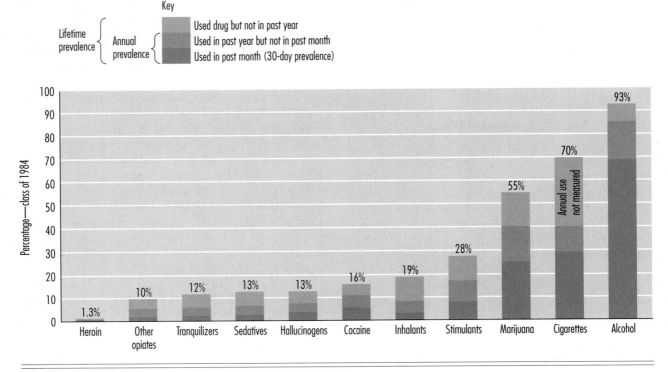

FIGURE 9.2 **Drug usage among high school seniors**   Source: Johnston, O'Malley, & Bachman, 1985, for the National Institute on Drug Abuse, Publication No. ADM 85-1394.

young people commit delinquent acts (Gold & Petronio, 1980). Most delinquent acts occur at around age 15 to 16 years. Delinquent acts are more common among boys than girls, but the rate of delinquency for girls has been increasing over the past several years.

A lot of delinquent behavior is related to status in the peer group. Delinquent acts are committed both with peers and for peers (Sigelman & Shaffer, 1991). Minor delinquent acts are considered normal and appear to be motivated by the desire to be liked by peers and to enhance one's sense of self esteem.

When deviant behavior occurs at early ages, the problem is seen as conduct disorder. However, when the behaviors lead to illegal acts by juveniles, then the problem is identified as delinquency. Research has found that

delinquency can be predicted from behavior displayed at early ages. For example, children who are identified as aggressive have a high probability of becoming delinquents in adolescence (Kazdin, 1987). It is important to understand that most criminals have a history of juvenile delinquency, but most individuals with a history of juvenile delinquency do not end up as criminals (Dryfoos, 1990).

Many studies have examined the antecedents of delinquency (Dryfoos, 1990). Delinquent adolescents often come from disturbed families where there is an absence of social and emotional support. This deficiency allows for negative peer influences to become more salient. Peer influence can lead to delinquent acts and ultimately to gang affiliation. Poor academic achievement is also related to delinquency. Young people who

TABLE 9.6   The Antecedents Associated with Delinquency

Antecedent	Association with Delinquency
Demographic	
Age	**Early initiation
Sex	**Males
Race/ethnicity	Conflicting and incomplete data
Personal	
Expectations for education	**Low expectations, little commitment
	*Low participation in school activities
School grades	**Low achievement in early grades, poor verbal ability
Conduct, general behavior, misconduct	**Truancy, "acting out," early stealing, lying
Religiosity	**Low attendance at church
Peer influence	**Heavy influence, low resistance
Conformity-rebelliousness	**Nonconformity, independence
Involvement in other high-risk behaviors	**Early, heavy substance use
	**Precocious sex
Psychological factors	**Hyperactivity, anxiety, aggressive behavior
Congenital defects	*Handicapping conditions
Family	
Household composition	*Inconsistent data
Income, poverty status	**Low socioeconomic status
Parent role	**Lack of bonding, repressive, abusive, low communication
Parental practice of high-risk behaviors	*Family history of criminality, violence, mental illness, alcoholism
Community	
Neighborhood quality	*Urban, high crime, high mobility
School quality	*Repressive environment
	*Tracking ability
	*Ineffective school management

* Several sources agree that this factor is a major predictor.

** Most sources agree that this factor is a major predictor.

Source: Dryfoos, 1990.

display limited problem-solving abilities and social skills are also more likely to be delinquent. Dryfoos (1990) summarizes the antecedents of delinquency based on numerous studies (see Table 9.6).

A survey conducted by the U.S. Department of Justice revealed that approximately 25,000 juveniles are in state correctional facilities. Characteristics of the juveniles in these facilities include the following: 93% are male, 40% African American, and 12% Hispanic; 75% are from divorced or single-parent families; over 50% have had a family member incarcerated; and 60% had already been in jail.

APPLYING THE FRAMEWORK

A Depressed Adolescent

Developmental History

Susie Lee, a 13-year-old Chinese American female, was brought to the agency by her biological parents. Susie's parents are third-generation Chinese Americans and live according to American cultural norms and values. Susie has two brothers and one sister, all younger than she.

Susie's parents discussed her early development, including pregnancy and childhood illnesses. Susie's mother reported that her pregnancy was normal with no complications. She also states that she was very careful throughout her pregnancy to avoid food, drink, medication, or illegal substances that could harm her developing fetus. The only medical problems out of the ordinary were Susie's seizures at the age of 5 as a result of influenza. Her mother reported no developmental delays and that Susie crawled, walked, and talked at the appropriate times.

Biophysical Considerations

Susie often has trouble sleeping at night and reports periodic nightmares (1 or 2 per month). She also has experienced *night eating syndrome*—being unable to sleep at night, she eats. Then by morning she does not feel like eating breakfast. She has a tendency to consume a large amount of food quickly and feels bad about having done that afterward. She does not eat a balanced diet. She denies any self-induced vomiting. This sequence of events often leads to severe self-criticism. Susie was an early-maturing female who had her first menses at 11 years of age. She has been diagnosed with *dysmenorrhea* (painful menstruation) and often complains about having stomach aches.

Psychological Considerations

Cognitive Development and Information Processing

Susie appears to be of average intelligence and performs well academically. Last year she had above-average grades of As and Bs. In discussing her self-criticism, Susie demonstrated abstract thinking ability as she commented introspectively about her own thought processes. She demonstrates complex thinking about the psychological processes she is experiencing. However, Susie is often unable to make simple decisions because she is literally thinking too much about a decision. Susie believes she is invulnerable—that no harm can come to her. Although this is an aspect of normal cognitive development, it can lead to negative outcomes if her thinking influences her behavior.

Communication

One of Susie's strengths is her ability to communicate her thoughts and feelings clearly and directly. She expresses concern about her eating habits and about feeling down and irritable much of the time.

Attitudes and Emotions

Susie expresses intense emotions that range from extreme anger to hopelessness. She describes feeling sad, irritable, touchy, "on edge," and depressed. She described some of her feelings as "I feel like I'm falling into a dark tunnel that I cannot climb out of; screaming all the way down but no one hears me." Sometimes she's deeply sad and spends a lot of time crying. Other days she's extremely irritable—everybody and everything bothers her. When asked about how she perceives herself, she reports feeling like the ugliest girl at school. She often looks in the mirror and sees a fat, ugly person. She is extremely preoccupied with how "bad" she thinks she looks. "I hate my body," she reports. A lot of her self-criticism is related to her binge eating and her negative body image. Susie scored in the depressed range on the Beck Depression Inventory. She admitted that she thought about suicide previously—especially after a friend had committed suicide. At present she denies any thoughts of suicide. She does not have access to a gun.

A Depressed Adolescent

Social Cognition and Regulation

Susie expresses strong egocentric thoughts. She is preoccupied with her feelings and behaviors in a self-conscious manner. This is demonstrated in her body perceptions—she is very concerned about how others are going to view her body and looks. She feels self-conscious about not having a boyfriend at the present time. This style of thinking is an entry to more intensely self-critical statements. She reports being quite concerned about what her peers are saying and doing and has difficulty expressing any independence around them. Her parents report that she "gives in to peer pressure all the time and that this gets her into a lot of trouble." Her mother expressed specific concern that she would not be able to say no to sexual advances by boys. In the one-to-one interview with Susie, she discussed having been sexually active with a previous boyfriend. She reports inconsistent use of birth control methods.

Social Considerations

Family Situation

Susie experiences serious family conflict, including a highly conflictual relationship and lack of closeness with her father. Indeed, her father still spanks her. Furthermore, Susie suffered a major loss when her favorite grandfather died last year of cancer. In addition, she stared junior high school this school year, and this has been a difficult transition for her.

Susie expressed concern over her inability to get along with her family. In particular, fairness is a big issue with Susie. She reports that her siblings are treated more fairly than herself. Her parents describe situations where Susie feels she is being treated unfairly and throws a temper tantrum. For example, last week she threw a tantrum because she found a box from a fast-food meal that had been her brother's lunch, stating that it wasn't fair that

he got one and she did not. She threw things around the living room, started yelling, and ran to her room crying. Susie reports being gruff and harsh with family members on a daily basis. Her oppositional behavior is also evident on a regular, but not daily, basis when she lies, loses her temper, argues with her parents, fights with her siblings, or refuses to do her chores. She says she "feels unimportant to this family" and that everyone sees her as a "bad" kid. She is angry at her father and believes he mistreats her—especially by spanking her. She also believes that her parents, particularly her father, do not love her.

Groups, Social Supports, and Contexts

Susie feels like an outsider at school although she has 3–4 friends she regularly interacts with. Recently Susie has found it difficult to go to school. When she is in school, she feels empty and dull. Although she used to be involved in after-school activities, she has no extracurricular activities now. When asked if she has an adult she is close to, she said there was no one for her to talk with, especially since her grandfather died. Her parents are frustrated with her and do not provide her with much emotional support.

Multicultural and Gender Considerations

Susie disclosed concern regarding her identity. Although her family is very acculturated, she has recently been questioning the significance of her Chinese American background since meeting a student at school who is very involved in the Chinese culture. She has expressed concern about how others may be viewing her. For example, at school she believes teachers expect more from her than other students when she turns in assignments or takes exams. She resents the additional pressure she feels from her teachers and her parents. She wants to be treated "just like everyone else." Her parents are frightened that they are loosing control over her, and Susie complains that her parents are not giving   (continued)

A Depressed Adolescent

(continued)   her enough freedom. Although Susie's family is highly acculturated, they are having a difficult time reconciling their family values with the values and norms of the dominant society.

Summary and Impressions

As a result of assessment, it is apparent that Susie has several problems that need to be addressed:

1. Depression
2. Irritable with extreme mood swings
3. Resentful behavior toward siblings
4. Uncontrolled anger outbursts
5. Poor family relationships
6. Possible unresolved grief
7. Adjustment issues involving her developmental stage (e.g., identity concerns)

8. High-risk behaviors such as unprotected sexual intercourse

Although the family members are experiencing difficulties, they do provide a stable, predictable living situation for Susie and her siblings. Susie's father earns a steady income that provides adequate resources. Susie's mother works part-time while the children are at school and states that she is usually home when they return from school. They have lived in the community for five years and have established a network of family friends and church support. In addition, both parents appear genuinely concerned and willing to evaluate their parenting techniques in order to work toward a positive outcome. Susie's strengths include her intellect and thoughtfulness, her good communication skills, and her desire for improved family relationships.

Chapter Summary
Developmental Themes

Adolescence represents a journey of discovery—a search to find out more about who you are. Peer approval is considered very important in early adolescence. By late adolescence, two developmental tasks are critical: independence from the family and the development of personal identity. Erikson refers to this stage as identity versus identity confusion.

Biophysical Dimension

Biophysical Growth and Development

Adolescents experience a growth spurt with rapid gains in height and weight. Biologically, adolescence begins with the onset of the pubertal process. This leads to hormonal changes in boys and girls. These physical and hormonal changes require psychological adjustment.

Psychological Dimension

Cognitive Development and Information Processing

Adolescence is a period of formal operations. Adolescents can now use complex and abstract thinking referred to as hypothetical-deductive reasoning. Formal operational thought includes two states: assimilation and accommodation.

Communication

In adolescence, communication skills become more advanced. For example, adolescents begin to use metaphors in their expressions and they delight in using satire. Adolescents can become very intent on expressing themselves, and many use journals to record their thoughts and ideas.

Attitudes and Emotions

Adolescence is a period of time for developing one's self-concept. They begin to assume greater independent decision making, feel less pressure to conform with peers, experience dating and awareness of their sexuality, and begin to consider major decisions that affect their adult life. In essence, they develop a more integrated self. Although adolescence used to be considered a time of crisis, this notion is now considered a myth. Adolescents do, however, cycle through moods rapidly. Adolescence is also a time for the development of identity. Identity status theory describes four different identity stages that adolescents experience: diffusion, foreclosure, moratorium, and achievement. Adolescents of color may need to establish an identity in two different cultural systems—their own ethnic values and the values of the majority culture. One aspect of achieving an identity is seeking independence from one's family.

Social Cognition and Regulation

Adolescents are continuing to develop their moral reasoning abilities. Kohlberg's theory of moral development suggests that adolescents are in stage 3, "interpersonal conformity"—their reason to be good is so that others will think well of them and they can think well of themselves. To do "what's right" is to be a nice person and live up to the expectations of others. By late adolescence, most young people move to stage 4, "responsibility to the system," and they reason that they should fulfill their responsibilities to the social system they are part of. Related to moral development is adolescent egocentrism, where young people are preoccupied with their behavior and thoughts in a self-conscious manner. There are two aspects of egocentric thought: the imaginary audience and the personal fable. Adolescents develop the ability to monitor their social thoughts—a conscious self-awareness.

Psychological Hazards

Adolescents can develop a number of behavior problems that are both externalzing and internalizing. One fairly common externalizing disorder is conduct disorder, or delinquent activity. Behavioral treatment approaches are commonly used with children who have delinquent behaviors.

Social Dimension

Families, Groups, Support Systems, and Contexts

Three key developmental tasks for the family include the development of autonomy, the resolution of parent-adolescent conflict, and parent-adolescent attachment. Three types of parenting styles have been identified: authoritative parenting, authoritarian, and laissez-faire (with two types: permissive indifferent and permissive indulgent). Research studies have supported the effectiveness of authoritative parenting. Adolescence and peer groups go hand in hand. Peer group interaction is a critical source of personal and social competence development for adolescents. Peer pressure and conformity are evident in the adolescent years. Friendships flourish, and adolescents become capable of sharing intimately with one another. Social skills training can be an effective method of addressing many problems that adolescents experience. Adolescent peer groups are usually organized according to cliques or crowds. Gangs have become an increasing problem for adolescents, and they appear to be related to the developmental need for young people to associate with peer groups. In adolescence, many young people of color become more aware of their ethnic minority status. Schools play a critical role in facilitating the development of adolescents. The social and organizational aspects of schools can influence adolescent development. Often the transition between schools (e.g., from an elementary school to a middle school) can be difficult for adolescents. Both middle schools and high schools could be better designed to meet students' needs. A serious problem in the schools is the high dropout rate.

Multicultural and Gender Considerations

There are special problems that must be overcome for the adolescent immigrant. Adolescents are becoming increasingly identified with their gender roles; however, there is more acceptance of androgyny, which is the combination of male and female behaviors in the same person. Adolescent girls face some difficult issues, and many lose their voice or sense of self. Depression is also more common for girls and often revolves around their body image. Sexual identity is a major task during this period. Adolescents discover their heterosexual or homosexual tendencies. By the end of high school, the majority of adolescents have had experience with sexual intercourse. There are four factors related to early sexual behavior: biological influences, history of sexual abuse, experiencing other problem behaviors, and normative expectations. AIDS prevention takes on special significance in the adolescent years.

Social Hazards

In understanding adolescents at risk, adolescent problem behavior theory is helpful. This theory identifies protective and risk factors that influence adolescent risk-taking behavior. A particular concern is adolescent pregnancy and childbirth. The consequences of adolescent pregnancy are significant for both the mother and the child. Adolescent fathers are being recognized as playing a more critical role in the adolescent pregnancy problem. A clear need exists in developing methods to reduce the incidence of adolescent pregnancy. There needs to be improved sex education and education about sexual assault for adolescent boys. An additional concern about adolescent sexual behavior is sexually transmitted diseases. Two additional social problems of great significance are alcohol and drug use and delinquency.

KEY TERMS

androgen
authoritarian parenting
authoritative parenting
care perspective
clique
concrete thinking
conduct disorder
connectedness
crowd
endocrine glands
estrogen
formal operational thought

gang
gonadotropins
hormones
human immunodeficiency virus
    (HIV)
hypothalamus
hypothetical-deductive reasoning
imaginary audience
individuation
justice perspective
laissez-faire parenting
menarche

moral development
obesity
ovaries
personal fable
psychological moratorium
puberty
rite of passage
social cognitive monitoring
social skills training
testes

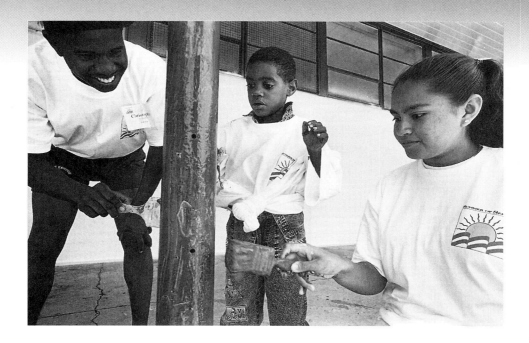

10

Young Adulthood

Developmental Themes

I want to be smart. I want to be somebody. I want to make money. I want to be a successful lawyer, but my personal life comes first. I want to be a lovely wife, do my husband's shirts, take Chinese cooking lessons, and have two children. . . . I want to have a briefcase in my hands. I want to look good and feel good and be happy in what I am doing.

—Nicole DiMarco—

The above quote from Ruth Sidel's (1990) book *On Her Own*, a study about young women today, represents the aspirations, challenges, and difficulties that many young adults face. Young adulthood, which is considered a major life transition, is a critical period that spans the ages of 22 to 34 years old. In young adulthood, significant life roles become established. Young people move from a preoccupation with the self to a focus on intimacy that often leads to marriage, children, and the need to establish a stable career path. In many ways, everything that has taken place before this stage can be considered preparation for adulthood.

Perhaps two of the most critical developmental tasks are economic independence and independent decision making. Often these two aspects are considered the hallmark of the transition from adolescence to young adulthood (Santrock, 1992). Economic independence occurs as young people move from high school or college into the workforce on a full-time basis. This movement represents major life changes, as the ability to live independently carries with it new responsibilities. Many of these new responsibilities lead to independent decision making. Where to work, where to live, how to budget income, what kind of dates to go on, when to get married—these examples depict the independent decisions that go along with adulthood.

White (1966) describes the following developmental tendencies in adulthood: the development of a stable ego identity, the freeing of personal relationships, the development and expansion of interests, the refinement and humanizing of values, and the development of caring. Unlike the preoccupation with self in adolescence, young adulthood moves toward the outside with a focus on social and intimate relationships with others. These tendencies are reflected in Erikson's (1974, p. 124) description of the young adult:

> In youth you find out what you care to do and who you care to be—even in changing roles. In young adulthood you learn whom you care to be with—at work and in private life, not only exchanging intimacies, but sharing intimacy. In adulthood, however, you learn to know what and whom you can take care of.

Levinson describes young adulthood as having a focus on choices in love, occupation, friendship, values, and lifestyle. Focus on Development describes the stages of adulthood according to Levinson.

FOCUS ON DEVELOPMENT

Levinson's Eight Stages of Adult Development

Levinson and his colleagues (1978) were instrumental in developing a theory of adult development. On the basis of intensive interviews with adult men at different stages in the life cycle, Levinson set forth his ideas about the stages adults go through. More recently he has expanded his theory to include adult women (Levinson, 1985, 1986). Levinson outlined eight developmental stages in young and middle adulthood. Fundamental to his theory is his notion of "life structure." A life structure represents a basic pattern of an adult's life at a particular time. A person's life structure reflects the choices a person makes, such as marriage, child-rearing, career, and so forth. According to Levinson, the stages of the adult life cycle alternate between stability and turmoil and transition. The stages are summarized as follows:

1. *Ages 17 to 22:* Leave adolescence; make preliminary choices for adult life.
2. *Ages 22 to 28:* Initial choices in love, occupation, friendship, values, lifestyle.
3. *Ages 28 to 33:* Change in life structure, either a moderate change or, more often, a severe and stressful crisis.

4. *Ages 33 to 40:* Establish a niche in society; progress on a timetable, both in family and in career accomplishments.

5. *Ages 40 to 45:* Life structure comes into question; usually a time of crisis in the meaning, direction, and value of each person's life; neglected parts of the self (talents, desires, aspirations) seek expression.

6. *Ages 45 to 50:* Choices must be made and a new life structure formed; the person must commit to new tasks.

7. *Ages 50 to 55:* Further questioning and modification of the life structure; men who did not have a crisis at age 40 are likely to have one now.

8. *Ages 55 to 60:* Build a new life structure; can be a time of great fulfillment.

Biophysical Dimension

Biophysical Growth and Development

Physical development in young adulthood represents both the peak of physical development and its slow decline as the body gets older. Our physical performance is usually the strongest during the early twenties. An easy way to assess the body's performance is to examine the average ages of the Olympic gold medalists. Only about 15% of Olympic medalists are over the age of 30 (Santrock, 1992). The peak of actual muscular strength occurs between age 25 and 30 years and decreases about 10% between age 30 and 60 years. As a result, the mid-twenties is a good age for speed and agility. However, professional athletes perform well into their thirties when they are competing in endurance-type sports, such as long-distance running and weight lifting. So if you are in young adulthood, enjoy your peak level of physical development—it's all downhill after this!

In young adulthood, many individuals begin a pattern of health-conscious behavior. Indeed, the workout frenzy is very popular among this age group. This is a particularly good time to begin a healthy lifestyle. Many individuals at this age start putting on weight and may be struggling to avoid excessive weight gain and obesity. During early adulthood, the percentage of body weight that is composed of muscle decreases. This represents not a loss of muscle but an increase in fat weight (Hay-

wood, 1986). It is recommended that body fat be 15% to 18% for men and 20% to 25% for women. Women typically have more fat deposits in the buttocks, thighs, breasts, and shoulders, whereas men distribute their fat more evenly. Body composition reflects an individual's overall physical health.

Fat in the body is stored in adipose cells. As these cells fill, your hunger is satisfied. If the cells are empty, then you are going to be hungry. As people gain weight, they increase the number of fat cells in the body—and at this point, it becomes difficult to get rid of them. Obese people have an excessive amount of fat cells in their bodies. One reason that we gain more weight as we age is that our **basal metabolism rate,** which is the minimum amount of energy that we use in our resting state, decreases as we get older. The implication of this decrease is that for us to keep the same weight as we had in the past, we would need to eat less to compensate for the decline in the basal metabolism rate.

Although restrictive diets are very popular, exercise combined with proper diet is a more effective means by which to lose weight. Exercise is important because it burns up calories and continues to raise the metabolic rate for several hours after the exercise. Exercise can be effective in weight loss because it lowers the body's set point for weight and makes it easier to maintain a lower weight. The most effective means to lose weight is to exercise *and* eat a low-fat, healthy diet. The American Dietetic Association recommends the following: 10–15 grams of fiber per day, limiting intake to 30% of daily calories from fat, and increasing to 50–60% the daily calories derived from complex carbohydrates (fruits, vegetables, and grains).

The Reproductive System During Early Adulthood

This stage of development is considered the best period for a woman to become pregnant. A woman in her early twenties has a mature reproductive system and is more likely to produce fertilizable eggs. Also, her hormone production is more regular. Because her physical abilities are at her peak and her uterus is more receptive to a pregnancy, this is an ideal time for a safe and healthy delivery of a baby (Schuster & Ashburn, 1992).

The Impact of Hormones on Women   Although hormones influence both men and women, their impact on women is stronger. As women progress through the **menstrual cycle,** their hormones fluctuate. In particular, estrogen levels rise to their highest point when a woman is ovulating and then begin to decline as she approaches her menstrual period. After ovulation, progesterone levels begin to increase. When progesterone production is at its highest, about ten days before the beginning of the menstrual cycle, some women experience the set of symptoms known as **premenstrual syndrome (PMS).** PMS is associated with breast tenderness, a bloated feeling, irritability, and negative moods occurring just prior to the menstrual period.

Although women are affected by PMS, most are not incapacitated. Nevertheless, in one study, a small portion of women, less than 10%, believed that their PMS symptoms could be considered severe (Woods, Most, & Dery, 1982). Some women report mild forms of these symptoms, but many women do not experience any symptoms at all.

One particularly fascinating study sheds some light on the social as well as the biological factors that influence premenstrual and menstrual symptoms. In a study of college women, Englander-Golden, Sonleitner, Whitmore, and Corbley (1986) found that women report more symptom changes over a month if they know that their menstrual cycles are being studied than if they are just reporting how they feel on certain days with no reference to their menstrual cycle. The implication from this research is that stereotypes of what women "should" experience during menstruation affect what they experience and subsequently report. Related to this research is the finding that women in more traditional roles report more negative emotions during premenstrual and menstrual cycles than do women in nontraditional occupations or women who are more highly educated (Brown & Woods, 1986; Woods, Most, & Dery, 1982). However, significant symptoms should not be discounted. In fact, DSM-IV, the classification system for psychiatric disorders, has included as a condition for further consideration the new diagnosis of Premenstrual Dysphoric Disorder. Some women suffering from this disorder may benefit from antidepressants.

Biophysical Hazards

An important health hazard of the reproductive system for both women and men is cancer. Women are encouraged to develop the habit of breast self-examination. During their lifetime, more than 1 in 10 women will develop breast cancer (Devita, Hellman, & Rosenberg, 1989). Conducting a self-examination is easy and can be a life saver. To conduct the exam, women should choose the same time each month, preferably after the menstrual period has ended. This time frame is important because the breasts vary in size and texture during the menstrual cycle, but after the menstrual period they are not swollen. Health professionals can provide guidance regarding how to conduct the exam, and the American Cancer Society has brochures that describe the procedure.

Men are also encouraged to conduct a self-examination of the testes. Testicular cancer is a common disease for men between 15 and 35 years old and is the most common cause of cancer death among early adult males. Self-examination is important because, when detected, it is second only to skin cancer in terms of successful cure rate. Like women, men should be taught by a health professional how to perform the exam.

Additional physical hazards include diseases such as AIDS and homicide—particularly for African American men, as described in Focus on Multiculturalism: Life and Death for African Americans. Also, in early adulthood many men and women suffer from the consequences of excessive drinking. Focus on Biophysics: To Drink or Not to Drink describes efforts being used to combat the abuse of alcohol by young people.

FOCUS ON MULTICULTURALISM

Life and Death for African Americans

The significance of life and death has become increasingly recognized as many media reports have profiled the dramatic increase in death rates for African American males. Consider the following statistics:

- Three African American males die (between the ages of 15 and 44) for every white American male.
- Homicide is the leading cause of death of African American males between the ages of 15 and 24.

- African American males contract AIDS at a rate of 29.9 per 1000, whereas for white Americans the rate is 9.7 per 1000.

These data graphically reveal that the life expectancy for the African American male is actually declining. These data are coupled with serious problems in health care coverage for African Americans. Almost one-quarter of all African Americans are not covered by private health insurance. As a result, African Americans have higher incidences of chronic disability and illness.

Source: Baruth & Manning, 1991.

FOCUS ON BIOPHYSICS

To Drink or Not To Drink: Is That *Really* the Question?

Loaded. Plastered. Tanked. Smashed. College entrance exam vocabulary? Guess again. These are colloquial terms for the all-too-familiar collegiate phenomenon of getting drunk. Although research indicates that most students successfully mature past the period of heavy drinking, the college period is one of heightened vulnerability to the pressures associated with alcohol consumption. Traditional prevention efforts have relied on educating the population about the potential dangers of abusing alcohol, assuming that the individual will apply this information to his or her own personal situation. Recently, prevention has taken on a new focus: affecting people's motivation and desire to drink. These efforts are being implemented on college campuses and in small towns.

From laboratory data collected over more than ten years, researcher Alan Marlatt has found that "peer pressure and expectancies about sexual arousal and social acceptance could increase the reported amount people drink" (Azar, 1995, p. 20). Marlatt also found factors that could decrease the reported amount people drink, including exercise, meditation, and community activities.

Marlatt is now using this information out in the field. His energies are aimed not at preventing drinking but at preventing development of drinking problems and the ensuing injuries in those individuals who already drink.

With this goal in mind, Marlatt developed a six-week cognitive-behavioral program that (1) challenges the glamorous portrayal of the effects of alcohol; (2) emphasizes awareness of one's drinking habits as a safety precaution; and (3) suggests plausible alternatives to drinking—exercise, nonalcoholic parties, and community work. A one-hour motivational interview with these areas emphasized was as effective in the preliminary studies as the six-week program: Results yielded a significant reduction in binge drinking among small groups of college students.

On the basis of this success, Marlatt and his colleagues began a longitudinal study in 1990, in which they followed 500 college students identified as high risk for problem drinking when they were high school seniors. Half of the sample received no treatment, and the other half received the one-hour motivational interview when they started college. Students whose drinking problems persisted received the six-week program, and any students who showed signs of severe drinking problems were taken out of the study and given a referral for treatment.

Annual evaluations, even after three years, show that the program makes a significant difference in helping to accelerate "maturing out of drinking behavior" (Azar, 1995, p. 20). Marlatt has now targeted fraternities and sororities with the hope that the group format will foster group pressure toward behavior change.

Source: Written by Julianne Azimov, based on Azar, 1995.

Psychological Dimension

Cognitive Development and Information Processing

According to Piaget, the ability of formal operational thinking that occurs in adolescence is the last stage of cognitive development. Therefore, young adulthood is characterized by the same mechanisms of formal operational thought. You will recall that Piaget (1972) believed

Alcohol consumption in college has many negative ramifications, including unwanted sexual activity, negative altercations, and automobile accidents.

that formal operational thought consists of conceiving abstract concepts, systematic thinking, and step-by-step logic. In late adolescence and young adulthood, people refine their formal operational approach to problem solving. The cognitive changes that take place in adulthood consist of cognitive operations that are applied to increasingly complex situations and problems.

Adults are better able to harness the formal operational thinking because of their reduced egocentrism, and therefore adults approach problems with greater objectivity. Adults are also able to more effectively access past experiences and education in using the cognitive operations that are present. In a similar manner, Labouvie-Vief (1985) suggests that a new integration in thought occurs in adulthood, but she believes that adulthood carries a pragmatic adaptive strategy that leads to less emphasis on the logical approach characterized in adolescence. Perhaps this pragmatic approach provides experience for adults in generating and considering more options and realistically hypothesizing the potential effects of each option—a facet of multidimensional thinking (Bornstein & Schuster, 1992).

Many people do not obtain formal operational thinking. This could be due to many factors, such as genetic limitations on their cognitive abilities or poor cognitive stimulation as children. However, given Piaget's theory, a serious problem is the large number of people who apparently do not reach the formal operational thinking stage. Studies have shown that only 60–75% of adolescents can solve any formal operational problems (Neimark, 1975) and no more than 30% of adults ever complete the transition to the highest levels of formal operational thought (Kuhn, Kohlberg, Langer, & Haan, 1977). This suggests that formal operational thinking is not universal and instead is only available in certain people who are perhaps trained in this type of thinking.

The Development of Postformal Thought

Labouvie-Vief (1985) used a scenario to examine the differences between adolescent and adult thinking. Read the following scenario and an adult and adolescent response and compare them. How is the thinking different between the two? Scenario (Labouvie-Vief, 1985, p. 13):

John is known to be a heavy drinker, especially when he goes to parties. Mary, John's wife, warns him that if he gets drunk one more time, she will leave him and take the children. Tonight John is out late and at an office party. John comes home drunk.

Does Mary leave John? How certain are you of your answer?

The adolescent response (Labouvie-Vief, 1985, pp. 17–18) would be:

It's a good chance that she would leave him because she warns him that she will leave him and take the children, but warning isn't an absolute thing. . . . And, I'd be absolutely sure that, well let's see. . . . I'm trying to go all the way. I'm trying to think of putting everything [together] so I can be absolutely certain of an answer. . . . It's hard to be absolutely certain. "If he gets drunk, then she'll leave and take the children." I want to say yes 'cause everything's in that favor, in that direction, but I don't know how I can conclude that she does leave John.

The adult response (Labouvie-Vief, 1985, p. 41) would be:

There was no right or wrong answer. You could get logically to both answers [yes or no]. . . . It depends on the steps they take to their answer. If they base it on what they feel, what they know, and they have certain steps to get an answer, it can be logical.

Which response seems more characteristic of formal operational thinking? In the adolescent response, there is an understanding of the ambiguity of the situation but also the need to search for the correct answer. The adult response does not search for a correct answer—there is tolerance of the ambiguity. It also presents a combination of logic and feeling in understanding the situation.

As Labouvie-Vief (1985) points out in this example, the adult would be scored as not having reached formal operational thought in this example. Does this mean that there is a decline in formal operational thought as one gets older? Perhaps it is not so much a decline as a qualitative shift in one's way of thinking.

Communication

In young adulthood, perhaps what is most pronounced about communication is the notion of *mis*communication—young men and women can become quite focused on the differences in the way they communicate. Indeed,

this notion is reflected in the popular culture. For example, Deborah Tannen's (1991) book *You Just Don't Understand: Women and Men in Conversation*, points out many of the significant ways in which women and men are quite different in their relationships with each other. Although important gender differences are emerging, much of our understanding about the differences between men and women boils down to sexual stereotyping. Often the prescription regarding differences is reduced to two conclusions: Men are in pursuit of power, and women are in pursuit of relationships. Such overgeneralizations have yet to be supported by good studies.

However, many people have written about the differences in communication between men and women. Women obtain a much greater level of intimate communication with each other than men do. Women discuss more intimate topics and confide about their personal lives more than men do. In fact, women often complain about their lack of intimate conversations with men. When men are with each other, they also do not maintain a very intimate conversation. Men do not confide with each other about their private lives the same way that women do.

Intimacy between a man and a woman does not always follow the pathway that seems most logical. It is not during a long drive to the country or during an evening's dinner that they speak intimately. Too often, it is only after a long fight or after one person explodes in frustration that they break through their normal communication and meet each other on a more intimate plane. Social workers need to understand communication with a diverse range of clients. The following Focus on Diversity section looks at communication with deaf individuals.

FOCUS ON DIVERSITY

Communicating with the Deaf Requires More Than Just Signs

Social workers who work with deaf clients know that just using an interpreter does not address the whole picture.

To be effective in working with deaf clients, social workers must understand the linguistic, cultural, educational, and service issues. Deaf people are different in that they represent a linguistic minority with a separate language—the ASL (American Sign Language). Research in psycholinguistics has found that signing is not just gestural but has its own syntax and is well formed like other languages. What makes social work practice with deaf clients difficult is that you are working in a language that is not your own. A common error in assessment of deaf individuals lies in not understanding that they often read and write English at a much lower level than hearing students at the same age level. For example, a deaf high school graduate may have a reading level of only the fourth grade. For social workers attempting to evaluate deaf clients, they need to know how to evaluate a person with poor reading skills. Writing is also very different for the deaf because ASL and English have very different structures, styles, and syntax. As a result, deaf people can appear mentally disoriented when in fact they are not. Professionals are needed who specialize in deafness, although there are very few programs that train professionals with a subspecialty in deafness.

Attitudes and Emotions

A major psychosocial task in young adulthood is the development of intimacy with others. Erikson referred to this stage as intimacy versus isolation. Indeed, many young adults become quite focused on building intimate relationships with others. Intimacy in this context refers to the ability to share one's true and deeper self—both the good and the bad parts. Developing intimacy involves taking a risk, sharing aspects about yourself while knowing that the other person can make judgments about what you share. Kiefer (1988, p. 131) describes the complexities involved in intimacy: "Any close relationship involves the exchange of demands and expectations, some of which are difficult and unpleasant. More importantly, getting to know someone intimately always involves hurt when illusions are dashed or expectations unfulfilled; and it always involves unpleasant insight into one's own weaknesses."

Experiences of intimacy may be quite different for men and women. Carol Gilligan (1982) has noted that whereas for men, identity precedes intimacy, for women, these tasks seem instead to be congruent. Intimacy occurs hand in hand with identity, as the female comes to know herself through her relationship with others. Although Gilligan believes that men have more of a focus on justice and women have more of a focus on caring and relationships, she does see these perspectives as converging. She believes that the perspective between fairness and care provides a better understanding of relations between the sexes and also provides a more comprehensive portrayal of adult work and family relationships (Gilligan, 1982).

The counterpoint to intimacy is isolation—the inability to share intimately with others. With a lack of such exchanges, you are robbed of the experience of having another person understand you from your point of view, insight and understanding about yourself, and support and encouragement about your actions and thoughts. Such isolation may lead to a deep sense of loneliness. The tasks of intimacy and isolation are discussed in more detail as we explore the outcomes of these tasks—love and loneliness.

Love

One of the most prevalent emotions in young adulthood is love. Love takes on particular significance for the young adult, who begins to experience many meaningful emotional relationships. Indeed, such emotions of love are likely to lead to marriage in young adulthood. Erik Erikson identifies the core task of the early adult years as intimacy. As the task of identity is addressed, the individual moves toward preparation for intimacy. Those who cannot effectively resolve the tasks of intimacy are left to isolation and lack the ability to form reciprocal exchanges based on understanding, empathy, and support. A major developmental task of the young adult is to develop emotionally satisfying relationships—to experience love.

But what is love? This is a critical question and one that is asked by many young adults. A typical young adult scenario is the following. A young couple meets and they begin seeing each other. As their interest and excitement grows, they become increasingly obsessed with the other. They want to spend increasing amounts of time with each other, and they cannot get their sexual desires fulfilled, no matter how much they try. And although they are sharing what seems to be immense parts of themselves with each other, they do not know if this is *really* love. They realize that to keep the relationship going means a certain amount of sacrifice and personal risk. They are unsure whether they should take the plunge and exclaim, "I love you" to each other. They face an extremely difficult question that is quite common for young adults: Is this love? How can I tell?

Is love something we can define and study? In the last 20 years, many researchers have set out to study love and bring a more exacting understanding of this emotion. Most researchers begin by differentiating romantic love from "true" love. Robert Solomon (1988) describes three features common to romantic love: (1) it is sexual in origin and motivation; (2) it is spontaneous and voluntary—and not directly under our control; and (3) it is an emotion appropriate only between equals (for example, not between a mother and child).

Hatfield and Walster (1985) describe several myths that have resulted from our idealized concept of love:

Myth 1: When you fall in love, you'll know it.
Myth 2: When love does hit, you have no control over it.
Myth 3: Love is a completely positive experience.
Myth 4: True love will last forever.
Myth 5: Love can conquer all problems.

Robert Solomon (1988, p. 17) describes the difficulty many of us have in understanding love: "The problem, the irony, is that in our obsession with love we have lost touch with what love is, and we have stopped thinking carefully about what it should be. Love, like happiness, may make itself more available to those who don't press it too hard, who don't expect too much, who aren't too impatient to see it through."

Some new theories of love may shed some light on how we can better understand this elusive concept. Sternberg's triangular theory of love (1988) suggests that love has three components: intimacy, passion, and commitment. In this theory, intimacy refers to the warmth and closeness shared in a relationship; passion refers to the intense feelings (included are both positive and negative) experienced in love relationships, including sexual desire; commitment refers to the decision and intent to maintain a relationship in spite of the difficulties encountered. The triangular theory of love posits eight types of relationships that emerge from the presence or absence of the three components of love (based on Sternberg, 1986):

Nonlove is the absence of any of the three components and reflects casual interactions.

Liking involves the experience of only one component of love—intimacy. We feel close but not passionate toward the other.

Infatuation involves the experience of only one component of love—passion. Such passion reflects a person who is loved as an idealized object rather than for who the person really is.

Empty love is the third component of the triangle that represents commitment. In this case there is commitment but none of the other essential ingredients of love.

Fatuous love is the combination of passion and commitment. An example is couples who become quickly and intensely involved with each other and decide to marry.

Romantic love is the combination of intimacy and passion. Romantic lovers are drawn to each other in an intimate way and have lots of passion, but there is no commitment. Romantic love may begin as infatuation.

Companionate love is the combination of intimacy and commitment. This type of love is observed in long-term marriages where passion is no longer present. Most romantic love relationships will eventually become companionate love relationships as passion fades.

Consummate love is the result of all three components of love—intimacy, passion, and commitment. Although most of us seek consummate love relationships, maintaining such relationships is quite difficult.

In a very different theory of love, Hazan and Shaver (1987) theorize that adult romantic love is very similar to attachments that occur in infancy. Infant attachment, the emotional bond between child and parent, and adult love share many similar features, such as intense preoccupation with the other person, distress at separation, and motivation to stay close and spend time together. Hazan and Shaver believe that our romantic relationships in adulthood parallel our attachments in infancy.

Attachments in infancy, as discussed in the chapter on infancy, are believed to be formed in part in response to the caregiver's style. For example, a warm/responsive parenting style leads to a secure attachment for the infant. In adulthood this is reflected as a secure attachment style. The adult is capable of intimate relationships with others and is comfortable depending on others. The cold/rejecting parenting style leads to the avoidant attachment in infants, which is characterized by little separation protest and a tendency to avoid the caregiver. In adulthood, the person develops an avoidant attachment style. The adult is uncomfortable being close to others and has a difficult time trusting. The ambivalent/inconsistent parenting style leads to an anxious/ambivalent infant attachment. Here there is a strong separation protest, and the child has a tendency to resist contact initiated by the parent. In the adult, the anxious/ambivalent attachment is reflected in reluctance to get close to others and feelings of insecurity.

Hazan and Shaver (1987) present some limited findings in support of their theory. In a survey of adults' love relationships, they found that adults can be classified according to the three attachment styles. In particular, they found that secure adults were represented by 56% of the participants, avoidant adults were represented

by 24% of the participants, and anxious/ambivalent adults were represented by 20% of the participants. These percentages are similar to the percentages of infants that have been classified into these attachment categories. Although this provides some limited support to their theory, longitudinal studies are needed to demonstrate a causal relationship between the infant attachment and adult attachment patterns.

George Levinger developed a scale designed to measure both the rewards and costs of a loving relationship. All relationships, although emotionally satisfying, have costs—they take time and can be emotionally draining as well. Levinger's Interpersonal Involvement Scale has respondents rate the positive and negative aspects of a given relationship. Some of the items are listed in Box 10.1.

The Counterpoint of Love: Isolation and Loneliness

Although many young adults are actively seeking emotionally satisfying friendships and romantic relationships, many others are experiencing feelings of loneliness. In fact, research on the prevalence of loneliness (1) identifies adolescents and young adults as the loneliest

BOX 10.1

An Interpersonal Involvement Scale

_____ 1. Doing things together
_____ 2. Having no secrets from one another
_____ 3. Needing the other person
_____ 4. Feeling needed by the other person
_____ 5. Accepting the other's limitations
_____ 6. Growing personally through the relationship
_____ 7. Helping the other grow
_____ 8. Having career goals that do not conflict

_____ 9. Understanding the other well
_____ 10. Giving up some of one's own freedom
_____ 11. Feeling possessive of the other's time
_____ 12. Taking vacations together
_____ 13. Offering emotional support to the other
_____ 14. Receiving affection from the other
_____ 15. Giving affection to the other
_____ 16. Having interests the other shares

Source: Levinger (no date).

TABLE 10.1   Cognitions and Behaviors That Lead to Loneliness

Cognitive Clusters	Behaviors
I'm undesirable. I'm dull and boring.	Avoidance of friendships
I can't communicate with others. My thoughts and feelings are bottled up inside.	Low self-disclosure
I'm not a good lover. I can't relax, be spontaneous, and enjoy sex.	Avoidance of sexual relationships
I can't seem to get what I want from this relationship.	Lack of assertiveness in relationships
I won't risk being hurt again. I'd screw up any relationship.	Avoidance of potentially intimate relationships
I don't know how to act in this situation. I'll make a fool of myself.	Avoidance of other people

Source: Young, 1982.

age group, and (2) finds that loneliness decreases with age, at least until late adulthood when marriage partners and friends begin to die (Peplau, Bikson, Rook, & Goodchilds, 1982; Rubenstein & Shaver, 1982).

Loneliness is a very subjective feeling, and it is associated with social isolation, but it is not the *same* as social isolation. **Loneliness** is best defined as having fewer interpersonal relationships than *desired*, or not obtaining the desired level of personal satisfaction from interpersonal relationships. Loneliness, therefore, is not the same as spending time alone. Many people experience loneliness even though they may have many personal "friendships." On the other hand, many people desire solitude and want few personal relationships.

Loneliness in not unidimensional, as it appears to occur in different areas of one's life. For example, you could be satisfied with your relationship with your partner but not personally satisfied with your friendships. Research (Schmidt & Weiner, 1988) has identified four key areas where loneliness can be a problem: (1) romantic/sexual relationships, (2) friendship relationships, (3) family relationships, and (4) community relationships. Therefore, knowing what areas of loneliness are particularly problematic suggests a different focus for learning how to best address feelings of loneliness.

Implications for Practice: Coping with Loneliness

Most of the interventions developed to help people cope with loneliness focus on three areas: cognitive restructuring or changing negative self-talk; reducing anxiety and increasing comfort to help people stay engaged in social situations; and teaching people social skills like starting and maintaining a conversation. The appropriate intervention depends on the particular cause of the loneliness (Weiten & Lloyd, 1994).

Young (1982) has identified a variety of different kinds of cognitions or self-talk that contribute to feelings of loneliness. His research has identified six clusters of cognitions that lead to different kinds of irrational cognitions and subsequent behaviors (see Table 10.1). Knowing what kind of thinking processes a client has can be helpful in planning different intervention strategies. The following Focus on Psychology section discusses the prevalence and nature of shyness that is associated with loneliness.

Shyness—Prevalence and Nature

Phillip Zimbardo (1987) and associates have conducted major research on shyness. In an important survey on the prevalence of shyness, Zimbardo found that shyness was experienced by a majority of the people surveyed. In fact, over 80% of the respondents reported being shy at least sometime during their lives. Almost half (40%) reported currently experiencing problems with shyness. Zimbardo believes that whether or not a person feels shy depends on the situation. In other words, a shy person may not be well represented by our stereotype of the person who is always overly timid. Zimbardo found that 60% of the people he surveyed said they were shy but that it was situationally specific—it depended on the people and situations. What factors were most likely to elicit a shy response? The researchers found that the three interactions most likely to make people shy were strangers, the opposite sex, and authorities, by virtue of their knowledge. The three situations that were most likely to make people shy were where they are the focus of attention, in large groups, and in positions where they have lower status than others.

Social Cognition and Regulation

Although intimacy is a primary focus in young adulthood, independence also becomes an important developmental task. Although young adults are exploring aspects of intimacy, they are also recognizing their need for independence and freedom. Maturity and growth are reflected in the ability to experience both intimacy and dependence and freedom and independence.

In adolescence, young people are working to *develop* their identity; in young adulthood they are trying to *establish* their identity. Keniston (1971) refers to this developmental phase as "the continuing quest to operationalize a sense of identity." This often takes place as

young adults begin to strengthen their own inner identity and clarify their beliefs and values. Still, it is common for people in this stage to struggle with doubts about independent decisions they must make. For example, they may be concerned about career choices they are making or commitments they are making in relationships.

This process of developing one's identity is often facilitated by how the young adult begins to shape a "Dream." According to Levinson (1978), such dreams reflect what a person would like to accomplish as an adult. These dreams often start out as concrete and overly simplistic and then mature into more clear and realistic visions. Men's dreams focus more on occupational goals—for example, having a career in the development of computer software programs. Women's dreams often include visions of both career and family (Levinson, 1986; Roberts & Newton, 1987).

Problems, however, can occur when people fail to establish their own identity. How can young people develop an independent identity when they are still dependent on their parents for financial, personal, and emotional needs? Such dependency may lead to problems in developing intimate relationships with others or in developing independent career opportunities.

Regulation

Kohlberg's theory of moral development was introduced in the chapter on adolescence. In young adulthood, moral development is further refined as young adults are able to address the cognitive complexities involved in resolving moral dilemmas.

Widely recognized in moral development theory is the controversy of whether or not there is a gender bias. Carol Gilligan (1982) is well-known for her criticism of Kohlberg. What disturbed Gilligan was that most of the interviews regarding morality were conducted with men; in addition, the results of the interviews showed that women reason more at stage 3, whereas men reason more at stage 4. Gilligan challenged this finding because it suggested that women are considered morally inferior to men.

But what could account for these differences between men and women in the nature of their moral thoughts? Gilligan considered the differences between how boys and girls are socialized. Boys are taught to be assertive, independent, and achievement oriented, and this may lead them to perceive moral dilemmas as the result of conflicts between the rights of different parties (representative of stage 4). Girls, on the other hand, are raised to be nurturant, concerned about the needs of others, and empathic, and this may lead them to perceive moral dilemmas as conflicts between individual needs and the needs and desires of others (representative of stage 3). Gilligan (1982) theorizes that these differences show a male perspective that emphasizes a justice perspective and a female perspective that emphasizes a care perspective. These contrasting views place a focus on morality in terms of laws that define rights and responsibilities as preeminent (male perspective) or in terms where the welfare of people is the most central (female perspective).

Gilligan first set out to examine women's morality in her study of pregnant women facing the dilemma of whether to keep their babies or have abortions. She identified a series of stages that women go through:

Stage 1. Self-interest is the key factor in decision making.
Stage 2. Sacrificing self-interest for the welfare of others is the deciding influence.
Stage 3. Avoiding hurting either the self or others is the guiding principle.

The last stage represents a morality of care or responsibility. An example of this stage of thinking would be:

> I would not be doing myself or the child a favor by having this child. . . . I don't need to pay off my imaginary debts to the world through this child, and I don't think that it is right to bring a child into the world and use it for that purpose. (Gilligan, 1977, p. 505)

The gender bias in moral thinking is still a controversy, and there has not been consistent support that Kohlberg's theory is biased against women (Sigelman & Shaffer, 1991). Some studies have found that women do reason in a similar manner to men (Thoma, 1986; Walker, 1989). Nonetheless, Gilligan's work has brought an awareness about the importance of considering gender in interpreting research results and has provided an important new direction in studying morality—an examination of both a morality of justice and a morality of care (Brabeck, 1983). For example, Gilgun (1995) recently examined the moral thinking of incest perpetrators using the concepts of both justice and care.

Psychological Hazards

Robert Havighurst (1972), a researcher who studies adulthood, has noted that the young adult years are one of the most difficult periods in a person's life. Indeed, young adults face many challenges during this period. They must make major decisions that include career and job, selecting a mate, extending education, and bearing and rearing children—these are major responsibilities for someone who is just entering adulthood. Many young adults become easily frustrated because they have not been adequately prepared for the life skills they now need. The large number of frustrations, coupled with immense responsibilities, often lead the young person to psychological problems. One devastating problem that a young person could have to face is learning to cope with a major mental illness.

Serious Mental Illness

Many of the major mental illnesses become evident in the late adolescent and early adulthood phase of life. In particular, **schizophrenia**, a serious mental illness, is usually a disorder of late adolescence and early adulthood. Those who suffer from schizophrenia can be grouped into three broad categories: treated successfully with a full recovery, a partial recovery with a reasonably normal life, and little or no recovery with repeated hospitalizations.

When a person does suffer from an illness like schizophrenia, what factors might be likely to produce a favorable prognosis? Lehmann and Cancro (1985) have identified four factors that suggest more promise for a recovery: (1) a sudden rather than a gradual onset, (2) an onset that occurs at a later age, (3) a good social and work environment prior to the onset of the disorder, and (4) an informal support system within their family.

What leads a person to develop a serious mental illness like schizophrenia? Most of the evidence points to heredity as the major explanation. Studies have shown that relatives of a person with schizophrenia have an increased risk for developing schizophrenia. Also, the

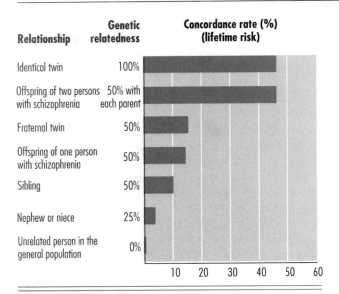

Relationship	Genetic relatedness	Concordance rate (%) (lifetime risk)
Identical twin	100%	
Offspring of two persons with schizophrenia	50% with each parent	
Fraternal twin	50%	
Offspring of one person with schizophrenia	50%	
Sibling	50%	
Nephew or niece	25%	
Unrelated person in the general population	0%	

FIGURE 10.1 Genetic vulnerability to schizophrenic disorders

Source: Nicol & Gottesman, 1983.

closer the relationship, the higher the risk. Figure 10.1 shows the association between the kind of relationship, the genetic relatedness, and the concordance rate or lifetime risk. Being an identical twin or the offspring of two schizophrenic parents creates almost a 50% risk for developing schizophrenia (Nicol & Gottesman, 1983).

What causes people to become schizophrenic? Many researchers now look to the influence of neurochemical factors. In particular, schizophrenia and other mood disorders are accompanied by changes in neurotransmitter activity in the brain. Most of the drugs that are effective in controlling the symptoms of schizophrenia act to restrain dopamine activity in the brain. Therefore, excess **dopamine** is believed to be the most likely cause of schizophrenia. Most recently, research (Davis, Kahn, Ko, & Davidson, 1991) has linked schizophrenia to excessively high dopamine activity in subcortical areas of the brain but abnormally low dopamine activity in the prefrontal cortex area.

The National Alliance for the Mentally Ill (NAMI) has become a powerful advocacy group that promotes the well-being of people with schizophrenia and their families. Formed from a grassroots organization in 1979, today NAMI has chapters in most cities across the country. The organization is designed to serve in an advocacy role, bringing problems and issues to the attention of local, state, and government agencies. NAMI promotes research and knowledge that can be helpful to persons with mental illness and their families. For example, NAMI is particularly interested in research that would identify new ways to help clients readjust to the community using the least restrictive environment as a guiding principle. NAMI is also very involved in working to find ways that would enable families to function more effectively and with less overall stress. The following Focus on Disability section discusses case management services, which can be critical in providing effective care for persons with serious mental illness.

FOCUS ON DISABILITY

Case Management and Better Tracking Are Keys to Providing Better Care for Persons with Serious Mental Illness

Although case management and tracking systems are not new concepts, they are receiving renewed attention in the struggle to provide adequate care for persons with serious mental illness. Case management refers to the process of "managing" a case—linking individuals with needed services and coordinating existing services. In many cases, past efforts at case management have failed because social workers were given extremely large caseloads and couldn't do the necessary advocacy work that would coordinate needed services. Today, many states are finding that their case management systems need an overhaul. For example, New York has an intensive case management program in which approximately 4000 adults with a history of inpatient care and poor follow-

Serious mental illness—from which people can suffer throughout their adult life—often makes its first appearance in young adulthood. Proper care and treatment for persons with mental illness are enhanced through case management services.

through have been assigned to the intensive unit. Here, the case managers have an average workload of about ten clients and are the single point of responsibility. In this model, caseworkers are responsible for providing the housing, job, and mental health care needs of the clients on a 24-hour basis. The state provides a total dollar amount of funds to be spent on each client's personal needs. This allows greater flexibility to meet the sometimes very special needs of clients. For example, the client may not be taking needed medication, but this failure could be due in part to a substance-abuse problem that needs to be addressed.

Oklahoma, recognizing similar problems with their system of care for persons with mental illness, has developed a centralized, statewide database to track its clients with mental illness. When clients enter the system, a confidential computer file is created that lists demographic data, diagnosis, treatment history, presenting problem, living arrangements, and payment source. All local community mental health centers and state hospitals can access the system. This system allows for greater continuity of care for the clients. For example, when a client is discharged from the hospital, staff transmit key data to the community mental health centers. The center can then watch for the client and begin a treatment plan based on the client's individual history. Also, the tracking system can provide data to "flag" clients who may need greater attention. For example, a report can be printed that lists all existing clients at each mental health center and identifies those clients who have not been seen for 40 days. Other reports that can be created include a list of clients discharged from hospitals and referred to community mental health centers, with clients identified who never showed up at the centers, or a monthly list of clients who were readmitted to the hospital within two weeks of discharge to identify clients who are not getting the services they need. The combination of improved case management and better tracking is paving the way to better and more effective help for persons with serious mental illness.

Source: Youngstrom, 1990.

Implications for Practice: Assessment of Clients with Mental Illness

Social workers are often called upon to provide the necessary services for clients with mental illness. Understanding the multifaceted aspects of mental illness is critical in designing and coordinating services. Box 10.2 presents some of the factors that social workers might want to consider in assessing the client and his or her social situation. Focus on Gender: Women and Depression looks at depression, one of the most common mental health problems for women in the United States.

Women and Depression

Depression is one of the leading mental health problems for women in this country. It is estimated that more than 7 million women have a diagnosable depression. Unfortunately, many of these women will go without proper treatment, in spite of new treatment technologies that have reduced depressive symptoms in women by 80–90%. Women, in contrast to men, constitute 70% of those with depression. Why do women experience such high rates of depression? This question, as you might imagine, generates a number of different explanations, including the following:

BOX 10.2

Factors to Consider for Assessment of Clients with Mental Illness

Physical Health Status
Physical functioning
Ability to perform activities for daily living
Extent of bodily pain
Quality of sleep
Level of energy and fatigue

Quality of Life
Access to resources and opportunities
Fulfillment of life's roles and tasks
Overall well-being or life satisfaction

Family and Peer Relationships
Ability to maintain and develop relationships with others

Ability to maintain and develop relationships with family members
Extent of the family's burden

Rehabilitation Status
Social skills
Vocational status
Independent living skills

Although not complete, the above aspects of assessment give some idea of the complexity involved in working with people with mental illness. Understanding and helping these clients involves assessing multiple aspects of the social environment.

Source: Adapted from the National Institute of Mental Health, 1991.

- Approximately 37% of women have been victims of physical or sexual abuse before the age of 21.
- Seventy-five percent of the nation's poor are women.
- It is estimated that depression is misdiagnosed 30–50% of the time.
- There has been a 250% increase in suicide among women aged 15–24.

Most experts now agree that depression in women can be explained only from a biopsychosocial perspective. Research has identified a multitude of factors that influence the prevalence of depression, such as personal styles of women characterized as avoidant, passive, and pessimistic. These characteristics are related to sex-role expectations and socialization experiences. Also, women who suffer from depression often focus on their feelings, neglecting to take action to gain a sense of control over the conditions that may be leading to the depression.

Additional research has found that being unhappily married increases the chances for depression. For women, in comparison with men, being in an unhappy marriage increases the likelihood of depression threefold. When there are young children to care for in the home, women are more likely to be depressed. Also, the more children women have, the greater the likelihood of depression.

Other factors include any physical and emotional abuse that a woman may have experienced. This abuse is likely to be directly linked to depression in women. Many women in this country live in extreme poverty. Such adverse economic conditions contribute to the persistent depression many women feel. Other women may be further marginalized or socially stigmatized by their age, ethnicity, sexual orientation, or drug dependence.

Source: Jones, 1990.

Social Dimension

Families, Groups, Support Systems, and Contexts

Marriage and the emergence of the "family" become one of the most significant life changes in young adulthood. The decision of whether to get married and whether to have children are fundamental struggles in this period. Newman and Newman (1995, p. 523) state that "the most important social factors contributing to the creation of a lifestyle are whether one marries, the characteristics of one's marriage or intimate life partner, whether one has children and the characterisitics of those children, and one's work. The extent to which one has a choice about each of these factors depends on cultural values and restrictions, societal norms and barriers, and socioeconomic factors, especially educational attainment. Each factor interacts with personality, interests, and life goals to shape a lifestyle."

Marriage—Forming a Family

Although the institution of marriage has changed considerably over the past 30 or 40 years, most Americans still opt for marriage at least sometime in their lives—in fact, throughout the 20th century, only about 7% of women have never married (Glick, 1984). Still, there are some very distinctive changes that have taken place with regard to marriage. Perhaps most significant is that young adults are postponing marriage until their late twenties. Consider the fact that the percentage of single women between the ages of 20 and 24 rose dramatically from 28% in 1960 to 78% in 1987 (U.S. Bureau of the Census, 1989). In addition to the increase in the number of single women, there has also been an increase in the number of couples who choose to cohabit and not get married. Data from the U.S. Bureau of the Census (1990) shows that the number of couples cohabiting increased fivefold between 1970 and 1990. The upward trend in the divorce rate has also changed the way we view marriage. Marriage now takes place within the context of each marriage partner's own personal growth. As a result, people are less willing to sacrifice for the sake of the marriage. Today there is less stigma associated with divorce than there was in the past, partly because of the sheer numbers of people who eventually end up divorced. It is estimated that two out of every three marriages will end in divorce or separation (Wisensale, 1992).

In spite of these trends, many people still have an idealized notion of the "nuclear" family: a married couple with two or more children, the husband as the primary breadwinner, and the woman as the homemaker (Weiten & Lloyd, 1994). Yet, it has been estimated that only 7% of American families match this idealized image (Otto, 1988). Our image of the American family needs to change. We need to recognize the influence of single-parent families, childless families, unwed parents, gay couples, and dual-career families, which reflect the reality of the diversity of families.

Selecting a Partner   Finding a partner to whom you are willing to make a serious commitment is usually a gradual process that involves moving through a series of phases that leads to a deepening attraction and commitment. Adams (1986) has identified four phases that lead to marriage:

Phase I: Opportunity, physical attraction, valued behaviors
Phase II: Positive self-disclosure, rapport, sexuality, value concerns, salient homogeneity, similarity
Phase III: Role compatibility, empathy
Phase IV: The "right one" relationship, commitment escalators
Marriage

In phase I, opportunity plays a critical role as a factor in determining who is available to choose from when selecting a partner. Opportunity will be influenced by the values of the young person's culture, family, and social class (Schuster & Ashburn, 1992). For example, such cultural influences may produce opportunities for selecting a partner based on attendance at private schools, church groups, sporting events, or local neighborhood events. In the early stages, physical attraction and behaviors that are valued (e.g., being outgoing) are also important determinants in the selection process.

By the time young people move to phase II, they are focusing on a process of more intimate discovery. They might reflect on such questions as, Who is this person, really? Is he (or she) similar to me? Through reciprocal self-disclosure, each person learns more about the other. The information gained is often assessed in terms of similarities. For example, many people would consider similarity in religious faith to be an important factor that would influence their selection of a mate.

The transition to phase III is similar but involves a deeper level of disclosure. Couples may share aspects about their sexual desires, personal fears, and fantasies. In this phase, there is more trust and a greater level of risk as one shares increasingly intimate aspects of the self. This sharing leads to two central processes: role compatibility and empathy. The couple learns about the extent to which they are truly compatible and deepen their level of understanding about each other.

Finally, the couple reaches phase IV, where each partner is persuaded that this is the "right" relationship, and both take steps to deepen their commitment to one another. Each partner has developed comfortable feelings and predictability. Furthermore, the couple is socially defined as being "together," so the costs of ending the relationship become much greater. The following Focus on Diversity section examines marriage for people with mental retardation.

FOCUS ON DIVERSITY

I Do, and I Will—Marriage as a Union of Souls and Determination

Getting to the church on time is the least of the obstacles facing Roger Drake Meyers and Virginia Rae Hensler on their wedding day, but you would never know it. Roger and Virginia, both born with mental retardation, are challenging the previously designated dependent role of adults with mental retardation. Their marriage is a reflection of their commitment to one another and their desire to free themselves from the often inaccurate labels society imposes on individuals with mental retardation.

Determination of mental retardation is frequently based on IQ and social adjustment; difficulties in both areas appear before age 18 in people determined to have some form of retardation. About 89% of individuals with mental retardation have mild retardation and can have, with some assistance, an independent lifestyle. Potential for this population may be enhanced by early intervention programs involving intellectual and motor stimulation.

Even with early developmental attention, how can we be sure that people like Roger and Virginia are ready for the rigors of marriage? In reality, we can never be sure that any couple, whatever its characteristics, is marriage-ready. The statistics suggest, however, that couples composed of individuals with mild retardation have as good a chance of navigating marriage as other couples. Marriage between such people occurs at roughly the same rate as marriage between members of any group within the nonaffected population. Couples' descriptions of their marriages are diverse: Some report creative, satisfying marriages; some describe a relationship characterized by poverty, depression, and violence; others see marriage as a "badge of normality and a way to 'pass' in to the nonretarded community" (Meyers, 1978, p. 107).

Roger and Virginia see marriage as one way of finding a place within the larger community. In working toward complying with societal norms, they face many difficult marital issues. For example, they must decide whether or not to have children. Because neither Roger nor Virginia has congenital retardation, their children would have as much of a chance of not having retardation as would a child born to parents who have no retardation. Other difficulties relate to handling the well-intentioned but troublesome interference of their in-laws. With the help of a counselor, Roger and Virginia are able to address these issues effectively.

Both individually and as a couple, Roger and Virginia are excellent models of learning to work with and around a disability. They demonstrate the power of developing an individual's potential, and of using personal strengths to move beyond societal labels.

Source: Written by Julianne Azimov, based on Myers, 1978.

Coming Together—Adjustment to Marriage   Once a person has found the "right" partner, both must come together and begin the process of making an adjustment to marriage. This adjustment can be challenging, as it includes adapting to myths and expectations of marriage, learning how to effectively communicate with one's spouse, deriving satisfaction from one's relationship and learning how

to deal with conflict, and accepting gender differences in how men and women relate to marriage.

Marital Expectations and Myths   Addressing marital expectations and myths is often a good place for couples to start adjusting to marriage. Too often, marriages go awry because one or both partners have unrealistic expectations. Larson (1988) found that many college students are influenced by myths about marriage, and he developed a marriage quiz to assess such myths. The quiz includes items that are evaluated as either true or false. Some sample questions from the quiz are:

1. A husband's marital satisfaction is usually lower if his wife is employed full-time than if she is a full-time homemaker.
2. In most marriages, having a child improves marital satisfaction for both spouses.
3. For most couples, marital satisfaction gradually increases from the first year of marriage through the childbearing years, the teen years, the empty-nest period, and retirement.

All of the above three items are false. Larson (1988) found that young adults answered almost half of the items on the marriage quiz incorrectly. These results confirm the notion that, indeed, young adults may not be properly prepared to enter marriage with a realistic point of view. Adjustment to a new marriage requires a new set of tasks for each person. The Focus on Family lists 20 of the new tasks a couple needs to address.

FOCUS ON FAMILY

Tasks Associated with Adjustment to a New Marriage

Entering into a marriage is more complex than it might seem. Although individuals may come into a marriage with a lot of experience dating others, marriage brings a new set of tasks that the couple must work out. Kelly (1979) has identified some 20 tasks that new couples face:

1. Establishing routines for daily living
2. Learning how to make purposeful decisions together
3. Building new friendships as a couple
4. Developing relationships with in-laws
5. Establishing a working family budget
6. Developing a "double-person" spending and shopping mentality
7. Establishing religious habits
8. Deciding on children and contraceptive methods
9. Learning how to negotiate conflicts
10. Learning the give and take of living together
11. Allocating responsibilities
12. Developing effective communication patterns
13. Establishing a shared core-value system
14. Identifying family "rules"
15. Creating common goals
16. Deciding on leisure-time activities and community involvement
17. Establishing financial credit
18. Developing a satisfying sex life
19. Establishing a balance between togetherness and respect for individuality
20. Establishing traditions as a family

Marital Communication and Adjustment   Communication is a critical part of our existence. We need to communicate to survive and succeed in our society. Couple communication has been the subject of many books and articles, in part because communication is a complicated phenomenon that has great impact on our lives. Communication is more than just sending and receiving messages. It involves processes such as encoding the message, interpreting the message, and responding to the intended message. The result of this process is that the message sent may not be the message received. A message is processed on two levels: an outer experience of what is being sent and an inner experience of how the message is being translated. A diagram (from Stuart, 1980, p. 215) helps illustrate this process:

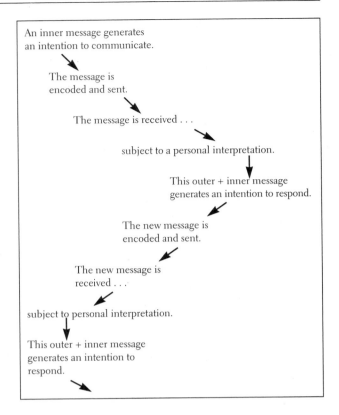

Nonverbal Communication May Be More Powerful Than You Think

In well-known studies of nonverbal communication, Mehrabian (1969) and others have shown that there are three dimensions represented in nonverbal expressions. (1) The *like-dislike* dimension is expressed through closeness or distance; for example, looking at or away from a person; (2) the *potency* dimension is expressed through one's expression; for example, standing straight rather than slumped or rapid-versus-slow movements; (3) the *responsiveness* dimension is expressed through one's facial movements, voice tone, and voice volume. Mehrabian (1972) is often noted for his observation that, of a total feeling conveyed in a message, 7% is verbal feeling, 38% is vocal feeling, and 55% is facial feeling. What's important about this observation is that although we may restrict what we say in words, it is often more difficult to restrict our feelings from entering our nonverbal responses.

Therefore, nonverbal responses may contradict our verbal message. It is the nonverbal part of the message that will qualify what we are attempting to communicate verbally.

Problems in communication are a particular concern to couples. Beck and Jones (1973) discovered that communication problems were the most frequently identified issue of couples seeking counseling. Research (Fowers & Olson, 1989) has also found that happy and unhappy couples can be distinguished on the basis on three aspects of communication: comfort in sharing information with the other person, willingness to recognize and resolve conflicts as they occur, and quality of the couple's sexual life.

In a study that attempted to predict the likelihood of divorce, Buehlman, Gottman, & Katz (1992) studied communication and interaction styles while the couples discussed problem areas. Primarily on the basis of how the couple related to each other, the researchers were able to predict, with an accuracy of 94%, which couples would divorce three years later.

Satisfaction and Conflict in Marriages   What factors predict marital satisfaction? Researchers have attempted to answer this question for years. It is difficult because notions such as marital "satisfaction" or "success" are difficult to define. However, researchers have generally found the following factors to correlate positively with marital satisfaction:

- People whose parents were divorced are more likely to experience divorce themselves (White, 1990).
- Couples who marry young have a higher divorce rate (White, 1990).
- The longer the courtship, the greater the likelihood of marital success (Grover, Russell, Schumm, & Paff-Bergen, 1985).
- Divorce is more common among the working and lower classes than among middle and upper classes, probably because of the greater financial stress of the working and lower classes (Conger et al., 1990).

Is compatibility critical to marital success? Is the reduction of conflict critical to saving troubled marriages? Although many social work practitioners would answer these questions with a "yes," recent research is finding a different answer. Research by Gottman (1994, p. 44) has

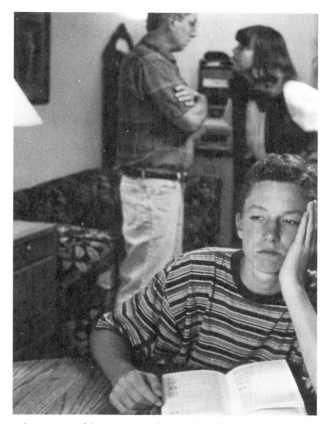

To have a successful marriage, couples must learn how to communicate and resolve conflict.

found that "it isn't the lack of compatibility that predicts divorce, but the way couples handle their inevitable *incompatibilities*, not whether they fight all the time or never fight at all, but the way they resolve conflicts and the overall quality of their emotional interactions." Indeed, Gottman and associates have discovered that what is critical in a marriage is the balance between the couple's positive and negative interactions—this is what determines their satisfaction. In fact, their research has discovered that you can quantify the ratio of positive to negative interactions needed to maintain a healthy marriage. Gottman (1994, p. 44) believes that "satisfied couples, no matter how their marriages stacked up against the ideal, were those who maintained a five-to-one ratio of positive to negative moments."

Conflict and fighting is an aspect of married life. All marriages, including good ones, have a degree of conflict. It may be that such negativity serves a function in that it keeps the marriage dynamic rather than static. Gottman (1994) suggests that anger, if it is directed at a specific issue and expressed without contempt, can be healthy for marriages. However, not all negativity is equal, and the four factors that seem to lead to the worst outcomes for married couples include criticism, defensiveness, contempt, and stonewalling. In a more functional marriage, anger and disagreements are directed at the other person's specific actions, whereas in a troubled relationship, criticism and contempt are focused more globally and directed at the person, rather than their actions. So it's not just the anger but the insulting manner in which the anger is directed that makes the difference.

The impact of such insulting remarks often leads to intense fighting, and the spouse is likely to then take up the other processes that contribute to the negativity, such as stonewalling. Gottman (1994) has found that about 85% of the stonewallers are male, and he believes this may be due to men's physiological reaction to conflict. When men face conflict, they get more intensely upset physiologically than women do. More specifically, they have an increased heart rate and blood pressure and remain upset for longer periods of time than women do. One explanation for this response difference is that it may have served some evolutionary survival benefits, whereby the male, in order to protect the female and her young, needed to remain physiologically responsive to external danger. However, this impact on today's marriages is not helpful. As Gottman (1994, p. 46) points out, "in modern life, the propensity to higher arousal is not nearly so adaptive; it feels terrible, and to avoid the acute distress it causes, men are likely simply to shut themselves down, refuse to respond, try, as much as possible, to turn themselves into unfeeling stone." This physiological gender difference may help us understand why men and women have such different approaches to conflict—women pursue the conflict with emotion and men avoid the conflict through rationalizations, the "silent" treatment, and physically withdrawing.

Gender Differences in Communication

Men and women are different. This difference becomes salient when we examine how men and women communicate, because gender differences in communication are often the source of much frustration and anger between men and women. Tannen (1991) describes how the process of socialization leads to many misunderstandings. Tannen believes that men are socialized to see the social world as basically hierarchical. As a result, men approach conversations as "negotiations in which people try to achieve and maintain the upper hand if they can and protect themselves from others' attempts to put them down and push them around" (p. 25). On the other hand, women are socialized to see the world as a community and to focus on their connections with others in the community. As a result, women approach conversations as "negotiations for closeness in which people try to seek and give confirmation and support, and to reach consensus. They try to protect themselves from others' attempts to push them away" (p. 25). The end result: Neither understands the other. What is it about men's and women's communication styles that makes them so different?

Some researchers identify men as using an instrumental style of communication and women as using an expressive style of communication. **Instrumental communication** refers to having a focus on identifying goals and finding solutions. **Expressive communication** involves the expression of emotions and having a perspective that is sensitive to how others feel. In general, men are more interested in having rational discussions and solving problems, and women are more interested in expressing emotions and feeling listened to and provided with support. The following scenario is a typical example of this kind of mismatch:

A young mother describes her worries and frustrations concerning appropriate child care for her son. She is using her expressive style and is most interested in having her partner listen to her and provide some support. However, the husband, using his instrumental style of communication, assumes she wants to solve a problem and begins to search for solutions. This mismatch in communication leads to serious problems. Because her husband is not listening to her and hence not providing her with the support she desires, she assumes he doesn't have any sympathy for her concerns. On the other hand, he is frustrated by what he perceives as her complaining and her inability to simply solve the problem.

This represents a classic mismatch because each person is talking at cross-purposes. Each person, in his or her own way, is attempting to respond appropriately. However, they are frustrating each other; she wants his sympathy and he wants to help her solve a problem. In this context, each partner assumes that they know what the other person wants, but clearly they do not.

Other differences in communication according to Tannen (1991) include women's use of **rapport talk,** which involves discussing similarities and matching experiences, and men's use of **report talk,** which involves discussing knowledge and displaying skill. What men and women talk about also varies considerably. Women usually prefer discussions about their personal lives and feelings, whereas men seem to prefer discussions about activities and events.

Differences also emerge in mixed-sex conversations, where women are more often *listeners* and men are more often *lecturers.* Tannen explains these differences by suggesting that this represents games that men and women learned to play in childhood. For men the game is "do you respect me?" and for women the game is "do you like me?" According to Tannen, mixed-sex conversation places women in a double bind because men's style of conversation is dominant in most situations. Because the male style is used as the norm against which the woman will be evaluated, she is placed in this double bind; she is evaluated negatively if she adopts either a male or a female style. Tannen (1991, p. 244) explains that "if they speak in ways expected of women, they are seen as inadequate leaders. If they speak in ways expected of leaders, they are seen as inadequate women."

Implications for Practice: Communication Skills for Men and Women

Communication Skills for Women   Often, in a discussion among men and women, men dominate the discussion. Women may need to "jump into" the conversation more forcefully than they are accustomed to doing. Good use of nonverbal behavior can be critical: making eye contact, using appropriate vocal tone and pitch, and maintaining good posture and orientation in space will command greater attention. When the content of a spoken message is inconsistent with the nonverbal message, the nonverbal message will have the greatest impact. Because nonverbal behavior can be so powerful, women should use both nonverbal and spoken messages to convey positive responses and should rely more on oral communication to express negative responses. Personal use of space can also affect the impact of a message. Many

women need to become more visible by obtaining a good position for interaction with others.

Women are often less comfortable than men in talking about themselves and their accomplishments. Women for whom this is a problem might want to script a short biography that describes their specific accomplishments and states their areas of expertise. To feel more comfortable about sharing their point of view, women can also practice expressing *opinions* on a variety of topics.

Communication Skills for Men   Because men often tend to dominate a conversation, they should observe their patterns of communication and evaluate their tendency to dominate. If this is a problem for them, they can learn to catch themselves interrupting and politely encourage the other person to continue with his or her thoughts. Men can sometimes be difficult to talk with because they don't "carry" enough of the conversation; for example, they might only provide short answers to questions. Some men also need to work at being more conversational. A good technique to use for improving conversational skill is the two-question rule (Stuart, 1980). This rule keeps the conversation focused on the other person it requires a speaker to ask an opening question and then to follow up that question with another inquiry. Often, people ask just one question, such as "How did you feel about that meeting?" and then proceed with their own analysis and reaction to the meeting. By contrast, asking a second, follow-up question demonstrates good listening and helps to keep the dominant person from launching into a lengthy monologue. In general, many men need to practice being good listeners. Too often, women feel "talked at" rather than "talked with." Good listening requires concentration and sustained effort. A good balance of conversational give-and-take will facilitate good communication between men and women.

Men who do not usually use an expressive communication style can practice discussing their interests, feelings, and thoughts. To do so, rather than approach a conversation as an interaction about events and activities, men can focus on their *feelings* about various subjects.

Diversity in Companionship

Although marriage is a major developmental task for many young adults, increasing numbers of young adults are choosing different alternatives to the traditional pathway of marriage and children. Many young adults choose to remain single, go through divorce and remarriage, become part of a stepfamily, develop a committed relationship with a partner of the same sex, or cohabit. There are many ways that young adults can meet their needs for companionship.

Remaining or Becoming Single

Although some young adults remain single throughout their lives, many become single after being widowed, separated, or divorced. Being single has increased dramatically over the last 25 years. In both the early twenties and mid to late twenties, the percentage of men and women who remain single has more than doubled. This trend is due to several factors. For example, young adults have increasingly delayed the age at which they marry, and this has increased the number of people who remain single before marriage. Also, the increased rate of divorce and separation has contributed to a larger number of men and women becoming single.

Many young adults who are single face difficult stereotypes and pressures. When the majority of the population marries, the question many single adults must confront is, why haven't you married? Often the stereotype conforms to two alternatives (Keith, 1986): the assumption is either that the single people are uncommitted so they can pursue promiscuity, or they are single because they were not "good enough" to capture a mate.

Research studies have attempted to examine the differences between single and married people. Overall, single people do rate themselves as less happy than married people (Lee, Secombe, & Shehan, 1991). This seems to reflect the social expectation that it is better to be married. However, it is interesting to note that these differences have narrowed in recent years. Also, research finds single women are more happy than single men (Glenn & Weaver, 1988).

Being single may require some special adaptations. For example, socializing often occurs in couples and the single person may feel left out. Many single people feel lonely because they lack the constant companionship available in a marriage or a committed relationship. Single people often complain about not wanting to go places or do things alone. A good network of friends can help eliminate many of these concerns.

Homosexual or Gay Relationships

Use of the term *homosexual* can be traced back to 1869 (Money, 1988). Today, the term *gay* is more often used and is related to the gay-rights movement of the past 20 years. The term *gay* refers to males and sometimes females; however, the term "lesbian" refers exclusively to female homosexuals.

In the late 1940s and early 1950s, Alfred Kinsey reported the sexual histories of thousands of Americans. His research found that 8% of men and 4% of women were exclusively homosexual for at least a period of three years. In addition, 4% of men and 2% of women were exclusively homosexual after adolescence. A much larger percentage of the population had some previous experience with homosexual behavior—37% of the men and 20% of the women reported at least one homosexual experience that led to orgasm.

More representative studies of the general population have found lower estimates of homosexual behavior than the early Kinsey studies. For example, one comparative analysis (Fay, Turner, Klassen, & Gagnon, 1989) found that in both 1970 and 1988 studies, the portion of homosexual men in the general population during the preceding year was 2%. In a recent review of studies, Seidman and Rieder (1994) estimated that 2% of men are exclusively homosexual and that an additional 3% are bisexual. Diamond (1993) examined homosexuality for men and women throughout the world and estimated that 6% of men and 3% of women have engaged in same-sex behavior since adolescence. However, many experts believe that these estimates are low because the tremendous amount of social prejudice against homosexuals would preclude many from self-reporting homosexuality. Indeed, many experts place the estimate of homosexuals as high as 10% for both sexes. Furthermore, how one defines homosexual behavior is going to have a large impact on how the prevalence is estimated.

Many different studies have been conducted to determine whether homosexuals have a greater degree of psychopathology when compared with heterosexuals. Most studies using various methodology have failed to find any differences (Gonsiorek, 1991). Furthermore, research on specific disorders, such as the sexual abuse of children, has not found an increased frequency of homosexual perpetrators (Groth & Birnbaum, 1978). This information has not provided support for the once-popular notion that detached or hostile fathers and castrating mothers are the link to male homosexuality. Indeed, most experts recognize that the origins of sexual orientation are multifactorial and diverse (Friedman & Downey, 1994).

There may be as many as 25 million gay people in the United States. How do gay couples differ from their heterosexual counterparts? In many respects, gay couples do not differ much from heterosexual couples. A study by Peplau (1991) compared homosexual and heterosexual men and women on what aspects of intimacy they valued and found that heterosexual men and women were quite similar to homosexual men and women. Gay couples, however, do have to face a different reality concerning their relationship. For example, in many states gay couples are prohibited from getting legally married. As a result, gay couples do not get the same economic benefits that heterosexual couples do (Rivera, 1991)—for example, shared health benefits or joint tax returns.

Homophobia   Homophobia is an irrationally negative attitude toward homosexual people. Homosexual people are often depicted in terms of negative stereotypes; however, this tendency may have recently begun to lessen (Friedman & Downey, 1994). A majority of people indicate that they would prefer to not be in a work setting with homosexual people (Herek, 1991). Factors that appear to be related to homophobia include authoritarian perspectives, highly religious views, being with others who share negative views toward homosexuals, and not having had any personal contact with gay or lesbian people. In recent years, homophobic attitudes as well as the fear of AIDS have lead to many gays being harassed or even assaulted (Herek & Berrill, 1990).

Homophobia exists in all aspects of society. Many homosexual professionals, including doctors, social workers, and lawyers, believe that they need to conceal their homosexual identity. One study (Wisniewski & Toomey, 1987) found that social workers, like many other professional groups, have evidence of homophobia. Although there are few studies available, clearly many homosexuals remain "in the closet," and their colleagues and clients do not know their sexual orientation. The following Focus on Diversity section looks at how

AIDS has surprisingly not influenced coming out for homosexuals.

FOCUS ON DIVERSITY

Coming Out in the Age of AIDS

Is AIDS changing the number of men coming out among homosexuals? A common fear in today's society is that young gay men are being discouraged from coming out because of the AIDS epidemic. This reluctance could lead to increased participation in unsafe sex and in sexual harassment. However, when Robert Marks (1988) interviewed 15 young gay men, he expected the AIDS era to have discouraged young gay men from claiming their sexual identity. He did not find this to be true. Today's young gay men continue to have a powerful gay identity that does not appear to be hampered by AIDS. In fact, Marks reports that in some ways AIDS has facilitated the process. The greater presence and visibility of gay people may be contributing to a greater willingness to come out. What has changed, according to Marks, is the *way* people come out. He believes that the past image of gay men descending on the gay bar scene in search of sex is giving way to a stronger desire by gay men for more long-lasting relationships.

Source: Written by Rebecca Melin; adapted from Dregni, 1989.

The Transition to Parenthood

Carrying the baby horizontally across my chest like a football usually calms him, and often puts him to sleep. But not tonight. He's still crying, cycling through his whole repertoire: the screechy fear cry; the lower, throaty demand cry; the pitiable gasping interspersed with slobbery whimpers. Kapa nursed him an hour ago at midnight, so he isn't hungry. Teething—always a suspect—doesn't seem to be the problem tonight: he isn't drooling much, nor is he clawing at his ears. I may give him a dropperful of Tylenol anyway, to help me relax. (Goodrich, 1995, p. 12)

As this scene depicts, the transition to parenthood brings many changes and new challenges. Consider all the adaptations the new parent must make. Parents must now accommodate changes in priorities, as they have less time to spend on career and personal interests. Indeed, the loss of free time appears to be one of the most difficult adjustments for parents. How will the new household tasks be divided between the parents? Many parents struggle to find the time and energy needed to keep their own relationship satisfying in terms of intimacy and companionship. The transition must also include their adaptation to a new role—that of parent. What makes a good parent? What kind of parents do they want to be?

These life changes are usually accompanied by a significant increase in stress. The crying baby and the new demands of diapers, bottles, and laundry combine to create a stressful environment for many new parents. Mothers can be uniquely affected, and they often enter parenthood exhausted from the birth process. For older mothers and working mothers, the transition to parenthood is often more difficult. Women are particularly vulnerable to distress when they are the major caretaker of the infant and when they have babies with difficult temperaments (Kalmuss, Davidson, & Cushman, 1992). Curran (1985) surveyed married couples and single mothers to identify what parents perceive as the most stressful aspects of their lives. He identified the following top ten stressors listed in order of priority:

1. Economics, finances, budgeting
2. Children's behavior, discipline, sibling fighting
3. Insufficient couple time
4. Lack of shared responsibilities in the family
5. Communicating with children
6. Insufficient "me" time
7. Guilt for not accomplishing more
8. Spousal relationships (communication, friendship, sex)
9. Insufficient family playtime
10. Overscheduled family calendar

Implications for Practice:
Preparing for the Transition to Parenthood

Given the types of stresses new parents experience, how can we make the transition to parenthood less stressful?

Jay Belsky (1985) has recommended that parents be given more realistic expectations about parental responsibilities. This recommendation is based on the finding that stress is highest in new mothers who have overestimated the benefits of their new mothering role and underestimated the difficulties associated with their new role. Mothers with optimistic perspectives about what it is like to be a parent tend to experience more distress, because their expectations need the greatest amount of realignment. Prospective parents could be greatly helped by better education about what parenting is like. Once parents understand that although children are "bundles of joy," that joy is accompanied by "bundles of stress," they can develop more realistic expectations and be in a better position to cope effectively with their new role as parents. The following Focus on Ethics section looks at the difficult issue of how to deal with parents of "crack babies."

FOCUS ON ETHICS

Parents of Crack Babies—Where Do We Draw the Line?

Jennifer Johnson of Florida was one of the first women convicted of child abuse as a result of her addiction to crack. She was sentenced to mandatory drug treatment and 15 years probation. As crack became increasingly popular, the media exposed the dramatic scenes of crack addiction known to many. Janee Chapman started using pot and alcohol when she was 12, and by the time she was 16, she was using cocaine. After her second pregnancy, she discovered crack. That caused social workers to remove her two children, but she still couldn't stop. Her crack baby was born with the "shakes," a common sign of drug exposure, and is developmentally delayed. Melinda East, a former crack addict, gave birth to a baby with the "shakes," but that did not stop her. She went back on the street as a prostitute to support herself and her habit. At times, she sold disposable diapers and milk back to the grocery store to obtain drug money.

The frustration and sadness of seeing crack babies has prompted many to ask, "When should we take their kids away?" The debate centers on at what point should child protective authorities remove a child from the home? Many states now have child abuse laws that consider it illegal for mothers to give birth to children with illegal drugs in their bloodstream. In some cases, this is considered delivering drugs to a minor. Frustrated policy makers have gone even further, some suggesting that female addicts be required to accept Norplant—a birth control implant that works for up to five years—if they want to avoid serving jail time. Many child advocates are impatient in considering the civil liberties of the mothers. They argue that the system is letting babies die, or at best, returning them to mothers who are ill equipped to parent them.

But what happens to the babies who are removed from their mothers? Many end up as wards of the court and are boarded in overcrowded hospitals. Other options include shifting the babies from one foster home to the next. Many experts believe many of these babies will end up suffering from the failure to thrive syndrome, where weight gain and normal development are negatively affected. Health policy officials are taking a closer look at the impact of such a punitive approach to dealing with these mothers. Because many of these women do get pregnant again after being treated so negatively, many of them will be even less likely to seek health care when they are pregnant. Many communities are changing their initial strategy of removing all crack babies. In Los Angeles, such an action would completely overwhelm the system. Instead, social workers must carefully assess the child's health and the mother's potential for rehabilitation when making court recommendations. Interestingly, one of the biggest factors in custody decisions is the presence of a grandmother. In some counties, grandmothers reportedly care for over half of all the crack babies.

Additional problems resulted from the policy to remove babies identified with drugs in their bodies. In a few cases there were mistaken assessments; for example, one mother had her child removed after she received drugs for a cesarean delivery, which led to a false positive drug test. Also at issue is that these social policies were implemented with women of color at public hospitals but not with white women in private hospitals. Such discrimination was exposed, which, along with the destruction of families

as a result of this approach to the crack problem, has led to renewed efforts to find other solutions.

What is making a difference is the combination of offering addicted mothers intensive wraparound services with the threat of legal sanctions. Addicted mothers need lots of help—detoxification, child pediatric services, counseling, social support, career and vocational help—backed up with the threat of legal intervention. For example, the Women and Infants Clinic in Boston offers comprehensive services but also requires women to submit to random urine tests each week. Other programs give mothers a choice: jail or treatment. Many believe that the ultimatum works well. Social workers are also finding new ways to provide treatment to these women. For example, many social services professionals believe that it is not helpful to confront women about their lying and behavior as is often done in drug rehabilitation programs. What may be different about addicted mothers as compared with other addicted individuals is that many of these women ended up in their situation because they were once sexually or physically abused or raped. This leads to a different treatment strategy than has typically been used in the past with addicts. The present approach is a combination of legal intervention and service delivery and the notion that in order to save the child, we must also save the mother.

Source: Based on Cronin & Gorman, 1991.

Voluntary Childlessness

An increasing number of married couples are choosing not to have children (Seccombe, 1991). A review of U.S. Census Bureau data shows an increase in the number of women without children for all age groups. For women aged 25–29 the percentage without children went from under 30% in 1970 to over 40% in 1990. This change is most likely due to women seeking career opportunities and marrying at a later age. The percentage of women who never expect to bear children is over 10% (U.S. Bureau of the Census, 1987). Approximately one-third of childless couples had decided to be childless prior to marriage (Veevers, 1980). In fact, many men and women decide while still adolescent to remain childless (Campbell, 1985).

When Couples Can't Conceive: Infertility

Infertility is defined as the inability to achieve pregnancy after one year of sexual intercourse with no contraception. The latest figures indicate that 20 to 25% of couples are infertile. This number is a significant increase over the 10% of couples unable to conceive only a generation ago. This rise in infertility is attributable to an increase in sexually transmitted diseases, which result in pelvic inflammation and adhesions, and also to the fact that couples now delay childbearing into their thirties. Female fertility decreases after age 30, and male fertility drops after age 45. Thus, couples who delay childbearing may pass up their most fertile years and later experience difficulties conceiving.

There are several causes of infertility. Male abnormalities contribute to 40% of the cases of infertility, female problems another 40%; in the remaining 20%, there is no ascertainable reason the couple cannot conceive. In males, the problems of infertility involve having a low sperm count, having abnormally formed sperm, or having sperm with low motility—that is, the sperm are unable to make the journey through the cervix and uterus to the fallopian tube.

In females, various problems contribute to an inability to conceive. Menstrual cycles result in infrequent or absent ovulation. Cervical mucus, which is hostile to sperm, can prevent migration of the sperm through the cervix. The fallopian tubes may become blocked, from past pelvic infection or inflammation from gonorrheal salpingitis or from the pelvic adhesions of endometriosis (a condition that arises when pieces of the lining of the uterus become attached to structures in the abdominal cavity including the fallopian tubes). Uterine problems such as fibroids, congenital malformations and intrauterine adhesions can keep a fertilized egg from implanting.

Implications for Practice: The Infertile Couple

Julie had always planned on having children. She had assumed she would get her degree, marry her boyfriend, work a while, and have a couple of children. After college, though, she went to graduate school and then began an exciting career. After eight years of an on-again, off-again relationship, her boyfriend left. After a couple of years of dating, at the age of 34, Julie fell in love, got married, and stopped taking birth control pills. Two years later, Julie
has not conceived. At first she attributed her failure to conceive to having taken the pill for so long. But now, each month when she gets her period, Julie is increasingly worried. An infertility workup disclosed that her husband has a low sperm count. The couple's relationship is becoming strained as they consider their options for having a child.

Couples who receive the diagnosis of infertility are in a crisis situation, and their emotions and reactions should be considered from this viewpoint. They are facing the loss of a lifelong dream—the end to their hopes and dreams of having a family. Often the first reaction is shock, followed by denial (this can't happen to us). The practitioner should allow the couple to express their feelings of isolation, guilt, depression, and anger. Because of the economic and emotional cost and low success rate, Paulson and Sauer (1991) urge that counseling the couple should, from the beginning, include the option to stop the treatment. The social worker should help the couple differentiate treatment failure from personal failure. The practitioner should reframe the meaning of infertility and the partners' view of themselves (Olshansky, 1992). Although the drive to become a biological parent may be strong, other options for fulfilling the need to nurture should be explored with the couple. The social worker should discuss the options of adoption and of leading a fulfilling life as a childless couple.

Ken Daniels feels that "social work, with its focus on the interaction of person/problem/situation, is ideally suited to respond to the psychosocial needs arising from infertility" (1993, p. 507). He notes that "a social worker providing counselling from a psychosocial perspective will be aware of the importance of the couple's network/support system and seek to enable them to utilize this vital source of support. This is in contrast to more traditional infertility counselling, where the focus is more likely to be on the individual or couple alone" (p. 509).

In addition to counseling for their emotional needs, the partners need assistance in using their social support system to help them through this crisis. The couple may have problems communicating with parents or employers at this time when they most need to talk with others. The social worker may need to hold sessions with the couple and with members of their extended family. Through role playing and problem solving, the social worker can also enable the partners to explain to employers work-related problems caused by the treatment. Focus on the Family: Some Babies Die examines what happens when a couple loses a baby.

FOCUS ON THE FAMILY

Some Babies Die

Mei Ling and Kim were thrilled when they learned that Mei Ling was pregnant. Mei Ling told everyone—her co-workers, her friends, neighbors, and family—that she was pregnant. The couple began to look at baby items in stores and to plan how they would decorate the nursery. Eleven weeks into the pregnancy, however, late one after-noon at work, Mei Ling experienced some lower abdom-inal cramping. After dinner that night, she felt increased cramping and began to have vaginal bleeding. Mei Ling called her doctor who told her to go to the hospital. There, later that evening, Mei Ling miscarried. Mei Ling and Kim were devastated by the loss, but their doctor as-sured them that they were young and could try again soon. The nurses gave Mei Ling a booklet about coping with fetal death, the number of a support group to call, and a satin-covered box containing a small gold ring. The couple was encouraged to name the baby and to have some kind of memorial. They hardly had time to cry. Kim returned to work two days later, and Mei Ling took a few days to recover. Two weeks after the loss, friends and family stopped asking Mei Ling how she felt. One month later, the couple had a major argument after Mei Ling accused Kim of not caring about their baby. After this blowup, they decided to attend the support group. Their first question was, "How long does this pain last?"

Often in a hospital or clinical setting, a social worker is called on to support families who suffer a fetal loss. To many couples, an early miscarriage can signify the loss of a child. Even at the beginning of pregnancy, most couples have dreamed of and planned for their ex-pected child. The mother, especially, has fantasized about the baby she will have, and the loss of that dream is very real and painful. At any stage of pregnancy, mourning a perinatal loss is difficult though, because

there is so little concrete evidence of the child's exis-tence. It is hard for a mother to identify with a child she has only interacted with through fantasy. It is hard for friends and family to understand the pain of the loss of someone they never knew. It is difficult to grieve for someone who never lived. As a consequence, many cou-ples who experience a fetal loss lose not only their dream but also their right to mourn.

Often, because this situation involves coping not only with one's own grief but that of one's spouse as well, partners experience at least one episode of intense con-flict following perinatal loss (Gilbert, 1989). Men and women grieve a fetal loss in different ways. Fathers report that intense grieving lasts less than one month, whereas mothers' intense grieving lasts up to one year (Hughes & Page-Lieberman, 1989). Because of the shortened pe-riod of intense grief fathers experience, mothers may feel that their partner is unfeeling and not adequately mourning the loss, and the father may feel that his part-ner is dwelling on her grief instead of getting on with life (Hughes & Page-Lieberman, 1989).

The couple needs to recognize that the fetal loss is the loss of a real baby and all the dreams and fantasies surrounding it. The couple should be encouraged to ad-equately mourn before attempting another pregnancy. Attempting to have a second pregnancy to replace a peri-natal loss is likely to result in unresolved grief, which could interfere with subsequent bonding to the next child (Leon, 1992). First, the couple should be encour-aged to see the body, name the baby, make a book of memories, and have a memorial service (Leon, 1986). The hospital can attempt to provide the family with evi-dence of the child's existence by providing a photograph, a lock of hair, a footprint, or whatever the couple wishes to keep. Most important, the couple should be allowed the time and opportunity to express their feelings about the loss. They should be helped to understand and ac-cept that each person grieves loss in his or her own way. But for some who ask, "How long will the pain last," the answer is often "A long time."

Work Life

In young adulthood, a person's career or job can become a significant part of the person's self-identity. Often a person's self-definition is related to what he or she does. Levinson (1978) describes the process of young adults entering an occupation whereby they must develop an occupational identity and establish themselves in the work world. Each job carries with it a set of components that must be adapted to for successful adjustment in the workplace. Newman and Newman (1995) describe four of these components: the use of technical skills; the development of authority relations; adapting to special demands and hazards; and the development of interpersonal relationships with peers. As young adults make important inroads to their career, they may also be starting a family. The balance between one's career, leisure, and family life is a developmental task that needs to be addressed during this period.

The psychological importance of what one does varies, and it is important to understand the difference between a job and a career. Many people pursue a job in order to earn a living. Therefore, their job may not have much value to them from a psychological perspective. Other people pursue a career more as a way of life. Their career may have significant value to them because it is a central aspect of their life. Not everyone has the opportunity to pursue a career, so adapting to young adulthood can be very different depending on whether one is entering the workforce for a "job" or a "career."

Pursuing either a job or a career requires exploration, planning, and decision making (Santrock, 1992). Studies have found that young people often approach job seeking with a high degree of uncertainty and ambiguity. Most disconcerting is that young adults are often neither systematic nor intentional in their planning (Super, Kowalski, & Gotkin, 1967). Yet, in one study (Hamdani, 1974) with disadvantaged youth, a specific course on career education and planning was developed, and the results showed an increase in the disadvantaged students' career planning, increased use of resources, and better decision making.

Women and Work   The role of women in the workplace has changed dramatically in recent decades. Today, over half of all women are either in the workforce or are seeking jobs. Although the role of women has changed dramatically, the reality is that the workplace is still quite different for men than for women. Discrimination and inadequate opportunities remain significant obstacles for women (Eccles, 1987). Particularly salient is that women still experience job segregation on the basis of gender. There are jobs that are considered "male" jobs and jobs that are considered "female" jobs. Many of the major professions—computer programming, electrical engineering, accounting, and law—are dominated by men. One implication of this inequity is less income. Employees in female-dominated professions earn less than employees in male-dominated professions, even when skill levels and responsibilities are similar (Rukeyser, Cooney, & Winslow, 1988).

Peer Relationships—Forming Mentorships   Levinson's theory of adult development describes the stage of entering the adult world. It is during this phase that the person begins to shape his or her "dream," or vision of what the person would like to accomplish as an adult. Often during this phase a special relationship is formed with a mentor—a person who serves as a role model, teacher, and adviser. This most often occurs in a work setting with a colleague. Mentors are usually about 10–15 years older than the individual and play a critical role in helping the young adult refine and achieve his or her dream. The use of mentors occurs more often for men than for women. Studies have found that, at least for career women, professional mentoring is less likely (Noe, 1988). This may be due to the lack of available mentors for young professional women. However, women have indicated that they often perceive older friends or relatives as role models.

Multicultural and Gender Considerations

Multicultural aspects of young adulthood are many and varied across the different cultures. However, the development of one's career or livelihood is an important task that has clear multicultural aspects. In particular, unemployment rates are critical for the African American, Hispanic, and Native American groups. Many young adults in these groups value the family but are frustrated in their attempts to provide for their families because of limited opportunities. Baruth and Manning (1991) describe the following additional issues among different cultures as their members face adulthood: alcoholism among Native Americans; acculturation of Asian Americans; the stereotype of the African American as violent; and the increasing significance of African American females as the head of household. Table 10.2 presents

TABLE 10.2 Challenges Confronting Ethnic or Racial Groups

Ethnic or Racial Group	Unique Challenges Confronting Adults
Native Americans	Many of their unique problems stem from a history of discrimination, broken treaties, and prejudice. Poor academic attainments (only 57% are high school graduates). Extremely high unemployment rates. Language problems have affected progress. Stereotypes promoted by TV and movies.
African Americans	Dialect differences have challenged them. The stereotype of the "violent Black" is influencing their social progress. Poor academic progress and lack of social progress. Social conditions that are detrimental to self-improvement like discrimination, racism, lack of opportunities.
Asian Americans	Language problems have been a challenge. The "model minority" stereotype. With acculturation, family roles and expectations can conflict with the white American culture. Value changes in family relationships can lead to a schism between younger and older generations.
Hispanic Americans	Language problems are critical because many Hispanics speak only Spanish. Poor academic progress and lack of social progress. Improvement in middle-paying and high-paying jobs. Lack of appropriate skills for coping in the dominant white society and with discrimination and prejudice.

Source: Adapted from Baruth & Manning, 1991.

some of the unique challenges that confront adults in Native American, African American, Hispanic American, and Asian American cultures.

Gender Roles

In young adulthood, women confront two very significant role expectations (Weiten & Lloyd, 1994). In particular, two mandates occupy the traditional female role: the marriage mandate and the motherhood mandate.

The marriage mandate says that to be a successful heterosexual female, you must find a marriage partner. In fact, part of being a young adult is that you have gotten married. Some researchers believe that the fact that a significant number of lesbians were previously married is evidence of the strength in the marriage mandate.

The motherhood mandate says that a successful adult woman also must bear children and become a mother. The mandate further suggests that it is important to have two children, with one of them being a son (Russo, 1979). The woman should also be a "good mother."

These are two mandates that adult women face. Although the expectation that a woman have a career is increasingly being accepted, it does not carry the weight of a mandate. Often the exclusive attention to dating and marriage leads women to feel less secure in their focus on a career. The social expectation that successful career women are not good wives and mothers is such that women associate high career achievement with social rejection (Cherry & Deaux, 1978).

What is it like for women who do stay home to take care of the house and children? Tavris and Wade (1984) refer to this scenario as the "housewife syndrome." Women who experience the housewife syndrome have been found to experience less happiness, feel more discouraged, and be more self-critical than are employed single or married women (Nickerson & Pitochelli, 1978). In general, women who stay at home have greater psychological adjustment problems when compared with either employed husbands or employed wives (Steil & Turetsky, 1987).

Two factors may help explain why women are less happy when they occupy the homemaker role. First, these women are socially isolated. It may be difficult, especially in our postmodern world, for them to find meaningful connections with others on a day-to-day basis. Second, the role of homemaker carries a negative connotation, and therefore the status of the homemaker is low. The important role of being a homemaker and good mother in the home is not very valued by our society, and this makes it difficult for those who occupy this role.

Gender expectations and stereotypes can be very negative and destructive for women and men. Many young adults are committed to ending such expectations, focusing instead on qualities that are valued by everyone. For example, Carol Tavris (1992), in her book *The Mismeasure of Women*, examines the dominant male viewpoint and challenges this as a standard for what is normal for both men and women. She argues for an expanded view of what it means to be human and recommends a move away from the typical "us/them" perspective used when discussing gender issues. The following Focus on Gender section looks at how men and women divide housework.

FOCUS ON GENDER

Housework—Are Men Doing Their Fair Share?

Because the roles men and women play in the family have changed dramatically in the last 30–40 years, many experts look to changes in child care and housework when assessing the significance of the changes. Do men share a greater role in child care and housework when compared with the past? Studies of the family in the late 1960s found that a husband's participation in family work was 1.1–1.6 hours per day compared with that of

housewives, who worked 7.6 to 8.1 hours per day. But what if the wives were working outside the house? In this case, husbands increased their participation 0.1 hours per day when their wives were employed (Robinson, 1977). A few changes were noted in the 1970s. For example, Pleck (1985) found that husbands did family work 1.8 hours per day and housewives did family work 6.8 hours per day; and employed wives did family work 4.0 hours per day. Studies have found that, yes, husbands have increased the amount of time they spend doing family work by about 25%. However, husbands' participation in family work continues to be about one-third of that of their wives.

Source: Levant, 1990.

The Impact of Mother's Work on Children's Development

As increasing numbers of women enter the workforce, an often-asked question is, "What affect does women's employment have on a child's development?" Hoffman (1987) has examined this question and pointed out two critical assumptions that are always made. First, it is assumed that the more time that mothers spend with their children, the better the outcome. Second, it is assumed that full-time housewives in the past devoted more time to their children than the contemporary mother. Hoffman points out that negative effects can result from too much time together—for example, the development of unhealthy dependency. Furthermore, the technological developments of the last 20–40 years may mean that mothers today can spend about the same amount of time with their children that mothers did in the past.

Nonetheless, it is a popular notion that a mother's employment has a negative effect on the child's development. Interestingly, this notion may be unfounded, as many studies have discovered that maternal employment is *not* harmful to children (Demmo, 1992). Studies (Chase-Lansdale, 1981; Easterbrooks & Goldberg, 1985) have examined whether a mother's employment affects the quality of infant-mother interactions and emotional attachment and found no connection. What may be more important is the attitude of the parents. When families are satisfied with the wife's role in the family, the children are most well-adjusted (Easterbrooks & Goldberg, 1985). Strong attachments and commitment to children can clearly occur for working mothers.

Indeed, some recent research suggests that in some cases the effect of maternal employment may be positive. Children of working mothers have been found to be particularly self-reliant and responsible. This appears to be more true for girls than for boys. Hoffman (1987) concludes that daughters of working mothers are higher in academic competence and career aspirations. The following Focus on Gender section looks at the changes that will be necessary worldwide in order for men and women to attain political and economic equality.

FOCUS ON GENDER

When Will Women and Men Be Equal?

According to the results of a new survey, it may take another 1000 years for women to match the political and economic clout of men. Based on the current rate of progress, it will take 500 years for women to hold equal managerial jobs and 475 years for women to reach equal political and economic status. These finding are based on the following types of statistical data:

- Women hold 41% of management jobs in the United States—11% high ranking and 3% top level.
- In other countries, women hold 40% of management jobs in Canada and Australia, 8.3% in Japan, and 4% in South Korea.
- Greece and Paraguay had a decrease in women managers.
- Only 6 of 179 members of the United Nations have a female head of state.
- Women occupy 3.5% of government cabinet posts worldwide.

Source: Sanchez, 1994.

Social Hazards

The William T. Grant Foundation (1988) became interested in examining how well American young people are making the transition from school to adult roles in work and family life. The results of their study found that the transition was particularly difficult for the forgotten half: the noncollege-bound youth. A major focus of the study was on the declining economic fortunes of young adults. A disturbing finding was that "virtually all young male workers, despite their educational achievements, are, on average, far worse off than they were a decade ago and minorities are substantially worse off than whites" (William T. Grant Foundation, 1988, p. 21). All males (except young African American college graduates) suffered substantial earnings losses. This decline in earnings is a result of changes in the economy that have created a deterioration in real earnings.

How can there be earnings losses for Americans? This happens when the amount of money someone earns does not keep up with living costs. It simply costs a lot more to live today than it did 10 and 20 years ago—and how much you can buy for your money is substantially less. Consider some of the following statistics:

- In 1974, low-income families spent 35% of their income on rent and utilities. In 1983, that percentage had risen to 46%—almost half of the family income.
- The average 30-year-old who owned a house in 1973 was spending about 21% of his or her monthly income on home mortgage payments. However, by 1983 that same person was spending 44% of earnings to pay the mortgage.
- From 1974 to 1983, average housing costs and utility costs rose by 35%.

This means that supporting a family is a lot harder for a larger percentage of American society today than it was in the past, particularly for young people who are not college bound. Coupled with this loss of earnings is the fact that opportunities are shrinking for these young people. For example, in 1974 almost half of all jobs held by young African Americans were blue-collar, craft, and operative occupations that paid enough to support a family. Only 12 years later, African Americans held only 25% of these jobs. For noncollege youth, supporting a family is extremely difficult given this sharp decline in earnings. This is the primary reason the percentage of minority families that are below the poverty line has increased so dramatically. High school dropouts and high school graduates earn substantially less than they did 10 and 20 years ago. And there are fewer jobs for noncollege youth; along with the decline in the economy has been a decline in jobs.

The implication of these findings is that American society needs to work toward better compensation for noncollege youth. The William T. Grant Foundation (1988, p. 24) concluded that "the American people should set as a conscious goal of public policy the improvement of employment and earnings levels for all workers, not the least those lacking college education." Although this recommendation seems logical, it is not without controversy. Congress did just pass an increase in the minimum wage, but many economists believe this will cost young people jobs even though it can increase their standard of living.

The Family That Has a Child with a Disability

Having a child with a disability in the family can require many special adaptations on the part of family members (Schuster & Ashburn, 1992). Indeed, the impact of caring for a child with a disability often restructures the family's intentions and plans. The mother, who perhaps was looking forward to returning to work, may now decide that she needs to stay home to provide special care for the child. This decision, in turn, affects the financial status of the family and may compel the father to seek additional work to compensate for the loss of income. However, the father may also feel a need to be more available to the family (McConachie, 1986). The family may decide that services are not adequate in the area they live in and may seek a new location that can better provide for the child. Many sacrifices are made as the family attempts to restructure and respond to the new demands placed on it.

The mother is often under enormous pressure and may become physically exhausted. She is often the person who must spend hours traveling to doctor's offices, following up on health insurance claims, seeking special education programs, and so forth. Going on a simple outing may require taking special equipment like a wheelchair, special eating utensils, and medications. Caring for a child with a severe disability is demanding

and often leaves the mother stressed, socially isolated, and exhausted from the hard work (Pahl & Quine, 1987). Much of the stress results from the mother's inability to develop interests beyond the child's care. Critical to successful adjustment is the emotional support she can receive from her husband or significant others.

Parents of children with disabilities can benefit from respite service, so the parents can leave the child with others and get some time away. However, these services are not always available. And some parents have had such little time that when they do get away, they don't know what to do (Schuster & Ashburn, 1992). The parents may spend their time fighting since they have not had any opportunity in their regular schedules to address their problems. For a good adjustment to take place, parents need to recognize their responsibilities to each other as a couple as well as their responsibilities to the child as parents (Simons, 1987).

Does the increased stress and pressure result in a higher divorce rate among couples with a child with a disability as compared to couples without such children? Although it would be logical to assume so, this is not the case. When divorce does occur, it is usually due to pre-existing problems (Simons, 1987). Thomas (1987), who has studied family adaptation, reports that a common response among parents of children with a disability is a strengthening of their relationship and a perception that the experience of raising a child with a disability has helped them grow as individuals.

Divorce

For over a century, the percentage of marriages that end in divorce has been steadily increasing. However, it is difficult to specify the percentage of marriages that end in divorce. The often-quoted ratio of marriages in a year to divorces is considered misleading by researchers studying divorce. Regardless of the statistic used, divorce is becoming a fairly common event in American society. Divorce experts Martin and Bumpass (1989) estimate that two-thirds of today's marriages will end in separation or divorce. Factors associated with a higher incidence of divorce include marriage at a young age, low educational attainments, and low income.

Whatever the cause of the divorce, the emotional consequences are often dire for both men and women. It

A family with a child who has a disability needs to make special efforts to provide the child with normal social experiences.

is a dramatic change in one's life to go from being married to being divorced. Consider the following statement from Weiss's (1975, p. 75) study on marital separation: "And then all of a sudden every goddamn thing, I'm back to zero. I have no house. I don't have a child. I don't have a wife. I don't have the same family. My economic position has been shattered. And nothing is recoverable. All these goals which I had struggled for, every goddamn one of them, is gone."

Research supports the negative impact of divorce on husbands, wives, and their children. Many studies have found that divorce is associated with depression, anxiety, and drug use (Gotlib & McCabe, 1990; Schaefer & Burnett, 1987). Indeed, separated and divorced men and women have higher rates of psychiatric disturbance and admission to psychiatric hospitals. Some differences between men and women have been noted; for example, divorced men lose emotional support and ties to friends and relatives, whereas divorced women lose income (Gerstel, Reissman & Rosenfield, 1985). One study (Kiecolt-Glaser & Glaser, 1988) found that in

comparison with married couples, individuals who were separated—and more stressed—had reduced their immune system's capacity to ward off infection and disease. Furthermore, studies have found that poor marital adjustment leads to depression and anxiety for women (Gotlib & McCabe, 1990). Therefore, sticking it out in a conflictual and unhappy marriage may also lead to negative outcomes.

Why do people divorce? Answers to this complex question must take into consideration a multitude of factors. One explanation has to do with the social changes that have occurred regarding the stigma associated with divorce. Divorce is not the evil phenomenon it was 50 years ago. Society as a whole has become increasingly tolerant of divorce—due in part to the increasing numbers of people who have experienced it. Other changes have probably influenced the divorce rate as well, for example, women are less dependent on men, and this makes divorce a more viable alternative. Families have changed as well, with a decline in fertility rates and smaller families enhancing the likelihood of divorce when problems arise. Legal barriers to divorce have been reduced, and men and women are more likely to seek their own self-fulfillment rather than make sacrifices for each other (Yankelovich, 1981). The following Focus on Diversity section explores the process of gay and lesbian couples' breaking up.

When Lesbian and Gay Couples Break Up

Surveys typically find about 60% of all gay and lesbian adults are in couple relationships. In our survey of 1266 couples, around three-quarters subscribed to a lifelong commitment, and most of the remainder were committed "for a long time"—not unlike heterosexual neighbors.

But lesbian and gay couples face many more obstacles than heterosexuals do in maintaining a relationship. Separating poses special burdens as well. Some couples must remain "invisible," a response to the threat of violence or lost jobs. Too often they enter relationships with problems, such as substance abuse and low self-esteem, that result from experiences of oppression.

Gay and lesbian couples also frequently lack support from immediate family. Instead of the typical blessings and presents awarded heterosexual unions, a same-sex wedding announcement may result in abandonment. Even the gay community has been slow to recognize family relationships. As one woman put it, "Gay friends I haven't seen in a while ask if we're still together—not 'How are you doing?'"

When relationships end, same-sex couples face the gender-blind pain of separation, property division, and lost contact with "in-laws" and common friends. Legally, they can mark the split-up by revising or destroying any documents that may have marked the relationship, such as powers of attorney, wills, or domestic partnership affidavits.

We believe lesbian and gay couples deserve the option to marry. Many already behave as married couples, but legalizing same-sex marriage would change the world around them and, we believe, make divorce less likely.

Source: Bryant & Demian, 1990.

Sexual Harassment

Sexual harassment is defined as unwelcomed sexually oriented behavior. The behavior in question may be glares or "checking someone out," or it may involve physical touching, pressuring someone into sex, or sexual assault. It is being increasingly recognized in society as a problem and extends beyond just the work setting—although this is where it usually occurs.

It is difficult to obtain accurate information about the prevalence of sexual harassment because many people don't recognize it and so hesitate to report it. However, it is estimated that as many as 50 to 75% of women have experienced sexual harassment on the job (Fain & Anderson, 1987), and 17 to 38% of women on college campuses report an experience with harassment (Dziech & Weiner, 1991).

From a legal viewpoint, there are two types of sexual harassment: **quid pro quo** and **environmental harassment**. *Quid pro quo* is Latin meaning that something is exchanged for something else. In the context of sexual harassment, a person in a position of power subjects a person of lower status to unwanted sexual advances. Furthermore, the person in power requires certain behaviors in exchange for a job, a promotion, a higher grade, and so forth. Fundamentally, an aspect of the person's job depends on her or his agreement to engage in some form of unwanted sex. Environmental harassment is when a hostile work environment is created by the person in power as a result of some unwanted sexual behavior. For example, telling work colleagues sexual jokes may create a hostile work environment.

Sexual harassment is not limited to just sexual acts like intercourse. It includes a wide range of unsolicited and unwelcome actions like flirting, comments about another person's dress or anatomy, intrusive questions about another person's personal life, and descriptions of the person's own sexual experiences. Unwanted physical contact also includes a wide range of unwelcome behaviors such as touching, hugging, pinching, and slapping. Fundamentally, sexual harassment is an abuse of power by someone in a position of authority.

Sexually Transmitted Diseases

STDs, or sexually transmitted diseases, are being increasingly recognized as a serious social problem for adolescents and young adults. Many people think of STDs as one of three diseases: AIDS, syphilis, and gonorrhea. Actually, there are approximately 20 sexually transmitted diseases. Some can be easily treated, others cannot. Most are transmitted through genital, oral-genital, or genital-anal contact; however, not all are, and some do not require intercourse for transmission. For example, yeast infections can develop even when partners are monogamous.

The rate of STDs is increasing, and there are more than 10 million new cases each year. Gordon and Snyder (1989) present the increase in prevalence in a more dramatic fashion: If you are between the ages of 15 and 55, your chance of developing an STD other than AIDS is 1 in 4 during your lifetime. Box 10.3 describes the common sexually transmitted diseases. Focus on Diversity: AIDS and Ethnicity looks at how AIDS affects one ethnic group—Hispanics.

FOCUS ON DIVERSITY

AIDS and Ethnicity— Implications for Hispanics

The impact of AIDS varies according to different ethnic groups. This is because different ethnic groups, like Hispanics, have cultural practices that affect the use of preventive actions. For example, cultural factors such as machismo, homophobia, and religious taboos associated with the Catholic church, seem to have limited Hispanics in taking specific actions that could prevent AIDS. Nonetheless, white and African American groups have much higher percentages of the overall AIDS cases, 58% and 26% respectively. Hispanics account for an additional 15% of the cases. The spread of AIDS among Hispanics occurs primarily through male intravenous drug use. This fact places Hispanic women at great risk for contracting the virus—they are 11 times more likely to contract AIDS than non-Hispanic women. A related factor is that Hispanics have greater reluctance than other groups to use condoms, which can prevent the spread of AIDS. A survey in Chicago revealed that as many as 80% of the Hispanic population did not want to use condoms.

Source: Written by Rebecca Melin, based on Baruth & Manning, 1991.

Rape and Sexual Assault

There is no justification in this world for hurting me, for taking away what he tried to take away from me. . . . I cried, I know what rage lives inside of me. It's always been there—it always will be. It's OK. I went out and danced and got plowed last night. . . . I was drained the rest of the day and felt cruddy cuz of my hangover. . . . Tonight is my first night alone and I battle the "caged in" feeling. . . . I screamed in a loud voice in my front yard, "I am mad at the whole world. . . . " (from the diary of a 26-year-old rape victim, personal communication)

The prevalence of rape is so high that it is likely to touch everyone sometime in their lives. It is now estimated that between 2 and 3 of every 10 women will be a victim of rape—that's more than one rape every 6 minutes (Parrot & Bechhofer, 1991). Other experts estimate that up to 50% of women in the United States will be raped or subjected to attempted rape in their lifetime (Muehlenhard & Linton, 1987). Over the past 20 years, the incidence of rape has increased over 20%, one of the largest increases for a major crime (Riesenberg, 1987); however, it is unclear whether the number of rapes is growing or the likelihood of reporting is growing. Victims of rape are more likely to be young, and only 20% of all rapes are committed by strangers.

Although the incidence of rape is alarming, the fear of rape has a direct effect on the quality of all women's lives. In their daily lives, women must take precautionary actions because of the fear. In particular, women must often isolate themselves—not go out after dark and certainly not go out alone.

Although women are predominately victims of rape, men can be victims. Men raped by other men suffer traumatic and long-term consequences, especially because they have never thought of themselves as possible rape victims. Also, rape is usually discussed in a heterosexual context, but homosexuals can also be victims of

BOX 10.3

Common Sexually Transmitted Diseases

STD/ Transmission/Symptoms

Acquired immune deficiency syndrome: Spread by sexual intercourse or anal intercourse. Can be spread by oral-genital sex, especially when semen is swallowed. Spread by nonsexual interaction through contaminated blood, for example, by sharing hypodermic needles used for drug injection. Typically there are no symptoms for approximately five years. After symptoms do begin, death occurs soon afterward.

Bacterial vaginosis: Most common is the transmission of *Gardnerella vaginalis* by sexual intercourse. Women experience a thin musty-smelling discharge. Most men are asymptomatic.

Candidiasis: This fungus accelerates growth when the chemical balance of the vagina is disturbed; it can be transmitted through sexual intercourse. Described as a white "cheesy" discharge from the vagina; irritation of the vaginal tissue.

Trichomoniasis: Can be transmitted through genital sexual contact or through less direct means, for example, from towels or bathtubs of an infected person. Vaginal discharge that is white or yellow; unpleasant odor; vagina is sore and irritated.

Chlamydial infection: The bacterium is transmitted primarily through sexual contact. It can be spread by fingers from one body part to another. For women, pelvic inflammatory disease can occur. This can disrupt the menstrual periods, elevate temperature, lead to abdominal pain, nausea, vomiting, and headaches. In men, discharge from the penis and a burning sensation during urination. May be accompanied by heaviness in the affected testicles, inflammation of the scrotal skin, and swelling at the bottom of the testicle.

Gonorrhea: The bacterium is spread through genital, oral-genital, and genital-anal contact. In women, a greenish/yellow discharge; however, it often goes undetected. At a later stage, pelvic inflammatory disease may develop. In men, discharge from the penis and burning sensation during urination. Untreated complications can include inflammation of the scrotal skin and swelling at the base of the testicle.

Syphilis: The bacterium is transmitted from open lesions during genital, oral-genital, or genital-anal contact. In the primary stage, a chancre appears where the spirochetes entered the body. In the secondary stage, the chancre disappears and a generalized skin rash appears. In the latent stages, there are often no observable symptoms. In the tertiary stage serious symptoms occur: heart failure, blindness, eventually death.

Pubic lice: Pubic lice are easily spread through body contact or through shared clothing or bedding. Lice invade the pubic hair area and cause persistent itching.

Herpes: The virus is transmitted primarily by genital, oral-genital, or genital-anal contact. An oral herpes virus is transmitted by kissing. Genital area develops small red, painful bumps. These papules are painful blisters that will rupture and form open sores.

Genital warts: The virus is spread primarily through genital, oral-genital, and genital-anal contact. Warts develop in the affected areas as hard yellow-gray bumps or soft, pinkish, cauliflower-like bumps in moist areas.

rape. And, increasingly, men have reported being raped by women.

Two types of rape have been distinguished, **acquaintance rape** and **date rape** (Weiten & Lloyd, 1994). Acquaintance rape occurs when a woman is raped by someone she knows, and date rape occurs when she is raped by someone she is dating. Date rape is different from the act of seduction. Seduction occurs when a woman is persuaded and *agrees* to have sex. Date rape occurs when a woman is forced into sexual intercourse without her consent. When a man attempts to seduce a woman and fails, date rape may be the consequence. Table 10.3 describes the characteristics of date rapists.

Both men and women often fail to acknowledge that date rape has occurred. In one study (Koss, Gidycz, & Wisniewski, 1987) of all the men who admitted forcing a woman to have intercourse, none perceived this act as rape. Of the women who indicated sexual aggression that constituted a legal definition of rape, only 27% actually said that they had been raped. Why is there such little recognition that rape has occurred? Part of the answer lies in the myth that for rape to occur, it has to be perpetrated by a stranger. However, stranger rape is less frequent than rape by acquaintances or by a person the victim is dating. Koss (1985) refers to this as a "hidden crime," noting that it helps men deny their responsibility and causes women who have been raped to question and doubt their intentions.

Implications for Practice: Rape Trauma Syndrome

Regardless of the type of rape women experience, a common reaction is the **rape trauma syndrome**. As the beginning quote reveals, women experience many intense emotions and reactions about being physically forced to do something against their will. The crime is life threatening, the victim is helpless, she experiences a loss of control, and she has become the object of another person's rage. These reactions lead to overwhelming feelings of fear and stress. Women may develop a number of fears: fear of being alone, fear of men, fear of trusting dating partners. Common feelings associated with rape include depression, anger, guilt, shame, and anxiety. Most rape survivors experience some of the following clusters of symptoms (Francis, 1993):

TABLE 10.3 Characteristics of Date Rapists

Sexual Entitlement	Power and Control	Hostility and Anger	Acceptance of Interpersonal Violence
Touching women with no regard for their wishes	Interrupting people, especially women	Showing quick temper	Using threats in displays of anger
Sexualizing relationships that are not appropriately sexual	Being a bad loser	Blaming others	Using violence in borderline situations
Engaging in conversation that is inappropriately intimate	Exhibiting inappropriate competitiveness	Transforming other emotions into anger	Approving observed violence
Telling sexual jokes at inappropriate times and places	Using intimidating body language		
Making inappropriate comments about women's bodies, sexuality, and so on	Game playing		

Source: Rozee, Bateman, & Gilmore, 1991.

- **Disorganization phase.** This phase reflects the woman's immediate expressed or controlled reactions, physical reactions, and emotional reactions to the trauma. Common feelings in this phase are most likely fright, anger, and disbelief. A common reaction is "second guessing," for example, "what could I have done to avoid this?" Such questioning can lead to intense feelings of guilt and self-blame.

- **Controlled reaction.** In this phase, the rape victim assumes a more composed and calm perspective following the trauma. Although some women react in a physically distressing manner by crying, shaking, and showing hysterical behaviors, other women do not react this way. Even though the woman is experiencing a controlled reaction, she is still suffering from the trauma.

- **Reorganization phase.** This phase reflects the adjustment and adaptation that is necessary following the rape. In one study (Burgess & Holmstromm, 1985) of rape victims followed up on four years after the rape, three-quarters of the women felt recovered. Half of the women felt recovered after several months; the other half indicated it took them years to recover following the trauma. A quarter of the women still did not feel recovered after four years. Reorganization needs to take place as women attempt to regain equilibrium in physical, psychological, social, and sexual areas. The recovery process follows a pattern similar to that of people who must adjust to grief. Francis (1993, p. 680) identifies four issues that are important to the rape victim during the reorganization process:

1. Regaining a feeling of physical well-being and safety
2. Working through fears and phobias
3. Coming to terms with losses, such as loss of self-esteem and loss of trust
4. Assimilating the event into one's sense of self

For many women, being in a support group is helpful because they can "tell their story" and begin the process of accepting what happened to them and learn how to assimilate their experience into their sense of self. However, many family therapists believe the family can be a critical aspect of a person's ability to recover from a trauma. For example, Pauline Boss notes that "I've come to believe that trauma survivors need more than to tell their story to the therapist . . . they have to tell it to some-one who matters to them, someone who is willing to validate their pain" (cited in Markowitz, 1991). Often that person is a family member. As Markowitz (1991, p. 32) notes, "the most powerful healing from a trauma comes from the love and support of family. Knowing they have someone they can count on, who loves them no matter what, helps survivors regain their confidence and trust in the world after a debilitating setback." The following Focus on Gender section examines an international perspective: the global war against women.

FOCUS ON GENDER

The Global War Against Women

Violence against women—including assault, mutilation, murder, infanticide, rape, and cruel neglect—is perhaps the most pervasive yet least recognized human rights issue in the world. It is also a profound health problem, sapping women's physical and emotional vitality and undermining their confidence—both of which are vital to achieving important social goals, especially in the Third World. Despite its invisibility, the dimensions of this problem are vast. In Bangkok, Thailand, a reported 50% of married women are beaten regularly by their husbands. In the barrios of Quito, Ecuador, 80% of women are said to have been physically abused. And in Nicaragua, 44% of men admit to beating their wives or girlfriends. Equally shocking statistics can be found in the industrial world. There are also less recognized forms of violence. In Nepal, female babies die from neglect because parents value sons over daughters; in Sudan, girls' genitals are mutilated to ensure virginity until marriage; and in India, young brides are murdered by their husbands when parents fail to provide enough dowry. This is not random violence. In all these instances, women are targets of violence because of their sex. The risk factor is being female. Most of these abuses have been reported in one or another country, at one or another time. But it is only when you begin to amass statistics and reports from around the world that the horrifying dimensions of this global war on women come into focus. For me, the revelation came only recently after talking with scores of women throughout the world. I never intended to investigate violence; I was researching maternal and child health issues overseas. But I would commonly begin my interviews with a simple question: What is your biggest problem? With unnerving frequency the answer came back: "My husband beats me."

Source: Heise, 1989.

Spouse Abuse in the Family

Spouse abuse is a serious problem in this country. Families, often suffering from intense stress, conflicts, and maladaptive coping, fall prey to acts of violence (see Box 10.4 on violence against women). Every year over 6 million family members are victims of physical abuse at the hands of spouses, parents, siblings, or children (Gelles, 1987). It is estimated that over the course of their lives, over 50% of women will at some point be a victim of battering. In many cases, the battering is life threatening; 2000 to 4000 women are beaten to death every year (Browne, 1987). Women, unlike men, are more likely to

BOX 10.4

Violence Against Women in the United States

Murder: Every day four women die as a result of domestic violence. This adds up to approximately 1400 women a year. The number of women murdered by intimate partners exceeds the number of soldiers killed in the Vietnam War.

Battering: There are 572,000 reports of assault by intimate partners each year. A conservative estimate is that 2 to 4 million women are battered each year. Approximately 170,000 of those violent acts are so severe that women seek hospitalization, emergency room visits, or need a doctor's assessment.

Sexual Assault: It is estimated that 132,000 women have been victims of rape or attempted rape and more than half will know their attackers. Anywhere from two to six times as many rapes are likely to happen but don't get reported. When one's former spouse or partner is the perpetrator, then there are approximately 1.2 million forcible rapes.

The Targets: Women are over ten times more likely to be victims of violence by an intimate. Women who are young, separated, divorced, single, low income, and African American are more likely to be victims of assault and rape. Poverty is a significant factor in domestic violence, and spouse abuse is twice as likely when the spouse is unemployed. Violent attacks on lesbians and gays are growing at a very fast rate.

Impact on Children: Violent juvenile offenders are four times more likely to have grown up in homes where there was a history of violence. Child witnesses of violence are reported to be five times more likely to commit or suffer violence when they become adults.

Impact on Health and Social Services: Battered women need more than twice the health care as nonbattered counterparts. Pregnant women who become battered (17% report being battered) are at risk for poor health outcomes such as miscarriages, stillbirths, and low-birth-weight babies.

Legislation: NOW, the National Organization for Women, helped secure passage of the Violence Against Women Act, which provides new revenue for addressing the issues of violence against women.

Source: National Organization for Women, 1995.

be killed by a husband, ex-husband, boyfriend, or acquaintance. Also, spouses and ex-spouses commit a much larger percentage of the homicides (18%) than do strangers (8.8%) (U.S. Department of Justice, 1995). Women aged 19 to 29 and women with incomes below $10,000 are more likely than other women to be victims of violence by a spouse or intimate (U.S. Department of Justice, 1995). Intimates causing the violence are more likely to injure women than strangers who victimize women. Such violence often leads to homelessness as women flee violent home situations. As many as one-third of homeless women have suffered domestic violence (National Council on Homelessness, 1995).

What would cause intimate spouses to resort to such gross mistreatment of each other? Of course, there are multiple factors related to family violence, including intergenerational transmission of violence, impact of poverty, social pressure and stress, social isolation and a lack of community involvement, serious personality problems, and psychopathology. When multiple risk factors are present, the family is vulnerable to maladaptive coping behaviors and the family's welfare becomes threatened. In addition to providing shelter to protect women from violence, many communities are attempting rehabilitation of the man. Focus on Gender presents an example from a group that works with men who batter.

APPLYING THE FRAMEWORK

Schizophrenia

Maria is a 24-year-old single woman who looks older than her stated age. She presented with symptoms of schizophrenia—prominent thought disorder, delusions, inappropriate affect or silly affect, and disorganized speech. The police brought Maria to the emergency room after neighbors complained of a young woman, who they feared might be dangerous, walking down the street laughing and talking to herself. Several days later, her brother called the police and reported Maria as a missing person. The police informed her brother that a young woman fitting his sister's description had been taken to the hospital and admitted to the psychiatric ward a few days ago.

Maria's family history revealed that she came from a problematic family. She was the second of three children and was often the victim of criticism and abuse from her father. Her father was abusive and often came home drunk. Maria's mother died when she was 13 years old, and Maria never "recovered." While she was living, Maria's mother had tried to protect the children from their father. Maria and her mother had been particularly close. When Maria's mother died, the children were placed in the custody of the state because of their father's

inability to take care of them. The children were separated on several occasions during their tenure in foster homes, but the impact of separation took its toll on Maria. Even when Maria was a young child, she would experience problems adjusting to minor changes and would withdraw from her normal activities. Her school records supported the problems Maria had in trying to adjust to school routines and how traumatic it was for Maria to leave home and go to school. She had to compete with different children of different age groups while living in foster homes. She was beaten by some of these children and by some of the foster parents. Even before the foster homes, Maria had a history of "bizarre behavior" and was highly withdrawn. Her mother was hospitalized twice before she died, according to Maria's older sister. She told the attending physician: "My mother had emotional problems and was sent away."

Developmental Considerations

Maria's problems started when she was very young—physical and psychological abuse, placement in foster homes, and lack of a sense of security. The first signs of

Groups for Men Who Batter

A group format offers the men a variety of models and sources of feedback for learning to self-observe, change cognitions, and interact differently. Although many men who batter express regret about their behavior, they are given mixed messages by those around them. The importance of having other men in the same situation saying, "I don't like what I am doing and I want to stop," supports a commitment to nonviolent behavior. In a follow-up

study of a program for men who batter, Gondolf (1989) found that men ranked the group support as the most important element in helping them to stop the violence.

Sam's group treatment had several goals. First, Sam had to take responsibility for his violent behavior. This required confronting his denial. Second, he needed to learn skills to help maintain nonviolence. The necessary skills include self-observation, time-out, cognitive restructuring, and interpersonal skills training. Third, Sam needed to examine and adjust his attitudes and expectations that encouraged his violence. Fourth, it was hoped that Sam would begin to explore his family of origin and other personal issues that may be related to his violence.

Source: Tolman & Bennett, 1992.

Schizophrenia

her disorder were not detected until adulthood. However, she had a number of developmental issues often noted in the histories of persons who developed schizophrenia. Her early childhood and adolescence indicates that she had issues involving trust versus mistrust, separation-individuation, evidence of possible bonding difficulties, and identity difficulties during adolescence. The loss of her mother had a profound impact on Maria because her mother was Maria's only support system. Maria's symptoms of schizophrenia were undetected before the presentation of active psychotic symptoms. Her history of poor functioning in school and at work, and her inability to adjust to life events contributed to Maria's disorder. Her disorder had an early and insidious onset. Given the characteristics of the onset, the changes that were taking place with Maria were untreated until she moved into the active phase of schizophrenia.

Biophysical Considerations

Maria's episode with schizophrenia may suggest that she had a predisposition for schizophrenia (genetic), which is supported by the finding that her mother had been

hospitalized for emotional problems. Also, structural changes in the brain are likely in neurotransmitter systems (namely dopamine). Further confirmation for biophysical hypotheses can be found if brain imagery techniques show evidence of cortical atrophy.

Psychological Considerations

Maria manifested some deficits in the cognitive, affective, and behavioral domains. During the active phase of her disorder, she presented with disorganized speech, distorted perceptions (delusions and hallucinations), and distorted thought processes in the cognitive area. Her affective state is best characterized as inappropriate or silly. She laughed inappropriately throughout the admission process.

Communication

The communication process within Maria's family is unclear. The family demonstrates some signs of restrictiveness in their communication abilities. Her bizarre behavior further aggravates her communication *(continued)*

Schizophrenia

(continued)   competence. She smiles inappropriately and does not demonstrate that she can share what she is experiencing.

Attitudes and Emotions

It is difficult at this time to assess Maria's attitudes and emotions; she is currently in the active phase of her illness, and the medication has not reduced her symptoms. Usually, her type of schizophrenia has a poor prognosis with a chronic course. Maria has isolated herself and rarely interacts with others. She does not appear to hold suspicious or bizarre delusions.

Family

Maria is 24. Before her mother died, Maria lived with her parents and two siblings. Maria's father was particularly abusive to her. The family believes that he singled her out because she looks like his paternal grandmother. Maria and her siblings lived in foster homes for about five years. Her sister, Ester, is 18 months her senior, and her brother, Marios, with whom she presently lives, is the youngest member of the family. She has no contact with her extended family.

Social Support

The most consistent support Maria ever had was her mother, who died when Maria was 13 years of age. Her mother's death undoubtedly contributed to many of Maria's problems in later life.

Summary and Impressions

Maria is experiencing the following:

1. She developed schizophrenia, and the symptoms are currently in the active phase.
2. She had a prolonged history of social and psychological problems.
3. She was a victim of physical and psychological abuse.
4. The course of her disorder suggests a poor prognosis.
5. Her responses to neuroleptic medications has been marginal at best.
6. Her past medical record was essentially unremarkable.

Maria is a young adult who contracted a severe mental disorder known as schizophrenia, disorganized type. Her prognosis is poor with a chronic course. Her disorder is associated with possible structural changes in the brain—Type II schizophrenia. The etiology is unknown at this time. She may have had a predisposition for this disorder, as indicated by her family history. Her problems had been exacerbated by the interaction of biological, social, and psychological factors. These factors proved too much for her to handle. She cannot cope with these changes nor handle many other demands.

In the event of her discharge, she will need supervision and social support. It is imperative that her medication is supervised closely by her physician and the physician informed of Maria's (change, relapse) by those in charge of her custody. Her caregivers should be educated about Maria's disorder and attend at least some of her group sessions. Finally, it is critical that Maria's cultural background be taken into account in planning support services.

Source: Written by Habert Johnston.

Chapter Summary

Developmental Themes

Young adulthood is considered a major life transition. Most young adults move from a preoccupation with the self to intimacy with others that leads to marriage, children, and a more stable career path. Two of the critical developmental tasks are economic independence and independent decision making.

Biophysical Dimension

Biophysical Growth and Development

Young adulthood represents the peak of physical development across the life span. During this time, a pattern of health-conscious behavior develops. Many young adults start putting on weight. This is because our basal metabolism rate decreases as we get older. Women are in the prime time for pregnancy. Hormones can have a strong impact on women; many women experience premenstrual syndrome (PMS).

Biophysical Hazards

A health hazard of the reproductive system for both men and women is cancer. Women are encouraged to do breast self-examinations, and men are encouraged to do testicular self-examinations. Schizophrenia is a major mental illness that occurs more frequently during this stage of life. There are many potential causes of schizophrenia; however, most researchers now look to the influence of neurochemical factors. Case management and tracking systems have received increased attention in their capacity to help coordinate needed treatment for those with a serious mental illness.

Psychological Dimension

Cognitive Development and Information Processing

The ability of formal operational thinking is typically present in young adulthood. The nature of formal operational thinking emphasizes problem solving that represents a more pragmatic adaptive strategy. Still, many young adults do not obtain formal operational thinking.

Communication

Young adulthood is focused more on *mis*communication—in particular, the notion that men and women communicate very differently. Women obtain more intimate communication with each other than do men.

Attitudes and Emotions

A major psychosocial task in young adulthood is the development of intimacy. The experience of intimacy may be quite different for men and women. Ultimately the experience of intimacy is likely to lead to love. Romantic love must be differentiated from "true" love. There are many different kinds of love; one researcher suggests three components: intimacy, passion, and commitment. Although many young adults are pursuing love, others must confront the pain of isolation and loneliness. Learning to cope with loneliness can be important. Certain types of thinking processes may lead to behaviors that contribute to loneliness. Searching for an identity and seeking independence is also an important developmental task.

Social Cognition and Regulation

Moral development is further refined in young adult women and men; women tend to emphasize a care perspective, and men may emphasize a justice perspective.

Psychological Hazards

Young adulthood is a period of making major life decisions and of taking on major responsibilities. Depression, a serious mental illness, is one of the leading mental health problems among adult women.

Social Dimension

Families, Groups, Support Systems, and Contexts

Marriage and the creation of a family most often occur in young adulthood. Many people still have an idealized vision of the "nuclear" family, when in fact families represent a great diversity of configurations. People go through four phases when selecting a partner to marry. Marriages often have problems because they are based on unreasonable expectations and myths. Adjustment to a new marriage requires a new set of tasks and good communication. Certain factors have been found to predict marital satisfaction. Also important is not the amount of conflict in a relationship but how couples handle their incompatibilities. Important gender differences exist in how couples communicate with one another—men are more instrumental and women are more expressive—this has implications for teaching couples better communication skills.

Marriage is not the only road to companionship; many individuals remain or become single, and others develop homosexual or gay relationships. When couples decide to raise children, the transition to parenthood can be difficult. An increasing number of couples find they cannot conceive and must face the issue of infertility. In addition to a family, a young adult's career or job is often a significant part of his or her self-identity. Unfortunately, many young adults have had to face declining economic benefits due to earnings losses. Women continue to face discrimination and inadequate opportunities in the workforce.

Multicultural and Gender Considerations

In young adulthood, women face two significant role expectations or mandates: They must marry and they must be mothers. Although many new mothers are not working, research is finding that it may not be as harmful to the child as originally thought. Ethnic or racial groups have unique challenges they must face as young adults. For example, Asian Americans must deal with the "model minority" stereotype.

Social Hazards

Some families may require special adaptation when they have a disabled family member. Just as young adults are building families, many are leaving families as a result of divorce. Divorce is a significant adjustment for all family members. Additional social hazards include sexually transmitted diseases, rape and sexual assault, and spouse abuse.

KEY TERMS

acquaintance rape
basal metabolism rate
controlled reaction
date rape
disorganization phase
dopamine
environmental harassment

expressive communication
infertility
instrumental communication
loneliness
menstrual cycle
premenstrual syndrome (PMS)
quid pro quo

rape trauma syndrome
rapport talk
reorganization phase
report talk
schizophrenia

Middle Adulthood

Developmental Themes

Many adults at midlife truly feel that they are at a crossroads, as aptly described by Margaret Atwood (1991) in her novel *Cat's Eye*:

> This is the middle of my life. I think of it as a place, like the middle of a river, the middle of a bridge, halfway across, halfway over. I'm supposed to have accumulated things by now: possessions, responsibilities, achievements, experience and wisdom. (p. 13)

Midlife is different from other developmental phases in that it is less affected by biological maturation. Indeed, adults are most affected by their own experiences—and how they time those experiences. For some, midlife involves launching children and focusing on career development; for others, it may involve beginning a family and postponing career development. The impact of chronological age seems to become a less reliable indicator of what men and women are like at various points in their lives. So variation is an important theme in middle adulthood because there is so much of it. Midlife is often considered to begin at age 35 and continue until age 60—a span of 25 years. However, midlife is different for men and women because of their differences in life expectancy. Therefore, more accurately, midlife is age 35 for men and age 39 for women (Baruch & Brooks-Gunn, 1984).

Adults at midlife are most typically characterized by a new perspective of who they are and a new perspective about their world—a new definition of self, new expectations about what they want to accomplish, and new satisfactions in living. Because there is so much diversity in midlife, many experts refuse to identify a timetable for adult development. However, Gail Sheehy's (1976) book *Passages* continued the notion that adult lives are predictable and based on age-linked stages. In fact, the profound influence of Sheehy's book was that it set out a normative expectation that in middle adulthood there is a "midlife crisis" phase. What led to the enormous success of *Passages?* Many people want predictability and could relate themselves to one of the phases Sheehy described. However, as midlife became increasingly studied, the picture of adulthood development grew more complex. Today, most experts see many of the problems seen in previous stage theories, and the idea of a universal midlife crisis has not found much empirical support.

Although stage theories have been very popular for examining the life course and midlife in particular, they are becoming increasingly less relevant (Goldstein & Landau, 1990). Many of the stages are simply not connected with the age ranges originally intended. "The identity crisis that Erikson thought should be resolved in adolescence now often persists well into the twenties; the bonding stage that is thought to typically occur in the mid-twenties may be delayed until the thirties, or experienced more than once" (Goldstein & Landau, 1990, p. 20). Furthermore, the changes for women have disrupted ideas of a life-stage approach. Women entering the workplace, delays in childbirth, changing patterns of career development—all these changes have wreaked havoc with attempts to generalize women's life patterns. Indeed, as Schlossberg (cited in Goldstein & Landau, 1990, p. 20) noted, "give me a room of 40-year-old women and you have told me nothing."

Complicating the picture even further is the work of Neugarten, who has focused on the importance of changing times and how different expectations influence various "cohorts"—groups of people who are born in the same year or time period. For example, if you were born during the Great Depression, your perspective on midlife may be different than if you were born during more optimistic times. Neugarten argues that the social environment of a particular cohort will influence the social timetable of when people expect to accomplish major life tasks, such as having children or selecting a career. The implication of this is that findings from one cohort may not apply to other cohorts. For this reason, it is difficult to make generalizations about people in middle age. In this chapter, then, we will attempt to explore the various ways individuals experience their middle years of life.

Biophysical Dimension
Biophysical Growth and Development

Although the leading causes of death during middle age are cancer and heart disease, evidence suggests that these illnesses may not be purely physiological in origin. What other factor could be so powerful that it influences how a disease presents itself? *Stress.* Stress can actually be linked to physical illness and may have an impact on how the illness affects an individual.

A classic study sought to discover the causes of coronary disease. Friedman and Rosenman (1974) found that some individuals who were in good physical shape and should have avoided heart disease didn't, and others who were in bad physical shape successfully avoided heart disease. Eventually, they discovered that physical shape in addition to personality factors influenced the course of heart disease. They found people are of two personality types: **Type A personality**—competitive, impatient, and sometimes hostile perfectionists; **Type B personality**—relaxed, easygoing, and generally amicable individuals. Type B personalities are less easily agitated than Type A personalities are. Also, Type A behavior has been more often associated with heart disease and other health problems.

Researchers have attempted to measure Type A personality through a variety of methods, including checklists and interviews. It is still unclear what is the best approach to assessing Type A personality. Friedman and Rosenman (1974) describe a series of questions to help assess Type A personality; for example:

1. Do you find it difficult to restrain yourself from hurrying others' speech (finishing their sentences for them)?
2. Do you often try to do more than one thing at a time (such as eat and read simultaneously)?
3. Do you often feel guilty if you use extra time to relax?
4. Do you tend to get involved in a great number of projects at once?
5. Do you agree to take on too many responsibilities?

Several potential explanations link Type A personalities with heart disease and other health problems: (1) Type A personalities are more easily emotionally engaged in situations; they are more quick to react, which affects their blood pressure and heart rate; (2) Type A individuals tend to push themselves beyond reasonable and healthy limits because of their perfectionistic nature; (3) Type A individuals rely less on supportive others and place more of the burden for a task on themselves; and (4) Type A individuals tend to have poor health habits. The reactive nature of the Type A personality, both psychologically and physiologically, puts the individual at increased risk for health problems.

More recent research on Type A personality is pointing to hostility as the primary factor related to increased coronary risk (Booth-Kewley & Friedman, 1987; Smith & Pope, 1990). In particular, people who can be identified with **cynical hostility,** who are resentful, moody, and generally distrusting, have more problems with coronary disease, hypertension, and early mortality. These individuals display a quick temper and easily criticize others.

An important criticism of the studies on Type A personality and heart disease is that they have been primarily limited to people who were already ill. As a result, it is not clear whether the personality led to the disease or the disease led to the development of the personality. Groundbreaking research by Ronald Grossarth-Maticek (cited in Eysenck, 1989) examined a large group of individuals by administering personality tests and following them for ten years or more to see what health problems they might develop. Identifying different personality types—type 1, cancer-prone; type 2, coronary heart disease–prone; and types 3 and 4, healthy individuals who cope with stress in a nondestructive fashion—this research uncovered a strong relationship between personality and various health outcomes. For example, Grossarth-Maticek (cited in Eysenck, 1989) was able to achieve 50% accuracy in predicting death from cancer. More specifically, he found that of the type 1 individuals who died, half died from cancer and fewer than one-tenth died from heart disease. Of the type 2 individuals, one-third died from cancer and one-fifth died from heart disease. However, individuals of types 3 and 4 showed very few deaths. These basic conclusions have been replicated in other studies.

If we can understand more about why certain individuals develop health problems, can we prevent them from happening? Eysenck and Grossarth-Maticek believe the answer is yes. They conducted an experimental study in which they taught cancer- and heart-disease-prone people to express their emotions more readily, use coping skills for stress, reduce their emotional dependencies, and become more self-reliant. In the study, they assigned 50 cancer-prone people to the therapy and 50 to a no-therapy condition. Their results showed a dramatic influence: In a 13-year follow-up, 45 of the original 50 in the therapy group were alive, but only 19 of the 50 in the no-therapy group were still living at the time of the follow-up. They replicated these results with heart-disease-prone individuals and then again with women who had terminal breast cancer.

Menopause

You know, it's kind of like when I was 10 years old, before puberty. I don't have to deal with all that female, sexual stuff anymore. I'm just me again.

—A woman discussing her experience of menopause—

Menopause occurs when a woman has not experienced a menstrual cycle for one year. Attitudes toward this event vary, depending on cultural connotations and on women's individual expectations. In societies where the woman's role is mostly reproductive, inability to bear any more children is a loss of status. In cultures where the wisdom and experience of older women is valued, menopause is seen as a positive life event (Dan & Bernhard, 1989). In general, young women and men view menopause more negatively, whereas women who have gone through the experience view it more positively. Individually, some women view the cessation of their monthly period as a sign of impending old age and mourn the loss of youth and beauty. Other women, as the one above, are glad to be rid of it.

Menopause occurs when the ovaries stop functioning and no longer produce the hormones estrogen and progesterone. It is a gradual process that can take from 5 to 20 years. During premenopause, the time when hormone levels begin to fall until menstrual cycles stop, a woman may notice several changes. Her menstrual cycles may become more irregular. She may experience a decreased monthly flow as well as more spotting. Symptoms of premenstrual tension such as breast tenderness and fluid retention may increase. The average age of menopause is 51.4 years; the vast majority of women reach menopause between 45 and 55 years of age (Schuster & Ashburn, 1992).

Falling estrogen levels affect the woman in different ways. The most universal symptom is the **hot flash,** in which a wave of heat rises from the woman's chest to her neck, face, and arms. This feeling of heat may last from a few seconds to a minute or more (Dan & Bernhard, 1989). Hot flashes frequently occur at night, earning the label "night sweats." Recurrent night sweats can interfere

with sleep. Another effect of estrogen loss is thinning and drying of the vaginal membranes. This problem occurs with less severity, though, if a woman stays sexually active. Loss of estrogen also affects the urinary tract and can result in an increase in the frequency of urination and in stress incontinence (this means that when a menopausal woman coughs, sneezes, or laughs she may inadvertently lose urine) (Schuster & Ashburn, 1992). Other physical changes include dry, itching skin and dry hair, and a heightened sense of touch (see Table 11.1). But the major physical effects of estrogen loss are cardiovascular changes, which put postmenopausal women at greater risk of heart disease, and increased bone loss, which puts them at risk of **osteoporosis** (thinning and weakening of bones). As a result of this bone loss, postmenopausal women are at higher risk of bone fractures, especially of the hip, and vertebral fractures (in the spine). Women most at risk of osteoporosis are white, slender, smokers with low calcium intake who don't exercise regularly. Although increased calcium intake can help, the amount of calcium the body can use is limited without estrogen. Psychological effects of menopause are unclear. Some women report increased energy, often referred to as postmenopausal zest (PMZ). Some attribute this increase in energy, confidence, and assertiveness not to biological events but to "the crisis and resolution of midlife women's psyche" (Apter, 1995, p. 201). In other words, menopausal women are struck by a sense of unmet goals or unfulfilled potential and experience "an increased capacity to resolve old conflicts and satisfy suppressed desires" (p. 202). On the other hand, menopausal women no longer have a monthly loss of blood and may experience increased iron stores. Plus they no longer have periodic hormonal fluctuations and no longer have to deal with premenstrual syndrome.

The big question, though, is, do women become depressed and irritable at menopause? Because menopause occurs at a time in life when women may feel they are "getting old," it is difficult to differentiate the effects of menopause from the effects of aging (Dan & Bernhard, 1989). Apter (1995) states, "Current research has found no significant changes in anger, anxiety, depression, self-consciousness, or worry about the body between women observed from the time they were premenopausal to the time they had become postmenopausal. This means that, in general, a woman's mood is not determined by meno-

TABLE 11.1 The Changes of Menopause

When	Symptom	Comments
Before menopause	Irregular periods	Cycle may shorten or lengthen; flow may increase or decrease.
During menopause	Periods stop	
	Hot flashes	Skin temperature rises, then falls. Accompanied by sweating and sometimes heart palpitations, nausea, and anxiety. Occur anywhere from once a month to several times an hour. May begin 12–18 months before menopause and continue for some years after.
	Insomnia	Sometimes caused by nightly bouts of hot flashes. Dream-rich REM sleep may also decrease, disturbing sleep.
	Psychological effects	Irritability, short-term memory loss, and problems with concentration are common. These symptoms may simply result from sleep deprivation.
After menopause	Changes in nervous system	The perception of touch can become more or less sensitive.
	Dry skin and hair	The skin can become thin, dry, and itchy. Hair may also thin out. Facial hair may increase.
	Incontinence	Tissue shrinkage in the bladder and weakening pelvic muscles may lead to problems with bladder control.
	Vaginal dryness	The mucosal membranes and walls of the vagina become thinner, which may lead to pain on intercourse and susceptibility to infections.
	Bone loss	Increases dramatically.
	Cardiovascular changes	Blood vessels become less flexible. Cholesterol and triglyceride levels rise.

Source: Adapted from Davis, 1989.

pause; but an individual woman may respond to it with increases in anger, anxiety, depression or self-consciousness because of how she experiences or perceives its meaning" (p. 215). Some argue that women who expect menopause to be a negative experience do find it to be a negative experience. And some women who have a lot of symptoms may become depressed over the symptoms (Adler, 1991). Others believe that depression may occur as a result of the changes in a woman's life rather than because of hormonal loss. Women who think that in order to be valued they must be young and beautiful may be depressed over menopausal changes. Some women may feel sad as their children grow up and leave home.

So, many researchers believe that women who are emotionally stable prior to menopause experience no increase in depression or irritability. However, estrogen affects the production of **endorphins,** substances produced in the brain that make you feel good. A drop in estrogen results in a drop in endorphins (Davis, 1989), which can be depressive. In addition, menopausal women may experience insomnia due to night sweats, itching skin, and urinary frequency. And when they do sleep, it is not as restful because REM sleep (dream sleep) is decreased. A sleep-deprived woman can be irritable and less able to concentrate and handle stress.

Some women pass through menopause with few symptoms or effects; others experience more severe problems. Although the occurrence of psychological changes at menopause is debatable, a woman experiencing any of these symptoms needs to believe that, whatever the cause, her complaints are being taken seriously and not being passed off as "all in her head." Women with physical symptoms may benefit from **estrogen replacement therapy (ERT),** in which synthetic estrogen is taken to replace that lost through menopause (see Focus on Biophysics).

FOCUS ON BIOPHYSICS

Estrogen Replacement Therapy

Recently, some literature has been encouraging women to accept menopause as a natural part of the life cycle. These writers claim the medical profession has described menopause as a deficiency disease for which medication is prescribed. Such authors suggest that the cessation of menstruation is not an illness that needs to be treated but a part of the rhythm and flow of a woman's life. Some even claim an evolutionary advantage to menopause in that women can stop bearing children when they are still young enough and energetic enough to participate in raising older children (Dan & Bernhard, 1989).

This attitude, however, overlooks the fact that just last century, the average life expectancy of a woman was 48 years. So women who experienced the natural process of menopause may not have lived many years beyond that experience. Today, a healthy woman undergoing menopause at 52 can expect to live another 30 or more years (Davis, 1989). And research is showing that as these years pass, the reduction in estrogen that occurs at menopause increases a woman's risk of heart disease, stroke, and osteoporosis. There is now overwhelming evidence that estrogen replacement therapy (ERT) or giving a woman estrogen to replace that which she has lost, greatly reduces her risk for all these problems (Ravn, Rosenberg, & Bostofte, 1994). ERT helps with the symptoms associated with menopause such as hot flashes and vaginal dryness, too, but many women find these symptoms to be mild and easily remedied without the addition of daily hormones.

But heart disease is the leading cause of death in postmenopausal women, and hormone therapy with estrogen results in marked reduction in this risk (Stevenson, 1995). In addition, estrogen therapy has been shown to prevent the bone loss of osteoporosis for at least 15 years after menopause (Langer & Barrett-Connor, 1994).

Yet, despite this promising evidence, only 20% of women have had ERT prescribed for them, and only 40% of those for whom it is prescribed use it for more than one year (Hammond, 1994). The main reason for this failure to use ERT may be fear. Many women fear the increased risk of endometrial cancer and breast cancer that has been publicized to occur with ERT. Yet researchers have found that using progesterone in addition to estrogen for ten days during the month (hormone replacement therapy or HRT) reduces the risk of endometrial cancer without affecting the benefits of estrogen (Ravn, Rosenberg, & Bostofte, 1994). (The drawback here is that adding progesterone to HRT causes some women to continue to menstruate. Plus, with the addition of progesterone, some women experience symptoms associated with PMS, including fluid retention, and must then add a diuretic to their daily medications.) Research is suggesting there is only a small risk, if any, of breast cancer from HRT, and then only after prolonged use of 15–20 years (Ravn, Rosenberg, & Bostofte, 1994). Ross and Whitehead (1995) contend that there are few medical reasons now to avoid HRT and that the choice should be up to the individual patient, depending on the severity of her symptoms and her risk of heart disease and osteoporosis. Women should also consider their personal risk of developing breast cancer when considering HRT. Each woman, then, needs to weigh the risks and benefits of hormone therapy, plus any potential side effects of the therapy, in order to get the most out of her postmenopausal years.

Sexuality in Middle Adulthood

Maggie Scarf (1992) describes how the midlife years can often lead to problems for marital couples who do not understand some of the changes they are going through. In particular, she notes the different physical changes that men and women go through during the middle years. A man's aging crisis is related to the pressure he feels to "make it," and a woman's aging crisis is related to concerns and anxiety she feels about her physical appearance.

These changes have direct implications for their sexual relationship. Scarf (1992) describes how such changes affect the **sexual response cycle,** which includes three phases: desire, excitement, and orgasm. First, desire, being sexually motivated, can be affected by aging. For example, the side effects of diseases (such as diabetes or hyperthyroidism), of psychological difficulties (such as depression), or of medical concerns (such as hypertension) that require drug treatment can all negatively affect the desire phase. In general, over time the sex drive declines, particularly for men. The male sex drive is also affected by a drop in testosterone, the male hormone.

Excitement, the second phase of the sexual response cycle, is the first physiological reaction to stimulation and results in blood engorgement of the genitals. As Scarf (1992, p. 54) points out, "while earlier the mere thought of having sex might have made him erect, later on in life he will often require both *psychological and tactile* stimulation." This can make the man feel more vulnerable to his partner. In fact, without successful adaptation, both partners may end up humiliated—the man who has to confront his slowed sexual response and the woman who may perceive his slowness as a sign of rejection—of less attractedness toward her.

The last phase of the sexual response cycle, orgasm, also changes dramatically with age, primarily in the area known as the **refractory period**—the time between one orgasm and the physical capability to achieve another orgasm. The adolescent male can have as many as two orgasms per minute, but the midlife male may need as long as 24 to 48 hours between orgasms.

For the midlife woman, the sexual profile is quite different. Indeed, erotic interest often increases in the desire phase, primarily in response to changes in her biological makeup. When estrogen, the female hormone, declines, it allows her testosterone to have more of an influence. During menopause, the ovaries continue to produce small amounts of testosterone, and with the decline of estrogen, the impact of the testosterone is greater, leading to a stronger sexual desire (Scarf, 1992). However, in the excitement phase, lack of estrogen often leads to problems with vaginal dryness. Without proper prevention for this dryness, the sexual experience can be adversely affected. With estrogen replacement therapy, the dryness is less problematic. During the last phase, the orgasm, the woman—unlike her male counterpart—has no refractory period and can have multiple orgasms. These can be difficult changes for sexual partners. As our sexual response system changes, we must be prepared to accommodate the changes and learn new ways of remaining sexually active.

Biophysical Hazards

One of the biggest health fears of middle-aged women is breast cancer. In 1994, 182,000 women were diagnosed with breast cancer, and 46,000 women died of this disease. Women who live to age 85 have a 1-in-9 chance of developing cancer of the breast in their lifetime (Winawer & Shike, 1995). Not only is this risk relatively high in itself, it also represents a dramatic increase in breast cancer risk. In 1970, the chance was 1 in 16. What is causing this alarming increase?

Some in the medical field believe the rise in risk is due to more awareness of and earlier detection of the disease. This explanation might account for the fact that, although the rate of breast cancer has increased, earlier detection of the disease allows for increased survival, so the mortality rate has remained stable or in some areas decreased (Winawer & Shike, 1995). Others argue that the increased incidence of breast cancer is due to environmental factors. Some support for this idea comes from the fact that women who move from an area with low breast cancer rates to an area with high breast cancer rates experience an increase in their personal risk. Environmental factors that have been suggested as contributing to breast cancer rates include a diet high in fat, the presence of pesticides and other toxic chemicals in food and water, exposure to radiation from nuclear testing in the 1950s, and lives with increased stress levels (Clorfene-Costen, 1993).

Several factors that increase a woman's personal risk for breast cancer have been identified. One is age. Although the overall chance of developing breast cancer is 1 in 9, this risk applies to an 85-year-old woman. A woman at age 30 has only a 1 in 2500 chance and a woman at menopause a 1 in 50 chance (Winawer & Shike, 1995). Other risk factors include having a family history of breast cancer, undergoing menarche (the onset of menstrual periods) before age 12 or menopause (the cessation of menstrual periods) after age 50, being childless or having a first child after age 30, being overweight, having a sedentary lifestyle, drinking alcohol, and eating a diet high in fat.

Women are now encouraged to decrease their risk of breast cancer by lowering their intake of dietary fat, by increasing their physical activity, performing monthly breast examinations, and having annual mammograms (screening X rays of the breasts) after menopause (Friedenreich, 1995; Kerlikowske et al., 1995; Vantveer, 1994).

Early detection of breast cancer allows for less extensive surgical intervention. In many instances, however, the treatment for breast cancer involves the surgical removal of part or all of the breast. Because of this potentially disfiguring treatment, a woman may perceive breast cancer as a threat to her sense of herself as a feminine, sexual, nurturing being (Winawer & Shike, 1995). The psychosocial/psychosexual adjustments to the disease may be more difficult for a woman than the actual physical recovery from the surgery (Winawer & Shike, 1995). Women with breast cancer need support for their emotional as well as their physical well-being. Many women may benefit from support groups for breast cancer patients. But some research suggests that the most important source of support is the family, in particular the woman's partner (Pistrang, 1995). The woman needs to be able to maintain good communication with her partner and to feel that her partner is empathic and will not withdraw from her because of potentially disfiguring treatments. To mediate the psychological stress of breast cancer, social workers can help couples to continue to communicate with and support each other. The implications of a diagnosis of breast cancer for women who lack a partner or other significant support are described in Focus on Biophysics: An African American Woman's Experience with Breast Cancer.

FOCUS ON BIOPHYSICS

An African American Woman's Experience with Breast Cancer

In July 1991, I was taking a shower, and all of a sudden there was this lump in my right breast. I'm fortunate because I only had a lumpectomy (the lump removed, instead of the whole breast). It just put a little crease in the upper part of my right breast. They also took 25 lymph nodes out. Only two of them were cancerous, which was absolutely great. Then, I was in a state of denial, thinking, I'm fine now. But the doctors said, "You have to have radiation and chemotherapy."

So I went for a bone scan. I'm looking up, and I see all these frigging signs that say, "You are now entering a radiation zone." That's when I became aware of what was really wrong with me. I started crying and could not stop. The doctor was totally detached. He was like: "What's wrong with you? Why are you crying?"

No one was with me. *Girlfriend, this whole thing has been by myself.* My mother had to work. My friends had to work. My daughter had to work. My children—two daughters and a son—couldn't really deal with it. I was dating a doctor at the time. He had been very supportive, but when I had my surgery, it took him an extra day to show up. I got out of the hospital, and he stopped communicating with me. I had to go through this alone.

I got angry, because I kept getting these calls to go to support groups out of my area. All the groups that were available to women in Los Angeles are either on Wilshire Boulevard, which is in the financial district, or in Santa Monica, which is a good 20 miles from South Central L.A., where I live. It takes two hours to get to Santa Monica on a bus.

My issues are different from the issues in the white community. My experience is, right now, all my bills are due. Some black women just started a job, won't get a paycheck for three weeks, and have no transportation. If women with children leave them at home, they have to pay someone.

During my treatment, I started the Women of Color Breast Cancer Survivors' Support Group, which now has four sites in Central and South Central L.A. Our groups have three facilitators and me, trained through the National Black Women's Health Project. I make presentations about prevention. In the underserved community, you have women whose health gets pushed to the side. I enlighten them. It's about care of one's body. They don't even know they're at risk.

And I want them to see my attitude. I'm overweight from the chemo, but you cannot tell I've had cancer, because everything about me exudes health, energy, and life.

Source: Adapted from Viviansayles, 1993.

A Family Systems Look at Couples and Illness

When one spouse is sick, is it a family affair?[1] It is, according to researchers Howard Liddle and Gail Dakov.

[1] This section was written by Julianne Asimov, based on McCarthy (1990).

Liddle and Dakov studied patterns of coping in couples in which one spouse had cancer. Contrary to popular belief, they found that openly talking about the illness is *not* always the best coping mechanism. Instead, Liddle and Dakov conclude that what is important is not *how much* the couple communicates about illness-related concerns, but how much "their desire to share is similar." This means that adjustment of partners who do *not* wish to discuss the illness is just as good as adjustment of spouses who wish to discuss concerns openly. Adjustment problems occur, however, when partners have different levels of desire to talk about the illness.

Liddle and Dakov note that couples' adjustment to cancer is not based solely on communication styles, but is related to other factors as well. Relationship history, for example, plays a role in how couples adjust to illness. In many troubled couples, partners showed hostility toward one another after diagnosis. In happier couples, diagnosis reportedly brought spouses closer together.

Other research on couples in which the husband had a heart attack six months earlier looked at the emergence of overprotectiveness within the relationship. Researchers found that overprotectiveness, commonly thought to be hostile in origin, is actually a response to the well partner's desire to help when illness threatens a close relationship. The illness becomes an integral part of the system and emphasizes the interdependence of partners as key in understanding the dynamics of the dyad. The following Focus on Gender section examines some of the dramatic health care changes that have occurred for women.

FOCUS ON GENDER

Women and Health Care: A Short History

Health care for women has changed dramatically over the last 25–35 years. Imagine the following: a woman being told that childbirth is better experienced in an unconscious state, natural childbirth being considered too dangerous to consider, and a friend—unexpectedly pregnant—having to fly to Mexico to obtain an abortion that is illegal in the United States. (Boston's Women's Health Book Collective, 1992). These are the kinds of events that led to the 1970 publication of *Our Bodies, Ourselves.* This now-classic book, first sold for 75 cents, sold over 250,000 copies before it was commercially published. Women embraced the idea that they could be experts on their own bodies regarding their own health care. They began to take action on policies that directly affected their health. For example, congressional hearings were disrupted as women voiced complaints about the side effects of the pill. This crusade led to the development of a self-help movement that sprung dozens of women-controlled health centers. These efforts were largely in the service of white, middle-class women, but by the 1980s, women of color began to use their voices for change. They addressed issues such as the high incidence of sterilization abuse against poor women, especially women of color. By 1981, Bylle Avery, an African American woman, was elected to the board of directors of the National Women's Health Network. Today, there are 150 chapters of the National Black Women's Health Project. Using an empowerment model, this early effort has grown with associations such as the National Latina Health Organization, the Native American Women's Health Education Resource Center, and the Asian Health Project. All projects are a grassroots effort to organize women at the community level with a commitment to self-help.

The results of this early movement led to changes that directly influence the lives of individual women. For example, midwives and nurse practitioners deliver babies in women's homes, the birth control pill no longer has excessive amounts of estrogen, women with breast cancer do not automatically lose their breasts, DES is no longer given during pregnancy (this was a drug that produced babies with birth defects), abortions are readily available, and silicone breast implants are being restricted.

Source: From Boston Women's Health Book Collective, 1992.

The Effects of Brain Injury on the Family System

In the popular movie *Regarding Henry*, a ruthless, high-priced lawyer suffers brain damage after being shot in

Serious accidents can lead to brain injury. The brain-injured person is often completely changed by the accident and must make considerable adjustments to adapt to a "new self."

the head.[1] Following the injury, he remembers little of his former self or life. He is a very different man—one who moves slower, thinks slower, and cannot even remember how to read. He is unable to take up his old life again. At one point he comments, "I thought I could go back to my life . . . But I don't fit in." Henry cannot function as before in his job and ultimately quits. He loses most of his old friends, who cannot get used to the new Henry. Commenting on his recovery, his friends whisper at a party, "One minute you're an attorney. The next you're an imbecile." Henry and his family must learn to cope with a very different life after the injury.

What is the best way to cope with the brain injury of a loved one? Research suggests that there is no simple answer to this question. According to Betsy Zeigler, families who adjust well to the situation learn to see the postinjury person as distinct from the individual they previously knew. They are then able to let go of the old image of the family member and to integrate the new person into the family system. Although this perspective provides a practical goal for the family, the nature of

brain injury makes this task difficult. The loss felt after a brain injury is in some ways harder to reconcile than the death of a loved one. Death is finite, but the extent and permanence of the loss with brain injury remains unclear. This fosters hope for recovery, but it also leaves family members in limbo: "After a death, you eventually get on with your life. [Brain injury] goes on forever and you're dealing with it in one stage or another for the rest of your life" (Souza, cited in Mitiguy, 1990).

Grief for family members may never quite be resolved, due to the unpredictable nature of the injury. The injured individual remains a constant reminder of loss for family members, but society may not recognize the family's grief because the injured individual remains present in a physically familiar form.

Familial responses of denial and hope parallel the meandering path of the grieving process. These responses can be helpful for the family. Availability and utilization of resources are important ways of perpetuating hope in

[1]This section was written by Julianne Azimov, based on Mitiguy, 1990.

families after brain injury. Programs and other types of support are seen as signs of hope for improvement.

Reactions to brain injury are not the same for any two individuals, but research suggests certain parental, sibling, son/daughter, and spousal similarities. For parents, children represent immortality through family traditions and values. Although returning to the role of caregiver for a child with brain injury may resonate with an earlier nurturing role, this change in dynamics may also lead to overprotectiveness on the parents' part. Responses of mothers and fathers may differ due to the differing nature of parent-child relationships. Injury can be both a binding and a divisive factor for parents.

Siblings' reactions to brain injury tend to be very individualized, based on a number of factors: age, prior relationship with the injured sibling, and role in the family. Sons and daughters of brain-injured parents also have diverse experiences, dependent upon age, relationship with both the healthy and the brain-injured parents, and role changes within the family. Spouses of brain-injured individuals face challenges associated with the emotional, social, and physical aspects of the marital bond.

Although these processes may not ever be completely resolved, many families do achieve a level of adjustment that incorporates a realistic perspective on the nature and duration of loss. This facilitates functioning of a family system that includes and changes with the brain-injured person.

Psychological Dimension

Cognitive Development and Information Processing

Researchers in the past have attempted to study cognitive development based on the seminal ideas of Piaget. However, more recently, researchers interested in adult development have discovered that using Piaget's child-oriented theory may not be the best approach for studying adult development. In fact, Piaget's work has contributed to the accepted social stereotype that childhood is the primary period for intellectual development (Willis, 1989). Childhood and adolescence have been seen as the time periods for acquiring the knowledge

needed to operate successfully in adulthood. For a long time, it was believed that cognitive development or intelligence peaked in late adolescence and early adulthood. Of course, this belief appeared logical because there is an obvious shift of biological aging in middle adulthood, noted most obviously by one's graying hair (Willis, 1989). A critical question in attempting to understand how cognitive development changes over the life course is: Do individuals' cognitive abilities decline after young adulthood, as some stereotypes would suggest?

A series of studies by Schaie (1983) has dramatically changed the way many people view cognitive development in middle adulthood. Schaie conducted longitudinal studies that discovered, for example, that verbal ability actually peaks in late middle age (Schaie & Strother, 1968). Figure 11.1 shows changes across the life span in five different aspects of cognitive ability: spatial visualization, reasoning, verbal ability, word fluency, and number ability. The overall conclusion from this data is that for all the abilities studied, intellectual functioning is stable in middle age. Decline in intellectual ability begins only after age 60. Other interesting findings suggest age-related declines occur earlier for some abilities—for example, numerical computations and spatial reasoning. The gender differences show that men perform at a somewhat higher level than women on spatial ability, but women perform at a somewhat higher level on reasoning ability. So, clearly these findings suggest that intellectual ability continues to develop throughout the middle years.

The results of these findings will probably be comforting to the many men and women at midlife who are required to perform at a very high level of intellectual competence. Adults in middle age are assuming major family, professional, and social responsibilities that demand sharp minds and the ability to acquire new skills and information (Willis, 1989). Schaie (1983) contends that this is why we must examine adult cognitive functioning in a different manner. Rather than using the child-focus, which involves how information is acquired, to study adult intellect, we need to examine how information is used. During adulthood, individuals are not exclusively concerned with acquiring skills but are concentrating more on achieving goals. This means that a majority of their cognitive abilities are focused on applying knowledge to real-world problems, which requires a new set of

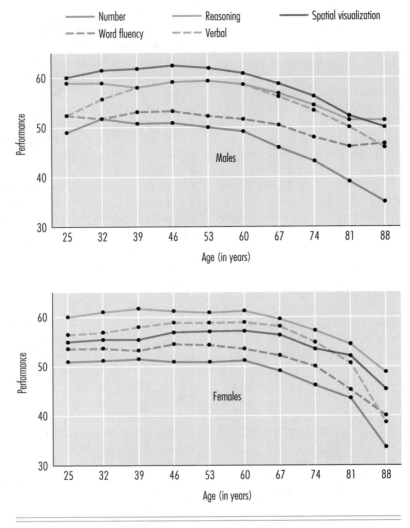

FIGURE 11.1   Intellectual performance across late adulthood   Source: Schaie, 1983.

cognitive abilities—social and abstract cognitive skills. Schaie (1983) argues that cognitive and social functioning merge dramatically in midlife, where tasks have what Schaie calls "role-related achievement potential." Adults perform better at these tasks because these tasks are strongly related to the roles adults are assuming. This merging of social and cognitive functioning is also related to adults at midlife who are assuming more responsibility for others. Many adults become increasingly involved in civic and community organizations. Schaie's theory suggests that young adults move from "What should I know?" to the middle adulthood focus of "How should I use what I know?" to later adulthood, when the emphasis is "Why should I know?" (Schaie, 1977, p. 135).

Impact of Professional Obsolescence

The concept of **professional obsolescence** may be particularly relevant during the midlife years (Willis, 1989).

Professional obsolescence refers to the use of information, theories, and technology that are less useful in performing tasks than what is currently available in one's field of practice. As Dubin (1972) points out, obsolescence is not related to age-related loss of ability but rather to an inability to learn and apply new information and techniques.

In our rapidly moving information society, it is critical to keep up with relevant knowledge. Adults in midlife have finished schooling but may need additional training to remain current on the job. As people's life span grows, so does their longevity in the workforce. As a result, special efforts to prevent professional obsolescence may be needed.

For example, almost all professional occupations now require some knowledge of computers. Few middle-aged adults received any formal training on how to use computers. As you can see, with rapid technological changes, adults will need new skills to remain competent in the workforce. Indeed, a person's **professional half-life** may be getting increasingly shorter as the knowledge explosion unfolds. A professional half-life is the time it takes for 50% of one's professional knowledge to become invalid or obsolete (Dubin, 1972). This varies according to one's career; for example, the professional half-life of a computer scientist is perhaps only two or three years (Willis, 1989). Such information attests to the notion that "learning is, indeed, becoming a lifelong process" (Willis, 1989, p. 109).

Communication

By midlife, the process of communication is clearly established. Communication at this stage is dominated by family and by friends. In terms of the family, this may be the period in life where one can truly reconnect with one's partner or spouse. After many years of raising children, many midlife adults are ready to establish more meaningful relationships with their spouse, adult children, and friends. Prior to this time, many adults are simply too busy managing family life to establish a strong network of friends. Also, as midlife adults begin the process of "life review," they may reflect on communications that they would like to mend or at least make better. Midlife adults are seeking more meaning in their life, and as a consequence, they are interested in communication on a deeper level. The friendships that are developed are based on values such as honesty, sincerity, closeness, and mutual support.

In fact, many adults may become increasingly interested in engaging in the process of forgiveness as they reflect on relationships that may not have developed the way they wanted. Beverly Flanigan (1992) has written a book on the topic, entitled *Forgiving the Unforgivable*. This book examines questions like the following: How long should a woman maintain anger at a husband who leaves her for a younger woman? Should she express rage toward the husband, and if so, for how long after their divorce? How can she make things right in her own life after this unforgivable act?

By midlife, many people have accumulated a history of harms from persons with whom they have had close relationships. We have all heard of individuals who are not communicating with a sister, brother, child, parent, or close friend because of some unforgivable act. Flanigan illustrates how forgiveness is an essential mechanism for righting such wrongs. Many people are not at peace with themselves for not having asked the forgiveness of a loved one. Others maintain anger at themselves for not being able to forgive a friend or relative for some harmful action. If practitioners desire to help clients with these forgiveness issues, Flanigan argues that they should have some understanding of the forgiveness process.

Flanigan (1992) has studied individuals who have "forgiven the unforgivable." From this research, she has identified six phases that appear to be involved in the journey of forgiving an unforgivable injury:

- *Phase one:* Naming the injury
- *Phase two:* Claiming the injury
- *Phase three:* Blaming the injurer
- *Phase four:* Balancing the scales
- *Phase five:* Choosing to forgive
- *Phase six:* The emergence of a new self

This process of forgiving begins with identifying and naming the injury and ends with the emergence of a new self. Although many people begin this process, all do not finish it. Forgiveness will not occur without a person making significant changes in his or her feelings and beliefs. "Forgiveness is a rational process; it is a conversion in the way you have thought about yourself and other people and about harm and vulnerability" (Flanigan, 1992, p. 72). At the end of this process, individuals do not wish any harm on their injurers and develop a new perspective about the causes of events in their lives.

The Illiterate Adult

Many of us take for granted our ability to communicate through writing, reading, and speaking. However, as many as 20% of the adults in our society are functionally **illiterate**—they cannot read and write well enough to participate in society. Kozol (1985) estimates that 35 million or more American adults do not possess the reading skills needed to function independently in society. As modern society becomes more complex, concerns about illiteracy become increasingly critical.

The notion of being **functionally literate** originated in World War I when the U.S. Army found that many soldiers could read and write but not to an extent that would make them effective soldiers (Radwin, 1993). Programs were started to teach soldiers how to be functionally literate.

Definitions of functional literacy vary widely and have changed over time. In the late 19th century, literacy was the ability to write one's name. The U.S. Bureau of the Census defines functional literacy as a sixth-grade reading level. The most common definition of functional literacy is the ability to perform everyday reading, writing, and arithmetic tasks. These different definitions produce different estimates of functional illiteracy that range from 13 to 50% (Radwin, 1993). Whatever the exact percent, we do know that illiteracy afflicts mainly people who are poor, uneducated, and undereducated and people of color. Many illiterate adults grew up in socioeconomically disadvantaged areas with family members who did not encourage reading skills and with no one else to help them learn essential literacy skills.

Where does the functionally illiterate adult come from? Most people who are illiterate completed elementary school, and many even received a high school diploma (Schuster & Ashburn, 1992). However, in school they did not learn some essential skills, such as writing letters, filling out applications, reading instructions on a package, reading the newspaper, or writing a check.

Functionally illiterate adults are often embarrassed that they do not understand essential communication.

They are often concerned that people will "discover" that they are illiterate, and therefore they hide their inability to read and write. Disabled persons may be illiterate because they had been denied proper educational services as a child. Parents may have lacked the confidence that the child could learn and inadvertently contributed toward his or her illiteracy (Schuster & Ashburn, 1992).

Non-English-Speaking Adults

In many respects, adults living in the United States who do not speak English may face similar difficulties. Often, immigrants who do not speak English face discrimination in employment. They may be highly educated and competent in their native language but unable to communicate in English, thus forced into low-paying jobs and lives of poverty (Schuster & Ashburn, 1992). The immigrant may not have important functional skills such as reading street signs, advertisements, newspaper want ads, and so forth. Being shut off from your surrounding world can lead to anger, frustration, and depression. Often non-English-speaking persons must become dependent on others to translate and communicate for them. This can lead to relationship problems and a difficult lifestyle when one cannot communicate with other people. "Feelings, fears, pleasures, observations must all be kept to oneself, creating a lonely, depressing existence" (Schuster & Ashburn, 1992, p. 596).

Attitudes and Emotions

Many theorists believe that a midlife identity change takes place for most adults. Adults may begin to ask themselves, "What do I want to spend the rest of my life doing?" or "Are my relationships giving me the kind of satisfaction I want?" Such questions reflect identity changes that can have a strong influence on our emotions. In particular, adults experience more depression and anxiety. Why would these emotions become prevalent in midlife?

Goldstein and Landau (1990) argue that at midlife there is a "coming apart" that takes place in the continued quest for identity. This process of coming apart is facilitated by a review of the self in relation to work and family and a re-examination of expectations and roles that may no longer be valid. Goldstein and Landau believe that for many adults, this process is linked to increased rates of depression and recognition of the reality of aging. And although many adults "come apart," this process ultimately leads to "coming together," where there is a renewal and reintegration of one's identity.

A significant part of this coming-apart process may be related to Levinson's (1978) notion of **de-illusionment,** which refers to the giving up of illusions from earlier periods of life and reflects the general loss of faith in people and ideas. In addition, many midlife adults experience what is referred to as the death of the hero. Many cultures emphasize hero myths (Campbell, 1988), and such heroes may provide us with important psychological benefits. For example, a hero provides a model to emulate. A hero may provide a mechanism for us to self-reflect upon our own achievements or may provide an example of making successful transformations from difficult times to periods of renewal. Goldstein and Landau (1990, p. 89) point out that "as we approach midlife, our youthful hero is running out of steam and his mission is questionable." They believe that for healthy adult development to proceed, the hero must die and eventually be replaced. This phenomenon may explain some of the depression and anxiety that is common in midlife.

Midlife as a Crisis

Given this intense focus on reflection, is there a midlife crisis? The answer to this question is complex. Levinson's (1978) theory of adult development suggests that the crisis is a normal part of adult development. However, work by Vallant (1977) found that only a small percentage of adults experience a midlife crisis. Apter (1995) adds to the literature on women in midlife and believes that at midlife a crisis is likely to occur that includes a period of reflection and self-questions. She suggests that men may no longer experience the midlife crisis but that women today engage in crisis as a normal developmental stage. Neugarten (1986) reminds us that development may be different, depending on the cohort; therefore, past studies may have been reflecting a cohort phenomenon rather than a stage. And although not all midlife adults will experience a "crisis," this period of life does seem to be a time for intense self-reflection.

So, particularly during middle age, adults are in a position to reflect on their lives. This reflection often influences important actions they may take. Levinson

The 50th birthday is a key marker in the life course for most middle adults. They often realize at this point that they have completed two-thirds of their life and have only one-third remaining.

(1978) has presented the most compelling theory about the influence of such reflection on the behavior of men at midlife:

> A profound reappraisal of this kind cannot be a cool, intellectual process. It must involve emotional turmoil, despair, the sense of not knowing where to turn or of being stagnant and unable to move at all. A man in this state often makes false starts. He tentatively tests a variety of new choices, not only out of impulsiveness but, equally, out of a need to explore, to see what is possible, to find out how it feels to engage in a particular love relationship, occupation, or solitary pursuit. Every genuine reappraisal must be agonizing, because it challenges the illusions and vested interests on which the existing structure is based. (p. 23)

In a similar manner, Vallant (1977) has built on the work of Erikson and suggests that an important stage of individuals at midlife is keeping the meaning versus falling into the rigidity, which can occur from 45 to 55 years of age.

Why do midlife adults reflect on the importance of meaning in their lives? The process begins with recognition that youthful qualities are being lost, bringing reminders that one's physical functioning is decreasing while contact with problems of illness and exposure to death are increasing. Levinson suggests that much of the cognitive processing is in response to a subtle reflection of one's mortality.

Midlife can become painful for adults as a result of the growing realization of their mortality. As they reflect on the fact that their life will eventually end, they feel a corresponding concern about its meaning. Reflecting back over their life, they have many questions and doubts about how meaningfully they have pursued it. An increased emphasis on spirituality is common. The following Focus on Multiculturalism section discusses how spiritual experience is integrated into the life of Native Americans.

FOCUS ON MULTICULTURALISM

The Spiritual Experience of American Indians

The spirituality of American Indian tribal people has sometimes been appreciated, but it is most often misunderstood; yet, this important fabric of Indian society will not be destroyed. A people's spiritual landscape serves to guide and give meaning and purpose to its existential being. Understanding the spirituality of American Indian tribal people, therefore, is essential to recognizing and understanding American Indian tribal communities. These communities have survived all attempts at their destruction. Their spiritual fiber is the latticework that forms the bulwark of their strength.

American Indian tribal peoples of North America helped to bring an understanding of humanity's place on this earth. It was not an attempt to divorce humans from nature or religious traditions. It enabled North American tribal people to be open to the transcendent reality that humanity has always faced. Thus, their spirituality encompassed the temple of nature and their relationship to the natural world. In short, it has always spoken to why we live. Their spirituality is central in comprehending and coming to terms with one's place on this earth.

The great mystery of life taught the many lessons needed to live. Nature was and is seen as divine revelation. The people's spirituality was that of reverence, allowing for humility, simplicity, and appreciation of beauty with an understanding of the miracle of the ordinary.

Spirituality through prayer and patience allowed for the teaching of a sense of honor, a life of service, beauty of generosity, order, etiquette, decorum, moral strength, respect for justice, friendship, bravery, courage, meaning of death, and a reality of psychic powers that can continue the visible life cycle. This cycle was often illustrated in the use of the circle in art, dance, and stories, which reflected the cyclical nature of life. This was important, for example, in assuring that death need not be feared as it is one of the elements of this cycle.

The natural world was a gift and everywhere is considered a mystery. Everything in nature embodied spiritual truth. The people lived a life that was surrounded by the remainder of their spiritual purpose. The tribal people saw that nature and humanity had a spiritual origin and meaning. The concept that the creator could breathe life only into humans and not everything else in nature, such as trees, plants, rocks, and lightning, was alien. Tribal peoples observed each phenomenon as a reflection of the creator. Lessons for spiritual living were reflected all around in sharp contrast to what was observed in the Christians who had come to civilize them. In essence, their spirituality was misjudged and devalued when, in reality, it was the basis for a strong society that valued contributions from all its members. The strength of their beliefs and observation of nature always turned them toward the divine. They lived in the cycle of rituals and seasons that were understood in the light of the sacred, and the eternal was everywhere present.

Source: Written by Edwin Gonzalez-Santin.

Social Cognition and Regulation

Although the preceding theories seem to suggest that at midlife there is a strong internal focus on oneself in which change is experienced as a crisis, Maas (1989) argues that midlife represents an increased opportunity to branch out and become involved in socially responsible activities. This branching out to more socially responsible behavior results from the natural transitions that occur in midlife. For example, children often leave the home, and spouses become increasingly removed from their roles as mother and father.

Most major theorists on adult development discuss this emphasis on social responsibility. Early on, Havighurst (1952) suggested that at midlife the major task was one of civic and social responsibility. Erikson's task of ego integrity reflects an emphasis on actions directed toward social causes. It is "an emotional integration which permits participation by followership as well as acceptance of the responsibility of leadership: both must be learned and practiced in religion and in politics, in the economic order and in technology" (Erikson, 1959, p. 97). Maslow (1962) describes the feelings of gratitude that arise following an individual's "peak experience," which often result in the person's desire to do something good for the world.

Maas (1989) defines the essence of social responsibility as based on two aspects. The first is the person's sense of obligation. Midlife adults can move beyond their narrow self-interest and begin to consider the general interest of others. "The obligation is based on a keen awareness of one's group memberships—ultimately, the human race—and of human interdependence in society" (Maas, 1989, p. 260). The second aspect of social responsibility is the person's ability to carry out his or her sense of obligation. By midlife, most adults have obtained a level of competence that allows them to be effective in undertaking their obligations. Over time, they develop the capacity to become socially responsible and fulfill their sense of obligation to society.

Psychological Hazards

As many of the adult development theories point out, midlife can be a difficult period of time, requiring many new adjustments. The new roles one must adapt to, the intense reflection about one's accomplishments, and the search for new meaning can lead to psychological hazards. In particular, alcohol and drug use may have progressed to the point of a serious addiction.

Alcohol and Drug Addiction

Alcoholism is the consumption of alcoholic beverages to the extent that major aspects of a person's life, such as work, family, and friends, are affected. Alcoholism is considered a disease by many, meaning that it follows a prescribed course of physical, psychological, and social symptoms. Alcoholism is a progressive problem that can lead to irreversible damage and, ultimately, death. When an alcoholic person abstains from drinking, he or she is said to be "recovering."

An estimated 10 million Americans are alcoholics (Caplan, 1993), and alcoholism reaches all age and all sociocultural and economic groups. It is currently estimated that of all alcoholics, the majority (75%) are men and a quarter (25%) are women. Alcoholism is one of the most serious social problems facing Americans. Weiten and Lloyd (1994) note that alcohol misuse is blamed in 64% of murders, 41% of assaults, 30% of suicides, 60% of child abuse, 45% of drownings, and 55% of arrests. It is estimated that as many as 1 family in 3 is affected in some way by a drinking problem (Caplan, 1993).

Identification and assessment of alcoholism is complex. Not all alcoholics drink every day, and many people who do have one or two drinks every day would not be considered alcoholics. Some people will react to a personal crisis and abuse alcohol as a means of coping for a period of time but not become alcoholics. Indeed, many young adults will abuse alcohol for a short time period but eventually develop a healthy pattern of social drinking. Distinguishing heavy drinking from the early stages of alcoholism can sometimes be difficult.

What patterns of behavior make a person an alcoholic? The National Council on Alcoholism has developed a self-test designed to help individuals recognize whether they are addicted. It is a series of questions to which you answer yes or no. The more "yes" answers you have, the more likely you may need help with substance abuse. The items include the following (adapted from the National Council on Alcoholism by *Newsweek*, 1989):

- Do you sometimes binge on alcohol or drugs?
- Do more people seem to be treating you unfairly without good reason?
- Do you try to avoid family or friends while you are drinking or using drugs?
- Are you secretly irritated when family or friends discuss your drinking or drug use?
- Do you sometimes feel guilty about your drinking or drug use?

- Do you often regret things you have done or said when drunk or high?
- Have you often failed to keep the promises you have made to yourself about controlling or cutting down your drinking or drug use?
- Do you eat very little or irregularly when you are drinking or getting high?
- Do you feel low after indulging, and sometimes miss work or appointments?
- Do you use more and more to get drunk or high?

Some common signs suggest someone is moving into the early stages of alcoholism. Many people increasingly use alcohol in order to cope with their personal problems. Other signs include memory lapses or "blackouts" while drinking, craving the alcohol, and an increase in the individual's tolerance for alcohol. In the middle stages of alcoholism, there is an increase in memory problems from blackouts, and the person becomes increasingly physically dependent on alcohol. This dependence is first suggested when the person experiences early morning tremors and agitation that require a drink for relief. In the later and final stages, there are regular drinking bouts. Also during this stage, alcoholics experience **delirium tremens (DTs),** a withdrawal syndrome with symptoms including agitation, tremor, hallucination, and sometimes seizures.

Researchers still do not understand the causes of this complex problem; however, it is likely to include a combination of biological, psychological, and social factors. Recent attention has been directed to the incidence of alcoholism in families. Studies have shown that 50–80% of all alcoholics have a close relative who is alcoholic (Littrell, 1991). As a result, researchers have begun to search for an inherited physical predisposition to alcohol addiction. Some research has suggested that alcoholism is related to a particular gene on chromosome 11. This gene is related to the production of receptor sites, on brain cells, of the neurotransmitter dopamine.

Many researchers have attempted to find a particular personality that would lead to the development of alcoholism, but results have not been encouraging. However, alcoholism does appear to be related to various types of emotional problems. For example, many alcoholics drink to help them cope with feelings of depression or anxiety. Other individuals drink as a means to release their inhibited feelings. Alcoholics may experience role conflicts in their work and family life.

Although much of the substance-abuse problem is related to alcohol in the United States, there are also serious consequences associated with drug dependence. Drug dependence, or drug addiction, is defined by three characteristics (Goode, 1993). First, drug dependence is related to the length of time a person has been using the drug. Just how long a time is required to develop dependence is difficult to say and is related to the particular type of drug and the particular user's characterstics. Second, individuals who are dependent find it difficult to stop using the drug. A lot of effort is consumed with continuing to use the drug, including such things as stealing to get needed money. Third, when dependent drug users do refrain from using, they experience physical pain or psychological stress, referred to as the withdrawal syndrome.

Drug dependence is associated with a large number of different drugs, ranging from nicotine found in tobacco products, Valium used as a sedative, angel dust (a street drug derived from horse tranquilizer), and hallucinogenic drugs (such as LSD and mescaline), to name only a few. There are six primary classifications of drugs: *narcotics*, like heroin and morphine; *sedatives*, like Seconal and Quaaludes, which include barbiturates and nonbarbiturates; *stimulants*, like amphetamines and cocaine; *hallucinogens*, like LSD and mescaline; *cannabis*, like marijuana and hashish; and *alcohol*, like wine and scotch.

Implications for Practice:
Addiction and AA's 12-Step Program

The 12-step approach to addiction is so popular that it is now referred to as a social movement (Herman, 1988). In the 12-step approach—the core of Alcoholics Anonymous (AA)—people follow 12 carefully devised steps on the road to recovery. What exactly is the 12-step program, and how does it work?

The 12-step program is very straightforward in its approach to alcoholism. Part of its success may be related to the clear model it sets out as necessary for the road to recovery. Essentially, members are expected to "work the steps." In the process, individuals must admit wrongdoing, admit their powerlessness, pray and meditate, and meet with sponsors outside of the group meetings. AA is

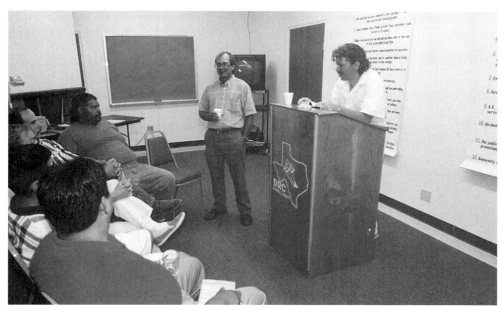

Twelve-step programs, which attract many people who are seeking help, offer a social context for addressing problems, a group setting for social support, and a clear structure.

famous for its helpful slogans, such as "live one day at a time" or "let go and let God."

The program is delivered through a series of weekly meetings. Members are encouraged to go to the meetings, and many people keep a daily schedule of meeting attendance. Most meetings begin with an opening statement, then a speaker addresses the group telling his or her own personal story, the members are invited to share, and then there is a closing statement. Members may speak about whatever they want, and the group must listen without interruption or subsequent comment.

Members are also encouraged to get involved with a sponsor. The sponsor is a kind of "buddy" who helps the member by providing advice and counsel about the program philosophy and structure. There is a strong emphasis on providing members with support. Sponsors and other members make themselves available 24 hours a day to help the person during times of crisis.

Although AA is recognized as one of the more effective approaches to alcoholism, it has come under increasing criticism. First, few studies have been able to clearly document AA's effectiveness, so many researchers are leery about its overall "success" rate. Equally critical are individuals who do not like AA's emphasis on religion and individual responsibility. For example, one of the 12 steps states, "[We have] made a decision to turn our will and our lives over to the care of God, *as we understood Him.*" Many individuals also do not like the emphasis of putting the alcoholic's addiction completely on the alcoholic's shoulders. Because AA accepts a disease concept of alcoholism, the responsibility for both the disease and recovery rests with the individual.

What other contextual factors might relate to people becoming addicted? Increasing research is providing some support for the notion that there may be a genetic predisposition toward alcoholism. These explanations are not consistent with the AA philosophy. Because AA members must admit to "powerlessness," it is difficult to promote notions of empowerment with AA members.

Critics offer additional questions for thought: "Can all human pain be collected into one big bundle labeled addiction? Should it be? What about the feelings of pleasure that people derive from food, drugs, alcohol, sex, and a host of other substances and activities?" (Herman,

1988, p. 59). This "movement" of disease-related addictions raises concerns about turning self-destructive behaviors into diseases and normal people (with problems) into victims rather than promoting empowerment of the individual as a socially responsible member of society. Some of the dissatisfaction with the AA model has sprung new, but related, approaches such as Rational Recovery, Secular Organization for Sobriety, and Women for Sobriety. Fingarette (1988), an outspoken critic of the AA model, argues that alcoholism is a mythical disease. He notes that "what seems to be compassion done in the name of a 'disease' turns out to subvert the drinker's autonomy and will to change, and to exacerbate a serious social problem" (Fingarette, 1988, p. 64). Fingarette spells out the social and political pressure that continue to define alcoholism as a disease.

If there are all these problems with AA's model of addiction, why do so many professionals believe that it is an effective alternative for alcoholics? Regardless of all of the criticism, AA does attract a large number of individuals who are looking for help and offers them something that appeals to their needs. There may be three primary reasons why AA works, at least for some people (Bufe, 1987; Herman, 1988):

1. *It provides a needed social context for addressing the problem.* In this social context is a safe haven for people to be understood and to be accepted for who they are. Many people in society are demoralized and lonely, and any program that can address those issues will be helpful to people.

2. *It provides a group setting for social support.* In most groups, a critical factor is having the feeling that you are not alone—that you are not unique. By expressing feelings and receiving emotional support, people gain confidence that they can take action to solve their problems.

3. *It provides a clear structure—a path to follow.* There is a self-determined behavioral routine that members follow, and this can be critical when your life is literally turned upside down. The steps provide a mechanism to focus one's energy.

Codependency

As part of the self-help movement, the codependency movement has become very popular—"the chic neurosis of our time" (Lyon & Greenberg, 1991, p. 435). The term *codependency* refers to a pattern of behavior in which a person's sense of self-worth is based on external referents. Codependents have a strong need for personal validation that is met by excessive caretaking of others, often to the neglect of their own best interests. The excessive caretaking often results in a preoccupation with the other person's feelings. The end result is excessive guilt when the codependent does not act assertive, fears of abandonment, and anxiety over not hurting another's feelings. The term *codependency* was originally applied to the wives of alcoholic husbands who got enmeshed in their spouses' addictions in ways that supported their addiction (Weiten & Lloyd, 1994). For example, a wife may lie to her husband's supervisor, who calls to find out why her husband has not yet arrived for work. In essence, she protects him from the natural consequences of his addiction. Today, the term *codependency* is used very broadly to refer to the general tendency to be preoccupied with another person's needs to the exclusion of one's own (Weiten & Lloyd, 1994).

Why would someone become codependent? The major theorists believe that codependents seek out dysfunctional relationships with troubled individuals so they can fulfill their need for excessive caretaking. Codependency is particularly a concern for women who have an overly strong need for affection and approval (Weiten & Lloyd, 1994). Haaken (1990) suggests that women are more vulnerable than men to codependency because they are socialized to value support, selflessness, and caretaking.

Similar to AA groups is Codependents Anonymous, a recovery program for people afflicted with codependency. In this context, codependency is seen as a disease, and recovery takes place when individuals admit that they have lost control over the disease (Weiten & Lloyd, 1994).

Weiten and Lloyd (1994) have reviewed literature on the codependency movement and summarized a number of criticisms that are worth noting:

1. There is no clear definition of codependency. In fact, Whitfield (1991) found 23 different definitions. The implication of the varying definitions is that it is difficult to determine who is codependent and who is not (Fischer, Spann, & Crawford, 1991).

2. At present, no good empirical studies exist to support many of the basic concepts of codependency

(Wright & Wright, 1991). Also, it is difficult to determine whether codependency is equally relevant across different types of problems. Does codependency operate the same for people who are addicted to food, love, or sex?

3. Kaminer (1992, p. 10) asserts that "every conceivable form of arguably compulsive behavior is classified as an addiction. We are a nation of sexaholics, rageaholics, shopaholics, and rushaholics." This perspective may demean the concept of addiction.

4. All problems end up being traced back to codependency. For example, Beattie's (1987) book *Codependent No More* lists 234 symptoms of codependency (Weiten & Lloyd, 1994). This is considered an oversimplification of a complex problem because it seems unlikely that everything can be explained by the processes of addiction and codependency.

5. Some women have raised concerns about the label of codependency as it is applied to women. It may contribute to a pattern of self-blame regarding their own suffering, problems with men, and their husband's problems (Tavris, 1992).

6. Although recovery groups are suggested as the only viable treatment, alternative further research may uncover additional treatment strategies that are helpful. Perhaps certain people will do better with recovery groups, and others will need to find alternative treatments.

Given these criticisms, is codependency a useful concept? Well, this depends on your perspective. However, it has helped practitioners to better understand complex relationships and how they are tied to addictive behaviors. Certainly, codependency is a popular concept, and to that extent it has accurately described the conflicts that many people feel. Furthermore, recovery groups, like AA groups, are likely to provide participants with needed social support to get further help or learn how to cope better with their problems. Part of that help may be obtained through professional guidance from a social worker or other health professional.

Implications for Practice: When to Seek Professional Help

In general, individuals should be encouraged to seek professional treatment when they are under serious psychological distress. First, consider that other forms of so-cial support may be helpful to the individual. These would include family members, church members, and personal friends. Sometimes a person's distress or conflict can be effectively dealt with through these types of natural helpers. However, other times it is best to encourage the person toward professional help. The type of help would vary—individual therapy, group therapy, or family therapy—depending on the nature of the concern. Some general guidelines for when to get help might include the following (Bruckner-Gordon, Gangi, & Wallman, 1988):

- There are no friends or acquaintances to discuss or help the person with his or her problem.
- The friends or acquaintances indicate that the person's problems are too difficult for them to handle.
- The person feels extremely overwhelmed and helpless.
- The person's daily life is affected by his or her psychological distress.

However, given the complexities we all face in modern life, individuals often seek professional help because they feel dissatisfied with life. The following Focus on Psychology section examines the controversial false memory syndrome, stimulated by the large number of women who sought help for having been sexually abused as a child.

FOCUS ON PSYCHOLOGY

False Memory Syndrome

One of the fascinating stories of the 1990s is the emergence of the False Memory Syndrome Foundation (FMSF). This foundation was established on the heels of hundreds of thousands of women who revealed that they had been sexually abused as children. In 1985, a *Los Angeles Times* poll reported that 22% of those sampled had been sexually abused before the age of 18. Many of these women sought refuge in *The Courage to Heal*, a self-help book that profiles over 100 interviews with survivors of sexual abuse. Although this revelation was shocking the country, a new development became equally shocking—the organization of a group of parents who believed that they had been falsely accused of sexual abuse. By 1992, more than 8000 accused parents were involved with the False Memory Syndrome Foundation. These parents claimed their innocence and were exasperated in their attempts to meet with their sons' and daughters' therapists to tell their part of the story. They were angry about having become completely ostracized by their children and sought some scientific evidence that might help explain their sons' and daughters' misperceived judgments. The interest in false memory syndrome intensified as several books were published, such as Elizabeth Loftus's *The Myth of Repressed Memory*, Richard Ofshe's *Making Monsters*, and (by a father accused of sexual abuse) Mark Pendergrast's *Victims of Memory*. As Butler (1995) describes it, "the 'incest recovery movement' turned into the 'recovered memory movement.'" Also contributing to the growing interest in the false memory syndrome (FMS) were the court cases won by the parents accused of sexual abuse against the therapists of women who recalled memories of sexual abuse. The therapists were found to have reinforced the false memories of their clients. By 1994, over 300 women and men had "recanted" accusations of parental sexual abuse and contacted the False Memory Syndrome Foundation. Not surprisingly, these events raised far more questions than answers. Butler (1995) asks: "Why are a relatively small group of accused parents so close to setting the clinical agenda for millions of genuine abuse survivors and eclipsing public awareness of the more than 130,000 children who are newly sexually victimized each year?" Butler believes these events may be due in part to a backlash against therapy—against the idea that anybody can be a victim. And although many therapists may be contributing to this backlash through their ineffective practice, incest cannot be explained by bad therapy alone. As Butler (1995, p. 79) argues, "it may be easier for the culture to focus its outrage on therapy than to face the larger issue—its failure to protect children, both yesterday's and today's, from real abuse."

Source: Adapted from Butler, 1995.

Social Dimension

Families, Groups, Support Systems, and Contexts

Family diversity was discussed in the chapter on young adulthood, the stage when many adults are beginning their families. Divorce was also addressed, but divorce often leads to new relationships and often to new marriages— with the end result of a **blended family.** A blended family is a newly formed unit consisting of a husband and wife, one or both of whom have children from a previous marriage. In middle adulthood, many divorces and remarriages take place and blended families are created. Adapting to a blended family may require facing unique tasks as many changes must be confronted.

Blended Families or Stepfamilies

As we have seen, divorce and subsequent remarriage is increasingly common, and 60% of couples who divorce have children and become single parents. However, most single parents do not remain so for long. Indeed, within five years of a divorce, three-quarters of single-parent families will become blended or **stepfamilies.** Stepfamilies are families whose kinship is determined by remarriage. Many stepfamilies will procreate their own children to add to the family.

Stepfamilies face significant changes as they must adapt to a new marital relationship, continue relationships with prior spouses, and help their children adjust to a difficult family transition. Although research has lagged behind in studies of stepfamilies in general, Visher and Visher (1988), in their book *Old Loyalties, New Ties*, have outlined the critical tasks stepfamilies face. Table 11.2 presents a summary of stepfamily characteristics and tasks.

As Table 11.2 makes clear, stepfamilies must face unique tasks in order to make a successful transition. Families must begin with acceptance of loss and changes, readjust expectations about what a family is, facilitate role adjustment for all family members, and coordinate a lifestyle that juggles two family households.

How do such changes affect the children in stepfamilies? Research is just beginning to shed light on this question. In general, following remarriage of their

TABLE 11.2 Stepfamily Characteristics and Tasks

Stepfamily Characteristics	Stepfamily Tasks
1. Starts in the context of many losses and changes	1. Dealing with loss and changes
2. Starting of a second family life cycle	2. Addressing different developmental needs
3. Family members bring expectations from previous families	3. Establishing new traditions
4. Parent-child relationships predate the new couple	4. Forming a strong marital bond
5. Biological parent living elsewhere	5. Creating a parenting coalition
6. Children adjusting to two households	6. Adapting to continual shifts from one household to another
7. Ambiguous or nonexistent legal relationship between stepparent and children	7. Risk of involvement without societal support

Source: Visher & Visher, 1988.

parents, many children develop behavior problems (Santrock, 1992). Behavior problems are more likely in boys, whereas girls often experience an increase in emotional problems. Adolescents can pose special problems for the stepfamily because they are moving toward independence, and the increased stress associated with the stepfamily may adversely affect them.

Of course, there are benefits associated with a stepfamily. Moving from a single-parent family to a family with a stepfather or stepmother can add a significant new relationship to the life of the child. In fact, boys seem to do less well in single-parent families, and when they gain a stepfather, they become less anxious, experience an increase in self-esteem, and make a better adjustment in general (Heatherington, 1987). Girls do not seem to benefit as much in gaining a stepfather. Still, over time both boys and girls make an adjustment to being part of a stepfamily.

Heatherington (1988) suggests that the stepfather is most likely to gain acceptance by his stepchildren if he refrains from directly controlling the child's behavior; this is better left to the mother of the child. "Instead, the new father should first work at establishing a relationship with the child and support the mother in her parenting" (Heatherington, 1988, p. 311). After a stronger relationship is established, then the stepfather can engage in more authoritative parenting.

Adapting to the new stepfamily can be complex and may be assisted by professional counseling services. Couples need to bolster their marital relationship and

work to adapt to the changes. Wald (1989, p. 560) believes that it is essential for social workers to "understand that the characteristics inherent in the stepfamily do not reflect pathological dynamics but rather normal and transitional adjustments to a new situation."

Marriage and Intimate Relationships at Midlife

From the life cycle perspective, many couples at midlife are launching their children into adulthood. For the couple who have been parents throughout much of their lives, this signals a very significant change—often referred to as the *empty nest syndrome*. However, this reference confers some outdated notions on this stage of life. Originally, the empty nest syndrome was a particular concern for the mother who had devoted herself full-time to raising children. Of course, that picture has changed with the large increase in the number of working mothers. Studies have found that rather than being "empty," this stage can be one of satisfaction for both men and women. So rather than seeing marital satisfaction decline, research has found that it begins a steady climb upward in the postchildbearing years (Sherman, 1987).

Why would satisfaction increase as children are launched into adulthood? Rollins (1989) believes that the stresses associated with children are due to "roles overload," whereby parents with children at home neglect their roles as married partners, and that this has a negative impact on marital satisfaction. Overload occurs in these families because communication and companionship are sacrificed in order to respond to the caregiving role as parents. The implication is that "professional helpers can be alert to marital problems of their clients at midlife that are related to poor communication and lack of companionship" (Hunter & Sundel, 1989, p. 181).

How do love and intimate relationships change at midlife? One common explanation is that the nature of intimacy changes and couples develop more affectionate and companionate love. Whereas, in young adulthood much of the focus on intimacy revolves around romantic love, physical attraction, and passion, by midlife many adults are more concerned about maintaining relationships from the perspective of mutual sharing, security, and loyalty (Reedy, Birren, & Schaie, 1981).

Is there such a thing as a good marriage that has survived? Judith Wallerstein (1995) notes that many people claim they have never seen a good marriage and cannot imagine how one would look. Her research examined the lives of affluent married couples who have experienced satisfying, enduring marriages. What she offers is confirmation that a good marriage requires a lot of hard work and dedication. Without a strong appreciation for the other person, a sense of companionship and loyalty, sexual attraction, and empathy, you are less likely to have a successful marriage.

Of course, for many middle adults, their lives move in different directions, and this creates greater distance between them. Each partner may be seeking different goals and commitments that make the development of mutual sharing difficult. For example, the wife may be seeking growth through work and other commitments, while the husband may be seeking stronger emotional support and shared activities. As Wallerstein (1995) points out, the survival of the marriage may depend on the commitment each spouse has attained over the years and each one's ability to appreciate and understand the other person's needs. In many respects, it is during middle adulthood that the couple may want to review and renew their commitment to the marriage. Although the couple face important changes, divorce is much less likely to occur at midlife than at an earlier point in life (Rollins, 1989).

In middle adulthood, many individuals are not married or connected to a significant other or partner. They may be lifelong singles or recently divorced or widowed. However, at midlife, these individuals also seek relationships that are mutual, loyal, and companionate. As Lindsey (1982) found, most single adults have at least one significant other of the same or opposite sex who is part of their "adopted" family. Such support is critical to the individual's life satisfaction and mental health (Lindsey, 1982). The following Focus on Multiculturalism section takes a closer look at marital satisfaction among African Americans.

FOCUS ON MULTICULTURALISM

Marital Satisfaction Among African Americans

Most of the research on marital satisfaction has been conducted with couples who are white, middle class, and affluent. However, African Americans have a higher divorce rate when compared with whites at every income level. Research by Broman (1993) sought to examine what factors predict marital quality among African Americans. Results found that for both husbands and wives, the perception that family income was adequate to meet the family's needs was predictive of marital satisfaction. For African American women, economic adequacy was related to how positively they assessed their husband's role performance. In addition to economic adequacy, the following factors were also considered important: Providing emotional support predicted marital satisfaction and harmony for both men and women; for African American men, having a smaller number of children was related to greater marital satisfaction, but for African American women, it wasn't the number of children but the degree of problems associated with raising the children; personal development and the opportunity to express individual freedoms were positively related to marital satisfaction for both husbands and wives; and for African American women, job satisfaction was correlated with marital satisfaction.

Source: Broman, 1993.

Extramarital Affairs   For many men and women who struggle with changes in midlife, an extramarital affair offers an opportunity to rediscover themselves. Married couples often have established routine patterns that become unexciting and boring. At midlife, they are often searching for something new and different, and an affair may offer them a unique opportunity to rediscover different aspects of themselves. Such affairs may be related to seeking greater fulfillment in personal relationships. An affair may emerge out of anxiety over physical aging and a need to perceive oneself as still attractive. For men, an affair may be an opportunity to deny their declining sexual performance. As Goldstein and Landau (1990, p. 189) aptly put it, "if either a man or a woman is haunted by the sense of time running out, if either abruptly realizes that they have spent much of their lives doing what others wanted them to do, then either one is a likely candidate to follow wherever a forbidden impulse leads."

Santrock (1989) describes how, for the next generation of midlife women, sexual relationships outside of marriage are likely to continue to increase because of such factors as greater acceptance of women as sexual beings, family changes that leave many women without men, men's shorter life expectancy, and the changing role of women in the workforce. "Extramarital sex will frequently occur in the transition out of marriage and into new sexual and marital arrangements" (Santrock, 1989, p. 471). Midlife women may be increasingly interested in extramarital sex, not because they are unhappy in their marriage but because they are seeking excitement and variety in their sex lives. By participating in the workforce, married women become more equal partners in the marriage, and single women increase their opportunity to access potential partners. In addition, Santrock believes that because of the above-mentioned changes, midlife women will enjoy solitary sex more frequently than their older sisters or mothers did.

How common are extramarital affairs or instances of nonmonogamy in couple relationships? Blumstein and Schwartz (1983), in their study of American couples, found that affairs are least likely to occur with wives; 21% reported having an extramarital affair since the beginning of a relationship. For men, the percentage was just 5% more; a total of 26% report having affairs. This represents almost one-quarter of all married relationships. For gay men, nonmonogamous relationships were extremely common—over 80% report instances of such

relationships. Lesbians were only a little more likely to have nonmonogamous relationships (28%) when compared with husbands and wives. Couples involved for 10 years or more have a greater incidence of nonmonogamy than do either couples involved 2–10 years or couples involved 0–2 years. The researchers also found differences in the intent of the nonmonogamous relationship. For men, the interest in outside sex was more likely to be variety and sexual excitement, whereas for women, the interest was more likely to be for a special relationship. In general, the range of sexual choices will continue to grow as we move into the next century.

Parent–Adult Child Relationships

Any discussion of the family in middle adulthood must address two aspects: how middle-aged parents relate to their adult children and how middle-aged parents relate to their aging parents. It is for this reason that middle adulthood is seen as the phase in life that provides continuity in the family's identity. Middle-aged adults become the critical link between their aging parents and their young adult children. They provide the foundation for the bridge that links the generations.

As in other stages in the family life cycle, the family continues to be a primary source of social support, with parents and their children providing important mutual assistance to one another (Lemme, 1995). The mutual support comes in a variety of ways; for example, parents may provide needed baby-sitting when grandchildren are small, and children may provide needed care to parents during times of illness or hospitalization. As Lemme (1995, p. 283) points out, "this reciprocal assistance may shift in direction over the life of the family, focusing more on children in the earlier stages and flowing more toward parents as they age." Social support is a critical link in the long-term relationship between middle-aged parents and their children and between middle-aged adults and their aging parents.

Middle-Aged Parents and Their Adolescent Children

When I was a boy of 14 my father was so ignorant I could hardly stand to have the man around. But when I got to be 21, I was astonished at how much he learnt in 7 years.

—Mark Twain—

Small children tend to see parents as all-powerful and all-knowing. When those children become adolescents, suddenly those parents no longer seem so competent or knowledgeable. Throughout this book, we have been concentrating on how parents influence their children's development; but how do children, especially adolescent children, influence their middle-aged parents?

Research by Laurence Steinberg (1995) has found that the most difficult time for parents is when their children are between the ages of 11 and 14. Steinberg states that parents' midlife crises develop most often when their children reach this age. In fact, 40% of parents experience a decrease in psychological well-being during their children's adolescence. Also, marital satisfaction declines during this time. What changes in the parents and children account for these midlife problems?

Santrock (1990) states that parents experience more economic problems during their children's adolescence because teenage children cost more. Parents may be dealing with career decisions and questioning life goals during this time. They also may be concerned with their health and appearance. Middle-aged parents may feel they are becoming less attractive while watching their adolescent become more attractive. One mother remarked, "You know you are a middle-aged woman when you go out in public and the men who used to flirt with you now flirt with your daughter."

Santrock (1990) explains that children are also going through changes at this time. Whereas younger children are more compliant and easy to handle, adolescent children become noncompliant, oppositional, and resistant to parental standards. They may question parental demands and challenge decisions. The child may become oversensitive to adult remarks. Adolescents begin to push for more independence and autonomy from parental control. Many adolescents become larger than their parents. A single mother may wonder how to control a son who towers over her.

All these changes lead to conflict and power struggles between adolescents and their middle-aged parents. And this conflict increases the stress level in the lives of these middle-aged adults. Steinberg has found that these problems occur in all family types. Single mothers have more problems with their sons, and they tend to let their sons go their own way when power struggles arise. In stepfamilies, more problems exist with daughters, who may feel a loss of closeness with the mother when she remarries. And in intact two-parent families, both parents may face a loss of control of their children, jealousy of their children's accomplishments, or fear of the children making the same mistakes the parents made (Dubin, 1994).

Steinberg has found that being involved in a satisfying career and having outside interests and activities help middle-aged parents cope with this difficult time in their life as parents. Santrock suggests patience and understanding when parenting adolescents. As Mark Twain noticed, as the children grow up, the parents amazingly regain their competence and knowledge.

Middle-Aged Parents and Their Adult Children   By midlife, many parents have raised their children to adults and must now shift their relationship from one of parent-child to one of parent-friend. In large part as a result of longevity, parents and their children are likely to grow old together. This change is positive, as most parents report an improved relationship with their sons and daughters as they become young adults. Most adult children feel "close" or "very close" to their parents. One study (Troll & Bengston, 1982) found that parents are more likely to view their young adult children as friends.

However, at midlife, parents are often in the ironic situation of addressing the difficulties of raising children and at the same time discussing shared difficulties with difficult and impossible parents. It is in this sense that middle-aged adults are often referred to as the *sandwich generation*. Although many parents may perceive their children as friends when they become adults, how important is a good relationship with one's parents on a young adult's psychological adjustment?

Baruch and Barnett (1983) studied middle-aged women to examine how a woman's overall well-being was related to her relationship with her mother. The results showed that middle-aged women are better adjusted psychologically when they have a positive relationship with their mothers. In particular, those women with positive relationships had greater self-esteem, were less anxious, and less depressed than women who did not have satisfactory relationships with their mothers.

Middle-aged women also play an important role as *kinkeeper*, keeping the ties between families. It often becomes the middle-aged woman's role to bring the family together for family traditions and celebrations. This role is probably related to the strong mother-daughter bond that is consistent over the life span (Troll, 1986). Adult daughters are more likely than adult sons to live nearby and to exchange help with their mothers (Cicirelli, 1983). Daughters are also more likely to be the keepers of family symbols, photographs, and heirlooms than are sons.

Middle-Aged Adults and Their Aging Parents

It is too late to turn back. I have set in motion events that are tumbling me along like a broken branch in floodtide. I have run out of choices. I look at my 94-year-old mother. Her thin, hunched body is dwarfed amid a welter of crates, cartons of books, piles of possessions to take to the Salvation Army, and other stacks of worthless items too precious to leave behind. Her expression matches the disheveled room. She doesn't know it yet, but by this time next week, she will be in a nursing home in Colorado, a thousand miles from here, whatever life remains to her drastically changed. The cost of dying, particularly if one does it slowly, is prohibitive in California. (Hartney, 1989, p. 39)

As the above quote points out, middle-aged adults must face the task of caring for their aging parents—a task that can sometimes be very difficult. With the increase in life expectancy, there is a greater need for adult children to care for their aging parents, who may need assistance with daily activities such as eating, dressing, housework, and finances. Since 1980, the number of individuals needing assistance has doubled (U.S. Bureau of the Census, 1990). Most often when an elderly parent needs some assistance, it is family members who provide the needed medical and personal care.

Not only has the number of older people who need caregiving increased, but the nature of caregiving required is also changing (Pearlin, Mullan, Semple, & Skaff, 1990). Because of rapid medical advances, individuals are much less likely to die from acute causes and instead are more likely to die from a chronic illness, like cancer (Lemme, 1995). Furthermore, when an individual gets a chronic illness, he or she is more likely to live longer than in the past. The implication for middle-aged adults is that the caretaking role is extended over a longer period of time. Therefore, adult children provide not only longer care to their parents but also more difficult care (Brody, 1985).

Providing needed assistance is a shared expectation of both adult children and their aging parents. Harmon and Blieszner (1990) found that over 85% of adult children agreed with the following responsibilities they should assume: help understand resources, give emotional support, talk over matters of importance, make room in home for emergency, sacrifice personal freedom, and be together on special occasions. Aging parents also endorsed these same responsibilities, but adult children had a greater sense of obligation than their parents expected of them.

Parent caring, as it is sometimes called, is most often left to the daughter in the family. In this culture, women are expected to assume the role of caretaker, managing and nurturing the family. Many women assume dual roles of both mother and grandmother, caring for elderly parents and helping adult children manage their families (Arlington & Troll, 1984). Indeed, women play an essential role in making sure family members receive proper health care, providing transportation, arranging and planning family gatherings, providing emotional support to aging parents, and talking with family members to keep everyone abreast of new developments in the family.

This picture of the adult child caring for elderly parents has been refuted by media reports, which too often have portrayed the adult child as neglecting or abandoning his or her parents. Gerontologists have pointed to research that shows children attending to parents' needs and providing essential caregiving functions (Brody, 1981).

It is also important to point out that, although caregiving is being emphasized, many older people are in good or excellent health. Only 5% of adults who are 65 years and older suffer from organic brain syndrome and only 10% show signs of dementia. Older persons like living alone and want to function quite independently (Lemme, 1995). In fact, research by Stueve and O'Donnell (1984) found that the notion of "caught in the middle" may be quite inaccurate for our understanding of parent-child relationships. This notion makes sense only in the context of a traditional life cycle approach, and, as these researchers found, many women today do not fit the typical life cycle stages. For example, many women in their forties and fifties may be parenting adolescent children, but an increasing number of women this age are also just beginning their families. Still, women are expected to provide care for elderly parents and often for other elderly kin as well—including parents-in-law (Stueve & O'Donnell, 1984).

In fact, Brody (1985) points out that parent care is only one aspect of a woman's **caregiving career**—a career that often includes caring for children, caring for elderly parents and relatives, and providing care for a dependent husband. The career aspect of this idea points out that caregiving is not simply a one-time, limited episode. Indeed, caregiving has important implications for women who provide this care without receipt of wages, pension benefits, or other resources (Lemme, 1995). How caregiving of middle-aged women is going to affect their participation in the labor force is an important consideration in the future. Beck (cited in Lemme, 1995) states that the average woman will spend 17 years caring for children and 18 years caring for aging parents.

Implications for Practice: Adjusting to the Role of Caregiver

Being a caregiver can be a stressful experience. Although being a caregiver is most often a satisfying experience, it is also the kind of experience that provides constant stress and often produces mental and physical consequences for the caregiver (Schulz, Visintainer, & Williamson, 1990). Because so many older people will need caregivers in the future, Peak and Toseland (1992) refer to caregiving as a social problem. As they note, many caregivers are unprepared for their role. Also, depending on the nature of the illness, caregivers may need to be prepared for rapid degeneration of the person. Daily routines such as helping with feeding, toileting, and lifting can become difficult. From a psychosocial perspective, caregivers often feel abandoned by their friends and family members and may have feelings of depression, anxiety, self-blame, and general stress (Peak & Toseland, 1992).

An important source of support for caregivers is a social support group. Such a group may provide needed emotional support, coping skills, and a reduction in anxiety and stress. Toseland and Rossiter (1989) suggest the following functions a support group can provide to caregivers:

- Provide a much-needed respite from caregiving
- Reduce isolation and loneliness
- Provide an opportunity to share feelings and experiences in a supportive atmosphere

- Affirm and validate feelings and thoughts about the caregiving situation
- Instill hope
- Educate caregivers about the effects of chronic disabilities and available community resources
- Encourage a mutual sharing of information about effective coping strategies
- Help caregivers to become motivated to use systematic problem-solving procedures and coping strategies to reduce or eliminate the stress they are experiencing

In caregiving support groups, social workers are expected to provide supportive interventions that stress such skills as ventilation of stressful experiences in an understanding and supportive environment, validation and confirmation of similar caregiving experiences, affirmation of members' ability to cope with the situation, praise for providing the care, and support and understanding when struggling with difficult situations (Peak & Toseland, 1992).

Grandparenthood

Many parents of adult children have the opportunity to be grandparents. Indeed, given the longevity of older adults, most will live long enough to be involved with grandchildren and some will live long enough to be involved with their great-grandchildren. Grandparents approach their new roles from very different perspectives. Some are interested mostly in being fun-seekers, having mostly informal and playful interactions, while others are surrogate parents, assuming major child-care responsibilities (Neugarten & Weinstein, 1964). Grandparents can serve as important role models of aging and integrity (Kivnick, 1986). They offer the family a sense of continuity.

The role shift to grandparents can require relearning old skills and adapting to new ways of parenting. Grandparents may be called on to help calm a fussy baby, change a diaper, heat a bottle of milk, and teach toilet training to a toddler. Often the grandparent's approach is different from that of the parent, and the differences between them need to be worked out. Being a grandparent, therefore, involves new roles that affect family relationships (Severino, Teusink, Pender, & Bernstein, 1986). Grandparenting can be very rewarding if it is approached with experience and wisdom.

The experience of being a grandparent may offer a sense of completion to the middle-aged adult. Being a grandparent may reflect a person's influence across the generations, providing to him or her an affirmation of values and a sense of general satisfaction (Cherlin & Furstenberg, 1986). Grandparents often are able to share their experience and wisdom in child-rearing, offer emotional support to the parents, and achieve satisfaction in their grandchildren's accomplishments (Neugarten & Weinstein, 1964). This new role offers new opportunities and new learnings. The tasks of grandparenting can lead to self-reflection of one's own parenting history and call for new competencies.

In general, grandparenting can play a critical role in adapting to the aging process. For many grandparents, this new role replaces impending retirement and concern over loss of responsibilities. Being a grandparent contributes to one's personal influences across the generations, and in this sense it may help grandparents become more comfortable with their own death. It provides an acceptable opportunity to pass on one's cultural heritage and communicate special meanings to grandchildren. Focus on Multiculturalism describes the role African American grandmothers play in multigenerational households, and Focus on Family discusses grandparents who are raising their grandchildren.

FOCUS ON MULTICULTURALISM

African American Grandmothers

What role do African American grandmothers play in multigenerational households? Research by Pearson, Hunter, Ensminger, and Kellam (1990) sought to answer this question by examining the role grandmothers play when living with their grandchildren. The researchers found the following results:

- One-third of all families in the study were extended families, and 10% of the households included grandmothers.
- Grandmothers were most involved in parenting functions where there was no mother in the home. In

general, parenting involvement differed as a function of family structure.
- Employment of the grandmother did not influence her participation in parenting.
- The types of roles grandmothers played in their parenting functions included both authoritarian and nurturing.

FOCUS ON FAMILY

Parents Again—Grandparents Raising Their Grandchildren

It's like turning back the clock to 20 years ago, yet we're a lot older. We're back to finding a sitter if we have to go out. We're back to having very little, or should I say, no time to ourselves.

I am too old for the young mothers and the people I grew old with do not have grandchildren with them all of the time. We have nothing in common anymore. This situation makes me feel like a misfit. I should be going to senior citizens' activities instead of parent-teacher meetings.

What worries me most is what should happen to him if I should die.

When young parents cannot care for their children because of such factors as substance abuse, mental illness, criminal activity, poverty, homelessness, or AIDS, frequently it is the grandparents who end up raising the children. Though many grandparents willingly accept the responsibility for their children's children, this responsibility often brings added stress. Kelly (1993) discusses the stress associated with the demands of parenthood at a later age:

- Older adults raising their children's children face increased family stress at all levels. These grandparents may worry about their own children, who may be in trouble with addiction or illness. These older adults may also be coping with their own elderly parents who need care. Now they have small children to raise who may have been abused or neglected. These children may need extra care and support.

- In general, social support mediates stress for parents. But grandparents raising their grandchildren may lose their support network. They are often isolated from their peers who are no longer raising children.
- The grandparents may worry about living long enough to raise their grandchildren or about becoming ill and being unable to care for their grandchildren.

Because of this increase in family stress, grandparents may experience problems in relating to their grandchildren. Such stress can lead to a decrease in caregiver-child interactions, which can then affect the children's development (Crnic & Greenberg, 1990).

Organizations such as the American Association of Retired Persons (AARP) have established formal support systems for grandparents raising grandchildren. AARP publishes a newsletter and offers a grandparent information center.

Source: Adapted from Kelly, 1993.

The Men's Movement

Almost everyone is familiar with the women's movement and its influence on American society, but we have only recently been exposed to the men's movement. Although the men's movement is indeed here, it has emerged in a very different way from the women's movement. In particular, the men's movement seems aimed more toward men's change rather than any kind of external change (Graham, 1992). Perhaps best known in the men's movement is Robert Bly's book *Iron John*. The story of Iron John is about a boy who helps a primitive man escape from the adults who are holding him captive and goes with him to a journey in the woods. Here the boy grows to manhood. This story is about the unavailability and the distance many men feel toward their fathers. Bly is addressing the influence of his own abusive and alcoholic father. Bly's concern is about the contemporary separation of boys from their fathers. He contends that many mothers look to their sons for the emotional satisfaction their husbands deny them. The son feels ashamed when he realizes he cannot soothe his mother, and at the same

time he distrusts his father and other men. Bly's book highlights how our culture contributes to the separation of boys from their fathers, which has led to an absence of appropriate masculine identity. His book has spawned a movement of men who are seeking to recover their lost manhood by denouncing contemporary culture and rediscovering their lost masculine identity.

In a similar thesis, Sam Keen's (1991) *Fire in the Belly* is about the process of being a man. Keen, like Bly, suggests that men must break free of cultural boundaries in order to reassert their masculinity and male role. Keen states than men's problems result from the "primal power that women wielded over men because of the imperfect separation of man from the mother." Many theorists believe that, in childhood, boys prematurely dissociate from their mothers and enter the aggressive, competitive world of men. The boy desires to turn to his father but finds him emotionally distant and unavailable. The result is that his developing masculinity is defined by turning away from anything feminine.

These two popular icons of the men's movement are much different from the previous image of the sensitive man. As Graham (1992, p. 840) notes, "the sensitive-man model was accepted and emulated by few men, and it did not seem that many women found it completely satisfying." To Bly, this image of the sensitive man is what has robbed men of their righteous anger and their ability to act with certainty and has disconnected them from their identity and their instincts toward manhood (Graham, 1992).

The interest in men's issues is also being examined within specific ethnic groups. For example, in 1990 the National Council of African American Men, an organization that fosters understanding of black males, was formed. More recently, there was the Million Man March, where African American men bonded together and marched in Washington, D.C. Particularly relevant is the impact of racism on gender-role development. One program receiving increasing attention is the Afrocentric socialization model—where black youth are matched with positive black male role models to help them develop more effective coping responses.

Implications for Practice: Men in Therapy

Male and female stereotypes of men can have a significant impact on a man's use of social services. As Sleek

(1994, p. 6) states, "men are about as comfortable in therapy as penguins in the desert." Men seek mental health services about half as frequently as women. When men do enter treatment, they often are uncomfortable with self-disclosure and emotional exploration. Bogard (1991), in her book *Feminist Approaches for Men in Family Therapy*, describes her experience of reaching an impasse with a defensive male client. She confronted her stereotype that "men can't do more" when a colleague confronted Bogard about why she stopped challenging the client. Bogard now argues that men's ability to grow is seriously untapped by mental health practitioners. Female practitioners often describe male clients as dependent, childlike, and distant. She found that often women do the emotional work for their male clients, rather than challenging the client to articulate his feelings.

Male practitioners also have negative stereotypes about their male clients. In a recent study by McPhee (cited in Sleek, 1994), therapists were asked to diagnose potential male and female clients of different jobs and income based on individual vignettes. Both male and female therapists diagnosed more serious problems—for example, affective or personality disorders—in the men than in the women, even though the vignettes described symptoms characteristic of adjustment disorder.

Mental health practitioners are now realizing the need to make treatment male-friendly. This can be accomplished through several avenues, such as helping the reluctant male client move toward instrumental changes rather than stressing emotional expression. And the process of seeking treatment can be reframed as a sign of strength. Also, many practitioners believe that men's therapy groups work better than individual therapy for many men.

Such attempts to make treatment more accessible to men may be critical to creating successful adjustment for many men. A recent program by Ivanoff ("High Rate," 1994) attempted to respond to the high rate of suicide among personnel of the New York police department. Because most police officers are male, Ivanoff had to respond to the resistance of the officers to seeking treatment. Indeed, Ivanoff found that officers are trained not to show signs of weakness and not to discuss problems or feelings. The project had to encourage officers who needed help to seek it. The method used to address the reluctant officers included viewing a film that examines the lives of three officers who considered suicide. The officers reported that they were more willing to seek help for themselves and for fellow officers after having viewed this film and participated in a training session.

Context: Career Development and Job Satisfaction

Consider the following comments from Kyle, a 51-year-old man (Bergoquist, Greenberg, & Klaum, 1993, pp. 120–121):

> I have come through the printing industry, from apprentice to journeyman, learning the trade and going through the changes we have experienced in the industry. It's been quite an experience. But my success was moving through the management part of the job, and this has been most rewarding to me. It certainly broadened my scope, and being part of the challenges of the future has been a great lesson. . . . I'm where I am today because of the way I do my job, and I feel I have been recognized for that. This job is a continuing learning process. I don't happen to think that, just because I have this job, I have reached the goal I set for myself in life. I feel that there is a lot more for me to do and still a lot more for me to learn.

Work and career development are major contexts for adult development (Newman & Newman, 1995). By middle adulthood, most individuals have entered the job market and have begun a career. Regardless of the nature of the work, unskilled or professional, it becomes a central focus around which adult life revolves. Indeed, work often provides a growing sense of satisfaction as we get older (Warr, 1992). Our jobs may mean more to us, and as a consequence, we are more serious about our work and derive more satisfaction from it—aptly described in the above quote.

Work as a Way of Life   What you do in your job is likely to have a major impact on your overall lifestyle. First, work is going to determine your **socioeconomic status.** Socioeconomic status is a common research variable that combines economic status or level of income, social status or level of education, and work status as measured by your occupation (Dutton & Levine, 1989). Our world is centered on our work—it determines where we live, who we socialize with, what schools we take our children to, and it contributes to our sense of self.

Our work also sets forth the kind of expectations that society has for us. It determines the social appropriateness of how we dress, behave, and evaluate ourselves (Lemme, 1995). So our work is certainly more than just a job; it gives direction to our overall lifestyle and is central to our identity. Studs Terkel (1974, p. xiii), who interviewed men and women about their work, concluded that work is "a search for daily meaning as well as daily bread, for recognition as well as cash, for astonishment rather than torpor; in short, for a sort of life rather than a Monday through Friday sort of dying. Perhaps immortality, too, is part of the quest."

Career Changes at Midlife   The idea that many individuals change their careers at midlife is quite popular. Indeed, many fascinating stories have been written about people who gave up their job making hundreds of thousands of dollars as a stockbroker to move to the country and reconsider their values. How accurate are such stories about persons who make such dramatic life changes? Estimates are that only about 10% of men and women change jobs at midlife. What are some of the reasons that men and women would be motivated to change careers?

Newman and Newman (1995) have identified five reasons that may lead to a change in work-related goals. First, some careers may just end during middle adulthood—the individual cannot perform the duties of the job—for example, professional athletes. The second reason reflects the popular stereotype of the midlife crisis—that adults decide that their work is not meaningful to them anymore and go in search of a different, more meaningful, career. Third, midlife career change can occur because the individual believes he or she has succeeded as much as possible in a job, perhaps because changing technology has created the need for specialized training to keep up with the job. Fourth, particularly for women, a career change may come when children are "launched" and there is more time to commit to a career. Also, women may become **displaced homemakers,** forced into the job market by the circumstances of divorce or widowhood. Fifth, due to economic pressures, the workforce may be restructured, requiring that some workers be laid off.

The idea of the midlife career change is a central thesis in Levinson's (1978) theory of adult development. Levinson suggests that many adults become reflective about their experience in a job and must reconcile their idealistic hopes with realistic possibilities. Given the amount of time left in a career, can the individual reach his or her goals? When this issue becomes a central focus for the adult, it is believed to be the motivating factor behind serious midlife changes, such as career changes, extramarital affairs, divorce, and alcoholism.

Gender, Work, and the Family: Different Pathways   Typically, men have pursued a narrow career pathway for most of their adult life. At midlife, they may begin to question their accomplishments at work, but they may also question their contribution to the family. At midlife, a common male reaction is to reevaluate their role in the family in relation to their commitment to their work. They may regret not having spent more time with their children. For example, the reflections of Alex, a 50-year-old, are common: "We had a good family. It could have been much better if I had put much more into it. I've learned to take the important things more seriously than I had before. Too many times my family took a back seat to my work" (Bergquist, Greenberg, & Klaum, 1993, p. 93).

For women, the potential for midlife career changes is greater because they have not had such a narrow career pathway. Many women have had an **interrupted career** that began before motherhood, was interrupted by child-rearing, and then reestablished when full-time work resumed (Golan, 1986). Other women start professional training while raising children and then move into a full-time career. The implication for this pattern is significant in terms of career progress and earning potential for later life (Hatch, 1990). Because retirement income is directly related to work history, women's earning potential has long-term economic consequences for them. This fact, coupled with the increasing caregiving functions, is likely to contribute to increased poverty among older women (Davis, Grant, & Rowland, 1990).

When a midlife career or schooling change does take place, it is likely to have special significance. There are a number of additional benefits for many women who return to or start a career. Apter (1995, p. 154), in her study of midlife women, explains it this way: "They not only learned new facts, but gained new perspectives. In learning how to run a business, for example, some women felt they were gaining access to an entire range of concepts that they had previously thought themselves incapable of mastering. In studying social theory or psychology or literature, they gathered new tools for reflecting on the problems that had long plagued them. Moreover, the new knowledge and new skills would, they hoped, lead to new opportunities for further friendships, further self-confirming experiences, and make further knowledge possible." Many women at midlife pursue schooling as a means for continued growth and change. The pursuit of learning is not just for an enhanced education. It reflects something more personal—an opportunity to rediscover their strengths and become more empowered (Hohman, 1995).

These kinds of changes may create conflict within the family. This may be particularly true when a husband is pulling back from his career and wanting to spend more time with his family and a wife is wanting to spend more time pursuing school or a career. Also, the woman's shift in direction may mean that she will put less emphasis on other more family-oriented roles. The degree to which work and family roles conflict depends in part on how the partners view each other's participation in the world of work (Newman & Newman, 1995). For example, in a traditional household, a husband may support his wife's new career to the extent that it is viewed as supplementary to his own career. Successful adaptation will depend on how the couple resolves the changes in roles and the flexibility with which they approach these changes.

Multicultural and Gender Considerations

Cavanaugh (1990, p. 351) raises the question, "to what extent is it important or beneficial to maintain ethnic identity across adulthood?" In many respects, the notion of ethnic identity is contrary to the idea of assimilation into the larger society (Cool, 1987). Research with older adults has found that ethnic identity can serve as a source of support for the individual. At the point in life when people are becoming increasingly removed from society, ethnic identity is likely to provide a strong source of support (Royce, 1982). Indeed, research by Luborsky and Rubinstein (1987) found that ethnic identity became more important later in life than it was in early adulthood. Qualitative interviews with older widows uncovered the manner in which ethnic identity became stronger as the individual aged. For example, individuals discussed how, after the death of a spouse, they adopted the role of family historian. As a consequence, they re-

flected on the importance of family heritage and traditions, which often led to a rediscovery of the significance of their ethnic roots. Also, individuals discussed how reexamining the past had to be integrated with their current selves. This process becomes increasingly important as people age and move toward an overall sense of integrity in their life. Focus on Multicultralism describes a Puerto-Rican American woman's experience of being a person of color who is a professional social worker.

FOCUS ON MULTICULTURALISM

Living in Two Worlds

It is strange to have lived in the country for almost 40 years and have someone I've just met ask me, "Where do you come from?" as if I had just arrived from the island. At those moments, I feel a sudden split in my being. How do I explain that I come from two worlds, and that most of the time I feel I am on a bridge shuttling back and forth between them? Despite my lush memories of growing up in Puerto Rico—the smell of the ocean, the sound of the breeze and the taste of cornmeal with coconut milk and ripe plantains—sometimes it seems I have become a *gringa* in the way I think and live my life. Yet, that question about where I come from always reminds me that others see me as a foreigner, as someone who doesn't belong. . . .

It was not until I was 26 that I finally realized that much of my life would not be lived fully in either world but on the bridge. Most Latinos marry early and have children right away and that was what my Puerto Rican fiancé wanted. Instead, I decided to go to graduate school, even though that meant abandoning rules I had learned growing up about being a Latina. Despite the shame I felt admitting to my fiancé—and myself—that I did not immediately want children and my mother's life, my choice marked my liberation from the world of my childhood and my embrace of the part of me that had become a *gringa*. . . .

While I can't remember experiencing outright discrimination as a professional because of my race or culture, I have felt the subtleties of prejudice and the discomfort of tokenism. When I am asked to present at national conferences, or to be active in professional organizations, it is never clear to me whether I'm being asked for myself or because I represent a "minority" group. Recently, while giving information about my professional experience over the phone to someone from a national professional organization, I had to explain over and over that my work as a family therapist wasn't limited to Latinos, and that I gained my expertise working with adolescents and their families while directing an adolescent day hospital at a major mental health center. . . .

What I offer beyond my skill as a therapist and my own experience of immigration, is my optimism. While never easy, I *know* it is possible to shuttle between these two worlds. When I help people construct the bridges they need for this journey between cultures, my own bridge becomes sturdier and wider.

Source: Garcia-Preto, 1994.

Gender Concerns

Perhaps nowhere in the life cycle is the issue of gender differences more pronounced than in middle adulthood. Part of the reason for this disparity is that the classical research in this area was based exclusively on men but was generalized to women. For example, Daniel Levinson's well-known work on adult development is based on a small sample of all men. Yet, the purpose of his study was to create an overarching conception of development that would encompass the biological, psychological, and social factors that influence adult development. Carol Gilligan, in her work on women's development, found that many well-known theories and ideas about adult development were based on studies of men. She found clear examples of sexual stereotypes that emphasized either love or work. Expressive capacities are assigned to women, whereas instrumental abilities are assigned to men.

What, if any, are the differences between women and men when they reach midlife? Apter (1995) believes that women experience a crisis at midlife that is a normal part of their developmental growth, whereas for men, the midlife crisis is relevant to only a minority of them. Although women must suffer through some doubt

and despair, a hope of new development sustains them. Apter (1995, p. 23) explains it this way: "When women are freed of the supposition that someone else has the answer, when they are no longer shadowed by a need to please a parent, when they are less anxious about standing in opposition to a partner, when the fantasy of the ideal of who they should be is shattered by the mature reflection in the mirror, they grow strong enough to listen to their own answers to the questions they pose." Therefore, even though there is a crisis, women become empowered to come up with their own answers. This newfound energy and self-assertion is what Apter refers to as the "secret path that women achieve at midlife."

A major difference between men and women is that men are often focused on their one primary role—whether it be worker, father, or lover—in midlife. They often find a new sense of relaxation about life, more expressiveness, and a general enjoyment of the fruits of their labor. In contrast, women's roles in midlife are characterized by their multiple roles—mother, wife, daughter, worker. Bateson (1990) refers to how women "compose a life" as they develop different themes. These themes result in more change over the life course in comparison with men. They move from their crisis to liberation and newfound energy as they confront a critical question: "Why did it take me so long to trust myself?" (Apter, 1995, p. 27).

To answer this question, women must do a lot of "midlife reconstruction." Men, on the other hand, appear not to have this need for the integration among the various parts of their selves. Their needs are less likely to conflict (Apter, 1995), whereas women must address conflicting needs—for example, pleasing self versus pleasing others and private time versus development of outside relationships.

From a more theoretical perspective, women at midlife may be dealing with role strain and role conflict. Since women are searching for greater integration, this is likely to reflect attempts to adapt to each role and to the many segments of each social circle subscribed to that role. Indeed, women are often committed to four major roles: wife, homemaker, mother, and employee. In addition, women must relate to other roles—such as daughter, daughter-in-law, neighbor, and friend—which can lead to role conflict (Bernard, 1975, 1981). Lopata and Barnewolt (1984) believe that women at midlife

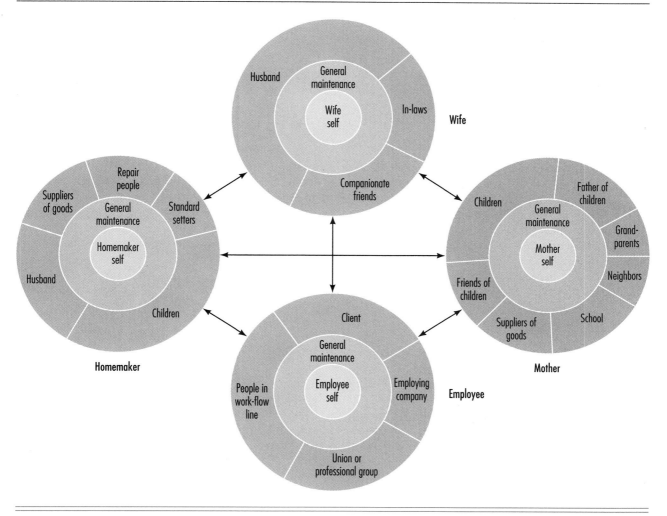

FIGURE 11.2   The four major social roles of women   Source: Lopata & Barnewolt, 1984.

must adapt to many conflicting social-role commitments. However, for many men and women, by midlife they are relinquishing the role of parents, and as the major duties of parenting decline, men and women are freer to break out of traditional sex roles. Figure 11.2 presents the four major social roles of women in American society.

Although many similarities exist between middle adult men and women of different ethnicities, there are some distinctions that can have important implications. For example, Spurlock (1984) discusses some of the similarities and differences between African American men and women and white men and women at midlife. For instance, she notes that because African Americans are more likely than whites to come from backgrounds of poverty, African Americans are more likely to age quickly and to be vulnerable to disorders related to poverty. Among all African Americans across lower- and upper-income classes, hypertension is a common disorder in the middle adult years.

The fate of African American men also has an impact on African American women. Because African American men are more likely to suffer from poor health, African American women are more likely than white women to face midlife as widows. Furthermore, African American women have fewer opportunities for remarriage when compared with their white counterparts. These factors, combined with others, means that many African American women are single.

Some additional differences are that for many African American women, midlife is a period of mothering—for her grandchildren or other children related to the extended family. Perhaps most significant is the fact that the "overwhelming majority of black women arrive at and live through the middle years burdened by economic problems" (Spurlock, 1984, p. 255). This is aptly summarized by poet Langston Hughes's (1970) statement that life "ain't no crystal stair."

Social Hazards

Employment is an important aspect of most adults' meaningful participation in life. Therefore, when adults become jobless, it can have significant physical, psychological, and social consequences. The individual's sense of worth and hope about the future declines. For men, employment has a strong cultural significance—this is how a man cares for his family. Loss of a job can be embarrassing and socially uncomfortable, especially given this country's emphasis on productivity. Joblessness can stimulate feelings of anger, guilt, and shame (Newman & Newman, 1995). African Americans and Hispanic/Latino Americans are more likely to experience unemployment—often chronic unemployment—when compared with white Americans.

The impact of joblessness affects the entire community. For example, one study (Janosik, 1986) found that a 1% increase in unemployment resulted in the following consequences for the community: 5% more suicides, 3–4% increase in hospitalizations for mental illness, 4–6% increase in homicides, 6–7% increase in prison incarcerations, and a 2% increase in the overall death rate. Braginsky and Braginsky (1975) conducted research that compared white-collar men who became unemployed with employed white-collar men. The results revealed the psychological impact of unemployment. The men felt unwanted and insignificant, lacking a role in society.

Many of the men harbored feelings of anger and bitterness. They felt isolated and looked down upon by their friends. Particularly revealing was the finding that even after becoming reemployed they continued to suffer from feelings of low self-esteem.

The impact of joblessness is not felt just by the unemployed individual. If a family is involved, members face problems of increased conflict, loss of morale, violence, feelings of deprivation, and loss of roles (Schuster & Ashburn, 1992). The family's ability to cope with adversity is tested. Children can also be affected because they may no longer have the money to participate in special events or buy new clothes. Children may become depressed at their situation or angry toward their parents for not being able to provide them with certain necessities.

Homelessness

Imagine what it would be like to be homeless—no permanent place to call home. For many people, "home" is a makeshift structure in a washout in the desert, a county jail cell, or even a storm drain. Yet, every night as many as 600,000 people are without a home and end up sleeping wherever they can—often in public parks, bus stops, homeless shelters, or just in the street (Task Force on Homelessness and Severe Mental Illness, 1992). According to U.S. Census Bureau statistics in 1990, there are an estimated 3 million homeless people in this country.

Who are the homeless? The homeless are a diverse group of men and women that includes youth, single men and women, families, adults with mental illness, and older adults. More specifically, they are often disabled or chronically sick individuals without support for housing, older persons on fixed incomes who have no family support, Vietnam veterans who have not adjusted to society, documented and undocumented immigrants, ex-prisoners without support for their return to society, and unemployed persons without adequate income (Peterson, 1993). According to studies conducted in homeless shelters, the majority of the homeless population is white, although African Americans and Hispanic/Latino Americans are overrepresented. Indeed, homeless people no longer fit the stereotype of the middle-aged alcoholic male; instead they are a heterogenous group (Connell, 1987). In fact, due in part to a poor economy over the last several years, families are the fastest-growing group among the homeless.

The problem of homelessness has grown in recent years. A wide range of people can become homeless; common reasons for homelessness include loss of job, lack of family support, avoidance of violence, substance abuse, and mental illness.

What factors contribute to homelessness? The reasons for homelessness are as diverse as the homeless population. In general, homeless people get to that state after a long series of crises, poor decision making, and missed opportunities (Bassuk, 1991). Common factors related to homelessness include lack of employment opportunities, need to flee from violence, lack of family support, substance abuse, and mental illness.

Mental illness among the homeless is a serious problem in this country. Many people with mental illness have become homeless through failures in the mental health care system, the disabling effects of their mental illness that have gone untreated, the combined influence of substance abuse and mental illness, and the inability of many people with mental illness to set realis-tic life goals. Also relevant is a loss of adequate income and diminished social supports. Many of the current problems of this segment of the homeless population are related to the effects of deinstitutionalization. When people with mental illness were categorically released from hospitals and care facilities, they were not provided adequate community support programs. E. F. Torrey (1988) has studied mental illness for years, and he describes many of the problems of deinstitutionalization:

- There are twice as many people living on streets and in shelters as there are in public psychiatric hospitals.
- There are increasing numbers of people with serious mental illness in the nation's jails and prisons.
- People with serious mental illness are regularly released from hospitals with little or no provision for aftercare or follow-up treatment.
- Violent acts perpetrated by people with untreated mental illness are increasing.
- Housing and living conditions for people with mental illness in the community are grossly inadequate.
- Community mental health centers, originally funded to provide community care so people with mental illness would no longer have to go to state psychiatric hospitals, are almost complete failures.
- Laws designed to protect the rights of people with serious mental illness primarily protect their right to remain ill.
- The majority of the people with mental illness who were discharged from hospitals have been officially "lost."

Predictors and Prevention in Inner-City Homeless Individuals

Between 1984 and 1986, a study funded by the National Institute of Mental Health (NIMH) engaged almost 400 homeless people in inner-city Los Angeles in extensive individual interviews (Koegel, 1989). Using this sample as representative of the skid row homeless population, researchers sought to gain insight into these individuals' experiences and characteristics, to learn the incidence of specific psychiatric disorders in this population, and to discover differences between homeless individuals with chronic mental illness and those who do not have mental illness.

Data from this study suggest that mental illness is more prevalent in the inner-city homeless population than in the greater Los Angeles community. About 28% of the targeted population suffered from "severe and chronic major mental illness," such as schizophrenia or bipolar disorder (Koegel, 1989, p. 16). Nearly half of these individuals were also chronic substance abusers. In addition, 34% of the population abused substances but did not have a major mental illness. This finding suggests an overall chronic substance abuse rate of 46%. Individuals who abused substances and/or had chronic mental illness were homeless more often and for longer duration than those without either condition.

Yet substance abuse and mental illness should not be isolated as solely responsible for homelessness. Urban demographics contribute as well: As the number of both employed and unemployed poor is increasing, the availability of low-income housing is decreasing. Poverty and the lack of affordable housing cause homelessness; mental illness and substance abuse increase vulnerability to homelessness.

This complex interaction of factors leading to homelessness suggests that effective intervention must take a comprehensive approach to helping this population. Mental health programs should take preventive steps on behalf of vulnerable individuals. In addition, attention must be given to the broader social issues that affect this population, such as social welfare and affordable housing. Effective outreach is critical to helping vulnerable populations. Focus on Gender describes the need for outreach programs for women at risk for AIDS.

FOCUS ON GENDER

Women at Risk for AIDS— Is There Hope?

"AIDS will become one of the four leading killers of women," reports Judith Cohen, an epidemiologist at the University of California, San Francisco. It is already the number one killer of African American women in New York and New Jersey. Cohen notes that over 70% of women with AIDS are African American or Hispanic/

Latino American. With experts suggesting that the number of female AIDS deaths is around 14,000, it is clear that programs intended to prevent AIDS in at-risk female populations need to be aggressive in their efforts.

Three years ago, the National AIDS Demonstration Research (NADR) program was launched with this aggressive outreach agenda in mind. With 63 sites in the continental United States and Puerto Rico, the program by last June had formally interviewed 8000 women. At least 40,000 at-risk women were contacted and often received some form of prevention services.

The best strategies for AIDS outreach include actively seeking these women out and addressing in some depth all the other issues that are affecting their lives. This outreach may involve services such as rape counseling, legal advocacy, or assistance with parenting issues. Another crucial element of the AIDS prevention program is a focus on empowering women as individuals, building self-esteem and other inner resources that will help the women initiate and sustain changes in their lifestyle. External resources, such as day care and other community support mechanisms, can also be cultivated to help women maintain these changes and reduce their risk for AIDS.

A six-month progress report on the NADR program showed significant decreases in overall drug injection frequency and in the frequency with which users shared injection equipment. The percentage of women who always use new needles doubled, and in the remaining women, incidence of needle-cleaning rose. Changes in sexual behaviors were also noted but were not as remarkable as the transformation in drug-related practices. With such positive results after only six months, it is clear that barriers to reaching this at-risk population are not insurmountable.

Source: Written by Julianne Azimov, based on Frelberg, 1990.

Implications for Practice: Adapting to Midlife

The experience of reaching midlife affects individuals in different ways, depending on their expectations and their own life experiences. Some may greet the approach of their later years with anxiety and dread as in the following quote from Apter (1995, p. 51): "From the very beginning of my awareness that this person who was 'me' would grow older, the prospect brought no eagerness, only dread. At some prehistory of the self, as I was attempting to adapt to a grotesquely conceived future, I plotted my escape from aging. The simple solution I came to was that when I discovered my first grey hair, I would pull it out and then kill myself. I imagined how I would lie, on the carpet of my childhood bedroom where this chill thought found me. I would be discov- ered, dead, before anyone could disclose the evil secret of my maturity."

Yet for others, for most, the prospect of maturity brings renewal and opportunity—not a last chance, but a continuing chance to develop and grow, to leave their mark in the world. In many instances, the old saying holds true: "Life begins at forty." As people's longevity increases, expectations of their productivity also increase, and they do more and demand more from midlife.

APPLYING THE FRAMEWORK

Alcoholism in Middle Age

Lee Park is a 54-year-old man who has an alcohol addiction. He began treatment at the Harborview Medical Center after his wife and children worked with a substance-abuse counselor who coached them in how to perform an "intervention" on Lee. The "intervention" consisted of a meeting between Lee, his wife, and their two children, in which they expressed to him their concern about his drinking and the negative consequences it had for them. Each family member spoke frankly about their fears and anxieties over Lee's drinking behavior. They gave carefully constructed examples of when he had acted inappropriately because of his drinking. They also pressured Lee to seek immediate treatment, and he agreed to go with them to the Harborview Medical Center that specializes in alcoholism treatment.

Developmental Considerations

Lee began drinking socially as a young adult. He enjoyed entertaining and being in the company of others. His social drinking continued and slowly, over time, grew to become more and more serious. Lee has also experienced bouts of depression. He becomes very withdrawn and loses all motivation for work. He becomes irritable and often does not get enough sleep during the night, and then he feels drowsy during the day.

Lee describes an eventful history that seems to have preceded his move into a serious drinking problem. Throughout his career, Lee had been loyal to one company and performed adequately as an electrical engineer. Slowly his job performance deteriorated, and although Lee still adequately conducted his job, his employer was unhappy with his results. Eventually Lee was "let go" from his job, and at 54 years of age, he did not have an easy time seeking new employment. Lee became unemployed for over one year. At that time, he desperately searched for a new position; however, it seemed that employers were only interested in hiring younger workers. Lee's frustration at not being able to find work led to an increase in his rate of drinking. Drinking became a way for him to calm his anxieties and move from very unpleasant feelings of worry and concern to more pleasant feelings associated with the drinking. Lee was able to successfully start a small business and it has been going well, although Lee reports feeling extremely nervous about his potential for continued success.

Biophysical Considerations

Lee's alcoholism has developed into a physical dependence. His abstinence from alcohol in the *(continued)*

Alcoholism in Middle Age

(continued)   hospital led to alcohol withdrawal, suggesting physical tolerance. He was observed to have coarse tremors of the hands. Family members report the presence of chemically induced alcoholic blackouts. Additional symptoms included insomnia and daytime drowsiness, increased psychomotor activity, and increased blood pressure.

Lee has been drinking for almost 30 years. He began drinking in his twenties, and it has gotten steadily more frequent and more intense. He drinks every day but most heavily on weekends. Lee primarily drinks Scotch but also consumes beer. He estimated his drinking to be about "a pint of scotch" a day.

In spite of a long history of drinking, Lee's general health was rated satisfactory by the physician. He has a tendency toward high blood pressure, but the doctor does not consider it to be a medical concern at this time. Lee is 25 pounds overweight, due primarily to a lack of exercise and excess calories obtained from drinking. All other indications suggest Lee does not have any other physical concerns.

Psychological Considerations

Cognitive Development and Information Processing

Lee is a college graduate with a B.A. degree in engineering. He presents himself as someone who has the capacity for good intellectual functioning. However, this is difficult to assess at times due to his lack of motivation and flat affect. In discussing his current work situation, Lee is able to articulate difficult business decisions he is grappling with. Moreover, he displays reasonable problem-solving abilities in relation to the tasks he is currently working on. For example, he recognizes that one of his difficulties is retaining good employees and keeping them motivated to work. Because he is feeling unmotivated, he is concerned about how his employees may be reacting to his lack of motivation. He has described several ideas for how to address this problem. In general, Lee's judgment about work issues shows careful consideration of consequences and forethought about the implications of his actions.

When discussing more personal issues, Lee appears to have difficulties with cognitive flexibility. In particular, he displays thinking styles characteristic of a depressed person. For example, when asked about how he could reach out to establish some new relationships with other men, he could think of no alternatives. And when asked about past relationships, he exclaimed, "I should have friends but no one really feels close to me." Such thoughts show minimization and all-or-nothing thinking patterns.

Communication

Lee has serious communication difficulties, particularly in the context of his family. He is reserved and has a timid, unassertive personality style. In family sessions, he often turns to his wife to let her speak for him. His wife describes frustrating attempts to simply "talk to Lee about what is going on with him." He recognizes this and describes difficulties in "expressing my thoughts to my wife and children." Because the children have recently moved out on their own, Lee and his wife are readjusting to more time by themselves and with each other. Lee's wife wants him to become more involved with social activities and is motivated to push him to confront his drinking problem so "they can return to a normal life."

Attitudes and Emotions

Although alcohol drinking has been consistent since young adulthood, it became more frequent and more intense after Lee lost his employment. This loss was significant for Lee, as he felt he no longer had a significant role in his family. He reports feeling guilty about not

Alcoholism in Middle Age

being able to provide for the family. Lee reported a general sense of failure and hopelessness about the future following his employment loss. Although he now has a financially stable business, he reports feeling anxious and nervous about his future. Lee complains often of "low energy" and believes he is depressed much of the time. He states, "I do not have anything to look forward to." Lee is also beginning to wonder what the meaning of his life has been. He describes much of his life to date as "a failure." When asked what he would like to accomplish, he responded, "I don't feel I have anything I can accomplish or look forward to."

Social Cognition and Regulation

Lee's sense of self, or self-concept, is quite negative. He is focused on his limitations and inadequacies and has a great deal of difficulty when asked to discuss any positive attributes. This is probably related to his depression as described above.

Lee is beginning to accept the notion that he has a drinking problem. In the past when confronted with concerns about his drinking, he immediately expressed denial of any problems. In the last five years, his wife has been increasingly concerned and confrontive about his drinking. About one year ago, Lee had an alcohol-related accident where, fortunately, no one was hurt. At one point, his wife challenged him to quit for three months to prove that he did not have a drinking problem. Lee was unable to meet the challenge. Also, family members, especially after working with a counselor, became better at letting Lee experience the consequences of his drinking behavior rather than covering up for him and assuming caretaking and enabling roles for him. Lee does acknowledge that his drinking is "a problem for other people in my family."

Lee does express much concern over "what he has left in his life." He appears concerned that family members and others perceive him as having made an impor-

tant contribution. With regard to this issue, he expresses intense dissatisfaction: "I want others to feel I have done right by them and I should get my act together for the benefit of others." He can express his frustration over wanting to "get more out of life," and it appears he is consistently thoughtful about what he wants to achieve in the future.

Social Considerations

Family

Lee has been married for 30 years and feels his marriage is one of convenience. He gets along with his wife, but she "isn't able to really understand my problems or help me." Although he presents the marriage in a negative light, he is observed to be caring and concerned with discussing his problems with his wife. She has been putting increasing pressure on Lee, which has resulted in an increasing conflict between them. She stated, "I told Lee I was tired of this and I did not want to live under these circumstances."

Lee's relationship with his children has also become increasingly strained. The children and his wife have been more confrontive, and this may explain the increase in family conflict. Lee believes the children should "stay out of this" and does not want them to be involved in his treatment. He appears embarrassed to admit that he has a problem and needs help. The children report feeling "cut off" from their father and "do not know how to separate who he is from his drinking problem."

Lee's parents live far away, and he has not been very involved with them in the past even though he is an only child. However, recently his father had a heart attack and he went to visit them. When he returned, he was "shocked" to see how old they were getting and realized that they may need help in the next several *(continued)*

Alcoholism in Middle Age

(continued)   years. He has felt additional stress from feeling this is not an additional burden he can take on right now.

Social Support

Lee's greatest social support is from his family. His wife and children are concerned about his behavior and are motivated to help him quit drinking. And even though he describes his relationships as strained, they are what he appears to care the most about. Lee has a strong sense of social responsibility toward his family, and he wants them to see him as a competent and effective husband and father.

Outside of his family, Lee has one business friend that he spends a lot of time with. He describes this person as his only friend. His wife has encouraged him to attend AA meetings in the past, and within the last six months, he did attend AA meetings for about a month. He quit going, complaining that they were too religious and that the people there were "too screwed up to be of any help to me."

Multicultural and Gender Considerations

Lee comes from a family that has always been accepting and open toward drinking. He can remember drinking with his family of origin when he was only 17 years old. Both of his parents drank alcohol, but he says neither of them had a drinking problem.

Lee also comes from a middle-class family that values success through hard work. It is difficult to determine exactly when Lee's drinking became serious enough to constitute alcoholism. However, his loss of employment was very significant in his life, and he describes his most serious problems as having begun when he lost his job. For Lee, work gave him an acceptable role to play in his family and helped him feel he was making a contribution to society. When he lost that ability, he was not able to cope effectively and turned to alcohol for relief.

Summary and Impressions

Lee is experiencing the following problems:

1. He has an alcohol addiction.
2. He has mild to moderate denial regarding the negative aspects of his alcohol use.
3. He is experiencing clinical depression.
4. He has serious self-doubts concerning his self-worth and experiences worry and anxiety over his future.
5. He needs to reestablish his relationship with his wife and children.
6. He has difficulty expressing himself and being assertive.

Lee is a high-functioning midlife male who has an alcohol addiction and is experiencing depression. It is difficult to assess the relationship between his feeling depressed and his drinking. He may have developed a serious drinking problem in his effort to use alcohol to cope with his depressive feelings. Lee's family is experiencing many concerns related to Lee's drinking and is actively involved in his treatment. They can offer him needed support and reassurance throughout his recovery. Although Lee has entered Harborview Medical Center for his alcoholism, he is still experiencing denial in relation to his alcohol use.

Exacerbating his problems are concerns that Lee has regarding his future and worries about his ability to succeed in life. He is increasingly concerned about his contribution in life. Lee's difficulties in communication and assertiveness make it difficult for him to make his needs known. Lee has some important strengths that will help his prognosis for treatment. He is an intellectually competent man with a successful business. His family is supportive and involved in his treatment. He is making progress on his denial and has agreed to a first step of seeking inpatient treatment.

Chapter Summary

Developmental Themes

Middle adulthood is different from other life stages because it is less affected by biological maturation and most affected by adults' own experiences. Such experiences represent great diversity in middle adulthood, although for many adults this life stage involves launching children and focusing on career development. At midlife, many adults develop a new perspective about who they are as they reflect on their past years.

Biophysical Dimension

Biophysical Growth and Development

The leading causes of death during middle age are cancer and heart disease. Stress, however, can have an influence on one's health, particularly if the person has a Type A personality. In middle age, women experience menopause. For some women this can lead to physical and psychological changes. These women may benefit from estrogen replacement therapy. Physical changes also lead to changes in the sexual response cycle.

Biophysical Hazards

During middle age, breast cancer becomes a significant concern for women.

Psychological Dimension

Cognitive Development and Information Processing

Intellectual functioning is stable in middle age. Adult intelligence is more related to adults performing role-related tasks. Professional obsolescence may become relevant during this life stage.

Communication

Communication patterns often change as adults reconnect with their partner or spouse. As adults move closer to doing a "life review," they reassess their communication with others. For some, this leads to engaging in the process of forgiveness. Many adults must adjust to the fact that they are functionally illiterate. Others must adapt as a non-English-speaking person.

Attitudes and Emotions

Midlife may bring about a midlife identity change, which requires a renewal and reintegration of one's identity. Although midlife does not necessarily result in a midlife crisis, midlife usually involves a period of reflection.

Social Cognition and Regulation

Midlife represents an increased opportunity to become involved in socially responsible activities. There is a stronger sense of one's obligation to society.

Psychological Hazards

One critical psychological hazard is the development of an alcohol or drug addiction. The 12-step program is a self-help method of treatment for alcohol and drug dependence. The notion of codependency has become popular in recent years. It is helpful to know when individuals should seek professional help.

Social Dimension

Families, Groups, Support Systems, and Contexts

Many middle-aged adults join blended or stepfamilies. Individuals in stepfamilies face significant change as they adapt to many new aspects of the family. Marital relationships can be positively affected as children leave the home and marriage partners develop more companionate love. However, as adults reflect on their lives, many seek new experiences that can sometimes lead to extramarital affairs. The relationship between middle-aged parents and their children changes as the children grow older. The adolescent years, when parents' general well-being decreases, can be especially difficult. As the children become adults, most families experience improvements in their relationships with one another. Middle-aged parents must also begin the process of caring for their aging parents. Many adults, particularly women, do a significant amount of caregiving for their elderly parents. Many caregivers are unprepared for this role. At the same time, many parents of adult children become grandparents. The experience of grandparenting can offer new roles and may be helpful in adapting to the aging process. The men's movement has provided new alternatives for how men see their roles and responsibilities. For many men, it has provided a new type of masculine identity. Male and female stereotypes of men can influence their use of social and psychological treatment. There is a growing sense of satisfaction as one grows older. An individual's career or work gives direction to one's overall lifestyle and identity. Career changes at midlife are not as common as often thought. One's work or career can lead to different pathways for men and women. Men are often stepping back from their work, whereas women may be investing time in a new job or returning to school.

Multicultural and Gender Considerations

Gender differences may be pronounced in middle adulthood. Many of the original theories of adult development were based exclusively on men. Men often focus on one primary role, whereas women often juggle multiple roles. These multiple roles may lead women to search for a sense of integration in midlife. People also may find that their ethnic identity provides a sense of support as they get older.

Social Hazards

Adults can face significant hazards during midlife. Joblessness can take a strong social and psychological toll. Often, joblessness results in homelessness. Although the homeless are a diverse group, many homeless adults have mental illness and face difficult adjustments in the community.

KEY TERMS

alcoholism
blended family/stepfamily
caregiving career
cynical hostility
de-illusionment
delirium tremens (DTs)
displaced homemakers
endorphins

estrogen replacement therapy (ERT)
functionally literate
hot flash
illiterate
interrupted career
menopause
osteoporosis
professional half-life

professional obsolescence
refractory period
sexual response cycle
socioeconomic status
Type A personality
Type B personality

12

Late Adulthood

Shirley Patterson

Developmental Themes

A social worker was speaking at a weekly social meeting of a senior citizens' group. All the participants were at least 70 years old. The subject of the talk was the needs of older adults. To begin his presentation, the social worker asked how many people present considered themselves "older adults." No one raised their hand.

The years from age 60 until death are considered late adulthood. Erikson termed this stage "old age," with the developmental task being to experience integrity or despair. People in their later years tend to reflect on their lives and their accomplishments. If they believe their life has been meaningful and rewarding, they experience satisfaction that their life has been worthwhile and develop integrity. If, however, they are disappointed because of missed opportunities and unresolved crises, they may regret what they have done with their lives and fall into despair.

But what exactly is "old age"? The answer to this question is becoming increasingly difficult for the simple reason that people are living longer. "Old" keeps getting older. These days, 70-year-olds may not consider themselves old. And the stage of "old age" keeps lasting longer. With increased life expectancy, it is not uncommon for individuals to live nearly a third of their lives in the arena of late adulthood. In the future, it may not be that uncommon for some individuals to spend almost half their lives in this span of development.

Many believe that Erikson's stages compress too many years into this life stage. For instance, Erikson's (1963) first six stages of psychosocial development cover a span of 34 years, whereas the other two stages, middle adulthood to old age, range from 35 years of age to death. Newman and Newman (1987) have revised Erikson's stages and have included two developmental descriptors for older persons: late adulthood (ages 60 to 75) and very old age (75 until death). Other theorists have divided the developmental stages into two to four subperiods, including the young-old, middle-old, old-old, and very old (Botwinick, 1984; Charness & Bosman, 1992; Neugarten, 1974).

Adding to the problem of defining the stage of late adulthood is the fact that when people live longer, they have more opportunities to develop differently. According to some theorists (Bornstein, 1992; Germain, 1991; Neu-

This older person is alert and vitally involved in life, enjoying new experiences while reflecting on past events.

garten, 1969), the amalgamation of a lifetime of forces (intrinsic and extrinsic) influences the development of people such that the longer they live, the more diverse they become. Hartford (1985) put it succinctly when she argued:

> There is a tendency to lump this entire age period into one set of characteristics called "old age." For no other age span have the social or behavioral sciences done this. Infancy, early childhood, later childhood, adolescence, young adulthood, middle age each cover a shorter period of time ranging from 3 or 4 years to a decade. The physiological changes, psychological changes, social experiences and personal characteristics of people beyond early 60's are as dramatic in 5 to 10 year age spans as they are earlier in life. (p. 45)

As a result of these factors (e.g., longevity and diversity), there is significant difficulty in distinguishing the developmental tasks of particular subperiods in late adulthood. An 80-year-old with a hearty genetic inheritance who has maintained a healthy lifestyle may still be gainfully employed. This individual has not had to confront changes related to age in his or her work role and status. On the other hand, a 65-year-old with a debilitating terminal illness has had to confront such losses as the work role, good health, changes in body image, and the immediacy of mortality. Although it is difficult to delineate the characteristics of older people in different subperiods of late adulthood, it is possible to suggest general characteristics for each subperiod (see Table 12.1). Practitioners, however, must look beyond these general characteristics and explore and identify the nuances of this population's diversity.

With the problem of late adulthood being such a lengthy stage with such divergent individuals, how can the tasks of this stage of life be defined? Butler, Lewis,

and Sunderland (1991) have observed that older people have some special characteristics "connected with the unique sense of having lived a long time and having accepted the concept of life as a cycle from birth through death" (p. 79). According to the authors, these characteristics include the following:

• A desire to leave a legacy through children, grandchildren, work, art, memories, possessions. The notion of "legacy" provides a sense of continuity with future generations.
• The "elder" function, which is closely associated with the notion of legacy in that older people have a predilection for sharing a wealth of accumulated knowledge, experience, and wisdom with the young.
• Attachment to familiar objects means an increasing emotional investment in familiar household objects, heirlooms, keepsakes, photo albums, and letters. Attach-

TABLE 12.1 General Characteristics of Older Adults by Subperiod

Subperiod	Characteristics
Young-old (65–74)	Many may still be employed full- or part-time because of the extension of mandatory retirement age or personal wishes to work; other, more affluent individuals may be retired and pursuing long-term interests and activities; the phenomenon of women outliving their spouses begins to emerge; the young-old typically remain active in the community and maintain strong ties with families and friends; some may increase their recreation, adult education, and voluntary activities. Retirement often means the beginning of facing a series of losses, including status and income, with resulting decrease in activities that are costly. Loss through death of mates, friends, family members, and co-workers becomes more frequent. Chronic illness may develop and/or become more debilitating and depression is not uncommon. This age group may assume or continue the assumption of the caregiver role to an elderly relative. Most individuals in this age group maintain a good capacity to cope and use their talents productively.
Middle-old (75–84)	More in this age group experience chronic disease (arthritis, cardiovascular, respiratory, circulatory); added stresses through death of mates (an even greater number of males die), friends, relatives, and adult children. Generally, people in this age cohort tend to experience more physiological changes in terms of impairments in vision or hearing; problems with balance that may lead to loss of mobility (e.g., walking, driving); slowing of response time and judgment of spatial relationships. These factors, combined with accrued losses, often have negative impacts on older adults with respect to a more constricted life space and may result in withdrawal, depression, disorientation, and pseudo-dementia. Growing numbers of people in this age range, however, continue to manage well and contribute to the arts, literature, science, and politics. They are socially and physically active, in better health, better educated, and better able to function independently. Because of the noticeably different rates of change of individuals in this age group, they are even more diverse from one another than are the young-old.
Old-old (85+)	Although the 85+ age group is the fastest-growing population of any age group, they represented only 3.4 million of the 32.8 million elderly in 1993. A predominant number of this group is dependent, frail, and experiencing more disabilities and chronic illnesses. Social isolation tends to become greater for this cohort because they have more physical decrements and are more vulnerable to accidents, disabling diseases, and environmental impacts. Mobility becomes even more limited, and very few are employed, though some work independently or use their creative capacities for fulfillment. Mental disorders increase with age—a small proportion (5 to 7% of the total population and up to 20% of the 85+ group) of elderly show evidence of brain disorders or some form of dementia. Those elderly who have survived well continue to maintain daily routines, and live independently or with families, although the ratio of women to men (256:100) is much greater.

Source: Based on Hartford, 1985.

ments to pets are characteristic particularly of old-old people and engender a sense of continuity, assist the memory, and provide both comfort and security.

• Change in the sense of time indicates that although middle-aged adults may be concerned with time running out, older adults tend to live in the present and experience a sense of time as "now" with children, friends, nature, and closeness (physical and emotional).

• Creativity, curiosity, and surprise suggest that with continued good health and adequate social and environmental supports, many older people retain a curiosity about life and all living things, and some develop or discover creative abilities. The adaptive qualities of curiosity, creativity, and surprise are likely to reflect lifelong personality traits that add richness to old age.

• A sense of consummation or fulfillment in life are those qualities of "serenity" and "wisdom" that emanate from a sense of having resolved one's personal conflicts and viewing one's life in a historical context that is generally positive and gratifying.

From these brief summaries, it is evident that chronological age has little to do with one's ability to survive, persevere, and achieve fulfillment in life. In fact, even through adversity, some persevere and make significant contributions to others. Take, for example, Esther E. Twente, a little-known social worker and educator from the rural Midwest. Beset with serious vision, hearing, and arthritic problems, Twente, between her mid-sixties and mid-seventies, was engaged in the following activities: directed a two-year Ford Foundation Project, one of seven funded across the United States; was coinvestigator of two sequential three-year research projects funded by the National Institute of Mental Health (NIMH); and published her first book, *Never Too Old* (1970), at age 75. Until six weeks before her death at age 76 from metastatic cancer, Twente continued to work on one of the NIMH research projects. Although Esther E. Twente is not a household name—even within her own profession of social work—she left a significant legacy to all who follow after her and to students and to colleagues who knew her. This legacy, among other things, includes contributions to the knowledge base of the "strengths perspective" in social work, particularly as this concept relates to older people. Twente was not a prolific writer, but she had a way of capturing the essence of ideas through her remarkable powers of personal observation.

Many older people have creative capacities. The re-

Esther Twente was a pioneer social work practitioner and educator who focused her writing on the capacities and potential of older people. *Never Too Old,* Twente's only book, was published when she was 75 years old, one year before her death.

peated evidence may even lead one to speculate that the creative urge may possibly become stronger as life draws to a close—like the push for life in the old apple tree that produces an especially bountiful crop just before its death. The farmer remarks, "It overworked itself." But perhaps it was just trying to satisfy that final big desire (Twente, 1965, p. 106). The following Focus on Narrative section, written by Esther Twente, is an example of the strengths perspective.

FOCUS ON NARRATIVE

Apple Trees, Strength, and Creativity

It was a cold, snowy day in January when I first met Mrs. Stanley. I was visiting old people because I thought they might be lonely. Mrs. Stanley is a 90-year-old widow. Her husband was a farmer, but like many others during the Depression, the Stanleys lost their land. They moved to a small town. Then Mr. Stanley died.

When I arrived, Mrs. Stanley was lying down. Her voice was weak. She was suffering from shingles in her face and she complained of dysentery. She was unhappy, neither the world nor anyone in it seemed to please her. After a while I said, "I hear you have a green thumb."

With that a great change came over her. Her expression brightened. Her voice became stronger. She told me of her interest in plants, her rare bulbs, the flowers she had furnished for three weddings, and her hopes for a garden for the coming summer. Then she said, "I have other interests."

"I am sure you have," I replied, for by now I sensed the creative capacity of the old lady.

She got up, spry and enthusiastic, and showed me her collection of vases. Then she said, "Would you like to see my embroidery?"

Of course I would. And there it was, drawers-full. Many of the designs were of her own making, and every piece was carefully done.

I have kept in touch with Mrs. Stanley. We have discussed international relations and the John Birch Society. I have seen her during the summer pulling weeds and tenderly touching one flower after another. She wrote letters to me telling me when this lily was in bloom and that rose was about to open. Her granddaughter and I took pictures of her garden. In the fall slides of her flowers were shown at a meeting of a newly organized group of older people. Proudly she told about each plant.

Spring is here again. The wind is still cold but Mrs. Stanley is in her garden carefully planting her bulbs. "I like the fresh air," she says.

Source: Twente, 1965, pp. 107–108.

Biophysical Dimension

Biophysical Growth and Development

Given successful treatment of illnesses and accidents, the potential life span of the human species could extend to 120 years of age (Schaie & Willis, 1986). Al-though **life span** represents the upper limit of human life, **life expectancy** refers to the number of years the average person may live who was born in a particular year (Santrock, 1995; Schaie & Willis, 1986). Moreover, due to such factors as healthier lifestyles, better nutrition, decreased mortality rates, and technological advances in medicine, life expectancy has increased significantly in the last several decades. Data drawn from the U.S. Bureau of the Census, the American Association of Retired Persons (AARP), and the Administration on Aging (AOA) (1994) indicate the following:

- People who reached age 65 in 1992 had an average life expectancy of an additional 17.5 years—19.1 years for females and 15.5 years for males.
- In 1993, the 65-and-older population numbered 32.8 million and represented 12.7% of the population in the United States.
- In 1993, approximately 1 in every 8 Americans were 65 and older.
- Because women tend to outlive men, the sex ratio of women to men increases with age, ranging from 122:100 at 65–69 to 256:100 after 85.
- It is estimated that by 2030 the older population will have grown to 70.2 million, nearly twice their number in 1993 and representing 20% of the total population.
- Between 2010 and 2030, the most rapid increase in population is expected when a generation of "baby boomers" reach age 65.
- By 2030, minority groups are projected to represent 25% of the older population, nearly double the percentage (13) in 1990. In fact, the total minority population will grow at a much faster rate than the white non-Hispanic population 65 and over (see Table 12.2).

There is as much variation among older people in the physical changes that occur with age as there is with their developmental tasks generally. Miller (1992) postulates that certain conclusions can be drawn from several biological theories of aging:

1. Biological aging occurs in all living organisms.
2. Biological aging is natural, inevitable, irreversible, and progressive with time.
3. The course of aging varies from individual to individual.
4. The rate of aging for different organs and tissues varies among individuals.

TABLE 12.2   Projected Rate of Growth of Ethnic Older People (65+) Between 1990 and 2030

Ethnic Older People	Percent
White non-Hispanic	93
Hispanic	555
Non-Hispanic Blacks	160
American Indians, Eskimos, Aleuts	231
Asians, Pacific Islanders	693

Source: Based on AARP & AOA, 1994.

5. Biological aging is influenced by nonbiological factors.
6. Biological aging processes are different from pathological processes.
7. Biological aging increases one's vulnerability to disease. (p. 804)

Because physical change and decline varies from individual to individual, chronological age cannot be used as a marker for biophysical change. Inevitably, however, physical change does occur in the following biological systems (see Table 12.3): skeletal, muscle, brain and nervous system, sensory, circulatory, respiratory, and integumentary (skin, hair, nails).

Sexuality

Large-scale research (Kinsey, Pomeroy, & Martin, 1948; Kinsey, Pomeroy, Martin, & Gebhard, 1953; Masters & Johnson, 1966; Starr & Weiner, 1982) on sexual behavior indicates that older adults maintain not only interest in but also activity in sexual relationships in later life. Prior to the sexual revolution of the 1960s, sexuality was not a common, everyday topic of conversation. Even today, when sexuality is more freely discussed, according to Butler and colleagues (1991), both young and old are amazed that 70-, 80-, or 90-year-olds are interested in making love. Members of this society assume that

> (1) older people do not have sexual desires, (2) they could not make love even if they did want to, (3) they are too fragile physically and it might hurt them, (4) they are physically unattractive and therefore sexually undesirable, and (5) the whole notion is shameful and decidedly perverse. (p. 219)

Physiological Changes and Sexual Activity   Physiological changes affect both female and male sexual activity to some extent. Most older women in good health can expect to continue sexual activities well into late life. As discussed in the last chapter, though, many older women may be coping with the postmenopausal changes brought on by estrogen depletion, including thinning and drying of the vaginal walls. This dryness may make intercourse more difficult for them. Estrogen creams and hormone replacement therapy can help alleviate the dryness. Plus, women who remain sexually active have less of a problem.

Similar to women, older men typically are able to engage in sexual activity well into their seventies, eighties, and beyond. Unless there is physical illness or emotional difficulties, older men do not lose their facility for erection with age. Manual stimulation of the penis, however, may be required to initiate sexual activity. A decrease in the pressure to ejaculate is caused by a reduction in the volume of seminal fluid. In turn, orgasms, although still pleasurable, are experienced in a shorter one-stage period rather than in two stages as experienced in earlier life. It may take from 12 to 24 hours for older men to achieve an erection following ejaculation. If older men lose interest in sexual activities or become impotent, a number of causes can account for these conditions, including extreme fatigue, alcohol abuse, overeating, boredom, depression, and fear of an inability to perform. Erectile dysfunction may be due to such physical causes as cardiorespiratory, atherosclerotic, neurological, genitourinary, endocrine, hematological, and infectious disorders. Impotence also has been induced by such drugs as antihypertensive medication, tranquilizers, and antidepressants. Intractable physical impotence may be cured through penile implants or prosthesis. Most erectile problems, however, may be dealt with effectively through sexual therapy or through individual, couple, or group counseling (Butler et al., 1991).

Implications for Practice: The Need for Sexual Expression in Late Adulthood

The capacity for sexual expression in late adulthood has been well documented. It may diminish to some extent because of ill health, widowhood, or lack of access to suitable partners. Butler and colleagues (1991) noted

TABLE 12.3   Age-Related Changes in Biological Systems

Skeletal system	Reduction in height of 2 to 4 cm per decade due to decline of spinal discs, osteoporosis, and other age-related changes; bones become less dense due to osteoporosis—a gradual loss of bone mass (bone loss in women more accelerated due to estrogen loss); joints are more restricted, resulting in a diminished range of motion in the upper arms, lower back, hips, knees, and feet; osteoarthritis, the most common form of arthritis, affects about 30% of older persons and is considered a universal aging phenomenon; foot problems (non-disease-related) may include bunions, heel spurs, hammer toes, and calluses.
Muscle system	Lean body mass decreases with the beginning of middle age, and body fat increases in males (50%) and females (33%); power and speed of muscular contractions gradually decreases with age; incontinence due to slowed reflexes; there is a gradual decline in muscle strength and endurance, which results in muscle fatigue after briefer periods of activity or exercise.
Brain and nervous system	With age there is a loss of neurons (estimated to be between 5 and 10% until the seventies—may accelerate subsequently), the basic cellular unit of the nervous system; unless the blood supply is blocked, there may be little functional change; if, for example, there is diminished flow of blood to the brain, neurotransmitter changes, accumulations of cholesterol, etc., these changes may affect reaction time and interfere with perception and cognition.
Sensory system	Gait and balance changes may occur due to combined effects of muscular, skeletal, and neurological changes, which may result in an increase in accidents and falls; due to toughening of the skin, older people experience a decrease in tactile sensitivity and develop a higher pain threshold; there is a decline in a sense of smell due to gradual degenerative changes in olfactory cells and a decrease in a sense of taste as a result of such factors as presence of dental or systemic disease, etc.; changes in vision increase with age, often due to a reduction of the quality or intensity of light reaching the retina; very old age may be accompanied by degenerative changes in the retina, impairing one's ability to see; the ratio of legal blindness is 100:100,000 in individuals under age 21, but it increases to 1400:100,000 in individuals age 69 and above; significant hearing impairment occurs with increasing age when degenerative changes affect the compartments of the ear and the auditory nerve pathway; high-pitched sounds are not heard as well, resulting in jumbled or distorted words and sentences.
Circulatory system	Age-related changes appear to include a slight enlargement of the left ventricle of the heart and thickening of the atrial endocardium and atrial ventricular valves; changes in the arteries (an increase in collagen and calcification of elastin fibers) make the arterial walls more vulnerable to disorders that cause their hardening and thickening (e.g., the most common form of arteriosclerosis); such factors as obesity, lack of exercise, anxiety, illness, and hardening of blood vessels may cause an increase in blood pressure; with increasing age, veins become less elastic, thicker, and more dilated, causing valves in the large leg vein to become less efficient in returning blood to the heart.
Respiratory system	Between the ages of 20 and 80, lung capacity decreases 40%, even in the absence of disease; lungs lose elasticity, the chest decreases in size, and the diaphragm weakens; mouth breathing and snoring is the result of connective tissue changes that cause the nose to have a retracted septum; although air volumes are altered due to changes in the chest wall and in lung elastic recoil, total lung capacity stays essentially the same due to compensatory mechanisms.
Integumentary system	Age-related changes in the skin make the skin look paler, thinner, and irregularly pigmented; skin has diminished moisture content and less turgor, resulting in easier injury to the skin's surface; other indicators of age-related changes include wrinkling, sagging, and mostly harmless growths and lesions; nails become increasingly soft, brittle, and are likely to split; because of trauma or poor circulation, toenails may thicken; graying hair and baldness (most frequently in males) occurs with age; loss of body hair is progressively experienced by men and women in the pubic and armpit area; coarse hair, due in part to hormonal changes, may grow on the upper lip and lower face of older women and the ears, nostrils, and eyebrows of older men.

Source: Based on Miller, 1992; Santrock, 1995; Zastrow & Kirst-Ashman, 1994.

that sex, a sense of self-esteem, and the self-image are closely related. Additionally, a study by Marsiglio and Donnelly (1992), which used a national probability sample that included 807 respondents 60 years of age or older, revealed that people's sense of self-worth/com-petence and partner's health status were significantly and positively related to the incidence of sex within the past month. To maintain good biopsychosocial health, older people need to recognize and understand the interrelationship of physical and emotional needs and capacities.

Biophysical Hazards

The processes of physiological aging increase the individual's vulnerability to various types of health problems. According to Santrock (1995), chronic disorders "are characterized by a slow onset and long duration. Chronic disorders rarely develop in early adulthood, increase during middle adulthood, and become common in late adulthood" (p. 521). Many older people have chronic conditions, and the older one becomes, the more likely one is to have multiple conditions (see Box 12.1).

Chronic Health Problems

The two most common types of chronic disorders are arthritis and hypertension. *Arthritis* is a broad term that describes a wide variety of disease entities, the most common of which include rheumatoid arthritis and osteoarthritis. Generally, arthritis is located in the connective tissues of the body, primarily tendons, ligaments, and cartilage (Cohen, 1982). The tissues become inflamed, causing pain and difficulty in movement (Santrock, 1995). Rheumatoid arthritis, which is more common in females than in males, may appear to be a disease of the immune system because it can stimulate inflammation in such parts of the body as the heart, nerves, spleen, liver, and blood vessels. Both emotional and physical stressors facilitate the occurrence of the disease (Bullock & Rosendahl, 1988). Although some people have some form of disability the remainder of their lives, this condition can be treated with medication or surgery. Osteoarthritis, a degenerative joint disease, is the result of repeated trauma or wear and tear on tissue, primarily in

---

BOX 12.1

Common Myths Associated with Mental Impairment

Myth: Changes in mental capability and behavior such as confusion, forgetfulness, and depression are just signs of growing older.

Fact: There are distinct differences between changes occurring with "normal" aging and those of mental disorders. However, mild levels of impairment can and do occur when a normally aging individual is under stress or has a physical problem. Factors such as sensory loss and decreased ability to cope with stresses may affect the normal aging person as well.

Myth: Old people who are forgetful or confused should never be left alone.

Fact: Older persons who exhibit symptoms of minimal impairment can and do function in the community. Constant surveillance and overprotective measures tend to reduce the older person's freedom and sense of self-control and should be held to a minimum,

short of endangering the individual or others. Adequate support systems must integrate the resources of family, health care providers, and community. Adaptations of the older person's environment may be all that is required.

Myth: Old people are uncooperative and unsociable.

Fact: Unusual behavior may often result from sensory deficits that can be corrected. The older person who cannot see or hear well is often unable to communicate effectively, and the resulting frustration may give rise to inappropriate behavior. Sadness or depression can also cause the older person to withdraw.

Myth: Inability to concentrate, impaired attention span, and memory loss in an older person are signs of aging.

Fact: Depression as well as an organic mental dysfunclarge joints such as the shoulder, knee, hip, and ankle. It involves the loss and destruction of cartilage that serves as a buffer between bones where they have contact with one another. Cartilage loss results in severe pain and impaired joint function (Burdman, 1986). Both rheumatoid and osteoarthritis symptoms begin in middle age and become more marked with age. Osteoarthritis affects men and woman equally. Gross or fine motor impairments, joint deformity, and posture changes represent the more severe forms of this condition (Miller, 1992).

Genetics is a factor in the development of hypertension (high blood pressure) (Bullock & Rosendahl, 1988). Hypertension predisposes older people to stroke and heart disease. It poses a substantial risk even in moderate form. Hypertension in older people is most commonly caused by arteriosclerosis (hardening of the arteries) or atherosclerosis (clogging of the arteries with fatty deposits) and may affect the kidneys and blood vessels. This condition is more common and severe in African Americans than in whites (Kent, 1980). Depending on the type and severity of the person's hypertension, as well as other medical problems, the condition may be treated by medication, by change in health habits, or by some combination of both (Tucker, 1980).

In 1992, 35% of all hospital admissions for chronic and acute disorders were attributed to older people. And once admitted, older people tend to stay longer in the hospital—on average, 8.2 days compared with 5.1 days for people under 65. In addition, those over 65 averaged more contacts with doctors. A disproportionate amount of total personal health care expenditures are attributable to this age group. Out of $162 billion in expendi-

Common Myths Associated with Mental Impairment

tion can cause these impairments of mood and thought. Depression is the most common affective disorder in older persons. Because depression responds well to treatment, it should be targeted even when the diagnosis is uncertain.

Myth: Older people should not be allowed to engage in work or activity that requires mental or physical effort.

Fact: Depriving older people of work or activity simply because of their age invariably results in a loss of self-esteem, which causes serious problems. Often older persons are patronized and/or excluded from significant social roles when in reality they have much to contribute. Allowing for responsibilities to match the abilities of older persons will enhance self-respect and help them to maintain a functional level well into later years.

Myth: Older people need eight hours of sleep every night.

Fact: Sleep patterns change over time. Many older persons function well on five to six hours of sleep a day. Some prefer to sleep less at night and to rest when they feel tired during the day.

Myth: Older people react to alcohol and drugs just as do younger adults.

Fact: The alteration in absorption, distribution, and excretion rates in older persons make them very sensitive to the actions of individual drugs. Also, older persons are prone to toxic reactions because of drug interactions. There is a need for conservative use of drugs, continuous monitoring to avoid side effects, and an awareness of the potential for alcohol-related problems.

Source: Burdman, 1986.

tures, an average of $5360 was spent per year on each older person, whereas an average of $1290 was spent on younger persons. The largest share of health care expenditures for older persons was hospital expenses (42%), followed by physicians (21%) and nursing home costs (20%). Older adults rely more on government programs to pay for their health care. About two-thirds (63%) of health care expenditures for older people are covered by government benefit programs, including Medicare and Medicaid, whereas only 26% of health care expenditures for people under 65 are subsidized by benefit programs (AARP & AOA, 1994).

Implications for Practice: Maintaining Good Health

Variations in age-related biophysical changes indicate the importance of having an adequate understanding of older people's health status. Thorough physical exams assist in discerning the biophysical needs and capacities of individuals within this age group. Good health and the maintenance of good health is dependent on such factors as exercise and better nutrition. Exercise has a salient effect on the heart, lungs, blood pressure, bones, muscles, and overall physical well-being of older adults. Moreover, exercise is positively associated with psychosocial health in terms of lessening depression, reducing stress, and enhancing intellectual functioning. Adequate nutrition promotes a higher level of wellness in late adulthood. Although the nutrient requirements of older adults are not that different from those of their middle-aged counterparts, it is crucial that they eat higher-quality foods that are lower in calories. Daily diets must include the major food groupings with adequate amounts of fiber and fluids (Miller, 1992; Santrock, 1995).

Psychological Dimension
Cognitive Development and Information Processing

Determining the nature of intellectual decline in late adulthood is a complex issue influenced by the types of studies used to measure this phenomena. Two major types of research strategies used are cross-sectional and longitudinal studies. On the basis of cross-sectional data, Horn (1982) concluded that although **crystallized intel-**

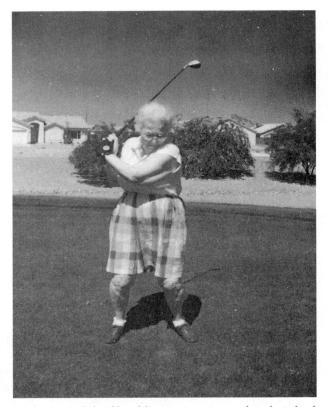

Regular exercise helps older adults maintain or improve their physical and mental well-being.

ligence (accumulated information and verbal skills) increases with age, **fluid intelligence** (abstract reasoning ability) decreases with age. On the other hand, Schaie (1983) has conducted longitudinal research that indicated that although moderate declines may occur for some, for others intellectual capacities may increase with age. Schaie (Schaie & Willis, 1986) criticized cross-sectional studies such as Horn's because the data collected compared different age groups (e.g., 30-year-olds and 70-year-olds). Also cross-sectional studies do not take into account **cohort** effects.

Cohort refers to any group of people born within a specified short period. For instance, people born in 1920, in 1945, and in 1960 constitute distinct cohorts. Snapshots of them at the same age would reveal marked differences not just in appearance but in many aspects of psychological functioning. Variation is inevitable because each cohort is exposed to a unique set of cultural and societal experiences as it travels through life (Belsky, 1990, p. 27).

Further, Belsky explains that older cohorts, compared with younger cohorts, have not been exposed to an environment that promotes better health practices and emphasizes education. Younger cohorts, therefore, have distinct advantages over older cohorts because of these types of cohort differences. Cross-sectional studies do offer more reliable information about age differences at any point in time, but they do not offer more reliable information about age changes over the life span.

In the longitudinal approach, which focuses on age changes, one or more age cohorts are chosen and tested periodically over a number of years. It is preferable that the same measures are used in this process. Although this research strategy yields valuable data on age changes, it is difficult to make universal assumptions about aging. Conclusions can be drawn only about the age cohort selected "because each cohort is unique, and it may show an idiosyncratic pattern of change as it ages" (Belsky, p. 28). Other problems that occur with longitudinal research include such factors as cost, amount of time consumed, and the dropout rate due to illness, disinterest, migration, and the like (Santrock, 1995).

In the Seattle Longitudinal Study (Schaie & Willis, 1986), five primary mental abilities of respondents were tested, including verbal meaning, reasoning ability, word fluency, numerical ability, and spatial visualization. Frequency distributions covering seven-year age ranges were prepared to determine the proportion of people likely to decline at a given age. Abilities varied greatly in areas tested; however, by age 67 there was no more than a 25% decline, by age 74 about 33% decline, and by age 81 decline had risen to about 40%. The investigators pointed out that the large proportion who remained stable and the few who increased performance on some measure was remarkable. Although the state of knowledge of intellectual decline is imperfect, it appears likely that decline is not a given with advancing age and that there is considerable variation in the loss of mental abilities.

Information Processing, Memory, and Learning

The speed of information processing to retrieve knowledge is dependent upon sensory inputs from the eye, ear,

and other sensory organs. With age, the eye's ability to focus on nearby objects decreases, the amount of light required to see increases, and there is impairment in the ability to adapt from light to darkness and back to light. The ability to hear, particularly high frequencies, also decreases (Burdman, 1986). With sensory deficits, age seems to affect the quality of perception and the ability to receive, process, and act on information. This tends to lead to a slowing of behavioral responses in late adulthood (Burdman, 1986; Salthouse & Coon, 1993).

There is an interrelationship between memory and learning; that is, memory is the ability to retain what has been learned. Difficulties or impairments in this area may be due to problems of perception, attention, or motivation. Burdman (1986) points out that the state of emotional and physical health can have significant impact on memory functions. These types of impairments may be misdiagnosed when, as is often the case, they are transitory or reversible (see Focus on Narrative: The Professor Prevails). In addition, a variety of drugs may affect memory function or mimic certain brain disorders (Butler et al., 1991).

FOCUS ON NARRATIVE

The Professor Prevails

Professor Frank Minkoff, a 70-year-old Russian immigrant with a university degree in engineering, was still teaching mathematics at an evening school. He was unmarried, was the only member of his family in the United States, and lived in an apartment crammed with books. Suddenly he became confused and disoriented. He was frightened and refused to leave his room. Concerned neighbors quickly called a doctor, who expressed his unwillingness to make a home visit, saying, "There is nothing I can do. He needs to be in a nursing home or a mental institution." The neighbors were unconvinced, remembering Mr. M.'s earlier good functioning. They pleaded with the doctor and, under pressure, he angrily complied and visited the home. While there, he again repeated his conviction that Mr. M. needed "custodial" care. Mr. M. was coherent enough to refuse, saying he would never voluntarily go to a nursing home or mental hospital. He did agree to be admitted to a medical hospital. Admission took place and studies resulted in the diagnosis "reversible brain syndrome due to acute viral infection." Mr. M. was successfully treated and released to his home in good condition in less than a week.

Source: Butler, 1975, p. 5.

In the normal aging process, long-term memory loss rarely occurs, although losses in short-term and recent memory occur much more frequently. It is possible that current events do not have the significance for the older person that events of the past have for them. Exercising and keeping the mind stimulated and active assist memory functioning (Burdman, 1986). The Seattle Longitudinal Study (Schaie, 1983) results showed that a significant number of older people do not decline intellectually even in their eighties. Schaie (1987) states there are several factors that characterize these octogenarians: they have no cardiovascular disease; they are average or above, economically; they are actively involved in life; and their self-reports indicate they have been flexible in attitudes and behavior since the middle years.

Implications for Practice: Changes in Mental Functioning

It is clear that intellectual capacity does not necessarily decline with age, although the speed of information processing tends to decline as a result of sensory and visuomotor changes. Problems with memory may be as a result of a number of factors, including health, perception, attention, or motivation. Other explanations may include differences in level of education and ability to reason abstractly (fluid intelligence) or both, instead of aging per se. Criticisms of testing methods (e.g., the requirement of completing trivial tasks in sterile laboratory settings) have been advanced as a barrier to performance. Studying how people complete practical tasks within their natural environments is a more salient approach (Santrock, 1995; Schaie & Willis, 1986).

Methods of retraining have been developed to assist older adults in sharpening their cognitive skills. Using a variety of training strategies (e.g., modeling, individual practice, feedback, and group discussion), Willis and Nesselroade (1990) taught older adults how to identify the rule or pattern in problem solution. Following the cognitive training, in this seven-year longitudinal study, 70- and 80-year-old adults performed at a higher level than they had in their late sixties.

Cognitive well-being is an overriding concern for older persons and their families. Mental decline or impairment poses a great threat to individuals as they age. Yet, some common beliefs associated with mental impairment must be dispelled (see Box 12.1).

Communication

The purpose of **reminiscence** as a part of the normal life review process was articulated by Butler (1963) in response to the widespread notion that reminiscence was associated with short-term memory loss and, therefore, it was an indicator of aging. He noted that reminiscence is a mental process that emerges when one realizes the inevitability of death. Reviewing one's life has the potential of bringing to consciousness past events, especially those in which conflicts have been unresolved and "that can be looked at again and reintegrated" (Butler et al., 1991, p. 112). The reintegration process serves the function of putting one's life in order and preparing for death. This process is seen as universal, spontaneous, and unselective. It occurs in other age groups but is most commonly observed in older persons who are near to death. Butler (1963) noted that it also may be more frequently observed in the aged because retirement allows time for reflection and contemplation. Reminiscence has the potential for assisting an older person to bring positive closure to life and, often, is a gift to the one who listens (see Focus on Development: Reminiscing with an Older Person).

FOCUS ON DEVELOPMENT

Reminiscing with an Older Person

I do not live in the past; it is the past which is alive in me.
—Rene Dubos—

Reminiscing, something we find ourselves doing more and more as we age, is normal and natural; it is part of the process of putting meaning to our lives. But there may be more to sharing memories for older people. In addition to helping them put their lives in order, reminiscence can be a socialization tool, as memories are shared with friends and relatives. It can help an older person orient to the present by getting a "good grip" on the past. As one reviews the events of one's life, past accomplishments and successes may be more appreciated in hindsight, whereas weaknesses and mistakes don't seem as serious as they were decades ago.

Reminiscence holds many rewards for the listener as well. We can gain great insight into "survivorship," the skills and traits developed over a lifetime to cope with adversity and life's challenges. If the speaker is a relative, the stories illustrate the characters of family members we may or may not have known, as well as the character of the family as a whole. We may learn the origins of the traditions and rituals we practice, gain clues to the way family members have been assigned roles within the family, and add to our sense of continuity, connectedness, and belonging.

Here are some tips for making the most out of listening to an older loved one's reminiscing:

- Suggesting a topic, such as family traditions, parent-child relationships, youthful passages, courtship and marriage, the Depression, war years, education, and professions may help trigger vivid memories.
- Don't be afraid to talk about past losses and the death of long-ago loved ones. This may give you valuable insight into the speaker's feelings regarding his or her own approaching death and wishes regarding life-sustaining measures and funeral arrangements.
- Don't trust your own memory; write down the stories you hear, or use a tape recorder or videotape. These will all become more priceless mementos than any material heirloom.
- Bookstores carry special bound volumes that are designed specifically for recording reminiscences and genealogical information.
- Even those suffering from dementia or other mental impairments have lucid moments when they can vividly recall the events of their life, and having an active and interested listener may help them feel less isolated and more anchored.

- Be an "audience" for older persons to whom you are not related, too. They may have no close family with whom to share the stories of their lives.
- Reminiscence is a gift to the listener and a chance for the older person to reinforce his or her part of the continuum of life and feel unique, precious, and cherished.

Source: Based on Richardson, 1988.

Attitudes and Emotions

Loss, and its attendant issues, is one of the dominant factors that characterize the common emotional problems of older adults. In every aspect of late life, losses occur from the micro to the macro: death of a loved one, decline in health, loss of status, prestige, and active involvement in communal life. Older adulthood is marked by the expending of physical and emotional energy on grieving, grief resolution, adaptation, and recovery from loss (Butler et al., 1991). Multiple losses at any one point in time are not uncommon. The variety of factors that may affect individual experience, overt behavior, and level of adaptation are outlined in Box 12.2.

Grief and Loss

Grief, associated with loss, is the normative emotional reaction experienced by people in late adulthood. Death, as loss, is viewed as the most profound loss human beings endure because the dying process and death is accompanied by such losses as the following: the loss of people, the loss of experiencing, the loss of control and competence, the loss of the body, the loss of the capacity to complete projects and plans, and the loss of life's dream (Kalish, 1985). Grief may be expressed physiologically and emotionally. Physiological expressions of grief often include emptiness in the pit of the stomach, a feeling of suffocation or shortness of breath, weak knees, and a tendency to deep sighing (Butler et al., 1991). Emotional expressions of grief may contain such reactions as depression, sorrow, sadness, relief, guilt, anger, and denial (Kalish, 1985). The loss of a spouse or partner and other loved ones through death may have a profound impact on survivors, partly because there is less likelihood that the lost relationships will be replaced. May Sarton, in a poem called "Mourning to Do," movingly expressed grief for the loss of a partner who experienced first dementia and then death (see Focus on Family: Grief for a Partner).

(see Focus on Family: Grief for a Partner)

FOCUS ON FAMILY

Grief for a Partner

Mourning to Do

The new year and a fresh fall of snow,
The new year and mourning to do
Alone in the lovely silent house,
Alone as the inner eye opens at last—
Not as the shutter of a camera with a click,

But like a gentle waking in a dark room
Before dawn when familiar objects take on
Substances out of their shadowy corners
And come to life. So with my lost love,
For years lost in the darkness of her mind,
Tied to a wheelchair, not knowing where she was
Or who she had been when we lived together
In amity, peaceful as turtledoves.
Judy is dead. Judy is gone forever.
I cannot fathom that darkness, nor know
Whether the true spirit is alive again.
But what I do know is the peace of it,
And in the darkened room before dawn, I lie
Awake and let the good tears flow at last,
And as light touches the chest of drawers
And the windows grow transparent, rest,
Happy to be mourning what was singular
And comforting as the paintings on the wall,
And that can now come to life in my mind,
Good memories fresh and sweet as the dawn—

BOX 12.2

Factors That May Affect Experience, Behavior, and Adaptation in Loss

Environmental or Extrinsic Factors

Personal losses or gain: marital partners; other loved and significant figures (friends, children)

Social forces (losses or gain): status changes, prestige changes: in social groups other than family and as paterfamilias

Socioeconomic adversities: income drop, inflation

Unwanted retirement: arbitrary retirement policies

Cultural devaluation of older persons: sense of uselessness, therapeutic pessimism, forced isolation, forced segregation

Intrinsic Factors

Nature of personality: character structure (defensive and integrative mechanisms), life history, survival characteristics

Physical diseases: disease of any organ system; perceptual decrements; sexual losses; disease of integrative systems (hormonal, vascular, and central nervous systems); brain damage; arteriosclerosis; senile dementia, etc.; physical limitations (such as arthritis)

Age-specific changes (largely obscure and mysterious, but inexorable with the passage of time): losses of speed of processes and response; involuntary processes; others (heredity, survival qualities); changes in body size and appearance ("slipping" and "shrinkage")

Experience of bodily dissolution and approaching death (subjective passage of time)

Source: Butler et al., 1991.

Judy drinking her tea with a cat on her lap,
And our many little walks before suppertime.
So it is now the gentle waking to what was,
And what is and will be as long as I am alive.
"Happy grieving," someone said who knew—
Happy the dawn of memory and the sunrise.

Source: Sarton, 1984.

The Importance of Mourning

Jill lost her husband, Robert, to cancer in 1987.[1] *He had been ill for three years, and his death was no surprise. At the time of his death, Jill was busy with funeral arrangements and with putting her financial affairs in order. After the death, she was active in her church and in community organizations and filled her days with various civic and volunteer activities. She rarely mentioned her husband, and her friends were amazed at her courage and fortitude. Over the years, several men asked her out on dates, but she refused, saying no one could ever replace Robert. Then, last week, her cat died. He had been her pet for 14 years, and now Jill finds that she cannot stop crying. In fact, she is in so much emotional pain that she is having difficulty sleeping and often finds herself wishing she were dead. She feels foolish for being so upset over an animal, but eight years after the death of her husband, she feels terribly lost and alone.*

William Worden (1991), in *Grief Counseling and Grief Therapy*, discusses the importance of working through grief. When people who experience the loss of a loved one do not deal with their pain and loss, problems can arise years down the road. Worden outlines four steps necessary in mourning a loss:

- *Accept the loss.* Initially, people deny the reality of a death, so the first task is to accept that the loved one is gone and will not return. Often people display searching behaviors, seeing the loved one in a crowd or hearing their voice.
- *Feel the pain.* Many ask after the death of a loved one, "When does this pain go away?" Many simply do not want to hurt so much, so they busy themselves in activities or go on a trip to avoid their feelings. But pain cannot be avoided, and if not dealt with at the time of death, it may resurface when another loss occurs (such as the death of a pet). Bereaved individuals need to exter-

nalize the pain by talking about the death and the loved one. Group therapy situations are helpful.

- *Adjust to a new environment.* The bereaved person needs to realize that he or she can live in a world where the loved one no longer exists.
- *Reinvest in new relationships.* Relationships are a risk. The bereaved person must work through grief before being able to enter new relationships and be willing to risk being hurt again.

How do you know when you have worked through the grief over loss of a loved one? When you can recall that person and it doesn't hurt.

Death and Dying

The process people go through when facing imminent death has been described in various ways by different investigators (see, e.g., Kastenbaum & Weisman, 1972; Kübler-Ross, 1969; Pattison, 1978). Perhaps the best-known investigator of the process of dying is Elisabeth Kübler-Ross, a Swiss-born psychiatrist who began a systematic study of death and dying at the University of Chicago's teaching-research hospital. After interviewing more than 200 dying patients, Kübler-Ross identified five stages (not necessarily sequential) in the dying process: (1) denial and isolation, (2) anger, (3) bargaining, (4) depression, and (5) acceptance.

1. *Denial and isolation* is the most common response in the initial stage of the process. It is characterized by feelings of shock, disbelief, and numbness. In the short run, denial serves as a healthy defense for dealing with a painful, difficult situation. As a buffer, denial provides a brief respite to people, allowing them opportunity to confront the reality of dying and to mobilize other less radical defenses.

2. *Anger* provides people with the chance to vent their rage and resentment about dying. It is not uncommon for anger to be displaced on loved ones and caregivers, both formal and informal. The displacement typically is not personal, but it is a cry of anguish, perhaps at the untimeliness of death, over enviousness of those who experience good health, or about all that will be left uncompleted and unfulfilled.

[1]Source: This section was adapted from Worden, 1991.

As a person prepares for dying, he or she must address the emotional pain, grief, and indignity that often accompanies death. The dying person must also grieve the loss of family and friends, as well as the loss of life.

3. *Bargaining* is an attempt to delay or postpone death's inevitability. Terminally ill people may believe they can bargain for an extension of life because rewards often follow good behavior (e.g., "I will quit smoking, drinking, and lose weight if I can live to see my granddaughter married").

4. *Depression* is characterized by a great sense of loss and consists of two types: reactive depression and preparatory depression. Reactive depression focuses on past losses and may be accompanied by guilt or shame (e.g., for not confronting issues of estrangement with loved ones). In contrast, preparatory depression takes into account all the impending losses to come: loss of self, loss of relationship, and all that one has ever known or loved.

5. *Acceptance* of mortality is not resignation but a state in which people have an opportunity to consider the end of life with some dignity. If enough time is available to confront death, this stage allows for the working through of prior emotional reactions. People during this stage may be weak, withdrawn, and uncommunicative

with others. Focus on Biophysics: The Dying Process discusses what actually happens when a person dies.

FOCUS ON BIOPHYSICS

The Dying Process

Death from a chronic illness does not usually come quickly; it may take weeks or months (Enck, 1992). Beginning one to three months before the actual death, several changes occur in dying individuals. First they begin to withdraw and turn inward. This is the first step in separating from the world. They begin to sleep more and to interact with friends and family less. There may be a drop in food consumption.

The actual dying process begins about one to two weeks before death occurs. The dying person becomes disoriented and confused. He or she may talk to long-deceased loved ones or become agitated and pick at the bedclothes. Sleep increases, and food consumption falls to very little. The dying person may perspire more, and his or her skin color may change to pale yellow with bluish hands and feet. Breathing and pulse become irregular.

Days or hours before the death, all these signs intensify. However, the dying person may experience a surge of energy and be more alert, eating and socializing—almost as if he or she were getting energy to say goodbye. Then the person usually slips into a coma. Hands, feet, and legs become blotchy and purplish. Pulse is weak and hard to find. Breathing becomes very irregular with long pauses between breaths. Then the dying person becomes unresponsive and breathing stops. . . .

> I am standing upon the seashore. A ship at my side spreads her white sails to the morning breeze and starts for the blue ocean. She is an object of beauty and strength. I stand and watch her until at length she hangs like a speck of white cloud just where the sea and sky come to mingle with each other.
>
> Then someone at my side says: "There, she is gone!"
> "Gone where?"
> Gone from my sight. That is all. She is just as large in mast and hull and spar as she was when she left my side and she is just as able to bear her load of living freight to her destined port.
>
> Her diminished size is in me, not in her. And just at the moment when someone at my side says: "There, she is gone!" there are other eyes watching her coming, and other voices ready to take up the glad shout: "Here she comes!"
>
> And that is dying. (Anonymous)

Source: Adapted from Karnes, 1986.

Causes of Death   The leading causes of death (in rank order) of Americans 65 years of age and older are (1) heart disease, (2) cancer, (3) cerebrovascular disease (stroke), (4) lung diseases, (5) pneumonia and influenza, and (6) diabetes (Santrock, 1995). In 1993, nearly half (48%) of noninstitutionalized older women (8.6 million) were widows, whereas only 14% of noninstitutionalized older men (1.8 million) were widowers, a ratio of nearly 5:1 (AARP & AOA, 1994). Although generalizations

were made earlier in this chapter with respect to grief reactions, patterns of grieving are not uniform. Widows and widowers, for example, may react or respond differently to the death of a spouse.

It is a myth that when one spouse dies, the other soon follows. In fact, the most recent research shows that although this might be somewhat true for widows under age 50, those aged 60–69 have the same mortality rate as married women, and those over 70 show only a slightly higher mortality rate. For men, however, mortality rates seem to be significantly higher among widowers (Hesling & Szklo, 1981).

Fear of Death   One of the most common human reactions to death and the process of dying is fear. Attitudes toward death and dying vary over the life span and have been a topic of study. Nagy (1959) conducted a study of death anxiety, interviewing 378 children between the ages of 3 and 10. She found that children 3 to 5 years of age did not know what death meant or have any sense of its reality; for those between 6 and 9, death was viewed as real but was perceived as relating to others rather than the self; and for those 9 and older, death was viewed as final and inevitable, even for the self.

In adolescence and early adulthood, it is difficult to confront one's mortality, and the fear of death, or death anxiety, is relatively low. The possibility that death will occur in the prime and vitality of youth almost is inconceivable to this age group (Puner, 1974). Yet, a study (Ewalt & Perkins, 1979) of high school students' experience of death showed that 90% (1303) reported they had seen a dead person, or had lost a family member or someone else they cared about through death. About 20% (283) of the students had been present when a death occurred, and 40% (591) had experienced the death of a friend their own age. Although death may be seen as remote by youth and treated with some casualness, "the normal identity crisis of adolescence may be exacerbated when coupled with grief reactions" (Cho, Freeman, & Patterson, 1982, p. 91).

In middle age, according to Neugarten (1968), men and women have developed an awareness of the finiteness of time. Moreover, their perceptions of time are different. In effect, time-left-to-live is a more salient perception than is distance-from-birth. Investigators (Kalish & Reynolds, 1976; Puner, 1974) have shown that the fear of death is a more prominent feature of middle age than it is in younger or older age groups. Middle age is a time when bodily changes begin to occur (for example, wrinkles, graying hair), chronic illnesses may begin to develop, concern for financing retirement becomes an issue, or a parent may die or suffer a terminal condition. These and other life events have power to generate fear and anxiety in the middle years.

Fear of death, or death anxiety, is relatively low in old age. Dying is more of an everyday topic of conversation among the old, and late adulthood appears to be a time of life when one deals more directly with life's end. Older people have experienced a range of losses, including death of a loved one. A heightened awareness of death and its attendant issues is the result of such factors as the increased sophistication of modern medical technology, discussions about euthanasia and physician-assisted suicide, and the passage of The Patient Self-Determination Act of 1990 (PSDA). The purpose of this act is twofold: (1) to encourage competent adults to execute advance directives (e.g., living wills, durable powers of attorney for health care) and (2) to identify previously admitted patients to acute or long-term care facilities who have completed advance directives. "Institutions that receive Medicare or Medicaid funding are required to ask patients about the presence of advance directives, to record responses, and to provide patients without such documents with information regarding their right to establish one" (Morrison, Olson, Mertz, & Meier, 1995, p. 478). The overall thrust of the Act is improved access to and increased execution of advance directives.

Several studies have provided support for lower death anxiety among older people compared with other adult age groups (see, e.g., Bascue & Lawrence, 1977; Bengston, Cuellar, & Ragan, 1977). A more recent study (Gesser, Wong, & Reker, 1987–88), designed to develop a multidimensional Death Attitude Profile (DAP), included the following dimensions:

1. Fear of Death (negative thoughts and feelings about the state of death)
2. Fear of Dying (negative thoughts and feelings about the process of dying)
3. Approach-Oriented Death Acceptance (death is viewed as a passageway to a happy afterlife)
4. Escape-Oriented Death Acceptance (death is viewed as an escape from a painful existence)
5. Neutral Acceptance (death is neither welcomed nor feared, but simply accepted as reality) (p. 115)

The DAP was administered to 50 young adults (MA = 21.4), 50 middle-aged adults (MA = 41.4), and 50 older adults (MA = 74.3) who were nearly equally divided by gender in each age grouping. The results indicated that older respondents showed less fear of death and more acceptance (approach, escape, and neutral) than did their younger or middle-aged counterparts.

In Western societies, death has often been viewed as an unnatural interruption of or deviance in relation to life. Other cultures, however, have viewed loss and death as a natural and not uncomfortable part of the process of life and living (see Focus on Narrative: A Native American Elder Contemplates Life's End). In the last several decades, societal changes have influenced attitudes toward death such that its inevitability and normality are more prevalent. Today, people express more concern about quality-of-life issues than about dying—a one-time experience.

FOCUS ON NARRATIVE

A Native American Elder Contemplates Life's End

Today is a very good day to die.
Every living thing is in harmony with me.
Every voice sings a chorus within me.
All beauty has come to rest in my eyes.
All bad thoughts have departed from me.
Today is a very good day to die.
My land is peaceful around me.
My fields have been turned for the last time.
My house is filled with laughter.
My children have come home.
Yes, today is a very good day to die.

Source: Wood, 1974, p. 31.

Widowhood

Because widowhood is more common for women—because they generally live longer and may marry older men—women may be better prepared for this life change. Or perhaps women cope better because they are more likely to have a good network of support. Still another possibility is that widowhood may actually signify a time for growth in women's lives. Silverman (1987) sees widowhood as a change in the life cycle, necessitating adjustments in the way a woman relates to herself and to others, and leading to a new identity: "When widowhood is seen as a stage in the life cycle, then it can also be understood not only as an ending but as a beginning as well" (p. 171).

Although widows of any age experience a period of bereavement and possible fear and uncertainty, they seem to emerge from their pain with new strengths: increased decisiveness and feelings of self-reliance, autonomy, and freedom. They may feel a void for the rest of their lives, but over time, "other selves and other relationships emerge that bring other satisfactions" (p. 180). Some may recognize that they have spent most of their lives meeting others' needs, seeing life through their husbands' eyes, and speaking their husbands' words. They begin to rediscover—or discover for the first time—their own voices.

Widows seldom remarry, which has often been attributed to the fact that there are four widows for every widower in the United States (Bremmer & van den Bosch, 1995). But one study suggests that widows often choose to remain single (Gentry, Rosenman, & Shulman, 1987). Women in this study were asked to cite the resources they used to cope with the problems that arise from widowhood; the most frequently cited resource was the woman herself. Even remarried widows cited themselves as their most important resource, indicating that widowhood brings increased feelings of self-reliance and decreased dependence on others. Forty percent of the women reported no wish to remarry, "because, despite the difficulties, they enjoyed the independence that life without a spouse gave them" (p. 170). Perhaps the widow, emerging slowly from her dark chrysalis of pain and grief, finds new identity—even rebirth—in her last stage of life, as colorful and free as a butterfly.

In some respects, older men may be more vulnerable and fragile when they experience the death of a spouse. It is almost as though the center of life has died with the loved one. Death, as an alternative to living without a loved one, may be a welcome choice. In his book *Diary of an Old Man*, Chaim Bermant's (1966) main character, Cyril, recounts the events leading to the death of a widowed friend (see Focus on Narrative).

FOCUS ON NARRATIVE

The Death of a Widower

They buried old Harry this morning. I don't know why I call him old Harry, but old Harry it's been for as long as I've known him. He was 74—tried to make out he was only 73, but he was 74 if a day, and a nice old soul, but he didn't wear well. Some men don't begin to straighten out till they get widowed—as if the wife kept them from the sun; others fall apart. Harry was a faller-apart. He used to say: "It's all right for you, Cyril. You lost your Elsie when you were still a young man. You had time to get used to your own company. But Deirdre and me have been together for thirty-eight years. It's a bit late at my age to get used to myself." He went up to his bed straight after her funeral and never came down, at least not on his own legs.

Source: From Bermant, 1966.

Other Related Emotions

Loneliness in late adulthood tends to be greater immediately following the death of a spouse or partner and may grow when there is an ever-diminishing circle of significant others who may not be replaced easily (Busse & Pfeiffer, 1977; Butler et al., 1991). Loneliness has been defined as "an awareness of an absence of meaningful integration with other persons or groups, a consciousness of being excluded from the system of opportunities and rewards in which other people participate" (Busse & Pfeiffer, 1977, p. 163). Although loneliness affects members of all age groups at some point in time, its presence may be especially poignant in the aged who fear they may have no one to whom they can relate.

There appears to be little research on loneliness and the aged, but one early study (Shanas et al., 1968) examined the relationship between subjectively experienced loneliness and social isolation. Only half of those living alone stated they felt lonely rarely or not at all, whereas three-fourths living with other people reported they were rarely or never lonely. Those who had been single all their lives were less lonely than those who were married, widowed, separated, or divorced. The investigators concluded that loss or desolation has a closer relationship with loneliness than isolation.

Nonetheless, when the old no longer have the rewards of work and family members do not live nearby, their social and emotional needs may not be met. Pets, acquaintances, church, and hobbies assist in ordering one's life but are not enough to meet intimacy needs. There are still individuals who are "independent-pull-yourself-up-by-your-bootstraps-people," living alone and pursuing daily routines without much connection to life. For these individuals, who need human contact, there is the cultural prescription of living alone and caring for oneself. Older people in more group- or collective-oriented cultures do not appear to have the same sense of loss of independence or self-esteem as those in this culture (Butler et al., 1991).

Guilt, a sense of impotence and helplessness, and rage are other emotional reactions that may occur in old age. Although this period of life often is a time for positive reflection and reminiscence for some, for others remembrances of past estrangements or conflicts may surface. Just as one is attempting to find some kind of holistic meaning for life, guilt feelings arise. It is important to resolve these kinds of issues in this stage of life (Butler et al., 1991). Age also may bring with it a sense of helplessness and impotence for those who once held positions of power. Lack of control over one's life is both depressing and anxiety provoking. Those affected by a feeling of powerlessness and loss of self-esteem as they age are of lower socioeconomic classes, women, and members of some ethnic groups. White upper-class men in their eighties, who have the highest suicide rates, are more likely to experience emotional disorders (Butler et al., 1991; Schaie & Willis, 1986). Feelings of rage and anger may be manifested in those who experience the indignities and neglect of the "society that once valued their productive capacities" (Butler et al., 1991, p. 95).

Implications for Practice: Coping with Loss

Longevity brings with it both joy and sadness. When people live long enough, there is a certainty that age will bring with it a series of losses that may evoke a range of common human emotions. These emotions will vary depending on such factors as the nature of the situation, the closeness of a relationship, the investment in a career, the commitment to a belief system, gender, ethnic background, and socioeconomic status. Being aware of the types of losses associated with aging, the emotions that may follow, and the diversity of expression of these emotions provides guidelines for assisting older people to come to terms with life. There is no formula for optimum aging in general, but one can help people in late adulthood find the formula that suits their own particular individuality.

Social Cognition and Regulation

A significant issue in the concept of sense of self for older adults is that they resist thinking of themselves as older adults (Schuster & Ashburn, 1992). "Old is always 15 years older than I am." Recall the senior citizens' group from the beginning of the chapter; none of this 70+ age group considered themselves "old." In fact, people begin to make the transition to defining themselves as old only when their health begins to fail. Yet even in that frail, failing body, the older adult is still a young adult inside.

Another concept in older adults' sense of self is that they tend to think of themselves in terms of their former occupation. When introduced, many state what job they retired from. They also tend to keep the same behavior patterns they developed over the years (Schuster & Ashburn, 1992).

Basically, as people age, they do not change their core sense of self. They do not become like other older adults but become more like themselves.

Theories of Successful Aging

What are the dimensions of adjustment in late adulthood that maintain, decrease, or increase life satisfaction? An assumption made by social gerontologists in the early 1940s and 1950s was that continued involvement in activities and maintenance of social roles was a prescription for higher morale, although little research supported this assumption. In the early 1960s, however, an alternative view suggested that levels of life satisfaction are associated with a diminution of activities and relationships. In the ensuing years, these rival theories fueled both debate and research.

Disengagement theory was introduced initially by Cumming and Henry (1961) in the Kansas City Study of Adult Life. This theory postulates that disengagement occurs in late adulthood through the process of mutual withdrawal of the person and society, and the process could begin from either end of the spectrum. People choose to withdraw when they recognize a lessening of their capacities and distance from death, whereas society withdraws to maintain equilibrium by making room for younger people in the social system. Withdrawal was not viewed as a uniform pattern—for example, some people might be forced to retire rather than choose to retire. Although the variability of disengagement might decrease morale initially, once people had an opportunity to reorganize their lives and priorities, a higher level of morale could be established. Moreover, even with cultural and individual variations in timing, the process of disengagement was seen as universal and inevitable. The controversy over a theoretical approach proposing that people, at a certain point in life, became self-preoccupied and less interested in relationships and societal involvement stimulated research on life satisfaction and activity.

Activity theory focuses on the relationship between social activity and life satisfaction in late adulthood. The loss of roles through retirement, death, and distance (e.g., grandparenting when children and their offspring live far away) deprives people of roles that have been a major source of stability throughout life. The central assumption of this theory was that the more activity one engaged in, the greater one's sense of life satisfaction would be (Lemon, Bengston, & Peterson, 1972). The researchers described three types of activities: (1) informal, which involved socializing with relatives, friends, and neighbors; (2) formal, including participation in voluntary groups; and (3) solitary, pursuing an activity independently, such as reading. Informal activities are the most intimate, followed by formal and then solitary activities. The hypothesis that informal activities would be the most reinforcing and would contribute to life satisfaction was partially supported by the research. A later replication of the study (Longino & Kart, 1982) provided substantial support for this hypothesis. Moreover, Longino and Kart found that informal activity was the type of activity most highly associated with life satisfaction. Informal (intimate) activity appears to reaffirm important roles and a sense of self-worth with others. This study showed that formal activity was associated with decreased morale, whereas solitary activity had no influence on life satisfaction. The major implication of this study is that not all activities carry equal weight in terms of adjustment in late adulthood. Quality, more than frequency, of activities is important.

Neither disengagement nor activity theory focuses on individual differences in adjustment to aging. Instead, both theories are broad and offer a variety of patterns one might follow. For instance, forced retirement would not increase life satisfaction, but choosing to retire and focusing on one's most cherished activities would provide an optimal pattern of aging.

Psychological Hazards

Traditionally, mental disorders in late adulthood have been classified in two ways: as functional (psychiatric) disorders, with no known physical causes, and organic disorders, for which there are documented physical causes (Belsky, 1990; Butler et al., 1991). According to Butler and colleagues (1991), there is a blurring of the boundaries of the organic and functional disorders of the aged because research with respect to the "biochemical underpinnings of the 'functional' psychiatric disorders, and behavioral research in the 'organic' disorders is revealing multiple psychological and social factors which strongly influence clinical outcomes" (p. 115). Two of the most serious mental disorders that appear to affect older people are **dementia** (impairment or loss of cognitive abilities)—especially dementia of the Alzheimer's type—and depression (Belsky, 1990; Butler et al., 1991; Santrock, 1995; Schaie & Willis, 1986). In late adulthood, a variety of factors (e.g., physical, cognitive, social, and emotional difficulties) may combine in such a way that diagnosis of a mental disorder may be confounded. Types of dementia, for instance, share common symptom presentation but have different etiologies. The DSM-IV (American Psychiatric Association, 1994) lists the following types:

1. Dementia of the Alzheimer's type
2. Vascular dementia
3. Dementia due to HIV disease
4. Dementia due to head trauma

5. Dementia due to Parkinson's disease
6. Dementia due to Pick's disease
7. Dementia due to Creutzfeldt-Jakob disease
8. Dementia due to other medical conditions
9. Substance-induced persisting dementia
10. Dementia due to multiple etiologies
11. Dementia not otherwise specified

In addition, for example, early-stage Alzheimer's might "look like" depression, and vice versa (Belsky, 1990; Gruetzner, 1988). Moreover, even quite skilled diagnosticians may vary in their diagnoses, both in terms of type and whether the person has a mental disorder at all (Gurland, Dean, Copeland, Gurland, & Golden, 1982). Psychological problems and symptoms may also appear to be different in old age than in younger ages (e.g., depression may be manifested by memory problems alone), and this cohort of people tend to underreport any negative symptoms (Belsky, 1990).

Alzheimer's Disease

Alzheimer's disease, as distinct from the normal processes of aging (Gruetzner, 1988), has been defined as a "progressive, irreversible brain disorder characterized by gradual deterioration of memory, reasoning, language, and eventual physical function" (Santrock, 1995). It is estimated that 2–5 million individuals in the United States have Alzheimer's disease (Butler et al., 1991; Gruetzner, 1988), and it is projected that by 2025, 7–9 million people will suffer from this disease (Butler et al., 1991). Alzheimer's occurs more frequently in women than in men, probably because of women's longer life expectancy (APA, 1994; Butler et al., 1991). Those who work with older people need to be conversant with the various forms of dementia, including the Alzheimer's type (see Box 12.3).

The most current research on Alzheimer's disease in terms of causes, diagnosis, and treatment is summarized here:

BOX 12.3

Diagnostic Criteria for Dementia of the Alzheimer's Type

A. The development of multiple cognitive deficits manifested by both memory impairment (impaired ability to learn new information or recall previously learned information) and one (or more) of the following cognitive disturbances:
1. *aphasia* (language disturbance)
2. *apraxia* (impaired ability to carry out motor activities despite intact motor function)
3. *agnosia* (failure to recognize or identify objects despite intact sensory function)
4. *disturbance in executive functioning* (i.e., planning, organizing, sequencing, abstracting)

B. The cognitive deficits in Criteria A1 and A2 each cause significant impairment in social or occupational functioning and represent a significant decline from a previous level of functioning.

C. The course is characterized by gradual onset and continuing cognitive decline.

D. The cognitive deficits in Criteria A1 and A2 are not due to any of the following: other central nervous system conditions that cause progressive deficits in memory and cognition (e.g., cerebrovascular disease, Parkinson's disease, Huntington's disease, subdural hematoma, normal-pressure hydrocephalus, brain tumor), systemic conditions that are known to cause dementia (e.g., hypothyroidism, vitamin B12 or folic acid deficiency, niacin deficiency, hypercalcemia, neurosyphilis, HIV infection), or substance-induced conditions.

E. The deficits do not occur exclusively during the course of a delirium.

F. The disturbance is not better accounted for by another Axis I disorder (e.g., Major Depressive Disorder, Schizophrenia).

Source: American Psychiatric Association, 1994.

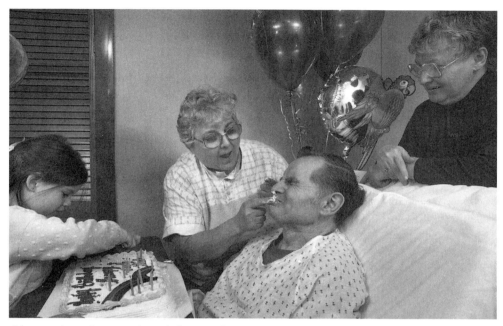

Alzheimer's disease brings significant challenges to the caregiver and family members because of the sufferer's extensive loss of memory, personality changes, loss of communication, and relinquishing of inhibitions.

Causes   Scientists have already found certain inherited abnormal genes that predispose an individual to early Alzheimer's (in the thirties or forties). Currently, there is extensive work being conducted in the field of genetics, trying to pinpoint a gene that may cause Alzheimer's disease in old age.

A recent study involving 678 older nuns indicates that the most highly educated and intellectually active of these subjects lived longer, maintained more agile brains, and seemed less likely to develop Alzheimer's, supporting a "use it or lose it" theory (Heilman, 1995).

Previous research that indicated a possible connection between aluminum exposure and Alzheimer's has not been supported by further study, and it appears unlikely that aluminum exposure is a factor.

Some scientists have suggested that Alzheimer's disease may be virally transmitted. There are some similarities between the disease and certain "slow" viruses—such as AIDS and Kuru, a neurological disorder documented in certain tribes in New Guinea—in which

symptoms appear a considerable length of time after infection (Hinrichsen, 1990).

Diagnosis   At this time, autopsy is the only definitive method of diagnosing Alzheimer's.

Diagnosis in a living patient requires a complex and costly battery of psychological and neurological tests whose combined results correctly diagnose Alzheimer's in about 90% of cases (Gordon, 1994), but new tests seem promising.

Researchers at UCLA reported in March 1995 that it seems possible to use brain-imaging scans to see signs of mental deterioration in people with abnormal genes many years before Alzheimer's symptoms appear (Heilman, 1995). Researchers at the National Institute of Mental Health have found that a form of magnetic resonance imaging (MRI) called frequency-shifted burst imaging, can detect the lowered blood flow in the brain that is characteristic of those with Alzheimer's. This type of imaging is quick, can be performed with an ordinary scanner, and does not require the use of radioisotopes, allowing the test to be performed frequently to monitor changes (Beardsley, 1995).

A simple eye test, using tropicamide to dilate the patient's pupils, may be the most promising diagnostic technique. Huntington Potter, a neurobiologist at Harvard University, looked for similarities between Alzheimer's sufferers and people born with Down syndrome (it was already known that those with Down syndrome often exhibit symptoms similar to Alzheimer's when they reach their thirties). Potter tested 58 people to see whether their eyes were as hypersensitive to the drug atropine (which comes from the belladonna plant) as are the eyes of those with Down syndrome. Nineteen of the subjects had probable diagnoses of Alzheimer's (the others had other dementias or no illness at all), and 18 of these showed a significantly wider and faster dilation of the pupil than that of the other subjects. It is hoped that further extensive testing of this method will begin soon, leading to commercialization of the test (Gorman, 1994).

Treatment The only drug currently approved by the Federal Drug Administration (FDA) is tacrine, which can minimize Alzheimer's symptoms. But tacrine helps only a few people for a short period of time, has possible serious side effects, and does not stop progression of the disease.

Some common drugs may affect development of Alzheimer's. There is some indication that postmenopausal women who are given estrogen replacement therapy are far less likely to get Alzheimer's than are those who are untreated. Also being researched are anti-inflammatory drugs and vitamins E and C.

Although President Clinton lifted the ban on fetal tissue research in 1993, the current political climate makes it unlikely that there will be significant federal funding for this research in the future. There had been high hopes that healthy fetal brain cells would reveal the substances that stimulate the brain to make the chemicals needed for its survival, leading to a synthesized form of these substances that could revitalize the brains of Alzheimer's patients.

CytoTherapeutics, a biotechnology company, is investigating implanting a natural body chemical (Nerve Growth Factor) into the brain to protect cells from dying. Research has also begun at the University of California at San Diego, in which skin or muscle cells are taken from a patient's own body, stimulated to produce a crucial missing chemical, and then injected directly into the patient's brain (Heilman, 1995).

Nature may hold the key to an Alzheimer's cure. A chemist has synthesized a neurotoxin found in marine worms to make GTS-21, a compound that ameliorates some symptoms of Alzheimer's. A drug derived from a plant called a Caucasian snowdrop mimics the effects of the drug tacrine without the liver damage that often accompanies this drug (Lipkin, 1995).

Mental Status Exam

A popular "bedside" measure of cognitive status, the mini-mental state exam (MMSE) measures the cognitive component of mental state (see Box 12.4). This standardized test is quick (5–10 minutes) and easy to administer, eliminating—or indicating a need for—more extensive and detailed assessment of a patient (Dick et al., 1984).

The maximum score of 30 represents the sum of the correct responses. A score of 23 or less is usually suggestive of cognitive impairment. An important aspect of the MMSE is the consistency of its scores over time, making the exam an ideal indicator of possible Alzheimer's or other dementia. For example, if a patient's score has dropped more than five points over a two-year period, there is a strong indication of neurological disorder (Mitrushina & Satz, 1991).

Implications for Practice: Alzheimer's and the Family

In people with Alzheimer's disease, the individual's behavioral alterations (e.g., physical and verbal aggression, delusions, suspiciousness, uncontrollable agitation, wandering) have an enormous impact on the family as well as on the individual. When the disease is not too advanced, individuals may show signs of depression, which tend to exacerbate cognitive deficits (Belsky, 1990). Group and individual counseling are available to persons with Alzheimer's and their caregivers. If the disease is not too advanced, the person with Alzheimer's might benefit from a support group to discuss feelings, problems, and ideas for coping. Individual sessions might consist of cognitive training or reality orientation to help people remember important information and be reoriented to time, date, and place. Caregiver support groups and family treatment assist all (partners, spouses, children, or close friends) who care for one who has Alzheimer's. The focus of either type of treatment might be on dealing with feelings and frustrations and providing practical tips for coping with the situation. Respite

BOX 12.4

The Mini-Mental Status Exam (Example)

ORIENTATION

What is the time?
    date?
    day?
    month?
    year?   5 points (_____)

What is the name of this ward?
    this hospital?
    the county?
    the town?
    the country?   5 points (_____)

REGISTRATION

Name three objects. Score up to 3 points if, at the first attempt, the patient repeats, in order, the three objects you have randomly named. Score 2 or 1 if this is the number of objects he or she repeats correctly. Endeavor, by further attempts and prompting, to have all three repeated, so as to test recall later.

                    3 points (_____)

ATTENTION AND CALCULATION

Ask the patient to subtract 7 from 100, and then 7 from the result. Repeat this five times, scoring 1 for each time a correct subtraction is performed.

                    5 points (_____)

RECALL

Ask for the three objects repeated in the registration test, scoring one for each correctly recalled.

                    5 points (_____)

LANGUAGE

Score 1 point for two objects (a pencil and a watch) correctly named.

                    2 points (_____)

Score 1 point if the following sentence is correctly repeated: "No ifs, ands, or buts."

                    1 point (_____)

Score 3 if a three-stage command is correctly executed, scoring 1 for each stage. For example, "With the index finger of your right hand, touch the tip of your nose and then your left ear," or "Take this piece of paper in your right hand, fold it in half, and place it on the floor."

                    3 points (_____)

On a blank piece of paper write, "Close your eyes" and ask the patient to obey what is written. Score 1 point if patient closes his or her eyes.

                    1 point (_____)

Ask the patient to write a sentence. Score 1 if the sentence is sensible and has a verb and a subject.

                    1 point (_____)

Construct a pair of intersecting pentagons, each side 1 inch long. Score 1 if this is correctly copied.

                    1 point (_____)

       TOTAL SCORE (30 points) (_____)

Source: Dick et al., 1984.

care consists of supervised adult daytime health care for the person with Alzheimer's and provides the caregiver with periods of rest and relief. In some communities, in-home respite care is available for evenings, weekends, or longer time periods (Hyman, 1987).

Depression

A relatively small percentage of older people have major depressive disorders as classified by the DSM-IV (APA, 1994). What is not clear is the prevalence of mild depressive symptoms in late adulthood. The estimate of its prevalence has ranged anywhere from 5% to more than 30% (Gurland, Dean, Cross, & Golden, 1980; Waxman, McCreary, Weinrit, & Carner, 1985). It has been pointed out that late-life depression may be characterized by the following paradox: "Although the prevalence of depressive symptoms increases with age, the prevalence of major depressive disorders does not" (Kennedy et al., 1989).

Generally, it is difficult to distinguish between levels of depression. Depression is not the same as the sadness or unhappiness felt by people confronting everyday life. Symptoms of depression may include feelings of sadness and emptiness, withdrawal, self-neglect, changes in appetite, loss of sexual desire, and sleeping problems (Gruetzner, 1988). In older people, depressive symptoms are often associated with medical conditions that tend to mask the depression itself. Medical conditions commonly associated with depression include (1) coronary artery disease—e.g., hypertension, myocardial infarction; (2) neurologic disorders—e.g., cerebrovascular accidents, Alzheimer's disease; (3) metabolic disturbances—e.g., diabetes, hypo- or hyperthyroidism; (4) cancer—e.g., pancreatic, breast, lung; and (5) other conditions—e.g., arthritis, sexual dysfunction, and deafness (Sunderland, Lawlor, Molchan, & Martinez, 1988). Another study (Kennedy et al., 1989), using a representative sample of 2137 older urban residents, found a hierarchy of characteristics associated with substantial levels of depressive symptoms: illness, disability, isolation, bereavement, and poverty.

Symptoms of depression have been treated through the use of both medication and counseling. According to Belsky (1990), medication may work well with those symptoms tied to physical signs of illness and less well when tied to events. Counseling is the treatment of choice when the focus is on changing the "depression-causing situation or modifying the person's depression-generating thoughts" (p. 276).

Implications for Practice: Assessing Depression in Older Persons

Physical health and functioning are key factors associated with depression in older people. Depression has a reverberating effect in that the process of recovery may be impeded if the person is not motivated to pursue adequate medical attention and rehabilitation, maintain medical regimens, or engage in self-care. This may be particularly true if there is no hope to regain previous levels of functioning (Berkman et al., 1986). Interestingly, in a rural study (O'Hara, Kohout, & Wallace, 1985) that consisted of 3159 older adults (aged 65 to 105 years), the data indicated that prevalence of significant depressive symptomatology (9%) was low for this sample. Those most at risk for depression were women, people who lived alone, and those with lower incomes. There was also evidence that those at lower risk for depression were married and had attained higher educational levels. The investigators speculated that high levels of social support available in rural communities may account for low levels of depression.

The latter research suggests that social work practitioners should assist depressed older people in restoring broken social support systems or acquiring new systems through voluntary activities or special-interest groups, for example. For the older person who lives alone, home-sharing with a younger person who can assist around the house might be an option. Supportive approaches that emphasize the uncovering and mobilization of an individual's strengths to help them remain connected with life can be very useful. There has been considerable success in using cognitive behavioral approaches that assist the depressed client in identifying and changing depression-generating thoughts or cognitions.

One "quick" method of assessing potential depression in older people is the Geriatric Depression Scale (GDS), a 15-item validated scale (Yesavage et al., 1983). In scoring the scale, assign one point for each answer given as follows: questions 1, 5, 7, 11, and 13 answered no and the remainder answered yes. A normal score is 0–5; above 5 suggests depression (see Box 12.5).

Suicide

Suicide is a significant problem in late adulthood. Furthermore, although only a small proportion of depressed people commit suicide, most serious suicide attempts are made by depressed people (Belsky, 1990). Committing suicide because of depression over a lifetime of accumulated losses, debilitating terminal illnesses, isolation, loneliness, lack of a sense of control, and the like is not so surprising. When depression is defined all inclusively, it has been estimated that nearly 100% of older people who attempt suicide have depressive symptoms (Stenback, 1980).

The prevalence of suicide in any age group is difficult to determine with accuracy because suicides may be masked, for instance, as accidents or natural causes. A study (Manton, Blazer, & Woodbury, 1987) analyzing cross-temporal data on suicide (between 1962 and 1981) from the National Center on Health Statistics found that the suicide rate was highest in older white males, followed by nonwhite males, white females, and nonwhite females (see Figure 12.1). Note that the suicide rate for white men also peaked in middle age, whereas the suicide rate was highest for white women in middle age. For nonwhite males, the suicide rate was higher in young adulthood. Over time, the suicide rate for nonwhite females decreases with minor peaks. Another study (Rich, Young, & Fowler, 1986) indicated that the suicide rate per 100,000 population was 31.9% for males and 15.9% for females 65 and older.

Butler and colleagues (1991) speculate that the most preventable suicides are those related to depression since suicide "in these cases is a passive, desperate giving up" (p. 131). There are those, however, who choose their time of death before dependency and complete lack of control engulfs them. Some even advocate for **assisted suicide** (helping to provide the means to end a person's life) (see Focus on Ethics: Assisted Suicide) or **euthanasia** (putting to death those with a painful or debilitating terminal illness) (see Focus on Sociology: Right to Die).

BOX 12.5

Geriatric Depression Scale (GDS): Short Form (Example)

CIRCLE THE BEST ANSWER FOR HOW YOU FELT OVER THE PAST WEEK.

Are you basically satisfied with your life?	yes/no
Have you dropped many of your activities and interests?	yes/no
Do you feel that your life is empty?	yes/no
Do you often get bored?	yes/no
Are you in good spirits most of the time?	yes/no
Are you afraid that something bad is going to happen to you?	yes/no
Do you feel happy most of the time?	yes/no
Do you often feel helpless?	yes/no
Do you prefer to stay at home, rather than going out and doing new things?	yes/no
Do you feel you have more problems with memory than most?	yes/no
Do you think it is wonderful to be alive now?	yes/no
Do you feel pretty worthless the way you are now?	yes/no
Do you feel full of energy?	yes/no
Do you feel that your situation is hopeless?	yes/no
Do you think that most people are better off than you are?	yes/no

Source: Yesavage et al., 1983.

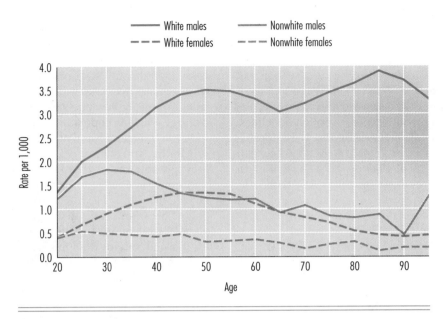

FIGURE 12.1   **Suicide rates**   Source: Manton, Blazer, & Woodbury, 1987.

FOCUS ON ETHICS

Assisted Suicide: Murder or Mercy?

Dr. Jack Kavorkian, known as "Dr. Death," may be news-worthy in the United States, but he's actually part of a tradition that has been operational in the Netherlands for more than a decade. Moved and concerned by the moral burden posed by participating in euthanasia and assisted suicide, the Royal Dutch Medical Association has recently proposed some refinements to existing euthanasia guidelines. The Association's present rules address several crucial areas. First, the patient's request for euthanasia must be made independently and voluntarily. In addition, the patient must have been well-informed about the alternatives and have a firm and lasting resolve to die. The patient's suffering must be experienced as hopeless and unbearable, with the physician concluding that the suffering cannot be remedied. The physician must have a consultation with at least one colleague familiar with euthanasia-related cases and issues; the proper written documentation, including the patient's medical history and the declaration that the above rules have been met, must be generated. The new guidelines, put together by lawyers and ethicists as well as doctors, appear in a 39-page policy document sent out in August 1995 to the 24,000 members of the Royal Dutch Medical Association. Although the new rules do not propose any fundamental changes, they do impose some restrictions on the existent guidelines. The first refinement suggests that whenever possible, doctors should have terminally ill patients administer their own fatal drugs, as opposed to a physician administering an intravenous drip or injection. Second, the new rules stipulate that the outside consultation must be with a physician who does not have a preexisting professional or family relationship with the patient or the attending doctor. Finally, although no doctor is required to perform euthanasia, he or she is obligated to inform patients of his or her moral position so that a patient wishing to die might contact another physician for assistance.

It is the position of the Association and its proponents that the patient's participation in the termination of his or her own life helps diminish, if only slightly, the difficult moral and emotional burden experienced by the assisting physician. Opponents of euthanasia and assisted suicide suggest a perversity in the euthanasia logic that refusing to kill someone is considered cruel, and that agreeing to kill the person is compassionate. One such opponent suggests that at the heart of the Netherlands' problem is a lack of facilities for palliative care, such as hospices, which could alleviate the pain and suffering that lead patients to wish to end their lives. But is this simply a way to ease the collective conscience of the living?

Source: Written by Julianne Azimov, based on Simons, 1995.

The Living Will and Medical Power of Attorney

If a person has a terminal illness that is not treatable or reversible, the **living will** allows that person to document that he or she does not want to be kept alive by artificial means but instead desires care only for comfort. The person states that he or she does not wish to be resuscitated if breathing stops or if his or her heart stops beating.

The **medical power of attorney** applies to a person with any illness (not necessarily a terminal one). If an ill person loses the ability to make medical decisions regarding his or her care, the medical power of attorney designates someone to have the authority to make those decisions for the ill person.

Many hospitals give the patient the option to make a living will or to designate medical power of attorney on admission. These documents do not require a lawyer or a notary; they require only a witness. These documents can be revoked in writing at any time.

FOCUS ON SOCIOLOGY

Right to Die

Two years ago my mother, who was then 83, told me that she planned to end her life by taking an overdose of pills.

Her health was failing rapidly and she was going blind. She didn't want to become weak and dependent. She had always been a fierce and active woman. She wrote her intentions in a letter to me—I was her only close family member—and she told two friends and her doctor. We all told her that we would not help her accumulate enough pills to do the job. And I think we all worked very hard to help her find new reasons to be happy to be alive. But finally I understood that she really wanted to do what she had planned, and in the end, after she gathered together enough pills and took them, I sat with her for the last 36 hours as she slipped away. I can't tell you how many of her friends and acquaintances told me how graceful my mother was in her life to the very end. For my mother, given her personality, staying in control of her own life made her graceful. (a 41-year-old woman)

Source: From Howell, Allen, & Doress, 1987.

Social Dimension
Families, Groups, Support Systems, and Contexts

Today's older people have experienced all the influences of neonatal development, infancy, childhood, adolescence, early adulthood, and middle age. The development and behavior of the young-old, the middle-old, and the old-old also have been shaped by different historic events over their life spans as well as by unique events that have influenced their lives positively or negatively. Development, however, does not stop with age. The contexts of older people's lives continues to influence their growth and development.

Families

Social work family theorists Hartman and Laird (1987) have defined two types of families, one that is created and one that is inherited: "A family [then] is created when two or more people construct an intimate environment that they define as a family, an environment in which they generally will share a living space, commitment, and a variety of roles and functions usually considered part of family life. The second family, common to all human beings and psychologically important whether or not close ties have been maintained, is the family of origin—that family of blood or **bloodlike ties** (such as those that occur in adoption), both vertical (intergenerational) and horizontal (kinship), living and dead, close and distant, known and unknown" (p. 576).

The behavior of older adults is influenced to some extent by the patterns present in their families of origin. To their created or chosen family forms, older people have brought with them certain sets of values, beliefs, and varied ways of interacting with others and with their environments. Created family forms in late adulthood are as diverse as they were in other periods of development. Some older adults live with their spouses of 40 years or more; others are newlyweds; some are widowed, single, or never married; and others are gay men or lesbians. In a sense, those who reside in nursing homes can count other residents and staff as family as well as adult children and other relatives. For noninstitutionalized older people, other relatives with whom they live may include parents, children, siblings, nieces, or nephews. Older people living with nonrelatives may include gay or lesbian partners, friends, or "roommates." Those who live alone may count as family a circle of friends, as well as children and other relatives. It is obvious that the configurations of created family forms among older people are both diverse and complex. For purposes of this discussion of family, however, we shall include only relationships between marital pairs, gay male and lesbian partnerships, parents and children, grandparents and grandchildren, and friends.

Couples   Most of the studies on satisfaction with marital relationships have used cross-sectional approaches, which tend to measure cohort differences rather than relationships over time. More longitudinal studies are needed to accomplish the latter. Early studies (Blood & Wolfe, 1960; Pineo, 1969) showed that marital satisfaction decreased over time, particularly after children were born. Later studies (Miller, 1976; Orthner, 1975; Rollins & Feldman, 1970), however, have shown that although marital satisfaction drops when children are born, it tends to rise to previous highs in the postparental period. Marital pairs have the opportunity to rediscover and renew their relationship and have the time to spend with one another in pursuit of joint interests. There is some

evidence (Atchley & Miller, 1983) that people with higher socioeconomic status and levels of education experience greater marital satisfaction than do those who are more impoverished and less well educated (Depner & Ingersol-Dayton, 1985). Marital satisfaction for those who remarry in old age appears to be quite high (McKain, 1972). These individuals typically are in good health and are seeking others with whom they can enjoy such activities as travel and leisure. Studies (Atchley & Miller, 1983; Duvall & Miller, 1985) have shown, though, that when one of the marital partners becomes ill, the other partner's morale declines. However, the illness does not appear to erode the bond between husband and wife (Johnson, 1983). Indeed, the healthy spouse becomes the primary caregiver and rarely seeks outside help (Cantor, 1983; Johnson, 1983). As with other age groups, satisfaction or happiness with marriage differs among the old; some remain close and in love and others do not. The following Focus on Diversity section looks at homosexuality and older adults.

FOCUS ON DIVERSITY

Homosexuality and Older Adults

According to Kimmel (1978), four conclusions can be drawn with respect to the present state of knowledge about adult gay male and lesbian development:

1. Little is known about life-span development for gay males and lesbians except for those who are white, relatively well educated, and financially stable.
2. Older gay males differ from younger gay males, but it is not clear whether this is due to normative processes of aging or history-graded influences. The likelihood is that this same question exists with respect to older and younger lesbians.
3. Stereotypes of lonely, depressed, sexually frustrated gay men are invalid for samples examined to date. One can draw the same conclusions about lesbians.
4. The unique concerns of lesbians and gay men are not known. Innovative research is needed to assess these special needs.

In the 17 years since Kimmel's article was published, the state of knowledge about lesbians and gay men has expanded, but not substantially. One study (Kehoe, 1989) of older lesbians included 106 respondents, 60 years of age and older, who were asked to respond to lifestyle issues, relationships, sexuality, life satisfaction, and so forth. From the data, Kehoe developed the following profile of the older lesbian.

The subject is white, 67 years of age, and overweight. She has never been married to a man and is childless. Her education and work experience are above average and place her in the professional category. She holds a graduate degree and is now retired. Her gross income in 1983 was between $25,000 and $50,000 a year. She does not smoke and is a social drinker only. She does not frequent bars, lesbian or otherwise, but does belong to a lesbian social group, and most of her friends are lesbians. Her self-image is good, and she feels very positive about being a lesbian. She has not been aware of being discriminated against because of her lifestyle. She is not currently involved with another woman and has always considered sex only "one important part" of any relationship. She believes in monogamy and has never wanted to change her sex. Her history indicates that she has been either exclusively homosexual, or homosexual with only incidental heterosexual episodes. She is not bisexual (based on Kehoe, 1989, pp. 75–76).

Older gay males are more likely to designate their relationship as one of being "roommates," similar to male heterosexual roommates (Diamond & Karlen, 1980). The relationship may be long-term, emotionally supportive, and include a division of responsibility for maintenance like any family. Sex may be sought outside the relationship. This behavior, however, does not differ much for some heterosexual males. Lesbians, on the other hand, tend to form long-term monogamous relationships and view sexual aggressiveness or immorality as offensive, similar to heterosexual females (Diamond & Karlen, 1980).

Quam and Whitford's (1992) study of 80 (39 women, 41 men) lesbians and gay men over age 50 showed that concerns for these groups included areas typical of all who age: loneliness, health, and income. The investigators also stated that previously or currently married respondents indicated another layer of special concerns for the future when they "wrote movingly of

fears of rejection by adult children and grandchildren when, as a parent or grandparent, they came out to their family" (p. 373). In terms of social work practice, Woodman and Lenna (1980) delineate some factors that place stressors on lesbian or gay male relationships: lack of familial support; legal issues with respect to child custody, survivor's benefits, and hospital visitation; and rejection and oppression by traditional formal support systems (e.g., religious institutions).

Parent-Child Relationships Increased health and longevity have further complicated parent-child relationships. In the normal course of events, cohort (generational) differences cause conflicts between parents and children over the life span. A younger adult child, for instance, may have little patience or understanding of the experience of a parsimonious older parent who lived through the Depression. The complexity of parent-child relationships increases even more when aging parents have older adult children. Children who themselves are approaching retirement age, with all its constraints and concerns (e.g., income, health), may have to care for older parents as well. Caregiving of elderly parents by aging children is a very common phenomenon in today's society. And for some aging children, responsibilities have not ceased for their own young adult children (e.g., financial, emotional). Caregiving, typically, is the responsibility of the adult daughter rather than the son. Brody (1981), a social worker, and her colleagues coined the phrase "women in the middle," which implies that such women are in middle age, in the middle from a generational standpoint, and in the middle in that the demands of their various roles compete for their time and energy. To an extent unprecedented in history, roles as paid workers and as caregiving daughters and daughters-in-law to dependent older people have been added to their traditional roles as wives, homemakers, mothers, and grandmothers (p. 471).

Caregiving of older parents is an issue that has had and will continue to have an enormous impact on families in the future. Current literature abounds on the intricacies of caregiving; for instance, a small list includes gender and caregiving (Baruch & Spaid, 1989; Young & Kahana, 1989), dementia and caregiving (Dura, Haywood-Niler, Kiecolt-Glaser, 1990; Hinrichsen & Ramirez, 1992), and stress and burden of caregiving (Cattanach & Tebes, 1991; Stephens, Kinney, & Ogrocki, 1991). Caregiving can be extraordinarily stressful for any adult children, but the burdens of homosexual and single adults caring for an older parent may have additional consequences if they have never been married nor had children of their own. Take, for example, the situation of a 57-year-old gay man who cares for his 90-year-old mother in the home.

Ricardo, as we shall call him, has schizophrenia, is stabilized on medication and supportive treatment, and has 15 years of sobriety from alcoholism. His mother is bedridden and needs constant personal care. According to his social worker, Ricardo and his mother live in the family home and are supported by their disability and social security income. Ricardo is a bright, well-read, articulate individual who cultivates a large vegetable garden each year and cares for his mother with tenderness and concern. Ricardo's caregiving role has kept him from pursuing other interests and relationships, but he does not complain. There are times when he speculates about what will happen after the death of his mother and when he reaches old age. There will be no one left in the family to call upon.

Because the issues of caregiving are so complex and overwhelming, it often is easy to view older people as always the recipients rather than the givers of help. A growing body of research (see, e.g., Cantor, 1979; Patterson, 1987; Quam, 1983) indicates older people provide a remarkable amount of help not only to relatives but also to friends and neighbors. In her study of natural helpers (relatives, friends, and neighbors to whom one turns in time of need), Patterson (1987) found that older respondents assisted relatives, friends, and neighbors with a range of life transitional, environmental, and interpersonal relationship difficulties. The relatives helped were not just adult children, grandchildren, and their own parents but also siblings, in-laws, and other relatives (aunts and uncles, nieces and nephews, cousins). Thus, the informal caregiving role should be expanded to include a wider variety of helpers (neighbors and friends) as well as the old themselves.

Grandparenthood   For many older people (80%), grandparenthood is a role in which they find joy in their relationships with grandchildren. Moreover, most view grandparenting as easier than it was to be a parent (Brubaker, 1985). Even if there are infrequent contacts with grand-

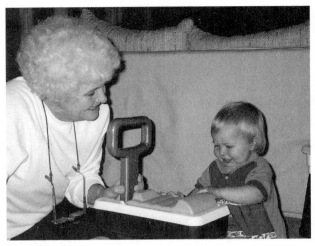

Grandparents can be important figures in a child's life and can play a significant role in transmitting cultural and family values to children.

children, grandparents state that being a grandparent has significant meaning in their lives (Wood & Robertson, 1978). According to Hagestad (1985), grandparenting has many meanings, some which are intangible:

> Grandparents serve as symbols of connectedness within and between lives; as people who can listen and have time to do so; as reserves of time, help, and attention; as links to the unknown past; as people who are sufficiently varied, flexible, and complex to defy easy categories and clear-cut roles. (p. 48)

Grandparenting appears to have different functions in some families, depending on such factors as ethnicity or culture. For instance, Hagestad (1985) found that grandmothers were closer to both their children and grandchildren than grandfathers and provided more personal advice to them. Robertson (1976) found that young adult working-class grandchildren perceived their grandparents positively and their primary expectation of the grandparents was to provide emotional gratification and nurturance. About two-thirds of the young adults viewed their responsibility toward the grandparents as helping without payment. In a study of African American, white, and Mexican American grandparenting relationships, Bengston (1985) found that Mexican American grandparents and grandchildren had closer relationships with one another than the white and African American respondents had with their grandchildren. Furthermore, these grandparents had more frequent contact with their grandchildren and assumed more supportive roles to them and their parents.

Friendships

Friends play an important, supportive role in old age (Crohan & Antonucci, 1989). Sandmaier (1995) states that the bond of friendship is elective, more fragile than ties with kin, and has no formalized rituals. And, she writes further, "as we move through our lives, the friends we've made and kept over time take on an increasingly vital role as curators of our emotional histories" (p. 34). Litwak and Szelenyi (1969) identified three types of primary group structures: kin, neighbors, and friends, each with different functions. Ties of kinship are characterized by the permanence of relationship and/or legal responsibility. Thus kin are more likely to exchange support and resources in situations requiring long-term commitment, such as the care of an aged member or financial aid during prolonged unemployment. Ties among neighbors are based on face-to-face contact and immediate proximity and, in urban life, tend to lack permanence in this era of geographic mobility. Thus neighbors are more likely to exchange resources and services that do not require a long-term commitment (such as short-term baby-sitting or transportation for shopping or medical appointments). Ties among friends lack, to some degree, the permanence of kinship ties and often the proximity of neighbors. But because friendship rests on mutual regard and often affection, friends are more likely to exchange guidance, advice, and emotional support. In her study of the support systems of 400 women over 50 (Mn = 66 years), Quam (1983) found that friends were most likely to be called upon for expressive support (e.g., listening to personal/family problems) and unlikely to be called upon for instrumental support (e.g., financial). Frauenhofer and colleagues (1987, p. 129) quote a 75-year-old woman who aptly describes the importance of social support in later adulthood.

> The greatest pleasure of growing old is remaining in contact with friends from church and in the community. I'm treasurer of the Older Women's League chapter here, and also the Black Caucus on Aging. I kept contact with my friends from childhood. I love people, all kinds of people. I don't give up a relationship easily. I only gave up one in

seventy-two years, someone who really, really hurt me. I am friends with my ex-husband's second wife and went to see her on my vacation. She was so glad to see me.

Friendships have a special salience for gay men, lesbians, single adults, and those who have moved to retirement communities, often some distance from children, grandchildren, and other relatives. For instance, one group, known as the Sun Citians evolved into a close-knit cadre of friends when they started a limerick group to "put a little humor in their lives." The group ranges in age from 52 to 92 and meets frequently for potluck dinners and limerick construction. Once a year, the group takes a trip together to such places as Santa Fe and San Diego, and one year they rented a houseboat on Lake Powell. The group has become emotionally close and supportive and has unlimited abilities to laugh at themselves. A 72-year-old member penned the following (V. Wood, 1996, personal communication):

> There was an old man in Sun City
> Who really was smart and quite witty,
>   But he was blind as a bat,
>   And so was his cat,
> How in the heck can we end such a ditty?

Nursing Homes

Long-term care can be defined as medical and social interventions for those who have chronic illnesses or impairments. These interventions are geared toward helping a patient live as satisfactorily as possible and may be provided in a number of settings, including normal private homes, supportive housing, and nursing homes or other institutions.

About 5% of older people live in long-term-care facilities, and many feel that a nursing home is a "last resort," when other resources have been exhausted or the situation has become desperate. Actually, nursing homes may be more realistically viewed as a specialized resource for those who need a higher level of care than can be provided at home.

The decision to move to assisted living can be a difficult one for families and individuals. Many older adults wish to remain independent as long as possible. Many family members wish to provide care for older relatives for as long as possible. Some older people have no one to provide needed care. When an older adult becomes confused and disoriented, wanders off without warning, is incontinent, or is bedridden, help becomes necessary. The problem then becomes finding appropriate placement. Custodial care of older people is not covered by most insurance. The cost of nursing homes or assisted living can be more than many older adults' monthly income from Social Security or a pension. Older adults living on a fixed income may have to exhaust their resources and savings to become eligible for state- or federal-government-funded placement. Social workers are often involved in helping older adults obtain adequate care at home or appropriate placement. The following Focus on Sociology section describes guidelines that can be used for choosing a nursing home.

FOCUS ON SOCIOLOGY

Choosing a Nursing Home

Although national standards have led to a high level of quality in most nursing homes, here are some guidelines for those seeking an excellent facility for a client or loved one:

- Be sure the nursing home is licensed. Medicare and Medicaid eligibility may also be an indication of basic quality, but some excellent facilities accept only private payments. Also check for membership in the American Health Care Association, which sets high standards for quality.
- Walk through the facility and smell the air. Occasional odors from incontinence and other medical conditions are unavoidable, but a persistently bad-smelling facility is probably poorly run.
- Check the fee schedule. Be sure you understand exactly what services are included, and beware of hidden charges.
- Request a full tour, including the kitchen. Be suspicious of any facility that denies this request.
- Talk to staff members at every level, especially the aides who have the most contact with residents. Watch them interact with residents.
- Ask about a backup plan for medical emergencies. If

the patient's regular doctor is not available, what happens?
- Observe the residents. Do they appear well cared for?
- Be sure the rules about visitors and residents leaving the vicinity for outside activities are reasonable and flexible.
- Ask about choices for residents. Are they allowed to choose activities, foods, furnishings? Can they bring treasured belongings from home?

Source: Adapted from Roth & Atherton, 1989.

Hospice

Up until World War II, death was a part of the human experience and of the life of the community. People died at home in the presence of friends and family. Everyone, including children, saw and experienced death as an integral part of life (Munley, 1983). Today, many people live in areas separated from extended family. Many adults have never seen a dying person or experienced a death.

In fact, modern medicine has almost made death an isolated phenomenon of older people. Those over 65 account for two-thirds of all deaths; and the majority of total deaths occur from diseases of older adults, such as stroke, cancer, and heart disease. Instead of occurring at home in the midst of loved ones, most of these deaths now occur in a hospital.

This movement of death from the home to the hospital occurred shortly after World War II. According to Kastenbaum (1981), attitudes toward death then changed, as though people were trying to pretend death did not exist. Efforts to provide an alternative to hospital death resulted in the **hospice** movement. Hospice became important in treating terminal patients when families, patients, and caregivers found hospitals were not meeting their needs. In contrast to the goals of a hospital, the aim of hospice is to care for and support the dying. Whereas the major focus of the hospital is to cure, the major focus of hospice is pain and symptom control.

Individuals are eligible for hospice when they have less than a six-month life expectancy and agree to give up seeking a cure for their illness. Hospice care is provided in the patient's home and sometimes in a special hospice unit in a hospital or community agency. Many hospice patients are older persons, and many are dying of cancer.

But, increasingly, hospice patients are young people with AIDS. The purpose of the hospice is to allow the patient to experience death, not in isolation, but in an atmosphere of love and acceptance.

Retirement

Retirement occurs when one leaves the workforce and begins living on some kind of pension. Often, retirement is thought of as the period at which people begin to receive social security or other pension benefits. Although most people think of retirement as occurring around age 65, it arrives earlier for many people. In fact, some people plan to retire in their fifties. This trend has been increasing as many companies are offering a package of early retirement to entice people to retire, often done to free up personnel money for new workers.

What would it be like to go from working on the same job or in a similar job for 30–40 years to becoming retired? No schedule to follow, no alarms to set, no need to be in rush-hour traffic, no performance or work reviews, none of the familiar behaviors that are associated with work. For many older adults, retirement can be a difficult period of adjustment. In fact, for a long time many theorists thought that retirement automatically led to a crisis. From this perspective, retirement was considered negative, hazardous to one's physical and mental health. Now research has found that this is not the case and that, although retirement may require some special adjustment, it does not have to be a crisis.

Still, retirement is a major shift in one's family roles, daily activity, social interactions, and financial resources. How one anticipates these changes can affect how successfully one retires. Atchley (1976) identifies a process of adjustment to retirement that moves through a series of changes. Individuals begin at the *preretirement phase*, which is an opportunity to begin to think and plan for retirement. Just after retirement, individuals often move into a *honeymoon phase*, where their newfound freedom is unleashed and they enjoy increased opportunities for visiting family and friends and enjoying leisure time, sports activities, gardening, and so forth. Not surprisingly, the honeymoon phase ends and leads to a *disenchantment phase*, where retirement does not seem as pleasant as before. Last, the individual moves to a *reorientation phase* and becomes more realistic about retirement and learns to make the necessary adaptations. Research (Ekerdt, Bossé, & Levkoff, 1985) has found that these phases are accurate. Men recently retired were satisfied and optimistic about the future, but 13 to 18 months later they were disenchanted with their lives, and men in long-term retirement were satisfied and reoriented.

Retirement is made more difficult for individuals who have little income to begin with and must then adjust to a reduction in income. Many older adults become embarrassed and uncomfortable with the notion that they have little money and cannot provide for their family as they may have done in the past. The following Focus on Multiculturalism section discusses how some cultures have no retirement.

FOCUS ON MULTICULTURALISM

Some Cultures Have No Retirement

If you were living among the !Kung San of the Kalahari Desert in Africa, you would not understand the concept of retirement. As adults get older, rather than being put into retirement they are considered important people who have respect among the community. They take on a number of critical roles for the community: (1) stewards of water rights and resources in the area; (2) keepers of knowledge, skills, and lore; (3) teachers and caretakers of children; (4) spiritual teachers and healers; and (5) privileged community members. In many respects, these roles are based on reciprocal obligations across the life cycle (Biesele & Howell, 1981). There is no retirement here. Men continue to perform hunting and healing functions, and women remain gatherers and healers. As they grow old, men move to less taxing responsibilities such as trapping, gathering, visiting, and telling stories. Women move to less physical activities as well, including child care and production of handicrafts.

Multicultural and Gender Considerations

Greene (1994) states that "members of an ethnic group think of themselves as a 'people' . . . with diverse life-style, languages, histories, and cultural strengths and supports" (p. 6). To work with different ethnic groups, social workers must acquire informed, competent, and culturally sensitive services. Because there is such diversity in minority groups, difficulties often are generated in health and mental health services as a result of inflexibilities in these systems. Successful service provision to minority older people (Cuellar, 1980) is dependent on whether services are located in the ethnic community and are easily accessible, have an informal and personalized environment, have a client-oriented staff that helps them get all the services needed, and have bilingual or indigenous outreach workers who are culturally sensitive and concerned about the people and the community they serve. One common factor that appears to be present in diverse Native American tribes is the concept of the extended family. This form of family may be influenced by residence (urban or reservation), acculturation, socioeconomic factors, and varied family circumstances. Younger family members seek both advice and support from their elders. In assuming a central role in the family, older Native Americans provide spiritual, cultural, and behavioral guidance for younger family members. Grandparenting is viewed as an important responsibility, and it is not uncommon for older people to take over complete child-rearing responsibilities for their adult children. In exchange for these kinds of help, older Native Americans are respected and cared for if they become unable to care for themselves (Shoemaker, 1989). Informal support is more plentiful on reservations than in urban areas because of the close proximity of family members.

In the past, there was a certain set of role behaviors expected of males and females in traditional Indian culture. It is likely that gender-role expectations are maintained among the oldest Native Americans. For instance, older women assumed responsibility for such expressive functions as "kin-keeping," whereas men retained the employment role. With rapid societal changes, impoverishment, and acculturation, more middle-aged to young-old women are assuming leadership roles than in the past (Hanson, 1980).

To understand African American families, it is critical to investigate an array of factors: African cultural influences, racial oppression, social class differences both within and between groups, and family and kinship networks (Dodson, 1988). For instance, in one study (John-son & Barer, 1990) of families and networks among older inner-city African Americans, the investigators found that both African Americans and whites used formal support systems when they needed help, but African Americans had more active informal support networks than whites did, despite the low incidence of child and spousal support. The investigators postulate that African American families expand their network membership through the creation of fictive kin, which can consist of friends, godparents, children in other families, church members, and the like. In effect, such individuals assume the rights and obligations found among kin. This phenomena was referred to by Hartman (1978) when she defined family of origin as that family of blood or "bloodlike" ties. Thus, family boundaries are broadened in African American cultures and reinforced by the use of such familial terminology as "brother," "sister," "aunt," and "uncle" when these individuals may not be related by blood.

There is a growing highly educated middle class emerging in the African American culture that is represented in high occupational ranks, yet a disproportionate number of African Americans are illiterate and impoverished, including older people (Markides & Mindel, 1987). African American men have been stereotyped in this country as irresponsible, criminalistic, and lacking in masculinity, whereas African American women have been viewed as the backbone or strong person in the marital dyad (Staples, 1988). Marital relationships have been influenced by socioeconomic and educational factors such that the divorce rate among African Americans is twice that of whites (Ho, 1987). Over time, middle-aged and older African American women have been a source of strength to their families. A qualitative study (Allen & Chin-Sang, 1990) has shown that within the context of lifelong work histories, older African American women have followed a pattern of unpaid agricultural work in childhood, paid domestic and service work as adults, and volunteer work in church and senior centers as retirees. By incorporating their lifetime of hard work into leisure activities and service to self and others, African American women have continued a history of self-reliance in old age.

The notion of extended family is a very strong orientation among all populations of Hispanics (Applewhite, 1988), although their migration histories differ (Gelfand & Barresi, 1987). The Hispanic family, which also includes close friends and godparents, is viewed as a warm, nurturing circle of people who foster a sense of belonging. Traditionally, the Hispanic family has designated certain family roles and functions by generation and sex. In terms of the male in the family, the nature of *machismo* has taken many varying forms, from head of the household, decision maker, breadwinner, authority over spouse and children to provider of protection and the one responsible for those who cannot care for themselves. The opposite tradition, *marianismo*, refers to the self-sacrificing female who, as wife and mother, complements the traditional male role. The period of the life cycle, coupled with individual personalities and degree of acculturation, determine the actual extent to which Hispanic men and women assume these roles (Applewhite, 1988).

Older people in Hispanic families are viewed as wise, knowledgeable, and deserving of respect from the young. Respect of elders emphasizes their past labor for the family and their providing continuity for its members over the life cycle. When they can no longer assume paid work roles, older Hispanics become transmitters of their culture, nurturers and protectors of small children, family historians, and teachers of the faith (Bacerra, 1988).

Gender Issues

Hess (1990) summed up the major issue with respect to gender and age: "Because the life course is played out within systems of stratification, sex and race distinctions will remain crucial to understanding the process of aging in any society as long as gender and racial equality remain distant goals" (p. 15). Women tend to have a longer life expectancy than men do but women experience more chronic and disabling diseases than do their male counterparts, who have more fatal diseases (Markides, 1990). As noted earlier, 17% of women, contrasted with 7% of men, live alone. This isolation, coupled with potential chronic disabilities, makes women prime candidates for institutionalization, whereas men with disabilities are most likely to be cared for by a spouse—55% compared with 18% of women (Hess, 1990). According to the U. S. Senate, Special Committee on Aging (1988), three out of four nursing home residents are women, three-fourths are over age 80, 84% are unmarried, and 93% are white. Women of color are more likely to be cared for by a relative. If nursing home placement is necessary, it is critical for social work practitioners and family members to thoroughly investigate the facility and its policies.

Social Hazards

The social hazards of late adulthood may take many forms. It is, for instance, a hazard to cross a busy intersection of a large metropolitan area during rush hour. Untold numbers of people are killed by careless or drunk drivers. Older people are particularly vulnerable to being victimized. Victimization may take a more violent form in terms of mugging or robberies, or it may take a more subtle direction in terms of fraudulent money "scams" or selling people goods and services that are unneeded. Two particular types of hazards older adults may experience are abuse and stereotyping.

Elder Abuse

Battering or abuse typically is perpetrated on older persons by family members and home-care workers or in institutions where they reside. Five different types of **elder abuse** have been identified and delineated by Wolf and Pillemer (1989): (1) physical abuse, causing pain or injury (e.g., broken bones, burns); (2) psychological abuse, causing mental or emotional anguish (e.g., threats, intimidation, shaming); (3) material abuse, illegal or improper use of the person's resources; (4) active neglect, refusal to care for the older person, deliberate attempt to place physical and emotional stress on the person (e.g., leaving an incontinent person alone, denial of food); and (5) passive abuse, refusal or failure to care for the older person because of inadequate knowledge or own disabilities.

As with any family secret, the prevalence of abuse is difficult to determine but may be as much as 4% a year. It has been estimated that as many as 1 million older people have been abused at some point. Spousal abuse is the most prevalent form of abuse, followed by abuse perpetrated by an adult child. Abuse often is associated with the caregiver's mental illness, chronic disease, or alcoholism. According to Breckman and Adelman (1988), the risk factors for mistreatment or abuse include the presence of one or more of the following:

- Presence of family member's mental illness, dementia, retardation, or drug or alcohol abuse

- A history of family violence
- Older person's dependency on others to meet all physical and emotional needs
- Older person's isolation from others and activities of choice
- Stressful life events such as financial loss, death, divorce
- Older person who lives with caregiver

Hooyman and Lustbader (1986) have outlined the areas of assessment social workers should cover when poor care is evident:

• *What has been the nature of the long-term relationship between family members and the older person?* Were the adult children physically or sexually abused earlier in life? When forced to be caregivers, those with unresolved resentments may consciously or unwittingly use the situation to get back at the parent. The power to withhold needed help to a physically vulnerable parent offers adult children a position of superior strength, which can play into past and current battles.

• *What current life problems unrelated to the care needs are pressuring family members?* Are financial constraints interfering with compliance with medical recommendations? Is the primary caregiver overwhelmed by demands from several dependent people at once? Job stresses, personal health limitations, and worries about their own children are examples of problems that may affect caregivers' capacities to meet care demands constructively.

• *What difficulties are resulting directly from the older person's care needs?* How much rest are caregivers getting? What personal sacrifices are caregivers making in order to serve the person's needs? How much constant surveillance is involved in the caregiving tasks? Is the care especially stressful or repugnant? How drastically has the older person's personality changed in response to illness? When difficult care needs are present, the availability of extra help and professional support become critical determinants of family members' ability to sustain nonabusive care (p. 104).

Stereotyping

Individual and family development occurs within a context influenced by economic, historical, cultural, and social factors. By examining these factors over time, we have seen the birth, growth, and development of ageism, sexism, and racism. It is highly likely that every American will experience one or more prejudiced acts if they reach late adulthood. On the basis of income and health alone, it is clear that older women of color are in triple jeopardy (Edmonds, 1990), carrying the burdens of **ageism,** racism, and sexism. Robert Butler (1990) called ageism a disease in which prejudices and stereotypes are applied to older people simply on the basis of their age. Despite the discriminatory assaults experienced by older adults, they tend to prevail and continue to enrich the lives of those around them.

Living on a Fixed Income

In 1993, though the median income of families headed by persons 65 and over was $25,821, the range in income was wide—approximately 21% of family households with an older person as head had incomes of less than $15,000, whereas 41% had incomes of $30,000 or more. And for non–heads of households, 45% of persons living alone or with nonrelatives had incomes below $10,000. In fact, approximately 3.8 million older people were below the poverty level (in 1993, $8740 for an older couple or household and $6930 for an individual), and another 2.3 million were classified as "near-poor." In 1993, 11% of whites, 28% of African Americans, and 21% of Hispanic older people were impoverished (AARP & AOA, 1994).

Many individuals in other stages of life can look to the future with the hope of increasing their income in various ways (promotion, new job, spouse returns to work, kids leave home). But for many older people, retirement means living on a **fixed income,** which does not increase from year to year. Often that income is reduced after retirement by one-third or one-half (Schuster & Ashburn, 1992). These older adults then need to adjust their lifestyle to cope with this reduced availability of financial resources. Adjustments range from eating out less often to substantially reducing their food intake; from moving to a smaller home to forgoing necessary home repairs and doing without heat and air conditioning. Even those who saved money for retirement may find their resources greatly reduced after a prolonged illness. For women, the problem may be even more severe because twice as many women as men tend to fall below the poverty level (Hess, 1990).

Many older adults live in poverty on a fixed income.

APPLYING THE FRAMEWORK

Depression in an Older Woman

Esther Rodriguez is a 77-year-old widow who broke her hip three months ago. After a two-week hospital stay for emergency hip replacement surgery and four weeks in a convalescent facility for strengthening and mobility training, she is staying in her daughter and son-in-law's home because she was not fully capable of caring for herself independently when her need for skilled services (and thus her Medicare coverage) ended at the convalescent facility. She was referred to Catholic Social Services by her daughter, who wanted help in making long-range plans for her mother's care.

Mrs. Rodriguez has lived in the same house for nearly 50 years. She raised two sons and a daughter there. Her husband, who died five years ago, worked for the railroad. Mrs. Rodriguez was primarily a homemaker, but she supplemented the family income by selling her homemade tortillas and tamales to neighborhood restaurants. Mrs. Rodriguez's older son died, at age 52, of cancer two years ago. Her younger son lives in another state with his second wife and their children. Mrs. Rodriguez's daughter, Ana Clark, 50, and Ana's husband, Joe Clark, are purchasing the modern   *(continued)*

Depression in an Older Woman

(continued)   townhouse that they moved into five years ago. It is located on the opposite side of town from Mrs. Rodriguez. Ana is a self-employed C.P.A. She and her husband own their own accounting firm. They have two grown children and three grandchildren. One of their sons, age 24, is living in their home while he seeks employment.

Developmental History

Mr. and Mrs. Rodriguez had made a comfortable adjustment to retirement and had about seven years together before his death five years ago. Mrs. Rodriguez's activities had not changed as much as her husband's, but she spent less time in church activities with the other women and more time gardening and working around the house with her husband. Once a week, however, she had lunch with three of her best high school friends while her husband played bingo with his retired friends at church. On Sundays, her daughter Ana and son-in-law Joe came for dinner. Her husband's death was very hard for her. It took her nearly two years before she felt she could wake up and not ache from feeling lonely. Following her son's death two years ago, she again had a very hard time. Ana reported that her mother never seemed to be her old self after that.

The current circumstances of Mrs. Rodriguez and her daughter's family are stressing the natural stages of family and individual life cycle development. Mrs. Rodriguez's role with her older son (wise parent, loving mother) has been prematurely interrupted as has his role with her and his sister (responsible son who can help with maintenance of family home, validation of parental wisdom and elder's value). Ana is just into the stage of launching children and moving on, but her son's return home and now her mother's living with her is requiring a return to more caretaking and home-management demands. Ana and her mother have been arguing daily about Mrs. Rodriguez returning to her own home. Ana is worried that her mother will forget to take her blood pressure medicine, fall down, or even wander away. She doesn't think her mother will bother with eating or, worse still, may forget to turn off the stove and set fire to her house. This role reversal with her mother (daughter taking more parental responsibility for adult parent and parent being more dependent) is magnified by the fact that her mother is living in Ana's home, and it is hard for Ana to learn to support her mother without overfunctioning for her. Their arguing represents what a considerable strain this is for both mother and daughter. Ana also has confessed that she and her husband have been arguing frequently. They are having to renegotiate their marital relationship to accommodate both the younger and older generation living in their family space. Ana also is feeling pressure to put in more hours at work as tax season is approaching, and her husband is expecting her to keep up with her part of their business.

Ana becomes tearful as she confesses to feeling "trapped." She is worried about her mother's current well-being, but she is also fearful that Mrs. Rodriguez may have an incurable problem, such as Alzheimer's disease, and that she will never be able to return to living in her own home. Ana seems to be feeling some resentment of the fact that she has become her mother's chief caretaker, even though she works full-time, has raised her own children, and has a brother who should be equally responsible for their mother. Ana has had several telephone conversations with her brother to discuss optional living arrangements for Mrs. Rodriguez. Her brother expresses concern, but he poses distance and his own family responsibilities as barriers to his being an integral part of any solution. He has offered some limited financial help and has given his approval to whatever plan his sister and mother work out.

Depression in an Older Woman

Biophysical Considerations

Mrs. Rodriguez is not frail and is of above-average intelligence. She had been completely independent in her own home before she broke her hip. She was able to do all her activities of daily living in her familiar environment. She needed partial help with only two instrumental activities of daily living. Following her husband's death, she had asked Ana to help her manage the lump-sum life insurance money from her husband's railroad life policy, and she needed help with transportation for shopping because she had never learned to drive.

Chronic medical problems for Mrs. Rodriguez include arthritis, hearing loss, high blood pressure, digestive difficulties, and osteoporosis. The osteoporosis was a major factor contributing to her broken hip. Whether she fell and the soft bone in her hip broke or whether the hip broke and caused her to fall is not known. But, either way, the brittleness of her bones puts her at great risk for further broken bones resulting from slight falls and for compression fractures in her spine, which can occur without provocation.

Mrs. Rodriguez is well-known to her family doctor, whose office is in her neighborhood. He has treated her for several years, since his father, who delivered her three children, died. A telephone conversation with the doctor has revealed that Mrs. Rodriguez has managed her chronic medical problems well. She has been compliant in taking her blood pressure medication and comes in for periodic checkups. Her chronic conditions are stable. However, since being at Ana's, Mrs. Rodriguez complains of chronic pain "all over." She frequently refuses to take her daily walk, citing pain in her (artificial) hip as the reason. She has frequent headaches and seems tired most of the time. Ana reports that the orthopedic surgeon who replaced her mother's hip states she is healing well and, with time and normal activity, the soreness in her hip should decrease. Because Mrs. Rodriguez is now so far away from her doctor's office, she has not seen her regular doctor since she left the hospital. Ana is trying to decide whether to find a doctor near her own home to take over her mother's care or to transport her mother across town to see her regular doctor.

Cognitive Development and Psychological Hazards

Ana reports that her mother "is just not with it." She had always enjoyed watching the news and discussing current events with others, but Ana can no longer engage her in discussion. Mrs. Rodriguez cannot seem to concentrate on the news stories, and she becomes agitated and frustrated when Ana tries to talk with her. "She just doesn't seem to care about anything," Ana says. Ana also reports that her mother has significant short-term memory deficits. She becomes upset with Ana if Ana is late getting home from work, even after Ana calls before leaving the office to tell her that she's stopping for groceries. She often asks what day it is, only to ask the same question 10 minutes later. She tells Ana that she ate the meal Ana left for her, although Ana finds it untouched in the refrigerator. Ana reports that her mother began exhibiting these memory problems a few weeks after she entered the nursing home.

In an effort to sort out whether Mrs. Rodriguez's cognitive difficulties are organic or more psychological and related to a significant depression, the social worker completed a Mini-Mental Status Exam. At first, Mrs. Rodriguez had difficulty comprehending what was being asked of her, but then the social worker decided that perhaps a part of the problem was Mrs. Rodriguez's hearing loss. The social worker began using a voice amplifier attached to earphones that Mrs. Rodriguez was asked to wear, and Mrs. Rodriguez responded much better to the questions and appeared much brighter. She scored 25 out of a possible 30 points. She had the most *(continued)*

Depression in an Older Woman

(continued)   difficulty with attention/calculation and re-call sections. This score is strongly suggestive of a pseudo-dementia caused by depression, rather than an organic, ir-reversible dementia.

When the social worker asked Mrs. Rodriguez to take the self-administered Geriatric Depression Scale, she scored 7, which suggests that depression may be the root of her cognitive and memory difficulties and her generalized physical pain.

Attitudes and Emotions

The significant losses that Mrs. Rodriguez has experi-enced in the last few years (losing her husband and el-dest son to death; another son to distance; her own hear-ing and now mobility) have taxed her abilities to adjust and cope. One coping strategy she has used is to main-tain a sense of normalcy by continuing to perform rou-tine activities of housekeeping, gardening, going to church, and visiting neighbors. These are now difficult for her because of her physical limitations and because she resides in a household that is not her own. The loss of her husband, though devastating, was more in the ex-pected process of life, whereas the son's death before her own is more unnatural. This fact may be making be-reavement more complicated for Mrs. Rodriguez. She often said she would much rather have gotten cancer herself and gone to be with her husband than for her son to have to leave this life so soon.

Ana believes that her son, who is recovering from substance abuse, may be using his grandmother as an ex-cuse to avoid looking for employment. However, Mrs. Rodriguez states that she has developed a "new" and close relationship with this 24-year-old grandson. They have shared a common struggle to recover from different difficulties, and both are concerned that the other suc-ceeds. They may be a newfound resource for each other to cope with loss and the new challenges in their lives.

Support Systems, Contexts, and Multicultural and Gender Issues

Mrs. Rodriguez's home is in a historic part of town, popu-lated by mostly Hispanic families. Many of these families have lived in the neighborhood for three or more genera-tions. Mrs. Rodriguez has many friends in the neighbor-hood, which remains largely intact with a corner grocery, a pharmacy, a school and an active Catholic church. Mrs. Rodriguez has enjoyed cooking with the church women who provide food for weddings, funerals, and special cele-brations. She still takes pride in her tortilla-making. She has a number of close neighbors who have known her for years. She has provided them with support (baby-sitting, cooking, emotional support) many times in the past.

The church remains a central focus for the life of this community as well as for Mrs. Rodriguez. Attending mass on Sunday and religious holidays has always been an important part of her self-identity. She considers the parish priest her adviser on all matters of living and has spoken to him several times about personal matters since her husband died.

Ana's husband is white. Ana has left much of her cul-tural upbringing behind but continues to attend a Catholic church near her current home. Ana's children have be-come even more assimilated into the dominant culture. Al-though Ana and her mother are bilingual, Ana rarely speaks Spanish to her mother because she feels this would be in-considerate of her husband and son, who speak only Eng-lish. These cultural differences make Ana's home unfamil-iar and, in many ways, uncomfortable for Mrs. Rodriguez. Mrs. Rodriguez's presence in Ana's home has brought up old conflicts for Ana around her Hispanic identity and her-itage that Ana thought she had put to rest long ago.

The Ecomaps demonstrate the changes in Mrs. Ro-driguez's life context from before her husband died (see Figure 12.2) to the present time (see Figure 12.3).

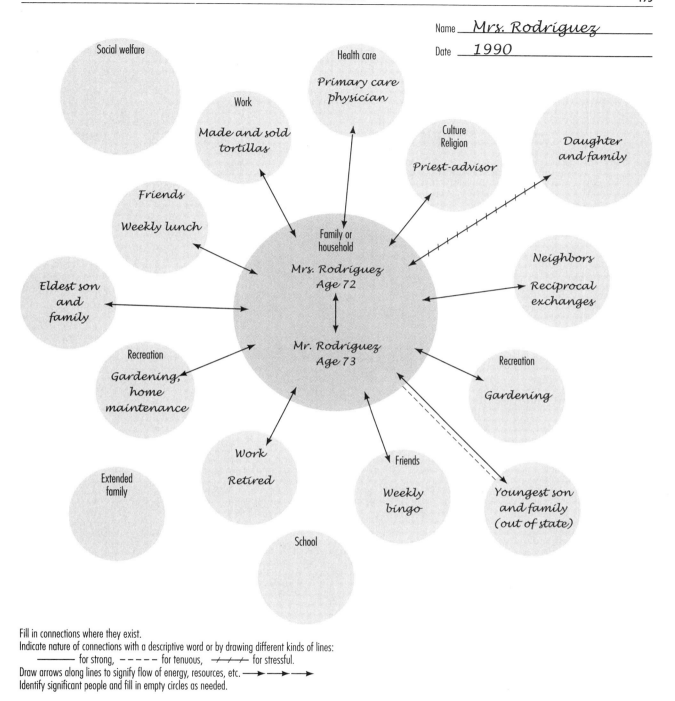

Name __Mrs. Rodriguez__

Date ___1990___

Fill in connections where they exist.
Indicate nature of connections with a descriptive word or by drawing different kinds of lines:
————— for strong, — — — — for tenuous, ⊬⊬⊬ for stressful.
Draw arrows along lines to signify flow of energy, resources, etc. ——→ ——→ ——→
Identify significant people and fill in empty circles as needed.

FIGURE 12.2   Ecomap prior to husband's death   Source: Hartman, 1978.

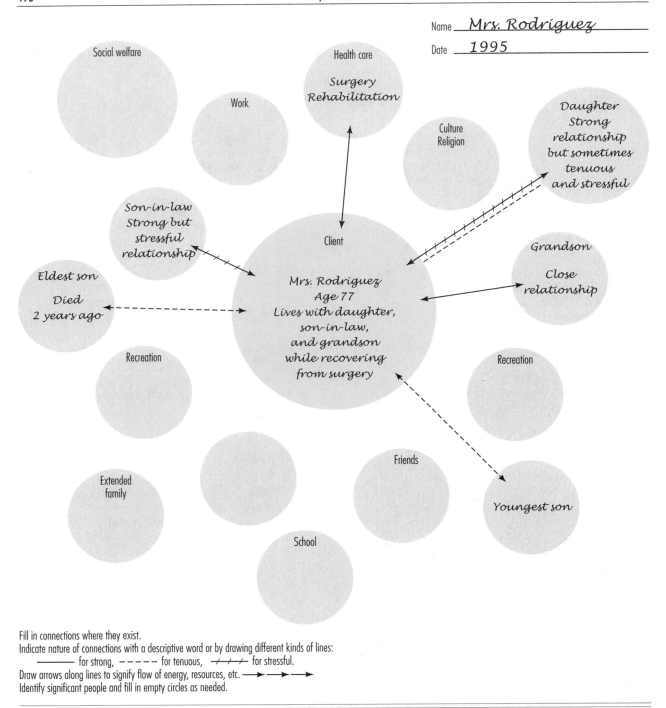

Name *Mrs. Rodriguez*

Date *1995*

Social welfare

Work

Health care
Surgery
Rehabilitation

Culture
Religion

Daughter
Strong
relationship
but sometimes
tenuous
and stressful

Client

Son-in-law
Strong but
stressful
relationship

Mrs. Rodriguez
Age 77
Lives with daughter,
son-in-law,
and grandson
while recovering
from surgery

Grandson
Close
relationship

Eldest son
Died
2 years ago

Recreation

Recreation

Extended
family

Friends

Youngest son

School

Fill in connections where they exist.
Indicate nature of connections with a descriptive word or by drawing different kinds of lines:
———— for strong, — — — — for tenuous, —/—/— for stressful.
Draw arrows along lines to signify flow of energy, resources, etc. ——▸ ——▸ ——▸
Identify significant people and fill in empty circles as needed.

FIGURE 12.3   Ecomap at present   Source: Hartman, 1978.

Depression in an Older Woman

(continued) This assessment tool shows the severe constriction of her life space since her husband's death and her surgery. Many nurturant support systems—priest, church, friends, neighbors—and activities are no longer a part of her everyday existence. These accumulated losses will add to her depression and confusion, and her current living situation will only exacerbate the stressful relationship between Mrs. Rodriguez and her daughter, Ana. Restoration of Mrs. Rodriguez to her home and neighborhood, with appropriate formal supports, is the preferred goal of treatment.

Social Hazards

Impoverishment may be a hazard for Mrs. Rodriguez. She owns her home and has several thousand dollars in a saving account, but her income is fixed and just meets her regular expenses. She has Medicare but has not felt she could afford the cost of a supplemental health insurance policy on her fixed income. She has been able to manage comfortably, but added expenses for a prolonged period could quickly deplete her savings and leave her home as her only financial asset.

Summary and Impressions

Problems needing intervention

- It is likely that depression has caused Mrs. Rodriguez's cognitive deterioration. Both medical and nonmedical interventions are suggested because there are important issues of loss and grief that Mrs. Rodriguez needs help in resolving, as well as physical signs of depression. With treatment for her depression, Mrs. Rodriguez should suffer less from "generalized pain," be motivated to continue rehabilitating her hip, and be able to make the necessary adjustments to continue her independent living, though with more supports.
- Hearing impairment may be creating more cognitive deficits and adding to Mrs. Rodriguez's depression.

This needs to be further evaluated through an audiology specialist.
- Confusion as to the source of Mrs. Rodriguez's memory and concentration problems has produced anxiety and catastrophic thinking in Ana and hindered her ability to have accurate information needed for appropriate planning for her mother's future needs.
- Mrs. Rodriguez will need help with certain activities of daily living, such as bathing, dressing, and heavy housework because her mobility is still limited from the hip surgery.
- Ana is experiencing increasing stress due to physical and time demands of caring for her mother and managing all of her other responsibilities.
- Ana's family is experiencing stress and role strain with the new demands on Ana at a time when the family is facing other demands in the business and needs of the younger son for emotional support to progress to the next stage in his life.
- Ana and Mrs. Rodriguez are experiencing role strain as Mrs. Rodriguez becomes more dependent.

Strengths identified

- There is a strong family bond and commitment to looking for solutions that address everyone's needs.
- Mrs. Rodriguez has been flexible in adapting to earlier changes in her life and has coping skills that should continue to help her adapt.
- Mrs. Rodriguez lives in a supportive, close, culturally homogeneous neighborhood where she feels safe and important.
- Mrs. Rodriguez has built many reciprocal relationships among her neighbors, which may make it more probable that they can help her in ways that can enable her to return to living in her own home.
- Mrs. Rodriguez has a close relationship with former high school friends with whom she enjoys leisure-time activities.

Chapter Summary

Developmental Themes

It is difficult to define the developmental themes of late adulthood because this period covers such a long span of years. In addition, people are living longer and old keeps getting older. As people live longer, they become more diverse. Erikson describes this stage as one of integrity versus despair.

Biophysical Dimension

Biophysical Growth and Development

Life expectancy has increased significantly in the last several decades. Physical change and decline vary from one person to another, but as the body ages, changes do occur in many biological systems. Older adults remain interested in and capable of sexual activity.

Biophysical Hazards

Aging can result in more chronic health problems. The most common disorders are arthritis and hypertension. Arthritis involves inflammation of the connective tissues in the joints of the body and results in pain and difficulty in movement. Hypertension or high blood pressure can lead to stroke and heart disease. Good nutrition and adequate exercise can contribute to wellness in late adulthood.

Psychological Dimension

Cognitive Development and Information Processing

Mental decline varies between individuals. Many older adults retain mental abilities into advanced ages. Sensory deficits in late adulthood contribute to a slowing of behavioral responses. Long-term memory loss is rare, and short-term memory loss is more frequent in older adults. Problems of memory may be due to several factors, including health, perception, attention, or motivation.

Communication

Reminiscing in old age may serve to put one's life in order and prepare one for death. Reminiscing with an older person helps the person bring closure to life and provides insight and rewards to the listener.

Attitudes and Emotions

Loss is a common theme for older adults. Grief is a normal reaction to loss, especially to loss that occurs due to death of a loved one. Kübler-Ross identified five stages in the dying process: denial and isolation, anger, bargaining, depression, and acceptance. The leading causes of death are heart disease, cancer, stroke, lung disease, pneumonia, influenza, and diabetes. Fear of death is stronger at younger ages than in older adulthood. Though widows experience a period of bereavement, many emerge with self-reliance and autonomy. Men who lose their wives have a more difficult adjustment than women who lose their husbands. With the loss of a partner and of other family members and friends, loneliness can be a problem for older adults. Life review may bring feelings of guilt and anger for some over missed opportunities and an increasing sense of powerlessness.

Social Cognition and Regulation

Older adults resist considering themselves old. They tend to continue thinking of themselves in terms of their former occupation. People's core sense of self does not change as they age. Rival theories explain the process of aging. Disengagement theory suggests that people tend to withdraw from society due to diminished capacities, while society withdraws from older individuals to make room for younger adults. Activity theory suggests that as people are deprived of former roles through the process of aging, they must become engaged in other activities to retain life satisfaction.

Psychological Hazards

Dementia and depression are two serious disorders for older adults. One form of dementia is Alzheimer's disease. This disease results in deterioration of memory, reasoning, language, and physical function. Cause of and effective treatment for the disease are still undetermined. The mini-mental status exam provides a quick assessment of an individual's cognitive status. Factors that may be associated with depression among older people include illness, disability, isolation, bereavement, and poverty. Helping an older adult expand available social support may help with depression. Suicide is a risk for older depressed adults. Some advocate for assisted suicide among the elderly with terminal illness. The living will allows a terminally ill person to document that he or she does not want to be kept alive by artificial means. The medical power of attorney appoints someone to make medical decisions concerning care for an ill person.

Social Dimension

Families, Groups, Support Systems, and Contexts

Forms of families are as diverse in older adulthood as in younger years. Marital pairs may become closer as partners have the opportunity to rediscover their relationship and pursue common interests. Some remain close, whereas others do not. With increased life expectancy, adults nearing retirement may be caregivers for their parents. Caregiving of older parents impacts the family significantly and may cause stress. Older adults can also be helpers to others. Grandparenthood can be a fulfilling role for older adults, but this role may vary between different cultures and ethnic groups. Friends play an important, supportive role in old age. Some older adults will require the additional care offered by nursing homes and adult-care facilities. Hospice is an alternative for individuals with less than a six-month life expectancy. Instead of focusing on cure, hospice provides symptom and pain control. For many older adults, retirement can be a difficult time of adjustment.

Multicultural and Gender Considerations

Women live longer than men but suffer more disabling diseases. These factors give women a higher chance of being institutionalized in late adulthood. Three out of four nursing home residents are women. Services for older people need to be sensitive to cultural and ethnic considerations. Extended family is important for many ethnic groups. Older Native Americans have more informal support on reservations than in urban areas. In the African American culture, family boundaries are broadened to include close friends as brother, sister, aunt, or uncle. Older persons are respected in the extended families of the Hispanic culture.

Social Hazards

Elder abuse may be perpetrated by family members, home-care workers, or workers in institutions. Abuse may include physical abuse, psychological abuse, material abuse, neglect, and passive abuse. Older people may be discriminated against on the basis of age. Many older people live on a fixed income. These adults may have to adjust their style of living to accommodate a lower income from year to year. Prolonged illness may deplete financial resources. Poverty can cause problems with options for care for older adults.

KEY TERMS

activity theory	disengagement theory	life expectancy
ageism	elder abuse	life span
assisted suicide	euthanasia	living will
bloodlike ties	fixed income	medical power of attorney
cohort	fluid intelligence	natural helpers
crystallized intelligence	grief	reminiscence
dementia	hospice	

Epilogue: The Journey of Life

We have now come to the final pages of this book—moving from birth to death. We hope that the framework and information we have provided can help you make some sense of this lifelong progression. And yet, on a deeper level, is it possible for us to make sense of life? After taking this journey, perhaps this is an appropriate time to pause and reflect on the meaning of life. What is the real sense of it all?

Great minds have struggled with this question. Kierkegaard informs us that "life is lived forward, but understood backwards." Socrates was cheerful in his answer to this question—we are here to be happy. And for Socrates, the path to happiness was through knowledge. Other philosophers, such as Epicurus, would simply state that our existence is to cultivate pleasures. Religious philosophers place the focus of our existence on faith. If we have faith, we can be assured to have a special place in God's kingdom. According to Lao-tzu, our existence should be focused on knowing the inner harmony of Nature's Way. Bob Dylan sings, ". . . all you can do is do what you must. You do what you must do and you do it well."

Though we can present the facts and theories of human development in the social environment, and philosophize at length, defining the purpose of life is a difficult task—maybe a lifelong task. In the end, perhaps it is up to us individually to make sense of our life and to make life something very real and very meaningful. As we pause, then our personal reflections on life may provide our own sense of meaning. These reflections might bring forth images about our origin and our start in life, our growth and struggles throughout life, our hopes and our fears, our achievements, our love, and ultimately our death:

We whisper a new baby's name to the rising sun,
we laugh as the child mistakes a cow for a dog,
we call each other "buttface,"
we learn and grow,
we dye our hair purple as we struggle to establish a
    unique identity,
we work and we love and sometimes we cry,
we stand at the crossroads and hesitate for just a moment
    before moving on,
we stare as the shoreline recedes and the ship sails away
    before finally turning to hear the voices calling from
    the other shore.

Appendix

Life-Span Stages of Development

Framework Features	Characteristics and Issues of Each Stage	
	Infancy	**Early Childhood**
Developmental Themes	Stage: trust vs. mistrust. Formation of attachments, acquisition of knowledge, development of a sense of self.	Stage: autonomy vs. shame. Development of greater autonomy, physical ability, and language skills; mastery of basic self-help skills; increased social skills.
Biophysical Dimension		
Biophysical Growth and Development	Physical growth, brain development. Normal development: rapid growth and physical development, from lying down to standing and walking. Atypical development: any developmental disability, such as Prader-Willi syndrome.	Ability to run, jump, climb, tumble, ride a tricycle, throw a ball; need for large muscle activity; increase in fine motor coordination; need for optimal nutrition.
Biophysical Hazards	Accidents, childhood illness and disease, lack of immunization, SIDS.	Asthma, leukemia.
Psychological Dimension		
Cognitive Development and Information Processing	Piaget's sensorimotor stage. Information processing techniques and ideas: attention, categorization, cross-modal transfer, memory.	Piaget's preoperational stage. Longer attention span; infantile amnesia; memory; increase in information processing speed; task analysis, developmental waves.
Communication	Infant gestural communication, infants' acquisition of language, adults' infant-directed speech.	Expansion of language abilities, syntax, grammar; increase in semantic skills; communication disorders.
Attitudes and Emotions	Development of emotions, stranger anxiety, separation anxiety; differences in infant temperament and goodness of fit, different attachment patterns.	Fears, aggression, anger management, altruism/empathy, fantasy.
Social Cognition and Regulation	Development of a sense of self, understanding of standards of right and wrong, learn to say "No."	Self-concept, self-control, sociability of preschoolers, social skills training for preschoolers.
Psychological Hazards	Separation and loss, disorders of attachment, failure to thrive, possible mental health issues.	Developmental disorders; diagnosis and assessment issues; elimination problems: enuresis, encopresis; anxiety disorders, depression, autism.
Social Dimension		
Families, Groups, Support Systems, and Contexts	Interactions between infants and their families, fathers, grandparents, siblings, adoptive family members, peers, day care workers.	Parenting, parenting styles, mother's role, father's role, sibling relationships, peer relationships, play, effects of TV. Education: value of preschool, kindergarten, Head Start.
Multicultural and Gender Considerations	Issues involve developmental assessment of minority infants, cultural considerations in assessment, gender differences, sex stereotyping.	Development of racial identity, gender role, and sexual identity role.
Social Hazards	Impoverished environment, poverty, infant abuse and foster care, lead poisoning, parents with mental illness, parents with a history of developmental delay, teen parents.	Marital conflict/divorce, child abuse, poverty, coping and resiliency.

(continued)

Life-Span Stages of Development   (continued)

Characteristics and Issues of Each Stage		
Middle Childhood	**Adolescence**	**Young Adulthood**
Stage: industry vs. inferiority. Adaptation to separation, greater interaction with peers, increased capacity to learn from others.	Stage: identity vs. identity confusion. Independence from parents, increased emphasis on peer-group relations, preoccupation with self, changing body image.	Stage: intimacy vs. isolation. Independence from parents; economic independence; friendships, career, and marriage; transition to parenthood.
Ability to throw and catch a ball (age 6 years), play baseball (8–10 years), team sports (10–12); slow and consistent growth until prepubertal years.	Increased intellectual and physical ability; stronger, greater coordination and endurance; development of secondary sex characteristics, onset of menstrual cycle/nocturnal emissions.	Changes in reproductive systems during early adulthood, the impact of hormones on women, peak of physical development, loss of muscle and increase in fat weight, and development of health patterns.
Greater risk for physical injury; potential for hearing and sight loss, physical abnormalities, and serious physical illness.	Obesity, acne, headaches, meeting the proper nutritional needs.	Health hazards, cancer and self-examinations, unhealthful lifestyle and life expectancy.
Concrete reasoning, mental reversal of operations, capacity to think about two objects at the same time, decrease in egocentric thinking.	Formal operations, more abstract thinking, hypothetical reasoning, logical consistency.	Formal thought, reduced egocentrism, abstract thinking, and postformal thought.
More correct and complex language, development of abstract connotations, reading and writing abilities refined.	Renewed interest in language, use of metaphors and satire, more organized communication, journal writing for more personalized communication.	Miscommunication, intimacy in communication, gender and communication, communicating with the deaf.
Development of a more differentiated self, better understanding of how others view them, evaluation of themselves against their peers to establish a sense of self, increase in sex-typed behaviors.	Identity formation, increased emotional intensity and fluctuations, changes in self-esteem, increased self-awareness and self-reflection, identity and independence.	Development of intimacy, opportunities for love, possibility of isolation and loneliness, shyness, search for an identity, commitment to a sense of identity in multiple contexts.
Development of self-reflective view, moral development moves from what's-in-it-for-me fairness to interpersonal conformity, cooperation and reciprocity in interpersonal awareness, at later stages (ages 11–13) role-taking skills can be evident, development of skills in friendship making.	Moral development moves from interpersonal conformity to responsibility to the system, egocentric thought evidenced by the imaginary audience and the personal fable, growth of social awareness.	Moral development, responsibility, morality of justice, morality of care.
Learning problems, physical or sexual abuse, loneliness and isolation.	Conduct disorder, antisocial behavior, depression, suicidal attempts or rumination, eating disorders.	Major life decisions, serious mental disorders, depression.
Greater independence from family/parents as primary role models. Development of peer relationships, friendship, reciprocity, sharing, more formalized peer groups, less dependence on parental authority, mastery of academic and school demands.	Family influences, control and autonomy within the parent-adolescent relationship, parenting styles, stronger peer-group affiliation, popularity, development of cliques and crowds, potential gang involvement, transition to middle schools, motivation in high school	Marriage, selecting a partner, coming together, adjustment to marriage, marital expectations and myths, being single, gay or lesbian relationships, transition to parenthood, work life, women and work.
Continued development of ethnic identification and gender roles.	Gender-role development, heterosexuality and homosexuality.	Gender roles, multicultural challenges, motherhood mandates, gender expectations and stereotypes, challenges for persons of color.
Poverty, family disruption, divorce, peer difficulties, school adjustment and learning difficulties.	Adolescents at risk, adolescent pregnancy, adolescent fathers, sexually transmitted diseases, alcohol and other drug use, delinquency.	Families with a disabled member, divorce, sexual harassment, sexually transmitted diseases, rape and sexual assault, spouse abuse and effects on the family.

Life-Span Stages of Development

Framework Features	Characteristics and Issues of Each Stage	
	Middle Adulthood	**Late Adulthood**
Developmental Themes	Stage: generativity vs. stagnation. Adaptation to physical changes, to transition from parenthood, to aging parents; confronting mortality, reflections on work and family.	Stage: Integrity vs. despair. Management of changing status and roles, cultivation of new roles, need to cope with physical and emotional changes of aging, and to confront own mortality.
Biophysical Dimension		
Biophysical Growth and Development	Adaptation to physical changes: changes in physical appearance, decrease in physical abilities, menopause, osteoporosis; possibility of need for estrogen replacement therapy.	Need to face age-related changes in physical decline, increased vulnerability to chronic health problems and life-threatening illnesses, changes in sexuality and sexual relations, and health-enhancing behaviors.
Biophysical Hazards	Adjustment to sexuality in adulthood, women's health care, breast cancer, brain injury, physical illness. .	Chronic health problems, arthritis, hypertension, and declining health.
Psychological Dimension		
Cognitive Development and Information Processing	Cognitive focus on achieving goals, applying knowledge to real-world concerns, role-related achievement potential, concern over professional obsolescence.	Fluid and crystallized intelligence, adjustment to changes in memory and learning.
Communication	Reconnection with one's partner or spouse, communication on a deeper level, establishment of new relationships with others, forgiveness, concerns about illiteracy, communication with nonspeaking adults.	Life review and communication of critical life events.
Attitudes and Emotions	Continued quest for identity, reexamination of expectations and roles, deillusionment, death of the hero, midlife as a crisis.	Grief and loss, mourning, death and dying, fear of death, widowhood, loneliness and other related emotions.
Social Cognition and Regulation	Development of caring and socially responsible behaviors, establishment of mentor relationships, assumption of leadership roles, reflection on one's mortality.	Maintenance of a stable sense of self, successful aging.
Psychological Hazards	Alcohol and drug addiction, codependency, need for professional help, twelve-step programs.	Alzheimer's disease, depression, suicide, assisted suicide.
Social Dimension		
Families, Groups, Support Systems, and Contexts	Blended families, launch of children into independence, empty nest syndrome, return to more intimate relationships, marital affairs, impact of adolescent children on middle-aged parents, changing relationships with adult children, addressing the needs of aging parents, caregiving, grandparenthood, the men's movement, men in therapy, satisfaction in work, balancing career and family.	Family relationships, couples, parent-child relationships, caregiving for and by older people, grandparenthood, friendship, nursing homes, hospice, retirement.
Multicultural and Gender Considerations	Problems with generalizing adult development theories to women, gender differences at midlife, role strain and role conflict for women, ethnic identity in adulthood, balancing life in two cultures.	Issues of gender and family minority groups.
Social Hazards	Unemployment or job loss, homelessness, mental illness and homelessness, women and AIDS.	Abuse and neglect—physical, psychological, and material; stereotyping: ageism, sexism, racism; living on a fixed income.

Glossary

Abstraction   The ability to recognize the meaning of symbols.

Accommodation   The cognitive process of modifying the existing cognitive schema to allow for the admission of new information.

Acquaintance rape   When a woman is raped by someone she knows.

Activity theory   A theory of aging that holds that older people who remain active and involved experience greater life satisfaction.

Adaptation   Refers to the ability to respond to the demands of the environment. Includes the processes of assimilation and accommodation.

Affect   A person's instant emotional state.

Ageism   Prejudice against and stereotypes applied to people on the basis of their age.

Aggression   Acts that intend to hurt another.

Alcoholism   The consumption of alcoholic beverages to the extent that major aspects of a person's life, such as work, family, and friends, are affected.

Allele   One of a pair of genes for a specific trait.

Alpha-fetoprotein blood screening   Blood test used to detect neural tube defects.

Altruism   Helpful behaviors that arise out of concern for the welfare of others, without regard for personal gain.

Amniocentesis   A prenatal screening procedure in which a needle is inserted through the mother's abdomen into the uterus to collect a sample of amniotic fluid for chromosome testing.

Androcentricity   A perspective whereby men are considered the norm.

Androgen   The hormone secreted from the testes.

Androgyny   A combination of masculine and feminine behaviors in the same person.

Angina pectoris   A coronary condition involving pain and tightness in the chest.

Animism   The belief that inanimate objects have lifelike qualities and abilities.

Anoxia   Insufficient oxygen to the fetus during delivery.

Apgar score   A newborn assessment scale developed by Virginia Apgar that looks at the newborn's adaptation to life in the first minutes after birth. Scores are recorded at 1 minute and 5 minutes after delivery.

Assimilation   The cognitive process of consolidation of new information into existing knowledge.

Assisted suicide   Helping to provide the means for an individual with a terminal illness to end his or her life.

Associationism   One of the oldest constructs in psychology that involves the formation of mental associations that are registered or stored in the mind.

Attachment   The process by which an infant forms a strong emotional tie to a caregiver.

Attention   The ability to focus on a specific stimulus without distraction by irrelevant stimuli.

Attention deficit hyperactivity disorder (ADHD)   A psychiatric disorder in which a person shows signs of developmentally inappropriate inattention, impulsivity, and hyperactivity.

Attitude   A learned evaluative response.

Authoritarian parenting   A parenting style based on low levels of warmth and a demanding, restrictive, and punitive approach.

Authoritative parenting   Encourages warmth and affection; encourages independence but with limits and controls on the child.

Autism   Pervasive developmental disorder in which children suffer psychological, cognitive, and social deficits that impair functioning in almost all areas of life.

Autosomes   Chromosomes other than sex chromosomes.

Avoidant disorder   Fear of strangers and strange or new situations.

Axons   Long fibers that carry impulses from the cell body of a neuron to other cells.

Babbling   Early communication in which a baby puts vowel and consonant sounds together and repeats them over and over.

Basal metabolism rate   The minimum amount of energy that we use in our resting state.

Behavioral intention   Our subjective estimate of how likely we are to engage in a specific behavior.

Beliefs   In social psychology, information about objects.

Bilingual   The ability to speak two languages.

Biophysical dimension   Refers to the biochemical, cell, organ, and physiological systems that represent the material substance of a person.

Blended family   A newly formed unit consisting of a husband and wife, one or both of whom have children from a previous marriage.

Bloodlike ties   Refers to different ethnic and cultural definitions of family, including situations such as adoption.

Brazelton Neonatal Assessment Scale (BNAS)   Newborn assessment used to measure the baby's muscle tone and reflexes and how the baby responds to and controls stimulation.

Bureaucracy   An organization that is ruled by officials.

Canalization   The process by which persons inherit general pathways that constrain their growth and developmental processes.

Caregiving career   Refers to the substantial caregiving functions women have that include caring for children, elderly parents, and a dependent husband.

Care perspective   Reasoning about moral dilemmas with a focus on the connectedness to others; concern for others is paramount.

Categorical self   Process by which preschoolers classify themselves, first according to age, then to gender, then to activities and possessions.

Categorization   The ability to place objects into groups on the basis of their similarities.

Central nervous system   The brain and spinal cord.

Cephalocaudal   Development that progresses from the head to the feet.

Cerebral palsy   Brain damage resulting from lack of oxygen during birth or from bleeding in the brain. Can cause paralysis, muscle weakness, and incoordination. Also may result in mental retardation and speech difficulties.

Cesarean section   Delivery of a baby through an incision in the mother's abdomen.

Child abuse   Child maltreatment that includes physical abuse, sexual abuse, physical neglect, educational neglect, and psychological abuse.

Cholinergic   Refers to any nerve that releases the neurotransmitter acetylcholine at its synapse.

Chorionic villus sample (CVS)   A prenatal screening procedure in which a catheter is inserted into the uterus through the vagina to obtain a piece of the developing placenta.

Circular influences   Process by which family interactions affect interactions with the infant and affect the infant's interactions with the caregivers, which then affects family interactions.

Classical conditioning   The strengthening of an association between a stimulus and a response through the presentation of a second stimulus.

Clique   Small interaction-based group with close relationships.

Codependency   A pattern of behavior in which a person's sense of self-worth is based on external referents.

Cognition   Obtaining, organizing, and utilizing sensory and perceptual information from activities such as plans and strategies.

Cohesive group   A group in which individual members have strong bonds with one another and to the group itself.

Cohort   A group of people of about the same age, born around the same time.

Communication patterns   How members of a group communicate verbally and nonverbally.

Concentration   A person's ability to sustain inner mental operations without disruption.

Concrete thinking   The ability to perform operations such as logical reasoning, which replaces intuitive thought as long as it is applied to concrete examples.

Conduct disorder   DSM-IV term that refers to a cluster of behaviors that reflect oppositional, noncompliant, and delinquent actions, such as stealing, robbery, and assault.

Connectedness   Refers to both a person's sensitivity to and respect for others' views and the person's openness and responsiveness to others' views.

Consciousness   Our awareness of internal and external stimuli.

Conservation   The recognition that properties of a substance do not change when its appearance is altered in some manner.

Continuity   Associations occurring in the mind because two events occur together in time or space.

Controlled reaction   A phase of rape trauma syndrome in which the rape victim assumes a more composed and calm perspective following the trauma.

Coping   Active efforts to master, reduce, or tolerate the demands created by stress.

Creolization   The process of maintaining original identities but incorporating customs and practices from other groups or cultures into the original identities.

Cretinism A chronic disease due to absence of, or deficiency in, normal thyroid secretion. Cretinism is characterized by physical deformity and dwarfism.

Cross-modal transfer The ability to transfer information gained from one sense to another sense. An example would be picking out a picture of something you had only felt with your hands.

Crossover A division process that involves an exchange of chromosome parts.

Crowd Larger than clique; reputation-based group of similar young people who do not necessarily spend a lot of time together.

Crystallized intelligence Accumulated information and verbal skills.

Culture A system of meanings and values shared by a population and transmitted to future generations.

Cynical hostility Tendencies toward being resentful, moody, and generally distrusting. Related to an increased tendency toward coronary disease, hypertension, and early mortality.

Cystic Fibrosis A serious disease of the exocrine gland that causes secretion of excess, thick body fluids.

Das-Luria model of cognitive functioning Understands cognitive functioning based on two modes of processing information: simultaneous meanings and successive processing.

Date rape When a woman is raped by someone she is dating.

De-illusionment The process of giving up illusions from earlier periods of life.

Delirium tremens (DTs) A withdrawal syndrome from alcoholism that includes agitation, tremor, hallucination, and sometimes seizures.

Dementia Impairment or loss of cognitive abilities, including memory impairment.

Dendrites The branched fibers on the cell body that bring messages to the cell body of the neuron.

Development The refinement or improvement of body components.

Developmental waves The idea that children learn in overlapping waves instead of in steps.

Diastolic pressure The measure of the blood's flow during the relaxation of the heart.

Differentiation theory Contends that all information needed to interpret sensory input is contained in the sensations themselves.

Difficult child A baby characterized by unpredictable daily habits, negative intense mood, and slow adaptability.

Discrimination Applying prejudice or bias to a person on the basis of some particular characteristic.

Disease Any classifiable set of symptoms and signs stemming from disturbed bodily function and associated with findings from laboratory and other tests.

Disengagement theory A theory of aging that holds that people and society withdraw from each other in old age—people because of their diminished capacity and society to make room for younger people.

Dishabituation The process by which an individual attends to a new stimulus after habituating to a previous stimulus.

Disorder A syndrome of behavioral, physical, or psychological dysfunctions less clearly defined than a disease primarily because etiology of the dysfunctions are unknown.

Disorganization phase A phase of rape trauma syndrome that reflects the woman's immediate expressed or controlled reactions, physical reactions, and emotional reactions to the trauma.

Disoriented states Whenever individuals experience significant deviations in their levels of awareness of time, place, and person.

Displaced homemakers Women who are forced into the job market because of divorce or widowhood.

Dominant gene A gene that is always expressed for a trait, in paired genes.

Dopamine A neurotransmitter whose generalized function is to activate other neurotransmitters and aid in exploratory and pleasure-seeking behaviors.

Easy child A baby characterized by regular, positive responses to new stimuli, high adaptability to change, and mild or moderately intense mood, which is usually positive.

Echolalia Repeating words, songs, and phrases heard in other people's communications.

Ecomap A tool used in social work to highlight the points of connection between systems influencing a person's life.

Ego According to Freud, the executive branch of one's personality that makes rational decisions.

Egocentrism Being unable to distinguish between one's own perspective and another's.

Elder abuse Maltreatment of older persons, which can include physical abuse, psychological abuse, material abuse, active neglect, and passive abuse.

Empathy Possessing the ability to understand the feelings and attitudes of others.

Encopresis Lack of bowel control after age 4.

Endocarditis An infection or other factor that damages the heart's valves.

Endocrine glands Glands, namely the pituitary gland and male and female gonads, that secrete chemicals into the bloodstream that help control bodily functioning.

Endorphins Substances in the brain that are related to feeling good.

Enrichment theory Contends that the information we receive through our senses is formless and we must augment this information to make sense of it.

Enuresis Lack of bladder control after the age of 5, which results in bedwetting or daytime accidents.

Environmental harassment Exists when a hostile work environment is created by the person in power as a result of some unwanted sexual behavior.

Epigenetic principle The biological blueprint that dictates how an organism grows and reaches maturity.

Estrogen The hormone secreted from the ovaries.

Estrogen replacement therapy (ERT) A synthetic estrogen that is given to women to replace that lost through menopause.

Euthanasia Assisting the death of those with painfully debilitating or terminal illness.

Exosystems The larger institutions of society that influence our personal systems.

Expressive communication The expression of emotions and having a perspective that is sensitive to how others feel.

Externalizing problems Problems of overcontrol, such as aggressive behavior, fighting, and overactivity.

Failure to thrive When the child's weight falls below the 5th percentile for age.

Family A composition of people who decide to live together.

Family structure The manner in which each family organizes itself into interactional patterns.

Fetal alcohol syndrome (FAS) A set of birth defects that occur when a pregnant woman consumes alcohol. It is the leading known cause of mental retardation. Physical signs include small head, small eyes, thin upper lip, short nose, flattened midfacial area, and poorly developed philtrum (the part of the face between the nose and upper lip).

Fixed income Income that does not increase from year to year though inflation and other factors may raise the cost of living.

Floating family A family with a formless array of familial relationships that are in a continuous state of flux.

Fluid intelligence Abstract reasoning ability.

Folkways Group ways of solving problems and of doing things.

Formal operational thought Thought processes characterized by adolescents' abilities to think about their own thought and to recognize both possibility and actuality.

Formal organization Any large social group that is designed to rationally achieve a specific objective.

Formed groups Groups created by an outside influence or intervention and convened for a particular purpose.

Fragile X syndrome A serious form of mental retardation that is identified in karyotype studies by a constriction at the end of the long arm of the X chromosome.

Frontal lobe The portion of the brain that participates in body movements, thinking, feeling, imagining, and making decisions.

Functionally literate Able to perform everyday reading, writing, and arithmetic tasks.

Gang "A collectivity consisting primarily of adolescents and young adults who (a) interact frequently with one another; (b) are frequently and deliberately involved in illegal activities; (c) share a common identity that is usually, but not always, expressed through a gang name; and (d) typically express that identity by adopting certain symbols and/or claiming control over certain 'turf'—persons, places, things, and/or economic markets" (Huff, 1993, p. 4).

Gender The social definitions of male and female.

Gender polarization The organizing of social life around male and female distinctions.

Genotype The actual genes an individual carries for a specific trait.

Gestation Length of time in the womb or fetal age. Full term is 38–41 weeks, premature is before 38 weeks, postmature is longer than 41 weeks.

Glia The supporting cells that make up the bulk of the brain.

Goal-directed behavior Putting together a series of actions to achieve a desired result.

Gonadotropins Hormones secreted by the pituitary gland that activate the testes and ovaries.

Goodness of fit Refers to how well the demands of the environment match the child's behavioral style.

Grief The normal, emotional reaction to loss.

Groupthink Occurs in a cohesive group that emphasizes consensus at the expense of critical thinking.

Growth A technical term that refers to the addition of new biophysical components such as new cells or an increase in body size.

Habituation The process by which an individual stops responding to a stimulus.

Hemophilia A condition that is due to a defective gene on the X chromosome that causes a deficiency in the blood coagulation factor VIII.

Heterozygous genes When two genes in a specific pair are different for a specific trait.

Hierarchy Dimension of social space that includes all the elements in a society's system of social stratification.

Holophrastic speech Using one word to express the meaning of a whole sentence.

Homeostasis in families The self-regulating mechanism of a family system.

Homophobia The fear and hatred of sex with a same-sex partner.

Homozygous genes When two genes in a specific pair are the same for a specific trait.

Hormones Chemical substances in the body that regulate various body organs.

Hospice An alternative to hospital care for terminally ill patients. Hospice focuses on comfort and relief of symptoms instead of cure.

Hostile aggression Behaviors designed to hurt another.

Hot flash A sudden feeling of heat experienced by some women during menopause.

Human immunodeficiency virus (HIV) A virus that destroys the human immune system and leads to the set of opportunistic infections commonly referred to as acquired immune deficiency syndrome, or AIDS.

Human relations school A school of organizational theory that focuses on understanding the influences of informal networks on all forms of organizational activities.

Huntington's chorea A disorder involving a dominant autosomal gene and characterized by progressive chorea (purposeless motions) and the eventual development of dementia (mental deterioration).

Hyperemesis gravidarum Persistent and unrelenting vomiting during pregnancy.

Hyperplasia The type of growth that involves an increase in the number of cells.

Hypertrophic growth The type of growth in which increases are observed in the size of cells.

Hypervigilance An excessive focus on outward factors in the environment.

Hypothalamus The part of the brain that controls the level of hormone secretion from the pituitary gland.

Hypothetical-deductive reasoning The problem-solving process that tests and evaluates hypotheses to find the best solution.

Id According to Freud, the instinctive component of personality that operates from the basis of the pleasure principle.

Ideal type An abstract description derived from real cases that were analyzed to determine their essential features.

Illiterate Inability to read and write well enough to participate in society.

Illness A person's subjective perception of being unwell.

Imaginary audience The belief that others are as preoccupied with an adolescent's behavior as he or she is.

Immediate memory Information retained for up to 10 seconds.

Individuation A process by which a person develops a stronger sense of autonomy.

Induction Use of explanation and/or rationalizing in an attempt to influence a child's actions.

Infantile amnesia Refers to the fact that children have little or no memory for specific events before the age of 3.

Infertility Inability to achieve pregnancy after one year of sexual intercourse with no contraception.

Information processing The theory that examines the uptake, selection, coding, and storage of information.

Instrumental aggression Behaviors designed to achieve a nonagressive end, which hurt someone in the process.

Instrumental communication Having a focus on identifying goals and finding solutions.

Intelligence quotient Mental age divided by chronological age, multiplied by 100.

Intentional means-end behavior The process by which a child takes several random activities and puts them together to achieve a goal.

Intention-cue detection Ability to correctly perceive another person's intention; for example, differentiating prosocial, accidental, or hostile acts.

Internalizing problems Problems of undercontrol, such as anxiety, loneliness, shyness, and/or social withdrawal.

Interrupted career Began as a regular career and was interrupted by child-rearing and then reestablished when full-time work resumed.

Intrauterine growth retardation (IUGR) Growth slowdown in the prenatal period. Occurs when the fetal weight falls below the 10th percentile for gestational age.

Invisible displacement In testing for object permanence, moving a toy from one hiding place to another without letting the baby view the process of moving the toy.

Justice perspective Reasoning about moral dilemmas with a focus on the rights of the individual to independently make moral decisions.

Klinefelter's syndrome A condition in which a male is born with an extra X chromosome (XXY).

Lability The rapid shift from one emotion to another within a very brief period of time.

Laissez-faire parenting A parenting style representing two types: permissive indifferent parenting and permissive indulgent parenting. Permissive indifferent parents are uninvolved in their child's life; they are neglectful and unresponsive. Permissive indulgent parents are warm, accepting, and responsive but are undemanding.

Learned helplessness Learning to attribute failures to luck or the difficulty of the task.

Lesch-Nyhan syndrome A disorder that involves a gene on the X chromosome and is characterized by mental retardation, spasticity, and self-mutilation.

Libido According to Freud, the energy that drives all human behavior.

Life expectancy The number of years the average person born in a particular year may expect to live.

Life span The upper limit of years humans can live.

Living will   A document that allows a terminally ill person to state that he or she does not want to be kept alive by artificial means.

Loneliness   A state of feeling as though one has fewer interpersonal relationships than desired or not obtaining the desired level of personal satisfaction from interpersonal relationships.

Long-term memory   Retention of information for days to months.

Love withdrawal   Involves withdrawing love when a child's behavior is viewed as inappropriate.

Macrosystem   Represents the larger subcultural and cultural contexts in which the microsystem, mesosystem, and exosystem are located.

Malignant tumors   Tumors that are not self-contained.

Malpresentation   Birth presentation other than head down (i.e., feet first, butt first, shoulder first).

Meconium aspiration   Inhalation of fetal waste in the amniotic fluid during delivery. May result in later respiratory problems.

Medical power of attorney   A document that allows an ill person to designate someone to have the authority to make decisions regarding medical care for the ill person.

Meiosis   The process of cell division that creates the sex cells.

Menarche   The first menstruation in pubertal females.

Menopause   When a woman stops experiencing a menstrual cycle for a continuous period of time; her ovaries stop functioning and no longer produce the hormones estrogen and progesterone.

Menstrual cycle   The series of changes in a nonpregnant female involving the preparation of the endometrium to receive a fertilized ovum, or, if no fertilization occurs, a portion of the endometrium is shed.

Mental age   An intelligence test score that indicates the chronological age at which a child functions cognitively.

Mesosystems   The network of personal settings in which we live our lives.

Metacognition   Knowledge about knowing. A person's awareness of self as a knower able to use and evaluate strategies.

Metalinguistic awareness   The ability to think about language and its properties.

Microsystems   Any systems that involve face-to-face or direct contact among the system participants.

Mitosis   The cellular process in which a body cell reproduces itself by dividing and producing two new daughter cells.

Mitral valve prolapse   A valvular disease of the heart involving the protrusion of one or both cusps of the mitral valve back into the left atrium.

Mood   A prevailing and enduring emotional state.

Moral development   The rules of conduct people use in their interactions with others.

Mores   Folkways that are considered the right or wrong way of doing things.

Morphemes   Represent the smallest unit of meaning in any language system.

Multiplex relationship   A relationship in which a person has more than one type of exchange with another person.

Munchausen's syndrome by proxy   Child abuse in which the caregiver induces symptoms of illness in the child.

Mutations   Random events that distort key characteristics in an organism's growth and development.

Myelinization   The process of coating the nerve cells with myelin, a substance that forms around neurons and acts as insulation, allowing faster and more efficient transmission of nerve impulses.

Myocardial infarction   The condition in which insufficient oxygen is directed to the heart's muscle.

Myocarditis   An infection or other factor that damages the heart's muscle.

Natural groups   Groups created by naturally occurring events, interpersonal attraction, or the mutual needs of the individuals involved.

Natural helpers   Relatives, friends, and neighbors to whom one turns in time of trouble or need.

Neural tube defects   Birth defects of the brain or spinal cord that include the following: spina bifida, in which one or more vertebrae do not close over the spinal cord—if the cord bulges through the opening the baby has a meningocele; hydrocephalus—excess fluid in the head resulting in a large head; microcephaly—a much smaller than normal head; anencephaly—absence of all or part of the brain.

Neurons   The cells in the nervous system involved in conveying information from one cell to another.

Neurotransmitters   Chemicals that are synthesized inside the neuron.

Night terrors   A sudden awakening from sleep with intense feelings of panic.

Norms   Expectations and beliefs about appropriate behavior in a group.

Obesity   Having a body weight 20% or more above the recommended weight for one's height.

Object permanence   The ability to hold an image of an object or person in one's mind.

Obligatory attention   Describes the fact that babies will attend to something they find interesting and not be distracted from it.

Occipital lobe   Located below the parietal lobe and involved in the receiving and sending of visual information.

Open adoption   Adoption in which the birth mother and sometimes birth father participate in choosing the adoptive family, and often remain in contact with the child after adoption.

Operant conditioning   The acquisition of new responses because of their effects on the environment.

Organization   According to Piaget, a tendency held by all species to systematize their processes into coherent systems.

Osteoporosis   The thinning or weakening of bones.

Ovaries   Part of the female reproductive system. The ovaries produce the ovum, or egg, and the female hormones estrogen and progesterone.

Overanxious disorder   Fears that have no specific focus. Children with this disorder worry that something will go wrong in almost any situation.

Overextension   Using one word to include a larger category. An example is referring to all furry creatures as a dog.

Parasympathetic nervous system   The branch of the nervous system that counteracts the activities of the sympathetic nervous system and conserves body resources.

Parietal lobe   Portion of the brain that is primarily involved in the process of integrating sensory information.

Peer group   A group of age-mates that is durable and composed of interactions based on an established set of social relationships.

Perception   The interpretation of information detected by the senses.

Perceptual set   Whenever people perceive objects as having only their most common or recent functional significance.

Pericardium   The thin sac that encloses the heart.

Peripheral nervous system   All those nerves that lie ouside the brain and spinal cord.

Personal fable   The adolescent's belief that he or she is indestructible and unique—so much so that no one can understand what it is like to be him or her.

Phenotype   The trait expressed by genes in the individual.

Phobias   Irrational fears.

Phonemes   The basic identifiable sounds in the language system.

Phonology   The component in language studies that examines the system of sound in languages.

Polyhydramnios   Excess amniotic fluid, the presence of which may indicate a problem with the fetus, such as anencephaly.

Power   In a group, a person's ability to obtain control through reward, coercion, expertise, personal characteristics, and legitimacy.

Power assertive discipline   A punitive style of discipline that includes physical punishment, threat of punishment, and/or attempts to control the child's behavior.

Pragmatics   The study of the rules that specify how language is used across social contexts.

Prejudice   A generalized negative attitude that is directed toward another person's membership in a socially defined group.

Prematurity   Birth before the 37th week of gestation.

Premenstrual syndrome (PMS)   A set of symptoms some women experience about ten days prior to their menstrual period. The symptoms may include breast tenderness, a bloated feeling, irritability, and negative moods.

Primary process thinking   Based on irrational, illogical, and fantasy-oriented notions.

Problem solving   The ability to sort out relevant from irrelevant information and to adopt a strategy or plan for completing the task.

Professional half-life   The time it takes for 50% of one's professional knowledge to become invalid or obsolete.

Professional obsolescence   The use of information, theories, and technology that are less useful in performing tasks than what is currently available in one's field of practice.

Prolonged labor   One lasting longer than 24 hours for a first-time mother or more than 12 hours for a woman who has previously given birth.

Protein   Any organic compound that has a large combination of amino acids.

Proximodistal   Development that progresses from the spine outward to the extremities.

Psychological dimension   The systems that contribute to the organization and direction of an individual's mental processes.

Psychological moratorium   A gap between childhood security and adult autonomy.

Puberty   A period in development that is characterized by maturation of physiological mechanisms, including reproductive capacity and the development of secondary sex characteristics.

Quid pro quo   Latin phrase meaning something is exchanged for something else.

Race   A large number of people who, for social or geographical reason, have interbred over a long period of time and developed visible physical characteristics and regard themselves and are regarded by others as a biological unit.

Racism   Any attitude, action, or institutional structure that subordinates a person because of his or her race.

Rape trauma syndrome   A cluster of symptoms experienced by rape victims.

Rapport talk A style of communication that involves discussing similarities and matching experiences.

Readiness Refers to the point in time when a child's developmental maturity allows him or her to quickly learn a needed skill or ability.

Recent memory Refers to the retention of information within the last 24 hours.

Recessive gene The gene that is not expressed in a trait unless paired with a similar or homozygous gene.

Reciprocal interaction An interaction in which both parties can influence each other. For example, an infant can influence its mother and the mother can influence the infant.

Refractory period The time between one orgasm and the physical capability to achieve another.

Relational space The degree of intimacy between people as indicated by factors such as number and type of interactions between them, the intensity and length of their relationship, and the nature of their ties.

Reminiscence The process of remembering the past and reviewing one's life that may arise when one realizes the inevitability of death.

Remote memory Retention of information occurring several weeks or months in the past.

Reorganization phase The adaptation and adjustment phase a rape victim experiences after a rape.

Repetition A factor in association that assumes that ideas are likely to be associated when they occur together often.

Report talk A style of communication that involves discussing knowledge and displaying skill.

Resiliency The ability to recover from or adjust to problems, adversities, and stress in life.

Reversibility The ability to reverse an action by mentally performing the opposite action.

Rh incompatibility Occurs when the mother has Rh negative blood and the fetus has Rh positive blood. The mother makes antibodies that attack the fetal blood cells, resulting in anemia and possible fetal death or brain damage.

Rickets A deficiency in either diet or sunshine that can induce permanent damage to the body, such as flat chest, deformed pelvis, or a crooked back.

Rite of passage A ritualized recognition of a person's transition from one life stage to another, such as childhood to adolescence.

Role A pattern of expected behavior that a person acts out in a group.

Role-taking ability The mutual ability to see things from another person's perspective. It involves the reduction of egocentric thought.

Schema An internal cognitive structure that facilitates adaptation.

Schizophrenia A psychological disorder marked by disturbances in thought that spill over to affect perceptual, social, and emotional processes.

Secondary process thinking Based on realistic and rational approaches to problem solving.

Semantics The area in language studies that deals with meaning.

Sensation The process in which receptors detect information that is transmitted to the brain.

Sensitive period Based on the idea that humans experience a period of time immediately following birth in which the mother and infant bond. Researchers now believe this postbirth bonding is not as important as once thought.

Separation anxiety Distress displayed by an infant in the absence of the primary caregiver. Usually begins around 8–10 months.

Separation anxiety disorder Severe anxiety about leaving home or separating from the primary caregivers.

Separation-individuation Developmental process proposed by Margaret Mahler in which the infant grows from having no sense of self as separate from the caregiver to being an autonomous, independent individual.

Sex The biological status of being female or male.

Sex-role stereotype How we can categorize people according to our impressions of what we consider "male" or "female."

Sex-typed behavior The developmental process by which culturally assigned values and behaviors are considered appropriate for members of that sex.

Sexual response cycle The three stages that culminate in sexual satisfaction: desire, excitement, and orgasm.

Shaken infant syndrome Infant abuse in which an adult shakes the infant, causing brain damage.

Short-term memory Memory of an event that can be maintained for about 20 to 30 seconds.

Signs Have a valid relationship with the thing for which they stand.

Similarity A factor in associationism that refers to associations being formed because events or ideas that occur close together have features that are similar.

Single-gene disorders Inherited dysfunctions or defects that result from dominant, recessive, or X chromosome–linked genes.

Slow-to-warm-up child A child who exhibits a sedate, less exuberant orientation to life. These babies are slow to adapt to new situations and many times have negative responses.

Social cognition The level of awareness one has regarding other peoples' thoughts, feelings, and intentions.

Social cognitive monitoring   A person's ability to monitor and make sense of his or her social thoughts; a conscious self-awareness.

Social dimension   The systems of social relationships that the person interacts with individually or in a group.

Social distance   The nearness in relationships between people.

Social functioning   All the factors influencing the performance of roles that enable individuals to achieve a reasonable degree of fulfillment and to function as productive and contributing members of society.

Social integration   The quantity of ties that a person has to major social institutions.

Social learning theory   Assumes that people can learn by observing events that they do not directly experience or perform.

Social marginality   The absence of ties to major social institutions.

Social referencing   The process by which an infant looks to others for emotional information about how to respond in an unfamiliar situation or to an unfamiliar person or object.

Social skills training   A treatment program that assumes problem behaviors can be understood in terms of not having the skills needed to cope with situational demands.

Social support systems   Continuing social aggregates that provide individuals with opportunities for feedback about themselves and for validations for their expectations about others, which may offset deficiencies in these communications in larger community contexts.

Socioeconomic status   The combination of one's economic status or level of income, social status or level of education, and work status as measured by one's occupation.

Status   The ranking of each member's position in a group relative to the other members.

Stepfamily   Families whose kinship is determined by remarriage.

Stereotypes   Oversimplified or prejudicial beliefs about a target group held by nonmembers of that group.

Stranger anxiety   Distress displayed by an infant at the sight of an unfamiliar face. Usually begins around 5–6 months.

Subjective norms   Beliefs about what important people or significant others think about an object.

Superego   According to Freud, the moral guidance that helps balance the drives associated with the id.

Symbols   Stand for other things or ideas, but do not have a direct relationship with them.

Sympathetic nervous system   The branch of the nervous system that mobilizes the body for emergencies.

Symptoms   Subjective complaints like "my head hurts."

Synaptic cleft   The space between any two neurons or between a neuron and another cell.

Syndactyly   The total fusion of fingers and toes.

Syndrome   Any cluster of signs and symptoms.

Syntax   The component of language studies that focuses on the rules that govern the way words are combined to form sentences.

System   Any set of elements that affect or influence one another.

Systolic pressure   A measure of the heart when it is constricting and pumping blood out and through the body.

Task analysis   A method of studying what children know by identifying the various components of the task the child is performing.

Task groups   Groups that have as their primary purpose to complete the work for which the groups were convened.

Tay-Sachs disease   A neurodegenerative disorder that is characterized by progressive mental and physical retardation.

Telegraphic speech   Using only words that are absolutely necessary to convey a message.

Temperament   The characteristic pattern by which an infant responds to and interacts with the environment.

Temporal lobe   The portion of the brain involved in emotions and human motivation.

Teratogens   Substances that cause birth defects and anomalies.

Testes   Part of the male reproductive system. The testes produce sperm and the male hormone testosterone.

Toxemia or eclampsia   A serious complication of pregnancy, which can result in maternal death, fetal death, or fetal brain damage. Early stages are referred to as preeclampsia. Symptoms include elevated blood pressure, swelling of hands and face, weight gain, protein in urine.

Transitional object   Something (a blanket, toy, or teddy bear) the infant uses for comfort in the absence of the primary caregiver.

Transracial adoption   Adoption in which the child is of a different race than the adoptive parents.

Treatment groups   Groups that seek to meet members' socioemotional needs.

Trial and error   The sequential application of possible solutions to problems.

Triangulation   Occurs in families when two family members experience conflict and "triangulate," or involve, a third member to regulate the stress and conflict between them.

Tumor   What is formed when cell growth leads to the buildup of masses of purposeless tissue.

Turner's syndrome   Occurs when a female is born with only one X chromosome (X0).

Type A personality   Competitive, impatient, and sometimes hostile perfectionists.

Type B personality   Relaxed, easygoing, and generally amicable individuals.

Ultrasound   A prenatal screening procedure in which high-frequency sound waves are passed through the mother's abdomen to form a picture of the developing fetus.

Uninformative messages   Messages that do not clarify the exact meaning being communicated.

Uniplex relationship   A relationship in which a person has one type of exchange with a person.

Vaginal bleeding   A complication of pregnancy that may be associated with spontaneous abortion or with placental complications.

Values   Abstract goals that do not have specific objects or reference points, such as beauty, freedom, or health.

Verbal control   The development of speech through three successive stages: other-external, self-external, and self-internal; the idea that self-verbalizations are related to self-guidance.

Vigilance   The capacity of sustaining outward attention over a prolonged period of time.

References

Abel, E., & Sokol, R. (1987). Incidence of fetal alcohol syndrome and economic impact of FAS-related anomalies. *Drug & Alcohol Dependence, 19,* 51–70.

Abel, R. L. (1982). *The politics of informal justice: Vol. 1. American experience.* New York: Academic Press.

Abramovitch, R., Corter, C., Pepler, D. J., & Stanhope, L. (1986). Sibling and peer interaction: A final follow-up and comparison. *Child Development, 47,* 217–229.

Abuelo, D. N. (1983). Genetic disorders. In J. L. Matson and J. A. Muilick (Eds.) *Handbook of Mental Retardation.* New York: Pergamon Press.

Achenbach, T. M. (1991). *Child Behavior Checklist.* Burlington, VT: Department of Psychiatry.

Achenbach, T. M., & Edelbrock, C. (1983). *Manual for the child behavior checklist and revised child behavior profile.* Burlington: University of Vermont Department of Psychiatry.

Achenbach, T. M., McConaughy, S. H., & Howell, C. T. (1987). Child/adolescent behavioral and emotional problems: Implications of cross-informant correlations for situational specificity. *Psychological Bulletin, 101,* 213–232.

Adams, B. N. (1986). *The family: A sociological interpretation* (4th ed.). San Diego: Harcourt Brace Jovanovich.

Adams, G. R., Abraham, K. G., & Markstrom, C. A. (1987). The relations among identity development, self-consciousness, and self-focusing during middle and late adolescence. *Developmental Psychology, 23,* 292–297.

Adams, G. R., & Gullotta, T. (1989). *Adolescent life experiences.* Pacific Grove, CA: Brooks/Cole.

Adler, H., Davies, S. P., Bane, F., Reeves, M., & Lewis, M. (1932). *Social Services Review, 6,* 429–451.

Adler, T. (1989, August). Shy monkeys are born, not made. *APA Monitor,* p. 5.

Adler, T. (1990, July). Genes and behavior: Old tune in a new key? *APA Monitor,* pp. 8–9.

Adler, T. (1990, December). Melody is the message of infant-directed speech. *APA Monitor,* p. 9.

Adler, T. (1991, July). Women's expectations are menopause villians. *APA Monitor,* p. 14.

Ainsworth, M.D.S., Blehar, M., Waters, E., & Wall, S. (1978). *Patterns of attachment.* Hillsdale, NJ: Erlbaum.

Ainsworth, M.D.S., & Eichberg, C. (1992). Effects of infant-mother attachment on mother's unresolved loss of an attachment figure or other traumatic experience. In P. Morris, J. Stevenson-Hinde, & C. Parkes (Eds.), *Attachment across the life cycle* (pp. 160–183). New York: Routledge.

Ajzen, I. (1987). Attitudes, traits, and actions: Dispositional prediction of behavior in personality and social psychology. In L. Berkowitz (Ed.), *Advances in experimental social psychology.* New York: Academic Press.

Alexander, J. F., & Parsons, B. V. (1982). *Functional family therapy.* Pacific Grove, CA: Brooks/Cole.

Alexander, W. M., & McErwin, C. K. (1989). *Schools in the middle: Progress* from 1968–1988. Reston, VA: National Association of Secondary School Principals.

Allen, K. R., & Chin-Sang, V. (1990). A lifetime of work: The context and meanings of leisure for aging black women. *The Gerontologist, 30,* 734–740.

Allport, G. W. (1935). Attitudes. In M. Murchison (Ed.), *Handbook of social psychology.* Worcester, MA: Clark University Press.

Als, H., Lawhon, G., Duffy, F., McAnulty, G., Gibes-Grossman, R., & Blickman, J. (1994). Individualized developmental care for the very low birth weight preterm infant: Medical and neurofunctional effects. *JAMA, 272,* 853–858.

American Association of Retired Persons & Administration on Aging. (1994). *A profile of older Americans.* Washington, DC: Author.

American Psychiatric Association. (1994). *Diagnostic and statistical manual of mental disorders* (4th ed.). Washington, DC: Author.

Ancelet, B. J. , Edwards, J. D., & Pitre, G. (1991). *Cajun country.* Jackson: University of Mississippi Press.

Andersen, M. L., & Collins, P. H. (1995). *Race, class and gender: An anthology.* Belmont, CA: Wadsworth.

Anderson, R. E, & Carter, I. (1984). *Human behavior in the social environment: A social systems approach (3rd ed.).* New York: Aldine.

Anderson, S. M., & Williams, M. (1985). Cognitive/affective reaction in the improvement of self-esteem: When thoughts and feelings make a difference. *Journal of Personality and Social Psychology, 49,* 1086–1097.

Andreason, N. C. (1984). *The broken brain: The biological revolution in psychiatry.* New York: Harper & Row.

Andreasen, N. C., & Black, D. W. (1991). *Introductory textbook of psychiatry.* Washington, DC: American Psychiatric Press.

Apgar, V. (1953). A proposal for a new method of evaluation in the newborn infant. *Current Research in Anesthesia and Analgesia, 32,* 260–267.

Aponte, H. J., & Van Deusen, J. M. (1981). Structural family therapy. In A. S. Gurman & D. P. Kniskern (Eds.), *Handbook of family therapy.* New York: Brunner Mazel.

Appetite suppressant found in brain, researchers say. (1996, January 4). *USA Today.*

Applewhite, S. R. (Ed.). (1988). *Hispanic elderly in transition.* New York: Greenwood Press.

Apter, T. (1995). *Secret paths: Women in the new midlife.* New York: Norton.

Arlington, D. E., & Troll, L. E. (1984). Social change and equality: The roles of women and economics. In G. Baruch & J. Brooks-Gunn (Eds.), *Women in midlife.* New York: Plenum.

Arrendondo, P. M. (1984). Identity themes for immigrant young adults. *Adolescence, 19,* 977–993.

Ashburn, S. S., Schuster, C. S., Grimm, W. A., & Goff, S. M. (1986). Language development during childhood. In C. Schuster & S. S. Ashburn (Eds.), *The process of human development: A holistic life-span approach* (pp. 257–276). Boston: Little, Brown.

Asher, J. (1987, April). Born to be shy? *Psychology Today,* pp. 56–64.

Asher, S. R., & Dodge, K. A. (1986). Identifying children who are rejected by their peers. *Developmental Psychology, 22,* 444–449.

Asher, S. R., & Renshaw, P. (1981). Children without friends: Social knowledge and social skill training. In S. R. Asher & J. M. Gottman (Eds.), *The development of children's friendships.* New York: Cambridge University Press.

Ashford, J. B. (1994). Child maltreatment interventions: Developments in law, prevention and treatment. *Criminal Justice Review, 19,* 271–285.

Atchley, R. (1976). *The sociology of retirement.* New York: Halsted Press.

Atchley, R. C., & Miller, S. J. (1983). Types of elderly couples. In T. H. Brubaker (Ed.), *Family relationships in later life.* Beverly Hills, CA: Sage.

Atwood, M. (1991). *Cat's eye.* London: Virago.

Avard, D. (1985). Risks and benefits of obstetric epidural analgesia: A review. *Birth: Issues in Perinatal Care and Education, 12,* 215–225.

Azar, B. (1995, May). Avoiding alcohol in real-world settings. *American Psychological Association Monitor,* p. 20.

Azar, B. (1995, June). Data released from child-care study. *APA Monitor,* p. 18.

Bacerra, R. M. (1988). The Mexican American family. In C. H. Mindel, R. W. Habenstein, & R. Wright (Eds.), *Ethnic families in America: Patterns and variations* (3rd ed.). New York: Elsevier.

Baillargeon, R. (1987). Object permanence in 3 1/2 and 4 1/2 month-old infants. *Developmental Psychology, 23,* 655–664.

Balaskas, J. (1992). *Active birth: The new approach to giving birth naturally.* Boston: Harvard Common Press.

Baldwin, J. R., & Hecht, M. L. (1995). The layered perspective of cultural (in)tolerance(s). In R. L. Waiseman (Ed.), *Intercultural communication theory.* Thousands Oaks, CA: Sage.

Bales, R. F. (1958). Task roles and social roles in problem-solving groups. In E. E. Maccoby, T. M. Newcomb, & E. L. Hartley (Eds.), *Readings in social psychology.* New York: Holt, Rinehart & Winston.

Ballenger, M. (1983). Reading in the kindergarten: Comment. *Childhood Education, 59,* 187.

Bandura, A. (1965). Influence of models' reinforcement contingencies on the acquisition of imitative responses. *Journal of Personality and Social Psychology, 1,* 589–595.

Bandura, A. (1971). *Social learning theory.* Englewood Cliffs, NJ: Prentice Hall.

Bandura, A. (1977). *Social learning.* Englewood Cliffs, NJ: Prentice Hall.

Bandura, A. (1989). Social cognitive theory. In R. Vasta (Ed.), *Annuals of child development: Vol. 6. Theories of child development: Revised formulations and current issues.* Greenwich, CT: JAI Press.

Bandura, A., Ross, D., & Ross, S. (1963). Vicarious reinforcement and imitative learning. *Journal of Abnormal and Social Psychology, 67,* 601–607.

Banton, M. (1994). *Discrimination.* Buckingham: Open University Press.

Barash, D. P., & Lipton, J. E. (1985). Sociobiology. In H. Kaplan and B. J. Sadock (Eds.), *Comprehensive textbook of psychiatry* (Vol. 4). Baltimore: Williams & Wilkins.

Barnes, K. E. (1971). Preschool play norms: A replication. *Developmental Psychology, 4,* 99–103.

Baron, R. A., & Byrne, D. (1984). *Social psychology: Understanding human interaction.* Newton, MA: Allyn & Bacon.

Barrett, D. E. (1979). A naturalistic study of sex differences in children's aggression. *Merrill-Plamer Quarterly, 25,* 193–203.

Bartlett, H. (1970). *The common base of social work practice.* Washington, DC: National Association of Social Workers.

Baruch, A. S., & Spaid, W. M. (1989). Gender differences in caregiving: Why do wives report greater burden? *The Gerontologist, 29,* 667–676.

Baruch, G. K., & Barnett, R. C. (1983). Adult daughters' relationships with their mothers. *Journal of Marriage and the Family, 45,* 601–606.

Baruch, G. K., & Brooks-Gunn, J. (1984). The study of women in midlife. In G. Baruch & J. Brooks-Gunn (Eds.), *Women in midlife.* New York: Plenum.

Baruth, L. G., & Manning, M. L. (1991). *Multicultural counseling and psychotherapy.* New York: Merrill.

Bascue, L. O., & Lawrence, R. E. (1977). A study of subjective time and death anxiety in the elderly. *Omega, 8,* 81–90.

Baskett, L. M., & Johnson, S. M. (1982). The young child's interactions with parents versus siblings. *Child Development, 53,* 643–650.

Basow, S. A. (1992). *Gender: Stereotypes and roles.* Pacific Grove, CA: Brooks/Cole.

Bassuk, E. L. (1991). Homeless families. *Scientific American, 265,* 66–74.

Bates, E. (1976). *The emergence of symbols.* New York: Academic Press.

Bateson, M. C. (1990). *Composing a life.* New York: Plume.

Baumgartner-Papageorgious, A. (1982). *My daddy might have loved me: Student perceptions of differences between being male and being female.* Denver: Institute for Equality in Education.

Baumrind, D. (1971). Current patterns of parental authority. *Developmental Psychology Monographs, 4* (1, Pt. 2).

Baumrind, D. (1989). Parenting styles and adolescent development. In J. Brooks-Gunn, R. Lerner, & A. C. Petersen (Eds.), *The encyclopedia of adolescence.* New York: Garland.

Baumrind, D. (1991). Effective parenting during the early adolescent transition. In P. A. Cowan & E. M. Hetherington (Eds.), *Advances in family research (Vol. 2).* Hillsdale, NJ: Erlbaum.

Baylor, B. (1977/1978). *The way to start a day.* New York: Macmillan.

Beal, C. R. (1987). Repairing the message: Children's monitoring and revision skills, *Child Development, 58,* 920–928.

Beardsley, T. (1995, February). Putting Alzheimer's to the tests. *Scientific American,* 12–13.

Beattie, M. (1987). *Codependent no more.* New York: Harper-Collins.

Beck, C. M., Rawlins, R. P., & Williams, S. R. (1988). *Mental health psychiatric nursing: Holistic life cycle approach.* St. Louis: C. V. Mosby.

Beck, D. F., & Jones, M. A. (1973). *Progress on family problems: A nationwide study of clients' and counselors' views on family agency services.* New York: Family Service Association of America.

Begley, S. (1988, March). All about twins. *Reader's Digest,* pp. 80–85.

Bellinger, D., & Needleman, H. (1985). Prenatal and early postnatal exposure to lead: Developmental effects, correlates, and implications. *International Journal of Mental Health, 14,* 78–111.

Belsky, J. (1980). Child maltreatment: An ecological integration. *American Psychologist, 35,* 320–335.

Belsky, J. (1981). Early human experience: A family perspective. *Developmental Psychology, 17,* 3–23.

Belsky, J. (1985). Exploring differences in marital change across the transition to parenthood: The role of violated expectations. *Journal of Marriage and the Family, 47,* 1037–1044.

Belsky, J., Gilstrap, B., & Rovine, M. (1984). The Pennsylvania infant and family development project: 1. Stability and change in mother-infant and father-infant interaction in a family setting at 1, 3, and 9 months. *Child Development, 55,* 692–705.

Belsky, J. K. (1990). *The psychology of aging: Theory, research, and interventions* (2nd ed.). Pacific Grove, CA: Brooks/Cole.

Belsky, J., & Rovine, M. (1988). Nonmaternal care in the first year of life and the security of infant-parent attachment. *Child Development, 59,* 157–167.

Bem, D. J. (1967). Self-perception: An alternative interpretation of cognitive dissonance phenomena. *Psychological Review, 74,* 183–200.

Bem, S. L. (1974). The measurement of psychological androgyny. *Journal of Consulting and Clinical Psychology, 42,* 155–162.

Bem, S. L. (1977). On the utility of alternative procedures for assessing psychological androgyny. *Journal of Consulting and Clinical Psychology, 45,* 196–205.

Bem, S. L. (1993). *The lenses of gender: Transforming the debate on sexual inequality.* Binghamton, NY: Vail-Ballou.

Benedict, H. (1979). Early lexical development: Comprehension and production. *Journal of Child Language, 6,* 183–200.

Bengston, V. L. (1985). Diversity and symbolism in grandparental roles. In V. L. Bengston & J. Robertson (Eds.), *Grandparenthood.* Beverly Hills, CA: Sage.

Bengston, V. L., Cuellar, J. B., & Ragan, P. K. (1977). Stratum contrasts and similarities in attitudes toward death. *Journal of Gerontology, 12,* 76–88.

Benson, P. L. (1990). *The troubled journey: A portrait of 6th–12th grade youth.* Minneapolis: The Search Institute.

Bergin, D. (1988). Stages of play development. In D. Bergin (Ed.), *Play as a medium for learning and development.* Portsmouth, NH: Heinemann.

Bergoquist, W. H., Greenberg, E. M., & Klaum, G. A. (1993). *In our fifties: Voices of men and women reinventing their lives.* San Francisco: Jossey-Bass.

Berkman, L. F., Berkman, C. S., Kasl, S., Freeman, D. H., Jr., Leo, L., Ostfeld, A. M., Cornoni-Huntley, J., & Brody, J. A. (1986). Depressive symptoms in relation to physical health and functioning in the elderly. *Journal of Epidemiology, 124,* 372–388.

Berko, J. (1958). The child's learning of English morphology. *Word, 14,* 150–177.

Berlyne, D. E. (1960). *Conflict, arousal, and curiosity.* New York: McGraw-Hill.

Bermant, C. (1966). *Diary of an old man.* Holt, Rinehart & Winston.

Bernard, J. (1975). *Women, wives, mothers: Values and options.* Chicago: Aldine.

Bernard, J. (1981). *The female world.* New York: Free Press.

Berndt, T. J. (1979). Developmental changes in conformity to peers and parents. *Developmental Psychology, 15,* 608–616.

Berndt, T. J., & Ladd, G. W. (1989). *Peer relations in child development.* New York: Wiley.

Berrick, J. D, & Gilbert, N. (1991). *With the best of intentions: The child sexual abuse prevention movement.* New York: Guilford Press.

Berrueta-Clement, J., Schweinhart, L., Barnett, W., Epstein, A., & Weikart, D. (1984). *Changed lives: Effects of the Perry Preschool Program on youths through age 19.* Ypsilanti, MI: High/Scope Press.

Berry, P. (1993). Pathological findings in SIDS. *Journal of Clinical Pathology, 45,* 11.

Besharov, D. J. (1985). Right versus rights: The dilemma of child protection. *Public Welfare, 42*(2), 19–27.

Bialystok, E. (1988). Levels of bilingualism and levels of linguistic awareness. *Developmental Psychology, 24,* 560–567.

Biesele, M., & Howell, N. (1981). The old people give you life: Aging among !Kung hunter-gatherers. In P. T. Amoss & S. Harrell (Eds.), *Other ways of growing old: Anthropological perspectives.* Stanford, CA: Stanford University Press.

Bjorklund, D. F., & Bjorklund, B. R., (1992). *Looking at children: An introduction to child development.* Pacific Grove, CA: Brooks/Cole.

Black, D. (1993). *The social structure of right and wrong.* San Diego: Academic Press.

Black, D. J. (1976). *The behavior of law.* New York: Academic Press.

Blakemore, J.E.O., LaRue, A. A., & Olejnik, A. B. (1979). Sex-appropriate toy preference and the ability to conceptualize toys as sex-role related. *Developmental Psychology, 15,* 339–340.

Blashfield, R. K. (1984). *The classification of psychopathology: Neo-Kraepelian and quantitative approaches.* New York: Plenum.

Block, R. D., & Moore, E. G. (1986). Advantage and disadvantage: A profile of American youth. Hillsdale, NJ: Erlbaum.

Blood, R. O., & Wolfe, D. M. (1960). *Husbands and wives.* New York: Macmillan.

Blumstein, P., & Schwartz, P. (1983). *American couples.* New York: Simon & Schuster.

Boehm, W. W. (1958). The nature of social work. *Social Work, 3,* 10–18.

Boehm, W. W. (1959). *Objectives of the social work curriculum of the future (Vol. 1).* New York: Council of Social Work, Education.

Bogard, M. (1991). *Feminist approaches for men in family therapy.* New York: Haworth Press.

Bogatz, G. A., & Ball, S. (1972). *The second year of* Sesame Street: *A continuing evaluation.* Princeton, NJ: Educational Testing Service.

Bonkowski, S., & Yanos, J. (1992). Infant mental health: An expanding field for social work. *Social Work, 37,* 144–148.

Bonvillian, J. D., Orlansky, M. D., & Novack, L. L. (1983). Development milestones: Sign language acquisition and motor development. *Child Development, 54,* 1435–1445.

Booth, C. L., Barnard, K. E., Mitchell, S. K., & Spieker, S. J. (1987). Successful intervention with multiproblem mothers: Effects on the mother-infant relationship. *Infant Mental Health Journal, 8,* 288–306.

Booth-Kewley, S., & Friedman, H. S. (1987). Psychological predictors of heart disease: A quantitative review. *Psychological Bulletin, 101,* 343–362.

Bootzin, R. E., & Acocella, J. R. (1988). *Abnormal psychology: Current perspectives.* New York: McGraw-Hill.

Bornstein, M., & Sigman, M. (1986). Continuity in mental development from infancy. *Child Development, 57,* 251–274.

Bornstein, R. (1992). Psychosocial development of the older adult. In C. S. Schuster & S. S. Ashburn (Eds.), *The process of human development: A holistic life-span approach* (3rd ed., pp. 831–850). New York: Lippincott.

Bornstein, R., & Schuster, C. S. (1992). Cognitive development during the adult years. In C. S. Schuster & C. Ashburn, *The process of human development.* New York: Lippincott.

Boston Women's Health Book Collective. (1992). When yogurt was illegal. *Ms., 3,* 38–39.

Botwinick, J. (1984). *Aging and behavior* (3rd ed.). New York: Springer.

Bouchard, T. J., Jr., Lykken, D. T., McGue, M., Segal, N. L., & Tellegen, A. (1990). Sources of human psychological differences: The Minnesota study of twins reared apart. *Science, 250,* 223–228.

Bourne, L. E., Ekstrand R. R., Dominowski, R. L. (1971). *The psychology of thinking.* Englewood Cliffs, NJ: Prentice Hall.

Bowen, M. (1978). *Family therapy in children practice.* New York: Jason Aronson.

Bower, T.G.R. (1982). *Development in infancy.* San Francisco: Freeman.

Bowlby, J. (1958). The nature of the child's tie to his mother. *International Journal of Psychoanalysis, 39,* 350–373.

Bowlby, J. (1969). *Attachment and loss: Vol. 1. Attachment.* New York: Basic Books.

Bowlby, J. (1980). *Attachment and loss: Vol. 3. Loss, sadness and depression.* New York: Basic Books.

Brabeck, M. (1983). Moral judgment: Theory and research on differences between males and females. *Developmental Review, 3,* 274–291.

Bradley, R. (1987). Providing a stimulating and supportive home environment for young children. *Physical and Occupational Therapy in Pediatrics, 7,* 77–89.

Bradley, R., & Brisby, J. (1990). Assessment of the home environment. In J. Johnson & J. Goldman (Eds.), *Developmental assessment in clinical child psychology* (pp. 219–250). New York: Pergamon Press.

Bradley, R., Caldwell, B., Rock, S., Casey, P., & Nelson, J. (1987). The early development of low-birthweight infants: Relationship to health, family status, family context, family processes and parenting. *International Journal of Behavioral Development, 10,* 301–318.

Bradley, R., Whiteside, L., Mundfrom, D., Casey, P., Kelleher, K., & Pope, S. (1994). Contribution of early intervention and early caregiving experiences to resilience in low-birthweight, premature children living in poverty. *Journal of Clinical Child Psychology, 23,* 425–434.

Braginsky, D. D., & Braginsky, B. M. (1975, August). Surplus people: Their lost faith in self and system. *Psychology Today, 9,* 68–72.

Brazelton, T. B. (1973). Neonatal behavioral assessment scale. In *Clinics in Developmental Medicine,* No. 50, Philadelphia: J. B. Lippincott.

Brazelton, T. B. (1992). *Touchpoints: Your child's emotional and behavioral development.* Reading, MA: Addison-Wesley.

Breckman, R., & Adelman, R. (1988). *Strategies for helping victims of elder mistreatment.* Newbury Park, CA: Sage.

Bremmer, J. (1988). *Infancy.* Great Britain: Page Bros.

Bremmer, J. N., & van den Bosch, L. (1995). *Between poverty and the pyre: Moments in the history of widowhood.* New York: Routledge.

Brennan, A. (1985). Participation and self-esteem: A test of six alternative explanations. *Adolescence, 20,* 445–466.

Bretherton, I., Fritz, J., Zahn-Waxler, C., & Ridgeway, D., (1986). Learning to talk about emotions. *Child Development, 57,* 529–548.

Brewer, W. (1995, June). New cognitive research makes waves. *American Psychological Association Monitor.*

Brieland, D. (1987). History and evolution of social work practice. In A. Minahan (Ed.), *Encyclopedia of social work* (18th ed.) (pp. 739–754). Silver Spring, MD: National Association of Social Workers.

Brim, O. (1975). Macro-structural influences on child development and the need for childhood social indicators. *American Journal of Orthopsychiatry, 45,* 516–524.

Brissett-Chapman, S. (1995). Child abuse and neglect: Direct practice. In *encyclopedia of social work* (19th ed.) Washington DC: NASW Press.

Brock, W. M. (1980). *The effects of day care: A review of the literature.* (ERIC Document Ed. 195–348) Los Alamitos, CA: Southwest Regional Laboratory for Educational Research and Development.

Brody, E. M. (1981). "Women in the middle" and family help to older people. *The Gerontologist, 21,* 471–480.

Brody, E. M. (1985). Parent care as a normative family stress. *The Gerontologist, 25,* 19–25.

Brody, J. E. (1987, January 21). Guidelines for parents on children's TV viewing. *New York Times.*

Broman, C. (1993). Race differences in marital well-being. *Journal of Marriage and the Family, 55,* 724–732.

Bromwich, R. (1985, December). Vulnerable infants and risky environments. *Zero to Three,* 7–12.

Bronfenbrenner, U. (1977). Toward an experimental ecology of human development. *American Psychologist, 32,* 513–531.

Bronfenbrenner, U. (1986). Ecology of the family as a context of human development: Research perspectives. *Developmental Psychology, 22*, 723–742.

Bronson, W. C. (1985). Developments in behavior with age mates during the second year of life. In M. Lewis & L. A. Rosenblum (Eds.), *The origins of behavior: Friendship and peer relations*. New York: Wiley.

Brooks-Gunn, J. (1986). Pubertal processes and girls' psychological adaptation. In R. M. Lerner & T. T. Foch (Eds.), *Biological psychosocial interactions in early adolescence: A life-span perspective*. Hillsdale, NJ: Erlbaum.

Brooks-Gunn, J., & Lewis, M. (1984). The development of early self-recognition. *Developmental Review, 4*, 215–239.

Brooks-Gunn, J., McCormick, M., & Heagarty, L. (1988). Preventing infant mortality and morbidity: Developmental perspectives. *American Journal of Orthopsychiatry, 58*, 288–295.

Brooks-Gunn, J., & Ruble, D. N. (1983). The experience of menarche from a developmental perspective. In J. Brooks-Gunn & A. C. Petersen (Eds.), *Girls at puberty*. New York: Plenum.

Brooks-Gunn, J. & Warren, M. P. (1985). The effects of delayed menarche in different contexts: Dance and nondance students. *Journal of Youth and Adolescence, 14*, 285–300.

Brooks-Gunn, J., & Warren, M. P. (1989, April). *How important are pubertal and social events for different problem behaviors and contexts*. Paper presented at the biennial meeting of the Society for Research in Child Development, Kansas City.

Brower, A. M., & Nurius, P. S. (1993). *Social Cognition and Individual Change*. Newbury Park: Sage.

Brown, B. B. (1990). Peer groups and peer cultures. In S. S. Feldman & G. R. Elliott (Eds.), *At the threshold: The developing adolescent* (pp. 171–196). Cambridge, MA: Harvard University Press.

Brown, B. B., & Mounts, N. (1989, April). *Peer group structures in single versus multi-ethnic high schools*. Paper presented at the biennial meeting of the Society for Research in Child Development, Kansas City, MO.

Brown, C. C. (1976, November). It changed my life. *Psychology Today*, 48–112.

Brown, L. M., & Gillian, C. (1992). *Meeting at the crossroads*. New York: Ballantine Books.

Brown, L. N. (1991). *Groups for growth and change*. New York: Longman.

Brown, M. A., & Woods, N. F. (1986). Sex role orientation, sex typing, occupational traditionalism, and premenstrual symptoms. In V. L. Olesen & N. F. Woods (Eds.), *Culture, society, and menstruation*. Washington, DC: Hemisphere.

Brown, P. & Elliott, R. (1965). Control of aggression in a nursery school class. *Journal of Experimental Child Psychology, 2*, 103–107.

Brown, R. (1958). *Words and things*. Glencoe, IL: Free Press.

Brown, R. H. (1994). Reconstructing social theory after the postmodern critique. In H. W. Simons & M. Billig (Eds.), *After postmodernism: Reconstructing ideology critique*. London: Sage.

Browne, A. (1987). *When battered women kill*. New York: Free Press.

Brubaker, T. H. (1985). *Later life families*. Newbury Park, CA: Sage.

Bruckner-Gordon, F., Gangi, B. K., & Wallman, G. U. (1988). *Making therapy work: Your guide to choosing, using, and ending therapy*. New York: HarperCollins.

Bryant, S., & Demian. (1990, May/June). When lesbian and gay couples break up. *Partners Newsletter for Gay and Lesbian Couples*.

Buehler, C. A., Hogan, M. J., Robinson, B. E., & Levy, R. J. (1985). The parental divorce transition: Divorce-related stressors and well-being. *Journal of Divorce, 9*, 61–81.

Buehlman, K. T., Gottman, J. M., & Katz, L. F. (1992). How a couple views their past predicts their future: Predicting divorce from an oral history interview. *Journal of Family Psychology, 5*, 295–318.

Bufe, C. (1987, November). AA: Guilt and god for the gullible. *The Match! An Anarchist Journal*. Excerpted in *Utne Reader* (1988, November/December), 54–55.

Bullock, B. L. & Rosendahl, P. P. (1988). *Pathophysiology: Adaptations and alterations in function* (2nd ed.). Glenview, IL: Scott, Foresman.

Burdman, G. M. (1986). *Healthful aging*. Englewood Cliffs, NJ: Prentice Hall.

Burgess, A. W., & Holmstromm, L. L. (1985). Rape trauma syndrome and post traumatic stress response. In A. W. Burgess (Ed.), *Rape and sexual assault: A research handbook* (pp. 46–60). New York: Garland.

Burton, L. (1990). Teenage childbearing as an alternative life-course strategy in multigenerational black families. *Human Nature, 2*, 123–143.

Busse, E. W. & Pfeiffer, E. (1977). *Behavior and adaptation in late life*. Boston: Little, Brown.

Butler, K. (1995, March/April). Caught in the crossfire. *Family Therapy Networker*, pp. 25–29.

Butler, R. M. (1970). *Social functioning framework: An approach to the human behavior and social environment sequence*. New York: Council on Social Work Education.

Butler, R. N. (1963). The life review: An interpretation of reminiscence in the aged. *Psychiatry, 26*, 65–76.

Butler, R. N. (1975). *Why survive? Being old in America*. New York: Harper & Row.

Butler, R. N. (1990). A disease called ageism. *Journal of the American Geriatric Association, 38*, 178–180.

Butler, R. N., Lewis, M., & Sunderland, T. (1991). *Aging and mental health: Positive psychosocial and biomedical approaches* (4th ed.). New York: Macmillan.

Cairns, R. B., Cairns, B. D., Neckerman, H. J., Ferguson, L. L., & Gariepy, J. L. (1989). Growth and aggression: Childhood to adolescence. *Developmental Psychology, 25*, 320–330.

Caldwell, B., & Bradley, R. (1984). *Home observation for measurement of the environment*. Little Rock: University of Arkansas Press.

Call, J. D. (1964). Newborn approach behavior and early ego development. *International Journal of Psychoanalysis, 45*, 286.

Calvert, S., & Calvert, P. (1992). *Sociology today*. London: Harvester/Weatsheaf.

Camp, B. W., Blom, G. E., Herbert, F., & Van Doorninck, W. J. (1977). "Think aloud": A program for developing self-control in young aggressive boys. *Journal of Abnormal Psychology, 5*, 167–169.

Campbell, E. (1985). *The childless marriage: An exploratory study of couples who do not want children*. New York: Tavistock.

Campbell, J., with Moyers, B. (1988). *The power of myth*. New York: Doubleday.

Cantor, M. H. (1979). Neighbors and friends: An overlooked resource in the informal support system. *Research on Aging, 1*, 434–463.

Cantor, M. H. (1983). Strain among caregivers: A study of the experience in the United States. *The Gerontologist, 23*, 597–604.

Cantwell, D. P. (1982). Childhood depression: A review of current research. In B. B. Lahey & A. E. Kazdin (Eds.), *Advances in child clinical psychology*. New York: Plenum.

Caplan, G. (1974). *Support systems and community mental health*. New York: Behavioral Publications.

Caplan, R. (1993). Alcoholism. *Grolier Electronic Encyclopedia*.

Carey, S. (1977). The child as word learner. In M. Halle, J. Bresman, & G. A. Miller (Eds.), *Linguistic theory and psychological reality*. Cambridge: Massachusetts Institute of Technology Press.

Carnegie Council on Adolescent Development. (1989). *Turning points: Preparing youth for the 21st century*. New York: Carnegie Corporation.

Carter, B., & McGoldrick, M. (1988). *The changing family life-cycle: A framework for family therapy* (2nd ed.). New York: Gardner.

Cartwright, D. (1968). The nature of group cohesiveness. In D. Cartwright & A. Zander (Eds.), *Group dynamics: Research and theory* (3rd ed.). New York: Harper & Row.

Caspi, A., Elder, G. H., & Bem, D. J. (1987). Moving against the world: Life-course patterns of explosive children. *Developmental Psychology, 23*, 308–313.

Cassell, C. (1984). *Swept away: Why women fear their own sexuality*. New York: Simon & Schuster.

Cattanach, L., & Tebes, J. K. (1991). The nature of elder impairment and its impact on family caregivers' health and psychosocial functioning. *The Gerontologist, 31*, 246–255.

Cavanaugh, J. C. (1990). *Adult development and aging*. Belmont, CA: Wadsworth.

Chaikin, A. E., Sigler, E., & Derlega, V. (1974). Non-verbal mediators of teacher expectancy effects. *Journal of Personality and Social Psychology, 30*, 144–149.

Chamberlain, D. (1994a). Intelligence before birth: Ethical implications for birth professionals. Manuscript submitted for publication.

Chamberlain, D. (1994b). Observations of behavior before birth: Current findings. Manuscript submitted for publication.

Chamberlain, P., & Patterson, G. R. (1985). Aggressive behavior in middle childhood. In D. Shaffer, A. A. Ehrhardt, & L. L. Greenhill (Eds.), *The clinical guide to child psychiatry*. New York: Free Press.

Chambliss, L. (1994, Fall). Domestic violence—What is the health care provider's responsibility? *Samaritan Airevac News for Physicians and Managers*, 1–3.

Chapkis, W. (1986). *Beauty secrets: Women and the politics of appearance*. Boston: South End Press.

Chapman, J., Siegel, E., & Cross, A. (1990). Home visitors and child health: Analysis of selected programs. *Pediatrics, 85*, 1059–1068.

Charness, N., & Bosman, E. A. (1992). Human factors in aging. In F.I.M. Craik & T. A. Salthouse (Eds.), *The handbook of aging and cognition*. Hillsdale, NJ: Erlbaum.

Chase, S. N., & Clement, P. W. (1985). Effects of self-reinforcement and stimulants on academic performance in children with attention deficit disorder. *Journal of Clinical Child Psychology, 14*, 323–333.

Chase-Lansdale, P. L. (1981). Maternal employment and quality of infant-mother and infant-father attachment (Doctoral dissertation, University of Michigan). *Dissertation Abstracts International, 42*, 2562B.

Chase-Lansdale, P. L., & Owen, M. (1987). Maternal employment in a family contest: Effects on infant-mother and infant-father attachments. *Child Development, 58*, 1505–1512.

Cherlin, A., & Furstenberg, F. F. (1986). *The new American grandparent*. New York: Basic Books.

Cherry, F., & Deaux, K. (1978). Fear of success versus fear of gender-inappropriate behavior. *Sex Roles, 4*, 97–102.

Chestang, L. (1980). Character development in a hostile environment. In M. Bloom (Ed.), *Life span development*. New York: Macmillan.

Chilman, C. (1979). *Adolescent sexuality in a changing American society: Social and psychological perspectives*. Washington, DC: Public Health Service, National Institutes of Mental Health.

Cho, S. A., Freeman, E. M., & Patterson, S. L. (1982). Adolescents' experience with death: Practice implications. *Social Casework, 63*, 88–94.

Chu, C. E., Cooke, A., Stephenson. J. B., & Tolmie, P. (1994). Diagnosis in Prader-Willi syndrome. *Archives of Disease in Childhood, 71*, 441–442.

Cicchetti, D., & Schneider-Rosen, K. (1986). An organizational approach to childhood depression. In M. Rutter, C. Izard, & P. B. Read (Eds.), *Depression in young people: Developmental and clinical perspectives*. New York: Guilford Press.

Cicchetti, D., & Wagner, S. (1990). Alternative assessment strategies for the evaluation of infants and toddlers: An organizational perspective. In S. J. Meisels and J. P. Shonkoff (Eds.), *Handbook of early childhood intervention* (pp. 246–277). New York: Cambridge University Press.

Cicirelli, V. G. (1983). Adult children and their elderly parents. In T. Brubaker (Ed.), *Family relationships in later life*. Beverly Hills: Sage.

Cintas, H. (1988). Cross-cultural variation in infant motor development. *Physical & Occupational Therapy in Pediatrics, 8*, 1–20.

Clark, K. B., & Clark M. K. (1939). The development of consciousness of self and emergence of racial identification in Negro preschool children. In R. Wilcox (Ed.), *The psychological consequences of being a black American: A sourcebook of research by black psychologists*. New York: Wiley.

Clarke-Stewart, K. A. (1978). And daddy makes three: The father's impact on mother and young child. *Child Development, 49*, 466–478.

Clarke-Stewart, K. A. (1989). Infant day care: Maligned or malignant? *American Psychologist, 44*, 266–273.

Clarke-Stewart, K. A. (1991). A home is not a school: The effects of environments on development. In M. Lewis & S. Feinman (Eds.), *Social influences and socialization in infancy* (pp. 41–61). New York: Plenum.

Clarke-Stewart, K. A., & Fein, G. G. (1983). Early childhood programs. In P. H. Mussen (Ed.), *Handbook of child psychology* (4th ed., Vol. 2). New York: Wiley.

Clasen, D. R., & Brown, B. B. (1987). Understanding peer pressure in middle school. *Middle School Journal, 19*, 21–23.

Clorfene-Costen, L. (1993, May/June). The environmental link to breast cancer. *Ms.*, 52–56.

Cohen, D. (1983). *Piaget: Critique and reassessment*. London: Croom Helm.

Cohen, D. (1988). Social work and psychotropic drug treatments. *Social Services Review, 62*(4), 576–599.

Cohen, G., Yeast, J., & Hu, D. (1994). Epidural analgesia in labor and cesarean delivery for dystocia. *Obstetrical & Gynecological Survey, 49*, 362–369.

Cohen, S. (1982). Arthritis—But what sort? *Geriatrics, 37*, 49–51.

Cohen, S., & Strauss, M. (1979). Concept acquisition in the human infant. *Child Development, 50*, 767–776.

Coleman, J. S. (1980). The peer group. In J. Adelson (Ed.), *Handbook of adolescent psychology*. New York: Wiley.

Coleman, J. S., Campbell, E., Hobson, C., McPartland, J., Mood, A., Weinfield, F., & York, R. (1966). *Equality of educational opportunity*. Washington, DC: U.S. Government Printing Office.

Coles, R. (1986). *The political life of children*. Boston: Little, Brown.

Coll, C., & Meyer, E. (1993). The sociocultural context of infant development. In C. Zeaneh (Ed.), *Handbook of infant mental health* (pp. 56–69). New York: Guilford Press.

Colletti, L. (1979). Relationship between pregnancy and birth complications and the later development of learning disabilities. *Journal of Learning Disabilities, 12*, 659–663.

Collins, A. H., & Pancoast, D. L. (1976). *Natural helping networks*. Washington, DC: National Association of Social Workers.

Comas-Diaz, L., & Greene, B. (1994). *Overview: An ethnocultural mosaic*. In L. Comas-Diaz & B. Greene (Eds.) *Women of color: Integrating ethnic and gender identities in psychotherapy*. New York: Guilford Press.

Combs, M. L., & Slaby, D. A. (1977). Social skills training with children. In B. B. Lahey & A. E. Kazdin (Eds.), *Advances in clinical child psychology*. New York: Plenum.

Committee on Economic Development (1987). *Children in need: Investment strategies for the educationally disadvantaged*. Washington, DC: Committee for Economic Development.

Condon, W. (1975). Speech makes babies move. In R. Lewin (Ed.), *Child alive!* (pp. 75–85). Garden City, NY: Anchor Books.

Condry, J. C. (1989). *The psychology of television*. Hillsdale, NJ: Erlbaum.

Conger, R., Elder, G., Lorenz, F., Conger, K., Simons, R., Whitbeck, L., Huck, S., & Melby, J. (1990). Linking economic hardship to marital quality and instability. *Journal of Marriage and the Family, 52*, 643–656.

Connell, S. (1987). Homelessness. In *Encyclopedia of social work* (pp. 789–795). Silver Spring, MD: National Association of Social Workers.

Conners, K. (1989). Conners' Teacher Rating Scale — 39-item version. (*CTRS–39*). North Tonawanda, NY: Multi-Health Systems.

Consortium for Longitudinal Studies (1983). *As the twig is bent.* Hillsdale, NJ: Erlbaum.

Constable, B. (1983). The individualized educational program: content, process, and the social worker's role. In B. Constable & J. Flynn (Eds.), *School social work: Practice and research perspectives.* Pacific Grove, CA: Brooks/Cole.

Cook, S. W. (1979). Social science and school desegregation: Did we mislead the Supreme Court? *Personality and Social Psychology, 5*, 418–428.

Cooke, T., & Apolloni, T. (1976). Developing positive social-emotional behaviors: A study of training and generalization effects. *Journal of Applied Behavior Analysis, 9*, 65–78.

Cool, L. E. (1987). The effects of social class and ethnicity on the aging process. In P. Silverman (Ed.), *The elderly as modern pioneers* (pp. 211–227). Bloomington: Indiana University Press.

Cooper, C. R., & Grotevant, H. D. (1989, April). *Individuality and connectedness in the family and adolescents' self and relational competence.* Paper presented at the biennial meeting of the Society for Research in Child Development, Kansas City, MO.

Corah, N., Anthony, E., Painter, P., Stern, J., & Thurston, D. (1965). Effects of perinatal anoxia after seven years. *Psychological Monographs, 79*, 3.

Coren, S., & Searleman, A. (1985). Birth stress and self-reported sleep difficulty. *Sleep, 8*, 222–226.

Costin, L., Bell, C., & Downs, S. (1991). *Child welfare: Policies and practices.* New York: Longman.

Cote, J. E., & Levine, C. (1988). A critical examination of the ego identity status paradigm. *Developmental Review, 8*, 147–184.

Cotterrell, R. (1984). *The sociology of law: An introduction.* London: Butterworths.

Council on Social Work Education. (1990). *Psychopharmacology in social work education.* Alexandria, VA. Authors.

Cowen, E. L., Pederson, A., Babigan, H., Izzo, L. D., & Trost, M. A. (1973). Long-term follow-up of early detected vulnerable children. *Journal of Consulting and Clinical Psychology, 41*, 438–446.

Creno, C. (1994, April 19). Bonding before birth: Child's mental health begins at conception, small-but-growing group insists. *The Arizona Republic*, p. E1.

Crnic, K. (1984). Maternal stress and social support: Effects on the mother-infant relationship from birth to eighteen months. *American Journal of Orthopsychiatry, 54*, 224–235.

Crnic, K., & Greenberg, M. (1990). Minor parenting stresses with young children. *Child Development, 61*, 1628–1637.

Crnic, K., & Harris, V. (1990). Normal development in infancy and early childhood. In J. Johnson & J. Goldman (Eds.), *Developmental assessment in clinical child psychology* (pp. 15–33). New York: Pergamon Press.

Crockenberg, S. (1981). Infant irritability, mother responsiveness, and social influences on the security of infant-mother attachment. *Child Development, 52*, 857–865.

Crockenberg, S., Lyons-Ruth, K., & Dickstein, S. (1993). The family contest of infant mental health: II. Infant development in multiple family relationships. In C. Zeanah (Ed.), *Handbook of infant mental health* (pp. 38–55). New York: Guilford Press.

Crohan, S. E., & Antonucci, T. C. (1989). Friends as a source of social support in old age. In R. G. Adams & R. Blieszner (Eds.), *Older adult friendships.* Newbury Park, CA: Sage.

Cronin, M., & Gorman, C. (1991, May 13). Should we take away their kids? *Time, 137*(19), 62–63.

Cronin, M., Ludtke, M., & Willwerth, J. (1991, May 13). Innocent victims. *Time, 137*(19), 56–60.

Csikszentmihalyi, M., & Larson, R. (1984). *Being adolescent.* New York: Basic Books.

Cuellar, J. (1980). *Minority elderly Americans: A prototype for area agencies on aging.* San Diego, CA: Allied Home Health Association.

Culbertson, J., & Gyurke, J. (1990). Assessment of cognitive and motor development in infancy and childhood. In J. Johnson & J. Goldman (Eds.), *Developmental assessment in clinical child psychology* (pp. 100–131). New York: Pergamon Press.

Cumming, E., & Henry, W. E. (1961). *Growing old: The process of disengagement.* New York: Basic Books.

Cummings, E. M. (1987). Coping with background anger in early childhood. *Child Development, 58*, 976–984.

Cummins, J., & Swain, M. (1986). *Bilingualism in education: Aspects of theory, research and practice.* London: Taylor & Fry.

Curran, D. D. (1985). *Stress and the healthy family.* Minneapolis: Winston Press.

Damon, W. (1995, May). Is self-esteem really all that important? *APA Monitor.*

Dan A., & Bernhard, L. (1989). Menopause and other health issues for midlife. In S. Hunter & M. Sundel (Eds.), *Midlife myths: Issues, findings and practice implications* (pp. 201–217). Newbury Park, CA: Sage.

Dangel, R. F., & Polster, R. A. (1988). *Teaching child management skills.* Elmsford, NY: Pergamon Press.

Daniel, W. A. (1983). Pubertal changes in adolescence. In J. Brooks-Gunn & A. C. Petersen (Eds.), *Girls at puberty.* New York: Plenum.

Daniels, K. (1993). Infertility counselling: The need for a psychosocial perspective. *British Journal of Social Work, 23,* 501–512.

Danziger, S. K., & Radin, N. (1989, April). *Absent does not equal uninvolved: Predictors of fathering in teen mother families.* Paper presented at the biennial meeting of the Society for Research in Child Development, Kansas City, MO.

Daro, D. (1991). Child sexual abuse prevention: Separating fact from fiction. *Child Abuse & Neglect, 15,* 1–4.

Darwin C. (1859/1958). *The origin of species by means of natural selection or the preservation of favored races in the struggle for life.* New York: New American Library (Mentor Books).

Darwin, C. (1872). *The expression of emotions in man and animals.* New York: Philosophical Library.

Das, J. P. (1984). Intelligence and information integration. In J. Kirby (Ed.), *Theory and research in learning disabilities.* New York: Plenum.

Davidson, E. (1992). Racial disparity in infant mortality. *New England Journal of Medicine, 327,* 1022–1023.

Davidson, M., & Jamison, P. W. (1983). The clinical social worker and current psychiatric drugs: Some introductory principles. *Clinical Social Work Journal, 71,* 134–150.

Davis, K., Grant, P., & Rowland, D. (1990). Alone and poor: The plight of elderly women. *Generations, 14,* 43–47.

Davis, K. L., Kahn, R. S., Ko, G., & Davidson, M. (1991). Dopamine in schizophrenia: A review and reconceptualization. *American Journal of Psychiatry, 148,* 1474–1486.

Davis, L. (1989). The myths of menopause. In L. Fenson & J. Fenson (Eds.), *Human development 90/91* (pp. 237–241).

De Ande, D. (1984). Bicultural socialization: Factors affecting minority experience. *Social Work, 29,* 172–181.

DeAngelis, T. (1995, January). How adoptees fare. *APA Monitor.*

Deaux, K., Dane, F. C., & Wrightsman, L. S. (1993). *Social psychology in the 90s.* Pacific Grove, CA: Brooks/Cole.

DeCasper, A. J., & Fifer. & W. P. (1980). Of human bonding: Newborns prefer their mothers' voices. *Science, 208,* 1174–1176.

Demmo, D. H. (1992). Parent-child relations: Assessing recent changes. *Journal of Marriage and the Family, 54,* 104–117.

Demmo, D. H., & Acock, A. C. (1988). The impact of divorce on children. *Journal of Marriage and the Family, 50,* 619–648.

Dempster, F. N. (1981). Memory span: Sources of individual and developmental differences. *Psychological Bulletin, 89,* 63–100.

Denisoff, R. S., & Wahrman, R. (1979). *An introducation to sociology* (2nd ed.). New York: Macmillan.

Dennis, W. (1960). Causes of retardation among institutional children: Iran. *Journal of Genetic Psychology, 96,* 47–59.

Dennis, W. (1973). *Children of the creche.* East Norwalk, CT: Appleton-Century-Crofts.

Dennis, W., & Dennis, J. (1940). The effect of cradling practices upon the onset of walking in Hopi children. *Journal of Genetic Psychology, 56,* 77–86.

Depner, C. E., & Ingersol-Dayton, B. (1985). Conjugal social support: Patterns in later life. *Journal of Gerontology, 40,* 761–766.

Dettwyler, K. (1989). Styles of infant feeding: Parental/caretaker control of food consumption in young children. *Research Reports, 91,* 696–703.

Devita, V. T., Hellman, S., & Rosenberg, S. A. (1989). *Cancer principles and practice of oncology* (Vol. 1, 3rd ed.). Philadelphia: Lippincott.

DeVitto, J. (1970). *The psychology of speech and language: An introduction to psycholinguistics.* New York: Random House.

Diamond, M. (1993). Homosexuality and bisexuality in different populations. *Archives of Sexual Behavior, 22,* 291–310.

Diamond, M., & Karlen, A. (1980). *Sexual decisions.* Boston: Little, Brown.

Dick, J.P.R., Guiloff, R. J., Stewart, A., Blackstock, J., Bielawska, C., Paul, E. A., & Marsden, C. D. (1984). Mini-mental status examination in neurological patients. *Journal of Neurology, 47,* 496–499.

Diener, C. I., & Dweck, C. S. (1980). An analysis of learned helplessness: II. The processing of success. *Journal of Personality and Social Psychology, 39,* 940–952.

DiMatteo, M. R., (1991). *The psychology of health, illness, and medical care: An individual perspective.* Pacific Grove, CA: Brooks/Cole.

Dinkmeyer, D., & McKay, G. D. (1982). *The parents handbook: STEP.* Circle Pines, MN: American Guidance Service.

Dinkmeyer, D., & McKay, G. D. (1983). *Systematic training for effective parenting: The parent's guide.* St. Paul, MN: American Guidance Service.

Dion, K., Miller, N., & Magnan, M. (1970). Cohesiveness and social responsibility as determinants of risk taking. *Proceedings of the American Psychological Association, 5,* 335–336.

Dlugokinski, E., & Firestone, I. J. (1974). Other centeredness and susceptibility to charitable appeals: Effects of perceived discipline. *Developmental Psychology, 10,* 21–28.

Dodge, K. A., Pettit, G. S., Murphy, R. R., & Buchsbaum, K. (1984). The assessment of intention-cue detection skills in children: Implications for developmental psychopathology. *Child Development, 55,* 163–173.

Dodson, J. (1988). Conceptualizations of black families. In H. P. McAdoo (Ed.), *Black families* (pp. 77–90). Beverly Hills, CA: Sage.

Dolgin, K. G., & Behrend, D. A. (1984). Children's knowledge about animates and inanimates. *Child Development, 55,* 1646–1650.

Dollinger, S. J., & Gasser, M. (1981). Imitation as social influence. *Journal of Genetic Psychology, 138,* 149–150.

Dornbusch, S. M., Carlsmith, J. M., Bushwall, S. J., Ritter, P. L., Leiderman, H., Hastorf, A. H., & Gross, R. T. (1985). Single parents, extended households, and the control of adolescents. *Child Development, 56,* 326–341.

Doyle, P. (1995, August 7). Custody fights in adoptions test Indian tribes' power. *Arizona Daily Star,* pp. 1, 8.

Dregni, M. (1989, September/October). Coming out in the age of AIDS. *Utne Reader,* pp. 19–20.

Dreykurs, R. (1964). *Children the challenge.* New York: Hawthorne Books.

Drucker, P. F. (1954). *The practice of management.* New York: Harper & Row.

Dryfoos, J. G. (1990). *Adolescents at risk: Prevalence and prevention.* New York: Oxford University Press.

Dubin, M. (1994). Aggravating adolescent years often will hit parents hard. *Arizona Daily Star,* p. 1D.

Dubin, S. (1972). Obsolescence or lifelong education: A choice for the professional. *American Psychologist, 17,* 486–498.

Dubos, R. (1978). Health and creative adaptation. *Human Nature, 1,* 74–82.

Dulcan, M. K. (1986). Comprehensive treatment of children and adolescents with attention deficit disorders: The state of the art. *Clinical Psychology Review, 6,* 539–569.

Dunker, K. (1945). On problem solving. *Psychological Monographs, 58*(5, Whole No. 270).

Dunn, J. (1991). Sibling influences. In M. Lewis & S. Feinman (Eds.), *Social influences and socialization in infancy* (pp. 97–109). New York: Plenum.

Dunn, J., & Kendrick, C. (1982). *Siblings.* Cambridge, MA: Harvard University Press.

Dunn, J., & Munn, P. (1986). Sibling quarrels and maternal intervention: Individual differences in understanding and aggression. *Journal of Child Psychology and Psychiatry, 27,* 583–597.

Dunst, C., Trivette, C., & Cross, A. (1986). Mediating influences of social support: Personal, family, and child outcomes. *American Journal of Mental Deficiency, 90,* 403–417.

Dura, J. R., Haywood-Niler, E., & Kiecolt-Glaser, J. K. (1990). Spousal caregivers of persons with Alzheimer's and Parkinson's disease dementia: A preliminary comparison. *The Gerontologist, 30,* 332–336.

Durham, W. H. (1991). *Coevolution: Genes, culture, and human diversity.* Stanford, CA: Stanford University Press.

Dusek, J., & Flaherty, J. (1981). The development of the self-concept during the adolescent years. *Monographs of the Society for Research in Child Development, 46*(Serial No. 191).

Dutton, D. B., & Levine, S. (1989). Overview, methodological critique, and reformulation. In J. P. Bunker, D. S. Gomby, & B. H. Kehrer (Eds.), *Pathways to health* (pp. 29–69). Menlo Park, CA: Henry J. Kaiser Family Foundation.

Duvall, E. M. (1971). *Family development* (4th ed.). Philadelphia: Lippincott.

Duvall, E. M., & Miller, B. C. (1985). *Marriage and family development* (6th ed.). New York: Harper & Row.

Dweck, C. S. (1986). Motivational processes affecting learning. *American Psychologist, 41,* 1040–1048.

Dweck, C. S., Davidson, W., Nelson, S., & Enna, B. (1978). Sex differences in learned helplessness: II. The contingencies of evaluative feedback in the classroom, and III. An experimental analysis. *Developmental Psychology, 14,* 268–276.

Dweck, C. S., & Reppucci, N. D. (1973). Learned helplessness and reinforcement responsibility in children. *Journal of Personality and Social Psychology, 31,* 674–685.

Dwyer, K. P. (1995, May). Is self-esteem really all that important? *APA Monitor.*

Dziech, B. W., & Weiner, L. (1991). *The lecherous professor: Sexual harassment on campus.* Urbana: University of Illinois Press.

Eagly, A. H., & Wood, W. (1991). Explaining sex differences in social behavior: A meta-analytic perspective. *Journal of Sex Research, 36,* 424–435.

Easterbrooks, M. A., & Goldberg, W. A. (1985). Effects of early maternal employment on toddlers, mothers, and fathers. *Developmental Psychology, 21,* 774–783.

Eberstadt, N. (1991). America's infant mortality puzzle. *The Public Interest, 105,* 30–47.

Eccles, J. S. (1987). Gender roles and achievement patterns: An expectancy value perspective. In J. M. Reinisch, L. A.

Roseblum, & S. A. Sanders (Eds.), *Masculinity/femininity*. New York: Oxford University Press.

Eccles, J. S., & Midgley, C. (1989). Stage/environment fit: Developmentally appropriate classrooms for early adolescents. In R. E. Ames & C. Ames (Eds.), *Research on motivation in education* (Vol. 3). New York: Academic Press.

Eckert, P. (1990). Cooperative competition in adolescent "girl talk." *Discourse Processes, 13*, 91–122.

Edelman, M. W. (1987). *Families in peril: An agenda for social change*. New York: Alan Guttmacher Institute.

Edmonds, M. (1990). The health of the Black aged female. In Z. Harel, E. A. McKinney, & M. Williams (Eds.), *Black aged*. Newbury Park, CA: Sage.

Edwards, C. (1984). The age group labels and categories of preschool children. *Child Development, 55*, 440–452.

Edwards, C., Johnson, A., Knight, E., Oyemade, U., Cole, O., Westney, O., Jones, S., Laryea, H., & Westney, L. (1994a). Maternal stress and pregnancy outcomes in a prenatal clinic population. *Journal of Nutrition, 124*, 1006–1022.

Edwards, C., Johnson, A., Knight, E., Oyemade, U., Cole, O., Westney, O., Jones, S., Laryea, H., & Westney, L. (1994b). Pica in an urban environment (African-American women and their pregnancies). *Journal of Nutrition, 124*, 9545–9554.

Edwards, D., Porter, S., & Stein, G. (1993). A pilot study of postnatal depression following caesarean section using two retrospective self-rating instruments. *Journal of Psychosomatic Research, 38*, 111–117.

Eisenberg, N. (Ed.). (1982). *The development of prosocial behavior*. New York: Wiley.

Eisendrath, S. J. (1988). The mind and somatic illness: psychological factors affecting physical illness. In H. H. Goldman (Ed.), *Review of general psychiatry*. East Norwalk, CT: Appleton & Lang.

Ekerdt, D. J., Bossé, R., & Levkoff, S. (1985). Empirical test for phases of retirement: Findings from the Normative Aging Study. *Journal of Gerontology, 40*, 368–374.

Elias, M. (1991). A multilevel action research perspective on stress-related interventions. In M. E. Colten & S. Gore (Eds.), *Adolescent stress*. New York: Aldine de Gruyter.

Elkind, D. (1976). *Child development and education: A Piagetian perspective*. New York: Oxford University Press.

Elkind, D. (1978). Understanding the young adolescent. *Adolescence, 13*, 127–134.

Elkind, D. (1981). *The hurried child*. Reading, MA: Addison-Wesley.

Elkind, D. (1987). *Miseducation: Preschoolers at risk*. New York: Knopf.

Elliot, D. S. (1993). Promoting the health of adolescents: New directions for the twenty-first century. In S. Millstein, A. C. Petersen, & E. O. Nightingale (Eds.), *Adolescent health promotion*. New York: Oxford University Press.

Ellis, S., Rogoff, B., & Cromer, C. C. (1981). Age segregation in children's social interactions. *Developmental Psychology, 17*, 399–407.

Emde, R. (1987). Infant mental health: Clinical dilemmas, the expansion of meaning, and opportunities. In J. Osofsky (Ed.), *Handbook of infant development* (pp. 1297–1320). New York: Wiley.

Emde, R. N., Plomin, R., Robinson, J., Corley, R., DeFries, J., Fulkner, D. W., Reznick, J. S., Campos, J., Kagan, J., & Zahn-Waxler, C. (1992). Temperament, emotion, and cognition at fourteen months: The MacArthur Longitudinal Twin Study. *Child Development, 63*, 1437–1455.

Emler, N. , Renwick, S., & Malone, B. (1983). The relationship between moral reasoning and political orientation. *Journal of Personality and Social Psychology, 45*, 1073–1080.

Emmerich, W. (1959). Parental identification in young children. *Genetic Psychology Monographs, 60*, 257–308.

Emmerich, W. (1966). Continuity and stability in early social development: II. Teacher's ratings. *Child Development, 37*, 17–27.

Enck, R. (1992, July/August). The last few days. *The American Journal of Hospice and Palliative Care*, pp. 11–13.

Englander-Golden, P., Sonleitner, F. J., Whitmore, M. R., & Corbley, G.J.M. (1986). Social and menstrual cycles: Methodological and substantive findings. In V. L. Olesen & N. F. Woods (Eds.), *Culture, society, and menstruation*. Washington, DC: Hemisphere.

Entwisle, D. R. (1990). Schools and the adolescent. In S. S. Feldman & G. R. Elliot (Eds.), *At the threshold: The developing adolescent* (pp. 197–224). Cambridge, MA: Harvard University Press.

Ephross, J. (1982). A social work perspective on families with infants who fail to thrive. In P. J. Accardo (Ed.), *Failure to thrive in infancy and early childhood* (pp. 331–347). Baltimore: University Park Press.

Erickson, J. (1996, May 6). Obstetric anesthesia safety called remarkable. *The Arizona Daily Star*, pp. 1B, 4B.

Erikson, E. (1959). Identity in the life cycle. [monograph 1]. *Psychological Issues, 1*.

Erikson, E. H. (1963). *Childhood and society* (2nd ed.). New York: Norton.

Erikson, E. H. (1968). *Identity: Youth and crisis*. New York: Norton.

Erikson, E. H. (1974). *Dimensions of a new identity*. New York: Norton.

Evans, C., & Dion, K. (1991). Group cohesion and performance. *Small Group Research, 22*, 175–186.

Ewalt, P. L., & Perkins, L. L. (1979). The real experience of death among adolescents. *Social Casework, 60,* 547–551.

Eyer, D. (1994). Mother-infant bonding: A scientific fiction. *Human Nature, 5,* 69–94.

Eysenck, H. J. (1989, December). Health's character. *Psychology Today,* pp. 28–32, 34–35.

Fagot, B. (1978). The influence of sex of child on parental reactions to toddler children. *Child Development, 49,* 459–465.

Fagot, B. (1989). The young child's gender schema: Environmental input, internal organization. *Child Development, 60,* 663–672.

Fagot, B. (1991). Observations of parent reactions to sex-stereotyped behaviors: Age and sex effects. *Child Development, 62,* 617–628.

Fagot, B. (1992). Gender labeling, gender stereotyping, and parenting behaviors. *Developmental Psychology, 28,* 225–230.

Fahey, M., & Phillips, S. (1981). The self-concept in middle childhood: Some baseline data. *Child Study Journal, 11,* 155.

Fahlberg, V. (1991). *A child's journey through placement.* Indianapolis, IN: Perspectives Press.

Fain, T. C., & Anderson, D. L. (1987). Sexual harassment: Organizational context and diffuse status. *Sex Roles, 17,* 291–311.

Fay, R. E., Turner, C. F., Klassen, A. D., & Gagnon, J. H. (1989). Prevalence and patterns of same-gender sexual contact among men. *Science, 243,* 338–348.

FBI: Racism cause of most hate crime. (1993, January 5). *Tempe Daily Tribune,* p. A3.

Feinbloom, R. (1993). *Pregnancy, birth and the early months: A complete guide.* Reading, MA: Addison-Wesley.

Feingold, B. (1975). *Why your child is hyperactive.* New York: Random House.

Feinman, S. (1991). Bringing babies back into the social world. In M. Lewis & S. Feinman (Eds.), *Social influences and socialization in infancy* (pp. 281–320). New York: Plenum.

Feld, S., & Radin, N. (1982). *Social psychology for social work and the mental health professions.* New York: Columbia University Press.

Feldman, R. A., Caplinger, T. E., & Wodarski, J. S. (1983). *The St. Louis conundrum: The effective treatment of antisocial youth.* Englewood Cliffs, NJ: Prentice Hall.

Fernald, A. (1987). Acoustic determinants of infant preference for motherese speech. *Infant Behavior and Development, 10,* 279–293.

Fernald, A. (1991). Prosody and focus in speech to infants and adults. *Developmental Psychology, 27,* 209–221.

Ferrante, J. (1995). *Sociology: A global perspective.* Belmont, CA: Wadsworth.

Feshbach, S. (1956). The catharsis hypothesis and some consequences of interaction with aggressive and neutral play objects. *Journal of Personality, 24,* 449–461.

Festinger, L. (1950). Informal and social communication. *Psychological Review, 57,* 271–282.

Festinger, L. (1957). *A theory of cognitive dissonance.* Stanford, CA: Stanford University Press.

Field, T. (1978). Interaction behaviors of primary versus secondary caretaker fathers. *Developmental Psychology, 14,* 183–184.

Field, T. (1981). Early development of the preterm offspring of teenage mothers. In K. Scott, T. Field, & E. Robertson (Eds.), *Teenage parents and their offspring* (pp. 145–175). New York: Grune & Stratton.

Field, T. (1983). High-risk infants "have less fun" during early interactions. *Topics in Childhood Special Education, 3,* 77–87.

Field, T., Schanberg, S., Scafidi, F., Bauer, C., Nitza, V., Garcia, R., Nystrom, J., & Kuhn, C. (1986). Tactile/kinesthetic stimulation effects on preterm neonates. *Pediatrics, 77,* 654–658.

Field, T. M., Woodson, R., Greenberg, R., & Cohen, D. (1982). Discrimination and imitation of facial expression by neonates. *Science, 218,* 179–181.

Figel, H. (1960). Mind-body, not a pseudoproblem. In S. Hook (Ed.), *Dimensions of mind: A symposium.* New York: New York University Press.

Fine, G. A. (1980). The natural history of preadolescent male friendship groups. In H. C. Foot, A. J. Chapman, & J. R. Smith (Eds.), *Friendships and childhood relations.* New York: Wiley.

Fingarette, H. (1988). *Heavy drinking: The myth of alcoholism as a disease.* Berkeley: University of California Press.

Finn, J. (1995). Computer-based self-help groups: A new resource to supplement support groups. *Social Work with Groups, 18,* 109–117.

Finn, J. (in press). Computer-based self-help groups: On-line recovery for addictions. *Computers in Human Services, 12.*

Fischer, J. L., Spann, L., & Crawford, D. W. (1991). Measuring codependency. *Alcoholism Treatment Quarterly, 8,* 87–100.

Fishbein, M., & Ajzen, I. (1975). *Belief, attitude, intention and behavior.* Reading, MA: Addison-Wesley.

Fivush, R. (1995). New cognitive research making waves. *APA Monitor.*

Fixsen, D. L., Phillips, E. L., Phillips, E. A., & Wolf, M. M. (1976). The teaching family model group home treatment. In W. E. Craighead, A. E. Kazdin, & M. J. Mahoney (Eds.), *Behavior modification.* Boston: Houghton Mifflin.

Flanigan, B. (1992). *Forgiving the unforgivable.* New York: Macmillan.

Flavell, J. H. (1979). Metacognition and cognitive monitoring: A new area of psychological inquiry. *American Psychologist, 34,* 906–911.

Flavell, J. H. (1981). Monitoring social cognitive enterprises: Something else that may develop in the area of social cognition. In J. H. Flavell & L. Ross (Eds.), *Social cognitive development: Frontiers and possible futures.* New York: Cambridge University Press.

Flavell, J. H. (1985). *Cognitive development* (2nd ed.). Englewood Cliffs, NJ: Prentice Hall.

Fong-ruey, L., & Brooks-Gunn, J. (1994). Cumulative familial risks and low-birthweight children's cognitive and behavioral development. *Journal of Clinical Child Psychology, 23,* 360–372.

Fontaine, P., & Toffler, W. (1991). Dorsal penile nerve block for newborn circumcision. *American Family Physician, 43,* 1327–1333.

Ford, M. E. (1986). A living systems conceptualization of social intelligence: Outcomes, processes, and developmental change. In R. J. Sternberg (Ed.), *Advances in the psychology of human intelligence* (Vol. 3). Hillsdale, NJ: Erlbaum.

Foster, R., Hunsberger, M., & Anderson, J. (1989). *Family-centered nursing care of children.* Philadelphia: Harcourt Brace Jovanovich.

Foster, R. L., Hunsberger, M. M. & Anderson, J. T. (1989). *Family-centered nursing care of children.* Philadelphia: Saunders.

Fowers, B. J., & Olson, D. H. (1989). ENRICH Marital Inventory: A discriminant validity and cross-validation assessment. *Journal of Marital and Family Therapy, 15,* 65–79.

Fraiberg, S. H. (1968). *The magic years: Understanding and handling the problems of early childhood.* London: Methuen.

Fraiberg, S. H. (1980). *Clinical studies in infant mental health.* New York: Basic Books.

Francis, S. (1993). Rape and sexual assault. In B. S. Johnson, *Adaptation and growth: Psychiatric nursing.* Philadelphia: Lippincott.

Frank, A. (1952). *The diary of a young girl.* Garden City, NY: Doubleday.

Frank, D., Silva, M., & Needlman, R. (1993, February). Failure to thrive: Mystery, myth, and method. *Contemporary Pediatrics,* pp. 114–133.

Frankel, M. (1983). Does mother know best? Mothers and fathers interacting with preschool sons and daughters. *Developmental Psychology, 19,* 694–702.

Frankenberg, W., & Dodds, J. (1967). Denver Development Screening Test. *Journal of Pediatrics, 71,* 181–191.

Frauenhofer, D., Scott, L., Doress, P. B., & Rosenthal-Keese, K. (1987). Relationships in middle and later life. In P. B. Doress, D. L. Siegel, & The Midlife and Older Women Book Project (Eds.), *Ourselves, growing older: Women aging with knowledge and power* (pp. 79–98). New York: Simon & Schuster.

Freeman, B. J. (1993). The syndrome of autism: Update and guidelines for diagnosis. *Young Children, 6,* 1–11.

Frelberg, P. (1990, November). Outreach helps women at risk for AIDS. *APA Monitor,* pp. 28–29.

French, J., & Raven, B. (1959). The bases of social power. In D. Cartwright (Ed.), *Studies in social power.* Ann Arbor: Institute for Research, University of Michigan.

Freud, A., & Dann, S. (1951). An experiment in group upbringing. *Psychoanalytic Study of the Child, 6,* 127–168.

Friedenreich, C. (1995). A review of physical activity and breast cancer. *Epidemiology, 6,* 311–317.

Friedman, M., & Rosenman, R. F. (1974). *Type A behavior and your heart.* New York: Knopf.

Friedman, R. C., & Downey, J. I. (1994). Homosexuality. *The New England Journal of Medicine, 331,* 923–930.

Friedrich, L. K., & Stein, A. H. (1973). Aggressive and prosocial television programs and the natural behavior of preschool children. *Monographs of the Society for Research in Child Development, 38.*

Frosh, S. (1987). *The politics of psychoanalysis: An introduction to Freudian and post-Freudian theory.* New Haven, CT: Yale University Press.

Furman, W., & Buhrmester, D. (1985a). Children's perceptions of their personal relationships in their social networks. *Developmental Psychology, 21,* 1016–1024.

Furman, W., & Buhrmester, D. (1985b). Children's perceptions of the qualities of sibling relationships. *Child Development, 56,* 448–461.

Galambos, N. L. & Almeida, D. M. (1992). Does parent-adolescent conflict increase in early adolescence? *Journal of Marriage and the Family, 54,* 737–747.

Galinsky, M., & Schopler, J. (1977). Warning: Groups may be dangerous. *Social Work, 22,* 89–94.

Garbarino, J., & Abramowitz, R. H. (1992a). Sociocultural risk and opportunity. In J. Garbarino, *Children and families in the social environment* (2nd ed.). New York: Aldine de Gruyter.

Garbarino, J., & Abramowitz, R. H. (1992b). The family as a social system. In J. Garbarino, *Children and families in the social environment* (2nd ed.). New York: Walter de Gruyter.

Garbarino, J., Burston, N., Raber, S., Russel, R., & Crouter, A. (1978). The social maps of children approaching adolescence: Studying the ecology of youth development. *Journal of Youth and Adolescence, 7,* 417–428.

Garbarino, J., Galambos, N. L., Plantz, M. C., & Kostelny, K. (1992). The territory of childhood. In J. Garbarino (Ed.), *Children and families in the social environment (2nd ed.)*. New York: Aldine de Gruyter.

Garcia-Preto, N. (1994, July/August). On the bridge. *Family Therapy Networker*, pp. 35–37.

Gardner, H. (1980). *Artful scribbles: The significance of children's drawings*. New York: Basic Books.

Garmezy, N., & Rutter, M. (Eds.). (1983). *Stress, coping, and development in children*. New York: McGraw-Hill.

Garrison, W. T., & McQuiston, S. (1989). *Chronic illness during childhood and adolescence*. Newbury Park, CA: Sage.

Gartner, A., & Riessman, F. (1977). *Self-help in the human services*. San Francisco: Jossey-Bass.

Garvin, C. D., & Seabury, B. A. (1984). *Interpersonal practice in social work*. Englewood Cliffs, NJ: Prentice Hall.

Gaylin, W. (1986). *Rediscovering love*. New York: Viking Penguin.

Gelfand, D. E., & Barresi, C. M. (Eds.). (1987). *Ethnic dimensions of aging*. New York: Springer.

Gelles, R. J. (1987). *Family violence*. Newbury Park, CA: Sage.

Gentry, M., Rosenman, L., & Shulman, A. D. (1987). Comparison of the needs and support systems of remarried and nonremarried widows. In H. Lopata (Ed.), *Widows: Vol. II. North America* (pp. 158–170). Durham, NC: Duke University Press.

Gerard, M., & Dukette, R. (1954). Techniques for preventing separation trauma in child placement. *The American Journal of Orthopsychiatry, 24*, 111–127.

Gergen, K. J. (1991, September/October). The saturated family. *Family Therapy Networker*, pp. 27–35.

Gerhart, U., & Brooks, A. (1993). The social work practitioner and antipsychotic drugs. *Social Work, 28*, 454–460.

Germain, C. B. (1991). *Human behavior in the social environment: An ecological view*. New York: Columbia University Press.

Geronimus, A. (1991). Teenage childbearing and social and reproductive disadvantage: The evolution of complex questions and the demise of simple answers. *Family Relations, 40*, 463–471.

Geronimus, A. (1992). Teenage childbearing and social disadvantage: Unprotected discourse. *Family Relations, 41*, 244–248.

Gerstel, N., Reissman, C. K., & Rosenfield, S. (1985). Explaining the symptomatology of separated and divorced women and men: The role of marital conditions and social network. *Social Forces, 64*, 84–101.

Gesser, G., Wong, P.T.P., & Reker, G. T. (1987–88). Death attitudes across the life-span: The development and validation of the death attitude profile (DAP). *Omega, 18*, 113–128.

Giannakoulopoulos, X., Sepulveda, W., Kourtis, P., Glover, V., & Fisk, N. (1994). Fetal plasma cortisol and B-endorphin response to intrauterine needling. *Lancet, 344*, 77–81.

Gibbs, J. T. (1985). City girls: Psychosocial adjustment of urban black adolescent females. *SAGE: A Scholarly Journal of Black Women, 2*, 28–36.

Gibbs, J. T. (1990). Mental health issues of black adolescents: Implications for policy and practice. In A. R. Stiffman & L. E. Davis (Eds.), *Ethnic issues in adolescent mental health*. Newbury Park: Sage.

Gibbs, J. T., & Huang, L. N. (1989). A conceptual framework for assessing and treating minority youth. In J. T. Gibbs & L. N. Huang (Eds.), *Children of color*. San Francisco: Jossey-Bass.

Gibson, E. (1984). Development of knowledge of visual-tactual affordances of substance. *Child Development, 55*, 453–460.

Giddens, A. (1989). *Sociology*. Cambridge, MA: Polity Press in association with Basil Blackwell.

Gilbert, K. (1989). Interactive grief and coping in the marital dyad. *Death Studies, 13*, 605–626.

Gilchrist, L. E., Schinke, S. P., & Blythe, B. J. (1985). Preventing unwanted adolescent pregnancy. In L. D. Gilchrist & S. P. Schinke (Eds.), *Preventing social and health problems through life skills training*. Seattle, WA: Center for Social Welfare.

Gilgun, J. F. (1995). We shared something special: The moral discourse of incest perpetrators. *Journal of Marriage and the Family, 57*, 265–281.

Gilligan, C. (1977). In a different voice: Women's conceptions of self and morality. *Harvard Educational Review, 47*, 481–517.

Gilligan, C. (1982). *In a different voice: Psychological theory and women's development*. Cambridge, MA: Harvard University Press.

Gilligan, C. (1985). *Response to critics*. Paper presented at the biennial meeting of the Society for Research in Child Development, Toronto.

Ginsburg, H. P. (1985). Jean Piaget. In H. I. Kaplan & B. J. Sadock (Eds.), *Comprehensive textbook of psychiatry*. (Vol. 4, pp.178–183). Baltimore: Williams & Wilkins.

Girgus, J. (1989, October). Body image in girls pushes rate of depression up. *American Psychological Association Monitor*, p. 33.

Glenn, N. D., & Weaver, C. N. (1988). The changing relationship of marital status to reported happiness. *Journal of Marriage and the Family, 44*, 317–324.

Glick, P. C. (1984a). American household structure in transition. *Family Planning Perspectives, 16*, 205–211.

Glick, P. C. (1984b). Marriage, divorce, and living arrangements: Prospective changes. *Journal of Family Issues, 5,* 7–26.

Golan, N. (1986). *The perilous bridge.* New York: Free Press.

Gold, M., & Petronio, R. J. (1980). Delinquent behavior in adolescence. In J. Adelson (Ed.), *Handbook of adolescent psychology.* New York: Wiley.

Goldberg, S. (1983). Parent-infant bonding: Another look. *Child Development, 54,* 1355–1382.

Goldenberg, R. (1991). Maternal psychological characteristics and IUGR. *Pre and Perinatal Psychology Journal, 6,* 129–134.

Goldson, E. (1991). The affective and cognitive sequelae of child maltreatment. *Pediatric Clinics of North America, 38,* 1481–1496.

Goldstein, E. G. (1984). *Ego psychology and social work practice.* New York: Free Press.

Goldstein, R., & Landau, D. (1990). *Fortysomething.* Los Angeles: Tarcher.

Gondolf (1989). *Men who batter: How they stop their abuse.* Paper presented at the second National Conference for Family Violence Researchers, Durham, NH.

Gonsiorek, J. C. (1991). The empirical basis for the demise of the illness model of homosexuality. In J. C. Gonsiorek & J. D. Weinrich (Eds.), *Homosexuality: Research implications for public policy* (pp. 115–137). Newbury Park, CA: Sage.

Goodchilds, J. D., & Zellman, G. L. (1984). Sexual signalling and sexual aggression in adolescent relationships. In N. M. Malamuth & E. D. Donnerstein (Eds.), *Pornography and sexual aggression.* New York: Academic Press.

Goode, E. (1993). Drug abuse. *Grolier Electronic Encyclopedia.*

Goodenough, F. (1931). *Anger in young children.* Minneapolis: University of Minnesota Press.

Goodrich, C. (1995, February). Fathering in the night. *The Sun,* pp. 12–14.

Goodwin, A. J., & Scott, L. (1987). Sexuality in the second half of life. In P. B. Doress, D. L. Siegel, & The Midlife and Older Women Book Project (Eds.), *Ourselves, growing older: Women aging with knowledge and power* (pp. 79–98). New York: Simon & Schuster.

Goodyear, I. M. (1990). *Life experiences, development, and childhood psychopathology.* New York: Wiley.

Gordon, M. R. (1994, November 6). In poignant public letter, Reagan reveals that he has Alzheimer's. *New York Times,* pp. 1, 47.

Gordon, S., & Gilgun, J. F. (1987). Adolescent sexuality. In V. B. Van Hasselt & M. Hersen (Eds.), *Handbook of adolescent psychology.* New York: Pergamon Press.

Gordon, S., & Snyder, C. W. (1989). *Personal issues in human sexuality: A guidebook for better sexual health.* Boston: Allyn & Bacon.

Gordon, T. (1970). *Parent effectiveness training.* New York: Wyden.

Gorman, C. (1994, November 21). An eye on Alzheimer's. *Time,* p. 89.

Gotlib, I. H., & McCabe, S. B. (1990). Marriage and psychopathology. In F. D. Fincham & T. N. Bradbury (Eds.), *The psychology of marriage: Basic issues and applications.* New York: Guilford Press.

Gottlieb, S., & Barrett, D. (1986). Effects of unanticipated cesarean section on mothers, infants, and their interaction in the first month of life. *Developmental and Behavioral Pediatrics, 7,* 180–185.

Gottman, J. M. (1994, May/June). Why marriages fail. *Family Therapy Networker,* pp. 41–48.

Graham, S. R. (1992). What does a man want? *American Psychologist, 47,* 837–841.

Grebb, J. A., Reus, V. I., & Freimer, N. B. (1988). Neurobehavioral chemistry & physiology. In H. H. Goldman (Ed.), *Review of General Psychiatry.* East Norwalk, CT: Appleton & Lang.

Green, J. W. (1995). *Cultural awareness in the human services: A multi-ethnic approach.* Boston: Allyn & Bacon.

Green, R. G., Beatty, W. W., & Arkin, R. M. (1984). *Human motivation.* Boston: Allyn & Bacon.

Greene, R. R. (1994). *Human behavior theory: A diversity framework.* New York: Aldine de Gruyter.

Greenspan, S., & Greenspan, N. (1985). *First feelings: Milestones in the emotional development of your baby and child.* New York: Viking Press.

Griffith, D. (1988). The effect of prenatal exposure to cocaine on the infant and on early maternal-infant interactions. In I. J. Chasnoff (Ed.), *Drugs, alcohol, pregnancy, and parenting.* Lancaster, U.K.: Kluwer.

Griffith, D. (1992, September). Prenatal exposure to cocaine and other drugs: Developmental and educational prognoses. *Phi Delta Kappan,* pp. 30–34.

Grinnell, R. M., Jr., Kyte, N. S., Bostwick G. J., Jr. (1981). Environmental modification. In A. N. Maluccio (Ed.), *Promoting competence in clients: A new/old approach to social work practice.* New York: Free Press.

Gross, M. D., Tofanelli, R. A., Butzirus, S. M., & Snodgrass, E. W. (1987). The effects of diets rich in and free from additives on the behavior of children with hyperkinetic and learning disorders. *Journal of the Academy of Child and Adolescent Psychiatry, 26,* 53–55.

Grossman, D. C., Milligan, C. B., & Deyo, R. A. (1991). Risk factors for suicide attempts among Navajo adolescents. *American Journal of Public Health, 81,* 870–874.

Groth, A. N., & Birnbaum, H. J. (1978). Adult sexual orientation and attraction to underage persons. *Archives of Sexual Behavior, 7,* 175–181.

Grover, K. J., Russell, C. S., Schumm, W. R., & Paff-Bergen, L. A. (1985). Mate selection processes and marital satisfaction. *Family Relations, 34,* 383–386.

Gruetzner, H. (1988). *Alzheimer's: A caregiver's guide and sourcebook.* New York: Wiley.

Grunwald, L., & Goldberg, J. (1993, July). The amazing minds of infants. *Life,* pp. 46–60.

Grusec, J., & Abramovitch, R. (1982). Imitation of peers and adults in a natural setting: A functional analysis. *Child Development, 53,* 636–642.

Grusec, J., & Lytton, H. (1988). *Social development: History, theory and research.* New York: Springer-Verlag.

Guernsey, J. (1993). *Abortion: Understanding the controversy.* Minneapolis: Lerner.

Gundara, J. S. (1993). Multiculturalism and the British nation-state. In J. Horton (Ed.), *Liberalism, multiculturalism, and toleration.* London: Macmillan Press.

Gunnar, M. (1984). Coping with aversive stimulation in the neonatal period: Quiet sleep and plasma cortisol levels during recovery from circumcision. *Child Development, 56,* 824–834.

Gurland, B. J., Dean, L. L., Copeland, J., Gurland, R., & Golden, R. (1982). Criteria for the diagnosis of dementia in the community elderly. *The Gerontologist, 22,* 180–186.

Gurland, B. J., Dean, L. L., Cross, P., & Golden, R. (1980). The epidemiology of depression and dementia in the elderly: The use of multiple indicators of these conditions. In J. O. Cole & J. E. Barrett (Eds.), *Psychopathology of the aged.* New York: Raven Press.

Haaken, J. (1990). A critical analysis of the co-dependence construct. *Psychiatry, 53,* 396–406.

Hagestad, G. (1985). Continuity and connectedness. In V. L. Bengston & J. Robertson (Ed.), *Grandparenthood.* Beverly Hills, CA: Sage.

Hahn, N. (1993). Why children and parents must play while they eat: An interview with T. Berry Brazelton, M.D. *Journal of the American Dietetic Association, 93,* 1385–1387.

Haith, M., & Canfield, R. (1991). Young infants' visual expectations for symmetric and asymmetric stimulus sequences. *Developmental Psychology, 27,* 198–208.

Haley, J. (1990). *Problem-solving therapy.* San Francisco: Jossey-Bass.

Hall, J. A., & Halberstadt, A. G. (1980). Masculinity and femininity in children: Development of the Children's Personal Attributes Questionnaire. *Developmental Psychology, 16,* 270–280.

Halpern, R. (1993). Poverty and infant development. In C.

Zeaneh (Ed.), *Handbook of infant mental health* (pp. 73–86). New York: Guilford Press.

Hamburg, B. A., & Dixon, S. L. (1992). Adolescent pregnancy and parenthood. In M. K. Rosenheim & M. F. Testa (Eds.), *Early parenthood and coming of age in the 1990s.* New Brunswick, NJ: Rutgers University Press.

Hamdani, R. J. (1974). *Exploratory behavior and vocational development among disadvantaged inner-city adolescents.* Unpublished doctoral dissertation, Columbia University, New York.

Hammond, C. B. (1994). Women's concerns with hormone replacement therapy—Compliance issues. *Fertility & Sterility, 62,* 157–160.

Hann, D. M., Osofsky, J. D., Barnard, K. E., & Leonard, G. (1990). Maternal emotional availability in two risk groups [Special ICIS issue]. *Infant Behavior and Development, 13,* 404.

Hansen, J. F. (1980). *Children's attachment to mother figures and the social development of black infants and young children.* Unpublished manuscript, University of California, Berkeley.

Hanson, W. (1980, October). The urban Indian woman and her family. *Social Casework,* pp. 476–483.

Harmon, R. R., & Blieszner, R. (1990). Filial responsibility expectations among adult child–older parent pairs. *Journal of Gerontology: Psychological Sciences, 45,* 110–112.

Harris, M. J., & Rosenthal, R. (1985). Mediation of interpersonal expectancy effects: 31 meta-analyses. *Psychological Bulletin, 97,* 363–386.

Harrison, L., Leeper, J., & Yoon, M. (1991). Preterm infants; physiologic responses to early parent touch. *Western Journal of Nursing Research, 13,* 698–713.

Harrison, L., & Woods, S. (1991, July/August). Early parental touch and preterm infants. *JOGNN,* pp. 299–305.

Harter, S. (1979). *The perceived competence scale.* Denver, CO: University of Denver.

Harter, S. (1982). The perceived competence scale for children. *Child Development, 53,* 87–97.

Harter, S. (1985). *Self-perception profile for children.* Denver, CO: University of Denver.

Harter, S. (1995, May). Is self-esteem really all that important? *APA Monitor.*

Hartford, M. E. (1985). Understanding normative growth and development in aging: Working with strengths. *Journal of Gerontological Social Work, 8,* 37–54.

Hartman, A. (1978). Diagrammatic assessment of family relationships. *Social Casework, 59,* 465–476.

Hartman, A., & Laird, J. (1983). *Family-centered social work practice.* New York: Free Press.

Hartman, A., & Laird, J. (1987). Family practice. In A. Minahan (Ed.), *Encyclopedia of social work* (18th ed., Vol. 1, pp. 575–587). Silver Spring, MD: National Association of Social Workers.

Hartney, L. L. (1989, September/October). My mother's keeper. *Family therapy networker*, pp. 38–41.

Hartup, W. W. (1974). Aggression in childhood: Developmental perspectives. *American Psychologist, 29*, 336–341.

Hartup, W. W. (1979). Peer relations and the growth of social competence. In M. W. Kent & J. E. Rolf (Eds.), *Primary prevention of psychopathology: Vol. 3. Social competence in children.* Hanover, NH: University Press of New England.

Hartup, W. W. (1983). Peer relations. In P. H. Mussen (Ed.), *Handbook of child psychology* (4th ed., Vol. 4). New York: Wiley.

Hartup, W. W. (1989). Social relationships and their developmental significance. *American Psychologist, 44*, 120–126.

Hastorf, A. H., & Isen, A. M. (1992). Social knowledge. In A. H. Hastorf & A. M. Isen (Eds.), *Cognitive Social Psychology.* New York: Elsevier/North Holland.

Hatch, L. R. (1990). Gender and work: At midlife and beyond. *Generations, 14*, 48–51.

Hatfield, E., & Walster, G. W. (1985). *A new look at love.* New York: University Press of America.

Haugh, S. S., Hoffman, C. D., & Cowan, G. (1980). The eye of the very young beholder: Sex-typing of infants by young children. *Child Development, 51*, 598–600.

Havighurst, R. J. (1952). *Developmental tasks and education.* New York: David McKay.

Havighurst, R. J. (1972). *Developmental tasks and education* (3rd ed.). New York: David McKay.

Hawkins, J., Pea, R. D., Glick, J., & Scribner, S. (1984). "Merds that laugh don't like mushrooms": Evidence for deductive reasoning by preschoolers. *Developmental Psychology, 20*, 584–594.

Hayes, N., Stainton, M., & McNeil, D. (1993). Caring for a chronically ill infant: A paradigm case of maternal rehearsal in the neonatal intensive care unit. *Journal of Pediatric Nursing, 8*(6), 355–360.

Haywood, K. M. (1986). *Life span motor development.* Champaign, IL: Human Kinetics.

Hazel, J. S., Schumaker, J. B., Sherman, J. A., & Sheldon-Wilder, J. (1981). The development and evaluation of a group skills training program for court-adjudicated youths. In D. Upper and S. M. Ross (Eds.), *Behavioral group therapy, 1981: An annual review.* Champaign, IL: Research Press.

Hazen, C., & Shaver, P. (1987). Romantic love conceptualized as an attachment process. *Journal of Personality and Social Psychology, 52*, 511–524.

Hearn, G. (1979). General systems theory and social work. In F. J. Turner (Ed.), *Social work treatment: Interlocking theoretical approches* (2nd ed.). New York: Free Press.

Heatherington, E. M. (1987). Family relations six years after divorce. In K. Pasley & M. Ihinger-Tollman (Eds.), *Remarriage and stepparenting today: Current research and theory.* New York: Guilford Press.

Heatherington, E. M. (1988). Parents, children, and siblings: Six years after divorce. In R. A. Hinde & J. Stevenson-Hinde (Eds.), *Relationships within families: Mutual influences* (pp. 311–331). New York: Oxford University Press.

Heatherington, E. M. (1989). Coping with family transitions: Winners, losers, and survivors. *Child Development, 60*, 1–14.

Heatherington, E. M., Cox, M., & Cox, R. (1979). Play and social interaction in children following divorce. *Journal of Social Issues, 35*, 26–49.

Hetherington, E. M., Cox, M., & Cox, R. (1982). Effects of divorce on parents and children. In M. Lamb (Ed.), *Nontraditional families: Parenting and child development.* Hillsdale, NJ: Erlbaum.

Hecht, M. (1993). *African American communication: Ethnic identity and cultural interpretation.* Newbury Park, CA: Sage.

Heilman, J. R. (1995, August 13). The good news about Alzheimer's. *Parade*, pp. 12–13.

Heiney, S., Hasan, L., & Price, K. (1993). Developing and implementing a bereavement program for a children's hospital. *Journal of Pediatric Nursing, 8*, 385–391.

Heise, L. (1989, March/April). The global war against women. *World Watch.*

Hepworth, D. H., & Larsen, J. A. (1989). *Direct social work practice* (3rd ed.). Belmont, CA: Wadsworth.

Hepworth, D. H., & Larsen, J. A. (1993). *Direct social work practice* (4th ed.). Pacific Grove, CA: Brooks/Cole.

Herek, G. M. (1991). Stigma, prejudice, and violence against lesbians and gay men. In J. C. Gonsiorek & J. D. Weinrich (Eds.), *Homosexuality: Research implications for public policy.* Newbury Park, CA: Sage.

Herek, G. M., & Berrill, K. (1990). Violence against lesbians and gay men: Issues for research, practice and policy. *Journal of Interpersonal Violence, 5.*

Herman, E. (1988, Summer). The twelve-step program: Cure or cover? *Out/Look: National Lesbian and Gay Quarterly.* Excerpted in *Utne Reader* (1988, November/December), pp. 52–63.

Hersch, P. (1990, July/August). The resounding silence. *Family Therapy Networker*, pp. 18–29.

Hesling, K., & Szklo, K. (1981). Mortality after bereavement. *American Journal of Epidemiology, 144*, 42–52.

Hess, B. B. (1990). Gender & aging: The demographic parameters. *Generations, XIV*, 12–15.

Hess, R. O., & Hollaway, S. D. (1984). Family and school as educational institutions. In R. D. Parke (Ed.), *Review of child development research: Vol. 7. The family*. Chicago: University of Chicago Press.

High rate of suicide among New York City police. (1994, November). *NASW News*, p. 9.

Hilgard, E. R. (1987). *Psychology in America: A historical survey*. San Diego: Harcourt Brace Jovanovich.

Hill, C. R., & Stafford, F. P. (1980). Parental care of children: Time diary estimate of quantity, predictability, and variety. *Journal of Human Relations*, 15, 219–239.

Hill, J. P., & Hombeck, G. N. (1986). Attachment and autonomy during adolescence. *Annals of Child Development*, 3, 145–189.

Hill, J. P., Hombeck, G. N., Marlow, L., Green, T. M., & Lynch, M. E. (1985). Pubertal status and parent-child relations in families of 7th grade boys. *Journal of Early Adolescence*, 5, 31–44.

Hinde, R. A., Titmus, G., Easton, D., & Tamplin, A. (1985). Incidence of "friendship" and behavior toward strong associates and nonassociates in preschoolers. *Child Development*, 56, 234–245.

Hinrichsen, G. A. (1990). *Mental health problems and older adults: Choices and challenges*. Santa Barbara, CA: ABC-CLIO.

Hinrichsen, G. A., & Ramirez, M. (1992). Black and white dementia caregivers: A comparison of their adaptation, adjustment, and service utilization. *The Gerontologist*, 32, 375–381.

Ho, M. K. (1987). *Family therapy with ethnic minorities*. Newbury Park, CA: Sage.

Hoff-Ginsberg, E. (1986). Function and structure in maternal speech: Their relation to the child's development of syntax. *Developmental Psychology*, 22, 155–163.

Hoffman, L. (1987). The effects on children of maternal and paternal employment. In N. Gerstel & H. Gross (Eds.), *Families and work*. Philadelphia: Temple University Press.

Hoffman, L. W. (1989). Effects of maternal employment in two-parent families. *American Psychologist*, 44, 283–293.

Hoffman, M. L. (1970). Moral development. In P. H. Mussen (Ed.), *Carmichael's manual of child psychology* (Vol. 2). New York: Wiley.

Hohman, M. (1995). *Self-efficacy and empowerment: A study of women in recovery from alcoholism*. Unpublished doctoral dissertation, School of Social Work, Arizona State University.

Holm, B. A., Cassidy, S. B., et al. (1993). Prader-Willi syndrome: Consensus diagnostic criteria. *Pediatrics*, 2, 398–402.

Honzik, M. (1976). Values and limitations of infant tests: An overview. In M. Lewis (Ed.), *Origins of intelligence* (pp. 59–95). New York: Plenum.

Hooyman, N. R. (1994). Diversity and populations at risk: Women. In F. G. Reamer (Ed.), *The foundations of social work knowledge*. New York: Columbia University Press.

Hooyman, N. R., & Lustbader, W. (1986). *Taking care: Supporting older people and their families*. New York: Free Press.

Horn, J. L. (1982). The theory of fluid and crystallized intelligence in relation to concepts of cognitive psychology and aging in adulthood. In F.J.M. Craik & S. Trehub (Eds.), *Aging and cognitive processes* (pp. 237–278). New York: Plenum.

Horton, J. (Ed.) (1993a). *Liberalism, multiculturalism, and toleration*. London: Macmillan Press.

Horton, J. (1993b). Liberalism, multiculturalism, and tolerance. In J. Horton (Ed.), *Liberalism, multiculturalism, and toleration*. London: Macmillan Press.

Horwitz, A. V. (1990). *The logic of social control*. New York: Plenum.

Hothersall, D. (1984). *History of psychology*. Philadelphia: Temple University Press.

Howard, D. V. (1983). *Cognitive psychology: Memory, language, and thought*. New York: Macmillan.

Howe, M. (1995, June). New cognitive developments make waves. *APA Monitor*.

Howell, M. C., Allen, M. C., & Doress, P. B. (1987). Dying and death. In P. B. Doress, D. L. Siegel, & The Midlife and Older Women Book Project (Eds.), *Ourselves, growing older: Women aging with knowledge and power* (pp. 392–403). New York: Simon & Schuster.

Hoyenga, K. B., & Hoyenga, K. T. (1988). *Psychobiology: The neuron and behavior*. Pacific Grove, CA: Brooks/Cole.

Huesmann, L. R., Eron, L. D., Lefkowitz, M. M., & Walder, L. O. (1984). Stability of aggression over time and generations. *Developmental Psychology*, 6, 1120–1134.

Huff, C. R. (1993). Gangs in the United States. In A. P. Goldstein & C. R. Huff (Eds.), *The gang intervention handbook* (pp. 3–20). Champaign, IL: Research Press.

Hughes, C. B., & Page-Lieberman, J. (1989). Totality of bereavement, 25–56-year-old fathers who experienced perinatal loss of infant. *Death Studies*, 13, 537–556.

Hughes, L. (1970). Mother to son. In A. Bontemps and L. Hughes (Eds.), *The poetry of the Negro, 1746–1970*. Garden City, NY: Doubleday.

Hunter, S., & Sundel, M. (Eds.). (1989). *Midlife myths: Issues, findings, and practice implications*. Newbury Park, CA: Sage.

Hyde, J. S. (1985). *Half the human experience: The psychology of women* (3rd ed.). Lexington, MA: Heath.

Hyman, J. (1987). Memory lapse and memory loss. In P. B.

Doress, D. L. Siegel, & The Midlife and Older Women Book Project (Eds.), *Ourselves, growing older: Women aging with knowledge and power* (pp. 380–391). New York: Simon & Schuster.

Ianniruberto, A., & Tajani, E. (1981). Ultrasonographic study of fetal movements. *Seminars in Perinatology, 5,* 175–181.

Infant Health and Development Program. (1990). Enhancing the outcomes of low-birthweight premature infants. *Journal of the American Medical Association, 263,* 3035–3042.

Izard, C. (Ed.). (1982). *Measuring emotions in infants and children.* London: Cambridge University Press.

Jackson, J. F. (1993). Multiple caregivers among African Americans and infant attachment: The need for an emic approach. *Human Development, 36,* 87–102.

Jackson, P. (1985, April). When the baby isn't perfect. *American Journal of Nursing,* pp. 396–399.

Jacobsen, T., Edelstein, W., & Hoffman, V. (1994). A longitudinal study of the relation between representations of attachment in childhood and cognitive functioning in childhood and adolescence. *Developmental Psychology, 30,* 112–124.

Jacobson, B. (1987). Perinatal origin of adult self-destructive behavior. *Acta Psychiatrica Scandinavica, 76,* 364–371.

Jaffe, M. L. (1991). *Understanding parenting.* Dubuque, IA: Wm. C. Brown.

James, W. (1884). What is emotion? *Mind, 19,* 188–205.

Janis, I. L. (1972). *Victims of groupthink.* Boston: Houghton Mifflin.

Janis, I. L. (1973, January). Groupthink. *Yale Alumni Magazine,* pp. 16–19.

Janis, I. L. (1982). *Groupthink: Psychological studies of policy decisions and fiascoes.* Boston: Houghton Mifflin.

Jannke, S. (1994). Mandatory drug testing of pregnant women. *Childbirth Instructor, 4*(4), 12–18.

Janosik, E. H. (1986). *Crisis counseling: A contemporary approach.* Boston: Jones & Bartlett.

Janzen, C., & Harris, O. (1986). *Family treatment in social work practice* (2nd ed.). Itasca, IL: Peacock.

Jason, J. & van de Meer, A. (1989). *Parenting your premature baby.* New York: Henry Holt.

Jencks, C. (1985). How much do high school students learn? *Sociology of Education, 58,* 128–135.

Jennings, K., Wisner, K., Conley, B. (1991). Serving the mental health needs of families with children under three: A comprehensive program. *Infant Mental Health Journal, 12,* 276–290.

Jessor, R. (1987). Problem-behavior theory, psychosocial development, and adolescent problem drinking. *British Journal of Addiction, 82,* 331–342.

Jessor, R. (1992). Risk behavior in adolescence: A psychosocial

framework for understanding and action. In D. E. Rogers & E. Ginzburg (Eds.), *Adolescents at risk: Medical and social perspectives* (pp. 19–34). Boulder, CO: Westview Press.

Johnson, C. L. (1983). Dyadic family relationships and family supports. *The Gerontologist, 23,* 377–383.

Johnson, C. L., & Barer, B. M. (1990). Families and networks among older inner-city Blacks. *The Gerontologist, 30,* 726–733.

Johnson, C. N., & Wellman, H. M. (1982). Children's developing conceptions of the mind and brain. *Child Development, 53,* 222–234.

Johnson, H. C. (1980). *Behavior, psychopathology, and the brain.* New York: Curriculum Concepts.

Johnson, H. C., Atkins, S. P., Battle, S. F., Hernandez-Arata, L., Hesselbrock, M., Libassi, M. F., & Parish, M. S. (1990, Spring/Summer). Strengthening the "bio" in the biopsychosocial paradigm. *Journal of Social Work Education,* pp. 109–123.

Johnson, J., & Goldman, J. (1990). *Developmental assessment in clinical child psychology.* New York: Pergamon Press.

Johnson, J., Johnson, M., Cunningham, J., Ewing, S., Hatcher, D., & Dannen, C. (1982). *Newborn death: A book for parents experiencing the death of a very small infant.* Omaha, NE: Centering Corporation.

Johnson, J. H., & Fennell, E. (1983). Aggressive and delinquent behavior in childhood and adolescence. In E. Walker & M. Roberts (Eds.), *Handbook of clinical child psychology.* New York: Wiley.

Johnston, L. D., O'Malley, P. M., & Bachman, J. G. (1988). *Illicit drug use, smoking, and drinking by America's high school students, college students, and young adults, 1975–1987.* Washington, DC: National Institute of Drug Abuse.

Jones, E., & McCurdy, K. (1992). The links between types of maltreatment and demographic characteristics of children. *Child Abuse and Neglect, 16,* 201–215.

Jones, J. (1990, November). APA report puts focus on women, depression, how to treat it. *APA Monitor,* p. 33.

Jones, S., & Raag, T. (1989). Smile production in infants: The importance of a social recipient for the facial signal. *Child Development, 60,* 811–818.

Jones-Witters, P., & Witters, W. (1986). *Drugs and society: A biological perspective.* Boston: Jones & Bartlett.

Jordan, C., & Franklin, C. (1995). *Clinical assessment for social workers.* Chicago: Lyceum Books.

Kaffman, M., & Elizur, E. (1977). Infants who become enuretics: A longitudinal study of 161 kibbutz children. *Monographs of the Society for Research in Child Development, 42.*

Kagan, J. (1978). On emotion and its development: A working paper. In M. Lewis & L. A. Rosenglum (Eds.), *The development of affect.* New York: Plenum.

Kagan, J. (1984a). The idea of emotion in human development. In C. E. Izard, J. Kagan, & R. B. Zajonc (Eds.), *Emotion, cognition, and behavior.* New York: Cambridge University Press.

Kagan, J. (1984b). *The nature of the child.* New York: Basic Books.

Kagan, J., Kearsley, R. B., & Zelazo, P. R. (1978). The effects of infant daycare on psychological development. *Evaluation Quarterly, 1,* 143–158.

Kalat, J. W. (1992). *Biological psychology.* (4th ed.). Pacific Grove, CA: Brooks/Cole.

Kalat, J. W. (1995). *Biological psychology* (5th ed.). Pacific Grove, CA: Brooks/Cole.

Kalish, R. A. (1985). *Death, grief, and caring relationships* (2nd ed.). Pacific Grove, CA: Brooks/Cole.

Kalish, R. A., & Reynolds, D. K. (1976). *An overview of death and ethnicity.* Farmingdale, NY: Baywood.

Kalmuss, D., Davidson, A., & Cushman, L. (1992). Parenting expectations, experiences, and adjustment to parenthood: A test of the violated expectations framework. *Journal of Marriage and the Family, 52,* 516–526.

Kalter, N. (1987). Long-term effects of divorce on children: A developmental vulnerability model. *American Journal of Orthopsychiatry, 57,* 587–600.

Kalter, N. (1990). *Growing up with divorce.* New York: Free Press.

Kalter, N., Kloner, A., Schreier, S., & Okla, K. (1989). Predictors of children's post divorce adjustment. *American Journal of Orthopsychiatry, 59,* 605–619.

Kalter, N., & Schreier, S. (1994). Developmental facilitation groups for children of divorce: The elementary school model. In C. W. LeCroy (Ed.), *Handbook of child and adolescent treatment manuals.* New York: Lexington Books.

Kaminer, W. (1992). *I'm dysfunctional, you're dysfunctional.* Reading, MA: Addison-Wesley.

Kaminski, H., Stafl, A., & Aiman, J. (1987). The effect of epidural analgesia on the frequency of instrumental obstetric delivery. *Obstetrics & Gynecology, 69,* 770–773.

Kanfer, F. H., Stifter, E., & Morris, S. J. (1981). Self-control and altruism: Delay of gratification for another. *Child Development, 52,* 674–682.

Kanter, R. M. (1977). Women in organizations: Sex roles, group dynamics, and change strategies. In A. Sergeant (Ed.), *Beyond sex roles.* St. Paul, MN: West.

Kantor, D., & Lehr, W. (1975). *Inside the family.* San Francisco: Jossey-Bass.

Karnes, B. (1986). *Gone from my sight: The dying experience.*

Kastenbaum, R. (1977). Death and development through the life span. In H. Feifel (Ed.), *New meanings of death* (pp. 18–45). New York: McGraw-Hill.

Kastenbaum, R. (1981). *Death, society and human experience.* St. Louis: C. V. Mosby.

Kastenbaum, R., & Weisman, A. D. (1972). The psychological autopsy as a research procedure in gerontology. In D. P. Kent, R. Kastenbaum, & S. Sherwood (Eds.), *Research planning and action for the elderly: The power and potential of social science* (pp. 214–216). New York: Behavioral Publications.

Katz, P., & Zalk, S. (1978). Modification of children's racial attitudes. *Developmental Psychology, 14,* 447–456.

Kaufman, A. S., & Kaufman, N. L. (1983). *Kaufman assessment battery for children: Interpretive manual.* Circle Pines, MN: American Guidance Service.

Kazdin, A. E. (1987). *Conduct disorders in childhood and adolescence.* Newbury Park, CA: Sage.

Kazdin, A. E., & Frame, C. (1983). Aggressive behavior and conduct disorder. In R. J. Morris & T. R. Kratochwill (Eds.), *The practice of child therapy.* New York: Pergamon Press.

Keating, D. P. (1980). Thinking processes in adolescence. In J. Adelson (Ed.), *Handbook of adolescent psychology.* New York: Wiley.

Keen, S. (1991). *Fire in the belly: On being a man.* New York: Bantam Books.

Kehoe, M. (1989). *Lesbians over 60 speak for themselves.* New York: Harrington Park Press.

Keith, P. M. (1986). The social context and resources of the unmarried in old age. *International Journal of Aging and Human Development, 23,* 81–96.

Kellner, D. (1990). The postmodern turn: Positions, problems and prospects. In G. Rutger (Ed.), *Frontiers of social theory* (pp. 255–286). New York: Columbia University Press.

Kelly, R. K. (1979). *Courtship, marriage, and the family* (3rd ed.). New York: Harcourt Brace Jovanovich.

Kelly, S. (1993). Caregiver stress in grandparents raising grandchildren. *IMAGE: Journal of Nursing Scholarship, 25,* 331–337.

Kendall, P. C., & Braswell, L. (1985). *Cognitive-behavioral therapy for impulsive children.* New York: Guildford Press.

Keniston, K. (1971). *Youth and dissent: The rise of a new opposition.* New York: Harcourt Brace Jovanovich.

Kennedy, G. J., Kelman, H. R., Thomas, C., Wisniewski, W., Metz, H., & Bijur, P. E. (1989). Hierarchy of characteristics associated with depressive symptoms in an urban elderly sample. *American Journal of Psychiatry, 146,* 220–225.

Kent, S. (1980). Advances in hypertension research. *Geriatrics,* 103–104.

Kerlikowske, K., Grady, D., Rubin, S., Sandrock, C., & Ernster, V. (1995). Efficacy of screening mammography: A meta-analysis. *Journal of the American Medical Association, 273,* 149–154.

Kiecolt-Glaser, J. K., & Glaser, R. (1988). Behavioral influences on immune function. In T. Field, P. McCabe, & C. Schneiderman (Eds.), *Stress and coping across development.* Hillsdale, NJ: Erlbaum.

Kiefer, C. W. (1988). *The mantle of maturity: A history of ideas about character development.* Albany: State University of New York Press.

Kiesler, S. (1978). *Interpersonal processes in groups and organizations.* Arlington Heights, VA: AHM Publishing.

Kietzman, M. L., Spring, B., & Zubin, J. (1985). Perception, cognition, information processing. In. H. I. Kaplan & B. J. Sadock (Eds.), *Comprehensive textbook of psychiatry* (Vol. 4, pp.157–178). Baltimore: Williams & Wilkins.

Kimmel, D. C. (1978). Adult development and aging: A gay perspective. *Journal of Social Issues, 34,* 113–130.

Kinsey, A. C., Pomeroy, W. B., & Martin, C. E. (1948). *Sexual behavior in the human male.* Philadelphia: Saunders.

Kinsey, A. C., Pomeroy, W. B., Martin, C. E., & Gebhard, P. H. (1953). *Sexual behavior in the human female.* Philadelphia: Saunders.

Kivnick, H. Q. (1986). Grandparenthood and a life cycle. *Journal of Geriatric Psychiatry, 19,* 39–55.

Klaus, M., & Kennell, J. (1976). *Maternal-infant bonding: The impact of early separation or loss on family development.* St. Louis: C. V. Mosby.

Klaus, M., Kennell, J., & Klaus, P. (1993). *Mothering the mother: How a doula can help you have a shorter, easier, and healthier birth.* Reading, MA: Addison-Wesley.

Klaus, M., & Klaus, P. (1985). *The amazing newborn.* Reading, MA: Addison-Wesley.

Kleigman, R. (1992). Perpetual poverty: Child health and the underclass. *Pediatrics, 89,* 710–713.

Kline, M., Tschann, J. M., Johnston, J. R., & Wallerstein, J. S. (1989). Children's adjustment in joint and sole physical custody families. *Developmental Psychology, 25,* 430–438.

Klinnert, M., Emde, R., Butterfield, P., & Campos, J. (1986). Social referencing: The infant's use of emotional signals from a friendly adult with mother present. *Developmental Psychology, 22,* 427–432.

Koegel, P. (1989). Mental illness among the inner-city homeless. *Journal of the California Alliance for the Mentally Ill, 1,* 16–17.

Kohlberg, L. (1969). Stage and sequence: The cognitive-developmental approach to socialization. In D. A. Goslin (Ed.), *Handbook of socialization theory and research.* Chicago: Rand McNally.

Konner, M. (1991). *Childhood: A multicultural view.* Boston: Little, Brown.

Koss, M. P. (1985). The hidden rape victim: Personality, attitudinal, and situational characteristics. *Psychology of Women Quarterly, 9,* 193–212.

Koss, M. P., Gidycz, C. A., & Wisniewski, N. (1987). The scope of rape: Incidence and prevalence of sexual aggression and victimization in a national sample of higher education students. *Journal of Consulting and Clinical Psychology, 48,* 460–468.

Kotelchuck, M. (1976). The infant's relationship to the father: Experimental evidence. In M. E. Lamb (Ed.), *The role of the father in child development* (pp. 329–344). New York: Wiley.

Kowalski, K. (1985, April). The impact of chronic grief. *American Journal of Nursing,* pp. 398–399.

Kozol, J. (1985). *Illiterate America.* Garden City, NY: Anchor Books.

Krown, S. (1974). *Threes and fours go to school.* Englewood Cliffs, NJ: Prentice Hall.

Krugman, R., Bays, J., Chadwick, D., Kanda, M., Levitt, L., & McHugh, M. (1994). Distinguishing SIDS from child abuse fatalities. *Pediatrics, 94,* 124–126.

Kubick-Balicheski, P., Martinez, R., & Walsh, B. (1994, January/February). Coordinating transitions in care for improved perinatal outcomes: The RIMM project. *Discharge Planning Update,* pp. 1–7.

Kübler-Ross, E. (1969). *On death and dying.* New York: Macmillan.

Kuhn, D., Kohlberg, L., Langer, J., & Haan, N. (1977). The development of formal operations in logical and moral judgment. *Genetic Psychology Monographs, 95,* 97–188.

Kupersmidt, J. B., & Coie, J. D. (1990). Preadolescent peer status, aggression, and school adjustment as predictors of externalizing problems in adolescence. *Child Development, 61,* 1350–1363.

Labouvie-Vief, G. (1986). Intelligence and cognition. In J. E. Birren & K. W. Schaie (Eds.), *Handbook on the psychology of aging* (2nd ed.). New York: Van Nostrand Reinhold.

Lagercrantz, H. (1986). The stress of being born. *Scientific American, 254,* 100–107.

Lamb, L. (1994, November/December). Selecting for perfection: Is prenatal screening becoming a kind of eugenics? *Utne Reader,* pp. 26–28.

Lamb, M. E. (1981). The development of father-infant relationships. In M. E. Lamb (Ed.), *The role of the father in child development* (2nd ed.). New York: Wiley.

Lamb, M. E. (1982). *Nontraditional families: Parenting and child development.* Hillsdale, NJ: Erlbaum.

Lamb, M. E., Easterbrooks, M. A., & Holden, G. W. (1980).

Reinforcement and punishment among preschoolers: Characteristics, effects, and correlates. *Child Development, 51,* 1230–1236.

Langer, R. D., & Barrett-Connor, E. (1994). Extended hormone replacement: Who should get it, and for how long? *Geriatrics, 49,* 20–29.

Langlois, J. H. (1986). From the eye of the beholder to behavioral reality: Development of social behaviors and social relations as a function of physical attractiveness. In C. P. Herman, M. P. Zanna, & E. P. Higgins (Eds.), *Physical appearance, stigma, and social behavior: The Ontario Symposium, Vol. 3.* Hillsdale, NJ: Erlbaum.

Langlois, J. H., & Downs, A. C. (1980). Peer relations as a function of physical attractiveness: The eye of the beholder or behavioral reality. *Child Development, 50,* 409–418.

Langlois, J. H., & Stynczynski, L. (1979). The effects of physical attractiveness on the behavioral attributions and peer preferences in acquainted children. *International Journal of Behavioral Development, 2,* 325–341.

Laosa, L. (1981). Maternal behavior: Socio-cultural diversity in modes of family interaction. In R. W. Henderson (Ed.), *Parent-child interaction: Theory, research and prospects.* New York: Academic Press.

Lapsley, D. K. (1985). Elkind on egocentrism. *Developmental Review, 5,* 227–236.

Lapsley, D. K. (1989). Continuity and discontinuity in adolescent social cognitive development. In R. Montemayer, G. Adams, & T. Gullota (Eds.), *Advances in adolescent research* (Vol. 2). Orlando, FL: Academic Press.

Lapsley, D. K., Harwell, M. R., Olson, L. M., Flannery, D., & Quintana, S. M. (1984). Moral judgment, personality, and attitude to authority in early and late adolescence. *Journal of Youth and Adolescence, 13,* 527–542.

Lapsley, D. K., & Power, F. C. (Eds.). (1988). *Self, ego, and identity.* New York: Springer-Verlag.

Lapsley, D. K., & Rice, K. G. (1988). The "new look" at the imaginary audience and personal fable: Toward an integrative model of adolescent ego development. In D. K. Lapsley & F. C. Power (Eds.), *Self, ego, and identity: Integrative approaches.* New York: Springer-Verlag.

Larson, J. H. (1988). The marriage quiz: College students' beliefs in selected myths about marriage. *Family Relations, 37,* 3–11.

Lasby, K., Newton, S., Sherrow, T., Stainton, M., & McNeil, D. (1994). Maternal work in the NICU: A case study of an "NICU experienced" mother. *Issues in Comprehensive Pediatric Nursing, 17,* 147–160.

Lawson, W. B. (1986). Racial and ethnic factors in psychiatric research. *Hospital and Community Psychiatry, 37,* 50–53.

Layder, D. (1994). *Understanding social theory.* London: Sage.

Lea, S. E. G. (1984). *Instinct, environment, and behaviour.* London: Methuen.

Leahey, T. H. (1987). *A history of psychology: Main currents in psychological thought.* Englewood Cliffs, NJ: Prentice Hall.

LeCroy, C. W. (1992). Promoting social competence in youth. In K. Corcoran (Ed.), *Structuring change* (pp. 167–180). Chicago: Lyceum Books

LeCroy, C. W. (1994). Social skills training. In C. W. LeCroy (Ed.), *Handbook of child and adolescent treatment manuals.* New York: Lexington Books.

LeCroy, C. W., & Milligan, K. B. (1996). Promoting social competence in the schools. In R. Constable, J. Flynn, & S. MacDonald (Eds.), *School social work: Practice and research perspectives.* Chicago: Lyceum Books.

Lee, G. R., Seccombe, K., & Shehan, C. L. (1991). Marital status and personal happiness: An analysis of trend data. *Journal of Marriage and the Family, 139,* 839–844.

Lefrancois, G. R. (1989). *Of children: An introduction to child development.* Belmont, CA: Wadsworth.

Lehmann, H. E., & Cancro, R. (1985). Schizophrenia: Clinical features. In H. I. Kaplan & B. J. Sadock (Eds.), *New perspectives in schizophrenia.* New York: Macmillan.

Lembau, J. R. (1988). Emotional sequelae of abortion: Implications for clinical practice. *Psychology of Women Quarterly, 12,* 461–472.

Lemeshow, S. (1982). *The handbook of clinical types in mental retardation.* Boston: Allyn & Bacon.

Lemme, B. H. (1995). *Development in adulthood.* Needham Heights, MA: Allyn & Bacon.

Lemon, B. W., Bengston, V. L., & Peterson, J. A. (1972). An exploration of the activity theory of aging: Activity types and life satisfactions among in-movers of a retirement community. *Journal of Gerontology, 27,* 511–523.

Leon, I. (1986). Psychodynamics of perinatal loss. *Psychiatry, 49,* 312–322.

Leon, I. (1992). Perinatal loss: choreographing grief on the obstetric unit. *American Journal of Orthopsychiatry, 62*(1), 7–8.

Leslie, G. R., Larson, R., & Gorman, B. L. (1973). *Order and change: Introductory sociology.* New York: Oxford University Press.

Lester, B. M. (1992). Infants and their families at risk: Assessment and intervention. *Infant Mental Health Journal, 13*(1), 54–66.

Levant, R. F. (1990). Men's changing roles. *The Family Psychologist, 6,* 4–6.

Levinger, G. (no date). *The interpersonal involvement scale.* University of Massachusetts, Amherst.

Levinson, D. J. (1978). *The seasons of a man's life*. New York: Knopf.

Levinson, D. J. (1985). The life cycle. In H. I. Kaplan & B. J. Sadock (Eds.), *Comprehensive textbook of psychiatry* (Vol. 4). Baltimore: Williams & Wilkins.

Levinson, D. J. (1986). A conception of adult development. *American Psychologist, 41*, 3–13.

Levinson, D. J., Darrow, C. M., Klein, E. G., Levinson, M. H., & Levitt, M. (1986). Social network relationships as sources of maternal support and well-being. *Developmental Psychology, 22*, 310–316.

Levitt, M. (1986). Social network relationships as sources of maternal support and well-being. *Developmental Psychology, 22*, 310–316.

Lewis, M. (1987). Social development in infancy and early childhood. In J. Osofsky (Ed.), *Handbook of infant development* (2nd ed., pp. 419–493). New York: Wiley.

Lewis, M. & Brooks-Gunn, J. (1979). *Social cognition and the acquisition of self*. New York: Plenum.

Libassi, M. F. (1990). Psychopharmacology in social work education (Contract No. 89MF700390ID). Washington, DC: National Institute of Mental Health.

Lickey, M. E., & Gordon, B. (1983). *Drugs for mental illness: A revolution in psychiatry*. New York: W. H. Freeman.

Lickona, T. (1983). *Raising good children*. New York: Bantam Books.

Lieberman, A. (1985). Infant mental health: A model for service delivery. *Journal of Clinical Child Psychology, 14*, 196–201

Lieberman, A. F. (1977). Preschoolers' competence with a peer: Relations with attachment and peer experience. *Child Development, 48*, 1277–1287.

Lieberman, A. F. (1993). *The emotional life of the toddler*. New York: Free Press.

Limbo, R., & Wheeler, S. (1986). *When a baby dies: A handbook for healing and helping*. LaCrosse, WI: Resolve Through Sharing.

Lindgren, H. C. (1969). *An introduction to social psychology*. New York: Wiley.

Lindsey, K. (1982). *Friends or family*. Boston: Beacon Press.

Linet, M. S., Stewart, W. F., Celentano, D. D., Ziegler, D., & Sprecher, M. (1989). An epidemiological study of headaches among adolescents and young adults. *Journal of the American Medical Association, 261*, 2211–2216.

Lipkin, R. (1995, April 8). Sea worms and plants spur new drugs. *Science News*, p. 212.

Lippa, R. A. (1994). *Introduction to social psychology*. Pacific Grove, CA: Brooks/Cole.

Lipsitz, J. (1980). *Sexual development in young adolescents*. Invited speech given at the meeting of the American Association for Moral Education, Pittsburgh, PA.

Little, R., & Ervin, C. (1984). *Alcohol problems in women*. New York: Guilford Press.

Littrell, J. (1991). *Understanding and treating alcoholism*. Hillsdale, NJ: Erlbaum.

Litwak, E., & Szelenyi, I. (1969). Primary group structures and their functions: Kin, neighbors, and friends. *American Sociological Review, 34*, 465–481.

Loney, J., & Ordona, T. (1975). Using cerebral stimulants to treat minimal brain dysfunction. *American Journal of Orthopsychiatry, 45*, 564–572.

Long, N., & Forehand, R. (1987). The effects of parental divorce and parental conflict on children: An overview. *Journal of Development and Behavioral Pediatrics, 815*, 292–296.

Longino, C. F., & Kart, C. S. (1982). Explicating activity theory: Formal replication. *Journal of Gerontology, 37*, 713–722.

Longres, J. F. (1995). *Human behavior in the social environment*. Itasca: Peacock.

Lonner, W. J., Thorndike, R. M., Forbes, N. E., & Ashworth, C. (1985). The influence of television on measured cognition abilities. A study with native Alaska children. *Journal of Cross-Cultural Psychology, 16*, 355–380.

Lopata, H. Z., & Barnewolt, D. (1984). The middle years: Changes and variations in social-role commitments. In G. Baruch & J. Brooks-Gunn (Eds.), *Women in midlife*. New York: Plenum.

Lozoff, B. (1983). Birth and bonding in non-industrial societies. *Developmental Medicine and Child Neurology, 25*, 595–600.

Luborsky, M., & Rubinstein, R. L. (1987). Ethnicity and lifetimes: Self-concepts and situational contexts of ethnic identity in late life. In D. E. Gelfand & C. M. Barresi (Eds.), *Ethnic dimensions of aging*. New York: Springer.

Ludington-Hoe, S. & Golant, S. (1993). *Kangaroo care: The best you can do to help your preterm infant*. New York: Bantam Books.

Ludwig, A. M. (1986). *Principles of clinical psychiatry* (2nd ed.). New York: Free Press.

Lukes, S. (1991). *Moral conflict and politics*. Oxford: Clarendon Press.

Lumsden, C. J., & Wilson, E. O. (1981). *Genes, mind, and culture: The coevolutionary process*. Cambridge, MA: Harvard University Press.

Lunneborg, P. (1992). *Abortion: A positive decision*. New York: Bergin & Garvey.

Luria, A. (1961). *The role of speech in the regulation of normal and abnormal behaviors*. New York: Liveright.

Lyman, D. R., & Selman, R. L. (1985). Peer conflict in pair therapy: Clinical and developmental analyses. In M. W. Berkowitz (Ed.), *Peer conflict and psychological growth*

(New directions for child development, No. 29). San Francisco: Jossey-Bass.

Lynch, M., Roberts, J., & Gordon, M. (1976). Child abuse: Early warning in the maternity hospital. *Developmental Medicine and Child Neurology, 18,* 759–766.

Lyon, D., & Greenberg, J. (1991). Evidence of codependency in women with an alcoholic parent: Helping out Mr. Wrong. *Journal of Personality and Social Psychology, 61,* 435–439.

Lyons-Ruth, K., Connell, D. B., Grunebaum, H. U., & Botein, S. (1990). Infants at social risk: Maternal depression and family support services as mediators of infant development and security of attachment. *Child Development, 9,* 225–235.

Lyons-Ruth, K., & Zeanah, C. (1993). The family context of infant mental health: I. Affective development in the primary caregiving relationship. In C. Zeanah (Ed.), *Handbook of infant mental health* (pp. 14–37). New York: Guilford Press.

Lyotard, J. F. (1984). *The postmodern critique: A report on knowledge* (G. Bennington and B. Massumi, Trans.). Minneapolis: University of Minnesota Press.

Lytle, L. D., Messing, R. B., Fisher, L., & Phebus, L. (1975). Effects of long-term corn consumption on brain serotonin and the response to electric shock. *Science, 190,* 692–694.

Maas, H. (1989). Social responsibility in middle age: Prospects and preconditions. In S. Hunter and M. Sundel (Eds.), *Midlife myths: Issues, findings, and practice implications.* Newbury Park, CA: Sage.

Maccoby, E. E. (1980). *Social development: Psychological growth and the parent-child relationship.* San Diego: Harcourt Brace Jovanovich.

Maccoby, E. E., & Jacklin, C. N. (1974). *The psychology of sex differences.* Palo Alto, CA: Stanford University Press.

Maccoby, E. E., & Martin, J. A. (1983). Socialization in the context of the family: Parent-child interaction. In P. H. Mussen (Ed.), *Handbook of child psychology* (4th ed., Vol 4). New York: Wiley.

MacDonald, K. (1987). Parent-child physical play with rejected, neglected, and popular boys. *Developmental Psychology, 23,* 705–711.

Macht, M. W., & Ashford, J. B. (1991). *Introduction to social work and social welfare.* New York: Merrill/Macmillan.

Madsen, M. C., & Shapira, A. (1970). Cooperative and competitive behavior of urban Afro-American, Anglo-American, Mexican-American, and Mexican village children. *Developmental Psychology, 3,* 16–20.

Main, M., & Solomon, J. (1986). Discovery of an insecure, disorganized/disoriented attachment pattern: Procedures, findings, and implications for the classification of behavior. In M. Yogman & T. B. Brazelton (Eds.), *Affective development in infancy* (pp. 95–124). Norwood, NJ: Ablex.

Main, M., & Solomon, J. (1990). Procedures for identifying infants as disorganized/disoriented during the Ainsworth Strange Situation. In M. T. Greenberg, D. Cicchetti, & E. M. Cummings (Eds.), *Attachment in the preschool years* (pp. 121–160). Chicago: University of Chicago Press.

Maluccio, A. N. (1981). *Promoting competence in clients—A new/old approach for social work practice.* New York: Free Press.

Manton, K. G., Blazer, D. G., & Woodbury, M. A. (1987). Suicide in middle-age and later life: Sex and race specific life table and cohort analyses. *Journal of Gerontology, 42,* 219–227.

Marcia, J. (1966). Development and validation of ego-identity status. *Journal of Personality and Social Psychology, 3,* 551–558.

Marcia, J. (1987). The identity status approach to the study of ego identity development. In T. Honess & K. Yardley (Eds.), *Self and identity: Perspectives across the lifespan.* London: Routledge & Kegan Paul.

Mare, R. D., & Winship, C. (1988). Ethnic and racial patterns of educational attainment and school enrollment. In G. D. Sandefur & M. Tienda (Eds.), *Divided opportunities* (pp. 173–195). New York: Plenum.

Marin, B. V., Holmes, D. L., Guth, M., & Kovac, P. (1979). The potential of children as eyewitnesses. *Law and Human Behavior, 3,* 295–305.

Markham, L. R. (1984). De dog and de cat: Assisting speakers of Black English as they begin to write. *Young Children, 39,* 15–24.

Markides, K. S. (1990). Risk factors, gender, and health. *Generations, 14,* 17–21.

Markides, K. S., & Mindel, C. H. (1987). *Aging and ethnicity.* Newbury Park, CA: Sage.

Markowitz, L. M. (1991, November/December). After the trauma. *Family Therapy Networker,* pp. 30–37.

Marks, R. (1988, Spring). Coming out. *Out/Look.*

Marlowe, M. (1985). Low lead exposure and learning disabilities. *Research Communications in Psychology, Psychiatry and Behavior, 10,* 153–169.

Marrale, J. C., Shipman, J. H., & Rhodes, M. L. (1986). What some college students eat. *Nutrition Today, 21*(1), 16–21.

Marsiglio, W., & Donnelly, D. (1992). Sexual relations in later life: A national study of married persons. *Journal of Gerontology, 46,* 334–338.

Martin, T. C., & Bumpass, L. L. (1989). Recent trends in marital disruption. *Demography, 26,* 37–51.

Martinez, F. (1996, May). *Can SIDS be prevented?* Presented at the Pediatric Specialty Conference, University Medical Center, Tucson, Arizona.

Maslow, A. H. (1962). *Toward a psychology of being*. Princeton, NJ: Van Nostrand.

Mason, J. (1991). Reducing infant mortality in the United States through Healthy Start. *Public Health Reports, 106*, 479–483.

Masten, A. S., Best, K. M., & Garmezy, N. (1991). Resilience and development: Contributions from the study of children who overcome adversity. *Development and Psychopathology, 2*, 425–444.

Masters, J. C., & Furman, W. (1981). Popularity, individual friendship selection, and specific peer interaction among children. *Developmental Psychology, 17*, 344–350.

Masters, W. H., & Johnson, V. E. (1966). *Human sexual response*. Boston: Little, Brown.

Matas, L., Arend, R. A., & Stroufe, L. A. (1978). Continuity of adaptation in the second year: The relationship between quality of attachment and later competence. *Child Development, 49*, 547–556.

Matejcek, A., Dytrych, Z., & Schuller, V. (1979). The Prague study of children born from unwanted pregnancies. *International Journal of Mental Health, 7*, 63–74.

Mawson, A. R., & Jacobs, K. W. (1978). Corn, tryptopha, and homicide. *Journal of Orthomolecular Psychiatry, 7*, 227–230.

Maxmen, J. S. (1986). *Essential psychopathology*. New York: Norton.

Maxmen, J., & Ward, N. (1995). *Essential psychopathology and its treatment*. New York: Norton.

Maxwell, M. (Ed.). (1991). *The sociobiological imagination*. Albany: State University of New York Press.

May, K., & Perrin, S. (1985). Prelude: Pregnancy and birth. In S. M. Hanson & F. W. Boxelt (Eds.), *Dimensions of fatherhood* (pp. 64–91). Beverly Hills, CA: Sage.

Maziade, M. (1987). Influence of gentle birth delivery procedures and other perinatal circumstances on infant temperament—Developmental and social implications. *Annual Progress in Child Psychiatry and Child Development*, 291–295.

Maziade, M., Caron, C., Cote, R., Merette, C., Bernier, H., Laplante, B., Boutin, P., & Thivierge, J. (1990). Psychiatric status of adolescents who had extreme temperaments at age 7. *American Journal of Psychiatry, 147*, 1531–1536.

McCamman, S., Rues, J., & Cannon S. (1988). Prader-Willi syndrome intervention approaches based on differential phase characteristics. *Topics in Clinical Nutrition, 3*, 1–8.

McCarthy, K. (1990, November). If one spouse is sick, both are affected. *APA Monitor*, p. 7.

McConachie, H. (1986). *Parents and young mentally handicapped children: A review of research issues*. Brookline, MA: Brookline Books.

McCord, J. (1990). Problem behaviors. In S. Feldman & G. R. Elliott (Eds.), *At the threshold: The developing adolescent*. Cambridge, MA: Harvard University Press.

McDavid, J. W., & Harari, H. (1973). Stereotyping in names and popularity in grade school children. *Child Development, 37*, 453–459.

McGrath, J. E. (1984). *Groups: Interaction and performance*. Englewood Cliffs, NJ: Prentice Hall.

McGregor, D. (1960). The human side of enterprise. New York: McGraw-Hill.

McIntosh, P. (1995). White privilege and male privilege: A personal account of coming to see correspondences through work in women studies. In M. L. Andersen & P. H. Collins (Eds.), *Race, class, and gender: An anthology*. Belmont, CA: Wadsworth.

McKain, W. C. (1972). A new look at older marriages. *The Family Coordinator, 21*, 61–69.

McKee, B. (1974). The psychosocial development of men in early adulthood and the midlife transition. In D. F. Ricks, A. Thomas, & M. Roff (Eds.), *Life history research in psychopathology* (Vol. 3). Minneapolis: University of Minnesota Press.

McLaughlin, B. (1983). Child compliance to parental control techniques. *Developmental Psychology, 19*, 667–673.

McLemore, S. D. (1991). *Racial and ethnic relations in America*. Boston: Allyn & Bacon.

McManus, M. C. (1991). Serving lesbian and gay youth. *Focal Point, 5*, 1–4.

McNeil, D. (1992). Uncertainties, waiting, and possibilities: Experiences of becoming a mother with an infant in the NICU. *Neonatal Network, 11*, 78.

Mehrabian, A. (1969). Significance of posture and position in the communication of attitude and status relationships. *Psychological Bulletin, 71*, 359–372.

Mehrabian, A. (1972). *Nonverbal communication*. Chicago: Aldine-Atherton.

Meilman, P. W. (1979). Cross-sectional age changes in ego identity status during adolescence. *Developmental Psychology, 15*, 230–231.

Melton, G. B., Petrila, J., Poythress, N. G., & Slobogin, C. (1987). *Psychological evaluations for the courts*. New York: Guilford Press.

Meltzoff, A., & Borton, R. (1979). Intermodal matching by human neonates. *Nature, 282*, 403–404.

Meltzoff, A., & Moore, M. (1977). Imitation of facial and manual gestures by human neonates. *Science, 198*, 75–78.

Meltzoff, A., & Moore, M. (1983). Newborn infants imitate adult facial gestures. *Child Development, 54*, 702–709.

Menaghan, E. G., & Lieberman, M. A. (1986). Changes in depression following divorce: A panel study. *Journal of Marriage and the Family, 45,* 371–386.

Meredith, H. V. (1978). Research between 1969 and 1970 on the standing height of young children in different parts of the world. In H. W. Reece & L. P. Lipsitt (Eds.), *Advances in child development and behavior* (Vol. 12). New York: Academic Press.

Meyers, J. S. (1972). *An orientation to chronic disease and disability.* New York: Macmillan.

Meyers, R. (1978, November). A couple that could. *Psychology Today,* pp. 99–108.

Mildred, S., & Hooper, C. R. (1993, July/August). The ancient Apache ceremony of changing woman. *Southwest Passages,* p. 64.

Miller, B. (1992). Adolescent parenthood: Economic issues and social policies. *Journal of Family and Economic Issues, 13,* 467–475.

Miller, B. C. (1976). A multivariate developmental model of marital satisfaction. *Journal of Marriage and the Family, 38,* 643–657.

Miller, B. C., McCoy, J. K., & Olson, T. D. (1986). Dating age and stage as correlates of adolescent sexual attitudes and behavior. *Journal of Adolescent Research, 1,* 361–371.

Miller, C. A. (1992). Biophysical development during late adulthood. In C. S. Schuster & S. S. Ashburn (Eds.), *The process of human development: A holistic life-span approach* (3rd ed., pp. 804–830). Philadelphia: Lippincott.

Miller, G. A. (1956). The magical number, seven, plus or minus two: Some limits on our capacity for processing information. *Psychological Review, 63,* 81–97.

Minnett, A. M., Vanell, D. L., & Santrock, J. W. (1983). The effects of sibling status on sibling interaction: Influence of birth order, age, spacing, sex of the child, and sex of the sibling. *Child Development, 54,* 1064–1072.

Minuchin, P. P. (1977). *The middle years of childhood.* Pacific Grove, CA: Brooks/Cole.

Minuchin, P. P., and Shapiro, E. K. (1983). The school as a context for social development. In P. H. Mussen (Ed.), *Handbook of child psychology: Vol. 4. Socialization, personality, and social development.* New York: Wiley.

Minuchin, S. (1974). *Families and family therapy.* Cambridge, MA: Harvard University Press.

Mitchell, J. (1993). *Pregnant, substance-using women.* Rockville, MD: U.S. Department of Health and Human Services, Substance Abuse and Mental Health Services Administration.

Mitiguy, J. S. (1990, Fall). Coping with survival. *Headlines: The Brain Injury Magazine,* pp. 2–8.

Mitrushina, M., & Satz, P. (1991). Reliability and validity of the mini-mental status exam in neurologically intact elderly. *Journal of Clinical Psychology, 47,* 537–543.

Money, J. (1988). Gay, straight, and in-between: The sexology of erotic orientation. New York: Oxford University Press.

Montemayer, R. (1983). Parents and adolescents in conflict: All families some of the time and some families most of the time. *Journal of Early Adolescence, 3,* 83–103.

Morris, R. (1996). The world is a box of crayons. In P. R. Popple & L. Leighninger (Eds.), *Social work, social welfare, and American society* (pp. 645–647). Boston: Allyn & Bacon.

Morrison, R. S., Olson, E., Mertz, K. R., & Meier, D. E. (1995). The inaccessibility of advance directives on transfer from ambulatory to acute care settings. *Journal of the American Medical Association, 274,* 478–482.

Mrazek, P. (1993). Maltreatment and infant development. In C. Zeaneh (Ed.), *Handbook of infant mental health* (pp. 73–86). New York: Guilford Press.

Muehlenhard, C. L., & Linton, M. A. (1987). Date rape and sexual aggression in dating situations: Incidence and risk factors. *Journal of Counseling Psychology, 34,* 186–196.

Mueller, E., & Lucas, F. (1975). A developmental analysis of peer interaction among toddlers. In M. Lewis & L. Rosenglum (Eds.), *Friendship and peer relations.* New York: Wiley-Interscience.

Mueller, E., & Vandell, D. (1979). Infant-infant interaction. In J. D. Osofsy (Ed.), *Handbook of infant development.* New York: Wiley.

Munley, A. (1983). *The hospice alternative.* New York: Basic Books.

Mussen, P. H. (1974). *Child development and personality* (6th ed). New York: Harper & Row.

Mutryn, C. (1993). Psychosocial impact of cesarean section on the family: A literature review. *Social Science and Medicine, 37,* 1271–1282.

Myers, B. (1982). Early intervention using Brazelton training with middle-class mothers and fathers of newborns. *Child Development, 53,* 462–471.

Myers, B., Jarvis, P., & Creasey, G. (1987). Infants' behavior with their mothers and grandmothers. *Infant Behavior and Development, 10,* 245–259.

Nagy, M. H. (1959). The child's view of death. In H. Feifel (Ed.), *The meaning of death* (pp. 79–98). New York: McGraw-Hill.

Nakagawa, M. (1993). Community leaders, police talk, hate crimes. *Asian Week,* p. 12.

Nash, M. (1989). *The cauldron of ethnicity in the modern world.* Chicago: University of Chicago Press.

National Center on Child Abuse and Neglect. (1994). *Child maltreatment 1992: Reports from the states to the National*

Center on Child Abuse and Neglect. Washington, DC: Government Printing Office.

National Council on Hopelessness. (1995). *Domestic violence and hopelessness.* National Council Fact Sheet on the Internet.

National Institute of Mental Health. (1991). *Caring for people with severe mental disorders: A national plan of research to improve services* (DHHS Publication No. ADM 91–1762). Washington, DC: U.S. Government Printing Office.

National Organization for Women. (1995). *Violence against women in the United States.* NOW home page on the Internet.

National Research Council. (1993). *Losing generations: Adolescents in high-risk settings.* Washington, DC: National Academy Press.

Neason, S. (1994). *Prader-Willi syndrome: A handbook for parents.* St. Louis, MO: Prader-Willi Syndrome Association.

Neimark, E. D. (1975). Longitudinal development of formal operational thought. *Genetic Psychology Monographs, 91,* 171–225.

Netting, F. E., Kettner, P. M., McMurtry, S. L. (1993). *Social Work Macro Practice.* White Plains, NY: Longman.

Neugarten, B. L. (1968). The awareness of middle age. In B. L. Neugarten (Ed.), *Middle age and aging* (pp. 93–98). Chicago: University of Chicago Press.

Neugarten, B. L. (1969). Continuities and discontinuities of psychological issues into adult life. *Human Development, 12,* 121–130.

Neugarten, B. L. (1974). Age groups in American society and the rise of the young-old. *Annals of the American Academy of Political and Social Science,* 187–198.

Neugarten, B. L. (1986). The aging society. In A. Pifer & D. L. Bronte (Eds.), *Our aging society: Paradox and promise.* New York: Norton.

Neugarten, B. L. & Weinstein, K. (1964). The changing American grandparent. *Journal of Marriage and the Family, 26,* 199–204.

Newberger, E., Barkan, S., Lieberman, E., McCormick, M., Yllo, K., Gary, L., & Schechter, S. (1992). Abuse of pregnant women and adverse birth outcome: Current knowledge and implications for practice. *Journal of the American Medical Association, 17,* 2370–2372.

Newcomb, M. D., Huba, G. J., & Bentler, P. M. (1986). Determinants of sexual and dating behaviors among adolescents. *Journal of Personality and Social Psychology, 50,* 428–438.

Newman, B. M., & Newman, P. R. (1987). *Development through life: A psychosocial approach* (4th ed.). Pacific Grove, CA: Brooks/Cole.

Newman, B. M., & Newman, P. R. (1991). *Development through life: A psychosocial approach* (5th ed.). Pacific Grove, CA: Brooks/Cole.

Newman, B. M., & Newman, P. R. (1995). *Development through life: A psychosocial approach* (6th ed.). Pacific Grove, CA: Brooks/Cole.

Newman, B. S. (1994). Diversity and populations at risk: Gays and lesbians. In F. G. Reamer (Ed.), *The foundations of social work knowledge.* New York: Columbia University Press.

Newman, L., & Buka, S. (1991, Spring). Clipped wings: The fullest look yet at how prenatal exposure to drugs, alcohol and nicotine hobbles children's learning. *American Educator,* pp. 27–42.

Newsweek (1988). December 5, pp. 24, 29.

Nickerson, E. T., & Pitochelli, E. T. (1978). *Learned helplessness and depression in married women: Marriage as a depressing life style for women.* Paper presented at the meeting of the Eastern Psychological Association, Washington, DC.

Nicol, S. E., & Gottesman, I. I. (1983). Clues to the genetics and neurobiology of schizophrenia. *American Scientist, 71,* 398–404.

Noe, R. A. (1988). Women and mentoring: A review and research agenda. *Academy of Management Review, 13,* 65–78.

Norton, D., Brown, E. F., Brown, E. G., Francis, E. A., Murase, K., & Valle, R. (1978). *The dual perspective: Inclusion of ethnic minority content in the social work curriculum.* New York: Council on Social Work Education.

Nuckolls, K. B., Cassel, J., & Kaplan, B. H. (1972). Psychosocial assets, life crises, and the prognosis of pregnancy. *American Journal of Epidemiology, 95,* 431–441.

Nurcombe, B., & Gallagher, R. M. (1986). *The clinical process in psychiatry: Diagnosis and management planning.* London: Cambridge University Press.

Oden, S., & Asher, S. R. (1977). Coaching children in social skills for friendship making. *Child Development, 48,* 495–506.

Offer, D., Ostrov, E., & Howard, K. (1981). *The adolescent: A psychological self-portrait.* New York: Basic Books.

O'Hara, M. W., Kohout, F. J., & Wallace, R. B. (1985). Depression among the rural elderly: A study of prevalence and correlates. *The Journal of Nervous and Mental Disease, 173,* 582–589.

Okun, B. F. (1984). *Working with adults: Individual, family, and career development.* Pacific Grove, CA: Brooks/Cole.

Olds, D., & Kitzman, H. (1990). Can home visitation improve the health of women and children at environmental risk? *Pediatrics, 86,* 108–116.

Olsen, J. (1980). Social and psychological correlates of pregnany resolution among adolescent women: A review. *American Journal of Orthopsychiatry, 50,* 432–445.

Olshansky, E. (1992). Redefining the concepts of success and failure in infertility treatment. *NAACOGS Clinic Issues in Perinatal and Women's Health Nursing, 3,* 313–319.

Olweus, D. (1980). Familial and temperamental determinants of aggressive behavior in adolescent boys: A causal analysis. *Developmental Psychology, 16,* 644–660.

Opie, I., & Opie, P. (1987). *The love and language of school-children.* New York: Oxford University Press.

Ornstein, P. (1995, January). New cognitive research making waves. *APA Monitor.*

Orthner, D. (1975). Leisure activity patterns and marital satisfaction over the marital career. *Journal of Marriage and the Family, 37,* 91–102.

Osofsky, J., Hann, D., & Peebles, C. (1993). Adolescent parenthood: Risks and opportunities for mothers and infants. In C. Zeaneh (Ed.), *Handbook of infant mental health* (pp. 106–119). New York: Guilford Press.

Ostrom, T. (1984). The sovereignty of social cognition. In R. S. Wyer & T. K. Srull (Eds.), *Handbook of social cognition* (Vol. 1, pp. 1–32). Hillsdale, NJ: Erlbaum.

Otto, L. B. (1988). America's youth: A changing profile. *Family Relations, 37,* 385–391.

Ouchi, W. (1981). *Theory Z: How American business can beat the Japanese challenge.* Reading, MA: Addison-Wesley.

Oyserman, D., Radin, N., Benn, R. (1993). Dynamics in a three-generational family: Teens, grandparents, and babies. *Developmental Psychology, 29,* 564–572.

Page, D. S. (1981). *Principles of biological chemistry* (2nd ed.). Boston: Willard Grant Press.

Pahl, J., & Quine, L. (1987). Families with mentally handicapped children. In J. Oxford (Ed.), *Treating the disorder, treating the family* (pp. 39–61). Baltimore: Johns Hopkins University Press.

Pancoast, D. L., & Collins, A. (1987). Natural helping networks. In *Encyclopedia of Social Work* (18th ed., 177–182). Silver Spring, MD: National Association of Social Workers.

Pancoast, D. L., Parker, P., & Froland, C. (1983). *Rediscovering self-help: Its role in social care.* Beverly Hills, CA: Sage.

Papousek, H., & Papousek, M. (1982). Integration into the social world: Survey of research. In P. M. Stratton (Ed.), *Psychobiology of human newborn* (pp. 367–390). New York: Wiley.

Papousek, H., & Papousek, M. (1987). Intuitive parenting: A dialectic counterpart to the infant's integrative competence. In J. Osofsky (Ed.), *Handbook of infant development* (2nd ed., pp. 669–720). New York: Wiley.

Papousek, H., & Papousek, M. (1992). Beyond emotional bonding: The role of preverbal communication in mental growth and health. *Infant Mental Health Journal, 13,* 43–53.

Papousek, M., Papousek, H., & Bornstein, M. H. (1985). The naturalistic vocal environment of young infants: On the significance of homogeneity and variability in parental speech. In T. Fields & N. Fox (Eds.), *Social perception in infants* (pp. 269–297). Norwood, NJ: Ablex.

Paris, S. C., & Lindayer, B. K. (1982). The development of cognitive skills during childhood. In B. B. Wolman (Ed.), *Handbook of developmental psychology.* Englewood Cliffs, NJ: Prentice Hall.

Parke, R. D., MacDonald, K., Beital, A., & Bhavangri, N. (1988). The interrelationships among families, fathers, and peers. In R. D. Peters (Ed.), *New approaches to family research.* New York: Brunner/Mazel.

Parke, R. D., & O'Leary, S. (1976). Family interaction in the newborn period: Some findings, some observations and some unresolved issues. In K. Riegel & J. Meacham (Eds.), *The developing individual in a changing world: Vol. 2. Social and environmental issues.* The Hague: Mouton.

Parke, R. D., & Slaby, R. G. (1983). The development of aggression. In P. H. Mussen (Ed.), *Handbook of child psychology* (4th ed., Vol. 4). New York: Wiley.

Parke, R. D., & Tinsley, B. (1987). Family interaction in infancy. In J. Osofsky (Ed.), *Handbook of infant development* (2nd ed., pp. 579–641). New York: Wiley.

Parker, B., McFarlane, J., Soeken, K., Torres, S., & Campbell, D. (1993). Physical and emotional abuse in pregnancy: A comparison of adult and teenage women. *Nursing Research, 42,* 173–177.

Parker, J. G., & Gottman, J. M. (1989). Social and emotional development in a relational context: Friendship interaction from early childhood to adolescence. In T. J. Berndt & G. W. Ladd (Eds.), *Peer relations in child development.* New York: Wiley.

Parrot, A., & Bechhofer, L. (1991). *Acquaintance rape.* New York: Wiley.

Parsons, J. E., Adler, T. F., & Kaczala, C. M. (1982a). Socialization of achievement attitudes and beliefs: Parental influences. *Child Development, 53,* 308–318.

Parsons, J. E., Adler, T. F., & Kaczala, C. M. (1982b). Socialization of achievement attitudes and beliefs: Parental influences. *Child Development, 53,* 322–329.

Parten, M. (1932). Social play among preschool children. *Journal of Abnormal and Social Psychology, 27,* 243–269.

The Patient Self-Determination Act of 1990, 4206, 4751 of the *Omnibus Reconciliation Act of 1990,* PL No. 101–508 (November 5, 1990).

Patterson, G. R. (1982). *A social learning approach to family in-*

terventions: Vol. 3. Coercive family process. Eugene, OR: Castalia.

Patterson, G. R. (1986). Performance models for antisocial boys. *American Psychologist, 41,* 432–444.

Patterson, G. R., DeBarsyshe, B. D., & Ramsey, E. (1989). A developmental perspective on antisocial behavior. *American Psychologist, 44,* 329–335.

Patterson, J. M., & McCubbin, H. I. (1987). Adolescent coping style and behaviors: Conceptualization and measurement. *Journal of Adolescence, 10,* 163–186.

Patterson, S. L. (1987). Older rural natural helpers: Gender and site differences in the helping process. *The Gerontologist, 27,* 639–644.

Patterson, S., Brennan, E., Germain, C., & Memmot, J. (1988). The effectiveness of rural natural helpers. *Social Casework, 69,* 272–279.

Pattison, E. M. (1978). The living-dying process. In C. A. Garfield (Ed.), *Psychosocial care of the dying patient* (pp. 145–153). New York: McGraw-Hill.

Paulson, R., & Sauer, M. (1991). Counseling the infertile couple: When enough is enough. *Obstetrics and Gynecology, 78,* 462–464.

Pavenstedt, E. (1965). A comparison of the child-rearing environment of upper-lower and very low lower-class families. *American Journal of Orthopsychiatry, 35,* 89–98.

Peak, T., & Toseland, R. W. (1992). Friends don't really understand: The therapeutic benefit of social group work for caregivers of older persons. In C. W. LeCroy (Ed.), *Case studies in social work practice.* Pacific Grove, CA: Brooks/Cole.

Pearlin, L. I., Mullan, J. T., Semple, S. J., & Skaff, M. M. (1990). Caregiving and the stress process: An overview of concepts and their measures. *The Gerontologist, 30,* 583–594.

Pearson, J. L., Hunter, A. G., Ensminger, M. E., & Kellam, S. G. (1990). Black grandmothers in multigenerational households: Diversity in family structure and parenting involvement in the Woodlawn community. *Child Development, 61,* 434–442.

Pecora, P. J., Whittaker, J. K., & Maluccio, A. N. (1992). *The child welfare challenge: Policy, practice and research.* New York: Aldine de Gruyter.

Pederson, F., Cain, R., & Zaslow, M. (1982). Variation in infant experience associated with alternative family roles. In L. Laosa & I. Sigel (Eds.), *The family as a learning environment.* New York: Plenum.

Pedro-Carroll, J. L., & Cowen, E. L. (1985). The children of divorce intervention program: An investigation of the efficacy of a school-based prevention program. *Journal of Consulting and Clinical Psychology, 53,* 603–611.

Pellegrini, D. S. (1990). Psychosocial risk and protective factors in childhood. *Developmental and Behavioral Pediatrics, 11,* 201–209.

Penfield, W., & Perot, P. (1963). The brain's record of auditory and visual experience. *Brain, 86,* 595–696.

Pennebaker, J. W., Hendler, C. S., Durrett, M. E., & Richards, P. (1981). Social factors influencing absenteeism due to illness in nursery school children. *Child Development, 52,* 692–700.

Peplau, L. A. (1991). Lesbian and gay relationships. In J. C. Gonsiorek & J. D. Weinrich (Eds.), *Homosexuality: Research implications for public policy.* Newbury Park, CA: Sage.

Peplau, L. A., Bikson, T. K., Rook, K. S., & Goodchilds, J. D. (1982). Being old and living alone. In L. A. Peplau & D. Perlman (Eds.), *Loneliness: A sourcebook of current theory, research, and therapy.* New York: Wiley-Interscience.

Perrow, C. (1978). The short and glorious history of organizational theory. In J. M. Shafritz & P. H. Whitbeck (Eds.), *Classics of organization theory* (pp. 313–323). Belmont, CA: Wadsworth.

Petersen, A. C. (1987, September). Those gangly years. *Psychology Today,* pp. 28–34.

Petersen, A. C., & Crockett, L. J. (1992). Adolescent sexuality, pregnancy, and child rearing: Developmental perspectives. In M. K. Rosenheim & M. F. Testa (Eds.), *Early parenthood and coming of age in the 1990s.* New Brunswick, NJ: Rutgers University Press.

Petersen, A. C., Kennedy, R. E., & Sullivan, P. (1991). Coping with adolescence. In M. E. Colten & S. Gore (Eds.), *Adolescent stress.* New York: Aldine de Gruyter.

Peterson, K. (1993). The homeless mentally ill. In B. S. Johnson (Ed.), *Psychiatric-mental health nursing* (3rd ed., pp. 589–601). Philadelphia: Lippincott.

Petri, H. L. (1986). *Motivation: Theory and research* (2nd ed.). Belmont, CA: Wadsworth.

Pettit, G. S., Dodge, K. A., & Brown, M. M. (1988). Early family experience, social problem-solving patterns, and children's social competence. *Child Development, 59,* 107–120.

Pfohl, B. (1995, May). Is self-esteem really all that important? *APA Monitor.*

Piaget, J. (1929). *The child's conception of the world.* New York: Harcourt Brace.

Piaget, J. (1967). *The child's conception of the world.* Totowa, NJ: Littlefield, Adams.

Piaget, J. (1972). Intellectual evolution from adolescence to adulthood. *Human Development, 15,* 1–12.

Piaget, J., & Inhelder, B. (1969). *The psychology of the child.* New York: Basic Books.

Pinderhughes, E. (1994). Diversity and populations at risk:

Ethnic minorities and people of color. In F. G. Reamer (Ed.), *The foundations of social work knowledge*. New York: Columbia University Press.

Pineo, P. (1969). Developmental patterns in marriage. *Family Coordinator, 18,* 135–140.

Pines, M. (1979). Head start in the nursery. *Psychology Today, 13,* 56.

Pines, M. (1979, January). Superkids. *Psychology Today,* pp. 53–63.

Pines, M. (1982, June). It's changing the lives of handicapped kids: Infant stimulation. *Psychology Today,* pp. 48–53.

Pipp, S., Easterbrooks, M. A., & Harmon, R. J. (1992). The relation between attachment and knowledge of self and mother in one-to-three-year-old infants. *Child Development, 62,* 738–750.

Pistrang, N. (1995). The partner relationship in psychological response to breast cancer. *Social Science and Medicine, 40,* 789–797.

Pleck, J. H. (1985). *Working wives/working husbands.* Newbury Park, CA: Sage.

Plomin, R. (1990). *Nature and nurture: An introduction to human behavioral genetics.* Belmont, CA: Wadsworth.

Plomin, R. (1994). Nature, nurture, and social development. *Social Development, 3* (1), 37–53.

Plomin, R., & Daniels, D. (1987). Why are children in the same family so different from each other? *Behavioral and Brain Sciences, 10,* 1–16.

Plomin, R., DeFries, J. C., & McClearn, G. E. (1990). *Behavioral genetics: A primer* (2nd ed.). New York: W. H. Freeman.

Powell, A. G., Farrar, E., & Cohen, D. K. (1985). *The shopping mall high school: Winners and losers in the educational marketplace.* Boston: Houghton Mifflin.

Power, T. G. (1985). Mother- and father-infant play: A developmental analysis. *Child Development, 56,* 1514–1524.

Power, T. G., & Shanks, J. A. (1989). Parents as socializers: Maternal and paternal views. *Journal of Youth and Adolescence, 18,* 203–220.

Pratt, M. W., McLaren, J., & Wickens, G. (1984). Rules as tools: Effective generalization of verbal self-regulative communication training by first-grade speakers. *Developmental Psychology, 20,* 893–902.

Pritchard, J., MacDonald, P., & Gant, N. (1985). *Williams obstetrics.* Norwalk, CT: Appleton-Century-Crofts.

Proshansky, H., & Newton, P. (1968). The development of Negro self-identity. In M. Deutsch, A. Jensen, & I. Katz (Eds.), *Race and social class in psychological development.* New York: Henry Holt.

Puner, M. (1974). *To the good long life: What we know about growing old.* New York: Universe Books.

Quam, J. K. (1983). Older women and informal supports: Impact on prevention. In S. Simson, L. B. Wilson, J. Hermalin, & R. Hess (Eds.), *Aging and prevention: New approaches for preventing health and mental health problems in older adults.* New York: Haworth Press.

Quam, J. K., & Whitford, G. S. (1992). Adaptation and age-related expectations of older gay and lesbian adults. *The Gerontologist, 32,* 367–374.

Quinn, P. (1992). Ethnographic-type techniques in life-span human development courses: Integrating information and developing skills. *Family Relations, 41,* 59–64.

Radke-Yarrow, M., Cummings, E. M., Kuczynski, L., & Chapman, N. (1985). Patterns of attachment in two- and three-year olds in normal families and families with parental depression. *Child Development, 56,* 884–893.

Radke-Yarrow, M., Zahn-Waxler, C., & Chapman, M. (1983). Children's prosocial dispositions and behavior. In P. H. Mussen (Ed.), *Handbook of child psychology* (Vol. 4). New York: Wiley.

Radwin, E. (1993). Literacy and illiteracy. *The new Grolier multimedia encyclopedia* [CD ROM].

Ragozin, A. S., Bashan, R. B., Crnic, K. A., Greenberg, M. T., & Robinson, N. M. (1982). Effects of maternal age on parenting role. *Developmental Psychology, 18,* 627–634.

Raine, A., Brennan, P., & Mednick, S. (1994). Birth complications combined with early maternal rejection at age one year predispose to violent crime at 18 years. *Archives of General Psychiatry, 51,* 984–988.

Ramirez, M. (1978). A mestizo world view and the psychodynamics of Mexican-American border populations. In S. Ross (Ed.), *Views across the border: The United States and Mexico.* Albuquerque: University of New Mexico Press.

Ramos, S. (1975). *Profile of man and culture in Mexico.* Austin: University of Texas Press.

Rapalje, J., Degelman, D., & Ashburn, S. S. (1986). Psychosocial development during the school-age years. In C. S. Schuster & S. S. Ashburn (Eds.), *The process of human development: A holistic life-span approach.* Boston: Little, Brown.

Rauch, J. (1988). *Genetic content for graduate social work education: Human behavior and the social environment.* Washington DC: Council of Social Work Education.

Ravn, S. H., Rosenberg, J., & Bostofte, E. (1994). Postmenopausal hormone replacement therapy—Clinical implications. *European Journal of Obstetrics, Gynecology, and Reproductive Biology, 53,* 81–93.

Reeder, S., Mastroianni, L., & Martin, L. (1983). *Maternity Nursing* (15th ed.). Philadelphia: Lippincott.

Reedy, M. N., Birren, J. E., & Schaie, K. W. (1981). Age and sex differences in satisfying relationships across the adult life span. *Human Development, 24,* 52–66.

Reiss, I. R. (1980). *Family systems in America* (3rd ed.). New York: Holt, Rinehart & Winston.

Reissland, N. (1988). Neonatal imitation in the first hour of life: Observations in rural Nepal. *Developmental Psychology, 24,* 464–469.

Remafedi, G., Farrow, J. A., & Deisher, R. W. (1991). Risk factors for attempted suicide in gay and bisexual youth. *Pediatrics, 87,* 869–875.

Rest, J. R. (1986). *Moral development: Advances in research and theory.* New York: Praeger.

Revelle, G. L., Wellman, H. M., & Karabenick, J. D. (1985). Comprehension monitoring in preschool children. *Child Development, 56,* 654–663.

Reynolds, B. C. (1942). *Learning and teaching in the practice of social work.* New York: Farrar & Rinehart.

Reynolds, R. E., & Ortony, A. (1980). Some issues in the measurement of children's comprehension of metaphorical language. *Child Development, 51,* 1110–1119.

Riccio, C. A., Hynd, G. W., Cohen, M. J., & Gonzalez, J. J. (1993). Neurological basis of attention deficit hyperactivity disorder. *Exceptional Children, 60,* 118–124.

Rich, C. L., Young, D., & Fowler, R. C. (1986). San Diego suicide study. *Archives of General Psychiatry, 43,* 577–582.

Richard, B. A., & Dodge, K. A. (1982). Social maladjustment and problem-solving in school-aged children. *Journal of Consulting and Clinical Psychology, 50,* 226–233.

Richardson, D. K. (1988). The importance of reminiscence and family tradition. In J. Norris (Ed.), *Daughters of the elderly: Building partnerships in caregiving* (pp. 32–36). Bloomington: Indiana University Press.

Richardson, J. G., & Simpson, C. H. (1982). Children, gender, and social structure: An analysis of the contents of letters to Santa Claus. *Child Development, 53,* 429–436.

Richardson, K. (1988). *Understanding psychology.* Philadelphia: Open University Press.

Richmond, J. B., Stipek, D. J., & Zigler, E. (1979). A decade of Head Start. In E. Zigler & J. Valentine (Eds.), *Project Head Start: A legacy of the War on Poverty.* New York: Free Press.

Richmond, M. (1917). *Social diagnosis.* New York: Russell Sage Foundation.

Ridgeway, C. L. (1983). *The dynamics of small groups.* New York: St. Martin's Press.

Riesen, A. (1947). The development of visual perception in man and chimpanzee. *Science, 106,* 107–108.

Riesen, A., Chow, K., Semmes, J., & Nissen, H. (1951). Chimpanzee vision after four conditions of light deprivation. *American Psychologist, 6,* 282.

Riesenberg, D. (1987). Treating a societal malignancy—Rape. *Journal of American Medical Association, 257,* 899–900.

Rigsby, L. C., & McDill, E. L. (1975). Value orientations of high school students. In H. R. Strub (Ed.), *The sociology of education: A sourcebook* (pp. 53–75). Pacific Grove, CA: Brooks/Cole.

Ritter, M. (1996, January 2). Genetic missing link to personality found. *The Arizona Daily Star,* pp. 1, 7.

Rivera, R. R. (1991). Sexual orientation and the law. In J. C. Gonsiorek & J. D. Weinrich (Eds.), *Homosexuality: Research implications for public policy.* Newbury Park, CA: Sage.

Roberts, P., & Newton, P. M. (1987). Levinsonian studies of women's adult development. *Psychology and Aging, 2,* 154–163.

Robertson, I. (1977). *Sociology.* New York: Worth.

Robertson, J. F. (1976). Significance of grandparents: Perceptions of young adult grandchildren. *The Gerontologist, 16,* 137–140.

Robertson, M. J., Ropers, R. H., & Boyer, R. (1985). *The homeless of Los Angeles County: An empirical evaluation.* Los Angeles: UCLA School of Public Health.

Robin, A. (1994). Problem-solving training. In C. W. LeCroy (Ed.), *Handbook of child and adolescent training manuals.* New York: Lexington Books.

Robinson, B. E., & Barret, R. L. (1985, December). Teenage fathers. *Psychology Today,* 66–70.

Robinson, J. P. (1977). *How Americans use time: A social-psychological analysis of everyday behavior.* New York: Praeger.

Robinson, W. P. (1965). The elaborated code in working-class language. *Language and speech, 8,* 243–252.

Robson, W. L., & Leung, A. K. (1992). The circumcision question. *Postgraduate Medicine, 91,* 237–242, 244.

Roedding, J. (1991). Birth trauma and suicide: A study of the relationship between near-death experiences and later suicidal behavior. *Pre- and Perinatal Psychology Journal, 6,* 145–169.

Roff, M. (1963). Childhood social interaction and young adulthood psychosis. *Journal of Clinical Psychology, 19,* 152–157.

Rogers, R. (1989). Ethnic and birth-weight differences in cause-specific infant mortality. *Demography, 26,* 335–341.

Rollins, B. C. (1989). Marital quality at midlife. In S. Hunter & M. Sundel (Eds.), *Midlife myths: Issues, findings, and practice implications.* Newbury Park, CA: Sage.

Rollins, B. C. & Feldman, H. (1970). Marital satisfaction over the life cycle. *Journal of Marriage and the Family, 32,* 20–28.

Roots of addiction. (1989, February 27). *Newsweek,* pp. 37–46.

Rose, S. (1991). Information processing at 1 year: Relation to birth status and developmental outcome during the first 5 years. *Developmental Psychology, 27,* 723–737.

Rose, S. (1992). Infant information processing in relation to six-year cognitive outcomes. *Child Development, 63*, 1126–1141.

Rose, S. D. (1989). *Working with adults in groups: A multimethod approach.* San Francisco: Jossey-Bass.

Rosen, R. (1979). Some crucial issues concerning children of divorce. *Journal of Divorce, 3*, 19–26.

Rosenberg, M., & Simmons, R. (1971). *Black and white self-esteem: The urban school child.* Rose Monograph Series. Washington, DC: American Sociological Association.

Rosenblatt, A. (1962). The application of role concepts to the intake process. *Social Casework, 43*, 8–14.

Rosenthal, R., & Jacobsen, L. (1968). *Pygmalian in the classroom.* New York: Holt, Rinehart & Winston.

Ross, D., & Whitehead, M. I. (1995). Selecting patients for HRT: Positive indications. *British Journal of Clinical Practice, 49*, 92–94.

Roth, L. L., & Atherton, C. R. (1989). *Promoting successful aging.* Chicago: Nelson-Hall.

Rothblum, E. D., & Franks, V. (1983). Introduction: Warning! sex-role stereotypes may be hazardous to your health. In V. Franks & E. D. Rothblum (Eds.), *The stereotyping of women: Its effects on mental health.* New York: Springer.

Rovee-Collier, C., Sullivan, M., Enright, M., Lucas, D., & Fagan, J. (1980). Reactivation of infant memory. *Science, 208*, 1159–1161.

Royce, A. P. (1982). *Ethnic identity: Strategies of diversity.* Bloomington: Indiana University Press.

Rozee, P. D., Bateman, P., & Gilmore, T. (1991). The personal perspective of acquaintance rape: A three-tier approach. In A. Parrot & L. Bechhofer (Eds.), *Acquaintance rape: The hidden crime.* New York: Wiley.

Rubenstein, C. M. & Shaver, P. (1982). The experience of loneliness. In L. A. Peplau & D. Perlman (Eds.), *Loneliness: A sourcebook of current theory, research, and therapy.* New York: Wiley.

Rubin, K. N., Fein, G. G., & Vandenberg, B. (1983). Play. In P. H. Mussen (Ed.), *Handbook of childhood psychology* (4th ed., Vol. 4). New York: Wiley.

Rubin, R. (1970). Cognitive style in pregnancy. *American Journal of Nursing, 70*, 502.

Rukeyser, L., Cooney, J., & Winslow, W. (1988). *Louis Rukeyser's business almanac.* New York: Simon & Schuster.

Ruse, M. (1991). Epistemology. In M. Maxwell (Ed.), *The sociobiology imagination.* Albany: State University of New York Press.

Rushdie, S. (1982, December). The new empire within Britain. *New Society*, p. 9.

Rushton, J. P. (1980). *Altruism, socialization, and society.* Englewood Cliffs, NJ: Prentice Hall.

Russo, N. (1979). Overview: Sex roles, fertility, and the motherhood mandate. *Psychology of Women Quarterly, 4*, 7–15.

Rutter, M. (1981). *Maternal deprivation reassessed.* Harmondsworth, Eng. Penguin Books.

Rutter, M. (1983). School effects on pupil progress: Research findings and policy implications. *Child Development, 54*, 1–29.

Rutter, M. (1985). Resilience in the face of adversity: Protective factors and resilience to psychiatric disorder. *British Journal of Psychiatry, 147*, 598–611.

Rutter, M., Graham, P., Chadwick, F., & Yule, W. (1976). Adolescent turmoil: Fact or fiction? *Journal of Child Psychology and Psychiatry, 17*, 35–56.

Rutter, M., Maughan, B., Mortimore, J., & Ouston, J., with A. Smith (1979). *Fifteen thousand hours: Secondary schools and their effects on children.* Cambridge, MA: Harvard University Press.

Ryan, W. (1971). *Blaming the victim.* New York: Vintage Books.

Sagi, A., Lamb, M. E., Lewkowicz, K. S., Shoham, R., Dvir, R., & Estes, D. (1985). Security of infant-mother, -father, and -metapelet attachments among Kibbutz-reared Israeli children. In I. Bretherton & E. Waters (Eds.), *Growing points of attachment theory and research* (pp. 257–275). Monographs of the Society for Research in Child Development, 50(1–2, Serial No. 209).

Saleebey, D. (1985). In clinical social work practice, is the body politic? *Social Service Review, 59*, 578–592

Saleebey, D. (1992a). Biology's challenge to social work: Embodying the person-in-environment perspective. *Social Work, 37*, 112–119.

Saleebey, D. (1992b). *The strengths perspective in social work practice.* New York: Longman.

Salthouse, T. A., & Coon, V. E. (1993). Influence of task-specific processing speed on age differences in memory. *Journal of Gerontology, 48*, 244–255.

Sameroff, A. (1993). Models of development and developmental risk. In C. Zeanah (Ed.), *Handbook of infant mental health* (pp. 3–13). New York: Guilford Press.

Sanchez, S. (1994). Equality of sexes? Give it 1000 years. *USA Today.*

Sandmaier, M. (1995, July/August). The gift of friendship. *The Family Therapy Networker*, pp. 23–34, 66–68.

Santrock, J. W. (1986). *Life-span development.* Dubuque, IA: Wm. C. Brown.

Santrock, J. W. (1989). *Life-span development* (3rd ed.). Dubuque, IA: Wm. C. Brown.

Santrock, J. W. (1990). *Adolescence* (4th ed.). Dubuque, IA: Wm. C. Brown.

Santrock, J. W. (1992). *Life-span development* (4th ed.). Dubuque, IA: Wm. C. Brown.

Santrock, J. W. (1995). *Life-span development* (5th ed.). Madison, WI, & Dubuque, IA: Brown & Benchmark.

Santrock, J. W., & Warshak, R. A. (1986). Development, relationships and legal considerations in father custody families. In M. E. Lamb (Ed.), *The father's role: Applied perspectives*. New York: Wiley.

Sarton, M. (1984). *Letters from Maine, new poems*. New York: Norton.

Sauerman, T. H. (1984). *Read this before coming out to your parents*. Washington, DC: Federation of Parents & Friends of Lesbians and Gays, Inc.

Saussure, F. D. (1966). *Course in general linguistics* (W. Baskin, Trans.). New York: McGraw-Hill.

Scarf, M. (1992, July/August). The middle of the journey. *Family Therapy Networker*, pp. 51–55.

Scarr, S., & McCartney, K. (1983). How people make their own environments: A theory of genotype-environment effects. *Child Development, 54*, 424–435.

Schachter, F. F. (1981). Toddlers with employed mothers. *Child Development, 52*, 958–964.

Schaefer, E. S., & Burnett, C. K. (1987). Stability and predictability of quality of women's marital relationships and demoralization. *Journal of Personality and Social Psychology, 53*, 1129–1136.

Schaie, K. W. (1977). Toward a stage theory of adult cognitive development. *Aging and Human Development, 8*, 129–138.

Schaie, K. W. (Ed.) (1983a). *Longitudinal studies of adult psychological development*. New York: Guilford Press.

Schaie, K. W. (1983b). The Seattle longitudinal study: A twenty-one-year exploration of psychometric intelligence in adulthood. In K. W. Schaie (Ed.), *Longitudinal studies of adult psychological development* (pp. 64–135). New York: Guilford Press.

Schaie, K. W. (1987). Intelligence. In G. L. Maddox (Ed.), *The encyclopedia of aging* (pp. 357–358). New York: Springer.

Schaie, K. W., & Strother, C. R. (1968). A cross-sequential study of age changes in cognitive behavior. *Psychological Bulletin, 70*, 671–680.

Schaie, K. W., & Willis, S. L. (1986). *Adult development and aging* (2nd ed.). Boston: Little, Brown.

Scheiber, B. (1981). *One step at a time*. Washington, DC: U.S. Government Printing Office.

Schein, E. H. (1980). *Organizational Psychology*. Englewood Cliffs, NJ: Prentice Hall.

Schilling, R., Gilchrist, L., & Schinke, S. (1984). Coping and social support in families of developmentally disabled children. *Family Relations, 33*, 47–54.

Schinke, S. P., & Gilchrist, L. D. (1983). Coping with contraception: Cognitive and behavioral methods with adolescents. *Cognitive Therapy & Research, 7*, 379–388.

Schinke, S. P., Schilling, R. F., Gilchrist, L. D., Barth, R., Bobo, J. K., Trimble, J. E., & Cvetkovich, G. T. (1985). Preventing substance abuse among American Indian youth. *Social Casework, 66*, 213–317.

Schmidt, G., & Weiner, B. (1988). Measuring loneliness in different relationships. *Journal of Personality and Social Psychology, 44*, 1038–1047.

Schoem, D., Frankel, L., Zuniga, X., & Lewis, E. A. (Eds.). (1993). *Multicultural teaching in the university*. Westport, CT: Praeger.

Schoen, J., & Fischell, A. (1991). Pain in neonatal circumcision. *Clinical Pediatrics, 30*, 429–432.

Schriver, J. M. (1995). *Human behavior and the social environment: Shifting paradigms in essential knowledge for social work practice*. Boston: Allyn & Bacon.

Schulz, R., Visintainer, P., & Williamson, G. M. (1990). Psychiatric and physical morbidity effects of caregiving. *Journal of Gerontology, 45*, 181–191.

Schuster, C. S., & Ashburn, S. S. (1986). *The process of human development: A holistic life-span approach* (2nd ed.). Boston: Little, Brown.

Schuster, C. S., & Ashburn, S. S. (1992). *The process of human development: A holistic life-span approach* (3rd ed.). Philadelphia: Lippincott.

Schwartz, S., & Johnson, J. H. (1985). *Psychopathology of childhood*. New York: Pergamon Press.

Schwitalla, A. M. (1930). Proceedings of the National Conference of Social Work (pp. 544–551). Chicago: University of Chicago Press.

Sears, R. R., Maccoby, E. E., & Leven, H. (1957). *Patterns of childrearing*. New York: Harper & Row.

Seccombe, K. (1991). Assessing the costs and benefits of children: Gender comparisons among child-free husbands and wives. *Journal of Marriage and the Family, 53*, 191–202.

Segal, J., & Yahraes, H. (1978). *A child's journey: Forces that shape the lives of our young*. New York: McGraw-Hill.

Segal, J., & Yahraes, H. (1978, November). Bringing up mother. *Psychology Today*, pp. 90–96.

Seidman, S. N., & Rieder, R. O. (1994). A review of sexual behavior in the United States. *American Journal of Psychiatry, 151*, 330–341.

Seifer, R., & Dickstein, S. (1993). Parental mental illness and infant development. In C. Zeanah (Ed.), *Handbook of infant mental health* (pp. 120–142). New York: Guilford Press.

Seitz, V., Rosenbaum, L. K., & Apfel, N. H. (1985). Effects of family support intervention: A 10-year follow-up. *Child Development*, 376–391.

Seligman, M. E. P. (1975). *Helplessness: On depression, development and death*. San Francisco: W. H. Freeman.

Seligman, M. E. P. (1995, May). Is self-esteem really all that important? *APA Monitor.*

Selman, R. L. (1980). *The growth of interpersonal understanding.* New York: Academic Press.

Selman, R. L. (1990). *Making a friend in youth: Developmental theory and pair therapy.* Chicago: University of Chicago Press.

Selman, R. L., Jaquette, D., & Lavin, D. (1977). Interpersonal awareness in children: Toward an integration of developmental and clinical child psychology. *American Journal of Orthopsychiatry, 47,* 264–274.

Seltzer, J. A., & Bianchi, S. M. (1988). Children's contact with absent parents. *Journal of Marriage and the Family, 50,* 663–677.

Sepkoski, C. (1992). The effects of maternal epidural anesthesia on neonatal behavior during the first month. *Developmental Medicine & Child Neurology, 34,* 1072–1080.

Severino, S. K., Teusink, J. P., Pender, V. B., & Bernstein, A. E. (1986). Overview: The psychology of grandparenthood. *Journal of Geriatric Psychiatry, 19,* 3–17.

Seymour, D. Z. (1974). Black children. Black speech. In F. Rebelsky & L. Dorman (Eds.), *Child development and behavior* (2nd ed.). New York: Knopf.

Shaffer, D. R. (1989). *Developmental psychology: Childhood and adolescence* (2nd ed.). Pacific Grove, CA: Brooks/Cole.

Shaffer, D. R., (1993). *Developmental psychology: Childhood and adolescence* (3rd ed.). Pacific Grove, CA: Brooks/Cole.

Shafritz, J. M., & Whitbeck, P. H. (1978). *Classics of organization theory.* Oak Park, IL: Moore.

Shanas, E., Townsend, P., Wedderburn, D., Friis, H., Milhoj, P., & Stehouwer, B. (1968). *Old people in three industrial societies.* New York: Atherton.

Shantz, C. U. (1983). Social cognition. In P. H. Mussen (Ed.), *Handbook of child psychology* (4th ed., Vol. 3). New York: Wiley.

Shatz, M., & Gelman, R. (1973). The development of communication skills: Modifications in the speech of young children as a function of the listener. *Monographs of the Society for Research in Child Development, 38*(5, Serial No. 52).

Shaw, M. E. (1981). *Group dynamics: The psychology of small group behavior.* New York: McGraw-Hill.

Shea, J. D. C. (1981). Changes in interpersonal distances and categories of play behavior in the early weeks of preschool. *Developmental Psychology, 17,* 417–425.

Sheehan, G. J., & Martyn, M. (1970). Stuttering and its disappearance. *Journal of Speech and Hearing Research, 13,* 279–289.

Sheehy, G. (1976). *Passages.* New York: Dutton.

Sherif, M., Harvey, O. J., White, B. J., Hood, W. R., & Sherif, C. W. (1961). *Intergroup conflict and cooperation: The Robber's Cave experiment.* Norman, OK: Institute of Group Relations, University of Oklahoma.

Sherman, E. (1987). *The meaning of midlife transitions.* Albany: State University of New York.

Shipman, G. (1968). The psychodynamics of sex education. *Family Coordinator, 17,* 3–12.

Shoemaker, D. J. (1989). Transfer of children and the importance of grandmothers among the Navajo Indians. *Journal of Cross-Cultural Gerontology, 4,* 1–18.

Shure, M., & Spivack, G. (1980). Interpersonal problem solving as a mediator of behavioral adjustment in preschool and kindergarten children. *Journal of Applied Developmental Psychology, 1,* 37–52.

Sidel, R. (1990). *On her own: Growing up in the shadow of the American dream.* New York: Viking Penguin.

Siegler, R. S. (1995, January). New cognitive research making waves. *APA Monitor.*

Sigelman, C. K., & Shaffer, D. R. (1991). *Life-span development.* Pacific Grove, CA: Brooks/Cole.

Sigelman, C. K., & Shaffer, D. R. (1995). *Life-span development.* Pacific Grove, CA: Brooks/Cole.

Sigman, M. (1991). Continuity in cognitive abilities from infancy to 12 years of age. *Cognitive Development, 6,* 47–57.

Silverman, P. R. (1987a). Mutual aid groups. In *Encyclopedia of Social Work* (18th ed., pp. 1171–1176). Silver Spring, MD: National Association of Social Workers.

Silverman, P. R. (1987b). Widowhood as the next stage in the life course. In H. Lopata (Ed.), *Widows: Vol. II. North America* (171–190). Durham, NC: Duke University Press.

Silverstein, B., & Krate, R. (1975). *Children of the dark ghetto: A developmental psychology.* New York: Praeger.

Simmons, R. G., & Blyth, D. A. (1987). *Moving into adolescence.* Hawthorne, NY: Aldine.

Simmons, R. G., Rosenberg, F., & Rosenberg, M. (1973). Disturbance in self-image at adolescence. *American Sociological Review, 38,* 553–568.

Simons, M. (1995, September 11). Dutch doctors to tighten rules on mercy killings. *New York Times International.*

Simons, R. (1987). *After the tears.* San Diego: Harcourt Brace Jovanovich.

Singer, D. G., & Singer, J. L. (1987). Practical suggestions for controlling television. *Journal of Early Adolescence, 7,* 365–369.

Sizer, T. R. (1983). High school reform: The need for engineering. *Phi Delta Kappan,* 679–683.

Skeels, H. M. (1936). The mental development of children in foster homes. *Pedagogical Seminary and Journal of Genetic Psychology, 49,* 91–106.

Skinner, B. F. (1953). *Science and human behavior.* New York: Macmillan.

Skinner, L. (1979). *Motor development in the preschool years.* Springfield, IL: Charles C Thomas.

Skodak, M. (1939). Children in foster homes: A study of mental development. *University of Iowa Studies in Child Welfare, 16*(1).

Skodak, M., & Skeels, H. (1945). A follow-up study of children in adoptive homes. *Journal of Genetic Psychology, 66,* 21–58.

Skodak, M., & Skeels, H. (1949). A follow-up study of one hundred adopted children. *Journal of Genetic Psychology, 75,* 85–125.

Skolnick, A. (1986). *The psychology of human development.* New York: Harcourt Brace Jovanovich.

Slaby, R. G., & Crowley, C. G. (1977). Modification of cooperation and aggression through teacher attention to children's speech. *Journal of Experimental Child Psychology, 23,* 442–458.

Sleek, S. (1994, November). Therapists, both male and female, fall victim to stereotypes of men. *APA Monitor,* pp. 6–7.

Smart, B. (1993). *Postmodernity: Key ideas.* London: Routledge.

Smetana, J. G. (1988). Adolescents' and parents' conceptions of parental authority. *Child Development, 59,* 321–335.

Smetana, J. G., Yau, J., Restrepo, A., & Braeges, J. L. (1991). Conflict and adaptation in adolescence: Adolescent-parent conflict. In M. E. Colten & S. Gore (Eds.), *Adolescent stress.* New York: Aldine de Gruyter.

Smilansky, S. (1968). *The effects of sociodramatic play on disadvantaged preschool children.* New York: Wiley.

Smith, P., & Daglish, L. (1977). Sex differences in parent and infant behavior in the home. *Child Development, 48,* 1250–1254.

Smith, P. K., & Connolly, K. J. (1980). *The ecology of preschool behavior.* New York: Cambridge University Press.

Smith, R. (1995, July). The adoption equation, minus race. *NASW News,* 3.

Smith, T. W., & Pope, M. K. (1990). Cynical hostility as a health risk: Current status and future directions. *Journal of Social Behavior and Personality, 5,* 77–88.

Solomon, R. C. (1988). *About love: Reinventing romance for modern times.* New York: Simon & Schuster.

Sonenstein, F., Pleck, J., & Ku, L. (1989). Sexual activity, condom use and AIDS awareness in a national sample of adolescent males. *Family Planning Perspectives, 21,* 152–158.

Southern Poverty Law Center. (1994). The intelligence report, August. Atlanta, GA: Southern Poverty Law Center.

Specht, R., & Craig, G. (1987). *Human development: A social work perspective.* Englewood Cliffs, NJ: Prentice Hall.

Spelke, E. (1985). Perception of unity, persistence, and identity: Thoughts on infants' conception of objects. In J. Mehler & R. Fox (Eds.), *Neonate cognition.* Hillsdale, NJ: Erlbaum.

Spelke, E. (1994). Initial knowledge: Six suggestions. *Cognition, 50,* 431–445.

Spencer, L. J. (1989). *Winning through participation.* Dubuque, IA: Institute of Cultural Affairs.

Spencer, M. B., & Dornbusch, S. M. (1990). Challenges in studying minority youth. In S. Feldman & G. R. Elliott (Eds.), *At the threshold: The developing adolescent.* Cambridge, MA: Harvard University Press.

Spitz, R. (1945). Hospitalism: An inquiry into the genesis of psychiatric conditions in early childhood. *Psychoanalytic Study of the Child, 1,* 53–74.

Spitz, R. A. (1966). *No and yes: On the genesis of human communication.* New York: International Universities Press.

Sprich-Buckminster, S. (1993). Are perinatal complications relevant to the manifestation of ADD? *Journal of the American Academy of Child and Adolescent Psychiatry, 32,* 1032–1037.

Spurlock, J. (1984). Black women in the middle years. In G. Baruch & J. Brooks-Gunn (Eds.), *Women in midlife.* New York: Plenum.

Stacey, N., Deardon, R., Pill, R., & Robinson, D. (1970). *Hospitals, children, and their families: The report of a pilot study.* London: Routledge & Kegan Paul.

Stainton, C., McNeil, D., & Harvey, S. (1992). Maternal tasks of uncertain motherhood. *Maternal-Child Nursing Journal, 20,* 113–123.

Stake, J. E., DeVille, C. J., & Rennell, C. L. (1983). The effects of assertiveness training on the performance self-esteem of adolescent girls. *Journal of Youth and Adolescence, 12,* 435–442.

Staples, R. (1988). The Black American family. In C. H. Mindel, R. W. Habenstein, & R. Wright (Eds.), *Ethnic families in America: Patterns and variations* (3rd ed.). New York: Elsevier.

Stark, E. (1989, October). Teen boys get condom sense. *Psychology Today,* p. 63.

Starr, B. D., & Weiner, M. B. (1982). *The Starr-Weiner report on sex and sexuality in the mature years.* New York: McGraw-Hill.

Staub, E. (1984). Steps toward a comprehensive theory of moral conduct: Goal orientation, social behavior, kindness, and cruelty. In W. M. Kurtines & J. L. Gewirtz (Eds.), *Morality, moral behavior, and moral development.* New York: Wiley.

Steil, J. M., & Turetsky, B. A. (1987). Is equal better? The relationship between marital equality and psychological symptomatology. In S. Oskamp (Ed.), *Family process and problems: Social psychological aspects.* Newbury Park, CA: Sage.

Stein, N. (1995, June). New cognitive research making waves. *APA Monitor.*

Steinberg, L. (1990). Autonomy, conflict, and harmony in the family relationship. In S. Feldman & G. Elliot (Eds.), *At the threshold: The developing adolescent* (pp. 255–276). Cambridge, MA: Harvard University Press.

Steinberg, L. (1995). *How your child's adolescence triggers your own crisis.* New York: Simon & Schuster.

Steinberg, L., & Silverberg, S. (1986). The vicissitudes of autonomy in early adolescence. *Child Development, 57,* 841–851.

Steiner, R. F., & Pomerantz, S. (1981). *The chemistry of living systems.* New York: Van Nostrand Reinhold.

Stenback, A. (1980). Depression and suicidal behavior in old age. In J. E. Birren & R. B. Sloane (Eds.). *Handbook of mental health and aging.* Englewood Cliffs, NJ: Prentice Hall.

Stephens, M.A.P., Kinney, J. M., & Ogrocki, P. K. (1991). Stressors and well-being among caregivers to older adults with dementia: The in-home versus nursing home experience. *The Gerontologist, 31,* 217–223.

Stern, D. (1985). *The interpersonal world of the infant: A view from psychoanalysis and developmental psychology.* New York: Basic Books.

Stern, D. (1990). *Diary of a baby.* New York: Basic Books.

Sternberg, R. J. (1986). A triangular theory of love. *Psychological Review, 93,* 119–135.

Sternberg, R. J. (1988). Triangulating love. In R. J. Sternberg & M. L. Barnes (Eds.), *The psychology of love.* New Haven, CT: Yale University Press.

Steur, F. B., Applefield, J. M., & Smith, R. (1971). Televised aggression and interpersonal aggression of preschool children. *Journal of Experimental Child Psychology, 11,* 442–447.

Stevenson, H. (1995, May). Is self-esteem really all that important? *APA Monitor.*

Stevenson, J. C. (1995). *British Journal of Clinical Practice, 49,* 87–90.

Stevenson, L. (1974). *Seven theories of human nature.* New York: Oxford University Press.

Stevenson, L. (1981). *The study of human nature: Readings.* New York: Oxford University Press.

Stewart, R. B. (1983). Sibling Interaction: The role of older child as teacher for the younger. *Merrill-Palmer Quarterly, 29,* 47–68.

Stewart, R. B, Mobley, L. A., Van Tuyl, S. S., & Salvador, M. A. (1987). The firstborn's adjustment to the birth of a sibling: A longitudinal assessment. *Child Development, 58,* 341–355.

Stipp, D. (1995, May 24). Our prehistoric past casts ills in new light, some scientists say. *The Wall Street Journal,* pp. 1, 5.

St. James, J. (1987). *Inside baby's head.* Burton, OH: Palamora.

Stoner, J.A.F. (1961). *A comparison of individual and group decisions involving risk.* Unpublished master's thesis, Massachusetts Institute of Technology, Cambridge.

Stott, D. (1971). The child's hazards in utero. In J. G. Howells (Ed.), *Modern perspectives in international child psychiatry.* New York: Brunner/Mazel.

Strahan, D. B. (1983). The emergence of formal operations in adolescence. *Transcendence, 11,* 7–14.

Strauss, M., Gelles, R., & Steinmetz, S. (1980). *Behind closed doors.* New York: Doubleday.

Strauss, M. A. & Gelles, R. J. (1986). Societal change and change in family violence from 1975 to 1985 as revealed in two national surveys. *Journal of Marriage and the Family, 48,* 465–479.

Streissguth, A., LaDue, R., & Randels, S. (1988). *A manual on adolescents and adults with fetal alcohol syndrome with special reference to American Indians.* Rockville, MD: U.S. Department of Health and Human Services.

Stringer, G. M., & Rants-Rodriguez, D. (1987). *So what's it to me?* Renton, WA: King County Rape Relief.

Stroufe, L. A., Fox, N. E., and Pancake, V. R. (1983). Attachment and dependency in developmental perspective. *Child Development, 54,* 1615–1627.

Stuart, R. B. (1980). *Helping couples change.* New York: Guilford Press.

Stueve, A., & O'Donnell, L. (1984). The daughter of aging parents. In G. Baruch & J. Brooks-Gunn (Eds.), *Women in midlife.* New York: Plenum.

Sumner, W. G. (1906/1960). *Folkways.* New York: New American Library.

Sunderland, T., Lawlor, B. A., Molchan, S. E., & Martinez, R. A. (1988). Depressive symptoms in the elderly: Special concerns. *Psychopharmacology Bulletin, 24,* 567–576.

Suomi, S., & Harlow, H. (1972). Social rehabilitation of isolate-reared monkeys. *Developmental Psychology, 6,* 487–496.

Super, D. E., Kowalski, R., & Gotkin, E. (1967). *Floundering and trial after high school.* Unpublished manuscript, Columbia University, New York.

Swanson, J. M., McBurnett, K., Wigal, T., Pfieffer, E. J., Lerner, M. D., Williams, L., Christian, D. L., Tamm, L., Willcut, E., Crowley, K., Clevenger, W., Khouzam, N., Woo, C., Crinella, F. M., & Fisher, T. D. (1993). Effect of stimulant medication on children with attention deficit disorder: A "review of reviews." *Exceptional Children, 60,* 154–162.

Symanski, M. (1992). Maternal-infant bonding: Practice issues for the 1990's. *Journal of Nurse-Midwifery, 37,* 67–73.

Takahashi, K. (1986). Examining the strange-situation procedure with Japanese mothers and 12-month-old infants. *Developmental Psychology, 22*(2), 265–270.

Takaki, R. (1993). *A different mirror: A history of multicultural America.* Boston: Little, Brown.

Tannen, D. (1991). *You just don't understand: Women and men in conversation.* New York: Morrow.

Task Force on Homelessness and Severe Mental Illness. (1992). *Outcasts on main street.* (DHHS Publication No. ADM 92–1904). Rockville, MD: Department of Health and Human Services.

Tavris, C. (1992). *The mismeasure of women.* New York: Simon and Schuster.

Tavris, C., & Wade, C. (1984). *The longest war: Sex differences in perspective.* New York: Harcourt Brace Jovanovich.

Taylor, F. W. (1947). *Scientific management.* New York: Harper & Row.

Taylor, I. (1976). *Introduction to Psycholinguistics.* New York: Holt, Rinehart & Winston.

Tedder, J. (1991). Using the Brazelton neonatal assessment scale to facilitate the parent-infant relationship in a primary care setting. *Nurse Practitioner, 16,* 26–36.

Tellegen, A., Lykken, D. T., Bouchard, T. J., Wilcox, K. J., & Rich, S. (1988). Personality similarity in twins reared apart and together. *Journal of Personality and Social Psychology, 54,* 1031–1039.

Terkel, S. (1974). *Working: People talk about what they do all day and how they feel about what they do.* New York: Pantheon Books.

Termine, N. (1988). Infants' responses to their mothers' expressions of joy and sadness. *Developmental Psychology, 24,* 223–229.

Thoma, S. J. (1986). Estimating gender differences in the comprehension and preference of moral issues. *Developmental Review, 6,* 165–180.

Thomas, A., & Chess, S. (1977). *Temperament and development.* New York: Brunner/Mazel.

Thomas, A., & Chess, S. (1989). Temperament and personality. In G. A. Konnstamm, J. E. Bates, & M. K. Rothbart (Eds.), *Temperament in childhood* (pp. 249–261). New York: Wiley.

Thomas, R. B. (1987). Family adaptation to a child with a chronic illness. In M. H. Rose & R. B. Thomas (Eds.), *Children with chronic conditions: Nursing in a family and community context* (pp. 29–54). Orlando, FL: Grune & Stratton.

Thornburg, H. D. (1981). Sources of sex education among early adolescents. *Journal of Early Adolescence, 1,* 171–184.

Timasheff, N. S. (1967). *Sociological theory.* New York: Random House.

Timberlake, E. M., Sabatino, C. A., & Hooper, S. N. (1982). School social work practice and P.L. 94–142. In R. T. Constable & J. P. Flynn (Eds.), *School social work: Practice and research perspectives.* Pacific Grove, CA: Brooks/Cole.

Tinsley, B., & Parke, R. (1987). Grandparents as interactive and social support agents for families with young infants. *International Journal of Aging & Human Development, 25,* 259–277.

Tizard, B., & Rees, J. (1974). A comparison of the effects of adoption, restoration to the natural mother, and continued institutionalization on the cognitive development of four-year-old children. *Journal of Child Psychology and Psychiatry and Allied Disciplines, 16,* 61–73.

Tolman, R. M., & Bennett, L. (1992). Group work with men who batter. In C. W. LeCroy (Ed.), *Case studies in social work practice.* Belmont, CA: Wadsworth.

Torrey, E. F. (1988). *Nowhere to go: The tragic odyssey of the homeless mentally ill.* New York: Harper & Row.

Toseland, R., & Hacker, L. (1982). Self-help groups and professional involvement. *Social Work, 27,* 341–347.

Toseland, R. W., & Rivas, R. F. (1995). *An introduction to group work practice* (2nd ed.). Needham Heights, MA: Allyn & Bacon.

Toseland, R. W., & Rossiter, C. (1989). Group interventions to support caregivers: A review and analysis. *The Gerontologist, 29,* 438–448.

Towle, C. (1945). *Common human needs: An interpretation for staff in public assistance agencies.* Washington, DC: U.S. Government Printing Office.

Towle, C. (1960). A social work approach to courses in growth and behavior. *Social Service Review. 34,* 402–414.

Troll, L. E. (1986). *Family issues in current gerontology.* New York: Springer.

Troll, L. E., & Bengtson, V. L. (1982). Intergenerational relations throughout the life span. In B. Wolman (Ed.), *Handbook of developmental psychology* (pp. 890–911). Englewood Cliffs, NJ: Prentice Hall.

Trotter, R. (1987, May). You've come a long way, baby. *Psychology Today,* 34–47.

Trout, M. (1995, October). Infant attachment: Assessment, intervention and developmental impact. Workshop presented by M. Trout, Director of the Infant Parent Institute, Tucson, AZ.

Tucker, R. M. (1980). Is hypertension different in the elderly? *Geriatrics, 35,* 28–32.

Turner, J. (1972). *Patterns of social organization: A survey of social institutions.* New York: McGraw-Hill.

Turner, J. (1991). *The structure of sociological theory.* Belmont, CA: Wadsworth.

Turner, R. J., & Avison, W. R. (1985). Assessing risk factors for problem parenting: The significance of social support. *Journal of Marriage and the Family*, 881–892.

Twente, E. E. (1965). Aging, strength, and creativity. *Social Work, 10*, 105–110.

Twente, E. E. (1970). *Never too old.* San Francisco: Jossey-Bass.

U.S. Bureau of the Census. (1987). *Annual report of fertility rates.* Washington, DC: U.S. Government Printing Office.

U.S. Bureau of the Census. (1989). *Statistical abstract of the United States, 1989.* Washington, DC: U.S. Government Printing Office.

U.S. Bureau of the Census. (1990a). Need for personal assistance with everyday activities. *Current population reports*, Series P-25, No. 19. (Publication No. S/N 803-044-00007-4). Washington, DC: U.S. Government Printing Office.

U.S. Bureau of the Census. (1990b). *Statistical abstract of the United States, 1990.* Washington, DC: U.S. Government Printing Office.

U.S. Bureau of the Census. (1991). *Statistical abstract of the United States: 1991.* Washington, DC: U.S. Government Printing Office.

U.S. Department of Justice. (1995). *Women usually victimized by offenders they know.* Bureau of Statistics, the Internet.

U.S. General Accounting Office. (1986). *School dropouts: The extent and nature of the problem."* Report to Congressional Requesters.

U.S. Senate, Special Committee on Aging. (1988). The long-term care challenge. *Developments in aging: 1987* (Vol. 3). Washington, DC: U.S. Government Printing Office.

Vale, J. R. (1980). *Genes, environment, and behavior: An interactionist approach.* New York: Harper & Row.

Vallant, G. E. (1977). *Adaptation to life.* Boston: Little, Brown.

Valzelli, L. (1980). *An approach to neuroanatomical and neurochemical psychophysiology.* Torino, Italy: C. G. Edizioni Medic. Scientifiche.

Van Den Bergh, N. (1986). Renaming: Vehicle for empowerment. In J. Penfield (Ed.), *Women and language in transition.* Albany: State University of New York Press.

Van Den Bergh, N., & Cooper, L. B. (1987). Feminist social work. In A. Minahan (Ed.), *Encyclopedia of social work.* Silver Spring, MD: NASW Press.

Van Ijzendoorn, M. H., & Kroonenberg, P. M. (1988). Cross-cultural patterns of attachment: A meta-analysis of the strange situation. *Child Development, 59*(1), 147–156.

Van Strien, J., Bouma, A., & Bakker, D. (1987). Birth stress, autoimmune diseases and handedness. *Journal of Clinical and Experimental Neuropsychology, 9*, 775–780.

Vantveer, P. (1994). Diet and breast cancer: Trial and error. *Annals of Medicine, 26*, 453–460.

Vasconcellos, J. (1927). *Indologia: Una interpretación de la cultura iberoamericano.* Barcelona: Agencia Mundial de Liberia.

Veevers, J. E. (1980). *Childless by choice.* Toronto: Butterworths.

Verdoux, H. (1993). A comparative study of obstetric history in schizophrenics, bipolar patients and normal subjects. *Schizophrenia Research, 9*, 67–69.

Vetter, H. J. (1969). *Language behavior and communication: An introduction.* Itasca, IL: F. E. Peacock.

Visher, E. B., & Visher, J. S. (1988). Old loyalties, new ties. New York: Brunner/Mazel.

Viviansayles, P. J. (1993, May/June). The politics of breast cancer. *Ms.*, pp. 54–55.

Vygotsky, L. S. (1962). *Thought and language.* Cambridge: Massachusetts Institute of Technology Press.

Wagner, D. A., & Stevenson, H. W. (1982). *Cultural perspectives on child development.* San Francisco: W. H. Freeman.

Wald, E. (1989). Family: Stepfamilies. In *Encyclopedia of social work* (pp. 555–561). Silver Spring, MD: National Association of Social Workers.

Walker, L. J. (1989). A longitudinal study of moral reasoning. *Child Development, 60*, 157–166.

Wallerstein, J. S. (1984). Children of divorce: Preliminary report of a ten-year follow-up of young children. *American Journal of Orthopsychiatry, 57*, 199–211.

Wallerstein, J. S. (1988). Children of divorce: Stress and developmental tasks. In N. Garmezy & M. Rutter (Eds.). *Stress, coping, and development in children.* Baltimore: Johns Hopkins University Press.

Wallerstein, J. S. (1995). *The good marriage: How and why love lasts.* Boston: Houghton Mifflin.

Wallerstein, J. S., & Blakeslee, S. (1989). *Second chances.* New York: Ticknor & Fields.

Wallerstein, J. S., Corbin, S. B., & Lewis, J. M. (1988). Children of divorce: A ten-year study. In E. M. Hetherington & J. Arasteh (Eds.), *Impact of divorce, single-parenting, and step-parenting on children.* Hillsdale, NJ: Erlbaum.

Warr, P. (1992). Age and occupational well-being. *Psychology and Aging, 7*, 37–45.

Warren, K. (1985). Alcohol-related birth defects: Current trends in research. *Alcohol Health and Research World, 10*, 4.

Waters, M. (1994). *Modern sociological theory.* London: Sage.

Watson, J. B. (1925). *Behaviorism.* New York: Norton.

Watts, T. (1985). Ethnomethodogy. In R. M. Grinnell (Ed.), *Social work research and evaluation* (pp. 357–369). Itasca, IL: F. E. Peacock.

Waxman, H. M., McCreary, G., Weinrit, R. M., & Carner,

E. A. (1985). A comparison of somatic complaints among depressed and non-depressed older persons. *The Gerontologist, 25*, 501–507.

Weideger, P. (1976). *Menstruation and menopause.* New York: Knopf.

Weinman, J. (1987). *An outline of psychology as applied medicine.* Bristol: John Wright.

Weinraub, M., Clemens, L. P., Sockloff, A., Ethridge, T., Gracely, E., & Myers, B. (1984). The development of sex-role stereotypes in the third year: Relationships to gender labelling, gender identity, sex-typed toy preferences, and family characteristics. *Child Development, 55,* 1493–1503.

Weiss, R. S. (1975). *Marital separation.* New York: Basic Books.

Weiten, W. (1992). *Psychology* (2nd ed.). Pacific Grove, CA: Brooks/Cole.

Weiten, W. (1995). *Psychology: Themes and variations.* Pacific Grove, CA: Brooks/Cole.

Weiten, W., & Lloyd, M. A. (1994). *Psychology applied to modern life* (4th ed.). Pacific Grove, CA: Brooks/Cole.

Weithorn, L. A. (1984). Children's capacities in legal contexts. In N. D. Reppucci, L. A. Weithorn, E. P. Mulvey, & J. Monahan (Eds.), *Children, mental health, and the law.* Beverly Hills, CA: Sage.

Wells, S. J. (1995). Child abuse and neglect overview. In *Encyclopedia of social work* (19th ed.). Washington DC: NASW Press.

Werner, E. E., & Smith, R. S. (1982). *Vulnerable but invincible: A longitudinal study of resilience and youth.* New York: McGraw-Hill.

Werry, J. S., & Quay, H. C. (1971). The prevalence of behavior symptoms in younger elementary school children. *American Journal of Orthopsychiatry, 41,* 136–143.

West, D. J., & Farrington, D. P. (1973). *Who becomes delinquent?* London: Heinemann.

Westinghouse Learning Corporation. (1969). *The impact of Head Start: An evaluation of the effects of Head Start on children's cognitive and affectional development.* Report to the Office of Economic Opportunity. Washington, DC: Learning House for Federal Scientific and Technical Information.

White, J. L. (1989). *The troubled adolescent.* New York: Pergamon Press.

White, L. K. (1990). Determinants of divorce: A review of research in the eighties. *Journal of Marriage and the Family, 32,* 904–912.

White, R. W. (1959). Motivation reconsidered: The concept of competence. *Psychological Review, 66,* 297–333.

White, R. W. (1966). *Lives in progress* (2nd ed.). New York: Holt, Rinehart & Winston.

Whitfield, C. L. (1991). *Co-dependence: Healing the human condition.* Deerfield Beach, FL: Health Communications.

Whiting, B. B., & Whiting, J. W. M. (1975). *Children of 6 cultures: A psychocultural analysis.* Cambridge, MA: Harvard University Press.

Whittaker, J. K., & Garbarino, J. (1983). *Social support networks: Informal helping in the human services.* Hawthorne, NY: Aldine.

Whol, T. (1963). Correlation of anxiety and hostility with adrenocortical function. *Journal of the American Medical Association, 183,* 133–144.

Whorf, B. L. (1956). *Language, thought, and reality.* New York: Wiley.

Widmayer, S., & Field, T. (1980). Effects of Brazelton demonstrations on early interactions of preterm infants and their teen-age mothers. *Infant Behavior and Development, 3,* 79–89.

Widom, C. S. (1989). Does violence beget violence? A critical examination of the literature. *American Psychologist, 106,* 3–28.

Wigfield, R. (1994). SIDS: Risk reduction measures. *Early Human Development, 38,* 161–164.

William T. Grant Foundation (1988). *The forgotten half: Non-college youth in America.* Washington, DC: Youth and America's future: The William T. Grant Foundation on Work, Family and Citizenship.

Williams, C. L., & Berry, J. W. (1991). Primary prevention of acculturative stress among refugees. *American Psychologist, 46,* 632–641.

Williams, J. B. W., Karls, J. M., & Wandrei, K. (1989). The person-in-environment (PIE) system for describing problems of social functioning. *Hospital and Community Psychiatry, 40,* 1125–1127.

Willinger, M., Hoffman, H., & Hartford, R. (1994). Infant sleep position and risk for sudden infant death syndrome: Report of meeting held January 13 and 14, 1994, National Institutes of Health, Bethesda, Md. *Pediatrics, 93,* pp. 814–819.

Willis, D., & Holden, E. (1990). Etiological factors contributing to deviant development. In J. Johnson & J. Goldman (Eds.), *Developmental assessment in clinical child psychology* (pp. 38–57). New York: Pergamon Press.

Willis, S. L. (1989). Adult intelligence. In S. Hunter and M. Sundel (Eds.), *Midlife myths: Issues, findings, and practice implications.* Newbury Park, CA: Sage.

Willis, S. L., & Nesselroade, C. S. (1990). Long-term effects of fluid ability training in old age. *Developmental Psychology, 26,* 905–910.

Wilson, E. O. (1985). *Sociobiology: The new synthesis.* Cambridge, MA: Harvard University Press.

Wilson, K. J. (1987). *Anatomy and physiology in health and illness.* New York: Churchill Livingstone.

Winawer, S., & Shike, M. (1995). *Cancer free: The comprehensive cancer prevention program.* New York: Simon & Schuster.

Wine, J. D., & Smye, M. D. (1981). *Social competence.* New York: Guilford Press.

Wise, M. G. (1986). Working with medicated clients: A primer for social workers. *Health and Social Work, 11,* 36–41.

Wise, P. (1992). Infant mortality as a social mirror. *New England Journal of Medicine, 326,* 1558–1559.

Wisensale, S. K. (1992). Toward the 21st century: Family change and public policy. *Family Relations, 41,* 417–422.

Wisniewski, J. J., & Toomey, B. G. (1987). Are social workers homophobic? *Social Work, 32,* 454–464.

Wolf, R. B., & Pillemer, K. A. (1989). *Helping elderly victims.* New York: Columbia University Press.

Wolfgang, C. H. (1977). *Helping aggressive and passive preschoolers through play.* Columbus, OH: Merrill.

Wood, N. (1974). *Many winters.* Santa Fe, NM: William Gannon.

Wood, V., & Robertson, J. F. (1978). Friendship and kinship interaction: Differential effect on the morale of the elderly. *Journal of Marriage and the Family, 40,* 367–375.

Wood, W. (1987). Meta-analytic review of sex differences in group performance. *Psychological Bulletin, 102,* 53–71.

Woodman, N. J., & Lenna, H. R. (1980). *Counseling with gay men and women: A guide for facilitating positive life-styles.* San Francisco: Jossey-Bass.

Woods, N. F., Most, A., & Dery, G. K. (1982). Prevalence of premenstrual symptoms. *American Journal of Public Health, 72,* 1257–1264.

Worden, W. (1991). *Grief counseling and grief therapy: A handbook for the mental health practitioner.* New York: Springer.

Wright, P. H., & Wright, K. D. (1991). Codependency: Addictive love, adjustive relating, or both? *Contemporary Family Therapy: An International Journal, 13,* 435–454.

Wyer, R. S., & Srull, T. K. (Eds.). (1984). *Handbook of social cognition* (Vol. 1). Hillsdale, NJ: Erlbaum.

Wynn, K. (1992). Addition and subtraction by human infants. *Nature, 358,* 749–750.

Yalom, I. (1985). *The theory and practice of group psychotherapy* (3rd ed.). New York: Basic Books.

Yankelovich, D. (1981). *New rules: Searching for self-fulfillment in a world turned upside down.* New York: Bantam Books.

Yesavage, J. A., Brink, T. L., Rose, T. L., et al. (1983). Development and validation of a geriatric depression rating scale: A preliminary report. *Journal of Psychiatric Research, 17,* 37–49.

Yogman, M. (1982). Development of the father-infant relationship. In H. Fitzgerald, B. Lester, & M. Uogman (Eds.), *Theory and research in behavioral pediatrics* (pp. 221–279). New York: Plenum.

Yogman, M. W., Cooley, J., & Kindlon, D. (1988). Fathers, infants, and toddlers. In P. Bronstein & C. P. Cowan (Eds.), *Fatherhood today: Men's changing role in the family.* New York: Wiley.

Young, J. E. (1982). Loneliness, depression and cognitive therapy: Theory and application. In L. A. Peplau & D. Perlman (Eds.), *Loneliness: A sourcebook of current theory, research, and therapy.* New York: Wiley.

Young, R. F., & Kahana, E. (1989). Specifying caregiver outcomes: Gender and relationship aspects of caregiving strain. *The Gerontologist, 29,* 660–666.

Young, V. H. (1970). Family and childhood in a southern Negro community. *American Anthropologist, 72*(2), 269–288.

Youngstrom, N. (1990, October). Seriously mentally ill need better tracking. *APA Monitor,* pp. 18–19.

Youngstrom, N. (1991, September). Drug exposure in home elicits worst behaviors. *APA Monitor,* p. 23.

Youngstrom, N. (1991, October). Warning: Teens at risk for AIDS. *APA Monitor,* p. 38.

Yule, W. (1981). The epidemiology of child psychopathology. In B. Lahey & A. Kazdin (Eds.), *Advances in clinical child psychology* (Vol. 4). New York: Plenum.

Yussen, S. R. (1977). Characteristics of moral dilemmas written by adolescents. *Developmental Psychology, 13,* 162–163.

Zajonc, R. B. (1980). Feeling and thinking: Preferences need no inferences. *American psychologist, 35,* 151–175.

Zajonc, R. B. (1984). On the primacy of affect. *American Psychologist, 39,* 117–123.

Zajonc, R. B., & Markus, G. B. (1975). Birth order and intellectual development. *Psychological Review, 82,* 74–88.

Zametkin, A. J., Nordahl, T., Gross, M., King, A. C., Semple, W. E., Rumsey, J., Hamburger, S., & Cohen, R. M. (1990). Cerebral glucose metabolism in adults with hyperactivity of childhood onset. *New England Journal of Medicine, 322,* 1361–1366.

Zastrow, C. & Kirst-Ashman, K. K. (1994). *Understanding human behavior and the social environment* (3rd ed.). Chicago: Nelson-Hall.

Zausmer, E. (1978). Gross motor developmental stimulation. In S. M. Pueschel (Ed.), *Down syndrome: Growing and learning* (pp. 88–105). New York: Andrews, McMeel & Parker.

Zeanah, C. H., & Emde, R. N. (1994). Attachment disorders in infancy and childhood. In M. Rutter, E. Taylor, & L.

Hersou (Eds.), *Child and adolescent psychiatry: Modern approaches* (pp. 490–504). Oxford: Blackwell Scientific.

Zelazo, R., Zelazo, N., & Kolb, S. (1972). "Walking" in the newborn. *Science, 176,* 314–315.

Zellman, G. L., & Eisen, M. (1984). Factors predicting pregnancy resolution decision satisfaction of unmarried adolescents. *Journal of Genetic Psychology, 145,* 231–234.

Zigler, E. (1973). Project Head Start: Success or failure? *Learning, 1,* 43–47.

Zigler, E., & Finn-Stevenson, M. (1992). Applied developmental psychology. In M. E. Lamb & M. Bornstein (Eds.), *Developmental psychology: An advanced textbook* (3rd ed.). Hillsdale, NJ: Erlbaum.

Zigler, E., & Stevenson, M. F. (1993). *Children in a changing world: Development and social issues* (2nd ed.). Pacific Grove, CA: Brooks/Cole.

Zigler, E., Taussig, C., & Black, K. (1992). Early childhood intervention: A promising preventive for juvenile delinquency. *American Psychologist, 47,* 997–1006.

Zigler, E., & Trickett, P. E. (1978). IQ, social competence, and evaluation of early childhood intervention programs. *American Psychologist, 33,* 789–798.

Zigler, E., & Valentine, J. (1979). *Project Head Start: A legacy of the War on Poverty.* New York: Free Press.

Zimbardo, P. G. (1987). *Shyness.* New York: Jove.

Zolotow, C. (1968). *My friend John.* New York: Harper & Row.

Index

Credits

Chapter 1: 6, Figure 1.1, from *The Dual Perspective*, by D. Norton et al. Copyright © 1978 Council on Social Work Education. Reprinted with permission.

Chapter 2: 26, Figure 2.2, from *Genetic Content for Graduate Social Work Education*, by J. Rauch, p. 138. Copyright © 1988 Council on Social Work Education. Reprinted with permission. **27,** Figure 2.3, from *Genetic Content for Graduate Social Work Education*, by J. Rauch, p. 140. Copyright © 1988 Council on Social Work Education. Reprinted with permission. **34,** Figure 2.4, from *Understanding Physical, Sensory, and Health Impairments: Characteristics and Educational Implications*, by K. Heller et al., p. 60, Brooks/Cole Publishing, 1996. **34,** Figure 2.5, from *Psychology*, by E. B. Goldstein, p. 96, Brooks/Cole Publishing, 1994. **36,** Figure 2.7, from *Psychology*, by E. B. Goldstein, p. 92, Brooks/Cole Publishing, 1994. **38,** Figure 2.8, from *Psychology*, by E. B. Goldstein, p. 88, Brooks/Cole Publishing, 1994. **39,** Figure 2.9, from *Psychology*, by E. B. Goldstein, p. 77, Brooks/Cole Publishing, 1994. **40,** Figure 2.10, from *Psychology: Themes and Variations*, Third Edition, by W. Weiten, p. 78, Brooks/Cole Publishing, 1995. **47,** Figure 2.12, from *Health Psychology*, Third Edition, by L. Brannon and J. Feist, Brooks/Cole Publishing, 1997. **48,** Figure 2.13, from *Introduction to Microbiology*, by J. L. Ingraham and C. A. Ingraham, Wadsworth Publishing, 1995. **49,** Figure 2.14, from *Psychology*, by E. B. Goldstein, p. 93, Brooks/Cole Publishing, 1994.

Chapter 3: 57, Figure 3.1, adapted from "Reflections on Dr. Borg's Life Cycle," by E. H. Erikson, in "Adulthood," *Dædalus, 105*, No. 2, Spring 1976, p. 43. Copyright © 1976 American Academy of Arts and Sciences. Adapted with permission. **61,** Figure 3.2, from *Psychology: Themes and Variations*, Third Edition, by W. Weiten, p. 256, Brooks/Cole Publishing, 1995. **62,** Figure 3.3, from *Psychology: Themes and Variations*, Third Edition, by W. Weiten, p. 120, Brooks/Cole Publishing, 1995. **63,** Figure 3.4, from *Psychology: Themes and Variations*, Third Edition, by W. Weiten, p. 143, Brooks/Cole Publishing, 1995. **69,** Figure 3.5, from *Cognitive Psychology: Memory, Language and Thought*, by D. V. Howard, p. 18. Copyright © 1983. Reprinted by permission of Prentice Hall, Upper Saddle River, NJ. **72,** Figure 3.7, from *Psychology: Themes and Variations*, Third Edition, by W. Weiten, p. 317, Brooks/Cole Publishing, 1995. **76,** Figure 3.8, from "Attitudes, Traits, and Actions," by I. Ajzen, 1987, *Advances in Experimental Social Psychology, 20*, 1–63. Copyright © 1987 Academic Press, Inc. Reprinted with permission.

Chapter 4: 86, Figure 4.1, adapted from C. B. Kopp and J. B. Krakow, *Child Development in the Social Context* (figure 12.1, p. 648). Copyright © 1982 by Addison-Wesley Publishing Company, Inc. Adapted by permission of Addison-Wesley Longman Publishing Company, Inc. Adaptation appears in *Life-Span Human Development*, Second Edition, by C. K. Sigelman and D. R.

Shaffer, p. 88, Brooks/Cole Publishing, 1995. **87,** Figure 4.2, from *Clinical Assessment for Social Workers,* by C. Jordan and C. Franklin, p. 23. Copyright © 1995 Lyceum Press. Reprinted with permission. **89,** Figure 4.4, from "Early Human Experience," by J. Belsky, 1981, *Developmental Psychology, 17,* 3–23. Copyright © 1981 American Psychological Association. Reprinted with permission. **91,** Table 4.1, adapted from *The Changing Family Lifecycle,* by B. Carter and M. McGoldrick, p. 15. Copyright © 1988 Allyn & Bacon. Adapted with permission. **92,** Figure 4.5, from "Marital Satisfaction over the Family Life Cycle," by B. C. Rollins & H. Feldman, 1970, *Journal of Marriage and the Family, 32,* 20–28. Copyright © 1970 National Council on Family Relations, 3989 Central Ave. NE, Suite 550, Minneapolis, MN 55421. Reprinted with permission. **93,** Figure 4.6, from *Clinical Assessment for Social Workers,* by C. Jordan and C. Franklin, p. 206. Copyright © 1995 Lyceum Press. Reprinted with permission. **98,** Table 4.2, from *An Introduction to Group Work Practice,* Second Edition, by R. W. Toseland and R. F. Rivas, p. 15. Copyright © 1995. All rights reserved. Reprinted by permission of Allyn & Bacon. **100,** Box 4.1, adapted from "Functional Roles of Group Members," by K. D. Benne & P. Sheats, 1948, *Journal of Social Issues, 4*(2), 41–49. Copyright © The Society for the Psychological Study of Social Issues. Used with permission. Adaptation appears in *Psychology Applied to Modern Life,* Fourth Edition, by W. Weiten and **M. A.** Lloyd, p. 211, Brooks/Cole Publishing, 1994. **102,** Box 4.2, reprinted with the permission of the Free Press, a division of Simon & Schuster, from *Decision Making: A Psychological Analysis of Conflict, Choice, and Commitment,* by Irving L. Janis and Leon Mann. Copyright © 1977 The Free Press. **107–108,** Focus on Theory, from *Modern Sociological Theory,* by M. Waters. Copyright © 1994 Sage Publications Ltd. Reprinted with permission. **110,** Table 4.3, from W. G. Ouchi, *Theory Z: How American Business Can Meet the Japanese Challenge,* p. 58, copyright © 1981 Addison-Wesley Publishing Company, Inc. Reprinted by permission of Addison-Wesley Publishing Company, Inc. **111,** excerpt from *Modern Sociological Theory,* by M. Waters. Copyright © 1994 Sage Publications Ltd. Reprinted with permission. **112,** excerpt from *Understanding Social Theory,* by D. Layder, p. 15. Copyright © 1994 Sage Publications Ltd. Reprinted with permission. **121,** Focus on

Multiculturalism, from *Social Work, Social Welfare, and American Society,* by P. R. Morris and L. H. Leighninger, pp. 645–647. Copyright © 1996 Allyn & Bacon. Reprinted by permission. **122–123,** excerpt from "White Privilege and Male Privilege," by P. McIntosh, 1988, *Working Papers Series,* Wellesley College Center for Research on Women. Copyright © 1988. Reprinted with the permission of Peggy McIntosh. **125,** Figure 4.7, from "Bicultural Socialization: Factors Affecting Minority Experience," by D. De Ande, 1984, *Social Work, 29,* 172–181. Copyright © 1984 National Association of Social Workers, Inc. Reprinted with permission. **127,** Figure 4.8, from *Social Psychology in the 90's,* Sixth Edition, by K. Deaux, F. C. Dane, and L. Wrightsman, p. 350, Brooks/Cole Publishing, 1993.

Chapter 5: 139, Table 5.1, from John W. Santrock, *Life-Span Development.* Copyright © 1983 Times Mirror Higher Education Group, Inc., Dubuque, Iowa. All rights reserved. Reprinted by permission. **140,** Figure 5.1, adapted from *Before We Are Born: Basic Embryology and Birth Defects,* Fourth Edition, by K. L. Moore. Copyright ©1989 by W. B. Saunders. Adapted by permission. Adaptation appears in *The Psychological Development of Children,* by F. B. Steuer, p. 148, Brooks/Cole Publishing, 1994. **149,** Figure 5.2, from *Children in a Changing World,* Second Edition, by D. F. Zigler and M. Finn Stevenson, p. 133, Brooks/Cole Publishing, 1993. **152,** Figure 5.3, from *Understanding Human Behavior and the Social Environment,* Second Edition, by C. Zastrow and K. K. Kirst-Ashman, p. 30. Copyright © 1990 Nelson-Hall Publishers. Reprinted with permission. **170,** Box 5.1, adapted from "Etiological Factors Contributing to Deviant Development," by D. Willis and E. Holden. In J. Johnson and J. Goldman (Eds.), *Development Assessment in Clinical Child Psychology,* p. 39. Copyright © 1990. All rights reserved. Adapted by permission of Allyn & Bacon.

Chapter 6: 179, Table 6.1, adapted from "The Denver Development Screening Test," by W. K. Frankenberg and J. B. Dodds, 1967, *Journal of Pediatrics, 71,* 181–191. Copyright © 1967 C. V. Mosby Company. Used with permission. Adaptation appears in *Developmental Psychology,* Fourth Edition, by D. R. Shaffer, p. 175, Brooks/Cole Publishing, 1996. **180,** Table 6.2, from *Family-Centered Nursing Care of Children,* by R. Foster, M. Hunsberger, and J. Anderson. Copyright © 1989

Harcourt Brace and Company. Reprinted with permission. **185,** Figure 6.1, reprinted with permission from *Nature,* 282, "Intermodal Matching by Human Neonates," by A. Meltzoff and R. Borton, 403–404. Copyright © 1979 Macmillan Magazines Limited. **187,** Table 6.4, adapted from "Etiological Factors Contributing to Deviant Development," by D. Willis and E. Holden. In J. Johnson and J. Goldman (Eds.), *Development Assessment in Clinical Child Psychology,* p. 5. Copyright © 1990. All rights reserved. Adapted by permission of Allyn & Bacon. **197,** Table 6.6, from "Disorders of Attachment," by C. Zeanah, O. Mammen, and A. Lieberman. In C. Zeanah, Jr. (Ed.), *Handbook of Infant Mental Health,* p. 346. Copyright © 1993 The Guilford Press. Reprinted with permission. **199,** Table 6.7, adapted from "Etiological Factors Contributing to Deviant Development," by D. Willis and E. Holden. In J. Johnson and J. Goldman (Eds.), *Development Assessment in Clinical Child Psychology,* p. 5. Copyright © 1990. All rights reserved. Adapted by permission of Allyn & Bacon. **209,** Focus on Sociology, adapted by Jane Wenk from an article by Tori DeAngelis for the *APA Monitor,* January 1995, p. 36. Copyright © 1995 American Psychological Association. Adapted with permission. **210,** Focus on Research, adapted by Jane Wenk from an article by B. Azar for the *APA Monitor,* June 1995, p. 18. Copyright © 1995 American Psychological Association. Adapted with permission. **214,** Box 6.2, adapted from *Pediatric Nursing,* 14(2), 1988, p. 98. Reprinted with permission of the publisher, Jannetti Publications, Inc., East Holly Avenue Box 56, Pitman, NJ 08071-0056; Phone (609) 256-2300.

Chapter 8: 268, Figure 8.1, from *Psychology: Themes and Variations,* Third Edition, by W. Weiten, p. 435, Brooks/Cole Publishing, 1995. **269,** Figure 8.2, from *Psychology: Themes and Variations,* Third Edition, by W. Weiten, p. 437, Brooks/Cole Publishing, 1995. **272,** Focus on Assessment, adapted from *Psychological Evaluation for the Courts,* by G. B. Melton et al. Copyright © 1993 The Guilford Press. Adapted with permission. **280,** Table 8.2, reproduced with permission from S. Harter, *Self-Perception Profile for Children,* University of Denver, 1985. **281,** Table 8.3, adapted from "Interpersonal Awareness in Children," by R. L. Selman, D. Jaquette, and D. Lavin, 1977, *American Journal of Orthopsychiatry,* 47, 264–274; and from *The Growth of*

Interpersonal Understanding, by R. L. Selman, copyright © 1980 Academic Press. Adapted with permission. **284,** Box 8.1, reprinted with permission from the *Diagnostic and Statistical Manual of Mental Disorders,* Fourth Edition, pp. 83–85. Copyright © 1994 American Psychiatric Association, Washington D.C. **285,** Box 8.2, from the *Conners' Teacher Rating Scale—39 Item Version (CTRS-39),* by Dr. C. K. Conners, copyright © 1989 Multi-Health Systems Inc., 908 Niagara Falls Blvd, North Tonawanda, NY, 14120-2060, (416) 424-1700. Reproduced by permission. **288,** Table 8.5, from *Parent Effectiveness Training,* by Dr. Thomas Gordon. Copyright © 1970 by Thomas Gordon. Reprinted by permission of David McKay, Co., a division of Random House, Inc. **290,** Figure 8.4, from "Age Segregation in Children's Social Interactions," by S. Ellis, B. Rogoff, and C. C. Cromer, 1981, *Developmental Psychology,* 17, 399–407. Copyright © 1981 American Psychological Association. Reprinted with permission. **294,** excerpt from *Life Experiences, Development and Childhood Psychopathology,* by I. M. Goodyer. Copyright © 1990 and reprinted by permission of John Wiley & Sons, Ltd. **310,** Figure 8.5, from the *Manual for the Child Behavior Checklist and Revised Child Behavior Profile,* by T. M. Achenbach. Copyright © 1991 T. M. Achenbach. Reproduced by permission.

Chapter 9: 316, Box 9.1, reprinted with permission from Colten, Mary Ellen and Gore, Susan (Eds.), *Adolescent Stress: Causes and Consequences* (New York: Aldine de Gruyter), "Coping with Adolescence," by Anne C. Petersen et al. Copyright © 1991 Walter de Gruyter, Inc., New York. **317,** Table 9.1, from *The Process of Human Development,* by C. S. Schuster and S. S. Ashburn. Copyright © 1992 J. B. Lippincott Company. Reprinted with permission. **324–325,** Focus on Multiculturalism, from *The Political Life of Children,* by Robert Coles. Copyright © 1986 Robert Coles. Used by permission of Grove/Atlantic, Inc. **325,** Table 9.3, from *Adolescent Life Experiences,* Second Edition, by G. R. Adams and T. Gullotta, p. 241, Brooks/Cole Publishing, 1989. **328,** Box 9.2, "The Stages of Moral Reasoning/Chart," from *Raising Good Children,* by Thomas Lickona, Ph.D. Copyright © 1983 Thomas Lickona. Used by permission of Bantam Books, a division of Bantam Doubleday Dell Publishing Group, Inc. **332–333,** Box 9.3, reprinted with permission from the *Diagnostic and Sta-*

tistical Manual of Mental Disorders, Fourth Edition. Copyright © 1994 American Psychiatric Association, Washington D.C. **344,** Box 9.5, from *Half the Human Experience: The Psychology of Women*, Third Edition, by J. S. Hyde. Copyright © 1985 D. C. Heath & Company. Reprinted with permission. **347,** Table 9.4, from *The Troubled Journey: A Portrait of 6th–12th Grade Youth*, by P. L. Benson. Copyright © 1990 The Search Institute. Reprinted with permission. **350,** Figure 9.1, from "Risk Behavior in Adolescence: A Psychosocial Framework for Understanding and Action," by R. Jessor. In D. E. Rogers and E. Ginzberg (Eds.), *Adolescents at Risk: Medical and Social Perspectives*, 19–34. Copyright © 1992 Westview Press. Reprinted with permission. **351,** Table 9.5, from "Adolescent Pregnancy and Parenthood," by B. A. Hamburg and S. L. Dixon. In M. K. Rosenheim and M. F. Testa (Eds.), *Early Parenthood and Coming of Age in the 1990s*. Copyright © 1992 Rutgers University Press. Reprinted with permission. **357,** Table 9.6, from *Adolescents at Risk: Prevalence and Prevention*, by Joy C. Dryfoos. Copyright © 1990 Joy C. Dryfoos. Reprinted by permission of Oxford University Press, Inc.

Chapter 10: 372, Box 10.1, from *The Interpersonal Involvement Scale*, by G. Levinger (no date), University of Massachusetts. Reprinted with permission. **373,** Table 10.1, from "Lonelinees, Depression and Cognitive Therapy: Theory and Application," by J. E. Young. In L. A. Peplau and D. Perlman (Eds.), *Loneliness: A Sourcebook of Current Theory, Research, and Therapy*. Copyright © 1982 John Wiley & Sons, Inc. Reprinted by permission of John Wiley & Sons, Inc. **376,** Figure 10.1, from "Clues to the Genetics and Neurobiology of Schizophrenia," by S. E. Nicol and I. I. Gottesman, 1983, *American Scientist*, 71, 398–404. Copyright © 1983 The Scientific Research Society. Reprinted with permission. **378,** Focus on Gender, from *The APA Monitor*, November 1990, p. 33. Copyright © 1990 American Psychological Association. Reprinted with permission. **392,** diagram from *Helping Couples Change*, by R. B. Stuart. Copyright © 1980 The Guilford Press. Adapted with permission. **398,** Focus on Diversity, from "When Lesbian and Gay Couples Break Up," by S. Bryant and Demian, 1990, *Partners Newsletter for Gay and Lesbian Couples*, May/June. Copyright © 1990 Partners Task Force for Gay & Lesbian Couples. Reprinted with permission. **401,** Table 10.3, from "The Personal Perspec-

tive of Acquaintance Rape," by P. D. Rozee, P. Bateman, and T. Gilmore. In A. Parrot and L. Bechhofer (Eds.), *Acquaintance Rape: The Hidden Crime*. Copyright © 1991 John Wiley & Sons, Inc. Reprinted by permission of John Wiley & Sons, Inc. **402–403,** Focus on Gender, reprinted from "The Global War Against Women," by Lori Heise in the March/April 1989 issue of *World Watch* magazine with permission of World Watch Institute, Washington, D.C., copyright © 1989. **403,** Box 10.4, from "Violence Against Women in the United States," copyright © 1995 National Organization for Women. Reprinted with permission.

Chapter 11: 413, Table 11.1, adapted with permission from "The Changes of Menopause," by Lisa Davis, *Hippocrates*, May/June 1989. Copyright © 1989 The Health Publishing Group. **416,** Focus on Biophysics, adapted with permission from "The Politics of Breast Cancer," by P. J. Viviansayles, *Ms.*, May/June, 1993, 54–55. Copyright © 1993 *Ms.* Magazine. **420,** Figure 11.1, from *Longitudinal Studies of Adult Psychological Development*, by K. W. Schaie. Copyright © 1983 The Guilford Press. Reprinted with permission. **431,** Table 11.2, from *Old Loyalties, New Ties*, by E. B. Visher and J. S. Visher. Copyright © 1988 Brunner/Mazel, Inc. Reprinted with permission. **435,** quotation from "My Mother's Keeper," by L. L. Hartney, *Family Therapy Networker*, Sept./Oct. 1989, 38–41. Copyright © 1989 The Family Therapy Networker. Reprinted with permission. **437–438,** Focus on Family, adapted from "Caregiver Stress in Grandparents Raising Grandchildren," by S. Kelly, 1993, *IMAGE: Journal of Nursing Scholarship*, 25, 331–337. Copyright © 1993 Sigma Theta Tau International. Adapted with permission. **441–442,** Focus on Multiculturalism, from "On the Bridge," by N. Garcia-Preto, *Family Therapy Networker*, July/Aug. 1994, 35–37. Copyright © 1994 The Family Therapy Networker. Reprinted with permission. **443,** Figure 11.2, from "The Middle Years: Changes and Variations in Social Role Commitments," by H. Z. Lopata and D. Barnewolt. In G. Baruch and J. Brooks-Gunn (Eds.), *Women in Midlife*, p. 85. Copyright © 1984 Plenum Publishing. Reprinted with permission.

Chapter 12: 458–459, Box 12.1, from *Healthful Aging*, by G. M. Burdman, pp. 67–71. Copyright © 1986. All rights reserved. Reprinted by permission of Allyn & Bacon. **464,** Box 12.2, from *Aging and Mental*

Photo Credits

Chapter 1: 1, Grant Faint/The Image Bank. **5,** Frank Siteman/Stock, Boston. **10,** Jean-Claude Lejeune/Stock, Boston. **24,** Lisco/Photo Researchers, Inc. **89,** Courtesy of Carol Germain.

Chapter 2: 20, Evan Johnson/Jeroboam. **32,** Courtesy of Prader-Willi Syndrome Association, U.S.A. **46,** Larry Shavelson/Impact Visuals.

Chapter 3: 54, Evan Johnson/Jeroboam. **57,** Jon Erikson. **64,** Elizabeth Crews/Stock, Boston. **78,** Erika/Photo Researchers, Inc. **80,** Michael Newman/PhotoEdit.

Chapter 4: 84, F. B. Grunzweig/Photo Researchers, Inc. **93,** Ellen B. Neipris/Impact Visuals. **115,** Jeff Greenberg/Photo Researchers, Inc. **118,** David Rae Morris/Impact Visuals. **131,** Ellis Herwig/Stock, Boston.

Chapter 5: 135, Garry Watson/Photo Researchers, Inc. **138,** D. W. Fawcett/Photo Researchers, Inc. **141,** Craig LeCroy. **142,** Craig LeCroy. **146,** Ansel Horn/Impact Visuals. **157,** Craig LeCroy. **177,** Craig LeCroy. **195,** R. Lee/Anthro Photo.

Chapter 6: 176, Robert Brenner/PhotoEdit. **184,** Craig LeCroy. **192,** Michael Newman/PhotoEdit. **205,** Craig LeCroy. **207,** Craig LeCroy. **217,** Evan Johnson/Impact Visuals.

Chapter 7: 223, Elizabeth Crews/The Image Works. **225,** Craig LeCroy. **226,** Craig LeCroy. **233,** Mary Kate Denny/PhotoEdit. **241,** Craig LeCroy. **248,** Craig LeCroy. **257,** Courtesy of the San Francisco Child Abuse Council, Inc.

Chapter 8: 265, Robert Clay/Jeroboam. **276,** Will/Deni McIntyre/Photo Researchers, Inc. **278,** Jim West/Impact Visuals. **291,** Tony Freeman/PhotoEdit. **298,** Michael Newman/PhotoEdit. **296,** Bob Daemmrich/Stock, Boston.

Chapter 9: 314, Craig LeCroy. **336,** Jeff Greenberg/Photo Researchers, Inc. **323,** Joseph Schuyler/Stock, Boston. **349,** Donna Binder/Impact Visuals. **352,** Gale Zucker/Stock, Boston.

Chapter 10: 363, Michael Emery/The Image Works. **368,** Craig LeCroy. **377,** Michael Newman/PhotoEdit. **381,** D. Young-Wolff/PhotoEdit. **397,** Jose Carillo/PhotoEdit.

Chapter 11: 409, Elizabeth Crews/The Image Works. **418,** Kenneth Murray/Photo Researchers, Inc. **423,** Craig LeCroy. **427,** John Boykin/PhotoEdit. **445,** N. R. Rowan/Stock, Boston.

Chapter 12: 451, Lisa Law/The Image Works. **452,** Craig LeCroy. **454,** Courtesy of the University of Kansas. **460,** Craig LeCroy. **466,** Alan Oddie/PhotoEdit. **473,** Kathy Seward-MacKay/Impact Visuals. **482,** Craig LeCroy. **489,** Joseph Schuyler/Stock, Boston.